Smith and Keenan's
English Law

Ninth edition

Denis Keenan

LLB(Hons), FCIS, DMA, CertEd
of the Middle Temple, Barrister-at-Law
Formerly Head of Department of Business Studies and Law
Mid-Essex Technical College and School of Art
(now Essex Institute of Higher Education)

Pitman

PITMAN PUBLISHING LIMITED
128 Long Acre, London WC2E 9AN

© Kenneth Smith and Denis Keenan, 1963, 1966
© Denis Keenan and Mrs K Smith, 1969, 1973, 1975, 1979, 1982
© Denis Keenan, 1986
© Denis Keenan, 1989

Ninth edition first published in Great Britain 1989

British Library Cataloguing in Publication Data
Smith, Kenneth, *1910–1966*
    Smith and Keenan's English law.—
    9th ed. *Denis Keenan*
    1. England. Law

    I. Title II. Keenan, Denis, *1926–*
    344.2

ISBN 0 273 03069 8

Produced by Longman Singapore Publishers (Pte) Ltd.
Printed in Singapore

Contents

Preface to ninth edition

This edition which takes the book into its twenty-sixth year as a leading students' text has, as always, been substantially rewritten and updated for the law never stands still.

The book is a little longer than the eighth edition, but in view of the fact that it contains some seventy new cases and fifteen major new Acts of Parliament this is to be expected.

Once again each case, or on occasion a group of cases, has introductory material which makes it possible to more effectively study the cases along with, or separately from the text. The intention is that the publication should be, in effect, a text and casebook combined.

A minor amount of essential updating is required to the text as follows—

(1) Compensatory awards (p. 74)
Section 104 of the Criminal Justice Act 1988 makes a number of changes to the power of the court to award compensation. It amends s. 35 of the Powers of Criminal Courts Act, 1973. The circumstances in which a compensation order may be made are expanded and a court is required to give reasons for not making such an order where they have a power to do so.

Home Office Circular 85/1988 (Guidelines on Compensation in the Criminal Courts) issued in September 1988 gives assistance to the court in the use and assessment of compensation orders, more particularly those involving personal injury. Recommended awards are: minor graze—up to £50; minor bruise—up to £75; black eye—£100; cut (no scar)—£75–£200; sprain—£100–£400; tooth (not front)—£50–£500; tooth (front)—£1000; small face scar—£550+; large face scar—£5000–£8000+; broken jaw—£1750; broken nose—£550–£1500; broken wrist—£1750–£2500+; broken finger—£750; broken leg/arm—£1750–£2500.

(2) Dismissal for failure to join a trade union (pp. 332 and 333)
Under the Employment Act 1988 dismissal for non-union membership is automatically unfair, whether or not there is a closed shop. This removes the remaining statutory support for the closed shop.

In the preparation of this edition the publishers and I have once again received the invaluable assistance of my wife in terms of the preparation of the indexes, together with the organisation of sources of new material since the last edition.

I must also express my thanks to Simon Lake and Howard Bailey of Pitman Publishing for their help throughout and also to those who set, printed and bound the book.

I hope the book will continue to be useful to the wide variety of students who use it, both here and overseas.

For the errors and omissions I am, of course, solely responsible.

Maenan,
Gwynedd.
January 1989

Denis Keenan

Table of Statutes

Table of Cases

Note The number of the case in the Appendix is printed in **bold** type; the page on which the case is cited is printed in ordinary type.

1 The development of English law

Our present legal system began, for all practical purposes, in the reign of Henry II (1154–1189). When he came to the throne justice was for the most part administered in local courts, i.e. by local lords to their tenants in the feudal courts, and by the County Sheriffs, often sitting with the Earl and the Bishop, in the courts of the Shires and Hundreds. They administered the law in their respective areas and decided the cases which came before them on the basis of local custom. Many of these customary rules of law were the same or similar in all parts of the country, but there were some differences. For instance, primogeniture, the right of the eldest son to inherit the whole of his father's land where there was no will, i.e. on intestacy, applied almost universally throughout England; but in Kent there existed a system of land-holding called gavelkind tenure whereby on intestacy all the sons inherited equally; while in Nottingham and Bristol, under the custom of Borough-English, the property passed to the youngest son. These customs were finally abolished by s. 1 and Part IV of the Administration of Estates Act, 1925, and replaced by the rule that land vests in those administering the deceased's estate for distribution to near relatives—in most cases spouse and children.

A Royal Court existed called the Curia Regis (King's Council) but this was in general available only to high-ranking persons to whom the King had granted interests in large estates.

In addition, the Curia Regis followed the person of the King and those wishing to complain to the court had to incur the expense, delay and frustration of pursuing the King in his constant movements about the country and abroad. It seems that one plaintiff followed the King through England and France for five years before his case was heard.

However, section 17 of the Statute of 1215, Magna Carta, provided that what is now the High Court should not follow the King but should be held 'in some certain place'. This turned out to be Westminster and so what is now the High Court became centred in London. It is now in the Strand.

Steps were also taken to ensure that royal justice would go out to the shires and be open to all. This began with the General Eyre which also was instrumental in unifying the law. This is considered below.

THE COMMON LAW

The administrative ability of the Normans began the process destined to lead to a unified system of law which was nevertheless evolutionary in its development. The Normans were not concerned to change English customary law entirely by imposing Norman law on England. Indeed, many charters of William I giving English boroughs the right to hold courts stated that the laws dispensed in those courts should be laws of Edward the Confessor, which meant that English customary law was to be applied.

Attempts were made to ensure a greater uniformity in English law and the chief means by which this was achieved was the introduction of the General Eyre whereby representatives of the King were sent from Westminster on a tour of the Shires for the purpose of checking on the local administration. During the period of their visit they would sit in the local court and hear cases, and gradually they came to have a judicial rather than an administrative function.

Henry II took steps to formalize the jurisdiction of the General Eyre by the Assize of Clarendon (1166) and the Assize of Northampton (1176). These provided that in relation to the criminal law there should be 12 men in every county to be responsible for presenting to the sheriff those suspected of serious crimes. The accused were then brought before the General Eyre when it arrived in the area. As regards the civil law, a new civil remedy called the Assize of Novel Disseisin was offered to persons who complained that their land had been wrongly seized. From this remedy grew a range of civil actions which were brought before the General Eyre. Thus royal and more uniform justice began to come to the country as a whole.

The General Eyre disappeared in the reign of Richard II (1377–99), but a system of circuit judges from what is now the High Court took its place, the first circuit commission being granted in the reign of Edward III (1327–77). By selecting the best customary rulings and applying these outside their county of origin, the circuit judges gradually moulded existing local customary laws into one uniform law 'common' to the whole kingdom. Thus, customs originally local ultimately applied throughout the whole of the realm. Even so, there was no absolute unification even as late as 1389, and in a case in what is now the High Court in that year, a custom of Selby in Yorkshire was admitted to show that a husband was not in that area liable for his wife's trading debts, though the common law elsewhere regarded him as liable.

Furthermore, the right to make a will of personal property, e.g. jewellery, was not universal in England until 1724 when it finally extended to the City of London. Before that time half of the personalty, 'the dead man's part', went to the church and the other half to the wife and children. Land could still not be left by will but descended to the heir at law, thought it later became possible, as it is today, to leave land by will.

However, many new rules were created and applied by the royal judges as they went on circuit and these were added to local customary law to make one uniform body of law called 'common law'. Thus the identity between custom and the common law is not historically true, since much of the common law in early times was created by the judges, who justified their rulings by asserting that they were derived from the 'general custom of the Realm'. Thus, in *Beaulieu* v. *Finglamm*, (1401), Y. B. 2 Hen. 4, f. 18, pl. 6, it was said that a man who by negligence failed to control a fire so that it spread to his neighbour's house was liable in damages according to 'the law and custom of the realm', though it is not easy to see which customary rule the court based its decision on.

The Royal Commissions

The circuit judges from what is now the Queen's Bench Division came eventually to derive their authority from Royal Commissions, the granting of which marked the real beginning of the assize system. The Commissions were—

Commission of oyer and terminer

This commission, which dates from 1329, directed the judges to 'hear and determine' all complaints of grave crime within the jurisdiction of the circuit.

General gaol delivery

This commission, which dates from 1299, gave the judges power to clear the local gaols and try all prisoners within the jurisdiction of the circuit.

Other criminal cases were heard by Justices of the Peace either summarily or sitting in quarter sessions (now abolished) and the circuit judges were also made Justices of the Peace so as to increase their jurisdiction.

Commission of Assize for Civil Actions

Civil actions were usually heard at Westminster but under the Statute of Westminster II, 1285, the circuit judges heard *civil cases* under provisions known as *nisi prius* which required the local sheriff to send a jury to London *unless before* the appointed time the royal justices came to hear the case locally, which in practice they always did. Thus civil cases were opened in London, tried by circuit judge and jury in the locality and the verdict recorded in London. This lasted until the nineteenth century when a Commission of Assize for Civil Actions was granted.

The Courts Act, 1971

The system, which lasted for many years, was brought to an end by the Courts Act, 1971, s. 1(2) which provided that all courts of assize were abolished and commissions to hold any court of assize would not be issued. (See p. 29.) This section, having achieved its purpose, was repealed by Sch. 7 of the Supreme Court Act, 1981.

Stare decisis

Initially the system was held together by the doctrine of *stare decisis*, or standing by previous decisions. Thus when a judge decided a new problem in a case brought before him, this became a new rule of law and was followed by subsequent judges. In later times this practice crystallized into the form which is known as the binding force of judicial precedent, and the judges felt bound to follow previous decisions instead of merely looking to them for guidance. By these means the common law earned the status of a system. Indeed it was possible for Bracton, Dean of Exeter and a Justice Itinerant of Henry III, to write the first exposition of the common law before the end of the thirteenth century—*A Treatise on the Laws and Customs of England*. There was also an earlier treatise ascribed to Ranulph de Glanvill in 1187, but this was not so comprehensive as the work of Bracton. Nevertheless, the number of writs which Bracton describes as being available in the Royal Courts is much in excess of those described by Glanvill and shows the rapid growth of the system in its first 100 years.

To sum up, the common law is a judge-made system of law, originating in ancient customs, which were clarified, *much* extended and universalized by the judges, although that part of the common law which concerned the ownership of land was derived mainly from the system of feudal tenures introduced from Europe after the Norman Conquest. It is perhaps also worth noting that the term 'common law' is used in four distinct senses, i.e. as opposed to (*a*) local law; (*b*) Equity; (*c*) statute law; and (*d*) any foreign system of law.

EQUITY

The growth of the common law was rapid in the thirteenth century but in the fourteenth century it ceased to have the momentum of earlier years. As a legal profession came into existence the judges came to be chosen exclusively from that profession instead of from a wider variety of royal officials as had been the case in the thirteenth century. The common law courts became more self-conscious about what they were doing and attempted to become more systematic. There was much talk about the proper way of doing things, of not being able to do this or that and much clever reasoning. Reports of cases in the Year Books, the nearest we have to law reports at this time, show a considerable concern with procedural points and niceties, a reluctance to depart from what had become established, a close attention to the observance of proper forms and much less concern with what the circumstances of a particular case demanded if it was to be settled in an appropriate way.

DEFECTS OF THE COMMON LAW

As a result of this hardening up of the system complaints were made by large numbers of people about the inadequacy of the service provided by the courts and the defects of the common law. The main defects were as follows—

(i) *The writ system*. Writs were issued by the clerks in the Chancellor's office, the Chancellor being in those days a clergyman of high rank who was also the King's Chaplain and Head of Parliament. In order to bring an action in one of the King's courts, the aggrieved party had to obtain from the Chancery a writ for which he had to pay. A writ was a sealed letter issued in the name of the King, and it ordered some person, Lord of the Manor, Sheriff of the County or the defendant, to do whatever the writ specified.

The old common law writs began with a statement of the plaintiff's claim, which was largely in common form, and was prepared in the Royal Chancery and not by the plaintiff's advisers as is the statement of claim today. Any writ which was novel, because the plaintiff or his advisers had tried to draft it to suit the plaintiff's case, might be abated, i.e. thrown out by the court. Thus, writs could only be issued in a limited number of cases, and if the complaint could not be fitted within the four corners of one of the existing writs, no action could be brought.

For example, the writ of trespass to land was available. However, trespass is a *direct* wrong, e.g. actually being on the land. *Indirect* activity affecting enjoyment of land was not covered, e.g. nuisance from smelly pigs or smoky bonfires. There was *at that time* no writ to redress this type of indirect harm. The common law came to expand its writs to cover an action for damages in this situation, but in the meantime equity had carved out a jurisdiction and had an ideal remedy to deal with nuisance, i.e. the issue of an injunction requiring the defendant to cease the activity on pain of a fine or imprisonment for contempt of court. Moreover, writs were expensive, and their cost could deprive a party of justice. In some cases the cost of the writ was more than the amount of the plaintiff's claim so he did not bother to sue.

However, a practice grew up under which the clerks in Chancery framed new writs even though the complaint was not quite covered by an existing writ, thus extending the law by extending the scope of the writ system. This appeared to Parliament to be a usurpation of its powers as the supreme lawgiver. Further, it took much work away from the local courts, diminishing the income of the local barons who persuaded Parliament to pass a statute called the Provisions of Oxford in 1258, forbidding in effect the practice of creating new writs to fit new cases. This proved so inconvenient that an attempt to remedy the situation was made by the Statute of Westminster II in 1285 which empowered the clerks in Chancery to issue new writs *in consimili casu* (in similar cases), thus adapting existing writs to fit new circumstances. The common law began to expand again, but it was still by no means certain that a writ would be forthcoming to fit a particular case, because the clerks in Chancery used the Statute with caution at first.

(ii) *Procedure*. Other difficulties arose over the procedure in the common law courts, because even the most trivial error in a writ would avoid the action. If X complained of the trespass of Y's mare, and in his writ by error described the mare as a stallion, his action could not proceed and he would have to start again. Furthermore, some common law actions were tried by a system called 'wager of law', and the plaintiff might fail on what was really a good claim if a defendant could bring more people to say that the claim was false than the plaintiff could muster to support it.

The system worked well in local courts where the witnesses (called 'oath helpers') knew the parties and circumstances of the case. However, in cases brought at Westminster it fell into disrepute because 'oath helpers' who would support any case could be hired outside court for a few pence a head.

(iii) *Defences and corruption*. In common law actions the defendant could plead certain standard defences known as *essoins* which would greatly delay the plaintiff's claim. For example, the defendant might say that he was cut off by floods or a broken bridge, or that he was off on a Crusade. He might also plead the defence of sickness which could delay the action for a year and a day. In early times these defences were verified by sending four knights to see the defendant, but at a later stage there was no verification and the defences were used merely to delay what were often good claims. There were also complaints about the bribery, corruption or oppression of juries, the partiality of sheriffs and the inability of a litigant to enforce a judgment or recover property from his more powerful neighbour.

(iv) *Remedies*. The common law was also defective in the matter of remedies. The only remedy the common law had to offer for a civil wrong inflicted on a plaintiff was damages, i.e. a payment of money, which is not in all cases an adequate compensation.

For example, if A trespasses each day on B's land, B is unlikely to be satisfied with damages. He would rather stop A from trespassing which equity could do by its remedy of injunction. The common law could not compel a person to perform his obligations or cease to carry on a wrong, though it is not true to say that the common law was entirely devoid of equitable principles, and even in early times there were signs of some equitable development; but generally the rigidity of the forms of action tended to stifle justice.

(v) *Trusts and mortgages*. Furthermore, the common law did not recognize 'the concept of the trust or use' and there was no way of compelling the trustee to carry out his obligations under the trust. Thus if S conveyed property to T on trust for B, T could treat the property as his own and the common law would ignore the claims of B. In addition, the main right of a borrower (or mortgagor) is the right to redeem (or recover) the land he has used as a security for the loan. Originally at common law the land became the property of the lender (or mortgagee) as soon as the date decided upon for repayment had passed, unless during that time the loan had been repaid. However, Equity regarded a mortgage as essentially a security, and gave the mortgagor the right to redeem the land at any time on payment of the principal sum, plus interest due to the date of payment. What is more important, this rule applied even though the common law date for repayment had passed. This rule, which still exists, is called the Equity of Redemption.

Many people, therefore, unable to gain access to the King's courts, either because they could not obtain a writ, or because the writ was defective when they got it, or because they were caught in some procedural difficulty, or could not obtain an appropriate remedy, began to address their complaints to the King in Council. For a time the Council itself considered such petitions, and where a petition was addressed to the King in person, he referred it to the Council for trial. Later the Council delegated this function to the Chancellor, and eventually petitions were addressed to the Chancellor alone.

The Chancellor appears to have been chosen because he was already involved in legal matters. His clerks were engaged in the issue of common law writs and so it was convenient to delegate this new function to him. The Chancellor had custody of the great seal of England which was used to authenticate writs and charters. His jurisdiction had nothing to do with his supposed position of Keeper of the King's Conscience, i.e. the person to whom the King confessed his sins. In fact a compilation of the King's Confessors reveals that not one of them was Chancellor, though it is true that the early Chancellors were clerics.

The Chancellor began to judge such cases in the light of conscience and fair dealing. He was not bound by the remedies of the common law and began to devise remedies of his own. For example, the Chancellor could compel a person to perform his obligations by issuing a decree of *specific performance* or could stop him from carrying on a wrong by the issue of an *injunction*. The Chancellor also recognized interests in property which were unknown to the common law, in particular the concept of the *use*, under which persons might be made the legal owners of property for the use or benefit of another or others. As we have seen, the common law did not recognize the interests of the beneficiaries under a trust (or use), but allowed the legal owner to deal with the property as if no other interests existed. Equity, however, enforced the beneficial interests. In order to bring persons before him the Chancellor issued a form of summons, called a *subpoena*, which did not state a cause of action but merely told the recipient to appear in Chancery. There were no rules of evidence and the Chancellor's Court did not sit in a fixed place; some hearings were even held in the Chancellor's private house. Equity was thus not cramped by anything analogous to the writ system or the excessive formality of the common law. Eventually as new Chancellors took over, and Vice-Chancellors were appointed to cope with the increasing volume of work, uncertainty crept into the system, conflicting decisions abounded, and it was said that 'Equity varies with the Chancellor's foot'.

At this stage in its development Equity also began to follow the practice of *stare decisis* which had proved so powerful a force in unifying the diverse systems of local custom under the common law. This was precipitated by the Reformation and by the appointment in 1530 of Sir Thomas More as Chancellor. More was a common lawyer and not a cleric. From then on non-clerical Chancellors were drawn from the ranks of the common lawyers and naturally followed the system of precedent which they had seen used in the common law courts. Lord Ellesmere (1596–1617) began to apply the same principles in all cases of the same type, and later, under Lord Nottingham (1673–1682), Lord Hardwicke (1736–1756) and Lord Eldon (1807–1827), Equity developed in scope and certainty.

Relationship of Law and Equity

Although Law and Equity eventually operated alongside each other with mutual tolerance, there was a period of conflict between them. This arose out of the practice of the Court of Chancery which issued 'common injunctions' forbidding a person on pain of imprisonment from bringing an action in the common law courts, or forbidding the enforcement of a common law judgment if such a judgment had been obtained.

Thus, if X by some unconscionable conduct, such as undue influence (see further p. 269), had obtained an agreement with Y, whereby Y was to sell X certain land at much below its real value, then, if Y refused to convey the land, X would have his remedy in damages at common law despite his unconscionable conduct. However, if Y appealed to the Chancellor, the latter might issue a common injunction which would prevent X from bringing his action at common law unless he wished to suffer punishment for defiance of the Chancellor's injunction. Similarly, if X had already obtained a judgment at common law, the Chancellor would prevent its enforcement by ordering X, on pain of imprisonment, not to execute judgment on Y's property.

However, the common law courts retaliated by waiting for the Chancellor to imprison the common law litigant for defiance of the injunction, and then the common law would release him by the process of *habeas corpus*.

This period of rivalry culminated in the *Earl of Oxford's* case in 1615,[1]* when Lord Coke offered a direct challenge to the Court of Chancery's jurisdiction. The challenge was taken up and James I, on the advice of Lord Bacon, then his Attorney-General and later Lord Chancellor, gave a firm decision that where common law and Equity were in conflict Equity should prevail. This principle now appears in s. 49 of the Supreme

---

* A superior number refers to the appropriate case number in the 'Cases and materials' section of this book.

Court Act, 1981, having appeared in a number of earlier Judicature Acts. Thereafter the two systems settled down and carved out separate and complementary jurisdictions. Equity filled in the gaps left by the common law, and became a system of case law governed by the binding force of precedent. By the same token, it lost much of its earlier freedom and elasticity. It is certainly no longer a court of conscience.

Many reforms were still to come. Equitable and legal remedies had to be sought in different courts, but this in due course was rectified by the Judicature Acts, 1873–1875, which brought about an amalgamation of the English Courts. Since then both common law and equitable remedies have been available to a litigant under the same action and in the same court.

Before leaving the topic, a final characteristic of Equity should be noted which is that Equity never says the common law is wrong but merely provides alternative solutions to legal problems. It is thus a gloss upon the common law and this is illustrated by certain cases in the Law of Contract. For example, the decisions in *Central London Property Trust Ltd* v. *High Trees House Ltd*, 1947 (see p. 589) and *Solle* v. *Butcher*, 1949 (see p. 614) show how modern Equity sometimes adopts a different solution to that provided by the common law.

LEGISLATION

In early times there were few statutes and the bulk of law was case law, though legislation in one form or another dates from A.D. 600. The earliest Norman legislation was by means of Royal Charter, but the first great outburst of legislation came in the reign of Henry II (1154–1189). This legislation was called by various names: there were Assizes, Constitutions, and Provisions, as well as Charters. Legislation at this time was generally made by the King in Council, but sometimes by a kind of Parliament which consisted in the main of a meeting of nobles and clergy summoned from the shires.

In the fourteenth century parliamentary legislation became more general. Parliament at first requested or prayed the King to legislate, but later it presented a bill in its own wording. The Tudor period saw the development of modern procedure, in particular the practice of giving three readings to a bill; and this was also the age of the *Preamble*, which was a kind of preface to the enactment, describing often at great length the reasons for passing it and generally justifying the measure.

From the Tudor period onwards Parliament became more and more independent and the practice of law making by statute increased. Nevertheless statutes did not become an important source of law until the last two centuries, and even now, although the bulk of legislation is large, statutes form a comparatively small part of the law as a whole. The basis of our law remains the common law, and if all the statutes were repealed we should still have a legal system of sorts; whereas our statutes alone would not provide a system of law but merely a set of disjointed rules.

Parliament's increasing incursions into economic and social affairs increased the need for statutes. Some aspects of law are so complicated or so novel that they can only be laid down in this form; they would not be likely to come into existence through the submission of cases in court. A statute is the ultimate source of law, and, even if a statute is in conflict with the common law or Equity, the statute must prevail. It is such an important source that it has been said—'A statute can do anything except change man to woman,' although in a purely legal sense even this could be achieved. No court or other body can question the validity of an Act of Parliament. (*Cheney* v. *Conn*, 1968.)[2]

Statute law can be used to abolish common law rules which have outlived their usefulness, or to amend the common law to cope with the changing circumstances and values of society. Once enacted, statutes, even if obsolete, do not cease to have the force of law, but common sense usually prevents most obsolete laws from being invoked. In addition, statutes which are no longer of practical utility are repealed from time to time by Statute Law Repeal Acts. Nevertheless, a statute stands as law until it is specifically repealed by Parliament. (*Prince of Hanover* v. *Attorney General*, 1957.)[3]

An Act of Parliament is absolutely binding on everyone within the sphere of its jurisdiction, but all Acts of Parliament can be repealed by the same or subsequent Parliaments; and this is the only exception to the rule of the absolute sovereignty of Parliament—it cannot bind itself or its successors. (*Vauxhall Estates Ltd* v. *Liverpool Corporation*, 1932.)[4]

The obligation of the British Parliament on entry to the European Economic Community was to ensure that Community law was paramount. The view of the European Court is that Community law overrides English law where the latter is inconsistent with it. Section 3 of the European Communities Act, 1972 binds our courts to accept this principle and talks of applying the principles of Community law with the idea that it prevails. Section 2(4) (*ibid.*) states that a UK statute should be construed so as to be consistent with Community law. However, many authorities on constitutional law see this obligation as a dilemma in the sense that Community law cannot be paramount when like the rest of our law it is at the mercy of any future Act of Parliament which must, under the fundamental rule of our constitution, prevail over any pre-existing law whatsoever. In other words, Community law is paramount as the result of the European Communities Act, 1972, which could be repealed by a future Act of Parliament. It would seem to be the duty of our courts to accept that repeal. Nevertheless, Parliament has a new role in relation to legislation emanating from the institutions of the Community and now has the right to send representatives to the European Parliament. (See further p. 123.)

DELEGATED LEGISLATION

Many modern statutes require much detailed work to implement and operate them, and such details are not normally contained in the statute itself, but are filled in from some other source. For example, much of our Social Security legislation gives only the general provisions of a complex scheme of social benefits, and an immense number of detailed regulations have had to be made by civil servants in the name of, and under the authority of, the appropriate Minister. These regulations, when made in the approved manner, are just as much law as the parent statute itself. This form of law is known as delegated or subordinate legislation.

CUSTOM

In early times custom was taken by the judges and turned into the common law of England, and it is still possible, even today, to argue the existence of a local or trade custom before the courts. Local customs consist in the main of customary rights vested in the inhabitants of a particular place to use, for various purposes, land held in the private ownership of another. For example, to take water from a spring (*Race v. Ward* (1855), 24 L.J.Q.B. 153) and for fishermen to dry their nets on private land (*Mercer* v. *Denne*, [1905] 2 Ch. 538). The existence of a trade custom is illustrated by *Hutton* v. *Warren*, 1836. (See p. 652.) As a present-day source of law, however, custom is of little importance.

THE LAW MERCHANT

Mercantile Law, or *Lex Mercatoria*, is based upon mercantile customs and usages, and was developed separately from the common law. The Royal Courts did not have a monopoly of the administration of justice and certain local courts continued to hear cases long after the Royal Courts were established. One notable area was that involving mercantile and maritime disputes. Disputes between merchants, local and foreign, which arose at the fairs where most important commercial business was transacted in the fourteenth century, were tried in the courts of the fair or borough, and were known as 'Courts of Pie Powder' (*pieds poudrés*) after the dusty feet of the traders who used them.

These courts were presided over by the mayor or his deputy or, if the fair was held as part of a private franchise, the steward appointed by the franchise holder. The rules applied were the rules of the European law merchant developed over the years from the customary practices of merchants and the jury was often made up of merchants. The fair or borough courts were supplemented for a time by 'Staple Courts' which sat in the staple towns. These towns, which were designated by Edward III (1327–1377) as the exclusive centres of trade for such commodities

11

as wine, wool, leather and tin, were required to hold courts to decide the trading disputes of merchants and again the customary practices of merchants were used.

Maritime disputes were heard by maritime courts sitting in major ports such as Bristol. These, too, applied a special European customary law developed from the customary practices of seamen.

The common law courts were slow to show an interest in dealing with commercial matters. In part this was due to the idea that their jurisdiction had a geographical limit and was restricted to matters which had arisen in England between English citizens. Foreign matters, and many of these commercial disputes did involve either a foreign merchant or a contract made or to be performed abroad, were left to some other body, especially if it could raise questions about the relations between the King and foreign sovereigns where the King's Council might be a more appropriate body. To some extent also it was due to the fact that the common law courts and the common law had come into existence at a time when land was the most important commodity and the procedures and concerns of the common law courts were adapted to problems arising from disputes about the possession and ownership of land. They were formal, slow and ill-adapted to the needs of merchants who required a speedier justice administered according to rules with which they were familiar.

When the Court of Admiralty developed, it took over much of the work of the merchant's courts, but from the seventeenth century onwards the common law courts began to acquire the commercial work, and many rules of the Law Merchant were incorporated into the common law. This was achieved partly by fiction. For example, to get over the fact that technically it still lacked jurisdiction over matters arising abroad the Court accepted allegations that something that had occurred abroad had in fact occurred in England within its jurisdiction, e.g. by using the fiction that Bordeaux was in Cheapside.

Lord Mansfield and Lord Holt played a great part in this development, in particular by recognizing the main mercantile customs in the common law courts without requiring proof of them on every occasion. Perhaps the most important mercantile customs recognized were that a bill of exchange was negotiable and that mere agreements should be binding as contracts. In this way the custom of merchants relating to negotiable instruments and contracts including the sale of goods became part of the common law, and later, by codification, of statute law in the Bills of Exchange Act, 1882, and the Sale of Goods Act, 1979.

CANON LAW

Before the Norman Conquest the then existing courts heard all suits, both lay and ecclesiastical, and the Bishop and the Earl sat as joint judges. These joint courts were disliked by the Papacy because of the quarrels which took place between the lay and ecclesiastical members of the various tribunals. Prior to his conquest of England, William I had promised to set up separate ecclesiastical courts in this country, in return for the Pope's blessing of his proposed campaign. After the Conquest, William carried out his promise and removed suits 'which belong to the government of souls' from lay to ecclesiastical courts, and thus began the separation of the two.

The ecclesiastical courts dealt not only with offences against doctrine and morality, but also with secular matters, e.g. matrimonial causes, legitimacy, and testamentary succession. Many of their rules were derived from Roman Law, and were inherited by the civil courts, to which the jurisdiction was transferred in 1857.

The Matrimonial Causes Act, 1857, transferred matrimonial causes to a new civil court called the Divorce Court. The Court of Probate Act, 1857, transferred suits concerning wills to a new court called the Probate Court. The Judicature Act, 1873, incorporated the Probate and Divorce Courts into a newly created Supreme Court of Judicature as part of the Probate, Divorce and Admiralty Division, which under s. 1 of the Administration of Justice Act, 1970, became the Family Division (see p. 31), and the legal principles evolved over the centuries were expressly incorporated in the laws of England. Section 5(1)(c) of the Supreme Court Act, 1981 now specifies the divisions of the High Court as including the Family Division.

The present position is that the church courts remain to deal with disciplinary and moral offences committed by the clergy and certain of the laity, e.g. parish clerks and churchwardens, of the Church of England, and certain other matters, e.g. decoration, alteration and use of churches.

The court of first instance is that of the diocesan chancellor, called a Consistory Court. He must be a member of the Church of England and is usually a practising barrister. Appeal lies from him to the Court of Arches in the province of Canterbury, and to the Chancery Court of York in the northern province. On matters concerning conduct, there is a further appeal to the Judicial Committee of the Privy Council and on other matters, e.g. the suitability of a Henry Moore altar in a Wren church (*Re St. Stephen Walbrook*, [1987] 2 All ER 578), there may be an appeal to the Court of Ecclesiastical Cases Reserved. The church courts are not courts of common law and the prerogative orders (see p. 97)—which operate as a valuable check on the abuse of power by other courts and tribunals—do not apply to them.

LEGAL TREATISES

One last source remains to be considered, namely legal treatises. Throughout the centuries great English jurists have written books, some in the nature of legal text-books, which have helped to shape the law and inform the legal profession.

We have already mentioned Bracton whose *Treatise on the Laws and Customs of England* was written in the thirteenth century and was probably based on the decisions of Martin de Pateshull, who was Archdeacon of Norfolk, Dean of St. Pauls and an Itinerant Justice from 1217 to 1229, and on those of William de Raleigh who was the Rector of Bratton Fleming in Devon and an Itinerant Justice from 1228 to 1250.

Sir Edward Coke, who lived from 1552 to 1634, is a celebrated name. His *Institutes* covered many aspects of law. For example, his *First Institute*, published in 1628, was concerned with land law. His *Second Institute*, published in 1642, was concerned with the principal statutes. The *Third Institute*, published in 1644, dealt with Criminal Law, while the *Fourth Institute*, also published in 1644, was concerned with the Jurisdiction and History of the Courts, this work containing bitter attacks on the Court of Chancery. During his lifetime Coke occupied the offices of Recorder of London, Solicitor-General, Speaker of the House of Commons, Attorney-General, and finally Chief Justice of Common Pleas.

Sir William Blackstone, who lived from 1723 to 1780, published his *Commentaries* in 1765. These are concerned with various aspects of law and are based on his lectures at Oxford. He was a Judge of the Common Pleas and was also the first Professor of English Law to be appointed in any English university.

In addition to older treatises such as those mentioned above, the works of modern writers, sufficiently eminent in the profession, are sometimes quoted when novel points of law are being argued in the Courts. (*Boys v. Blenkinsop*, 1968.)[5]

2 The courts of law

The Royal Courts of Westminster developed out of the *Curia Regis* (or the King's Council). The Court of Exchequer was the first court to emerge from the *Curia Regis* and dealt initially with disputes connected with royal revenues. The Court of Common Pleas was set up in the time of Henry II to hear disputes between the King's subjects. The Court of King's Bench was last to emerge and initially was closely associated with the King himself, hearing disputes between subjects and the King.

As the system developed the Court of Chancery was added and there was also a Court of Admiralty. The Court of Probate and the Divorce Court developed from the old ecclesiastical courts which formerly dealt with these matters. Each of these courts had its own jurisdiction, sometimes overlapping and sometimes conflicting. This was particularly true with regard to the common law courts and the Court of Chancery. For example, in *Knight* v. *Marquis of Waterford*, (1844) 11 Cl. & Fin. 653, the appellant was told by the House of Lords after 14 years of litigation in Equity, that he had a good case but must begin his action again in a common law court. It is useful to refer at this point to *Wood* v. *Scarth*, 1858 (see p. 628). This case is a further illustration of the delays which resulted from the administration of law and equity in separate courts. Anyway, this was how the English legal system entered the nineteenth century and it was this inheritance that the Victorians set out to rationalize into the form with which we are familiar.

THE SUPREME COURT OF JUDICATURE

In order to rationalize the system the Supreme Court of Judicature was established. Under the Judicature Acts, 1873–1875 the High Court was divided into five divisions: Queen's Bench, Common Pleas, Exchequer, Chancery, and Probate, Divorce and Admiralty, the number being reduced to three by an Order in Council in 1881 when the Common Pleas and Exchequer Divisions were merged into the Queen's Bench Division. The Court of Appeal was given jurisdiction over appeals.

The House of Lords

The House of Lords was not included in the Supreme Court of Judicature by the Judicature Acts because of Parliament's opposition to its hereditary character. Its jurisdiction as a final court of appeal was established by the Appellate Jurisdiction Act, 1876 which also provided the House with trained judges, i.e. Life Peers with legal training. The Judicature Acts, 1873–1875 were consolidated in the Supreme Court of Judicature (Consolidation) Act, 1925. This Act is now repealed by the Supreme Court Act of 1981, s. 1 of which reaffirms the previous position by providing that the Supreme Court of England and Wales shall consist of the Court of Appeal, the High Court of Justice and the Crown Court, and that the Lord Chancellor shall be President of the Supreme Court. The Restrictive Trade Practices Court and the Employment Appeal Tribunal are not included even though they are staffed in part by High Court judges and appeals lie to the Court of Appeal.

THE COURTS TODAY

In recent times far-reaching changes have been made in the structure and jurisdiction of the civil and criminal courts by various reforming statutes. The present system of courts exercising both civil and criminal jurisdiction is set out on pp. 18 and 19.

Magistrates' courts

Although, as we shall see, the Crown Court tries the most serious criminal cases (all those in fact which are tried on indictment with a jury), the great bulk of the criminal work of the country is performed in the magistrates' courts.

Types of magistrates

Magistrates may be of several kinds as follows—

(a) *Lay magistrates*. These are appointed by the Lord Chancellor by instrument on behalf of, and in the name of, the Queen. (See s. 6(1), Justices of the Peace Act, 1979, as amended by s. 65 of the Administration of Justice Act, 1982.) The Lord Chancellor is advised by a local advisory committee.

(b) *Stipendiary magistrates*. These are full-time magistrates who sit in certain commission areas. The area to which an appointment is made is entirely a matter for the Lord Chancellor. They are appointed by the Queen on the recommendation of the Lord Chancellor and must be barristers or solicitors of at least seven years' standing. At the present time there are 13 stipendiary magistrates in the provinces, appointments having been made, e.g. in West Midlands, Greater Manchester, and Merseyside. Metropolitan stipendiary magistrates are the counterpart in

London of the stipendiary magistrates in the provinces and are appointed in the same way. Currently there are 48 such magistrates, not including the Chief Metropolitan Magistrate, working, for example, in courts such as Bow Street and Tower Bridge.

(c) *Ex-officio magistrates*. Persons can become magistrates by holding another office. For example, the Lord Mayor and aldermen of the City of London are ex-officio magistrates.

The clerk

Each bench of lay magistrates has a salaried clerk, who is usually employed whole time. He assists the magistrates on questions of procedure and law whenever the magistrates ask for his help, though he can, as in *R* v. *Uxbridge Justices, ex p. Smith* [1985] Crim. L. R. 670, offer advice on *law* unasked and may leave the court to give it to the magistrates after they have retired to consider their decision, though he cannot lawfully advise on the *decision*. The clerk is also responsible for the administration of the court.

Certain functions of the magistrates may be delegated to the clerk. For example, s. 28 of the Justices of the Peace Act, 1979, gives power to make rules delegating to the clerk the functions of a single justice. This includes issuing summonses and granting legal aid. The clerk is appointed by the Magistrates' Courts Committee for the relevant area from barristers or solicitors of not less than five years' standing though some clerks hold office by reason of a length of service qualification, i.e. having regularly acted as a court clerk for not less than five years prior to 1 January 1980.

The duty solicitor

Under s. 1 of the Legal Aid Act, 1982 the Law Society takes responsibility for introducing Duty Solicitor Schemes in all magistrates' courts. Local solicitors attend on a rota basis to advise defendants who have no solicitor of their own. The duty solicitor, who is entitled to be paid under the Legal Aid Scheme specifically for acting as such, can advise on the plea, i.e. guilty or not guilty. If the plea is not guilty he can apply for bail and ask for an adjournment to apply for legal aid and prepare a defence. If the plea is guilty he can put in a 'plea in mitigation' (see further p. 53) in the hope of influencing the magistrates to give a lighter sentence.

The role of the duty solicitor was made more important when s. 58 of the Police and Criminal Evidence Act, 1984 gave persons held in custody at a police station a right of access to legal advice. Since then duty solicitors have been available on a 24 hour basis to go to police stations to give advice paid for by legal aid.

Commission areas

The Commission areas for which magistrates sit are metropolitan districts, metropolitan counties, non-metropolitan counties, London

Commission Areas and the City of London. Of these, metropolitan districts and non-metropolitan counties may be divided into petty sessional areas or divisions.

Magistrates' courts committees

These are appointed for the various Commission areas. The functions of these committees are limited to making recommendations to the Home Secretary regarding proposed Petty Sessional Area or Divisional Boundary changes, the provision of courthouses, the appointment of justices' clerks and their staff, and the training of magistrates, which is compulsory, and their clerks' staff under the supervision of the Judicial Studies Board. This Board also supervises the training of judicial chairmen and members of tribunals. It also provides training on matters such as the reviewing of sentencing cases and the drug problem for assistant recorders, registrars of county courts and their deputies, and circuit judges, who also hear family and civil cases in the county court.

SYSTEM OF COURTS EXERCISING CIVIL JURISDICTION

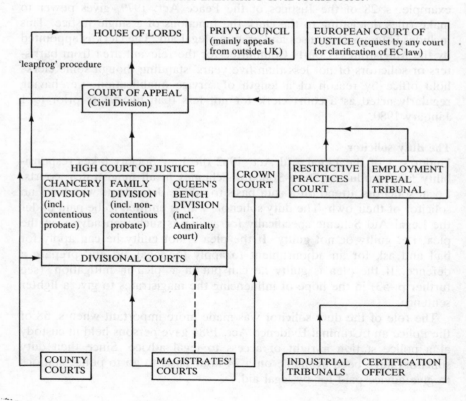

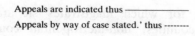

Appeals are indicated thus ─────────
Appeals by way of case stated.' thus ────────

SYSTEM OF COURTS EXERCISING CRIMINAL JURISDICTION

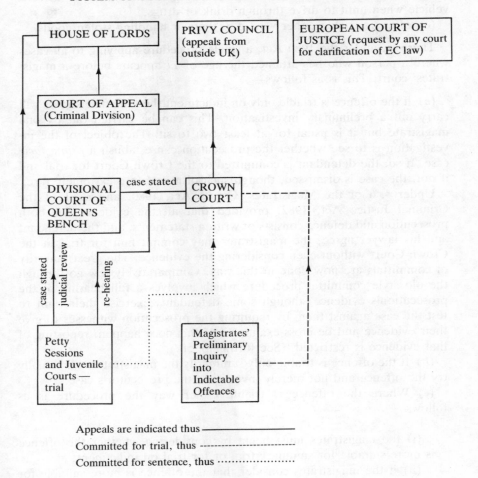

Appeals are indicated thus ——————

Committed for trial, thus - - - - - - - - - - - -

Committed for sentence, thus · · · · · · · · · · · · · · ·

The administration of a magistrates' court is a matter for the Clerk to the Justices and his magistrates.

Classification of criminal offences

Before discussing the powers of magistrates in regard to criminal prosecutions it is necessary to classify criminal offences for procedural purposes. Proceedings are regulated by the Magistrates' Courts Act, 1980. Criminal jurisdiction falls into three classes of offence listed in the Criminal Law Act, 1977 as—

 (a) offences triable only on indictment before a jury, e.g. murder and manslaughter;

 (b) offences triable only summarily by the magistrates, e.g. most road traffic offences, such as, for example, driving or attempting to drive a vehicle when unfit to drive through drink or drugs;

(*c*) offences triable either way, e.g. theft or handling stolen goods.

There is, under the 1980 Act, a single procedure applying to all cases where a person who has attained the age of 17 appears before a magistrates' court. This is as follows—

(*a*) if the offence is triable only on indictment then the magistrates will carry out a preliminary investigation. This can be carried out by one magistrate but it is usual for at least two to sit. The object of the investigation is to see whether the prosecution can establish a *prima facie* case. If so, the defendant is committed to the Crown Court for trial and if not, the case is dismissed, though such dismissals are extremely rare.

Under s. 6 of the Magistrates' Courts Act, 1980, and s. 61 of the Criminal Justice Act, 1982, provided that all the evidence for both prosecution and defence consists of written statements, and the defendant and his lawyer agree, the magistrates may commit him for trial in the Crown Court without even considering the evidence. The great majority of committals are now done in this way. Comparatively few go through the old style committal procedure which involves a full hearing of the prosecution's evidence, though some defendants exercise their right to test the case against them by requiring the prosecution witnesses to give their evidence and be cross-examined. If this does happen, reporting of that evidence is restricted. (See further p. 58.)

(*b*) If the offence is triable only summarily the magistrates will actually try the offence and not merely investigate the prosecutor's case.

(*c*) Where the offence is triable either way the procedure is as follows—

(i) the magistrates must begin by considering whether the offence is more suitable for summary trial or for trial on indictment;

(ii) if the magistrates consider that the offence is more suitable for summary trial the accused must be asked whether he consents to be tried summarily or wishes to be tried by a jury. If he consents to be tried summarily the court proceeds with summary trial; if he does not so consent the court proceeds as examining justices.

(iii) If the court considers that the offence is more suitable for trial on indictment the accused must be given an opportunity to make representation that he should be tried summarily and the court is then to decide whether to proceed to summary trial or as examining justices.

(iv) Where the magistrates have begun to try a case summarily and the offence in question is triable either way the court may at any time before the conclusion of the prosecution evidence change from summary trial to committal proceedings. Similarly, if the court has begun to inquire into the information as examining justices, it may, after representations by the prosecution or accused and having regard to all the circumstances of the case, change to summary trial.

However, once it has been decided that the matter is suitable for a summary trial and the defendant has elected for this and pleaded guilty, the magistrates cannot, according to the decision of the House of Lords in *Chief Constable of West Midlands Police* v. *Gilliard*, [1985] 3 All E.R. 634, subsequently commit the defendant for trial in the Crown Court but can only commit for sentence under s. 38 of the Magistrates' Courts Act, 1980.

As regards offences triable either way, SI 1985/601 introduces rules under s. 48 of the Criminal Law Act, 1977 requiring advance disclosure of the prosecution's case to defendants. This was not a requirement before the passing of the Statutory Instrument.

The rules apply *in either way cases only* and under the rules a prosecutor may withold information if he thinks that it could lead to the intimidation of a witness or to an interference with the course of justice.

The rules do not oblige the police to take statements from witnesses but merely to disclose any which they have. The purpose of the disclosure requirements is that advance knowledge of the case for the prosecution will often reveal its strength and lead to more guilty pleas. Some of the busiest courts have independently introduced various forms of pre-trial review which also lead to an increase in the number of guilty pleas when the strength of the case against the defendant is reviewed.

Sentencing
The maximum penalty which the magistrates may impose for any offence is in most cases six months' imprisonment. The maximum fine for any one offence may now be as much as £2000. In addition the magistrates can make compensation orders requiring a defendant to compensate the victim of his crime, up to a maximum figure of £2000 per offence. There are also restitution orders under which the defendant can be required to return stolen property and, in addition, the magistrates may make supervision orders which operate to some extent like probation, and community service orders under which the defendant may be required to carry out some useful service within the community. In addition, it should be noted that if the magistrates are trying an indictable offence summarily and feel that the circumstances are such that the defendant should be given a greater sentence than can be given in a Magistrates' Court, they may commit the defendant to the Crown Court for sentence under s. 38, of the Magistrates' Court Act, 1980.

Bail and remand
In addition to committals, trials and sentencing, magistrates also make vital decisions on whether to grant bail to the defendant or remand him to prison to await his trial.

Civil jurisdiction
The magistrates also have a civil jurisdiction which includes the making of affiliation orders, confirming the paternity of the father of an illegiti-

mate child and requiring him to pay maintenance, and domestic proceedings, under which applications for matrimonial relief such as separation and maintenance orders may be made, by women who do not initially on breakdown of marriage opt for divorce. They can also deal with questions concerning the custody and adoption of children and matters relating to licensing of pubs, restaurants, betting shops and casinos and the enforcement of rates, and may consent to the marriage of a minor of 16 or 17 years of age who is not a widow or widower.

There is also power to order a violent spouse to leave the home in order to protect the other spouse and children (if any). Where a foreign state wants an alleged criminal living in England to be returned, the request for extradition is heard under the provisions of the Criminal Justice Act, 1988 by a Metropolitan stippendiary magistrate.

Appeals

Appeals from the magistrates in domestic proceedings are to the Divisional Court of the Family Division. As regards criminal offences, appeal may be to the Crown Court or to the Divisional Court of Queen's Bench as follows—

(a) *Crown Court*. An appeal to the Crown Court may be made by the accused only, provided he did not plead guilty. The appeal may be against conviction or sentence on law or fact and no permission is required. If he pleaded guilty he may appeal against sentence only. An appeal against conviction takes the form of rehearing in the Crown Court and although the Crown Court may give greater punishment than the magistrates in fact gave, it is limited to a prison sentence of not more than six months or a fine of not more than £2000. When the Crown Court is reviewing sentence it must hear the antecedents of the person making the appeal and consider all the relevant reports on him together with affording him an opportunity to address the court in mitigation.

(b) *Divisional Court of Queen's Bench*. An appeal to the Divisional Court of Queens's Bench may be made by either the accused or the prosecution by means of *case stated*. This means that the magistrates must set out in writing the reasons for their decision. The appeal questions the decision of the magistrates on the ground that it is wrong in *law*. Issues of *fact* should not be appealed against by way of case stated (*James* v. *Chief Constable of Kent, The Times*, 7 June, 1986). It is available to a person who has pleaded guilty. If the Divisional Court or the House of Lords gives leave, there may be a further appeal to the House of Lords but the Divisional Court must certify that the case raises a matter of law of public importance.

(c) *Judicial Review*. Whenever a court, including, obviously, a magistrates' court, acts without jurisdiction, or fails to observe the rules of natural justice, or makes an important procedural error, any person aggrieved, and obviously a defendant, may apply to the High Court to review the decision of the magistrates and issue an order of *certiorari*.

(See further p. 97.) These types of defects in a magistrates' court must be challenged by judicial review and not by case stated. (*R.* v. *Wandsworth Justices, ex parte Read*, [1942] 1 All E.R. 56.)

If a decision of the magistrates is quashed because of their error in arriving at it, they may be sued for damages by a person wrongfully imprisoned because of it. However, s. 53 of the Justices of the Peace Act, 1967 provides for their indemnification out of local funds (*R.* v. *Manchester City Justices ex p. Davies, The Independent*, 17 November, 1987).

(*d*) *The European Court*. The magistrates may refer matters to the European Court. Thus in *R.* v. *Marlborough Street Stipendiary Magistrate, ex parte Bouchereau*, [1977] 3 All E.R. 365, the magistrate indicated that he proposed making a recommendation for the deportation of B, whereupon it was contended that the magistrate had no such power since B was a migrant worker protected by Article 48 of the Treaty of Rome. The magistrate decided to refer the matter to the European Court under Article 177 of the Treaty and this was held to be in order by a Divisional Court which decided also that legal aid legislation allows a magistrates' court to order legal aid for the purposes of proceedings before the European Court of Justice.

(*e*) *Rectification of mistakes by the magistrates themselves*. Section 142 of the Magistrates' Courts Act, 1980 provides an alternative to appeal to the Crown Court or Divisional Court. The section gives magistrates the power to re-open a case to rectify their mistake but only if the defendant has been found guilty; not if he has been acquitted. The power may be used, e.g. to deal with a sentence passed in excess of the court's powers and also where the defendant asks for a review of his sentence on the grounds that it is too harsh. The prosecution or the defence may institute a review and it would seem that the magistrates may do so of their own volition.

The juvenile court

The magistrates also have a part to play in regard to children over ten but under 14 and young persons who are over 14 but have not attained the age of 17. Criminal proceedings cannot be brought against a person under the age of ten. For this purpose the magistrates sit as a juvenile court. This court must sit in a different building or room from that in which other courts are held or else must sit on a different day. The court consists of three magistrates who are drawn from a special panel of persons under 65 years of age and it is usual for one or more female magistrates to be present. The public is excluded from these courts. Juvenile courts have a range of sentences at their disposal including custodial measures. (See further p. 56).

The county court

The magistrates' courts deal with most of the less serious criminal matters in this country. At something like the same level, but dealing exclusively with civil cases, is the county court. County courts were created by the County Courts Act, 1846, to operate as the chief lower courts for the trial of civil disputes, and a large number of cases are heard in these courts annually. They are now governed by the County Courts Act, 1984. Section references are to that Act unless otherwise stated.

A county court is presided over by a circuit judge appointed by the Crown on the advice of the Lord Chancellor. (S. 5 and see p. 29.) The judge usually sits alone, though, under ss. 66 and 67, there is provision for a trial by a jury of eight persons in some cases, e.g. where fraud, libel, slander, malicious prosecution, or false imprisonment is alleged. Under s. 77 appeal lies direct to the Court of Appeal (Civil Division). The judge is assisted by a Registrar who is appointed by the Lord Chancellor from solicitors of at least seven years' standing. (Ss. 6 and 9.) The Registrar acts as Clerk of the Court, and may try certain cases where the amount involved does not exceed £500 and no objection is raised by any of the parties. If the parties agree, his jurisdiction extends to any action or matter within the general jurisdiction of the court. Under ss. 7 and 9 the Lord Chancellor may, with the agreement of the Treasury as to numbers and salaries, appoint in connection with any court such Assistant Registrars as he considers necessary for carrying out the work of the court. The appointment is from solicitors of at least seven years' standing and the Assistant Registrar is capable of discharging any of the functions of the Registrar. Under ss. 8 and 9 the Lord Chancellor may also appoint a solicitor of at least seven years' standing to be a Deputy Registrar as a temporary measure to dispose of business in the County Court. The Deputy Registrar has the same powers as the Registrar.

Jurisdiction
Regarding the jurisdiction of the court, there are limitations as to place, and as to the nature and amount of the claim. The general rule is that the plaintiff must bring his action in the court of the district where the defendant dwells or carries on business, or that for the district in which the cause of action wholly or mainly arose. Where land is involved, the action is generally brought in the court of the district in which the land is situated. Under s. 22 the county court has the same jurisdiction as the High Court to grant an injunction or a declaratory judgment setting out the rights of the parties, in respect of, or relating to, any land or the possession, occupation, use or enjoyment of any land. This jurisdiction applies only where the net annual value for rating of the relevant land does not exceed the county court limit on jurisdiction (currently £1000).

Apart from this, a county court has power to grant an injunction under s. 38 if it is ancillary to some other claim, e.g. for damages, which is properly before the court in its specific jurisdiction. Thus an employer who is suing his employee for damages for breach of a covenant in restraint of trade (see further p. 277) may be granted an interlocutory injunction pending trial to prevent breach of the contract. (*Hatt & Co. v. Pearce* [1978] 2 All E.R. 474.)

The general jurisdiction of county courts and the procedure therein are governed by the County Courts Act, 1984, and the County Court Rules. The latter are in the form of delegated legislation and are set out in an annual volume known as the County Court Practice. In general terms, the extent of the jurisdiction is as follows—

(i) *Actions founded on contract and tort* with a limit of £5000 unless the parties agree to waive the limit. For certain torts (i.e. libel and slander) the court has no jurisdiction unless both parties agree.

(ii) *Equity matters*, e.g. mortgages and trusts where the amount involved does not exceed £30,000, unless the parties agree to waive the limit. Under this heading would be found requests for repossession orders by building societies against mortgage defaulters.

(iii) *Actions concerning title to land, and actions for recovery of possession of land*, where the rateable value of the land does not exceed £1000. There is unlimited jurisdiction in cases within the Rent Acts or by agreement between the parties.

(iv) *Bankruptcies*. Here there is unlimited jurisdiction, but not all county courts have bankruptcy jurisdiction. The Lord Chancellor is empowered by s. 374 of the Insolvency Act, 1986 to exclude any county court from having such jurisdiction. Bankruptcy cases in the London insolvency district are heard in the Bankruptcy Court of the High Court. Appeal from the county court in bankruptcy matters is to the Divisional Court of the Chancery Division.

(v) *Company winding up*, where the paid-up share capital of the company does not exceed £120,000, if the court has a bankruptcy jurisdiction (s. 117 Insolvency Act, 1986).

(vi) *Probate proceedings*, where the value of the deceased's estate is estimated to be £30,000 or less.

(vii) *Admiralty matters*. Some county courts in coastal areas have Admiralty jurisdiction which is limited to £5000 except in salvage cases where the limit is £15,000. The parties may by agreement waive these limits.

(viii) *Matrimonial causes*. The jurisdiction of county courts in matrimonial causes is derived from s. 33 of the Matrimonial and Family Proceedings Act, 1984.

A county court designated by the Lord Chancellor as a 'divorce county court' has jurisdiction in certain matters relating to any undefended matrimonial cause, but may *try* such a cause only if further designated as a court of trial. Every matrimonial cause must be commenced in a divorce county court and is to be heard and determined there, unless transferred to the High Court e.g. under s. 39 of the 1984 Act, i.e. on the application of a party or on the court's own motion.

Divorce county courts may make orders for ancillary relief and the protection of children and may deal with wilful neglect to maintain and the variation of maintenance agreements (s. 34 of the 1984 Act). They may also hear applications made before presentation of the petition which relate to arrangements made between parties (s. 35 of the 1984 Act). The Lord Chancellor may assign particular circuit judges to matrimonial proceedings (s. 36 of the 1984 Act).

The Government has prepared a Consultation Paper advocating changes under which the family jurisdiction of the various courts would be merged into a new court which might be called the Family Court. (See further p. 31.)

(ix) *Arbitration.* In order to strengthen the county court as a tribunal for the determination of small claims, county court rules, which will in future be made under s. 64 of the County Courts Act, 1984, prescribe that where a claim does not exceed £500 the Registrar *shall* upon receipt of the defence, refer the case for arbitration. In such cases therefore the Registrar will *automatically* refer the case to arbitration. *In other cases an order of the judge is necessary.*

Usually the arbitrator will be the Registrar, but in cases involving larger sums of money, where the parties have agreed to arbitrate, the judge may act as arbitrator. However, if both parties agree, someone else other than the judge or Registrar may be appointed. The Registrar may, on the application of any party *rescind* the reference to arbitration if he is satisfied (*a*) that a difficult question of law or a question of fact of exceptional complexity is involved; or (*b*) that a charge of fraud is in issue; or (*c*) that the parties are agreed that the dispute shall be tried in court; or (*d*) that it would be unreasonable for the claim to proceed to arbitration having regard to its subject matter, the circumstances of the parties, or the interests of any other person likely to be affected by the award. (See *Pepper* v. *Healey*, 1982.)[6] There is an appeal to the judge on the issue of rescinding the arbitration and from him to the Court of Appeal (see *Pepper* v. *Healey*, 1982)[6] and to the House of Lords with leave. The arbitration arrangements are not confined to any particular class of case but are likely to be especially appropriate in consumer disputes.

A major advantage of arbitration is that the proceedings are heard in private and the Registrar or judge is unrobed. Thus no litigant present in person need feel deterred by having to appear in public in strange surroundings when he brings or defends an action. The precise terms on which the arbitration is to take place are settled by the court according to the circumstances of the individual case. In general the strict rules of evidence are dispensed with so that, for example, hearsay, may be admitted; and, if the parties agree, the arbitrator can be authorized to decide the case on the basis of statements and documents submitted by the parties. However, when one of the parties is legally represented the lawyer concerned is allowed to cross-examine the unrepresented party. It is then the duty of the arbitrator, without taking sides, to make sure that the unrepresented party puts his points properly to the other side (*Chilton* v. *Saga Holidays plc*, [1986] 1 All E.R. 841).

Either party may ask for arbitration and in certain circumstances, as we have seen, it is automatic. The plaintiff can include in his particulars of claim a request for arbitration if the defendant contests the case and the form supplied to the defendant with the summons enables him to say, if he does not admit the claim, whether he wishes the case to be arbitrated. It is also open to a party to ask for arbitration at a later stage, e.g. at a pre-trial review (see below).

The award of the arbitrator is entered as the judgment in the proceedings. A party may appeal from the Registrar or other arbitrator, to the county court judge to set aside the award.

County court rules also extend the power to refer questions to experts for enquiry and report. The Registrar can order this in cases of up to £500 or with the consent of the parties. Consumer cases often depend on an expert opinion about a piece of equipment alleged to be faulty. To enable such reports to be more easily obtained the Government has invited the co-operation of competent bodies such as trade associations and the Weights and Measures Inspectorate with a view of ensuring that the services of suitable experts are available at a reasonable fee.

When a case is referred to arbitration the court will indicate how the costs are to be dealt with but in general terms they will be left to the discretion of the arbitrator. However, where a claim does not exceed £500 no lawyers' fees are normally recoverable. Thus the plaintiff does not face the prospect of paying his own and the defendant's lawyer's fees, if he loses. However, if the plaintiff wins he cannot, in general, get the other side to pay his lawyer's fees. The 'no costs' rule for legal representation is not always an advantage. (See *Newland* v. *Boardwell*, 1983.)[7] However, if the court considers that costs have been incurred through the unreasonable conduct of the opposite party, it may order them to be paid to a successful litigant. In addition, a party who loses will usually be required to pay the winner's out-of-pocket expenses, e.g. expert or other witness fees, and loss of wages. This could be a sum in excess of £100.

These provisions in county court rules do not exclude legal representation where the claim does not exceed £500, either in ordinary county court proceedings or in cases referred to arbitration. However, in such cases the employment of solicitors and barristers is likely to be discouraged unless there is a special reason for it. In arbitration proceedings a litigant in person will usually be allowed to take a friend or relative along with him to help him present his case. The action in a small claim can be commenced by using special and simple forms and not by writ.

(x) *Pre-trial review*. It should also be noted that a *pre-trial review* by the Registrar is now a regular feature of ordinary actions in the county court and also in default actions, i.e. cases in which a fixed sum of money, such as a debt, is claimed. A major advantage of the pre-trial review is that the parties may compromise the claim and settle, thus saving time and money involved in going to trial. However, if there is no compromise then at the conclusion of the review the date of trial is fixed or the action is adjourned for the hearing to be fixed at a later date. If the defendant does not attend the review the plaintiff may be given a judgment if adequate documentary evidence is presented by him.

(xi) *Miscellaneous matters*. The county court derives an important part of its jurisdiction from social legislation, e.g. adoption of children, guardianship of infants, legitimacy, race relations, and the enforcement of legislation concerning landlord and tenant.

Although in many matters the county court has concurrent jurisdiction with the High Court, there are certain matters over which the county courts have *exclusive* jurisdiction so that actions concerning them cannot be commenced in the High Court, e.g. regulated consumer credit agreements or hire agreements where the fixed sum credit does not exceed £15,000 or, in a running account, the credit limit does not exceed £15,000, though the court's jurisdiction in proceedings relating to extortionate credit agreements under s. 139 of the Consumer Credit Act, 1974, is limited to £5000. Furthermore, where the lender on mortgage is seeking to take possession of land and the mortgage includes a dwelling house and no part of the land is in Greater London, the county court has exclusive jurisdiction provided the rateable value does not exceed £1000. (S. 21, County Courts Act, 1984.) In addition, the Attachment of Earnings Act, 1971, s. 1 gives the county court alone the power to order attachment of earnings for ordinary civil debt.

A *plaintiff* may ask for an action to be transferred to the High Court. Thus in contract and tort an order transferring the action will be made if the plaintiff can establish that there are reasonable grounds for believing that the damages will exceed £5000 if the action is transferred to the High Court. (*Stiffel* v. *Industrial Dwellings Society Ltd*, [1973] 2 All E.R. 1131.)

Provision is also made for actions to be *transferred* to the High Court if the *defendant* objects to the case being tried in the county court, provided, e.g. that the judge certifies that in his opinion some important question of law or fact is likely to arise, and the defendant gives security for the amount claimed and the costs of the trial in the High Court. Thus in *Bethall* v. *Sabena*, [1983] 3 C.M.L.R. 1, the judge at Wandsworth County Court transferred a claim for £50 to the High Court at the request of the defendants. The action was for alleged overcharging of fares and was part of a campaign to reduce European air fares by Lord Bethall which would involve important issues of fact and law.

Similarly if an action *is begun* in the High Court for a sum of not more than £5000 the defendant may apply to have the case transferred to a county court and it will be transferred if the judge or master who hears the application thinks fit. If in an action brought in the High Court a sum of less than £600 is recovered, the plaintiff will not be entitled to costs. If he recovers £600 or more, but less than £3000, he will only be awarded costs on the county court scale unless it appears to the judge or master that there was reasonable ground for supposing that he would recover more than he could have claimed in the county court or if they are satisfied that there was sufficient reason for bringing the action in the High Court or, of course, if the defendant objected to the case being transferred to a county court. If he recovers £3000 or more High Court costs are awarded.

Appeal

Appeal from a decision of a county court judge lies direct to the Court of Appeal (Civil Division). (S. 77, County Courts Act, 1984.)

The Crown Court

The Crown Court is a superior court of record created by the Courts Act, 1971. The Crown Court system replaced Courts of Assize and Quarter Sessions. It deals in the main with criminal work, though appeals from magistrates' courts in matters of affiliation, betting, gaming, and licensing now lie to the Crown Court.

Constitution

The jurisdiction and powers of the the Crown Court are exercised by the following—

(a) *High Court judges*. Certain cases are not appropriate for trial in a Crown Court by a circuit judge or recorder but are reserved for trial in that court by a High Court judge. All offences have been divided for the purpose of trial into four classes and, for example, Class 1 offences must be tried by a High Court judge. These include murder and treason. On the other hand, offences such as wounding or causing grievous bodily harm would normally be tried by a circuit judge or recorder.

(b) *Circuit judge*. Circuit judges are appointed by the Queen on the recommendation of the Lord Chancellor from barristers of at least ten years' standing, or from recorders who have been in post for at least three years. Unlike High Court judges who are *invited* to take appointment, those wishing to become circuit judges *apply* to the Lord Chancellor.

(c) *Recorder*. This is a part-time appointment made by the Queen on the recommendation of the Lord Chancellor from barristers or solicitors of at least ten years' standing. Since a solicitor may be appointed as a recorder, he may after three years in post become a circuit judge, and a number of appointments of solicitors to the position of circuit judge have been made. Again, those who wish to become Recorders apply to the Lord Chancellor.

(d) *Magistrates*. When the Crown Court is hearing an appeal or a committal for sentence from the Magistrates' Court between two and four justices sit with the judge or recorder. Where a judge of the High Court, Circuit Judge, or Recorder, sits with Justices of the Peace, he presides and—

(i) the decision of the Crown Court may be a majority decision; and

(ii) if the members of the court are equally divided, the judge of the High Court, circuit judge, or recorder shall have a casting vote. (S. 73(3), Supreme Court Act, 1981.)

Jurisdiction

All indictable offences are triable in the Crown Court. The Court also hears appeals from magistrates and committals for sentence from the magistrates. It also hears appeals from juvenile courts and for this purpose forms a juvenile appeals court. This consists of a circuit judge plus two magistrates drawn from the juvenile court panel.

Central Criminal Court

Before leaving the subject of the Crown Court special mention should be made of the Central Criminal Court, otherwise referred to as the 'Old Bailey'. This court continues as a Crown Court sitting in the City of London, though its constitution is slightly different in that the Lord Mayor and any alderman of the City may sit with any judge of the High Court or any circuit judge or recorder.

The High Court

Under s. 4(1)(e) of the Supreme Court Act, 1981, the High Court is staffed by a maximum of 85 judges (when all posts are filled) known as *puisne* judges (pronounced 'puny'). The *puisne* judges of the High Court are styled 'Justices of the High Court'. The number of *puisne* judges may be increased by Order in Council. Appointment is by the Queen on the advice of the Lord Chancellor and the qualification is being a barrister of at least ten years' standing. (S. 10(3)(c), *ibid.*)

The Queen's Bench Division has the largest staff, of some 50 *puisne* judges. The Court is presided over by the Lord Chief Justice. As regards jurisdiction, every type of common law civil action, e.g. contract and tort, can be heard by the Queen's Bench Division at the Royal Courts of Justice in the Strand. In addition, the judges of this division staff the Crown Court and sit in the Court of Appeal (Criminal Division) as well as the Divisional Court of Queen's Bench and the Central Criminal Court. Admiralty business is now assigned to a separate court called the Admiralty Court within the Queen's Bench Division. The same is true of commercial business which is heard by a separate court called the Commercial Court within the Queen's Bench Division. The Commercial Court also provides an arbitration service. (See p. 32.)

The Chancery Division currently has 12 *puisne* judges and is presided over by the Lord Chancellor. However, he is nominal head only and does not try cases. A Vice-Chancellor is now appointed to perform organizational and administrative functions as deputy to the Lord Chancellor. The Vice-Chancellor also hears cases. Under s. 10(3)(a) of the Supreme Court Act, 1981, the appointment is by the Queen from persons qualified to be a Lord Justice of Appeal. Company business is assigned to a separate court called the Companies Court within the Chancery Division. Apart from company work the Chancery Division deals with partnership matters, mortgages, trusts, revenue matters, rectification of deeds and documents, the administration of estates of deceased persons and contentious probate. The bulk of the bankruptcy work of the Chancery Division is performed by Registrars in Bankruptcy who deal with cases arising in the London insolvency district, provincial bankruptcies being dealt with by the local county court. The Patents Court forms part of this Division.

The Family Division has 16 *puisne* judges and is presided over by the President of the Division. The Court deals with all business which concerns marriage, family property and children, including adoption and wardship.

Reform

The Report of the Committee on One-Parent Families (the Finer Report), Cmnd 5629, in 1974 contained a proposal that there should be a comprehensive Family Court to bring the jurisdiction of the various matrimonial courts together. The Lord Chancellor then issued a Consultation Paper on the family jurisdiction of the various courts. The outcome may be the setting up of a new Family Court for family cases on the lines of the Crown Court for criminal cases. This is the most radical option in the Consultative Paper which is called the Interdepartmental Review of Family and Domestic Jurisdictions May 1986.

An interesting comment on the jurisdiction of the divisions of the High Court was made by the Court of Appeal in *Barclays Bank plc* v. *Bemister, The Times*, 15 December, 1987. It might be time, the Court said, to unify the High Court. This would be most useful as between Queen's Bench and Chancery especially where one court (often Queen's Bench) is overloaded. Delays could be avoided by assigning cases traditionally brought in Queen's Bench to Chancery and vice versa if necessary.

Divisional courts

Each of the three divisions of the High Court has divisional courts. These are constituted by not less than two judges.

(*a*) *Divisional Court of Queen's Bench.* This hears appeals on points of law on cases stated by magistrates and the Crown Court. It also has a supervisory jurisdiction under which it exercises the power of the High Court to discipline inferior courts and to put right their mistakes by means of judicial review through the orders of *mandamus, certiorari*, and *prohibition*. It can also deal with the writ of *habeas corpus* and *election petitions*.

(*b*) *Divisional Court of the Chancery Division.* This court hears appeals in bankruptcy cases from county courts outside London, the Bankruptcy Court of the Chancery Division hearing bankruptcy appeals from London.

(*c*) *The Divisional Court of the Family Division.* This court hears appeals from magistrates' courts in matrimonial cases.

The Commercial Court

Since 1964 the High Court has operated a Commercial Court. Section 6 of the Supreme Court Act, 1981 now constitutes, as part of the Queen's Bench Division, a Commercial Court for the trial of causes of a commercial nature, e.g. insurance matters. The judges of the Commercial Court are such High Court Judges as the Lord Chancellor may from time to time nominate to be Commercial Judges. They are, in practice, drawn from those who have spent their working lives in the commercial field.

They combine the general work of a Queen's Bench Judge with priority for commercial cases. The Act merely continues formal independence to the Commercial Court. Commercial litigation has since 1895 been dealt with in the Queen's Bench Division on a simplified procedure and before a specialist judge, the intention being to overcome the reluctance of commercial men, who prefer the privacy of arbitration, to resort to the machinery of the courts.

Two specific steps were proposed in the Administration of Justice Bill, 1970 to attract such customers: first a power was to be taken to allow the court to sit in private and to receive evidence which would not normally be admissible in an ordinary court, and secondly High Court judges were to be allowed to sit as arbitrators. The first of these proposals was rejected by the House of Commons at the Report Stage but the second was passed into law and s. 4 of the Administration of Justice Act, 1970 enables a judge of the Commercial Court to take arbitrations. Before doing so he must obtain clearance from the Lord Chief Justice that the pressure of work in the High Court and Crown Court will enable him to be made available for this purpose, but in practice this is unlikely to cause difficulty.

Thus, although in theory the Court has no wider power than other courts, of the Queen's Bench Division, there is, in practice, a general discretion for departures in procedure and admission of evidence where the parties consent or where the interests of justice demand it or where it is necessary to expedite business. The power to hold hearings in private is restricted but s. 12 of the Administration of Justice Act, 1960, gives a power which could be used if, for example, trade secrets were involved. Commercial cases may be tried by a judge alone, or by a judge and a jury. It was once a special jury in that it consisted of persons who had knowledge of commercial matters. An ordinary jury is now used since s. 40 of the Courts Act, 1971, abolished special juries. All actions in the Commercial Court are tried in the City of London. The work of the Commercial Court now probably consists of a greater number of cases which arise in some way out of arbitrations than cases which are taken direct to the Court.

The Arbitration Act of 1979 introduced radical reforms in the area of judicial review of arbitration awards. Section 21 of the Arbitration Act 1950 (now repealed) allowed a party to an arbitration in which a question of law arose, to request the arbitrator to state a special case for the decision of the court, or, if the arbitrator refused, the court could make an order that he should do this. This special case procedure has been abolished by s. 1(1) of the Arbitration Act, 1979.

The 1979 Act further provides that the court cannot set aside an award on the ground of error of fact or of law on the face of the award itself. However, the Act provides that if the award does not set out the reasons for its making, the court may order the arbitrator to give reasons in detail adequate to enable the court to decide whether it should allow the appeal to the court on a point of law. (S. 1(5), 1979 Act.) If the court is of the opinion that the rights of the parties will be substantially affected without an appeal, then the court may allow the appeal. (S. 1(4), 1979 Act.)

Nevertheless, the above procedure for judicial review may be excluded by the parties in an exclusion agreement in writing. (S. 3(1), 1979 Act.) However, in arbitrations over disputes arising in England and Wales this cannot be done until after the arbitration has commenced (s. 3(1), 1979 Act), though the parties can include what is known as a *Scott* v. *Avery* clause, from the case of that name which is referenced (1856) 25 L.J. Ex. 308, to provide that no action shall be brought in court until after the award is made.

Where a judge of the Commercial Court is acting as an arbitrator he sits in private and in any place convenient to the parties. There is no requirement for such arbitrations to take place in the Law Courts. The conduct of the hearing should be as informal as any other arbitration. In addition, the award is made privately to the parties and not published like a judgment.

The Companies' Court

This is really a court of the Chancery Division where company matters are tried before a single judge whose special concern is with company work. The work of the court is divided into company liquidation proceedings, and other company matters.

The Bankruptcy Court

The bulk of the bankruptcy work of the Chancery Division is performed by Registrars in Bankruptcy who deal with cases arising in the London insolvency district, provincial bankruptcies being dealt with by those county courts with bankruptcy jurisdiction.

The Court of Protection

This court is concerned to protect and administer the property and effects of those who are by reason of mental disorder not able to manage these matters for themselves.

Part VII of the Mental Health Act, 1983 deals with Court of Protection matters. The judges of the Chancery Division are nominated under

s. 93(1) to act. There is also a Master and Assistant Masters nominated under s. 93(4).

The usual remedy is to appoint a receiver to look after the patient's property and affairs. It is usual for a near relative, e.g. a spouse, to apply and be appointed.

The Restrictive Practices Court

This superior court of record was set up by the Restrictive Trade Practices Act, 1956. Following a consolidation of restrictive trade practices legislation the registration and judicial investigation of restrictive trading agreements is now covered by the Restrictive Practices Court Act, 1976, the Restrictive Trade Practices Act, 1976 and the Resale Prices Act, 1976. These Acts, which are further discussed in the chapter on the law of contract (see p. 285), are designed to prevent manufacturers entering into agreements which restrict free competition and tend to fix prices in regard to *goods*. The court investigates agreements which may be of this nature to see whether they are contrary to the public interest.

The court has power to enforce its rulings by injuction, but in practice business men do not try to implement an agreement which the court has not sanctioned. The court also deals with the question of resale price maintenance agreements under the Resale Prices Act, 1976 (see p. 286) and acquired an additional jurisdiction under the Fair Trading Act, 1973 (see now Restrictive Trade Practices Act, 1976) to consider restrictive agreements in regard to *services* (see p. 285). In addition, as we are a member of the EEC, the competition rules laid down in the Treaty of Rome have been since the 1st January 1973 part of our own law. Two Articles of the Treaty of Rome provide for common rules of competition (Articles 85 and 86) and the court may be required to consider these from time to time. Under s. 5 of the Restrictive Trade Practices Act, 1976 the Restrictive Practices Court may postpone or defer taking decisions under the provisions of the Restrictive Trade Practices Act, 1976, where this would conflict with Community law.

The court consists of the following judges—one of whom is appointed by the Lord Chancellor to be President of the Court; three *puisne* judges of the High Court nominated by the Lord Chancellor; one judge of the Court of Session of Scotland nominated by the President of that Court; one judge of the Supreme Court of Northern Ireland nominated by the Lord Chief Justice of Northern Ireland. The judges are assisted by up to ten laymen appointed by the Queen on the recommendation of the Lord Chancellor, as being persons with knowledge of, or experience in, industry, commerce or public affairs. The court may sit in divisions, each division being constituted by one judge and two laymen. The judges decide matters of law but matters of fact are decided by a majority of the members of the court. Where the proceedings involve only issues of law the court may consist of a single member, that member being a judge.

The Court of Appeal

The Court of Appeal consists of two divisions—

(*a*) *the Civil Division* which exercises the jurisdiction formerly exercised by the former Court of Appeal, and

(*b*) the *Criminal Division* which exercises the jurisdiction formerly exercised by the Court of Criminal Appeal.

Civil Division

The work of the Civil Division is carried out by a maximum of 28 Lords Justices of Appeal. This number can be increased by Statutory Instrument. The Court is presided over by the Master of the Rolls, who is appointed by the Prime Minister who is in turn advised by the Lord Chancellor. A normal court consists of three judges but there may on occasion be a full court of five or seven. The qualification for a Lord Justice of Appeal is 15 years' standing as a barrister or having been a *puisne* judge. (S. 10(3)(b), Supreme Court Act, 1981.) They are appointed by the Queen on the advice of the Prime Minister and the Master of the Rolls. It should be noted that also included in the judiciary in the Civil Division are the Lord Chancellor, ex-Lord Chancellors, Law Lords, the Lord Chief Justice, and the President of the Family Division. The Lord Chancellor may also request judges of the High Court to sit. However, under s. 56 of the Supreme Court Act, 1981 a judge may not sit on an appeal to the Court of Appeal if he sat at the hearing of the case in the lower court. This applies to both civil and criminal cases.

As regards jurisdiction, the Civil Division hears appeals from any division of the High Court and from the County Court and from orders of Judges in Chambers or Masters in Chambers regarding pre-trial matters. The court may on appeal uphold or reverse the lower court or substitute a new judgment. Exceptionally, it may order a new trial as where evidence has been improperly admitted or rejected.

The Supreme Court Act, 1981 made changes in the organization of the business of the Court of Appeal, Civil Division. The object was to speed up the rate at which appeals are heard and prevent a long backlog.

First, it created the office of Registrar of Civil Appeals. (S. 88 and Sch. 2.) The Registrar relieves the judges of the need to deal with some judicial matters, e.g. applications for leave to serve notice of appeal out of time. He also deals with administrative matters, e.g. he ensures that the parties to an appeal and their advisers have given the court all the necessary documents so that there will be no confusion or delay when the appeal comes on for hearing. (See s. 58.)

Secondly, it allows appeals in cases prescribed by the Lord Chancellor with the agreement of the Master of the Rolls to be heard by a two-judge court. If they do not agree the case must be re-argued before a court of at least three judges. (S. 54.) While fullest use of the two-judge court will be made, it will sometimes be in the public interest that three judges should sit, as where the issus are complex. In such cases counsel should apply to the registrar for the hearing to take place before a court of three (*Coldunell Ltd.* v. *Gallon, The Times*, 21 November, 1985).

Finally, county court legislation has been amended and under s. 77(2) of the County Courts Act, 1984 the Lord Chancellor may, by order, prescribe classes of proceedings in the county court, e.g. according to the amount of the claim, in which there is no right of appeal without leave of the judge of the county court or of the Court of Appeal.

Criminal Division

The work of the Criminal Division is carried out by the Lord Chief Justice and the same 28 Lords Justices of Appeal, as a maximum, who also sit in the Civil Division. It should also be noted that the Lord Chief Justice may ask any judge of the High Court to sit in the Criminal Division. The normal court consist of three judges but sometimes a full court of five or seven will sit if the case is a difficult one. Under s. 55 of the Supreme Court Act, 1981 a court of two may sit to deal with appeals against sentence. A single judge may carry out some functions, e.g. grant leave to appeal. (See s. 31, Criminal Appeal Act, 1968.) The success rate in terms of the ordinary prisoner seeking leave to appeal against *conviction* is negligible, though thousands of appeals against *sentence* are heard annually.

As regards jurisdiction, the Criminal Division hears appeals from the Crown Court against conviction and sentence and may dismiss or allow the appeal. In addition the Home Secretary may refer a case to the Criminal Division so that, for example, a sentence might be reviewed where the accused was under a disability (Criminal Appeal Act, 1968, s. 17). Furthermore, the Attorney-General may refer for an opinion on a point of law arising from a charge which resulted in an acquittal (s. 36(1) Criminal Justice Act, 1972). An example is to be found in *Attorney-General's Reference* (*No. 2 of 1982*), [1984] 2 W.L.R. 447, where two directors, A and B, were alleged to have committed theft of the company's property leaving it without funds to pay its creditors. They were also the only shareholders. Since theft requires a taking from some other person without that person's consent, the trial judge held that the offence of theft had not been committed and A and B were acquitted. On the reference of the Attorney-General the Court of Appeal held that since a company was a separate person at law (see further p. 171), A and B could steal from it. Furthermore, although the consent of the directors would often be imputed to the company, it was irrational to do so here when A and B were alleged to be acting dishonestly in relation to the company. The Court of Appeal was of the opinion that A and B could be legally charged with theft.

In the past the Court of Appeal has not been able to increase a sentence. The Criminal Justice Act, 1988 allows the Attorney-General to refer a case for increased sentence if it appears that the judge in the Crown Court has been too lenient.

The court may order a new trial under s. 7 of the Criminal Appeal Act, 1968 as amended by the Criminal Justice Act, 1988. However, this power can only be used in cases where there is fresh and credible evidence and the court considers that it is in the interests of justice to receive it even though it was available and admissible at the trial.

There is also a power to order a new trial at common law where there has been a fundamental defect in the trial so that it was a nullity. Thus, in *R*. v. *Ishmael*, [1970] Crim. L.R. 399, the accused had been sentenced to life imprisonment having pleaded guilty at his trial to an offence under s. 3 of the Malicious Damage Act, 1861 (arson of buildings, punishable by life imprisonment) thinking he was charged with an offence under s. 7 of the 1861 Act (arson of goods, punishable by 14 years' imprisonment). The Court of Appeal held that he must be tried again.

Under s. 3(3) of the Supreme Court Act of 1981, the Lord Chancellor may appoint one of the ordinary judges of the Court of Appeal as Vice-President of both Divisions of that court, or one of those judges as Vice-President of the Criminal Division and another of them as Vice-President of the Civil Division. The Vice-President will preside in the absence, for example, of the Lord Chief Justice or the Master of the Rolls.

Assistance for transaction of judicial business in the Supreme Court

Section 9 of the Supreme Court Act, 1981 brings together a number of provisions enabling assistance to be given by judges, former judges and deputy judges in terms of the business of the Supreme Court.

A judge of the Court of Appeal is competent to act on request in the High Court and the Crown Court. A person who has been a judge of the Court of Appeal is competent to act in the Court of Appeal, the High Court and the Crown Court. A *puisne* judge of the High Court is competent to act in the Court of Appeal. A person who has been a *puisne* judge of the High Court is competent to act in the Court of Appeal, the High Court and the Crown Court. A circuit judge is competent to act in the High Court.

By reason of s. 58 of the Administration of Justice Act, 1982 a Recorder is competent to act in the High Court. This includes Solicitor-Recorders.

Under s. 9(4) of the Supreme Court Act, 1981, if it appears to the Lord Chancellor that it is expedient as a temporary measure to make an appointment in order to facilitate the disposal of business in the High Court or the Crown Court, he may appoint a person qualified for appointment as a *puisne* judge of the High Court to be a deputy judge of the High Court during such period or on such occasions as the Lord Chancellor thinks fit.

House of Lords

Constitution
The court is constituted by the Lord Chancellor and Lords of Appeal in Ordinary (or Law Lords). There are at any one time between 9 and 11 Law Lords, two of whom normally come from the Scottish judiciary. The Law Lords are life peers and each of them is appointed by the Queen on the Prime Minister's advice, who is in turn advised by the Lord Chancellor, from among barristers of at least 15 years' standing or from *puisne* judges who have held office for at least two years. Normally the appointments are made from the Lords Justices of Appeal.

Jurisdiction
(a) *Civil*. On the civil side the House of Lords hears appeals from the Court of Appeal (Civil Division), the Court of Session in Scotland, when one or two Scottish Law Lords sit, and the Supreme Court of Northern Ireland when a Law Lord from Northern Ireland sits. In all cases the lower court must certify that a point of law of general public importance is involved and either the lower court or the Appeal Committee of the House of Lords consisting of three Law Lords must give leave. In addition, there is a direct appeal from the High Court or Divisional Court to the House of Lords by what is referred to as the 'leapfrogging method'. This phrase is used because the appeal goes straight to the House of Lords and not through the Court of Appeal. All parties must consent and the appeal must raise a point of law of public importance relating wholly or mainly to a statute or statutory instrument. The trial judge must certify the importance of the case and the House of Lords must give leave. This 'leapfrogging' procedure is most likely to be used in revenue appeals and patent matters where construction of statutes is often very involved.

(b) *Criminal*. On the criminal side the Court hears appeals from the Court of Appeal (Criminal Division) and the Divisional Court of Queen's Bench. In both cases the lower court must certify that a point of law of general public importance is involved and either the lower court or the Appeal Committee of the House of Lords must give leave. The House of Lords is not a final appellate tribunal for Scotland in criminal matters, but the Scottish Court of Criminal Appeal is.

The proceedings in the House of Lords are surprisingly informal. The Law Lords are not robed but sit in dark suits in panels of five at a table in one of the committee rooms in the Houses of Parliament at Westminster.

The Judicial Committee of the Privy Council

The Privy Council is a lineal descendant of the ancient King's Council, and was originally a sort of cabinet advising the Crown. The Judicial Committee, which is not part of the Supreme Court, is a final court of appeal in civil and criminal matters from the courts of some Commonwealth and Colonial territories, but the changes which have taken place in the Commonwealth have restricted the number of cases coming before it, many Commonwealth countries preferring to hear appeals within their own judicial systems. However, some aspects of this jurisdiction survive. For example, Malaysia and New Zealand have retained the Privy Council as a final appeal court in spite of their constitutional independence. The Australia Act Commencement Order of 1986 abolished appeals to the Privy Council from Australia.

The court is still the final court of appeal from the Channel Islands and the Isle of Man, and also from those islands and colonies, such as Gibraltar, Hong Kong and Belize, whose independence is not a viable proposition. There is strictly speaking no right of appeal, but it is customary to petition the Crown for leave to appeal. It is also the final court of appeal from English ecclesiastical courts, and here it is assisted by the Archbishops of Canterbury and York who, as assessors, advise on ecclesiastical matters. In wartime it hears appeals from the Admiralty Court on matters concerning prize. It also hears appeals from disciplinary bodies for dentists, opticians, and professions relating to medicine.

The Judicial Committee is comprised of the Lord Chancellor, the Lords of Appeal in Ordinary, and all Privy Councillors who have held high judicial office in the United Kingdom, together with Commonwealth judges who have been appointed members of the Privy Council. It does not actually decide cases, but advises the Crown which implements the advice by an Order in Council. This advice used to be unanimous, but since March, 1966, dissenting members of the Privy Council who were present at the hearing of the appeal may express their dissent, giving reasons therefor. The Court is not bound by its own previous decisions.

Employment tribunals

These are considered in detail in Chapter 4 which is concerned with tribunals and the legal profession.

The Court of Justice of the European Community

This court, which is often referred to as the European Court, sits in Luxembourg, and is charged with ensuring that Community law is observed in regard to the interpretation and implementation of the Treaties. Its decisions must be accepted by the courts of member states and there is no right of appeal. Matters before the court are disposed of in front of all the judges, though some preliminary (or interlocutory) matters can be dealt with by a division of three judges.

The court consists of a President of the whole court, a First Advocate-General, the Presidents of the First, Second, Third, Fourth and Fifth Chambers (3 persons in all) together with nine judges, five Advocates-General, and a Registrar; 20 persons in all. There is no requirement of professional law practice and the court consists of professional judges, academic lawyers and public servants. A judge may be removed only by unanimous decision of the other judges.

Procedure

There is more emphasis upon submissions in writing (pleadings) rather than oral argument. The proceedings are more inquisitorial and the judges play a more active role in terms of asking questions during hearings.

As we have seen, there is a First Advocate-General and five Advocates-General. They assist the court and they give an independent view of the proceedings *at the end of the case*.

The court gives a single judgment and no dissenting views are given. Enforcement of judgments is through the national courts of member states. The language in which the case is heard is a matter for the plaintiff, except where the defendant is a member state when it will be in the language of that state.

An important function of the court is to hear references from national courts for a ruling on the interpretation of provisions of Community law. Other than that, the court is mainly concerned with actions alleging failure to fulfil the obligations of the Treaty, e.g. by member states.

The European Communities (Amendment) Act, 1986 ratified the Single European Act under which a new court of first instance is to be created. It will be competent to hear certain classes of actions and procedures as may be decided.

Role of the European Court at Luxembourg

It was decided by the Court of Appeal in *Bulmer* v. *Bollinger*, [1974] 2 All E.R. 1226 that the High Court and the Court of Appeal have a jurisdiction to interpret Community law and that they are not obliged to grant a right of appeal to the European Court of Justice. However, if the case goes to the House of Lords on appeal, the House of Lords is bound to refer the matter to the European Court of Justice if either or both of the parties wishes this. The decision in *Bulmer* was based upon an interpretation of Article 177 of the Treaty, which provides, in effect, that although any court or tribunal of a member state *may* ask the European Court to give a ruling, only the final court of appeal, in our case the House of Lords, is *bound* to ask for a ruling if a party requests it.

In the case Bulmers had marketed products for many years under the name of 'Champagne Cider' and 'Champagne Perry'. Bollingers claimed that this was contrary to an EEC regulation which restricted the use of the word 'champagne' to wine produced from grapes grown in the Champagne district of France. The Court of Appeal decided that since cider was made from apples and perry was made from pears, there was no infringement of the regulation. The court also refused to refer the matter to the European Court.

In the course of his judgment Lord Denning, M.R., laid down certain guidelines to assist judges in deciding whether to refer a case to the European Court or not. The main guidelines are as follows—

(i) *The time to get a ruling.* The length of time which may elapse before a ruling can be obtained from the European Court should always be borne in mind. The average length of time at present seems to be between six and nine months. It is important to prevent undue protraction of proceedings. The English judge should always consider this delay and the expense to the parties. However, in *Customs & Excise Commissioners* v. *A.P.S. Samex*, [1983] 1 All E.R. 1042, Bingham, J., while accepting that a reference should not be made in, say, the High Court, simply because if it was not made one of the parties would go on making appeals, it might be that if the High Court did make the reference, thus preventing further appeals to English courts, it would be cheaper for the parties in the long run.

(ii) *The European Court must not be overloaded.* In this connection it should be borne in mind that all the judges must sit on a reference from a national court and they cannot split up into divisions of, say, three or five judges. Thus, if there are too many references, the court would not be able to get through its work.

(iii) *The reference must be on a question of interpretation only of the Treaty.* It is a matter for the national courts to find the facts and apply the Treaty, though the way in which the national court has interpreted the Treaty can then be a matter for reference.

(iv) *The difficulty of the question of Community law raised.* Lord Denning was of opinion that unless the point raised was 'really difficult and important' it would be better for the English judge to decide it himself. However, in *A.P.S. Samex* (above) Bingham, J. took the view that in some cases, even though the point raised might not be of great difficulty, the European Court should receive a reference because it was in a better position, among other things, to make the sort of decision which would further the orderly development of the Community. These statements by Bingham, J. in this case are to be welcomed because they show a greater willingness in the judiciary to take matters to Luxembourg and not to make too many decisions themselves thus to some extent shutting out the European Court.

In regard to criminal matters, a circuit judge presiding over a criminal trial on indictment has a discretion conferred on him by Article 177 of the Treaty of Rome to refer any question of interpretation of the Treaty to the European Court. It was held by the House of Lords in *R.* v. *Henn*, [1980] 2 All E.R. 166 that it can seldom be a proper exercise of the presiding judge's discretion to seek a preliminary ruling before the facts of the alleged offence have been ascertained, since this could result in proceedings being held up for nine months or more. It is generally better, said the House of Lords, that the judge should interpret the Treaty himself in the first instance and his interpretation can be reviewed thereafter if necessary through the hierarchy of the national courts, any of which may refer to the European Court.

In general terms, therefore, the House of Lords has an obligation to make a reference under Art. 117. Lower courts *may* do so but if they think that the relevant community law is sufficiently clear to be applied to the case straightaway they will not refer. This is known as the doctrine of *acte clair*.

The European Court of Human Rights

This court, which sits in Strasbourg, was set up by the Convention for the Protection of Human Rights and Fundamental Freedoms to ensure the observance of the engagements undertaken by contracting states under the Convention. The United Kingdom is one of the states which have accepted the Court's jurisdiction. The jurisdiction of the court in contentious matters extends to all cases concerning the interpretation and application of the Convention. It cannot be approached directly. All alleged breaches of the Convention must go first to the European Commission of Human Rights. Since its creation in 1959 it has dealt with a wide variety of problems, including compulsory sex education in state primary schools in Denmark, where it was found that there was no violation of the Convention, and punishment by birching in the Isle of Man, where one or more breaches of the Convention were found to exist. More recently, the court decided against Britain by regarding the caning of schoolchildren against the wishes of their parents as a breach of the Convention. The court has power to grant 'just satisfaction' of a pecuniary nature to the injured party.

Removal and retirement of judges

Section 17(4) of the Courts Act, 1971 contains the only formal power to remove a judge. The power relates to circuit judges and states that the Lord Chancellor may, if he thinks fit, remove a circuit judge from office on the ground of incapacity or misbehaviour. Recorders, Assistant Recorders, and Magistrates are governed by similar provisions. Other judges can only be removed by a motion approved by both Houses of Parliament.

As regards retirement, the Judicial Pensions Act, 1959 provides for retirement at 75 years of age except in the case of circuit judges and recorders where the age is 72, but the Lord Chancellor may extend this to 75.

3 Criminal and civil procedure

Having described the system of major civil and criminal courts existing in England and Wales, we shall before looking at other courts and tribunals, consider the procedure in those major courts which leads to a prosecution for crime or to an action for, say, damages at civil law.

CRIMINAL PROCEDURE

The system of trial in this country is accusatorial in that a trial is a contest between two persons. As regards crime, these persons are normally the Queen (on behalf of the community) and the person accused of the crime.

Barristers (called counsel) representing the prosecution and the defence each put forward evidence to the court so that a decision may be made on the question before the court which is, did the accused commit the offence with which he is charged?

It should also be noted in particular that a person accused of crime is presumed innocent until proved guilty and is given certain protections in regard to the proof of his guilt as follows—

(a) *The Code of Practice for the Detention, Treatment and Questioning of Persons by the Police*. This Code, which was prepared by the Home Office under powers given by the Police and Criminal Evidence Act, 1984, ensures that a person cannot be trapped by questioning into an admission of guilt. The main safeguard of the Code is that once an investigating police officer has grounds to believe that the person being questioned has committed an offence, whether he has admissible evidence to that effect or not, questioning *about the offence* can continue, but only after the suspect has been 'cautioned'. This involves telling the suspect that he need not say anything but that, if he does, what he says may be written down and given in evidence. At any subsequent trial anything said by the person while a suspect may be used for or against his case.

If questioning is interrupted the Code states that the caution should be given afresh each time questioning is resumed. It also provides that a person who is not under arrest when he is cautioned, e.g. a person cautioned over a minor traffic offence, should be so informed.

(b) *The burden of proof.* Once in court the prosecution must prove its case beyond all reasonable doubt. The magistrates or jury need not be *certain* of the accused's guilt, but they must in effect be *sure* that he has committed the crime. (And see *Woolmington* v. *DPP*, 1935 at p. 875).

The prosecutor

The Prosecution of Offences Act, 1985 establishes a national prosecution service for England and Wales. The service separates the *prosecution* of offences from the police service which is concerned with *detection and investigation.*

The police continue to decide whether to prosecute, caution, or take no further action in the first instance. However, if they do decide to prosecute, the case is handed over to the Crown Prosecutors. The Crown Prosecution Service has power to advise the police at this stage. However, they have no right to be informed of cases and cannot insist that any advice they give is accepted until the police decide to prosecute. This is a major weakness in the Act.

The Director of Public Prosecutions (see further p. 45) is in charge of the Crown Prosecution Service under the general superintendence of the Attorney-General. The Service conducts all police prosecutions except minor motoring matters. Thus Crown Prosecutors are able to take the decision to continue or drop a case without consulting the police and may in that sense override the wishes of the police. However, withdrawal of charges in court is another matter. A Crown Court judge may refuse to allow a case to be dropped. (*R.* v. *Broad* (1979), 68 Cr. App. R. 281.) However, s. 23 *ibid.*, allows Crown Prosecutors to discontinue any proceedings in the magistrates' courts (before the opening of a contested trial) without the prior permission of the court. The situation in the Crown Court remains unchanged.

The staff of the Crown Prosecution Service, called Crown Prosecutors, are appointed by the DPP and must be qualified as barristers or solicitors. The senior prosecuting officer in the various areas is called a Chief Crown Prosecutor. The DPP may, however, employ barristers and solicitors who are not members of the Crown Prosecution Service.

The Act also gives the Secretary of State power to set limits on the time for the opening of criminal proceedings and under it cases must be brought to court within time limits to be specified in regulations.

The right of persons to institute private prosecutions is retained and the DPP may take over the prosecution at any time (s. 6 *ibid.*). Amendments to the Supreme Court Act of 1981 control and restrict vexatious proceedings, whether civil or criminal.

Private prosecutions are only instituted where the police are reluctant to be involved, as in an assault summons between neighbours. However, there have been more spectacular cases, e.g. the prosecution of *Gay News* for blasphemy by Mrs Mary Whitehouse. It is unfortunate, however, that a Queen's Bench Divisional Court decided in *R* v. *D.P.P. ex parte Hallas, The Times*, 11 December, 1987 that a private citizen mounting a prosecution has no right of access to police statements, reports or photographs held by the Crown Prosecution Service. Mrs Hallas was trying to set up a prosecution for causing death by reckless driving against the allegedly drunk driver of the car which had killed her son. Section 6 *ibid.* gives no right to these materials.

A private individual who is of opinion that the police are failing to prosecute in a particular case may ask the High Court to compel them to do so. Thus, in *R.* v. *Commissioner of Police of the Metropolis, ex parte Blackburn, (No. 3)*, 1973 (see p. 519), Mr Blackburn sought an order of *mandamus* requiring the Commissioner of Police of the Metropolis to secure the enforcement of the law against pornography upon various publishers and booksellers, and to reverse his decision that no prosecution should be undertaken. It was held by the Court of Appeal that although the evidence showed that pornography was widely available, this was not a proper case for the Court to interfere with the discretion of the police. Except in an extreme case, the Court said, the police have a discretion in carrying out their duty of enforcing the law with which the courts will not interfere.

Government departments, such as the Inland Revenue, also employ a staff of prosecutors to bring prosecutions for offences in connection with the department's activities, for example fraudulent tax evasion.

The Director of Public Prosecutions

The Director of Public Prosecutions may also become involved. The office of Director of Public Prosecutions was created by the Prosecution of Offences Act, 1879. He is appointed by the Home Secretary from among barristers or solicitors of not less than ten years' standing but acts under the superintendence of the Attorney-General, who is formally answerable to Parliament for his actions. The Director prosecutes through his own staff and on some occasions through Treasury Counsel.

Sometimes an offence *must* be referred to the Director before prosecution. For example, under s. 329 of the Companies Act, 1985 (as amended by the Financial Services Act, 1986) a company whose shares are quoted on a recognised investment exchange, e.g. the Stock Exchange, is required to inform that Exchange of the purchase of shares in the company by its own directors. Failure to give such information can lead to the prosecution of the company and its directors but such a prosecution can only be brought with the consent of either the Secretary of State for Trade and Industry or the Director of Public Prosecutions.

Even if the offence is not one which must be referred to the Director, his advice through the Crown Prosecution Service is often sought by police authorities where, for example, they are not sure whether there is sufficient evidence to warrant the institution of criminal proceedings in a particular case.

Prosecuting fraud

The Criminal Justice Act, 1987 reforms the law relating to trials for fraud following the Report of the Roskill Committee on Fraud Trials 1986.

Section 1 sets up a Serious Fraud Office under a Director, who is supervised by the Attorney-General, to investigate and prosecute complex and/or serious frauds. Sections 4–6 which are aimed at simplifying fraud trials allow a case of alleged fraud to be transferred to the Crown Court without the need for committal proceedings in front of magistrates. Sections 7–11 reinforce the simplifying theme by providing for Preparatory Hearings before a judge sitting alone to be held when the trial first begins so as to simplify the issues which will eventually go to the jury.

Involvement of Attorney-General

In some cases the consent of the Attorney-General is required before prosecution. This applies, for example, in the case of prosecutions under the Official Secrets Acts.

Getting the person accused into court

With the exception of fraud, all persons accused of crime appear first in the magistrates' court. The appearance of the person accused is obtained by a summons or charge following arrest without a warrant. Arrest under a warrant signed by a magistrate is not common today. The main use of warrants is to arrest those who, having been bailed, do not turn up for trial.

To get a summons the prosecutor must give a short account of the alleged offence, usually in writing, to the magistrates or their clerk (a process called laying an information). The information may be substantiated by a police officer swearing as to its truth before a magistrate and must be so substantiated if it is used as the basis for a warrant for arrest. A summons setting out the offence is then issued and served upon the person accused either in person or, for minor offences, through Recorded Delivery or Registered post.

Arrest without warrant occurs where a police officer arrests a person whom he reasonably suspects has committed, or is committing, or is about to commit, for example, an arrestable offence under s. 24 of the Police and Criminal Evidence Act, 1984. This is, e.g. an offence punishable with five years' imprisonment or more. Most crimes of theft under the Theft Act are arrestable offences. Powers of arrest without warrant under the 1984 Act are more fully considered on p. 378.

Under s. 30, *ibid.*, a person who has been arrested should be taken to a police station as soon as practicable unless his presence is required elsewhere for the effective investigation of crime. Under s. 34(1), *ibid.*, a person arrested for an offence may be held at a police station only if certain detention conditions apply. He must be released if they cease to apply.

The relevant conditions are set out in ss. 37 and 38, *ibid.* Before a person is charged there is only one condition which is that there are reasonable grounds for believing that the detention is necessary to secure or preserve evidence of, or relating to, the offence for which the person was arrested, or to obtain such evidence by questioning him. (S. 37(2).) After charge there are a number of detention conditions, e.g. that the defendant's name and address are not known, or it is reasonably thought that he may have given a false name and address, or that he may not be long enough at his address for a summons to be served. (S. 38(1).) Under s. 36, *ibid.*, every police station must have a custody officer who is responsible for supervising the detention and proper treatment of the detained person. Section 40, *ibid.*, provides for periodic review of the validity of the detention, the first to be made within six hours of detention. Subsequent reviews must be at intervals of not more than nine hours.

Section 41, *ibid.*, provides that holding a suspect for more than 24 hours without a charge requires the approval of a person of the rank of superintendent (or above) for a further 12 hours and after that of a magistrates' court. The magistrates can approve any period provided it is not longer in total than 96 hours after which time the suspect must be charged or released. If the magistrates' permission is refused the suspect must be either charged or released at that point in time. There may, of course, be a duty to release earlier if there are not reasonable grounds under s. 37(2), *ibid.*, for detention. There are some exceptional cases where the above rules do not apply. These are set out in s. 51, *ibid.*, and include terrorist offences.

Section 56, *ibid.*, and the relevant Code of Practice provide that when a suspect arrives at a police station he is entitled to have someone informed that he is under arrest. This is expressed to be one friend or relative, or other person who is known to him or who is likely to take an interest in his welfare. Such person must be told of the arrest without delay and of the whereabouts of the suspect. Under s. 58, *ibid.*, a person held in custody is entitled, if he so requests, to consult a solicitor privately. Under the Code suspects should be given a written notice of this right to request a consultation e.g. with the Duty Solicitor, by the custody officer who is also required to confirm the right orally. However, if a suspect is alleged to have committed a serious arrestable offence e.g. rape, a superintendent may postpone the right for 36 hours. It was decided by the Court of Appeal in *R.* v. *Samuel, The Times*, 19 December, 1987 that the right to see a *particular* solicitor can be refused if the police officer concerned has reason to believe that the solicitor will e.g. alert other suspects. Obviously this will be rare and even when it occurs the detainee must be allowed to see a different solicitor.

If a solicitor has been called, the Code provides that the police must wait for his arrival before questioning the suspect unless he has agreed to questioning in writing or an officer of the rank of superintendent or above has reasonable grounds to believe that delay will, e.g. harm the process of investigation. The above rules do not apply to those detained for alleged terrorist crimes. Those detained for offences which are not serious arrestable offences have an unqualified right to see a solicitor.

Under s. 46, *ibid.*, a person who has been charged and is being held in custody must be brought before magistrates as soon as practicable. Under s. 46(2) he must be brought before a magistrates' court as soon as practicable and in any event not later than the first sitting after he is charged with the offence. If no sitting is due on the day of the charge or the next day, the custody officer must inform the clerk to the justices for the area of the situation. (S. 46(3).) The clerk must then arrange for the court to sit not later than the day next following the relevant day. (S. 46(6).)

Bail

(*a*) *By police.* Under s. 47 of the Police and Criminal Evidence Act, 1984 the custody officer (see above) must, after charges have been laid, consider whether the detention conditions (see above) apply. If not, he must order the release of the accused on bail in accordance with the Bail Act, 1976 (see below) or without bail. An accused who is not released must be brought before the magistrate as soon as practicable. (See above.)

(*b*) *By magistrates.* When an accused person comes before magistrates, e.g. on a preliminary hearing, the magistrates have to decide at the end of the hearing whether to remand the accused in custody, in one of the remand prisons for persons awaiting trial, or release him on bail. Bail should also be considered at remand appearances but following the decision of the Divisional Court of Queen's Bench in *R.* v. *Nottingham Justices, ex parte Davies*, [1980] 2 All E.R. 775, the magistrates' duty is only to consider new circumstances or circumstances not previously before them and not to review matters previously considered. This seemed out of line with the spirit of the Bail Act, 1976 (see below) which was intended to encourage more bail and the Criminal Justice Act, 1988 requires the court to consider bail at every hearing. A remand in custody before sentence can be for a maximum of eight days. However, under s. 59 and Sch. 9 of the Criminal Justice Act, 1982 there is no need for a court appearance every time a remand is necessary. With the consent of an accused person of 17 or over, for whom a solicitor is acting, up to three remands in custody may be made in his absence. He must be present at the fourth remand when if he consents the whole procedure can start again. Under s. 22 of the Prosecution of Offences Act, 1985 (and rules made thereunder) the custody time limits are laid down, e.g. in cases of trial on indictment between first appearance in court and committal for trial to a limit of 84 days (SI 1988/164).

The granting of bail is covered by the Bail Act, 1976, which is applied also to those in customs detention by the Criminal Justice Act, 1988. Section 4 of the 1976 Act contains a statutory presumption in favour of granting bail. Under the section a person accused of crime must be granted bail unless—

(a) he is charged with, or convicted of, an offence which is punishable with imprisonment and the court is satisfied there are good grounds for believing that, if released on bail, he would fail to appear at a subsequent hearing or commit an offence while on bail or obstruct the course of justice by intimidating witnesses; or

(b) the court is satisfied that he ought to remain in custody for his own protection, or if he is a juvenile, for his own welfare; or

(c) there has not been enough time to obtain information about the defendant for the court to reach a decision; or

(d) the defendant has been convicted of an imprisonable offence and remanded for enquiries or, say, a medical report, and it seems to the court that it is not practical to complete the enquiries or make the report unless the defendant is kept in custody.

Where the defendant is charged with, or convicted of, an offence which is not punishable with imprisonment, the grounds for refusing bail are much more restricted. However, such a person can be refused bail if he has previously failed to answer bail and if the court believes, in view of that failure, that he will again fail to surrender to custody if released on bail. Conditions may be imposed on the granting of bail, e.g. the handing in of a passport or regular reporting to the police.

The Criminal Justice Act, 1988 provides that when the prosecution opposes bail, the court will have to give reasons for granting it where a person is charged with murder, attempted murder, manslaughter, rape or attempted rape.

As regards appeals, an unconvicted defendant can, under s. 22 of the Criminal Justice Act, 1967, appeal to a High Court judge against a refusal by the magistrates to grant bail. Under s. 60 of the Criminal Justice Act, 1982 he may, as an alternative to the High Court judge, go to a Crown Court judge in chambers for bail. Section 29, ibid., gives the Crown Court power to grant bail pending an application to the Court of Appeal for leave to appeal against sentence, or pending an appeal thereto against conviction or indictment.

Section 3 of the 1976 Act imposes a duty upon a person granted bail to surrender to custody. This duty is enforceable by the creation of the offence of absconding in s. 6. Security for surrender into custody and sureties may not be required nor conditions imposed on the grant of bail except as provided by the section. Thus security may be required of a defendant only if it appears likely that he will leave Great Britain. The court may ask for sureties other than the defendant to provide an additional guarantee to secure the defendant's surrender to custody. As regards conditions, the section makes it plain that these are only to be imposed to ensure the defendant's surrender to custody, that he does not commit a further offence while on bail, that he does not interfere with the course of justice, as by intimidating witnesses, and that he makes himself available for the purposes of enabling enquiries or a report to be made. The section also provides for the parent or guardian of a juvenile to stand as surety in a sum not exceeding £50 to ensure that the juvenile complies with the requirements attached to the grant of bail.

Section 6 also creates the offence of failing, without reasonable cause, to surrender at the time and place appointed. The offence is punishable in a Magistrates' Court by a maximum of three months' imprisonment and/or a fine, and in a superior court, such as a Crown Court, with 12 months' imprisonment and/or a fine. Section 7 provides for the arrest of a defendant who fails to surrender himself to custody at the appointed time and place or who breaches any of the conditions attached to the grant of bail.

If the court requires sureties under s. 3, then s. 8 provides for the first time in statutory form some matters which should be taken into account in deciding the suitability of sureties. The list, which is neither mandatory nor exhaustive, relates to the financial resources, character (including previous convictions) and proximity to the defendant (in terms of blood relationship, dwelling, or otherwise) of the proposed surety. In addition, the section enables a person who is not accepted as a surety to apply to a court to have the matter reconsidered. Section 9 creates the offence of agreeing at any time and regardless of whether or not a person in fact becomes a surety, to indemnify that person against his liability as a surety. Thus, if A asks B to stand as a surety for C and tells B that he (A) will pay to B any sum which B has to pay into court because C absconds, then A commits this s. 9 offence. The penalties for this offence are the same as those for the offence of absconding. No proceedings may be instituted under this section without the consent of the Director of Public Prosecutions.

Section 11 provides for the granting of legal aid on a wider basis than before for defendants who wish to be represented in actions relating to whether they are entitled to bail or not.

The three major weaknesses of the Act are as follows—

(a) it does not place any duty on the court to find out the defendant's personal circumstances so that there continues to be the risk that the court will hear only the police view on the bail/custody issue.

(b) The Act does not deal with the duration of remands in custody. Remands in custody are frequently made because of a police objection to bail on the basis that there are further police enquiries to be made. There are those who think that this should not stand as a distinct ground for refusing bail and that the court should question the police more closely when they object to bail on these grounds. However, the Act makes no reference to this problem.

(c) The problems arising from the decision in *R.* v. *Nottingham Justices ex parte Davies*, 1980, now improved by the 1988 Act (see p. 48).

Before leaving the subject of bail, the provision of bail hostels is worthy of consideration. These hostels, which are provided by the probation service, are growing in number and provide an accused person with an address so that he need not necessarily be remanded in custody because he has no fixed abode which is still a ground under s. 1(4) of the Magistrates' Courts Act, 1980, though persons of no fixed abode are not bound to be refused bail. The Secretary of State is given power to approve bail hostels and to provide a system of inspection under s. 49 of the Powers of Criminal Courts Act, 1973 (as amended by the Criminal Justice Act, 1982). Before this statutory measure there were only a limited number of such hostels provided by voluntary organizations.

Summary trial before magistrates (other than juvenile offenders)

Since the majority of summary trials before magistrates relate to motoring offences, such an offence has been chosen as an example of the form of summary trial.

The alleged offence
Let us suppose that on 29 March, 1989, Freda Jones was driving her car along George Road, Barchester and that her attention was distracted by the sun so that she ran into the back of a stationary delivery van which was parked at the kerbside in an area where no parking restrictions were in force.

The summons
The police are intending to bring a prosecution against Freda under the Road Traffic Act, 1972, for careless driving. Freda will receive a summons as follows.

BARCHESTER MAGISTRATES' COURT
To Freda Jones
12 Acacia Avenue, Barchester, Barchestershire.
You are hereby summoned to appear on 7 June, 1989 at 2.00 p.m. before the Magistrates' Court at 14 High Street, Barchester to answer to the following information laid on 29 March, 1989 that you at George Road, Barchester, did drive a motor vehicle without due care and attention contrary to s. 3 and Sch. 4 of the Road Traffic Act, 1972.

Informant	Police Constable Peter Green
Address	Barchester Police Station
Date	3 April, 1989
Signed	J. Bloggs
	Justices' Clerk

STATEMENT OF FACTS
IF YOU INFORM THE CLERK of the Court that you wish to plead
guilty to the offence set out in the summons above, without appearing
before the Court, and the Court proceeds to hear and dispose of the
case in your absence under s. 12 of the Magistrates' Courts Act, 1980,
the following Statement of Facts will be read out in open Court before
the Court decides whether to accept your plea. If your plea of guilty
is accepted the Court will not, unless it adjourns the case after
convicting you and before sentencing you, permit any other statement
to be made by or on behalf of the prosecutor with respect to any facts
relating to the offence.

On 29 March, 1989 at 10.00 hours you were the driver of Mini Metro
FEY 856Y travelling north on George Road, Barchester. On
approaching the junction with Marks Road you collided with a Ford
delivery van C113 PJC which was parked at the kerbside. When asked
by the Police Reporting Officer what had happened you said: 'I had
the sun in my eyes. I did not see the van.'
Signed   Peter Green
            (on behalf of the Prosecutor)

Freda will be advised that her driving licence must be at the Court by
the date of the hearing and that failure to comply could lead to the
suspension of the licence and a fine.
   Freda is unlikely to get legal aid for a lawyer to defend her. Many
magistrates are reluctant to give legal aid in motoring offences. This
contrasts with persons pleading not guilty in the Crown Court. They are
likely to get legal aid whatever the offence.

The trial

Freda could plead guilty by letter. However, on the assumption that
Freda is to attend court and plead not guilty, the procedure is as set out
below.
The charge. Freda appears in answer to the summons and the first thing
that happens is that the Clerk to the Magistrates reads out the offence
with which she is charged.
Election to trial by jury. This does not arise in Freda's case because the
offence of careless driving under s. 3 of the Road Traffic Act, 1972,
cannot be tried on indictment before a jury. If, however, the police had
decided to charge her with reckless driving under s. 2 of the Road Traffic
Act, 1972 (as substituted by s. 50 of the Criminal Law Act, 1977) the
question of trial on indictment would have arisen because the offence is
triable either way.
Freda's plea. Since Freda's case will be dealt with summarily by the
magistrates, the next step is that the clerk will ask her whether she pleads
guilty or not guilty. If Freda pleads guilty such a plea in itself constitutes
a conviction and the magistrates have the power to sentence her without

hearing evidence, though they also have the power to decide that even on a guilty plea it is desirable in the circumstances to hear evidence on oath.

The prosecution's case. Since we know that Freda will plead not guilty, the prosecution will have to prove its case. The prosecutor will give a summary of the evidence which he proposes to call and of the effect of that evidence on the charge. He will then call his witnesses and ask questions of them (called examination-in-chief). It is then open to Freda or her solicitor to cross-examine the witnesses for the prosecution.

The defence. When the case for the prosecution has been presented the defence may—

(*a*) submit that there is no case to answer; or
(*b*) proceed to open the case for the defence.

The choice in (*a*) above could be taken where, for example, the witnesses for the prosecution had broken down under cross-examination and changed or partly changed their evidence, or contradicted each other. Freda's solicitor may support his submission of no case to answer by a speech in which he may draw the attention of the court to inconsistencies and omissions in the prosecution's case. Since these are matters of law the prosecution may reply.

The court will then consider the submission and may retire in order to do so. Should the court accept the submission the case is dismissed. If they find that there is a case to answer then the defence proceeds. On the assumption that the court does not accept the submission of no case to answer, oral evidence is given by witnesses for the defence and by the defendant, who are in turn examined by the prosecution, and there may be a speech by or on behalf of the defendant, either before or after the evidence is heard, or if the court permits, both before and after and the prosecution may call witnesses in reply. If there are two speeches by or on behalf of the defendant the prosecution has a right to make a speech in reply. Should there be no witnesses for the defence other than the defendant there may be a speech by or on behalf of the defendant, either before or after the defendant has given evidence.

Otherwise the prosecution has no right to address the court in reply unless a point of law is raised in which case the prosecution can present arguments in relation to the law.

Decision and sentence. When the case for the defence is closed and after hearing witnesses for the prosecution who may have been called in reply, the court must consider whether to convict the defendant or dismiss the information. The court decides by a majority and lay justices do not normally give reasons for their findings, though some stipendiaries do. There is no need for unanimity and if magistrates are equally divided a new trial is ordered. The justices may ask their clerk to give them advice privately on matters of law (and see *R.* v. *Uxbridge Justices ex p. Smith*, 1985 at p. 17) but they must not ask for or listen to the views of the clerk on issues of fact, and it is certainly improper for them to ask the clerk to retire with them when no issues of law arise in the case.

If the magistrates decide to convict they will then enquire whether the accused has any previous convictions recorded against her and may hear both the prosecution and the defence as to her character. The defence may also address the court in what is called mitigation. This could consist, for example, of an address outlining the defendant's domestic stress, perhaps in Freda's case, that her boyfriend had recently been severely injured in a road accident. The court will then decide upon the sentence and announce it. Once the court has done this, or has dismissed the summons, it will not normally change its decision. However, as we have seen, magistrates' courts are given the power to re-open a case to rectify a mistake in any order they have made within 14 days. The court on the second occasion must be constituted in the same way as it was on the first occasion or with a majority of the same justices. This procedure could be used, for example, where the magistrates had omitted to order the endorsement of a defendant's driving licence. (See also p. 23.)

If Freda's defence has failed, the magistrates can fine her or, in the case of a second or subsequent conviction, may sentence her to imprisonment for three months or fine her, or both. They have a discretion as to whether to disqualify her from driving, though an endorsement of her licence is obligatory. Freda will also be ordered to make a contribution to the legal costs.

Trial in a juvenile court

Those aged ten and under 17 *who are charged with a criminal offence* appear before a juvenile court as either a child (if aged ten to 14) or a young person (if over 14 and under 17). Minors under ten years of age are by presumption of law incapable of any crime. However, it is thought that children under ten, if caught in the act of damaging property, could be restrained by the police under their common law power to protect property or detained under s. 28(2) of the Children and Young Persons Act, 1969, on the grounds that they were beyond the control of their parents or guardians, for the purposes of s. 1(2)(d), *ibid.*

In addition to criminal proceedings, there are *care proceedings* which may be brought by the officers of a local authority, the police or other persons, for example, an inspector of the National Society for the Prevention of Cruelty to Children.

Care proceedings
These may be brought because a minor of any age up to 17 is thought to be in some sort of trouble short of the commission of crime, as where he is not attending school or is beyond the control of parents or guardians.

However, care proceedings can be used even where an offence has been committed and, it is the intention of the law that so far as children and young persons are concerned, criminal proceedings should be brought only as a last resort.

In order to illustrate the procedure in care proceedings we shall take the case of Philip Green, aged 14, who has had a history of not attending school for periods of time and of violence within the school involving attacks on other pupils and, more recently, on a teacher. Philip's father is dead and his mother finds difficulty in preventing this sort of conduct. Let us assume that all of this has resulted in the county council making application for a care order, on the ground that Philip is beyond his mother's control for the purposes of s. 1(2)(d) of the 1969 Act.

Care proceedings are civil in character and Philip will be eligible for legal aid. It is usual for the child to be legally represented no matter how young. Since 1983 when legal aid became available for parents in their own right they are often legally represented. This helps them to meet allegations which may be made against them.

Philip arrives at the court accompanied by his mother. Parents are asked to be present and if they do not attend the court may adjourn the hearing until one of them does. If the parent or guardian refuses to attend, the Court may issue a warrant to ensure his or her participation. Philip will find that there are no formalities. The bench in juvenile courts consists of not more than three persons of whom one must be a woman and one a man. The hearing is whenever possible held in an ordinary room and not in a court room.

Before the case starts Philip and his mother will be invited to enter the room and sit on chairs facing the magistrates' table.

The clerk will explain that the county council alleges that Philip is beyond the control of his mother and that his proper development will be prevented unless a care order is made. Philip and his mother will then be asked if they understand the county council's allegations.

A lawyer for the county council will then go through the details of Philip's difficult behaviour and may call witnesses, e.g. Philip's headmaster. Philip will be invited to ask questions of the witnesses and in any case Philip's own lawyer will cross-examine the witnesses. In addition to evidence as to the facts evidence will also be given by experts, e.g. those employed by child guidance clinics who would normally have seen Philip over the period of his difficult behaviour and have formed a view as to the best method of dealing with the problem.

When all the witnesses have been examined and cross-examined Philip will be asked to make a statement which is mainly designed to see whether he disagrees with what has been said about him. Philip's mother will also be asked to make a statement.

After this the magistrates retire, and let us assume that they find that the county council has proved its case. If so, and the court feels that there is no alternative, it will put Philip into the care of the county council, by means of a care order, which means that he will live, for example, in a community home, until he is 18, though if he responds well the county council may go back to the juvenile court and ask that the order be revoked before he reaches 18. He may also be placed in a foster home or with prospective adopters. The care order gives the local authority the powers and duties of a parent. It is not of necessity a custodial or residential order and not all juveniles are removed from their homes.

Parents may appeal against a care order to the Crown Court or ask the juvenile court at a later date to revoke the order, as where the home circumstances have improved.

Criminal proceedings

Where children or young persons are found guilty of a criminal offence in a juvenile court the magistrates may still make a care order, even though the proceedings are not care proceedings.

Under the Criminal Justice Acts, 1982 and 1988, persons under 21 years of age found guilty of a criminal offence in a juvenile court if under 17, or in a magistrates' or Crown Court if between 17 and 21, *cannot be sent to prison for any offence*. The possibilities open to the court are fines and the following—

(*a*) *Supervision orders*. These have replaced probation orders and when such an order has been made the child continues to live at home under the supervision of the local authority social services department, though in the case of persons of 14 years and over, the Probation Service carries out the supervision.

(*b*) *Attendance centre orders*. As we have seen, these require a young offender to spend a specific number of hours (up to a maximum of 24 in all) at an attendance centre, usually on a Saturday afternoon. The regime is one of vigorous exercise and instruction in recreational activities.

(*c*) *Custodial sentences—generally*. The Criminal Justice Act, 1988 moves to a single custodial sentence for young offenders (except in the circumstances outlined in (*d*) below). The new sentence is known as 'detention in a Young Offenders Institution' and replaces Youth Custody Orders and Detention Centre Orders. The sentence may, if for a short period, be served under the old detention centre regime, e.g. programmes founded on work, basic education, physical education, parades and inspection. Longer periods will be served under the old Youth Custody arrangements. The Secretary of State may direct detention in a prison for some temporary purpose.

The 1988 Act achieves the above arrangements by adding to the Criminal Justice Act, 1982 s. 12(1) and 1(A). The provisions appear contrary to the European Convention on Human Rights in terms of sex discrimination in that males are eligible at 14 but females only at 15.

(*d*) *Crimes attracting imprisonment for life*. Under s. 8 of the Criminal Justice Act, 1982 a person under 21 who is convicted of an offence for which the sentence is fixed by law as imprisonment for life must be sentenced to custody for life, though a child or young person under 18 who is convicted of murder must be detained during Her Majesty's pleasure. (Children and Young Persons Act, 1933, s. 53(1).) A person aged 17 or over but under 21 who is convicted of any other offence carrying up to life imprisonment, e.g. robbery under s. 8 of the Theft Act, 1968, may be sentenced to custody for life.

A criminal trial of a person under 21 in the juvenile court or a magistrates' or higher court, as appropriate, proceeds in the usual way with the prosecution opening its case and witnesses being examined-in-chief and cross-examined. Then the case for the defence is presented and the magistrates retire to make a decision. If they decide that the young person is guilty his previous convictions, if any, are made known to the court.

However, for persons under 21 the court must, under s. 2(1) of the Criminal Justice Act, 1982 obtain and consider a Social Inquiry Report (SIR) before imposing a custodial sentence. If the court is of the opinion that it is unnecessary because of the circumstances of the case (s. 2(3), *ibid.*) it may pass a custodial sentence without an SIR. However, the reason for this opinion must be stated in open court, in the court register, and on the warrant of commitment to an institution for custodial sentence. (S. 2(6) and (7), *ibid.*)

There are statutory powers to fine young offenders and to order payment by a parent or guardian, unless e.g., it would be unreasonable to do so, as where the offender's finances are better than those of the parent or guardian.

Juveniles in adult courts

Sometimes a person under 17 may appear in an adult court. The circumstances are as follows—

(*a*) when the young person is charged jointly with a person over 17 and the magistrates think they should be tried together, as where they are members of a gang;

(*b*) when a child or young person is charged, for example, with murder or some other serious offence, he will be sent for trial to the Crown Court. Possible sentences have already been considered.

Trial on indictment in the Crown Court

Persons appearing in the Crown Court for trial on indictment have committed rather serious offences. They will have appeared before a magistrates' court and been committed for trial by that court after a preliminary hearing in which the prosecution has made out a *prima facie* case against the person accused. That is, the prosecution has shown that there is sufficient evidence against the accused to make a full trial necessary.

Before the preliminary hearing the accused will no doubt have appeared before the magistrates and may have been remanded. Issues of bail or no bail will have been decided and the accused will have been instructed how to apply for legal aid and given the necessary form. The usefulness of the duty solicitor at this stage has already been described. (See p. 17.)

Legal aid

Legal aid in criminal proceedings is given only to those charged with offences and is not available to persons wishing to bring a prosecution.

The criteria for granting legal aid include cases involving complex points of law or where the defendant has language difficulties. The most important however, is whether a defendant is at serious risk of losing his liberty, his job, or his reputation. A very large percentage of those appearing before the Crown Court get legal aid. Many of those who appear before magistrates are not legally represented.

Reporting of committal proceedings

In general, the only evidence given at committal proceedings is by the prosecution, the accused merely reserving his defence for the actual trial. If full reporting of committal proceedings was allowed, the accused could be prejudiced because by the time his trial occurred the general public, including probably the jury, would have read only one side of the case and might have reached the conclusion that the accused was guilty. However, this need not happen because under s. 8(4) of the Magistrates' Courts Act, 1980, newspaper, television, and radio reports of committal proceedings are restricted to the following matters—

(a) the name of the court and the names of the justices;

(b) the names, addresses, ages and occupations of the prosecutor, defendants, and witnesses;

(c) the offences under consideration;

(d) the names of the advocates;

(e) the decision of the court;

(f) where a committal is ordered, the charges involved;

(g) the name of the higher court to which the committal is ordered;

(h) in the case of an adjournment, the date and place to which the hearing is adjourned;

(i) any order as to bail and whether or not legal aid was granted.

On conviction for an offence against the above provisions, editors and publishers of newspapers and periodicals, together with their counterparts in the field of broadcasting, are liable to a maximum fine not exceeding £1000. (Magistrates' Courts Act, 1980, s. 8(5)(c).)

Under s. 8(2) of the Magistrates' Courts Act, 1980, as amended by the Criminal Justice (Amendment) Act, 1981, where there are two or more accused and one objects to the making of an order by the magistrates lifting the reporting restrictions, then the magistrates must hear representations which any of the accused may wish to make and will make an order lifting the restrictions if, and only if, satisfied that it is in the interests of justice to do so. In general terms, the reasons for lifting reporting restrictions must have some relevance to the issue to be considered at the trial, such as the prejudice of the police against the accused and not, as in *R.* v. *Leeds Justices, ex parte Sykes*, [1983] 1 All E.R. 460, because an accused person wishes to give publicity to the conduct of the police who at first said they would not bring charges for conspiracy to rob but later decided to do so. There was no evidence of police prejudice in that conduct.

There is no restriction on reporting if the magistrates decide not to commit for trial. After the trial of the defendant (or the last if there is more than one defendant) reporters can mention in detail matters raised in committal proceedings.

When a preliminary hearing changes into a summary trial reporters can report fully the committal proceedings which took place before the summary trial.

Liability may be incurred under the Magistrates' Courts Act, 1980, where a report of committal proceedings contains *any* details other than those permitted by s. 8(4), *ibid.*, and quite irrespective of whether or not the details are potentially prejudicial in nature. (*The Eastbourne Herald Case*, 1973.)[8] This distinguishes the s. 8(4) offence from the offence of contempt of court under the Contempt of Court Act, 1981. If there is to be a contempt, the material published must be likely to be prejudicial to a fair trial. The reporting of *trials*, as distinct from *committal proceedings*, is governed by the Contempt of Court Act, 1981. (See further p. 69.) However, s. 4 of the Contempt of Court Act, 1981 makes it clear, for the avoidance of doubt, that no action for contempt can be brought against those who comply with s. 8 of the 1980 Act.

Alibi
Section 11 of the Criminal Justice Act, 1967, is designed to prevent the use of 'sprung' or late alibis which were once so widespread in criminal trials. The section provides that, in general, notice of alibi must be given in advance of a trial on indictment. This is not required in summary trials because of the ease with which the prosecution can ask for an adjournment where the defendant 'springs' an alibi on the prosecution at the last moment.

The following warning (or one similar to it) must be given during the course of committal proceedings, usually by the clerk.

'You must understand that at your trial at the Crown Court you will not be allowed to give evidence in support of an alibi which means that you were somewhere else when the offence was committed unless you have given notice to the prosecution giving the particulars of the alibi. You can either give those particulars now or your solicitor can send them to the prosecution within the next seven days.'

Although this warning need not be given if it seems unnecessary having regard to the nature of the offence charged, it should as a general rule be given where there is any doubt, because the Act provides that failure to give it will allow the defendant to introduce a last-minute alibi at his trial. Where an unrepresented defendant does not appear to understand what is meant by 'alibi', the word must be explained to him.

There is a discretion in the trial judge to allow alibi evidence to be heard even though particulars of it were not given within seven days, provided the prosecution has been given time to investigate the alibi before the trial started. (*R.* v. *Sullivan*, [1970] 2 All E.R. 681.)

Place and time of trial

Under s. 7 of the Magistrates' Courts Act, 1980, a magistrates' court committing a person to trial on indictment to the Crown Court has to specify the Crown Court centre at which he is to be tried and in selecting that centre must have regard to—

(*a*) the convenience of the defence, the prosecution and the witnesses;
(*b*) the expediting of the trial;
(*c*) any directions regarding the distribution of Crown Court business given by the Lord Chief Justice or by an officer of the Crown Court with the concurrence of the Lord Chancellor under the Supreme Court Act, 1981.

Under s. 76 of the Supreme Court Act, 1981 the Crown Court may alter the place of any trial on indictment by varying the decision of the magistrates or a previous decision on the matter made by the Crown Court. Under the 1981 Act the defendant or the prosecutor, if dissatisfied with the place of trial as fixed by the magistrates or by the Crown Court, may apply to the Crown Court to vary the place of trial. The Crown Court may deal with the application as it sees fit. An application under the 1981 Act must be heard in open court by a High Court judge.

The above provisions are designed to bring an accused person to trial as quickly as possible. However, the prosecutor and the accused and his advisers must be given time in which to prepare the case properly. Accordingly, s. 77 of the Supreme Court Act, 1981 (as amended) provides for the laying down under Crown Court Rules of the minimum period from the date of committal when the trial shall commence. These minimum periods cannot be *shortened* without the consent of the accused and the prosecutor or *lengthened* without an order of the Crown Court.

The offence and indictment

Let us suppose that Jim Green has recently and successfully objected to the granting of planning permission to Fred Brown, his neighbour, which has prevented Fred from using part of his land for car-breaking. Let us also suppose that on the evening of 25th February, 1988, Jim left home for work and shortly afterwards in a lane not far from his home he was attacked by Fred who was wearing a black balaclava over his head. Fred attacked Jim with a knife. Jim suffered serious injuries requiring five stitches in his cheek, six on his right hand, and 16 in his stomach. Jim was detained in hospital for several days.

Fred is now to be tried on indictment for the offence. An indictment is a printed accusation of crime made at the suit of the Queen and read out to the accused at the trial. In Fred's case the main contents of the indictment will state the court of trial and set out the following—

Fred Brown is charged as follows—

Statement of Offence—WOUNDING contrary to s. 18 of the Offences Against the Person Act, 1861.

Particulars of Offence—Fred Brown on the 25th February, 1988, in the County of Barchestershire, wounded Jim Green with intent to cause grievous bodily harm.

In this case there is only one offence but if there had been more each would have appeared in a separate paragraph. Each paragraph is referred to as a 'count'.

There may be a motion by the defence to quash the indictment. This is quite rare because such a motion is appropriate only where there is an error apparent on the face of the indictment. A possible ground to quash the indictment is that a count set out in it is bad for duplicity, as where assault and theft are charged in the same count.

Arraignment

When the day of Fred's trial arrives the clerk of the court will confirm Fred's identity, read out the indictment and ask Fred whether he is guilty or not guilty. This is called the arraignment.

If Fred pleads guilty counsel for the prosecution will give the court a summary of the evidence together with details of Fred's background and record. The defence will put in a plea for mitigation of sentence and sentence will then be passed.

Fred may, while intending to plead 'not guilty' to the s. 18 offence, be prepared to plead 'guilty' to a lesser offence which is not on the indictment. In this case Fred may be prepared to plead guilty to unlawful wounding under s. 20 of the Offences Against the Person Act, 1861. This carries a maximum period of five years' imprisonment, whereas the s. 18 offence carries a maximum term of imprisonment for life. This change of plea may arise because of a bargain reached between Fred's lawyer and the prosecution's lawyer, often with the judge's approval. This is known as 'plea-bargaining'.

If the prosecution refuses to accept the plea to the lesser offence then the trial will continue and if Fred is acquitted he cannot be sentenced on the basis of his guilty plea to the lesser offence (*R.* v. *Hazeltine*, [1967] 2 All E.R. 671); which is regarded as withdrawn if not accepted by the prosecution. It should be noted that a trial judge may allow a defendant to change his plea to not guilty at any time before sentence is passed, even though a formal verdict of guilty has been returned by the jury on the direction of the judge after the trial has begun (*R* v. *Drew*, [1985] 1 WLR 914).

We will assume that Fred pleads not guilty and in this case a jury must be sworn in.

Membership of the jury

Under the Juries Act, 1974, a person is eligible for jury service if he or she is not less than 18 and not more than 70 and is included on the Register of Electors for parliamentary and/or local government elections, and has been resident in the United Kingdom, the Channel Islands, or the Isle of Man for at least five years since the age of 13. As regards exemptions and disqualifications, these include members of the judiciary, those concerned with the administration of justice, such as barristers and solicitors, police and prison officers, the clergy, and persons receiving treatment for mental illness. The 1974 Act makes it an offence for anyone in these categories to serve as a juror. In addition, penalties are imposed upon persons who are eligible and have been duly summoned but fail to attend or are unfit through drink or drugs. Under the Juries Act, 1974 anyone imprisoned for more than three months and up to five years is disqualified for jury service for ten years, and anyone imprisoned for a term of over five years or for life is disqualified for life. Nevertheless, under the 1974 Act criminals could sit on juries. For example, those put on probation were not barred. However, the Juries (Disqualification) Act, 1984 disqualifies from jury service anyone who has served a custodial sentence of any kind or has had such a sentence suspended, or has been put on probation or placed under a community service order. The disqualification period is ten years, but only five years for those placed on probation. Those punished by fines can, of course, still sit on a jury.

Certain persons, although not ineligible for jury service, can if asked to serve, claim to be excused 'as of right'. These include members of Parliament, full-time serving members of H.M. Forces, and those in medical or similar professions. In addition, the 1974 Act provides that a person summoned for jury service may be excused for good reasons whether he is in one of the special classes or not. The Act also provides for exemptions to be granted administratively for previous jury service; before only the trial judge could grant exemption. Under s. 5 of the Juries Act, 1974 the defence has a right to see the names, and in London the addresses as well, of the jury panel. This could assist 'jury nobbling' but it remains a right at the present time.

As regards summoning and excusal, each summons for jury service is accompanied by details of the provisions for eligibility, disqualifications, and excusals as of right. A person receiving a summons will be asked to complete a form telling the court whether he or she is qualified for jury service and, if so, whether it is the person's wish to be excused either 'as of right' or for any other reason, e.g. because of personal circumstances, such as a mother with very young children, or a person running a one-man business. Much depends upon the Clerk of the Court; some are more difficult than others in terms of the acceptance of personal reasons for not serving.

Under s. 61 of the Administration of Justice Act, 1982 questions may be put to a prospective juror to ascertain whether he is qualified for jury service *at any time*, and not just when he attends following a jury summons. If a juror refuses without reasonable excuse to answer, or knowingly or recklessly gives a false answer to the questions which are customarily set out in the jury summons, he will commit an offence punishable with a fine. This applies also to a juror who pretends to have a disqualification which he does not have in order to try to avoid jury service.

As regards disabilities, the 1974 Act provides that the court may also exclude anyone from jury service because physical disability or insufficient understanding of English makes his ability to act effectively as a juror doubtful. However, s. 18 provides that no judgment after verdict should be reversed by reason, amongst other things, that any juror was unqualified or unfit to serve. Thus in *R.* v. *Chapman*, (1976) 63 Cr. App. R. 75 where, after a trial at which both defendants had been found guilty by a unanimous verdict, it was discovered that one juror had been deaf so that he was unable to follow the proceedings, it was held that that did not make the verdict unsafe or unsatisfactory and was a situation covered by the Juries Act, 1974, s. 18.

Under s. 3 of the 1974 Act the responsibility for summoning jurors is placed upon the Lord Chancellor, though the court's administration at each centre acts as summoning officer. Juries are paid travelling and subsistence allowances and are compensated for loss of earnings and other expenses.

Advantages and disadvantages of jury trial

Some take the view that the verdict of a jury is more acceptable to the public than the verdict of a judge, and certainly the jury system gives ordinary persons a part to play in the administration of justice. It is perhaps better that lay men and women should decide matters of fact and the credibility of witnesses. The jury system also tends to clarify the law, in that the judge has to explain the more important points arising at the trial in clear and simple terms, so that the jury may arrive at a proper verdict.

On the other hand, juries may be too easily swayed by experienced counsel and the random method of selection sometimes produces a jury which is not as competent in intellectual terms as it might be in weighing the evidence and following the arguments presented. It has been suggested that trial by (say) three judges would be better, particularly where difficult issues are involved.

All indictable offences are triable before a jury of 12 persons. A panel of more than 12 jurors is brought into court and the clerk will select 12 jurors by a ballot.

Challenge

The names of the jury as selected by the clerk's ballot are called out on selection and each person goes into the jury box to be sworn. Under s. 110 of the Criminal Justice Act, 1988 the right to challenge jurors without cause (reasons), in proceedings for the trial of a person on indictment, is abolished.

Now a challenge must be supported by reasons. A man may, for example, challenge the inclusion of a woman juror where his case involves wife-assault on the grounds that she will be less tolerant of that sort of conduct. The prosecution can also challenge jurors but must give reasons.

However, they have, in effect, a right to challenge without cause under the 'stand by' procedure. Prosecuting counsel may call on a juror to 'stand by for the Crown', i.e. to be excluded unless it is impossible for a jury to be empanelled without calling on him. In practice they are not called again.

Jury vetting

Following judicial decisions, particularly perhaps that of the Court of Appeal in *R*. v. *Mason*, [1980] 3 All E.R. 777, that it was not only lawful but necessary and a 'commonsense' precaution, for the police to vet jurors' criminal records and pass information to the prosecution so that challenge could be made, the Attorney-General has issued guidelines on jury checks. In the first place the guidelines state that a person will in general be disqualified or ineligible for a jury only as provided by the Juries Act, 1974 and the Juries (Disqualification) Act, 1984. However, where the case involves national security and part of the evidence is likely to be heard *in camera* (i.e. court closed to public and news media), or in terrorist cases, extra precautions may be necessary. However, no check on the records of police special branches will be made except on the authority of the Attorney-General following a recommendation from the D.P.P. Furthermore, checks involving so-called strong political motives will not be made except in terrorist cases or where national security is involved and the court is expected to sit *in camera*. There is, of course, no reason why routine police checks on criminal records for the purpose of ascertaining whether or not a jury panel includes any person disqualified under the Juries Act, 1974 should not continue.

The oath

The 12 persons who survive the selection procedure are then sworn, by each holding a Bible in his right hand and reading the following oath—

'I swear by Almighty God that I will faithfully try the defendant and give a true verdict according to the evidence'.

The affirmation which jurors may select if non-Christian is as follows—

'I do solemnly, and sincerely and truly declare and affirm that I will faithfully try the defendant and give a true verdict according to the evidence'.

The jury is then addressed by the clerk who explains the charges and tells them that having heard the evidence they must decide whether the defendant is guilty or not, and the trial begins officially at this point (*R v. Tonner*, [1985] 1 All E.R. 807).

The judge

Criminal offences are divided into four classes for the purpose of trial in a Crown Court. In broad terms the position is that *Class 1* offences, e.g. murder, treason and spying, are tried by a High Court judge. *Class 2* offences, e.g. manslaughter, rape, infanticide and sexual intercourse with a girl under 13, are tried by a High Court judge unless a particular case is released as suitable for a circuit judge by or on the authority of the Circuit Presiding Judge (see p. 114) as where the circumstances of the offence are not of unusual gravity. *Class 3* offences, i.e. all indictable offences other than those in Classes 1, 2 and 4, e.g. arson, perjury, corruption of Government or local government officers, may be tried by a High Court judge or a circuit judge or recorder. *Class 4* offences are all offences which are triable summarily or on indictment, e.g. reckless driving, plus certain others, e.g. causing death by reckless driving, burglary and wounding or causing grievous bodily harm with intent. These may be tried by a High Court judge but will normally be listed for trial by a circuit judge or recorder, or assistant recorder.

Thus it is likely that Fred will be tried by a circuit judge or recorder, or assistant recorder.

Trial and evidence

The barrister appearing for the prosecution will make an opening speech outlining his case to the Court and will then call witnesses to confirm the facts. However, before doing so he must tell the jury that the burden of proof rests on the prosecution to establish that the defendant is guilty beyond a reasonable doubt. A witness will first take the oath appropriate to his religion or affirm if he has no religious belief. The Christian oath is most often used. It is: 'I swear by Almighty God that the evidence I shall give shall be the truth, the whole truth and nothing but the truth'. Contrary to popular belief it does not end with 'so help me God'.

During the examination-in-chief, counsel for the prosecution must not lead his witnesses, i.e. must not suggest a particular answer to his question. Thus counsel for the prosecution cannot ask one of his witnesses, say, a police officer, 'did the defendant punch you when you arrested him?' He must instead say 'what happened when you arrested the defendant'?

Also, in examination-in-chief counsel must not contradict his own witness by referring to a prior inconsistent statement made in, say, committal proceedings, unless the witness becomes 'hostile', i.e. as where he is now showing bias against the person calling him. In addition hearsay evidence is not admissible. A witness must give evidence only as to what he himself saw or heard. Thus evidence given by a witness either for the prosecution or the defence in the form 'Alice told me that she saw Bill in the pub on Wednesday' would be inadmissible.

After counsel for the prosecution has carried out his examination-in-chief of a witness counsel for the defence can cross-examine the witness. In this situation he can lead and say, for example, 'my client was upset by the circumstances of his arrest, wasn't he? There was no need to have called him a lying swine, was there?' Counsel for the prosecution can also refer to prior inconsistent statements of the witness.

When the prosecution has called all its witnesses the defence will present its case and call witnesses to support it. These witnesses are examined-in-chief, cross-examined, and sometimes re-examined. More rarely, defence counsel may, before calling his witnesses, try to bring the trial to an end by endeavouring to persuade the judge that there is no case to answer, i.e. that the prosecution has not produced sufficient evidence to warrant the trial proceeding. This argument takes place without the jury. If the judge agrees with defence counsel he will call the jury back and tell them to give a formal acquittal. Otherwise the trial proceeds.

The defendant may give evidence on oath or by affirmation on his own behalf, though he is not obliged to give evidence at all. Section 72 of the Criminal Justice Act, 1982 abolishes the right of an accused person to make an unsworn statement from the dock without being subject to cross-examination. However, the accused may address the court or jury if he has no legal representation and may make a statement in mitigation of sentence without being sworn. If he gives evidence on oath in the ordinary way he may be cross-examined but there can be no cross-examination where a mere statement is made, though the making of a statement in this way often leads to the suggestion that the defendant has something to hide.

After the defence witnesses have been heard the prosecution makes its closing speech, followed by the defence, which always has the last word. (Criminal Procedure (Right of Reply) Act, 1964.)

Summing up

The judge will then explain his role to the jury. He will say that he will tell them what the law is and that the law is a matter for him but that they are the only judges of the facts in the case. He will repeat that it is for the prosecution to prove guilt. The judge will them sum up the evidence on both sides and will define the law of the offence. If he misleads the jury on this the accused may well have grounds for a successful appeal. The judge will also explain that although Fred is charged under s. 18 of the Offences Against the Person Act, 1861 of wounding with intent to cause grievous bodily harm, the jury may acquit him of that offence and yet find him guilty of the lesser offence of unlawful wounding under s. 20

of the Offences Against the Person Act, 1861. The judge may then explain to the jury that they must endeavour to reach a unanimous verdict (but see below), though whether he does so or not is a matter of discretion (*R.* v. *Watson, The Times*, 10 March, 1988). The judge will then leave the court and the jury, escorted by a bailiff, will retire to a jury room where they must stay until they reach a verdict. If a verdict is not reached on the day the jury retire they will be taken to an hotel to spend the night.

The verdict

If the jury is unanimous in finding Fred guilty they will tell the jury bailiff that they are ready to come back into court. The judge and counsel return and the jury files in. A court usher will ask the foreman of the jury what their verdict is. We assume that they have found Fred guilty of the s. 18 offence; the foreman says so.

At this stage Fred's previous convictions, if any, will be handed to the judge who may refer to some of them openly in court. Counsel for the defence will then normally put in a plea in mitigation, saying, perhaps, that Fred has not been in trouble before or at least not for some time, according to his record, in the hope that this plea will lead to a lighter sentence.

The judge will then address the defendant and pass sentence, which in view of the violence involved in Fred's case, is likely to be a term of imprisonment.

Majority verdicts

The Juries Act, 1974, provides for majority verdicts of juries in criminal proceedings. Section 17 provides that the verdict of the jury in criminal proceedings need not be unanimous if—

(*a*) in a case where there are not less than *eleven* jurors, *ten* of them agree on the verdict. In the case of an ordinary jury of twelve this means that the judge can accept a verdict of eleven to one or ten to two; and

(*b*) in a case where there are *ten* jurors, *nine* of them agree on the verdict.

A court must not accept a majority verdict of guilty unless the foreman of the jury has stated in open court the number of jurors who respectively agreed to and dissented from the verdict. No such statement is required if the verdict is one of not guilty so that it will not be known that a verdict of not guilty was by a majority.

Furthermore, a court must not accept a majority verdict unless it appears to the court that the jury have had not less than two hours' deliberation or such longer period as the court thinks reasonable, having regard to the nature and complexity of the case.

The judge cannot accept a majority verdict after less than two hours' deliberation and if the jury is not unanimous after two hours he should send them back, at least once more, to try to reach unanimity. If they still cannot he should send them back to see if they can reach a decision by the necessary majority, having directed them on the law relating to majority verdicts.

When the jury returns to the courtroom the judge will ask whether the required majority has agreed on a verdict. If they have, the verdict is accepted *provided*, according to a Practice Direction made on 11 May, 1970, that at least two hours and *ten minutes* have elapsed between the time at which the last juror left the jury box to go to the jury room and the time when the judge asked whether the jury had reached a verdict by the required majority.

Before the judge asks whether the jury has reached a majority verdict the senior officer of the court present must announce the deliberation time which the jury has had. The extra ten minutes was added in order to reduce the number of appeals made to the Court of Appeal on the ground that majority verdicts had been accepted although the deliberation time had been less than two hours, as for example, where the jury had returned to put a question to the court during the deliberation period.

The majority provision is, of course, a controversial one because the principle of the unanimous decision was an old and much-respected feature of English law. The main reason for the change was the growing problem of deliberate corruption or intimidation of jurors to secure an acquittal. The majority of ten to two was chosen because it was felt that it would be difficult to find more than one or two who were susceptible to bribery or intimidation, particularly in view of the fact that those with criminal records are excluded from jury service under the Juries Act, 1974 and the Juries (Disqualification) Act 1984. It should be noted that what happens in a jury room is not supposed to be disclosed. This is now reinforced by s. 8 of the Contempt of Court Act, 1981. This makes it an offence for a juror to reveal the discussions in the jury room and for a newspaper or any other organization or person to try to find out by interviewing a juror.

Alternative verdicts

The common law, as re-stated by s. 6(3) and (4) of the Criminal Law Act, 1967, provides for alternative verdicts, which means that a jury can convict an accused of an offence other than the one with which he is charged. Although the wording of s. 6 appears wider then the common law rule, subsequent cases seem to indicate that a jury cannot convict of an offence different in *character* from the offence charged. The power is limited to a conviction for an offence involving *the same criminal act* but with a lesser degree of aggravation. As we have seen, in Fred's case it would have been possible for the jury to bring in a verdict of unlawful wounding under s. 20 of the Offences Against the Person Act, 1861 although the charge was wounding with intent to cause grievous bodily harm under s. 18, *ibid*.

Where there exists an alternative and less serious offence to the one charged, the judge *must* direct the jury on the lesser offence if there is evidence to support it (*R* v. *Fairbanks*, [1986] 1 WLR 1202).

Number of jurors

The number of jurors will normally be 12 unless the number has been reduced in accordance with s. 16 of the Juries Act, 1974. The section provides for the continuation of criminal trials where a juror dies or is discharged by the court, whether through illness or for any other reason.

If the number of members of the jury is not reduced below nine, the trial may proceed and the verdict may be given accordingly.

However, on a trial for any offence punishable with death, e.g. treason, this rule only applies if assent in writing is given by or on behalf of both the prosecution and the accused, or each of the accused if there is more than one.

Moreover, the court has discretion in any criminal trial to discharge the jury if it sees fit to do so when its numbers are depleted. If a trial has continued under the above provisions with nine jurors, s. 17 of the Juries Act, 1974, does not apply and the verdict must be unanimous.

Committal to Crown Court for sentence

As we have seen, there are times when the Crown Court sits to sentence persons convicted of offences before the magistrates. This happens where the magistrates have found a particular defendant guilty and then have had access to his previous convictions showing, shall we say, a very bad record, and feel that the defendant should receive a greater sentence than they can give. In such a situation they will commit the defendant to the Crown Court for sentence.

The Crown Court may sit solely for the purpose of sentencing and if so consists of a judge (either a High Court judge or circuit judge or recorder) and not less than two nor more than four magistrates. The decision as regards the sentence is by a majority and if there is an equality of voting the judge has a casting vote.

Appeals in criminal cases

A person who has been convicted and sentenced by a criminal court has rights of appeal. These have already been considered in chapter 2 (see p. 19).

Contempt of Court Act, 1981

Under s. 4 of the 1981 Act the trial judge may make an order imposing restrictions on the reporting of a trial in, e.g. newspapers. The section gives the court power to order the postponement of publication of reports of a trial or part of a trial where it appears necessary to avoid a substantial risk of prejudicing that trial or other proceedings pending or imminent, as where witnesses or potential witnesses might be intimidated.

Section 11 gives the court power to prohibit the publication of any name or other matter in connection with the proceedings where the court has allowed the name or other matter to be withheld from the public when the proceedings were before the court.

Sentencing

Before considering the range of sentences a criminal court can now give, it may be advantageous to state in broad terms the purposes which are, or were, behind certain types of sentence. These are as follows—

(a) The philosophy of retribution. This is based on the idea of atonement. Retribution emphasizes the position of the social group against which the criminal offends rather than that of the criminal himself. By imposing punishment society exacts retribution. The science of criminal law has gradually moved away from this philosophy.

(b) The philosophy of deterrence. This emphasizes the social objective. Punishment must be designed so as to deter, as far as possible, the commission of similar offences in terms both of deterring an actual offender and other members of society who have not yet committed crimes. This philosophy still prevails in modern criminology.

(c) The philosophy of reformation. This involves the use of, for example, educational methods, either in addition to, or in substitution for, punishment proper. In general terms the increasing attempt to understand the social and psychological causes of crime has led to a growing emphasis on this philosophy.

Underlying all of the above philosophies is, of course, the need to protect society from the criminal and this leads on occasions to sentences which are *preventive* in aim such as, for example, long prison sentences and disqualification from driving.

(d) Reparation. In modern times the principle of requiring the criminal to make reparation to his victim and/or to the community is increasingly the motive behind sentencing policy. The principle is expressed, for example, in sentences involving compensation orders and community service orders.

Types of sentence

The death penalty is still available for treason but the Murder (Abolition of Death Penalty) Act, 1965, abolished the death penalty for murder. The sentence is now life imprisonment but the trial judge may recommend a minimum period for which the convicted person should be detained before the Secretary of State considers the release of the defendant on licence. In addition, there is no power to administer corporal punishment upon an offender. Sentences which are available are set out below.

(*a*) *Custodial sentences.* The punishment for most crimes is laid down by Acts of Parliament. The usual provision lays down a maximum fine and/or imprisonment, leaving the court to decide what sentence to give up to that maximum.

Persons who are serving life imprisonment may be released on licence by the Home Secretary at any time. Others are entitled to a reduction of sentence of up to one-third for good behaviour. In addition, those who have served one-third of their sentences, provided that this has involved at least six months in prison, may be released on licence or parole. The licence may be revoked by the Home Secretary, e.g. for failure to co-operate with the supervising officer, or by the Crown Court or a Magistrates' Court if there is a conviction of crime. The sentences available to the magistrates in juvenile courts have already been considered (see p. 56).

The Powers of Criminal Courts Act, 1973, provides for the system of suspended sentences. The essential features of the system are as follows—

(i) any court which passes a sentence of imprisonment for a term of not more than two years *may* order the sentence as a suspended sentence and announce the *operational period*, i.e. the length of the term of suspension, i.e. 'nine months suspended for two years'. The maximum operational period is two years and the minimum one year. (S. 22(1).) If the offender commits another offence within the stated period the original sentence can, at the discretion of the court, be activated and the offender made to serve it after any sentence imposed for the subsequent offence.

(ii) a sentence of imprisonment must be appropriate in the circumstances of the case even though the defendant will not in fact go to prison unless he offends again. (S. 22(2).) The court is now required to consider other forms of sentence before passing a suspended sentence of imprisonment.

Section 47 and Sch. 9 of the Criminal Law Act, 1977 (as amended by s. 30 and Sch. 14 of the Criminal Justice Act, 1982) provide for a *partially suspended sentence* under which part of the sentence is served immediately in prison and part is suspended. If during the *whole* period of the sentence, i.e. the custodial as well as the suspended part, the offender commits an imprisonable offence, e.g. in the custodial part against a fellow prisoner or prison officer, he will be liable on conviction to be ordered to serve the whole or part of the suspended period in prison.

The minimum sentence of imprisonment which may be partly suspended is three months and the maximum two years. The minimum imprisonment to be served immediately is 28 days. It was held in *Re Dobbs, The Times*, 8 November, 1983 that the courts have no power to suspend a sentence of what is now detention in a young offenders institution, either in whole or in part.

(*b*) *Fines*. These are available for every offence except murder and treason. Any criminal court may order the payment of a sum of money by an offender, in general up to a maximum laid down by statute. In general terms this is up to a maximum of £2000 in a magistrates' court, and unlimited in a Crown Court. Failure to pay can lead to imprisonment but the court will first enquire into the offender's ability to pay.

The fine is a most appropriate sentence to give against a corporation and company legislation often provides for default fines on registered companies and their officers, e.g. for failure to file returns with the Registrar of Companies.

(*c*) *Probation*. An offender may be placed under the supervision of a probation officer for a period not exceeding three years. Regular contact with a probation officer is required and conditions may be imposed, e.g. that the offender must have medical treatment. Under s. 65 of the Criminal Justice Act, 1982 the court may impose attendance at a Day Centre as a condition of probation.

(*d*) *Absolute and conditional discharge*. A court may give an absolute discharge where the accused is in breach of the law but the court considers that there are mitigating factors. These are, e.g. no previous criminal record and sometimes unemployment or old age, or a conditional discharge which means that the court will not pass sentence on the offender unless he commits another offence during a specified period not exceeding three years. In which case he can be sentenced also for the original offence.

(*e*) *Community Service Orders*. With the offender's consent the court may make a 'Community Service Order' to be performed at given times but not interfering with educational or work routines. A report by a probation officer or by a local authority social worker must be considered. The total number of hours is between 40 and 240 to be served within a year. The service is prescribed by the Home Secretary and consists of such things as building playgrounds, gardening, helping elderly or disabled people or repairing vandalized property. The Community Service Order may be made for breach of probation or instead of committal to prison for failure to pay a fine. (S. 6 and ss. 14–17 of the Powers of Criminal Courts Act, 1973, and s. 49(1) of the Criminal Justice Act, 1972.) Proceedings for breach of a Community Service Order may be initiated by probation officers through the supervising magistrates' court either by summons or warrant.

(*f*) *Miscellaneous sentences*. These include binding over to keep the peace with the sanction that a sum of money will be forfeited if there is a breach; endorsement of driving licence and disqualification from driving.

The following provisions relating to sentencing are also of interest—

(1) Any person of 21 years of age or over shall not be sentenced to imprisonment if he has not been sentenced to imprisonment previously

unless no other method of dealing with him appears appropriate. A suspended sentence which has not been activated does not count as a previous imprisonment, nor does a previous sentence of detention as a young offender. (Powers of Criminal Courts Act, 1973, s. 20.)

Section 62 of the Criminal Justice Act, 1982 requires a court to get a social enquiry report before imposing a sentence of imprisonment on a person who has not previously served such a sentence. If a *magistrates' court* does impose a sentence of imprisonment on an offender who has not served one before, but without a social inquiry report, the magistrates must state their reasons for this in open court and record them in the warrant of commitment to prison.

(2) If the accused is a 'first offender' in the above sense and is not legally represented at a summary trial, he must not be sentenced to imprisonment, or detention as a young offender, unless either he failed in his application for legal aid on the ground that he had sufficient means, or he refused or failed to apply for legal aid (Powers of Criminal Courts Act, 1973, s. 21).

(3) Crown Courts and magistrates' courts are given power to defer sentence for six months to see how the offender behaves after conviction, e.g. whether he has made any reparation for his offence. The consent of the offender is required before sentence can be deferred (Powers of Criminal Courts Act, 1973, s. 1).

(4) The court has power to order forfeiture of *any* property in the offender's possession which was used or intended for use for the purpose of committing or facilitating the commission of *any* offence, provided the offender has been convicted of an offence punishable on indictment by two years or more imprisonment. (Powers of Criminal Courts Act, 1973, s. 43.) This section is intended to cover property such as motor vehicles and radio equipment as well as the traditional tools of the criminal's trade.

(5) On a conviction similar to that set out in (4) above the court may order the offender to be disqualified from driving if a vehicle was used for the purpose of committing or facilitating the commission of an offence. (Powers of Criminal Courts Act, 1973, s. 44.) The person disqualified need not have been the driver.

(6) Under s. 3 of the Immigration Act, 1971 both a Crown Court and a magistrates' court may recommend deportation of non-patrials given that certain conditions regarding notice have been fulfilled.

(7) Under the Drug Trafficking Offences Act, 1986 the Crown Court, when sentencing for any drug trafficking offence, may make a confiscation order. The Court is required to determine whether the defendant has benefited from drug trafficking and, if so, how much is to be ordered by way of confiscation. The maximum order will be the value of the defendant's proceeds of drug trafficking or the amount of his realisable property whichever is the greater.

(8) Under ss. 32–33 of the Criminal Justice Act, 1988 the Attorney-General may refer to the Court of Appeal cases in which it appears to

him that the sentence has been too lenient. The Court of Appeal may then pass such sentence as it thinks appropriate and which it was in the power of the lower court to pass.

Compensatory awards

In order to avoid the need for a victim of crime to bring an action in a civil court for compensation there is some power in criminal courts to give monetary compensation. Sections 35 to 38 of the Powers of Criminal Courts Act, 1973, provide for reparation by the offender. *Compensation orders* are available for any 'personal injury, loss or damage resulting from' an offence of which the offender is convicted or which he asks to have taken into consideration in sentence. Compensation is not available to dependants of a person killed as a result of a crime, nor is it for 'loss or damage due to an accident arising out of the presence of a motor vehicle on a road'. Where property which is the object of an offence under the Theft Act, 1968 is damaged the offender may be ordered to pay compensation however and by whomsoever the damage was caused. Compensation for victims of theft and burglary is the main use of s. 35.

Magistrates' courts are limited to a total of £2000 in respect of one conviction, i.e. the offence of which the person is convicted and any other offences which he asks to have taken into consideration. In making an order the court must consider the offender's means. There is no limit to the amount which a Crown Court can order. However, the amount should not be so great that the offender has no hope of paying it, or which will take too long to pay, say more than two years. These compensation orders operate alongside the scheme for compensation for criminal injuries out of public funds (see below).

The compensation order can be appealed against (s. 36) or reviewed by the magistrates' court having the function of enforcing it (s. 37). It can be reviewed if the property to which it relates has been recovered or if civil damages have been awarded which are less than the amount of the order but there is no provision for the person compensated to pay the excess in either case.

Section 38 provides that in civil proceedings no account shall be taken of the compensation order in assessment of damages, but the civil judgment cannot be enforced in respect of the amount paid under the order. Leave of the court must be obtained to enforce the outstanding amount of the civil judgment which corresponds to the outstanding amount of the order. It should be noted that compensation orders can be made by the court without application by the person aggrieved.

Although in the past a compensation order could only be made *in addition* to another sentence for crime, s. 35 of the Powers of Criminal Courts Act, 1973, as substituted by s. 67 of the Criminal Justice Act, 1982, allows a court to make a compensation order in its own right, i.e. *instead of* imposing another sentence for crime. The same section now allows a compensation order to be made even though the *precise* amount of the loss or damage has not been proved. A reasonable estimate can be made from evidence called by the prosecution.

Restitution orders may also be made in regard to property which is the object of an offence under s. 28(1)(c) or (3) of the Theft Act, 1968 and under s. 6 of the Criminal Justice Act, 1972. Restitution orders may also be made in respect of an offence which the accused asks to have taken into consideration. A restitution order and a compensation order may be made in respect of the same goods if recovered in a damaged condition.

The compensatory awards set out above are ineffective if the offender is never caught or if when caught he has no money or property with which to pay compensation. In consequence there is, under ss. 100–9 and Scheds. 6 and 7 of the Criminal Justice Act, 1988, a scheme of state compensation operated by the Criminal Injuries Compensation Board.

The Board may make discretionary payments to those suffering personal injury which is attributable to certain criminal offences e.g. rape and assault under s. 47 of the Offences Against the Person Act, 1861. Payments are not made for offences against property. Dependants of a person who dies as a result of a relevant crime may claim. There are rights of appeal. The Board can, having made an award, seek to reimburse itself by a claim against the offender. Those who cannot show the need for this sort of compensation may, of course, make an application under s. 35 of the Powers of Criminal Courts Act, 1973 if possible. (See p. 74.) In addition, it should be noted that motoring offences, except where the vehicle has been used as a means of injury, and offences committed against members of the offender's family are excluded. The above restrictions exclude a large number of criminal injuries from the scheme.

Rehabilitation of Offenders Act, 1974

The provisions of this Act are an attempt to give effect to the principle that when a person convicted of crime has been successful in living down that conviction and has avoided further criminal activities, common justice demands that his efforts should not be prejudiced by the unwarranted disclosure of that earlier conviction.

All sentences are subject to rehabilitation except imprisonment for life and custodial sentences of more than 30 months. After the expiry of certain defined periods the offender is rehabilitated. For example, if it was a custodial sentence for a term exceeding six months but not exceeding 30 months, rehabilitation is after ten years; if for a term not exceeding six months, it is seven years, or if the sentence was a fine, it is five years. In the case of those who were under 17 at the date of conviction, the rehabilitation periods are halved.

So far as the employment of persons with previous convictions is concerned, it should be noted that any questions seeking information as to a person's previous convictions shall be treated as not relating to spent convictions and any obligation on any person to disclose matters shall not require him to disclose a spent conviction, and a spent conviction or failure to disclose a spent conviction is not a proper ground for dismissing or excluding a person from or prejudicing him in any occupation or employment. There is an exception (see S.I. 1986/1249) where the employment allows contact with persons under 18 e.g. in care, leisure and recreational activities. Here questions can be asked designed to reveal spent convictions particularly those with a sexual connotation. Such spent convictions are a ground for dismissal which will not, for that reason alone, be unfair.

It should be noted that the above provisions do not affect the admission of evidence relating to a person's previous convictions in any criminal proceedings (*R. v. Smallman* [1982] Crim. L.R. 175) or in proceedings relating, for example, to adoption, guardianship, custody or care and control of any minor. However, in practice the courts do not usually consider 'spent' offences. The defendant's record supplied for the purposes of sentence contains all previous convictions, but those which are spent are as far as possible marked as such. A person may, moreover, consent to the admission of evidence of his own spent convictions.

The provisions of the Act apply to convictions, whether by courts in Great Britain or outside, and they also apply to persons dealt with in service disciplinary proceedings.

The Act also covers actions for libel or slander brought by a rehabilitated person. If the defendant imputed, for example, in a reference, that the plaintiff had a conviction and that conviction was at the time of publication a spent conviction, the defendant may still successfully plead justification, i.e. the truth of his statement, unless the plaintiff can prove malice.

CIVIL PROCEDURE

We shall consider the way in which a civil action is brought and concluded in the High Court.

For the purposes of our High Court action we shall deal with a case of breach of contract under which John, a miller operating as a sole trader, was to sell to Nature Foods Ltd 1000 tons of special high quality stone-ground flour in accordance with a sample shown to an agent of Nature Foods at the time, the price being £45 per ton. John claims that flour in accordance with the sample was delivered and that he has not been paid.

It appears that Nature Foods have not paid because the flour had defects in terms of quality not revealed by a reasonable examination of the sample. They will counterclaim for damages for breach of contract by John.

Bringing a civil action to trial

John's claim is too high in monetary terms to be brought in the County Court, either before a judge or in arbitration, unless Nature Foods agree which we shall assume they will not. Therefore John's action must be brought in the High Court. If John is wealthy no problems arise in terms of his ability to pay for the service of lawyers. If he is not wealthy then this position is much more difficult. If the claim against Nature Foods proceeds to trial and John is successful then he will receive most of his costs from Nature Foods. However, if he fails in his claim he may have to pay his own and most of Nature Foods' costs.

Legal aid

It is unlikely that John will be able to claim legal aid because legal aid in civil proceedings is only for persons of very limited means. The qualifying capital and income limits are revised at intervals but John is unlikely to qualify. However, the provisions are useful to persons of very limited means in some instances, say employment disputes, since legal aid is available, for example, for proceedings before the Employment Appeal Tribunal. In civil proceedings a person of limited means can get two kinds of legal aid: advice and assistance from a solicitor and legal aid for civil court proceedings. There is also, as we have seen, Criminal legal aid which provides for payments to lawyers to represent a person charged before the court with a criminal offence.

Attempt to settle

On the assumption that John has sufficient funds to proceed and has duly consulted a solicitor, the next step is to attempt an early settlement, and the solicitors of each party will correspond on this. If this fails then John's solicitor must consider going to court (or litigation) and whether or not an action by John would be successful.

On this issue John's solicitor may rely on his own view but in a difficult case will usually consult counsel. Counsel will give a written opinion and on the assumption that this is favourable, proceedings are commenced.

Nevertheless, in view of the costs of litigation, John's solicitor will continue, even after service of the writ and before trial, to seek a settlement. A number of cases are settled on the steps of the court itself on the day of the trial to avoid further costs.

The writ

The first step is to issue a writ (the equivalent in the county court is called a summons). The writ is drafted by John's solicitor or counsel and filed in the court office where it is also sealed and returned to the plaintiff. The writ is then served on the defendant, or his solicitors, but in the case of Nature Foods, which is a corporation, service will be at its registered office or solicitors, personally by the plaintiff or his agent or by ordinary first class mail.

The writ tells the defendants, Nature Foods, that the plaintiff, John, has a claim against them and sets out briefly its nature, and the relief or remedy required, by way of what is called an indorsement of claim. It calls on Nature Foods to satisfy the claim or return to the Central Office of the Supreme Court, or a District Registry if the writ was issued by a District Registry, the accompanying Acknowledgement of Service.

Acknowledgement of service

On the assumption that Nature Foods wish to contest John's case, their solicitor will inform the court that this is so. This is done by completing and returning the form of Acknowledgement of Service received with the writ.

This should be done within 14 days of service of writ. If Nature Foods do not give notice of intention to defend John will be entitled to judgment. John is claiming a liquidated sum, i.e. £45,000, and if Nature Foods fail to give notice of intention to defend John may enter *final* judgment for that sum plus interest (see p. 319) and costs. However, if John's action had been for an unliquidated sum, e.g. damages for negligence, *final* judgment could not have been obtained because the damages would have to be assessed. In such a case John would have obtained an interlocutory judgment, the amount of damages being then assessed by a Master (see p. 113). The defendant may attend the hearing before the Master in person or by solicitor or counsel to dispute the amount of damages. After this procedure has been followed the plaintiff may enter *final* judgment.

Statement of claim

If Nature Foods give notice of intention to defend, then John, through his lawyers, must deliver a 'statement of claim'. This may have been done with the writ but if not, it is delivered separately. In this case it would seem to have been reasonable to endorse the statement of claim on the writ. However, in a more complex case it might be reasonable to serve a separate statement of claim.

A separate statement sets out in detail the facts which the plaintiff alleges support his claim and the defendant receives a copy. All material facts must be set out and the plaintiff will not be allowed at the trial to introduce material of which the defendant has not been given notice.

The evidence supporting John's claim need not be stated and there need be no mention that the facts set out reveal an alleged breach of contract because this is obvious, both to the court and Nature Foods' lawyers.

The facts must be given in sufficient *detail* to enable the defendants to prepare a defence. Places and dates must be given so that the defendant may try to show that the event did not happen or, if it did, to give a different version of it.

Striking out

If a statement of claim is alleged to disclose no cause of action, e.g. a claim in negligence where the defendant alleges no duty of care (see p. 393) or is too vague or so full of irrelevant matter as to prejudice a proper defence at the trial, the defendant can apply to a Master (see p. 113) to have it 'struck out'. If the application is successful the plaintiff must deliver a new statement of claim.

In addition, a plaintiff's claim may be struck out under Rules of Supreme Court. Examples are for failing to serve a statement of claim or to comply with requirements relating to further and better particulars, discovery of documents (see p. 81), and interrogatories (see p. 82). However, the court has an inherent power to strike out a claim if, as the Court of Appeal decided in *Allen* v. *Sir Alfred McAlpine & Sons Ltd*, [1968] 1 All E.R. 543, there has been inordinate and inexcusable delay which gives rise to a substantial risk that a fair trial is not possible. These principles were approved by the House of Lords in *Birkett* v. *James*, [1977] 2 All E.R. 801. Furthermore, it was held by the Court of Appeal in *Janov* v. *Morris*, [1981] 3 All E.R. 780 that in an appropriate case of delay the court may even strike out a second claim made by a second writ within the limitation period, thus effectively preventing the plaintiff from ever receiving the relief claimed.

Further and better particulars

A statement of claim which merely fails to give sufficient detail will not be struck out but the defence may ask for 'further and better particulars', and the plaintiff must then supply the details required of the allegations he has made. He may not allege totally new matters.

The request for particulars is made initially by letter but if the plaintiff fails to give the necessary details, either properly or at all, the defendant may apply to a Master who may order the plaintiff to comply with the request. Failure to comply with these requirements may result in the striking out of the plaintiff's claim.

The defence

When the defence is satisfied that it understands the allegations in the statement of claim and the detail given in the particulars, then it must put forward its version of the dispute. The document in which this is done is called a 'defence'.

The defence sets out the facts as the defendant sees them and the allegations he makes. If an allegation in the statement of claim is denied, the defence must say so. If it is not denied the court will assume that it is admitted.

A defence which is vague or irrelevant may be struck out, and one which does not give sufficient detail gives the right to the plaintiff to ask for further and better particulars of it.

Reply

If the plaintiff merely wishes to deny the defendant's allegations he need do nothing more. If, however, he wants to raise further allegations in order to answer a point in the defence, he pleads these in a further document called a 'reply'. This process may continue, replies being exchanged, until each party has raised every point which is considered relevant.

Counterclaim

In many cases only a statement of claim and a defence are necessary. However, sometimes the defendant says that not only is the plaintiff's claim unfounded, but that it is he who has a claim against the plaintiff. Where this is so the defendant sets out his claim in a separate part of his defence, called a 'counterclaim'. This is, in effect, a reverse statement of claim to which the plaintiff will deliver a reply containing a 'defence to counterclaim'. Nature Foods will deliver a counterclaim in regard to the alleged breach of contract by John.

Payment into court

A payment in, as it is usually called, is a sum of money which the defendant pays into the Pay Office of the Central Office of the Supreme Court in London or a District Registry in a city outside London. A note of the payment is sent to the plaintiff, or to the defendant in the case of a payment in by a plaintiff in respect of a counterclaim by a defendant, and to any co-defendants or co-plaintiffs, as the case may be. A payment in, which is allowed in all actions for debt and damages, may be made at any time, even after service of writ and during the trial, but not after the judge has started to sum up.

A payment in, e.g. by a defendant, is intended to put pressure on the plaintiff. If Nature Foods were to pay in a sum of money less than £45,000, say, £30,000 representing what they thought to be a fair settlement of the claim, John must decide either to take the sum paid in or go on to trial or with the trial if it has commenced.

The snag is that if John refuses the offer and the judge at the trial awards less, even a penny less, than the £30,000 paid in, John will have to pay his own costs *and* those of Nature Foods incurred after payment in, and may be left with little, if anything of whatever sum the judge has awarded him. Normally, as a winning plaintiff, John would have had his costs paid by Nature Foods.

The judge is not told that there has been a payment in until *all* questions of liability and the amount of debt or damages to be awarded have been decided. If the judge is, e.g. by some mistake by a solicitor for a party, made aware of a payment in, he has, according to *Millensted* v. *Grosvenor House Ltd*, [1937] 1 K.B. 717, a discretion whether to continue to try the case or to order a retrial by another judge.

The pleadings

Thus, in our case the statement of claim will allege that on a given date the parties signed a written contract under which John was to supply 1000 tons of flour in accordance with sample at a price of £45 per ton; that the flour was duly delivered but the price has not been paid.

Nature Foods will admit the contract and the non-payment but say that the flour did not conform with the sample. In addition, because of John's failure to perform the contract properly, Nature Foods were unable to bake sufficient high quality bread to fulfil all their contracts with health food shops. Nature Foods, having become liable to pay damages to their customers counterclaim for those damages plus compensation for loss of goodwill. John then delivers a reply denying the allegations made in the defence and saying that he delivered flour which did conform with the agreed sample.

The various documents are referred to as 'pleadings' and when the plaintiff and the defendant do not wish to plead any additional facts, the pleadings are said to be closed.

The precise matters now in dispute are clear to both sides so that they can now prepare their evidence accordingly. In addition, a judge will see clearly from the pleadings the matters which he is called upon to decide.

Drafting the pleadings

All the documents forming the pleadings are usually drafted by counsel so that papers, e.g. letters, must be sent to counsel and returned after drafting and delivery to the other party. All of this takes time and leads to the delays which occur before trial.

Discovery

Although every fact relied upon by a party must be disclosed to the other, the evidence which will be used to prove those facts in court need not be disclosed until it confronts the other party at the trial.

To this there is a major exception which is that each party can be required to disclose to the other the *documentary evidence* which he has whether it *assists or impedes his case*. The opponent may take copies of the documents which may include any kind of writing, however informal, e.g. bills and rent books. The method of exchanging documents after close of pleading is called 'discovery'. Discovery is available only against a party to an action and not against a witness.

There may be objections to disclosure. If so, the court can, if it thinks fit, order production. However, a person cannot be required to produce privileged documents, e.g. confidential communications passing between a client and his solicitor.

During recent years there have been a number of cases on *public interest immunity* where the issue has been the necessity for the proper administration of public services for public authorities to refuse to disclose documents.

It appears that the court will uphold public interest immunity unless disclosure is fundamental to a particular litigant's case. Thus in *Campbell* v. *Tameside Metropolitan Borough Council*, [1982] 2 All E.R. 791 the Court of Appeal decided that C, who had been seriously assaulted by an 11-year-old child at the school where she was a teacher, could have discovery of the local authority reports on the child by teachers and psychiatrists to assess the local authority's knowledge of his previous violent behaviour which was vital as a ground for her claim against the authority.

A party to civil litigation and his solicitors who have obtained by discovery documents belonging to the other party must not use them for any purpose of their own apart from the action as a result of which discovery was granted.

In *Home Office* v. *Harman*, [1982] 1 All E.R. 532 the House of Lords held that it was a civil contempt of court for the solicitor of a litigant in an action against the Home Office for alleged unlawful confinement in a prison 'control unit' isolated from the rest of the prison system, to allow a journalist access to documents obtained by discovery to write an article highly critical of the Home Office and the control unit. This was civil contempt, said the House of Lords, even though the documents concerned had been read out at the trial.

Advice on evidence
The next step is to ask counsel to use his ability and experience to decide how to use the rules of procedure before trial to get John into the best possible position and what evidence should be called at the trial.

This stage is most important because cases are often won or lost by the way in which the evidence is prepared and presented.

Interrogatories
If a fact essential to success cannot be proved by a party because those facts are peculiarly within the knowledge of his opponent, the problem may be overcome by the use of 'interrogatories'.

These are questions which one side may require the other to *answer on oath*. The answer may then be read at the trial. Whether a particular question may or may not be asked is a matter to be decided by a Master.

Remember that particulars are designed to make clear the opponent's allegations which, if he fails to prove, will lose him his case. Discovery and interrogatories are concerned with evidence. If they fail to provide the evidence required then other methods of proof may be used. However, each party is tied to the pleadings and if he cannot establish the facts there set out no other facts will do, unless, of course, in his pleadings he sets out two fact situations on which he may rely.

Thus, Nature Foods may be asked for particulars as to why the delivery of flour failed to conform with the sample, but not whether there is any record in, say, a stock book. That should have been dealt with on discovery. Nor may Nature Foods be asked for particulars relating to whether they told one of their customers by telephone prior to delivery of the flour that they did not want it. Such a question might be asked as an interrogatory.

Notice to admit

A party faced on the pleadings with the problem of proving a particular fact, e.g. that a letter was in fact written by the person whose signature it appears to bear, may serve a notice on his opponent requiring him to admit that fact in order to save the expense of producing the necessary evidence.

If the other party refuses to admit then, when costs are being considered, the party asking for the admission may try to convince the judge or Master that refusal to admit was unreasonable and that his opponent must pay the cost of proving that point, whatever the result of the case.

Notice to produce a document

If either party wishes at the trial to refer to a document which is in his opponent's possession he must serve on his opponent a Notice to Produce the Document. This notice does not make the opponent produce it at the trial but it gives him warning that its contents may be brought into question so that he has a reasonable opportunity of bringing the document to the trial in order to prove his own version of what it contains.

Setting down for trial

The case may now be 'set down' to wait a time for hearing.

There is much criticism of the time taken to get a case into court and reforms may be desirable. However, the procedure outlined above is important because the most costly part of any civil action is the actual proceedings in court so that it is vital that the pre-trial procedure should ensure that the precise issues at stake are clear and that no time in court will be wasted on irrelevant matters. Also, it would be most unjust if pre-trial procedure did not ensure that both parties had fair warning of the case which each has to meet and of the facts and documents which will be put in question.

The trial

The parties and their witnesses will assemble for the trial. If a witness refuses to appear a 'subpoena' may be issued. This is a summons to appear and give evidence on condition that reasonable expenses are offered by the party calling the witness. Those who ignore a subpoena are in contempt of court and may be punished by fine or imprisonment.

Often the case will not be heard at the time stated in the list. The court must not be kept waiting and so cases are listed in such a way as to cope, for example, with actions which, as we have seen, are settled out of court at the last moment. If this does not happen, however, there is a trial and others are kept waiting.

When the action is 'called on' counsel for the plaintiff begins. He explains the matters in dispute to the judge, goes through the pleadings and outlines the plaintiff's case, indicating how it will be supported by evidence. Then he calls his witnesses.

The court requires that evidence be given on oath (or affirmation by a person who objects to swearing on the Bible). Documentary evidence such as a letter is not normally admissible and the writer must be called and give evidence on oath unless it is difficult or impossible to call him.

As in a criminal trial counsel for the plaintiff cannot ask his own witnesses 'leading questions' nor is hearsay evidence admissible. After the examination-in-chief the witnesses for the plaintiff may be cross-examined by counsel for the defence, the object being to discredit their evidence. After cross-examination counsel for the plaintiff may re-examine a witness.

Sometimes a witness will give an account of events which is totally different from that which he told to the plaintiff's solicitors; counsel for the plaintiff is not allowed to discredit his own witness unless the judge gives leave as he may do if he feels that the witness is prejudiced against the person who called him. Such a witness is called a hostile witness and his examination-in-chief is more like a cross-examination since it is designed to discredit his evidence.

At the end of the plaintiff's case it is the turn of counsel for the defence to produce evidence to refute it. The plaintiff does not have to prove his case beyond a reasonable doubt, as the prosecution in a criminal trial does but must show that what he alleges is probably the right version, i.e. proof on a balance of probabilities. The court must be satisfied that it is more likely than not (or more probable than not) that the relevant fact is established. (*R.* v. *Swaysland, The Times*, 15 April, 1987.)

The defence need not necessarily produce evidence. If the plaintiff's case is weak the defence may submit to the judge that there is no case to answer. If the judge agrees the action is finished and judgment is given for the defence. However, if the judge does not accept the submission of no case to answer he will immediately give judgment for the plaintiff, so counsel for the defendant will not easily take this course of action.

If there is no submission of no case to answer the defence will call its witnesses who will be examined, cross-examined and re-examined.

Counsel for the defence then makes a closing speech showing how in his view the plaintiff's case has failed. The plaintiff's counsel then presents his view. Both will give an indication of what they think the damages should be.

The judge will have remained largely silent during the trial, though he may have asked for an obscure point to be clarified. However, during the closing speeches he will indicate to counsel what he regards as the weaknesses in their respective cases so that they can answer the judge on them.

After the closing speeches the judge considers the evidence and will then give judgment stating the grounds on which it is based, though if a judge requires more time to consider the case he may reserve judgment and give it at a later date. The judge will also decide the amount of damages.

Civil jury

Section 69 of the Supreme Court Act, 1981 gives the court discretion with regard to juries in civil cases, though a jury must be empanelled at the request of the defendant where fraud is alleged, or at the request of either party in cases of libel, slander, malicious prosecution and false imprisonment. If the trial is likely to involve long and detailed examination of documents or accounts or scientific evidence, the court has the discretion to refuse a jury trial even in these cases.

However, libel actions involving issues or persons of national importance should be tried with a jury, even if complex documents are involved. (*Rothermere* v. *Times Newspapers*, [1973] 1 All E.R. 1013.) The percentage of jury trials in civil actions is very small.

Juries are not used in Admiralty cases but there is a power to summon a jury in the Chancery Division. This power is, in practice, neglected.

A civil jury consists of 12 persons, though the parties may, in a particular case, agree to proceed with less. There is a right, under s. 66 of the County Courts Act, 1984, to ask for a jury of eight persons in a county court, where the case is an appropriate one, as where fraud, libel, slander, malicious prosecution, or false imprisonment are alleged. These rights are rarely exercised. In addition, a coroner must, under s. 13(2) of the Coroners' (Amendment) Act, 1926 (as amended by s. 62 of the Administration of Justice Act, 1982), summon a jury of seven to eleven persons in some cases, e.g. where the deceased was in police custody, or death was the result of an injury caused by a police officer in the purported execution of his duty, and may accept the verdict of the majority if the dissentients are not more than two. Where there is no jury the judge determines the facts as well as the law.

Apart from a coroner's jury a civil jury had formerly to be unanimous. However, under s. 17 of the Juries Act, 1974, the verdict of the jury in civil proceedings in the High Court need not be unanimous if—

(*a*) where there are not less than eleven jurors, ten of them agree on the verdict; and

(*b*) where there are ten jurors, nine of them agree on the verdict.

The verdict of a jury of eight persons in a county court need not be unanimous if seven of them agree on the verdict. The two hours deliberation necessary for a jury before a majority verdict is permissible is not required for a civil jury. It is enough if it appears to the court that the jury had such period of time for deliberation as the court thinks reasonable, having regard to the nature and complexity of the case. In civil cases the court may accept a verdict by *any* majority so long as both parties consent. (S. 17(5), *ibid*.)

Appeals

Consideration has already been given in Chapter 2 to the rights of appeal in civil cases (and see p. 18).

Enforcing a judgment

Let us assume that the judge has given judgment for John on his claim and to Nature Foods on their counterclaim for sums of money thought appropriate in the circumstances of the case. Let us suppose that neither party is prepared to pay these sums. How can a party to an action get the money the court has awarded him? Some of the more important methods are set out below.

(a) The writ of fi fa (fieri facias). A plaintiff can ask the High Court for this writ which orders the sheriff of the county in which the debtor's goods are located to seize through bailiffs the defendant's goods and sell them if necessary in order to pay the plaintiff. In the County Court there is a similar procedure but it is based upon a warrant of execution.

(b) The charging order. The court may make such an order over, say, the defendant's land or other property such as shares. If the money is not paid the plaintiff can have the property sold and recover his damages from the proceeds of sale. The Charging Orders Act, 1979 defines the type of property in respect of which a charging order may be made. The 1979 Act widened the scope of property which may be made the subject of an order so that, for example, a charging order may now be made over a debtor's beneficial interest under a trust.

(c) The garnishee order. If the creditor knows that the debtor is owed money by a third party—where, for instance, there is a credit balance on the debtor's bank account—the creditor may wish to divert the payment away from the debtor to himself. This can be done by applying to the court for a garnishee order *nisi*. The order is addressed to the third party, e.g. the bank, forbidding it to pay the debt to the debtor and requiring a representative to attend before the court to show why the money (or part of it) should not be paid over to the judgment creditor.

The order is served at least seven days before the next court hearing on the matter and if at that hearing no cause has been shown as to why payment should not be made to the judgment creditor, the court can make a garnishee order absolute, requiring payment by the bank to the judgment creditor.

(*d*) *Attachment of earnings.* Where the defendant is in employment the plaintiff can obtain an attachment of earnings order through the county court. Under such an order the defendant's employer is required to deduct a specified sum from the defendant's wages or salary and pay the money into court for the plaintiff. Attachment is not available against the profits of the self-employed.

(*e*) *Equitable execution.* The court may appoint a *receiver* where, for example, the defendant owns property. The receiver can take over income such as rent and apply it in order to pay the plaintiff. The judgment creditor of a person who is a partner can, under s. 23 of the Partnership Act, 1890, obtain an order charging that partner's interest in the partnership property and profits with payment of the judgment debt. If the judgment creditor feels that he will experience difficulty in getting the firm to pay over, e.g. the profit share of the partner concerned, he can ask for the appointment of a receiver.

The enforcement of a non-money judgment, such as an injunction, is by means of the offence of contempt of court. If a defendant fails to obey an injunction he is in contempt of court and the court may, if the plaintiff applies, punish him. It may make, for example, an order for committal under which if the defendant still refuses to comply with the injunction, he may be imprisoned. Alternatively, the court may issue a writ of sequestration. This writ, which is directed by the court to commissioners, usually four in number, commands them to enter the lands and take the rents and profits and seize the goods of the person against whom it is directed. Thus the court can in effect take control of the defendant's property until the plaintiff has complied with the Court's order.

4 Other courts and tribunals and the legal profession

All of the famous writers on constitutional theory have drawn attention to the dangers of any system which takes away from the citizen, in his dealings with government and other officials, the protection of the law functioning in its traditional setting, i.e. the courts of law, which were considered in a previous chapter.

However, one of the most significant developments of this century is the considerable increase in what might be called broadly administrative justice dispensed in special courts outside of the ordinary system.

This has arisen from the great extension in the functions of government which has taken place, particularly in the last forty years. For example, the government pays pensions to various classes of persons, and a wide variety of social security benefits. In order to further schemes of social welfare, it is often necessary for a public body to acquire land by compulsory purchase, and it has also been necessary to establish a system of controlling the rents of dwellings, so that the free operation of the laws of supply and demand might be restricted.

Obviously disputes arise between individuals and the State. A person may claim a benefit which the State suggests he is not entitled to, and landowners are often aggrieved by the compulsory purchase of their land and the compensation offered for it. The settlement of such disputes might have been given over to the ordinary courts of law, but instead increasing use has been made of an administrative court of one kind or another.

Lord Denning, in *Freedom under the Law*, has said of these tribunals—

They are a separate set of courts dealing with a separate set of rights and duties. Just as in the old days there were ecclesiastical courts dealing with matrimonial cases and the administration of estates and just as there was the Chancellor dealing with the enforcement and administration of trusts so in our day there are the new tribunals dealing with the rights and duties between man and the State.

It should not be assumed, however, that all administrative tribunals are concerned with disputes between man and the State. Some deal with disputes between individuals. The Rent Assessment Committees which when acting to resolve disputes are known as Rent Tribunals (see s. 72, Housing Act, 1980) set up to deal with rent and other questions arising under statutory provisions relating to the letting of houses, are an example of a situation in which the Government has provided a specialized court to deal with certain disputes between landlord and tenant rather than give the particular jurisdiction to the ordinary courts of law.

Furthermore, administrative justice is not always meted out in a permanent independent tribunal. For example, the local planning authority may grant planning permission with or without conditions or may refuse permission or fail to notify their decision within the period laid down. In the case of a grant with conditions, or a refusal to grant, or delay in notification, the applicant may appeal to the Secretary of State through the Department of the Environment. The applicant and the local planning authority each have the right to be heard by a person approved by the Department of the Environment. The decision of the Secretary of State is final, though there may be an appeal by the authority or the applicant to the High Court on the grounds set out in s. 245 of the Town and Country Planning Act, 1971, e.g. that the order is not within the provisions of that Act.

In addition, there are some cases in which no machinery is provided for appeal to a tribunal or a local enquiry. For example, there is no appeal against withdrawal of a passport by the Foreign Office.

We shall now consider in more detail the way in which certain of these tribunals work.

ADMINISTRATIVE TRIBUNALS

It is not appropriate in a book of this nature to deal with all the tribunals in this field but consideration will be given to some important ones as examples.

(a) Social security tribunals

The procedure is governed by Sched 8, of the Health and Social Services and Social Security Adjudications Act, 1983 and the Social Security Act, 1975 (as amended by the 1983 Act). Where a person wishes to make a claim for benefit under social security legislation, including unemployment benefit, the claim must in the first instance be made to a local officer attached to the local Social Security office who may authorize payment, or refuse payment, or refer the claim to a local tribunal.

If payment is refused, application can be made to the local adjudication officer to review his decision. If payment is still not made the person claiming can appeal to a local Social Security Appeal tribunal which has three members, two non-lawyers, one drawn from a panel of persons representing employers and the self-employed, and one drawn from a panel of persons representing employees. The third member is usually a lawyer, for example a local solicitor appointed by the Secretary of State to be chairman.

If the tribunal allows the appeal the adjudication officer may appeal against that decision to a Social Security Commissioner. The same route of appeal is given to the person making the claim where the tribunal does not decide in his favour. Leave to appeal is required in all cases.

Social Security Commissioners are appointed by the Crown from amongst barristers and solicitors of not less than ten years' standing. There is an appeal from a Commissioner to the Court of Appeal with leave of the Commissioner or the Court of Appeal and ultimately to the House of Lords. This procedure effectively supersedes the former one whereby an application could be made by the DHSS or the claimant to the High Court for judicial review.

(b) Valuation and use of land tribunals

Another important tribunal is the *Lands Tribunal* which deals with disputes arising over the valuation and compensation payable on compulsory acquisition of land by public authorities under a variety of statutes, together with appeals from local valuation courts on the value of property for various purposes. The tribunal has a President, who is either a person who has held high judicial office or a barrister of at least seven years' standing, and other members, who must be solicitors or barristers of like standing, or persons experienced in the valuation of land. The jurisdiction of the tribunal may be exercised by any one or more of its members. Procedure is governed by rules made by the Lord Chancellor, and these are published by Statutory Instrument. The tribunal ordinarily sits in public and travels round the country, and there is a right of audience and legal representation. The decisions of the tribunal are written and reasoned, and appeal lies to the Court of Appeal on points of law. Either party can require the tribunal to state a case for consideration by the Court of Appeal. Legal aid, and by implication legal representation, is available in respect of proceedings in the Lands Tribunal.

(c) Conciliation and employment tribunals

(i) Conciliation.
The Advisory, Conciliation and Arbitration Service (ACAS) is, under the Employment Protection (Consolidation) Act, 1978, given a role in settling matters which are, or could be, the subject of proceedings before an industrial tribunal.

When a complaint or claim is presented to an industrial tribunal, say for equal pay or sex discrimination, a copy is sent to the conciliation officer. It is his duty to try to settle the dispute so that it need not go to an industrial tribunal. He can do this if asked to by the person making the complaint or the person against whom it is made, or even on his own initiative where he thinks there is a good chance of a settlement.

During the course of conciliation the parties can speak freely with the conciliation officer because anything which is said to the conciliation officer during the course of an attempted settlement is not admissible in evidence if the matter goes to an industrial tribunal unless the person who made the statement agrees.

(ii) Industrial tribunals.

The jurisdiction of these tribunals includes, for example, disputes arising out of the contract of employment or unfair dismissal, redundancy, equal pay and sex discrimination. (See further p. 322.)

The chairman of each tribunal is a barrister or solicitor of not less than seven years' standing, appointed by the Lord Chancellor and he sits with two other members selected by the President of Industrial Tribunals who is himself appointed by the Lord Chancellor. The selection is made from a panel of persons compiled by the Secretary of State for Employment on the basis of knowledge or experience of employment problems in industry or commerce. The tribunals sit at suitable centres throughout the United Kingdom.

If a sum of money awarded by a tribunal is not paid over to the claimant he can apply to the county court for a warrant of execution. (See p. 86.)

Legal aid is not available for a lawyer to represent a claimant before a tribunal but legal advice may be given in respect of employment matters. This can include the drafting of documents in relation to the proceedings and assistance with the way in which the case is to be presented to the tribunal. A legal aid lawyer can attend the tribunal hearing with his client but cannot speak or argue on his behalf. If legal representation is required at the hearing, the party concerned must take responsibility for payment subject to recovery of costs, which are only exceptionally awarded.

Written applications for the case to be heard by an industrial tribunal can be made on an originating notice of application form available from local Job Centres. The person against whom the claim is made will receive a copy of the application from the tribunal secretariat and should enter an appearance through the secretariat within 14 days of receiving it.

Industrial tribunals have power to request the parties to give each other further particulars of the grounds which are relied upon and to grant discovery of documents.

Hearings before industrial tribunals normally take place in public though there may be a private hearing where, in the opinion of the tribunal, this would be appropriate, as where evidence is to be presented which relates to national security.

As regards costs, an industrial tribunal does not make an award but may do so where in its opinion a party to any proceedings has acted frivolously or vexatiously, as where, for example, an employer refuses to take any part in the proceedings.

The decision is made by a majority and is given orally at the meeting or, if necessary, reserved and given at a later date. In any case it is recorded in a document which is signed by the chairman and contains reasons for the decision. The parties each receive a copy. It should also be noted that where an employee has died tribunal proceedings may be started or continued by his personal representatives.

An industrial tribunal can review and change its decision afterwards where, for example, new evidence has become available which could not have been known of or foreseen at the original hearing.

(iii) The Employment Appeal Tribunal.

Appeal from an industrial tribunal lies only on questions of law. The determination of the facts by an industrial tribunal cannot be challenged on appeal and it is therefore most important that the facts are properly presented to the tribunal at the hearing. Under s. 136(3) of the Employment Protection (Consolidation) Act, 1978 it will also hear an appeal from the ACAS Certification Officer by a trade union aggrieved by his refusal to issue it with a certificate that it is independent. The major legislative privileges are given to those trade unions which are independent of the employer and not, for example, to employer-dominated staff associations. The Certification Officer adjudicates upon the matter of independence under s. 8 of the Employment Protection Act, 1975.

The Employment Appeal Tribunal is a superior court of record with an official seal. Although the central office of the tribunal is in London, it may sit at any time and in any place in Great Britain. It may also sit in one or more divisions.

Appeals are usually heard by a judge of the High Court or a judge of the Court of Appeal and either two or four appointed members who do not belong to the judiciary but have special knowledge or experience of industrial relations, either as representatives of employers or workers. The reason why the judge will sit with either two or four appointed members is so that in either case there are an equal number of persons whose experience is as representatives of employers and of workers. The decision need not be unanimous but may be by a majority. Each member of the court, including the judge, has a vote so that the judge could be outvoted, but this is extremely rare. Exceptionally, if the parties to the proceedings consent, a case may be heard by a judge and one appointed member.

Appeals to the Employment Appeal Tribunal are commenced by serving on the tribunal within 42 days of the date on which the document recording the decision or order appealed against was sent to the person appealing, a notice of appeal. The appropriate form is set out in the Employment Appeal Tribunal Rules.

The hearing will normally take place in public but the tribunal may sit in private to hear evidence where, for example, it relates to national security or could cause substantial injury to an organization appearing before it, as where a company's trade secrets might be revealed. Legal aid is available for proceedings in the Employment Appeal Tribunal.

The Employment Appeal Tribunal may review and change any order made by it on a similar basis to the provisions already mentioned in regard to industrial tribunals. Appeal lies on any question of law, decision, or order of the Employment Appeal Tribunal, either with leave of the Tribunal or of the Court of Appeal to the Court of Appeal. Legal aid would be available on such appeal according to the usual rules. There may then be a further appeal to the House of Lords under the usual rules.

Administrative inquiries

As we have seen in some areas of administrative action, e.g. planning, there is in general no right of appeal from the initial decision of the Government or a local authority to an independent tribunal. The relevant Acts of Parliament normally provide for an opportunity to put a case against the decision at a public inquiry conducted before an inspector who is normally a Ministry official. The inspector makes a report to the Ministry concerned and the decision is made by the Minister himself or a senior civil servant on his behalf.

Advantages of tribunals

As a method of deciding disputes tribunals and administrative inquiries have advantages. For example, the tribunals and inquiries generally specialize in a particular field, and can thus acquire a detailed knowledge of disputes in that field. The procedure of tribunals is simple and informal, and it is often suggested that this puts those appearing before them at ease so that they are better able to present their case. Certainly such justice is cheaper and there are in general no court fees and costs, though if the assistance of a lawyer is required he will have to be paid and there is as yet no legal aid in this field except in the Lands Tribunal and the Employment Appeal Tribunal.

However, appellants who are not represented by lawyers may take full advantage of the rights of appeal given, though sometimes this results in references to tribunals which are frivolous by nature. Generally speaking, administrative tribunals and inquiries give quick decisions, and appellants are not subjected to the delays which are sometimes met with in ordinary courts of law. Tribunals and inquiries are usually local by nature; they are therefore able to acquaint themselves with local conditions, and can carry out inspections of property and sites where this would assist them in their decision.

The Tribunals and Inquiries Acts

Criticism of administrative tribunals led to the setting up of a Committee on Administrative Tribunals and Inquiries under the chairmanship of Sir Oliver Franks which reported in 1957. The main areas of disquiet were that tribunals did not give reasons for their decisions and furthermore that those decisions were not subject to appeal to the High Court on a point of law.

The majority of the proposals of the Franks Committee were accepted by Parliament and enacted in the Tribunals and Inquiries Act, 1958. This Act, together with certain changes and additions in subsequent legislation has been re-enacted as the Tribunals and Inquiries Act, 1971.

The implementation of Franks led to the following main changes—

(1) A Council on Tribunals now gives advice to the Lord Chancellor on the working of tribunals and reports to Parliament from time to time on its work.

(2) The chairmen of the various tribunals are selected by the ministers in whose fields they work from a panel of persons appointed by the Lord Chancellor. The chairmen are usually lawyers.

(3) A tribunal must normally allow a party who wants it to have a lawyer to represent him.

(4) All material facts are disclosed to all parties before a tribunal hearing and the hearing is in public unless, e.g. public security is involved.

(5) Reasons for decisions are given if requested.

(6) Appeals lie from most tribunals to the Divisional Court of Queen's Bench.

Unfortunately, Governments have often set up new tribunals without proper consultation with the Council on Tribunals to see whether an existing tribunal might take on the work. This has resulted in a proliferation of tribunals with a bewildering multiplicity of separate jurisdictions. That apart, the implementation of most of the Franks' recommendations means that there are no longer any major reasons for dissatisfaction with the powers and duties of tribunals.

There are those who continue to argue for appeal to a special Administrative Division of the High Court. Such a division has not been set up. However, a special panel of judges of the Queen's Bench Division has been created to sit in the Divisional Court when a case involving administrative law is taken before it. This goes some way to meet the arguments of those who advocate a special Administrative Division.

Legal aid

Legal aid in tribunals has been reviewed from time to time by the Legal Aid Advisory Committee which has felt it appropriate to recommend that legal aid should be extended to the Lands Tribunal only, though more recently it has been extended to proceedings before the Employment Appeal Tribunal. Many still regard the present position as unreasonable.

In particular it is felt that legal aid is appropriate in cases heard before e.g. the Social Security Commissioners. In addition there is no reason why legal aid should not be extended to some of the domestic tribunals, e.g. in respect of hearings before the Disciplinary Committee of the Law Society and the General Nursing Council.

Domestic tribunals

Another area in which persons or groups of persons or other public agencies exercise judicial or quasi-judicial functions over others is to be found in the system of domestic tribunals. These are, in general, disciplinary committees concerned with the regulation of certain professions and trades, some having been set up by statute and others merely by contract between members and the association concerned. Examples of tribunals regulating professions are what might be referred to broadly as the disciplinary committees of the General Medical Council, Architects' Registration Council, The Law Society, the General Nursing Council, and the Inns of Court. As regards the regulation of the investment industry and the City of London, there is the Securities and Investments Board set up by the Financial Services Act, 1986 and the Panel on Take-Overs and Mergers, together with recognised investment exchanges e.g. The Stock Exchange.

There are also certain trade organizations which are corporate bodies set up under statute. They represent the producers and distributors of particular commodities, and they control the production and sale of those commodities mainly by fixing prices. They are able to enforce their instructions by levying fines on members or excluding them from the scheme, and are mainly concerned with agriculture. Each Board has a Disciplinary Committee which has a chairman who is generally a lawyer. The parties are normally entitled to an oral hearing in public, and the Committee may subpoena witnesses and take evidence on oath. One of the most important Boards is the Milk Marketing Board.

It is not possible to control domestic tribunals by means of the prerogative orders, e.g. *certiorari*, because they are not *public* authorities. They are regarded by the courts as *private associations based on contract*. At one time members were bound by the rules no matter how unreasonably or unfairly in effect these might operate. For example, if the rules allowed expulsion there was no remedy against this even though a person so expelled might be unable to work if he was not a member of the association.

The breakthrough came in the decision of the Court of Appeal in *Lee* v. *Showmen's Guild of Great Britain*, [1952] 1 All E.R. 1175 which brought domestic tribunals under the control of the courts. Mr Lee ran a roundabout. He occupied the same pitch each year at Bradford Summer Fair. Another Guild member, Mr Shaw, claimed the pitch and a committee of the Guild found that Mr Shaw was entitled to have it and that Mr Lee was guilty of unfair competition. They fined Mr Lee £100. He then brought an action claiming a declaration that the committee's decision was invalid. The Court of Appeal upheld Mr Lee's claim in the main because it was at last accepted that the contract associations could not by that contract rule out the jurisdiction of the court because no contract intended to bind the parties to it could oust that jurisdiction. (See further p. 276.)

Since that time the courts have intervened to see that the rules of these associations are correctly interpreted and that the principles of natural justice (see further p. 98) are observed. They have developed a jurisdiction to redress wrongful expulsion; wrongful refusal to admit to membership; refusal to admit women and restrictive activities in terms of what members can do. Thus in *Pharmaceutical Society of Great Britain* v. *Dickson*, [1968] 2 All E.R. 686 the House of Lords decided that the Society could not by its rules restrict chemists in terms of what they sold in their shops.

In *R.* v. *Panel on Take-Overs*, [1987] 1 All E.R. 564, the Court of Appeal decided that having regard to the public consequences of non-compliance with the code, e.g. that a bid by one company for another could be declared invalid if the procedures of the code were infringed, an application for judicial review of its decisions would be available in an appropriate case.

It should be noted, however, that the courts cannot control domestic tribunals by means of judicial review leading to the issue of a prerogative order, e.g. *certiorari* or *mandamus*. (*Law* v. *National Greyhound Racing Club Ltd*, [1983] 3 All E.R. 300.) A person aggrieved by the decision of a domestic tribunal can, however, ask the court for the remedy of a *declaration* of his rights or an *injunction*. These have proved quite powerful remedies as a means of controlling domestic tribunals.

JUDICIAL CONTROL OVER INFERIOR COURTS AND TRIBUNALS

We must now consider what *control* the ordinary courts of law have over administrative action as expressed in the decisions of tribunals and inquiries and what *methods* are used to exercise that control.

Control by the judiciary is exercised as follows—

(*a*) by statutory rights of appeal from the tribunal;
(*b*) by application of the doctrine of *ultra vires*;
(*c*) by the use of the principal administrative law remedies, i.e. injunctions, declarations, and the prerogative orders of *certiorari*, prohibition, and *mandamus*, through an application under Rules of Supreme Court for judicial review.

These methods of control will now be considered in more detail.

Statutory right of appeal

Where, as in the case of the Lands Tribunal, the Act of Parliament setting up or controlling the tribunal gives a right of appeal to the ordinary courts of law, the courts are entitled to re-hear the whole case and are not limited to a consideration of the reasons given by the tribunal for its decision. The court can consider the whole matter afresh, and can substitute a new decision for that of the tribunal.

Ultra vires

No public authority may lawfully make a decision and take action on it unless it is authorized by law to do so or the act is construed as being reasonably incidental to its authorized activities. An act which does not conform with the above is treated by the courts as void under the doctrine of *ultra vires* (beyond the powers of).

The doctrine applies to bodies and individuals such as ministers exercising judicial, quasi-judicial, legislative or administrative functions, including local authorities, tribunals, Government departments and other public authorities, though Parliament's legislative powers are unlimited. (See p. 10.)

Typically, the *ultra vires* method of control is used where the decision taken is unauthorized by the powers given to the authority. (*Attorney-General* v. *Fulham Corporation*, 1921.)[9] However, even when the authority acts within its powers, the court can review the decision if it is unreasonable to a high degree (*Associated Provincial Picture Houses Ltd* v. *Wednesbury Corp.*, [1947] 2 All E.R. 680).

Prerogative orders and judicial review

Where no right of appeal is given it may be possible to challenge the decision of an inferior court or public tribunal by having recourse to the supervisory jurisdiction of the High Court.

This jurisdiction is exercised by the Queen's Bench Division of the High Court by means of the prerogative orders known as *certiorari*, prohibition, and *mandamus*. These orders, which are not available as of right but at the discretion of the court, were formerly prerogative writs, which a subject might obtain by petitioning the Crown.

The Sovereign has no such power today, the control being exercised by the Queen's Bench Division, the former writs being now called orders. (S. 29, Supreme Court Act, 1981.)

A person cannot normally invoke the supervisory jurisdiction of the High Court if other more appropriate procedures for appeal exist. (R. v. *Brighton Justices ex parte Robinson* 1973).[10]

Order 53 of the Rules of Supreme Court introduces a comprehensive system of judicial review. A statutory basis for this procedure also appears in s. 31 of the Supreme Court Act, 1981. It allows an application to cover under one umbrella, as it were, all the remedies of *certiorari*, *mandamus*, and prohibition, and also declaration and injunction. There is no need to apply for one of these remedies individually. Any combination of them is available under the one claim for judicial review. Damages may also be claimed on an application for judicial review.

(S. 31(4), *ibid.*) No application for judicial review may be made without leave. Application is made for this to a single judge.

There have been difficulties in the past as to whether a person had the necessary *locus standi*, i.e. interest, to bring an action for one of the administrative remedies. *Locus standi* is dealt with in Order 53 and s. 31(3), *ibid.*, which lay down a simple test which is that the applicant must have 'a sufficient interest in the matter to which the application relates'. The test is, of course, rather vague, but Lord Denning, in discussing the remedy of judicial review in *The Discipline of Law* states: 'The court will not listen to a busybody who is interfering in things which do not concern him, but it will listen to an ordinary citizen who comes asking that the law should be declared and enforced, even though he is only one of a hundred, or one of a thousand, or one of a million who are affected by it. As a result, therefore, of the new procedure, it can I hope be said that we have in England an *actio popularis* by which an ordinary citizen can enforce the law for the benefit of all—as against public authorities in respect of their statutory duties'. However, the House of Lords decided in *I.R.C.* v. *Federation of Self-Employed and Small Businesses Ltd*, 1981[11] that a taxpayer has no sufficient interest in asking the court to investigate the tax affairs of another taxpayer.

Furthermore, it should not be assumed that judicial review is available to redress any decision which might be regarded in a broad sense as 'unfair'. The House of Lords made it clear in *Puhlhofer* v. *Hillingdon L.B.C.*, [1986] 1 All E.R. 467—an attempt to challenge a decision not to house the applicant—that persons seeking judicial review must base their case on one of the accepted principles of review e.g. *ultra vires* or procedural irregularity.

Grounds on which *certiorari* lies
The only ground on which *certiorari* lies are as follows—

(i) Want or excess of jurisdiction. This exists where the inferior court or body has adjudicated on a matter which it had no power to decide, i.e. where it is acting beyond its powers (*ultra vires*) (*R.* v. *London County Council, ex parte Entertainments Protection Association*, 1931.)[12]

Certiorari is not the only remedy which may be used to control *ultra vires* acts. Note, for example, the use of an injunction in the *ultra vires* situation seen in *A.-G.* v. *Fulham Corporation*, 1921.[9]

(ii) Denial of natural justice. The principle is that although a tribunal should not be required to conform to judicial standards, but should be free to work out its own procedures, nevertheless it must observe the rules of natural justice, i.e. there must be no bias and both sides should be heard.

(*a*) *Bias.* This may be pecuniary bias (*Dimes* v. *Grand Junction Canal*, 1852),[13] but other forms of bias are relevant (*R.* v. *Bingham Justices, ex parte Jowitt*, 1974).[14]

(b) *The right to be heard*. There is no inherent right to an oral hearing; written evidence may be acceptable. However, the right to be heard (*audi alteram partem*) implies that notice of the hearing or other method of stating one's case must be given together with notice of the case which is to be met (see *R.* v. *Wear Valley D.C. ex p. Binks*, (1985) and *R.* v. *Board of Governors of London Oratory School ex p. R*, (1988) at p. 517). In addition, though the law is not entirely free from doubt, it is the better view that a reasonable opportunity to cross-examine witnesses is part of the *audi alteram partem* principle. Thus in *Nicholson* v. *Secretary of State for Energy* (1977), 76 L.G.R. 693, the right of cross-examination at a public inquiry into the siting of an opencast mine was upheld on the basis that the denial of that right was a breach of natural justice.

Legal representation is also part of the *audi alteram partem* principle. Public tribunals under the Tribunals and Inquiries Act, 1971 will normally allow a party who wants it to have a lawyer to represent him. As regards a domestic tribunal, the Court of Appeal in *Enderby Town Football Club Ltd* v. *The Football Association Ltd*, 1971[15] laid down the following broad principles—

(a) There is no inherent right to legal representation, though if the case involves difficult points of law legal representation, should be allowed. A rule forbidding legal representation absolutely and in any circumstances is probably invalid;

(b) Cases involving difficult points of law should not in general be decided by domestic tribunals. The parties should ask the ordinary courts for a declaratory judgment setting out their rights. The ordinary courts are better equipped to deal with cases of legal difficulty and to follow the arguments of lawyers.

However, it seems that in *disciplinary cases* where it is necessary to reach decisions quickly, it might well be appropriate to refuse legal representation. Thus, in *Maynard* v. *Osmond*, [1977] 1 All E.R. 64, the Court of Appeal held that natural justice did not require that a police constable should have legal representation at a hearing before the chief constable on a disciplinary matter involving an allegation that a sergeant had falsely stated that P.C. Maynard had been asleep while on duty. Furthermore the House of Lords decided in *R.* v. *Board of Visitors of the Maze Prison ex p. Hone and McCarten, The Times*, 22 January, 1988 that a prisoner charged with a disciplinary offence is not entitled, as of right, to legal representation at the disciplinary hearing.

Whether a decision is judicial, quasi-judicial or administrative, or disciplinary, the rules of natural justice need not necessarily be applied if national security is involved (*R.* v. *Secretary of State for Home Department, ex parte Hosenball*, 1977.)[16]

(iii) *Effect of failure to comply with rules*. In recent times the courts have made it clear that anything done by a tribunal in breach of natural justice (or *ultra vires*) is void as in *Ridge* v. *Baldwin*, 1963.[17] If action has been taken on the decision of a tribunal which is void that action is also void. If the decision was merely voidable action taken on it prior to the court quashing it would be valid.

(iv) Error of law on the face of the record. *Certiorari* lies to quash a decision the record of which discloses an error of law. According to Lord Denning in *R.* v. *Northumberland Compensation Appeal Tribunal, ex parte Shaw*, [1952] 1 All E.R. 122, the record consists of 'the document which initiates the proceedings, the pleadings (if any), and the adjudication, but not the the evidence or the reasons unless the tribunal chooses to incorporate them.' As we have seen, the Tribunals and Inquiries Act, 1971 requires reasoned decisions in cases coming before tribunals and inquiries so that there should now normally be a record giving reasons which will assist the High Court in exercising its supervisory jurisdiction. In addition, if a reasoned decision is required by the 1971 Act the order of *mandamus* lies to compel the tribunal or inquiry to give one.

However, the above provisions do not apply to magistrates' courts. If an order of a magistrates' court does not contain reasons for the making of the order, then, provided the magistrates have stayed within their jurisdiction and observed the rules of natural justice, *certiorari* does not lie on the order under this heading.

Prohibition lies to prevent an inferior tribunal from exceeding its jurisdiction, or infringing the rules of natural justice. It is governed by similar principles to *certiorari*, except that it does not lie when once a final decision has been given (*certiorari* is then the appropriate order). The object of prohibition is to prevent an inferior tribunal from hearing and deciding a matter which is beyond its jurisdiction. Prohibition and *certiorari* are available against the Crown and public authorities but not against private persons or bodies, e.g. the big industrial conglomerates and trade unions.

Applications for *certiorari* and prohibition are often brought together, e.g. to quash a decision already made by a tribunal, and to prevent it from continuing to exceed or abuse its jurisdiction.

The order of *mandamus* may be issued to any person or body (not necessarily an inferior court, since it might be issued to a local authority). It commands him or them to carry out some public duty. Once again, it is not available against private persons or bodies.

It might be used to compel an administrative tribunal to hear an appeal which it is refusing to hear, or to compel a local authority to carry out a duty lying upon it, e.g. to produce its accounts for inspection by a rate-payer. (*R.* v. *Bedwellty U.D.C.*, [1943] 1 K.B. 333.) *Mandamus* lies to compel the exercise of a duty and of a discretionary power, though in the case of the latter not in a particular way (*R.* v. *Commissioner of Police of the Metropolis, ex parte Blackburn*, 1973).[18]

It is not available against the Crown itself; but it may issue against

Ministers (*R. v. Secretary of State for Social Services, ex parte Grabaskey*, 1972)[19] or other Crown servants to enforce a personal statutory duty.

The High Court has power to issue prerogative orders under s. 29(3) of the Supreme Court Act, 1981 in respect of all decisions of the Crown Court, with the exception of matters relating to trial on indictment, where such orders are normally appropriate, e.g. where an error of law appears on the face of the record in, say, a licensing decision. (*R. v. Exeter Crown Court, ex parte Beattie*, [1974] 1 All E.R. 1183.) Appeals from trials on indictment are to the Court of Appeal, Criminal Division.

Injunction and declaratory judgment

The High Court can also exercise control over the decisions of inferior tribunals by granting, at its discretion, an injunction to prevent, for example, the implementation of a decision made by an inferior tribunal which does not observe the rules of natural justice. The remedy is not available against the Crown. Defiance of an injunction amounts to contempt of court. In many ways the remedy is like prohibition. However, it is rarely used against public tribunals. It is more commonly brought into play against domestic tribunals.

A *declaratory judgment* may be asked for by a person aggrieved by the decision of an inferior tribunal so that the High Court·can state the legal position of the parties. Defiance of a declaratory judgment is not a contempt of court and there is no method by which it can be enforced, but parties usually observe it. It is particularly useful in respect of complaints against the actions of government departments (*Laker Airways* v. *Department of Trade*, 1977)[20] and ministers (*Congreve* v. *Home Office*, 1976).[21].

Damages

Although a public authority has acted unlawfully in the sense of being *ultra vires*, a person affected, such as Shell U.K. in *R. v. Lewisham B.C. ex parte Shell U.K.* (see p. 514), cannot recover damages unless he bases his claim on breach of contract, or a tort or alleges infringement of a property right (*O'Reilly* v. *Mackman*, [1983] 2 AC 237).

OTHER CONTROLS ON DECISION MAKING

Ministers of the Crown

Sometimes an Act of Parliament places a minister in a supervisory role over, for example, the decisions of local authorities, and where this is so he must act judicially and not administratively in respect of that supervisory role. If he does not exercise the supervisory role in the way envisaged by the Act which gave it to him, the Minister's directions are themselves subject to review by the court. (*Secretary of State for Education and Science* v. *Tameside Metropolitan Borough Council*, 1976.)[22]

The Parliamentary Commissioner for Administration

A further check on abuse of power by government departments was created by the appointment of the Parliamentary Commissioner for Administration (or 'Ombudsman') under the provisions of the Parliamentary Commissioner Act, 1967. The Commissioner is appointed by the Crown and has the same security of tenure as a judge of the Supreme Court. He is also a member of the Council on Tribunals. His function is to investigate complaints relating to the exercise of administrative functions. However, investigation of Central Government departments is made only at the request of a Member of Parliament and a citizen who wishes to have a complaint investigated must first bring it to the notice of an M.P.

Unfortunately, the Commissioner is very often limited to a consideration of the *administrative procedures* followed and is powerless to act if the correct procedure has been followed even though the decision is bad. Furthermore, he cannot investigate personnel matters. Nevertheless, each year sees a steady rise in the number of complaints referred to him, though the Commissioner and his functions are still not well enough known and he is at the present time less effective than his counterparts in other countries. In fact Britain is alone among the countries with national Ombudsmen in not allowing the Ombudsman to initiate his own investigations. Most of the complaints involve government departments in constant contact with the public, more complaints being levied against the Department of Health and Social Security, followed by the Inland Revenue, than any other department. The Commissioner's jurisdiction under the Act of 1967 is limited to certain aspects of Central Government administration but the Parliamentary Commissioner (Consular Complaints) Act, 1981 extends the jurisdiction of the Parliamentary Commissioner to complaints about the conduct of United Kingdom consular officers abroad. The Parliamentary and Health Service Commissioners Act, 1987 extends the jurisdiction of the Parliamentary Commissioner to non-departmental bodies etc. listed in Sched. 1 e.g. the Data Protection Registrar.

There is now a Health Service Commissioner for England and Wales to investigate complaints about certain aspects of the National Health Service. The Commissioner is the present Parliamentary Commissioner who therefore combines the two offices.

In addition, there are two Commissions for Local Administration in England and Wales each consisting of Local Commissioners appointed by the Secretary of State plus the Parliamentary Commissioner. A Local Commissioner may investigate a written complaint made by a member of the public who claims to have sustained injustice in consequence of maladministration in connection with action taken by or on behalf of local authority, joint board, police authority or water authority, being action taken in the exercise of administrative functions. The complaint will normally be made in writing either through a member of the local authority complained against *or* with evidence that a member has been asked to refer it but has not done so. Furthermore it must be made within a time limit of 12 months. Any one of the Local Commissioners has the same powers as the High Court to require the attendance of witnesses and production of documents when he is conducting an investigation. He must report the results of any investigation to the person who referred the complaint to him, to the complainant and to the authority concerned which must make copies available for public inspection. If he finds that injustice has been caused, the authority concerned must consider his report and notify him of what action they have taken. The greatest number of complaints relates to activities of local housing and planning authorities. Certain matters, such as the conduct of legal proceedings, action taken to prevent crime, or action concerning the giving of instruction or discipline in schools, are excluded from the jurisdiction of a Local Commissioner.

Under the Act of 1967 the Parliamentary Commissioner is given discretion whether to investigate a complaint or not. In consequence, the order of *mandamus* will not issue to him since he has no duty to hear a complaint (*Re Fletcher's Application*, [1970] 2 All E.R. 527). Furthermore, there is no way of enforcing the findings of the Ombudsman and there are those who feel that it would improve matters if the courts had power to enforce these findings. Judicial review is not available against the decisions of local commissioners (see *R.* v. *Local Commissioner for Administration for the South, the West, the West Midlands etc., The Independent*, 22 July, 1987).

More recently, a Banking Ombudsman, (see p. 499) an Insurance Ombudsman and a Building Society Ombudsman have been appointed to deal, on a limited basis, with disputes in those industries. The Council of the Stock Exchange has also appointed an Ombudsman to mediate in disputes between investors and stockbrokers.

CORONERS' COURTS

These courts, which commenced in 1194, are amongst the oldest English courts still in existence. Their chief function is to inquire into cases of violent, unnatural or suspicious death, together with cases of sudden death without apparent cause. They also inquire into deaths in prison and deaths by hanging—which is still a possible punishment, for example, for the crime of treason.

A coroner has jurisdiction to hold an inquest on a body lying within his jurisdiction even though the death and cause of death has not occurred in England and Wales. Thus in *R.* v. *West Yorkshire Coroner, ex parte Smith*, [1982] 3 All E.R. 1098 the Court of Appeal decided that the coroner was obliged under s. 3(1) of the Coroners' Act, 1887 to hold an inquest into the death of a nurse who had died in Saudi Arabia but whose body had been brought back to this country. However, the coroner faces special difficulties in such a case because he cannot summon witnesses from abroad or request the production of documents. (See further p. 81.)

The procedure is that of an inquest or inquiry; it is not a trial. The object is to find out the identity of the deceased, the cause of his death, and where the death took place. The coroner's officer, a serving police officer, collects evidence before the inquest begins. All witnesses are under oath, but the rules of evidence are not applied as strictly as they are in other courts. The coroner decides what constitutes relevant and admissible evidence, and has much discretion at all stages of the investigation.

In cases such as suspected murder or death in prison, the coroner may summon a jury of from seven to eleven persons, and he may accept the verdict of the majority so long as there are not more than two dissentients. He is required to summon a jury under s. 13(2)(e) of the Coroners Amendment Act, 1926 where the death with which he is concerned occurred in circumstances, the continuance or possible recurrence of which is prejudicial to the health or safety of the public or any section of the public. This arises from the decision of the Court of Appeal in *R.* v. *Hammersmith Coroner, ex parte Peach*, [1980] 2 All E.R. 7, where it was held that the suspicious or unauthorized use by a police officer of a lethal weapon was a matter coming within s. 13 (*ibid*), and accordingly it was compulsory to have a jury. Section 62 of the Administration of Justice Act, 1982 requires a coroner to summon a jury where the deceased was in police custody or death resulted from an injury caused by a police officer in the purported exercise of his duty.

The Coroners's Juries Act, 1983 provides that a person is not qualified to serve as a juror at an inquest held by a coroner unless he is for the time being qualified to serve as a juror in the Crown Court, the High Court, and the county court. (See further p. 62.) The Act also provides criminal penalties for evasion of service on a coroner's jury.

The coroner can require a *post mortem*, and the attendance of medical and other witnesses who may be examined on oath.

If the court finds that a death was a result of murder, manslaughter or infanticide, this does not operate to convict the person said to be responsible, and a coroner can in no case charge a person with those offences.

If on an inquest regarding a death the coroner, before the conclusion of the inquest—

(*a*) is told by the clerk of a magistrates' court that some person has been charged before a magistrates' court with the murder, manslaughter or infanticide of the deceased, or with an offence under s. 1 of the Road Traffic Act, 1972 (as substituted by s. 50 of the Criminal Law Act, 1977), of causing death by reckless or dangerous driving, or with an offence under s. 2(1) of the Suicide Act, 1961 consisting of aiding, abetting, counselling, or procuring the suicide of the deceased; or

(b) is informed by the Director of Public Prosecutions that some person has been charged before examining justices with an offence not mentioned in (a) above but alleged to have been committed in circumstances connected with the death of the deceased, and is requested by the Director to adjourn the inquest,

then, the coroner must adjourn the inquest until after the conclusion of the relevant criminal proceedings and if he has summoned a jury he may, if he thinks fit, discharge them. This is to prevent inquests turning into, in effect, murder trials as they sometimes did in the 1920s.

After the conclusion of the relevant criminal proceedings the coroner may resume the adjourned inquest if, in his opinion, there is sufficient cause to do so. If he does resume an inquest then the finding of the inquest as to the cause of death must not be inconsistent with the outcome of the relevant proceedings. (Criminal Law Act, 1977, Sch. 10.)

Under s. 220 of the Local Government Act, 1972 the appointment of coroners falls to county councils, the Greater London Council and the Common Council of the City of London (in respect of appointments in the City and the Temples). They are barristers, solicitors or medical practitioners having five years' standing in their profession. The appointment is generally part-time and a coroner can be dismissed for inability or misbehaviour. The Lord Chief Justice and the judges of the High Court are coroners *ex officio*.

The coroner also retains jurisdiction in treasure trove. Treasure trove is money, coin, manufactured gold, silver plate or bullion deliberately hidden in the earth or other private place, the owner being unknown. Such property belongs to the Crown. The coroner is concerned to establish that the property was deliberately hidden because, if it was not, but merely lost, the finder, not the Crown, acquires a good title to it, except as against the true owner. However, if the finder makes prompt report of his discovery of treasure trove, the present practice of the Crown is to restore the article to him, or if it is required for a museum, to pay him its value. Nevertheless, the Crown has no prerogative right to treasure trove if the objects are not of gold or silver, and in *Attorney-General of the Duchy of Lancaster* v. *Overton (G.E.) (Farms)*, [1982] 1 All E.R. 524, the Court of Appeal held that 7811 third century Roman coins of debased silver, containing only 0.2% to 18% silver found in a field at Coleby, Lincs, were not treasure trove and therefore not the property of the Crown.

Reform. The coroner's court has a number of major weaknesses, particularly where the death has occurred in controversial circumstances. It cannot subpoena witnesses and those witnesses who attend voluntarily cannot be compelled to answer questions under oath, nor can they be made to submit to cross-examination. Furthermore, there is no power of discovery of documents. This has led to suggestions that, at least in controversial cases, there should be a tribunal of inquiry headed by a High Court judge with the usual rules of evidence and procedure available so that the truth of the matter may be better arrived at.

ARBITRATION

(a) Arising from contract. Not uncommonly commercial contracts, for example contracts of insurance, contain a provision under which the parties agree to submit disputes arising under the contract to an arbitrator who need not be a lawyer but might in, say, a building dispute, be a surveyor who has knowledge and experience of the subject matter of the dispute.

Arbitration proceedings are better than court proceedings in only two main ways: firstly, they are private in that there need be no publicity, (e.g. a public hearing followed by a law report), and secondly, the arbitrator will have special experience of the particular trade or business which a judge would not have. Privacy is usually the determining factor in the choice by the parties of commercial arbitration rather than litigation.

Arbitration is no longer cheap since experienced arbitrators can command daily fees of several hundred pounds, and the lawyers who appear before the arbitrators charge the same fees as for litigation in the courts. There is no guarantee of a quick resolution because it may be several months before the parties can agree upon the identity of the arbitrator(s) and also the parties are dependent in arranging the arbitration on the availability of the arbitrator, whose diary may be as full as the waiting lists in the ordinary courts.

Arbitration proceedings are governed by the Arbitration Acts, 1950 and 1979 and the award of an arbitrator, if properly arrived at, will be enforced if a judge of the High Court gives leave in the same way as a judgment (see p. 86).

(b) Arbitration in the High Court and County Court. This has already been considered on pp. 32 and 26.

THE LEGAL PROFESSION

The legal profession in England has two branches. There are barristers and solicitors. Each profession has developed independently, and each has its own controlling body. No person may practise in both capacities at the same time.

Barristers

Barristers conduct cases in court, and generally draft the pleadings which outline the manner in which the case is to be conducted. They also give opinions on difficult legal problems. Barristers have a right to be heard in every court in our legal system.

There is, of course, nothing to stop a party presenting his own case, though when it comes to an appeal to the House of Lords, unless leave has been granted by the Court of Appeal, it is necessary for two Queen's Counsel to certify that it is reasonable to bring the case to appeal.

Call to the English Bar is the prerogative of the four Inns of Court—Lincoln's Inn, Gray's Inn, the Inner Temple and the Middle Temple. The Inns of Court are unincorporated societies governed by Masters of the Bench, who are judges or senior barristers, and Call to the Bar is by the Benchers.

Council of Legal Education

The Council of Legal Education is responsible for the education and examination of students at later stages of qualifying and holds lectures which are conducted by leading academic and practising lawyers.

Once a student has passed the examinations and 'kept terms' by dining in the hall of his Inn a set number of times, he must (if he wishes to practise), become the pupil of a senior barrister, often referred to as a pupil master, for a period of 12 months. A barrister must then find chambers from which to practise and some fail to do so and forsake the Bar for careers in industry and commerce. Since 1981 it has been possible to follow a commercial pupillage, i.e. a period spent in employment under the guidance of an approved barrister in industry or commerce which will count towards the compulsory period of pupillage which barristers must undergo before practising on their own.

Circuits

After call, a barrister intending to practise will join a circuit and he will then practise within that circuit though he may take cases on others. There are six circuits in England and Wales, i.e. Midland and Oxford; North Eastern; Northern; South Eastern; Wales and Chester; and Western.

There are no partnerships at the Bar, and one barrister cannot employ another, but it is usual for counsel to group together in chambers and employ a clerk who is responsible for the administration of the chambers, fees, appointments and instructions. There is, however, no objection to what is called 'purse-sharing' under which a particular chambers pools all its fees and each barrister draws the same monthly 'salary'. Some of what remains can go to make payments to pupil barristers.

Queen's Counsel

Experienced barristers may apply to the Lord Chancellor to 'take silk,' i.e. to become Queen's Counsel which gives the entitlement to wear a silk gown in court. The Lord Chancellor recommends suitable applicants to the Queen who makes the appointment. After appointment as Queen's Counsel a barrister will not in general appear without a junior, i.e. another barrister who is not a Q.C., and his practice henceforth tends to be restricted to the more important cases requring two counsel, i.e. a junior to deal with less difficult but time-consuming procedural matters and the drafting of pleadings, leaving the Q.C. to concentrate on advocacy.

Until 1977 the rules of conduct laid down by the Bar *prevented* a Q.C. from working without a junior. The rule was dropped following a report by the Monopolies Commission that the practice was contrary to the public interest. However, most Q.C.s still claim that they need the assistance of a junior.

Briefing and negligence

A barrister will not normally deal directly with a client but must be briefed by a solicitor, and he cannot sue for his fees, though a solicitor who fails to pay over to counsel fees received from a client is liable to disciplinary action.

As regards fees, barristers are entitled to a 'brief fee' which covers preparation of the case plus the first day of the trial (if any). Added to this is a sum called a 'refresher' payable for the second and each subsequent day of the trial for however long it continues. The costs of one side for a week in court on, say, a contested personal injury case with a Q.C. can run into several thousands of pounds on top of which fees are also payable to the firm of solicitors involved in preparatory work.

As a result of the decisions of the House of Lords in *Saif Ali* v. *Sydney Mitchell & Co*, 1978[23] and *Rondel* v. *Worsley*, 1967[24] it may be said that as regards professional negligence, a barrister has immunity in terms of his conduct and management of litigation. However, a barrister may be sued for advice given or work done negligently before a case comes to trial, and it is only where the pre-trial work is so intimately connected with the conduct of the case in court that it can fairly be said to be a preliminary decision affecting the way the case is to be conducted at the actual hearing that a barrister can claim immunity.

Etiquette

In matters of etiquette, counsel is under an obligatory duty to conduct his case in a proper manner. He must inform the court of all the relevant statutes and precedents, and, where a legal authority is against his argument, he must not suppress it, though he may attempt to distinguish or criticize it. He must also ensure that his client has a fair hearing. If a prosecuting counsel in a criminal case is aware of facts which support the case for the accused, or lessen the gravity of the offence, he must state them. Counsel may not plead guilty for a client, but may persuade him to do so if it is in the client's interest.

The bar and the bench

So far as claims to sit on the bench are concerned, Lords of Appeal in Ordinary are chosen only from barristers as are Lords Justices of Appeal and High Court Judges. Circuit judges are chosen from barristers or from those who have held the office of recorder for three years and recorders from barristers and solicitors of at least ten years' standing. Thus a solicitor can now become a circuit judge if he has previously been a recorder.

Stipendiary magistrates are chosen from barristers and solicitors. Masters of the Queen's Bench Division must be barristers, though Masters of other divisions may be solicitors. The National Insurance Commissioner and the National Insurance (Industrial Injuries) Commissioner are barristers as is the President of the Lands Tribunal.

Solicitors

The profession of solicitor is derived from three former branches of the legal profession. The early stages of litigation in the King's Bench and Common Pleas was conducted by *attorneys*; in the Court of Chancery by *solicitors*, so called because cases in Chancery could go on for years and the only way of getting the case moving was to employ a person to '*solicit*' or cajole the court into action, and in the Ecclesiastical Courts and Admiralty by *proctors*. These three branches fused in 1831 to form the Law Society, though their functions were not fused under the one name of solicitor until 1875. The Law Society is responsible for prescribing the qualifications and setting the examinations, issuing practising certificates and preserving minimum standards of behaviour. It also runs a compensation fund for those who have suffered from the wrongful acts and defaults of solicitors, supervises the charges made by solicitors for their work and provides a complaints system.

Today a solicitor is in some respects a business man who advises his clients on legal, financial and other matters. His work is not all of a legal nature, but most of it requires legal training. Much of the work of a solicitor is concerned with property. He investigates title to land, prepares contracts of sale, conveyances and wills, and often acts as executor and trustee. He also assists promoters in company formation. Since the passing of the Administration of Justice Act, 1985 practising solicitors no longer have a monopoly of conveyancing which may now be done also by licensed conveyancers who are not qualified as solicitors.

There is a Practice Rule forbidding a solicitor from acting for both parties to a transaction though there are exceptions, e.g. where both parties are established clients. Solicitors are commissioners for oaths and any person who is required to sign a document and swear as to the truth of the statements in it may go to a solicitor so that the latter can declare that he has witnessed the taking of the oath. Some documents, e.g. statutory declarations required on the formation of companies, must be sworn before a solicitor who is also a 'notary public.'

The distinction between solicitors and barristers is quite marked in the matter of litigation. The solicitor's function is to prepare the case, ascertain the facts, and arrange for the presence of the necessary witnesses and any documents which may be required. He also conducts any disputes over costs which have been awarded after judgment. Regarding advocacy, a solicitor has a right to be heard in county courts and magistrates' courts. He may also be heard in bankruptcy matters in the High Court and Divisional Court, and in interlocutory proceedings in the House of Lords, the Court of Appeal and the High Court. The Lord Chancellor may under the Supreme Court Act, 1981, issue directions regarding the right of audience of solicitors in the Crown Court. Directions have been made under which a solicitor may appear, conduct, defend and address the court in criminal or in civil appeals or committals where he or his partner or employee appeared for the defendant in the magistrates' court. In addition to the cases in which solicitors already have rights of audience and without prejudice to the discretion of a judge to allow a solicitor to represent his client in open court in an emergency, a solicitor may appear in the Supreme Court in formal or unopposed proceedings, i.e. those proceedings where, by reason of the agreement of the parties, there is unlikely to be any argument and the court will not be called upon to exercise a discretion. This would enable, for example, a solicitor to read a statement in open court on behalf of his client who was either a plaintiff or defendant in a defamation action. As we have seen, it is also possible for solicitors to be eligible for appointment to the circuit bench. (See pp. 29 and 109.)

In order to qualify as a solicitor it is necessary to complete the examinations of the Law Society as appropriate and serve a period under training with a solicitor. A degree is not essential but the vast majority of entrants are graduates, though not necessarily in law. After this application must be made to the Law Society for admission as a solicitor, and admission must be approved by the Master of the Rolls, since a solicitor is an officer of the court. A person may then practise alone, or as a member of a partnership, though every practising solicitor must take out an annual practising certificate. A number of solicitors and barristers are employed in local and central government departments and by commercial firms.

In conclusion, the Solicitors Act, 1974 provides for the appointment of Lay Observers to receive complaints from the public of the handling by the Law Society of complaints against solicitors. The Lord Chancellor appointed a Lay Observer in 1975 with offices in the Royal Courts of Justice in the Strand. His annual reports list complaints made to him and the nature of those complaints.

Legal executives

The Institute of Legal Executives which was established in 1963 gives professional status to the unadmitted staff employed in solicitors' offices.

There are two examinations: the first leads to Associate membership of the Institute and the second, which is of higher standard, leads to Fellowship. Senior unadmitted employees are known as managing clerks and they frequently carry heavy responsibilities in connection with the business of the firm. A great deal of the routine work in connection with, e.g. conveyancing, also falls on them. Section 61 of the County Courts Act, 1984 enables the Lord Chancellor to confer on legal executives and other solicitors' employees limited rights of audience in the County Court. Under this power, so far as exercised, Fellows of the Institute have a right of audience in regard to an unopposed application for an adjournment and an application for judgment by consent where there is no question as to the applicant's entitlement to the judgment or its terms.

Reform

It has often been suggested that members of the public would be able to obtain cheaper legal services if the two branches of the profession, i.e. barristers and solicitors, were to merge. This is to some extent true in that only one person would be employed throughout the case doing both the pre-trial work and acting as advocate in court.

However, there are disadvantages involved in an amalgamation, some of which are as follows—

(a) Independence. Since a barrister is not involved to a great extent or at all with the client in pre-trial work, he is better able to treat the case when preparing it for trial with detachment as regards, for example, the personality and social background of the client. He sees the case as a legal problem requiring solution and this attitude of detachment is regarded by many as necessary if the court is to reach sound and unemotional decisions.

(b) Availability. At the present time the services of a barrister who is an expert in a particular branch of law are available to the clients of all solicitors, subject only to the ability to pay. Fusion of the profession would be likely to lead to larger firms of lawyers, some specializing in pre-trial work, and some in advocacy and opinions in special areas. The services of these specialists would unfortunately tend to be available, in the main, to clients of the particular firm and not to others.

(c) Relationship of Bench and Bar. Since the judiciary is for the most part selected from members of the Bar a special relationship of trust exists between judge and advocate. This can and does result in the speeding up of trials since the judge can accept more readily the method of dealing with the case which the advocates on both sides have agreed upon. This may mean, for example, that certain witnesses are not heard on the ground that the point which their evidence would make is accepted by both sides.

111

The Royal Commission on Legal Services, which reported in 1979, was, however, uncompromising against any change in the present position and none is likely for the time being.

Information and advice from non-lawyers

Those in business can obtain information and advice on legal matters from non-lawyers. Accountants are highly competent in the law of taxation and also in company law and government departments can be helpful—for example the Department of Employment is prepared to advise on employment legislation, as the Inland Revenue is on tax, and as the Customs and Excise are on VAT regulations. There are also Government sponsored organizations which provide information and advice such as the Equal Opportunities Commission on sex discrimination. Those in business may also obtain useful information and advice from a relevant trade association and of course from their own professional institutes and associations. Advice on social matters such as rent reduction, security of tenure of property and social benefits can be obtained from Citizen's Advice Bureaux.

SOME IMPORTANT JUDICIAL OFFICERS

The Lord Chancellor

The Lord Chancellor is the Speaker of the House of Lords and the ultimate head of the Judiciary in that he is the chief judge in the country, and controls the administration of the courts of law. He is also the Chairman of the Judicial Committee of the Privy Council. He advises the Crown on the appointment of High Court judges, and circuit judges. He is responsible for the appointment of Justices of the Peace, and advises on the appointment of recorders, stipendiary magistrates and Metropolitan stipendiaries. He is also the custodian of the Great Seal, which represents the signature of the Crown in its corporate capacity. Unlike the Speaker of the House of Commons, he may take part in debates and may vote in all divisions, but has no casting vote. The office is political, and the holder is usually a Cabinet Minister. However, the Prime Minister could appoint as Lord Chancellor a person who was not a politician. The one essential requirement is that he must be a barrister. His position serves to support the contention that there is no separation of judicial, legislative and executive powers in the British Constitution.

The Attorney-General and the Solicitor-General

The Attorney-General and the Solicitor-General are known as the Law Officers. The appointments are political and change with the Government. As a rule the Law Officers are not members of the Cabinet.

The Attorney-General is appointed by Letters Patent under the Great Seal, and is usually a member of the House of Commons. He represents the Crown in civil matters and prosecutes in important criminal cases. He is the Head of the English Bar, and points of professional etiquette are referred to him. He also advises government departments on legal matters, and advises the court on matters of parliamentary privilege. He can institute litigation on behalf of the public, e.g. to stop a public nuisance or the commission of a crime and to enforce or regulate public charitable trusts, because he acts on behalf of the public as a whole. Individuals do not have sufficient interest (or *locus standi*) to bring actions in these cases.

Where a person does not have sufficient *locus standi* to initiate proceedings himself, he may ask the Attorney-General to take proceedings. If the Attorney-General does act at the relation of a private individual, the action is known as a 'relator action' and the relator is responsible for the costs incurred. If the Attorney-General refuses to act no court can compel him to do so. (*Gouriet* v. *Union of Post Office Workers*, 1977.)[25]

The Solicitor-General is the subordinate of the Attorney-General, and sometimes gives a joint opinion with him when asked by government departments. In spite of his title he is a barrister, and he need not, strictly speaking, be in the House of Commons. His duties are similar to those of the Attorney-General and he is in many ways his deputy. Both Law Officers are precluded from private practice. The Law Officers Act, 1944, provides that any functions authorized or required to be discharged by the Attorney-General may be discharged by the Solicitor-General, if the office of Attorney-General is vacant, or if the Attorney-General is unable to act because of absence or illness, or where the Attorney-General authorizes the Solicitor-General to act in any particular matter.

Masters

Many matters arise for decision between the time of issue of the writ and the trial of the action, e.g. what documents must be shown by one side to the other; what time should be allowed for putting in statements of claim and defences; what is the most convenient and proper place for the trial to be held. These will usually be dealt with by a master, but sometimes by a judge.

Queen's Bench and Chancery Masters are salaried officials of the High Court the former being appointed from among barristers of not less than ten years' standing and the latter from solicitors of not less than ten years' standing.

Taxing Masters are salaried officers of the Supreme Court, being solicitors of at least ten years' standing. They fix the costs which one party is directed to pay to the other. In most important provincial towns there is a District Registry under the supervision of a *District Registrar* who performs the same functions as a master in London.

Official referees

Cases which involve detailed examination of books and documents, e.g. lengthy building disputes, are referred separately for trial, and are known as Official Referee's Business. Section 68 of the Supreme Court Act, 1981, as amended by s. 59 of the Administration of Justice Act, 1982, provides that the Lord Chancellor may nominate circuit judges, deputy circuit judges, and recorders, including solicitors, to deal with Official Referee's business.

The Official Solicitor

The Official Solicitor is an officer of the Supreme Court who acts in litigation to protect the interests of persons suffering under mental disability. He is also concerned to protect the interests of children in adoption matters and those of persons imprisoned for contempt of court.

Circuit administrators

The Royal Commission on Assizes and Quarter Sessions (Beeching Commission) recommended the appointment of a Circuit administrator in each of the six Circuits into which England and Wales was divided. A legal qualification is not essential, but if the applicant is legally qualified he must be a barrister or solicitor of at least 10 years' standing during which time he or she must have been in practice or had substantial experience in the courts. Their function is to a large extent managerial and they took over from Clerks of Assize, Clerks of the Peace, and other officers of the numerous different courts who previously had to try to provide the public and the legal profession with a court service. There is now one person at each High Court and Crown Court Centre to whom all involved can turn in respect of administrative problems.

Circuit administrators must as far as possible ensure prompt hearings for civil and criminal cases at their centres. Their function in the new High Court and Crown Court Centres is to decide whether cases should be heard by High Court judges or Circuit judges.

Presiding Judges

The Lord Chief Justice with the agreement of the Lord Chancellor appoints two High Court judges known as Presiding Judges who are assigned to each of the six Circuits in England and Wales. The appointment is not a statutory one. They take it in turn to spend substantial periods of time in the area and have general responsibility for the local

High Court and Crown Court Centre. They see to the convenient and efficient distribution of judges in the area, and give support and guidance to the Circuit administrator on these matters.

The Lord Chief Justice also appoints a Lord Justice as a Senior Presiding Judge to oversee all the Circuits. His function is to provide the Presiding Judges with a Senior Lord Justice to whom they can turn for advice rather than to the Lord Chief Justice himself, and to relieve the Lord Chief Justice of some of the administrative work in which he would otherwise be involved both in and out of London.

5 Law in action

The word 'source' has various meanings when applied to law. One may treat the word 'source' as referring to the *historical or ultimate origins of law* and trace the *development* of the common law, equity, legislation, delegated legislation, custom, the law merchant, canon law and legal treatises, as we have done in Chapter 1. But on the other hand one may treat the word 'source' as referring to the *methods by which laws are made or brought into existence*, and consider the current processes of legislation, delegated legislation, judicial precedent and, to a limited extent, custom. In this chapter we shall be concerned with the *methods by which laws are made*, i.e. the *active* or *legal* sources of law.

LEGISLATION

It is common knowledge that much of our law is contained in Acts of Parliament. Parliament consists of two chambers—the House of Commons and the House of Lords. The House of Commons contains 650 members, each of whom represents a geographical area in the country called his constituency. Members of Parliament (M.P.'s) are elected *en bloc* at general elections. Casual vacancies, occurring through the death or withdrawal of a member, are filled separately at by-elections. The House of Lords, on the other hand, consists in the main of hereditary peers, though under the provisions of the Life Peerages Act, 1958, there has been added a number of distinguished people from various walks of life who hold life peerages, but whose descendants will have no right to a seat when the life peers are dead. In addition to the Lords Temporal there are also the Lords Spiritual, e.g. the Archbishops of Canterbury and York, and certain other bishops. Over 1000 people are eligible to sit in the House of Lords but many do not exercise their right to do so.

An Act of Parliament begins as a Bill, which is the draft of a proposed Act.

Types of Bills

A Session of Parliament normally lasts for one year commencing in October or November. During that time, a large number of Bills become law, most of which are *Government Bills*. The Government is formed by the parliamentary party having an overall majority, or at least the greatest number, of members in the House of Commons, or more rarely by a formal coalition of, or more informal arrangement between two or more parties who between them can command such a majority. The Government is led by a Prime Minister who appoints a variety of other Ministers such as the Chancellor of the Exchequer, the Home Secretary, the Foreign Secretary, and others to manage various departments of State. A small group of these Ministers, called the Cabinet, meets frequently under the chairmanship of the Prime Minister and formulates the policy of the Government, and an important part of this policy consists of presenting Bills to Parliament with a view to their becoming law in due course. Such Bills are usually presented by the Minister of the department concerned with their contents.

The legislative intentions of the Government are given in outline to Parliament at the commencement of each session in the Queen's Speech. This is read by the Queen but is prepared by the Government of the day. Most Government Bills are introduced in the House of Commons, going later to the House of Lords and finally for the Royal Assent. However, some of the less controversial Government Bills are introduced in the House of Lords, going later to the Commons and then for the Royal Assent. Money Bills, i.e. those containing only provisions relating to finance and taxation, e.g. the annual Finance Bill, and other Bills with financial clauses must start in the Commons.

Members of either House whether Government supporters or not have a somewhat restricted opportunity to introduce *Private Members' Bills*. Such Bills are not likely to become law unless the Government provides the necessary Parliamentary time for debate. Some, however, survive to become law, for example, the Murder (Abolition of Death Penalty) Act, 1965. Those that are lost usually fail to be debated fully because influential and anonymous objectors work behind the scenes to ensure that they are taken towards the end of the session when Parliamentary time is at a premium. In addition, the severe restriction of debating time for Private Members' Bills makes such time as is available an ideal stamping ground for the determined filibuster who wishes to talk the bill out. At present certain Fridays are set aside by the Leader of the House for Private Members' Bills.

A session of Parliament is of about one year's duration. It is brought to an end by the Monarch by prorogation and a Bill which does not complete the necessary stages and receive the Royal Assent in one Session will lapse. It can be introduced in a subsequent Session but must complete all the necessary stages again. Bills also lapse when Parliament is dissolved prior to a General Election. The above provisions do not apply to *Private Bills* (see below) which because of the eosts involved in promotion can complete their remaining stages in a new session. The sittings of Parliament within a session are divided by periods of 'recess'. Bills do not lapse when Parliament goes into recess.

Bills are also divided into *Public* and *Private* Bills. *Public Bills*, which may be Government or Private Members' Bills, alter the law throughout England and Wales and extend also to Scotland and Northern Ireland unless there is a provision to the contrary. A *Private Bill* does not alter the general law but confers special local powers. These Bills are often promoted by local authorities, where a new local development requires compulsory purchase of land for which a statutory power is needed. Statutory bodies have no power to amend their own constitution, unlike a limited company which may do so, subject to the Companies Act (see p. 171). Enactment of these Bills is by a different Parliamentary procedure.

The Speaker of the House of Commons rules whether a Bill is public or private if there is doubt as where, e.g. the Bill might affect areas beyond that of the local authority concerned, as would be the case if a seaport authority forbade the export of live animals from the port.

Enactment of Bills

A Public Bill and a Private Members' Bill follow the same procedure in Parliament. These Bills may be introduced in either House; though, as we have seen, a money Bill, which is a public Bill certified by the Speaker as one containing only provisions relating to taxation or loans, must be introduced in the Commons by a Minister and not a Private member. The following procedure relates to a Public or Private Members' Bill introduced in the Commons.

On its introduction the Bill receives a purely formal first reading. Only the title of the Bill is read out by the Clerk of the House. The purpose of this stage is to tell Members that the Bill exists and that they can now get printed copies. Later it is given a second reading, at which point its general merits may be debated, but no amendments are proposed to the various clauses it contains. There is an alternative procedure for the second reading stage of *Public Bills in the Commons*, which is designed to save Parliamentary time. A Minister may move that the Bill be referred to a Standing Second Reading Committee of between 30 to 80 M.P.s. They report to the Commons recommending with reasons whether or not the Bill should be read a second time. The report of the Committee must be put to the House for a vote without debate or amendment. This procedure does not apply if 20 Members rise in their seats to object. Private Members' Bills are automatically referred to the Second Reading Committee.

Having survived the second reading, the Bill passes to the Committee stage. Here details are discussed by a Standing Committee of fifteen to twenty members chosen in proportion to the strength of the parties in the House of Commons. Amendments to the clauses are proposed, and, if not accepted by the Government, are voted on, after which the Bill returns to the House at the Report stage. The Committee mentioned may be a Committee of the Whole House, if the legislation is sufficiently important. Certain Bills in the Commons may be sent to a Special Standing Committee which is given power to hear evidence from outsiders, thus following to some extent the procedure for Private Bills. (See below.)

At the Report stage the amendments may be debated, and the Bill may in some cases be referred back for further consideration. It is then read for the third time, when amendments may strictly speaking be moved but in practice only verbal alterations are taken.

After passing the third reading, the Bill is said to have 'passed the House'. It is then sent to the House of Lords where it goes through a similar procedure and must pass through all stages successfully *in the same Session of Parliament*. If the Lords propose amendments, the Bill is returned to the Commons for approval. At one time the House of Lords had the power to reject Bills sent up by the Commons. Now, under the provisions of the Parliament Acts, 1911 and 1949, this power amounts to no more than an ability to delay a Public Bill (other than a money Bill) for a period of one year; a money Bill may be delayed for one month only. The supremacy of the Commons stems from the fact that it is an elected assembly, responsible to its electors and coming periodically at intervals of not more than five years before the public for re-election. The Lords may veto a Private Bill and have retained the power to reject a Bill which attempts to extend the duration of Parliament beyond five years.

Private Bills—a judicial stage

The main difference between the enactment of a *Private Bill* and a *Public Bill* is that the committee stage of a Private Bill may be judicial. Any person whose interests are specifically affected by the Bill, normally in relation to property or business interests, may lodge a petition against the Bill in accordance with the procedure set out in Standing Orders. In such a situation the Bill is referred to an Opposed Committee consisting of four M.P.s of all parties appointed by the House. They must be entirely disinterested in a material sense, in the matters with which the Bill is concerned. The Committee hears both the petitioner and the promoter, who usually appear by counsel. If the petition succeeds the Bill is amended to take account of it. There is no appeal against the decision of the Committee. Since this is a somewhat lengthy procedure, some statutes allow ministers to grant special powers to local authorities by what is called a Provisional Order. Such an order does not take effect unless and until it is embodied (usually along with others) in a Provisional Order Confirmation Bill which is passed by Parliament and given the Royal Assent.

When a Bill has passed through both the Commons and the Lords, it requires the Royal Assent. It is not customary for the Monarch to consent in person and in practice consent is given by a committee of three peers, including the Lord Chancellor. The Royal Assent Act, 1967, provides that an Act is duly enacted and becomes law if the Royal Assent is notified to each House of Parliament, sitting separately, by the Speaker of that House or acting Speaker.

The former Bill is then referred to as an Act or a Statute, and may be regarded as a *literary* as well as a *legal* source of law. However, an Act may specify a future date for its coming into operation, or it may be brought into operation piecemeal by ministerial order. The courts have no power to disregard an Act of Parliament, whether public or private, nor have they any power to examine proceedings in Parliament in order to determine whether the passing of an Act has been obtained by means of any irregularity or fraud. (*British Railways Board* v. *Pickin*, 1974.)[26]

Short title—numbering and citation

It should be noted that, as well as having a title setting out what its objects are, each Act has, under the provisions of the Short Titles Act, 1896, a short title to enable easy reference to be made. Each Act has also an official reference. The Law of Property Act, 1925, is the short title of an Act whose official reference is 15 & 16 Geo. 6, c. 20, which means that the Law of Property Act, 1925, was the twentieth statute passed in the Session of Parliament spanning the fifteenth and sixteenth years of the reign of George the Fifth.

The Acts of Parliament Numbering and Citation Act, 1962, provides that chapter numbers assigned to Acts of Parliament passed in 1963 and after shall be assigned by reference to the calendar year and not the session in which they are passed. For example, the official reference of the Sale of Goods Act, 1979 is 1979, c. 54.

Statute law and case law distinguished

The essential differences between statute law and case law are apparent from the definition of a statute. It is—

an express and formal laying down of a rule or rules of conduct to be observed in the future by the persons to whom the statute is expressly or by implication made applicable.

Thus a statute openly creates new law, whereas a judge would disclaim any attempt to do so. Judges are, they say, bound by precedent and merely, select existing rules which they apply to new cases. (But see p. 138.) A statute lays down general rules for the guidance of future conduct; a judgment merely applies an existing rule to a particular set of circumstances. A judgment gives reasons and may be argumentative; a statute gives no reasons and is imperative.

Parliament and the European Community

Because Britain is a member of the European Economic Community, Parliament has had to adapt to a new role in regard to legislation emanating from the institutions of the Community. There are three principal types of Community legislation. *Regulations* which are of general application in the member countries and, under Art. 189 of the Treaty of Rome in theory, become part of domestic law without the need for UK legislation to implement them. In practice, however, some may give rise to consequential subordinate legislation or require the repeal or amendment of existing Acts. *Decisions* are of more particular application, and are also immediately operative. Decisions may be addressed to a state or to an individual or a corporation and an example of a decision would be a Commission ruling that a company was adopting restrictive practices in its operations within the Market contrary to Arts 85/86 of the Treaty. (See p. 288.) Such a Decision could also impose a fine. Decisions have the force of law but affect the recipient only. *Directives* are under Art. 189 binding in principle, but it is left to the member countries to decide upon the means of giving them legal and administrative effect usually within a given time scale. In Britain this is dealt with by s. 2 of the European Communities Act, 1972, and the most common method of incorporating directives into British law will be by statutory instruments, subject to annulment by 'negative' resolution of Parliament. (See p. 126.) However, the UK's response to the First Directive on Company Law is included in various sections of the Companies Act, 1985. (See p. 224.) Nevertheless, fundamental obligations in a directive, such as free movement of workers, which are not subject to any exception or conditions may have immediate effect without the need for legislation in the UK. (*Van Duyn* v. *The Home Office*, 1974.)[27]

As regards the provisions of the Treaty of Rome itself, these are enforceable in the High Court under s. 2 of the European Communities Act, 1972, provided the High Court can ascertain from the words of the Treaty itself what right has been infringed. (See *Van Duyn* v. *The Home Office*, 1974.)[27] If this is not possible, as where a person claims relief against sex discrimination generally on the basis of an article of the Treaty which deals merely with discrimination on the grounds of pay, no 'enforceable Community right' is created. (*Amies* v. *ILEA*, 1977,[28] contrast *Macarthys Ltd* v. *Smith*, 1981[29]).

There is also the additional problem that many articles of the Treaty are expressed in general terms making it difficult to judge precisely what rights are conferred, so that in many cases the Treaty provides only the bones of suggested rights and is not enforceable in the absence of a UK Act of Parliament which expresses clearly the *detailed* rights conferred in the UK as a response to the *general* requirements of the Treaty. In any case an industrial tribunal cannot take into account an 'enforceable Community right' since it was set up by a UK Act of Parliament to administer only UK Acts of Parliament dealing with specific industrial matters. (*Amies* v. *ILEA*, 1977.)[28]

The E.C. Treaties

There are three Treaties setting up three European Communities as follows—

(a) The European Coal and Steel Community, (ECSC), established by the Treaty of Paris 1951 with the object of managing a common market in coal and steel;

(b) The European Atomic Energy Community (Euratom), established by the second Treaty of Rome 1957 to develop a common market in nuclear energy and the distribution of power produced thereby;

(c) The European Economic Community (EEC), established by the first Treaty of Rome 1957. The EEC has broader objectives. An immediate aim is economic integration of the member states and, in the longer term, political integration into a European Community. This will be further advanced under the European Communities (Amendment) Act, 1986 which ratifies the Single European Act which was approved by the Council in December 1985 and signed in 1986. The aim is to produce a single market by 1992 with the lifting of tariff barriers and with common passports, together with a new European Court of first instance (see p. 40).

The institutions

There are three main institutions dealing with the functions of the communities. The Commission proposes legislation, the Parliament advises, and the Council of Ministers enacts.

The Commission

This consists of commissioners nominated by member states. A president is appointed from the commissioners. The Commission is charged with implementing the Treaty, with bringing to the Council proposals for furthering the aims of the Community, and with supervising the adherence to the Treaty by the member states.

The term of office of a commissioner is five years, though they may resign or be compulsorily retired for misconduct by the Court of Justice before that period expires. In addition, a vote of censure carried by a two-thirds majority in the European Parliament results in the compulsory retirement of the whole Commission. Commissioners must not take instructions from their national governments but must act independently in the interests of the communities. Individual commissioners have special responsibilities, e.g. for agriculture and transport.

The Commission initiates most Community legislation and places it before the Council of Ministers for enactment. In some areas, e.g. agriculture, the Commission can enact legislation itself because the Council has delegated power to the Commission to do so.

The Commission can bring any member state or commercial undertaking before the Court of Justice where it feels community obligations are not being carried out and in the case of breach of restrictive practices and anti-monopoly provisions, the Commission operates quasi-judicially and, as we have seen, can issue a decision on the matter and impose a fine.

Council of ministers

The council is composed of one representative from each of the member states. The representative is usually the Foreign Secretary but others may attend where a matter of importance in a particular field is involved, e.g. if agriculture, the Minister of Agriculture.

There is a Committee of Permanent Representatives consisting of the various ambassadors to the member states which assists the Council in preliminary discussions designed to clarify issues before they reach the Council.

The Council enacts legislation on proposals from the Commission. The representatives of the larger countries have more votes than others and in most cases more than a simple majority is required. Thus for the admission of a new member state the Council must approve unanimously. However, under the European Communities (Amendment) Act, 1986, more matters will be decided by a simple majority vote with less need than before for unanimity.

European Parliament

This represents the peoples of the member states. Seats are allocated to member states on the basis of population. The members, who tend to act in political rather than national groups, are elected by the electorate of the state which they represent. In the UK the relevant legislation is the European Assembly Elections Act, 1978.

The Parliament does not legislate, but advises. However, it is invariably consulted on proposals for legislation. It provides a place where community problems can be discussed and questions put to the Council and Commission. As we have seen, an important power is to remove the Commission members from office by a vote of censure passed by a majority of two-thirds. This is a sanction which the Parliament has if the Commission fails to propose what Parliament has advised. In addition, it has power to veto the annual Community budget which in effect freezes the activities of the Community.

Introduction of Community law

As we have seen, s. 2 of the European Communities Act, 1972, provides that the Treaties and all secondary legislation, such as regulations, intended to take effect in member states shall become part of our law. This includes legislation made before and after our entry into the Community and gives what are referred to as 'enforceable Community rights'. Directives must in general be implemented by legislation in the member states, but see *Van Duyn* v. *The Home Office*, 1974.[27]

Community law is now part of English law and if there is any inconsistency Community law prevails. It does not supplant English law but is part of it and overrides any other part which is inconsistent with it. As we have seen, individuals may plead Community law before English courts. (See, e.g. *Van Duyn* v. *The Home Office*, 1974[27] and *Macarthys Ltd* v. *Smith*, 1981.)[29]

Control over Community law

The bulk of Community law (some 90 per cent) is made by the European Commission in its day-to-day administration of the common agricultural policy. Much of this law is trivial and is not published in draft so that such scrutiny as is both necessary and feasible falls within the responsibility of the European Parliament to which Britain sends representatives.

The more substantial kinds of Community law come from the Council of Ministers acting usually on proposals put forward by the Commission and published in draft months or sometimes years before the final decision is taken. Such legislative proposals must be referred to the European Parliament before the Council takes the final decision.

Thus all important legislative proposals are published in draft at an early stage, and this gives the legislatures of member countries a chance to exert influence at the formative stages of law making. Of course, in the case particularly of directives there is a second opportunity when the appropriate instrument or Bill comes before the domestic Parliament for endorsement. There is clearly a considerable potential for effective scrutiny, perhaps even for control, but whether that potential is realized in practice depends upon a number of factors: firstly, the willingness of governments to make information available and to accept responsibility for Community decisions; secondly, the enthusiasm of parliamentarians, already operating under some strain, for working in unfamiliar territory, and finally, the provision of adequate parliamentary machinery to assist them in their new tasks.

The UK Parliament has set up Select Committees in the Commons and in the Lords to scrutinize and report on Community proposals. (See further p. 130.)

It should be noted that although U.K. courts may interpret E.C. legislation and ask the European Court for a ruling, only the European Court can declare Community legislation void (*Foto-Frost* v. *Hauptzollamt Lübeck-Ost*, *The Times*, 30 December, 1987).

LAW REFORM

It should be noted that a number of official bodies exist to consider and make proposals for *law reform*, and the work of these bodies can have a considerable influence on the development of statute law. The most important of these bodies is the Law Commission, which was set up by the Law Commissions Act, 1965. Section 1 of the Act establishes the Commission to promote the reform of English Law and deals with the constitution of the Commission. The Lord Chancellor appoints the members of the Commission, on a full-time basis, from among persons holding judicial office, experienced barristers and solicitors and university teachers of law. Section 3 states the duty of the Commission to be to keep under review the whole of English law with a view to its systematic development and reform, including the codification of such law, the elimination of anomalies, the repeal of obsolete enactments and generally the simplification and modernization of the law. The present programme of the Law Commission includes the codification of the law of contract. The Criminal Law Act, 1967, which abolished the distinction between felonies and misdemeanors and certain obsolete crimes, resulted from proposals made by the Commission.

In arriving at its programme the Commission consults with the chairmen of the Criminal Law Revision Committee and the Law Reform Committee, which are bodies set up on a part-time basis by the Home Secretary to consider specific matters of law reform which he may refer to them in the fields of criminal and civil law respectively. The work of the Commission and the Committees may be regarded as a source of law in that it is an *historical source* of the law contained in the statute which implements its proposals. Thus the proposals of the Law Commission may be regarded as an historical source of the Criminal Law Act, 1967.

DELEGATED LEGISLATION

Modern statutes may require much detailed work to implement and operate them. In such a case the Act is drafted so as to provide a broad framework, the details being filled in by ministers by means of delegated legislation. For example, much of our Social Security legislation gives only the general provisions of a complex scheme of social benefits and an immense number of detailed regulations have had to be made by civil servants in the name of and under the authority of the appropriate minister. These regulations when made in the approved manner are just as much law as the parent statute itself. This form of law is known as *delegated* or *subordinate* legislation.

Advantages

A number of advantages are claimed for delegated legislation as follows.

(a) It saves Parliamentary time in that ministers are left, with the civil service, to make the detailed rules, Parliament concerning itself solely with the broad framework of the legislation.

(b) Speed. The Parliamentary procedure for enacting bills is slow whereas rules and orders can be put more rapidly into law, particularly in a time of national emergency.

(c) Parliament cannot foresee all the problems which may arise after an Act has become law. Delegated legislation can deal with these if and when they arise.

(d) Delegated legislation is less rigid in that it can be withdrawn quickly if it proves impracticable by another statutory instrument.

(e) The aptitude of the legislature is limited and experts in the Departments of State can better advise a minister on the technicalities of a certain branch of law. It would be difficult to give this kind of advice to the Lords or Commons as a whole.

Disadvantages

However, there are disadvantages as follows—

(a) Parliamentary control over legislation is undoubtedly reduced. However, the power to make delegated legislation must be given by an Act of Parliament (sometimes referred to as the enabling statute) and so Parliament is to that extent in broad control because it must pass the enabling statute.

Beyond that much depends upon what the enabling statute says about reference to Parliament when instruments are made. There are different requirements and the inclusion of one rather than another in an enabling statute does not appear to be based upon any detectable principle.

The enabling Act may require—

(i) that the instrument be merely laid before Parliament. If so M.P.s and Peers have no right to change it but laying before Parliament does, at least, inform them that the instrument exists. In some cases the instrument is already in force. However, Members may ask Parliamentary questions about instruments laid for information only;

(ii) that Parliament may annul the instrument, e.g. within 40 days of laying. Where this is so a resolution of either House to annul the instrument is effective, but if there is no such resolution the instrument passes into law. However, whether there is a debate leading to a resolution to annul the instrument is entirely dependent upon the initiative of an M.P. or Peer to engineer the debate since the Government is not obliged to find time for it;

(iii) that each House of Parliament must pass a resolution approving the instrument. Where this is so the Government must obviously find time for a debate and a resolution approving the instrument must be made in each House, otherwise it will not become law;

(iv) that the instrument be laid in draft before Parliament and may only be issued if an affirmative resolution is passed by each House in its favour;

(v) that the instrument be laid in draft without reference to affirmative resolutions, in which case by s. 6 of the Statutory Instruments Act of 1946 it may be made law after a period of 40 days if no resolution is passed during that period by either house against it.

It should be noted that if it is essential that an instrument come into operation before copies of it can be laid before Parliament, then it may do so provided notification is sent to the Lord Chancellor and the Speaker of the House of Commons explaining why copies could not be laid before the instrument came into operation.

There are also other controls both by the judiciary and by Parliament itself. (See below.)

(b) It is said that there is too much delegated legislation so that it is difficult to know what the law is, particularly in view of the fact that little publicity is given to statutory instruments whereas most important Acts of Parliament are referred to at one time or another in the Press. The difficulty is that a defendant's *ignorance of the law is no excuse*, though s. 3(2) of the Statutory Instruments Act of 1946 protects a person in respect of a crime contained in a statutory instrument *if the instrument has not been published*, unless it is proved that reasonable steps have been taken for the purpose of bringing the content of the instrument to the notice of the public or of persons likely to be affected by it or the person in fact charged. The section does not protect if the instrument has been published but a particular defendant does not know of its existence.

(c) The dangers of sub-delegation are on occasions quite real. One can find in some cases a pedigree of four generations of instruments emanating from a statute as follows—

(i) regulations made under the statute;
(ii) orders made under the regulations;
(iii) directions made under the orders;
(iv) licences issued under the directions.

When this happens it does reduce very seriously the control by Parliament of the making of new laws since Parliament would only see the parent statute and the first set of regulations.

Types of delegated legislation

In modern statutes delegated powers are exercisable by four main vehicles as follows—

(a) Statutory instruments. Most powers conferred on ministers in modern statutes are exercisable by ministerial or departmental regulations or orders, called collectively statutory instruments.

(b) Orders in Council. Powers of special importance relating to constitutional issues, e.g. emergency powers, are conferred on the Queen in Council. These powers are in fact exercised by the Cabinet who are all Privy Councillors by means of an order in council.

(c) Bye-laws of Local Authorities. These are made by local authorities under powers given to them in Acts of Parliament and require the approval of the appropriate Minister.

(d) Rules of the Supreme Court and county court. These are made by Rules Committees set up by statute specifically to make rules concerning the practice and procedure of the courts.

Judicial control

Delegated legislation takes effect as if it were part of the enabling statute. Therefore it has statutory force and, as we have seen, the courts cannot declare a statute *ultra vires*. However, delegated legislation does not acquire statutory force unless it is *intra vires*, i.e. properly made in accordance with the terms of the enabling Act. The courts can declare delegated legislation *ultra vires* in this sense. There are two approaches to the *ultra vires* rule as regards delegated legislation as follows—

(a) Substantive ultra vires. This means that the Minister has exceeded the powers given to him in the parent statute. If a Minister is authorized to make regulations as to road traffic, clearly if he purports to make regulations under the same parent statute concerning rail traffic, they would be held by the courts to be *ultra vires* and invalid. (See *Hotel and Catering Industry Training Board* v. *Automobile Proprietary Ltd* (1969).)[30]

(b) Procedural ultra vires. This means that the instrument is invalid because the minister has failed to follow some mandatory procedural requirement specified in the parent Act. For example, much Social Security legislation requires the minister to consult various advisory bodies before making rules and orders. If a rule or order was made without the necessary consultation, then it would be *ultra vires* in procedural terms and invalid.

It should be noted that the courts will not examine the internal proceedings of Parliament in order to invalidate delegated legislation. (*R.* v. *Immigration Appeal Tribunal, ex parte Joyles*, 1972.)[31] However, it was decided by the Court of Appeal in *R.* v. *HM Treasury, ex parte Smedley*, [1985] 1 All E.R. 589 that the courts are entitled to examine questions of law in relation to a draft order, in this case whether it was *ultra vires*, while it is still before Parliament and has not been approved.

Henry VIII (or ouster) Clauses

Sometimes a section of an Act will give a minister or the Queen in Council very wide powers so that it is difficult to say that any instrument made or decision taken under it is *ultra vires*. These are referred to as 'Henry VIII Clauses' after the way in which that monarch used to legislate in arbitrary fashion by a proclamation. A more modern expression is an 'ouster clause', i.e. a clause attempting to prevent a decision being reviewed by the court. For example, s. 4(7) of the Parliamentary Constituencies Act, 1986 provides that 'The validity of any Order in Council purporting to be made under this Act—shall not be called in question in any legal proceedings whatsoever.' It was at one time thought that the courts were powerless to intervene to review any order made under such a provision. However, in more recent times the courts have taken power to overcome ouster clauses by saying, in effect, that if the exercise of such a power is not in accordance with the law, as where it is, e.g. *ultra vires* or made by misinterpreting the power given, the minister or tribunal has lost jurisdiction and the court can intervene. In other words the jurisdiction is to decide correctly but not incorrectly. (See *Anisminic Ltd* v. *Foreign Compensation Commission*, 1969, p. 525.)

Parliamentary control

As regards Parliamentary control there is a Joint Committee on Statutory Instruments between the House of Commons and the House of Lords. The predecessors of this Joint Committee were the Lords' Special Orders Committee and the Commons' Statutory Instruments Committee. The Joint Committee is appointed to consider statutory instruments with a view to determining whether the special attention of Parliament should be drawn to the legislation on various grounds. The grounds, briefly, are as follows; that the legislation—

   (i) imposes a tax on the public;
   (ii) is made in pursuance of an enactment containing specific provisions excluding it from challenge in the courts;
   (iii) purports to have retrospective effect where there is no express authority in the enabling statute;
   (iv) has been unduly delayed in publication or laying before Parliament;
   (v) has come into operation before being laid before Parliament and there has been unjustifiable delay in informing the Speaker of the delay under s. 4(1) of the Statutory Instruments Act, 1946;
   (vi) is of doubtful *vires* or makes some unusual or unexpected use of the powers conferred by the enabling statute;

(vii) calls for any special reason of form or purport for elucidation;
(viii) is defective in its drafting.

The older House of Commons Select Committee on Statutory Instruments remains to consider legislation which is to be laid before and subject to proceedings in the House of Commons *only*. In addition, the Commons has set up the Select Committee on European Secondary Legislation and the Lords has set up the Select Committee on the European Communities. The Committees have the task of bringing to the attention of Parliament the more important Community proposals. The Commons Committee reports to the House on Community matters every six months. Provided matters are drawn to the attention of Parliament in time there can be a debate on the matters concerned in Parliament before the Council of Ministers makes a final decision.

Bye-laws of local authorities

These must be *intra vires*; i.e. within the powers given to the local authority in the enabling statute and also reasonable. Thus, in *Kruse* v. *Johnson* [1898] 2 Q.B. 91 a local authority bye-law making it an offence to sing within 50 yards of a dwelling house was upheld but the court decided that unreasonableness could be a ground for invalidating bye-laws. This can occur where the bye-law is partial and unequal in its operation as between different classes or if it involves oppressive and gratuitous interference with the rights of persons subject to it so that it cannot be justified in the minds of reasonable men. (And see *Denithorne* v. *Davies*, 1967.)[32]

CASE LAW OR JUDICIAL PRECEDENT

Case law still provides the bulk of the law of the country, although Parliament is becoming much more active in making new laws and statute law may come to dominate the common law. This trend is, of course, encouraged by the existence of the Law Commission which is constantly putting forward proposals to codify the law by statute. Some case law enunciates the law itself, and some is concerned with the interpretation of statutes. We will examine first the case law which is law in its own right. Case law is built up out of precedents, and a precedent is a previous decision of a court which may, in certain circumstances, be binding on another court in deciding a similar case. This practice of following previous decisions is derived from custom, but it is a practice which is generally observed. As Park, C.J., said in *Mirehouse* v. *Rennell* (1833), 1 Cl. & Fin. 527, 'Precedent must be adhered to for the sake of developing the law as a science.' In more modern times attention to precedent is essential because without it no lawyer could safely advise his client and every quarrel would lead to a law suit. Even in early times the itinerant judges adopted the doctrine of *stare decisis*, and this doctrine has been developed in modern times so that it means that a precedent binds, and must be followed in similar cases, subject to the power to distinguish cases in certain circumstances.

The modern doctrine of the binding force of judicial precedent only fully emerged when there was (*a*) good law reporting; and (*b*) a settled judicial hierarchy. By the middle of the nineteenth century law reporting was much more efficient, and the Judicature Acts, 1873–1875, created a proper pyramid of authority which was completed when the Appellate Jurisdiction Act, 1876, made the House of Lords the final Court of Appeal. Judicial precedents may be divided into two kinds—

(1) Binding Precedents
(2) Persuasive Precedents

but before we elucidate the precise meaning of these terms, we have still to ascertain where these precedents are to be found. The answer is in the law reports; and as we have seen the doctrine of judicial precedent depends upon an accurate record being kept of previous decisions.

Law reports

Bracton was the first person to compile cases (some two thousand of them) in his Notebook which appeared before the Year Books. The latter were gossipy and fragmentary notes of cases, written in Anglo-Norman, and covering a period of two and a half centuries from the reign of Edward I to that of Henry VIII—that is from the thirteenth century to about the middle of the sixteenth. The Year Books are little used by the modern practitioner because of their many inaccuracies, because of the language in which they are written, and because they do not always report the *ratio decidendi* of the case, but they were studied by the law apprentices in the Inns of Court.

Access to court records was only allowed to lawyers acting on behalf of the Crown. Hence we get the private reports, one of the first sets being Dyer's Collection, 1513–1581. Like the Year Books, many early private reports are of doubtful quality being inaccurate and gossipy. For example, it was said of Barnardiston who was a King's Bench reporter from 1726 to 1734 'that he was accustomed to slumber over his notebook and the wags in the rear took the opportunity of scribbling nonsense in it.' The following are among the most notable and accurate early collections: Plowden's Reports, Coke's Reports, and Burrow's Reports. The last-named runs from 1756–1772, and is the first attempt to report in the modern sense of the word, an effort being made to report arguments and judgments. Other good collections are those of Barnewell & Cresswell, and Meeson & Welsby.

Since 1865 law reports have been published under the control of what is now called the Incorporated Council of Law Reporting, which is a joint committee of the Inns of Court, The Law Society, and the Bar Council.

They are known simply as the Law Reports, and they have priority in the courts because the judge who heard the case sees and revises the report before publication. Nevertheless private reports still exist, and of these the All England Reports, published weekly and started in 1936, are the only *general* reports existing in the private sector. These reports are now revised by the judge concerned with the case, though this was not always so and differences do appear between the version of a case in the official reports and that in the unrevised All England Reports. In addition, there is some judicial editing of the transcript of the trial prior to publication in the reports. This has extended beyond minor textual amendments and in some cases the report states rules of law which were not in fact laid down in the judgment given at the trial. In 1953 the Incorporated Council began to publish reports on a weekly basis and these are known as the Weekly Law Reports. *The Times* newspaper publishes summarized reports of certain cases of importance and interest on the day following the hearing, as do other newspapers e.g. *The Financial Times, The Independent* and *The Guardian*, and there are also certain specialized series of reports covering, for example, the fields of taxation, shipping, company law and employment law. It is not absolutely essential that a case should have been reported in order that it may be cited as a precedent, and occasionally oral evidence of the decision by a barrister who was in court when the judgment was delivered may be brought.

The issue of the citation of unreported cases was raised by Lord Diplock in the House of Lords in *Roberts Petroleum* v. *Bernard Kenny*, [1983] 1 All E.R. 564, and Sir John Donaldson, M.R. in *Stanley* v. *International Harvester, The Times*, 7 February, 1983. These have become readily available since the Lexis Computer Retrieval System came into use. Lexis records, for example, 3000 Court of Appeal decisions a year. Of these only some 350 are reported in any of the major series such as All England, and Weekly Law Reports. These, as we have seen, are edited by the judge(s). Both judges seemed determined to discourage the growing resort by counsel to unreported cases. Indeed, in the Stanley case the view was that counsel should be beware of citing to the courts cases which are of no great novelty or authority, but which are supplied in unnecessary profusion by computers.

Decided cases are usually referred to as follows: *Smith* v. *Jones*, 1959. This means that, in a court of first instance, Smith was the plaintiff, Jones the defendant, and that the case was published in the set of reports of 1959, though it may have been heard at the end of 1958. This is called the Short Citation. A longer citation is required if the report is to be referréd to, and might read as follows: *Smith* v. *Jones*, [1959] 1 Q.B. 67 at p. 76. The additional information means that the case is to be found in the First Volume of the Reports of the Queen's Bench Division, the report commencing on page 67, the number 76 being used to indicate the page on which an important statement is to be found. Where the date is cited in square brackets it means that the date is an essential part of the reference, and without the date it is very difficult to find the report in question. For many years now the Incorporated Council's reports have been written up in a certain number of volumes each year. It will be seen that a mere reference to Vol. 1 of the Queen's Bench Division will not be sufficient unless the year is also quoted. The same procedures are followed in the All England Reports.

The early reports by the Incorporated Council and other collections did not use the year as a basic item of the citation, but continued to extend the number of volumes regardless of the year. So a case may be cited as follows: *Smith* v. *Jones*, 17 Ch. D. 230. It can be found by referring to Vol. 17 of the Chancery Division reports, and it is not necessary to know the year in which the report was published, though this will be ascertained when the report is referred to. Where the date is not an essential part of the citation it is quoted in round brackets. The abbreviations used in the Official Reports for the various divisions are: Q.B. for Queen's Bench; Ch. for Chancery; P. for Probate, etc.; Fam. for Family; and A.C. for the House of Lords and Privy Council (Appeal Cases). The reports of decisions of the Court of Appeal appear under the reference of the division in which they were first heard. As regards the case title petitions for leave to appeal and appeals to the Court of Appeal carry the same title as that which obtained in the court of first instance. This results in the plaintiff being shown first in the title whether he or she be the petitioner/appellant or respondent in the Court of Appeal. Since a Practice Note of 1974 ([1974] 1 All E.R. 752), this is now true of the House of Lords so that appeals to the House of Lords now carry the same title as that which obtained in the court of first instance, though in the Official Reports the reference A.C. is still used in House of Lords and Privy Council cases.

Precedents

We are now in a position to refer to a decided case but we still have to ascertain where the precedent is to be found, since the whole of the case is reported, and the judge may have said things which are not strictly relevant to the final judgment. We must know what to take as precedent, and what to ignore, so that we can find what is called the *ratio decidendi*. The doctrine of precedent declares that cases must be decided in the same way when their *material* facts are the same. The *ratio* is therefore defined as the *principle* of law used by the judge to arrive at his *decision* together with his *reasons* for doing so. In this connection it is worth noting the remarks of Sir George Jessel in *Osborne* v. *Rowlett* (1880), 13 Ch. D. 774, that 'the only thing in a judge's decision binding as an authority upon a subsequent judge is the principle upon which the case was decided.' To take an example from contract law, in *Household Fire Insurance Company* v. *Grant*, (1879) (see p. 560) the court *decided* that a letter of acceptance took effect when it was posted, the *reason* behind this *principle* being that the Post Office was the common agent of the parties.

The *ratio decidendi* of a decision may be narrowed or widened by a subsequent judge before whom the case is cited as an authority. Although a judge will give reasons for his ruling, he is neither concerned nor obliged to formulate *all* the possibilities which may stem from it. Thus the eventual and accepted *ratio decidendi* of a case may not be the *ratio decidendi* that the judge who decided the case would himself have chosen, but the one which has been approved by subsequent judges. This is inevitable, because a judge, when deciding a case, will give his reasons but will not usually distinguish in his remarks, in any rigid or immutable way, between what we have called the *ratio decidendi* and what are called *obiter dicta*. The latter are things said in passing, and they do not have binding force. Such statements of legal principle are, however, of some persuasive power, particularly the *dicta* of cases heard in the House of Lords.

The reason why *obiter dicta* are merely persuasive is because the prerogative of judges is not to make the law by formulating it and declaring it (this is for the legislature) but to make the law by applying it to cases coming before them. A judicial decision, unaccompanied by judicial application, is not of binding authority but is *obiter*. A judge does sometimes indicate which of his statements are *obiter dicta*. For example he may say: 'If it were necessary to decide the further point, I should be inclined to say that . . .' What follows is said in passing.

It may therefore be said that the *ratio decidendi* of any given case is an abstraction of the legal *principle* from the *material* facts of the case, and, the *decision* which the judge made thereon together with his *reasons* for so doing. Of course, the higher the level of abstraction, the more circumstances the *ratio decidendi* will fit. Let us take the following fact situation—'At 12 noon on a Saturday A, a woman aged 30, drove a car through the centre of Manchester at 80 mph. She mounted the pavement and injured B, an old man of 90. B sued A and the judge found that she was liable.' If a subsequent judge feels that the principle in *B* v. *A* should be restricted he will tend to retain many of the facts of the case as material. If he feels that the principle should be extended he will not regard many of the facts of the situation as material and so produce a broad principle of wide application. Thus, a very narrow *ratio* would be as follows 'If a woman aged 30 by the negligent driving of a car injures an old man of 90, she is liable to compensate him in damages.' However, the law of negligence is a much wider principle and the ratio is—'If A, by negligence injures B, A is liable to compensate B in damages.'

The same principles of abstraction apply when a judge chooses to follow *obiter dicta*. This is well illustrated by the way in which the decision of the House of Lords in *Donoghue* v. *Stevenson*, 1932 was developed to produce the modern doctrine of negligence. (See further p. 392.)

Binding force

It is now necessary to examine which precedents are binding, and this depends upon the level of the court in which the decision was reached.

House of Lords
Starting with the highest authority, the House of Lords, we find that this body was bound by its own decisions (*London Street Tramways* v. *London County Council*, [1898] A.C. 375), except, for example, where the previous decision had been made *per incuriam*, i.e. where an important case or statute was not brought to the attention of the court when the previous decision was made. However, in July, 1966, the House of Lords abolished the rule that their own decisions on points of law were absolutely binding upon themselves. The Lord Chancellor announced the change on behalf of himself and the Lords of Appeal in Ordinary in the following statement—

Their Lordships regard the use of precedent as an indispensable foundation upon which to decide what is the law and its application to individual cases. It provides at least some degree of certainty upon which individuals can rely in the conduct of their affairs, as well as a basis for orderly development of legal rules.

Their Lordships nevertheless recognize that too rigid adherence to precedent may lead to injustice in a particular case and also unduly restrict the proper development of the law. They propose therefore to modify their present practice and, while treating former decisions of this House as normally binding, to depart from a previous decision when it appears right to do so.

In this connexion they will bear in mind the danger of disturbing retrospectively the basis on which contracts, settlements of property and fiscal arrangements have been entered into and also the special need for certainty as to the criminal law.

This announcement is not intended to affect the use of precedent elsewhere than in this House.

A practice direction issued in March, 1971, by the Appeal Committee of the House of Lords requires lawyers concerned with the preparation of cases of appeal to state clearly in a separate paragraph of the case any intention to invite the House to depart from one of its own decisions.

The use by the House of Lords of the declaration of 1966 to depart from one of its own decisions is illustrated by *Schorsch Meier Gmbh* v. *Hennin*, 1975[33] and *Miliangos* v. *George Frank (Textiles) Ltd*, 1975.[34] However, in *Fitzleet Estates Ltd* v. *Cherry (Inspector of Taxes)*, [1977] 3 All E.R. 996, which was a case concerned with the tax treatment of interest paid on a loan used to buy property, the House of Lords refused to depart from its previous decision in *Chancery Lane Safe Deposit and Offices Co Ltd* v. *Inland Revenue Commissioners*, [1966] 1 All E.R. 1 and stated that in the absence of a change of circumstances, it would require more than doubts as to the correctness of an earlier opinion of the House, or even a majority only of the House, to justify departing from it. It will be noted that in the *Miliangos* case the circumstances were very different from those which pertained when the House of Lords decided the case of *Re United Railways of Havana*, [1960] 2 All E.R. 332. The situation regarding currency stability had, so the House of Lords said, substantially changed since that time and that justified a departure from its previous decision in the *Havana* case.

The declaration was not used for over 20 years to overrule decisions in the field of criminal law. It has now been used in the context of crime. For example, in *R* v. *Howe*, [1987] 2 W.L.R. 568, the House of Lords overruled its previous decision in *D.P.P. for Northern Ireland* v. *Lynch*, [1975] 1 All E.R. 913 which had decided that duress could be a defence in a prosecution for murder. *R* v. *Howe* removes the defence of duress from the law relating to murder altogether so that the defence is now never available to any participant in murder.

It should be noted that the House of Lords decided in *Wilson* v. *Colchester Justices*, [1985] 2 All E.R. 97 that the grant or refusal by an Appeal Committee of the House of Lords of leave to appeal to the House is in no way to be taken as implying disapproval or approval of the decision and judgments of the court below.

Appeal Courts

On the next rung of the hierarchy there is the Court of Appeal (Civil Division), and this court is bound by its own previous decisions, and those of its predecessors of co-ordinate jurisdiction as well as by those of the House of Lords. (*Young* v. *Bristol Aeroplane Co.* [1944] 2 All E.R. 293.) The Court of Appeal is not bound by a previous decision, if that decision cannot stand with a decision of the House of Lords, or the Judicial Committee of the Privy Council. Thus *Re Polemis*, 1921, (see p. 768) which was a decision of the Court of Appeal, was disapproved of by the Judicial Committee of the Privy Council in *The Wagon Mound*, 1961 (see p. 769) and *Re Polemis* was not followed by the Court of Appeal in *Doughty* v. *Turner Manufacturing Co*, 1964 (see p. 771).

On the criminal side, the Court of Appeal (Criminal Division) is bound by the decisions of the House of Lords and normally by its own decisions and those of the former Court of Criminal Appeal and the earlier Court for Crown Cases Reserved. However, an ordinary court of three judges in the Criminal Division may deviate from previous decisions more easily than the Civil Division because different considerations apply in a criminal appeal where the liberty of the accused is at stake (*R.* v. *Gould*, 1968),[35] and in any case a full court of the Criminal Division can overrule its own previous decisions. A full court generally consists of five judges instead of three as is usual in an ordinary sitting. A decision of the Civil Division is not binding on the Criminal Division and vice versa.

It is perhaps worth noting that Lord Denning in *Davis* v. *Johnson*, [1978] 1 All E.R. 841 took the view that the Court of Appeal should take for itself guidelines similar to those taken by the House of Lords in 1966 to depart from a previous decision of its own where that decision was clearly wrong. However, Lord Denning does not appear to have received sufficient support for this view and a declaration on the lines he suggests has not been made.

However, it was decided in *Williams* v. *Fawcett*, [1985] 1 All E.R. 787 that the Court of Appeal could depart from one of its own previous decisions where that decision was felt to be wrong in law and there was unlikely to be an appeal to the House of Lords by a person whose liberty was at stake.

Divisional Courts

Divisional Courts are, in civil cases, bound by the decisions of the House of Lords, the Court of Appeal (Civil Division) and generally by their own previous decisions, unless convinced that the previous decision was wrong (*Hornigold* v. *Chief Constable of Lancashire*, [1985] Crim. L.R. 792). In criminal cases there is, under ss. 12–15 of the Administration of Justice Act, 1960, an appeal from the Divisional Court of the Queen's Bench Division straight to the House of Lords, and the Divisional Court is not bound by the decisions of the Criminal Division of the Court of Appeal and those of its predecessors of co-ordinate jurisdiction.

High Court

At the next lower stage, a High Court judge, although bound by the decisions of the Court of Appeal and the House of Lords is not bound by the decisions of another High Court judge sitting at first instance. (*Huddersfield Police Authority* v. *Watson*, [1947] 2 All E.R. 193.) Nevertheless such a judge will treat previous decisions as of strong persuasive authority. The present High Court is not bound by the decisions of the old courts of Common Pleas, Queen's Bench or Exchequer.

It was stated by Lord Goddard, C.J., in *Huddersfield Police Authority* v. *Watson*, [1947] 2 All E.R. 193 that a High Court judge is bound to follow 'the decisions of the Court of Appeal, the House of Lords and Divisional Courts'. It is, however, sometimes disputed whether decisions of Divisional Courts are binding on High Court judges. It appears that a Divisional Court cannot overrule the decision of a High Court judge; and that a High Court judge may properly prefer a decision of one of his brethren to that of a Divisional Court. On the other hand, the Divisional Court professes *normally* to be bound by its own decisions (see *Huddersfield Police Authority* v. *Watson* above) and it is therefore odd if such decisions are binding on two or more judges sitting in a Divisional Court but not on one judge sitting alone.

Crown Court

A judge sitting in the Crown Court, the jurisdiction of which is largely confined to criminal cases, is bound by decisions made in criminal matters by the House of Lords and Court of Appeal (Criminal Division) but not apparently by decisions of the Divisional Court of the Queen's Bench Division. (*R.* v. *Colyer*, [1974] Crim. L.R. 243.) The Crown Court is a branch of the Supreme Court, having equal status with the High Court. A judge sitting in the Crown Court and exercising a civil jurisdiction, e.g.

licensing, is bound by the decisions of the House of Lords, Court of Appeal and the High Court.

Employment Appeal Tribunal

As regards this Tribunal only the decisions of the Court of Appeal and the House of Lords on matters of law are binding, though the decisions of the earlier Industrial Relations Court and the High Court in England are of great persuasive authority and the Tribunal would not lightly differ from the principles which are to be found in those decisions. (Per Bristow, J. in *Portec (UK) Ltd* v. *Mogensen*, [1976] 3 All E.R. 565 at p. 568.) These remarks remain valid even though the *Portec* case was overruled in terms of its decision by *Wilson* v. *Maynard Shipbuilding Consultants A.B.*, [1978] 2 All E.R. 78. Nevertheless, Wait, J. who as President of the EAT presided in *Anandarajah* v. *Lord Chancellor's Department*, [1984] I.R.L.R. 131, ruled that no assistance could be derived from precedent in deciding whether a dismissal was unfair. (See further p. 331.)

Judicial Committee of the Privy Council

The decisions of the Judicial Committee of the Privy Council are not binding, either on the Committee itself or on other English courts save the Ecclesiastical and Prize Courts. Its decisions are technically only of persuasive authority in English law, and this derives from the fact that the Judicial Committee hears appeals from overseas territories. Thus, when it hears an appeal from Hong Kong, it may not apply a rule of law used (say) in a previous appeal from the Channel Islands.

As regards the relationship of the Judicial Committee and the House of Lords, where the law applicable to the case is English, the Committee will feel bound to follow a relevant decision of the House of Lords but not otherwise (*Tai Hing Cotton* v. *Liu Chong Bank*, [1985] 2 All E.R. 947).

Exceptions to the rule of binding precedent

Having examined the relationship of the above courts with regard to the doctrine of binding precedent, it should be noted that a court is not always bound to follow a precedent which according to the rules outlined above ought to be binding on it. It is by avoiding the following of precedents that judges can, and do, make law.

Thus, when the court in question is invited to follow a binding precedent, it may refuse to do so—

(i) by *distinguishing* the case now before it from the previous case *on the facts*. A case is *distinguished* when the court considers that there are points of difference between the case now before it and a previous decision which it is being invited to follow. As Lord Halsbury said in *Quinn* v. *Leatham*, [1901] A.C. 495—

Every judgment must be read as applicable to the particular facts proved, or assumed to be proved, since the generality of the expressions which may be found there are not intended to be expositions of the whole law but govern and are qualified by the particular facts of the case in which such expressions are found.

This process of narrowing down the implications of the *ratio decidendi* of a previous case by 'distinguishing' is a device often used by a court which does not wish to follow an earlier decision which would otherwise be binding on it.

If a court feels that an earlier case was wrongly decided but cannot overrule it because the *ratio decidendi* of the case now before it does not cover all the matters raised in the earlier case, it may, by way of *obiter dictum*, disapprove the earlier case which is then to some extent affected as a precedent. Examples of distinguishing are to be found by comparing the decisions in *Phillips* v. *Brooks*, 1919, *Ingram* v. *Little*, 1961 and *Lewis* v. *Averay*, 1971; (See pp. 619–20).

(ii) by refusing to follow the previous case because its *ratio* is *obscure*. Thus in *Harper* v. *NCB*, [1974] 2 All E.R. 441 the Court of Appeal refused to follow the decision of the House of Lords in *Central Asbestos Co* v. *Dodd*, [1972] 2 All E.R. 1135 because the majority of three to two judges who found for Dodd left behind no discernible *ratio*. It was unclear whether the decision that Mr Dodd, who brought an action against his employers because he contracted an industrial disease in the course of his employment after the time limit of three years had elapsed, succeeded (1) because he knew that the injury arose from his employment but did not know that he could sue; or (2) that he knew he could sue but not that the disease arose from his employment;

(iii) by declaring the previous case to be in *conflict with a fundamental principle of law*, as where, for example, the court in the previous case has not applied the doctrine of privity of contract (see *Beswick* v. *Beswick*, 1967, p. 581);

(iv) by finding the previous decision to be *per incuriam*, i.e. where an important case or statute was not brought to the attention of the court (see view of Bristow, J. in *Miliangos*[34]) when the previous decision was made;

(v) by declaring the principle or *ratio* of the previous decision to be *too wide*, and regarding some of it as *obiter* and therefore not binding. (Compare, for example, *Bridges* v. *Hawksworth*, 1851, p. 790, and *South Staffordshire Water Co* v. *Sharman*, 1896, p. 791);

(vi) because the previous decision is one of several *conflicting decisions* at the same level. (*Tiverton Estates Ltd* v. *Wearwell Ltd*, 1974.)[36] In this connection the comments of Nourse, J. in *Colchester Estates* (*Cardiff*) v. *Carlton Industries*, [1984] 2 All E.R. 601 are of interest. He said that as a general rule, a judge faced with two conflicting authorities of judges of the same rank should feel himself bound by the later of them. This would not, however, be the rule if it appeared to the judge deciding the case that the later judgment was wrong in not following the first, as for example, where some other binding authority had not been cited to the earlier judge or judges;

(vii) because the *previous decision* had been *overruled by statute.*

Cases heard in the county court and in the magistrates' courts are not generally reported, and for this reason do not create binding precedents. It would not be desirable to report such cases, for English law already possesses such a large number of reported cases that decisions are sometimes made in which relevant precedents are not cited or considered, and may therefore be *per incuriam.* Some judges feel that this position is exacerbated by unreported cases stored in computers. (See p. 132.) Moreover decisions on civil matters in the former assize courts are sometimes criticized and not regarded as binding, since time did not always allow for full consideration of the points involved.

Persuasive precedents

These consist of decisions made in lower courts, and in the Judicial Committee of the Privy Council of *obiter dicta* at all levels and also decisions of Irish, Scottish, Dominion, and United States courts, the reason being that these nations also base their law on the common law of England, though some parts of the law of Scotland are derived from Roman law. Cases coming to the House of Lords from Scotland do not bind English courts. They are only persuasive unless the legal principles involved are the same in both systems of law. The House of Lords normally gives a directive as to the binding nature of such decisions; for example, *Donoghue* v. *Stevenson*, 1932 (see p. 740), which is a fundamental case on the law of negligence, is binding in both jurisdictions, although it was an appeal from the Scottish Court of Session.

In the absence of any persuasive authority from the above sources the court may turn to text-books and sometimes to Roman law. The weight which a court will give to persuasive authority may depend upon the standing of the judge whose decision or dictum it was and whether it was a reserved judgment, i.e. a case in which the court took time to consider the judgment. Reserved judgments are highly regarded. Undefended cases in which the issues have not been fully argued on both sides do not carry great weight.

Declaratory and original precedents

One further classification of precedents must be noted. They may be either 'declaratory' or 'original'—

A declaratory precedent is one which is merely the application of an existing rule of law.

An original precedent is one which creates and applies a new rule. Original precedents alone develop the law; declaratory precedents are merely further evidence of it. Thus, if a judge says: 'The matter before us is not covered by authority and we must decide it on principle . . .' an original precedent is indicated.

Reversing, overruling and *res judicata*

It often happens that when a case has been decided in (say) the High Court, a decision is taken to appeal to an appellate court, in this case the Court of Appeal. The Court of Appeal will re-examine the case and, if it comes to a different conclusion from the judge in the High Court, it reverses his decision. Reversal, therefore, applies to a decision of an appellate court in the same case. Sometimes, however, the case which comes before the appellate court has been decided by following a previously decided case, the judge having followed precedent. In this case, if the appellate court decides to differ from the decision reached in the lower court, it is said to overrule the case which formed the basis of the precedent.

Reversal affects the parties, who are bound by the decision of the appellate court, and it affects precedent because lower courts will in future be bound to follow the decision. *Overruling affects precedent*, but does not reach back to affect the parties in the original case, now regarded as wrongly decided, and it is not necessary, for example, for a successful plaintiff to return his damages. Furthermore, the case could not be tried again because the doctrine or *res judicata* would apply. So the doctrine of *res judicata* (a matter which has been adjudicated on) protects defendants against a multiplicity of actions in regard to the same issues.

If a judge of the High Court refuses to follow a previous decision on a similar point of law, the law reports will contain two decisions by judges of equal authority, and the cases will remain in conflict until the same point of law is taken to an appeal before a higher tribunal whose decision will then resolve the position. (And see also *Colchester Estates* (*Cardiff*) v. *Carlton Industries*, 1984, at p. 139.)

Advantages and drawbacks of case law

The system of judicial precedent has several *advantages*. Up to a point it can claim the *advantage of certainty*, since it is possible to predict the ruling of a court because judicial decisions tend to be consistent. Nevertheless judges have a habit of distinguishing cases on the facts, or of limiting the application of a principle which had formerly been thought to be of wider scope, and *vice versa*. This means that the claim to certainty has to be taken with reservations. Another claim put forward in favour of case law is its *power of flexibility and growth*. New decisions are constantly being added as new cases come before the courts. In this way the law tends to keep pace with the times and can adapt itself to changing circumstances. Judicial precedent covers a *wealth of detail*.

There is a case in point for every rule, and there is a *practical character* to judicial rulings. Legal rules are made only as the need arises, and the law is not made in advance on the basis of theory. When a case arises, a decision is taken and the ruling is usually recorded, so that when a similar case arises again the law will be there to be applied.

Case law has certain *drawbacks*. These drawbacks are in some cases merely the converse aspects of the advantages. For example, Jeremy Bentham criticized *the principle of the 'law following the event'*, and applied the epithet 'dog's law' to the system. 'It is,' he says, 'the judges that make the common law. Do you know how they make it? Just as a man makes laws for his dog. When your dog does something you want to break him of, you wait till he does it and then beat him. This is the way you make laws for your dog: this is the way the judges make law for you and me.'

A further criticism is that *the binding force of precedent limits judicial discretion*. It has been said that judges are engaged in 'forging fetters for their own feet.' This can be illustrated by the doctrine of common employment, which was laid down by the House of Lords in *Priestley* v. *Fowler* (1837), 3 M. & W. 1. This doctrine said that if an employee was injured by a fellow employee whilst both were acting within the scope of their employment, their employer was not liable vicariously for that negligence. The rule operated in a most unjust fashion during the period of great industrial development, but it continued to bind judges for over a century until it was finally abolished by the Law Reform (Personal Injuries) Act, 1948. All the judges could do in the meantime was to try to limit its scope.

Limiting the scope of a decision may lead to the court's making *illogical distinctions*. Judges and counsel pay attention to differences in cases which are fundamentally similar, in order to uphold the doctrine of precedent and still not feel bound to follow an inconvenient rule. Often these distinctions have real substance, but occasionally they are illogical and serve to complicate the law.

Difficulties of the kind outlined above may not now arise in such an acute form because, as we have seen, the House of Lords is no longer bound by its own decisions, though this tends to detract from the element of certainty.

A further criticism must be noted—that of *bulk and complexity*. The number of reported cases is so large that the law can be ascertained only by searching through a large number of reports. This search has been eased somewhat where case law has been codified by statute in order to produce a rational arrangement. The Bills of Exchange Act, 1882, the Sale of Goods Act, 1893 (now 1979), and the Law of Property Act, 1925, have to a large extent produced order in what might have been called chaos, but case law still tends to develop even around a codifying statute, and its sections soon have to be read in the light of interpretative cases.

Finally, it is a major criticism of our system of case law that only the House of Lords gives the ultimate authoritative judicial ruling on a matter. However, whether this happens depends upon the litigants footing the bill to get to the House of Lords or the Legal Aid Fund doing so. It would be an improvement if we had a system under which the High Court or Court of Appeal could refer a question of law to the House of Lords at public expense, rather on the lines of Art. 177 of the EEC Treaty which allows reference to the Court of Justice by domestic courts on matters involving Community Law.

Case law in the European Court
In line with the normal Continental approach, there is no doctrine of binding precedent, though the body of decisions which the court is making in the interpretation of the Treaty are having strong persuasive influence. These decisions are cited before the court in argument and are also quoted in judgments.

INTERPRETATION OF STATUTES BY THE JUDICIARY

The main body of the law is to be found in statutes, together with the relevant statutory instruments, and in case law as enunciated by judges in the courts. But the judges not only have the duty of declaring the common law, they are also frequently called upon to settle disputes as to the meaning of words or clauses in a statute.

Parliament is the supreme lawgiver, and the judges must follow statutes. Nevertheless there is a considerable amount of case law which gathers round important Acts of Parliament, since the wording sometimes turns out to be obscure. Statutes were at one time drafted by practising lawyers who were experts in the particular branch of law of which the statute was to be a part. Today, however, statutes are drafted by parliamentary counsel to the Treasury, and, although such persons are skilled in the law, the volume of legislation means that statutes are often obscure and cases continue to come before the courts in which the rights of the parties depend upon the exact meaning of a section of a statute. When such a case comes before a judge, he must decide the meaning of the section in question. Thus even statute law is not free from judicial influence.

The judges have certain recognized *aids to interpretation*, and these are set out below.

Statutory aids

Judges may get some guidance from statute law.

(*a*) The Interpretation Act, 1978, which is itself a statute, defines terms commonly used in Acts of Parliament. (*Hutton* v. *Esher U.D.C.*, 1973.)[37]

(*b*) A complex statute will normally contain an interpretation section, defining the terms used in the particular Act, e.g. ss. 735–44 of the Companies Act, 1985 define, among other things, 'accounts' and 'director', and the judges have recourse to this.

(*c*) Every Act of Parliament used to have what was known as a preamble, which set out at the beginning the general purpose and scope of the Act. The preamble was often quite lengthy and assisted the judge in ascertaining the meaning of the statute. Modern public Acts do not have this type of preamble, but have instead a long title which is not of so much assistance in interpretation. For example, the Sex Discrimination Act, 1975, which contains 87 sections and a number of schedules, says merely: 'An Act to render unlawful certain kinds of sex discrimination and discrimination on the grounds of marriage, and establish a Commission with the function of working towards the elimination of such discrimination and promoting equality of opportunity between men and women generally; and for related purposes.' All private Acts must have a preamble setting out the objects of the legislation, and this preamble must be proved by the promoters at the Committee stage in the House of Lords. So far as private Acts are concerned the preamble may be of considerable assistance.

General rules of interpretation evolved by judges

There are a number of generally recognized rules or canons of interpretation, and some of the more important ones are now given.

The mischief rule
This was arrived at in *Heydon's* case, (1584), 3 Co. Rep. 7a. Under this rule the judge will look at the Act to see what was its purpose and what mischief in the common law it was designed to prevent. As was said in *Heydon's* case—

> Four things are to be discussed and considered: (i) What was the common law before the making of the Act? (ii) What was the mischief and defect for which the common law did not provide? (iii) What remedy hath Parliament resolved and appointed to cure the disease of the commonwealth? (iv) What is the true reason for the remedy? Judges shall . . . make such construction as shall suppress the mischief and advance the remedy.

Broadly speaking, the rule means that where a statute has been passed to remedy a weakness in the law the interpretation which will correct that weakness is the one to be adopted.

An example of the use of the rule can be seen in *Gardiner* v. *Sevenoaks R.D.C.*, 1950.[38]

The literal rule
According to this rule, the working of the Act must be construed according to its literal and grammatical meaning whatever the result may be. The same word must normally be construed throughout the Act in the same sense, and in the case of old statutes regard must be had to its

contemporary meaning if there has been a change with the passage of time.

The Law Commission, in an instructive and provocative report on the subject of interpretation (Law Com. 21), said of this rule that 'to place undue emphasis on the literal meaning of the words of a provision is to assume an unattainable perfection in draftsmanship.'

The rule, when in operation, does not always achieve the obvious object and purpose of the statute. A classic example is *Whiteley* v. *Chappell* (1868–9), 4 L.R.Q.B. 147. In that case a statute concerned with electoral malpractices made it an offence to personate 'any person entitled to vote' at an election. The defendant was accused of personating a deceased voter and the court, using the literal rule, found that there was no offence. The personation was not of a person entitled to vote. A dead person was not entitled to vote, or do anything else for that matter. A deceased person did not exist and could therefore have no rights. It will be seen, however, that the literal rule produced in that case a result which was clearly contrary to the object of Parliament.

The golden rule
This rule is to some extent an extension of the literal rule and under it the words of a statute will as far as possible be construed according to their ordinary plain and natural meaning, unless this leads to an absurd result. It is used by the courts where a statutory provision is capable of more than one literal meaning and leads the judge to select the one which avoids absurdity, or where a study of the statute as a whole reveals that the conclusion reached by applying the literal rule is contrary to the intentions of Parliament.

Thus, in *Re Sigsworth*, [1935] Ch. 89 the court decided that the Administration of Estates Act, 1925, which provides for the distribution of the property of an intestate amongst his next of kin, did not confer a benefit upon the person (a son) who had murdered the intestate, (his mother) even though the murderer was the intestate's next of kin, for it is a general principle of law that no one can profit from his own wrong.

It follows also that a statute will not normally be interpreted so as to allow a person to permit and legalize his own wrong. (*Keene* v. *Muncaster*, 1980.)[39] Consideration has also been given to *Prince of Hanover* v. *Attorney-General*, 1957[3] to which reference could usefully be made again at this point.

The ejusdem generis rule
This is a rule covering things of the same genus, species or type. Under it, where general words follow particular words, the general words are construed as being limited to persons or things within the class outlined by the particular words. So in a reference to 'dogs, cats, and other animals,' the last three words would be limited in their application to animals of the domestic type, and would not be extended to cover

animals such as elephants and camels which are not domestic animals in the U.K. (And see *Lane* v. *London Electricity Board*, 1955.)[40]

Expressio unius est exclusio alterius

(The expression of one thing implies the exclusion of another.) Under this rule, where specific words are used and are not followed by general words, the Act applies only to the instances mentioned. For example, where a statute contains an express statement that certain statutes are repealed, there is a presumption that other relevant statutes not mentioned are not repealed. (And see *R.* v. *Immigration Appeals Adjudicator, ex parte Crew*, 1982.)[41]

Noscitur a sociis

(The meaning of a word can be gathered from its context.) Under this rule words of doubtful meaning may be better understood from the nature of the words and phrases with which they are associated. (*Muir* v. *Keay*, 1875.)[42]

Other considerations and presumptions

In addition to the major rules of interpretation, there are also several other considerations which the judge will have in mind. He will concern himself only with the wording of the Act, and will not go to *Hansard* to look up reports of the debates during the passage of the Act.

There is here some conflict with the mischief rule, since it might be thought that there is no better way to ascertain what mischief the Act was designed to prevent than by reference to the Parliamentary debates in Hansard. Nevertheless, the Law Commission in their deliberations on the matter of statutory interpretation decided against the use of Hansard since they doubted the reliability of statements made in Parliamentary debates.

The House of Lords decided in *Davis* v. *Johnson*, [1978] 1 All E.R. 1132 that it is now permissible for the court to refer to reports by such bodies as the Law Commission and committees or commissions appointed by the Government or by either House of Parliament from which the reform of the law stems.

A statute is presumed not to alter the existing law unless it expressly states that it does. There is also a presumption against the repeal of other statutes and that is why statutes which are repealed are repealed by specific reference.

In the absence of any express indication to the contrary, a contruction which would exclude retrospective effect is to be preferred to a construction which would not. Thus in *Alexander* v. *Mercouris*, [1979] 3 All E.R. 305, where the plaintiff sued the defendant for alleged defective workmanship in the conversion of two flats, the plaintiff tried to bring his case under the Defective Premises Act, 1972 (see further p. 406) which came into force on 1 January, 1974. However, it appeared that the defendant commenced the work in November, 1972 and it was held by the Court of Appeal that no claim could be brought under the Act as the Act could not be construed as having retrospective effect. Some Finance Acts do have retrospective effect in terms of taxation.

When a statute deprives a person of property, there is a presumption that compensation will be paid. Unless so stated it is presumed that an Act does not interfere with rights over private property. There is a presumption against alteration of the common law. Any Act which presumes to restrict private liberty will be very strictly interpreted, though the strictness may be tempered in times of emergency. It is presumed that an Act does not bind the Crown on the ground that the law, made by the Crown on the advice of the Lords and Commons, is made for subjects and not for the Crown. Furthermore, as we have seen, the courts lack the power to examine proceedings in Parliament in order to determine whether the passing of an Act has been obtained by means of any irregularity or fraud. (*British Railways Board* v. *Pickin*, 1974.)[26]

However, the Law Commissioners have recommended that more emphasis should be placed on the importance of interpreting a statute in the light of the general purposes behind it and the intentions of Parliament. This is referred to as a purposive interpretation. Thus in *Fletcher* v. *Budgen*, [1974] 2 All E.R. 1243 the Divisional Court of Queen's Bench decided that under the Trade Descriptions Act, 1968, a buyer of goods, in this case a car dealer, could be guilty of the offence of falsely describing goods when he told a private seller that his car was almost worthless, bought it, repaired it and sold it at a considerable profit. Lord Widgery, C.J. said that although he had never thought of the Act as applying to buyers of goods, it was necessary in the public interest that it should, at least in the case of expert buyers, and that in his view such decision '. . . is not in any sense illogical and is not likely to run counter to any intention which Parliament may have had.'

However, as Lord Scarman said in *Shah* v. *Barnet London Borough Council*, [1983] 1 All E.R. 226 at p. 238: 'Judges may not interpret statutes in the light of their own views as to policy. They may, of course, adopt a purposive interpretation if they can find in the statute read as a whole or in material to which they are permitted by law to refer as aids to interpretation an expression of Parliament's purpose or policy.'

Rules of interpretation tend to some extent to cancel each other. Thus by using one or other of these rules judges can be narrow, reformist, or conservative. In fact Pollock, in his *Essays in Jurisprudence and Ethics*, suggests—

English judges have often tended to interpret statutes on the theory that Parliament generally changes the law for the worse and that the business of the judges is to keep the mischief of its interference within the narrowest possible bounds.

It must be said that this comment applies particularly to judicial interpretation of welfare law where they have sometimes been reluctant to fill in gaps in order to make the law work, whereas if the Act is in the field of 'lawyers' law then they have been prepared to do precisely this in order, for example, to convict a guilty person of crime. This is, however, not surprising since judges are the product of a legalistic training and are clearly ill-equipped to pronounce upon welfare law, whereas in crime, for example, they are dealing with rules which they better understand so that they feel less reluctant to fill in gaps.

Interpretation of European treaties and instruments

English courts now face on an increasing basis, problems in connection with the interpretation of Community treaties and instruments. In this connection s. 3(1) of the European Communities Act, 1972, as amended by the European Communities (Amendment) Act, 1986, makes any question of interpretation of Community treaties or instruments a matter of law which, if not referred to the European Court, is for interpretation in accordance with principles laid down by any relevant decision of the European Court or any court attached to it. Article 177 of the EEC Treaty provides for reference to the European Court for a preliminary ruling on any matter of interpretation of the treaties or instruments in order to ensure uniform interpretation. Thus an English court faced with a problem of interpretation of a treaty or instrument can dispose of it by a reference to the European Court. However, this does of course carry with it the problem of costs and could lead to delays. (See further pp. 40–42.)

Interpretation of enactments by the European Court

In terms of the interpretation of legislation, the European Court has much broader powers than those which English courts have. There is no question of being restricted, for example, to the words of the Treaty or regulations. The Court may consider the reasons for enactment and the general objectives and policy of the Communities. It can have regard to *travaux préparatoires*, i.e. statements and publications made prior to enactment and *doctrine*, i.e. views of learned writers as to what the law should be.

6 Law of persons and fundamental concepts

NATURAL AND LEGAL PERSONS

A *person* in law possesses certain rights and owes certain duties. There are two categories of persons as follows—

(a) Natural persons. These are human beings who are referred to as natural persons. An adult human being has in general terms a full range of rights and duties. However, even in regard to human beings, the law distinguishes between certain classes and gives to them a *status* which may carry with it a more limited set of rights and duties than are given to the normal adult. These classes are minors, persons of unsound mind, bankrupts and aliens, and the significance of belonging to these categories will be more fully examined in connection with the chapters on substantive law, such as Contract and Tort. Non-human creatures are not legal persons and do not have the full range of rights and duties which a human being acquires at birth. However, animals may be protected by the law for certain purposes, e.g. conservation. (See Wildlife and Countryside Act, 1981).

(b) Juristic persons. Legal personality is not restricted to human beings. In fact various bodies and associations of persons can, by forming a corporation to carry out their functions, create an organization with a range of rights and duties not dissimilar to many of those possessed by human beings. In English law such corporations are formed either by charter, statute or registration under the Companies Act, 1985 or previous Acts; there is also the common law concept of the Corporation Sole.

NATURAL PERSONS

We can divide this section, for the purpose of exposition, into two parts, i.e. general legal concepts applicable to all natural persons and legal rules designed to deal with nationality and immigration and prevent discrimination on the grounds, e.g. of sex and race.

General legal concepts

These are set out below.

Domicil

The basis of jurisdiction and the law to be applied in many matters coming before English courts, e.g. wills, matrimonial causes and taxation, may depend on the domicil of the parties. (See, e.g. *IRC* v. *Bullock*, 1976.)[43] A person's domicil is the country which he regards as his permanent home, and thus contains a dual element of actual residence in a country and the intention of remaining there. Where a country has within its national boundaries several jurisdictions, the person's domicil must be determined with reference to a particular jurisdiction, e.g. there is no such thing as domicil in the United States of America, though a person may be domiciled in a particular State. England and Wales, Scotland, Northern Ireland, the Channel Islands, and the Isle of Man are distinct jurisdictions within the British Isles. A person must always have a domicil, and he can only have one domicil at a time. It should be noted that the concepts of domicil and nationality are, as appropriate, applied to corporate bodies.

Domicil of origin

The domicil of origin of a child is that of its father at the date of the child's birth if the father is alive at that date and is married to the child's mother, i.e. if the child is legitimate (for example, the Nova Scotia domicil of Mr Bullock in *IRC* v. *Bullock*, 1976).[43] If the child is illegitimate or, though legitimate, the father is not alive when it is born, it takes its domicil of origin from that of its mother at the date of the child's birth. Foundlings take their domicil of origin from the place where they were found.

Dependent domicil

The concept of dependent domicil applies as follows—

(a) *Minors*, i.e. persons under the age of 18 years

(i) *At common law*. The domicil of a legitimate, legitimated or adopted child is dependent on, and changes with, that of its father or adoptive father, and after the father's death with that of its mother or adoptive mother. The domicil of an illegitimate child depends on, and changes with, that of its mother.
(ii) *Under statute*. Ss. 3 and 4 of the Domicile and Matrimonial Proceedings Act, 1973 are concerned with the domicil of minors. Where previously the domicil of a minor had to follow that of his father until the age of majority, a minor can under the Act acquire an independent domicil at the age of 16, or under that age if he marries before then. This latter principle cannot of course apply to any marriages in this country,

but it may apply to those in this country, e.g. Nigerians, who may be married under 16 according to their domiciliary law. The provision referred to above, which is in s. 3 of the Act, avoids the previous possibility of a father leaving this country and establishing a domicil elsewhere, thus changing the domicil of his minor son who had remained in this country. Furthermore, it had always been uncertain whether, after the divorce of the parents, a child's domicil continued to follow his father's or followed that of his mother with whom the child was living. Now s. 4(2) of the 1973 Act provides that the child's domicil where he is under 16 or has not set up an independent domicil and his father and mother are alive but living apart shall be that of his mother if—

(*a*) he then has his home with her and has no home with his father; or

(*b*) he has at any time had her domicil by virtue of (*a*) above and has not since had a home with his father.

The section also deals with other possible situations, for example where the mother is dead and the child has not returned to his father, he will keep the domicil he acquired under s. 4(2).

(b) Married women

By s. 1 of the Domicile and Matrimonial Proceedings Act, 1973, the domicil of a married woman is not bound to be determined by that of her husband, as was the case at common law. She is capable of acquiring a separate domicil in exactly the same manner as her husband. By s. 1(2) of the 1973 Act a married woman is treated as retaining the domicil of her husband (as a domicil of choice if it is not one of origin) at the coming into force of the Act unless and until it is changed in accordance with common law rules for determining such change.

Certain consequences regarding jurisdiction in divorce proceedings follow from the general principles enacted by the above section. As a wife can now acquire a separate domicil from that of her husband, jurisdiction is now based upon the domicil of either party in England and Wales at the time of the proceedings or on the ground that either party was habitually resident in those countries for one year prior thereto. Similar rules apply to proceedings for nullity and presumption of death. As a corollary to the above principles, the court has power to stay proceedings where courts in two countries have jurisdiction. This would prevent, for example, divorce proceedings being taken in an English court and a Scottish court contemporaneously as where the husband had an English domicil but his wife had acquired one in Scotland.

Domicil of choice

A person, other than a minor under 16, can change his domicil of his own volition. To do so he must be in the new country, and have a 'fixed and settled intention' to abandon his domicil of origin or choice, and to settle instead in the new country.

A person retains his domicil of origin until he acquires a domicil of choice, and since a person must always have a domicil, there can be no abandonment of the domicil of origin unless a domicil of choice is acquired instead. However, having acquired a domicil of choice, a person who abandons it without acquiring a fresh domicil of choice, reverts to his domicil of origin. (*Tee* v. *Tee*, 1973.)[44]

The country in which a person resides is on the face of it the country of his domicil. Where it is claimed that a domicil of origin has been changed for one of choice, the onus of proof is on the party claiming that such a change has taken place. Examples of evidence which suggest a change of domicil are oral or written declarations to this effect, letters, wills (*IRC* v. *Bullock*, 1976)[43], the adoption of a new name, as where a German living in England changes his name to Richmond from Reichman, an application for naturalization (*Steiner* v. *IRC*, 1973)[45], the purchase of land, or a grave, or of a home or a business (*Steiner*)[45] in the new country. It is not enough merely to express an intention *eventually* to live and work in the new country nor to intend to marry a person resident in the new country at some time in the future even where the intention to marry is reciprocated (*Plummer* v. *I.R.C, The Times*, 24 October, 1987 and *Cramer* v. *Cramer, The Times*, 15 May, 1986).

Residence

The residence of a person is important for certain purposes, e.g. liability for Income Tax. Furthermore the jurisdiction of magistrates in matrimonial matters is based on the residence of the parties and not their domicil, as is the right to vote in a particular constituency at an election under s. 1(1) of the Representation of the People Act, 1983. On the other hand the jurisdiction of the High Court in matrimonial proceedings is based either on domicil or habitual residence for one year. (S. 5, Domicile and Matrimonial Proceedings Act, 1973.) Domicil must, therefore, be distinguished from residence.

The term residence imports a certain degree of permanence, and must not be casual or merely undertaken as a traveller. In *Fox* v. *Stirk*, [1970] 3 All E.R. 7, the Court of Appeal decided that two undergraduates were resident at their universities and entitled to have their names on the electoral register for that constituency although their parental homes were elsewhere. On the other hand in *Scott* v. *Phillips*, 1973 S.L.T. (Notes) 75 it was held that the plaintiff who lived mainly at his house in Inveresk but had a cottage on lease in Berwickshire in which he spent $3\frac{1}{2}$ months each year, was not resident in Berwickshire and therefore not entitled to have his name included on the electoral roll for that county. Obviously, residence can be changed at any time by moving to a new home. Temporary absences abroad while on holiday or on business do not create a gap in the period of residence, which is determined on the facts of the case.

Husband and wife

Although marriage is in essence a form of contract, it has special features in that it alters the status of the parties. Persons under the age of sixteen cannot be married nor can persons who are too closely related.

Regarding property, the status of a married woman was low during the nineteenth and early twentieth centuries and in particular all the wife's personal property passed to the husband on marriage. However, their emancipation was brought about by a series of statutes culminating in the Law Reform (Married Women and Tortfeasors) Act, 1935, so that today their status is the same as that of a *feme sole* (single woman).

Since the Law Reform (Husband and Wife) Act, 1962, husband and wife have been able to sue each other in tort. (See p. 344.)

Parents and legitimate children

At common law a child is legitimate only if his parents are lawfully married to each other at the time of his conception or birth or at any intervening time between the two, though, where the marriage is void, e.g. in the case of a bigamous marriage, the child will be legitimate only if at the time of its conception or, if later at the time of celebration of the 'marriage', both or either parent reasonably believed that the marriage was valid. (S. 1(1), Legitimacy Act, 1976.) Section 1(1) only applies where the father of the child was domiciled in England and Wales at the time of the birth or, if he died before the birth, was so domiciled immediately before his death.

A legitimate child has a right to succeed to the property of his father and mother where they die without having made a will (i.e. intestate).

Illegitimate children

A child which cannot satisfy the tests of legitimacy outlined above is illegitimate. Where the mother is unmarried the child must be illegitimate, subject of course to the provisions of s. 1 of the Legitimacy Act, 1976, which relate to void marriages (see above). If the mother is married, then a presumption that her husband is the father of the child arises. This is a presumption of legitimacy and must be rebutted if illegitimacy is to be established. In the past the standard of proof offered in rebuttal had to be very strong; generally speaking, proof beyond a reasonable doubt. However, s. 26 of the Family Law Reform Act, 1969, now provides that the presumption of legitimacy may be rebutted on a balance of probabilities.

Section 27 of the Family Law Reform Act, 1987 deals with artificial insemination and provides that a child born following artificial insemination by a donor (A.I.D.), who is not the woman's current husband, will be deemed the legitimate child of the woman and her husband if the latter consented to A.I.D.

Legal position of the illegitimate child

Two main areas are important in business—

(a) Fatal Accidents Act. The Fatal Accidents Act, 1976, gives the dependants of a person who is killed as a result of a tort, a right of action
against the tortfeasor. (See p. 349.) Dependants include an illegitimate
child. (Section 1(3)(e), 1976 Act, as substituted by s. 3, Administration
of Justice Act, 1982.)

(b) Succession. The Family Law Reform Act, 1987 does not abolish the
concept of illegitimacy or the rules which make a person illegitimate
outlined above. However, under ss. 1 and 18 illegitimacy is irrelevant for
the purposes of succession on the death of either of the natural parents.
The rights are for all practical purposes the same as those possessed by
legitimate children.

In addition, s. 18 of the Family Law Reform Act, 1969 brings illegitimate dependants within the scope of the Inheritance (Provision for
Family and Dependants) Act, 1975. These Acts apply where a deceased
person has not made reasonable provision by his will or on intestacy for
those who were dependent upon him during his lifetime, as where he has
left his property outside the family or has given it away during his lifetime, leaving an inadequate estate. Such persons may make application
to the court for financial provision from the estate, which will affect the
entitlement of those who are beneficiaries under the estate, or from lifetime gifts.

Legitimation

A person may be legitimated *by and from* the date of the subsequent
marriage of his or her parents provided the father is domiciled in England
and Wales (s. 2, Legitimacy Act, 1976), and this is so whether or not the
birth arose out of adultery, as where either or both of the parents were
married to another person.

Effect of legitimation

Once a person has been legitimated he has the same rights (in respect
of settlements made and death occurring on or after 1 January, 1976) as
if he had been born legitimate though as regards rights under the Fatal
Accidents Act, 1976 and in terms of the law of succession (see above)
these would be available anyway, to an illegitimate child under the
Family Law Reform Act, 1987. However, some persons may still prefer
the legitimation process.

Application for a declaration of legitimacy may be made to the High
Court or in some circumstances to the county court, and persons who
may be affected, e.g. in matters of succession to titles may oppose the
application.

Adoption

Adoption was not possible in England until the passing of the Adoption
of Children Act, 1926. The rules relating to adoption are now governed
by the Adoption Act, 1976, to which section references relate, and

adoption may be effected by order of a magistrates' court, a county court or the High Court (s. 62), though different procedures are involved. A court order is essential. A mere agreement by a parent to transfer his or her rights and duties to someone else is ineffective. (S. 1(2), Guardianship Act, 1973.)

Effect of adoption
An adopted child qualifies as a child of the adoptive parents' marriage. (S. 39.) This principle applies in interpreting wills, settlements made during lifetime and intestacies which take effect on or after 1 January, 1976. Where questions of seniority arise s. 42 provides that the adopted child is deemed to have been born on the date of the adoption and if adoptive parents adopt two or more children on the same day they are regarded as born on that day in the order of the actual dates of their births. For example, we may take a gift in the will of a testator 'to the eldest son of X'. Suppose that X had a natural child (A) in 1975 and in 1976 adopted a child (B) then aged 10, it appears that the natural child (A) takes the gift although B is biologically the elder.

However, the above rules do not affect a document where there is reference to the age of a child. (S. 42(2)(b).)

Thus if a testator gave his estate 'to the children of X at 25' it is clear that an adopted child would take the gift when he in fact attained that age and not 25 years after his adoption. It also seems that a gift to 'the first son of X to attain 25' would go to an adoptive child if he attained 25 before X's natural born children, although, as we have seen, he would not take as X's 'eldest son' in the example given above.

Adopted persons may, on reaching the age of 18, have a copy of their birth certificate as of right and not as formerly only by leave of the court. (S. 51 Adoption Act, 1976).

Adoptions in other countries
The Adoption Act, 1976, s. 72(2) enables adoptions authorized in other countries to be effective in the UK by giving legal recognition to adoption orders made in certain countries outside the UK.

Minors
The Family Law Reform Act, 1969, s. 1(1) reduced the age of majority from twenty-one to eighteen years. There is also a provision in the Act which states that a person attains a particular age, i.e. not merely the age of majority, at the first moment of the relevant birthday, though this rule is subject to any contrary provision in any instrument (i.e. a deed) or statute. (S. 9.)

Section 1(2) provides that the age of eighteen is to be substituted for twenty-one wherever there is a reference to 'full age', 'infant', 'infancy', 'minor', 'minority' in—

(a) any statutory provision made *before or after* 1 January, 1970;

(b) any deed, will or other instrument made *on or after* that date.

This subsection draws a distinction between *statutory provisions* and *private dispositions*. In the case of the former the new age of eighteen is substituted. Thus, in s. 164 Law of Property Act, 1925 which uses the word 'minority' to deal with restrictions on the accumulation of income in a trust, references to 'minority' will be construed as applying to persons under eighteen years of age. However, in the case of private dispositions such as deeds, wills and settlements the Act does not apply retrospectively. Accordingly, if in a deed made before 1 January, 1970, a person X is to take property 'on attaining his majority,' he will take it at age twenty-one years. If the deed was on or after 1 January, 1970, he would take it at eighteen years. The reason for this rule is that where persons in the past have arranged their affairs in reliance on the law as it stood, it would be unjust to interfere.

The law has always regarded minors as being in need of protection, and consequently they enjoy certain immunities and are subject to certain disabilities at law. We have dealt with the legal position of minors with regard to domicil (see p. 150) and nationality is considered on p. 159, and we shall be giving fuller consideration to their position in contract, tort, and property in the chapters which follow. However, certain general matters may be considered at this point.

(i) A minor cannot contract a valid marriage under the age of sixteen years and requires the consent of his parents or if the parents are divorced or separated, the one with custody, or if one parent is dead, the survivor (or on failure that of a magistrates' court) to marry under eighteen years of age.

(ii) A person under eighteen years cannot vote at elections and must be 21 before he can sit in Parliament or be a member of the council of a local authority.

(iii) With regard to civil litigation, a minor sues through a 'next friend', i.e. an adult who is liable for the costs (if any) awarded against the minor in the action, though the minor must indemnify him. A minor defends an action through a 'guardian *ad litem*' who is not liable for costs. The minor's father or mother usually acts as 'next friend' or 'guardian *ad litem*'.

In criminal matters the minor himself is the person prosecuted and may defend himself or be represented by a solicitor or counsel.

(iv) For the purposes of criminal liability minors are divided into three classes—

(*a*) *Those under ten years*. It is presumed that minors under ten years of age are incapable of any crime, and the presumption is irrebuttable. (Children and Young Persons Act, 1963, s. 16.) However, it is thought that children under ten who are caught in the act of damaging property could be restrained by the police under their common law powers to protect property, or detained under s. 28(2) of the Children and Young Persons Act, 1969, on the grounds that they were beyond the control of their parents or guardians.

(*b*) *Those between ten and fourteen years.* The presumption which is wholly dependent on the common law is that a minor is incapable of forming a guilty intent, but this can be rebutted by proving 'mischievous discretion', i.e. knowledge that what was done was morally wrong. Evidence as to this must be before the court before a conviction can properly be made. (*H.* v. *Chief Constable of South Wales, The Times*, 5 July, 1986). Thus in *York* (1748) Fost. 70, C.C.R., a boy aged ten was convicted of murder on evidence which showed that, after he had killed a five-year-old girl, he concealed the body and then told lies about what had happened.

More recently in *McC* v. *Runeckles, The Times*, 5 May, 1984, a girl of 13 was convicted of assault occasioning actual bodily harm contrary to s. 47 of the Offences Against the Person Act, 1861. She stabbed another girl with a broken milk bottle and ran away when police officers arrived. She hid in a garden where she was apprehended. These acts indicated to the court that she knew that what she had done had gone beyond childish mischievousness.

(*c*) *Minors of fourteen years and over* are fully liable for crimes, but there are certain differences as to procedure and punishment, as we have seen at p. 56.

The following additional matters relating to minors are of interest—

(*a*) A person of sixteen or over can give valid consent to medical treatment and it is not necessary as before to obtain the consent of a parent or guardian. (Family Law Reform Act, 1969 (s. 8).)

(*b*) The Tattooing of Minors Act, 1969, makes it an offence, punishable by fine, for a person other than a duly qualified medical practitioner to tattoo a person under the age of eighteen. The person charged with the offence will have a defence if he can show that at the time he had reasonable cause to believe that the person tattooed was eighteen years of age or over.

Persons suffering from mental disorder

We shall be giving fuller consideration to the position of mentally disordered persons in contract and tort in the chapters which follow. However, the position in criminal law is worth noting at this point and is to some extent governed by the following rules which arise from the case of *R.* v. *M'Naghten* (1843), 10 Cl. & Fin. 200.

(i) Every defendant is presumed to be sane until the contrary is proved.

(ii) To establish a defence on the ground of insanity, it must be clearly proved that, at the time of the committing of the act, the party accused was labouring under such a defect of reason, from disease of mind (*R.* v. *Kemp*, 1956),[46] as not to know the nature and quality of the acts he was doing; or, if he did know it, that he did not know he was doing what was wrong. It is a question of the party's knowledge of right and wrong in respect of the very act with which he is charged.

(iii) If the accused labours under a partial delusion only, he must be considered in the same situation as to responsibility as if the facts with respect to which the delusion exists were real.

If a man suffering from a delusion supposes another man to be in the act of killing him, and he kills this man, as he supposes, in self-defence, he would be exempt from punishment. If the delusion was that the victim had inflicted a serious injury to his character and fortune, and the accused killed him in revenge for such a supposed injury, he would be liable to punishment.

If the defence of insanity is successful, the verdict is 'Not guilty by reason of insanity', as provided for in s. 2(1) of the Trial of Lunatics Act, 1883. The judge is then required by reason of s. 5(1) of the Criminal Procedure (Insanity) Act, 1964 to order the defendant to be detained in a special hospital, e.g. Broadmoor. If the defence is unsuccessful the accused has a right of appeal on the same conditions applicable to criminal appeals generally. The right to raise the issue of insanity at a trial is a matter for the defence and not the prosecution. However, it was held by the Court of Appeal in *R.* v. *Dickie*, [1984] 3 All E.R. 173, that exceptionally the trial judge may raise it and leave the decision to the jury if the evidence suggests that the accused was insane.

In *R.* v. *Sullivan*, 1983 (see p. 537) the House of Lords held that the definition of insanity in *M'Naghten* could extend to a person suffering from epilepsy, although epileptics are not regarded as insane by medical criteria.

Diminished responsibility. By virtue of s. 2 of the Homicide Act, 1957, this defence is now available in respect of a murder charge only. The burden of proof is on the defence, and if the defence is successfully established, it reduces the conviction for murder to one of manslaughter.

The defence must show that the accused 'was suffering from such abnormality of mind (whether arising from a condition of arrested or retarded development of mind, or any inherent causes, or induced by disease or injury) as substantially impaired his mental responsibility for his acts and omissions in doing, or being a party to, the killing'.

It should be noted that s. 1 of the Mental Health Act of 1983 gives a comprehensive and more enlightened definition of mental disorder which deals with mental disorder, severe mental impairment, mental impairment, and psychopathic disorder. It is not appropriate for a judge to direct the jury that only partial or borderline insanity amounts to diminished responsibility. (*R.* v. *Seers*, [1984] 79 Cr. App. R. 261.)

A killing arising from drink or drugs is not covered, because the condition is self-induced, and jealousy, hate and rage are not covered because they are ordinary human frailties which the defendant is expected to control. The merit of diminished responsibility for the offender before 1965 was that it enabled him to escape the death penalty. Since 1965 it has enabled him in many cases to escape the fixed life imprisonment (the only sentence for murder) or indefinite detention following an insanity verdict.

The accused's sanity or mental disorder is also relevant—

(a) *When he is put up for trial*. Although there may be no doubt that the accused was sane when he did the act with which he is charged, he may be too insane to stand trial or as it is usually put—'unfit to plead'. If this is found to be so by a jury, he will be detained during the Queen's pleasure until he recovers. He could then be tried but in practice never is.

(b) *On conviction*. Here the accused's mental condition is relevant to punishment. Under the Mental Health Act, 1983, the court can make a variety of hospital and guardianship orders though not in the case of murder.

(c) *After sentence*. If the accused is found to be suffering from mental disorder after receiving a sentence of imprisonment he may be transferred to a mental hospital under the Mental Health Act, 1983.

If a person suffering from mental disorder goes through a ceremony of marriage but cannot understand the nature of marriage, i.e. the responsibilities and change of status involved, the marriage will be void.

In connection with mental disorder, it is of interest to note the existence of the Court of Protection which is concerned with proper management of a mental patient's property. The Court operates through receivers who are, in many cases, close relatives of the patient.

Nationality and discrimination

Nationality

The main importance of nationality today is in the realms of public law, since aliens and nationals are treated similarly in most matters of civil law. However, matters such as allegiance, the right to vote at elections and sit in Parliament are governed by the nationality of the person concerned. A wholesale reform of nationality was brought into effect by the British Nationality Act, 1981. The broad general principles relating to the acquisition of British citizenship are set out below.

(a) *British citizenship*. A child born in the United Kingdom will be a British citizen if the father or mother is a British citizen and is settled in the UK which implies an entitlement to stay here *indefinitely*.

(b) *Citizenship by descent*. A mother or father can transmit his or her British citizenship to a child born outside the UK. However, under s. 2(1)(a) of the 1981 Act this applies to one generation only. Where the parent himself or herself is a British citizen by descent further requirements of registration and residence must be complied with by the child. (See s. 3(2), *ibid*.)

(c) Registration. Certain persons, e.g. British Dependent Territories' citizens who are those living in the remaining colonies, e.g. Hong Kong, and British overseas citizens, e.g. a citizen of a former British colony who retained British citizenship on independence, are entitled to be *registered* as a British citizen if they are settled in the UK and have been resident here for five years. (S. 4, *ibid.*)

(d) Naturalization. This is available to anyone and continues to be at the Home Secretary's discretion on the basis of five years' residence with requirements of knowledge of the English language, good behaviour and intention to live in the UK. (S. 6, *ibid.*)

British citizens have full rights of entry into the UK and to residence here.

Aliens

An alien cannot acquire property in a British ship or aircraft, save as a member of a limited liability company if the company itself is British, nor can he become the master of a British ship. Aliens cannot vote at elections or become members of Parliament. They also require work permits if they wish to take up employment here and may be deported if convicted of certain crimes. Citizens of the Republic of Ireland are not treated as aliens and may vote at elections and become members of Parliament. These are, of course, matters of civic and political rights, rather than nationality matters, but they may have to be dealt with by legislation at some stage, particularly since the Republic of Ireland does not reciprocate these rights in favour of British citizens.

Powers of internment and deportation are provided for by statute (see *Hosenball.*)[16] There is also legislation to control immigration to the United Kingdom. These provisions were considerably strengthened by the Immigration Acts of 1971 and 1988. Aliens who are here for more than six months are required to register with the police.

Racial discrimination

The Race Relations Act, 1976 and the Public Order Act, 1986 are designed to deal with discrimination on racial grounds and with relations between different racial groups. It should be noted before considering the main provisions of the Acts that under s. 72 of the 1976 Act a term in a contract which purports to exclude or limit any provisions of that Act is unenforceable by any person in whose favour the term would operate.

The Race Relations Act, 1976

Discrimination to which the Act applies. Section 1 provides that it is *direct discrimination* to treat a person less favourably on racial grounds and *indirect discrimination* where there is some requirement or condition, e.g. of employment, which, although it applies to all potential employees, is discriminatory since a smaller proportion (or none) of black applicants can comply with it than can white. Thus a rule insisting that bus conductors wear company caps could be *indirect discrimination* against Sikh applicants, who were held to be a protected ethnic group by the House of Lords in *Mandla* v. *Dowell Lee*, [1983] 1 All E.R. 1062.

Section 2 deals with *discrimination by way of victimization* of a person who has, for example, brought or given evidence in proceedings under the Act against a discriminator or alleged discriminator. Thus if A brings proceedings against his employer, B, for alleged discrimination and as a consequence A's landlord, C, will not allow A to use a goods lift provided for common use in the block of flats where A lives, then C could be guilty of victimization under s. 2. Under s. 3 'racial grounds' means colour, race, nationality, or ethnic or national origins, and 'racial group' means a group of persons defined by reference to colour, race, nationality, or ethnic or national origin. The Act still permits discrimination on grounds of religious belief unless that constitutes racial discrimination, as it would if the religion was Jewish but not if it is Catholic or Protestant since the last two named are not matters of race.

Discrimination in employment. The provisions of the Act which relate to discrimination in employment are set out below. These provisions are supplemented by the Commission for Racial Equality's Code of Practice on Racial Equality in Employment.

(*i*) *Offers of Employment.* Under s. 4(1) it is unlawful for a person in relation to employment by him at an establishment in Great Britain (other than a private house) to discriminate against another person on the grounds of colour, race, nationality, or ethnic or national origins; (i) in the arrangements he makes for the purpose for deciding who should be offered the job; or (ii) in the terms on which the job is offered; or (iii) by refusing or deliberately omitting to offer him the job. (*Johnson* v. *Timber Tailors* (*Midlands*), 1978.)[47]

'Arrangements' is a wide expression covering a range of recruitment techniques, e.g. asking an employment agency to send only white applicants. Discriminatory advertisements are unlawful (s. 29) as is discrimination by employment agencies (s. 14).

(*ii*) *Terms of the contract of employment.* Section 4(2) makes it unlawful to discriminate against an employee (other than a person employed in a private household, though even here discrimination by victimization applies) in terms of the employment which is given to him or in terms of access to opportunities for promotion, transfer or training, or to any other benefits, facilities or services, or by dismissing him or subjecting him to any other detriment. Section 4(4) makes unlawful discrimination in regard to matters such as privileged loans and mortgages by banks and building societies and discounts on holidays given to employees of travel firms.

(*iii*) *Exceptions*

(*a*) *Genuine Occupational Qualifications.* Section 5 gives a list of circumstances in which it is lawful to discriminate because it is a genuine occupational qualification (GOQ) for the job that the person appointed belongs to a particular racial group, e.g. employment of a West Indian social worker or probation officer to deal with problems relating to young West Indians. Other instances are dramatic performances or other entertainment, artists' or photographic models, and employment in places serving food or drink to be purchased *and consumed* on the premises by the public. Thus, being Chinese is a GOQ for employment in a Chinese restaurant but not in a 'take-away'.

(*b*) *Training*. Section 6 allows discrimination in regard to the training in this country of persons from overseas. Thus if a person allocates a number of employment-for-training places on the basis of nationality, there is clearly discrimination against other people who might do the job. However, s. 6 protects an employer against an action for discrimination in this situation.

(*iv*) *Contract workers*. Previous legislation did not apply to contract workers but s. 7 plugs this gap. The discrimination provisions now apply to workers supplied by a third party so that temporary staff supplied by an agency are covered. In addition it is unlawful under s. 14 for an employment agency to discriminate.

(*v*) *Local authorities*. When local authorities enter into a contract with private sector companies they are bound by a general duty to eliminate unlawful racial discrimination and promote equality of opportunity and good relations between persons of different racial groups (s. 71). Section 18 of the Local Government Act, 1988 allows local authorities to ask questions, as specified by the Secretary of State, of contractors in relation to the racial policy of the organisation seeking a contract.

Partnerships. Section 10 extends protection against discrimination to partnerships as regards failure to offer a partnership or the terms on which it is offered, including benefits, facilities and services, except where a GOQ applies. The section applies only to firms of six or more partners, though there is a power in s. 73 to reduce this number. The provision as it stands will allow discrimination in the majority of medical practices but not, e.g. in the larger firms of accountants and solicitors. The section also covers discrimination in cases where persons are preparing to form themselves into a partnership.

Trade unions. Section 11 renders unlawful discriminatory practices by trade unions, employers' associations and professional trade bodies. Surprisingly, individual discriminatory action by shop stewards is not covered by the Act. Thus if a shop steward discriminates with the authority of his union, the union will be liable, but if he acts without authority, no one is liable. This appears to be a defect in the Act since it is well known that white organized labour has in several areas of the country held back black development in employment.

Qualifying bodies. Section 12 provides that it is unlawful for an authority or body which can confer an authorization or qualification which is needed for, or facilitates employment in, a particular trade or profession to discriminate against a person in terms of conferring that authorization or qualification.

Miscellaneous. The Act does not apply to those whose work is wholly or mainly outside Great Britain (s. 8) though it does apply in relation to employment concerned with the exploitation of petroleum fields in foreign sectors of the Continental Shelf (Oil and Gas (Enterprise) Act, 1982, Sch. 3. para. 36). Discrimination is allowed against foreign seamen recruited abroad (s. 9) since the *immediate* abolition of the right to employ seamen recruited overseas at lower rates of pay than those applicable in the UK would cause serious difficulties for the UK shipping industry. However, shipowners are required to make early and visible progress towards eliminating the practice of paying lower wages to foreign (mainly Asian) seamen, otherwise the Government will intervene. Section 13 and 15 apply the Act to vocational training bodies such as the remaining industrial training boards and to the Training Commission. Section 16 covers discrimination in terms of employment in the police force.

Victimization. This may arise in employment because, as we have seen, s. 2 provides that it is unlawful to victimize a person, i.e. treat him less favourably than others, because he has, for example, exercised or proposed to exercise his rights under the Act.

Discrimination in education. Sections 17–19 make it unlawful for responsible bodies, e.g. governing bodies of educational establishments including both State and private schools, to discriminate on racial grounds as regards, for example, allocation of places.

Discrimination in provision of goods, facilities or services. Under s. 20 discrimination by, for example, shops, hotels, boarding houses and banks is outlawed as is discrimination in clubs which have 25 or more members. When membership of a club reaches 25 or more a licence to serve intoxicating liquor must be sought. Clubs with membership of less than 25 members are excluded and may discriminate.

Discrimination in the disposal or management of premises. Section 21 states that discrimination on racial grounds by a seller of property in terms of the buyer or by, say, a brewery in terms of who shall manage a public house, is unlawful. The section does not apply to owner-occupiers of houses who sell the property without employing an estate agent or advertising it for sale. (S. 21(3).) There is also an exemption for the letting of accommodation in premises where the occupier or a near relative of his resides and intends to continue to reside on the premises which are 'small premises' under s. 22(2), e.g. where there is not room for more than six persons in addition to the occupier and members of his household. Section 23 provides for exemptions allowing discrimination where a person takes into his home and treats as a member of his family a child, an elderly person or a person requiring a special degree of care and attention. Thus discrimination on racial grounds in the choice of foster children is not unlawful. Section 24 provides that where a tenant requires the licence or consent of the landlord to assign or sublet to another person it is unlawful for that licence or consent to be withheld in a discriminatory way, as where a landlord will not allow a tenant to assign to a black tenant.

As we have seen, discrimination in clubs with 25 or more members is unlawful but s. 26 provides an exemption for organizations whose main object is to confer benefits on ethnic or national groups and does not exclude others. Thus the London Welsh Club is still a lawful association but must not exclude black Welshmen.

By s. 27 the Act applies only to benefits, facilities and services in Great Britain. However, it does extend outside Great Britain in some cases. For example, discrimination in Great Britain in regard to the provision of facilities for travel is unlawful even though the facilities are to be supplied outside Great Britain.

Discriminatory practices. Under s. 28 there may be a discriminatory practice, even where there is no victim. Thus a factory which has discriminatory recruiting procedures may be regarded as discriminating even during a recession when there has been no recruitment for some time. However, proceedings under s. 28 can be brought only by the Commission for Racial Equality.

Advertisements. Section 29 makes discriminatory advertisements unlawful unless, as in an employment advertisement, there is, for example, a GOQ.

Instructions, pressure or inducement to discriminate. Under ss. 30 and 31 it is unlawful to instruct a person to discriminate or to put pressure on a person to discriminate in a way which the 1976 Act makes *unlawful*. The act must be unlawful so instructions by a landlord to his tenant not to take black foster children would not be unlawful. (But see *Commission for Racial Equality* v. *Imperial Society of Teachers of Dancing*, 1983.)[48] Under s. 32 an employer is vicariously liable (see p. 351) together with the offending employee for any act done by the employee in course of employment, whether the act was done with the knowledge or approval of the employer or not. Similarly, principals will be liable for the *authorized* acts of their agents but in neither case does vicarious liability extend to criminal proceedings. An employer (not a principal) is given a defence if he can show that he took such steps as were reasonably practicable to prevent his employee doing discriminatory acts. Under s. 33 those who assist others to do unlawful acts are also liable.

Charities. Section 34 makes it clear that any provision in an existing or future charitable instrument, e.g. a trust, which confers benefits on persons of a different colour is void. Further, it is unlawful to do any act in Great Britain to give effect to such a provision.

General exceptions. Certain general exceptions from liability are set out in Part IV of the Act. Under s. 35 acts done to meet the special needs of racial groups with regard, for example, to education, training and welfare, such as special language training for groups whose first language is not English, are not unlawful; there is some overlap here with s. 6. Sections 37 and 38 allow positive discrimination in favour of particular racial groups by training bodies, employers and trade unions, employers' associations, and professional and trade associations, by encouraging members of those groups to take work by giving special talks and guided tours of factories and premises. Under s. 39 the selection of sports teams on the basis of nationality, place of birth, and length of residence is exempted from the provisions of the Act. Thus a county cricket club may, if that is a rule, continue to select teams from among those born in the county but cannot refuse to select a person otherwise willing and able, who was born in the county of, say, Pakistani parents.

The Commission for Racial Equality. Section 43 sets up the Commission (CRE) which is to work towards the elimination of discrimination; to promote equality of opportunity; good relations between different racial groups and to keep under review the working of the Act. Under s. 47 the CRE has the power to issue codes of practice giving guidance on ways of achieving equality of opportunity and eliminating discrimination in the employment field. Sections 48–52 give the CRE power to conduct formal investigations, for example, into alleged discriminatory employment practices in order to carry out its duties. The court may prevent such an investigation going ahead on the grounds, e.g. that the concern to be investigated has not been given an opportunity to make representations of its own position. (*R.* v. *Commission for Racial Equality, ex parte Prestige Group plc*, [1983] I.R.L.R. 408.)

Enforcement. The enforcement provisions which are set out in Part VIII are of two types—

(a) *Complaints by an individual* who is the subject of unlawful conduct other than 'discriminatory practices', advertising or pressures or instructions to discriminate. In employment cases the complaint goes to an industrial tribunal (s. 54) (see below). Complaints of discrimination in education and in the provisions of goods, facilities and services and in housing may be made to the county court. (S. 57.) Complaints that a responsible body in an educational establishment has discriminated must be notified to the Secretary of State for Education who must be given a maximum of two months to consider the matter before court proceedings can be commenced. (S. 57(5).) It should be noted that an individual is given direct access to courts and tribunals for the first time in race relations matters; under previous legislation only the Race Relations Board (now abolished) could institute proceedings.

(b) *Enforcement by the CRE.* This involves—(i) the issuing of a non-discrimination notice (s. 58); (ii) proceedings in the county court or industrial tribunal where there are discriminatory practices, advertisements or pressures or instructions to discriminate (s. 63); (iii) proceedings in the county court for an injunction where there has been persistent discrimination (s. 62); (iv) assisting individual complainants in certain matters of principle or complexity or other special considerations (s. 66).

It should be noted that a non-discrimination notice will require a person not to commit any further discriminatory acts and, where in order to comply with this it is necessary to change practices or arrangements, to inform the CRE that the changes have been effected and bring these changes to the attention of other persons concerned. There is a right of appeal within six weeks against such a notice to an industrial tribunal which may modify or quash the notice (s. 59). If an appeal against a notice is dismissed, the notice becomes final and is entered on the CRE's Register of Notices (s. 61).

(c) *Enforcement in the employment field.* Section 55 provides for conciliation by the Advisory, Conciliation and Arbitration Service to try to help the parties to settle the matter without going to a tribunal.

That failing, complaints in the employment field are, with the exception of those relating to discrimination by certain qualifying bodies under s. 12 (see below), heard by industrial tribunals (s. 54). The complaint must be brought within three months of the occurrence of the act complained of (s. 68(1).) There is no legal aid but the CRE may arrange for legal advice or assistance (s. 66).

Where a person is refused a qualification he may take the matter to an industrial tribunal unless there is already another statutory right of appeal. Thus appeals against the Law Society will continue to be to the Court of Appeal and doctors will appeal, as before, to the Privy Council.

(d) *Remedies in the employment field.* Under s. 56 a tribunal may make—

(i) an order declaring the rights of the parties with the intention that this should be observed; (ii) an order to pay compensation for loss of earnings and other losses, including prospective loss of earnings and injured feelings (s. 57(4)); (iii) a recommendation that the person discriminating take action for the purpose of obviating or reducing the adverse effect on the person complaining of the act of discrimination. If the person discriminating fails to comply with the recommendation the tribunal may increase the amount of compensation or make an order for compensation if such an order could have been made but was not.

The Public Order Act 1986
Part III of the Act makes it an offence to stir up racial hatred by use of words or behaviour or display of written material (s. 18); by publishing or distributing written material (s. 19); by the public performance of plays (s. 20); by distributing, showing or playing a recording (s. 21); by broadcasting or including a programme in a cable service (s. 22); by possessing racially inflammatory material (s. 23). There are powers of police entry and search of premises to discover material (s. 24) and a power of forfeiture under s. 25. Nothing in the Act applies to fair and accurate reports of Parliamentary proceedings, nor to law reports (s. 26).

Institution of proceedings requires the consent of the Attorney-General. The maximum sentence is 2 years imprisonment and/or an unlimited fine (s. 27). If a corporation is found guilty any director or other officer who consented to or connived at the offence is also guilty (s. 28).

Sex discrimination
The three main Acts of Parliament involved here are the Sex Discrimination Acts, 1975 and 1986 and the Equal Pay Act, 1970, to which amendments have been made by the Equal Pay (Amendment) Regulations, 1983.

Sex Discrimination Act, 1975. The form of drafting used in the Race Relations Act, 1976, was based on the Sex Discrimination Act, 1975, and the reader will recognize many similar features.

Under the Act of 1975 it is unlawful to treat anyone, on the grounds of sex, less favourably than a person of the opposite sex is or would be treated in the same circumstances. Once again, a term in a contract which purports to exclude or limit any provision of the Act is unenforceable by any person in whose favour the term would operate (s. 73(3)).

Sex discrimination defined. There are two kinds of discrimination as follows—

(a) Direct discrimination which involves, for example, treating a woman less favourably than a man because she is a woman or because of marital status;

(b) Indirect discrimination which occurs where conditions are applied which favour, quite unjustifiably, one sex more than the other, as where a firm advertises for clerical workers who must be six feet tall. (And see *Price* v. *The Civil Service Commission*, 1977.)[49]

It should be noted that although the Act is written in terms of discrimination against women, it applies equally to discrimination against men either because they are men or because of marital status.

167

Areas of discrimination

These are exactly the same as those covered by the Race Relations Act, 1976, as follows—

(a) Employment. Employers may not discriminate because of sex in their recruitment of employees or in the treatment of them once in employment. This also applies to promotion and training.

Except in rare situations employers may not label jobs as being 'for men' or 'for women', though there are a number of exceptions. For example, in jobs where a person's sex is a genuine occupational qualification, as in acting. In employment it is also unlawful to discriminate because a person is married. Again, such discrimination may be *direct*, as where a person is treated, on the grounds that he or she is married, less favourably than a single person of the same sex; or *indirect* where there is a condition or requirement which fewer married people than single people of the same sex can comply with, e.g. a refusal by an employer to promote employees with children. The Sex Discrimination Act, 1986 makes certain changes. The 1975 Act excluded private households and undertakings employing five or less people from its provisions. The 1986 Act removes that exemption unless the work, in the case of a household, involves intimate contact with the employer, so that, e.g., a bedridden woman would be able to discriminate in favour of a woman to take care of her. Discrimination in employment is also considered at p. 325, where the rules of the 1986 Act regarding small partnerships and retirement are dealt with.

(b) Education. Co-educational schools, colleges, and universities may not discriminate in the provision of facilities or in their admissions. Thus it would be unlawful to refuse a girl admission to a metalwork class because she is a girl. In addition, the Careers Service must not discriminate in the advice and assistance offered to girls and boys, though single-sex schools are still permissible.

Local education authorities are required to provide secondary education without discriminating on the grounds of sex. In *R.* v. *Birmingham City Council ex parte Equal Opportunities Commission, The Times*, 15 October, 1987 it appeared that the Council provided considerably fewer grammar school places for girls than for boys. McCullough, J. granted a declaration that the Council's arrangements were unlawful.

(c) Housing, goods, facilities and services. In general, no-one providing housing, goods, facilities or services to the public may discriminate because of sex. There are some exceptions where discrimination will not be unlawful; these include, for example, situations where it is necessary to preserve decency and privacy, e.g. public lavatories.

Discrimination must not be used in the buying or renting of accommodation and an hotel, boarding house or restaurant may not refuse accommodation or refreshment on the grounds of sex. (See *Gill* v. *El Vino Co. Ltd*, 1983.)[50]

In addition, a bank, building society, finance house or other credit business must offer credit, a mortgage or loan on the same terms that it would offer the facilities to someone of the opposite sex. (See *Quinn* v. *Williams Furniture Ltd*, 1981.)[51]

(d) Advertising. Advertisements with job description such as 'salesgirl, waiter, stewardess, postman' are deemed to discriminate unless they contain an indication that both men and women are eligible, though it should be noted that only the Equal Opportunities Commission (EOC) can bring proceedings in matters to do with advertising.

Victimization. The provisions here are the same as those set out in the Race Relations Act, 1976, so that the law will protect a person if they are victimized for bringing a complaint under the Sex Discrimination Act, 1975.

The Equal Opportunities Commission. The Equal Opportunities Commission was set up to ensure effective enforcement of the Sex Discrimination Act and the Equal Pay Act (see below) and to promote equal opportunity between the sexes. The Commission has power to hold formal investigations, and if satisfied that practices are unlawful, can issue non-discrimination notices requiring that they cease. When holding a formal investigation, either on its own initiative or because it has been asked to do so by the Secretary of State the Commission has power to require any person to furnish information and to attend hearings to give evidence.

The Commission has power to help individuals in the preparation and conduct of complaints in both courts and tribunals and as well as investigating areas of inequality between the sexes, the Commission has a duty to make recommendations to the Government about the operation of existing law. It is also empowered to undertake or assist others to undertake research and educational work and generally to advise people as to their rights.

The Race Relations Act, 1976, makes minor amendments in the Sex Discrimination Act. In particular, the EOC is given power to issue codes of practice giving practical guidance on equality of opportunity and the elimination of discrimination in the employment field between men and women, i.e. powers matching those given to the CRE. This is achieved by adding s. 56A to the Sex Discrimination Act, 1975.

Enforcement. The provisions, which are similar to those of the Race Relations Act, 1976, are as follows—

(a) Individuals' rights. Complaints in the employment field may be made to industrial tribunals in exactly the same way as complaints in relation to race. Again, a conciliation officer of ACAS has a duty to help

the parties to reach a settlement without the need for a tribunal hearing. If there is a hearing before a tribunal the remedies are exactly the same as those available for discrimination on the grounds of race (see p. 165).

Complaints in all other fields may be made to a county court and if the court finds in favour of the complainant it may award—(i) an order declaring the rights of the parties as, e.g. in *Gill* v. *El Vino Co. Ltd*, 1983;[50] (ii) an injunction; or (iii) damages which may include loss of earnings and also compensation for injured feelings.

(*b*) *The Equal Opportunities Commission.* The functions of the EOC in regard to enforcement are as follows—

(i) the Commission may conduct formal investigations into any matter in order to carry out its duties and where it discovers conduct which contravenes the Sex Discrimination Act or the Equal Pay Act it is empowered to issue a non-discrimination notice. The result of issuing such a notice is the same as that under the Race Relations Act, 1976 (see p. 166);

(ii) the Commission can institute legal proceedings in respect of persistent discrimination, including judicial review (*R.* v. *Birmingham City Council ex parte E.O.C.*, (1987). See p. 168).

(iii) the Commission has the sole right to institute legal proceedings in respect of discriminatory practices in advertisements, and instructions and pressure to discriminate;

(iv) the Commission has power to assist individual complainants in preparing their case on, e.g. difficult aspects of the law.

(*c*) *Qualifying bodies.* Where a qualifying body is required by law to satisfy itself as to the good character of an applicant for the authorization or qualification it can confer, it must have regard, in deciding whether or not to issue, renew, or extend the authorization or qualification, to any evidence tending to show that the applicant, or any of his past or present employees or agents has practised unlawful discrimination in, or in connection with, the carrying on of any profession or trade. Discrimination by persons who require such authorizations or qualifications to carry on their profession or trade may therefore be drawn to the attention of the appropriate qualifying body, e.g. the Law Society. An additional example would be an allegation against a person in the consumer credit or hire business, for which a licence from the Director-General of Fair Trading is required. Such an allegation may be referred to the Director-General who is required to have regard to evidence of discrimination when considering the fitness of a person to hold a licence under the Consumer Credit Act, 1974.

Equal pay

The Equal Pay Act, 1970 seeks to eliminate discriminatory treatment between men and women in pay and other terms and conditions in employment. The Act applies to all kinds of work, both manual and non-manual, full-time or part-time, whether in factories, offices, shops, or anywhere else. The topic is considered in more detail at p. 325.

JURISTIC PERSONS

As we have seen, the concept of personality is not restricted to human beings and we shall now consider corporate personality in terms of the nature and types of corporations.

The joint stock company

The enormous increase in industrial activity during the industrial revolution made necessary and inevitable the emergence of the joint stock company and the concept of limited liability. For the first time it was possible for the small investor to contribute to the capital of a business enterprise with the assurance that, in the event of its failure, he could lose no more than the amount he had contributed or agreed to contribute. The principles of 'legal entity' and 'perpetual succession' apply, whereby the joint stock company is deemed to be a distinct legal person, able to hold property and carry on business in its own name, irrespective of the particular persons who may happen to be the owners of its shares from time to time. (*Salomon* v. *Salomon*, 1897.)[52]

The concept of corporate personality is capable of abuse and where, for example, the concept has been used to evade legal obligations, the courts have been prepared to investigate sharp practice by individuals who are trying to hide behind a company front. Thus in *Gilford Motor Co.* v. *Horne*, [1933] Ch. 935 a former employee bound by a restraint of trade set up a company in order to evade its provisions, claiming that he as a person might be bound by the restraint but the company, being a separate entity, could not be. An injunction was granted against both him and his company which the court described as 'a device, a stratagem . . . a mere cloak or sham'.

Joint Stock Companies are formed by registration under the Companies Act, 1985 or previous Acts. The main current controlling statute is the Companies Act, 1985. It provides for two types of registered companies: the Public Limited Company and the Private Company. A registered company is fully liable for its debts but the liability of the members may be limited either to the amount unpaid on their shares, i.e. *a company limited by shares*, or to the amount they have agreed to pay if the company is brought to an end (wound up), i.e. *a company limited by guarantee*. Some companies are *unlimited* and the members are fully liable for the unpaid debts of the company if, and only if, the company goes into liquidation.

The allotted capital of a public limited company, which must before it can trade or borrow money be at least £50,000 with 25% of the nominal value and the whole of any premium paid up, is usually raised by the public subscribing for its shares, which are issued with varying rights as to dividends, voting powers, and degrees of risk. Shares are freely transferable and are almost invariably listed on a recognised investment exchange such as the Stock Exchange. When making a public issue of shares, the company is under a statutory obligation to publish full particulars of the history, capital structure, loans, profit record, directors, and many other matters calculated to assist the intending shareholder to assess the possibilities of the company. Such a document is called a Prospectus, and the directors are liable to penalties for fraud, misrepresentation or failure to disclose the material information as required by Part IV (Listed Securities); and Part V (Unlisted Securities) of the Financial Services Act, 1986, together with the rules of a recognised investment exchange such as the Stock Exchange.

The minimum number of members is two, but there is no upper limit. Incorporation is achieved by lodging with the Registrar of Companies certain documents of which the following are the most important—

(a) *The Memorandum of Association* is a document which defines the constitution of the company, and sets out in the Objects Clause the powers of the company. This clause governs the activities into which the company can legally enter (but see p. 224) and it may be said that the memorandum governs the company's relations with the outside world. In the memorandum one also finds the company's name, together with a statement that the liability of the members is limited (where this is the case); the situation of its Registered Office, i.e. England or Wales or Scotland (this governs the company's nationality and domicile); the amount of its Authorized Capital; and an Association Clause in which the subscribers ask for incorporation and agree to take at least one share. Under s. 1 of the Companies Act, 1985 the memorandum of a public limited company has a clause stating that that is what it is.

(b) *The Articles of Association* contain the regulations governing the relationship between the company and its members, and thus cover the internal or domestic affairs of the company. Such matters as alteration of shareholders' rights, powers of directors, conduct of meetings, and resolutions, are contained in the Articles.

The directors of a company stand in the fiduciary position of agents towards the company whose money they control, and many of the provisions of the Companies Act, 1985 are framed to ensure the maximum possible degree of disclosure by the directors of information calculated to keep the members acquainted with the affairs of the company.

The Memorandum and Articles of Association are public documents which must be deposited with the Registrar of Companies, and are open to public inspection along with other records relating to charges on the company's property, and copies of important resolutions. Each year the company's Annual Return, giving particulars of share capital, debentures, mortgages and charges, list of members, particulars of directors and secretary, must be filed with the Registrar. In addition, the company's accounts and the directors' and auditors' reports must be laid before a general meeting of the company and filed with the Registrar within ten months (private company) and seven months (public company) of the end of the accounting period to which they relate. Any person may inspect the Register of Members at the Registered Office of the company.

The private company, which has a minimum of two members and no maximum number is now a firmly established feature of the present day business world. The private company is barred by s. 170 of the Financial Services Act, 1986 from going to the general public for subscriptions for its shares.

Dissolution of a registered company usually takes place by the company being put into liquidation, as a result of the process of winding up.

Other types of corporation

Incorporation may also be achieved by a *Royal Charter* granted by the Crown. The procedure is for the organization desiring incorporation to address a petition to the Privy Council, asking for the grant of a charter and outlining the powers required. If the Privy Council consider that the organization is an appropriate one, the Crown will be advised to grant a charter. Charter companies were formerly used to further the development of new countries, e.g. the East India Company and the Hudson Bay Company, but now they are usually confined to non-commercial corporations, e.g. the Institute of Chartered Accountants in England and Wales and the Institute of Chartered Secretaries and Administrators. Universities are also incorporated in this way. It is possible for the liability of members to be limited, and a chartered company, sometimes known as a 'Common Law Corporation,' has the same powers as an individual person in spite of limitations in its charter. However, it is said that the Crown may forfeit the charter if the company pursues *ultra vires* activities, and certainly a member can ask the court to grant an injunction preventing the company from carrying out *ultra vires* activities. (*Jenkin v. Pharmaceutical Society*, 1921.)[53]

Companies may be created by special Act of Parliament, and are governed by their special Acts and also by Acts which apply to statutory companies generally, which are known as 'Clauses Acts'. These Acts together define and limit their activities. The purpose of statutory companies is to promote undertakings of the nature of public utility services, e.g. water supply, where monopolistic powers and compulsory acquisition are essential to proper functioning. The liability of members may be limited. Many of the former statutory public utility companies have now been nationalized by other statutes and are operated on a national basis, e.g. British Coal.

All the forms of incorporation which we have discussed have one feature in common, i.e. they produce corporations aggregate having more than one member. However, English law recognizes the concept of the *Corporation Sole*, i.e. a corporation having only one member. A number of such corporations were created by the common lawyers. They were concerned because land did not always have an owner, and there could be a break, however slight, in ownership. Church lands for example were vested in the vicar of the particular living, and at higher levels in other church dignitaries, such as the bishop of the diocese. When such persons died, the land had no legal owner until a successor was appointed, so the common lawyers created the concept of the corporation sole whereby the office of Vicar or Bishop was a corporation, and the present incumbent the sole member of that corporation. The death of the incumbent had thereafter no effect on the corporation, which never dies, and each successive occupant of the office carries on exactly where his predecessor left off. The Bishop of London is a corporation sole, and the present holder of the office is the sole member of the corporation. The Crown is also a corporation sole.

It does not seem likely that any further corporations sole will be created by the common law, but they may still be created by statute. For example, the Public Trustee Act, 1906, sets up the office of Public Trustee as a corporation sole. The Public Trustee is prepared to act as executor or trustee, when asked to do so, and much property is vested in him from time to time in the above capacities. It would be most inconvenient to transfer this property to the new holder of the office on the death or retirement of the current one, and so the person who holds the office of Public Trustee is the sole member of a corporation called the Public Trustee, and the property over which he has control is vested in the corporation, and not in the individual who is the holder of the office.

UNINCORPORATED ASSOCIATIONS

Having considered juristic personality, we will now turn to organizations which have no personality separate and distinct from the members. Many groups of people and institutions exist which carry on their affairs in much the same way as incorporated associations, but which are in fact non-charitable unincorporated associations. Examples are cricket clubs, tennis clubs, and societies of like kind. Such associations have no independent legal personality, and their property is treated as the joint property of all the members. The main areas of legal difficulty arising in regard to these associations are as follows—

Liability of members in contract. This rests on the principles of the law of agency. Thus a member who purports to make a contract on behalf of his club is usually personally liable. The other members will only be liable as co-principals if they had authorized the making of the contract. This would be the case if, for example, the rules of the club so provided. Alternatively, the members may ratify the contract after it is made. However, it appears that no member has authority to make a *purchase on credit* (*Flemyng* v. *Hector* (1836), 2 M & W 172) unless he is specifically authorized to do so. Membership of a club usually involves payment of an annual subscription and nothing more. Consequently it is expected that everything needed by the club will be paid for from existing funds. If more money is needed a meeting of members should be called so that subscriptions might be raised rather than pledge the credit of the members.

Liability of members in tort. A person is liable if he committed the tort and in addition may be liable vicariously for the tort of his employee (see p. 351). These principles have been applied to clubs in two main types of case, viz.—

(*a*) Where a person has been injured as a result of the dangerous condition of the club premises. The tendency here is to hold all the members liable as 'occupiers' and not merely the club's officers or a committee or trustees. (*Campbell* v. *Thompson*, [1953] 1 Q.B. 445.)

(*b*) Where a person has been injured as a result of the negligence of an employee of the club. The tendency here is to find that the employee is employed by the officer or committee or trustees who appointed him. (*Bradley Egg Farm Ltd* v. *Clifford*, [1943] 2 All E.R. 378.)

Rights of members in the assets of the association. While a club is functioning the individual members have no separate rights in its property. They do, however, acquire realizable rights when the club is dissolved. On dissolution the general rule is that the assets are sold and after liabilities have been discharged any surplus is divided equally among those persons who are members regardless of length of membership or of subscriptions paid *at the time of dissolution* (*Re GKN Bolts & Nuts Ltd Sports & Social Club, Leek and Others* v. *Donkersley and Others*, [1982] 2 All E.R. 855), subject, of course, to any contrary provision in the rules of the club. It should be noted that a club is not dissolved simply because it changes its name and constitution with the express or implied consent of the members. (*Abbatt* v. *Treasury Solicitor*, [1969] 3 All E.R. 1175.)

Rights of members under the rules. The rules of an unincorporated association constitute a contract between the members of the association and the court will grant an injunction to a member who is denied a right given under the rules, e.g. the right to vote at meetings (*Woodford* v. *Smith*, [1970] 1 All E.R. 1091), or if he is expelled either where there is no power of expulsion under the rules, or if the power exists it has not been exercised properly as where the principles of natural justice have not been observed.

Procedure. If only a few of the members are liable no problems arise since they can all be sued personally. If, however, it is intended to allege that all the members are liable this procedure is impracticable since all would have the right to be individually defended and represented. In this sort of case a representative action is available. Under the Rules of Supreme Court and the county court rules the plaintiff may ask for a *representative order* to be made against certain members of the association and sue them. If he is successful these members will be liable to pay the damages but may also be entitled to an indemnity from the funds of the association, and in this way the plaintiff is in effect paid from the association's funds. Similarly some members of an unincorporated association can sue for wrongs done to the association by means of the representative order procedure.

Trade unions

As regards the status of trade unions, s. 2(1) of the Trade Union and Labour Relations Act, 1974, provides that a trade union shall not be treated as if it were a body corporate but it is capable of making contracts; the property of the trade union is vested in trustees on trust for the union; it is capable of suing and being sued in its own name, whether in proceedings relating to property or founded on contract or tort or any other cause of action whatsoever; proceedings for any offence alleged to have been committed by it or on its behalf may be brought against it in its own name and any judgment made in proceedings of any description brought against a trade union are enforceable, e.g. by way of execution against the property held in trust for the union as if the union were a body corporate.

Section 3(1) of the 1974 Act extends the identical provisions to an employers' association where it is unincorporated. However, an employers' association may be a body corporate.

Under s. 15 of the Employment Act, 1982 the liability of trade unions is as follows:

Industrial action against the employer of its members (primary action)
In an official strike the union is liable for torts committed during the dispute. The most usual tort is interfering with contracts of employment by organizing the strike. There may be other torts, e.g. damage to the employer's property.

A trade union has immunity in regard to the tort of interference with contracts of employment only if the industrial action is preceded by a ballot of members and the action is commenced within four weeks of the ballot taking place. The majority of those voting must vote in favour of the action. Under the Employment Act, 1988 the ballot must be secret and there must be separate ballots for each place of work. An official scrutineer must supervise the way in which voting papers are drawn up and sent to members to prevent ballot-rigging.

If there is no ballot the union can be sued for an injunction and damages which are limited (see below).

Action which is not against the employer (secondary action).
The union is liable for torts including interfering with contracts of employment and there is no immunity by reason of a ballot. An injunction and damages may be awarded.

In cases of primary and secondary action damages are limited in any one case to £10,000 (membership less than 5000); £50,000 (membership between 5000 and 25,000); £125,000 (membership between 25,000 and 100,000) and £250,000 if membership is 100,000 or more.

Contracts made by a trade union are normally enforceable in accordance with the general principles of the law of contract. However, under s. 18 of the Trade Union and Labour Relations Act, 1974 collective agreements, i.e. with an employer in regard to wages, hours and conditions of work of a group of workers, are presumed *not* to be intended to be legally enforceable *unless* they are in writing and contain a provision to that effect.

The partnership

A partnership is defined in s. 1 of the Partnership Act, 1890, as 'the relationship which subsists between persons carrying on a business in common with a view of profit'. It will be noted that there must be a business; that it must be carried on in common by the members (whether by all of them, or by one or more of them acting for the others, will depend on the agreement subsisting between them); and that there must be the intention to earn profits. An association of persons formed for the purpose (say) of promoting some educational or recreational object to which the whole of the funds of the association shall be devoted, and from which no advantage in the nature of a distribution of a profit shall accrue to the members, is not a partnership.

Participation in the profits of a business may be regarded as *prima facie* evidence of a partnership, but it is not conclusive—the intention of the parties must be examined. Thus, an employee whose remuneration is based on a share of profits, or the widow or child of a deceased partner receiving an annuity in the form of a share of profits, would not legally be deemed to be partners. Neither does the common ownership of property constitute a partnership (see further p. 435), nor the lending of money in consideration of an agreement to pay the interest, or to repay the capital, as a share or percentage of profits as they accrue. (But in such a case the lender should take the precaution of having the agreement embodied in writing, signed by all the parties, and setting out clearly the fact that he is not to be considered a partner.)

The question of citation as a partner is of great importance because the existence of a partnership, if such is proved, will involve all parties cited as partners in unlimited liability for the debts of the firm. Partners are agents for the firm, and can bind the other partners in contracts concerning the business of the firm whether they are specifically authorized to make them or not.

Two or more persons can combine to form a partnership, which can be brought into existence in a highly formal or a very casual manner. *No legal formalities are essential*, but it is desirable and usual for the rights and liabilities of the partners to be defined in a formal Deed of Partnership, or at least in a written Partnership Agreement. On the other hand, a mere oral agreement is equally binding, and in extreme cases a relationship of partnership may be inferred from the conduct of the parties. The partners are at liberty to vary the arrangements made between them, and where the conduct of the parties has for a lengthy period been inconsistent with the terms as originally agreed, it will be presumed that they intend that the new arrangements shall be binding on them. The Partnership Act makes provisions as to contribution of capital, division of profits, rights of partners to participate in active management, and so on, but these only apply in so far as they are not varied by agreement between the partners.

Section 716 of the Companies Act, 1985, prohibits the formation of a partnership consisting of more than twenty persons for the purpose of carrying on any business for gain. The Banking Act of 1979, s. 51(2) and Sch. 7 applies the usual limit of 20 to banking partnerships.

However, certain partnerships of solicitors, accountants and stockbrokers are exempted from this prohibition by s. 716 of the Companies Act, 1985. Regulations made by the Department of Trade and Industry exempt from the prohibition in s. 716 of the Act of 1985 certain other partnerships, e.g. patent agents and also certain partnerships of surveyors, auctioneers, valuers and estate agents.

There is no limitation on the activities of partners provided these are legal; nor is there any limit to the liability of the individual partners for the debts of the firm, each partner being liable to the full extent of his personal estate for any deficiencies of the partnership. However, provision is made for the introduction of limited partners whose liability is limited to the amount of capital they have introduced, though there must always be at least one general partner who is fully liable for the debts of the firm. Such a partnership must be registered as a limited partnership under the Limited Partnerships Act, 1907.

The partnership was the normal form of business organization for operations on a fairly large scale before the advent of the joint stock company, but it is now largely restricted to the type of enterprise requiring intimate personal collaboration between the members, or where incorporation is not possible or desirable, as among doctors, solicitors and accountants, though the increasing control over companies including, in particular, private companies, may see some revival of the partnership as a more general business organization. However, in the legal and accounting professions particularly, negligence liability is encouraging a move towards incorporation of firms to achieve limited liability.

One of the defects of the partnership is its lack of continuity. On the death of a partner the continuing partners must account to his personal representatives for the amount of his interest in the firm. This difficulty may be met to some extent by providing funds out of the proceeds of an insurance policy on the deceased partner's life, or by arranging for the balance of his capital account to be left in the business as a loan, but failing these measures the sudden withdrawal of a large amount of capital may well cause serious dislocation of the smaller business, or even end its operations. The most serious defect of a partnership, however, is the difficulty of providing additional funds for expansion, and this may induce partners to admit new members for the sake of their capital, regardless of their fitness for taking an active part in controlling the business.

A partnership firm is not a persona *at law*; a partnership is an aggregate of its members. In the matter of procedure the Rules of Supreme Court make it possible for the firm to sue and be sued in its own name, but this does not confer upon it a legal personality as is possessed by a corporation. This makes the holding of property more difficult in the partnership. For example, land cannot be conveyed to the firm. Instead it is conveyed to some or all of the partners as legal owners who declare a *trust for sale* for all the partners in equity.

THE CROWN

The Crown consists of the Monarch and her Ministers, together with the Central Government departments staffed by civil servants, the armed forces, and the Privy Council which retains some powers, e.g. to arrange for the coronation of the Monarch. The police are not servants of the Crown, nor are the nationalized industries, e.g. British Coal, part of the Crown.

Until 1947 the Crown was not liable for the tortious acts of its servants, and was liable only to a limited extent in contract, though the actual tort-feasor could be sued and the Crown often stood behind him and paid the damages against him. Actions in contract could only be started by a cumbrous procedure known as a Petition of Right, with the consent of the Crown given on the advice of the Attorney-General.

The rather anomalous position at common law which has been outlined above arose out of the ancient maxim, 'The King can do no wrong,' which was extended to cover the activities of the Departments of State and their servants. The Crown Proceedings Act, 1947, and the Rules of the Supreme Court (Crown Proceedings) Act, 1947, which were required to support the Act in the matter of procedure, came into force together on 1 January, 1948, to rectify the matter.

The general effect of this legislation is to abolish the rule that the Crown is immune from legal process, though s. 40 preserves the immunity of the Monarch in a personal capacity from any liability in law, and to place the Crown as regards civil proceedings in the same position as a subject. Proceedings by Petition of Right are abolished, and all claims which might before the Act have been enforced by Petition of Right can be brought by ordinary action in accordance with the Act.

The Crown is now liable in contract where a Petition of Right could have been brought before, and also in tort. Regarding contractual claims, there are some limitations upon the rights of the other party, viz.—

(a) Executive necessity
In *Rederiaktiebolaget Amphitrite* v. *R.*, [1921] 3 K.B. 500, a neutral shipowner's vessel was detained in England although the British Legation in Stockholm had given an undertaking that it would not be. The basis of Rowlatt, J's., decision for the Crown was that the Government cannot by contract hamper its freedom of action in matters which concern the welfare of the State. This statement has been regarded as much too wide and is probably of very limited application.

The main result of the ruling of Rowlatt, J. is that contracts with the Government normally contain cancellation clauses which provide for compensation. In practice the Crown does not invoke the *Amphitrite* rule to avoid liability for such compensation.

(b) Parliamentary funds
In *Churchward* v. *R.*, [1865], 1 Q.B. 173, a contract to carry mail for eleven years was terminated by the Crown in the fourth year. Shee, J., in deciding for the Crown, held that it was a condition precedent of the contract that Parliament would allocate funds and if they chose not to there was no claim. This decision came under criticism in subsequent cases and the better view is that it is limited to cases where Parliament has *expressly* refused to grant the necessary funds.

This rule does, of course, cause hardship to contractors with the Government but it must be continued if the control of Parliament over public expenditure is to be maintained.

(c) Freedom to legislate
In *Reilly* v. *R.*, [1934] A.C. 176, a barrister who was employed by the Canadian Government had his contract terminated by legislation. The Privy Council found for the Crown on the ground that the Crown cannot by contract restrict its right to legislate.

(d) Contracts of employment
Here the position is as follows—

(i) *Military personnel.* Military employees cannot successfully claim against the Crown for breach of contract (*Dickson* v. *Combermere* (1863), 3 F. & F. 527) nor can they claim arrears of pay. (*Leaman* v. *R.*, [1920] 3 K.B. 663.)

(ii) *Civil servants.* At common law civil servants are dismissible at pleasure (*Shenton* v. *Smith*, [1895] A.C. 229) but can claim arrears of pay. (*Kodeeswaran* v. *A.G. of Ceylon*, [1970] 2 W.L.R. 456.) Furthermore, *dicta* in *Reilly* v. *R.*, [1934] A.C. 176 suggest that even at common law an express promise to employ for a definite period, the contract to be determinable only 'for cause', e.g. misconduct, overrides the implied term relating to dismissal at pleasure. The general rule that those in Crown service may be dismissed at the Crown's pleasure may be varied by legislation. A well-known example is the provision under which judges of the High Court and the Court of Appeal hold their offices during good behaviour. (S. 11(3), Supreme Court Act, 1981.)

However, the provisions of the Employment Protection (Consolidation) Act, 1978 which protect employees against unfair dismissal by actions before industrial tribunals apply to civil servants but not to military personnel. Civil servants have no action against the Crown in the ordinary courts of law in respect of dismissal. However, the practical effect of the provisions of the 1978 Act is that the Crown can only rarely be legally entitled to exercise its right to dismiss at pleasure without paying compensation of one sort or another.

Actions in tort will lie against the Crown for the torts of its servants or agents committed in the course of their employment; for breach of duty owed at common law by an employer to his servants; for breach of the duties attaching to the ownership, occupation, possession or control of property; and for breach of statutory duties, e.g. breaches of the duty of fencing dangerous machines under factory legislation.

The law as to indemnity and contribution under the Civil Liability (Contribution) Act, 1978 applies to Crown cases, so if the Crown is a joint tortfeasor, it can claim a contribution from fellow wrongdoers, which may, under s. 2(2) of the 1978 Act be a complete indemnity, so that where the Crown is led into publishing a libel, it may claim an indemnity against the party responsible. (See further p. 348.) The Law Reform (Contributory Negligence) Act, 1945, also applies to Crown cases. (See further p. 398.)

Under s. 10 of the Crown Proceedings Act, 1947 both the Crown and any member of the Armed Forces were immune from liability in tort in respect of the death of, or personal injury to another member of the Armed Forces on duty, provided that the death or injury arose out of service which ranked for the purpose of pension. This section was repealed in regard to acts or omissions causing injury after May 15, 1987 (See Crown Proceedings (Armed Forces) Act, 1987).

Actions under the Act may be brought in the High Court or a county court, and under ss. 17 and 18 of the 1947 Act the Treasury is required to publish a list of authorized government departments for the purposes of the Act, and of their solicitors. Actions by the Crown will be brought by the authorized department in its own name, or by the Attorney-General. Actions against the Crown are to be brought against the appropriate department, or, where there is doubt as to the department responsible or appropriate, against the Attorney-General.

In any civil proceedings by or against the Crown, the court can make such orders as it can make in proceedings between subjects, except that no injunction or order for specific performance can be granted against the Crown. The court can, in lieu thereof, make an order declaratory of the rights of the parties in the hope that the Crown will abide by it. No order for the recovery of land, or delivery up of property, can be made against the Crown, but the court may instead make an order that the plaintiff is entitled as against the Crown to land or to other property or to possession thereof. No execution or attachment will issue to enforce payment by the Crown of any money or costs. The procedure is for the successful party to apply for a certificate in the prescribed form giving particulars of the order. This is served on the solicitor for the department concerned, which is then required to pay the sum due with interest if any. The above exceptions show that, in spite of the Act, the rights of the subject against the Crown are still somewhat imperfect.

For historic, constitutional, and procedural reasons also, the Crown cannot be prosecuted for crime. Once again a nominated defendant is put forward; e.g. for a road traffic offence, such as using a lorry with a defective tyre, the principal transport officer of the Department concerned would probably be nominated. Unfortunately, this practice results in the officer concerned acquiring a long record of motoring convictions in a personal capacity. Accordingly, in *Barnett* v. *French*, [1981] 1 W.L.R. 848, the Court of Appeal suggested the use of the name 'John Doe' for the nominated defendant who, for the purpose of criminal records, would be shown as having a date of birth 'circa 1657'. The name 'John Doe' was used in civil actions from about that time onwards as part of a very elaborate procedure to prove the title to land. The procedure is no longer in use.

The general rule that statutes do not bind the Crown unless by express words or necessary implication is contained in s. 40 of the 1947 Act. It produced an absurd result when it was decided that public health and hygiene legislation did not apply to National Health Service hospital kitchens. This anomaly was abolished by the National Health Service (Amendment) Act, 1986 though the general immunity in other areas given by s. 40 was preserved.

Crown privilege in civil proceedings

As we have seen, either party to a civil action can, amongst other things, ask the court to order the other party to produce any relevant documents for inspection. (See p. 81.) Under s. 28 of the Crown Proceedings Act, 1947, this right lies against the Crown though the Crown could refuse to obey the order if production of the document(s) would be injurious to the public interest. It had been felt for some time that ministers whose departments were involved in civil litigation had abused this right. Undoubtedly, some plaintiffs failed in an action against the Crown because even the judge could not obtain access to documents necessary to support the claim. As a result of a number of cases of this kind, the House of Lords decided in *Conway* v. *Rimmer*, [1968] 1 All E.R. 874, that even though a minister certifies that production of a particular document would be against the public interest the judge may nevertheless see it and decide whether the minister's view is correct. If the judge cannot accept the minister's decision he may overrule him and order disclosure of the document to the party concerned. Thus the decision of the minister is no longer conclusive though it is unlikely that a judge would order disclosure if there was a danger of real prejudice to the national interest.

However, despite *dicta* in *Conway* v. *Rimmer* that claims to privilege on grounds of confidentiality could not expect sympathetic treatment, the courts vary in their interpretation of this view. (*Norwich Pharmacal Co.* v. *Commissioners of Customs and Excise*, 1973;[54] *Alfred Crompton Amusement Machines* v. *Customs and Excise Commissioners*, 1973.)[55]

Privilege in civil proceedings—the public interest ground

In the *Alfred Crompton* case the House of Lords was of opinion that 'Crown privilege' was not the best phrase to use in this context and that the phrase 'privilege on the ground of public interest' was more appropriate. That this is so is illustrated by the fact that privilege extends beyond cases against the Crown. Thus in *D.* v. *NSPCC*, [1977] 1 All E.R. 589 the House of Lords held that the NSPCC or a local authority is entitled to privilege from disclosing the names of its informants in relation to child neglect or ill-treatment.

The House of Lords decided in *British Steel Corporation* v. *Granada Television*, [1980] 3 W.L.R. 774 that the information media and their journalists do not have immunity from the obligation to disclose their sources of information when disclosure is necessary in the interests of justice. Their Lordships went on to say, however, that the remedy is equitable and may be withheld in the public interest.

Public interest privilege has really replaced the older Crown privilege. However, the latter has been included as a separate head of privilege to show the historical development.

SOME FUNDAMENTAL LEGAL CONCEPTS

Before entering into a more detailed study of the various branches of substantive law we must first of all examine certain fundamental legal concepts and classifications.

Private and public law

Private law is concerned with the legal relationships of ordinary persons in everyday transactions. It is also concerned with the legal position of corporate bodies and associations of persons the first of which are endowed with a special form of legal personality. Private law includes contract and commercial law, the law of tort, family law, e.g. divorce, adoption and guardianship, trusts and the law of property which involves a consideration of the rights which can exist in property and how property can be transferred.

Public law is concerned with the constitution and functions of the many different kinds of governmental organizations, including local authorities,

English Law

such as county and district councils, and their legal relationship with the citizen and each other. These relationships form the subject matter of constitutional and administrative law. Public law is also concerned with crime which involves the State's relationship with the power of control over the individual.

There is also a division into *criminal and civil law*. Criminal law is concerned with legal rules which provide that certain forms of conduct shall attract punishment by the State, e.g. homicide and theft. Civil law embraces the whole of private law and all divisions of public law except criminal law.

In order to understand the various branches of substantive private law which are considered in detail later, it is necessary to be able in particular to distinguish the following—

Contract

A contract is an agreement made between two or more persons which is intended to have legal consequences. Thus, if there is a breach of contract, the parties can go to court and obtain a remedy. We shall see in the chapter on contract which agreements the courts will enforce, under what conditions they are enforceable, and what remedies are available to injured parties. It should be noted that the parties to a contract enter voluntarily into their obligations; the function of the law is merely to enforce or adjudicate on such agreements.

Tort

A tort, on the other hand, is a civil wrong independent of contract. It arises out of a duty imposed by law, and a person who commits a tortious act does not voluntarily undertake the liabilities which the law imposes on him. There are many kinds of tort with a common characteristic; injury of some kind inflicted by one person on another. Nuisance, trespass, slander and libel are well-known civil wrongs. The typical remedy in this branch of the law is an action for damages by the injured party against the person responsible for the injury. Such damages are designed not to punish the wrongdoer but to compensate the injured party.

Crime

A crime is in a different category. It is difficult to define a crime, but it is a public offence against the State, and, while an individual may be injured, the object of a criminal charge is to punish the offender, not to compensate the victim though under the provisions of the Powers of Criminal Courts Act, 1973, compensation orders can now be made. (See p. 74.) Criminals are prosecuted, usually by a Crown Prosecutor, and if found guilty receive the appropriate punishment.

Trusts

A trust arises where one person holds property for the benefit of another. Suppose a man wishes to provide for his children when he dies; he may

184

leave them some of his property on trust, particularly if they are minors, i.e. under age 18 years. He will appoint trustees in whom the property will be vested (legally owned), but they will not benefit from the proceeds, since the income arising from the trust property will have to be devoted to the purposes of the trust; in this case for the benefit of the children, who are called the beneficiaries or the *cestuis que trust* (pronounced 'setty que trust'). Trusts may also be set up by living persons. The characteristics of a trust are that the trustees own the property but the *cestuis que trust* get the benefits.

It must not be assumed that all acts fall into these tidy categories. Certain breaches of trust are also criminal offences. Some activities may be both torts and crimes, and an act which is a breach of contract is often a tort. Thus, if a taxi-driver drives dangerously and injures a passenger, he is liable to that passenger for breach of contract and negligence. He may also have committed the crime of dangerous driving for which he may be prosecuted.

Some common legal relationships

The law recognizes and defines certain common relationships. The following, in particular, have relevance to the various branches of substantive law dealt with in later chapters.

Agency

It is quite common to find parties having the relationship of principal and agent. Sometimes a person (the principal) wishes to have certain tasks carried out—he may wish to sell a house or buy shares in a company. He therefore employs an estate agent or a stockbroker to carry out his purposes. Sometimes an agent is a specialist who carries out a limited range of duties, e.g. an auctioneer who sells a wardrobe put into an auction. Sometimes he has wider powers, and may even be able to bind the principal in all the ways the principal could bind himself, as where the agent has a power of attorney.

An agent may be specifically appointed as such, but in some cases an agent acquires his status without specific authority being given to him, and such an agent may bind his principal by what is called usual authority. If P appoints A to be the manager of an hotel, A may be able to bind P in a contract although he had no actual authority to make it, for the law is not solely concerned with the actual authority of an agent but regards him as having the usual powers of an agent of his class. It follows that the usual powers of an hotel manager will be relevant in deciding the sort of agreement which A can make on behalf of P. The doctrine of usual authority does not apply where the third party knows that the agent has no authority to make the contract.

An agent's powers may also be extended in an emergency. If A is a carrier of perishable goods for P, he may be able to sell them on behalf of P if the goods are deteriorating and he cannot get P's instructions with regard to disposal. A becomes an agent of necessity for the purpose of sale, though his actual authority is to carry the goods. Agency may also arise out of conduct resulting in apparent authority. If a husband pays the debts which his wife incurs with a local dressmaker, he may be liable to pay for an expensive article of clothing which she buys without his consent, because the husband has, by his conduct, led the dressmaker to believe that the wife has power to bind her husband in contracts of this nature. This type of agency is not peculiar to the relationship of husband and wife and could arise wherever P holds out A as having authority to make contracts on P's behalf. It is also possible in certain circumstances for a principal to ratify, i.e. adopt, the contracts of his agent, even though the agent had no actual authority when making the contract.

At one time, if a person appointed an agent to manage his or her affairs, the appointment became invalid when the person making the appointment lost mental capacity. However, under the Enduring Powers of Attorney Act, 1985 it is possible to enter into an agency agreement which does not terminate on the principal's loss of mental capacity.

Bailment

A bailment arises when one person (the bailor) hands over his property to the care of another (the bailee). The reasons for such a situation are many. The bailee may have the custody of the property by way of loan or for carriage. The article may be pledged, or left with another to be repaired or altered. Sometimes the bailee has the mere custody of the goods; sometimes he may use the property, as when he 'purchases' a radio set under a hire-purchase (or consumer credit) agreement or borrows a lawn mower. In all cases of bailment, the property or ownership remains with the bailor; the possession with the bailee.

A bailment is an independent legal transaction and need not necessarily originate in a contract. When X hands his goods to Y under a bailment Y has certain duties in regard to the care of the goods even though the bailment is not accompanied by a contract. Thus Y may be held liable for negligent damage to the goods even though he had not been promised any money or other benefit for looking after them. Bailment is considered in more detail on p. 428.

Lien

A lien is a right over the property of another which arises by operation of law and can be independent of any contract. In its simplest form it gives a creditor, such as a watch repairer, the right to retain possession of a debtor's property, in this case his watch until he has paid or settled the debt, incurred in this case as a result of repairing the watch. Lien is considered in more detail on p. 461.

7 The law of contract

A contract may be defined as an *agreement*, enforceable by the law, between two or more persons to do or abstain from doing some act or acts, their intention being to create *legal relations* and not merely to exchange mutual promises, both having given something, or having promised to give something of *value as consideration* for any benefit derived from the agreement.

The definition can be criticized in that some contracts turn out to be unenforceable and, in addition, not all legally binding agreements are true contracts. For example, a transaction by deed under seal derives its legally binding quality from the special way in which it is made rather than from the operation of the laws of contract, e.g. a deed is enforceable even in the absence of valuable consideration. In consequence, transactions under seal are not true contracts at all. Nevertheless, the definition at least emphasizes the fact that the basic elements of contracts are (i) an agreement, (ii) an intention to create legal relations, and (iii) valuable consideration.

THE ESSENTIALS OF A VALID CONTRACT

The essential elements of the formation of a valid and enforceable contract can be summarized under the following headings—

(i) There must be an offer and acceptance, which is in effect the agreement.

(ii) There must be an intention to create legal relations.

(iii) There is a requirement of written formalities in some cases.

(iv) There must be consideration (unless the agreement is under seal).

(v) The parties must have capacity to contract.

(vi) There must be genuineness of consent by the parties to the terms of the contract.

(vii) The contract must not be contrary to public policy.

In the absence of one or more of these essentials, the contract may be void, voidable, or unenforceable.

CLASSIFICATION OF CONTRACTS

Before proceeding to examine the meaning and significance of the points enumerated above the following distinctions should be noted.

Void, voidable and unenforceable contracts

A *void* contract has no binding effect at all and in reality the expression is a contradiction in terms. However, it has been used by lawyers for a long time in order to describe particular situations in the law of contract and its usage is now a matter of convenience. A *voidable* contract is binding but one party has the right, at his option, to set it aside. An *unenforceable* contract is valid in all respects except that it cannot be enforced in a court of law by one or both of the parties should the other refuse to carry out his obligations under it. However, as we shall see, an unenforceable contract does have some life because it can be used as a *defence to a claim*. (See further p. 217.)

Executed and executory contracts

A contract is said to be *executed* when one or both of the parties have done all that the contract requires. A contract is said to be *executory* when the obligations of one or both of the parties remain to be carried out. For example, if A and B agree to exchange A's scooter for B's motor cycle and do it immediately, the *possession* of the goods and the *right* to the goods are transferred *together* and the contract is *executed*. If they agree to exchange the following week the *right* to the goods is transferred but not the *possession* and the contract is *executory*. Thus an *executed* contract conveys a *chose in possession* (see p. 424), while an *executory* contract conveys a *chose in action* (see p. 424).

Specialty and simple contracts and contracts of record

Specialty contracts are also called contracts under seal, or deeds. All the terms of such contracts are reduced to writing and then the contract is signed, sealed and delivered. However, in *First National Securities Ltd v. Jones*, [1978] 2 All E.R. 221, the Court of Appeal decided that a document could be regarded as a deed even though not sealed where the parties clearly intended it to operate as a deed. In that case the parties intended to create a legal charge over land which requires a document under seal. (See further p. 449.) The legal charge was not in fact sealed but operated as if it had been in giving the lenders of money a legal charge over the property used as security since this was clearly the intention of the parties.

The above case is likely to be followed where the parties have given consideration as where a deed is used for a contractual obligation such as a security for a loan. However, where there is no consideration, as in a deed of gift, a seal would probably be required.

The signature is usually attested, i.e. witnessed. A deed operates from the date of delivery, though a deed is presumed to have been delivered on the day of the date of the deed, unless this can be rebutted by evidence to the contrary. Delivery may be (*a*) *actual*, where the deed is handed over to the other party, or (*b*) *constructive*, where the party delivering the deed touches the seal with his finger and says: 'I deliver this my act and deed!' This is then construed as delivery and the deed becomes operative. In many cases, however, there is no delivery, actual or constructive, and once a deed has been signed by the parties, it will be extremely difficult for either of them to show that the deed was not delivered. (*Per* Danckwerts, J., in *Stromdale and Ball Ltd* v. *Burden*, [1952] 1 All E.R. 59.)

The general law of contract *requires* a deed in the case of a lease of more than three years, which must be under seal if it is to create a legal estate. In addition a transfer of property, e.g. a conveyance, which imposes covenants (or agreements) in regard, for example, to the use of the land, is a contract and must also be by deed. In addition, a conveyance is an *agreement* by the vendor of land to convey his title or ownership and the *agreement* of the purchaser to take it.

Sometimes a deed is delivered subject to a condition, e.g. that is not effective until the purchase money has been paid; or is delivered now, but is not to become operative until some future time. In these cases, the deed is not operative until the condition is carried out or the stipulated time has elapsed and such a deed has the special name of 'escrow'.

There are two forms of escrow—

(i) Where the deed is delivered to a third party who delivers to the other party when the condition is fulfilled.

(ii) Where the deed is delivered to the other party directly, but is not operative until the condition is fulfilled.

An escrow is useful where a person is selling property but will be abroad before completion. He may sign and deliver an escrow before leaving the country so that the deal can be completed if the conditions are carried out.

A deed has certain characteristics which serve to distinguish it from a simple contract—

(a) Merger. If a simple contract is afterwards embodied in a deed made between the same parties, the simple contract merges into, or is swallowed up by the deed, for the deed is the superior document. But if the deed is only intended to cover part of the terms of the previous simple contract, there is no merger of that part of the simple contract not covered by the deed.

(b) Limitation of actions. The right of action under a specialty contract is barred unless it is brought within twelve years from the date when the cause of action arises on it, i.e. when the deed could first have been sued upon. Time does not run from the date of making the deed. A similar right of action is barred under a simple contract after only six years. (See further p. 304.)

(c) Consideration is not essential to support a deed, though specific performance will not be granted if the promise is gratuitous. (See p. 316.) Simple contracts must be supported by consideration.

(d) Estoppel. Statements in a deed tend to be conclusive against the party making them, and although he might be able to prove they were not true, the rule of evidence called 'estoppel' will prevent him from doing this by excluding the very evidence which would be needed. In modern law, however, a deed does not operate as an estoppel where one of the parties wishes to bring evidence to show fraud, duress, mistake, lack of capacity, illegality, or that the deed is an escrow. In addition, where a deed is rectifiable (see p. 233) the doctrine of estoppel by deed does not bind the parties to it. (*Wilson* v. *Wilson*, 1969.)[56]

Simple contracts form the great majority of contracts, and are sometimes referred to as parol contracts. This class includes all contracts not under seal, and for their enforcement they require consideration. Simple contracts may be made orally or in writing, or they may be inferred from the conduct of the parties; but no simple contract can exist which does not arise from a valid offer and a valid acceptance supported by some consideration. When these elements exist, the contract is valid in the absence of some vitiating element such as lack of capacity of one of the parties, lack of reality of consent, or illegality or impossibility of performance.

THE FORMATION OF CONTRACT

In order to decide whether a contract has come into being it is necessary to establish that there has been an *agreement* between the parties. In consequence it must be shown that an *offer* was made by one party (called the offeror) which was *accepted* by the other party (called the offeree) and that *legal relations* were intended.

OFFER AND ACCEPTANCE

A contract is an agreement and comes into existence when one party makes an offer which the other accepts. The person making the offer is called the offeror, and the person to whom it is made is called the offeree. An offer may be express or implied. Suppose X says to Y—'I will sell you this watch for £5,' and Y says—'I agree.' An express offer and acceptance have been made; X is the offeror and Y the offeree.

Alternatively Y may say to X—'I will give you £5 for that watch.' If X says—'I agree,' then another express offer has been made, but Y is the offeror and X is the offeree. In both cases, the acceptance brings a contract into being. In order to find out who makes the offer and who the acceptance, it is necessary to examine the way in which the contract is negotiated.

Offer

An offer is an undertaking by the offeror that he will be bound in contract by the offer if there is a proper acceptance of it. An offer may be made to a specific person or to any member of a group of persons, and in cases of an offer embracing a promise for an act designed to produce a unilateral contract, to the world at large (*Carlill* v. *Carbolic Smoke Ball Co.*, 1893),[57] though sometimes what looks like an offer may be no more than an invitation to make an offer, or, as it is sometimes called, an *invitation to treat*. If I expose in my shop window a coat priced £50, this is not an offer to sell. It is not possible for a person to enter the shop and say: 'I accept your offer; here is the £50.' It is the would-be-buyer who makes the offer when tendering the money. (*Pharmaceutical Society of Great Britain* v. *Boots Cash Chemists Ltd*, 1953.)[58] If by chance the coat has been wrongly priced, I shall be entitled to say: 'I am sorry; the price is £100,' and refuse to sell. An invitation to treat is often merely a statement of the price and not an offer to sell.

The same principles have been applied to prices set out in price lists, catalogues, circulars, newspapers and magazines (*Spencer* v. *Harding*, 1870,[59] and *Partridge* v. *Crittenden*, 1968),[60] and a prospectus issued by a company in order to invite the public to subscribe for its shares is an invitation to treat so that members of the public make an offer to buy the shares when they make application for them and the company is the acceptor in so far as shares are alloted to a subscriber.

In other cases, such as automatic vending machines, the position is doubtful, and it may be that such machines are invitations to treat. However, it is more likely that the provision of the machine represents an implied offer which is accepted when a coin is put into it. However, it does seem that if a bus travels along a certain route, there is an *implied offer* on the part of its owners to carry passengers at the published fares for the various stages, and it would appear that when a passenger puts himself either on the platform or inside the bus, he makes an *implied acceptance* of the offer, agreeing to be bound by the company's conditions and to pay the appropriate fare: *per* Lord Greene *obiter* in *Wilkie* v. *London Passenger Transport Board*, [1947] 1 All E.R. 258.

With regard to negotiations for the sale of land, the same principles are again applied with perhaps this difference, that in a case involving the sale of land where *specific performance is a possible remedy* the court may be reluctant to grant that remedy unless the intention to contract is very clear. (*Harvey* v. *Facey*, 1893,[61] and *Clifton* v. *Palumbo*, 1944.)[62]

Problems relating to contractual offers have risen in the case of *auction sales* but the position is now largely resolved. An advertisement of an auction is not an offer to hold it. (*Harris* v. *Nickerson*, 1873.)[63] At an auction the bid is the offer; the auctioneer's request for bids is merely an invitation to treat. (*British Car Auctions* v. *Wright*, 1972.)[64] The sale is complete when the hammer falls, and until that time any bid may be withdrawn. (*Payne* v. *Cave*, (1789) 3 Term Rep. 148.)

The position when the auction is without reserve is not absolutely certain because it has never been clearly decided whether an advertisement to sell articles by auction without any reserve price constitutes an offer to sell to the highest bidder. It is at any rate clear that s. 57(2) of the Sale of Goods Act, 1979 prevents any *contract of sale* coming into existence if the auctioneer refuses to accept the highest bid. There remains the possibility once the auction of an item has begun that the auctioneer may be liable in damages on the basis of a breach of warranty that he has authority to sell, and will sell, the goods to the highest bidder. This device appears to be sanctioned by the decision of the Court of Exchequer Chamber in *Warlow* v. *Harrison*, (1859) 1 E & E 309.

Acceptance

Once the existence of an offer has been proved, the court must be satisfied that the offeree has accepted the offer, otherwise there is no contract. An agreement may nevertheless be inferred from the conduct of the parties. (*Brogden* v. *Metropolitan Railway*, 1877.)[65]

The person who accepts an offer must be aware that the offer has been made. Thus if B has found A's lost dog and, not having seen an advertisement by A offering a reward for its return, returns it out of goodness of heart, B will not be able to claim the reward. He cannot be held to accept an offer of which he is unaware. However, as long as the acceptor *is aware* of the making of the offer, his motive in accepting it is immaterial. (See *Carlill* v. *Carbolic Smoke Ball Co.*, 1893.)[57]

It should be noted that an acceptance brings the offer to an end because the offer then merges into the contract.

Conditional assent

An acceptance must be absolute and unconditional. One form of conditional assent is an acceptance 'subject to contract.' The law has placed a special significance on these words, and they are usually construed as meaning that the parties do not intend to be bound until a formal contract is prepared. (*Winn* v. *Bull*, 1877[66] and *Tiverton Estates Ltd* v. *Wearwell Ltd*, 1974.)[36]

In other cases of conditional assent, i.e. where the words 'subject to contract' are not used, the attitude of the court is not so predictable, but it would seem that if the court decides that the further agreement of the parties is not a condition precedent to the formation of the contract, but is merely part of the performance of an already binding agreement, the court will enforce the contract. (*Filby* v. *Hounsell*, 1896[67] and *Michael Richards Properties* v. *Corporation of Wardens of St. Saviour's Parish, Southwark*, 1975.)[68]

A potential purchaser can generally recover any deposit paid if he does not continue with a 'subject to contract' purchase. (*Chillingworth* v. *Esche*, 1923.)[69]

The effect of the use of the words 'without prejudice' in letters forming the basis of negotiations between parties to a contract was considered by the court in *Tomlin* v. *Standard Telephones and Cables Ltd*, 1969.[70] It was decided that the words meant 'without prejudice to the position of the writer of it if the terms which he proposed therein were not accepted.' If the terms were accepted a binding contract was established.

Incomplete (or inchoate) agreements

While considering the matter of conditional assent, it is convenient to deal briefly with an additional problem which may face a court in certain of these cases.

A contract will not be enforced unless the parties have expressed themselves with reasonable clarity on the matter of essential terms. A situation may therefore exist in which the parties have gone through a form of offer and acceptance but this has left some terms unclear so that if either party wishes to avoid the contract he may claim to do so on the basis that he does not know precisely what to do in order to perform his part of it. The concept of the inchoate contract normally arises as a defence to an action for breach of contract.

In such a case it may be possible for the court to complete the contract by reference to a *trade practice* or *course of dealing* between the parties. (*Hillas* v. *Arcos*, 1932.)[71] Sometimes the agreement itself may provide a method of completion. (*Foley* v. *Classique Coaches Ltd*, 1934[72] and *Brown* v. *Gould*, 1971.)[73] However, if the court cannot obtain assistance from these sources, it will not usually complete the contract for the parties, and the contract, being *inchoate*, cannot be enforced. (*Scammell* v. *Ouston*, 1941.)[74] However, a covenant in a conveyance that the purchaser should be given 'the first option of purchasing . . . at a price to be agreed upon' certain adjoining land imposes an obligation on the vendor at least to offer the land at a price at which he is willing to sell. (*Smith* v. *Morgan*, [1971] 2 All E.R. 1500.)

However, it is necessary to distinguish between a term which has yet to be agreed by the parties and a term on which they have agreed but is in the event meaningless or ambiguous. In the first case, no contract exists unless the deficiency can be made good by the methods outlined above. In the second case, it may be possible to ignore the term and enforce the contract without it. (*Nicolene* v. *Simmonds*, 1953.)[75] However, if, as in *Scammell* v. *Ouston*, 1941,[74] the term is still being negotiated the contract will be inchoate and unenforceable. In addition, the term must be *clearly* severable from the rest of the contract, i.e. it must be possible to enforce the contract without it, which was the case in *Nicolene*[75] but not in *Scammell*.[74]

Counter-offer

A counter-offer is a rejection of the original offer and in some cases has the effect of cancelling it. Where the counter-offer *introduces a new term*, the original offer is cancelled (*Hyde* v. *Wrench*, 1840,[76] and *Northland Airlines Ltd* v. *Dennis Ferranti Meters Ltd*, 1970),[77] though the counter-offer may be accepted either expressly or by implication as in *Butler Machine Tool Co.* v. *Ex-cell-O Corp.* (*England*), 1979.[78] However, a simple request for information where the offeree merely *tries to induce a new term* may not amount to an actual counter-offer. (*Stevenson* v. *McLean*, 1880.)[79]

Retrospective acceptance

Acceptance may be retrospective, i.e. the parties may carry out certain acts on the assumption that a contract will eventually be made. When the acceptance is eventually made, it is capable of operating retrospectively, thus giving legal effect to everything that has been done before. That the contract is to operate retrospectively may be provided for by an express term in the contract or may be inferred from conduct as in *Trollope and Colls Ltd* v. *Atomic Power Constructions Ltd*, 1962.[80]

In the case of an invitation to submit tenders for the purchase of specific goods, as in *Spencer* v. *Harding*, 1870,[59] the person or company which asks for the tender will usually be regarded as making an invitation to treat. The tender is the offer and the person who asks for it may accept it or reject it as he thinks fit. If tenders are asked for an indefinite amount of goods, e.g. 'coal as required during 1989 not exceeding 100,000 tonnes' the 'acceptance' of such a tender results in a standing offer by the supplier to supply the goods set out in the tender as and when required by the person accepting it. Each time the buyer orders a quantity, there is a contract confined to that quantity; but if the buyer does not order any of the goods set out in the tender, or a smaller number than the supplier quoted for, there is no breach of contract. Conversely, if the person submitting the tender wishes to revoke his standing offer, he may do so, except in so far as the buyer has already ordered goods under the tender. These must be supplied or the tenderer is in breach of contract. (*Great Northern Railway* v. *Witham*, 1873.)[81]

Methods of acceptance

An acceptance may be made in various ways. It may be made in writing or orally, or at an auction by the fall of the hammer, but it must in general be communicated and communication must be made by a person authorized to make it. (*Powell* v. *Lee*, 1908.)[82] Silence cannot amount to acceptance (*Brogden* v. *Metropolitan Railway*, 1877)[65], except sometimes where there is the prior consent of the offeree which is, for example, implied in circumstances such as those in *Carlill's* case.[57] Thus if P says to Q: 'If I do not hear from you before noon tomorrow, I shall assume you accept my offer,' he will find he is unable, at least without Q's consent to this method of making a contract, to bind Q in this way, and Q need take no action at all. (*Felthouse* v. *Bindley*, 1862[83] and *Fairline Shipping Corporation* v. *Adamson*, 1974.)[84]

This rule of the common law goes some way towards preventing inertia selling, though protection is now given by the Unsolicited Goods and Services Acts, 1971 and 1975. The Acts provide for fines to be made on persons making demands for payment for goods which they know are unsolicited. If the demand is accompanied by threats a higher scale of fines applies. Furthermore, under s. 1 of the 1971 Act, unsolicited goods may be kept by the recipient without payment *after a period of 30 days* provided the recipient gives notice to the sender asking that they be collected, or *after six months* even if no such notice has been given.

There are some cases in which the offeror is deemed to have waived communication of the acceptance. This occurs in the case of *unilateral contracts* such as promises to pay money in return for some act to be carried out by the offeree. Performance of the act operates as an acceptance, and no communication is required. (*Carlill* v. *Carbolic Smoke Ball Co.*, 1893.)[57]

The offeror may stipulate a method of acceptance and where this is done it would seem that, if the offeror makes it clear that one method only will suffice, then there is no contract unless the offeree accepts by the method prescribed. Nevertheless, in such a case the offeror could waive his right to have the acceptance communicated in a given way and agree to the substituted method. Apart from the American case of *Eliason* v. *Henshaw*, 1819,[85] which takes a rather strict view of the method of communication, it seems that if the offeror has stipulated a method of acceptance *but does not make it clear that only one method will suffice*, then a quicker or equally expeditious method will be effective, since there is no prejudice to the offeror if he learns that the offer has been accepted sooner than, or at the same time as he would have known had the offeree used the prescribed method. (*Manchester Diocesan Council for Education* v. *Commercial and General Investments Ltd*, 1969[86] and *Yates Building Co.* v. *R.J. Pulleyn & Sons* (*York*), 1975.)[87] Certainly an offer by telemessage is good evidence of the offeror's desire for a quick reply so that a reply by letter would probably be ineffective.

If the offeror has not stipulated a method of acceptance, the offeree may choose his own method, though where acceptance is by word of mouth it is not enough that it be spoken, it must actually be heard by the offeror. In this connection an interesting development occurs with the use of the telephone and teleprinter. Since these are methods of instantaneous communication, it is held that the contract is not complete unless the apparent communication takes place. (*Entores Ltd* v. *Miles Far East Corporation*, 1955.)[88]

Use of post and telemessages

The general rule is that acceptance must be communicated to the offeror and that the contract is made *when* and *where* the acceptance is received by the offeror. (*Entores Ltd.* v. *Miles Far East Corporation*, 1955.)[88]

However, if the post is the proper method of communication between the parties then acceptance is deemed complete immediately the letter of acceptance is posted, even if it is delayed or is lost or destroyed in the post so that it never reaches the offeror. (*Household Fire Insurance Co.* v. *Grant*, 1879.)[89] Nevertheless, the letter of acceptance must be properly addressed and properly posted (*Re London and Northern Bank, ex parte Jones*, 1900),[90] and the court must be satisfied that it was within the contemplation of the parties that the post might be used as a method of communicating acceptance. Thus in *Henthorn* v. *Fraser*, [1892] 2 Ch. 27 the post was the proper method of accepting an offer, which the offeror had, in fact, handed to the offeree, because the parties lived in different towns.

The rule relating to acceptance by post is a somewhat arbitrary one seeming to favour the offeree and is in practice kept within narrow confines. If the statements of the parties or the provisions of a statute appear to exclude the rule then the court will not apply it. (*Holwell Securities Ltd* v. *Hughes*, 1974.)[91] Where there is a misdirection of the letter containing the offer, then the offer is made when it actually reaches the offeree, and not when it would have reached him in the ordinary course of post. (*Adams* v. *Lindsell*, 1818.)[92] In contrast with the rule regarding acceptance by post, a letter of revocation is not effective until it actually reaches the offeree, whereas a letter of acceptance is effective when it is posted. (*Byrne* v. *Van Tienhoven*, 1880.)[93] A telemessage is effective as an acceptance when it is given to the Telecom operator. (*Cowan* v. *O'Connor*, (1880) 20 Q.B.D. 640 decided this was so with the telegram, which was the predecessor of the telemessage.)

The better view is that, in English law, an acceptance cannot be recalled once it has been posted even though it has not reached the offeror. Thus, if X posted a letter accepting Y's offer to sell goods, X could not withdraw the acceptance by telephoning Y and asking him to ignore the letter of acceptance when it arrived, and Y could hold X bound by the contract if he wished to do so. This is obvious, the rules being what they are, since otherwise Y would be bound when the letter was posted, and X would be reserving the right to withdraw his acceptance during the transit of the letter even though Y was still bound. However, by Scots law the effect of an acceptance can be altered after posting. (*Dunmore (Countess)* v. *Alexander*, 1830.)[94]

There is some controversy as to whether agreement can result from *identical cross-offers*. For example, suppose X by letter offers to sell his bicycle to Y for £50, and Y, by means of a second letter, which crosses X's letter in the post, offers to buy X's bicycle for £50. Can there be a contract? The matter was discussed by an English court in *Tinn* v.

Hoffman, (1873) 29 L.T. 271, and the court's conclusion was that no contract could arise, though this is regarded as too strict a view of the position. The matter is still undecided by the judges and it is possible to hold the view that today a contract would come into being where it appears that the parties have intended to create a legally binding agreement on the same footing.

Revocation of offer

The general rule is that *an offer may be revoked at any time before* it is accepted. (*Payne* v. *Cave*, (1789) 3 Term Rep. 148.) Once an offer has been accepted it cannot be withdrawn merely because the offeror made a mistake, provided the offeree was not aware of that mistake. Thus in *Centrovincial Estates* v. *Merchant Investors Assurance, The Times*, 8 March, 1983 it was held by the Court of Appeal that a landlord who offered to grant a tenancy at a stated rent of £65,000 which the tenant accepted, could not withdraw the offer merely because he made a mistake in the offer and had intended to ask for a rent of £126,000. If the offeree knows that the offeror is mistaken the contract may be void for unilateral mistake. (See p. 231.)

Sometimes there is what is known as an option attached to the offer, and time is given to the offeree in which to make the decision whether to accept the offer or not. If the offeror agrees to give seven days, then the offeree may accept the offer at any time within seven days, or he need not accept at all. However, the offeror need not keep the offer open for seven days but can revoke it (*Routledge* v. *Grant*, (1828),[95] unless the offeree has given some consideration for the option.

The consideration need not be adequate. For example, let us suppose that on Monday Fred offers to sell Joe his house for £30,000 and Joe says 'Give me until Friday to think it over and I will buy you a pint'. The purchase of the pint for Fred or the promise to buy him a pint is enough to give Joe an enforceable option on the house. Again, in *Mountford* v. *Scott*, 1974 (see p. 734) the Court of Appeal held that a West Indian who signed an agreement in consideration of £1 giving the plaintiff an option to purchase his house for £10,000 within six months, was bound by that option in spite of the fact that only £1 was given for it.

The option is really a separate contract to allow time to decide whether to accept the original offer or not. It was thought at one time that, where the option to buy property was not supported by consideration, the offer could be revoked by its sale to another, but in modern law it is necessary for the offeror to communicate the revocation to the offeree either himself, or by means of some reliable person. (*Stevenson* v. *McLean*, 1880.)[79]

Before leaving the topic of options, it should be noted that the Law Commission in Working Paper No. 60 entitled 'Firm Offers' and published in 1975 criticized the present position under which a promise to keep an offer open will not be binding on the offeror unless consideration for the promise is given by the offeree (though of course this is not necessary where the option is made in a deed), on the grounds that it is contrary to business practice and also contrary to the law of most foreign countries. The Law Commission make a provisional recommendation that 'an offeror who has promised that he will not revoke his offer for a definite time should be bound by the terms of that promise provided that the promise has been made in the course of business'.

Revocation, to be effective, must be communicated to the offeree before he has accepted the offer. The word 'communication' merely implies that the revocation must have come to the knowledge of the offeree. (*Byrne* v. *Van Tienhoven*, 1880.)[93]

Presumably the offeree cannot ignore facts suggesting an attempt to communicate a revocation. If A offers B a car and before B accepts A posts a letter of revocation which B receives but, recognizing A's handwriting, does not open until he has written and posted a letter of acceptance, it would seem unfair to regard A as bound in contract and he would probably not be. In addition, it appears from statements made in the House of Lords in *Eaglehill Ltd* v. *J. Needham* (*Builders*) *Ltd*, [1972] 3 All E.R. 895 (see further p. 863), where their Lordships were discussing notice of dishonour of a bill of exchange, that an offer would be revoked when the letter of revocation 'was opened in the ordinary course of business or would have been so opened if the ordinary course of business was followed'.

Communication may be made directly by the offeror or may reach the offeree through some other reliable source. Suppose X offers to sell a car to Y and gives Y a few days to think the matter over without actually giving him a valid option. If, before Y has accepted, X sells the car to Z and Y hears from P that X has in fact sold the car, it will be of no avail for Y to purport to accept and try to enforce the contract against X, provided P is a reliable source. (*Dickinson* v. *Dodds*, 1876.)[96]

Where the offer consists of a promise in return for an act, as where a reward is offered for the return of lost property, the offer, although made to the whole world, can be revoked as any other offer can. It is thought to be enough that the same publicity be given to the revocation as was given to the offer, even though the revocation may not be seen by all the persons who saw the offer.

A more difficult problem arises when an offer which requires a certain act to be carried out is revoked after some person has begun to perform the act but before he has completed it. If, for example, X offers £1000 to anyone who can successfully swim the Channel, and Y, deciding he will try to obtain the money, starts his swim from Dover, can X revoke his offer from a helicopter when Y is half-way across the Channel? One view is that he cannot on the grounds that an offer of the kind made by X is two offers in one, namely (i) to pay £1000 to a successful swimmer and (ii) something in the nature of an option to hold the offer open for a reasonable time once performance has been embarked upon, so that the person trying to complete the task has a reasonable time in which to do so.

Other lawyers reach the same conclusion by distinguishing between the acceptance of the offer and the consideration necessary to support it. As regards the latter, the completion of the act involved is necessary before the offeror can be required to pay any money because until the act is completed the necessary consideration has not been supplied. However, acceptance may be assumed as soon as the offeree has made a beginning on the performance of the contract and proof of the fact that he has made a beginning makes revocation impossible. The problem could have arisen in *Carlill's* case[57] if the company had tried to revoke its offer after Mrs Carlill had started to perform the contract by using the Smokeball.

The matter also came before the Court of Appeal in *Errington* v. *Errington*, [1952] 1 All E.R. 149. In that case a father bought a house for his son and daughter-in-law to live in. He paid the deposit but the son and daughter-in-law made the mortgage payments after the father gave the building society book to the daughter-in-law, saying 'Don't part with this book. The house will be your property when the mortgage is paid.' The son left his wife who continued to live in the house. It was held by the Court of Appeal that neither the father nor the plaintiff, his widow, to whom the house was left by will, could eject the daughter-in-law from the property. As Lord Denning said: 'The father's promise was a unilateral contract—a promise of the house in return for their act of paying the instalments. It could not be revoked by him once the couple entered on the performance of the act, . . .' The Court went on to decide that the son and daughter-in-law would be fully entitled to the house once they had made all the mortgage repayments.

Lapse of time

If a time for acceptance has been stipulated, then the offer lapses when the time has expired. If no time has been stipulated, then the acceptance must be within a reasonable time. What is reasonable is determined by the court from the circumstances of the case. (*Ramsgate Victoria Hotel Co.* v. *Montefiore*, 1866,[97] and *Manchester Diocesan Council for Education* v. *Commercial and General Investments Ltd*, 1969.)[86] However, where the offer is made by telemessage it is likely to lapse very quickly.

Conditional offers

An offer may terminate on the happening of a given event if it is made subject to a condition that it will do so, e.g. that the offer is to terminate if the goods offered for sale are damaged before acceptance. Such a condition may be made expressly in the contract as where, e.g. a seller offers to sell goods by tender from time to time subject to a condition that the seller can himself obtain adequate supplies. It may also be implied from the circumstances. (*Financings Ltd* v. *Stimson*, 1962.)[98]

Effect of death of a party

The effect of death would appear to vary according to the type of contract in question, whether the death is that of the offeror or offeree, and whether death takes place before or after acceptance.

(a) Death of offeror before acceptance
It would seem that if the contract envisaged by the offer is not one involving the personality of the offeror, the death of the offeror may not, until notified to the offeree, prevent acceptance. (*Bradbury* v. *Morgan*, 1862.)[99] However, there is a contrary point of view based on the judgment of Mellish, L.J. in *Dickinson* v. *Dodds*, 1876[96] where he said 'it is admitted law that, if a man who makes an offer dies, the offer cannot be accepted after he is dead . . .'. If the contract envisaged by the offer does involve a personal relationship, such as an offer to act as agent, then the death of the offeror certainly prevents acceptance.

(b) Death of offeree before acceptance
Once the offeree is dead, there is no offer which can be accepted. His executors cannot, therefore, accept the offer in his stead. The offer being made to a living person can only be accepted by that person and assumes his continued existence. The rule would seem to apply *whether the proposed contract involves a personality relationship or not*. (*Re Cheshire Banking Co., Duff's Executors' Case*, 1886.)[100]

(c) Death of parties after acceptance
Death after acceptance has normally no effect unless the contract is for personal services, when the liability under the contract ceases. Thus, if X sells his car to Y and before the car is delivered X dies, it would be possible for Y to sue X's personal representatives for breach of contract if they were to refuse to deliver the car. But if X agrees to play the piano at a concert and dies two days before the performance, one could hardly expect his personal representatives to play the piano in his stead.

Offer and acceptance not identifiable

Sometimes the usual processes of offer and acceptance are not easily identifiable and yet a contract is deemed to exist. (See *The New Zealand Shipping Co. Ltd* v. *A.M. Satterthwaite & Co. Ltd*, 1974 at p. 664.) There are also situations of collateral contract. These derive from another main contract, and for purposes of illustration reference should be made to *Clarke* v. *Dunraven*, 1897[101] where the main contract was with the yacht club, and *Rayfield* v. *Hands*, 1958[102] where the main contract was with the company through the memorandum and articles.

INTENTION TO CREATE LEGAL RELATIONS

The law will not necessarily recognize the existence of a contract simply because of the presence of mutual promises. Some agreements are not intended to be the subject of legal actions, and if the parties expressly declare, or clearly indicate in their agreement, that they do not intend to assume contractual obligations, then the law accepts and implements their intention. There are many promises made which are of such a nature that no reasonable person could imagine that there was any intention to create legal relations. If P invites Q to dinner, he does not also invite an action for damages if he fails to keep the appointment.

In deciding the question of intention the courts have regard to two main presumptions: (i) that domestic agreements are unenforceable without proof of intention to create legal relations and (ii) that commercial agreements are enforceable in the absence of clear proof that legal relations were not intended.

The subject can be considered under three headings—

(i) Cases where the parties have not expressly denied their intention to create legal relations

(a) Advertisements
It is commonplace in business to advertise goods by making extravagant claims as to their efficacy, often supported by promises or assurances of a vague character if the goods do not live up to expectations. The construction placed by the courts on such statements depends on the circumstances, but where a company deposits money in the bank against possible claims, then the court is likely to hold that legal relations were contemplated. (*Carlill* v. *Carbolic Smoke Ball Co.*, 1893.)[57] But not all advertisements are treated as serious offers, and advertising 'puffs' are often treated as mere sales talk; otherwise the courts would be perpetually passing judgment on the vaguely expressed merits or demerits of a host of products. It is unlikely, for example, that a statement such as 'you will not go far wrong with a Roma camera' would be regarded as contractual.

In addition, of course, advertisements are generally regarded as invitations to treat and not offers unless the advertisement can result in a unilateral contract when it may be regarded as an offer. (See *Carlill's* case.)[57]

(b) Family agreements
Many of these cannot be imagined to be the subject of litigation, but some may be. The question is basically one of construction, and the court looks at the words and the surrounding circumstances. With regard to agreements between husband and wife, it is difficult to draw precise conclusions from the decided cases. However, it seems that the courts will not enforce these agreements where—

(i) the husband and wife were living together even though the relationship was strained when the agreement was made—on the ground perhaps that in the view of the court it would be unseemly and distressing to use legal proceedings for settling marital differences (*Balfour* v. *Balfour*, 1919).[103] However, where husband and wife were not living together when the agreement was made the court may enforce it, particularly where the agreement is intended to deal with a break-up of the marriage. (*Merritt* v. *Merritt*, 1970.)[104]

(ii) the words used by the parties were uncertain—on the ground perhaps that uncertainty in deciding upon important terms of the agreement leads to the conclusion that there was no intention to create legal relations. Thus in *Gould* v. *Gould*, [1969] 3 All E.R. 728, where a husband on leaving his wife said that he would pay her £15 per week 'so long as I can manage it', it was held that there was no contractual intention because this had been negatived by the vague, uncertain, or discretionary terms of the arrangement.

An agreement between husband and wife is much more likely to be enforced if it is clear and unequivocal. This might be achieved if the parties made an agreement supported by a simple note or memorandum setting out the terms and preferably prepared by a solicitor.

It should be noted that agreements of a non-domestic nature made between husband and wife may be enforceable, e.g. a husband may be his wife's tenant.

In family agreements other than those between husband and wife, the court will more readily reach the conclusion that legal relations can be inferred and the injured party may be given a remedy. (*Simpkins* v. *Pays*, 1955[105] and *Snelling* v. *John G. Snelling Ltd*, 1972.)[106] This is particularly true where one of the parties has altered his position to his detriment in reliance on the promises of the other (*Parker* v. *Clark*, 1960),[107] or where the family relationship has been destroyed by disagreements. (*Snelling*. v. *John G. Snelling Ltd*, 1972.)[106] However, the terms must be certain otherwise the court will conclude that there was no contractual intent. (*Jones* v. *Padavatton*, 1969.)[108]

(iii) *Other cases*. In other situations whether there is an intention to create legal relations must be deduced by the court from the circumstances of the case. Thus in *Peck*. v. *Lateu*, (1973) 117 S.J. 185, two ladies attended bingo sessions together and had an arrangement to pool their winnings. On one of them winning an additional 'Bonanza' prize of £1107, and claiming that it was not covered by the sharing arrangement, it was held, by Pennycuick, V.C., that the arrangement was in the circumstances legally binding and therefore the plaintiff was entitled to share in the prize.

However, in the case of clubs and societies, many of the relationships which exist and promises which are made are enforceable only as moral obligations. Thus, if a person competes for a prize in a local golf competition and is the winner, he or she may not be able to sue for the prize if it is not otherwise forthcoming.

It should also be borne in mind that quotations and estimates may be passed from one person to another without any intention that they should be legally binding *at that stage*.

(ii) Cases where the parties expressly deny any intention to create legal relations

Some types of agreement, which would normally be the subject of a contract, are expressly taken outside the scope of the law by the parties' agreeing to rely on each other's honour. (*Jones* v. *Vernon's Pools Ltd*, 1938.)[109] In such cases there is a standardized agreement and the advantage of excluding legal action appears to be predominantly in favour of one of the parties. However, as the judges appear to recognize, the pools companies are particularly susceptible to fraud by those who would try to conceal late entries made after the games had finished and it is probably for this reason that the courts accept honour clauses which the pools companies can invoke where they suspect that an investor is fraudulent, rather than to go to court over the matter. It has been pleaded, but without success, that standardized agreements which exclude the possibility of legal redress are against public policy, and clearly if such procedures become widespread Parliament may have to intervene.

There is no such objection where businessmen reach agreements at arm's length, and if the parties expressly declare or clearly indicate that they do not wish to assume contractual obligations, then the law accepts and implements their decision, though the agreement is enforceable so far as it has been acted upon. (See *Rose and Frank Co.* v. *Crompton and Brothers Ltd*, 1925.)[110]

As we have seen, it is also well settled that an agreement to sell land which is made 'subject to contract' is not a binding contract and that the effect of these words is to negative any contractual intention.

(iii) Statutory provisions

Sometimes an Act of Parliament renders an agreement unenforceable. Thus under s. 1 of the Law Reform (Miscellaneous Provisions) Act, 1970, a contract of engagement which is, in effect, an agreement to marry, is not enforceable at law since there is a statutory presumption that there was no intention to create legal relations. Thus actions for breach of promise are no longer possible.

Furthermore, under the Post Office Act, 1969, the acceptance of letters and packets for transmission does not give rise to an enforceable contract between the Post Office and the sender. (See p. 345.)

Finally, under s. 18 of the Trade Union and Labour Relations Act, 1974, collective agreements between trade unions and employers (or employers' associations) concerning industrial conditions (hours, wages, holidays, procedures in disputes, and so on) are presumed *not* to be intended to be legally enforceable *unless* they are in writing and contain a provision to that effect.

CONSIDERATION

Definition and related matters

Consideration, which is essential to the formation of any contract not made under seal, was defined in *Currie* v. *Misa*, (1875) L.R. 10 Ex 153 as—

> Some right, interest, profit or benefit accruing to one party, or some forbearance, detriment, loss or responsibility given, suffered or undertaken by the other.

Paying (or promising to pay) money in return for the supply of goods or services constitutes the most common form of consideration.

Consideration may be *executory*, where the parties exchange promises to perform acts in the future, e.g. C promises to deliver goods to D and D promises to pay for the goods; or it may be *executed*, where one party promises to do something in return for the act of another, rather than for the mere promise of future performance of an act. Here the performance of the act is required before there is any liability on the promise. Where X offers a reward for the return of his lost dog, X is buying the act of the finder, and will not be liable until the dog is found and returned.

The definition in *Currie* v. *Misa* suggests that consideration always refers to the type called executed consideration since it talks of 'benefit' and 'detriment', whereas in modern law executory contracts are enforceable. Perhaps the definition given by Sir Frederick Pollock is to be preferred—

> An act of forbearance of one party, *or the promise thereof*, is the price for which *the promise* of the other is bought, and *the promise* thus given for value is enforceable.

This definition which was adopted by the House of Lords in *Dunlop* v. *Selfridge*, 1915,[111] fits executory consideration as well as executed. The 'promise for a promise' concept really means that consideration can consist in a promise to act in the future, e.g. to deliver goods or to pay for goods.

CONSIDERATION IN RELATION TO FORMATION OF A CONTRACT

There are a number of general rules governing consideration in terms of the *formation* of a contract—

(a) Simple contracts must be supported by consideration. This has a long history, but in practical terms it is the common law's way of limiting the number of agreements which can be brought before the courts for enforcement. Other legal systems have required, e.g. part performance by one or other of the parties or some kind of formality. The effect of the consideration rule is that in English law an agreement, even if the parties intend legal relations, is not a contract unless it is supported by consideration or made under seal.

(b) Consideration need not be adequate, but must have some value, however slight. The courts do not exist to repair bad bargains, and though consideration must be present, the parties themselves must attend to its value. (*Thomas* v. *Thomas*, 1842[112] and *Mountford* v. *Scott*, 1974.) (See p. 734.) However, where the consideration for a transaction is of very small value, it may raise a suspicion of fraud, duress or undue influence on the part of the person gaining the advantage. However, what is offered by way of consideration must be capable of expression in terms of economic value or at least the giving up of some right. (See *White* v. *Bluett*, 1853.)[113] That apart, acts or omissions even of a trivial nature may be sufficient to support a contract. (*Chappell* v. *Nestlé*, 1959.)[114]

Although there were once arguments to the contrary, it is now accepted that forbearance to sue may be adequate consideration. It is not necessary to show that the action would have succeeded but merely that if it had been brought to trial it might have done. (See *Horton* v. *Horton*, 1961.)[115] Thus the court would be unlikely to accept that a bookmaker could supply consideration by forgoing a claim against a client for stake money. Such an action, being based on an illegal transaction, could have no hope of success.

A self-seeking act in itself may not suffice, and in the case of *Carlill* v. *Carbolic Smoke Ball Co.*, 1893,[57] the consideration was provided not by using the smoke ball to cure influenza, but by the unpleasant method of its use. A gift promised conditionally may be binding, if the performance of the condition causes the promisee trouble or inconvenience, e.g. 'I will give you my old car if you will tow it away.' So too may a gift of property with onerous obligations attached to it, e.g. a promise to give away a lease would be binding, if the donee promised to perform the covenants to repair and pay rent. A promise to give away shares which were partly paid up would be good, if the donee promised to pay the outstanding calls.

The concept of *bailment* gives rise to problems because a person may be held liable for negligent damage to or loss of goods in his care, although he received no money or other consideration for looking after them. (*Coggs* v. *Bernard*, 1703,[116] and *Gilchrist Watt and Sanderson Pty.* v. *York Products Pty.*, 1970.)[117] However, confusion can best be avoided by regarding bailment as an independent transaction, which has characteristics of contract and tort but is neither. It seems that when X hands his goods to Y under a bailment Y has certain duties in regard to the care of the goods, whether the bailment is accompanied by a contract or not.

Of course the court may be invited to refuse a claim on the contract by a person who has given inadequate consideration by invoking the doctrine of inequality of bargaining power. (See further p. 271.) However, at the present time the basis of this doctrine, which has been applied in particular by Lord Denning, is somewhat vague and has not, as yet, received much direct judicial support.

(c) Consideration must be sufficient. Sufficiency of consideration is not the same thing as adequacy of consideration. The concept of sufficiency arises in the course of deciding whether the acts in question *amount to consideration at all*. This situation arises where the consideration offered by the promisor in an act which he is already bound to carry out. Thus, the discharge of a *public duty* imposed by law is not consideration (*Collins* v. *Godefroy*, 1831);[118] nor is the performance of a *contractual duty* already owed to the defendant (*Vanbergen* v. *St Edmund's Properties Ltd*, 1933;[119] *Stilk* v. *Myrick*, 1809).[120] However, where the contractual duty is not precisely coincident with the public duty but is in excess of it, performance of the contractual duty may provide consideration (*Glasbrook Bros Ltd* v. *Glamorgan County Council*, 1925[121] and *Ward* v. *Byham*, 1956)[122] and the actual performance of an outstanding contractual obligation may be sufficient to support a promise of a further payment by a third party. (*Shadwell* v. *Shadwell*, 1860.)[123]

(d) Consideration must be legal. An illegal consideration makes the whole contract invalid. (See further p. 272.)

(e) Consideration must not be past. Sometimes the act which one party to a contract puts forward as consideration was performed before any promise of reward was made by the other. Where this is so, the act in question may be regarded as *past consideration* and will not support a contractual claim. This somewhat technical rule seems to be based on the idea that the act of one party to an alleged contract can only be regarded as consideration if it was carried out in response to some promise of the other. Where this is not so, the act is regarded as gratuitous, being carried out before any promise of reward was made. (*Re McArdle*, 1951.)[124]

However, there are exceptions to this rule—

(i) Where services are rendered at the express or implied request of the promisor in circumstances which raise an implication of a promise to pay. (*Re Casey's Patents, Stewart* v. *Casey*, 1892.)[125] This exception is not entirely a genuine one since the promisor is assumed to have given an implied undertaking to pay at the time of the request, his subsequent promise being regarded as deciding merely *the actual amount to be paid*. In this situation the act, which follows the request but precedes the settling of the reward, is more in the nature of *executed consideration* which, as we have seen, will support a contract.

(ii) A debtor or his duly authorized agent can make a written acknowledgement of the debt to the creditor or his agent (s. 29 Limitation Act 1980). Time begins to run again from the date of acknowledgement. However, once a debt is statute barred it cannot be revived in this way (s. 29(7) *ibid.*). (See further p. 304). Again, this exception is not wholly genuine since the Limitation Act, 1980, does not provide that past consideration will support the subsequent acknowledgement of debt. The Act simply states that *no consideration of any kind* need be sought.

(iii) Section 27 of the Bills of Exchange Act, 1882, provides that an antecedent debt or liability will support a bill of exchange. (See further p. 471.) This genuine exception was probably based on a pre-existing commercial custom.

(f) Consideration must move from the promisee, i.e. the person to whom the promise is made (the promisee) must give some consideration for it to the promisor. From this arises the doctrine of privity of contract which is considered below.

Privity of contract

This means that in general third parties cannot sue for the carrying out of promises made by the parties to a contract. Thus, if a contract between A and B requires B to benefit C, the privity rule prevents C from suing B. However, A may sue B if B breaks the contract, and the court may award A damages (*Jackson* v. *Horizon Holidays*, 1975)[126] or may grant a decree of specific performance under which B must perform the contract for the benefit of C. (*Beswick* v. *Beswick*, 1967.)[127] If A and C are, in fact, both parties to the contract with B then C still cannot sue B unless he has provided some consideration. Merely being a party to the contract is not enough. Even though C may be named in the document, if any, which records and constitutes the contract between A and B, or may be a party to their oral deliberations, if he does not undertake anything in return for a promise from A or indeed from B, then he is not participating in a bargain with A and/or B and is not a party to the contract. This view is based upon the belief that the 'privity' rule is merely an aspect of the rule that 'consideration must move from the promisee'. The application of the rule is illustrated by *Tweddle* v. *Atkinson*, 1861,[128] *Dunlop* v. *Selfridge*, 1915,[111] and *Dunlop* v. *New Garage and Motor Co. Ltd*, 1915.[129]

However, there are cases in which a person is allowed to sue upon a contract to which he is not a party—

(a) A principal, even if undisclosed, may sue on a contract made by an agent. This exception is perhaps more apparent than real, because in fact the principal is the contracting party who has merely acted through the instrumentality of the agent.

(b) Attempts have been made to modify the rule of privity by invoking the equitable doctrine of the constructive trust. Thus, if A and B agree for consideration that B should confer a benefit on C, it may be possible to regard B as a constructive trustee for C of the benefit of the contract. C would then have an action against B if the latter had received the benefit and would not pass it on to C, or against A. However, if A were sued, B would be joined in the action, as a co-plaintiff if he consented or as a co-defendant if he did not. The application of this principle has always been uncertain and limited, and the courts do not seem eager to extend it. However, one aspect of this equitable doctrine has been established in the commercial world, and was recognized by the House of Lords in *Les Affréteurs Réunis Société Anonyme* v. *Walford*, 1919.[130]

(*c*) The assignee of a debt or chose in action may, if the assignment is a legal assignment, sue the original debtor. (See further p. 464.) In addition, contractual rights may be transferred by the original debtor where he gives a *recognition* or *acknowledgement* of the fact that a fund which he holds for the original creditor is available for payment to a third party. (*Shamia* v. *Joory*, 1958.)[131]

(*d*) The holder for value of a bill of exchange can sue prior parties and the acceptor. (See p. 470.)

(*e*) Under the Resale Prices Act, 1976, s. 26, the supplier of goods is given a statutory cause of action, so that he may enforce against a person not a party to the contract of sale a condition as to a minimum re-sale price. However, the re-sale price agreement must have been approved under the provisions of the Resale Prices Act, 1976, otherwise there can be no enforcement of it. (See p. 286.) Books are one of the few items approved for this purpose. (See *Net Book Agreement*, 1957, [1962] 3 All E.R. 751.)

(*f*) Certain other exceptions are to be found in statute, e.g. s. 11 of the Married Women's Property Act, 1882, provides that if a man insures his life for the benefit of his wife and/or children, or a woman insures her life for the benefit of her husband and/or children, a trust is created in favour of the objects of the policy, who, although they are not parties to the contract with the insurance company, can sue upon it. In addition the policy moneys are not liable for the deceased's debts.

(*g*) The position in land law is that benefits and liabilities attached to or imposed on land may in certain circumstances follow the land into the hands of other owners. (*Smith and Snipes Hall Farm* v. *River Douglas Catchment Board*, 1949,[132] and *Tulk* v. *Moxhay*, 1848.)[133]

(*h*) As regards bankers' commercial credits, it is common commercial practice for an exporter, E, to ask the buyer of the goods, B, to open, with his banker, a credit in favour of E, the credit to remain irrevocable for a specified time. B agrees with his banker that the credit should be opened and, in return, promises to repay the banker, and usually gives him a lien over the shipping documents. The banker will also require a commission for his services. B's banker then notifies E that a credit has been opened in his favour, and E can draw upon it on presentation of the shipping documents.

It will be seen that E and B's banker are not in privity of contract. It might be thought that this could give rise to problems in the unlikely event that the banker did not pay. However, this is not so. In fact the buyer/customer of the bank cannot stop payment. In *Malas* (*Hamzeh*) v. *British Imex*, [1958] 1 All E.R. 262 the plaintiffs, who were buyers of goods, applied to the court for an injunction restraining the sellers (who were the defendants in the case) from drawing under a credit established by the buyer's bankers. The Court of Appeal refused to grant this injunction and Jenkins, L.J. said: 'The opening of a confirmed letter of credit constitutes a bargain between the banker and the vendor of the goods which imposes on the banker an absolute obligation to pay . . . .' Sellers, L.J. said that there could well be exceptions where the court could exercise a jurisdiction to grant an injunction, as where there was a fraudulent transaction. However, in other situations the binding nature of the banker's commercial credit is an exception to the doctrine of privity of contract.

There are also similar developments in the field of performance bonds. These are illustrated by *Edward Owen Engineering Ltd* v. *Barclays Bank International Ltd*, 1977.[134]

(*i*) Attempts have also been made to modify the rule of privity by an appropriate interpretation of s. 56(1) of the Law of Property Act, 1925.

The subsection provides that 'a person may take an immediate or other interest in land or other property, or the benefit of any condition, right of entry, covenant or agreement over or respecting land or other property, although he may not be named as a party to the conveyance or other instrument.'

Section 205(1) of the 1925 Act provides that 'unless the context otherwise requires, the following expressions have the meanings hereby assigned to them . . . (xx) "property" includes any thing in action and any interest in real or personal property.'

Section 56(1) certainly applies to provisions in covenants concerning land. Thus, if X derives his title to real property under a conveyance of, say, 1977, he can enforce a restrictive covenant regarding the use of the land made in an earlier conveyance between other parties. However, some judges, including Lord Denning, have been of the opinion that the word 'property' in s. 56(1) should be interpreted as covering all things in action, even contractual rights in a contract not concerned with land. This interpretation would open the door to claims formerly barred by the rule of privity, and would do away with the rule in *Tweddle* v. *Atkinson*, 1861,[128] and similar cases.

The matter came before the House of Lords in *Beswick* v. *Beswick*, 1967,[127] and their Lordships could not accept the wider interpretation of s. 56(1) advocated by Lord Denning and others in previous cases, but regarded the subsection as being limited to cases concerning real property.

(*j*) As a result of the decision in *Snelling* v. *John G. Snelling Ltd*, 1972[106] it would appear that if A makes a contract with B for the benefit of C, as where C is A's employee and A has included an exemption clause in a contract with B which excludes the liability of A and C, then if there is an action between B and C, say, for C's negligence, C will not be able to claim the benefit of the contract as such by way of defence but A can apply for an injunction to prevent the action between B and C coming to trial, or if it has come to trial, apply for a stay of proceedings under the Supreme Court Act, 1981. In either case if all parties are before the court and B's case would, if pursued, fail, then the court may dismiss the claim and not merely stop the action.

CONSIDERATION VIEWED IN RELATION TO THE DISCHARGE OR VARIATION OF A CONTRACT

All that has so far been said in regard to consideration relates to the *formation* of a contract. As we have seen there must be offer, acceptance, consideration and intention to create legal relations in order to bring a contract into existence. The rules are rather different where a contract is to be *discharged* or *varied*. There are a number of ways in which a contract may be discharged, all of which will be dealt with later. However, the one with which we are now concerned is *discharge by agreement* under which contract A is to be discharged by a new contract, B, the question being to what extent does contract B require consideration? The attitude of the common law is different from that of equity, as we shall see.

Common law—the doctrine of accord and satisfaction

At common law if A owes B £10 and wishes to discharge that obligation by paying B £9 he must—

(i) obtain the agreement (accord) of B; and
(ii) provide B with some consideration (satisfaction) for giving up his right to £10 unless the release is under seal.

This is the common law doctrine of accord and satisfaction. The doctrine is an ancient one and an early example of it is to be found in the judgment of Brian, C.J. in *Pinnel's Case*, (1602), 5 Co. Rep., 117a. Pinnel sued Cole in debt for what would now be £8.50 which was due on a bond on 11 November, 1600. Cole's defence was that at Pinnel's request he had paid him £5.12 on 1 October and that Pinnel had accepted this payment in full satisfaction of the original debt. Although the court found for Pinnel on a technical point of pleading, it was said that—

(*a*) payment of a lesser sum on the due day in satisfaction of a greater sum cannot be any satisfaction for the whole; but

(*b*) payment of a smaller sum at the creditor's request before the due day is good consideration for a promise to forego the balance for it is a benefit to the creditor to be paid before he was entitled to payment and a corresponding detriment to the debtor to pay early.

The first branch of the rule in *Pinnel's Case* was much criticized but was approved by the House of Lords in *Foakes* v. *Beer*, 1884[135] and the doctrine then hardened because of the system of binding precedent. However, the practical effect of the rule is considerably reduced under common law by the following exceptions which have been made to it—

(i) Where there is a dispute as to the sum owed. If the creditor accepts less than he thinks is owed to him the debt will be discharged. For example, A says that B owes him £11. B says it is only £9. A agrees to take £10. Then, even if it can be proved that A was owed £11, he cannot recover the £1. He has compromised his claim.

(ii) Where the creditor agrees to take something different in kind, e.g. a chattel, the debt is discharged by substituted performance. Thus, if A gives B a watch worth £5 and B is agreeable to taking it, then the debt of £10 will be discharged. The legal theory here seems to be that the article given may be worth more than the balance of the debt and the court is not prepared to be a valuer. In this connection it should be noted that a cheque for a smaller sum no longer constitutes substituted performance. (*D. & C. Builders Ltd* v. *Rees*, 1965.)[136]

(iii) The payment of a smaller sum before the larger is due gives the debtor a good discharge. This is the second branch of the rule in *Pinnel's Case*.

(iv) If a debtor makes an arrangement with his creditors to compound his debts, e.g. by paying them 85p. in the £1, he is satisfying a debt for a larger sum by the payment of a smaller sum. Nevertheless, it is a good discharge, the consideration being the agreement by the creditors with each other and with the debtor not to insist on their full rights. (*Good* v. *Cheesman*, 1831[137] and see *Snelling* v. *John G. Snelling Ltd*, 1972.)[106]

(v) Payment of a smaller sum by a third party operates as a good discharge. (*Welby* v. *Drake*, 1825.)[138]

Equity—the doctrine of promissory estoppel

There has always been some dissatisfaction with the common law rule of accord and satisfaction. After all, if A owes B £10 and B agrees to take £9, as he must before there can be any question of discharging the obligation of A to pay £10, why should B be allowed afterwards to break his promise to take £9 and succeed in an action against A simply because A gave him no consideration?

It was to deal with this sort of situation that the equitable doctrine of promissory estoppel was propounded, first by Lord Cairns in *Hughes* v. *Metropolitan Railway*, (1877) 2 App. Cas. 439 and later by Denning, J. (as he then was) in the *High Trees Case*, 1947[139] and later by the House of Lords in *Tool Metal Manufacturing Co. Ltd* v. *Tungsten Electric Co. Ltd*, 1955.[140]

The doctrine of estoppel is basically a rule of evidence under which the court, surprisingly enough, is not prepared to listen to the truth.

It occurs at common law out of physical conduct. Suppose A and B go into a wholesaler's premises and A asks for goods on credit. The wholesaler, who knows that B is creditworthy, but has no knowledge of A, is not prepared to give credit until A says 'do not worry, you will be paid, B is my partner.' If B says nothing and A receives the goods on credit and does not pay, then B could be sued for the price, even though he can produce evidence that he was not in fact A's partner. This evidence will not be admitted because the wholesaler relied on a situation of partnership created by B's conduct.

Promissory estoppel in Equity is very little different except that the estoppel arises from a *promise*, not *conduct*. The common law does not recognize an estoppel arising out of a promise.

As a result of the above decisions and others (as indicated below) the doctrine of promissory estoppel has the following ingredients—

(*a*) It arises from a promise made with the intention that it should be acted upon.

(*b*) It was once thought that the person who had received the promise must do something to show that he had relied on it. If A, a landlord, said B could pay only half his usual rent while he was unemployed, it was thought that B would have to show, for example, that he had spent what should have been the rent money on travelling expenses to find work in the district. Reliance upon the promise in this way is not, it would appear, a necessary requirement. All that would seem to be necessary is that the debtor has made the part-payment; he need not do anything else. (*Alan* v. *El Nasr*, 1972.)[141]

(*c*) It relates only to variation of a contract by agreement and does not affect the requirement of consideration on formation of contract. (*Combe* v. *Combe*, 1951.)[142]

(*d*) So far as the rule has been developed in cases, it merely *suspends* rights but does not totally discharge them because it does not preclude enforcement of the original contract after reasonable notice has been given. Thus it does not create a binding variation for the future. (*Tool Metal Manufacturing Co. Ltd* v. *Tungsten Electric Co. Ltd*, 1955.)[140]

(*e*) The promise must be freely given and not extorted by threats. (*D. & C. Builders Ltd* v. *Rees*, 1965.)[136]

(*f*) Of considerable importance is a *dictum* by Lord Denning in *D. & C. Builders* v. *Rees*, 1965[136] that the rule could be developed to the point at which it operated, not merely to suspend rights, but to preclude enforcement of them. If this point is reached, then if A owes £10 and B agrees to take £9, A will be discharged from his obligation to pay £10 without the need for consideration.

Such a situation would involve a virtual overruling of *Foakes* v. *Beer*, 1884[135] and would put an end to the first branch of the rule in *Pinnel's Case* which is that payment of a lesser sum on the due day in satisfaction of a greater sum cannot be any satisfaction for the whole. Although in the past a number of *dicta* by Lord Denning have been incorporated into the *rationes* of subsequent decisions, the position outlined in (*f*) above has not as yet been reached. If that position is reached, then *Foakes* v. *Beer* would be applied only to extorted promises.

The rule of equitable estoppel has relevance in discharge of a contract by performance. (See p. 711.) Although the agreed date of delivery must usually be complied with in a contract of sale, the buyer may waive the condition relating to the date of delivery and accept a later date. Such a waiver may be binding on him whether made with or without consideration. It was held by Lord Denning in *Charles Rickards Ltd* v. *Oppenhaim*, 1950 (see p. 711) that the binding nature of a waiver without consideration might be based on the *High Trees Case*[139] (i.e. a promissory estoppel to accept a later delivery date). Alternatively, the seller may rely on s. 11(2) of the Sale of Goods Act, 1979, which states: 'Where a contract of sale is subject to any condition to be fulfilled by the seller, the buyer may waive that condition.'

Equitable estoppel—other applications

The principle of Equity on which promissory estoppel is based is one of general application and may be applied whenever the court feels it is necessary in the interests of justice to do so. For examples of its use in situations not concerned with discharge or variation of contract see *Durham Fancy Goods* v. *Michael Jackson* (*Fancy Goods*) *Ltd*, 1968.[143]

FORMALITIES

We have already discussed the main differences between contracts under seal and simple or 'parol' contracts. In most cases, it does not matter which of the various forms of simple contract is used and a contract made orally or by conduct will usually be just as effective as a written one. Exceptionally, however, written formalities are required.

Contracts which must be made by deed

A lease of more than three years should be made by deed, otherwise no legal estate is created. If there is no deed then there is in equity a contract for a lease. This is an estate contract under s. 2(3)(iv) of the Law of Property Act, 1925. It is enforceable against third parties who acquire the freehold from the landlord only if it has been registered at the Land Registry. Registration gives notice to the whole world. Failure to register makes the contract void against a later purchaser of the freehold from the landlord for a consideration, even though in fact the purchaser *knows* the lease exists. (S. 199(1), Law of Property Act, 1925.) The purchaser could turn out the tenant if the lease was not registered. However, where it is registered the tenant is protected. (See further p. 457.)

As we have already seen at p. 188, it was decided in *First National Securities Ltd* v. *Jones*, [1978] 2 All E.R. 221 that a document given for consideration can operate as a deed even without a seal, provided that the evidence established that the document was executed as a deed.

Contracts which must be in writing

The following simple contracts are required by statute to be in writing—

(*a*) cheques, other bills of exchange and promissory notes (see p. 468);

(*b*) contracts of marine insurance. A contract of marine insurance is inadmissible in evidence unless embodied in a written policy in accordance with the Marine Insurance Act, 1906, ss. 22 and 24, and signed on behalf of the insurers. The policy may be executed when the contract is made or afterwards, even after the property is lost. (*Mead* v. *Davison* (1835), 3 Ad. & El. 303.)

(*c*) acknowledgements of debt (see p. 304).

Consumer credit transactions under £15,000, including hire-purchase and moneylending, must be in writing and properly executed. Where this is not so the agreement is *unenforceable* by the creditor or the owner, against the debtor or the hirer unless the court thinks, in the circumstances, it is fair to allow enforcement of the contract by the creditor or owner. (Consumer Credit Act, 1974, ss. 61, 65, and 127.)

The reason why the consumer credit provisions require writing is mainly so that the document can contain information which the Act and government regulations require as part of consumer protection. In addition, the writing is a protection for the consumer in the sense that it gives him a written statement of the terms of the contract should there afterwards be any dispute about it. For similar reasons under s. 1 of the Employment Protection (Consolidation) Act, 1978 employees have to be given written particulars of the terms of the contract of service which they have entered into. (See further p. 323.)

Contracts which must be evidenced in writing

In two cases writing, though not essential to the formation of a contract, is needed for evidential purposes, and in its absence the courts will not enforce the agreement. These two special cases are—

(i) contracts of guarantee, and

(ii) contracts for the sale or other disposition of land or any interest in land.

The Statute of Frauds, 1677, originally set out six classes of contracts which required this evidential writing. The provision concerning land was embodied in s. 40 of the Law of Property Act, 1925, as part of the consolidation of the law of property. The provision regarding guarantees remained after the Statute of Frauds was largely repealed by the Law Reform (Enforcement of Contracts) Act, 1954, which, having served its purpose, was itself repealed by the Statute Law (Repeals) Act, 1974.

Even in these cases the writing need not be in the form of a contract, but may be the exchange of letters or other memoranda; and where one party has partly performed his side of the contract, the courts may dispense with the need for written evidence. Further, the absence of a memorandum must be specially pleaded by the party seeking to rely on its absence, otherwise the court will hear oral evidence to prove the contract.

These rules apply to contracts of guarantee but they do not apply to contracts of indemnity. It is necessary, therefore, to distinguish between these two. In a contract of indemnity, the person giving the indemnity makes himself primarily liable by using such words as, 'I will see that you are paid.' In a contract of guarantee, the guarantor expects the person he has guaranteed to carry out his obligations, and the substance of the wording would be, 'If he does not pay you, I will.' An indemnity does not require writing because it does not come within the wording of the Statute of Frauds; a guarantee requires a memorandum. (*Mountstephen* v. *Lakeman*, 1871.)[144]

In this connection it should be noted that it is an essential feature of a guarantee that the person giving it is totally unconnected with the contract he guarantees except by reason of his promise to pay the debt. Thus, a *del credere* agent who for an extra commission promises to make good losses incurred by his principal in respect of the unpaid debts of third parties, introduced by the agent, may give a guarantee but because his undertaking to reimburse his principal is part of a wider transaction, i.e. agency, writing is not required.

Difficulties have arisen in the application of the provisions concerning land in cases dealing with the sale of crops. A distinction must be made between *fructus naturales* (natural products of the soil, or the products of things which do not have to be sown each year) and *fructus industriales* (crops produced annually by man). Thus, an agreement to sell growing timber or grass must be evidenced in writing, but an agreement to sell growing potatoes need not be. (*Parker* v. *Staniland*, (1809) 11 East, 362.) However, if the *fructus naturales* are to be cut at once by either party and therefore *no further benefit is to be derived from the soil* the contract is regarded as one for the sale of goods and no memorandum is required. (*Marshall* v. *Green*, (1875) 1 C.P.D., 35.)

The memorandum

The memorandum in writing, to satisfy the courts in the two cases where it is now required, need not be made when the contract is made, but must exist before the action is brought. This illustrates clearly that writing is not required in order to form the contract but merely as evidence of it.

Thus a written memorandum obtained after the contract was made orally will be enough to make it enforceable.

There are four main requirements of the memorandum—

(i) It must contain the names or a sufficient description of the parties. It must state which is the buyer and which is the seller, and it is not sufficient to call the seller the vendor, since the court wishes to ascertain the owner and not the person who purports to sell. It is sufficient if they are described so as to be capable of identification, even if this involves the admission of some oral evidence (*Carr* v. *Lynch*, 1900)[145] and the fact that one of the parties is misnamed will not prevent the contract being enforced if he can be identified by reference to characteristics other than his name. (*F. Goldsmith (Sicklesmere) Ltd* v. *Baxter*, 1969.)[146]

(ii) The subject matter of the contract must be described so that it can be identified, and all the material terms of the contract must be stated. However, the subject matter may be sufficiently described without going into great detail, e.g. a memorandum recording the sale of '24 acres of land at Totmanslow in the parish of Draycott, in the County of Stafford', was held sufficient on proof that the seller had no other land there. (*Plant* v. *Bourne*, [1897] 2 Ch. 281.) The absence of a material term may make the memorandum ineffective (*Tweddell* v. *Henderson*, 1975),[147] though not if it is beneficial to only one party and the other party agrees to carry it out or the party to benefit agrees to waive it. (*Hawkins* v. *Price*, 1947,[148] and *Scott* v. *Bradley*, 1971.)[149]

(iii) The consideration must appear, except in contracts of guarantee. In the latter case s. 3 of the Mercantile Law Amendment Act, 1856, dispenses with the necessity for setting out the consideration, but it must exist. The consideration for a guarantee is usually the extension of credit. It follows that the guarantee must be given before the credit was extended, otherwise it is for past consideration, and is unenforceable unless made under seal.

(iv) The memorandum must contain the signature of the party to be charged or his agent properly authorized to sign. This means in effect that there may be cases where one party has a sufficient memorandum to found an action, whereas the other may lack the necessary signature. The rule is made less rigid by a somewhat liberal interpretation of the word signature, and it may take any form so long as it was intended to be a signature. (*Caton* v. *Caton*, 1867.)[150] It may be printed, typed, or stamped, and mere initials or an identifying mark will suffice. It need not be at the end of the document, but may be in the middle or at the beginning. In the case of an auction sale, the auctioneer or his clerk signs for both buyer and seller.

(v) The memorandum must not be made 'subject to contract'. As a result of the judgments in *Tiverton Estates* v. *Wearwell Ltd*, 1974[36] it would now appear that any writing which denies that there was any contract; does not admit that there was any contract; says that the parties are in negotiation; or says that there was an agreement 'subject to contract' does not satisfy s. 40 of the Law of Property Act, 1925, because none of them contains any recognition or admission of the existence of a contract.

The rigidity of the writing requirements of s. 40 of the 1925 Act is mitigated by the fact that the memorandum need not be a single document, but may consist of a number of connected documents. Oral evidence will be admitted to connect them if *(a)* one refers to the other; or *(b)* the documents are *prima facie* connected, since in the latter case proof of connection is not entirely oral. (*Pearce* v. *Gardner*, 1897,[151] and *Timmins* v. *Moreland Street Property Ltd*, 1958.)[152]

Effect of absence of memorandum

In the absence of a memorandum the contract is not void at common law but is unenforceable, although it may sometimes be relied upon as a defence. Thus, if X orally agrees to let Y dig for gravel on X's land, Y would not commit a trespass if he entered on the land to dig. If, however, X asks him to leave and Y refuses, then he may become a trespasser in spite of the contract, since it was at best a licence which has now been withdrawn. It follows that if the contract is not void, money paid or property transferred under it cannot be recovered, unless there is a total lack of consideration. For example, where a purchaser pays a deposit on the sale of land it cannot be claimed back so long as the vendor is ready and willing to perform the contract. (*Monnickendam* v. *Leanse*, 1923.)[153]

Although the common law requires a written memorandum, there may still be equitable remedies, and equity will grant specific performance in suitable cases where the plaintiff has partly performed his agreement. This remedy, which is stated by s. 40(2) of the Law of Property Act, 1925 to be available, is particularly appropriate in contracts for the sale or other disposition of land. The basis of this equitable jurisdiction probably stems from the maxim: 'Equity will not allow a statute to be used as an engine of fraud.'

The following conditions must exist before the doctrine can operate—

(a) The contract must be one of which specific performance will be granted. Specific performance is a discretionary remedy and it follows that; 'He who comes to Equity must come with clean hands.' It will not be granted where the court thinks damages are an adequate remedy, and not normally in the case of contracts with minors. (See p. 317.) This seems in the context of written memoranda to confine the remedy to contracts concerning land, because Equity will not specifically enforce a guarantee.

(b) Relationship of the act(s) of part performance to the alleged contract.
The plaintiff's part performance need not be unequivocally or exclusively
referable to the contract alleged. It is sufficient if it proves the existence
of some contract and is consistent with the contract which the plaintiff
claims exist. This principle was applied by Stamp, J., in *Wakeham* v.
MacKenzie, 1968[154] and by the Court of Appeal in *Steadman* v.
Steadman, 1973.[155]

However, acts of part performance may still be ineffective if they are
explainable on grounds other than the existence of a contract. (*Re Gonin
(deceased)*, 1977.)[156]

*(c) There must be adequate oral evidence of the terms of the contract, and
the act of part performance must be the act of the plaintiff.* It is said that
a mere payment of money is not a sufficient act of part performance,
because money has no exclusive nature; such a payment raises no equity
except the right to recover the money. This is certainly true of the
payment of purchase money in a sale of land. In other situations a
payment of money may be enough (see *Steadman* v. *Steadman*, 1973).[155]
Occupation of property is usually considered a sufficient act of part
performance and is the most common one.

The acts of part performance may also be those of a plaintiff who is
the vendor and not the buyer. Thus in *Rawlinson* v. *Ames*, [1925]
Ch. 96 the vendor of a lease of a flat (R) made improvements in the flat
at the request and under the supervision of the intended tenant (A).
When A refused to take the lease R got specific performance on the basis
of the acts of part performance.

CAPACITY TO CONTRACT

Adult citizens have full capacity to enter into any kind of contract, but
certain groups of persons, and corporations or unincorporated groups,
have certain disabilities in this connection.

Aliens

They normally have full capacity to contract, but they cannot acquire
property in a British ship (Merchant Shipping Act, 1894, s. 1), save as
a member of a limited liability company if the company itself is British.
However, contracts with *enemy aliens* during the period of hostilities are
illegal and void. The term 'enemy alien' includes not only aliens, but
British subjects voluntarily resident or carrying on business in the
enemy's country or in a country occupied or controlled by the enemy.
The test is not nationality, but the place where the person resides or
carries on business.

An enemy alien who is in England during the period of hostilities *may
be sued* in the English courts but he cannot himself *bring an action* in

those courts. (*Porter* v. *Freudenberg*, [1951] 1 K.B. 857.) However, an enemy alien present in England by licence of the Crown, as where he is registered under relevant legislation such as the Aliens Restriction Acts, may sue and be sued in the English courts and may make valid contracts even during hostilities.

Contracts made during peace with persons who later become enemy aliens by reason of outbreak of war and which require continuous business relations or are prejudicial to this country, e.g. armaments contracts, are treated as follows—

(a) The contract gives no rights after the outbreak of war. It is thus cut short and enforcement of the contract will relate only to the part which was *executed* before the war, the *executory* rights and duties being cancelled. Thus, if A and B enter into a contract under which A charters a ship from B for ten years, then if after two years B becomes an enemy alien, the contract will be cut in effect to two years and the parties released from all obligations arising under the charter after the outbreak of war. This is so even though hostilities may cease before the eight years remaining under the charter have elapsed.

(b) The rights and duties outstanding in respect of performance before the outbreak of war are not destroyed though they cannot be enforced until hostilities cease. Thus a debt due under a contract before the outbreak of war would survive the hostilities and be enforceable on the return of peace. (*Arab Bank Ltd* v. *Barclays Bank*, [1954] A.C. 495.) Where the contract does not involve commercial intercourse with the enemy alien or prejudice to this country, the rights and duties are merely suspended and not destroyed. Thus, in a separation agreement made between husband and wife before the outbreak of hostilities the husband would be liable after the war to pay to the wife sums falling due by way of maintenance during the period of hostilities even though the wife became an enemy alien for that period. (*Bevan* v. *Bevan*, [1955] 2 Q.B. 227.)

Foreign sovereigns and diplomats are in a privileged position, since they cannot be sued at civil law or prosecuted in this country unless they submit to the jurisdiction of our courts.

The law relating to the privileges and immunities of sovereigns and heads of states, their families and retinue, and of diplomatic representatives in the United Kingdom is now laid down by the Diplomatic Privileges Act, 1964 and the State Immunity Act, 1978.

The certificate of the Foreign Secretary is conclusive as to the entitlement of a person to any privilege or immunity and cannot be challenged in court. (*R.* v. *Secretary of State for Foreign and Commonwealth Affairs ex parte Trawnik, The Times*, 21 February, 1986). Diplomatic privilege may be waived, though in the case of an ambassador or other head of a mission, waiver must be with the consent of his Sovereign. In other cases waiver must be by the head of the mission.

It should be noted that a foreign state's unilateral action in appointing a diplomatic agent does not confer immunity on him. Until this country has accepted and received him, i.e. until he has been officially accredited to the Court of St. James, he is not immune from proceedings in the English courts. (*R.* v. *Pentonville Prison Governor, ex parte Teja*, [1971] 2 W.L.R. 816.)

State trading corporations

The growth of foreign state trading corporations and the spread of international commerce, taken together with the United Kingdom rules of sovereign immunity, caused great difficulties for private UK litigants, particularly in the field of commerce. For example, where a foreign state corporation failed to perform a contract it might claim immunity from suit if an action was brought against it. The courts were beginning to develop a doctrine that commercial transactions were not immune from suit in the English courts but the matter is now covered by the State Immunity Act, 1978.

Under s. 1 of the Act 'A state is immune from jurisdiction of the courts of the United Kingdom' except as provided in the Act. The main exceptions are—

(i) proceedings in respect of which the foreign state has submitted to the courts of the UK;

(ii) commercial transactions which are defined in s. 3. Thus it was held by the House of Lords in *Alcom Ltd* v. *Republic of Colombia*, [1984] 2 All E.R. 6 that an unpaid seller of goods could obtain a garnishee order (see p. 86) on a bank account used for the purposes of commercial transactions but not on an account used for paying the day-to-day running expenses of a diplomatic mission;

(iii) contracts to be performed wholly or partly in the UK. (S. 3.);

(iv) contracts of employment made or to be performed in the UK. (Ss. 4 and 16.);

(v) claims in respect of:

(*a*) death or personal injury, or

(*b*) damage to, or loss of, tangible property caused (in either case) by an act or omission in the UK. (S. 5.);

(vi) claims in arbitration. (S. 9.);

(vii) claims in respect of ships used or intended to be used for commercial purposes. (S. 10.);

(viii) claims for Customs or Excise duty and VAT.

Minors

The Family Law Reform Act, 1969, s. 1(1) reduced the age of majority from 21 to 18 years. There is also a provision in the Act which states that a person attains a particular age, i.e. not merely the age of majority, at the first moment of the relevant birthday, though this rule is subject to any contrary provision in any instrument (i.e. a deed) or statute. (S. 9.) However, the common law rule that the age is attained at the first moment of the day preceding the birthday is at least repealed.

With regard to procedure, a minor sues through a 'next friend', i.e. an adult who is liable for the costs (if any) awarded against the minor in the action, though the minor must indemnify him. A minor defends an action through a 'guardian *ad litem*', who is not liable for costs. It should be noted that a parent is not liable for his child's debts unless the child is an agent of the parent in respect of the transaction concerned, in which case the parent is liable for the debt the child incurs on his behalf. (*Mortimore* v. *Wright*, (1840) 6 M. & W. 487.)

Contracts made by minors were governed by the common law (including parts of sale of goods legislation) as amended by the Infants Relief Act, 1874 and the Betting and Loans (Infants) Act, 1892. The Minors' Contracts Act, 1987 repealed the relevant parts of the 1874 and 1892 Acts so that minors' contracts are now governed by the rules of common law (including the Sale of Goods Act, 1979) as amended by the Minors' Contracts Act, 1987.

Valid contracts

These are as follows—

(*a*) *Executed contracts for necessaries.* These are defined in s. 3(3) of the Sale of Goods Act, 1979 as 'Goods suitable to the condition in life of the minor and to his actual requirements at the time of sale and delivery.'

If the goods are deemed necessaries the minor may be compelled to pay a reasonable price which will usually, but not necessarily be, the contract price. The minor is not liable if the goods, though necessaries, have not been delivered. This, together with the fact that he is only required to pay a reasonable price, illustrates that a minor's liability for necessaries is only quasi-contractual.

If the goods (or services) have a utility value, such as clothing, and are not merely things of luxury, e.g. a diamond tiara, then they are basically necessaries. Whether the minor will have to pay a reasonable price for them then depends upon:

(i) the minor's income which goes to his condition in life. If he is wealthy then quite expensive goods and services may be necessaries for him provided they are useful;

(ii) the supply of goods which the minor already has is also relevant. If the minor is well supplied with the particular articles then they will not be necessaries even though they are useful and are well within his income. (See *Nash* v. *Inman*, (1908)[157] and *Elkington* v. *Amery*, (1936)[158]).

(b) *Contracts for the minor's benefit.* These include contracts of service, apprenticeship, and education. (*Roberts* v. *Gray*, (1913)[159]). However, the modern tendency *may* be not to restrict the concept of the beneficial contract to these particular categories, but to interpret the word 'benefit'

more broadly, and to include contracts which are analogous to contracts
of service in that they enable the minor to make a living, e.g. as an
author. (*Chaplin* v. *Frewin*, (1965)[160]).

However, trading contracts of minors are not enforceable no matter
how beneficial they may be to the minor's trade or business. The theory
behind this rule is that when a minor is in trade his capital is at risk and
he might lose it, whereas in a contract of service there is no likelihood
of capital loss. (*Mercantile Union* v. *Ball*, (1937)[161]).

It should be noted that the subject-matter of the contract is not decisive. A contract, which as regards its subject-matter, is in the category
of contracts for the minor's benefit, will not be enforced if its terms are
onerous and the court will look at the whole contract, not merely at
isolated terms, and will arrive at its decision on the total effect of the
agreement. (*De Francesco* v. *Barnum* (1890)[162] and *Clements* v. *L. &
N.W. Railway*, (1894)[163]).

Contracts not binding unless ratified (voidable A)
These are as follows—

(a) *Loans.* These are not binding on the minor unless he ratifies the
contract of loan after reaching 18 which he may now legally do. No fresh
consideration is now required on ratification.

(b) *Contracts for non-necessary goods.* Again, these are not binding on
the minor unless he ratifies the contract after reaching 18 as he may now
legally do. Once again, no fresh consideration is required on ratification.

It should be noted that in spite of the fact that the contracts in (a) and
(b) above are not enforceable against the minor, he gets a title to any
property which passes to him under the arrangement and can give a good
title to a third party as where, e.g. he sells non-necessary goods on to
someone else (who takes in good faith and for value). This was decided
in *Stocks* v. *Wilson*, (1913).[164] Furthermore, any money or property transferred by the minor under the contract can only be recovered by him if
there has been a total failure of consideration (see below).

Contracts binding unless repudiated (voidable B)
These are usually contracts by which the minor acquires an interest of
a permanent nature in the subject-matter of the contract. Such contracts
bind the minor unless he takes active steps to avoid them, either during
his minority or within a reasonable time thereafter. Examples of voidable
contracts are shares in companies, leases of property and partnerships.
(*Steinberg* v. *Scala*, (1923)[165]; *Davies* v. *Beynon-Harris*, (1931)[166] and
Goode v. *Harrison*, (1821)[167]).

Consequences of the contracts of minors
As we have seen, contracts entered into by minors will, if defective, be
voidable A or voidable B. The effect of the term 'voidable' in this context
is untypical and must be considered here—

(a) *Recovery by minor of money paid under a voidable contract of type A or B*. When a minor has paid money under such a contract, he cannot recover it unless he can prove a total failure of consideration, i.e. that he has received no benefit at all under the contract. The court is reluctant to find that no benefit has been received and this can be seen in the context of a voidable A contract in *Pearce* v. *Brain*, (1929)[168] and a voidable B contract in *Steinberg* v. *Scala*, (1923)[165]. However, if there has really been no consideration at all a minor will be able to recover his money. (*Corpe* v. *Overton*) (1833)[169].

(b) *Effect of purchase by minor of non-necessary goods*. As we have seen, the minor acquires a title to the goods and can give a good title to a third party who takes them *bona fide* and for value (*Stocks* v. *Wilson*, (1913)[164]). The tradesman who sold the goods to the minor cannot recover them from the third party.

However, as regards recovery from the minor, if he still has the property, s. 3 of the Minors' Contracts Act, 1987 provides that the court can order restitution, e.g. of non-necessary goods to the tradesman, where the minor is refusing to pay for them. As we know, he cannot be sued for the price.

The question of recovery in any particular case is left to the court which must regard it as just and equitable to allow recovery, though a restitution order can be made whether the minor is fraudulent, as where he obtained the goods by overstating his age, (*Leslie* v. *Sheill*, (1914)[170]), *or not*. Fraud is no longer a requirement for restitution. Money will be virtually impossible to recover because it will normally be mixed with other funds and not identifiable. However, the minor could be made under s. 3 to offer up any goods acquired in exchange for the non-necessary goods. The tradesman recovers the goods in the state he finds them and cannot ask for compensation from the minor if they are, e.g. damaged.

(c) *Guarantees*. Section 2 of the Minors' Contracts Act, 1987 provides that a guarantee by an adult of a minor's transaction shall be enforceable against the guarantor even though the main contractual obligation is not enforceable against the minor. Thus if a bank makes a loan to a minor or allows a minor an overdraft and an adult gives a guarantee of that transaction, then although the loan or overdraft cannot be enforced against the minor, the adult guarantor can be required to pay. This section overrules cases occurring in circumstances such as those in *Coutts* v. *Browne-Lecky*, (1947)[171].

Married women

A married woman has the same contractual capacity as an unmarried woman (*feme sole*) or a man. However, a husband is not liable for his wife's contracts unless she is his agent for the particular transaction and she can no longer be an agent of necessity in respect of domestic transactions. (See p. 186.)

Corporations

Corporations are another special case of capacity to contract. A corporation aggregate may be a body incorporated by Royal Charter, a corporation formed by a special Act of Parliament, or a company registered under the Companies Act, 1985, or previous Acts.

The contractual capacity of a corporation is limited—

(a) *By natural impossibility*, which arises from the fact that it is an *artificial* and not a *natural* person. Thus it can only make contracts through an agent and in consequence cannot fulfil contractual obligations of a *personal nature*. It is obviously impossible for a corporation to marry and it cannot as yet act as a solicitor, doctor or accountant, nor can it act as the treasurer of a friendly society which is a personal office. (*Re West of England and South Wales District Bank* (1879), 11 Ch. D. 768.)

(b) *By legal impossibility*, since corporations are subject to what is called the *ultra vires* rule, which limits what they can legally do. A corporation can only act within its powers, and actions outside this scope are called *ultra vires*, or beyond its powers.

Parliamentary approach to *ultra vires*

Limited protection for persons dealing in good faith with a registered company is given by s. 35 of the Companies Act, 1985. The section is the United Kingdom's response to the first directive issued by the Council of Ministers of the European Communities for the harmonization of company law in the member states. Section 35 provides that in favour of a person dealing in good faith (see *International Sales & Agencies Ltd* v. *Marcus*, 1982 at p. 608) with a company any transaction decided on by its directors shall be deemed to be within the capacity of the company to enter into validly, and the other party to the transaction shall not be bound to enquire about the capacity of the company to engage in it and shall be presumed to have acted in good faith unless the contrary is proved.

The *ultra vires* rule is not abolished because the subsection merely allows the other party to an *ultra vires* transaction with a company to enforce it against the company if the necessary conditions are fulfilled.

Thus the subsection does not—

(a) prevent a member of the company from obtaining an injunction to restrain the company and its directors from entering into an *ultra vires* transaction; or

(b) absolve the directors from liability for any loss they cause the company by carrying out such a transaction, though of course there may be no loss since the *ultra vires* contract may be very profitable to the company; or

(c) make the transaction enforceable by the company but only against it; thus the other party can raise the defence of *ultra vires* (see *Bell Houses Ltd* v. *City Wall Properties Ltd*, 1966 at p. 612) if sued by the company. However, if the other party sues the company it could plead defences and make counter-claims, e.g. if the company was sued for the value of goods supplied under an *ultra vires* contract, the company could plead, in order to reduce the claim, that they were defective. Furthermore, if the other party accepts benefits under the transaction or allows the company to incur expense in connection with it he may be estopped from denying the validity of the transaction.

Unfortunately s. 35 applies only if the transaction has been 'decided on by the directors'. Few transactions of public companies are formally resolved upon at board meetings and the subsection would seem to apply only where the transaction has been authorized, effected, or ratified by a resolution of a board meeting or by all the directors assenting to it. It does not seem to extend to transactions entered into by one director acting under broad delegated powers because the precise nature of the transaction is not a matter upon which the directors decide. However, if the board has decided, say, that A, a director, shall negotiate for a lease in the City of London for 99 years at a named price, so that A is merely left to negotiate minor details, the lease may be regarded as a transaction 'decided on by the directors' and enforceable by the landlord if the lease happened to be beyond the company's powers.

However, s. 35 applies and an *ultra vires* transaction is binding on the company where it is made on behalf of the company by a director to whom all actual authority to act for the board has effectively been delegated. This rule of the sole effective director will apply only in private companies. (*International Sales & Agencies Ltd* v. *Marcus*, 1982.)[172] It seems that not all *ultra vires* transactions of public companies will be validated by s. 35. Some will remain invalid and be covered by the common law rules set out below. For the time being, therefore, plaintiffs will probably reinforce actions for breach of *ultra vires* contracts by asking in the alternative for one or more of the secondary remedies, e.g. subrogation and tracing, in case they cannot rely on s. 35, and the usual contractual remedies are therefore denied to them.

As regards subrogation, where a company has used an *ultra vires* loan to pay off *intra vires* debts the lender is subrogated to the rights of the creditors so paid. Thus if X lends £5000 to the Y Company Ltd, the loan being *ultra vires*, X will not be able to recover the loan as such. But if the company has used the money to pay off (say) £3000 worth of enforceable debts, X may stand in the shoes of the creditors paid off, and sue the company as the creditors could have done if they had not been paid, and X will have an action for £3000. (*Sinclair* v. *Brougham*, [1914] A.C. 398.)

As regards tracing, property passing under an *ultra vires* transaction which can be traced into any particular asset of the company, or the proceeds of sale of that asset, can be claimed, the company being deemed to hold that asset as a trustee for the person from whom it was obtained. Thus if X sells tractors to a company which does not have power to buy them then he cannot sue for his debt in contract, but can recover the tractors if the company still has them. If the tractors have been sold he can trace the proceeds of sale but here the proceeds would generally be in a mixed account, e.g. the company's bank account and there may be difficulties in ascertaining what part of that account belongs to X. However, subject to this quite serious practical difficulty, X has a tracing remedy.

As we have seen, s. 35 would seem to validate a large number of *ultra vires* contracts made by *private* companies. So many of these are 'one man' companies in which everything is decided by the one man in his capacity as sole director.

It is interesting to note that the Conservative Government's Companies Bill of 1973 provided in Clause 5 that a transaction between a company and another party shall not be repudiated by the company on the ground that it was beyond the capacity of the company or the powers of the directors unless the other party had actual notice of that fact. Such a provision would have been much more effective in validating *ultra vires* transactions with both types of registered companies.

At the time of writing Dr Dan Prentice of Oxford University has been appointed by the Government to examine the *ultra vires* rule in terms of its legal and commercial implications with a view to its abolition.

Charter and statutory companies and the *ultra vires* rule

Charter corporations may contract as an ordinary person can, and even though the Charter may impose limitations on the corporation's contractual capacity, any contracts which it makes beyond those limitations are nevertheless good. (*Baroness Wenlock* v. *River Dee Co.* (1887), 36 Ch. D. 674.) The Crown may in such a case forfeit the Charter, or a member of the corporation may ask the court to restrain the corporation by injunction from doing acts which are *ultra vires*. (*Jenkin* v. *Pharmaceutical Society*, 1921.)[53]

Statutory corporations have powers contained in the statute setting them up, and these powers are sometimes increased by subsequent statutes or by delegated legislation. Any acts beyond these powers are *ultra vires* and void.

Registered companies and the *ultra vires* rule

Registered companies possess powers determined by the objects clause of their memorandum of association, and an act in excess of the powers given in this memorandum is *ultra vires* and void. Thus an *ultra vires* contract is unenforceable against the company unless it is one which was 'decided on by the directors' under s. 35, Companies Act, 1985. (*Ashbury Railway Carriage and Iron Co.* v. *Riche*, 1875,[173] and *Re Jon Beauforte*, 1953.)[174] Corporations may carry out acts 'fairly incidental' to the specified objects (*Deuchar* v. *Gas, Light and Coke Co.*, 1925)[175] though whether an activity was fairly incidental has hitherto been a matter for the court to decide. However, the rule has been so uncertain in its operation that it has become customary for legal draftsmen to draft objects clauses which are extremely wide in scope and, in addition, include a provision that each specified object or power should be considered separate and distinct and in no way ancilliary to, or dependent upon, any other object (*Cotman* v. *Brougham*, 1918).[176] In this way, the severe limitations placed on a company's business by the *ultra vires* rule have been mitigated. However, in 1966 the Court of Appeal made a decision which seems, in effect, to allow the decisions of the directors of a company to usurp the courts in deciding what is reasonably incidental to the company's stated objects, and even allow them to bind the company to an activity which cannot conveniently be combined with the existing objects, and ought therefore to be regarded as *ultra vires*. (*Bell Houses Ltd* v. *City Wall Properties Ltd*, 1966).[177]

In addition, in 1985 the Court of Appeal made an important decision which went further along the road of abolition of the rule. (See *Rolled Steel Products Ltd* v. *British Steel Corporation*, 1985.)[178]

Contracts of companies—formalities

At common law contracts made by corporations had to be under seal. The requirement of sealing would have been extremely onerous but for the exceptions allowed, e.g. contracts of trifling importance and or daily necessity were not required to bear the company's seal.

The above rules have been amended by statute. The Companies Act, 1985, provides in s. 36 that a registered company need not contract under seal except where an ordinary person would have to do so, and the Corporate Bodies' Contracts Act, 1960, extends this privilege to all companies, no matter how formed.

Unincorporated bodies

In addition to corporations there are certain types of unincorporated bodies, such as tennis clubs and other societies. The liability of the members in contract has already been considered (see p. 174).

Persons suffering from mental disorder

Contracts made by a person of unsound mind are valid, but if the other party knew that he was contracting with a person who, by reason of the unsoundness of his mind, *could not understand the nature of the contract*, then the contract is voidable at the option of the insane party. The person of unsound mind must prove (*a*) the unsoundness of mind at the time of the contract, and (*b*) that the other party knew of it. (*Imperial Loan Co.* v. *Stone*, [1892] 1 Q.B. 599.) In *Hart* v. *O'Connor*, [1985] 2 All E.R. 880 the Privy Council refused to set aside an agreement to sell farmland in New Zealand because although the seller was of unsound mind, his affliction was not apparent. The price paid was not unreasonable. If it had been the Privy Council said that the contract could have been set aside for equitable fraud as an unconscionable bargain. If necessaries are supplied to a person of unsound mind he, like a minor, is bound to pay a reasonable price under s. 3(2) of the Sale of Goods Act, 1979.

A person of unsound mind can make a valid contract during a lucid interval, even though the other party knew that he was of unsound mind at times. Further, a contract made during a period of unsoundness of mind can be ratified during a lucid interval.

There seems to be no reason why persons suffering from some forms of mental disorder should not make valid contracts for non-necessary goods and services even where the other party knows of the disorder. Provided the person concerned understands the *nature* of the transaction a contract resulting from it could be binding. For example, a person who suffers under an insane delusion that he is Napoleon may nevertheless understand the nature of a commercial transaction such as the purchase of a watch. Where this is so he may be bound by a contract to buy the watch even though the seller knew of the delusion. (*Birkin* v. *Wing*, (1890) 63 L.T. 80.) Nevertheless, it is likely that the court would regard the contract as voidable if there was evidence to show that the person suffering from the delusion had been overreached as where the price asked for the watch was extortionate.

The above rules of law relating to persons of unsound mind must now be read in the light of the provisions of the Mental Health Act, 1983. Part VII of the 1983 Act contains provisions which give the Court of Protection power to appoint a receiver (often a near relative) to administer the affairs of the patient on behalf of the court in which the patient's property is vested. From then on the patient cannot make valid contracts. The receiver acts under the direction of the court and, subject to the powers given to him by the court, the receiver may bind the patient's estate in contract.

However, persons of unsound mind whose property is not subject to the control of the court are governed in contractual matters by the common law rules given above.

Drunkards

Similar common law rules apply to contracts made by drunkards. The contract is voidable at the option of the party who was drunk at the time it was made, if he can show (i) that he was drunk, and (ii) that the other party knew this. (*Gore* v. *Gibson* (1845), 14 L.J. Ex. 151.) A contract made by a person when drunk can be ratified by him when he is sober. (*Matthews* v. *Baxter* (1873), L.R. 8 Ex. 132.) Drunken persons have a quasi-contractual liability to pay a reasonable price for necessaries supplied to them. (Sale of Goods Act, 1979, s. 3(2).)

REALITY OF CONSENT

A contract which is regular in all other respects may still fail because there is no real consent to it by one or both of the parties. There is no *consensus ad idem* or meeting of the minds. Consent may be rendered unreal by mistake, fraud, misrepresentation, duress and undue influence.

MISTAKE

Mistake may affect the validity of a contract, and a mistake which has this effect is called an operative mistake, and must be one of fact and not of law. (*Sharp Bros. and Knight* v. *Chant*, 1917.)[179] An operative mistake renders the contract void. It will be operative only if it *induces* the contract. Thus if A orders goods from B's shop which is, unknown to A, now owned by C, then A has made a fundamental mistake, but so long as he gets his goods it will not affect the contract between A and C. A change of ownership would, however, affect the contract if, as in *Boulton* v. *Jones* (1857), 21 H. & N. 564, A was owed money by B and intended to set off B's debt against the price of the goods. In *Boulton* it was held that there was no contract between A and the new owner, C.

The concept of mistake has a somewhat technical meaning, and what would be considered a mistake by the layman will not always amount to an operative mistake. For example, errors of judgment are not operative mistakes. So if A buys a watch thinking it is worth £100 when in fact it is worth only £50, the contract is good and A must bear the loss if there has been no misrepresentation by the seller. This is what is meant by the maxim '*caveat emptor*' (let the buyer beware). In such a case there would be no claim by A for unilateral mistake because the mistake is as to the quality of the watch only. A mistake by one party as to his power to perform the contract is not an operative mistake. Where X agrees to build a house by 1 July, and finds he cannot complete the job before 1 September, he will be liable to an action for damages.

Operative mistake

Operative mistakes may be classified into the following categories—

(1) Documents mistakenly signed.
(2) Unilateral mistake, i.e. a mistake made by one party only.
(3) Bilateral mistake, i.e. where both parties make a mistake, and subdivided into (*a*) Common mistake; (*b*) Mutual mistake.

These categories are helpful, but students find considerable difficulty in distinguishing between common and mutual mistake because the words are frequently confused, or used synonymously, even in law reports. This can be illustrated by the case of *Solle* v. *Butcher*.[180] Bucknill, L.J., in the course of his judgment is reported in the *All England Reports*, [1949] 2

All E.R. at page 1116 as saying: 'In my opinion, therefore, there was a *mutual* mistake of fact on a matter of fundamental importance.'

In the *Law Reports*, [1950] 1 K.B. at page 686 this is rendered as: 'In my opinion, therefore, there was a *common* mistake of fact on a matter of fundamental importance.'

In *Cooper* v. *Phibbs*, (1867)[181] at page 170, Lord Westbury says: '. . . but if the parties contract under a *mutual* mistake and misapprehension as to their relative and respective rights, the result is, that that agreement is liable to be set aside as having proceeded upon a *common* mistake.' (And see also *Amalgamated Investment and Property Co. Ltd* v. *John Walker & Sons Ltd*, 1976, p. 621.)

We therefore propose to use words more self-identifying than common or mutual in order to assist the reader to understand and remember the categories. Common mistake occurs where *both* parties have made the *same* mistake and will be called, alternatively, *identical bilateral* mistake. Mutual mistake occurs where *both* parties make a *different* mistake and will be called *non-identical bilateral* mistake. These will be the clearly differentiated between themselves and contrasted with *unilateral* mistake.

Documents mistakenly signed

This form of *unilateral mistake* occurs if a person signs a contract in the mistaken belief that he is signing a document of a totally different nature. In this situation there will be a mistake which avoids the contract, and he will be able to plead *non est factum* (it is not my deed). However, as a result of the decision of the House of Lords in *Saunders* v. *Anglia Building Society*, 1970[182] the plea of mistake is available in such circumstances only if the person signing under a mistake can show that he was not negligent in so doing as in *Foster* v. *Mackinnon*, 1869.[183]

As between the immediate parties to what is always in effect a fraud, there is, of course, no difficulty in avoiding the contract or transaction mistakenly entered into. The rules set out above are relevant only where the contract or transaction mistakenly entered into has affected a third party, as where he has, as in *Saunders*[182] lent money on an interest in land obtained by fraudulent assignment under circumstances of mistake.

The principles set out in *Saunders*[182] apply also to those who sign blank forms as well as to those who sign completed documents without reading them. Thus if as in *United Dominions Trust Ltd* v. *Western*, [1975] 3 All E.R. 1017 A takes a car from B, a dealer, on hire purchase and signs a finance company's blank form of proposal leaving the dealer to fill it in for him, then if the dealer fills in the price of the car as greater than it was, A cannot avoid paying the finance company the additional sum on the grounds of *non est factum*.

Thus it will be seen that a person of full age and sound mind will only rarely be able to establish the defence of *non est factum*. However, the burden of disproving negligence could perhaps be discharged where a person was asked to witness a confidential document and had no reason to doubt that the document was as described. The old case of *Lewis* v. *Clay*, (1897) 67 L.J. Q.B. 224 provides a possible illustration. In that case Lord William Nevill produced to Clay documents completely covered with blotting paper except for four blank spaces which had been cut in it. Nevill told Clay that the hidden documents were concerned with a very private family matter and that Clay's signature was required merely as a witness. Clay signed his name in the blank spaces and it was later discovered that the documents underneath the blotting paper were promissory notes to the value of £11,113 signed by Clay in favour of a person called Lewis. On the faith of these notes Lewis had advanced money to Lord William Nevill. It was held in an action between Lewis and Clay that the promissory notes were not binding on Clay.

Unilateral mistake

Apart from documents mistakenly signed, unilateral mistake occurs whenever one of the parties to a contract, X, is mistaken as to some fundamental fact concerning the contract and *the other party Y, knows or ought to know this*. (*Legal and General Assurance Society Ltd* v. *General Metal Agencies Ltd*, 1969.)[184] This latter requirement is important because if Y does not know that X is mistaken, the contract is good. (*Higgins* v. *Northampton Corporation*, 1927.)[185]

Effect of unilateral mistake at common law
The cases are mainly concerned with mistake by one party as to the *identity* of the other party. Thus, a contract may be void if X makes a contract with Y, thinking that Y is another person, Z, and if Y knows that X is under that misapprehension. Proof of Y's knowledge is essential, but since in most cases Y is a fraudulent person, the point does not present great difficulties. (*Cundy* v. *Lindsay*, 1878.)[186]

It is also essential that there should exist in the mind of the party who has been misled some other person (or entity) with whom the contract could have been made, as in *Cundy* v. *Lindsay*, 1878.[186] If Jones contracts with Brown by leading Brown to believe that he (Jones) is Green, the contract *will not be void* for mistake if Brown has never heard before of either Jones or Green. It *may be voidable* for fraud but the difference may vitally affect the interests of third parties. (*King's Norton Metal Co. Ltd* v. *Edridge, Merrett & Co. Ltd*, 1897.)[187] However, even where there are two entities, the court may still find, *on the facts of the case*, that the contract is not void for mistake. (*Phillips* v. *Brooks, 1919,*[188] *Ingram* v. *Little*, 1961[189] and *Lewis* v. *Averay*, 1971.)[190]

Effect of unilateral mistake in Equity
If the plaintiff is asking for an equitable remedy, such as rescission of the contract or specific performance of it, then equitable principles will apply. As far as unilateral mistake is concerned Equity follows the law and regards a contract affected by unilateral mistake as void, and will rescind

it or refuse specific performance of it. (*Webster* v. *Cecil*, 1861.)[191] Rectification of the contract is also available.

Bilateral mistake

A bilateral mistake arises when both parties to a contract are mistaken. They may have made a *common* or *identical* mistake; or a *mutual* or *non-identical* mistake.

(a) Common or identical mistake

This occurs when the two parties have reached agreement but both have made an identical mistake as to some fundamental fact concerning the contract. Suppose, for example, that X sells a particular drawing to Y for £5000 and all the usual elements of agreement are present including offer and acceptance and consideration, and the agreement concerns an identified article. Nevertheless, if both X and Y think that the drawing is by Rembrandt, when it is in fact only a copy worth £25, then the agreement is rendered imperfect by the *identical* or *common* mistake. The circumstances giving rise to the mistake must exist at the time the contract is made. (*Amalgamated Investment & Property Co Ltd* v. *John Walker & Sons Ltd*, 1976.)[192]

Effect of identical bilateral mistake at common law. At common law a mistake of the kind outlined above has no effect on the contract, and the parties would be bound in the absence of fraud or misrepresentation. There are only two cases in which the common law appears to regard an *identical bilateral* mistake as a vitiating element, and even these cases are probably examples of precedent impossibility rather than mistake. The two categories of case are—

(*a*) *Cases of Res Extincta*

 (i) *Identical bilateral mistake as to the existence of the thing contracted for.* If X agrees to sell his car to Y, and unknown to them both the car had at the time of the sale been destroyed by fire, then the contract will be void because X has innocently undertaken an obligation which he cannot possibly fulfil. (*Couturier* v. *Hastie*, 1856.)[193] There are, however, cases in which the court may assume from the circumstances that the seller is warranting the existence of the goods. (*McRae* v. *Commonwealth Disposals Commission*, 1951.)[194]

 If the goods are lost after the sale takes place then the contract is good, and the loss lies with the buyer if the property in the goods has passed to him; if not the loss lies with the seller. The goods must also be specific or ascertained, otherwise the property will not normally pass, and the seller must supply similar goods or be liable in breach of contract.

 (ii) *Identical bilateral mistake as to the existence of a state of affairs forming the basis of the contract.* If A and B, believing themselves to be married, enter into a separation agreement and later learn that they are not validly married, the agreement is void, as in *Galloway* v. *Galloway*, (1914) 30 T.L.R. 531.

(*b*) *Cases of Res Sua.* These occur where a person makes a contract to buy something which already belongs to him. Such a contract is, at any rate in Equity, void though the remarks of Knight Bruce, L.J. in *Cochrane* v. *Willis*, 1865[195] suggest that the common law view is the same.

Apart from cases of *res extincta* and *res sua* the common law does not seem to recognize an *identical* bilateral mistake as having any effect on a contract. (*Bell* v. *Lever Bros Ltd*, 1932,[196] and *Leaf* v. *International Galleries*, 1950.)[197]

Effect of identical bilateral mistake in Equity. Where an equitable remedy is sought the position is as follows—

(*a*) *Cases of Res Extincta and Res Sua.* Equity treats these in the same way as the common law, regarding the agreement as void. Consequently Equity will not grant specific performance of such an agreement (*Jones* v. *Clifford*, 1876)[198] and will rescind it. (*Cooper* v. *Phibbs*, 1867.)[181]

(*b*) *Other cases.* Equity will apparently regard an agreement affected by *identical* bilateral mistake as *voidable* even though the case is not one of *res extincta* or *res sua*. This remedy is a discretionary one and the party seeking it may be put on terms, i.e. since the remedy is a discretionary one the parties seeking it may be required to accept other solutions to the problem which the court puts forward. (*Solle* v. *Butcher*, 1949,[180] *Grist* v. *Bailey*, 1966.)[199]

(*c*) *Rectification.* Equity has power to rectify agreements affected by *identical bilateral* or common mistake.

If the parties are agreed on the terms of their contract, but by mistake write them down incorrectly, the court may order equitable rectification of the contract. In order to obtain rectification it must be proved—

(i) that there was agreement in the contractual sense on all the terms of the contract or at least some outward expression of agreement between the parties *on the term in question*, even though that agreement was not in fact a contract. (*Joscelyne* v. *Nissen*, 1970.)[200]

(ii) that the agreement continued unchanged until it was reduced into writing (for if the parties disputed the terms of the agreement, then the written contract will be taken to represent their final agreement); and

(iii) that the writing does not express what the parties had agreed. (*Rose* v. *Pim*, 1953.)[201]

The power of the court to rectify agreements is generally confined to identical bilateral and not to unilateral mistake. (*Higgins* (*W.*) *Ltd* v. *Northampton Corporation*, 1927.)[185] In the case of unilateral mistake, rectification will only be granted in cases of fraud, misrepresentation or wrongful concealment.

Thus in *Thomas Bates & Son* v. *Wyndhams* (*Lingerie*), [1981] 1 All E.R. 1077 landlord and tenant entered into a lease which should have provided for the settlement of disputes as to rent by arbitration. No arbitration clause was inserted in the lease and the tenant knew this before he signed it, but concealed the fact from the landlord. Thus there was in effect a unilateral mistake, but the Court of Appeal held that the lease could be rectified in order to contain an arbitration clause.

Furthermore, the court can correct a misnomer or clerical error even if there has been no previous agreement on the point. It would appear that in such cases the strict rules of rectification do not apply. Thus in *Nittan* (*UK*) v. *Solent Steel Fabrications; Cornhill Insurance Co* (*third party*), [1981] 1 Lloyd's Rep. 633, N had sued SSF in respect of the malfunctioning of an electronic programmer. N had recovered £28,000. SSF then claimed upon their product liability policy with C and C sought to avoid that policy because by error the policy had been made out in the name of Sargrove Electronic Contractors, being a firm whose business SSF had acquired. The policy should therefore, have been in the name of SSF but by mistake it was in the name of Sargrove. It was held by the Court of Appeal that this was a misnomer that was clear to all and the Court had power to correct it. It was wrong to allow advantage to be taken of an error such as this, even though it did not fall within the rectification requirements, i.e. that there be a previous agreement which is incorrectly written down.

(b) Mutual or non-identical mistake

This occurs where the parties are both mistaken as to a fundamental fact concerning the contract but each party has made a *different* mistake. Thus if X offers to sell Car A, and Y agrees to buy thinking X means Car B, there is a bilateral mistake which is *non-identical*. This may prevent a contract coming into being between the parties because of *defective offer and acceptance*, and may result from the negligence of a third party. (*Henkel* v. *Pape*, 1870.)[202] It will be remembered that in the previous category the mistake was bilateral but both parties had made an *identical* mistake.

Effect of non-identical bilateral mistake at common law. The contract is not necessarily void because the court will try to find the 'sense of the promise', i.e. the sort of bargain which the reasonable man looking at the dealings of the parties would have thought had been made. This usually occurs where, although the parties are at cross-purposes, *the contract identifies* an agreement.

In many cases of *non-identical mistake* the court has been able to ascertain the 'sense of the promise' and has decided that an enforceable contract has been made *on the terms understood by one of the parties.* (*Wood* v. *Scarth*, 1858.)[203] If the circumstances are such that the court cannot find the 'sense of the promise', then the contract is void not so much because of mistake as because of uncertainty. If the parties are at cross-purposes and *the contract does not identify* their agreement, it is void. (*Raffles* v. *Wichelhaus*, 1864.)[204]

Effect of non-identical bilateral mistake in Equity. Equity also tries to find the 'sense of the promise', thus following the law in this respect. (*Tamplin* v. *James*, 1880.)[205] However, equitable remedies are discretionary, and even where the 'sense of the promise' can be ascertained, Equity will not necessarily insist on performance, particularly if this would cause hardship to the defendant. (*Wood* v. *Scarth*, 1858.)[203]

MISREPRESENTATION

Representation—meaning of

A representation is an inducement only and its effect is generally to lead the other party merely to make the contract. A representation must be a statement of some *specific existing* and *verifiable* fact or *past event* and in consequence the following are excluded.

(*a*) *Statements of law*.

(*b*) *Statements as to future conduct or intention*. In some cases, however, a statement of intention may, in effect, be a representation of existing fact. (*Edgington* v. *Fitzmaurice*, 1885.)[206]

(*c*) *Statements of opinion*. However, if it can be shown that the person making the statement had no such opinion, it may be considered in law to be a misstatement of existing fact. (*Smith* v. *Land and House Property Co.*, 1884.)[207]

(*d*) *Mere 'puffing', as in advertising or sales talk, or what is called these days 'hype'*. Not all statements amount to representations. Some of them are obviously of the nature of sales talk and cannot be relied upon. If a salesman says: 'This polish is as good as Snook's Polish,' this is a mere statement of opinion. If he says: 'This is the finest polish in the world,' this is mere sales talk. However, if he says: 'This polish has as much wax in it as Snook's Wax Polish,' he is making a statement of specific verifiable fact. The first two of these statements have no effect on the contract whether true or untrue; the third if untrue will amount to a misrepresentation.

(*e*) *Silence*. Silence or non-disclosure by one or both of the parties does not normally affect the contract. However, it may do so—

(i) *where the statement is a half-truth*—if the statement made is true but *partial*, so that a false impression is created, it may be regarded as an actionable misrepresentation (*Curtis* v. *Chemical Cleaning and Dyeing Co.*, 1951);[208]

(ii) *where the statement was true when made but became false before the contract was concluded*—where a statement is made in the course of negotiating a contract and that statement, though true when it was made, becomes false because of a change in circumstances, there is a duty on the party making the statement to disclose the change, otherwise the contract may be rescinded (*With* v. *O'Flanagan*, 1936);[209]

(iii) *where statute requires disclosure*, as does the Financial Services Act, 1986 under which a number of specified particulars must be disclosed in an advertisement/prospectus issued by a company to invite the public to subscribe for shares or debentures. The particulars must give all such information as investors and their professional advisers would reasonably require and reasonably expect to find in the advertisement/prospectus for the purpose of making an informed assessment as to whether to buy the securities.

(iv) *where the contract is uberrimae fidei* (of utmost good faith) such as a contract of insurance (see p. 267);

(v) *in cases of concealed fraud* following the case of *Gordon* v. *Selico Co Ltd*, (1986) 278 E.G. 53. In that case a flat in a block of flats which had recently been converted by a developer was taken by the plaintiff on a 99-year lease. Soon after he moved in dry rot was discovered. Goulding, J, who was later upheld by the Court of Appeal, decided that deliberate concealment of the dry rot by the developer could amount to fraudulent misrepresentation whereupon damages were awarded to the plaintiff. Silence can, therefore, amount to misrepresentation in the case of concealed fraud.

(vi) *where there is a fiduciary or confidential relationship between the parties*—the equitable doctrine of *constructive fraud* may be applied whenever the relationship between the parties to a contract is such that one of them has a special influence over the other.

In such a case, the person having the special influence cannot hold the other to the contract unless he can satisfy the court that it was advantageous to the other and that there was full disclosure of all material facts.

This branch of the law is closely akin to undue influence (see p. 269) which occurs, for example, in certain relationships such as parent and child. However, the doctrine of constructive fraud is wider and according to Lord Chelmsford in *Tate* v. *Williamson*, 1866[210] may be applied—

Whenever two persons stand in such a relation that, while it continues, confidence is necessarily reposed by one, and the influence which naturally grows out of that confidence is possessed by the other, and this confidence is abused, or the influence is exerted to obtain an advantage at the expense of the confiding party, the person so availing himself of his position will not be permitted to retain the advantage, although the transaction could not have been impeached if no such confidential relation had existed.

Thus it may be that while undue influence is the proper term to use of influence between certain established and accepted relationships, such as parent and child, trustee and beneficiary, when the influence is shown to exist outside of these relationships the true basis of the action is probably constructive fraud.

Inducement—meaning of

In order to operate as an inducement the representation must—

(a) be made with the intention that it should be acted upon by the person misled (*Peek* v. *Gurney*, 1873);[211]

(b) induce the contract so that the person making the claim to have been misled must not have relied on his own skill and judgment (*Redgrave* v. *Hurd*, 1881);[212]

(c) be material in the sense that it affected the plaintiff's judgment (*Smith* v. *Chadwick* 1884);[213]

(d) be known to the plaintiff. The plaintiff must always be prepared to prove that an alleged misrepresentation had an effect on his mind, a task which he certainly cannot fulfil if he was never aware that it had been made. Thus in *Re Northumberland & Durham District Banking Co.*, *ex parte Bigge*, (1859) 28 L.J. Ch. 50 a person who bought shares in a company asked to have the purchase rescinded because the company had published false reports as to its solvency. Although these reports were false, the claimant failed because, among other things, he was unable to show that he had read any of the reports or that anyone had told him what they contained.

Types of actionable misrepresentation

In cases which have come before the courts judges speak of two types of misrepresentation only: innocent misrepresentation, by which they mean innocent of fraud, and fraudulent misrepresentaion, which involves dishonesty. Innocent misrepresentation is then further subdivided into innocent statements made negligently, i.e. without reasonable grounds for believing them to be true and wholly innocent statements where the maker has reasonable grounds for believing them to be true.

However, for purposes of exposition we discuss three types of misrepresentation, i.e. innocent, negligent, and fraudulent. This should not cause any practical difficulty provided the above paragraph is understood. Thus an *innocent misrepresentation* is a false statement made by a person *who had reasonable grounds* to believe that the statement was true not only when he made it but also at the time the contract was entered into.

A *negligent misrepresentation* is a false statement made without dishonesty by a person *who had no reasonable grounds* for believing the statement to be true. A *fraudulent misrepresentation* is a false representation of a material fact made knowing it to be false, or without belief in its truth, or recklessly, not caring whether it be true or false. (*Derry* v. *Peek* 1889.)[214]

English Law

Agent's breach of warranty of authority

Under the law of agency, where an agent represents himself as having authority he does not possess, the third party may sue the agent for breach of warranty of authority if he suffers loss by not obtaining a contract with the principal, the action being based on quasi-contract. (See p. 319.)

Compensation under the Financial Services Act, 1986

Section 150(1) of the 1986 Act places express liability on those responsible for the listing of particulars issued in connection with a public flotation of shares, in regard to material mis-statements, omissions and misleading opinions. The directors of the company will e.g. be liable under s. 150.

Negligence at common law

The House of Lords ruled in *Hedley Byrne* v. *Heller and Partners*, 1963[215] that where there is a sufficient 'special relationship' between the maker of the statement and the person who is to rely on it, the former owes the latter a duty of reasonable care in making the statement and may be liable in damages in tort for negligence to the recipient if the statement contains false information given negligently rather than intentionally.

The remedy in negligence is useful where the parties concerned were *not* in a pre-contractual relationship when the statement was made because if they were not s. 2(1) of the Misrepresentation Act, 1967, will not apply.

However, in *Esso Petroleum* v. *Mardon*, [1976] 2 All E.R. 5 the Court of Appeal held that the principle in *Hedley Byrne*[215] could apply even where the parties concerned were in a pre-contractual relationship, and in addition that the person who had made the statement need not necessarily be in business to give advice, as had once been thought. Mr Mardon was awarded damages for a negligent misstatement by a senior sales representative of Esso in regard to the amount of petrol he could expect to sell per year from a petrol station in Southport which he was leasing from Esso. The facts of *Mardon* pre-dated the 1967 Act and the court could not use it. The decision is obviously important but where the facts have occurred since 1967 the Misrepresentation Act is likely to prove more popular with plaintiffs since they can ask the representor to show he was not negligent. In *Hedley Byrne*[215] claims the burden of proof is on the plaintiff to prove negligence. There is growing support for the view that this form of liability can be based on a wider principle of foresight so that a 'special relationship' exists whenever it is reasonable for one party to rely on the other's skill and judgment in making a statement. (See further p. 400.)

REMEDIES

There are the following possible remedies for misrepresentation—

(a) Rescission of the contract is a possible remedy in all cases of misrepresentation whether fraudulent, negligent or innocent.

(b) The refusal of the injured party to perform his part of the contract if he has not already done so. He can then raise the misrepresentation as a defence to an action for specific performance, debt or damages.

(c) An action for damages in the case of fraud. In this case the plaintiff sues not on the contract but on the tort of deceit.

The object of damages in fraud which is an action in tort rather than contract is to put the plaintiff in the position he would have been in if the tort (in this case fraud) had never been committed. This usually leads the court to the view that the buyer of goods or of a business would not have bought at all, so that all the damages flowing from the purchase are recoverable. (*Doyle* v. *Olby* (*Ironmongers*) *Ltd*, 1969.)[216] Aggravated damages (see further p. 311) may be given but it has not been finally decided whether an award of exemplary damages may be made. (*Mafo* v. *Adams*, 1969.)[217] This contrasts, for example, with damages for breach of a term of the contract where only damage which was in the contemplation of the parties is recoverable. This is not necessarily all of the plaintiff's loss. (See further p. 308.)

(d) Where the misrepresentation is negligent the person making the false statement is liable in damages and the onus of proving that the statement was not made negligently, but that there were reasonable grounds for believing it to be true, is on the maker of the statement (or representor). (Misrepresentation Act, 1967, s. 2(1).) The manner in which damages for negligent misrepresentation are assessed is discussed at p. 242.

In addition a principal can be affected by his agent's negligent misstatement of which he, the principal, is wholly unaware. (*Gosling* v. *Anderson*, 1972.)[218]

(e) A purely innocent misrepresentation may be remedied by an award of damages but these cannot be claimed as such. The person seeking relief must ask for rescission of the contract and the court may, in its discretion, award damages instead. (Misrepresentation Act, 1967, s. 2(2).)

Rescission

This remedy is available to a party misled by innocent, negligent, or fraudulent misrepresentation. It releases *the aggrieved party* from his obligations to accept performance and to carry out future obligations under the contract, e.g. a buyer who rescinds an instalment contract does not have to accept or pay for future deliveries but he must pay for past deliveries unless they were defective and were lawfully rejected. It also releases *the party in default* from future obligations to perform the contract, e.g. a landlord who validly rescinds a lease because the tenant has failed to pay rent, cannot sue the tenant for rent becoming due after the date of rescission of the lease. However, rescission does not excuse the party in default from liability in damages if his failure to perform the contract was in fact a breach. For example, in *Buckland* v. *Farmer and Moody*, [1978] 3 All E.R. 929 A had sold land to B and B failed to complete. A rescinded the contract and an award of damages in respect of his loss on the resale of the property to C was upheld by the Court of Appeal.

Rescission dates from the time when the party misled notifies his repudiation of the contract to the other party, or does any other act indicating repudiation. (*Car & Universal Finance Co.* v. *Caldwell*, 1963.)[219] A contract induced by fraud or misrepresentation (innocent or negligent) is voidable at the option of the party misled. The ways in which an injured party may lose the right of rescission are set out below.

(i) *If the injured party affirms the contract, he cannot rescind.* He will affirm the contract if, with full knowledge of the misrepresentation, he *expressly* affirms it by stating that he intends to go on with it, or if he does some act from which an implied intention may properly be deduced. (*Long* v. *Lloyd*, 1958.)[220]

Lapse of time, or delay in asking for the remedy, is evidence of affirmation and can defeat an action for rescission. This is sometimes known as the doctrine of *laches*, and it is based on the maxim: 'Delay defeats equities'. (*Leaf* v. *International Galleries*, 1950.)[197] However, as *Leaf's* case shows, lapse of time is an independent bar to rescission because in that case Leaf's claim was barred by lapse of time even though he had acted promptly when he discovered that the picture was a copy and so in that sense he could not be regarded as having affirmed. Lapse of time has no effect on rescission where fraud is alleged as long as the action is brought within six years of the time when the fraud was, or with reasonable diligence could have been, discovered. (Limitation Act, 1980, s. 32.) (*Applegate* v. *Moss*, 1970 and *King* v. *Parsons*, 1973; see p. 721.)

(ii) *Rescission will not normally be granted if the parties cannot be restored to their original positions.* (*Clarke* v. *Dickson*, 1858.)[221]

(iii) *It cannot be obtained where third party rights have accrued.* Rescission of a contract to take shares in a company cannot be obtained if the company has gone into liquidation because creditors' rights are paramount. Further, if X obtains goods from Y by fraud and pawns them with Z, Y cannot rescind the contract on learning of the fraud in order to recover the goods from Z, nor can he sue Z in conversion. (*Phillips* v. *Brooks Ltd*, 1919,[188] and *Lewis* v. *Averay*, 1971.)[190]

The equitable right of rescission is preserved even where the representation has been incorporated in the contract. (Misrepresentation Act, 1967, s. 1(a).) Although the section says 'Where . . . the misrepresentation has become a *term* of the contract,' it is not thought that there is a right to rescind for breach of warranty but only for a representation *incorporated in* the contract. If this is so, the availability of a remedy as drastic as rescission for a misrepresentation of minor importance when mere damages are available for a more serious breach of warranty is anomalous. Possibly, if the court is asked to rescind a contract for misrepresentation of minor importance, it will exercise its discretion under s. 2(2) of the 1967 Act to award damages in lieu of rescission.

Furthermore, a person is not prevented from asking for rescission merely because the contract has been performed. (Misrepresentation Act, 1967, s. 1(b).)

Certain problems are raised by the provisions of this section which are illustrated by the following example. A buys a drawing from B having been told by B, in innocence, that it is by Constable though it is in fact a fake. This assertion is then written in the subsequent contract as a condition of sale. If A wishes to reject the goods, he must do so within a reasonable time otherwise conditions become warranties for the purposes of remedies and A will have only an action for damages for the breach of condition. However, it seems that under s. 1(b) of the 1967 Act, A may ask for rescission for the innocent misrepresentation made by B. It would seem illogical to allow a person to rescind for innocent misrepresentation when his right to reject for breach of condition is barred. The problem may be solved by treating performance of the contract as *evidence* of the plaintiff's intention to treat the contract as subsisting, leaving him with an action for damages for the misrepresentation.

Damages for non-fraudulent misrepresentation

Damages are obtainable for non-fraudulent misrepresentation in the following cases—

(1) Innocent misrepresentation
(*a*) Section 2(2) of the Misrepresentation Act, 1967, provides that—

Where a person has entered into a contract after a misrepresentation has been made to him otherwise than fraudulently, and he would be *entitled*, by reason of the misrepresentation, to rescind the contract, then, if it is claimed, in any proceedings arising out of the contract, that the contract *ought to be* or has been rescinded, the court or arbitrator may declare the contract subsisting and award damages in lieu of rescission, if of opinion that it would be equitable to do so, having regard to the nature of the misrepresentation and the loss that would be caused by it if the contract were upheld, as well as to the loss that rescission would cause to the other party.

This subsection seems to be designed to give the court discretion to treat a contract as subsisting and award damages to the injured party in those cases where the misrepresentation is of a minor nature. However, damages cannot be awarded unless the party seeking them would have been *entitled* to rescind. Presumably, therefore, if a bar to rescission exists, e.g. delay, then damages cannot be awarded either. However, the subsection also uses the words 'ought to be . . . rescinded' and this may give the court a discretion to award damages even when a bar to rescission exists. For example, A sells a car to B, innocently representing that it is a 1988 model whereas it is a 1986 model. Six months later B discovers this fact and asks for rescission. Presumably, B is not *entitled* to rescind on grounds of delay, but whether he can obtain damages or not will depend upon which of the two constructions outlined above is adopted by the court.

A claim for damages in lieu of rescission under s. 2(2) of the 1967 Act appears to be independent of fault and any contractual intention. In these circumstances it is not clear whether damages will be assessed either in contract or in tort.

(*b*) *Agency*. Where an agent in good faith represents himself as having authority he does not possess, as where his principal is, unknown to the agent, dead, the third party may sue the agent for breach of warranty of authority if he suffers loss by not obtaining a contract with the principal, the action being based on quasi-contract.

(2) Negligent misrepresentation

(*a*) Section 2(1) of the Misrepresentation Act, 1967, provides that—

Where a person has entered into a contract after a misrepresentation has been made to him by another party thereto and as a result thereof he has suffered loss, then, if the person making the misrepresentation would be liable to damages in respect thereof had the misrepresentation been made fraudulently, that person shall be so liable notwithstanding that the misrepresentation was not made fraudulently, unless he proves that he had reasonable grounds to believe and did believe up to the time the contract was made that the facts represented were true.

Whether or not a representor can show reasonable grounds for believing his statement to be true will depend on what steps he has taken to *verify* what he has said. However, a representor particularly if not a dealer will normally be able to show reasonable grounds for believing his representation to be true if he was induced to buy the goods by the same misrepresentation. (See *Humming Bird Motors* v. *Hobbs*, 1986, p. 640). Presumably, the representor must have reasonable grounds for believing the statement to be true when he made it and right up to the time the contract was made. Thus, if a person makes a representation honestly and reasonably believing it to be true, and before contract receives additional information, which makes his belief unreasonable, he may be liable for negligent misrepresentation if he does nothing to correct his statement.

Damages for misrepresentation under s. 2(1) of the 1967 Act are assessed on the same principles as damages in tort. (*Chesneau* v. *Interhome Ltd*, 1983.)[222]

The subsection recognizes only a claim for damages and says nothing as to rescission. However, in *Mapes* v. *Jones*, (1974) 232 E.G. 717, a property dealer contracted to lease a grocer's shop to the plaintiff for 21 years but did not in fact have sufficient interest in the property himself to grant such a lease, the maximum period available to him being 18 years. Despite constant requests no lease was supplied as originally promised and the plaintiff shut the shop and elected to treat the contract as repudiated. Willis, J. held that the plaintiff was entitled to rescission for the misrepresentation under s. 2(1) of the 1967 Act. He also found that the defendant's delay in completion was a breach of condition allowing the plaintiff to repudiate the contract.

(*b*) Under s. 151 of the Financial Services Act, 1986 those responsible for publishing listing particulars containing false statements made innocently, will have to pay compensation unless—

(i) they had reasonable grounds for believing the statement to be true;

(ii) the statements were made on the authority of an expert who was thought to be competent; or

(iii) the statements were a copy of an official document;

(iv) If (i) to (iii) above cannot be proved, that they published a correction or took reasonable steps to see that one was published and reasonably believed it had been.

Experts, such as accountants, are also liable under the section for false statements in their reports which are included in the prospectus. The defence of lack of responsibility is available as where the expert has not consented to the inclusion of his report in the prospectus. However, given that he accepts responsibility for the inclusion of his report, he has a defence if he can show that he had reasonable grounds for believing his statement to be true. Presumably, he could sustain this defence by showing an appropriate standard of verification of his statements or that the false statement came from an official document.

(*c*) *Negligence at Common Law.* As we have seen, where the parties concerned were not in a pre-contractual relationship when the statement was made s. 2(1) of the Misrepresentation Act, 1967 will not apply. However, an action for damages for negligence will lie in tort provided the false statement is made negligently and a special relationship exists between the parties. (*Hedley Byrne & Co. Ltd* v. *Heller and Partners Ltd*, 1963.)[215] (But see p. 400.)

(3) Misrepresentation may raise an estoppel

If a person has relied on a mis-statement and has altered his previous position because of it, he may be able to resist a defence to an action for damages by raising an estoppel. (*Henderson* v. *Williams*, 1895.)[223]

It is also possible to recover a monetary indemnity for some losses caused by misrepresentation. This remedy can be asked for along with rescission where the court decides it will not award damages. Section 2(2) of the Misrepresentation Act, 1967, gives the court power to award damages instead of rescission but it cannot award both. Thus, if the court decides to grant rescission it is limited in its monetary award to that amount of loss for which Equity would give an indemnity. (*Whittington* v. *Seale-Hayne*, 1900.)[224]

Criminal penalties

In addition to the civil law remedies set out above the Trade Descriptions Act, 1968, makes it a criminal offence for a person to describe goods falsely or misleadingly.

The main offence relating to goods which are falsely described is set out in s. 1(1) of the 1968 Act which states 'Any person who, in the course of a trade or business, applies a false trade description to any goods or supplies or offers to supply any goods to which a false trade description is applied shall be guilty of an offence.' Car dealers in particular have fallen foul of this section. Successful prosecutions have been brought against dealers who have had cars displayed for sale whose odometers (mileometers) recorded fewer miles than the car had actually travelled.

A person who offends can be fined up to £2000 by magistrates and if tried on indictment before the Crown Court he can be fined an unlimited amount or face a sentence of imprisonment of up to two years. Additionally, the court can make a 'compensation order' in favour of the person who has been misled by the false description. The maximum amount of such orders is £2000 and they are made under s. 35 of the Powers of Criminal Courts Act, 1973. If no compensation order is made or if in the event it does not cover the whole loss, then civil proceedings can still be brought for the balance. In addition, any compensation paid under a compensation order made by a criminal court will be taken into account in later civil proceedings so that the person making the false description is not liable twice over. (S. 38, Powers of Criminal Courts Act, 1973.)

THE CONTENTS OF THE CONTRACT

Even where it is clear that a valid contract has been made, it is still necessary to decide precisely what it is the parties have undertaken to do in order to be able to say whether each has performed or not performed his part of the agreement.

In order to decide upon the terms of the contract it is necessary to find out what was said or written by the parties. Furthermore, having ascertained what the parties said or wrote, it is necessary to decide whether the statements were mere inducements (or representations) or terms of the contract itself, i.e. part of its actual contents.

EXPRESS TERMS

The statements of the parties

As we have seen, in order to decide upon the *express terms* of the contract it is necessary to find out what was said or written by the parties.

Where the contract is wholly oral this is a matter of fact to be decided by the court from the evidence presented to it and may give rise to problems where the evidence is conflicting and difficult to substantiate.

In the case of a written contract it is usually obvious what the parties have written down though there may be problems of interpretation arising, for example, from ambiguity, which the court may have to resolve. In addition it should be noted that where the terms of a contract have been written down the court may, to promote certainty, refuse to allow oral evidence to be admitted if it has the effect of adding to, varying or contradicting the written agreement. This rule is, however, subject to the following exceptions—

(*a*) *Oral evidence may be admitted to prove a trade custom or usage.* This will usually have the effect of adding a term or terms to the agreement. (See *Hutton* v. *Warren*, p. 652.)

(*b*) *Oral evidence may be admitted to show that the contract has not yet become effective.* This is not truly an exception since the contents of the contract are not varied, added to or contradicted. (*Pym* v. *Campbell*, 1856.)[225]

(*c*) *Oral evidence may be admitted where the court is of the opinion that the written document contains part only of the agreement.* This device is quite frequently used by the courts and represents a major exception to the rule relating to the admission of oral evidence. (*Quickmaid Rental Services* v. *Reece*, 1970.)[226]

Representation and terms

Having ascertained what the parties said or wrote it is necessary to decide whether the statements are representations or terms. Representations are statements which merely induce a contract whereas terms are part of the contract itself and make up its contents. The distinction is, of course, less important than it was since before the Misrepresentation Act, 1967, which created an action for damages for negligent misrepresentation, there was often no remedy for a misrepresentation which was not fraudulent. There was no possibility of damages for innocent misrepresentation and rescission was, as now, quite easily lost as a remedy. In such a case the plaintiff's only hope of obtaining a remedy was to convince the court that the defendant's statement was not a mere inducement but a term of the contract of which the defendant was in breach.

Whether a statement is a representation or a term of the contract is an issue of fact and no hard and fast rules can be laid down; however, certain broad tests may be applied—

(i) The court is always concerned to implement the *intentions of the parties* as they appear from statements made by them. Where, in a written contract, the parties have by their words indicated that a particular provision is to be considered as a term of the contract, then the court will normally follow that intention. Statements in written contracts are usually terms. In *Gill & Duffus SA* v. *Société pour l'Exportation des Sucres SA*, [1985] 1 Lloyd's Rep. 621 the defendants agreed to sell sugar to Gill. A term of the contract (not specified as a condition or warranty) said that the defendants were to name a port at which the sugar was to be loaded by November 14 'at latest'. The defendants did not nominate a port by that time and so Gill refused to take any sugar from the defendants and regarded the contract as cancelled. The defendants then tried to make a nomination of a port but Gill refused to accept it saying that they had repudiated the contract because of the defendants' breach of condition (or repudiatory breach). Following a decision unfavourable to them at arbitration, Gill appealed. Leggatt, J said that there were no words in the English language by which a deadline could be appointed more concisely, more precisely, or with more finality than 'at latest'. They meant what they said and the judge had no doubt that the intention of the parties as gathered from the contract itself, would be best carried out by treating the promise not as a mere warranty but as a condition precedent by the failure to perform which the other party was relieved of liability. Gill's contention was accepted. There was a repudiatory breach of condition.

Where the statement is an oral one, the court will decide the question by trying to ascertain the intentions of the parties and may come to the conclusion that the circumstances suggest that the statement was intended to be a term.

(ii) An oral statement is likely to be an inducement rather than a term if the person making the statement asks the other party to check or verify it, e.g. 'The car is sound, but I should get an engineer's report on it.'

(iii) An oral statement is likely to be a term if it is made with the intention of preventing the other party from finding any defects, and succeeds in doing this, e.g. 'The car is sound; you need not look it over.'

(iv) If an oral statement is so *important* that the aggrieved party would not have made the contract without it, then the statement will generally be a term of the contract. (*Bannerman* v. *White*, 1861.)[227]

(v) An oral statement made during *preliminary negotiations* tends to be an inducement. Where the interval between the making of the statement and the making of the contract is distinct, then the statement is almost certain to be an inducement. However, the interval is not always so well marked, and in such cases there is difficulty in deciding whether the statement is an inducement or a term. However, a college prospectus containing an outline of the syllabus of a course of study may form part of a contract between the college and a student who enters the college intending to follow that course. (*D'Mello* v. *Loughborough College of Technology*, 1970.)[228]

If the statement was oral and the contract was afterwards reduced to writing then the terms of the contract tend to be contained in the writing, and all oral statements tend to be pre-contractual inducements.

(vi) Where one of the parties has *special knowledge or skill* with regard to the subject-matter of the contract, then such a party can more easily give warranties to the other, and will find it difficult to convince the court that warranties have been given to him. (*Oscar Chess Ltd* v. *Williams*, 1957.)[229]

Conditions and warranties

Having decided that a particular statement is a term of the contract and not a mere inducement, the court must then consider the importance of that statement in the context of the contract as a whole. Not all of the obligations created by a contract are of equal importance and this is recognized by the law which has applied a special terminology to contractual terms in order to distinguish the vital or fundamental obligations from the less vital, the expression *condition* being applied to the former and the expression *warranty* to the latter.

A *condition* is vital term which goes to the root of the contract. It is an obligation which goes directly to the substance of the contract, or is so essential to its very nature that its non-performance may be considered by the other party as a substantial failure to perform the contract at all.

A *warranty*, on the other hand, is subsidiary to the main purpose. A warranty has been variously defined, but it may be said to be an obligation which, though it must be performed, is not so vital that a failure to perform it goes to the substance of the contract. It should be noted that the word 'warranty' is sometimes used in a different way, e.g. by a manufacturer of goods who gives a 'warranty' against faulty workmanship offering to replace parts free. The term 'warranty' is used by the manufacturer as equivalent to a guarantee. We are concerned in this book with its use as a term of a contract.

The distinction is important in terms of remedies. A breach of condition is called a repudiatory breach and the injured party may elect either to repudiate the contract, i.e. refuse to accept performance, or claim damages and go on with the contract. The plaintiff must go on with the contract and sue for damages if he has affirmed the contract after knowledge of a breach of condition. He may do this expressly, as where he uses the goods, or by lapse of time as where he simply fails to take any steps to complain about the breach for what in the court's view is an unreasonable period of time. A breach of warranty is not repudiatory and the plaintiff must go on with the contract and sue for damages. An interesting contrast is provided in *Poussard* v. *Spiers & Pond*, 1876[230] and *Bettini* v. *Gye*, 1876.[231]

Whether a term is a condition or a warranty is a question of the intention of the parties, and this is deduced from the circumstances of the case. Furthermore, the words used by the parties, while not conclusive, may be followed. They may have called a particular term a condition or a warranty, or even have used less specific terms whose intention is clear. In some cases where the parties state the effect of a breach, it becomes clear whether a condition or warranty was intended. (*Harling* v. *Eddy*, 1951.)[232] If there is no such indication, the court must decide the legal result of the breach, e.g. by addressing itself to the commercial importance of the term. (*Behn* v. *Burness*, 1863[233]: compare *Hong Kong Fir Shipping Co. Ltd* v. *Kawasaki Kisen Kaisha*, 1962.)[234] However, the mere fact that a commercial contract describes one of its terms as a 'condition' does not compel the court to hold that that term is a condition in the strict sense; the question must be decided by construing the contract as a whole. (*L. Schuler A.G.* v. *Wickham Machine Tool Sales*, 1973.)[235]

Before leaving the topic of conditions and warranties, the concept of the *intermediate or innominate term* should be noted. There are terms called intermediate or innominate terms which the parties may have called conditions or warranties. The effect of these on the contract depends upon how serious the breach has turned out to be *in fact*. If the breach has turned out to be serious the court will then treat the term as a condition so that the contract can be repudiated. If *in fact* the breach has not had a serious effect on the contract the court will treat it as a breach of warranty so that the parties must proceed with the contract, though the injured party will have an action for damages. (*Cehave NV* v. *Bremer Handelsgesellschaft, mbH—The Hansa Nord*, 1975.)[236]

Waiver of express terms

A person who is trying to enforce a contract may waive terms which have not been carried out but only if they are for his own exclusive benefit. This will rarely be the case. (*Heron Garage Properties Ltd* v. *Moss*, 1974.)[237]

IMPLIED TERMS

In addition to the *express* terms inserted by the parties and referred to above a contract may contain and be subject to *implied* terms. Such terms are derived from custom or statute. Furthermore, a term may be implied by the court where it is necessary in order to achieve the result which the parties obviously intended the contract to have.

Customary implied terms

A contract may be subject to customary terms not specifically mentioned by the parties. (*Hutton* v. *Warren*, 1836.)[238] However, customary terms will not be implied if the express terms of the contract reveal that the parties had a contrary intention.

Statutory implied terms—sale of goods and hire purchase

In a contract for the sale of goods the Sale of Goods Act, 1979, ss. 12–15, and in the case of a contract of hire purchase, the Supply of Goods (Implied Terms) Act, 1973, ss. 8–11, (as amended by Sched. 4, Part 1 para. 35 to the Consumer Credit Act 1974) settle the matter of implied terms. These terms, which are now broadly identical in both types of contract are as follows—

Title

There is a condition that the seller has the right to sell the goods (which in the case of hire purchase means at the end of the hiring period when the property is to pass) plus two warranties relating to the fact that the goods are free from encumbrances *known to the supplier* and that the buyer/hirer will have quiet possession of the goods. (*Rowland* v. *Divall*, 1923[239] and *Microbeads A.C.* v. *Vinhurst Road Markings*, 1975.)[240]

A seller who is not sure of his title may take advantage of a provision in s. 12(3) of the Sale of Goods Act, 1979 under which the sale of a limited interest is possible. Goods taken in execution by the sheriff (see p. 86) are usually sold with such a title as the seller may have because, although the bailiffs will try to ascertain that goods taken in execution are owned by the debtor, they may not in fact be and there is always the possibility that the real owner will dispossess the purchaser.

However, even where the sale is of a limited title under s. 12(3), there is an implied warranty that all charges or encumbrances known to the seller and not known to the buyer have been disclosed to the buyer before the contract is made. If this is not so and the buyer is dispossessed of the goods he would have an action for damages against the seller. (See s. 12(4), *ibid.*) Furthermore, there is an implied warranty that the buyer's quiet possession of the goods will not be disturbed by the seller or by a third person unless that third person has a charge or encumbrance on the goods which the seller has disclosed or which is known to the buyer before the contract is made. (See s. 12(5), *ibid.*) There can be, however, no claim by the buyer unless and until his quiet possession is disturbed.

Description

There is an implied condition that the goods shall correspond with the description. This is obviously of great importance where the goods are not seen before purchase as in a mail order sale. If an order were placed with a mail order firm for pink blankets as shown in the catalogue then the firm would be in breach of contract if it sent blue blankets. However, the condition also applies even where the goods are seen before purchase. (*Beale* v. *Taylor*, 1967.)[241]

Fitness for the purpose

There is an implied condition that the goods shall be reasonably fit for the purpose for which they are required. Breach of this implied condition usually means that the article is, because of its construction or design, not fit for the purpose for which it is required, so that no amount of adjustment or repair will ever make it so. In other words, it is the wrong article, but a perfect article. Thus in *Baldry* v. *Marshall*, [1924] 1 K.B. 260 a buyer went to a car salesman and asked for a car 'suitable for touring the Continent'. The salesman agreed to supply such a car and the contract was made. However, some days later the salesman delivered a car which was in fact a single-seater racing Bugatti. Although, obviously, the car was merchantable since it was totally free from defect, it was not fit for its purpose, i.e. for touring the Continent, and in that sense offended the implied condition of fitness.

Merchantable quality

There is an implied condition that the goods shall be of merchantable quality. An article is usually not merchantable because of some manufacturing defect. The situation is one in which a perfect article would serve the purpose but the one supplied will not because of an inherent defect. In other words, it is the right article but is a faulty one. Suppose, for example, that a purchaser goes to some showrooms and asks to buy a large gas cooker to cater for a large family. Let us suppose that he is shown a particular cooker which is demonstrated and that he orders a new cooker of that type. If, when it is delivered it will not work because of a faulty part, then although the cooker is fit for its purpose in the sense that a perfect cooker of that type would do the job of cooking for the large family, it offends the condition as to merchantable quality because it will not work. (See *Godley* v. *Perry*, 1960.)[242]

The condition of merchantable quality does not apply to defects drawn to the customer's attention before the contract is made or which any previous examination by the customer *ought to have revealed*, even if it has not.

Sale by sample

There are three implied conditions in a transaction by sample—

(a) the bulk must correspond with the sample in quality, (b) the buyer shall have a reasonable opportunity of comparing the bulk with the sample, and (c) the goods shall be free from any defect rendering them unmerchantable which would not be apparent on reasonable examination of the sample. (See *Godley* v. *Perry*, 1960.)[242]

Nature of liability

An action for damages based upon breach of a statutory implied term is against the retailer of the goods and not the manufacturer. Privity of contract prevents a *direct* action against the manufacturer, though the retailer will normally join the manufacturer so that the latter will end up paying the damages. Liability for breach of a statutory term is also strict in the sense that it does not depend upon fault, e.g. the retailer is liable even though he is not responsible for the contents of, say a packet of goods which he is selling. However, damage may in some cases be too remote.

If, for example, a retailer sells goods which are faulty and in breach of s. 14, he is obliged to indemnify the purchaser if the faulty goods injure a third party to whom the purchaser is found liable. No such indemnity is payable if the purchaser has continued to use the goods having become aware that they are faulty and dangerous. (*Lambert* v. *Lewis*, 1981.)[243] Product liability in negligence is considered at p. 392.

Statutory implied terms—supply of goods and services

As we have seen, those who buy goods have the protection of the implied terms of the Sale of Goods Act, 1979. Those who take goods on hire purchase are similarly protected by the Supply of Goods (Implied Terms) Act, 1973 (as amended).

As regards contracts for work and materials, e.g. the repair of a car in a garage where work is done and materials supplied, Part I of the Supply of Goods and Services Act, 1982 applies to the materials used. The services supplied (or the work element) are governed by Part II of the 1982 Act.

Contracts of exchange or barter, hire, rental, or leasing, are governed by Part I of the 1982 Act, while contracts for services only, e.g. a contract to carry goods or advice from an accountant or solicitor, are governed by Part II of the 1982 Act. The main provisions of the Act are dealt with below.

THE SUPPLY OF GOODS—PART I

Contracts for the transfer of property in goods

The contracts concerned are dealt with in s. 1(1) which provides that a contract for the transfer of goods means a contract under which one person transfers, or agrees to transfer to another, the property in goods, unless the transfer takes place under an excluded contract. These excluded contracts are set out in s. 1(2). They are, for example, contracts for the sale of goods and hire-purchase contracts. Transfer of property rights in goods by way of mortgage, pledge, charge, or other security are excluded, as are pure gifts.

There must be a contract between the parties. If not, the statutory implied terms cannot be relied upon if the goods supplied prove to be defective. Thus a chemist supplying harmful drugs under a National Health Service prescription will not come within the Act. This is because the patient does not provide consideration. The chemist collects the prescription charge for the Government and not for himself. The payment to the chemist does not come from the patient unless it is a private prescription where the patient has paid the full amount. Otherwise an action against the chemist will have to be framed in the tort of negligence.

As regards promotional free gifts, e.g. the giving away of a radio to a purchaser of a television set, the free gift would appear to be within the 1982 Act. In *Esso Petroleum Co. Ltd* v. *Commissioners of Customs and Excise*, [1976] 1 All E.R. 117, Esso supplied a 'World Cup' coin depicting a footballer with every four gallons of petrol. If the supply was a sale Esso were liable to purchase tax (now abolished). The House of Lords held that the sale of the petrol being for money was obviously a contract for sale. However, the coins were supplied under a collateral contract. The consideration for this was the making of a contract to buy four gallons of petrol. Thus it was not a money consideration and so not a sale of goods. However, since the House of Lords found that the coins were supplied under a collateral contract for which there was consideration, presumably the implied terms of the 1982 Act can be implied into that collateral contract. Thus, normally the distributor of the goods would be liable under the Act if the goods are defective but if the manufacturer sells the goods direct he will be liable under a collateral contract in respect of any accompanying promotional gifts.

The contracts covered by Part I

These are contracts for work and materials, exchange and barter, and hire.

Contracts for work and materials

It is impossible to provide a complete lists of contracts for work and materials but they fall under three broad heads as follows—

(1) *Maintenance contracts.* Here the organization doing the maintenance supplies the labour and spare parts as required. An example would be a maintenance contract for lifts.

(2) *Building and construction contracts.* Here the builder supplies labour and materials. An example would be the alteration of an office or workshop involving the insertion of new windows and extending the central heating.

(3) *Installation and improvement contracts.* Here the contractor does not have to build or construct anything but, e.g. fit equipment into an existing building, or apply paint to it. Examples are the fitting of an air-conditioning system, or painting and decorating an office or workshop.

The terms implied

These are similar to those in the Sale of Goods Act, 1979 as regards the materials supplied, i.e. s. 2 deals with title; s. 3 with description; s. 4(2) with merchantable quality; s. 4(5) with fitness for the purpose; and s. 5 with sample.

Remedies

Insofar as the implied terms are conditions and are broken by the supplier, then the customer can treat the contract as repudiated. The customer is discharged from his obligation to pay the agreed price and may recover damages. The breach of implied warranties gives the customer only the right to sue for damages.

Exchange and barter

The most likely transactions to emerge here are the exchange of goods for vouchers and coupons as part of promotional schemes. Part I of the 1982 Act applies and the retailer who supplies the goods under a contract to the customer is the one who is liable if they are in breach of, e.g. the implied terms of fitness and/or merchantable quality. The manufacturer will be liable to the retailer, of course.

An exchange transaction in which goods are simply exchanged is not a sale but is covered by the 1982 Act. Where part of the consideration is money, as in a part-exchange of an old car for a new one with a cash difference, the contract is presumably a sale of goods because money is at least part of the consideration and this is necessary if it is to be a sale of goods. It does not really matter now whether it is a sale or a supply because the implied terms are almost identical.

Often where there has been a sale of faulty goods the seller exchanges them for other goods of the same type, although he is under no legal duty to do so unless a particular contract expressly provides. What happens if the other goods are faulty? The substitute goods must comply with the implied terms as to title, description, quality and fitness, and there is no longer any point in going into legal niceties as to whether the exchange is a sale or supply.

The terms implied

The implied terms in exchange or barter are the same as those implied in a contract for work and materials as regards the goods supplied, i.e. s. 2 (title), s. 3 (description), s. 4(2) (merchantable quality), s. 4(5) (fitness), and s. 5 (sample).

Contracts for hire of goods

The main areas of hiring (or renting or leasing) are as follows—

(1) *office equipment*, e.g. office furniture and a variety of machines, including telephones;

(2) *building and construction plant and equipment*, e.g. cranes and JCB's;

(3) *consumer hiring*, e.g. cars, television and video.

Under s. 6(1) a contract for the hire of goods means a contract under which one person bails, or agrees to bail, goods to another by way of hire. There must be a contract, so that when the next-door neighbour makes a free loan of his lawnmower the Act does not apply. Also excluded are hire purchase agreements. A contract is a contract of hire whether or not services are also provided. This would be the case where a supplier rented a television to a customer and also undertook to service it.

The terms implied

Section 7 deals with title. It reflects s. 2 except that being a contract of hire there is provision only for the transfer of possession and not ownership. As regards description, s. 8 is the equivalent of s. 3. Section 9 enacts the same provisions for hiring contracts in regard to quality and fitness as s. 4 does for contracts for work and materials and exchange and barter. Section 10 applies to sample and is in line with s. 5 which applies to contracts of work and materials and exchange and barter.

Before leaving the topic of implied terms under the Sale of Goods Act, 1979, the Supply of Goods (Implied Terms) Act, 1973, and the Supply of Goods and Services Act, 1982, it should be noted that the implied terms regarding merchantable quality and fitness for the purpose apply only to those who supply goods in the course of a business.

THE SUPPLY OF SERVICES—PART II

The main areas of complaint in regard to service have been the poor quality of service, e.g. the careless servicing of cars; slowness in completing work where complaints have ranged over a wide area, e.g. from building contractors to solicitors, and, finally, the cost of the work, i.e. overcharging. Part II of the Act is concerned to deal with these matters.

The contracts covered

Under s. 12(1) a contract for the supply of a service means a contract under which a person agrees to carry out a service. A contract of service (i.e. an employment contract) or apprenticeship, is not included, but apart from this no attempt is made to define the word 'service'. However, the services provided by the professions, e.g. accountants, architects, solicitors, and surveyors, are included. Section 12(4) gives the Secretary of State for Trade and Industry power to exempt certain services from the provisions of Part II. Of importance here is the Supply of Services (Exclusion of Implied Terms) Order, 1982 (SI 1982/1771) which retains the common law liability in negligence of lawyers by exempting barristers and solicitors when acting as advocates before various courts and tribunals. It also exempts services rendered by a director to his company, thus retaining the existing common law liability in this area, too. This is largely because more time is needed to consult the relevant interests and decide what sort of liability there should be in the areas referred to.

Part II applies only to contracts. If there is no contract there cannot be implied terms. This will exclude work done free as a friendly gesture by a friend or neighbour. If, however, injury is caused to a person who is not in a contractual relationship with a supplier as a result of the negligence of the supplier, there may be an action in the tort of negligence at common law. (See *Junior Books Ltd* v. *Veitchi Co. Ltd*, 1982, p. 804.)

Duty of care and skill

This duty applies to contracts which are purely for service, e.g. advice from an accountant or solicitor, and also to the service element of a contract for work and materials. Section 13 provides that where the supplier of a service is acting in the course of a business there is an implied term that the supplier will carry out that service with reasonable skill and care. This means that the service must be performed with the care and skill of a reasonably competent member of the supplier's trade or profession. In other words, the test is objective, not subjective. Thus an incompetent supplier may be liable, even though he has done his best. A private supplier of a service, e.g. a milkman who is 'moonlighting' by doing the odd bit of decorating, will not have this duty.

There is no reference to conditions and warranties in regard to this implied term. Generally, therefore, the action for breach of the term will be one for damages. In a serious case the repudiation of the contract may be possible. This is rather like the intermediate term concept discussed at p. 248.

Cases such as *Woodman* v. *Photo Trade Processing Ltd*, 1981 and *Waldron-Kelly* v *British Railways Board*, 1981, which were brought on the basis of the common law tort of negligence would now be brought under the 1982 Act. (See further p. 262.)

Time for performance

Section 14 provides that the supplier will carry out the service within a reasonable time. This term is only implied where the time for performance is not fixed by the contract, left to be fixed in a manner agreed by the contract, or determined by the dealings of the parties. Section 14 states that what is a reasonable time is a question of fact. A plaintiff can claim damages for unreasonable delay. Of course, if a time for performance is fixed by the contract, it must be performed at that time and the question of reasonableness does not arise. Time is the essence in commercial contracts unless the parties expressly provide otherwise or there is a waiver. (See further p. 295.)

The charges made for the service

Under s. 15 the customer's obligation is to pay 'a reasonable charge' which is again a matter of fact. This is not implied where the charge for the service is determined by the contract, left to be determined in a manner agreed by the contract, or determined by the dealings of the parties. The section in essence enacts the common law rule of *quantum meruit* (see p. 314): it protects both supplier and customer.

Judicial implied terms

The court may imply a term into a contract which is not inchoate but complete and enforceable without the implied term, whenever it is necessary to do so in order that the express terms decided upon by the parties shall have the effect which was presumably intended by them. This is often expressed as the giving of 'business efficacy' to the contract, the judge regarding himself as doing merely what the parties themselves would have done in order to cover the situation if they had addressed themselves to it. For example, a contract to employ a lorry-driver must contain an implied term that he has the necessary licence.

The operation of the doctrine is illustrated by *The Moorcock*, 1889,[244] and *Lister* v. *Romford Ice and Cold Storage Co. Ltd*, 1957.[245] It should be noted that the court will not improve a contract which the parties have made, however desirable the improvement might be. If the express terms are perfectly clear and free from ambiguity, and there is no choice to be made between different possible meanings, the clear terms must be applied. (*Trollope & Colls Ltd*, v. *North West Metropolitan Regional Hospital Board*, 1973.)[246]

Conditional agreements

The expression 'condition' may also be used to denote *an event on which the operation or continued operation of the contract depends*. Such conditions, which are referred to as conditions *precedent* or *subsequent* must be distinguished from conditions which are an *essential term of the contract*, breach of which will give rise to a right to repudiate. Essential terms have already been considered under the headings 'Express and Implied Terms' above.

As an example, let us suppose that A agrees to take a lease of B's house, provided B puts it in good repair. The fact that B must put the house in good repair is a condition precedent to A's obligation to take the lease (and see also *Pym* v. *Campbell*, 1856.)[225] If the lease contains the normal covenants by the tenant to repair and a condition allowing the landlord to re-enter and determine the lease if at any time during the period of the lease the tenant does not repair, then this is a condition subsequent so that the tenant's failure to repair would entitle the landlord to put an end to the lease.

EXCLUSION CLAUSES

A contract may contain express terms under which one or both of the parties excludes or limits liability for breach of contract or negligence. Although such express terms are permissible, both the courts and Parliament have been reluctant to allow exclusion clauses where they have been imposed on a weaker party, such as an ordinary consumer, by a stronger party, such as a person or corporation in business to supply goods or services.

The attitude of the courts

The judges have protected consumers of goods and services against the effect of exclusion clauses in two main ways i.e. by deciding that the exclusion clause never became part of the contract and by construing (or interpreting) the contract in such a way as to prevent the application of the clause.

1. Was the clause part of the contract?
The court will require the person wishing to rely on an exclusion clause to show that the other party agreed to it at or before the time when the contract was made, otherwise it will not form part of the agreement.

The Unfair Contract Terms Act, 1977 (see below) provides, broadly speaking, that an exclusion clause will not operate unless it is reasonable. Nevertheless, the rules set out below are still of importance because a reasonable clause may fail if it has not been communicated.

(a) Where a contract is made by signing a written document the signer will in general be bound by everything which the document contains, even if he has not read it (*L'Estrange* v. *Graucob*, 1934),[247] unless the signature was induced by misrepresentation as to the effect of the document. (*Curtis* v. *Chemical Cleaning and Dyeing Co.*, 1951.)[208] An exception is the rule of *non est factum* provided the signer is not negligent.

(b) Where the terms are contained in an unsigned document, the person seeking to rely on an exclusion clause must show that the document was an integral part of the contract which could be expected to contain terms. (*Chapelton* v. *Barry U.D.C.*, 1940.)[248] However, if the document is contractual in the sense outlined above the clause may apply even though the plaintiff did not actually know about the exclusion clause in the sense that he had not read it. Communication may be constructive so long as the document adequately draws the attention of a reasonable person to the existence of terms and conditions. (*Thompson* v. *L.M.S. Railway*, 1930[249] and *Richardson Steamship Co. Ltd* v. *Rowntree*, 1894.)[250] However, the rule will not be applied if it would be unduly burdensome for the party affected by it (see *Interfoto Picture Library Ltd* v. *Stiletto Visual Programmes Ltd*, 1987 at p. 661).

(*c*) Where the defendant has not given the plaintiff a copy of conditions or drawn his attention to them when making a particular contract, constructive notice may not apply, at least in consumer transactions, to enable the defendant to rely on previous communications in previous dealings. (*McCutcheon* v. *David MacBrayne*, 1964.)[251] For non-consumer transactions see *British Crane Hire Corporation* v. *Ipswich Plant Hire*, 1974.[252]

(*d*) Any attempt to introduce an exclusion clause *after* the contract has been made is ineffective because the consideration for the clause is then past. (*Olley* v. *Marlborough Court Ltd*, 1949.)[253]

(*e*) The doctrine of privity of contract may also prevent the application of an exclusion clause. Thus, if A, the owner of a bus company, excludes his own and his employees' liability for damage to property of passengers by a properly communicated clause, an employee who causes damage to property will be liable, although his employer will not be, because the employee is not a party to the contract which is between his employer and the passenger. (But see *Snelling* v. *J. G. Snelling*, 1972[106] and *The New Zealand Shipping Co. Ltd* v. *A. M. Satterthwaite & Co. Ltd*, 1974.)[254]

It should be noted that where there is no contract between the parties there can be no contractual assent to damage inflicted. In such a case the defendant can only hope to show that the plaintiff has voluntarily assumed risk, i.e. plead the defence of *volenti non fit injuria* (see p. 361). (*Burnett* v. *British Waterways Board*, 1973.)[255]

2. Construction of exclusion clauses

If an exclusion clause has been communicated and become part of the contract, the party who wishes to rely on it must show that the breach and the loss are covered by the clause, or in other words are within its scope. Rules of construction (i.e. interpretation) of contract may, when applied, prevent the application of an exclusion clause by cutting down its scope. The major rules of construction are as follows—

(*a*) *The contra proferentem rule.* Under this rule if there is any ambiguity or room for doubt as to the meaning of an exclusion clause the courts will construe it in a way unfavourable to the person who put it into the contract. An example of the application of this rule is to be seen in *Hollier* v. *Rambler Motors*, 1972 (p. 662) and *Alexander* v. *Railway Executive*, 1951.[256]

(*b*) *The repugnancy rule.* This rule says in effect that the exemption clause is in direct contradiction to another term of the contract and is therefore repugnant to it. Where such repugnancy exists the exemption clause can be struck out. Thus, to take an extreme case, if A makes a contract to supply oranges to B but includes a clause which allows him to supply any sort of fruit, the clause is repugnant to the main purpose of the contract and could be struck out. Thus, A would be liable in breach of contract if he supplied B with apples and could not rely on the clause to excuse his breach of contract. (And see *Pollock* v. *Macrae*, 1922[257] and *Karsales (Harrow) Ltd* v. *Wallis*, 1956.)[258]

The rule also applies to the construction of a main contract with a collateral one as *Mendelssohn* v. *Normand Ltd*, 1969[259] and *Evans* v. *Merzario*, 1976[260] illustrate.

(c) *The four corners rule.* Under this rule exemption clauses only protect a party when he is acting within the four corners of the contract. Thus he is liable for damage which occurs while he is deviating from the contract and he would not be protected by any exclusion clause. (See *Thomas National Transport (Melbourne) Pty Ltd and Pay* v. *May and Baker*, 1966.)[261]

3. The doctrine of fundamental breach

The doctrine of fundamental breach was developed, particularly by the Court of Appeal, (see *Karsales (Harrow) Ltd* v. *Wallis*, 1956)[258] as a weapon with which to attack exclusion clauses which had in fact been properly communicated. It was repudiated by the House of Lords in the *Suisse Case*, [1966] 2 All E.R. 61 and then revived by the Court of Appeal in *Harbutt's Plasticine Ltd* v. *Wayne Tank & Pump Co Ltd*, [1970] 1 All E.R. 225. It was finally demolished by the House of Lords in *Photo Production Ltd* v. *Securicor Transport Ltd*, 1980.[262]

The doctrine of fundamental breach said that an exclusion clause could not, *as a matter of law*, protect a party from liability for a serious breach of contract, even if, as a matter of construction, the words of the clause did apply to the breach which had occurred. The House of Lords in *Photo Production*[262] said that the doctrine of fundamental breach had played a useful part in protecting consumers but that there was no need for it now that the Unfair Contract Terms Act was coming into force.

As regards exclusion clauses now, the matter is firstly whether the clause has been communicated, secondly whether as a matter of construction of the contract the clause covers the breach and the loss, and thirdly, if it does, one turns to the Unfair Contract Terms Act of 1977 to see whether the clause is struck down by the provisions of that Act. The only surviving aspect of the fundamental breach cases is that particularly in transactions with consumers (see below) the more serious the breach and its consequences, the more likely the court is to find that an exemption clause does not cover the breach. The *Photo Production* case indicates that an exclusion clause can excuse a fundamental breach in a non-consumer situation, i.e. where both parties are in business.

The approach of Parliament

Legislation affecting exclusion clauses is as set out below—

The Unfair Contract Terms Act, 1977

Generally

The Act is concerned with exclusion and restriction of *business liability* (s. 1(3)), though 'business' includes the practising of a profession and the activities of departments of local government and public authorities. (S. 14.) The main protection of the Act is in respect of those who deal as 'consumers', i.e. those who do not make the contract in the course of business in circumstances where the other party is contracting in the course of a business.

However, in *R & B Customs Brokers Co. Ltd* v. *United Dominions Trust Ltd, The Times*, 28 December, 1987 the Court of Appeal decided that when a business buys goods it may still take advantage of consumer law applying to an ordinary member of the public if the transaction concerned is not a regular one. The facts of the case were that R & B Customs bought a car for the use of a director. The contract excluded an implied term under s. 14(3) of the Sale of Goods Act 1979 that the goods be fit for the purpose. Such an exclusion does not operate if the sale is between a person in business and a consumer. It was held that R & B Customs must be treated as a consumer. The purchase of the car was not a frequent transaction and unless regularity could be established the transaction could not be regarded as an integral part of the business and was not therefore in the course of business. Furthermore, where goods are supplied they must be of a type usually supplied for private use or consumption. (S. 12(1)(c).) Thus it will be seen that in the sale of, e.g. a radio between a private seller and a private buyer the Act will not in general apply and exclusion clauses will be allowed to operate.

The Act extends to, and prevents, the imposition of short time limits on claims or restrictions on the way in which claims must be made, and also the restriction of rights or remedies, e.g. not allowing repudiation for breach of condition, but allowing instead only damages. (S. 13(1).) However, a written agreement to take disputes to arbitration is not regarded as excluding or restricting liability. (S. 13(2).)

Invalid exclusions

The Act renders wholly ineffective any terms of a contract or a notice by which a person acting in the course of a business (whom we may call B)—

(i) *Excludes or restricts liability for death or personal injury arising from negligence.* (S. 2(1).) However, in *Thompson* v. *Lohan*, [1987] 1 W.L.R. 649 A hired plant together with operatives to B. The contract contained a clause stating that B was liable for the negligence of the operatives who were A's employees. This clause was held by the Court of Appeal not to be contrary to s. 2 of the Unfair Contract Terms Act. It was not designed to restrict or exclude liability to those who might be injured by the negligence of the operatives but merely decided whether A or B was to bear the liability.

(ii) *Includes an exclusion clause in a manufacturer's guarantee of goods supplied for consumer use.* (S. 5.) Such a guarantee cannot effectively exclude or restrict liability for loss or damage resulting from defects in the goods while they are being used by a consumer and arising from negligence in manufacture or distribution, e.g. in the way in which the goods, such as cars, are prepared for sale by the distributor.

Section 5 is concerned with actions, either in negligence or on the collateral contract which the guarantee can create, against the manufacturer who is not the seller of the goods to the customer. The section is not concerned with the contractual relationship between the seller and the customer which is governed by ss. 6 and 7 (below). Thus a manufacturer's 12-month guarantee which said that the goods would, if defective, be replaced or repaired free of charge, but ended with a phrase such as: 'This guarantee is in lieu of, and expressly excludes all liability to compensation for loss or damage howsoever caused' would not prevent a claim by the purchaser against the manufacturer if the purchaser was, e.g. electrocuted by a vacuum cleaner (see *Donoghue* v. *Stevenson*, 1932, p. 740) or possibly for defective performance not causing physical injury. (See *Junior Books Ltd* v. *Veitchi Co. Ltd*, 1982, p. 804.)

(iii) *Attempts to exclude or restrict liability for breaches of terms implied by law in a consumer transaction.* (Ss. 6(2) and 7(2).) It will be recalled that in contracts of sale and hire purchase terms are implied by statute (see p. 248). As regards sale and hire purchase contracts, the implied terms as to title cannot be excluded, even in private transactions. (S. 6(1) and (4).)

Section 11 of the Supply of Goods and Services Act, 1982 applies the provisions of the Unfair Contract Terms Act, 1977 to exclusion clauses in work and materials, barter and exchange, and hiring contracts. The effect of this is set out below.

(*a*) *Consumer transactions.* In a contract covered by Part I of the Act the rights given by the implied terms under ss. 3–5 and ss. 8–10 of the 1982 Act cannot be excluded or restricted.

(*b*) *Business contracts.* In these circumstances the supplier can only rely on an exclusion clause if it is reasonable. However, the obligations relating to title in s. 2 of the 1982 Act cannot be excluded in a business dealing relating to work and materials and barter and exchange any more than they can in a consumer dealing. (See s. 7, Unfair Contract Terms Act, 1977, as amended by s. 17(2) of the 1982 Act.) However, the term in s. 7 relating to the right of possession in the case of a hiring can be excluded in a consumer or business contract if reasonable.

(iv) *Attempts to exclude or restrict civil liability under the Consumer*

Safety Act, 1978. Sometimes regulations made under the Act only affect the manufacturer, e.g. those which are concerned with design. Other regulations may affect the manufacturer, the wholesaler, and the retailer, e.g. those which require safety information to be supplied with the goods. If a trader, whether a manufacturer, wholesaler or retailer, infringes any of the regulations provided that they apply to him and causes damage or loss to a consumer by reason of the infringement, that person may sue for damages. It is not necessary to prove negligence. An action may be brought directly against the manufacturer even though the goods were not bought from him and even though the goods were not bought at all by the person injured, as where they were received as a gift. The Consumer Safety (Amendment) Act, 1986 extends the Government's power to enforce the provisions of the Consumer Safety Act, 1978.

Clauses effective if reasonable

Certain exclusion clauses are allowed to take effect provided they are *reasonable*. The party claiming that the clause is reasonable has the burden of proving that this is so. (S. 11(5).) The position is as follows—

(i) *Negligence liability other than death and personal injury.* The requirement of reasonableness applies to clauses seeking to exclude liability for negligence in regard, e.g. to damage to goods or loss of property. (S. 2(2).)

This aspect of the Act came up for consideration in two county court cases which it is believed were the first to be brought under the Act. In *Woodman* v. *Photo Trade Processing*, heard in the Exeter County Court in May, 1981, Mr Woodman took to the Exeter branch of Dixons Photographic for processing a film which carried pictures of a friend's wedding. The film was of special value because Mr Woodman had been the only photographer at the wedding, and he had said he would give the pictures as a wedding present. Unfortunately, the film was lost and when Dixons were sued they relied on an exclusion clause which, it appeared, was standard practice throughout the trade. The clause read as follows: 'All photographic materials are accepted on the basis that their value does not exceed the loss of the material itself. Responsibility is limited to the replacement of film. No liability will be accepted, consequential or otherwise, however caused'. The county court judge found that the customer had no real alternative but to entrust his film to a firm that would use such an exclusion clause and that, furthermore, Dixons could have foreseen that the film might be irreplaceable, and although Dixons could argue that the exclusion clause enabled them to operate a cheap mass-production technique, it could not be regarded as reasonable that all persons, regardless of the value of their films, should be required to take their chance of the system losing them. The judge therefore granted compensation of £75 to Mr Woodman and held that the exclusion clause was unreasonable.

In *Waldron-Kelly* v. *British Railways Board*, [1981] C.L.Y. 303, the plaintiff delivered a suitcase to Stockport railway station so that it could be taken to Haverfordwest station. The contract of carriage was subject to the British Railways Board general conditions 'at owner's risk' for a price of £6. A clause exempted the Board for any loss, except that if a case disappeared then the Board's liability was to be assessed by reference to the weight of the goods, which in this case was £27, and not to their value, which in this case was £320. The suitcase was lost whilst it was in the control of British Rail. Judge Brown, in the Stockport County Court, held that the plaintiff succeeded in his contention that the exclusion clause was unreasonable and therefore of no effect. The judge held that in the case of non-delivery of goods the burden of proof to show what had happened to the goods was on the bailee. British Rail had failed to show that the loss was not their fault and in any case the fault and loss were not covered by the exclusion clause because it did not satisfy the test of reasonableness.

Further, in *Stag Line Ltd* v. *Tyne Ship Repair Group Ltd*, [1984] 2 Lloyd's Rep. 211 Staughton, J., in finding that exclusion clauses inserted into the contract by the defendants were not fair and reasonable, said: 'The courts would be slow to find clauses in commercial contracts made between parties of equal bargaining power to be unfair or unreasonable, but a provision in a contract, which deprived a ship owner of any remedy for breach of contract or contractual negligence unless the vessel were returned to the repairer's yard for the defect to be remedied would be unfair and unreasonable because it would be capricious; the effectiveness of the remedy would depend upon where the ship was when the casualty occurred and whether it would be practical or economic to return the vessel to the defendants' yard.' Also in *Rees-Hough Ltd* v. *Redland Reinforced Plastics Ltd*, (1984) 134 N.L.J. 706 His Honour Judge Newey, QC, decided that it was not fair and reasonable for the defendants to rely on an exclusion clause in their standard terms and conditions of sale. They had sold pipes to the plaintiffs which were not fit for the purpose for which the defendants knew they were required, nor were they of merchantable quality under the Sale of Goods Act, 1979 and the clause excluded liability for this. Clearly, then it is difficult to apply exclusion clauses which try to prevent liability for supplying defective goods.

Where there is no contract, as in the *Hedley Byrne* situation where a bank used a 'without responsibility' disclaimer, s. 2(2) of the Act applies the reasonable test to the disclaimer.

(ii) *Clauses excluding or restricting liability in regard to terms implied by statute*. These may be allowed to operate so as to exclude, e.g. fitness for the purpose and merchantable quality in a non-consumer transaction, provided they are reasonable. (Ss. 6(3) and 7(3).) (See *Mitchell (George) (Chesterhall) Ltd* v. *Finney Lock Seeds Ltd*, 1983.)[263]

(iii) *Clauses excluding breach of contract generally*. Where a contract is made by B with a consumer, or where a contract is made by B with a consumer or non-consumer on B's written standard terms, the clause may be allowed to operate if reasonable. (S. 3(1) and (2)(a).)

The Act applies to failure to perform or the rendering of a different type of performance. (S. 3(2)(b).) Thus if a holiday contract with a tour operator, apparently for a 14-day holiday in Corfu, contained a clause allowing the operator to substitute ten days at a different price, or a different location, or cancel the contract, the clause would apply only if reasonable.

Terms allowing one party to refuse to perform or continue to perform on failure of the other party to carry out his obligations would seem to be legal and outside the provisions of the Act, as would clauses restricting the duty to perform in certain circumstances, e.g. if there is a strike.

(iv) *Contracts of indemnity.* Suppose B, a builder, agrees to repoint the house of a consumer, C, and the contract contains a clause that C will reimburse B for any damage which B has to pay to A, who is injured by reason of B's operations, as where a scaffold collapses on to the road, then the promise by C to reimburse B will apply only if reasonable. (S. 4.) Such clauses are unlikely to be found reasonable and B will have to cover himself by insurance. The section does not cover non-consumer situations and the indemnity found in *British Crane Hire* (see p. 663) would still be enforceable (and see *Thompson* v. *Lohan*, 1987 at p. 260).

(v) *Contracts on standard terms.* The requirement of reasonableness applies to an exclusion clause in a contract which is on 'written standard terms of business'. Examples include a wide variety of printed documents, tickets, quotations, catalogues, price lists, and notices, setting out conditions of one sort or another on which the supplier's customers are expected to contract.

(vi) *Misrepresentation liability.* There can be no exclusion of liability for misrepresentation or inducement liability unless reasonable. (S. 8.) The section also applies to non-business liability. A private seller cannot exclude his liability for misrepresentation unless he can show that the exclusion clause concerned satisfied the test of reasonableness. Thus, if one found in an estate agent's particulars a phrase such as the following 'notwithstanding any statement of fact included in these particulars, the vendor shall be conclusively deemed to have made no representation within the Misrepresentation Act', the clause would be of no effect unless reasonable. (*Walker* v. *Boyle*, 1982.)[264]

However, we should note the case of *Overbrook Estates Ltd* v. *Glencombe Properties Ltd*, [1974] 3 All E.R. 511 where conditions of sale contained in an auction catalogue stated that neither the auctioneers nor any person in their employ, had any authority to make or give any representations or warranty in relation to any particular property. Brightman, J. held that this clause was quite valid. It would not fall within the Unfair Contract Terms Act, 1977 because the Act prevents a person excluding liability for statements amounting to misrepresentation made by a duly authorized agent in circumstances where the agent has authority to make the statement. It does not prevent persons from cutting down the authority of their agents to make statements at all. Thus if the agent has authority to make the statement and it is false, liability cannot be excluded unless reasonable. If, however, the agent has no authority to make the statement at all, the 1977 Act does not apply, and the principal will not be liable for what the agent says to a person who knew that the agent had no authority to make the statement or had no reasonable grounds to believe that he had authority.

Meaning of reasonableness
The court which will decide the issue of reasonableness must consider—

(i) the clause in the context of the conditions prevailing when the contract was made. Subsequent changes of circumstances should not be allowed to influence the decision.

(ii) Where the clause is partial, i.e. restricts liability to a certain amount of money, regard must be had by the court to the resources of the person including the clause and the extent to which it was open to him to cover himself by insurance. (S. 11(4).) The object of this rule is to encourage persons to insure against liability in the sense that failure to do so will go against them if any exclusion clause which they have is before the court. However, in some cases it may be right to allow limitation of liability, e.g. in the case of professional persons such as solicitors and accountants where monetary loss may be caused to an horrendous amount following negligence and be beyond their power to insure against.

(iii) Where the contract is for the supply of goods, s. 11(2) and Sch. 2 lay down the following guidelines which the judge can bear in mind—

(a) the strength of the bargaining position of the parties;

(b) the availability of other supplies;

(c) the inducements to agree to the clause, as where the goods are offered for £9 with the clause, and £10 without it so that the purchaser pays for full liability in the seller;

(d) the buyer's knowledge of the clause, which implies that there must be honest disclosure and no concealment of it;

(e) customs of the trade and previous dealings;

(f) where the goods have been made or adapted to the order of the buyer it is possible for the supplier to exclude his liability if he feels that the design or adaption is not a sound one.

These guidelines will not, of course, eliminate some uncertainty which may arise from judicial discretion to interpret them. Although the above criteria are strictly speaking confined to exclusion of statutory implied terms in, e.g. the Sale of Goods Act, 1979, they are being applied in other situations. For example, Judge Clarke in *Woodman* v. *Photo Trade Processing* (see p. 262) felt it was right to use them where what was at issue was a negligent service.

It should be noted in particular that a term which is not reasonable will not apply even though the contract has been affirmed. (S. 9(2).)

Exclusion of Part II, Supply of Goods and Services Act, 1982
Section 15 of the 1982 Act applies the provisions of the Unfair Contract Terms Act, 1977 to exclusion clauses in regard to services. Section 2 of the 1977 Act is, as we have seen, concerned with liability for negligence. There can be no exclusion of liability if death or personal injury is caused. In other cases an exclusion clause may apply if reasonable.

Section 3 of the 1977 Act is concerned with liability for breach of contract. Broadly speaking, as we have seen, there can be no exclusion of liability for breach of contract, or a different performance or non-performance unless reasonable. The terms implied by the 1982 Act cannot be excluded in a consumer transaction. They can in a non-consumer deal if reasonable. The criteria relating to bargaining power and so on apply only to the exclusion of implied terms in a non-consumer transaction relating to goods, but they will no doubt be applied by analogy to the service element of contracts under the 1982 Act.

Other restrictions on evasion of the Act
The following points should be noted—

(i) If a term excluding or restricting liability is contained not in the main contract but in a separate one, the Act makes that separate or secondary contract ineffective so far as it tries to take away rights in the main contract, which under the Act cannot be excluded or restricted. (S. 10.) This is a complicated anti-avoidance provision but is aimed at the sort of case where a plaintiff who has a heating system installed by Company A is recommended to go to Company B for service of the system, Company B being a subsidiary of Company A. In these circumstances the service contract with company B may provide that the plaintiff will surrender his rights against Company A. In such a case the provision in the service contract is unenforceable.

(ii) If the contract contains a clause which makes it subject to the law of another country merely because one of the parties wishes to include an exemption clause which would be struck down by the 1977 Act but could well survive in another jurisdiction, then the Act will apply to the contract even though it contains such a clause provided the court is satisfied that it was imposed wholly or mainly to evade the 1977 Act.

Transactions not covered by the Act
The Act does not apply to contracts of insurance, nor to any contract for the transfer of an interest in land, so that house purchase is not covered. (S. 1(2) and Sch. 1, para 1(a) and (b).) The Act does not apply to contracts for the international supply of goods. (S. 26(1).) Finally, it would not apply to a contract which was international by nature and where the parties had no substantial connection with English law but the contract is, by reason of one of its provisions, said to be governed by English law. (S. 27(1).) Foreign businessmen who wish to use our courts to settle their differences are not required to comply with the 1977 Act.

Fair Trading Act, 1973

Under ss. 13 and 17 of this Act the Director-General of Fair Trading can in the course of investigating consumer trade practices deal in particular with 'terms and conditions on which or subject to which goods or services are supplied'. This, of course, concerns exemption clauses being used in consumer transactions. If after investigation the Director-General feels that a particular practice in terms of exemption clauses should cease he will make a report to the minister who may pass a statutory instrument to stop the practice. For example, the Consumer Transactions (Restrictions on Statements) Order, 1976 (No. 1813) as amended by S. I. 1978/127 prohibits persons who, in the course of business, sell goods to consumers or supply them under hire purchase or trading stamp agreements from purporting by means, amongst other things, of notices in shops to apply terms which are void by reason of the Unfair Contract Terms Act, 1977, and from supplying statements about the consumer's rights against the supplier relating to quality and fitness without at the same time notifying the consumer that his statutory rights are not affected.

CONTRACTS *UBERRIMAE FIDEI*

There is generally no obligation on a contracting party to enlighten the other party even where he knows or suspects there is a misapprehension. For example, X offers to sell a watch to Y, and Y, thinking it is a gold watch, offers £1000 for it. X, knowing the watch is not gold, accepts Y's offer without enlightening him. The contract is binding provided X made no representation in the matter. There is no unilateral mistake because the mistake is merely as to quality.

The maxim in such cases is *caveat emptor* (Let the buyer beware). This rather harsh rule is modified in certain circumstances, e.g. in the case of sales by persons privately or in a business, the Sale of Goods Act, 1979 imports into all contracts for the sale of goods certain implied conditions and warranties, which cannot be excluded in consumer sales but may be if it is fair and reasonable to do so in non-consumer sales.

However, there are certain contracts in which disclosure of material facts is required by law. They are called contracts *uberrimae fidei* or contracts of the utmost good faith. Here silence can amount to misrepresentation, in the sense that non-disclosure of some material fact by one of the parties to the contract will give rise to a remedy in the injured party. The following contracts are of this type—

(i) Contracts of insurance. There is a duty on the person insured to disclose to the insurer all facts which might affect the premium. Failure to do so renders the contract voidable at the option of the insurer, so that the insurance company need not meet the claim but must return the

premiums. Regarding disclosure, a person wishing to enter into a contract of insurance must disclose, for example, any refusal of previous insurance, or in the case of a life policy, illnesses, physical or mental, or in the case of a policy relating to theft, previous thefts from him.

In addition, most proposals for insurance require the proposer to sign a declaration in which he warrants that the statements he has made are true and agrees that they be incorporated into the contract as terms. Where this is so any false statement which the proposer makes will be a ground for avoidance of the contract by the insurance company even though the statement was not material in terms of the premium. (See *Dawsons* v. *Bonnin*, 1922.)[265]

(ii) Contracts to take shares in a company under a prospectus. As regards contracts to take shares in a company, there is a duty on the directors or the company's promoters, under the Financial Services Act, 1986 to disclose various matters essential to an informed assessment as to whether an investor should purchase the securities. These provisions, and those in earlier statutes which preceded them, had to be put into the law by Parliament because the judiciary had always refused to regard the sale of securities by a company as a contract *uberrimae fidei*. They did not, therefore, require the advertisement or prospectus under which the shares were issued necessarily to disclose all the material facts.

(iii) Family arrangements. In contracts and dealings between members of a family, each member must disclose all material facts within his knowledge. (*Gordon* v. *Gordon*, 1819.)[266]

(iv) Contracts for the sale of land. The vendor is under a duty to disclose all defects in his title if they are known to him, and also the extent of any restrictive covenants affecting the land.

(v) Suretyship and partnership contracts. There is a duty on partners to disclose all matters within their knowledge which affect or may affect the business. However, this duty arises only when the partners are partners so that disclosure is not required during the negotiations leading to the admission of a partner. Similarly there is some duty of disclosure between a creditor and the person who guarantees the debt due from the principal debtor.

Probably, contracts of insurance are the only true contracts *uberrimae fidei*. The others are analogous thereto, but are based more on the equitable concept of fiduciary relationship. The question of disclosure in the case of company prospectuses is, of course, statutory. A contract of service does not give rise to duties of disclosure. (*Bell* v. *Lever Bros Ltd*, 1932.)[196]

DURESS

Duress will affect all contracts and gifts procured by its use. Duress, which is a common law concept, means actual violence or threats of violence to the person of the contracting party or those near and dear to him. (*Welch* v. *Cheesman*, 1974.)[267] The threats must be calculated to produce fear of loss of life or bodily harm.

A contract will seldom be procured by actual violence but threats of violence are more probable. The threat must be illegal in that it must be a threat to commit a crime or tort. Thus to threaten an imprisonment, which would be unlawful if enforced, constitutes duress (*Cumming* v. *Ince*, 1847)[268] but not, it is said, if the imprisonment would be lawful. However, the courts are unlikely to look with favour on a contract obtained by threatening to prosecute a criminal. A contract procured by a threat to sue for an act which was not a crime, e.g. trespass, would not be affected by duress.

It is said that the concept is not applicable to threats to property. Thus in *Skeate* v. *Beale*, (1840), 11 Ad. & El. 983, a tenant owed what would now be £19.50 p and agreed to pay £3.37½ p immediately and the remaining £16.12½ p within a month if his landlord would withdraw a writ of distress under which he was threatening to sell the tenant's goods. The tenant later disputed what he owed and the landlord tried to set up the agreement and sued for the remaining £16.12½ p. It was held that the landlord was entitled to £16.12½ p under the agreement which was not affected by duress since the threat was to sell the tenant's goods.

However, recent cases suggest that it is not only duress to the person which will invalidate a contract. It was said, for example, in *The Siboen and the Sibotre*, [1976] 1 Lloyd's Rep. 293 that a person could plead duress where he was forced by another to enter into a contract by the threat of having a valuable picture slashed or his house burnt down.

A contract affected by duress is voidable not void. (*Pao On* v. *Lau Yiu Long*, [1979] 2 All E.R. 65.) Thus if B procures goods from A by duress and sells the goods to C who is a purchaser for value with no knowledge of the duress, he gets a good title to the goods and cannot be dispossessed by A.

UNDUE INFLUENCE

The doctrine of undue influence was developed by Equity. The concept of undue influence is designed to deal with contracts or gifts obtained without free consent by the influence of one mind over another.

Equity has given relief where an agreement has been obtained by pressure of one sort or another which is not within the common law definition of duress. Thus contracts obtained by threats to prosecute the person making the promise or his spouse or a close relative for a criminal offence have been set aside on the basis of undue influence. (See *Kaufman* v. *Gerson*, 1904, p. 678.)

Equity has also given relief even though no undue influence has necessarily been exercised, provided the relationship between the parties is such that one of them is able to take an unfair advantage of the other.

Where such a confidential or fiduciary relationship exists between the parties, the party in whom the confidence was reposed must show that undue influence was not used, i.e. that the contract was the act of a free and independent mind. It is desirable, though not essential, that independent advice should have been given.

There are several confidential relationships which are well established in the law, viz. parent and child, solicitor and client, trustee and beneficiary, guardian and ward and religious adviser and disciple. (*Allcard* v. *Skinner*, 1887.)[269] In these cases undue influence is presumed. There is no presumption of such relationship between husband and wife, nor, according to the Court of Appeal in *Mathew* v. *Bobbins*, (1980) 124 S.J. 479, between employer and employee. The fiduciary relationship between parent and child ends usually, but not necessarily, on reaching 18 or on getting married (but see *Lancashire Loans Ltd* v. *Black*, 1934.)[270]. If there is no special relationship between the parties undue influence may exist, but must be proved by the person seeking to avoid the contract. (*Williams* v. *Bayley*, 1866.)[271]

Effect on the contract

Undue influence renders the contract voidable so that it may be rescinded. However, since rescission is an equitable remedy, there must be no delay in claiming relief after the influence has ceased to have effect. Delay in claiming relief in these circumstances may bar the claim since delay is evidence of affirmation. (*Allcard* v. *Skinner*, 1887.)[269]

Effect on third parties

A contract procured by undue influence cannot be avoided by rescission against third parties who acquire rights for value without notice of the facts, but it may be avoided against third parties for value with notice of the facts and also against volunteers (i.e. persons who have given no consideration) even though they were unaware of the facts. For example, if B procures goods from A by undue influence and B gives the goods to C, A can recover them from C, who is a volunteer. If, on the other hand, B sells the goods to C, who takes them without knowledge of the undue influence, C can keep the goods but A may trace the proceeds of sale into B's assets.

ECONOMIC DURESS AND UNCONSCIONABLE BARGAINS

Apart from the old concepts of duress and undue influence, the courts are developing in modern times wider rules to protect persons against improper pressure and inequality of bargaining power as it affects contracts. This development was perhaps best described by Lord Denning in *Lloyds Bank* v. *Bundy*, [1974] 3 All E.R. 757 at p. 765 where he said, having discussed duress and various forms of undue pressure in contract: 'Gathering all together, I would suggest that through all these instances there runs a single thread. They rest on an "inequality of bargaining power". By virtue of it, the English Law gives relief to one who, without independent advice, enters into a contract on terms which are very unfair or transfers property for a consideration which is mostly inadequate, where his bargaining power is grievously impaired by reason of his own needs or desires, or by his own ignorance or infirmity, coupled with undue influence or pressures brought to bear on him by or for the benefit of the other.'

Economic duress is within this concept. Suppose A agrees to build a tanker for B by an agreed date and at an agreed price and B enters into a contract with C under which the tanker is to be chartered to C from the agreed completion date or shortly afterwards. If A then threatens not to complete the contract by the agreed date unless B pays more, and B makes an extra payment because he does not want to be liable in breach of contract to C, then the extra payment may be recovered from A by B on the grounds of economic duress. This is so in spite of the fact that the usual remedy for duress is to rescind the contract on the basis that it is voidable. (See below.)

The decision of the House of Lords in *Universe Tankships Inc of Monrovia* v. *International Transport Workers' Federation*, [1982] 2 All E.R. 67 is instructive in that it affirms the existence of the doctrine of economic duress. In that case a ship called the *Universe Sentinel*, which was owned by Universe Tankships, was 'blacked' by the respondent trade union, the ITF, which regarded the ship as sailing under a flag of convenience. ITF was against flag-of-convenience ships and refused to make tugs available when the ship arrived at Milford Haven to discharge her cargo. The 'blacking' was lifted after Universe Tankships had made an agreement with ITF regarding improvements in pay and conditions of the crew and had paid money to ITF which included a contribution of $6480 to an ITF fund known as The Seafarers' International Welfare Protection and Assistance Fund. Universe Tankships sued for the return of the $6480 on the basis of economic duress, and the House of Lords held that they were entitled to recover it. It appears from the judgments that the effect of economic duress is to make the contract voidable and to provide a ground for recovery of money paid as money had and received to the plaintiff's use—a form of quasi-contractual claim. (See further p. 319.)

The decision in *Universe Tankships* was applied by the Court of Appeal in *B & S Contracts & Design* v. *Victor Green Publications*, (1984) 128 S.J. 279 where A agreed to erect stands for B who was doing a presentation at Olympia. A's employees threatened to strike unless they received extra money which they had demanded and to which they were not entitled.

A said that the contract could not proceed unless the extra sums were paid by B as an increase in the contract price. B paid the extra sums to get the work done and then recovered them in this action. The money was paid under economic duress.

Further examples of inequality of bargaining power may be found in *Clifford Davies Management* v. *WEA Records*, [1975] 1 All E.R. 237 where A, an experienced manager, obtained a contract with a pop star, B, who had little or no business experience, under which B gave A the copyright in all his compositions for a period of years. It was held that B could avoid the contract because A had exploited his superior bargaining power. The concept has also applied to a guarantee of a bank loan obtained from the borrower's father by a bank manager in whom the father placed his trust. (*Lloyds Bank* v. *Bundy*, 1974.)[272]

However, there is no rule of law which states that a fair price must be paid in *all* transactions and some unfair contracts will be held binding provided the parties were of equal bargaining strength. In *Burmah Oil Ltd* v. *The Governor of the Bank of England*, [1979] 3 All E.R. 700 Burmah was in financial difficulties and sold a large holding of shares which it had in British Petroleum to the Government at a price below the Stock Exchange price. Burmah then brought an action to set the contract aside. The court refused to do so. Although there was authority to set aside a transaction where one party had acted without independent advice, or where the bargaining strength of one party was grievously impaired, neither of those situations existed in this case. The relationship was purely commercial and the contract for the sale of shares must stand.

CONTRACTS AND PUBLIC POLICY

Freedom of contract must always be subject to overriding considerations of public policy. In all actions brought in England the contract is subject to English rules of public policy even though the proper law of the contract is not English law. (*Kaufman* v. *Gerson*, 1904.)[273]

Public policy has been ascertained as follows—

(i) *At common law by the judiciary*. At one time the judiciary had wide powers of discretion in the matter of creating new categories of public policy but this view is now unacceptable. In *Fender* v. *Mildmay*, [1937] 3 All E.R. 402 the House of Lords declared against the extension of the heads of public policy, at least by the judiciary. However, up to 1938 the judiciary had created a number of categories of public policy. These fell into two areas as follows—

(a) *Illegal contracts*. These involve some degree of moral wrong and contracts to commit crimes or to defraud the revenue fall into this category.

(b) *Void contracts*. In these cases there is not in any strict sense blameworthy conduct; the contracts are rendered void because if enforced by the courts they could produce unsatisfactory results on society. Examples are contracts in restraint of trade, e.g. an agreement under which an employee covenants with his employer that on the termination of his contract he will not work for a rival firm or start a competing business, and contracts prejudicial to marriage, e.g. a contract under which a person promises not to marry at all.

(ii) *By Parliament*. Parliament expresses its view as to what is public policy by Acts of Parliament and rules and orders made by ministers under Acts of Parliament. Again, statute law in this area falls into two categories as follows—

(*a*) *The creation of illegal contracts*. This happens where the Act of Parliament actually makes the contract *unlawful*. Thus s. 1 of the Resale Prices Act, 1976, declares unlawful all *collective* agreements between suppliers of goods to 'blacklist' retailers who sell below the minimum resale price agreed by the suppliers.

(*b*) *The creation of void contracts*. Here there is no suggestion that the contract is unlawful in the strict sense or that moral blame attaches. There are two main areas as follows—

(1) Wagering contracts, which will be dealt with later, and
(2) The prevention of restrictive practices. Thus agreements by suppliers to fix prices or restrict supplies are void under the Restrictive Trade Practices Act, 1976, unless the parties can prove to the Restrictive Practices Court that their agreement is beneficial and in the public interest.

Public policy—the contribution of the judiciary

Illegal contracts
These contracts involve some form of moral weakness which society in general seeks to control. They are as follows—

(a) Contracts to commit crimes (see *Dann* v. *Curzon*, 1911)[274] or civil wrongs
Thus a contract between an agent and his client whereby the agent was to receive a double commission would be illegal because it has as its object the commission of a fraud on the principal, since if the agent takes a double commission there is a conflict of interest.

(b) Contracts involving sexual immorality
Agreements for future illicit cohabitation are void, because the promise of payment might encourage immoral conduct in a person who otherwise would not have participated. However, a contract under which a person promises to pay another money in return for past illicit cohabitation is not illegal because it does not necessarily encourage future immorality between the parties. Such a contract will, however, be unenforceable

unless made under seal because it is for past consideration. Furthermore, contracts which are on the face of it legal may be affected if *knowingly* made to further an immoral purpose. Immorality seems to refer only to extra-marital sexual intercourse. (*Pearce* v. *Brooks*, 1866.)[275]

It may be asked whether legally enforceable rights of maintenance may be created by a contract between cohabitants, i.e. persons who live together as husband and wife though unmarried. Certainly, a contract could be made, but its enforceability is doubtful. It was the view of the House of Lords in *Fender* v. *St. J. Mildmay*, [1937] 3 All E.R. 402 that the courts could not enforce an immoral promise between a man and a woman such as the payment of money or some other consideration in return for an immoral association. However, much depends upon the view a court would now take of this. The older cases, such as *Fender*, tended to regard the payment of money as a reward for and to induce the sexual aspect of the relationship. It may be that the courts would enforce a maintenance agreement which was entered into as part of a stable relationship between cohabitants, and which could not be seen as mere payment for a sexual relationship.

Nevertheless, in *H* v. *H, The Times*, 22 April, 1983, the court refused to enforce maintenance support provisions in what was in effect a wife-swopping contract intended by the four parties to be permanent. Thus the matter of enforceable maintenance by contract must remain doubtful in terms that it may be contrary to public policy. In addition, the court may not enforce it on the basis that the parties did not intend to create legal relations; a concept which may affect contracts between members of a family or friends.

(c) Contracts prejudicial to good foreign relations
This category includes contracts to carry out acts which are illegal by the law of a foreign and friendly country, since to enforce such contracts would encourage disputes. (See *Regazzoni* v. *K. C. Sethia Ltd*, 1958.)[276]

(d) Contracts prejudicial to the administration of justice
Thus, a contract tending to defeat the bankruptcy laws is illegal at common law. (See *John* v. *Mendoza*, 1939.)[277]

(e) Contracts tending to corruption in public life
A contract to procure a title or honour is illegal under this head. (See *Parkinson* v. *College of Ambulance*, 1925.)[278]

(f) Contracts to defraud the Revenue
This applies to frauds in connection with national taxes or local rates. (See *Napier* v. *National Business Agency Ltd*, 1951.)[279]

Consequences

The consequences of illegality in the above cases depend upon whether the contract was unlawful on the face of it, i.e. there was no way in which lawful performance could be achieved or whether the contract was lawful on the face of it, i.e. it could have been performed in a lawful manner.

(i) Contract unlawful on face of it
This includes all the categories mentioned above except some contracts involving sexual immorality. The consequences where the contract is unlawful on the face of it are as follows—

(a) The contract is void and there is no action by either party for debt (*Dann* v. *Curzon*, 1911),[274] damages, specific performance or injunction.

(b) Money paid or property transferred to the other party under the contract is irrecoverable. (*Parkinson* v. *College of Ambulance*, 1925.)[278] Unless—

(1) The plaintiff is relying on rights other than those which are contained in the contract. Thus if A leases property to B for five years and A knows that B intends to use the property as a brothel, then A cannot recover rent or require any covenant to be performed without pleading the illegal lease. However, at the end of the term A can bring an action for the return of his property as *owner* and not as a landlord under an illegal lease. (And see *Bowmakers Ltd* v. *Barnet Instruments Ltd*, 1944.)[280] In addition, if the action is to redress a wrong which, although in a sense connected with the contract, can really be considered independent of it, the law will allow the action. (*Edler* v. *Auerbach*, 1950.)[281]

(2) The plaintiff is not *in pari delicto* (of equal wrong). Where the contract is unlawful on the face of it, equal guilt is presumed but this presumption may be rebutted if the plaintiff can show that the defendant was guilty of fraud, oppression or undue influence. (See *Hughes* v. *Liverpool Victoria Legal Friendly Society*, 1916.)[282]

(3) The plaintiff repents provided that the repentance is genuine (*Bigos* v. *Bousted*, 1951.)[283] and performance is *partial* (*Taylor* v. *Bowers*, 1876)[284] and not *substantial*. (*Kearley* v. *Thomson*, 1890.)[285]

It should be noted that collateral transactions *between the same parties* are void. (*Fisher* v. *Bridges*, 1854.)[286] Where *a third party* enters into a collateral contract with one or both of the parties to the original transaction his rights will depend upon whether he knew or not that the original transaction was illegal. (*Southern Industrial Trust* v. *Brooke House Motors*, 1968.)[287]

(ii) Contract lawful on face of it
The result here is as follows—

(a) Where both parties intended the illegal purpose. There is no action by either party for debt, damages, specific performance or injunction (*Pearce* v. *Brooks*, 1866)[275] or to recover money paid or property transferred under the contract.

(b) Where one party was without knowledge of the illegal purpose.

The innocent party's rights are unaffected and he may sue for debt, damages, specific performance, or injunction (see *Fielding and Platt Ltd* v. *Najjar*, 1969)[288] or to recover money paid or property transferred.

Where a contract is prohibited by statute some judges have advanced the argument that even a party who was innocent of this fact may not be able to sue on the contract. (See further p. 283.)

(c) The party who would have performed the contract in an unlawful manner has no action on it (*Cowan* v. *Milbourn*, 1867[289] and *Ashmore, Benson, Pease* v. *A. V. Dawson Ltd*, 1973)[290] nor can he recover property delivered to the other party under the contract. (*Berg* v. *Sadler and Moore*, 1937.)[291] However, it is necessary to show that the plaintiff had knowledge of the illegal transaction and participated therein, though such knowledge may be imputed to the plaintiff even if he remains inactive as in *Ashmore, Benson, Pease*.[290]

Public policy and the judiciary—void contracts

These contracts do not involve any type of moral weakness but are against public policy because they are inexpedient rather than unprincipled. The contracts concerned are contracts to oust the jurisdiction of the courts, contracts prejudicial to the status of marriage, and contracts in restraint of trade. These are dealt with individually below.

Contracts to oust the jurisdiction of the courts

A contract which has the effect of taking away the right of one or both of the parties to bring an action before a court of law is void, though it may be possible to *sever* the offensive part of the contract and enforce the rest. (*Goodinson* v. *Goodinson*, 1954.)[292] This rule does not make void honourable pledge clauses because in such cases the parties do not intend to be bound by the contract at all. If the contract is to be binding, however, then the parties cannot exclude it from the jurisdiction of the courts. Furthermore, arbitration clauses are not affected. Many commercial contracts contain an arbitration clause, the object being to provide a cheaper or more convenient remedy than a court action. An arbitration clause in a contract is not void if the effect of it is that the parties are to go to arbitration *first* before going to court. An arbitration clause which denies the parties access to the courts completely is, of course, invalid.

Contracts prejudicial to the status of marriage

A contract in absolute restraint of marriage, i.e. one in which a person promises not to marry at all, is void. Partial restraints, if reasonable, are said to be valid, e.g. a contract not to marry a person of certain religious faith, or not to marry for a short period of time. However, there are no recent cases and it may be that even a partial restraint would be regarded as void today. Marriage brokage contracts, i.e. contracts to introduce men and women with a view to their subsequent marriage, are also void on the grounds that third parties should not be free to reap financial profit by bringing about matrimonial unions.

As regards separation agreements, these are invalid if made for the future, as where a husband promises that he will make provision for his wife if she should ever live apart from him, unless the agreement is made as part of a reconciliation arrangement. In this case the agreement is valid, although it may make provision for a renewed future separation. If the parties are not living in amity or are actually separated, then a separation agreement is valid. Once it is apparent that the parties cannot live together in amity it is desirable that a separation which has become inevitable should be concluded upon reasonable terms.

Contracts in restraint of trade

Originally all contracts in restraint of trade were regarded as void but in the 17th century the courts began to allow certain of them to operate if reasonable, apparently because of the reluctance of masters to train apprentices unless they were able to restrain those apprentices in some way on the completion of the apprenticeship.

In modern law such contracts are *prima facie* void and will only be binding if reasonable. Thus the contract must be reasonable between the parties which means that it must be no wider than is necessary to protect the interest involved in terms of the area and time of its operation. Mere competition is not an interest entitled to protection in this way. (*Morris* v. *Saxelby*, 1916.)[293]

Finally, the issue of reasonableness is a matter of law for the judge on the evidence presented to him which would include, for example, such matters as trade practices and customs. Once again it may be possible to sever offensive parts of the contract and enforce other valid restraints contained within it.

Voluntary contractual restraints

There are four categories of voluntary contractual restraints as follows—

(a) Restraints imposed upon employees
In this connection it should be noted that there are only *two* things an employer can protect—

(i) *Trade secrets*. A restraint against competition is justifiable if its object is to prevent the exploitation of trade secrets and/or confidential information learned by the employee in the course of his employment. (See *Forster & Sons Ltd* v. *Suggett*, 1918.)[294]

The court cannot redraft a restraint clause because it is too wide but it can, as a matter of construction, reach the conclusion that the parties intended to limit the clause to what it is legitimate to protect. Thus in *Littlewoods Organisation Ltd* v. *Harris*, [1978] 1 All E.R. 1026 the Court of Appeal considered the validity of a restraint which prohibited an employee of Littlewoods for a period of 12 months from working for any company in the Great Universal Stores Group. Littlewoods were trying to protect confidential information in regard to their mail order business which Mr Harris had acquired during his employment with them. Objection was taken by the defence in particular to the fact that the GUS group operated world-wide, whereas Littlewoods operated only in the UK, and also because the activities of the GUS Group included, but were not restricted to, the mail order business. Mr Harris had been offered employment by GUS and Littlewoods were seeking an injunction to prevent him taking that employment up.

Lord Denning, in the Court of Appeal together with Lord Justice Megaw, was of the opinion that limiting words ought to be read into the clauses as a matter of construction so as to confine it to that part of the business of the GUS group which operated within the United Kingdom and to that part of their business for which Littlewoods could reasonably be expected to be entitled to protection, i.e. the mail order business. Many would regard such an approach to the construction of contracts as being extraordinary, if not to say revolutionary. However, there is some support for Lord Denning's method of interpretation in earlier cases, particularly in the judgment of Lindley, M.R. in the case of *Haynes* v. *Doman*, [1899] 2 Ch. 13.

The restraint must be restricted to the sphere of activity in which the employee has been engaged. (*Commercial Plastics Ltd* v. *Vincent*, 1964.)[295]

(ii) *Business connection.* Sometimes an employer may use a covenant against *solicitation* of persons with whom the employer does business. The duration must be reasonable and the covenant confined to areas in which the employee has had customer contact. (*Home Counties Dairies* v. *Skilton*, 1970.)[296] In order to enforce a covenant in restraint of solicitation it is normally necessary to show that the business has recurring customers. (*Scorer* v. *Seymour Jones*, 1966.)[297]

As regards the enforcement of post-employment restraints, Denning, L.J. (as he then was) said in *M. & S. Drapers* v. *Reynolds*, [1956] 3 All E.R. 814 at 820: 'During the last 40 years the courts have shown a reluctance to enforce covenants of this sort. They realise that a servant has often very little choice in the matter . . . he is very much at the mercy of his employer.' However, recent decisions of the Court of Appeal show a change of attitude which may result in employer/employee restraints being more readily enforceable by the employer, at least in regard to *solicitation* covenants. (See *Home Counties Dairies* v. *Skilton*, 1970;[296] *White (Marion) Ltd* v. *Francis*, 1972[298] and *Lucas* v. *Mitchell*, 1972.)[299]

It must also be remembered that a covenant in restraint of trade is merely part of a larger contract of employment so that if the employer unjustifiably terminates the contract, as by wrongfully dismissing his employee, or the employee is, in the circumstances, justified in terminating his employment, the restraint will be unenforceable. (*General Billposting Co.* v. *Atkinson*, 1909.)[300]

Furthermore, an employer cannot enforce a contract restraining his employee from entering a particular field of business activity on the ground that the employer *may at a later date* wish to set up business in that field. (*Bromley* v. *Smith*, 1909.)[301] It should also be noted that a restraint may be applied even where an employee forms a limited company to carry on business in defiance of a restraint. Corporate status cannot be used for such a purpose. Thus in *Gilford Motor Co.* v. *Horne*, [1933] Ch. 935 a former employee bound by a restraint of trade set up a company in order to evade its provisions, claiming that he as a person might be bound by the restraint but the company, being a separate entity, could not. An injunction was granted against both him and his company which the court described as 'a device, a stratagem . . . a mere cloak or sham'.

The *duty of fidelity* of employees is also of interest, since it is possible to prevent an employee from using trade secrets or business connections without any specific contract in restraint of trade. Certain activities by employees are regarded by the law as breaches of the duty of faithful service which an employee owes to his employer. Breaches of the duty of fidelity will sometimes be prevented by the court, so a person who retains secret processes in his memory can be restrained from using them to his employer's disadvantage. However, the employee's knowledge of trade secrets must be readily separable and not merely part of the total experience gained from employment. (*Printers and Finishers Ltd* v. *Holloway*, 1964.)[302]

An employee who copies names and addresses of his employer's customers for use after leaving his employment can be restrained from using the lists without any express restriction in his contract. (*Robb* v. *Green*, 1895.)[303] In connection with the duty of fidelity; it should be noted that it does not matter who initiates the infidelity and, although in most cases the employee approaches the customer, the rule still applies even where the customers approach the employee. (*Sanders* v. *Parry*, 1967.)[304] The case of *Hivac Ltd* v. *Park Royal Scientific Instruments Ltd* 1946[305] is also of interest since it shows that skilled men with access to their employer's secrets may not be able to work for a rival firm *even in their spare time*.

Finally, a servant is under no implied obligation not to disclose information concerning his employer's misconduct if it ought in the public interest to be disclosed to a person having a proper interest to receive it. (*Initial Services* v. *Putterill*, 1967.)[306]

(b) Exclusive service contracts
There have been very few cases dealing with the extent of a restraint of an employee during the currency of his employment. However, it is now clear that an agreement between employer and employee can be declared

an unreasonable restraint of trade even during the existence of the employment but in normal circumstances this appears to be unlikely. It is probable that the courts would be reluctant to interfere with such agreements in the absence of special circumstances, such as where the contract is contrary to normal trade practice or where it is totally one-sided. (*A. Schroeder Music Publishing Co. Ltd* v. *Macauley*, 1974.)[307] However, even if the restraint is not invalid the employer would still face difficulties in regard to a suitable remedy. The employer can, of course, always dismiss the employee but it is doubtful how far he can go to prevent the employee from working for a third person. The appropriate remedy in such a case is an injunction. However, there are a number of limitations on the availability of that remedy in respect of service contracts, for instance the restriction must be worded negatively. (*Warner Bros.* v. *Nelson*, 1937; see p. 732.) In addition, the current trend seems to be against enforcing covenants of exclusive service either on the ground of restraint of trade or on the ground of the unavailability of an injunction.

(c) Agreements between partners
Clauses restricting an outgoing or retiring partner from practising within a defined area are frequently found in partnership agreements between professional persons. Such clauses will not be enforceable if they are wider than is reasonably necessary for the protection of the practice. However, protection *against competition* as such is to some extent allowed and this distinguishes professional practice restraint from employer and employee restraint, though the test of reasonableness still applies. (*Lyne-Pirkis* v. *Jones*, 1969.)[308]

(d) Restraints imposed on the vendor of a business
Such a restraint will be void unless it is required to protect the business sold and not to stifle competition. (*British Concrete Co.* v. *Schelff*, 1921.)[309]

(e) Restraints arising from agreements between manufacturers and traders
This branch of law is now largely regulated by statute, i.e. the Restrictive Trade Practices Act, 1976. Nevertheless, it is necessary to consider the common law position because not all restrictive agreements are covered by the above legislation and where it does not apply, the common law on the topic may be invoked. For example, the restrictive agreement which was at the root of *Kores Manufacturing Co.* v. *Kolok Manufacturing Co. Ltd*, 1959[310] was not covered by the Act which is not concerned with agreements between traders in regard to their employees and was decided on common law principles. These principles are that the agreement must be reasonable between the parties and reasonable in the public interest. Both of these points arose in *Kores*, the Court of Appeal holding that the agreement was unreasonable as between the parties and

also that it was contrary to the public interest though the *ratio* is based on the fact that the agreement was unreasonable as between the parties.

(f) Restrictions accepted by distributors of merchandise

A manufacturer or wholesaler may refuse to make merchandise available for distribution to the public unless the distributor accepts certain conditions restricting his liberty of trading. This is the main purpose of the solus agreement used by petrol companies. Such agreements are void unless reasonable. (See *Esso Petroleum Co. Ltd* v. *Harper's Garage (Stourport) Ltd*, 1967.)[311] It should be noted that there is a distinction as regards the duration of the restraint between a garage proprietor who is already in possession of the land before he ties himself to the oil company and a person who is out of possession and is let in by the oil company. A longer period of restraint may be allowed against a garage proprietor who is let into possession by the oil company. (*Cleveland Petroleum Co. Ltd* v. *Dartstone Ltd*, 1969.)[312]

Involuntary restraints

We have so far considered restrictions against trading contained in contracts. However, the doctrine is not confined to these voluntary restraints. It extends to involuntary restraints imposed by trade associations or professional bodies upon their members. Such restraints are void unless reasonable. (*Pharmaceutical Society of Great Britain* v. *Dickson*, 1968.)[313]

Contracts restraining the liberty of the individual other than contracts of service

These also may be illegal (see *Horwood* v. *Millar's Timber Co.*, 1917)[314] though such restrictions may be valid for certain purposes. (*Denny's Trustee* v. *Denny*, 1919.)[315]

Consequences

Where a contract is rendered void by the judiciary it is unenforceable only in so far as it contravenes public policy. Thus—

(*a*) money paid or property transferred is recoverable. (*Hermann* v. *Charlesworth*, 1905);[316] and

(*b*) lawful promises may be severed and enforced. Thus a contract of service which contains a void restraint is not wholly invalid and the court will sever and enforce those aspects of it which do not offend against public policy. Thus an employee who has entered into a contract of service which contains a restraint which is too wide can recover his wages or salary. (*Wallis* v. *Day*, 1837[317] and see also *Goodinson* v. *Goodinson*, 1954.)[292]

The court will not add to a contract or in any way redraft it but will merely strike out the offending words. What is left must make sense without further additions otherwise the court will not sever the void part in order to enforce what is good. (*Attwood* v. *Lamont*, 1920.)[318]

It should be noted that, even where severance is possible, the court is not bound to sever and the court will not sever a contract unless the provisions left leave the contract substantially what it was before. Severance will not be allowed if it alters the nature of the contract. (*Kenyon* v. *Darwin Cotton Manufacturing Co.*, 1936.)[319]

Illegal contracts—the contribution of Parliament

Some contracts are prohibited by statute in terms that they are illegal, the word 'unlawful' being used in the statute concerned. In this context 'statute' includes the orders, rules and regulations that ministers of the Crown and other persons are authorized by Parliament to issue.

The statutory prohibitions with which we are concerned may be express or implied.

(a) Implied prohibition

In these cases the statute itself does not say expressly that contracts contravening its provisions are necessarily illegal. The statute may affect the formation of a particular contract as where a trader does business without taking out a licence. In some cases the statute may affect the manner of performance of the contract as where a trader is required to deliver to a purchaser a written statement such as an invoice containing, for example, details of the chemical composition of the goods.

In either case whether failure to comply with a statutory provision renders the contract illegal is a matter of construction of the statute and is for the judge to decide.

If, in the opinion of the judge, the Act was designed to protect the public then the contract will be illegal. Thus in *Cope* v. *Rowlands*, (1836) 2 M. & W. 149 an unlicenced broker in the City of London was held not to be entitled to sue for his fees because the purpose of the licencing requirements was to protect the public against shady dealers. Furthermore, in *Anderson Ltd* v. *Daniel*, [1924] 1 K.B. 138 a seller of artificial fertilizers was held unable to recover the price of goods which he had delivered because he had failed to state in an invoice the chemical composition of the fertilizers which was required by Act of Parliament. (And see *Ashmore, Benson, Pease & Co. Ltd* v. *A. V. Dawson Ltd*, 1973.)[290]

On the other hand, if in the opinion of the judge the purpose of the legislation was mainly to raise revenue or help in the administration of trade, contracts will not be affected. Thus, in *Smith* v. *Mawhood*, (1845) 14 M. & W. 452 it was held that a tobacconist could recover the price of tobacco sold by him even though he did not have a licence to sell it and had not painted his name on his place of business. The purpose of the statute involved was not to affect the contract of sale but to impose a fine on offenders for the purpose of revenue. This rule is also applied where the legislation is designed to punish offenders against the law. (*Shaw* v. *Groom*, 1970.)[320] In addition, in *Archbolds (Freightage) Ltd* v. *Spanglett Ltd*, [1961] 1 Q.B. 374 a contract by an unlicensed carrier to carry goods by road was held valid because the legislation involved was only designed to help in the administration of road transport.

In the case of statutory illegality, it may be that the object of the statute is to protect a class of person and the plaintiff is within that class. If so, the plaintiff may be able to recover money or property transferred under the contract, for he is not deemed to be in *pari delicto*. (*Kiriri Cotton Co. Ltd* v. *Dawani*, 1960.)[321]

There are cases in which the innocent party to a contract affected by a statutory prohibition may not be able to sue upon it. This seems hard to justify but occasionally the court may reach the conclusion that it will advance the objects of the legislation if even an innocent party is denied a remedy. Thus in *Bedford Insurance Co.* v. *Institutio De Ressaguros Do Brasil, The Times*, 18 November, 1983, Parker, J. decided that because the Insurance Companies Act, 1974 prohibits certain types of insurance business, e.g. insurance of aviation risks, without the Department of Trade and Industry authority, an insurer who had carried on business for which he had no authority could keep the premiums he had received and refuse payment of claims.

However, in *Stewart* v. *Oriental Fire and Marine Insurance, The Times*, 9 May, 1984, Leggatt, J, allowed a Lloyds underwriter to enforce a reinsurance contract under which he had passed some risk under an aviation insurance to a reinsurer who was not authorized by the Department of Trade and Industry to take insurance of aviation risks. The underwriter did not know this and the judge said that he should not be penalized when he had acted innocently.

(b) Express prohibition

In a book of this nature it would be inappropriate to deal in detail with all statutes which render contracts illegal but a modern example is found in the Resale Prices Act, 1976, s. 1. One particular type of agreement, namely an agreement for the collective enforcement of conditions regulating the price at which goods may be sold is prohibited and made unlawful.

Such agreements were not usually regarded as illegal at common law but the doctrine of privity of contract prevented enforcement of the resale price agreement by a manufacturer against a retailer. Consequently, manufacturers not having access to the ordinary courts of law often brought the retailer before a secret and possibly unjust trade association tribunal which might put the retailer quite unreasonably on a stop list so that he was denied supplies.

Under Part I of the Resale Prices Act, 1976, *collective* agreements by two or more persons regulating the price at which goods may be resold are unlawful. There is no criminal penalty but the Crown may institute civil proceedings in the High Court and obtain, for example, an injunction to prevent the practice.

It is important to note that *individual* agreements between one manufacturer and his retailers are sanctioned by s. 26 of the Resale Prices Act, 1976, so that such a manufacturer now has access to the ordinary courts of law to enforce his agreement. The action may be for damages or an injunction, though it is important to note that s. 26 only applies if the resale price agreement has been approved by the Restrictive Practices Court under the Resale Prices Act, 1976. In fact very few such agreements have been approved although an example is the *Net Book Agreement*, (1964) L.R. 4 R.P. 484, under which publishers can enforce *minimum* resale price maintenance agreements in respect of books. In that case the court thought that abolition of resale price maintenance would lead to fewer stockholding book-sellers (because, e.g. supermarkets would stock and sell more cheaply the best-selling books) and fewer new titles, particularly of slow-selling but useful books on specialist topics which would not be stocked by supermarkets. All of this the court thought would be detrimental to the public interest. The case was decided under earlier legislation before there was a separate Act concerned with resale price maintenance. All suppliers can enforce *maximum* price agreements to see that they are not exceeded.

Void contracts—the contribution of Parliament

There are certain classes of contracts which are expressly declared by statute to be void. It would not be appropriate in a book of this nature to deal with all of them and therefore only those with a commercial connotation are described.

Wagering contracts

In essence for a wager to exist it must be possible for one party to win and one party to lose and there must be two persons or two groups opposed to each other in their views as to a future event. Thus, where X, Y and Z each put £5 into a fund to be given to the party whose selected horse wins a given race, there is no wager. The only commercial importance of the concept of wagering and the only reason why it is introduced in a book of this nature relates to insurance. A contract is not a wager if the person to whom the money is promised on the occurrence of the event has an interest in the non-occurrence of that event, e.g. where a person has paid a premium to insure his house against destruction by fire. Such an interest is called an *insurable interest* and is not a wager. However, to insure someone else's property would be a wager and not a valid contract of insurance.

The Gaming Act of 1845 renders wagering contracts void so that there is no action for the bet or for the winnings. However, it should be noted that if the bet or the winnings have actually been paid over they cannot be recovered. Payment operates as waiver of the Act and the payment over of money confers a good title to that money upon the person to whom it is paid.

Contracts affected by the Restrictive Trade Practices Act, 1976

Under the Act of 1976 collective agreements between two or more persons designed to fix prices and/or regulate supplies of *goods* must be registered with the Director-General of Fair Trading. Once an agreement has been reported to the Director-General of Fair Trading he may test its validity by bringing proceedings before the Restrictive Practices Court where the agreement will be declared void unless the parties to it can prove that it is in the public interest. This might be done, for example, where the parties can show that the agreement is designed to maintain the export trade. If the parties attempt to operate the agreement in spite of the fact that it has not been approved by the Restrictive Practices Court, the Director-General of Fair Trading may ask for an injunction to prevent the operation of the agreement.

However, it is rare that such action has to be taken because in most cases the firms concerned have not attempted to operate an agreement (or enter into similar agreements) if it has been rejected by the court. However, in *Re Galvanized Tank Manufacturers' Association's Agreement*, [1965] 2 All E.R. 1003, the court imposed under earlier legislation fines amounting to £102,000 on eight members of the Association for contempt of court in breaking their undertakings to the court that they would not enforce or give effect to restrictions in a price fixing agreement which the court had declared to be contrary to the public interest six years before. Again, in *Re an agreement between members of the British Concrete Pipe Association, The Times*, 18 December, 1980 the British Steel Corporation was fined £50,000 for breach of an undertaking given to the court that it would not enter into new restrictive agreements regarding orders for and the sale price of concrete pipes.

This Act also allows the Director-General of Fair Trading to investigate restrictive practices in regard to services. If necessary the matter can be brought before the Restrictive Practices Court which has a jurisdiction in respect of restrictive agreements relating to *services. Ravenseft Properties Ltd* v. *Director-General of Fair Trading*, 1977.)[322]

The Restrictive Practices Court may approve modifications to a registered agreement or may make an order under s. 4(1) of the Restrictive Trade Practices Act, 1976 on the application of the Director-General of Fair Trading, allowing the Director to approve modifications where the variation is not a substantial one. (See *re Building Employers' Confederation's Application*, [1985] I.C.R. 167).

The Resale Prices Act, 1976

Resale price maintenance agreements are presumed void under the 1976 Act unless the supplier can prove to the Restrictive Practices Court that the restriction is in the public interest. This might be done, for example, by showing that after sales service would be reduced or non-existent unless the resale price maintenance agreement was enforced. (And see *Re Chocolate and Sugar Confectionery Reference*, 1967.)[323] Except as regards agreements which have been approved, a supplier cannot legally withhold supplies to outlets selling at below a recommended price. However, if the supplier has other reasons for withholding supplies, as where the dealer owes him money, then the supplier will not be treated as withholding supplies of goods for the purposes of the Act. In *Oxford Printing Ltd* v. *Letraset*, [1970] 2 All E.R. 815, when Letraset were sued by the plaintiffs for an injunction to prevent withholding of supplies, it was held by Plowman, J. that the defendants had a good defence when they showed that their reason for withholding supplies was that the plaintiffs were, in addition to cutting the price, also using the defendants' products to promote the sales of a rival firm. The injunction was refused.

We have already seen that if a resale price maintenance agreement is approved by the Restrictive Practices Court it can be enforced regardless of the doctrine of privity of contract under the Resale Prices Act, 1976, s. 26.

The Fair Trading Act, 1973

This Act gives wide powers to the Office of Fair Trading under the Director-General of Fair Trading by reason of which it can deal with monopolies, mergers, restrictive practices, and the protection of consumers against trading practices which are considered unfair. The Office of Fair Trading is perhaps best known for its duty to vet mergers between parties having a large share of the relevant market and to recommend to the Department of Trade and Industry whether they should be referred to the Monopolies and Mergers Commission. The Government is not bound to take the advice of the Office of Fair Trading regarding reference. The Office of Fair Trading has, however, a much wider brief under the following main pieces of legislation: the Consumer Credit Act, 1974; the Competition Act, 1980 (*see below*); and, as we have seen, the Restrictive Trade Practices Act, 1976 and also the Resale Prices Act, 1976.

As regards consumer protection and surveillance of traders it works with local Trading Standards Consumer Protection departments and advice agencies and gives information on consumer rights. It can obtain assurances of future obedience to the law from traders under the Fair Trading Act, 1973 and under the Consumer Credit Act, 1974 it vets the fitness of traders offering credit and resolves disputes over the accuracy of information on people which is given by credit reference agencies.

The competition legislation brings monopolies and mergers and other trade practices which restrict, distort, or prevent competition in the UK under the surveillance and control of the Office of Fair Trading.

The Competition Act, 1980

The main significance of this Act is that it brings within the scope of investigation the practices of single firms which are neither monopolies in the statutory sense, nor in collusion with other enterprises for the purposes of the Restrictive Trade Practices Act, 1976.

The Act provides a two-stage inquiry process. First of all, the Director-General of Fair Trading can initiate a preliminary inquiry into a practice of a firm or firms and is required to report publicly his findings as to whether it constitutes an anti-competitive practice and if so, whether he feels it is right to refer the matter for investigation to the Monopolies and Mergers Commission. A company may volunteer an undertaking in regard to the abandonment of its restrictive or monopolistic practices to the Director-General at this stage and he may accept this instead of taking the matter to the Monopolies and Mergers Commission. The Director-General can, of course, monitor these undertakings to see whether they are being carried out.

If the matter goes to the Commission, the Commission must assess and report whether the practice is anti-competitive and, in addition, whether it has operated, or may be expected to operate, against the public interest.

Where the conclusion of the Commission is adverse, the Secretary of State may make an order under s. 10 requiring the company to desist from, or amend the practice concerned, or ask the Director-General of Fair Trading to seek undertakings from the company which the Director-General can subsequently monitor.

There is no list of anti-competitive practices in the Act. However, a not uncommon restrictive practice which the 1980 Act seeks to deal with is where manufacturers restrict or refuse to supply their goods to certain outlets, e.g. discount traders such as Argos and Tesco. Some of the inquiries under the new Act, e.g. the one concerning the supply of Raleigh bicycles, have been in this field.

In addition to the anti-competition provisions the Act provides for prices to be investigated by the Director-General of Fair Trading if the price is a matter of major public concern. There are however, no follow-up powers by which any recommendations could be enforced. It also allows the Monopolies and Mergers Commission to carry out 'efficiency audits' into the activities of public bodies. A number of these have been done, e.g. in connection with the London and South-Eastern commuter service of British Rail.

European Community

Under Arts. 85 and 86 of the Treaty of Rome all agreements between firms which operate to prevent or restrict competition in the Market are void. Under s. 5 of the Restrictive Trade Practices Act, 1976, the Director-General of Fair Trading and the Restrictive Practices Court and other courts as necessary are to take Arts. 85 and 86 into account—

(a) on the issue of registration of a particular agreement, and
(b) if the agreement comes before the Court for adjudication.

RESTRICTIVE TRADING AGREEMENTS AND THE TREATY OF ROME

We have considered above the position under English domestic law in regard to restrictive trading agreements. Some consideration must now be given to the position under Community Law.

Policy and source of law

The provisions of the Treaty, which have been part of our law since January, 1973, are based, as UK law is, on the protection of the public interest. The basis of the competition policy is to be found in Arts. 85 and 86 of the Treaty. These ban practices which distort competition between members of the Community, e.g. cartels (Art. 85) (see generally *Re German Ceramic Tiles Discount Agreement*, 1971,)[324] and prohibit the abuse of a monopolistic, or dominant, position by an organization within the market (Art. 86). There is an additional aim of raising living standards.

The result of a breach of the Treaty is that the agreement or decision concerned becomes void unless specifically exempted by the Commission in Brussels or the European Court of Justice in Luxembourg, or a national court. Additionally, the Commission may impose fines.

Powers of investigation

The Directorate-General for Competition is the Department of the European Commission which investigates suspected infringement of Articles 85 and 86 (the Competition Rules), and then if there is sufficient evidence prosecutes the organizations concerned and passes judgment upon them. There are powers of entry into premises for the purposes of an inquiry. There is also a power in the Treaty to ask for information from governments and from companies in order to pursue inquiries.

The development of the objectives of the Treaty can best be appreciated by looking at some of the major decisions which have been made under Articles 85 and 86.

Article 85

(a) Use of trade marks to restrict competition

One of the most famous decisions is that of *Consten and Grundig*, [1966] C.M.L.R. 418. Grundig set up a network of exclusive distributors for its products throughout the Community and appointed a French firm, Consten, to be its exclusive distributor in France. Consten, in common with all other Grundig distributors was not permitted to sell either directly or indirectly outside France, and to make certain that none of the other distributors violated Consten's exclusive territorial rights, Consten was permitted to register the trademark G.I.N.T. (which stands for Grundig International) as its French trademark. A third party imported Grundig products into France and Consten brought an action against the importer for infringement of trademark. The case went to the European Court of Justice and it was held that the purpose of the trade-mark agreement between Grundig and Consten was to guarantee complete territorial protection to Consten in the sale of Grundig products in France. That agreement was prohibited by Art. 85 as its purpose was to hamper the importing into France of Grundig products by other firms, so restricting competition, and in these circumstances the agreement was void.

(b) Cartel arrangements

A classic illustration of cartel arrangements is to be seen in the *Quinine* cartel, [1969] C.M.L.R. D.41. In that case an agreement had been made between the six manufacturing companies holding a dominant position on European and world markets by which they agreed to charge the same prices for quinine and a drug extracted from quinine and also set up export quotas in respect of imports from other member countries. The companies involved had received legal advice to the effect that their arrangement infringed Art. 85 but nevertheless they continued to apply it and took precautions to keep it secret, instructing their members to destroy any compromising documents. However, mainly as a result of an investigation by the US Senate Anti-Trust Monopolies Sub-Committee, the European Commission opened its investigations of the companies' headquarters in the Community and this led them to impose fines ranging from $10,000 up to $210,000, the fines being set in relation to each company's market position and its responsibility for the arrangements.

In the *Dyestuffs* cartel, [1969] C.M.L.R.D.23, the Commission's investigations were commenced on the basis of information which they received from trade organizations of industrial users. The investigations revealed that the ten major manufacturers of dyestuffs had made uniform, and for all practical purposes, simultaneous price increases between 1964 and 1967 on the sale of their goods. This price-fixing agreement led to the imposition of fines of $50,000 on the companies involved.

(c) The use of patent rights to restrict competition

An illustration of the attitude of the European Court on this issue is to be found in *Parke-Davis* v. *Probel*, [1968] C.M.L.R. 47. The Parke-Davis company, based in Detroit, held certain Dutch patents for an antibiotic. Another company imported the drug into Holland without the permission of the patent holder, Parke-Davis, and they brought an action against the other company for breach of the patent. It appeared that the defendant company had purchased the drug in Italy, where there was no patent protection in medicines, and had then imported it into Holland. Thus Parke-Davis had been unable to take out patents in Italy in order to protect their rights because there was a gap in Italian law as regards patents. In these circumstances Parke-Davis took the only action they could by suing the defendant company. The defendant company pleaded that the action was in breach of competition rules and the Dutch court referred the matter to the European Court of Justice. The European Court recognized the existence of the patent rights and that the exercise of those rights to prevent goods being imported into Holland from a country where such patent rights did not exist was a wholly proper action and did not constitute a restriction on competition. However, if the goods had been imported from another country where patent rights were in existence, an attempt to prevent their importation would probably have constituted an infringement of Art. 85.

(d) Other anti-competition infringements of Article 85

Of interest here is the case of *Cutsforth* v. *Mansfield Inns*, [1986] I.C.M.L.R. 1. C supplied coin-operated machines to 57 Humberside public houses owned by Northern County Breweries. M acquired Northern and requested all the tenants of the old Northern public houses to operate equipment supplied by M's list of nominated suppliers. M refused to put C on that list. This was held to be an infringement of Art. 85 and an injunction was granted preventing M from interfering with C's agreements with the tenants of the 57 public houses and from taking any action to limit the freedom of those tenants to order machines from C. M were not infringing Art. 86 because they were not in a dominant position in the market.

Article 86

In order that Act. 86 shall be applicable it must be shown firstly that a dominant position is held by some undertaking, and that secondly there has been an abuse of that domination and thirdly, that the abuse has had an effect on trade between member states. The attitude of the Commission and the European Court to the abuse of Art. 86 is illustrated by the *Continental Can Case*, [1972] C.M.L.R. D.11. The Continental Can Company was an American company producing packing materials, e.g. meat tins, fish tins, and metal lids for glass jars. In 1969, through a Belgian subsidiary, it took control of the largest German producer of packaging and in 1970 followed this up by acquiring a majority holding in a Dutch company which was the leading manufacturer of packing materials in the Benelux countries. In the opinion of the Commission the situation arising from this concentration within the market of light packings in the North-West region of the Common Market constituted the necessary conditions for an abuse of a dominant position within Art. 86. The Commission asserted that Continental Can, by acquiring control of the largest packaging manufacturers in the Benelux countries, had virtually eliminated in a major part of the Common Market all competition in meat cans, fish cans, and tin-plate caps. The finding of the Commission was set aside by the European Court on a technical ground that the Commission had failed to define which market was abused, whether it was that of meat tins, fish tins, metal lids for glass jars or all three. However, the Court stressed that Art. 86 would have been infringed on a definition of the market abused so that the mergers would have been void.

An illustration of the application of Art. 86 in the House of Lords is *Garden Cottage Foods Ltd* v. *Milk Marketing Board*, 1983.[325]

Relationship with UK law

National legislation on restrictive trade practices and monopolies applies alongside Community law unless it conflicts with Community law as interpreted by the Commission or the European Court of Justice. Therefore, if a restrictive agreement or merger threat affects only the UK market, the matter will remain subject exclusively to UK legislation. Thus a solus agreement between a petrol company and its retailers applying only in the UK would be covered by the UK rules which have already been considered in this chapter. (*Esso Petroleum Co. Ltd* v. *Kingswood Motors (Addlestone) Ltd*, [1973] 3 All E.R. 1057.) If such agreement affects trade between two or more member states then to that extent national law is excluded by Community law. Furthermore, if there is an overlap between Community and national law, Community law predominates. Therefore, once an agreement with inter-Market effect has been exempted by the Commission under Art. 85, it will from then on be immune from attack under United Kingdom restrictive practices or resale prices legislation. If the agreement has already been regarded as invalid under that legislation the invalidation will cease to be effective if the Commission exempts it under Art. 85. Additionally, if the restrictive practice has been approved by a UK court its approval will lapse if the agreement turns out to infringe the provisions of Art. 85.

However, steps have been taken to avoid possible conflict. A measure of discretion is given in the Restrictive Trade Practices Act, 1976 to the Restrictive Practices Court and the Director-General of Fair Trading. The former is given the discretion to refrain from declaring an agreement contrary to the public interest where it would infringe UK law but not Art. 85 or 86 of the Treaty of Rome. The latter is given a discretion not to bring agreements before the court which are approved under EEC law.

Procedure for notification of potentially restrictive agreements

If an agreement is thought to infringe Art. 85, the contracting parties may take one of three courses of action.

(i) The agreement may be amended by the deletion of the offending provisions thereby taking it outside the provisions of the Article altogether.

(ii) The parties may leave the agreement as it stands and run the risk of the practice coming to the notice of the Commission with the possible imposition of a fine.

(iii) The parties may register or notify the agreement to the Head of the Competition Department of the Commission in Brussels (i.e. the Directorate-General for Competition). Once registered the agreement obtains provisional validity at civil law and protection from fines until such time as the Commission declares it to be unlawful, or grants an exemption.

There is no need for notification of an agreement when all the parties are from one member state and the agreement does not relate either to import or export between member states.

There is no need to notify agreements in which only two enterprises participate, regardless of the member states to which they belong, provided the agreements are only concerned to fix prices or conditions of trading in the resale of goods which have been acquired from the other party to the contract; or where the restrictions are concerned with a licence to use industrial property rights or restrictions in terms of manufacturing processes or knowledge.

In addition, two enterprise agreements which are concerned, for example, with joint research and development, need not be notified.

There is nothing to stop the parties in case of doubt from notifying agreements in order to satisfy their own minds as to their legality and to cover the possible risk of misinterpretation of the agreement.

DISCHARGE OF A CONTRACT

A contract is discharged when the obligation created by it ceases to be binding on the promisor, who is then no longer under a duty to perform his part of the agreement. Discharge may take place in various ways.

Discharge by agreement

A contract is made by agreement; and it is also possible to end it by a subsequent agreement if there is new consideration for the discharge, or if the discharge is under seal. Where the contract is executory, i.e. a promise for a promise, and there has been no performance, the mutual release of the parties provides the consideration and is called bilateral discharge. But where the contract is executed, i.e. where it has been performed or partly performed by one party, then the party to be released must provide consideration, unless the agreement to abandon the contract is under seal. In other words, there must be *accord and satisfaction*, the agreement to discharge being the accord and the new consideration being the satisfaction. This method of discharge is called unilateral discharge. Where the discharge by agreement takes the form of the substitution of a new contract, the substitution is called a novation.

Sometimes a contract makes provision for its own discharge. It may make the completion of the contract subject to the fulfilment of a *condition precedent or warranty*. Thus, if I say I will buy your car if you fit new tyres to it, I shall incur no liability unless the tyres are so fitted. Similarly a contract to purchase land subject to planning permission being obtained can be rescinded if planning permission is refused. (*Hargreaves Transport Ltd* v. *Lynch*, [1969] 1 All E.R. 455.) Furthermore, in a contract of sale of land the payment of a deposit by the purchaser may be treated as a condition precedent of the contract of sale so that payment by cheque, which is later dishonoured, entitles the vendor to withdraw. (*Myton Ltd* v. *Schwab-Morris*, [1974] 1 All E.R. 326.)

A contract may provide that it shall be discharged by a *condition subsequent*, i.e. upon the occurrence of a certain subsequent event. An example of this is found in pre-incorporation contracts which company promoters make on behalf of a company in process of formation. The law does not allow them to act as agents for the company which, until incorporation, is a non-existent principal. Further, the company is not allowed to ratify the contract after incorporation, but must enter into a new contract or novation if it is to become liable. In addition, promoters incur personal liability under what is now s. 36 of the Companies Act, 1985. In order to avoid this, promoters' contracts may provide that they shall be discharged if the company is not incorporated at all, or within a reasonable time, or if the company when formed does not accept the contract by novation.

Contracts of employment usually provide for their own discharge by agreement but it should be noted that s. 49 of the Employment Protection (Consolidation) Act, 1978, provides for certain minimum periods of notice to be given by and to employees whose contracts are terminable by notice. The minimum notice to be given by an employee is one week, irrespective of the period of employment, provided he has been employed for at least one month. As regards employers, they must give one week's notice after one month's service, two weeks after two years' service and an additional week for each year of service up to 12 weeks after 12 years' service.

Longer periods of notice can, of course, be provided for expressly in particular contracts.

With regard to the form of discharge, a contract which is made in writing may be rescinded or varied by an oral agreement. A contract under seal may be rescinded or varied by a simple contract. However, while a contract required by statute to be evidenced in writing can be totally discharged by an oral agreement (*Moore* v. *Marrable*, 1866),[326] a partial discharge or variation must be in writing. (*Goss* v. *Nugent*, 1833.)[327]

It is also possible to discharge a contract by release. At any time before a contract is due to be performed, or after a breach of contract has taken place, a release of the obligations under the contract may be granted by deed. Such a deed dissolves the contract and is binding, whether or not it is based on consideration. No new contract is made; the old obligations are simply released.

Discharge by performance

A contract may be discharged by performance, the discharge taking place when both parties have performed the obligations which the contract places upon them. The court may construe a contract in such a way that the manner of performance must comply exactly with the terms of the contract. (*Moore & Co.* v. *Landauer & Co.*, 1921.)[328] The strict application of this rule would mean that all contracts would be *entire* so that no payment could be obtained for partial performance. The law assumes a contract between X and Y to be entire when it appears on construction of the contract that X has undertaken his obligations on the express or implied condition that he will not be obliged to perform those obligations unless Y completes or is willing to complete his obligations fully and exactly. (*Sumpter* v. *Hedges*, 1898.)[329]

However, there are *certain exceptions* to the rule of precise performance—

(i) *Where the contract is divisible*. Although there is a presumption in favour of entire contracts, the court may sometimes find that a contract is a divisible one, a usual instance being the contract between landlord and tenant. This means that the tenant cannot refuse to pay the rent even though the landlord is not carrying out the covenants of the lease, e.g. a covenant to repair. The tenant can sue the landlord for breach of covenant but must continue to pay.

(ii) *Where a partial performance has been accepted*. Where one of the parties to the contract has only partially carried out his obligations under the contract but the other party appears from his conduct to have accepted the benefit of the partial performance, the court may infer a promise to pay for the benefit received, and allow an action on a *quantum meruit* to the party who has partly performed the contract. If, for example, S agrees to deliver 3 dozen bottles of brandy to B and delivers 2 dozen bottles only, then B may exercise his right to reject the whole consignment. But if he has accepted delivery of the 2 dozen bottles he must pay a reasonable price for the bottles retained, and S's *quantum meruit* will normally be the agreed contract price per bottle.

However, the mere conferring of a benefit on one party by another is not enough; there must be evidence of the acceptance of that benefit by the party upon whom it was conferred. (*Sumpter* v. *Hedges*, 1898.)[329]

(iii) *Where performance is prevented by one party.* Here the party who cannot further perform his part of the contract may bring an action on a *quantum meruit* against the party in default for the value of work done up to the time when further performance was prevented. (*De Barnardy* v. *Harding*, 1853.)[330]

(iv) *Where there has been substantial performance.* The doctrine of substantial performance is based on the notion that precise performance of every term of the contract by one party is not required in order to make the other party liable to some extent on it. If the court, as a matter of construction, decides that there has been substantial performance, the plaintiff may recover for work done under the contract, though the defendant can, of course, counter-claim for any defects in performance. (*Hoenig* v. *Isaacs*, 1952[331] and *Bolton* v. *Mahadeva*, 1972.)[332]

In this connection it should be noted that where a contractor is employed under the Royal Institution of British Architects' standard form of contract, an architect's final certificate that the work has been carried out properly is conclusive evidence in any proceedings. (*Hosier & Dickinson* v. *P. & M. Kaye*, [1972] 1 All E.R. 121.)

In construing a contract to see whether a particular term must be fully performed or whether substantial performance is enough, the distinction between conditions and warranties is relevant. A condition must be wholly performed, whereas substantial performance of a warranty is enough. (*Poussard* v. *Spiers & Pond*, 1876,[230] and *Bettini* v. *Gye*, 1876.)[231]

A contract may provide for optional methods of performance. (*Narbeth* v. *James, The Lady Tahilla*, 1967.)[333]

Time for performance

The time for performance may in some cases be *of the essence of the contract* and in others it may not. At common law, where the parties have fixed a time for performance, time is the essence of the contract, even though the parties have not expressly said so in the contract. The rule may be applied even where performance is earlier than the contract specifies. (*Bowes* v. *Shand*, 1877.)[334]

However, Equity took a different view, and where the plaintiff was asking for an equitable remedy, e.g. for specific performance of a contract to sell land, the failure of either the vendor or the purchaser to complete exactly to time did not prevent a claim for specific performance so long as no injustice was done to either party. *Time was of the essence even in Equity:* (*a*) where the parties had stipulated a time for performance in the contract and had in addition indicated that this time was in the nature of a condition; (*b*) where time was not originally of the essence but had been made so by the aggrieved party giving notice to this effect (*Rickards (Charles) Ltd* v. *Oppenhaim*, 1950);[335] or (*c*) where from the circumstances of the case it appeared that the contract should be performed at the agreed time.

The sale of a short lease or of a reversionary interest would come into this last category. Suppose property is left by will to X for life with remainder to Y, then if Y sells his remainder, as he may do, it is obvious that the contract of sale should be completed at the agreed date, for delay will mean that the life tenant T is growing older and the value of the reversion is therefore increasing. Similarly in the sale of a business, Equity will generally take the view that the contract should be completed on time so that uncertainties regarding a change of owner should not be so prolonged as to affect adversely the goodwill of the business. Further, it was held in *Hare* v. *Nichol*, [1966] 1 All E.R. 285, that time is the essence of the contract where the property concerned is shares of a highly speculative nature. In addition, there is a presumption that time is of the essence of all mercantile contracts such as sale of goods unless the circumstances show otherwise. (*Elmdore Ltd* v. *Keech*, 1969.)[336]

Where the contract is capable of specific performance, the equitable rule still applies, even though the plaintiff may in fact be asking for damages. In other cases, the common law rule that time is of the essence of the contract prevails. (S. 41, Law of Property Act, 1925.)

Tender

With regard to the manner of performance, the question of what is good tender arises. *Tender is an offer of performance which complies with the terms of the contract.* If goods are tendered by the seller and refused by the buyer, the seller is freed from liability, given that the goods are in accordance with the contract as to quantity and quality. A tender of money which is refused does not discharge the tenderer, but if he pays the money into court without delay he will have a good defence to an action brought against him, and the debt will not bear interest.

As regards the payment of money, this must comply with the following:

(a) It must be in accordance with the rules relating to legal tender. By s. 1(2) and (6) of the Currency and Bank Notes Act, 1954 a tender of a note or notes of the Bank of England expressed to be payable to bearer on demand is legal tender for the payment of any amount. A tender of notes of a bank other than the Bank of England is not legal tender, though the creditor may waive his objection to the tender if he wishes. As regards coins, s. 2 of the Coinage Act, 1971, as amended by the Currency Act, 1983, provides that coins made by the Mint shall be legal tender as follows:

(i) gold coins for payment of any amount;
(ii) coins of cupro-nickel or silver of denominations of more than 10 pence, i.e. 20 p, 50 p, £1 and £2 coins are legal tender for payment of any amount not exceeding £10;

(iii) coins of cupro-nickel or silver of denominations of not more than 10 pence (in practice, the 5 p and 10 p coins) are legal tender for payment of any amount not exceeding £5;

(iv) coins of bronze, i.e. the 2 p and 1 p coins are legal tender for payment of any amount not exceeding 20 pence.

There is power by proclamation to call in coins which then cease to be legal tender or to make other coins legal tender.

(b) There must be no request for change.

Tender by cheque or other negotiable instrument is not good tender unless the creditor does not object; and the debt is discharged when the instrument is honoured, not when it is received. If the instrument is dishonoured, the creditor may sue for his money under either the contract or on the instrument. The tender must be unconditional, and must comply with the terms of the contract as to time, place and mode of performance. A payment of the amount due under a contract is a discharge, but the payment of a smaller sum is no discharge unless made earlier than it is due or by a third party. (See p. 210.)

Receipts

A receipt may be given on payment, but a receipt is only *prima facie* and not conclusive evidence of payment. A payment may be proved orally in cases where a receipt is lost or no receipt is given. Furthermore, s. 3 of the Cheques Act, 1957 provides that an unindorsed cheque which appears to have been paid by the banker on whom it has been drawn is evidence of the receipt by the payee of the sum payable by the cheque.

If money is sent by post it is not good payment if the letter is lost in the post unless the creditor requested payment in this way. Even a request to pay through the post does not absolve the debtor from paying in a reasonable manner and according to business practice, e.g. by registered cash. Where there is such a request, payment is established by proof of posting, even though the letter is lost in transit, and delay in the post excuses late payment.

It is important to consider the *rules governing appropriation of payments*. Certain debts are barred by the Limitation Act, 1980, and money which has been owed for six years under simple contracts or twelve years under specialty contracts, without acknowledgement, may not be recoverable by an action in the courts. Where a debtor owes several debts to the same creditor and makes a payment which does not cover them all, there are rules governing how the money should be appropriated—

(*a*) The debtor can appropriate the payment expressly, as where he says which debt he is paying, or by implication. If he owes two debts, one of £50 and one of £25, and sends a cheque for £25, there is an implied appropriation to the second debt.

(*b*) If there is no appropriation by the debtor, the creditor can appropriate the payment to any of the debts at any time, even to a statute-barred debt, since such a debt has not been extinguished; only the right of action in court has been lost. However, if the statute-barred debt is, say, £50 and the creditor appropriates a payment of £25 to it, the balance of the debt is not revived and cannot be sued for. (*Mills* v. *Fowkes*, (1839) 5 Bing, N.C. 455.)

(*c*) Where there is what is called a current account, appropriation follows the rule in *Clayton's* case (1816), 1 Mer. 572. Bank current accounts provide a good example of accounts to which this rule applies. *Clayton's* case says that, in the absence of a contrary intention, the money first paid in is to be regarded as the money which is first withdrawn (*Deeley* v. *Lloyds Bank Ltd, 1912*)[337] or that the first item on the debit side of the account is discharged or reduced by the first item on the credit side.

Discharge by breach

A breach does not of itself discharge a contract, but it may in some circumstances give the innocent party the right to treat it as discharged if he so wishes.

There are several forms of breach of contract—

(*a*) Failure to perform the contract is the most usual form, as where a seller fails to deliver goods by the appointed time, or where they are not up to standard as to quality or quantity.

(*b*) Express repudiation arises where one party states that he will not perform his part of the contract. (*Hochster* v. *De La Tour*, 1853[338] and *Gorse* v. *Durham County Council*, 1971.)[339]

(*c*) Some action by one party which makes performance impossible. (See *Omnium D'Entreprises* v. *Sutherland*, 1919.)[340]

Any breach which takes place before the time for performance has arrived is called an anticipatory breach.

The remedies where a contract has been discharged by breach are an action for damages if any have been suffered, or, if the parties have stipulated the damages to be payable on breach, an action for that sum which is called liquidated damages. Not every breach entitles the innocent party to treat the contract as discharged. It must be shown that the breach affects a vital part of the contract, i.e. that it is a breach of condition rather than a breach of warranty (*Poussard* v. *Spiers and Pond*, 1896[230] and *Bettini* v. *Gye*, 1876),[231] and that what has happened is not excused by the terms of the contract.

Thus, a charterparty (a contract under which a shipowner agrees to place his vessel at the disposal of another—the charterer—for the carriage of goods by sea) normally imposes a duty on the charterer to provide a cargo as agreed so that the shipowner can earn the freight. However, the contract may contain an exception under which the charterer is excused from doing this in circumstances which are not his fault, as in *The Angelia*, [1973] 2 All E.R. 144. Where this is so, the charterer's failure to provide a cargo will not amount to a breach of contract.

In the case of anticipatory breach, the innocent party may treat the contract as discharged at once and sue for damages, though the court may have regard to whether the contract could have been carried out by the plaintiff at the time scheduled for performance. (*The Mihalis Angelos*, 1970.)[341] Alternatively he may ignore the breach and wait until the time for performance arrives. It may be dangerous to wait since the contract may later become impossible of performance, so providing the party who was in breach with a good defence to an action. (*Avery* v. *Bowden*, 1855.)[342]

Where one party to a contract wrongfully repudiates it and the other party refuses to accept the repudiation, it seems that the contract survives and the rights of the innocent party are preserved. He may, if it is within his power, perform his part of the contract and recover on that basis, for there is no duty on him to vary the contract at the request of the other party so as to deprive himself of its benefit. (*White and Carter (Councils) Ltd* v. *McGregor*, 1961.)[343]

It should also be noted that where a person is entitled to repudiate his liability under a contract by reason of the other party's breach his delay in so doing will not operate against him unless other parties are prejudiced or the delay is so long as to indicate to the court that he has accepted liability. (*Allen* v. *Robles* (*Compagnie Parisienne de Garantie, Third Party*), 1969.)[344]

Regarding leases it appears that since a lease conveys an estate in land it does not necessarily come to an end by repudiation and acceptance of repudiation as an ordinary contract would. (*Total Oil Great Britain Ltd* v. *Thompson Garages (Biggin Hill) Ltd*, 1971.)[345]

Other matters

Two further points arise in connection with breach of contract. The first is that the concept of contributory negligence does not apply. In *Basildon District Council* v. *J. E. Lesser (Properties) Ltd*, [1985] 1 All E.R. 20 the plaintiff sued for breach of contract in regard to the building of dwellings which had become unfit for habitation without repair. There was a defence that the damages payable should be reduced on the basis that the Council's officers were guilty of contributory negligence. It was said that they should have noticed the lack of appropriate depth in foundations on seeing the building contractors' original drawings. It was decided by the High Court that the defence of contributory negligence did not apply in contract but only in tort.

It should be noted, however, that the obligation in the above case was entirely contractual. If the plaintiff could have sued, either in contract or in tort, as where the damage arises from a breach of contract and a tort, then even if the injured party decides to sue only for breach of contract, the damages can be reduced if he is contributorily negligent. (See *Forsikrings Vesta* v. *Butcher*, *Financial Times*, 3 November, 1987.)

Secondly, the Drug Trafficking Offences Act, 1986 in s. 24 brings in what is called a 'laundering' offence under which anyone knowingly assisting with the retention, control, or investment of drug trafficking proceeds could be liable to a maximum of 14 years' imprisonment. Banks, building societies, accountants, solicitors, and other advisers are given protection by the Act if they disclose their suspicions about their client's finances if these seem to be connected with drug trafficking. However, the Act ensures that they cannot be sued for breach of contract if they pass on to the appropriate authorities their suspicions that any funds or investments may be connected with drug trafficking.

Discharge by frustration (or subsequent impossibility)
If an agreement is impossible of performance from the outset, it is no contract. Sometimes, however, parties may make a contract which at the time is possible of performance but subsequently becomes impossible to carry out in whole or in part. The view of the early common law judges was that such eventualities should be provided for in the contract, and if this was not done the party liable for the performance of an impossible undertaking would be obliged to pay damages to the other party for such non-performance.

This rule was gradually modified and made less rigorous, but even now the courts are not anxious to give remedies for eventualities which could have been foreseen, e.g. if a strike prevents performance this could have been provided for in the contract. (And see *Davis Contractors Ltd* v. *Fareham U.D.C.*, 1956.)[346]

The present doctrine is that if performance was possible when the contract was made, subsequent impossibility may discharge it in the following cases—

(*a*) If the impossibility is due to changes in law or operation of law, the contract is discharged. (*Re Shipton, Anderson & Co. and Harrison Brothers' Arbitration*, 1915.)[347]

(*b*) If the contract is for personal services, it becomes discharged by the death or incapacity of the person who has to perform it. Temporary illness or other incapacity will not in most cases discharge a contract (*Storey* v. *Fulham Steel Works*, 1907,[348] *Mount* v. *Oldham Corporation*, 1973,[349] and *Hare* v. *Murphy*, 1975)[350] but if the illness or other incapacity goes right to the root of the contract, it will (*Poussard* v. *Spiers and Pond*, 1876).[230]

(*c*) If the performance depends upon the existence of a certain thing, or a state of affairs which ceases to exist, the contract is discharged. (*Taylor* v. *Caldwell*, 1863,[351] and *Krell* v. *Henry*, 1903.)[352] But it must be shown that the contract will be substantially affected by the new circumstances. (*Herne Bay Steam Boat Co.* v. *Hutton*, 1903.)[353]

(*d*) A contract is also discharged when its commercial purpose is frustrated, often because its completion would be so delayed as to make the performance, when it occurred, of little or no value. (*Joseph Constantine*

Steamship Line Ltd v. *Imperial Smelting Corporation Ltd*, 1942,[354] and *Jackson* v. *Union Marine Insurance Co. Ltd*, 1874.)[355] In terms of frustration, increased cost of performing the contract is rarely sufficient reason for invoking the defence.

The doctrine will not apply—

(i) where the parties have made express provision for the event which has occurred. In such a case, the provisions inserted into the contract by the parties will apply. Thus in some of the coronation seat cases, e.g. *Clark* v. *Lindsay* (1903), 19 T.L.R. 202 the contracts provided that if the procession was postponed the tickets would be valid for the day on which it did take place or that the parties should get their money back with a deduction for the room owner's expenses. These took effect to the exclusion of the principles of frustration;

(ii) where the frustrating event is self-induced (*Maritime National Fish Ltd* v. *Ocean Trawlers Ltd*, 1935);[356]

(iii) where the contract is one concerning land then, although it seems that a contract for the sale of land can be frustrated (*Amalgamated Investment & Property Co. Ltd* v. *John Walker & Sons Ltd*, 1976),[192] it is not frustrated by destruction of the property before completion. The purchaser will normally insure the property when he enters into a binding contract.

It would seem also that in spite of doubts and difficulties in past cases, a lease of land can be frustrated. Thus in *National Carriers* v. *Panalpina (Northern)*, [1981] 1 All E.R. 161, National Carriers leased a warehouse in Hull to Panalpina for ten years. The Hull City Council closed the only access to it because a listed building near the warehouse was in a dangerous condition. The access road was closed for 20 months and Panalpina refused to pay rent. The House of Lords held that they must pay rent; a lease could be frustrated but 20 months' lack of use out of ten years was not enough in the circumstances to frustrate it. Thus even though a court may be prepared to apply the doctrine of frustration to leases it would not often apply to longer leases because the break would rarely be long enough.

The Law Reform (Frustrated Contracts) Act, 1943

An important modern statute has laid down the conditions which will govern the rights and duties of the parties when certain contracts are frustrated. This measure is the Law Reform (Frustrated Contracts) Act, 1943. Before this Act it was the law that when subsequent impossibility discharged a contract, it did not discharge it *ab initio* (from the beginning), but only from the time when the event making the contract impossible of performance actually occurred. Thus any loss lay where it fell. Money not due at the time could not be claimed. Money due and not paid could be claimed. Money paid under the contract before it became impossible could not be recovered. (*Chandler* v. *Webster*, 1904.)[357]

The statute has amended the common law and provides what shall happen if the contract becomes discharged by frustration—

(i) All money paid before discharge is recoverable.

(ii) Money which was payable ceases to be payable.

(iii) The court will allow the parties to recover sums of money paid out on expenses incurred in connection with the contract, or to retain such sums from money already received under the contract.

(iv) It is also possible to recover, on a *quantum meruit*, a reasonable sum of money as compensation where one of the parties has carried out acts of part performance before frustration, i.e. where one party has received what the Act calls 'a valuable benefit' under the contract other than a money payment. There are difficulties in regard to the expression 'valuable benefit', particularly where the work is destroyed since the Act is not clear as to whether a sum can be recovered by the person conferring the benefit where there has been destruction of his work.

It all depends upon whether the court looks at benefit before the frustrating event or afterwards. In *Parsons Bros* v. *Shea* (1965), 53 D.L.R. (2d) 86, a Newfoundland court held, when interpreting the same provision, that the carrying out of modifications to a heating system in an hotel subsequently destroyed by fire could not be regarded as conferring 'benefit' upon the owner. However, in *B.P. Exploration Co. (Libya)* v. *Hunt (No. 2)*, [1982] 1 All E.R. 125, B.P., the plaintiffs, were engaged to develop an oil field on the defendant's land and were to be paid by oil from the wells. After the wells came on stream, but before B.P. had received all the oil which the development contract provided they should have, the wells were nationalized by the Libyan Government which gave the defendant some compensation. The contract was obviously frustrated but the House of Lords gave B.P. a sum of $35 million as representing the 'benefit' received by the defendant prior to the frustrating event.

There clearly was some benefit to the defendant here because without the development on his land he would not have obtained the oil which he did extract before nationalization and, of course, he may have received little, if anything, by way of compensation on nationalization unless there had been a successful development of the oil-bearing rock.

It would appear, therefore, that there is no need for the benefit conferred to survive the frustrating event. The court can make an award provided benefit was once conferred. The fact that it did not survive the frustrating event can be taken into account by the court when assessing (and probably reducing) how much it gives to the plaintiff.

The Act does not apply to contracts for the carriage of goods by sea or to contracts of insurance. If X insures against sickness on 1 January, and dies on 1 February, his executors cannot recover eleven-twelfths of the premium paid, even though the contract is now impossible of performance.

The Act also excepts from its provisions certain *sales* of *specific* goods which have *perished* the effect of which is, broadly speaking, as follows—

(*a*) *The goods must be specific and not unascertained.* Section 61 of the Sale of Goods Act, 1979, states that specific goods are goods identified and agreed upon at the time the contract of sale is made. Thus a contract to sell 'my 1982 Mini' is a contract to sell specific goods, whereas a contract to sell 'one of my two cars' would be a contract for the sale of unascertained goods since it is not certain which of the two cars will be sold.

(*b*) *The goods must have perished.* Goods are regarded as having perished—

(i) where they have been physically destroyed, say by fire; or
(ii) where although they physically exist they are so damaged that they cannot reasonably be regarded as the goods actually purchased, e.g. apples contaminated by sewage.

(*c*) *The contract must be a sale and not an agreement to sell.* A *contract of sale* is one in which the property (normally ownership) in the goods is transferred to the buyer at the time when the contract is made. In an *agreement to sell*, ownership is transferred to the buyer at a future date after the making of the contract. It should be noted that in English law the transfer of ownership does not depend upon *delivery* of the goods. Where the goods are specific and in the absence of any contrary intention, the property in the goods passes to the buyer when he accepts the seller's offer, even though the seller physically retains the goods.

The application of these concepts may be illustrated by the following examples—

(1) If A offers to sell the only car he has, which is at his home, to B for £800 and B accepts the offer, the contract will be for the sale of specific goods and ownership (and normally risk) will pass to B when he accepts A's offer regardless of actual delivery of the vehicle. Ordinarily A will deliver the car to B and all will be well; but let us suppose that the car is destroyed by fire before delivery, so that A cannot perform the contract. In such circumstances the legal position would appear to be as follows—

(*a*) If the car was destroyed *before* B accepted A's offer the contract is rendered *void* by s. 6 of the Sale of Goods Act, 1979. Thus A need not pay damages for non-performance nor is B obliged to pay for the car. Furthermore, if B had made a payment to A it could be recovered.

(*b*) If the car was destroyed *after* B accepted A's offer B would have become owner of the car and would have to pay A £800 for it even though the car could never be delivered.

(*c*) If in the course of selling the car to B it was agreed that ownership should not pass for one week, then if the car was destroyed before the week had elapsed the position would be as follows—

(i) A would have to bear the loss of the car; and
(ii) the contract would be avoided by s. 7 of the Sale of Goods Act,

1979, so that A would not be liable in damages for failure to perform the contract—B would not be required to pay for it and could recover any money paid to A.

(2) If the goods were *unascertained*, as where A sold to B 100 bags of wheat from a warehouse containing 150, then if more than 100 bags, say 120, were destroyed, e.g. by fire, the Act of 1943 would operate. Money payable would cease to be; money paid would be recoverable. The seller would be excused from performance of the contract. Presumably, if, say, 20 bags only were destroyed, the seller would be expected to carry out the contract.

(3) If the goods were *specific* but had *not perished* as where A's only car was requisitioned by the Crown in an emergency, then the Act of 1943 and the rules thereunder would also apply.

Before leaving the topic of frustration, it should be noted that the Act of 1943 does not apply to contracts governed by foreign law, and also that it can be excluded by a contrary agreement between the parties. For example, in some of the coronation seat cases the contract provided that if the procession was postponed, tickets were valid for the day on which it did take place or the parties should get their money back with a deduction for the room owner's expenses. These provisions took effect to the exclusion of the principles of frustration and would today be abided by rather than the Act being applied to the situation.

Discharge by lapse of time

Contracts entered into for a specified time are discharged when that period of time has elapsed. In other cases time is of no effect as regards discharge, but lapse of time may render contracts unenforceable in a court of law as evidence becomes less reliable with the passage of time.

The Limitation Act, 1980, provides that actions on simple contracts are barred after six years from the date upon which the plaintiff could first have brought his action. Actions on specialty contracts are barred after twelve years from the cause of action. However, if the time expires on a day when the court offices are not open the period is extended to the next working day. (*Pritam Kaur* v. *S. Russell & Sons Ltd*, [1973] 2 W.L.R. 147.)

The Limitation Act does not truly discharge a contract, which is why it has been dealt with separately here. The Act merely makes the contract unenforceable in a court of law and if the defendant does not plead the statutes of limitation, the judge will enforce the contract. In addition, where the contractual claim is not for damages but for a debt or other liquidated (i.e. ascertained) demand, time for making a claim can be extended by a subsequent payment of money not appropriated by the debtor, because, as we have seen, the creditor can appropriate it, or by the debtor or his duly authorized agent making a written acknowledgment of the debt to the creditor or his agent (s. 29 (*ibid.*).) Time begins to run again from the date of the acknowledgment. However, once a debt is statute-barred it cannot be revived in this way (s. 29(7) (*ibid.*).)

Such an acknowledgment need not have been written for the purpose and is effective if it indicates that a debt is due even if it does not state the amount. Thus, a statement of liabilities to 'sundry creditors' in a company balance sheet was held to be enough provided a particular creditor can establish by evidence that he is one of the sundry creditors and that his debt is included in the total: *Jones* v. *Bellgrove Properties Ltd*, [1949] 2 K.B. 700. The acknowledgment of the debt is as at the date on which the balance sheet was made up even though the date on which it was signed was later. (*Re Gee & Co. (Woolwich) Ltd*, [1974] 1 All E.R. 1149.) A statement of affairs prepared by the directors of a company in a receivership or liquidation and setting out a list of creditors can probably also operate as an acknowledgment of their debts, even though the statement is prepared under a Companies Act obligation and is not, in a sense, voluntary. (*Re Overmark Smith Warden Ltd*, [1982] 3 All E.R. 513.)

However, a debtor does not acknowledge a claim by denying liability and alleging that he has a set-off or cross-claim against the creditor. (*Surrendra Overseas* v. *Government of Sri Lanka*, [1977] 2 All E.R. 481.) A right of action 'accrues' from the moment when the breach occurs, not from the date when the contract was made. Thus if money is lent today for four years under a simple contract the creditor's right to recover it will not expire until ten years from today.

Where the plaintiff is a minor or person of unsound mind, the period of limitation does not run against him until his contractual disability ends, i.e. at eighteen or on becoming sane. But once time has started to run, any subsequent incapacity will not stop it running.

The defendant's fraud may also prevent his pleading the Statutes of Limitation. Section 32 of the Limitation Act, 1980, provides that where a right of action is concealed by the fraud or concealment of a cause of action of or by the defendant or his agent, the period of limitation does not begin to run until the plaintiff has discovered the fraud or could with reasonable diligence have discovered it. The same is true where the action is for relief from the consequences of a mistake. (*Lynn* v. *Bamber*, 1930.)[358] In this connection it should be noted that 'fraud' is not used in the common law sense. It is used in the equitable sense to denote conduct by the defendant or his agent such that it would be 'against conscience' for him to avail himself of the lapse of time.

Where the plaintiff's claims include a claim for damages in respect of personal injuries the limitation period is three years. However, a person may suffer personal injury the extent of which only comes to light more than three years after the breach of contract which caused it. For example, A is a passenger on B's coach and B's careless driving causes an accident as a result of which A suffers injury consisting of bruising of the face. Four years later A goes blind as a result of the accident. Under the Limitation Act, 1980, A has three years from his knowledge of his blindness to sue B and the court's permission is not required. The court may extend this period at its discretion, though in this case application must be made to the court for the extension. The implications of the Limitation Act, 1980 on this point, are dealt with in greater detail on p. 374.

Discharge by operation of law

This may occur in certain cases—

(a) Merger
A simple contract is swallowed up, or merged into, a subsequent deed covering the same subject matter, and in such circumstances an action lies only on the deed. Similarly a judgment, which is a contract of record, merges the contract debt on which the action was brought, so that all future actions are based on the judgment.

(b) Material alteration
An alteration of a material part of a deed or written contract, made by one party intentionally and without the consent of the other party, will discharge the contract. The alteration must alter the legal effect of the contract, and the mere alteration of a misdescription of one of the parties, or the insertion of the true date, will not operate as a discharge.

(c) Death
Death will discharge a contract for personal services. Other contractual rights and liabilities survive for the benefit, or otherwise, of the estate.

(d) Bankruptcy
A right of action for breach of contract possessed by a debtor, which relates to his property and which if brought will increase his assets, will pass to his trustee in bankruptcy, e.g. a contract with a third party to deliver goods or to pay money to the debtor. The right to sue for injury to the debtor's character or reputation does not pass to the trustee, even though it arises from a breach of a contract. (*Wilson* v. *United Counties Bank*, 1920.)[359]

With regard to contracts for personal services, it depends upon the date of the breach whether the debtor's right to sue remains with him or passes to his trustee. If the breach occurs before the commencement of the bankruptcy, the right of action passes to the trustee; if it occurs after this date, the debtor may sue, but the trustee may intervene and deduct from the sum recovered such sums as are not required for the reasonable maintenance of the bankrupt and his family. A trustee cannot force the debtor to carry out contracts involving personal service by him.

REMEDIES FOR BREACH OF CONTRACT

When there is a breach of contract the following remedies may be available—

(i) A right of action for damages at common law (the most common remedy).

(ii) A right of action on a *quantum meruit*.

(iii) A right to sue for specific performance or for an injunction.

(iv) A right to ask for rescission of the contract.

(v) A refusal of any further performance by the injured party.

(vi) A right at common law when paying the contract price to deduct damages due in respect of breaches committed by the other party and, if sued, to set up against the plaintiff such breaches of contract in diminution or extinction of the price. This right can be expressly excluded by the terms of a particular contract. However, there is a presumption that parties to contracts do not intend to abandon any remedies for breach of contract arising by operation of law and clear express words must be used in order to rebut this presumption. (*Gilbert-Ash (Northern) Ltd v. Modern Engineering (Bristol) Ltd*, [1973] 3 All E.R. 195.)

Damages

Assessment of damages

Damages are the common law remedy consisting of a payment of money and are intended as compensation for the plaintiff's loss and not as punishment for the defendant. The plaintiff should not be put in a *better* position than if the contract had been properly performed. The aim is to put the injured party in the *same* financial position as he would have been if the contract had been performed according to its terms. (*B. Sunley & Co. Ltd v. Cunard White Star Ltd*, 1940.)[360] This may involve taking into account the plaintiff's liability to taxation. (*Beach v. Reed Corrugated Cases Ltd*, 1956.)[361] Expenses incurred prior to the date of contract may be recovered if they were within the contemplation of the parties as a likely result of the breach. In *Anglia Television Ltd v. Reed*, [1971] 3 All E.R. 690, A Ltd engaged R to act in a film having previously spent £2750 in employing a director and designer. R repudiated the contract and A Ltd recovered £2750 from him.

It was at one time thought that damages could not be recovered for inconvenience or injured feelings. In *Hobbs v. London & South Western Railway Co.*, (1875) L.R. 10 Q.B. 111, Mellor, J. said 'For the mere inconvenience, such as annoyance and loss of temper, or vexation, or for being disappointed in a particular thing which you have set your mind upon, without real physical inconvenience resulting, you cannot recover damages . . .' Later in *Addis v. Gramophone Co. Ltd*, [1909] A.C. 488, the House of Lords held that a wrongfully dismissed employee could not recover damages in respect of injured feelings. However, the rule in

Addis is now subject to so many exceptions that little, if any, of it remains. For example, the court has awarded damages for injured feelings against tour operators who did not provide holiday accommodation to the contract standard (*Jarvis* v. *Swans Tours Ltd*, [1973] 1 All E.R. 71), and for injured feelings to an employee who was upset by a demotion in breach of contract by the employer, although he suffered no loss of income until he left the employment. (*Cox* v. *Philips Industries Ltd*, [1976] 3 All E.R. 161.)

Again, in *Heywood* v. *Wellers*, [1976] 1 All E.R. 300 (see also p. 708) the court awarded some damages to the plaintiff representing her mental distress and upset at the additional molestation inflicted upon her by a solicitor's failure to enforce an injunction against the man concerned. Damages for distress and upset were also awarded against a surveyor who negligently failed to draw the attention of his client to defects in a house which the client later purchased for his own use. The defects covered, e.g. defective woodwork and septic tank, the latter giving off offensive smells and infringing public health legislation. (See *Perry* v. *Sidney Phillips & Son*, [1982] 3 All E.R. 705.)

In view of these decisions, it seems safe to say that damages for injured feelings and aggravation of one sort or another will no longer be refused merely because the plaintiff bases his claim on a breach of contract. However, *Addis* may still be applied in actions for wrongful dismissal unless *Cox* v. *Philips* (above), which was about demotion, can be extended also to dismissal.

Damages for injury to feelings as above are not punitive (or exemplary). The plaintiff is said to need them in order that he may be properly compensated. Punitive (or exemplary) damages (see further p. 311) which are intended as a punishment to the defendant rather than compensation to the plaintiff, cannot be awarded in a purely contractual claim. They are still available to a limited extent in tort claims. (See p. 311.)

Finally, it should be noted that difficulty in assessing damages is not necessarily a bar to a claim. Damages may be awarded for the loss of a chance. This is not prevented by the rule that the plaintiff must not be better off. (*Chaplin* v. *Hicks*, 1911.)[362]

Remoteness of damage

Apart from the question of assessment, the question of *remoteness of damage* arises. The consequences of a breach of contract may be far reaching, and the law must draw the line somewhere and say that damages incurred beyond a certain limit are too remote to be recovered. Damages in contract must therefore be proximate. The modern law regarding remoteness of damage in contract is founded upon the case of *Hadley* v. *Baxendale*, 1854[363] as further explained in *The Heron II*, 1967.[364] These cases are authority for the statement that damages in contract will be too remote to be recovered unless they arise naturally i.e. in the usual course of things. Or, if they do *not* arise naturally, they are such that the defendant, as a reasonable man, would have had them in contemplation as likely to result. Damage which does not arise naturally and which would not have been in the contemplation of the reasonable man, may be recovered only if the defendant was made aware of the possibility of such damage and agreed to accept the risk of loss. (*Horne* v. *Midland Railway Co.*, 1873).[365] Notice of possible loss can be constructive as well as actual. (*Pinnock Bros.* v. *Lewis and Peat Ltd*, 1923.)[366]

As regards judgments given in foreign currency, it was until recently a fundamental principle of English Law that an English court could not give judgment for an amount in foreign currency, and a debt which was expressed and damages which were calculated in a foreign currency had to be converted into sterling for the purposes of litigation in England, irrespective of the place in which they were payable and the law governing the substance of the obligation. However, the decision in *Miliangos* v. *George Frank (Textiles) Ltd*, 1975[34] in which, as we have seen, the House of Lords overruled its previous decision in *Re United Railways of Havana*, [1960] 2 All E.R. 332 which was the decision which had established the judgment in pound sterling rule, established a new principle, *at least in so far as judgments for payments of a debt in foreign currency are concerned*, and provided the opportunity for an extension of that principle to other forms of judgment.

Since the decision of the House of Lords in *Miliangos* the rule has been extended and can now be regarded as of general application. It has been applied to a claim for unliquidated damages for breach of contract which may be given in a foreign currency (*The Folias*, [1979] A.C. 685) and in tort (*The Despina R*, [1979] A.C. 685). Thus in *Hoffman* v. *Sofaer*, [1982] 1 W.L.R. 1350, the plaintiff, who was a resident of the United States, was injured through the negligence of the defendant and asked for damages for loss of future earnings in US dollars. Talbot, J., applying the test laid down in *The Despina*, i.e. that the court may award damages for negligence or for breach of contract in the currency which best expresses the plaintiff's loss, held that as the plaintiff would make dollar payments to meet the expenses occasioned by his disability in the future, the US dollar was the currency with which the loss was most closely linked and judgment would be given in that currency.

As regards the rate of conversion, the position is that where a judgment for debt or damages is asked for, either in contract or tort, and is given in a foreign currency, the debtor must pay the sterling equivalent *at the actual date of payment* to the creditor, if the debtor pays voluntarily, or at the date when the creditor applies to enforce the judgment, e.g. by writ of *fi. fa.*, if it is not paid voluntarily.

Mitigation of loss

It must be understood that, when a breach occurs, the party suffering from the breach must do all he can to reduce his loss, and he cannot recover damages which have resulted from his *unreasonable* failure to do so. (*Brace* v. *Calder*, 1895[367] and *Moore* v. *D.E.R. Ltd*, 1971.)[368] Thus if a person cancels an hotel booking, the hotel proprietor must try to relet the rooms and if a seller refuses to deliver goods, the buyer must attempt to obtain supplies elsewhere. In the latter case, where there is an available market, the damages might amount to no more than the difference between the contract price and the market price on the day appointed for delivery, together with incidental expenses.

Useful examples of how these rules operate in practice may be drawn from three cases concerning motor car sales. If the plaintiff is a car dealer, *and being in a situation where demand for cars exceeds the supply*, has been able to find someone else to buy at the same price or a higher price the same car as has been wrongfully rejected by the defendant, he will not normally be entitled to damages other than, perhaps, nominal damages. The argument that he might have been able to sell a *different* car to that other purchaser was rejected by the Court of Appeal in *Charter* v. *Sullivan*, 1957[369] (in regard to a new car) and more recently in *Lazenby Garages Ltd* v. *Wright*, 1976[370] (in regard to a used car). However, in *Thompson* v. *Robinson (Gunmakers) Ltd*, 1955[371] the argument that it might have been possible to sell a different car to the other purchaser was accepted though in rather special circumstances, *where the supply of the particular car concerned exceeded the demand for it*. In the course of mitigating his loss a person may actually aggravate the damages and yet recover them (see *Hoffberger* v. *Ascot International Bloodstock Bureau*, 1976.)[372] The principle of mitigation also applies in the law of tort. (*Luker* v. *Chapman*, 1970.)[373]

As regards mitigation of loss in a situation of anticipatory breach, see *White & Carter (Councils) Ltd* v. *McGregor*, 1961[343] and subsequent cases noted with it.

Victim's default

The event causing loss may be brought about partly by the conduct of the plaintiff. For example, A hires a van with defective brakes from B and A is injured in a crash caused partly by this and partly by his own bad driving. Can B if sued by A for breach of the contract of hiring raise the defence of contributory negligence against A under the Law Reform (Contributory Negligence) Act, 1945 as he could if A was suing in tort? (See further p. 398.)

It was decided in *Basildon District Council* v. *J. R. Lesser (Properties) Ltd, The Times*, 15 February, 1984 that the answer was no. However, A's damages could be reduced by applying the normal principles of causation. We have already seen that in *Lambert* v. *Lewis* 1981[243] it was held that a dealer who supplied a defective trailer coupling was not liable for an accident caused by the customer's continued use of the coupling *after* he knew that it was defective.

Classification of damages

It is possible to classify damages under a number of headings, and this classification applies to both contract and tort.

(a) Ordinary damages

These are damages assessed by the court for losses arising naturally from the breach of contract; and in tort for losses which cannot be positively proved or ascertained, and depend upon the court's view of the nature of the plaintiff's injury. For example, the court may have to decide what to award for the loss of an eye, there being no scale of payments; and this is so whether the action is in tort or for breach of contract.

(b) Special damages

These are awarded in tort for losses which can be positively proved or ascertained, e.g. damage to clothing; garage bills, where a vehicle has been damaged; doctor's fees; and so on. However, where it is difficult to determine the exact proportions of a claim for special damages, e.g. loss of profit not supported by accurate figures the court must do its best to arrive at a fair valuation. (*Dixons Ltd* v. *J. L. Cooper Ltd* (1970), 114 S.J. 319.) In contract, the term covers losses which do not arise naturally from the breach, so that they will not be recoverable unless within the contemplation of the parties as described above.

(c) Exemplary and aggravated damages

The usual object of damages both in contract and tort is to compensate the plaintiff for loss which he has incurred arising from the defendant's conduct. The object of *exemplary* (*or punitive*) *damages* is to punish the defendant, and to deter him and others from similar conduct in the future. Thus, it was at one time thought that, if the court had arrived at a sum of money which would sufficiently compensate the plaintiff, it could award a further sum, not as compensation for the plaintiff, but as a punishment to the defendant, the exemplary damages being in the nature of a fine. An award of exemplary damages had always confused the functions of the civil and criminal law, and it would appear that since the judgment of Lord Devlin in *Rookes* v. *Barnard*, 1964 (see p. 312), an award of exemplary damages should only be made in certain special cases. (See below.)

Aggravated damages, on the other hand, can be awarded (generally only in tort) where the defendant's conduct is such that the plaintiff requires more than the usual amount of damages to *compensate him* for the unpleasant method in which the tort was committed against him. However, an award of aggravated damages is still *compensatory*.

The state of the law after *Rookes* v. *Barnard*, 1964, may perhaps be illustrated by taking a hypothetical case. Suppose a tenant T is evicted from his flat by the landlord L before T's term has expired, and that in order to evict T the landlord uses excessive violence. The court may decide that in an ordinary case of trespass and assault T would be adequately compensated by an award of damages of (say) £500. However, if the court considers that L used particularly violent and unpleasant methods to achieve this eviction, it may award a further sum (say) £100 as aggravated damages because, on the facts of the case, this is necessary to compensate T. It would appear that the court cannot now go on and make a further award to T in order to punish and deter L. (And see *Ansell* v. *Thomas*, 1973.)[374]

Exemplary or punitive damages were sometimes awarded in contract for breach of promise of marriage, particularly where a female plaintiff had allowed the defendant to have sexual intercourse with her on the promise of marriage. This action is now abolished by the Law Reform (Miscellaneous Provisions) Act, 1970, s. 1 and examples of exemplary damages would seem in the main to be confined to actions in tort. However, an action may lie where a promise to marry is made by a man *who is already married* on the grounds of breach by the man of an implied warranty that he is in a position to marry. That such an implied warranty exists in the circumstances was decided by the Court of Appeal in *Shaw* v. *Shaw*, [1954] 2 Q.B. 424. Damages for breach of such a warranty could be, and possibly still can be, exemplary. Although the award of exemplary damages is for all practical purposes confined to actions in tort, it is perhaps convenient to deal with them here.

Subject to what has been said above and as a result of Lord Devlin's judgment in *Rookes* v. *Barnard*, 1964, exemplary damages can be awarded only—

(i) *Where there is arbitrary or unconstitutional action by servants of the State*, e.g. an unreasonable false imprisonment or detention by State authorities.

(ii) *Where the defendant's conduct has been calculated by him to make a profit for himself which may well exceed the compensation payable to the plaintiff*. Thus a newspaper may decide that the increased sales of the paper containing a libel will more than compensate for any damages which may have to be paid to the person libelled. In such a case exemplary damages may be awarded to the plaintiff, though the intention to profit must be proved. It is not enough that the newspaper has been sold and some profit necessarily made. An example of the application of this head is to be seen in *Cassell & Co. Ltd* v. *Broome*, [1972] 1 All E.R. 801 where the House of Lords upheld an award of £25000 exemplary damages against defendants who published a book containing defamatory passages where the right circumstances appeared to exist and a defence if raised, would have failed.

(iii) *Where exemplary damages are expressly authorized by statute.*

Having apparently restricted the number of situations in which exemplary damages might be awarded, Lord Devlin said at one point in his judgment in *Rookes* v. *Barnard*, 1964 that 'Exemplary damages can properly be awarded whenever it is necessary to teach a wrongdoer that tort does not pay.' The ramifications of this statement, which could have the effect of extending the power to award exemplary damages to torts such as deceit or negligence where exemplary damages have not previously been awarded, were considered in regard to the tort of deceit in *Mafo* v. *Adams*, 1969.[217]

The House of Lords in *Cassell & Co. Ltd* v. *Broome*, [1972] 1 All E.R. 801 held that *Rookes* v. *Barnard*, 1964 had correctly formulated the principles of law governing the circumstances in which exemplary damages might be awarded to a plaintiff in the case of certain torts.

Lord Hailsham and Lord Diplock were of the opinion that the decision in *Rookes* v. *Barnard*, 1964 did not have the effect of extending the power to award exemplary damages to torts such as deceit or negligence where exemplary damages could not have previously been awarded and to this extent disapproved the dictum of Lord Widgery, L.J. in *Mafo* v. *Adams*, 1969.[217]

Thus it would appear that the broader statement of Lord Devlin (see above) is not to be taken as indicating that exemplary damages can be awarded except in the three areas set out above.

(d) Nominal damages
Sometimes a small sum (say £2) is awarded where the plaintiff proves a breach of contract, or the infringement of a right, but has suffered no actual loss.

(e) Contemptuous damages
A farthing was sometimes awarded to mark the court's disapproval of the plaintiff's conduct in bringing the action. Such damages may be awarded where the plaintiff has sued for defamation of character in spite of the fact that he has engaged in defamatory activities against the defendant. Since farthings are no longer legal tender, the decimal penny would now be used.

(f) Liquidated damages
These are damages agreed upon by the parties to the contract, and only a breach of contract need be proved; no proof of loss is required. Damages in tort are not normally liquidated.

(g) Unliquidated damages
Where no damages are fixed by the contract it is left to the court to decide their amount. In such a case the plaintiff must produce evidence of the loss he has suffered, as is normal in the case of tort.

Liquidated damages must appear to be a genuine pre-estimate of loss, not a *penalty* inserted to make it an ill bargain for the defendant not to carry out his part of the contract. The court will not enforce a penalty, but will award damages on normal principles. It will be seen, therefore, that the term 'penalty clause' is a misnomer in that a clause which is truly penal will not be enforced. Nevertheless, this terminology is often used in commercial contracts but such a clause is unenforceable unless it defines a method of calculating liquidated damages.

Certain tests are applied in order to decide whether or not the provision is a penalty. Obviously extravagant sums are generally in the nature of penalties. Where the contractual obligation lying on the defendant is to pay money, then any provision in the contract which requires the payment of a larger sum on default of payment is a penalty, because the damage can be accurately assessed. Thus in *Kemble* v. *Farren* (1829), 6 Bing. 141 the defendant entered into an agreement with the plaintiff under which the defendant was to appear at Covent Garden for four seasons at £3.6s.8d. a night. The contract contained a provision that if either party refused to fulfil the engagement or any part of it he should pay the other £1000 as liquidated damages. The defendant refused to act during the second season and when the plaintiff sued him for £1000 it was held that the stipulation was a penalty. Looked at from the point of view that the defendant might have sued for £1000 if the plaintiff had not paid him £3.6s.8d. on, say, one occasion, meant that the provision relating to the payment of £1000 was quite obviously a penalty.

Where the sum provided for in the contract is payable on the occurrence of any one of several events, it is probably a penalty; for it is unlikely that each event can produce the same loss (*Ford Motor Co. (England) Ltd* v. *Armstrong*, 1915),[375] though the rule is only a presumption and is not always applied. (*Dunlop* v. *New Garage and Motor Co. Ltd*, 1915.)[129] If a sum is agreed by the parties as liquidated damages, it will be enforced as agreed, even though the actual loss is greater or smaller. (*Cellulose Acetate Silk Co. Ltd* v. *Widnes Foundry Ltd*, 1933.)[376]

Quantum meruit

This remedy means that the plaintiff will be awarded as much as is earned or deserved. In the event of a breach of contract, the injured party may have a claim other than the one for damages. He may have carried out work or performed services and for such he may be entitled to claim on a *quantum meruit*. He will be awarded what the court thinks the work or services are worth. This action is quite distinct from an action for breach of contract and is in the nature of restitution for work done. The remedy can be used contractually or quasi-contractually, and, although the topic cannot be treated fully, examples of the use of the remedy are given below—

(a) Contractually

Here it may be used to recover a reasonable price or remuneration where there is a contract for the supply of goods or services, but the contract does not fix any precise sum to be paid. It may also be used where the original contract has been replaced by a new one, and a payment is required under the new agreement, e.g. X orders 20 bottles of brandy from Y at a certain price, and Y sends 18 bottles of brandy and 2 bottles of whisky. X is not, of course, bound to take delivery, but if he does he must pay a reasonable price for the whisky on a *quantum meruit*.

(b) Quasi-contractually

Here the remedy may be used to recover a sum of money for work done under a contract discharged by the defendant's breach. This is really an alternative to a claim for damages for breach of contract, but it does enable the court to award whatever it thinks the plaintiff has earned by his work, and this may be greater than the contract price. The remedy is also available when a contract is void, since for breach of a void contract no damages can be awarded (*Craven-Ellis* v. *Canons Ltd*, 1936);[377] and sometimes where the contract is frustrated. (*Davis Contractors Ltd* v. *Fareham U.D.C.*, 1956.)[346] The remedy is also available where there never was a contract. However, if a plaintiff has made an agreement to work for the defendant in return for a specified fee and then sued on a *quantum meruit* for extra work done, he must be in a position to show the court that the original agreement has been discharged. He must have finished with the old contract before he can start a new one (*Gilbert and Partners* v. *Knight*, 1968.)[378]

Specific performance and injunction

These are equitable remedies and are not available as of right, as is the case with damages, but at the discretion of the court. Formerly these remedies would have had to be sought in the courts of Equity, (see *Wood* v. *Scarth*, 1858),[203] but since the Judicature Acts, 1873–1875 these remedies, as well as damages, are available in any court.

A decree of *specific performance* is an order of the court, and constitutes an express instruction to a party to a contract to perform the actual obligation which he undertook under its terms. It is often granted in contracts connected with land. This is because each piece of land is unique in its own geographical situation. Thus damages are not an adequate remedy; land of a similar kind cannot be manufactured in the same way as, say, a car can. Furthermore, under s. 195 of the Companies Act, 1985, a contract to take debentures in a company can be specifically enforced, though normally specific performance of a loan would not be granted. However, the remedy is available in appropriate circumstances to enforce a payment of money. (See *Beswick* v. *Beswick*, 1967.)[127] In the case of contracts for the sale of goods, specific performance is not usually given, unless the goods are unique and cannot be purchased easily in the market, such as Ming vases which, like land, are not made any more, or where their value is difficult to assess, or in any other case where damages would not be an adequate remedy. See *Sky Petroleum Ltd* v. *VIP Petroleum Ltd*, 1974,[379] in which an injunction was granted in circumstances where it would operate like specific performance.

An *injunction* is an order of the court whereby an individual is required to refrain from the further doing of the act complained of. It may be used to prevent many wrongful acts, e.g. torts, but in the context of contract the remedy will be granted to enforce a negative stipulation in a contract in a case where it would be unjust to confine the plaintiff to an action for damages. 'The standard question in relation to the grant of an injunction, are damages an adequate remedy? might perhaps, in the light of the authorities of recent years, be re-written: is it just, in all the circumstances, that a plaintiff should be confined to his remedy in damages?' per Sachs, L.J. in *Evans Marshall* v. *Bertola SA*, [1973] 1 All E.R. 992 at p. 1005. Its application may be extended to contracts where there is no actual negative stipulation but where one may be inferred. (*Metropolitan Electric Supply Co.* v. *Ginder*, 1901.)[380] In a proper case an injunction may be used as an indirect method of enforcing a contract for personal services, but in that case a *clear* negative stipulation is required. (*Whitwood Chemical Co.* v. *Hardman*, 1891,[381] and *Warner Bros Pictures Incorporated* v. *Nelson*, 1937.)[382] However, the breach of contract which it is sought to redress by injunction must have resulted in a continuing wrong, the proper remedy to put right past wrongs being damages. (*Desk Advertising Co. Ltd* v. *Société Civile De Participations Du Group S.T. Dupont and Others*, 1973.)[383] Furthermore, the obligation to be enforced must be certain. (*Bower*, v. *Bantam Investments Ltd*, 1972.)[384]

Injunctions may be (*a*) Interlocutory, (*b*) Perpetual, (*c*) Prohibitory, (*d*) Mandatory. An *interlocutory injunction* is granted before the hearing of the action, the plaintiff undertaking to be responsible for any damage caused to the defendant if in the subsequent action the plaintiff does not succeed. The decision of the House of Lords in *American Cyanamid* v. *Ethicon*, [1975] 1 All E.R. 504 puts forward the following legal propositions in regard to interlocutory injunctions: (i) an applicant for an interlocutory injunction need no longer show that he has a *prima facie* case, but rather the court should consider the balance of convenience unless the material before the court fails to disclose that the plaintiff had any real prospect of succeeding at the full trial; (ii) that in deciding the balance of convenience the court should consider—(*a*) whether if no injunction were awarded and the plaintiff succeeded at the full trial, damages would adequately compensate him for loss suffered in the meantime (see *Garden Cottage Foods Ltd* v. *Milk Marketing Board*, 1983)[325], and (*b*) whether if the injunction were granted would the plaintiff's undertakings as to damages be sufficient to compensate the defendant for loss suffered in the meantime if the defendant finally won.

There is a form of interlocutory injunction called *quia timet* (because he fears). This may be granted, though rarely, even though the injury has not taken place but is merely threatened. (*Hooper* v. *Rogers*, 1974.)[385] A *perpetual injunction* is granted after a trial, and when the point at issue has been finally determined. A *prohibitory injunction* orders that a certain act shall not be done; a *mandatory injunction* orders that a certain positive act shall be done e.g. an order to pull down a wall erected in breach of covenant.

Since specific performance is an equitable remedy, it will be granted only when certain conditions apply—

(i) Consideration must exist, since 'Equity will not assist a volunteer.' (But see *Mountford* v. *Scott*, 1974.)[386]

(ii) The court must be able to supervise the performance. Specific performance will not be granted if constant supervision is necessary to ensure that the defendant complies with the decree. (*Ryan* v. *Mutual Tontine Westminster Chambers Association*, 1893.)[387]

(iii) It must be just and equitable that the remedy be granted. If the court considers that damages are an adequate remedy, it will not grant an equitable one, nor must there be undue hardship on the person against whom the remedy is granted. (See *Wood* v. *Scarth*, 1858.)[203]

(iv) Both parties must be able to obtain the remedy. The courts will not grant equitable remedies to a minor because his contracts cannot in general be enforced against him and those which can are in the nature of contracts of personal service. Equity requires equality or mutuality as regards its remedies and this does not exist in minors' contracts.

(v) The plaintiff must show that he was in a position to carry out his part of the bargain at the time fixed for performance.

(vi) The plaintiff's own conduct in the matter must be above reproach: for it is said that 'He who comes into Equity must come with clean hands.'

A contract for personal services will not be specifically enforced because—

(*a*) it would be undesirable to force persons to work together if they did not wish to do so; and

(*b*) it would be impossible to ensure that the contract was properly carried out unless the defendant was under the constant supervision of the court. The decision of the Court of Appeal in *Hill* v. *Parsons*, 1971[388] suggests to the contrary but the decision is now regarded (even by Lord Denning himself in *Chappell* v. *Times Newspapers Ltd* [1975] 2 All E.R. 233) as so unusual as to constitute no real precedent.

However, as we have seen, the court may *encourage* but not *compel* performance of a contract of personal service by means of an injunction. (*Whitwood Chemical Co.* v. *Hardman*, 1891,[381] and *Warner Bros Pictures Incorporated* v. *Nelson*, 1937.)[382] If the effect of an injunction would be to *compel* performance it will not be granted. (*Page One Records Ltd* v. *Britton*, 1967.)[389]

The court will not, however, grant an equitable remedy where to do so would lead to further litigation (*Wroth* v. *Tyler*, 1973),[390] or in a breach of another obligation. (*Warmington* v. *Miller*, 1973.)[391]

Defiance of the court's order granting an equitable remedy constitutes contempt of court, which is punishable by fine or imprisonment or a writ of sequestration which issues against a person defying the court's order and allows persons appointed by the court, e.g. accountants, to take possession of his property until he complies with the order. It is therefore usual for the court order to be obeyed. Some equitable remedies must be asked for within a given time by statute, but otherwise they must be asked for within a reasonable time, since 'Delay defeats Equities'. What is a reasonable time is determined by the court from the circumstances.

An Anton Piller Order

In *Anton Piller KG* v. *Manufacturing Processors Ltd*, [1976] 1 All E.R. 779 the Court of Appeal affirmed the inherent jurisdiction of the High Court to make what was to become known as an Anton Piller Order. It permits the plaintiff's representatives to enter the defendant's premises for the purposes of inspecting and removing vital material or evidence such as books and documents which the defendant might dispose of or destroy so as to frustrate the ends of justice.

Although it is in the nature of a civil search warrant, it does not authorize forced entry, though a defendant who refused entry would be in contempt of court. The most frequent use of an Anton Piller Order in the past has been to seize material which infringes copyright. The jurisdiction is now s. 72 of the Supreme Court Act, 1981.

A Mareva injunction

This remedy, which can be of assistance to a party suing for breach of contract, has developed considerably over recent times. In general terms, a court will not grant an injunction to prevent a person disposing of his property merely to assist a person suing, for example, for a debt, to recover his money. However, the Mareva injunction is an exception to that general rule and is granted, e.g. when litigation is pending to restrict removal of assets outside the jurisdiction by a foreign defendant where this is a real and serious possibility. It is clearly a valuable addition to existing contractual remedies, particularly when business is now so often conducted on an international scale.

The power of the High Court to issue Mareva injunctions is recognized by s. 37 of the Supreme Court Act, 1981. It is not confined to foreign-based defendants.

Rescission

This is a further equitable remedy for breach of contract. The rule is the same when the remedy is used for breach as it is when it is used for misrepresentation. If the contract cannot be completely rescinded, it cannot be rescinded at all; it must be possible to restore the *status quo*. All part payments must be returned on rescission and cannot be retained as security against future damages, but there are circumstances where part payment is regarded as a guarantee for the due performance of the payer's obligations, and, if this is so, it will be forfeited if he does not go on with the contract, although Equity will sometimes grant relief against forfeiture of deposits. It would appear that a plaintiff can combine a claim for rescission with a claim for damages (see further p. 240). In addition, a plaintiff with a right to rescind is not bound to do so but may claim damages, e.g. for fraud, instead. (*Archer* v. *Brown*, 1983, see p. 639.)

Refusal of further performance

If the person suffering from the breach desires merely to be quit of his obligations under the contract, he may refuse any further performance on his own part and set up the breach as a defence if the party who has committed the breach attempts to enforce the contract against him. Even so, he may, if he wishes, reinforce his position by bringing an action for rescission.

The recovery of interest on debt and damages

Under the provisions of s. 15 and Sched. 1 of the Administration of Justice Act, 1982 which inserted s. 35A of the Supreme Court Act, 1981 the court has power to award interest on debt or damages at the end of the trial or where judgment is obtained in default, i.e. where there is no defence and no trial. Interest may also be awarded where the defendant settles after service of writ but before judgment. Interest is not available where a person settles *before* service of writ no matter how long he has kept the other party waiting. The interest payable is at such rate as the court thinks fit or as rules of court may provide. The rate currently payable on judgment debts under s. 17 of the Judgments Act, 1838, which is likely to be a guideline, is 15 per cent per annum (S.I. 1985/437). The interest is tax-free (s. 74. Administration of Justice Act, 1982.)

QUASI-CONTRACTUAL RIGHTS AND REMEDIES

Quasi-contract is based on the idea that a person should not obtain a benefit or an unjust enrichment as against another merely because there is no obligation in contract or another established branch of law which will operate to make him account for it. The law may in these circumstances provide a remedy by implying a *fictitious promise* to account for the benefit or enrichment. This promise can then form the basis of an action in quasi-contract. (*Greenwood* v. *Bennett*, 1972.)[392] The main areas in which quasi-contractual remedies have been used are as follows—

Actions for money paid

Where A has a secondary and B has a primary *legal liability* to a third person and A has paid over money which B was in the ultimate liable to pay, an action will lie in quasi-contract to enable A to recover from B. (*Brook's Wharf and Bull Wharf Ltd* v. *Goodman Bros*, 1936.)[393]

It is essential to the claim that B should have been under a *common and legal obligation to pay*. (*Metropolitan Police District Receiver* v. *Croydon Corporation*, 1957.)[394]

Actions for money had and received

An action for money had and received by the defendant to the use of the plaintiff lies in the following circumstances—

(a) Total failure of consideration
The plaintiff must prove that there has been a *total* and not a *partial* failure of consideration. A partial failure of consideration may result in an action for damages. A *total* failure will result in recovery of all that was paid. A common reason for total failure of consideration arises where A, who has no title, sells goods to B and B has to give up the goods to the true owner. (*Rowland* v. *Divall*, 1923.)[239]

In addition the action is based on *failure* of consideration not its *absence*. Thus, money paid by way of a gift cannot be recovered in quasi-contract.

(b) Mistake of fact
Where there is a fundamental and material mistake of fact which results in a payment of money, there may be an action in quasi-contract to recover the sums so paid either in whole or in part according to the effect of the mistake. (*Cox* v. *Prentice*, 1815.)[395]

(c) Mistake of law
Money paid as a result of a mistake of law cannot generally be recovered since ignorance of the law is no excuse. However, as we have seen, it is not easy to distinguish a mistake of law from a mistake of fact, and legislation relating to rents and security of tenure has produced some interesting cases showing the different results obtainable according to the category into which the mistake is put. (See *Sharp Bros and Knight* v. *Chant*, 1917,[179] *Solle* v. *Butcher*, 1949,[180] and *Grist* v. *Bailey*, 1966.)[199] It appears that a mistake as to a person's legal rights can be construed, at least in Equity, as a mistake of fact thus giving rise to a remedy. (*Cooper* v. *Phibbs*, 1867.)[181]

There may be another ground for recovering money paid in circumstances of mistake of law, e.g. as in the case of an oppressed party to an illegal contract not *in pari delicto* with the other. Where this is so, the plaintiff will not be prevented from succeeding simply because he has made a mistake of law. (*Kiriri Cotton Co.* v. *Dawani*, 1960.)[321]

(d) Duress and extortion
Money paid under threats of physical violence or undue influence, i.e.

moral duress, is not paid voluntarily and may be recovered in quasi-contract.

(e) Money received from a third person
An application of this aspect of quasi-contract is to be found in insurance. If an insurance company pays out a sum of money to A (the insured) in respect of loss or damage to himself or his property and A later recovers additional money in respect of the loss from another, e.g. the person causing the loss, the insurance company may sue A in quasi-contract to recover the sums received from the third person. (*Darrell* v. *Tibbitts* (1880), 5 Q.B.D. 560.)

In addition, where A has received money from B with instructions to pay it to C, then C may sue A in quasi-contract if A refuses to pay the money over. (*Shamia* v. *Joory*, 1958.)[131]

(f) Waiver of tort
If A steals B's car which is valued at £2000 and sells it to a dealer C for £2200, then B may sue A or C for wrongful interference with goods but can if he wishes waive his right to sue in tort and recover the money in quasi-contract. The action in quasi-contract has some advantages over the action in tort, e.g. A may prove in a winding-up or bankruptcy for the sum of £2200 which he cannot do if his claim is in tort and has not reached judgment.

Claims on a *quantum meruit*

Where a plaintiff has done work for the defendant but no specific sum is owing, the plaintiff can recover a reasonable sum of money on a *quantum meruit*. This aspect of quasi-contract is dealt with on page 314.

Accounts stated

If A gives B an IOU for £10, the IOU operates as an admission of the debt and gives a separate cause of action in quasi-contract. An IOU is not conclusive and A may prove the debt is void for want of consideration or illegal or that he gave the IOU under circumstances of mistake. Nevertheless, A has the burden of proving these matters and, if he cannot, B will succeed on the IOU.

Furthermore, if A (a debtor) and B (a creditor) have an account recording a number of transactions and agree to strike a balance at an agreed figure, this operates as an account stated and B can sue in quasi-contract for the amount. This is a separate source of action and would enable B to recover even in respect of debts which were formerly statute barred.

LEGISLATION RELATING TO THE CONTRACT OF EMPLOYMENT

An ever-increasing feature of contract law is the way in which particular contracts are controlled by legislation to which the general principles of contract law yield; nowhere is this more obvious than in the contract of employment. Accordingly, the main features of this legislation, which are so important in all walks of business life, are given below. The statutes concerned are abbreviated so that the Employment Protection (Consolidation) Act, 1978 becomes the EPCA; the Sex Discrimination Act, 1975 the SDA; the Race Relations Act, 1976 the RRA; the Trade Union and Labour Relations Act, 1974 the TULRA; the Health and Safety at Work Act, 1974 the HASAWA; the Employment Act, 1980, the EA, 80 and the Employment Act, 1982, the EA, 82.

Recruitment and selection of employees

Here the employer must take account of race relations and sex discrimination legislation. The RRA establishes a Commission for Racial Equality with a duty to work towards the elimination of discrimination on the grounds of race. Its powers are much the same as those of the Equal Opportunities Commission set up under the SDA. It is unlawful for an employer to discriminate between applicants for jobs on the grounds of colour, race, nationality, or ethnic or national origins. It is also unlawful to publish an advertisement which could be interpreted as discriminatory.

Under the SDA it is unlawful for a person to discriminate against another on grounds of sex or marital status when determining who will be offered a job and in regard to the terms and conditions of the job e.g. privileged loans. There are exceptions where the sex or marital status of the person required is a genuine occupational qualification (GOQ), e.g. for reasons of physiology (as in the employment of a model) or for reasons of decency or privacy (as in the case of single-sex establishments such as schools and prisons) or where the job is one of two held by a married couple.

It should be noted that it is unlawful for a firm of six or more partners to discriminate in regard to the selection of new partners and benefits facilities, or services given to partners, unless a GOQ applies. Thus race (but not sex) discrimination would be allowed in e.g. the majority of medical practices but not in the major accounting and law firms. The Sex Discrimination Act, 1986 ruled out altogether sex discrimination in partnerships.

As regards enforcement, those who believe they have been discriminated against may complain to an industrial tribunal within three months of the date of the act complained of. A conciliation officer of the Advisory Conciliation and Arbitration Service will try to settle the complaint without the need for a tribunal hearing. If this is not possible and the matter goes to a tribunal, the tribunal may make an order declaring the rights of the parties in relation to the complaint. In addition, it may make an order for compensation which could cover loss of prospective earnings and injured feelings. It may also recommend that the employer take, within a specified period, action which appears to the tribunal to be practicable for the purpose of obviating or reducing the adverse effect of any act of discrimination on which the complaint is based. Proceedings (relating for example to discriminatory advertisements and instructions to discriminate) may only be instituted by the Commission for Racial Equality or the Equal Opportunities Commission, as the case may be.

During employment

The contract of employment

The EPCA provides that an employee is entitled to one week's notice after one month's service. After two years' service, the minimum notice is increased to two weeks, and for each year of service afterwards it is increased by one week, to a maximum of 12 weeks after 12 years' service. The statutory minimum period of notice which an employee must give is one week, irrespective of the period of employment, provided he has been employed for at least one month.

In addition, an employer must give his employee written information about the terms of employment not later than 13 weeks after the employment has commenced. This statement must contain the names of the employer and the employee; the date when the employment began; whether employment with a previous employer is to be counted as part of the employee's 'continuous period of employment' and, where this is so, the date on which it began (this is important to the employee, for example, in terms of redundancy payments); the title of the job; the scale or rate of remuneration or the method of calculating remuneration; the intervals at which remuneration is paid; any terms and conditions relating to the hours worked, entitlement to holidays and holiday pay, sickness or injury and sick pay, pensions and length of notice; there must also be a note specifying any disciplinary rules, the name of a person to whom the employee can apply in case of any disciplinary decision or grievance; and the disciplinary and grievance procedures, where these are laid down. The rules for calculating continuous employment, normal hours and a week's pay are in the EPCA.

An employee who does not receive particulars or who wants to dispute their accuracy or sufficiency may refer the matter to an industrial tribunal. The tribunal may then make a declaration that the employee has a right to a statement and what particulars should be included in it or amended within it. The statement approved by the tribunal is then deemed to have been given by the employer to the employee and will form the basis of his rights.

Pay

Under the EPCA, an employee is entitled to an itemized pay statement, containing the gross amount for wages or salary; the amounts of any variable and fixed deductions and the reasons for them; and the net amount of wages or salary payable. As only gross and net amounts and deductions are required, it is apparently unnecessary for workers to be informed as to details of their basic rates, overtime payments or shift premiums. The fixed deductions can be aggregated so long as the employee is issued with a statement of fixed deductions which is re-issued every 12 months, and he is notified of any alterations when they are made. If an employee does not receive a pay statement or if he receives one that is inadequate, he may refer the matter to an industrial tribunal. The industrial tribunal will make a declaration which will include answers to questions relating to the employer's failure to give particulars or his failure to give accurate amounts. The declaration then determines these matters. Where there have been unnotified deductions for pay during the previous 13 weeks, the tribunal may order the employer to pay to the employee a sum not exceeding the total unnotified deductions.

There is no presumption that a contract of employment contains an implied term that sick pay will be paid. (*Mears* v. *Safecar Security*, 1982 see p. 658).

Employers are required to provide what is called *statutory sick pay* on behalf of the Government. The law is to be found in the main, in the Social Security and Housing Benefit Act, 1982 and the Social Security Act, 1985. It is not necessary in a book of this nature to go into detail in regard to the statutory sick pay scheme but the main principles are that when an employee falls sick he or she gets a weekly amount from the employer and not from the Department of Health and Social Security. The employer recovers the amount paid as statutory sick pay from his overall liability for employers' National Insurance contributions.

This goes on for 28 weeks and since the vast majority of employees are not sick for anything like as long as this, employee sickness benefit is, in effect, now paid by the employer. It is not possible to avoid the statutory sick pay provisions and any clause in a contract of employment which sets out to do this is void.

Method of payment and deductions from pay

Under the Wages Act, 1986 employees no longer have a right to be paid in cash. The Truck Acts, 1831–1940, which used to give this right, were repealed by the 1986 Act. Payment may still, of course, be made in cash, but an employer can if he wishes pay the employee, for example, by cheque or by crediting the employee's bank account.

Deductions from pay are unlawful unless they are (a) authorized by Act of Parliament, such as income tax and National Insurance deductions; (b) or contained in a written contract of employment, and as regards (b) deductions from the wages of workers in the retail trade, e.g. petrol station cashiers, for stock and cash shortages are limited to ten per cent of the gross wages. These provisions are enforceable by the employee against the employer in industrial tribunals.

Equal treatment in terms and conditions of employment as between men and women in the same employment

The Equal Pay Act, 1970, as amended by the SDA, implies a term into women's contracts of employment which requires equal treatment in terms of pay, holidays, sick pay, and hours of work.

The Equal Pay Act, 1970 provides that the contracts of employment of all women are regarded as containing an equality clause which operates on pay when a woman is employed on 'like work' or on work 'rated as equivalent' to that of a man, e.g. by a job evaluation study.

Under the Equal Pay (Amendment) Regulations, 1983, there is a further instance when equality is to have effect, i.e. where a woman is employed on work which is, in terms of the demands made on her, for instance under such headings as effort, skill, and 'decision', of equal value to that of a man in the same employment. In addition, under the Regulations a complaint may go before an industrial tribunal, even if the two jobs under comparison have already been shown to be unequal in the job evaluation study. However, there will have to be reasonable grounds for saying that the evaluation study discriminated on the grounds of sex.

A woman who believes she is not being treated equally may complain to an industrial tribunal, which may award arrears of remuneration or damages.

Discrimination in the treatment of employees

Under the SDA and RRA, it is unlawful to discriminate against a person on grounds of race, sex or marital status as regards opportunities for promotion, training or transfer, or in the provision of benefits, facilities or services or by dismissal or any other disadvantages. However, the EPCA allows women to receive special treatment when they are pregnant, and employers have in the past been able to provide different retiring ages based on sex. There is no discrimination where the sex or marital status of the employee is a genuine occupational qualification.

As regards retirement ss. 2 and 3 of the Sex Discrimination Act, 1986 provide that employers can no longer have policies which set different compulsory retirement dates for men and women in comparable positions. Furthermore although race discrimination is not unlawful where the employment is in a private household, sex and marital discrimination is unlawful under the 1986 Act even in private households.

If an unlawful act of discrimination is committed by an employee, such as a personnel officer, the employer is held responsible for the act along with the employee unless the employer can show that he took all reasonable steps to prevent the employee from discriminating. If he can do this, only the employee is responsible. As regards enforcement by employees, those who believe that they have been discriminated against may make a complaint to an industrial tribunal within three months of the date of the act complained of. It is then the duty of a conciliation officer to see whether the complaint can be settled without going to a tribunal. If, however, a tribunal hears the complaint, it may make an order declaring the rights of the employee and employer in regard to the complaint, the intention being that both parties will abide by the order for the future. The tribunal may also give the employee money compensation, and may additionally recommend that the employer take, within a specified period, action appearing to the tribunal to be practicable for the purpose of obviating or reducing discrimination.

Sexual harassment does not specifically constitute a breach of the SDA but comes under the head of subjection 'to any other detriment' occuring in s. 6(2)(b) of the SDA. (*Porcelli* v. *Strathclyde Regional Council*, [1986] I.C.R. 564).

Disclosure of information

The Employment Protection Act, 1975 requires employers to disclose information necessary for the purposes of collective bargaining and for purposes of good industrial relations to representatives of trade unions. The Advisory Conciliation and Arbitration Service has published a code of practice indicating the sort of information that should be disclosed.

If a union representative asks for information for collective bargaining purposes and the employer fails to disclose it, a complaint may be made to the Central Arbitration Committee. Conciliation may be attempted at this stage. If it fails, or is not attempted, the Committee will hear the complaint and may make a declaration upholding it and pass on the necessary information obtained from the employer to the union representative. If the employer continues to fail to disclose information, a further complaint may be lodged, and if this is upheld after another hearing, it allows the Committee to force arbitration on an employer if the union presents a claim.

Guarantee payments

Employees with not less than four weeks' continuous service are entitled to a guarantee payment, currently £11.30 per day, if they are not provided with work on a normal working day (EPCA). This guarantee is, under the EA, 80, limited to five days in any three-month period. The provisions do not apply if the failure to provide work is due to a trade dispute, or if the employee has been offered suitable alternative work but has refused it.

An employee may present a complaint to an industrial tribunal that his employer has failed to pay the whole or any part of a guarantee payment to which the employee is entitled. The industrial tribunal may make an order to pay the employee the amount of guarantee payment which it finds is due to him.

Suspension from work on medical grounds

An employee with not less than four weeks' continuous service who is suspended from work under the provisions of an Act of Parliament (e.g. the HASAWA) or a code of practice, not because he is ill but because he is exposed to a health hazard at his work and may become ill if he continues at work, is entitled to be paid normal wages while suspended for up to 26 weeks (EPCA).

An employee may present a complaint to an industrial tribunal that his employer has failed to pay the whole or any part of remuneration to which he is entitled on suspension, and the tribunal may order the employer to pay the employee the remuneration due to him.

Maternity provision

(a) *For ante-natal care*. Under the Employment Protection (Consolidation) Act, 1978, as amended by the Employment Act, 1980, a pregnant employee who has, on the advice of a doctor, registered midwife, or registered health visitor, made an appointment to get ante-natal care must have time off to keep it and she must also be paid. The employer can ask for proof of the appointment in the form, for example, of an appointment card, but this does not apply to the first appointment. The employer who does not give the employee these rights can be taken to a tribunal by the employee but this must normally be during the three months following the employer's refusal. Compensation may be given to the employee. Part-time employees are entitled to this time off and it does not make any difference how many hours they work each week. However, an employer might be able to show in the case of a part-time worker that he had reasonably refused her time off because she could make the appointment during non-working hours. There is no minimum qualifying period of employment for the enjoyment of this right.

(b) *For maternity pay*. Part V of the Social Security Act, 1986 made major alterations to the maternity payment scheme. Prior to the Act a woman who qualified received maternity pay under the Employment Protection (Consolidation) Act, 1978, ss. 33–44 from which was deducted the State maternity allowance. Maternity pay was then recouped by the employer from the Maternity Pay Fund. The Social Security Act, 1986 repealed ss. 33–44 and the Maternity Pay Fund has been wound up.

Under the Social Security Act, 1986 the old provisions are replaced by statutory maternity pay (SMP) payable through the employer who will recoup it from National Insurance contributions (on the model of the statutory sick pay scheme). To qualify the woman must have worked for her present employer for at least six months. If so, she will be entitled to a payment at the lowest rate of statutory sick pay (at present £31.60 per week) for 18 weeks. Women who have been with the employer for two years or more will receive SMP of 90 per cent of earnings for the first six weeks of the maternity leave.

Women are able to choose when to take their paid maternity leave. Thirteen weeks of the leave must be taken to cover the period of six weeks before the baby is due and the seven weeks after it is born, but women will be free to choose when to take the other five weeks.

(c) *The right to return to work.* The employee must comply with certain formalities in order that she may have the right to return to work. These are that she must give her employer at least 21 days written notice before her absence begins:

(i) giving the reason why she will be absent and the expected week of confinement; and

(ii) of her intention to return to work if this is what she is going to do.

The employer may require the employee to produce a medical certificate giving the expected date of confinement.

Although a woman gives notice of her intention to return to work she is not forced to do so. This leaves the employer in a state of some uncertainty. The 1978 Act, as amended by the Employment Act, 1980, allows the employer to check what the situation is. The employer is allowed to make a request for information from the employee. The employer cannot do this until seven weeks have passed from the beginning of the expected week of confinement. The employer's request must be writing and will ask the employee to confirm her intention to return.

An employee intending to return must confirm the fact in writing within 14 days of receiving the request or as soon as reasonably practicable, otherwise the right to return is lost. However, confirmation does not oblige the employee to return.

In order actually to get back to work, the woman must give written notice to the employer at least 21 days before the notified date of return, that date being not later than 29 weeks after the beginning of the week in which the birth occurred. The return to work can be postponed by either the employer or the employee by up to four weeks from the date notified. The employer can postpone it for any reason so long as those reasons are notified to the employee. The employee can only postpone if she is ill and cannot work and has a medical certificate to that effect. If there is, for example, industrial action, so that the woman cannot return on the date notified, then she may return when the interruption is over or as soon as is reasonably practicable afterwards.

If the employee carries out all the formalities for return to work but the employer refuses to allow her to return, she will be regarded as dismissed and the employer will have to show that this was not unfair dismissal. (See p. 331.)

If because of a reorganization in the firm during the woman's absence her job is no longer available, the employer must offer her suitable alternative employment. If there is such employment and it is not offered to her she can claim unfair dismissal. If no such work is available she is redundant and can claim a redundancy payment. If she refuses to take suitable alternative work she will have no claim on the employer.

Small employers are specially protected because they cannot easily cope with a long absence by an employee. So, if there are not more than five employees counted together with those of an 'associated employer' (e.g. in a holding and subsidiary company situation you would have to count the employees in the holding company together with those of the subsidiary company in deciding whether the figure was five or less), at the time when the employee left, and it is not reasonably practicable for the employer to take the employee back or to offer alternative work, then the employer is not liable if he does not take the employee back.

The Government white paper *Building businesses . . . not barriers* sets out the Government's plans to change the entitlement period for unfair dismissal (see p. 331) redundancy (see p. 336) and maternity reinstatement (*see above*) to 20 hours per week for two years or 12 hours per week for five years, and proposes also to exempt those companies, firms and sole traders who employ fewer than ten employees from the maternity reinstatement provisions.

Time off

Time off with pay must be granted by employers to trade union officials to carry out their trade union duties and to receive training both on and off the premises (EPCA). Employees are also entitled to unpaid time off to take part in union activities (other than industrial action). The Advisory Conciliation and Arbitration Service has issued a Code of Practice as to what is reasonable. Reasonable unpaid time off must also be given to employees who hold certain public offices, e.g. as JPs or local councillors. Redundant employees must be given reasonable paid time off to look for work or arrange training for a job.

In addition the Health and Safety Commission has approved a Code of Practice to govern the exercise of the right of safety representatives appointed by recognized trade unions to have time off with pay to undergo training in health and safety matters. Furthermore, as we have seen, under the EA, 80, there is a right for pregnant employees to take time off to attend ante-natal clinics. Unreasonable refusal to allow time off or to pay for time taken off gives the employee grounds to complain to an industrial tribunal.

Insolvency of employer

An employee whose employer becomes insolvent is entitled to obtain payment of certain debts which are owed to him through the Redundancy Fund (EPCA). The legal rights and remedies in respect of the debts covered are transferred to the Secretary of State for Employment so that he can try and recover from the assets of the insolvent employer the cost of any payments made. Employees must apply for payment to the employer's representative, e.g. administrative receiver or liquidator, who, if unable to pay the claim in the near future, will submit the application to the Secretary of State for payment from the Redundancy Fund. Debts included are arrears of pay up to £164 per week for a period not exceeding eight weeks; holiday pay up to £164 per week with a limit of six weeks in the last 12 months of employment; payment in lieu of notice for the minimum statutory period, up to £164 per week; any outstanding payment in regard to an award by an industrial tribunal of compensation for unfair dismissal; reimbursement of the fees of an apprentice or articled clerk.

The above amounts are reviewed annually by ministerial order.

Health and safety at work

The HASAWA lays down certain general duties of employers to their employees in the field of health and safety. There is a general duty on employers to ensure as far as is reasonably practicable the health, safety and welfare of all employees while at work. However, in particular, the employer must provide and maintain plant and equipment and safe systems of work; avoid risks to safety and health in handling, storing and transporting articles and substances; provide and maintain safe premises and safe means of entering and leaving them; provide and maintain adequate welfare facilities and arrangements; provide information, training and supervision as required in order to ensure the safety and health of employees; prepare and/or revise policy statements on the safety and health of employees and give proper publicity to these; consult in these matters with safety representatives appointed by trade unions; establish safety committees where union representatives ask for this.

An employer must also conduct his undertaking in such a way that so far as is reasonably practicable those who are not his employees are not exposed to risk. Additionally, an employer must ensure so far as is reasonably practicable that premises which are open to others not employed by him are safe. There is also a duty to use the best practical methods to prevent noxious or offensive substances going into the atmosphere.

Directors are required to set out in their annual reports what their companies are doing in safety and health matters, and regulations will be issued specifying the classes of company that will have to comply with this provision and the kind of information which should be included.

Employees must take reasonable care of their own and other people's health and safety and co-operate with the employer in the carrying out of his duties. The Act also states that no person shall intentionally or recklessly interfere with or misuse anything which is provided in the interests of health, safety and welfare, e.g. safety equipment, and no employer may charge any employee for anything done or provided to comply with the employer's statutory duties.

Finally, those who design, manufacture, import, or supply equipment, machinery and plant must ensure that the design and construction is safe.

Enforcement is in the hands of the inspectorate of the Health and Safety Executive set up by the Act. Inspectors may issue a prohibition notice if there is a risk of serious personal injury. This operates to stop the activity concerned until remedial action specified in the notice has been taken. They may also issue an improvement notice if there is a contravention of any of the relevant statutory provisions, under which the employer must remedy the fault within a specified time. They may prosecute any person contravening the relevant statutory provision instead of or in addition to serving a notice. Failure to comply with a prohibition notice could lead to imprisonment though there is an appeal to an industrial tribunal.

Trade unions

An employee must not be penalized (i.e. action taken against him short of dismissal) by his employer for joining or trying to join a trade union or for playing a part in its activities at appropriate times. An employer must not penalize an employee in order to compel him to join a trade union. (EA, 82.)

Unfair dismissal

Before a person can ask an industrial tribunal to consider a claim that another has unfairly dismissed him or her, it is essential to establish that the relationship of employer and employee exists between them. In this connection the EPCA provides that an employee is a person who works under a contract of service or apprenticeship, written or oral, express or implied. (*Massey* v. *Crown Life Insurance Co*, [1978] 2 All E.R. 576.)

Under the EPCA, as amended by the EA, 80, employees with 52 weeks or more of continuous service have a right not to be unfairly dismissed. For employees whose employment began on or after 1 October, 1980, the period of continuous employment must exceed two years where the employer, together with any associated employer, employed 20 employees or less throughout the period. Those who started work on or after 1 June 1985 must complete two years' service regardless of the size of the firm. This does not apply where the dismissal is automatically unfair. Thus, there is no qualifying period where the dismissal is alleged to have been for an inadmissible reason, e.g. membership of a trade union or sex or race discrimination, and the period continues to be four weeks where the dismissal is on medical grounds in compliance with a health and safety requirement.

The EPCA also states that no account is to be taken of employment during any period when the hours of employment are normally less than 16 hours a week. After five years' employment the figure is reduced to eight hours. However, the requirements of 16 and eight hours do not apply to dismissals which are automatically unfair. The following matters should be noted:

(1) What is dismissal?
A dismissal means the termination of an employee's contract of service by the employer. Constructive dismissal is included, as where the employee is forced to terminate the contract because the employer breaks, or proposes to break, the contract, e.g. by changing, or proposing to change, the nature of the employment, the place of employment, or important terms of the contract such as pay.

In fixed-term contracts, as where a person is employed for, say, five years, there is a dismissal if the contract is not renewed when the fixed term ends, though this is not so where the fixed term is one year or more and the employee has agreed not to complain of unfair dismissal.

(2) Reasons justifying dismissal
Dismissal may be justified if an employee is dismissed because of—

(a) *Lack of capability*. An example would be where a bricklayer cannot lay a level or straight line of bricks. This would usually arise at the beginning of employment, where it becomes clear at an early stage that the employee cannot do the job in terms of lack of skill or mental or physical health. The longer a person is in employment, the more difficult it is to establish lack of capability.

(b) *Conduct*. This is always a difficult matter to deal with, and much will depend upon the circumstances of the case. However, incompetence and neglect are relevant, as are disobedience and misconduct, e.g. by assaulting fellow employees. Immorality and habitual drunkenness could also be brought under this head, as could the falsification of claims for expenses.

(c) *Redundancy*. Where a person is redundant, his employer cannot be expected to continue the employment, although there are safeguards in the matter of unfair selection for redundancy (see below).

(d) *Dismissal for failure to join a trade union*. This will be fair if it is the practice in accordance with a union membership agreement for employees of the same class to belong to one (or more) independent trade unions, and the only or principal reason for the dismissal was that the employee ceased to be a member of, or refused to join, or proposed to refuse to join or remain a member of the union in accordance with the union agreement, provided the union membership agreement has been approved by ballot and that a ballot has been held within five years of the notice of dismissal. (See preface.)

Under the EA, 82, if a union membership agreement is to be effective for the purposes of a fair dismissal, there must have been a ballot within the five years before dismissal. The ballot must have been approved by not less than 80 per cent and, in some situations 85 per cent, of all those entitled to vote.

Dismissal for failure to belong to a trade union will, however, become *unfair* even though there has been a requisite ballot if—

(i) the employee has an objection to being a member of the union on grounds of conscience or other deeply held personal conviction.

(ii) The employee holds qualifications necessary for the job which are subject to a code of practice which precludes him from taking part in industrial action, including strikes, and he is expelled, or refused membership of the union because of that code. This is particularly important in the Health Service, or

(iii) he has been unreasonably expelled or excluded from the union and a tribunal has so declared under the provisions of the EA, 80.

(e) *Statutory restriction placed on employer or employee.* If, for example, the employer's business is found to be dangerous and was closed down under an Act of Parliament or ministerial order, the employees would not be unfairly dismissed. Furthermore, a lorry driver who was banned from driving for 12 months could be dismissed fairly.

(f) *Other grounds.* Apart from the specific grounds mentioned above, whether the dismissal is fair depends in the last analysis on whether the employer can satisfy an industrial tribunal that it was reasonable to dismiss the employee in all the circumstances of the case. It is difficult to generalize from the cases, most of which depend upon their own facts. For example, the dismissal of an employee absent through sickness may be regarded as unfair in most situations, but has been held to be fair where the employee concerned was the sole driver of a business operating deliveries with only one van. It is also essential that proper procedures are followed. A dismissal for redundancy where there was no consultation could become an unfair dismissal, even if it later emerged that the employee, because of the financial difficulties of the company, became redundant anyway. (*Polkey* v. *A.E. Dayton Services Ltd*, [1987] 3 W.L.R. 1153.)

(3) Employee's contributory fault

This can reduce the compensation payable to the employee by such percentage as the tribunal thinks fit. Suppose an employee is often late for work and one morning his employer, who can stand it no more, sacks him. The dismissal is likely to be unfair in view of the lack of warning but a tribunal would very probably reduce the worker's compensation to take account of the facts.

Principles of natural justice also apply; it is necessary to let the worker state his case before a decision to dismiss is taken. Furthermore, reasonable inquiry must be made to find the truth of the matter before reaching a decision. Failure to do this will tend to make the dismissal unfair.

(4) Unacceptable reasons for dismissal

These are as follows—

(a) *Trade union membership.* Under the EA, 82 if the only (or principal) reason for the dismissal is as set out below, the dismissal will be automatically unfair.

(i) Because the employee was, or proposed to become a member of an independent trade union; or

(ii) because he had taken part, or proposed to take part in the activities of an independent trade union at an appropriate time; or

(iii) because he was not a member of a trade union, or had refused or had proposed to refuse to join or remain a member, unless (in which case the dismissal will be fair) there is a properly balloted closed shop, or unless (in which case dismissal will become unfair) the employee has an objection to being a member of the union on the grounds of

conscience or other deeply held personal conviction, or he holds qualifications necessary for his job which make him subject to a code of
practice precluding him from taking part in industrial action, including
strikes, and he has been expelled from or refused membership of the
union because of that code. The dismissal is also unfair if he has been
unreasonably expelled or excluded from the union and a tribunal has
so declared under the EA, 80. (See preface.)

(*b*) *Unfair selection for redundancy*. Even an employee dismissed for
redundancy may complain that he has been unfairly dismissed if he is of
the opinion that he has been unfairly selected for redundancy, as where
the employer has disregarded redundancy selection arrangements, e.g.
'last in, first out'. Ideally, all employers should have proper redundancy
agreements on the lines set out in the Department of Employment
booklet, 'Dealing With Redundancies'.

However, even though there is in existence an agreed redundancy
procedure, the employer may defend himself by showing a 'special
reason' for departing from that procedure, e.g. because the person
selected for redundancy lacks the skill and versatility of a junior
employee who is retained.

There is, since the decision of the Employment Appeal Tribunal in
Williams v. *Compair Maxam*, [1982] I.R.L.R. 83, an overall standard of
fairness also in redundancy arrangements. The standards laid down in the
case require the giving of maximum notice; consultation with unions, if
any; the taking of the views of more than one person as to who should
be dismissed; a requirement to follow any laid down procedure, i.e. last
in, first out; and finally, an effort to find the employees concerned
alternative employment within the organization. However, the EAT
stated in *Meikle* v. *McPhail (Charleston Arms)*, [1983] I.R.L.R. 351 that
these guidelines would be applied less rigidly to the smaller business.

(*c*) *Transfer of business*. The Transfer of Undertakings (Protection of
Employment) Regulations, 1981 (SI 1981/1974), apply to transfers of
business which take place on or after 1 May, 1982. Under the Regulations
if a business or part of it is transferred and an employee is dismissed
because of this, the dismissal will be treated as automatically unfair.
However, the person concerned is not entitled to the extra compensation
given to other cases of automatically unfair dismissals.

If the old employer dismissed before transfer or the new employer
dismissed after the transfer, either will have a defence if he can prove
that the dismissal was for 'economic, technical, or organizational' reasons
requiring a change in the workforce and that the dismissal was reasonable
in all the circumstances of the case.

(*d*) *Lock-outs and strikes*. If an employee is dismissed during a lock-
out or a strike, that dismissal will not be regarded as unfair unless other
employees involved were not dismissed or, if dismissed, were afterwards
offered re-engagement.

(*e*) *Pressure on employer to dismiss unfairly*. It is no defence for an
employer to say that pressure was put upon him to dismiss an employee

unfairly. Thus, if other workers put pressure on an employer to dismiss a non-union member so as, for example, to achieve a closed shop, the employer will have no defence to a claim for compensation for the dismissal if he yields to that pressure. However, the EA, 82 now gives the right to an employer to join a union or person as a third party to proceedings for unfair dismissal in a situation where he was pressurized to dismiss by the calling, organizing, procuring, or financing of a strike, or a threat to do so. This applies where the pressure was exercised because the employee was not a member of any trade union or of a particular trade union. If the industrial tribunal finds the employer's complaint well-founded the union or person concerned may be ordered to contribute towards the employee's compensation. If necessary this can be 100% indemnity.

(5) Complaints of unfair dismissal

Employees may make a complaint of unfair dismissal to an industrial tribunal at any time from the date on which they receive notice until three months after the date of dismissal.

(a) *Conciliation*. An industrial tribunal will usually not hear a complaint until a conciliation officer has had a chance to see whether he can help. A copy of the complaint made to the industrial tribunal is sent to the conciliation officer, and if he is unable to settle the complaint, nothing said by employer or employee during the process of conciliation will be admissible in evidence before the tribunal.

(b) *Remedies*. If a complaint of unfair dismissal is upheld, there are the following possibilities—

(i) *Reinstatement or re-engagement*. The power to order reinstatement or re-engagement is discretionary and in practice rarely exercized. Reinstatement means taken back by the employer on exactly the same terms and seniority as before; re-engagement is being taken back but on different terms.

(ii) *Compensation*. If the tribunal does not make an order of reinstatement or re-engagement, or makes one which the employer does not comply with, although it would have been practicable and reasonable for him to do so, the tribunal must make a basic award of compensation and may make, in addition, a compensatory award. The basic award is calculated according to the formula for redundancy payments, i.e. for each year of service up to a maximum of 20 years a number of weeks' pay up to a maximum of £164 per week as follows—

18 but under 22, ½ week's pay.
22 but under 41, 1 week's pay.
41 and over, 1½ week's pay.

The basic award is reduced after age 64 (men) and 59 (women). See further p. 337.

There is no minimum age limit for unfair dismissal claims as there is for redundancy, so a person of, say, 17 who was unfairly dismissed, could use a '17 but under 22' formula and get half a week's pay. Any contributory fault of the employee, e.g. a history of lateness for work, is taken into account and will reduce the money he obtains.

(iii) *Dismissal for union membership or activities*. An employee who is of the opinion that he has been unfairly dismissed for a reason connected with his trade union membership or activities may apply to an industrial tribunal for an order for reinstatement or re-engagement, or if this is not possible, for an order that he be suspended on full pay until his complaint is settled. The application must be made within seven days of dismissal, and has to be supported by a signed certificate from an official of the relevant trade union, stating that there are reasonable grounds for believing that the dismissal was for trade union reasons.

(6) Unfair dismissal, redundancy and frustration of contract

In cases appearing before industrial tribunals there is a certain interplay between the common law rules of frustration of contract (see p. 300) and the statutory provisions relating to redundancy and unfair dismissal. At common law a contract of service is frustrated by incapacity, e.g. sickness, if that incapacity makes the contract substantially impossible of performance at a particularly vital time, or by a term of imprisonment. (See *Hare* v. *Murphy Bros*, 1974.)[350] If a contract has been so frustrated then a complaint of unfair dismissal or a claim for a redundancy payment is not available because the contract has been discharged on other grounds, i.e. by frustration. Thus termination of a contract of service by frustration prevents a claim for unfair dismissal or redundancy.

Redundancy

The EPCA gives an employee a right to compensation by way of a redundancy payment if he is dismissed because of redundancy.

(1) Meaning of redundancy

Redundancy occurs where the services of employees are dispensed with because the employer ceases, or intends to cease, carrying on business, or does not require so many employees to do work of a certain kind. Employees who have been laid off or kept on short time without pay for four consecutive weeks (or for a broken series of at least six weeks in a period of 13 weeks) are entitled to terminate the employment and apply for a redundancy payment if there is no reasonable prospect that normal working will be resumed.

(2) Eligibility

Employees who have completed two years' continuous service since reaching the age of 18 are eligible for a redundancy payment. Additionally, they must work 16 hours or more per week (or eight hours or more where the employment has been for five years or more).

An employee who accepts an offer of suitable alternative employment with his employer is not entitled to a redundancy payment. Neither is an employee who is offered new employment on the same terms by the same employer, or an associated employer, e.g. a subsidiary company, and unreasonably refuses; or on different terms in a different place, and after a reasonable trial period of not less than four weeks, also unreasonably refuses.

(3) Amount of redundancy payment

As we have seen, those aged 41 to 65 (60, women) receive $1\frac{1}{2}$ weeks' pay (up to a maximum of £164 per week) for each year of service up to a maximum of 20 years. In other age groups, the above provisions apply except that the week's pay changes, i.e. for those aged 22 but under 41, it is one week's pay, and for those aged 18 but under 22, it is a half-week's pay.

Employees over 64 (59 women) have their redundancy payment reduced progressively, so that for each complete month by which the age exceeds 64 (or 59) on the Saturday of the week in which the contract ends, the normal entitlement is reduced by one-twelfth. Thus, a man aged 64 years and three months would have three-twelfths of the award deducted. These provisions are not affected by reason of the equal retirement ages for men and women in the Sex Discrimination Act, 1986. Complaints by employees in respect of the right to a redundancy payment, or questions as to its amount, may be made to an industrial tribunal which will make a declaration as to the employee's right which forms the basis on which payment can be recovered from the employer.

(4) Rebates for employers

It should be noted that employers of ten or more persons who have made a redundancy payment can no longer claim a rebate from Government funds. (Wages Act, 1986.)

(5) Procedure for handling redundancies

This is as follows—

(a) *Notification.* Employers must notify the Department of Employment of redundancies being planned which would involve the dismissal of more than 10 employees in a period of 30 days or less. The minimum notification period is 30 days, before the first dismissals take effect.

(b) *Consultation.* Employers are required to consult with trade union representatives (if any) as soon as possible even though only one person is to be made redundant. The period of consultation, if 100 or more employees are to be dismissed within a period of 90 days or less, is not less than 90 days before the first redundancies take effect, or 30 days if 10 or more employees are to be dismissed in a period of 30 days or less.

Consultation involves the employer in telling the unions the reason for the proposals, together with number and type of employees to be dismissed, the total number of employees of that type at the establishment involved, the proposed method of selection and of carrying out the dismissals.

Representations made by the unions must be received and replied to. If this is not done, an industrial tribunal may, on the complaint of a trade union (or in a multi-union situation, by any one of them) make a declaration of the tribunal's findings, and the tribunal may make a 'protective award' under which the employees will be kept in employment and paid for not more than a period corresponding to the minimum time required for prior consultation, i.e. 90 or 30 days as the case may be. If an employee is not paid during all or part of the period for which the protective award applies, he may apply to an industrial tribunal, which will issue an order to the employer to pay the amount of remuneration due to the employee.

(*c*) *Collective agreements on redundancy.* The Secretary of State may, on the application of the employer and unions involved, make an order modifying the requirements of redundancy pay legislation if he is satisfied that there is a collective agreement which makes satisfactory alternative arrangements for dealing with redundancies. The provisions of the agreement must be 'on the whole at least as favourable' as the statutory provisions, and must include, in particular, arrangements allowing an employee to go to independent arbitration or to make a complaint to an industrial tribunal.

Minimum period of notice

As we have seen under the EPCA, an employee is entitled to one week's notice after four weeks' service; after two years' service the minimum entitlement is increased to two weeks, and for each year of service after that it is increased by one week up to a maximum of 12 weeks' notice after 12 years' service. An employee who is engaged for a specific job on a 12-week or shorter contract is not entitled to any notice unless in the event the contract is extended or he is retained for a period longer than 12 weeks.

Three matters should be noted. Firstly, the legislation does not affect the common law right of an employer to dismiss an employee summarily without notice for misconduct, e.g. disobedience, neglect or drunkenness. Secondly, the legislation does not prevent employer and employee from agreeing to longer periods of notice to be given by the employer. Thirdly, such longer periods of notice may be implied by law or custom, and an industrial tribunal will not necessarily consider the minimum period of notice laid down by legislation as sufficient. Consideration will be given to the employee's length of service, his age, and the possibility of his finding alternative employment.

Breach of the provisions relating to minimum period of notice do not involve an employer in any penalty, but the rights conferred by the Act will be taken into account in assessing the employer's liability for breach of contract. Thus an employer who has dismissed his employee without due notice is generally liable for the wages due to the employee for the appropriate period of notice at the contract rate.

Offences by corporations

The EPCA provides that where an offence under that Act is committed by a body corporate, and it is proved that the offence was committed with the consent or connivance of, or neglect by, any director, manager, secretary or similar officer of the body corporate, or any person who was purporting to act in such capacity, that person as well as the body corporate shall be equally guilty of the offence and may be punished accordingly.

8 The law of torts

It is difficult to give a satisfactory definition of a tort. According to Professor Winfield 'tortious liability arises from a duty primarily fixed by law: this duty is towards persons generally and its breach is redressible by an action for unliquidated damages'.

THE NATURE OF A TORT

It is a matter of dispute whether there should be a law of tort or a law of torts: there are two schools of thought. One maintains that there should be a law of tort, i.e. that all harm should be actionable in the absence of just cause or excuse. If there was merely a law of specific torts, then no new torts could be created by the courts and the categories of tortious liability would be closed. It is urged that under the flexibility of case law new torts have come into being, and in no case has an action been refused simply because it was novel. This is called the *general principle of liability theory*. The other view is that there should be a law of torts—that there should be only specific torts and unless the damage suffered can be brought under a known or recognized head of liability, there should be no remedy. This view is supported by modern cases where an attempt has been made, unsuccessfully, to establish a purported tort of eviction (*Perera* v. *Vandiyar*; 1953,[396] and a tort of perjury. (*Hargreaves* v. *Bretherton*, 1958[397] and *Roy* v. *Prior*, 1969.)[398] Thus the courts have refused to create new torts even when given the opportunity. This is particularly unfortunate in the case of perjury. Perjury is not merely an offence against the State, as it has been traditionally regarded by the courts. It can cause an individual great loss or hardship and many feel that the victim should have a civil remedy in damages.

In addition, there is a danger in modern society of a serious invasion of privacy resulting from the increasing availability and use of electronic and other devices as a means of surreptitious surveillance and the accumulation of personal information about individuals in data banks, computers and credit registers. Apart from e.g. the law of defamation which protects against the publication of falsehoods, the common law of tort does not appear to be capable of extending to a remedy for invasion of privacy as such.

There is, yet, no general legislation on the matter of privacy, but the Data Protection Act, 1984 deals with information stored on computers. The details of the Act are beyond the scope of a book of this nature but the job of safeguarding the privacy of the individual in terms, e.g. of the information kept on him and the uses to which it is put, falls under the Act to the Data Registrar who is appointed by the Crown. He supervises a central register on which all data users must enter details of data banks and their purposes. The Registrar and 'data subjects', the latter through the courts, have access to records on computers.

Hence we may conclude that at the present there is no general principle of liability in tort. Nevertheless, if judges have not created new torts, they have applied old cases to new situations. This has resulted in an extension of the old torts and there is a tendency to expand the area of liability, particularly in the field of negligence. (See p. 392.) If this continues, the law may reach a stage approximating to a general liability for wrongful acts, for, as Lord Macmillan said in *Donoghue* v. *Stevenson*, 1932,[399] 'the categories of negligence are never closed'.

DAMAGE AND LIABILITY

The law distinguishes between two concepts—(1) *Damnum*, which means the damage suffered, and (2) *Injuria*, which is an injury having legal consequences. Sometimes, but not always, these two go together. For instance, if I negligently drive a car and injure a person, he suffers *damnum* (the hurt) and *injuria* (because he has a right of action to be compensated). There are, however, cases of *damnum sine injuria* (damage suffered without the violation of a legal right), and *injuria sine damno* (the violation of a legal right without damage).

The mere fact that a person has suffered damage does not entitle him to maintain an action in tort. Before an action can succeed, the harm suffered must be caused by an act which is a violation of a right which the law vests in the plaintiff or injured party. (*Best* v. *Samuel Fox & Co. Ltd*, 1952.)[400] Damage suffered in the absence of the violation of such legal right is known as *damnum sine injuria*. Furthermore a person who suffers *damnum* cannot receive compensation on the basis of *injuria* suffered by another. (*Electrochrome Ltd* v. *Welsh Plastics Ltd*, 1968.)[401] The concept of *damnum sine injuria* is not the same as that concerning whether there is a law of tort or a law of torts because under the concept of *damnum sine injuria* a person may suffer harm and have no claim even though the harm was suffered *as a result of a known tort*.

The fact that the defendant acts with malice, i.e with the intention of injuring his neighbour, does not give rise to a cause of action unless a legal right of the plaintiff is infringed. (*Bradford Corporation* v. *Pickles*, 1895,[402] and *Langbrook Properties* v. *Surrey County Council*, 1969.)[403] On the other hand, whenever there is an invasion of a legal right, the person in whom the right is vested may bring an action and recover damages (though these may be nominal) or, what may be more important, obtain an injunction, although he has suffered no actual harm. For example, an action will lie for an unlawful entry on the land of another (trespass) although no actual damage is done. Furthermore, in *Ashby* v. *White* (1703), 2 Ld. Raym. 938, it was held that an elector had a right of action, for a form of nuisance or disturbance of rights, when his vote was wrongly rejected by the returning officer although the candidate for whom he tried to vote was elected. This is known as *injuria sine damno*.

Motive

It is important to be clear on the mental element or the question of malice in tort. The law of torts is concerned more with the effects of injurious conduct than the motives which inspired it. Hence, just as a bad intention will not necessarily make the infliction of damage actionable (*Bradford Corporation* v. *Pickles*, 1895),[402] so an innocent intention is usually no defence. (*Wilkinson* v. *Downton*, 1897.)[404] However, there are circumstances in which malice is important. Thus where a person puts in motion the criminal law against another, this is actionable if malice is shown to be present and is known as the tort of malicious prosecution. Furthermore, the question of malice may be raised when certain *defences* are pleaded. Thus in the law of defamation the defences of qualified privilege and fair comment are allowed only where the defendant has not been malicious. Finally, in regard to the tort of nuisance, certain acts which would not necessarily be a nuisance may be regarded as such if they are exercised unreasonably. Malice is sometimes regarded as evidence of conduct which is unreasonable. (See *Christie* v. *Davey*, 1893, p. 795.)

PARTIES IN THE LAW OF TORTS

It is now necesary to consider certain categories of persons whose capacity in connection with tortious acts is limited.

Minors

A minor can sue in tort as a plaintiff in the ordinary way except that, as in contract, he must sue through an adult as next friend. He cannot compromise his action except by leave of the court, unlike an adult, who does not require such permission.

At common law there was a doubt as to whether a child had a cause of action for personal injuries caused before its birth. The matter is now covered by the Congenital Disabilities (Civil Liability) Act, 1976. Section 1 establishes civil liability where a child is born disabled in consequence of the intentional act or the negligence or the breach of statutory duty of some person before the child's birth. There can be no liability unless the child is born alive.

It was held in *C* v. *S*, [1987] 1 All E.R. 123 that a foetus has no right of action unless it is subsequently born alive. If it is stillborn the parents might have an action, e.g. for nervous shock. Causation must be proved which may be difficult in the case of pre-natal injuries. A mother cannot be liable under s. 1 for causing injury to the child by her own negligence, except where the injury is caused by the mother's negligence in driving a motor vehicle when she knows, or ought reasonably to know that she is pregnant. Barristers and judges, among others, have been strongly opposed to children being given a cause of action against their mothers, recognizing the danger of inter-family disputes, and, subject to what has been said about motor vehicle liability where the action is in effect against an insurance company and not really against the mother, their view has prevailed in the Act. The liability of a father is not, however, excluded and he can be liable to his child for injuries caused by his own negligence.

The section also distinguishes between matters arising *before* conception (where the injury can be to *either* parent) and matters arising when the child's mother is pregnant or during the actual process of childbirth (where the injury can *only* be to the mother). Thus the injury could result, for example, from irradiation which damages the progenitive capacity of the father. It also covers physical damage to the child during childbirth as by the negligent handling of instruments by those attending the mother. The injuries must be caused during the pregnancy and there could be problems in dating the beginning of this in some cases. The defendant is presumed to take the mother as he finds her and thus cannot say that he did not know she was pregnant nor that the damage to her child was not foreseeable.

The common law defence of *volenti non fit injuria* is applicable and in this sense if the mother is *volenti* so is the child. It is recognized that this may penalize the child but it was thought that any other solution would prejudice the position of women in society because organizations worried that a woman might be pregnant may refuse to enter into a wide variety of contracts with her. Incidentally, so far as the consent which the child is deemed to give results from an exemption clause in a contract made by the mother, then s. 1 creates a new exception to the doctrine of privity of contract. Section 1 also provides that the child's damages awarded against the defendant are to be reduced by any contributory negligence of the mother. Finally, s. 1 provides that professional persons, such as doctors, are under no liability for treatment or advice given according to prevailing professional standards of care. This codifies the common law rule in *Roe* v. *Minister of Health*, 1954 (see p. 810).

Section 3 clarifies the compensation provisions of the Nuclear Installations Act, 1965, where damages results from a nuclear incident and provides for compensation under the Act in the case of a child born subsequently with disabilities attributable to the incident.

Finally, it should be noted that the Act is not retrospective but applies to births after 22 July, 1976.

A minor is liable as defendant for all his torts except in a limited number of instances. Where the tort alleged requires a mental ingredient, the age of the minor (in cases of extreme infancy) may show an inability to form the necessary intent. In cases of negligence, a very young child cannot be expected to show the same standard of care as an older person though in *Williams* v. *Humphrey*, 1975[405] a boy of nearly 16 was held liable in negligence. Nor can a minor be made liable on contracts which do not bind him, unless he ratifies them, by the device of suing him in tort. (*Leslie* v. *Sheill*, 1914.)[170] However, if the act complained of is associated with a contract but is independent of it, then the minor can be made liable. (*Burnard* v. *Haggis*, 1863. See p. 607.)

A minor is liable for wrongful interference by conversion if he hires goods and fails to return them. (*Ballett* v. *Mingay*, 1943.)[406]

Basically children are liable for their own torts, but a father may be liable vicariously, if the relationship of employer and employee exists between him and the child or if there is the relationship of principal and agent. Simply as a father he is not liable unless the injury is caused by his negligent control of the child (*Donaldson* v. *McNiven*, 1952),[407] and so when he is liable, it is really for his own tort, i.e. negligence in looking after the child. (*Bebee* v. *Sales*, 1916.)[408] Such a liability may extend to other persons (not being parents) who have control of children, e.g. teachers and education authorities, and, if such persons or authorities act negligently, they may be held responsible for the harm caused by children under their care or control. Nevertheless, the basis of the action is negligent control or supervision. (*Carmarthenshire C.C.* v. *Lewis*, 1955,[409] and *Butt* v. *Cambridgeshire and Isle of Ely County Council*, 1969.)[410]

Persons suffering from mental disorder

In criminal law a person of unsound mind has considerable exemption from criminal liability (see p. 157), but these rules have never been applied to civil injuries. This is understandable if it is borne in mind that the aim of the law of torts is to compensate the injured party, not to punish the offender. In the light of this, any exemptions accorded to a person of unsound mind should be narrow, and he should be liable unless his state of mind prevents his having the necessary intent (where a mental ingredient is part of the tort) and in extreme cases where no voluntary act is possible. (*Morriss* v. *Marsden*, 1952.)[411]

Husband and wife

The rule used to be that a married woman was liable for her torts only to the extent of her separate property and that beyond this the husband was fully liable. Since the Law Reform (Married Women and Tortfeasors) Act, 1935, the wife is fully liable for her torts and the husband as such is no longer held responsible, unless, as in the case of a minor, there is a relationship of employer and employee or principal and agent.

The old common law rule whereby one spouse could not sue the other in tort has now been altered. The Law Reform (Husband and Wife) Act, 1962, provides that each of the parties to a marriage shall have the like right of action in tort against the other as if they were not married, but where the action is brought by one of the parties to the marriage against the other during the subsistence of the marriage, the court may stay the action if it appears—

(a) that no substantial benefit would accrue to either party from the continuation of the proceedings; or

(b) that the question or questions in issue could more conveniently be disposed of on an application made under s. 17 of the Married Women's Property Act, 1882. (This provides for the determination of questions between husband and wife regarding title to or possession of property by a summary procedure.)

It should also be noted that under s. 2(a), Administration of Justice Act, 1982 a husband has no right of action against a person who by a tortious act deprives him of the society and services of his wife, i.e. loss of consortium. A wife has no such right by reason of case law in respect of loss of consortium. (*Best* v. *Samuel Fox & Co. Ltd*, 1952.)[400]

The Crown and its servants

Prior to 1947 the Crown had considerable immunity in the law of tort and contract stemming from the common law maxim: 'The King can do no wrong.' We have already seen that, by the Crown Proceedings Act, 1947, the Crown is, in general, now liable in the same way as a subject. (See further p. 179.)

The Crown is not liable for torts committed by the police nor is the local authority which appoints and pays them. However, the Police Act, 1964, s. 48(1), provides that the chief officer of police for any police area is liable for the torts of police officers, e.g. wrongful arrest. The Act also provides that any damages and costs awarded against the chief officer shall be payable out of police funds.

Postal and telecommunications authorities

The Post Office is a public authority but is not an agent of the Crown. It is liable, subject to limitations set out in the Post Office Regulations, for loss of or damage to inland registered postal packets. (S. 30, Post Office Act, 1969.) Apart from this, neither the Post Office nor any of its servants, officers, or sub-postmasters is liable for anything done or omitted to be done in regard to anything in the post or for failure to collect the post. (S. 29(1) and (2).) Thus in *Harold Stephen & Co. Ltd*

v. *Post Office*, [1978] 1 All E.R. 939, the Court of Appeal refused to grant an injunction against the Post Office to companies in the Cricklewood area of London whose businesses were in jeopardy because they were receiving no mail through the Post Office closing the local sorting office and suspending post office workers who refused to handle mail in support of workers employed in the private sector.

Persons engaged in the carriage of mail or their servants, agents or subcontractors, are not liable for loss or damage in regard to the post. (S. 29(3).) Thus in *American Express Co.* v. *British Airways Board*, [1983] 1 All E.R. 557, the plaintiffs gave a postal packet containing travellers' cheques to the Post Office for delivery abroad. The Post Office gave it to the defendants and it was stolen by one of their employees. The plaintiffs claimed damages for breach of bailment. Lloyd, J. held that the defendants were not liable; they were exempted by s. 29(3) of the 1969 Act.

Since the enactment of the Telecommunications Act, 1984 British Telecom provides its telecommunications service under standard service contracts and is liable in the ordinary way for breach. However, the contracts concerned have exclusion clauses e.g. in the case of failure to repair equipment during an industrial dispute.

Judicial immunity

A judge has absolute immunity for acts in his judicial capacity, and this probably applies to justices of the peace when acting within their jurisdiction. (*Law* v. *Llewellyn*, 1906.)[412] Counsel and witnesses have immunity in respect of all matters relating to the cases in which they are concerned. This is mainly of importance in connection with possible actions for slander.

Foreign sovereigns and ambassadorial staffs

This heading includes all the categories of persons already enumerated in the chapter on Contract as having diplomatic immunity, and their liability is outlined on p. 219. However, it should be noted that if persons with immunity remain after finishing their duties, they may become liable even if the tort was committed before. They may, of course, voluntarily submit to the jurisdiction of our courts, since immunity is from suit and not from liability. (*Dickinson* v. *Del Solar*, 1930.)[413]

Aliens

Enemy aliens, including British subjects who voluntarily reside or carry on business in an enemy state, cannot bring an action in tort, although they themselves can be sued. Other aliens have neither disability nor immunity.

Corporations

A corporation can, as a plaintiff, sue for all torts committed against it. Obviously certain torts, such as assault, cannot by their nature be committed against corporations, but a corporation can maintain an action for injury to its business. (*D and L Caterers Ltd* v. *D'Anjou*, 1945.)[414] Section 35 of the Companies Act, 1985 does not apply to tortious activities and in cases where the corporation is the defendant we must consider separately tortious acts which are *intra vires* (within its powers) and *ultra vires* (outside its powers).

(a) *Intra vires* activities

Where a servant or agent of the corporation commits a tort while acting in the course of his employment in an *intra vires* activity, then the corporation is liable. Although it has been said that any tort committed on behalf of a corporation must be *ultra vires* (since Parliament does not authorize corporations to commit torts) this view is fallacious, since a corporation can have legal liability without legal capacity. A corporation is liable under the principles of vicarious liability for the torts of its employees or agents committed on *intra vires* activities.

(b) *Ultra vires* activities

Here we have to distinguish between express and non-express authority. A corporation will not be liable if a servant engages in an *ultra vires* activity without express authority. Thus, if a corporation has not got authority and has not given it, you cannot infer it. (*Poulton* v. *L. & S.W. Railway*, 1867.)[415] On the other hand, where a tortious action is *ultra vires* but has been expresssly authorized, the courts have taken the view that the *ultra vires* doctrine is irrelevant, and the corporation is liable for it. (*Campbell* v. *Paddington Borough Council*, 1911.)[416]

Unincorporated associations

These have already been considered in Chapter 6 and their position in tort is set out on p. 175.

Trade unions

These have already been considered in Chapter 6 and their position in tort is set out on p. 176.

Joint tortfeasors

Formerly there was no right of contribution between joint tortfeasors, but under the Law Reform (Married Women and Tortfeasors) Act, 1935, it was laid down that, if one joint tortfeasor was sued and paid damages, he could claim a contribution from fellow wrongdoers. The relevant provisions are now contained in the Civil Liability (Contribution) Act, 1978. Thus, if damage is caused by two or more persons *jointly*, e.g. employer and employee (*Lister* v. *Romford Ice and Cold Storage Co.*, 1957),[245] or *severally*, but at the same time, as where the negligent driving of A *and* B causes injury to C, one tortfeasor has a right of contribution against the other or others. However, there can be no contribution where the person claiming it is liable to *indemnify* the person from whom it is claimed. For example, an auctioneer is entitled to be indemnified by a client who has instructed him to sell goods to which, as it subsequently appears, the client does not have a title. (*Adamson* v. *Jarvis*, (1827) 4 Bing. 66) Therefore if the true owner sues the client for wrongful interference and the client pays the damages, he has no right to a contribution against the auctioneer although the auctioneer is also liable for wrongful interference because the auctioneer is a person whom the client would have had to indemnify if the true owner had chosen to sue the auctioneer. The amount of the contribution is settled by the court on the basis of what is just and equitable given the responsibility of each party for the injury and may be the full amount of the damages originally awarded against the person claiming the contribution.

In connection with the right of contribution the Law Reform (Husband and Wife) Act, 1962, has an important effect. Where a spouse A is injured by the joint negligence of the other spouse B and of a third party C, e.g. in a car accident, if C is sued by A, he can now claim a contribution from the negligent spouse B, since B is now a person liable for the purposes of the Act of 1978.

Executors and administrators

(a) General effect of death

Section 1(1) of the Law Reform (Miscellaneous Provisions) Act, 1934 (as amended by the Law Reform (Miscellaneous Provisions) Act, 1970) provides that all causes of action subsisting against or vested in a person at the time of his death shall survive against, or as the case may be, for the benefit of his estate.

This does not apply to actions for defamation. Furthermore, damages, recoverable in an action by the representatives of the deceased shall not include exemplary damages. The right of a person to claim for bereavement under s. 1A of the Fatal Accidents Act, 1976 (see below) does not survive for the benefit of his estate. (S. 4(1), Administration of Justice Act, 1982, amending s. 1(2)(a) of the Act of 1934.) No damages may be awarded for loss of income in respect of any period after the death of an injured person. (S. 4(2)(b), Administration of Justice Act, 1982, amending s. 1(2)(a) of the Act of 1934.)

Under the Proceedings Against Estates Act, 1970 all actions against the personal representatives of a deceased person, whether founded in contract or tort, are now subject to the normal three-year (personal injuries) or six-year (other injuries) limitation period.

(b) Fatal accident

If, as a result, e.g. of negligence, a person is killed, there are two sorts of claim against the person responsible. The executors of the deceased may wish to go ahead with any claim *which the deceased would have had if he had lived*. There may also be relatives who wish to claim because they have suffered as a result of the death.

Claim by the estate. As we have seen, under the Law Reform (Miscellaneous Provisions) Act, 1934, most causes of action in tort subsisting at the time of a person's death survive for (or against) his estate.

As regards a fatal accident, the estate can claim damages for the period between the injury and death, e.g. for pain and suffering and loss of amenity, as where an arm is amputated before death. Damages may be awarded for earnings lost and medical expenses incurred up to the time of death.

There is no claim for loss of expectation of life (s. 1(1)(a), Administration of Justice Act, 1982), nor is there a claim for lost earnings in respect of the period between the actual death and the cessation of notional working life (i.e. the lost years). Section 4(2), *ibid*, now states that no damages may be awarded for loss of income after death.

If the injured person died immediately the estate has no claim except for funeral expenses. (S. 1(2)(c), *ibid*.) If, e.g. a relative, pays the funeral expenses but was not dependent on the deceased and so has no general claim under the Fatal Accidents Act, 1976, that dependent may claim those funeral expenses under the 1976 Act.

Claims by dependants. These are brought under the Fatal Accidents Act, 1976. The claim is independent of the one made by the estate under the 1934 Act (as amended). Two awards of damages may therefore be made, one for the executors on behalf of the estate, and the other to the executors collectively for the dependants.

Under the provisions of the Fatal Accidents Act, 1976 a person whose negligence has caused the death of another may be liable to certain relatives of the deceased who have suffered financial loss because of the death. The following persons are entitled to claim *but only if they were dependent on the deceased*—husband, wife, children, grandchildren, parents, grandparents, brothers, sisters, aunts, and uncles, and their issue; the relationship may be traced through step-relatives, adoption, or illegitimacy, and relatives by marriage have the same rights as the deceased's own relatives. Under s. 1(3)(b) of the 1976 Act, as amended by the Administration of Justice Act, 1982, any person who was living with the deceased in the same household for two years or more before the death and was living for all of the time as the husband or wife of the deceased, may claim. This allows unmarried cohabitants to claim.

A single action must be brought on behalf of all eligible dependants and the total damages apportioned according to their dependancy. The action may be brought by the personal representatives of the deceased, but if there are none, or they fail to bring the action within six months of the death, the dependants may bring it.

If the deceased was guilty of contributory negligence or was a volunteer (see p. 361), the damages awarded will be reduced or extinguished, according to the degree to which the deceased was at fault or was a volunteer. Ordinarily, also, if more than three years have elapsed between injury and death, no Fatal Accidents Act claim can be brought. (S. 11(1), Limitation Act, 1980.) However, it is open to the personal representatives to ask the court to exercise the discretionary provisions of s. 33 of the Limitation Act, 1980 to override the limitation period. (See further p. 374.) Furthermore, if the plaintiff dies before the limitation period has expired, a new limitation period runs under s. 11(5) of the Limitation Act, 1980. This period is three years from either the date of death, or from the date of the personal representative's knowledge that there is a cause of action, whichever is the later.

The probability of pecuniary loss is a matter for the plaintiff to prove and the court to decide as a matter of fact. However, it should be noted that the object of the Fatal Accidents Act is to provide maintenance for relatives who have been deprived of maintenance by the death.

There is also now an award of £3500 for bereavement. (S. 1A(3), Fatal Accidents Act, 1976, as amended by the Administration of Justice Act, 1982.) This sum will be increased as appropriate by statutory instrument. It is in favour of a wife or husband or the parents of the deceased if he or she was under 18 and unmarried, or the mother of a child under 18 and unmarried who was illegitimate. (S. 1A(2)(b), Fatal Accidents Act, 1976.)

Section 4 of the Fatal Accidents Act, 1976 as amended by the Administration of Justice Act, 1982, provides that in assessing damages any benefits which have arisen, or will arise, or may arise to any person as a result of the death are to be disregarded. Thus friendly society or trade union benefits, pensions, or gratuities accruing to a relative would be ignored, even though the pecuniary loss was in a sense thereby reduced.

Partners, principals and agents generally

Partners are jointly and severally liable for the torts of other partners committed in the ordinary course of business, or with the authority of co-partners. A principal is liable for the torts of his agent committed within the scope of his authority, whether by prior authority or subsequent ratification.

VICARIOUS LIABILITY

While the person who is actually responsible for the commission of a tort is always liable, sometimes another person may be liable although he has not actually committed it. In such a case both are liable as joint tort-feasors. This is the doctrine of vicarious liability, and the greatest area of this type of liability is that of master and servant. A master is liable for the torts of his servant committed in the course of his employment, and so wide is the risk that it is commonly insured against. Under the Employers' Liability (Compulsory Insurance) Act, 1969, an employer *must* insure himself in respect of vicarious liability for injuries caused by his employees to their colleagues. Insurance is not compulsory in respect of injuries to persons other than employees.

Who is a servant?

According to Salmond on Torts, a servant may be defined as 'any person employed by another to do work for him on the terms that he, the servant, is to be subject to the control and direction of his employer in respect of the manner in which his work is to be done.' This definition was approved by the court in *Hewitt* v. *Bonvin*, [1940] 1 K.B. 188. In most cases the relationship is established by the existence of a *contract of service*, which may be express or implied and is usually evidenced by such matters as, for example, the power to appoint, the power of dismissal, the method of payment, the payment of National Insurance by the employer, the deduction of tax under PAYE, and membership of pension schemes (if any).

However, in deciding whether the relationship of employer and employee exists, the courts have not restricted themselves to cases in which there is an ordinary contract of service but have often stated that the right of *control* is the ultimate test. In *Performing Right Society Ltd* v. *Mitchel and Booker (Palais de Danse) Ltd*, [1924] 1 K.B. 762 at p. 767, McCardie, J., said—

> The nature of the task undertaken, the freedom of action given, the magnitude of the contract amount, the manner in which it is paid, the powers of dismissal, and the circumstances under which payment of the reward may be withheld, all these bear on the solution of the question. But it seems clear that a more guiding test must be secured . . . It seems . . . reasonably clear that the final test, if there be a final test, and certainly the test to be generally applied, lies in the nature and degree of detailed control over the person alleged to be a servant. This circumstance is, of course, one only of several to be considered but it is usually of vital importance.

The learned judge then went on to decide that the defendants, who employed a dance band under a written contract for one year, were liable for breaches of copyright, which occurred when members of the band played a piece of music without the consent of the holder of the copyright, because the agreement gave the defendants 'the right of continuous, dominant and detailed control on every point, including the nature of the music to be played'.

The existence of the control test means that where an employer (X) lends out his employee (Y) to another employer (Z), then Z may be liable for the wrongs of Y even though there is no contract of service between Y and Z, though such liability is rare.

An employer also owes certain duties to his employees, e.g. to provide proper plant, equipment and premises,and this is a further reason for deciding whether Z has become the master by virtue of the control test. (*Garrard* v. *Southey*, 1952.)[417] There is a presumption that control remains with X and the onus is upon him to provide that control has passed to Z. The burden is a heavy one and the temporary employer will not often become liable. (*Mersey Docks and Harbour Board* v. *Coggins and Griffiths (Liverpool) Ltd*, 1947.)[418] Nevertheless, transfer of control may be more readily inferred where a man is lent on his own without equipment (*Garrard* v. *Southey*, 1952),[417] or where he is unskilled.

Transfer of control is often a convenient method of making the temporary employer liable to, and for, the employee and does not affect the contract of service. A contract of service is a highly personal one and it cannot be transferred from one employer to another without the consent of the employee. However, where there is a contract for hire of plant and the loan of an employee to operate it, the contract of hiring may provide that the hirer shall indemnify the owners for claims arising in connection with the operation of the plant by the employee. (*Wright* v. *Tyne Improvement Commissioners*, 1968.)[419]

The control test was an appropriate one in the days when a master could be expected to be superior to his servant in knowledge, skill and experience. However, in modern times it is unreal to say that all employers of skilled labour can tell employees *how* to do their work. Accordingly the test has been modified in recent cases, the court tending to look for the power to control in incidental or collateral matters, e.g. hours of work and place of work. The existence of this sort of control enables the court to decide whether a person is part of the *organization* of another, and it might be called a '*when and where*' test (*Cassidy* v. *Ministry of Health*, 1951[420] and see also *Ferguson* v. *John Dawson & Partners (Contractors)*, 1976.)[421]

The control test also gives rise to difficulties in the case of the employees of companies. Subordinate employees are controlled by superior employees and some control is obviously present if the management is regarded as 'the company'. However, when one considers the position of directors and top management it is difficult to see how the company, being inanimate, can exercise control. In the case of 'one-man' companies, where the managing director is also virtually the sole shareholder, the reality of the situation is that the servant controls the company and not vice versa. Nevertheless, directors of companies, even 'one-man' companies, are regarded as employees, presumably because the usual incidents of a contract of service are present and despite the absence of genuine control. (*Lee* v. *Lee's Air Farming Ltd*, 1960.)[422]

Although control is the ultimate test in establishing the relationship of master and servant, it is also necessary to deal briefly with other circumstances which may be taken as evidence of the existence of the relationship. In *Short* v. *J. W. Henderson Ltd*, (1946) 62 T.L.R. 427, Lord Thankerton regarded the power to select or appoint, the power to dismiss, and the payment of wages, as relevant in establishing the existence, or otherwise, of a contract of service.

The power to select or appoint

The absence of a power to select or appoint may prevent the relationship of employer and employee arising. Thus, in *Cassidy* v. *Ministry of Health*, 1951[420] Denning, L. J., as he then was, made it clear that a hospital authority is not liable for the negligence of a doctor or surgeon who is *selected* and *employed* by the patient himself. The employer need not make the appointment himself, and an appointee may be an employee even though the employer *delegated* the power of selection to another employee, or even an independent contractor, such as a firm of management consultants, or was *required by law to accept* the employee, e.g. Ministers of State often have power to appoint members of statutory bodies who become the employees of those bodies.

The power to dismiss

An express power of dismissal is strong evidence that the contract is one of service. Many public bodies have a restricted power of dismissal in the sense that rights of appeal are often provided for, but such rights do not prevent a contract of service from arising, nor does the fact that these authorities cannot dismiss certain of their employees without the approval of the Crown or a Minister.

Payment of wages or salary

A contract of service must be supported by consideration which usually consists of a promise to pay wages, or a salary. Where the amount of remuneration or the rate of pay is not fixed in advance, this suggests that the contract is not one of service, but is for services. The employer usually pays his employees directly, but in *Pauley* v. *Kenaldo Ltd*, [1953] 1 All E.R. 226, at p. 228, Birkett, L.J., said, '. . . . a person may be none the less a servant by reason of the fact that his remuneration consists solely of tips.'

An employee may be employed on terms that his remuneration is to consist wholly or partly of commission which the employer pays directly, the commission being a method of assessment of the amount of the remuneration.

Salaries are paid to people who are certainly not employees, e.g. Members of Parliament, whereas payment of wages generally indicates a contract of service. However, little, if anything, turns on the distinction between wages and salaries, and we may conclude that the terms used to describe the way in which a person is paid have little bearing on the relationship between himself and the person who pays him.

In addition to the above indications of a contract of service the following matters have also been regarded as relevant in deciding difficult cases of relationship.

Delegation

In the normal contract of service the employee performs the work himself, and *power to delegate performance of the whole contract* to another is some indication that there is no contract of service. However, the fact that delegation is forbidden does not show *conclusively* that the contract is one of service, for agreements with independent contractors may forbid delegation.

Exclusive service

The fact that an employer can demand the *exclusive services of another* is a material factor leading to the inference of a contract of service and in some cases it has been the deciding factor. However, in the absence of an express contractual provision an employer cannot usually require the exclusive services of his employee, and cannot complain if the employee works for someone else in his spare time, though *Hivac Ltd v. Park Royal Scientific Instruments Ltd*, 1946,[305] is an exceptional case. This being so, a employee and independent contractor are usually both able to work for more than one person, and the exclusive service test may not help in deciding difficult cases of relationship. However, it is true to say that the typical employee works for one person, and the typical independent contractor works for many.

Place of work

If the services are always rendered on the *employer's premises* this is some evidence of the existence of a contract of service, though it is not conclusive. Similarly, the fact that a person works at his home or other premises is some evidence of a contract for services.

It may also be a material factor whether the services are rendered by a person having a *recognized trade or profession*, e.g. a surveyor, or a consulting engineer, which he is exercising in a business because such persons tend to be independent contractors rather than employees and persons not exercising a particular calling may more easily be regarded as the employees of those who employ them.

Plant and equipment

Provision of large-scale plant and equipment by the employer is an indication of the existence of a contract of service and a person who supplies his own large-scale plant and equipment is often an independent contractor. However, provision of minor equipment, such as tools, carries little weight as a test of relationship, for many employees provide their own tools.

Obligation to work

A contract of service and one for services usually *impose an obligation to do the work concerned* and an obligation to work is not helpful in the matter of relationships. However, persons such as salesmen who are paid entirely by commission, and who are not obliged to work at all are probably not working under a contract of service.

Hours of work and holidays

The right to control the *hours of work and the taking of holidays* is also regarded as evidence of the existence of a contract of service. Further an independent contractor is usually engaged for a specific job, whereas an employee is usually employed for an indefinite time.

Employees and independent contractors

An employee is a person whose work is at least *integrated* into the employer's business organization, whereas an independent contractor merely *works for* the business but is *not integrated* into it. Thus, firms of builders, architects, and estate agents are usually regarded as independent contractors, while factory and office workers are usually regarded as employees.

An employee works under a contract of service, whereas an independent contractor's contract is said to be one 'for services' under which he is to carry out a particular task or tasks. Although he may be sued for breach of contract if he fails to carry out his contract properly, the purchaser of his services has no other control over the manner of his work.

Nature of vicarious liability

The doctrine seems at first sight unfair because it runs contrary to two major principles of liability in tort, viz.—

(a) that a person should be liable only for loss or damage caused by his *own acts or omissions*; and

(b) that a person should only be liable where he was at *fault*.

The doctrine of vicarious liability is a convenient one in the sense that employers are, generally speaking, wealthier than their employees and are better able to pay damages, though the doctrine is often justified on the grounds that an employer *controls* his employee. However, it should be noted that control is not in itself a ground for imposing vicarious liability, e.g. parents are not vicariously liable for the torts of their children. It is also said that vicarious liability is a just concept because the employer profits from the employee's work and should therefore bear losses caused by the employee's torts. Again, the employer *chooses* his employee and there are those who say that if he chooses a careless employee he ought to compensate the victims of the careless employee's torts. Further, employer and employee are often identified in the sense that the act of the employee is regarded as the act of his employer and this theory that an employer and his employee are part of a *group* in much the same way as other associations of persons, e.g. companies, is expressed in the often quoted maxim *qui facit per alium facit per se* (he who does a thing through another does it himself). However, in practice the employer does not really suffer loss because he commonly insures against the possibility of vicarious liability and usually the cost of this insurance is put on to the goods or services which he sells. This has the effect of spreading the loss over a large section of the community in much the same way as welfare state benefits.

Course of employment

In order to establish vicarious liability it is necessary to show that the relationship between the defendant and the wrongdoer is that of employer and employee, and that when the employee committed the wrong he was in the *course of his employment*. It is sometimes difficult to decide whether a particular act was done during the course of employment, but the following matters are relevant.

Acts personal to the employee

Some acts done by an employee while at work are so personal to him that they cannot be regarded as being within the scope of employment. Employees do not generally have authority to use violence against third parties, and the use of such violence will usually be beyond the scope of employment, and the employer will not be liable. Thus in *Warren* v. *Henlys Ltd*, [1948] 2 All E.R. 935, the employer of a petrol pump attendant was held not liable for the latter's assault on a customer committed as a result of an argument over payment for petrol. However, where such authority exists, e.g. in the case of door-keepers at dance halls, the employer will be liable if the employee ejects a troublemaker but uses excessive force.

Improper performance of acts within scope of employment

The employer may be liable where the tort committed by the employee is not a personal or independent act but is merely an improper way of performing an act which is within the scope of employment. (*Century Insurance Co.* v. *Northern Ireland Road Transport Board*, 1942.)[423]

The tortious acts for which an employer may be liable must arise out of the employee's employment, but the employer may be liable in such circumstances even if the act is one which he has expressly forbidden his employee to do. The point has arisen in cases in which employees have given lifts to third parties in the employer's vehicle. In *Twine* v. *Bean's Express Ltd*, [1946] 1 All E.R. 202, a driver employed by the defendants gave a lift to a third person who was killed by reason of the employee's negligent driving. Instructions that employees were not to give lifts were displayed in the van. The court held that the employers were not liable because in giving a lift to a third person the driver went *beyond the scope of his employment*.

However, if the express prohibition only affects the *way* in which the employee is to perform his work and is not regarded as affecting the *scope* of his employment, the employer may be liable. (*Limpus* v. *London General Omnibus Co.*, 1962[424] and *Rose* v. *Plenty*, 1976.)[425]

Emergencies
Where the employee takes emergency measures with the intention of benefiting his employer in cases where the latter's property appears to be in danger, the employer will tend to be liable even though the acts of the employee are excessive. Thus in *Poland* v. *John Parr & Sons*, [1927] 1 K.B. 236, a boy was injured by a carter who knocked the boy off the back of his cart to protect his employer's property from theft. It was held that the carter's action was within his implied authority and his employers were liable. If, however, the employee's act is not merely *excessive* but *outrageous* as in *Warren* v. *Henlys Ltd*, [1948] 2 All E.R. 935, the employer will not be liable.

Employee mixing employer's business with his own
The cases under this heading have arisen largely out of the use of motor vehicles, and since it is clear that there can be no vicarious liability if the employee's wrong is not the result of his carrying out his contract of service, the employer will not be liable if he lends his vehicle to his employee entirely for the employee's own purpose. (*Britt* v. *Galmoye*, 1928.)[426]

However, a more difficult situation arises where the activity is basically an authorized one but the employee deviates from it in order to execute some business of his own. The mere fact of deviation will not prevent the employer being liable and this was made clear in the judgment of Cockburn, C.J., in *Storey* v. *Ashton* (1869), L.R. 4 Q.B. 476, when he said—

> I am very far from saying that, if the servant when going on his master's business took a somewhat longer road, that, owing to this deviation he would cease to be in the employment of the master so as to divest the latter of all liability; in such cases it is a question of degree as to how far the deviation could be considered a separate journey. Such a consideration is not applicable to the present case, because here the carman started on an entirely new and independent journey which had nothing to do with his employment.

However, if the journey is unauthorized the employee does not render his employer liable merely by performing some small act for his employer's benefit during the course of it. Thus in *Rayner* v *Mitchell* (1877), 2 C.P.D. 257, a brewer's vanman, without permission, took a van from his employer's stables for personal reasons, namely to deliver a coffin to a relative's house. On the way back he picked up some empty beer barrels and then was involved in an accident injuring the plaintiff. It was held that the brewer was not liable.

Employee using his own property on employer's business

The mere fact that an employee is using his own property in carrying out his employer's business will not prevent the employer from being liable for torts arising out of the use of the employee's property. The decided cases are largely concerned with methods of travel, and in *McKean* v. *Rayner Bros Ltd (Nottingham)*, [1942] 2 All E.R. 650, an employee who was told to deliver a message by using the firm's lorry was held to be in the course of his employment when he performed the task by driving his own car, contrary to his instructions. However, if the employee's act is unreasonable, as where an employee who is authorized to travel by car charters an aeroplane and flies it himself, then the act will be unauthorized and the employer will not be liable if the employee, or a third party, is injured.

Effect of contractual exceptions clauses

Cases may arise in which the employer has attempted to exempt himself from the wrongs of his employee by means of an exemption clause in a contract with a third person who is injured. Such clauses will be effective to exempt the employer from liability if they are properly communicated to the third person. However, they will not protect the employee against his personal liability at common law because he has not usually given any consideration to the third person and is not in privity of contract with him. Statute may extend the protection of an exemption clause in the employer's contract to his employees.

For example, the Carriage of Goods by Sea Act, 1971 provides that an employee or agent of a carrier by sea, but not an independent contractor, shall be entitled to avail himself of the same defences and limits of liability as the carrier. As regards an independent contractor, note *New Zealand Shipping Co.* v. *A. M. Satterthwaite & Co.*, 1974[254] where stevedores, who were independent contractors, took the benefit of an exemption clause in a contract between the carrier and the owner of the goods. However, the principle of privity will apply in other situations, e.g. to an employee of a carrier of goods by road who would not be protected by an exclusion clause in the contract between his employer and the owner of the goods being carried. However, in such circumstances note the device for protecting the employee which was apparently sanctioned in *Snelling* v. *J. G. Snelling*, 1972.[106]

Fraudulent and criminal acts

In early law the courts would not accept the principle of vicarious liability in fraud but gradually the concept was extended, first to cases in which the employee's fraud was committed for his employer's benefit, and later even to cases where the fraud was committed by the employee entirely for his own ends. The leading case is *Lloyd* v. *Grace, Smith & Co.*, [1912] A.C. 716. The defendants were solicitors and employed a clerk in their conveyancing department. The clerk fraudulently induced the plaintiff to transfer some property to him and later sold that property at a profit for his own purposes. Nevertheless, the defendants were held liable for the plaintiff's loss. The liability, however, still depends upon the employee having actual or apparent authority to undertake work or carry out duties of the sort which have enabled him to commit fraud, and obviously if the fraud is committed outside the course of employment then the employer will not be liable.

Criminal conduct on the part of an employee may be regarded as being in the course of his employment so that the employer will be liable at civil law for any loss or damage caused to a third person by the employee's criminal act. (*Morris* v. *C. W. Martin and Sons Ltd*, 1965.)[427]

Casual delegation

If Y lends his car to X for X's own purposes, then Y is not liable, even if in a general way X is his employee. (*Britt* v. *Galmoye*, 1928.)[426] Nevertheless, if Y has a purpose and X also has a purpose, and X is driving a car of Y's partly for his own and partly for Y's purposes, then Y would apparently be liable if X committed a tort. (*Ormrod* v. *Crosville Motor Services*, 1953.)[428] This is known as a case of casual delegation of authority. In these cases of casual delegation, the courts are guided by the doctrine of the *de facto* employee, and by using this doctrine they have extended the vicarious liability of the employer into the area of principal and agent. In fact the person actually committing the wrong is often called the agent. The result is to extend the area of operation of the doctrine of vicarious liability since it is easier to find the relationship of principal and agent than it is to establish the relationship of employer and employee. (See, for example, *Vandyke* v. *Fender*, 1970;[429] contrast *Nottingham* v. *Aldridge*, 1971.)[430]

However, merely giving permission to use the vehicle is not enough to make the owner liable (*Morgans* v. *Launchbury*, 1972),[431] nor is he liable merely because he is the owner (*Rambarran* v. *Gurrucharran*, 1970),[432] and there will, of course, be no vicarious liability in the owner where he did not consent to the taking of the vehicle. (*Klein* v. *Calnori*, 1971.)[433]

LIABILITY FOR TORTS OF INDEPENDENT CONTRACTORS

An independent contractor is by definition a person whose methods and modes of work are not controlled by the person who employs him, and this being so it would be unfair to give an employer general liability for the torts of such a contractor. However, there are circumstances in which a person may be liable for the torts of an independent contractor employed by him and these are set out below. However, it should be borne in mind that the circumstances listed below are not truly examples of vicarious liability. Instead they are based on the idea that the employer himself is in breach of a primary duty which he owes the plaintiff, as where, e.g. he undertakes hazardous operations.

(*a*) *Where the employer authorizes or ratifies the torts of the contractor.* If, for example, an employer authorizes, or afterwards, with knowledge, approves the conduct of an independent contractor in tipping the employer's industrial waste material on another's land, both the employer and the contractor will be liable in trespass as joint tortfeasors.

(*b*) *Where the employer is negligent himself*, as where he selects an independent contractor without taking care to see, as far as he can, that he is competent to do the work required, or gives a competent contractor imperfect instructions or information, as where, for example, he knows that his land is liable to subsidence and fails to tell a contractor who erects something on the land which slips and causes damage to another.

(*c*) *Where liability for the tort is strict, so that responsibility cannot be delegated.* Thus, an employer is liable for injuries to workmen resulting from failure to fence dangerous machinery securely. This duty is laid down by safety legislation, and it is no defence that the employer has delegated the task of fencing to an independent contractor who has failed to do the job properly. Moreover, liability under the rule in *Rylands* v. *Fletcher*, 1868 (see p. 420), cannot be avoided by employing an independent contractor. It seems also that liability is strict where there is interference with an easement of support. (*Bower* v. *Peate*, 1876.)[434]

(*d*) Finally there is a miscellaneous group of cases in which an employer has been held liable for the torts of an independent contractor and the principle which seems to run through them all is that the work which the employer has instructed the independent contractor to undertake is extra hazardous. Thus, work *on or under* the highway is attended with some risk if due precautions are not taken, though work *near* the highway is not for that reason alone regarded as extra hazardous. (See *Salsbury* v. *Woodland*, 1969.)[435] In *Pickard* v. *Smith*, (1861) 10 C.B., N.S. 470, the defendant who was the tenant of a refreshment room at a railway station was held liable when a coal merchant's servant left the coal cellar flap open while delivering coal to the defendant and a passenger on railway premises fell into the cellar and was injured. Again in *Honeywill & Stein Ltd* v. *Larkin Bros Ltd*, [1934] 1 K.B. 191, the plaintiffs had received permission from the theatre owner to take photographs in a theatre on which the plaintiffs had recently done work. A firm of photographers was employed by the plaintiffs and in order to take indoor photographs had, in those days, to use magnesium flares with the result that the theatre curtains caught fire and much damage was caused. The plaintiffs paid for the damage, and sued the photographers for an indemnity to which the court said they were entitled. It also emerged that the plaintiffs would have been liable if they had been sued by the theatre owner.

Where an employer is held liable to a third person for the torts of an independent contractor he will, in most cases, be able to claim an indemnity from the contractor. It should also be noted that an employer is not liable for what are called the *collateral* wrongs of his contractor, but only for wrongs which necessarily arise in the course of the contractor's employment. Thus, if A employs B, an independent contractor, to do some excavation work on his land, A will be liable if, say, his neighbour's greenhouse is damaged by the excavations but A will not be liable for loss caused by B's servants making off with the plants. (And see *Padbury* v. *Holliday*, 1912.)[436]

GENERAL DEFENCES

Some torts have special defences which can be raised in a particular action, but there are certain general defences which can be raised in any action in tort if they seem to be appropriate—

Volenti non fit injuria

(To one who is willing no harm is done.) This is alternatively called the doctrine of the assumption of risk. There are two main aspects of this defence—

(a) Deliberate harm.
(b) Accidental harm.

In the first case the plaintiff's assent may prevent his complaining of some deliberate conduct of the defendant which would normally be actionable. If A takes part in a game of rugby football, he must be presumed to accept the rough tactics which are a characteristic and *normal* part of the game, and any damage caused would not give rise to an action (*Simms* v. *Leigh Rugby Football Club*, 1969),[437] although if the same tactics were employed in the street, an action could be sustained. Similarly, although to stick a knife into a person would normally be actionable, if a surgeon does it with the consent of the patient it is not so.

In this connection cases have come before the courts in recent times in which the issue of *informed consent* has been raised. For example, in *Sidaway* v. *Bethlem Royal Hospital Governors*, [1984] 1 All E.R. 1018, the plaintiff gave her consent for an operation to relieve pain in her neck. The surgeon did not tell her of the possibility of damage to the spinal cord, which was in any case remote. However, there was such damage to the plaintiff's spinal cord and she sued the surgeon regarding her consent as nullified because not all possible risks had been disclosed to her before she gave it. Her claim failed in the Court of Appeal. The risk of spinal cord injury was in any case too remote to found a claim in negligence. As regards the doctor's duty of disclosure prior to a valid consent, Sir John Donaldson, M.R. said it was 'giving or withholding information as is reasonable in all the circumstances . . ., including the patient's true wishes, with a view to placing the patient in a position to make a rational choice.' This test was satisfied here and the plaintiff's consent was valid.

The plaintiff may *impliedly* consent to run the risk of accidental harm being inflicted upon him. Thus one of the risks incidental to watching an ice-hockey match is that the puck may strike and injure you (*Murray* v. *Harringay Arena Ltd*, 1951)[438] or in attendance at a motor race, that cars may run off the track for various reasons, injuring spectators. (*Hall* v. *Brooklands Auto-Racing Club*, 1933.)[439] These are possible hazards unless spectators are to be so fenced or walled in that they cannot see the sport and the maxim *volenti non fit injuria* would apply.

In addition, the plaintiff may be *expressly* put on notice that he undertakes a particular activity at his own risk. However, it is essential for the defendant to show as a matter of fact that the plaintiff agreed to *accept* the risk. This means, for one thing, that he must have had a choice and if a contract, e.g. of employment, forces him to accept the risk, there is no true assent. (*Burnett* v. *British Waterways Board*, 1973.)[255] A plea of *volenti* is open to a defendant against a plaintiff who is a minor. (*Murray* v. *Harringay Arena Ltd*, 1951.)[438]

If a person's assent to harm being inflicted upon him is purely contractual, it can only operate within the limits allowed by the law of contract; the doctrine of privity of contract applies. Thus if a carrier by road puts an exclusion clause in the contract with the customer excluding liability for damage to the goods, the customer could sue the driver if his negligence caused damage to the goods. The driver could not raise the exclusion clause in his defence because he was not a party to the contract in which it was contained. Sometimes a non-contractual agreement excluding liability for negligence has been upheld. (*White* v. *Blackmore*, 1972.)[440]

The defendant must show that the plaintiff knew of the risk. (*White* v. *Blackmore*, 1972.)[440] He must then go on to show that the plaintiff agreed to accept the risk. It does not follow that because a person has knowledge of a potential danger he assents to it. The rule applies equally to cases of *implied volenti* (*Baker* v. *James*, 1921,[441] *Dann* v. *Hamilton*, 1939[442] and *Smith* v. *Baker*, 1891)[443] and to cases of *express volenti*. (*Burnett* v. *British Waterways Board*, 1973.)[255] This principle, i.e. that knowledge is not assent, is most often exemplified in the employer and employee cases and in the rescue cases, and has restricted the application of the defence.

Where the danger is inherent in the job, as in the case of a test pilot, the maxim applies; but where the danger is not inherent, then the defence will rarely succeed. (*Smith* v. *Baker*, 1891.)[443] In instances where an employee expressly assumes a risk, and is even paid extra for doing so, the harm resulting will hardly ever be laid at the door of the employer, unless there is evidence that the employer was negligent and created a risk which was not normally present even in a job inherently dangerous.

The doctrine of *volenti non fit injuria* cannot be pleaded by an employer in an action for damages based on breach of a statutory duty, e.g. to fence machinery under safety legislation. The reason is that the object of the statute, to protect workmen, cannot be defeated by a private agreement between employer and employee.

However, where an employee is in breach of a statutory duty and the employer is not, then if the party injured by the breach of statutory duty seeks to make the employer vicariously liable for the tort of the employee, the employer can plead the defence if the circumstances are appropriate. (*I.C.I. Ltd* v. *Shatwell*, 1964.)[444]

The rescue cases
A different situation arises in what are known as the *rescue cases*. In these the plaintiff is injured while intervening to save life or property put in danger by the defendant's negligence. If the intervention is a reasonable thing to do for the saving of life or property, then this does not constitute the assumption of risk, nor does the defence of contributory negligence apply (*Haynes* v. *Harwood*, 1935,[445] and *Baker* v. *Hopkins*, 1959);[446] but if it is not reasonable then the defences of *volenti* and contributory negligence could apply. (*Cutler* v. *United Dairies*, 1933.)[447] A person may take greater risks in protecting or rescuing life than in the mere protection of property, though even in protecting property reasonable risks may be taken. (*Hyett* v. *G.W. Railway*, 1948.)[448]

Duty to rescuers
The duty of care owed to a rescuer is an original one and is not derived from or secondary to any duty owed to the rescued person by another. Thus a rescuer may recover damages even though no duty was owed to the person rescued. (*Videan* v. *B.T.C.*, 1963.)[449] In addition, the person rescued may be liable in negligence to the rescuer. In *Harrison* v. *British Railways Board*, [1981] 3 All E.R. 679, Mr Harrison, a guard, jumped off his train as it left the platform to rescue a fellow-employee, A, who was negligently trying to board the moving train, but had slipped and was hanging on to a carriage door. The driver, who was unaware of the incident, was not in any way negligent but A was held liable to Mr Harrison in negligence in regard to the injuries which Mr Harrison sustained when he jumped off the train in order to rescue A.

Furthermore, it is important to remember that the question whether the plaintiff has assented to the possibility of harm being inflicted upon him does not arise until it has been shown that the defendant has committed a tort against the plaintiff. If the harm is not tortious the defence is irrelevant. (*Wooldridge* v. *Sumner*, 1962[450] and *Wilks* v. *Cheltenham Home Guard Motor Cycle and Light Car Club*, 1971.)[451]

Finally, Parliament has in s. 148(3) of the Road Traffic Act, 1972 legislated to prevent exclusion of liability to passengers in motor vehicles on the basis of *volenti*. This certainly covers cases of express *volenti* where a person is given a lift in a car in which there is a notice saying that passengers are at their own risk. Whether it covers cases of implied *volenti* such as *Dann* v. *Hamilton*, 1939[442] is more doubtful. A passenger who knows that a driver is under the influence of drink or drugs may, if he is injured, be barred from recovering damages on the grounds of *public policy* since he is aiding and abetting a criminal offence. (See *Nettleship* v. *Weston*, 1971.)[452] For this reason there is doubt as to the correctness of the decision in *Dann* v. *Hamilton*, 1939[442] where the public policy principle was not considered.

Section 148 of the 1972 Act does not prevent the driver from pleading contributory negligence if this is appropriate.

Inevitable accident

The mere fact that the damage caused is accidental cannot itself be a defence if there is a duty to avert the particular consequences, but there are occasions where the defence of inevitable accident can be raised. Such an accident would be one which was not avoidable by any precautions a reasonable man could have been expected to take. (*Stanley* v. *Powell*, 1891[453] and *National Coal Board* v. *Evans*, 1951.)[454] It should be noted, however, that most so-called accidents have a cause, and this defence is of comparatively rare occurrence.

Act of God

This is something which occurs in the course of nature, which was beyond human foresight, and against which human prudence could not have been expected to provide. It is something in the course of nature so unexpected in its consequences that the damage caused must be regarded as too remote to form a basis for legal liability. (*Nichols* v. *Marsland*, 1876.)[455] It arises always from the course of nature and has no human causation. This distinguishes it from inevitable accident.

Necessity

This defence is put forward when damage has been intentionally caused, either to prevent a greater evil or in defence of the realm. Such damage is justifiable if the act was reasonable. (*Cresswell* v. *Sirl*, 1948.)[456] Thus where a whole area is threatened by fire, the destruction of property not yet alight with a view to stopping the spread of the flames would be damage intentionally done but reasonable in the circumstances. (*Cope* v. *Sharpe*, 1912.)[457] Furthermore, in *Leigh* v. *Gladstone*, (1909) 26 T.L.R. 139 the forcible feeding of a suffragette in prison was held justified by the necessity of preserving her life. This decision, which has been much criticized means that it is not an assault for prison officials to take reasonable steps to preserve the health and life of those in custody.

However, duress does not appear to be a defence and in *Gilbert* v. *Stone* (1647), Aleyn 35, the defendant was held liable for trespass although he entered the plaintiff's house only because twelve armed men had threatened to kill him if he did not do so.

Mistake

It is normally no defence in tort to say that the wrongful act was done by mistake. Even if the consequences of an act were not fully appreciated, everyone is presumed to intend the probable consequences of his acts. A mistake of law is no excuse, and this is usually true of a mistake of fact, unless it is reasonable in the circumstances, e.g. in a case of wrongful arrest. (*Beckwith* v. *Philby*, 1827.)[458]

However, the defence of unintentional defamation under s. 4 of the Defamation Act, 1952 is to some extent based on mistake. (See further p. 418.)

Act of State

Sometimes the State finds it necessary to protect persons from actions in tort when they have caused damage whilst carrying out their duties. (*Buron* v. *Denman*, 1848.)[459] This defence cannot be raised in respect of damage done anywhere to British subjects (*Nissan* v. *Att. Gen.*, 1967)[460] or where the court holds that damage has been done to a friendly alien. (*Johnstone* v. *Pedlar*, 1921.)[461]

Statutory authority

The acts of public authorities, e.g. local authority councils, are often carried out under the provisions of a statute. This statutory authority to act may give the public authority concerned a good defence if an action in tort arises as a result. However, much depends upon the wording of the relevant statute. *Statutory authority may be absolute* in which case the public authority concerned has a *duty* to act. Alternatively, *statutory authority may be conditional*, in which case the public authority concerned has the *power* to act but is not bound to do so.

If the authority given is *absolute*, then the body concerned is not liable for damage resulting from the exercise of that authority provided it has acted reasonably and there is no alternative way of performing the act. (*Vaughan* v. *Taff Vale Railway*, 1860.)[462]

On the other hand, if the authority given is *conditional*, the body concerned may carry out the relevant act only if there is no interference with the rights of others. (*Penny* v. *Wimbledon, U.D.C.*, 1899.)[463]

Whether statutory authority is *absolute* or *conditional* is a matter of construction of the statute concerned, though statutory powers are usually conferred in *conditional* or permissive form. The basic rules of construction in these cases appear to be as follows—

(i) Is the authorized act of such public importance as to override private interests?

(ii) If it is not, statutory powers are probably conferred subject to common law rights.

In addition, the matter of statutory compensation may be relevant. If the statute provides for compensation for loss resulting from an authorized act there may be no other claim even though the maximum compensation allowed by the statute is less than the actual loss. (*Marriage* v. *East Norfolk Rivers Catchment Board*, 1950.)[464] On the other hand, if there is no provision for compensation in the statute there is a presumption that private rights remain and that an action in respect of any infringement of these rights may be brought.

It should be noted that the above principles also apply where the act done is authorized by delegated legislation.

Justification or self defence

Where a person commits a tort in defence of himself or his property, he will not be liable provided the act done in such defence is reasonable or proportionate to the harm threatened, though no provocation by words can justify a blow. (*Lane* v. *Holloway*, [1967] 3 All E.R. 129.) The defence extends to acts in defence of the members of one's family and probably to acts in defence of persons generally.

Illegality

It would appear that an action in tort may be defeated on the ground that the plaintiff was committing an illegal or immoral act when the tort occurred. Thus in *Ashton* v. *Turner*, [1980] 3 All E.R. 870 three men committed a burglary after an evening's drinking and sought to escape in a car owned by one of them. The car crashed and a passenger was injured. He claimed damages alleging negligence against the driver and the car owner. It was held by Ewbank, J. dismissing the claim, that as a matter of public policy the law might not recognize a duty of care owed by one participant in a crime to another for acts done in the course of that commission, and in any case *volenti non fit injuria* was a defence open to the driver. Again in the Irish case of *Hegarty* v. *Shine*, (1878) 4 L.R. Ir. 288 the plaintiff, an unmarried woman, brought an action for trespass on the grounds that she had contracted venereal disease following her relationship with the defendant over a period of some two years. Palles, C.B. denied her a remedy, saying 'the cause of action here is a *turpis causa* incapable of being made the foundation of an action. The cause of action is the very act of illicit sexual intercourse'. It would appear, therefore, that the maxim *ex turpi causa* is not confined solely to contract. (For the contractual application see p. 275.)

REMEDIES

The remedies available to a person who has suffered injury or loss by reason of the tort of another are *damages*, the granting of an *injunction*, and in some cases an order for *specific restitution* of land or chattels of which the plaintiff has been dispossessed.

Damages

As we have seen in the chapter on the law of contract, damages may be nominal, contemptuous, punitive (or exemplary), aggravated or compensatory (which includes special damages).

Usually the damages awarded are *compensatory* and the underlying principle is that of *restitutio in integrum*, i.e. the damages awarded are designed to put the plaintiff in the position he would have been in if he had not suffered the wrong.

In the case of *personal injuries*, e.g. loss of a limb, damages obviously cannot restore the plaintiff to his previous position. However, damages for personal injuries may be awarded under the following heads—

    (i) pain and suffering;
    (ii) loss of enjoyment of life, or of amenity, as where brain damage causes permanent unconsciousness;
    (iii) loss of earnings, both actual and prospective.

As regards earnings, *Oliver* v. *Ashman*, [1962] 2 Q.B. 210 decided that where a tortious act had reduced the life expectancy of the plaintiff he could recover a sum representing loss of earnings for the reduced number of years for which he was likely to live but not for the lost years. In *Pickett* v. *British Rail Engineering Ltd*, [1979] 1 All E.R. 774 the House of Lords overruled *Oliver* and decided that earnings during the lost years should be taken into account, less of course, taxation, (see *Gourley* below) and the deduction of an estimated sum to represent the victim's probable living expenses during those years. Thus if A, aged 30, is injured by negligence and would have lived to 70 before but since the accident only to 50, then earnings from age 30–50 and 50–65 (the lost years) must now be taken into account.

Although s. 1(1)(a) of the Administration of Justice Act, 1982 has abolished the claim for *damages for* loss of expectation of life, it leaves unchanged the right to claim *income for* the 'lost' years.

Deductions—tax

The House of Lords decided in *British Transport Commission* v. *Gourley*, [1955] 3 All E.R. 796, that the fact that the plaintiff would have paid tax on his earnings must be taken into account so as to reduce the damages awarded in regard to earnings. The money is not paid to the Revenue so it is a benefit either to the defendant or his insurance company.

However the rule has some logic on the grounds that damages are *compensatory*, and gross salary must be reduced to net salary to achieve true compensation.

Deductions—collateral benefits

Under the Law Reform (Personal Injuries) Act, 1948, s. 2, one-half of the value of certain Social Security benefits, e.g. benefits payable for sickness and/or disablement received by the plaintiff or likely to accrue to him for five years after the accident occurred, must be deducted, though if the plaintiff did not know that he had a right to a particular form of national insurance benefit, and had not acted unreasonably in failing to claim it, the sum which he might have received will not be deducted from the damages awarded. (*Eley* v. *Bedford*, [1971] 3 All E.R. 285.)

Many cases have come before the courts on the matter of deduction of a wide variety of collateral benefits. In general the policy is one of non-deduction and sums received from other forms of insurance are not taken into account, nor is a disability or state retirement pension (*Parry* v. *Cleaver*, [1969] 1 All E.R. 555 and *Hewson* v. *Downes*, [1969] 3 All E.R. 193.)

Remoteness of damage

The consequences of a defendant's wrongful act or omission may be endless. Even so a plaintiff who has established that the defendant's wrong caused his loss may be unable to recover damages because his loss is not sufficiently connected with the defendant's wrong to make the latter liable. In other words, the loss is too remote a consequence to be recoverable. The principles which determined at what point damage became too remote used to be as follows—

(a) Regarding culpability or responsibility for the harm

All that the law required was that the reasonable man would have foreseen that his act would have caused the plaintiff *some* harm.

(b) Regarding liability to compensate the plaintiff

Given that the defendant would, as a reasonable man, have foreseen some harm as likely to result from his act, he became liable for all the *direct* consequences of the act even though such consequences could not possibly have been foreseen.

This test can be seen in operation in *Re Polemis and Furness Withy & Co*, 1921.[465]

This method of establishing liability was rather hard on the defendant because he was often made liable for damage which he could not possibly have foreseen, and certain inroads into the doctrine were made (see for example *Liesbosch* v. *Edison*, 1933),[466] though the general principles of *Re Polemis*[465] were never overruled. However, the decision of the Judicial Committee of the Privy Council in *Overseas Tankship (UK) Ltd* v. *Morts*

Dock and Engineering Co. Ltd, 1961[467] (generally referred to as *The Wagon Mound*), laid down a new test for remoteness of damage in tort which is as follows—

(i) Regarding culpability or responsibility for the harm

The test is still an objective test rather than a subjective one, because the law substitutes for the defendant a hypothetical reasonable man, and then proceeds to make the defendant only responsible for the damage which the reasonable man would have foreseen as a likely consequence of his act.

(ii) Regarding liability to compensate the plaintiff

The law now requires the defendant to compensate the plaintiff only for the foreseeable result of his act. The defendant is no longer liable for all the direct consequences of his act, but only for those which, as a reasonable man, he should have foreseen. However, it appears from more recent decisions that the *precise* nature of the injury suffered need not be foreseeable: it is enough if the injury was of a *kind* that was foreseeable even though the form it took was unusual. (*Hughes* v. *Lord Advocate*, 1963,[468] *Bradford* v. *Robinson Rentals*, 1967[469] and *Weiland* v. *Cyril Lord Carpets Ltd*, 1969.)[470] Nevertheless difficulties still exist in regard to the application of the principles laid down in *Hughes*[468] and *Bradford*[469] These difficulties are illustrated by the decisions reached in *Doughty* v. *Turner Manufacturing Co. Ltd*, 1964,[471] and *Tremain* v. *Pike*, 1969.[472]

Status of *The Wagon Mound*

Certain problems were raised by the decision in *The Wagon Mound*.

(1) Being a decision of the Judicial Committee of the Privy Council, it was not binding on English courts but was persuasive only. The decision in *Re Polemis* was made by the Court of Appeal which is bound by its own decisions, and ought therefore to have followed the decision in *Re Polemis* in future similar cases, rather than the decision in *The Wagon Mound*.

In the event the Court of Appeal in *Doughty* v. *Turner Manufacturing Co. Ltd*, 1964,[471] and the House of Lords in *Hughes* v. *Lord Advocate*, 1963,[468] treated the decision in *The Wagon Mound* as a correct statement of the law, subject in *Hughes'* case to an additional principle that the precise chain of circumstances need not be envisaged if the consequence turns out to be within the general sphere of contemplation and not of an entirely different kind which no one can anticipate. In addition the High Court has expressly stated in *Smith* v. *Leech Braine & Co. Ltd*, 1962[473] that *Polemis* is no longer law and that the principles laid down in *The Wagon Mound* are the governing authority.

(2) Before *The Wagon Mound* there was a well-established principle called the 'unusual plaintiff' rule. For example, if X strikes Y a puny blow

which might be expected merely to bruise him, but in fact Y has a thin skull and dies from the blow, the law has regarded X as liable for Y's death. The same rule has been applied where the plaintiff is a haemophiliac, i.e. a person with a constitutional tendency to severe bleeding. This rule squares with *Re Polemis* but cannot be reconciled with the decision in *The Wagon Mound*.

However, the courts have held that this principle is not affected by *The Wagon Mound* and remains as an exception to it. (See *Smith* v. *Leech Braine & Co. Ltd*, 1962.)[473] The rule that a victim is to be taken as he is found was not necessarily valid where the loss was economic rather than physical. (*Liesbosch* v. *Edison*, 1933.)[466] However, a more recent decision suggests that loss caused by impecuniosity is not necessarily too remote. (*Martindale* v. *Duncan*, 1973.)[474] Furthermore, the 'unusual plaintiff' rule seems to apply only to disabilities existing before the accident and not to disabilities arising afterwards. (*Morgan* v. *T. Wallis*, 1974.)[475]

The test of remoteness of damage in tort as laid down in *The Wagon Mound* relies upon the foreseeability of a reasonable man both in respect of culpability and liability to compensate. It appears, therefore, that the law of remoteness of damage is not the same as in the law of contract. In the *Heron II*, 1967[364] it will be recalled that the House of Lords decided that a party to a contract is not liable for all foreseeable damage.

Finally, it is perhaps worth noting that *damage which is intended* is never too remote and in this connection there is an inference that a man intends the natural consequences of his acts. (*Scott* v. *Shepherd*, 1773.)[476]

Novus actus interveniens

(A new act intervening.) A loss may be too remote a consequence to be recoverable if the chain of causation is broken by an extraneous act. The scope of this concept is as follows—

(*a*) When the act of a third person intervenes between the original act or omission and the damage the original act or omission is still the direct cause of the damage, if the act of the third person might have been expected in the circumstances (*Scott* v. *Shepherd*, 1773)[476] or did not materially cause or contribute to the injury. (*Barnett* v. *Chelsea and Kensington Hospital Management Committee*, 1968[477] and *Robinson* v. *The Post Office*, 1973.)[478] There is a duty to guard against a *novus actus interveniens*. (*Davies* v. *Liverpool Corporation*, 1949.)[479]

(*b*) If the act of the third person is such as would not be anticipated by a reasonable man, the chain of causation is broken, and the third party's act and not the initial act or omission will be treated as the cause of the damage. (*Cobb* v. *Great Western Rly*, 1894.)[480]

(*c*) The *novus actus* may be the act of the plaintiff and in these cases liability will turn on the precise facts. (*Sayers* v. *Harlow U.D.C.*, 1958,[481] and *McKew* v. *Holland and Hannen, and Cubitts (Scotland) Ltd*, 1969.)[482]

(*d*) In order to establish the liability of the intervenor, it is essential to show that he consciously intended to carry out the act. (*Philco Radio Corporation* v. *Spurling*, 1949.)[483]

Nervous shock
Damages for illness brought on by nervous shock are not necessarily too remote and may be recoverable where the nervous shock causes physical illness and—

(*a*) the defendant *intended* the shock (*Wilkinson* v. *Downton*, 1897)[404], or

(*b*) where the shock arises from negligence the plaintiff was 'foreseeable'. The shock will be foreseeable if the defendant's negligent act puts the plaintiff in fear of his or her safety (*Dulieu* v. *White*, 1901)[484] or if it threatens or actually injures some person who has a relationship with the plaintiff such as a family relationship (*Hambrook* v. *Stokes*, 1925[485] and *Hinz* v. *Berry* 1970)[486] including the relationship of rescuer and rescued. (*Chadwick* v. *British Railways Board*, 1967.)[487]

Protection may even be given to a person who has witnessed some awful spectacle even though neither the life nor limb of any third party has been imperilled. (*Owens* v. *Liverpool Corporation*, 1939.)[488]
However, damages will not be recoverable unless—

(i) the defendant *owed a duty of care* to the plaintiff (*Bourhill* v. *Young*, 1943);[489]

(ii) the shock was caused by *actually witnessing or hearing the accident* and not by *the account of others after the event* (*Hambrook* v. *Stokes*, 1925[485] and *Hinz* v. *Berry*, 1970),[486] though following the decision of the House of Lords in *McLoughlin* v. *O'Brian*, 1982 (see p. 778) this would not appear to be necessary in all cases, e.g. those involving accidents to near relatives.

Furthermore, damages for nervous shock following damage to property may be recovered. (See *Attia* v. *British Gas plc*, 1987 at p. 778.)

The above rules were developed because of the following problems inherent in actions for nervous shock—

(*a*) the difficulty of proving the degree of suffering involved and the possibility of fraudulent claims; thus, only where a known physical or mental condition is manifest are damages awarded;

(*b*) the difficulty which might arise if the number of possible claims, e.g. from persons not present at the accident, was not limited; thus, the rule of foreseeability requires that the person claiming should at least have seen or heard the accident or witnessed its aftermath, as in *Chadwick* v. *British Railways Board*, 1967[487] and *McLoughlin* v. *O'Brian*, 1982 (see p. 778).

Damage after successive accidents
If a second event, e.g. injury or illness, which is not connected with the tortious accident comes on before the trial and makes the injury worse,

damages are reduced to the extent of the loss caused by the further injury or illness. (*Jobling* v. *Associated Dairies*, 1980.)[490] If the second event is a tortious accident then no deduction is made. (*Baker* v. *Willoughby*, 1969.)[491]

A defendant who injures a plaintiff *who has already* been injured will be liable only in so far as his tortious act increases or exacerbates the pre-existing injury. (*Performance Cars Ltd* v. *Abraham*, 1961,[492] and *Cutler* v. *Vauxhall Motors Ltd*, 1970.)[493]

Provisional damages

Under Rules of Supreme Court there can be an award of provisional damages. Suppose A loses the sight of one eye in an accident caused by B's negligence. There is a risk that he might lose the sight of the other eye. If an award of damages is increased because of this possibility and it does not occur, then the damages were too much. If the sight of the other eye is affected the damages might be too small because the *precise* nature of the injury was not before the court. The judge can now make an award of provisional damages on the basis that the risk will not develop and specify a period during which a 'further award' can be made if it does.

Injunction

An injunction may be granted to prevent the commission, continuance or repetition of an injury, and there is a form of interlocutory injunction called *quia timet* (because he fears) which may be granted, though rarely, even though the injury has not taken place but is merely threatened. As we have seen, injunctions are discretionary remedies and cannot be obtained as of right. Furthermore, an injunction will not be granted where damages would be an adequate remedy. However, it is no defence to say that it will be costly to comply with the injunction, though the court may, as in *Pride of Derby and Derbyshire Angling Association Ltd* v. *British Celanese Ltd*, [1953] 1 All E.R, 179, where expensive alterations to sewage plant were required to prevent the pollution of a river, grant an injunction and suspend its operation for such time as may seem necessary to enable the defendant to comply with the order.

Other remedies

The court may order *specific restitution* of land or goods where the plaintiff has been deprived of possession and a plaintiff may be given an order for an *account* of profits received as a result of a wrongful act. Thus where a company or other business organization carries on business under a name calculated to deceive the public by confusion with the name of an existing concern, it commits the tort of *passing off* and can be restrained by injunction from doing so. In addition, the existing concern may be given an order for an *account* of profits received by the offending concern as a result of the deception.

CESSATION OF LIABILITY

Liability in tort may be terminated by *death* (see p. 348), and also by *judgment, waiver, accord and satisfaction* and *lapse of time*.

Judgment

Successive actions cannot be brought by the same person on the same facts and if a competent court gives a final judgment in respect of a right of action that right of action is *merged* into the judgment. Thus in *Fitter* v. *Veal*, (1701) 12 Mod. Rep. 542, the plaintiff sued the defendant for assault and battery and obtained a judgment for £11. After some years he discovered his injuries were worse than he had thought and he had to have part of his skull removed. It was held that he could not sue for further damages.

However, there are certain exceptional cases, for example, where two separate rights have been infringed. Thus in *Brunsden* v. *Humphrey* (1884), 14 Q.B.D. 141, the Court of Appeal held that a cab driver who had brought a successful action for damage to his cab caused by the defendant's negligence was able to bring a further action for personal injuries. One action was for damage to *property*, the other for injury to the *person*.

Waiver

The same conduct by the defendant may sometimes represent two separate and distinct torts or causes of action. If the plaintiff obtains judgment and satisfaction by electing to sue on tort A rather than tort B he cannot later sue in respect of tort B. However, the mere bringing of the action will not operate as an election: there must be judgment and satisfaction. (*United Australia Ltd* v. *Barclays Bank Ltd*, 1941.)[494] Furthermore, *adoption* of the transaction giving rise to the tort operates as a waiver. (*Verschures Creameries Ltd* v. *Hull and Netherlands S.S. Co. Ltd*, 1921.)[495]

Accord and satisfaction

A person may surrender a right of action in tort by deed or an agreement for consideration.

Lapse of time

In actions for damages for negligence, nuisance, or breach of duty, e.g. the statutory duty of an employer to fence a dangerous machine, where damages consist of, or include, damages for personal injury, the limitation period is three years. (S. 11(1), Limitation Act, 1980) (see *Letang* v. *Cooper* 1964.)[496] Under s. 2 of the 1980 Act the period in all other actions in tort is six years. However, actions in respect of registered postal packets under s. 30(1) of the Post Office Act, 1969 must be brought within 12 months.

The period of limitation generally begins from the date when the tort was committed, e.g. the date of a trespass to land. However at one time an action in negligence arose only when the harm was suffered but not, apparently, when it was detected. Thus in *Pirelli General Cable Works Ltd* v. *Oscar Faber & Partners Ltd*, [1983] 1 All E.R. 65 the defendants designed a chimney for the plaintiff. It was in the event a negligent design. Cracks were discovered by the plaintiffs in 1977 but evidence showed that they had appeared in 1970. When the plaintiffs sued in 1978 for negligence the House of Lords held that their claim was statute-barred.

The Latent Damage Act, 1986 now applies and the limitation period is either six years from the date on which the cause of action accrued or three years from the earliest date upon which the plaintiff had sufficient knowledge to sue. The Act imposes a 'long-stop' period of 15 years from the negligent act or omission or the occurrence of the damage whether or not the damage was discovered or even discoverable by then. No action can be brought after this time.

The above rules were also rather harsh in personal injury cases where, for example, the plaintiff did not know that he had a claim or the extent of that claim, as where he had contracted a dust disease and was not aware of its onset. Furthermore, if X had been run down by Y's negligent driving, and unknown to X the injuries inflicted on him at the time of the accident caused him to go blind (say) four years after the accident, then X's cause of action in respect of his blindness was barred before he knew it existed, since it was formerly held that once damage had occurred the cause of action accrued and that time began to run against the plaintiff even though he was unaware or mistaken as to the consequences of the damage.

The matter is now covered by the Limitation Act, 1980. The Act applies only to claims for personal injury arising out of negligence, breach of contract or breach of statutory duty. The basic limitation period of three years is retained but time runs from the date of accrual of the cause of action or the 'date of the plaintiff's knowledge if later'. The 'date of the plaintiff's knowledge' is the date on which the plaintiff first had knowledge that his injury was significant and that it was attributable in whole or in part to the act or omission which constitutes the alleged negligence, or breach of duty.

The action may be brought by dependants or on behalf of the estate of a deceased person. Thus actions may be brought within three years of the date of death or of the date on which the personal representatives or dependants, as the case may be, acquired a knowledge of the relevant facts.

If the tort is of a continuing nature, as in the case of nuisance or possibly trespass, an independent cause of action arises on each day during which the tort is committed, and the aggrieved party can recover for such proportion of the injury as lies within the limitation period, even though the wrong was first committed outside the period.

Where the plaintiff is a minor or person suffering from mental disorder, the period of limitation does not run against him until his disability ends, i.e. on becoming eighteen or on becoming sane or on death. But once time has started to run, any subsequent disability will not stop it running.

However, a minor was only regarded as being under a disability if he was not in the custody of a parent when the cause of action accrued. If he was in the custody of a parent the parent was expected to commence an action within the limitation period and if he did not the minor's action would be statute-barred. The Act of 1980, s. 8, abolishes that rule so that periods of limitation do not run against a minor whether he is in the custody of a parent or not.

Special periods of limitation

The periods of limitation in respect of actions against the estate of a deceased tortfeasor have already been considered on p. 348. However, it should be noted that the Limitation Act, 1980, does not operate to extend the time within which an action must be brought against a deceased tortfeasor's estate. So far as the death of an injured party is concerned, the ordinary six or three-year periods apply. They run from the accrual of the cause of action as if no death had occurred. As we have seen, personal representatives or dependants may ask for an extension of time under the provisions of the Limitation Act, 1980.

Other special periods of limitation are as follows—

(i) Actions arising out of collisions at sea; two years, subject to extension by the court. (Maritime Conventions Act, 1911, s. 8.)

(ii) Proceedings against air-carriers; two years. (Carriage by Air Act, 1961, s. 1(1).)

(iii) A joint tortfeasor who wishes to recover a contribution must bring the action within two years from the date on which he admitted liability or judgment was entered against him. (Limitation Act, 1980, s. 8.)

(iv) Actions in respect of damage arising from nuclear incidents; thirty years. (Nuclear Installations Act, 1965, s. 15.)

Public authorities and their officers have no special position and actions against them are governed by the same rules as any other action in tort.

It should also be noted that by s. 32 of the Limitation Act, 1980, the defendant's *fraud* or *negligent concealment* may prevent his pleading that the claim is statute-barred. (*Beaman* v. *A.R.T.S.*, 1949.)[497]

Assignment

It is against the rules of public policy to allow the assignment of rights of action in tort, since actions for damages should not become a marketable commodity. However, since rights may pass to others by operation of law in the following circumstances—

(i) *Death*. Rights and liabilities in tort survive for the benefit or otherwise of the estate, except actions for defamation unless damage to the deceased's estate has resulted.

(ii) *Bankruptcy*. Rights of action in tort possessed by a debtor which relate to his *property* and which if brought will increase his assets will pass to his trustee in bankruptcy. Actions for *personal torts*, e.g. defamation, remain with the bankrupt.

(iii) *Subrogation*. An insurance company which compensates an insured person under a policy of insurance can step into his shoes and sue in respect of the injury.

SPECIFIC TORTS

We shall next examine certain specific torts, beginning with those affecting the person.

TORTS AFFECTING THE PERSON

Trespass to the person

This has several aspects:

(a) Assault

An assault is an attempt or offer to apply unlawful force to the person of another. There must be an apparent present ability to carry out the threat, the basis of the wrong being that a person is put in present fear of violence. On general principles, pointing even an unloaded weapon or a model gun at another, who does not know that it is unloaded or a model, would amount to an assault.

It is often said that mere words cannot constitute an assault but this is a doubtful proposition. In *Ansell* v. *Thomas*, 1974[374] the assault seems to have consisted in the words threatening forcible ejectment if the plaintiff did not leave voluntarily. A threat to use force at some time in the future is not an assault, but it seems that it is enough if the threat is to use force if the person addressed does not immediately do some act. In *Read* v. *Coker*, (1853) 138 E.R. 1437, it was held that an assault was committed where the defendants threatened to break the plaintiff's neck if he did not leave the premises. Words, however, may prevent an assault coming into being. (*Turbervell* v. *Savage*, 1669.)[498]

As regards the unauthorized taking of a photograph, the position is somewhat complicated. It may be that where a flash is used the simple taking of the photograph without more is unlawful, since it is probably a battery to project light onto another person in such a manner as to cause personal discomfort. Where no flash is used, it is hard to see how, by itself, the taking of a photograph can amount to a battery, an assault or any other trespass.

(b) Battery

Intentionally to bring any material object into contact with the person of another is enough application of force to give rise to a battery. Thus to throw water on a person (*Pursell* v. *Horn*, (1838) 8 A&E. 602), or to apply a 'tone-rinse' to the scalp of a customer which was not ordered and caused damage, i.e. a skin rash is enough. (*Nash* v. *Sheen, The Times*, 13 March, 1953.) Substantial damages will be awarded when the battery is an affront to personal dignity, e.g. the wrongful taking of a finger-print. The mere jostling which occurs in a crowd does not constitute battery, because there is presumed consent and in any case there is normally no hostility which is also a requirement. Thus in *Wilson* v. *Pringle*, [1986] 2 All E.R. 440, one schoolboy had intentionally pulled a schoolbag off another boy's shoulder. However, this was only a form of horseplay and in the absence of a hostile intention there was no battery. It should be noted that there may be a battery without an assault, as where a person is attacked from behind.

In considering the defence of *volenti* there has already been some consideration of informed consent in an action for alleged negligence. (See *Sidaway* v. *Bethlem Royal Hospital Governors*, [1984] 1 All E.R. 1018 at p. 361.) A similar issue was raised in *Freeman* v. *Home Office*, [1984] 1 All E.R. 1036. The plaintiff was serving a sentence of life imprisonment. He was given drugs by a medical officer employed by the Home Office. He claimed that the drugs were given to discipline and control him and not as medical treatment, which he thought. He claimed that the medical officer had committed battery upon him and that his consent was negatived because it was not informed. The Court of Appeal decided that since the doctrine of informed consent formed no part of English law, the sole issue was whether on the facts the plaintiff had consented to the administration of the drugs and on that issue the trial judge had found that the plaintiff had so consented. His claim therefore failed.

In general there will be some active conduct constituting the assault. However, in *Fagan* v. *Metropolitan Police Commissioner*, 1968[499] the court appears to have accepted that a battery can arise from an omission.

Defences

There are certain defences to an action, brought for assault or for battery—

(i) *Self-defence*. This is not merely the defence of onself but also of those whom one has a legal or moral obligation to protect. It also applies to the protection of property, but no more than reasonable force must be used.

(ii) *Parental or similar authority*. Moderate chastisement inflicted on children by parents, and school masters by way of delegation of the parent's authority, is not actionable.

(iii) *Volenti non fit injuria*. As in the case of the players in a rugby match. (*Simms* v. *Leigh Rugby Football Club*, 1969.)[437]

(iv) *Judicial authority*. This includes the right to inflict proper punishment and to make lawful arrests.

(v) *Necessity*. This is not favoured as a defence but may be allowed if the defendant can prove that he committed the battery in order to prevent the happening of a greater harm. Thus in *Leigh* v. *Gladstone*, (1909) 26 T.L.R. 139, the forcible feeding of a suffragette in prison was held justified by the necessity of preserving her life.

(vi) *Prosecution in a magistrates' court*. Assault and battery is a crime as well as a civil wrong. If the wrongdoer is prosecuted, and *summary* proceedings are taken and the accused is convicted and punished, or the case is dismissed and the magistrates award a certificate of dismissal, no further action or civil proceedings may be taken in respect of the particular wrong. (Offences against the Person Act, 1861, ss. 44–45.)

It is now clear that trespass to the person is not actionable in itself; the plaintiff must prove intention or negligence (*Fowler* v. *Lanning*, 1959)[500] though he need not prove damage. It is also settled that where the interference is *unintentional* the plaintiff's only cause of action lies in negligence. (*Letang* v. *Cooper*, 1964.)[496]

(c) False imprisonment

This is the infliction of unauthorized bodily restraint without lawful justification. It is not necessarily a matter of bars and bolts, but any form of unlawful restraint might turn out to be false imprisonment. The imprisonment must be total, and if certain ways of exit are barred to a prisoner, but he is free to go off in another way, then there is no false imprisonment. (*Bird* v. *Jones*, 1845.)[501] If a person is on premises and is not given facilities to leave, then this does constitute false imprisonment, unless the refusal is merely the insistence on a reasonable condition. (*Herd* v. *Weardale Steel, Coke & Coal Co.*, 1915.)[502] It is not even essential that the plaintiff should be aware of the fact of his imprisonment, provided it is a fact. (*Meering* v. *Grahame White Aviation Co.* 1919.)[503] *Volenti non fit injuria* is defence to false imprisonment, as where a prison visitor agrees to be locked in a cell with the prisoner.

Arrest and the tort of trespass to the person

An arrest or other restraint of a person, as by stopping and searching him, will be unlawful and actionable as a trespass in civil law unless the following requirements are met.

Arrestable offences

The basic rule is that offences are arrestable if they carry a sentence of five years or more (s. 24(1)(b), Police and Criminal Evidence Act, 1984) or are offences for which the sentence is fixed by law, e.g. murder. (S. 24(1)(a), *ibid*.)

A private person may arrest without a warrant anyone who is, or whom he, with reasonable cause, suspects to be, *in the act* of committing an arrestable offence. (Police and Criminal Evidence Act, 1984, s. 24(4).) Where an arrestable offence *has been committed*, any person may arrest without warrant anyone who is, or whom he, with reasonable cause, suspects to be, guilty of the offence. (S. 24(5), *ibid.*)

A police constable is protected in respect of arrests made under the authority of a warrant. He may arrest without a warrant in the situations mentioned above. Furthermore he may arrest someone who is or is suspected, on reasonable grounds, to be *about to commit* an arrestable offence, and someone whom he suspects, on reasonable grounds, to be guilty of an arrestable offence even though the offence has *not* been committed. (S. 24(7), *ibid.*)

General powers of arrest
Section 25 of the 1984 Act gives the *police* a new general power of arrest *for any offence* if certain circumstances apply, as where the person arrested will not give his name and address, or the policeman thinks he has given a false one, or to prevent physical harm and damage to property or obstruction of the highway or to protect a child or other vulnerable person.

Section 28 of the 1984 Act requires that the person arrested should be told that he is and the grounds therefore, even if it is obvious, as where a thief is apprehended in the act of theft. (*Christie* v. *Leachinsky*, 1947[504] and *R.* v. *Kulynycz*, 1970.)[505] However, an arrest made without these formalities is not unlawful if the arresting officer cannot comply with them because of the condition or behaviour of the person arrested. (*Wheatley* v. *Lodge*, 1971.)[506]

Under s. 32 of the 1984 Act a person arrested may be searched for a weapon or evidence relating to the alleged offence. The power of search extends to any premises on which the arrest took place. In addition, s. 1 of the 1984 Act gives the police power to stop and search persons. The Act gives the police the power to search any person or vehicle *found in a public place* for stolen or prohibited articles, e.g. a gun, and to detain a person or vehicle for the purpose of such search. A person can be ordered to stop for the purpose of such a search and any stolen or prohibited article found in the course of such a search may be seized.

The matter of cautioning on arrest and procedure to be followed before the person arrested reaches court have already been considered. (See p. 43.)

The *remedies* available against false imprisonment are self-help, i.e. breaking away, the writ of *habeas corpus* and an action for damages. This prerogative writ of *habeus corpus* is designed to provide a person, who is kept in confinement without legal justification, with a means of obtaining his release. If he can show a *prime facie* case that he might be unlawfully detained, he (or often a friend or relative) will apply to a divisional court of the Queen's Bench Division, though application may be made to any judge of the High Court during vacation times. The person detained applies, through counsel, for the writ to be issued, the facts alleging unlawful detention being set out on an affidavit supporting the application. If the writ is issued the effect is to cause the alleged captor to 'bring the body' of the prisoner before the court which will then decide on the merits of the case whether there are any legal grounds for detention of the prisoner. If not, he is set free by the court.

TORTS AFFECTING PROPERTY

Trespass to land

Trespass to land is interference with the possession of land. It is not enough that the plaintiff is the owner; he must also have possession. So where land is leased for a term of years, the lessee is the person entitled to sue in trespass, though the lessor may bring an action if the damage is such as to affect his reversion when the lease ends. However, when a person signs a contract for the purchase of land, he becomes entitled to possession of it, and if a trespass takes place before he actually takes possession, then he can sue in respect of that trespass when he does. His right to sue relates back to the date on which he became entitled to the land under the contract.

Interference with the possession of land may take many forms but it must be direct. (*Southport Corporation* v. *Esso Petroleum Co.*, 1954.)[507] For example, an unauthorized entry on land is a trespass. It is trespass to place things on land e.g. leaving a dead cat in a neighbour's garden. To remain on land after one's authority is terminated constitutes a trespass. So, if a friend invites you into his house for a meal, tires of your company and asks you to leave, then if you refuse you are a trespasser. If you abuse the purpose for which you are allowed to be on land you become a trespasser. In *Hickman* v. *Maisey*, [1900] 1 Q.B. 752, where the highway was used for making notes of the form of racehorses being tried out on adjoining land, this constituted a trespass, since the proper use of a highway is for passing and re-passing.

While trespass usually takes place above the surface, it may be underneath by means of tunnelling or mining. With regard to trespass in the air-space above land, the position is doubtful, since there is no good authority. It is probably only a trespass if it is either within the area of ordinary user, or if it involves danger or inconvenience. (*Kelson* v. *Imperial Tobacco Co.*, 1957,[508] and *Woollerton and Wilson Ltd* v. *Richard Costain (Midlands) Ltd*, 1969).[509]

Section 76 of the Civil Aviation Act, 1982 provides that, subject to the exception of aircraft belonging to, or exclusively employed in the service of Her Majesty, no action lies in respect of trespass or nuisance by reason only of the flight of an aircraft over any property at a height above the ground, which having regard to weather and the other circumstances of the case is reasonable. (*Bernstein* v. *Skyviews & General*, 1977.)[510]

Subject to the same exception in regard to aircraft in the service of Her Majesty, the owner of an aircraft is liable for all material loss or damage to persons or property caused by that aircraft, whether in flight, taking off, or landing, or by a person in it, or articles falling from it, without proof of negligence or intention, or other cause of action.

Trespass to land or goods will not be unlawful and actionable at civil law if it is by the police who follow the provisions laid down in the Police and Criminal Evidence Act, 1984. Broadly speaking, s. 17(1) of the Act gives the police power to enter premises without a warrant in certain circumstances, e.g. to make an arrest. Section 8 gives the police a power to enter premises to search under a warrant from a J.P. Section 19 gives power to seize articles found on the premises unless they are exempt articles if the officer concerned reasonably believes that it is evidence in relation to an offence which he is investigating or any other offence; and that it is necessary to seize it in order to prevent its 'concealment, loss or destruction'. Section 19(6) states that items exempted from seizure are those subject to legal professional privilege.

Revocation of licences

Problems have arisen where a plaintiff has entered the premises by virtue of a licence, contractual or otherwise, because at one time it was not certain whether this licence could be revoked so as to make the plaintiff a trespasser and permit his ejection.

The common law view was that, where a person paid for admission to premises, his licence to be on those premises could be revoked at any time, in spite of valuable consideration, so that he could then be ejected as a trespasser, the defendant being liable for breach of contract, but not for assault. (*Wood* v. *Leadbitter*, 1845.)[511]

On the other hand, Equity took the view that, if there was on enforceable contract not to revoke, express or implied, as where valuable consideration had been given, the licence could not be revoked so that if the plaintiff had been ejected he could sue for assault; he could not be made a trespasser by a mere attempt at revocation. (*Hurst* v. *Picture Theatres*, 1915.)[512]

The equitable view gave rise to certain problems because it seemed to confuse rights over land with mere contracts, but the matter may now be regarded as settled. In *Winter Garden Theatre* v. *Millennium Productions Ltd*, 1948,[513] it was held by the House of Lords that, although a licence for value is contractual in its nature and cannot create a right over land itself (or a right *in rem* which will run with the land and affect third parties), yet, as between the parties to the contract it may be implied, even if it is not expressed, that the licence cannot unreasonably be revoked during the period for which the parties intended it to continue. This rule was applied in *Hounslow London Borough* v. *Twickenham Garden Developments*, 1970.[514]

There are certain extra-judicial remedies available to a person injured by a trespass. For example, *distress damage feasant* is the right to seize chattels which have done damage on land. There is no right to use or sell the chattels but merely to detain until the owner offers compensation. The remedy does not lie against Crown property, and the right to sue in trespass is postponed until the chattel is returned. Livestock may be detained (subject to notice to the owner and police) for compensation supported by a right of sale. (S. 7, Animals Act, 1971.) These provisions apply only to damage caused by straying animals; they do not give powers of detention in the case of other forms of damage by animals, e.g. damage caused by negligent control where the animal has not in fact strayed.

There is further extra-judicial remedy, often referred to as *self-help*, whereby the person in possession of the land may eject the trespasser, using such force as is reasonably necessary. The trespasser must be asked to depart peacefully and given time in which to quit the land. (*Hemmings* v. *Stoke Poges Golf Club*, 1920.)[515] A trespasser who enters by *force* may be removed immediately and without a previous request to depart.

Trespass to land is actionable *per se* (in itself) and it is not necessary for the plaintiff to show actual damage in order to commence his action, although the damages would be nominal in the absence of real loss. Nevertheless it is possible to obtain an injunction without proof of loss. Trespass upon property is not normally a criminal offence. The law does penalize by statute a trespass on particular property, e.g. railway property and also the law punishes trespass on property for the purpose of committing, e.g. theft or rape.

Part V of the Public Order Act, 1986 is now relevant in terms of criminal trespass. Section 39 gives senior police officers power to direct trespassers to leave land. The officer concerned must reasonably believe that two or more persons, having entered land as trespassers, are present with the common purpose of residing there, that reasonable steps have been taken on behalf of the occupier to ask them to leave and either that any of the persons has caused damage to property there or has used threatening, abusive or insulting words or behaviour to the occupier or his family, or that the trespassers have brought at least twelve vehicles on to the land. Failure to comply with a direction is a criminal offence. The Act is aimed mainly at groups of hippies.

Squatters

Apart from these statutory exceptions the criminal law dealt with entering or remaining on property by means of the Statutes of Forcible Entry which were a confusing and archaic set of laws. The fact that trespass is not generally a crime has led to difficulties, particularly in times of acute housing shortage where the civil law is not adequate to deal with the growing activities of 'squatters'. The Criminal Law Act, 1977, s. 6, now creates the offence of using or threatening violence to secure entry to premises on which there is another person who opposes entry. The offence can be commited by a person, notwithstanding he has some interest or right in the premises as where he is a landlord, but the offence cannot be committed by a displaced residential occupier, i.e. a person whose residential occupation of the premises has been interrupted by the occupation of the premises by a trespasser, or someone acting for a displaced residential occupier. Section 7 makes it a summary offence for a trespasser to fail to leave premises when required to do so by a displaced residential occupier. Section 8 makes it an offence for a person who is a trespasser on any premises which he has entered as a trespasser to have with him a weapon of offence. Section 9 makes it an offence to enter or be upon as a trespasser diplomatic or consular premises or the premises or residence of any body or person having diplomatic immunity in respect of its or his premises or residence. Section 10 creates a summary offence of resisting or intentionally obstructing a court officer seeking to execute an order for possession of premises, while s. 11 gives to a constable a power of entry and search for the purpose of exercising a power of arrest under that part of the Act which relates to offences of entering and remaining on property (i.e. Part II). Section 13 abolishes the common law offences of forcible entry and detainer and repeals related statutes.

Wrongful interference with goods

We propose to discuss the tort of wrongful interference by outlining the basic features of it, i.e. the relationship between the plaintiff and the goods, the conduct of the defendant which the plaintiff must prove, and the principle of liability, bearing in mind that the Torts (Interference with Goods) Act, 1977 defines, in s. 1, wrongful interference with goods as including conversion of goods, trespass to goods, negligence or any other tort so far as it results in damage to goods or to an interest in goods.

(a) Wrongful interference by trespass to goods

(i) *The relationship between the plaintiff and the goods*. Wrongful interference by trespass to goods is a wrong against the possession of goods. Possession in English law is a difficult concept which is considered more fully on p. 426. For the moment it will suffice to say that a person possesses goods when he has some form of *control* over them and has the *intention to exclude* others from possession and to hold the goods on his own behalf.

Possession must exist at the moment when the wrongful interference is alleged to have been committed. Thus a bailee of goods can sue for a wrongful interference to them, but a bailor cannot because, although he is the owner of the goods, he does not possess them at the time. Where there is a *bailment at will*, i.e. one which can be determined at any time, both bailee and bailor have possession so that either can sue for a wrongful interference to the goods. Possession does not necessarily involve an actual grasp of the goods; often a lesser degree of control will suffice. (*The Tubantia*, 1924.)[516]

Difficulties have arisen over the requirement of the intention to exclude others as a necessary ingredient of possession, in regard to things found under or on land.

The rules were dealt with by the Court of Appeal in *Parker* v. *British Airways Board*, 1982.[517] It was held that where goods were not attached to land it was necessary to distinguish between a finding in a place over which the occupier had shown a clear intent to control exclusively, and finding in a place to which the finder had access as a matter of course. In the latter case the finder's possessory title took precedence over that of the occupier.

However, an occupier of land or a building has superior rights to those of a finder in regard to goods in or attached to the land or building. (See *South Staffordshire Water Co.* v. *Sharman*, 1896[518] and the cases noted with it.)

Although the plaintiff relies on possession and not on ownership or title, the defendant can set up the *jus tertii* (right of a third party), under s. 8(1) of the Torts (Interference with Goods) Act, 1977. Under that section the defendant is entitled to show in accordance with rules of court that a third party has a better right than the plaintiff as respects all or any part of the interest claimed by the plaintiff and any rule of law (sometimes and formerly called *jus tertii*) to the contrary is abolished. Under s. 8(2) rules of court relating to proceedings for wrongful interference require the plaintiff to give particulars of his title; to identify any person who to his knowledge has or claims any interest in the goods; to authorize the defendant to apply for directions as to whether any person should be joined in the action with a view to establishing whether he has a better right than the plaintiff, or has a claim as a result of which the defendant might be doubly liable. If a party refuses to be joined the court may deprive him of any right of action against the defendant for the wrong, either unconditionally or subject to such terms or conditions as the court may specify.

(ii) *The conduct of the defendant which the plaintiff must prove.* In wrongful interference by trespass there must be a *direct* interference with the goods, and this may consist of moving a chattel or the throwing of something at it. A person who writes with his finger in the dust on the back of a car commits wrongful interference, as does a person who beats another's animals or administers poison to them.

(iii) *The principle of liability.* In wrongful interference by trespass to goods the liability would not now appear to be strict. The defence of inevitable accident would presumably be available to a defendant (*National Coal Board* v. *Evans*, 1951)[454] and it is possible that, since *Letang* v. *Cooper*, 1964,[496] the interference with the possession of goods must be intentional. Mere negligence may not suffice. This would follow a similar development in the tort of trespass to the person which began with the decision in *Fowler* v. *Lanning*, 1959.[500]

(b) Wrongful interference by conversion

(i) *The relationship between the plaintiff and the goods.* It is often said that the right to sue for wrongful interference by conversion depends on ownership, but this is not really true. To be able to sue for wrongful interference the plaintiff must have had either possession or the immediate right to possess at the time the wrong was committed. Mere ownership without one of the above rights is not enough. Nor is the mere right to possess unless it is coupled with ownership. (*Jarvis* v. *Williams*, 1955.)[519]

As in wrongful interference by trespass to goods so in wrongful interference by conversion, the defendant can set up the right of a third party and s. 8(1) and (2) of the 1977 Act apply.

(ii) *The conduct of the defendant which the plaintiff must prove.* In wrongful interference by conversion the defendant must do something which is a complete denial of, or is inconsistent with, the plaintiff's title to the goods; a mere interference with possession is not enough. (*Fouldes* v. *Willoughby*, 1841.)[520] Furthermore, wrongful interference by conversion need not be a trespass. (*Oakley* v. *Lyster*, 1931.)[521]

Generally the conduct of the defendant must be an act rather than a failure to act. Thus, although the plaintiff may base his case on a demand for the goods followed by a refusal, he must still show a denial of title in the defendant. If, therefore, the defendant can show that he was retaining the goods in the exercise of a lien for (say) repair charges unpaid, the plaintiff will fail in his action. A defendant may also refuse temporarily to give up the goods while he takes steps to check the title of the plaintiff.

(iii) *The principle of liability.* In general, liability in wrongful interference by conversion is strict and it is not necessary for the plaintiff to prove that the defendant had a wrong intention. Normally it is not a defence for the defendant to say that he acted honestly. (But see *Elvin and Powell* v. *Plummer Roddis Ltd*, 1933.)[522] Where the defendant has lost the goods by *negligence* there was no wrongful interference by conversion but the plaintiff may now sue under the provisions of the Torts (Interference with Goods) Act, 1977 for damage to goods caused by negligence.

Detention of goods

Section 2(1) of the Torts (Interference with Goods) Act, 1977, abolishes the old tort of detinue which was a tort relating to detention of goods. The Act substitutes statutory provisions. Under s. 2(2) the tort of wrongful interference by conversion is substituted for the old action of detinue. Thus mere detention can now amount to conversion. In other words, detinue and conversion are merged.

As regards the form of judgment where goods are detained, s. 3 provides that in proceedings for wrongful interference against a person who is in possession or in control of the goods relief may be given if appropriate in accordance with s. 3(2). Under s. 3(2) the relief is—

(a) an order for delivery of the goods, and for payment of any consequential damages, or

(b) an order for delivery of the goods, giving the defendant the alternative of paying damages by reference to the value of the goods, together in either alternative with payment of any consequential damages, or

(c) damages.

Section 3(2) provides that subject to rules of court relief should be given under only one of paragraphs (a), (b) and (c) above and relief under paragraph (a) is at the discretion of the court though the claimant may choose between the others. If it is shown to the satisfaction of the court that an order under (a) above has not be complied with the court may revoke the order or the relevant part of it and make an order for payment of damages by reference to the value of the goods. Where an order is made under (b) above the defendant may satisfy the order by returning the goods at any time before execution of judgment, but without prejudice to liability to pay any consequential damages. An order for delivery of the goods under (a) or (b) may impose such conditions as may be determined by the court or pursuant to rules of court and in particular where damages by reference to the goods would not be the whole of the value of the goods, may require an allowance to be made by the claimant to reflect the difference. For example, a bailor's action against the bailee may be one in which the measure of damages is not the full value of the goods, and then the court may order delivery of the goods, but require the bailor to pay the bailee a sum reflecting the difference. Under s. 3(7) the court may make an allowance in respect of any improvements made to the goods by the defendant whilst they were in his possession.

Remedies

Reference has already been made to the form of judgment where goods are detained. So far as wrongful interference by trespass and by conversion are concerned, the remedy is damages. The value of the goods is usually determined at the date of conversion. When a plaintiff has a claim for conversion he cannot delay the issue of his writ and the duty to mitigate loss operates. If the goods decrease in value between the date of the conversion and the time the court gives judgment, the plaintiff will normally still recover the value at the date of conversion. (*Rhodes* v. *Moules*, [1895] 1 Ch. 236.)

Section 5 of the 1977 Act makes it clear that a plaintiff's title to the goods is not extinguished by a judgment for damages but only when the judgment has been paid. The judgment as such does not affect title.

Under s. 6 an allowance is available for an improvement in the goods. For example, where a person in good faith buys a stolen car and improves it he is entitled to an allowance for that improvement, and where a person in good faith buys the car from the improver and is sued in conversion by the true owner, the damages may be reduced to reflect the improvement. Section 7 deals with double liability, providing in particular that where as the result of enforcement of a double liability the claimant is unjustly enriched to any extent he shall be liable to reimburse the wrongdoer to that extent. For example, if a converter of goods pays damages first to a finder of the goods and then to the true owner, the finder is unjustly enriched unless he accounts over to the true owner, which he is required to do, and then the true owner is unjustly enriched and becomes liable to reimburse the converter of the goods.

Special damage for conversion may be awarded. Thus a carpenter whose tools are converted can recover his loss of wages. (*Bodley* v. *Reynolds*, (1846) 8 Q.B. 779.) Furthermore, in *Hillesden Securities Ltd* v. *Ryjack Ltd, The Times*, 21 January, 1983 the defendant converted a Rolls Royce car which he had hired from the plaintiff. It was held that he remained liable for the hiring charge until he returned it. This was £13,000, although the value of the Rolls Royce at the date of conversion was only £7500.

Finally, s. 2(3), Limitation Act, 1980 provides that once the six-year period of limitation has expired the plaintiff's title to the goods is extinguished. The Act also provides that if there are successive conversions over the same goods, whether by the same person or not, the cause of action is extinguished six years from the first conversion (S. 3(1), Limitation Act, 1980.)

Recaption

A person who is entitled to the possession of goods of which he has been wrongfully deprived may retake them after a demand for their return but must not use more than reasonable force. It is not clear whether he may enter upon the land of an innocent third party in order to recover the goods. It would seem lawful only after explanation and permission.

Replevin

Goods which have been taken by what is alleged to be unlawful distress, e.g. by a landlord for unpaid rent which is alleged by the tenant to have been paid, may be recovered by the owner giving security to the registrar of the county court that he will immediately bring an action to determine the legality of the distress. The registrar issues a warrant for the restitution of the goods.

NUISANCE

The tort of nuisance is of two types—public and private.

Public nuisance

This is some unlawful act or omission endangering or interfering with the lives, comfort, property, or common rights of the public, e.g. the obstruction of a highway (*A-G* v. *Gastonia Coaches*, 1976),[523] or the keeping of dangerous premises near a highway. A public nuisance is a crime for which the remedy is criminal proceedings brought by the Attorney-General. But it is actionable as a tort at the suit of a private individual if he has suffered peculiar damage over and above that suffered by the public as a whole. (*Campbell* v. *Paddington Borough Council*, 1911[416] and see *A-G* v. *Gastonia Coaches*, 1976.)[523]

Obstructions to the highway occur daily in our cities and towns, e.g. road repairs and scaffolding. However, these obstructions, being for reasonable purposes, are lawful unless they last for an excessive time. *Dangerous activities* carried on near to the highway may amount to a nuisance. Thus in *Castle* v. *St Augustine's Links*, 1922,[524] damages were awarded against a golf club to a taxi-driver who lost an eye when a golf ball was sliced from the course on to the highway; the hole being sufficiently close to the highway to constitute a public nuisance. With regard to *projections* on to the highway there is no liability for *things naturally on land*, e.g. trees, unless the person responsible for them knew, or ought to have known, that they were in a dangerous condition, as where a branch of a tree is rotten. However, liability appears to be strict in the case of *artificial projections*. (*Tarry* v. *Ashton*, 1876.)[525] However, where an action is brought for damages for personal injuries arising out of other forms of obstruction on the highway, it appears that fault is essential to liability. (*Dymond* v. *Pearce*, 1972.)[526] Thus in this respect the torts of nuisance and negligence are being drawn together.

Private nuisance

This is an unlawful interference with a man's use of his property or with his health, comfort or convenience, and such interference may vary according to the standard existing in his neighbourhood. It is a wrongful act causing material injury to property or sensible personal discomfort. In this connection injuries to *servitudes* may amount to private nuisance as where the defendant obstructs a right of way, or interferes with the plaintiff's water supply, access of air, light or support.

In considering whether an act or omission is a nuisance, the following points are relevant.

(i) There need be no direct injury to health
It is enough that a person has been prevented to an appreciable extent from enjoying the ordinary comforts of life.

(ii) The standard of comfort must be expected to vary with the district
There is no uniformity of standard between Park Lane and Poplar, although there may be common ground in some matters, e.g. light, since it requires the same amount of light to read in either place. However, where the alleged nuisance has caused *actual damage to property* it is no defence to show that the district concerned is of any particular type.

(iii) A person cannot take advantage of his peculiar sensitivity to noise and smells
There must be some give and take, and people cannot expect the same amenities in an industrial town as they might enjoy in the country.

(iv) The utility of the alleged nuisance has no bearing on the question
Pigstyes and breweries may be regarded by the community as very necessary, but if they infringe a man's right to the ordinary comforts of life, they are nuisances. Consent cannot be implied from the fact that the plaintiff came to the premises knowing that the nuisance was in existence. (*Bliss* v. *Hall*, 1838.)[527] Nor is the fact that the nuisance arises out of the conferment of a public benefit a defence in the ordinary way. (*Adams* v. *Ursell*, 1913[528] and *Dunton* v. *Dover District Council*, 1977.)[529]

(v) The modes of annoyance are infinitely various
They may include such things as bell-ringing, circus performing, the excessive use of the radio, spreading tree roots, opening a sex shop in a residential area (*Laws* v. *Florinplace*, [1981] 1 All E.R. 659) and many others. (See *Christie* v. *Davey*, 1893.)[530] It should also be noted that picketing a highway may be actionable as a nuisance and an injunction may be granted to prevent it. (*Hubbard* v. *Pitt*, 1975.)[531]

(vi) A nuisance may result from the acts of several wrongdoers
Any one of them may be proceeded against, and he cannot plead in excuse that the nuisance was a joint effort, although he has a right of contribution against joint tortfeasors for the damages which might be assessed against him.

(vii) Duration of the act
Although the acts complained of in nuisance are usually continuous, e.g. the constant emission of pungent smells from a factory, an act may constitute a nuisance even though it is temporary or instantaneous as in the case of an explosion. (*British Celanese* v. *Hunt*, 1969.)[532] The duration of the act complained of has a bearing upon the remedy which is appropriate and the court will not often grant an injunction in respect of a temporary nuisance because damages are an adequate remedy. Furthermore, a temporary nuisance may be too trivial to be actionable.

(viii) Sometimes malice or evil motive may become the gist of the offence
Malice or motive may be evidence that the defendant was not using his property in a lawful way. (*Hollywood Silver Fox Farm* v. *Emmett*, 1936.)[533]

(ix) It is possible to acquire the right to create a private nuisance by prescription
That is by twenty years' continuous operation since the act complained

of first constituted a nuisance. There is no corresponding right in respect of a public nuisance. Since a public nuisance is a crime, no length of time will make it legitimate.

Nuisance is primarily a wrong to property, but even where there is no physical damage the court can award compensation for annoyance and discomfort. (*Bone* v. *Seale*, 1975.)[534] A claim in private nuisance cannot be based solely upon personal injury, where an action would be in negligence. Claims for personal injuries can be made in public nuisance, though as we have seen in *Dymond* v. *Pearce*, 1972,[526] *fault* in the defendant is generally required which makes the action in nuisance similar to that in negligence.

Furthermore, the tort of nuisance refers to the unreasonable use of property and is not a matter of reasonable care (compare negligence). Thus the defendant's use of his property may be offensive and constitute a nuisance no matter how careful he is.

Parties to sue or be sued

The occupant of the property affected by the nuisance is the person who should bring the action (*Malone* v. *Laskey*, 1907),[535] but a landlord may sue if the nuisance is effecting a permanent injury to his property e.g. where the defendant is erecting a building which infringes the landlord's right to ancient lights.

Regarding liability, it is a general rule that the person who creates the nuisance is liable, and this will generally be the occupier. But a landlord may be liable, as a joint tortfeasor with his tenant, (*a*) if he created the nuisance and then leased the property (*Wilchick* v. *Marks*, 1934,[536] and *Mint* v. *Good*, 1951),[537] or (*b*) where the nuisance was due to the landlord's authorizing the tenant expressly or impliedly to create (*Harris* v. *James*, 1876[538] and *Smith* v. *Scott*, 1972)[539] or continue (*Brew Bros* v. *Snax (Ross)*, 1969)[540] the nuisance; or (*c*) where the landlord knew or ought to have known of the nuisance before he let the premises. An occupier must abate a nuisance which was on the premises before he took them over, or is placed there afterwards, even by trespassers, provided that the occupier knows or ought to have known of the nuisance. (*Sedleigh-Denfield* v. *O'Callagan*, 1940.)[541] An occupier is also liable for nuisance arising out of the operations of an independent contractor engaged in work on the premises where there is a special danger of nuisance arising from the nature of the works being carried out, e.g. extensive tunnelling operations. (*Bower* v. *Peate*, 1876,[434] and *Padbury* v. *Holliday*, 1912.)[436].

Remedies

The remedies for nuisance are three in number—

(*a*) The injured party may abate the nuisance, that is, remove it, provided that no unnecessary damage is caused, that no injury arises to an innocent third party, e.g. a tenant, and that, where entry on the defendant's land is necessary, a notice requesting the removal of the nuisance has first been given.

(b) He may sue for damages.

(c) He may seek an injunction if (i) damages would be an insufficient remedy; and (ii) the nuisance is a continuing nuisance, e.g. smoke frequently emitted from a chimney. Where a continuing actionable nuisance is proved, only in exceptional circumstances should the court award damages in lieu of an injunction. (*Kennaway* v. *Thompson*, 1980.)[542]

Defences

Certain defences are available to a person who is charged with committing the nuisance—

(a) The injury is trivial. The legal maxim is: *De minimis non curat lex.* (The law does not concern itself with trifles.) Such a case would be an extremely short exposure to fumes from road repairs.

(b) The so-called nuisance arose from the lawful use of the land. (*Bradford Corporation* v. *Pickles*, 1895.)[402]

(c) The nuisance was covered by statutory authority, under the general principles elucidated under the defence of statutory authority.

(d) The person committing the alleged nuisance has acquired a prescriptive right through twenty years' user to do what is complained of. (*Sturges* v. *Bridgman*, 1879.)[543]

(e) The character of the neighbourhood is such that the act, while it might be a nuisance elsewhere, cannot be regarded as such in that particular district.

(f) Consent of the plaintiff is a possible defence but consent will not be implied simply because the plaintiff came to the premises knowing that the nuisance was in existence. (*Bliss* v. *Hall*, 1838.)[527]

Remoteness of damage

For the purpose of deciding problems of remoteness of damage the Privy Council held in *The Wagon Mound* (No. 2), [1966] 2 All E.R. 709 (see p. 769), that in a case of nuisance, as of negligence, it is not enough that the damage was a direct result of the nuisance if the injury was not *foreseeable*. Thus in *Lamb* v. *Camden London Borough Council*, [1981] 2 All E.R. 408 the plaintiffs owned a house which had been let furnished but because of local council work a water main nearby was broken and escaping water severely damaged the house. The tenant left and the house was then unoccupied. While it was empty squatters entered and caused extensive damage before they were evicted. The defendants admitted liability in nuisance and on the issue of the squatters' damage the Court of Appeal held that it was too remote to form part of any damages. (See also *British Celanese* v. *Hunt*, 1969[532] and *Page Motors* v. *Epsom and Ewell Borough Council*, 1981, p. 800.)

Statutory intervention

We have been discussing the civil law of nuisance. However, there is also the Public Health (Recurring Nuisances) Act, 1969, which can be effective in suppressing noisy parties and the like. Under the Act a Public Health Inspector can be asked to visit the premises and issue a Prohibition Notice. If the situation is unchanged after two hours the local council may initiate a prosecution.

In addition, the most satisfactory way of tackling a noise nuisance is usually under s. 59 of the Control of Pollution Act, 1974. This section allows a complaint to be made to a magistrates' court. If the complaint is proved the magistrates will make an abatement order. If that order is not complied with, an offence is committed, attracting a fine of up to £2000 and up to £50 for each day after conviction on which the offence continues. Alternatively, use may be made of s. 58 of the 1974 Act. This gives local authorities power to deal with noise from fixed premises, including land, which they consider amounts to a statutory nuisance. The powers apply not only to control existing noise but also where a noise is expected to occur or recur. For legal purposes 'noise' also includes vibration. A complaint is initiated through the environmental health department of the local authority.

Furthermore, since it is uncertain whether the common law has any rules controlling the spread of weeds (see *Giles* v. *Walker* 1890, p. 834) reference should be made to the Weeds Act, 1959. Where any one of five specified weeds is out of control the Minister of Agriculture can call on the occupier of the land concerned to take action to stop them from spreading. The Minister can get the work done himself if the occupier defaults, and prosecute the occupier.

NEGLIGENCE

In ordinary language negligence may simply mean not done intentionally, e.g. the negligent publication of a libel. But while negligence may be one factor or ingredient in another tort, it is also a specific and independent tort with which we are now concerned.

The tort of negligence has three ingredients and to succeed in an action the plaintiff must show (i) the existence of a duty to take care which was owed to him by the defendant, (ii) breach of such duty by the defendant, and (iii) resulting damage to the plaintiff.

(i) The duty of care

Whether a duty of care exists or not is a question of law for the judge to decide, and it is necessary to know how this is done. The law of contract dominated the legal scene in the nineteenth century and this affected the law of torts. The judges, influenced by the doctrine of privity of contract, used it to establish the existence of a duty of care in negligence in those cases where a contract existed by laying down the principle that, if A is contractually liable to B, he cannot simultaneously be liable to C in tort for the same act or omission. (*Earl* v. *Lubbock*, 1905.)[544]

The House of Lords in *Donoghue* v. *Stevenson*, 1932,[399] dispelled the confusion caused by the application of the doctrine of privity of contract where physical injury is caused to the plaintiff by the defendant's negligent act. In this case Lord Atkin formulated what has now become the classic test for establishing a duty of care when he said—

> You must take reasonable care to avoid acts or omissions which you can reasonably foresee would be likely to injury your neighbour. Who then is my neighbour? The answer seems to be persons who are so closely and directly affected by my act that I ought reasonably to have them in contemplation as being affected when I am directing my mind to the acts or omissions which are called in question.

It will be seen, therefore, that the duty of care is established by putting in the defendant's place a hypothetical 'reasonable man' and deciding whether the reasonable man would have foreseen the likelihood or probability of injury, not its mere possibility. The test is objective not subjective, and the effect of its application is that a person is not liable for every injury which results from his carelessness. There must be a duty of care. (*Bourhill* v. *Young*, 1943.)[489]

Nevertheless, new duties are established from time to time by case law. As we have seen, Lord Macmillan stated in *Donoghue* v. *Stevenson*, 1932[399] 'the categories of negligence are never closed'. However, there is always the requirement of foresight, i.e. the plaintiff must be within the area of foreseeable danger. (*Bourhill* v. *Young*, 1943.)[489]

Furthermore, there is, in general terms, no liability for failure to act, i.e. for omissions. (*Argy Trading Development Co. Ltd* v. *Lapid Developments Ltd*, 1977.)[545] (But see negligent exercise of statutory powers, below.)

As regards more recent developments the tendency has been to widen liability in negligence to the point where it is more a matter of public policy whether a particular defendant is liable. The view has been, in some cases, that the court can assume objective foresight and then see whether there is anything to prevent the defendant from being liable, e.g. a very wide liability which is currently not insured against may not be imposed as contrary to public policy.

One major development in this direction is the judgment of Lord Reid in *Home Office* v. *Dorset Yacht Club Co. Ltd*, (1970)[550]. This was an action by the owner of a yacht which was damaged by runaway Borstal boys who escaped while the three officers in charge of them were, contrary to instructions, in bed. In holding that the Home Office owed a duty of care to the owner of the yacht, Lord Reid made the following general comment regarding duty of care. '*Donoghue* v. *Stevenson* may be regarded as a milestone . . . It will require qualification in new circumstances. But I think that the time has come when we can and should say that it ought to apply unless there is some justification or valid explanation for its exclusion.'

Further progress along these lines came in *Anns* v. *London Borough of Merton*, (1977)[551]. In that case, the plaintiffs held a lease of a block of flats built in 1962. Later, considerable settlement caused cracks and the tilting of floors. The plaintiffs blamed the builders and also the local council because, it was alleged, the council had not inspected the flats during building as the bye-laws required, so their shallow foundations were not detected. Their Lordships found that the local authority had a duty of care to the plaintiffs and made general comments on the duty of care.

Lord Wilberforce, in particular, took the remarks of Lord Reid (as mentioned) a stage further when he said: '. . . the position has now been reached that in order to establish that a duty of care arises in a particular situation, it is not necessary to bring the facts of that situation within those of previous situations in which a duty of care has been held to exist. Rather the question has to be approached in two stages.

First, one has to ask whether, as between the alleged wrongdoer and the person who has suffered damage there is a sufficient relationship of proximity or neighbourhood such that, in the reasonable contemplation of the former, carelessness on his part may be likely to cause damage to the latter, in which case a *prima facie* duty of care arises.

Second, if the first question is answered affirmatively, it is necessary to consider whether there are any considerations which ought to negate, or reduce or limit the scope of the duty or the class of person to whom it is owed or the damages to which any breach of it may give rise.'

It should be noted however that the Privy Council in *Yuen Kun Yeu* v. *A.G. of Hong Kong*, [1987] 2 All E.R. 705 and the House of Lords in *Curran* v. *Northern Ireland Co-Ownership Housing Association*, [1987] 2 W.L.R. 1043 pointed out the danger of assuming that the comments of Lord Wilberforce in *Anns* lead to a rule that objective foreseeability of itself automatically leads to a duty of care and that a defendant with objective foresight is therefore liable unless there are reasons, e.g. public policy, why he should not be so. The tendency since these cases will perhaps be less assumption of foresight and therefore duty of care.

Economic loss. An area of some difficulty, and in which there has been much development, is in the field of economic loss. Is there a duty to avoid causing foreseeable economic loss? The position is as follows—

(a) *Careless mis-statements*. These are considered in greater depth at p. 400. However, broadly speaking, a person who makes a careless statement which causes economic loss to a plaintiff within the area of his *foresight* may be liable to compensate that plaintiff for economic loss.

(b) *Parasitical damages*. Damages for economic loss may be awarded if there is foreseeable physical injury to the plaintiff or his property, though issues of public policy still govern where the line is to be drawn. (See *Weller & Co.* v. *Foot and Mouth Disease Research Institute*, 1965,[546] *SCM (UK) Ltd* v. *W. J. Whittall & Sons Ltd*, 1970,[547] *Spartan Steel & Alloys Ltd* v. *Martin & Co. Ltd*, 1972,[548] and *Electrochrome Ltd* v. *Welsh Plastics Ltd*, 1968.)[401]

(c) *The Junior Books case*. In *Junior Books Ltd* v. *Veitchi Co. Ltd*, 1982[549] the House of Lords decided that the plaintiffs could recover economic loss which was not parasitical because in that case there was no physical injury to the plaintiff or his property, but merely faulty work.

However, it would be unwise to assume that injury to person or property is now never necessary. There was a very close proximity in terms of foresight of injury between the parties in *Junior Books* and as a matter of public policy it may still be necessary to restrict liability in cases such as *Weller*[546] where liability was potentially endless. There have, in more recent times, been a considerable number of restrictions placed on *Junior Books* almost confining it to its own facts. (See p. 806.)

Negligent exercise of statutory powers. There has been some development of the duty of care in this area. It seems that failure by a public authority to exercise a power may give rise to an action for damages. This is a form of liability for an omission. (See *Home Office* v. *Dorset Yacht Co. Ltd*, 1970[550] and *Anns* v. *Merton London Borough Council*, 1977.)[551]

(ii) Breach of the duty

If a duty of care is established as a matter of law, whether or not the defendant was in breach of that duty is a matter to be decided by the judge on the facts of the case, though the standard required, i.e. that of acting as a reasonable man, is a *legal standard*.

Here we are concerned with how much care the defendant must take. It is obvious that if motorists did not take out their cars many lives would be saved, and yet it is not negligent to drive a car. Once again the test is to place the 'reasonable man' in the defendant's position. It is an objective test and was thus stated by Baron Alderson in *Blyth* v. *Birmingham Waterworks Co.* (1856), 11 Ex. 781

> Negligence is the omission to do something which a reasonable man guided upon those considerations which ordinarily regulate the conduct of human affairs would do, or doing something which a prudent and reasonable man would not do.

The standard required is not that of a particularly conscientious man but that of the average prudent man in the eyes of the court. (*Daniels* v. *White and Sons*, 1938[552] but see *Hill* v. *J. Crowe*, 1977.)[553] It has been said that the reasonable man is the man on the Clapham omnibus, but it should not be thought that the average prudent man has a low standard of care. Most of us behave unreasonably from time to time, and if during one of these lapses a person suffers injury, it will be no good our pleading that we are usually reasonable men.

When a person has undertaken a duty which requires extraordinary skill, he will be expected to use a higher standard of care. For example, one would expect from a builder the degree of skill appropriate to a reasonably competent member of his trade (*Greaves & Co.* v. *Baynham Meikle & Partners*, 1974)[554] and from a doctor or surgeon, accountant or solicitor also an objective standard of competence. Such a person may, therefore, be negligent even though he does his best.

However, in the case of medical practitioners it seems that because allegations of negligence in the medical context are more frequent and serious, a high standard of proof of negligence is required so that an error of clinical judgment does not of itself amount to negligence. Thus in *Whitehouse* v. *Jordan*, [1981] 1 All E.R. 267 the plaintiff was born with severe brain damage following a difficult birth and sued the defendant, a senior hospital registrar, for damages. The defendant had used forceps to assist delivery of the plaintiff and it was alleged that he pulled too hard and too long. It was held by the Court of Appeal and later by the House of Lords that if the damage had indeed been caused by the defendant's use of forceps the most that could be said with the benefit of hindsight was that he had made an error of clinical judgment which did not of itself amount to negligence, so that the plaintiff's claim failed.

Barristers provide an exception to the above rule because no action lies against them for negligence in conducting a case (*Rondel* v. *Worsley*, 1967)[24] though it does in respect of preparatory work or advice unless it is pre-trial work intimately connected with the trial itself. (*Saif Ali* v. *Sydney Mitchell & Co.*, 1978.)[23] In other cases public policy may also require a higher standard of care than the defendant possesses so that again he may be negligent even though he does his best. Thus in *Nettleship* v. *Weston*, 1971[452] the plaintiff, who was a non-professional driving instructor, was injured when he was a passenger in the defendant learner-driver's car which crashed into a lamp-standard. The Court of Appeal held that the defendant was liable to the plaintiff for negligence and both Lord Denning and Megaw, L.J. said that the standard of care in such circumstances was the same as that owed by a non-learner-driver to the injured passenger, i.e. the standard of the experienced and competent driver. This, apparently, was essential to avoid a doctrine of 'varying standards' per Megaw, L.J. at p. 592. According to Lord Denning, public policy was also involved. In the course of his judgment he said: 'The high standard thus imposed by the judges is, I believe, largely the result of the policy of the Road Traffic Acts. Parliament requires every driver to be insured against third party risks. The reason is so that a person injured by a motor car should not be left to bear the loss on his own, but should be compensated out of the insurance fund. . . . But the injured person is only able to recover if the driver is liable in law. So the judges see to it that he is liable, unless he can prove care and skill of a high standard. . . .' Lord Denning's words have even more point now that passenger risk insurance is compulsory by law.

It should be noted that if precautions are taken which would have been reasonable in the case of persons possessed of the usual faculties of sight and hearing, this will be sufficient to absolve a person who does injury to those not possessed of such faculties, so long as he was not aware of their infirmity. (*Paris* v. *Stepney Borough Council*, 1951.)[555] However, persons engaged on operations on the *highway* must act reasonably so as not to cause damage to those who are using the highway, including blind people. (*Haley* v. *London Electricity Board*, 1964.)[556] Furthermore, the court will take into account the importance of the object which the defendant was trying to achieve (*Watt* v. *Hertfordshire County Council*, 1954)[557] and whether it was practicable and necessary for the defendant to have taken the precautions which the plaintiff alleged should have been taken. (*Latimer* v. *A.E.C. Ltd*, 1953.)[558]

(iii) Resulting damage to the plaintiff

It is necessary for the plaintiff to show that he has suffered some loss, since negligence is not actionable *per se* (in itself). A breach of contract with no loss will at least give an action for nominal damages but not so in tort. The major problem arising here is the question of remoteness of damage which was dealt with earlier in the chapter. The judge decides the measure of general damages.

Res ipsa loquitur

Although the burden of proof in negligence normally lies on the plaintiff, there is a principle known as *res ipsa loquitur* (the thing speaks for itself), and where the principle applies the court is prepared to lighten his burden. The principle applies wherever it is so unlikely that such an accident would have happened without the negligence of the defendant that the court could find, without further evidence, that it was so caused. It seems also to be a commonsense rule in that there is no point in asking the plaintiff to prove negligence because he has no view of what happened. If two cars collide on a public road, at least the drivers have a view of what happened prior to the crash but when, for example, a barrel falls out of a warehouse on to A he has no view at all of the happenings leading to the impact.

However, two conditions must be satisfied—

(*a*) the thing or activity causing the harm must be wholly under the control of the defendant or his servants (*Easson* v. *L.N.E. Rly Co.*, 1944)[559] and

(b) the accident must be one which would not have happened if proper care had been exercised. (*Byrne* v. *Boadle*, 1863[560] and *Scott* v. *London & St Katherine Docks Co.*, 1865.)[561]

There is no value in the principle where there is no indication of who is the person likely to have been negligent, as where the events leading up to the accident were, or might well have been, under the control of others besides the defendant. (*Roe* v. *Minister of Health*, 1954.)[562]

It should be noted that just because the principle *res ipsa loquitur* applies, it is not certain that the plaintiff will succeed; the court is not bound to find the defendant negligent. The defendant may be able to prove how the accident happened and that he was not negligent. (*Pearson* v. *North Western Gas Board*, 1968.)[563] He may not know how the accident happened but he may be able to prove that it could not have arisen from his negligence. Finally, he may suggest ways in which the accident could have happened without his negligence, and the court may find his explanations convincing. If a tile falls off Y's roof and injures X who is lawfully on the highway below, this would probably be a situation in which *res ipsa loquitur* would apply. But if Y can show that at the time an explosion had occurred nearby and this had probably dislodged the tile, and the court is impressed by this explanation of the event, the burden of proof reverts to X. However, it is not enough to offer purely hypothetical explanations (*Moore* v. *R. Fox and Sons*, [1956] 1 All E.R. 182), nor is it sufficient to explain how the accident happened unless the explanation also shows that the defendant was not negligent. (*Colvilles* v. *Devine*, [1969] 2 All E.R.53.)

If the defendant successfully rebuts the presumption of *res ipsa loquitur* the plaintiff has to establish his case by positive evidence. He will probably be unable to do this by the very nature and cause of the accident and the chances are that he may lose his claim. If he had had such positive evidence he would probably have adduced it in the first place and not relied on the maxim at all.

Contributory negligence

Sometimes when an accident occurs, both parties have been negligent and this raises the doctrine of *contributory negligence*. At one time a plaintiff guilty of contributory negligence could not recover any damages unless the defendant could, with reasonable care, have avoided the consequences of the plaintiff's contributory want of care. Thus the courts were often concerned to find out who had the last chance of avoiding the accident, and this led to some unsatisfactory decisions.

Now, however, under the Law Reform (Contributory Negligence) Act, 1945, liability is apportionable between plaintiff and defendant. The claim is not defeated but damages may be reduced according to the degree of fault of the plaintiff. A person may contribute to the *damage* he suffers although he is not to *blame* for the accident. Thus failure by a plaintiff to wear a crash helmet on a motor cycle or moped may reduce the damages he obtains on the ground of contributory negligence. (*O'Connell* v. *Jackson*, 1971.)[564] Similarly, failure by a plaintiff to wear a seat belt in a motor car may also reduce damages on the grounds of contributory negligence. (*Froom* v. *Butcher*, [1975] 3 All E.R. 520. (See below)). The defence of contributory negligence also applies to an action brought under the Fatal Accidents Act. Thus a wife whose husband failed to wear a seat belt and was thrown out of the van he was driving and killed had her damages reduced by one-fifth. (*Purnell* v. *Shields*, [1973] R.T.R. 414.)

Where the defendant is insured against the injury he has caused, which is often the case, the effect of a finding of contributory negligence is in a sense to punish the plaintiff. There have been suggestions in case law that the rule should be abolished where the defendant is insured since the doctrine merely saves the insurance company money. However, in *Froom* v. *Butcher*, [1975] 3 All E.R. 520, Lord Denning disapproved of these cases and held that where injuries resulting from a road accident would have been prevented or lessened if a fitted seat belt had been worn, the failure to wear a seat belt amounted to contributory negligence on the part of the plaintiff and damages awarded should therefore be reduced. In consequence Lord Denning has produced an additional definition of contributory negligence so that there are two, *viz.*—

(i) to contribute to the accident, which is the old view of contributory negligence; and

(ii) to contribute to the resulting damage, which is a new concept. Furthermore in *Froom* Lord Denning laid down a rather precise formula for contributory negligence in order to introduce as much certainty as possible in road traffic cases and reduce the number of trials, by saying that if failure to wear a seat belt by a front seat passenger or driver would have made no difference, then nothing should be taken off the damages. If it would have prevented the accident altogether the damages should be reduced by 25%, and if the accident would have been less severe the damages should be reduced by 15%, though exemptions would be made, said Lord Denning, for pregnant women and those who were very fat.

Since 1983 it has been a criminal offence for the driver and front-seat passenger not to wear seat belts. The courts may therefore reduce still further the damages where a seat belt is not worn. It is thought unlikely that they will refuse to give damages altogether because the plaintiff is breaking the law, i.e. the defence will probably not be able to raise *ex turpi causa* (see p. 275) as a complete defence.

It should be mentioned that a young child will seldom, if ever, be guilty of contributory negligence (*Jones* v. *Lawrence*, 1969.)[565] Furthermore, the contributory negligence of an adult who happened to be with the child is no defence to an action brought by the child. (*Oliver* v. *Birmingham Bus Co.*, 1932.)[566]

Furthermore, it was held in *Yianni* v. *Edwin Evans & Sons*, [1981] 3 All E.R. 592 that a house buyer who relies on a valuation of the property he is buying prepared by a building society surveyor is not contributorily negligent because he has not had the property surveyed by another independent surveyor employed by himself.

The doctrine of alternative danger or the 'dilemma principle'
It sometimes happens that a person is injured in anticipating negligence. If a passenger jumps off a bus which he believes to be out of control, and breaks his leg in so doing, he is not prejudiced by the fact that the driver later regains control and the anticipated accident is averted. He is not deprived of his remedy. This is sometimes referred to as the *doctrine of alternative danger*, and an act done in the agony of the moment cannot be treated as contributory negligence. Thus in *Jones* v. *Boyce*, (1816) 1 Starkie 493, in a coach accident, the plantiff was placed by the negligence of the defendant in a perilous alternative either to jump or not to jump. He jumped off the coach and was injured and it transpired that had he kept his seat he would have escaped. However, he was able to recover from the defendant because he had acted reasonably and in the apprehension of danger.

Statutory duties

Sometimes a particular duty of care is laid upon a person by statute, e.g. the duty laid on an employer as to guarding machinery under safety legislation. Such duties are high and very often absolute, though the employer can plead contributory negligence as a defence. In addition, where there is a breach of a statutory duty, it must be shown that the duty is owed to the plaintiff personally and not to the public as a whole. (*Atkinson* v. *Newcastle Waterworks Co.*, 1877.)[567]

A conditional statutory power saying that the person upon whom it is conferred may act, cannot be converted into a statutory duty which says he must act. Thus in *East Suffolk Rivers Catchment Board* v. *Kent*, [1940] 4 All E.R. 527, a river catchment board, which had a power to repair river banks, could not be sued successfully for failing to do so on the grounds that a statutory duty had been breached. However, this does not preclude an action in negligence if failure to exercise a power falls foul of a common law duty to conduct oneself with reasonable care so as not to injure persons liable to be affected by one's conduct. (See *Anns* v. *Merton London Borough Council*, 1977.)[551] However, where a statute prescribes provision to prevent damage, if an action is brought, the harm resulting from the breach of duty must be of the type contemplated by the statute. (*Gorris* v. *Scott*, 1874,[568] and *Lane* v. *London Electricity Board*, 1955.)[40]

LIABILITY FOR MIS-STATEMENTS

We have already considered the major principles of the *tort of deceit* in Chapter 7 (p. 237) but it is perhaps worth repeating that deceit occurs where there is a false statement of fact made knowing it to be false, or believing it to be false, or recklessly not caring whether it be true or false. If it is made with the intention that it should be acted upon by another and is so acted upon there are grounds for an action. It will be recalled that the definition of deceit (or fraud) and the requirement of intention were laid down in *Derry* v. *Peek*, 1889)[214]

It should also be noted that fraudulent misrepresentations as to a person's *credit* are not actionable unless they are in writing and signed by the defendant. (Lord Tenterden's Act, 1828.) However, the Act does not apply to negligent mis-statements. (*Anderson (W.B.) & Sons* v. *Rhodes (Liverpool)*, 1967.)[569]

Where monetary loss results from the defendant's negligent mis-statements rather than his acts, it was, but is now no longer, necessary to prove the existence of a contract or fiduciary relationship in order to establish a duty of care (*Candler* v. *Crane, Christmas & Co.*, 1951,[570] *Hedley Byrne & Co. Ltd* v *Heller & Partners Ltd*, 1963[215] and *Anderson (W.B.) & Sons* v. *Rhodes (Liverpool)*, 1967)[569] and the same is true if the plaintiff receives physical injuries as a result of the defendant's careless instructions. (*Clayton* v. *Woodman & Son (Builders) Ltd*, 1961.)[571]

However, both under *Candler*[570] and *Hedley Byrne*[215] the parties were required to be in a 'special relationship'. This meant in practice that the defendant had to *know* that his careless statement would be relied upon by a *known* plaintiff, as was the case in *Candler* and *Hedley Byrne*.

For a while, also, it was thought that liability could be placed only upon those who were in business to advise or had, or claimed, a special skill in a particular area, such as solicitors and accountants. (See *Mutual Life Assurance* v. *Evatt*, 1971.)[572] This restriction was removed by the decision in *Esso Petroleum* v. *Mardon*, 1976.[573]

Furthermore, in *JEB Fasteners* v. *Marks Bloom & Co.*, 1981[574] the law moved from a test of *knowledge* to a test of *foresight* and increased the scope of potential liability for careless mis-statements.

The need for the plaintiff to be a person who *has relied on the statement* was removed in *Ross* v. *Caunters*, [1979] 3 All E.R. 580 where a solicitor who had drafted a will for a testator failed to warn him that it should not be witnessed by the spouse of the beneficiary. (This causes the gift to fail.) The will was attested by the husband of the plaintiff who was a beneficiary and she lost her gift. It was held that the solicitor was liable in negligence to the plaintiff for economic loss. The solicitor's duty was not merely to the testator.

The rule also applies to render a local authority liable in damages when erroneous information is given to a person asking for search of the local land register. (*Coats Patons (Retail)* v. *Birmingham Corporation*, (1971) 69 L.G.R. 356). An arbitrator is generally thought to enjoy the same immunity as a judge, at least when he is exercising the judicial function of deciding a dispute rather than merely answering a question. A valuer, e.g. an auditor who on a sale negligently values shares in a private company, may also be immune if the parties who appoint him so agree, though otherwise he is liable. However, the House of Lords held in *Sutcliffe* v. *Thackrah*, (1974)[575] that when an architect issues an interim certificate stating that building work has been satisfactorily done, he does not act as an arbitrator and can therefore be made liable. Furthermore a statement will not be actionable under *Hedley Byrne* unless it amounts to *advice*. (*McInerny* v. *Lloyds Bank*, 1973.)[576]

Excluding and avoiding liability

As we have seen the maker of the statement can avoid liability by an express disclaimer. (*Hedley Byrne & Co. Ltd* v. *Heller and Partners Ltd*, 1963.)[215] However, since the Unfair Contract Terms Act, 1977 applies to exclusion of liability in situations where there is not necessarily a contract between the parties, a disclaimer may not be effective unless it is regarded by a court as reasonable in the circumstances of the case. (See *Smith* v. *Bush*, (1987) at p. 636.)

The most practical suggestion that can be made in terms of avoiding liability is for a professional person e.g. an accountant, to follow strictly the recommendations of the professional bodies in the field, e.g. the many accounting standards and other published material. If this is done the accountant or other professional person will at least have the advantage of the judgment of McNair, J. in *Bolam* v. *Friern Hospital Management Committee*, [1957] 2 All E.R. 118. He said in connection with doctors: 'A doctor is not guilty of negligence if he has acted in accordance with a practice accepted as proper by a responsible body of medical men skilled in that particular art . . . merely because there is a body of opinion who would take a contrary view'. The statement is, of course, equally applicable to other professions.

We have already seen in Chapter 7 (p. 241) that damages for negligent mis-statements are also obtainable—

(i) under the Misrepresentation Act, 1967, provided the parties are in a pre-contractual relationship;

(ii) where the parties are in a fiduciary relationship, e.g. solicitor and client;

(iii) under s. 150 of the Financial Services Act, 1986 directors and others are liable for negligent mis-statements in prospectuses, though they have certain defences under s. 151. (See p. 243.)

Injurious falsehood, which is concerned with such matters as slander of goods, is briefly considered on p. 420.

OCCUPIERS' LIABILITY

The question of the liability of occupiers of premises to persons suffering injury thereon may be regarded as a further aspect of negligence. The occupier is the person who has *de facto* control of the premises or the possession of them; it is a question of fact in each case and does not depend entirely on title. It should also be noted that occupation may be *shared* between two or more persons, (*Wheat* v. *E. Lacon & Co. Ltd*, 1966)[577] and that an employer may be vicariously liable for the torts of an employee who is acting within the scope of his employment. Thus in *Stone* v. *Taffe*, [1974] 3 All E.R. 1016, the owner of an hotel was liable when the manager failed to ensure that there was adequate lighting on the premises so that a guest fell and was killed.

The Occupiers' Liability Act, 1957

A common duty of care is owed to all lawful visitors to premises, 'visitor' being a term which includes anyone to whom the occupier has given, or is deemed to have given, an invitation or permission to use the premises. It includes some persons who enter the premises by right of law, such as inspectors, but not those who cross land in pursuance of a public or private right of way. These are governed by the Occupiers' Liability Act, 1984 (see p. 404).

Implied permission to enter premises is a matter of fact to be decided in the circumstances of each case, and the burden of proof is upon the person who claims implied permission. However, persons who enter upon premises for purposes of business which they believe will be of interest to the occupier, as where they wish to sell him a product, have implied permission to enter even though their presence is distasteful to the occupier.

Under the Act, an occupier of premises owes to all visitors the duty to take such care as, in all the circumstances of the case, is necessary to see that the visitor will be reasonably safe in using the premises for the purpose for which he is invited or permitted to be there. If the visitor uses the premises for some other purpose, the occupier does not owe him the same duty; such a person is in effect a trespasser, and liability to him falls to be decided on that basis. (See below).

Under s. 2(1) of the 1957 Act the occupier may restrict or exclude his liability, by giving adequate warning or by contract. However, this section must be looked at in the light of the Unfair Contract Terms Act, 1977, which states that the common law duty of care in regard to liability for death or personal injury cannot be excluded in relation to business premises. In addition, liability for other loss or damage occurring on such premises can only be excluded where it is reasonable to do so.

Where the accident has arisen through the defective work of an independent contractor, the occupier can avoid liability by showing that he behaved reasonably in the selection of the contractor. (*Cook* v. *Broderip*, 1968.)[578]

The defence of *volenti non fit injuria* is available to the occupier, though he must show that the entrant assented to the risk, not that he merely knew of it: the entrant's knowledge is no longer a defence. (*Bunker* v. *Charles Brand & Son*, 1969.)[579]

The occupier may also raise the defence of *contributory negligence* by the entrant which, though not defeating his claim, may reduce damages.

Trespassers

The main case on an occupier's liability to a trespasser was *British Railways Board* v. *Herrington*, [1972] 1 All E.R. 749 in which the House of Lords was unanimous in deciding that there could be liability to a trespasser. Unfortunately the five judges concerned reached that decision in different ways and the matter was referred to the Law Commission. Eventually Parliament passed the Occupiers' Liability Act, 1984 which now governs the position of trespassers and certain other non-visitors.

Section 1 deals with the duty of an occupier to persons other than his visitors—this includes trespassers and persons entering land without the consent of the owner, but in exercise of a private right of way or public access. In these cases the occupier owes a duty, if he is aware of the danger which exists, or has reasonable grounds to believe that it exists. He must also know, or have reasonable grounds to believe that the non-visitor concerned is in the vicinity of the danger—whether he has lawful authority for being in that vicinity or not. Furthermore, the risk must be one which in all the circumstances of the case it is reasonable to expect the occupier to offer the non-visitor some protection against. It was held, for example, in *Proffit* v. *British Railways Board, The Times*, 4 February, 1984 that British Rail had no *general* duty to erect or maintain fences sufficient to keep trespassers out.

The duty is to take such care as is reasonable in all the circumstances of the case to see that the non-visitor does not suffer injury because of the danger concerned. The duty may be discharged by giving warning of the danger or taking steps to discourage person from incurring risk. Thus the defence of *volenti* is preserved.

Access to the countryside

Section 2 of the Occupiers' Liability Act, 1984 is designed to encourage access to the countryside. The Unfair Contract Terms Act, 1977 had discouraged landowners with, say, a mountain crag, or potholes on their land, from admitting the public thereto because of the difficulty of excluding liability which might result. Under the 1984 Act they can exclude liability for the dangerous state of the land provided they are prepared to allow the public to come on to it for nothing. So long as the actual letting in of the public is not part of a business, as where access for recreational or educational purposes is charged for, the letting in of the public for nothing will not constitute running a business for the purposes of the 1977 Act.

Children on premises

Dealings with children always demand a high degree of care, whether a person is sued in the capacity of an occupier of premises or not (*Yachuk* v. *Oliver Blais & Co. Ltd*, 1949.)[580] However, in the case of an occupier of premises, the duty towards children was rather different from the corresponding duty to adults. If, with knowledge of the trespass of children on his land, the occupier made no reasonable attempt to prevent such trespass, e.g. by repairing fences, and a child was injured by something on the land which was especially alluring to children e.g. turntables, escalators, bright and poisonous berries, then the occupier in general was liable, even though the child was on the face of it a trespasser. (*Gough* v. *National Coal Board*, 1954.)[581] The difference owed to child trespassers is no longer so great in view of the broader rules laid down in the Occupiers' Liability Act, 1984. However, it should be noted that what is adequate warning to an adult might not be so to a child. (*Mourton* v. *Poulter*, 1930[582] and *Pannett* v. *McGuinness & Co*, 1972.)[583] These rules will presumably apply to the warnings which the 1984 Act allows the occupier to give.

As regards landlord and tenant, s. 4 of the Occupiers' Liability Act, 1957, provided that a landlord would be liable to his tenants' visitors who were injured or whose goods were damaged on the demised premises because of some defect which resulted from his failure to repair. However, s. 4 only applied where the landlord was under an obligation express, implied or statutory to repair, but the Defective Premises Act, 1972 repeals s. 4 and places liability on a landlord who has merely reserved a right to enter and repair. A landlord who does not repair where he has no obligation to do so, nor a power of entry, has no liability, under the Act or at common law.

Thus, now that s. 4 of the 1957 Act is repealed, the landlord's liability is similar to his liability in nuisance. Of course, only an occupier can sue in nuisance but under the Defective Premises Act, 1972, the landlord is liable to all persons who might reasonably be expected to be affected by defects in the state of the premises. This covers not only the tenant, his family and his visitors, but also neighbours, passers-by and trespassers.

Furthermore, under the 1957 Act it became established that a landlord was only liable to his tenants' visitors if he had been notified of the defect by the tenant. However, s. 4(2) of the 1972 Act provides that the duty is owed where the landlord knew or ought to have known of the relevant defect, so notice given by the tenant is no longer essential. Where the lease or tenancy expressly imposes on the tenant a duty to inform the lessor of defects but the tenant fails to do so with the consequence that a third party is injured, then the landlord can still be sued provided it can be shown that he ought to have known of the defect but in this case he will have a right of indemnity against the tenant for what that may be worth.

Where the person injured is the tenant himself the 1972 Act allows a tenant to sue his landlord for breach of his statutory duty but then the lessor would be able to allege contributory negligence in that the tenant failed to notify him of the defect. Where, however, the defect was due to a tenant failing to carry out an obligation expressly imposed on him by the lease or tenancy, the landlord does not owe the tenant any duty, although he would still owe a duty to third parties if they were injured but in these circumstances could recover an indemnity or contribution from the tenant who would be a joint tortfeasor.

There is little a landlord can do to exclude or restrict his liability. Section 6(3) of the 1972 Act renders void any exclusion clause in a lease or tenancy agreement.

HIGHWAY AUTHORITIES

A highway authority is liable for damage which is caused by its *active misfeasance* and, under the Highways Act, 1980, for damage which arises from its failure to repair.

In an action for damages against a highway authority based upon its failure to repair, it is a defence to prove that the authority has in all the circumstances taken reasonable care to ensure that the highway was not dangerous. (*Griffiths* v. *Liverpool Corporation*, 1966.)[584]

DEFECTIVE PREMISES ACT, 1972

This Act brought about three major changes. In the first place a landlord's liability for defects in demised premises was increased. This has already been dealt with in occupiers' liability (see p. 405). Secondly, much of the common law immunity of a vendor or landlord for negligence was abolished. Thirdly, there is a statutory duty on those concerned with providing dwellings to do the work properly. Section 1 places a duty on builders and developers, sub-contractors, architects and local authorities to see that building contracts are carried out in a workmanlike, or where appropriate, professional manner with proper materials so that the dwelling is fit for habitation. It should be noted that this statutory duty is owed not merely to the immediate client but to everyone who acquires a legal or equitable interest in the dwelling. The liability does not, of course, last for ever. It is subject to the Limitation Act, though s. 1(5) of the 1972 Act provides that a cause of action accrues at the time when the dwelling was completed, but where further work has to be done to put right a fault then the cause of action accrues only when the further work is completed. This means that from that date a plaintiff has six years to start an action or three years where the defect has caused death or personal injury. Section 6(3) of the 1972 Act renders void any term of an agreement which purports to exclude or restrict this statutory duty.

Under s. 1(3) a mere agreement by a client to a particular design or specification being used does not discharge the builder or other persons involved from this statutory duty. Section 2 offers an alternative by providing that no action can be brought where a State-approved scheme has conferred rights on the first sale or letting to those who have or will have an interest in the property in respect of defects in the state of the dwelling. Such schemes can be approved or withdrawn by the Secretary of State by statutory instrument.

The National Housebuilders Registration Council scheme is approved under these arrangements and where an N.H.R.C. scheme is in operation it applies rather than the Act. The advantage of an N.H.R.C. scheme over the Act is that if the builder becomes bankrupt the Council compensates the claimant. Section 3 of the Act sweeps away most of the old common law immunity from liability for negligence which was formerly enjoyed by sellers of property and lessors of property; they are now liable within the wider rule of *Donoghue* v. *Stevenson*, 1932.[399] Thus under the 1972 Act the maxim *caveat emptor* no longer provides a defence to a claim of negligence against a vendor or lessor in respect of defects in the premises sold or let and this liability extends beyond the immediate purchaser or lessee and can be brought by others who buy or rent the property within the constraints of the Limitation Act, 1980 and s. 1(5) of the 1972 Act. Thus there is now a law against building or letting tumbledown properties.

EMPLOYER'S NEGLIGENCE

Where an employee's case is based on his employer's negligence *at common law*, he will have to prove that his injury was the result of the employer's breach of a duty of care. The employee is assisted in this task because certain specific duties of an employer were laid down by the House of Lords in the leading case of *Wilsons and Clyde Coal Co.* v. *English*, [1938] A.C. 57, and an employer must take reasonable care to provide—

  (i) *proper and safe plant and appliances* for the work;
  (ii) *a safe system of work* with adequate supervision and instruction;
  (iii) *safe premises*; and
  (iv) *a competent staff* of fellow employees.

The employer's duty is a personal one so that he remains liable even though he has delegated the performance of the duty to a competent independent contractor. Thus in *Paine* v. *Colne Valley Electricity Supply Co. Ltd*, [1938] 4 All E.R. 803, an employer was held liable for injuries to his employee caused by the failure of contractors to install sufficient insulation in an electrical kiosk.

However, in *Davie* v. *New Merton Board Mills*, [1958] 1 All E.R. 67, the House of Lords decided that an employer was not liable for damage caused by a defective implement purchased from a reputable manufacturer. The employee was thus left to sue the manufacturer and this could prove difficult where the manufacturer had left the country or gone out of business or could not for any other reason be identified. Now the Employer's Liability (Defective Equipment) Act, 1969, provides that an employee who is injured because of a defect in his employer's equipment can recover damages from the employer if he can show that the defect is due to the fault of some person, e.g. the manufacturer but if no one is at fault damages are not recoverable. Agreements by employees to contract out are void, and rights under the Act are *in addition* to common law rights. Thus, an injured employee can sue a third party such as a manufacturer if he wishes, e.g. as where the employer is insolvent, though the Employer's Liability (Compulsory Insurance) Act, 1969, requires employers to insure against their liability for personal injury to their employees. The injury must result from equipment provided for the employer's *business*. Thus, domestic servants injured by household equipment would not be covered.

There are numerous statutes which are designed to protect the health, and provide for the welfare and safety of employees. The relevance of such statutes for our present purposes is that where the breach of a statutory duty, e.g. failure to fence a dangerous machine, has caused injury to a worker, he may be able to sue his employer for damages by using the breach of statutory duty to establish the duty of care under the principles already discussed. (*Millard* v. *Serck Tubes Ltd*, 1969.)[585]

TORTS AGAINST BUSINESS INTERESTS

It is a tort knowingly to induce a person to *break his contract* with a third party whereby that party suffers damage. It is also an actionable wrong for two or more persons to combine together (*or conspire*) for the purpose of wilfully causing damage to the plaintiff. There is also an action for *passing off* which occurs where A represents his goods or services to be those of B.

Inducement of breach of contract

If A induces B to break his contract with C, C can sue A. (*Lumley* v. *Gye*, 1853[586] and *Daily Mirror Newspapers* v. *Gardner*, 1968.)[587]

Trade union activity often involves interference with contract and the position as regards the immunity or otherwise of trade unions in this context has already been considered at p. 176.

Conspiracy

Where two or more persons act without lawful justification for the purpose of wilfully causing damage to the plaintiff and actual damage results, they commit the tort of conspiracy. The tort was fully considered in *Crofter Hand Woven Harris Tweed Co. Ltd* v. *Veitch*, 1942,[588] where the following principles were laid down—

    (i) the tort covers acts which would be *lawful if done by one person*;
    (ii) the combination will be justified if the predominant motive is self-

interest or protection of one's trade rather than injury to the plaintiff;
  (iii) damage to the plaintiff must be proved.

Passing off

Any person, company or other organization which carries on or proposes
to carry on business under a name calculated to deceive the public by
confusion with the name of an existing concern, commits the civil wrong
of *passing off* and will be restrained by injunction from doing so. Other
examples of passing off are the use of similar wrappings, identification
marks, and descriptions. Thus in *Bollinger* v. *Costa Brava Wine Co. Ltd*,
[1959] 3 All E.R. 800, the champagne producers of France objected to
the use of the name 'Spanish Champagne' to describe a sparkling wine
which was made in Spain and they were granted an injunction to prevent
the use of that term. The remedies other than an injunction are an action
for damages or for an account of profits.

DEFAMATION

Defamation is the publication of a statement which tends to lower a
person in the estimation of right-thinking members of society generally,
or which tends to make them shun or avoid that person. (*Byrne* v. *Deane*,
1937.)[589] In order to constitute a tort the statement must be false and
capable of bearing a defamatory meaning. Lord Reid in *Lewis* v. *Daily
Telegraph Ltd*, [1964] A.C. 234 at p. 258 indicated how a trial judge
might proceed in deciding whether words in their ordinary and natural
meaning are capable of bearing a defamatory meaning. 'What the ordinary man would infer without special knowledge has generally been
called the natural and ordinary meaning of the words. But the expression
is rather misleading in that it conceals the fact that there are two elements
in it. Sometimes it is not necessary to go beyond the words themselves,
as where the plaintiff has been called a thief or a murderer. But more
often the sting is not so much in the words themselves as in what the
ordinary man will infer from them, and that is also regarded as part of
their natural and ordinary meaning. . . . In this case it is, I think, sufficient to put the test in this way. Ordinary men and women have different
temperaments and outlooks. Some are unusually suspicious, and some
are unusually naive. One must try to envisage people between these two
extremes and see what is the most damaging meaning they would put on
the words in question.' In consequence the ordinary and natural meaning
of words is to be gathered not only by considering a strictly literal
interpretation but also from the inference which would be drawn by the
ordinary person who heard or read the words. Statements of *opinion* may
be defamatory; defamation is not confined to statements of fact. Thus in
Slazengers Ltd v. *Gibbs (C) & Co.* (1916), 33 T.L.R. 35 the defendants
stated during the First World War with Germany that the plaintiffs were

a German firm and would, in their opinion, be closed down. This statement of opinion was held to be defamatory of the plaintiffs.

Publication

The essence of the tort is the publication or communication of the falsehood to at least one person other than the person defamed, and other than the author's own husband or wife. Obviously publication to the plaintiff's spouse is defamatory. (*Wenman* v. *Ash*, (1853) 13 C.B. 836.) Every successive repetition of the statement is a fresh commission of the tort. Hence a defamatory statement written upon a postcard is published by the sender not only to the ultimate recipient but also to the postal officials through whose hands it may pass, and to every individual who legitimately handles the message, e.g. the secretary of the sender or the receiver. Similarly a libel contained in a newspaper is published by the reporter or author, and by the editor, the printer, the publisher, the proprietor, the wholesaler and the retail seller of that newspaper.

However, mere *mechanical distributors*, e.g. news vendors, booksellers, libraries, and the like, are not liable for their acts if they are unaware of the libel. However, if, as in *Vizetelly* v. *Mudie's Select Library Ltd*, [1900] 2 Q.B. 170, the library has overlooked a publisher's circular requesting return of copies of a libellous book, then there is liability. Persons lending books gratuitously or making gifts of them and tape and record dealers are also protected if unaware of the defamation. There is, of course, no need to consider the liability of the Post Office because it is exempt from any liability in tort in regard to postal packets. Nor is there any need to consider the liability of British Telecommunications because, although the telecommunications service is run under contract, there are excluding terms.

A defendant is not liable when a father opens his son's letter, (*Powell* v. *Gelstone*, [1916] 2 K.B. 615), or the butler opens the unsealed letter of his employer (*Huth* v. *Huth*, [1915] 3 K.B. 32). However, a correspondent should expect that clerks of the plaintiff, if a businessman, might in the ordinary course of business open letters addressed to him at his place of business and not marked 'personal' or 'private', etc., and such a correspondent is responsible for publication of a libel. It should also be noted that marking the communication 'private', 'personal', etc. may not prevent publication in the case of a very busy public figure such as the Prime Minister.

The third person who receives the defamatory statement must be capable of appreciating its significance. A written defamatory statement cannot be published to a blind man except in Braille. It is not publication to repeat a defamatory statement in a foreign language in the presence only of persons who cannot understand the tongue. But if X writes a defamatory statement to Y in (say) German, knowing that Y cannot understand it, X will be responsible for the publication which results from

Y's showing it to a linguist for the purpose of translation. In addition, to constitute publication, the person to whom the statement is communicated must understand that it refers to the plaintiff.

Who may be defamed?

No action lies at civil law for defaming a dead person, no matter how much it may annoy or upset his relatives. There may possibly be a prosecution for criminal libel if the necessary or natural effect of the words used is to render a breach of the peace imminent or probable.

As regards criticism of a trader, it is not defamatory merely to criticize his goods so long as the trader himself is not attacked. To say that a trader is bankrupt or insolvent is defamatory, but to say that he has ceased to be in business is not, for it does not reflect on his reputation (*Ratcliffe* v. *Evans*, [1892] 2 Q.B. 254). As we have seen, the law of defamation applies to corporations as its does to private individuals (*D & L Caterers Ltd.* v. *D'Anjou*, 1945).[414]

Libel and slander

The form of publication determines whether the tort committed is libel or slander. *Libel* is defamation in some permanent form; *slander* is a statement of a like kind in transient form. Pictures, effigies, writing and print are clearly libel. Speech is slander, and probably gestures and facial mimicry also. It has been held that a defamatory sound film was a libel (*Youssoupoff* v. *Metro-Goldwyn-Mayer Pictures*, 1934),[590] and legislation states that the broadcasting of defamatory matter is libel, whether sound or visual images are transmitted. (Defamation Act, 1952, s. 1.) (See also Theatres Act, 1968, p. 419.)

It is necessary to determine whether a tort is libel or slander for two reasons—

(i) Libel may be a crime as well as a tort;

(ii) Libel is actionable without the plaintiff having to prove special damage, i.e. pecuniary loss, whereas the plaintiff in an action for slander must as a general rule prove such special damage.

Slander is actionable *per se*, i.e. without proof of special damage in the following cases—

(a) Where there is an imputation that the plaintiff has been guilty of a criminal offence punishable with imprisonment, e.g. a statement such as 'I have enough information to put John in gaol'.

(b) Where there is an imputation of unchastity to any woman or girl (Slander of Women Act, 1891). This probably includes the case where a woman is alleged to have been the victim of rape (*Youssoupoff* v. *Metro-Goldwyn-Mayer Pictures Ltd*, 1934)[590], and seems to include a false allegation of lesbianism. (*Kerr* v. *Kennedy*, [1942] 1 K.B. 409).

(*c*) Where there is an imputation that the plaintiff is suffering from venereal disease and possibly other contagious diseases, e.g. leprosy or plague, which might cause him to be shunned and avoided. To say that a person *has suffered* from these diseases is not actionable *per se*.

(*d*) Where there have been words calculated to disparage the plaintiff in any office, profession, business or calling, by imputing dishonesty, unfitness or incompetence. (Defamation Act, 1952, s. 2.) However, it is not necessary for the plaintiff to show, e.g. that he has lost his job as a result, but the remark must be one likely to lower his standing in his trade or profession. Presumably, therefore, the old case of *Lumbe* v. *Allday*, (1831) 1 Cr. & J. 301 is still good law. In that case the court decided that a statement that a clerk employed by a gas company associated with whores was not actionable *per se* because his quality as a clerk would be in no way diminished by his association with prostitutes.

A suggestion, therefore, that a clergyman has been guilty of immoral conduct, or that a solicitor knows no law is actionable without proof of special damage. Spoken words in a broadcast are now actionable *per se* since they are regarded as libel. (Defamation Act, 1952, s. 1.)

It is not enough that the words are abusive. Thus to say of A, a bricklayer, that he is a legal ignoramus is not defamatory, though the same words would be defamatory if said of B, a solicitor. Difficulties might arise if the words were said of a chartered accountant who is required to have a knowledge of certain branches of the law.

To resolve problems such as these, two questions must be answered—

(i) Are the alleged words capable of bearing a meaning which is defamatory of the plaintiff? (This is a matter of law and is decided by the judge.)

(ii) If so, in this particular case are the words in fact defamatory of the plaintiff? (This is a matter of fact to be decided by the jury.)

What is special damage?

Some material loss is required, e.g. refusal of persons to enter into contracts with the plaintiff, or the loss of hospitality from friends who have provided food or drink on former occasions. (*Storey* v. *Challands*, (1837) 8 C. & P. 234.) Illness resulting from mental suffering is probably special damage. There were some early cases which said that it was not, but the better view is that these would not be followed now.

Innuendo

Cases may arise where the words are not at first sight defamatory, and only appear as such when the surrounding circumstances have been explained. Again a statement may be ironical, or accompanied by a wink or a gesture, or it may be ambiguous, e.g. the statement that 'X drinks'. In such a case the plaintiff must show that the words contain an innuendo or hidden meaning and that reasonable persons could, and in fact would, interpret the *words* used in a defamatory sense. (*Cassidy* v. *Daily Mirror*

Newspapers Ltd 1929.)[591] However, a newspaper article may be defamatory of a person whom readers only identify from their own knowledge of extrinsic facts. The defamation need not arise from words themselves. (*Morgan* v. *Odhams Press*, 1971.)[592] The judge decides as a matter of law whether the words are capable of bearing the innuendo alleged by the plaintiff, and the jury decides whether in fact the words do bear that meaning. (*Tolley* v. *Fry & Sons*, 1931.)[593] The meaning sought to be placed upon the words by the innuendo pleaded must be reasonable, and the court will not read into a statement a defamatory sense which is not there on a reasonable interpretation. (*Sim* v. *Stretch*, 1936.)[594] Furthermore, a plaintiff who claims that the innuendo to be drawn by those with special knowledge of the facts from a publication is libellous is bound to particularize those readers of the publication whom he alleges to have such special knowledge. (*Fulham* v. *Newcastle Chronicle and Journal*, 1977.)[595]

Where a plaintiff relies on an innuendo he must prove that the words were published to a specific person who knew *at the time of the publication* of specific facts enabling that person or persons to understand the words in the innuendo sense. Facts which come into existence afterwards do not make a statement defamatory. (*Grappelli* v. *Derek Block (Holdings)*, 1981.)[596]

Reference to the plaintiff

If the judge decides that the words are capable of bearing a defamatory meaning, he must then consider whether the words are capable of referring to the plaintiff. This again is a question of law. If he finds the answer to be yes, he must leave to the jury the question: 'Do the words in fact refer to the plaintiff?' This is a simple matter where the plaintiff has been referred to by name, and until recently the rule was that an author used a name at his peril if it turned out that it could reasonably be taken to refer to the plaintiff. Indeed the more obscure the name selected, the greater the chance of success of a plaintiff who bore that name should he sue for libel. (*Hulton & Co.* v. *Jones*, 1910.)[597] It is not uncommon to attach a disclaimer at the beginning of a work of fiction: 'The persons and events described in this book are wholly imaginary,' but it is doubtful whether this affects the author's liability.

The practical restriction on so-called 'gold-digging' actions was the power of the jury to award contemptuous damages of a farthing (when that coin was in existence), but the costs involved in defending an action might well lead a defendant to settle out of court for a substantial sum. The position has been modified by the Defamation Act, 1952, s. 4, which provides for an offer of amends which will be dealt with later.

It sometimes happens that a whole class of persons is the subject of a defamatory statement. Here a member of the class may only sue if he can show that he himself is the person pointed out by the defamatory statement. (*Knupffer* v. *London Express Newspaper Ltd*, 1944[598] and

Schloimovitz v. *Clarendon Press*, 1973.)[599] (But see *Farringdon* v. *Leigh*, 1987 at p. 828.)

Words may, of course, be defamatory of the plaintiff without his being mentioned by name, if the statement can be shown to apply to him. (*Youssoupoff* v. *M.G.M.*, 1934.)[590]

The defendant's motives are generally immaterial. The most laudable motives will not by themselves prevent a defamatory statement from being actionable. But where the defendant puts his motives in issue, as where he pleads fair comment or qualified privilege, or relies on s. 4 of the Defamation Act, 1952 (unintentional defamation), the plaintiff may then prove the malice of the defendant, or improper motive, to rebut the defence.

Defences

There are certain special defences which are peculiar to an action for defamation, but these defences do not preclude a defendant from denying in addition that the words are defamatory, or asserting that they do not refer to the plaintiff, or that they were not published.

Justification

There is no burden of proof on the plaintiff to establish that the defendant's statement is untrue; all the plaintiff has to do is to prove publication plus the defamatory nature of the statement. However, as the essence of defamation is a false statement, a defendant may always plead the truth of the statement as a defence in civil proceedings (but not in an action for criminal libel, where the rule is: 'The greater the truth, the greater the libel,' since true libels are more likely to influence passions). If the statement is true, no injury is done to the plaintiff's reputation; it is simply reduced to its true level. It does not matter that the statement was made maliciously or even that the defendant did not believe it to be true; so long as it is true the defence of justification is complete.

In the defence of justification the defendant asserts that the statements are 'true both in substance and in fact'. He must show not merely that the words are literally true, but also that there are no significant omissions which would affect the truth of the statement taken as a whole. If, however, the statement is essentially true, an incidental inaccuracy will not deprive the defendant of his right to justify. (*Alexander* v. *N.E. Railway Co.*, 1865.)[600] However, that which is proved to be true must tally with that which the defendant's statement is interpreted to mean. Thus in *Wakley* v. *Cooke* (1849), 4 Exch. 511 the defendant called the plaintiff 'a libellous journalist'. The defendant proved that the plaintiff had had one judgment against him for libel but the court held that the statement meant that the journalist habitually libelled people and so the defendant had not justified it.

The defence of justification really amounts to a positive charge against the plaintiff, and if it fails the damages may be increased, since the original wrong has been aggravated. The defendant's honest belief that the statement is true is no justification, though it may reduce damages. Nor is it a justification to prove that a quoted statement was made, if the quotation cannot be proved to be true. Suppose a statement is made: 'Mrs A tells me that Dr B has been committing adultery with a woman patient.' It is no justification to show that Mrs A made the statement to the defendant; he must show that Dr B is actually guilty of the conduct alleged.

In connection with this defence, it is important to note s. 5 of the Defamation Act, 1952, which provides that in an action for libel and slander in respect of words containing two or more distinct charges against a plaintiff, a defence of justification shall not fail by reason only that the truth of every charge is not proved if the words not proved to be true do not materially injure the plaintiff's reputation having regard to the truth of the remaining charges.

In connection with justification it should be noted that under s. 8 of the Rehabilitation of Offenders Act, 1974 (see further p. 75) a plaintiff who proves that the defendant has maliciously published details of a spent conviction may recover damages. However, the section does not affect the defences of absolute or qualified privilege and fair comment. Thus an employer will, in the absence of malice, still be protected if he writes a reference which mentions a spent conviction. It was decided in *Herbage* v. *Pressdram*, [1984] 2 All E.R. 769 by the Court of Appeal that a rehabilitated offender who seeks an interlocutory injunction to prevent publication of his conviction, is in the same position as a person against whom a defence of qualified privilege is raised. An injunction will only be granted if there is overwhelming evidence of malice in the publication or some irrelevant, spiteful, or improper motive.

Fair comment on a matter of public interest
Here the defendant must show that the statement alleged to be defamatory is in fact legitimate comment. The defence is designed to cover criticism of matters of public interest in the form of comment upon true, or privileged, statements of fact, such comment being made honestly by a person who did not believe the statements to be untrue and who was not otherwise actuated by malice. The malice element makes the defence similar to that of qualified privilege. (See p. 417.) The statement must be comment, i.e. the speaker's opinion of a true state of affairs; it must not be an assertion of facts, but a comment on known facts. (*London Artists* v. *Littler*, 1969.)[601]

Comment is the individual reaction to facts, and the court and the jury require to be satisfied only of the defendant's honesty. The test is; 'Would any honest man, however prejudiced he may be, however exaggerated or obstinate his views, have said that which this criticism has said of what is criticized?' If the answer is, 'yes', the comment is fair for the purposes of raising this defence.

The matter upon which the comment is made must be one of legitimate public interest such as the conduct of Parliament, the Government, local authorities and other public authorities, or the behaviour of a trade union whose actions affect supplies and services to the public. Further, a matter may become the subject of public interest because the plaintiff has voluntarily submitted himself and his affairs to public criticism. A person who makes a public speech, or publishes a book, or presents a play thereby submits the subject matter of such thing for public comment, and cannot complain if the comment is adverse.

It should also be noted that the facts relied on to support a plea of fair comment must be facts existing at the time of the comment and not facts which have occurred some time before the comment was made. (*Cohen* v. *Daily Telegraph*, [1968] 2 All E.R. 407.)

It is important to distinguish fair comment from the defence of justification. In fair comment it is not necessary to prove the truth of the comment but merely that the opinion was honestly held; if justification is pleaded in regard to matters of opinion, the defendant must prove not merely that he honestly held the views expressed but that they were correct views. Thus, if we take the following statement—'X's speech last night was inconsistent with his profession of Liberalism', in a plea of justification the defendant must prove that it was inconsistent, but in a plea of fair comment the defendant need only show that he honestly held this opinion of X's speech.

Privilege

This defence protects statements made in circumstances where the public interest in securing a free expression of facts or opinion outweighs the private interests of the person about whom the statements are made. Privilege may be absolute—such a statement is never actionable—or qualified, when privilege may be defeated by proof of the defendant's malice.

Absolute privilege. The Bill of Rights, 1689, protects statements in both Houses of Parliament. The Parliamentary Papers Act, 1840, affords a similar protection to reports, papers, etc., published by order of either House, e.g. *Hansard* and Government White Papers. The Defamation Act, 1952, s. 9, protects verbatim broadcasts and newspaper reports of Parliamentary proceedings but Parliament itself can fine or imprison those who abuse this privilege. Members of the European Parliament also have immunity for statements made during sessions of the European Parliament *even if it is not actually sitting*. (*Wybot* v. *Faure, The Times*, 24 July, 1986.)

With regard to the courts, statements by the judge, members of the jury, counsel, and the parties or witnesses are absolutely privileged, as are Orders of Court. Thus an Order of Court for divorce, including a finding of adultery against a woman, is not actionable even though reversed on appeal. A statement made by a witness is not actionable even though the judge finds it untrue and malicious. The abuse of the above privilege is checked by (*a*) the law of perjury (in the case of untrue statements by witnesses), (*b*) the power of the judge to report improper behaviour on the part of counsel to the Benchers of his Inn, and (*c*) the judge's power to commit persons to prison for contempt of court.

Communications between senior and responsible public officers in the course of their duty are absolutely privileged.

Qualified privilege. Where such privilege exists, a person is entitled to communicate a defamatory statement so long as he does so honestly and reasonably with regard to the words used and the means of publication, and without malice. Qualified privilege has been held to arise in the following cases—

(i) Common interest, i.e. where a statement is made by a person who is under a legal or moral duty to communicate it to a person who has a similarly legitimate interest in receiving it. This covers testimonials or references to prospective employers, or to trade protection societies whose function it is to investigate the creditworthiness of persons who are the objects of their enquiry. (*London Association for the Protection of Trade* v. *Greenlands*, 1916.)[602]

(ii) Statements in protection of one's private interests are privileged. (*Osborn* v. *Thos Boulter and Son*, 1930.)[603]

(iii) Statements by way of complaint to a proper authority, e.g. petitions to Parliament and complaints to officials of local authorities and professional bodies. (*Beach* v. *Freeson*, 1971.)[604] It was decided in *Graff* v. *Panel on Take-Overs and Mergers, Financial Times*, 11 October, 1980 that the Panel had a moral duty to investigate alleged breaches of the Code and that it followed from this that if the Panel had learned of an alleged breach of the Code and had circularized copies of an article— which was the subject of this libel action—in order to establish or to demolish the allegations, the Panel was protected by the defence of qualified privilege.

(iv) Professional confidential communications between solicitor and client on legal advice.

(v) Newspaper reports on various public matters. The Defamation Act, 1952, s. 7, confers qualified privilege upon fair and accurate newspaper reports of various matters of public interest and importance. These are of two classes—

(*a*) Those which are privileged without any explanation or contradiction being issued, e.g. reports of public proceedings of colonial or dominion legislatures, reports of public proceedings of the United Nations Organisation, of the International Court of Justice, or of British courts martial, and fair and accurate copies of and extracts from British public registers and notices.

(*b*) Those which are privileged only if the newspaper concerned is prepared, on the plaintiff's request, to publish a reasonable letter or statement in explanation or contradiction of the original report, e.g. semi-judicial findings of the governing bodies of learned societies, professional and trade associations, or authorities controlling games and sports. This also applies to fair and accurate reports of public meetings, meetings of local and public authorities, and the meetings of public companies.

(vi) Fair and accurate reports of Parliamentary proceedings are the subject of qualified privilege whether contained in a newspaper or not. (*Cook* v. *Alexander*, 1973.)[605]

(vii) Fair and accurate reports of public judical proceedings are privileged. This does not protect reports of proceedings in domestic tribunals, e.g. The Law Society, unless the report is in a newspaper. Such reports will not be privileged if the court has forbidden publication, as is often done in cases affecting children, or if the matter reported is obscene or scandalous. It is also a criminal offence to report indecent matter relating to judicial proceedings. (Judicial Proceedings (Regulation of Reports) Act, 1926; Domestic and Appellate Proceedings (Restriction of Publicity) Act, 1968.)

Qualified privilege may be rebutted by proof of malice or some improper motive, and proof of actual spite or illwill in the publication will defeat it. An improper motive may be inferred from the tone of the statement or from the circumstances attending its publication, and malice may also be inferred from abuse of the privilege, such as the giving of excessive publicity to statements protected by qualified privilege. However, the gross and unreasoning prejudice of the defendant will not defeat the defence of privilege if the defendant honestly believed that what he published was true. (*Horrocks* v. *Low*, 1972.)[606] But where a person without malice joins with a malicious person in publishing a libel in circumstances of qualified privilege, the person without malice is not liable to the person defamed. (*Egger* v. *Viscount Chelmsford*, 1964.)[607]

Where there is a pressing obligation to communicate defamatory matter, a person may communicate it, although he does not believe it to be true, and still claim qualified privilege. Thus an accountant who, on going through the books of a firm, finds evidence that the cashier has embezzled money, may communicate that view to authority and still claim qualified privilege, even though the accountant does not believe that the cashier has, in fact, embezzled the money.

Offer of amends

The Defamation Act, 1952, provides that the publisher of 'innocent defamation' may make an offer of amends as defined in the Act. (S. 4.) The words shall be treated as published innocently if the words were not defamatory on the face of them, and if the publisher did not know of circumstances by virtue of which they might be understood to be defamatory of the plaintiff, and if reasonable care was exercised in relation to the publication. Given that the above circumstances exist the defendant can apparently make an offer of amends, supported by an affidavit setting out the facts relied on to show that his publication was innocent.

An offer of amends requires the publication of a suitable apology to the party aggrieved and a suitable correction. The offeror must also take steps to notify persons to whom copies have been distributed that the words used are alleged to be defamatory of the party aggrieved. The High Court decides how the offer shall be carried into effect unless the parties have agreed on the matter.

It is a defence in any proceedings for defamation that the defendant's offer (i) has been accepted and performed, or (ii) that it has been refused, after having been made as soon as practicable after the defendant received notice that the words were or might be defamatory of the plaintiff, and that the offer has not been withdrawn.

If the plaintiff rejects the offer because he does not think the publication was innocent, or because the section of the Act has not been complied with, and fails to establish this at the trial, there seems no way of later enforcing the offer of amends.

Consent of the plaintiff to publication
If the plaintiff has agreed to publication, he cannot subsequently sue in respect of that statement. (*Chapman* v. *Lord Ellesmere*, 1932.)[608] Consent may be given in respect of a particular publication, or it may be general.

Theatres Act, 1968

Section 4 of the Theatres Act, 1968, amends the law of defamation (including the law relating to criminal libel) by providing that the publication of words (including pictures, visual images, gestures, and the like) in the public performance of a play shall be treated as publication in permanent form, i.e. libel. Performances given on a domestic occasion in a private dwelling house are exempt (s. 7(1)) and so are rehearsals and performances for broadcast or recording purposes (s. 7(2)) provided such rehearsals and performances are attended only by the persons *directly* connected with the giving of them.

Section 5 of the Act creates an offence of incitement to racial hatred by presenting or directing the public performance of a play though again, rehearsals and performances attended only by persons directly concerned are exempt. Prosecution under s. 5 is with the consent of the Attorney-General (s. 8).

It is of interest to note also that s. 1 of the Act abolishes the power of the Lord Chamberlain to censor plays.

Damages

Although many slanders are actionable only on proof of special damage to the plaintiff, actual damages awarded by the court will not be confined to the special damage so proved. For example, if as a result of defamation a man loses his employment, he can prove special damage in this connection, but the actual damages awarded may take in much more than this particular loss. Damages for defamation tend to be high. Juries are often used in such cases, and they are concerned with the *quantum* of damages. The damages awarded for loss of reputation may often be higher than damages awarded for the loss of life. However, damages should be compensatory and not punitive (*Davis* v. *Rubin*, 1967),[609] though they may be *aggravated* by mental suffering arising from the defamation, or *mitigated* by a full apology, provocation by the plaintiff, or the plaintiff's bad reputation.

Injunctions

Apart from damages a defamed person may seek an injunction restraining further publication. Such injunctions are of two kinds—

(*a*) *A perpetual injunction*, which is usually granted at the trial, and

(*b*) *an interim injunction* (or interlocutory injunction), which is granted pending the trial, and may be *quia timet*, that is before the wrong is actually done.

However, publication of an article will not be restrained merely because it is defamatory where the defendant says he intends to justify it or make fair comment on a matter of public interest, or claim privilege and the plaintiff cannot show that the defence(s) concerned will be likely to fail. (*Harakas* v. *Baltic Mercantile and Shipping Exchange Ltd*, [1982] 2 All E.R. 701.)

Before concluding the tort of defamation we should notice also the separate tort of *injurious falsehood*. Just as defamation is an attack on a man's reputation, so injurious falsehood is an attack on his goods. To say that A's goods are inferior in quality to B's may be an injurious falsehood. To say that A sells inferior goods as goods of superior quality may, on the other hand, be a defamatory statement.

Time limits for claims

Under s. 57 of the Administration of Justice Act, 1985 (amending the Limitation Act, 1980) the period for bringing claims for libel and slander is reduced from 6 years to 3 years from the cause of action, with the ability to apply to the court to sue out of time for one year after becoming aware of the facts, it these were not known within the 3 year period.

THE RULE IN *Rylands* v. *Fletcher*

This celebrated rule was stated in the case of *Rylands* v. *Fletcher*, 1868—

Where a person for his own purposes brings and keeps on land in his occupation anything likely to do mischief if it escapes, he must keep it in at his peril, and if he fails to do so he is liable for all damage naturally accruing from the escape.

The rule has been held to apply whether the things brought on the land be 'beasts, water, filth or stenches'. The rule also applies to fire. (*Emanuel* v. *Greater London Council*, 1970.)[610] It does not apply to the pollution of beaches by oil because, *inter alia*, the oil does not escape from *land* but from the sea. (*Southport Corporation* v. *Esso Petroleum Co.*, 1954.)[507]

The duty is an absolute one and does not depend on negligence provided the use of the land is not natural use. (*British Celanese* v. *Hunt*, 1969.)[532] In the case which gave rise to the rule, the defendant had constructed a reservoir on his land, employing competent workmen for the purpose. Water escaped from the reservoir and percolated through certain old mine shafts, which had been filled with marl and earth, and eventually flooded the plaintiff's mine. The defendant was held liable in that he had collected water on his land, the water not being naturally there, and it had escaped and done damage. Since the defendant employed competent workmen, it follows that the liability is absolute and does not depend on negligence, and in any case the defendant's action was quite innocent as there was no reason why he should know of, or even suspect the existence of, the disused shafts.

In order for the rule to apply, there must be an escape of the thing which inflicts the injury from a place over which the defendant has occupation or control to a place which is outside his occupation or control. (*Read* v. *Lyons*, 1947.)[611]

The rule is not confined to wrongs between owners of adjacent land and does not depend on ownership of land (*Charing Cross Electricity Supply Co.* v. *Hydraulic Power Co.*, 1914),[612] but the plaintiff must have some interest in the land. (*Weller* v. *Foot and Mouth Disease Research Institute*, 1965.)[546] Neither is it confined to the escape of water, but may cover the escape of any offensive or dangerous matter arising out of abnormal use of land provided the defendant has control of it. (*Attorney-General* v. *Corke*, 1933[613] and *Smith* v. *Scott*, 1972.)[539] It seems doubtful at the moment how far the rule extends to personal injuries, and it may be that proof of negligence is always necessary in an action of this kind. (*Read* v. *Lyons*, 1947,[611] and *Perry* v. *Kendricks Transport*, 1956.)[614]

In general there is no liability under the rule for damage caused by the escape of things naturally on the land (*Giles* v. *Walker*, 1890),[615] though there may be an action in nuisance (*Davey* v. *Harrow Corporation*, 1957)[616] or in negligence.

Although *Rylands* v. *Fletcher* imposes strict liability, the following defences are still open to the defendant—

(*a*) That the escape was the plaintiff's fault. It should also be noted that there is no reason why the Law Reform (Contributory Negligence) Act, 1945, should not apply where the plaintiff is partly to blame.

(*b*) That it was an Act of God (*Nichols* v. *Marsland*, 1876),[455] though the defence is not often successfully pleaded. (*Greenock Corporation* v. *Caledonian Railway Co.*, 1917.)[617]

(*c*) That the escape was due to the wrongful act of a stranger. (*Rickards* v. *Lothian*, 1913,[618] and *Emanuel* v. *Greater London Council*, 1970.)[610]

(*d*) That the damage was caused by artificial works done for the common benefit of the plaintiff and the defendant. (*Peters* v. *Prince of Wales Theatre (Birmingham) Ltd*, 1943.)[619]

(*e*) That there was statutory authority for the act of the defendant, provided that the defendant was not negligent. It should be noted that the defence of statutory authority is not available in respect of reservoirs. (Reservoirs Act, 1975, s. 28 and Sch. 2.)

9 The law of property

English law divides property into real property and personal property. Real property includes only freehold interests in land, and personal property comprises all other proprietary rights, whether in land or chattels. This classification is not identical with the obvious distinction between immoveables and moveables, and this is the result of the attitude of early law to the nature of a lease.

THE NATURE OF PROPERTY

Actions in respect of property fall into two kinds: actions *in rem* or real actions, and actions *in personam* or personal actions. An action *in rem* in English law is an action in which a specific thing is recovered; an action *in personam* gives damages only.

It so happened that in early days the courts would allow a real action or *actio realis* only for the specific recovery of land. If an owner was dispossessed of other forms of property, the person who had taken the property had a choice; he could either restore the property taken or pay damages to the rightful owner. Hence land became known as real property or *realty*, and all other forms of property were called personal property or *personalty*. So far the distinction corresponds to that between moveables and immoveables, but this convenient classification was disturbed by the lease for a term of years.

Although a lease of land was an interest in immoveable property, the real action was not available to the dispossessed tenant. Leases did not fit into the feudal system of landholding by tenure but were regarded as personal business arrangements whereby one man allowed another the use of the land for a period in return for a rent.

These transactions were personal contracts and created rights *in personam* between the parties, and not rights *in rem* which could affect feudal status. It was not an uncommon form of investment to buy land and let it out on lease to obtain an income on capital invested, and such transactions were more akin to commercial dealings than to landholding as it was understood in early days. Moreover the system had its advantages, since a lease was immune from feudal burdens and could be bequeathed by will at a time when dispositions by will of other land were still not permitted.

Leaseholds, therefore, come under the heading of personal property or chattels, but because they partake so strongly of the character of land, they are often referred to as *chattels real* to distinguish them from pure personalty, e.g. a watch or a fountain pen. Since the property legislation of 1925 this distinction has lost much of its importance, but it is still true that if in his will a testator says 'All my personalty to P and all my realty to R,' P would get the leaseholds.

Pure personalty itself comprises two different kinds of property known as *choses in possession* and *choses in action*. Choses in possession denote chattels, such as jewellery and furniture, which are tangible objects and can be physically possessed and enjoyed by their owner. Choses in action are intangible forms of property which are incapable of physical possession, and their owner is usually compelled to bring an action if he wishes to enforce his rights over property of this kind. Examples of choses in action are debts, patents, copyrights, trade marks, shares, and negotiable instruments.

Up to now we have been considering in the main rights which one has in one's own things. However it is possible to have rights over the things of another. We have already mentioned the lease, which is the right to possess another's land for a term in return for a rent, but in addition it is possible to become the owner of a *servitude* over the land of another, e.g. a right of way, a right of light, or a right to the support of buildings. A servitude may also be a right to take something from the land of another, e.g. the right to fish or collect firewood. Rights of the first class are called *easements*, and of the second *profits à prendre*. Further, a person may raise a loan on the security of his property either real or personal, and the lender has certain rights over the property so used as a security if the loan is not repaid.

OWNERSHIP

Ownership is a term used to express the relationship which exists between a person and certain rights which are vested in him. Ownership is the greatest right or collection of rights—the ultimate right—which a person can have over or in a thing.

For example, X may own a fee simple in Blackacre and may lease the land to Y, so giving up possession. But however long the lease, the ultimate right of ownership is in X, and eventually the right to possess, which he has for the moment forfeited, will return to him or to his estate if he is dead. Z may have a right of way over Blackacre. This is not ownership of Blackacre, but is ownership of a right over it which limits X's enjoyment of the land. B may have lent money to X on the security of the land, so that B is a mortgagee and, therefore, the owner of a right in Blackacre, but this does not constitute ownership of the land; it is a mere encumbrance attached to it, limiting X's enjoyment to the extent of the rights given to B as mortgagee. Nevertheless the supreme right is vested in X, and this right is called ownership of Blackacre.

Ownership is a *de jure* relationship; there is no need to possess the thing. Possession tends to be *de facto*, i.e. evidenced by physical possession, although, as we shall see, physical possession is not necessary in order to have legal possession.

It may be said that in a general sense all rights are capable of ownership, which is of many kinds—

(a) Corporeal
That is, the ownership of a thing or chose in possession such as a watch or a fountain pen.

(b) Incorporeal
That is, the ownership of a right only, e.g the right to recover a debt of £20 from X by an action at law, or the ownership of a chose in action. A share certificate is a chose in action, and ownership of it is incorporeal, for it is ownership of certain rights: the right to dividends as and when declared, the right to vote at meetings, and so on.

(c) Sole ownership
That is, as where X is the sole owner of Blackacre.

(d) Co-ownership
That is, as where X and Y are simultaneously owners of Blackacre, as joint tenants or tenants in common. (See further p. 435.)

(e) Legal or equitable ownership
A grant giving X the fee simple absolute in possession of Blackacre constitutes him the legal owner. But a grant giving X a life interest only constitutes him as equitable owner, whose interest can exist only behind a trust, the legal estate being vested in trustees.

(f) Trust or beneficial ownership
In the grant set out above giving X a life interest, the trustees hold the legal estate but not beneficially; the beneficial interest is in X and Equity will protect it.

(g) Vested or contingent ownership
In a grant to X for life with remainder to Y, X and Y have equitable interests and both are vested. Admittedly Y will not become entitled in enjoyment until X dies, but his interest is, nevertheless, vested, and if Y were to die before X the property would descend through Y's estate on X's death.

In a grant to X for life, with remainder to Y if he attains the age of eighteen years, X's interest is equitable and vested, Y's interest is equitable and contingent since he must satisfy the requirement of majority before his interest vests.

POSSESSION

The physical control of a thing by a person is what is normally known as possession, and if the idea of possession had remained wedded to physical control, the position would have been simple enough. But the widening sphere of legal activity made it necessary to attribute to persons who were not actually in physical control some or all of the advantages enjoyed by persons who were.

There are three possible situations at law—

(i) A person can have physical control without legal possession, as in the case of a porter carrying a traveller's suitcase in a station.

(ii) A person can have possession and its advantages without actual physical control, e.g. a person may have books at home which are still in his possession even when he is away on holiday.

(iii) A person can have both physical control and possession, e.g. a watch in his pocket or a pen in his hand.

Possession, therefore, has acquired a technical legal meaning, and the separation of possession from physical control has given the concept a high degree of flexibility.

The old theory of possession, derived from the Roman Law, relies upon (i) *corpus*, i.e. physical control, and (ii) *animus*, i.e. the intention to exclude others. But although these concepts help in deciding possession, they do not provide the complete answer. In fact English law has never worked out a completely logical and exhaustive definition of possession. The handing over of a key may be sufficient by itself to pass the possession of the contents of a room or box if it provides the effective means of control over the goods.

Wrongful interference

In the law of torts, wrongful interference to property is an invasion of possession. The policy of this branch of the law is to compensate the party whose interests have been affected, and in order to enable such persons to recover, the court has contrived to attribute possession to them.

A bailee is a person who gets possession of a chattel from another with his consent. A bailment may be at will, i.e. revocable by the bailor at any time, or it may be for a term, i.e. for a fixed period of time, as by hiring a television set for six months. Where a bailment is at will, the bailee, who by definition has possession, can sue a third party for wrongful interference. Since the bailment is revocable at will, the bailor also has an interest worth protecting, and in order that he too may bring an action for wrongful interference, his right to possess is treated as possession itself. Where, on the other hand, the bailment is for a term, only the bailee can bring an action for wrongful interference and not the bailor, although, where the bailee brings the action, he will have to account to the bailor for any damages obtained. If a third person destroys or permanently injures the chattel while it is in the bailee's possession, the bailor may have an action against the third party for injury to his reversionary interest. (*Mears* v. *L.S.W. Railway*, [1862] 11 C.B. (N.S.) 850.)

Where an employer has temporarily handed a thing to his employee, possession remains with the employer and the employee takes only custody. Thus an employer can sue for wrongful interference for an injury to the goods by a third party.

A person who loses a thing retains his ownership in it, and for the purpose of suing for wrongful interference someone who has taken it, his right to regain possession will suffice. But for the purpose of claiming from an insurance company for loss, he will be regarded as having lost possession, within the terms of the contract, if the thing cannot in fact be found.

Trespass to land by relation is another example of the artificial manipulation of the concept of possession to provide a remedy in trespass to one who needs to be compensated. When a person, with a right to possess, enters in pursuance of that right, he is deemed to have been in possession from the time when his right originally accrued, e.g. from the time when he made the original contract for a purchase or a lease. He can, therefore, sue for any trespass that has been committed between the accrual of the right and the actual entry.

As we have seen, difficulties have arisen over the requirement of the intention to exclude others as a necessary ingredient of possession where property of one sort or another has been found on the land of a person who was not its owner. (See *Parker* v. *British Airways Board*, 1982[517] and *South Staffordshire Water Co.* v. *Sharman*, 1896[518] and the cases noted with it.)

However, it should be noted that *unless an owner* of chattels can be shown to have *abandoned* or *sold* them he remains their owner and has a better title than a finder or a person on whose property they are found. (*Moffat* v. *Kazana*, 1968.)[620]

Adverse possession

A person may sometimes acquire the ownership of land by adverse possession. This arises from the occupation and use of land without the permission of, or any interference from, the true owner, as where a stranger encloses and cultivates a portion of a neighbour's land or occupies another's house. Adverse possession for a period of twelve years will give the possessor a title (*Hayward* v. *Challoner*, 1967),[621] but such adverse possession must take the form of overt acts which are inconsistent with the title of the owner, and in this case possession is viewed much more strictly than in the others we have been considering above. (*Littledale* v. *Liverpool College*, 1900.)[622] Whether adverse possession necessarily involves inconvenience to the true owner is not clear. In *Wallis's Caton Bay Holiday Camp* v. *Shell-Mex & B.P.*, [1974] 3 All E.R. 575, the defendants had purchased land for development, though they had no immediate use for it. The plaintiffs used it for 12 years for the purposes of grazing cattle on it and cultivating it. The Court of Appeal held that the plaintiffs had not established a good possessory title because what they had done was of no inconvenience to the defendants who had no immediate use for the land. However, in *Treloar* v. *Nute*, (1976) 120 S.J. 590, the plaintiff owned freehold land for which he had no immediate use and which was left derelict. The defendants bought land adjacent and occupied part of the derelict land for a period of 12 years. In holding that the defendants had a good possessory title to that land the Court of Appeal said it was not necessary to import into the definition of adverse possession a requirement that the owner must be inconvenienced or affected by that possession.

Where a tenant, during the currency of his tenancy, takes possession of other land belonging to the landlord, the land is presumed to have been taken as part of the holding comprised in the tenancy, and the tenant cannot acquire a good possessory title unless he communicates to his landlord some disclaimer of the landlord's title. (*Smirk* v. *Lyndale Developments Ltd*, 1974.)[623]

BAILMENT

Bailments are concerned with pure personalty and not with real property.

The bailment may or may not originate in a contract (*Fairline Shipping Corporation* v. *Adamson*, 1974)[84] and a minor may be a bailee of goods even though he obtained them under an unenforceable contract. (*Ballett* v. *Mingay*, 1943.)[406]

Possession

An essential feature of a bailment is the transfer of possession to the bailee. There is no precise definition of possession, but the basic features are *control* and *an intention to exclude others*. However, a person can have possession of chattels which he does not know exist (*South Staffordshire Water Co.* v. *Sharman*, 1896).[518] An employee who receives goods from his employer to take to a third party has mere *custody*; possession remains with the employer and the employee is not a bailee. If a third party hands goods to a employee for his employer the employee obtains possession and is the bailee.

In a bailment for a fixed term the bailee has possession to the exclusion of the bailor, and is, therefore, the only person who can sue a third party for wrongful interference. In a bailment at will, i.e. one which the bailor can terminate at will, the bailor retains either possession or an immediate right to possess and an action for wrongful interference is available to him as well as to the bailee (see also p. 426). A bailee can sue a third party in tort for loss of or damage to the goods even though the bailee is not liable to the bailor for the loss or damage. (*The Winkfield*, 1902.)[624]

Bailment and licence

The problem of distinguishing between bailment and licence has arisen mainly in connection with the parking of vehicles. If a vehicle is parked on land, either gratuitously or even on payment of a charge, the transaction may amount to a mere licence and not a bailment which gives rise to duties of care. (*Ashby* v. *Tolhurst*, 1937.)[625] The decisions in *Ultzen* v. *Nicols*, 1894,[626] and *Deyong* v. *Shenburn*, 1946,[627] are illustrative of the problems involved in distinguishing bailment and licence.

Finders and involuntary recipients

To constitute a bailment, the person who is given possession of goods must be entrusted with them for a particular purpose, e.g. to use and return as in the case of loan or hire, or to take from one place to another as in carriage. A banker is not a bailee of money paid into a customer's account, for his obligation is to return an equivalent sum and not the identical notes and coins. However, a banker is a bailee of property deposited with him for safe custody.

A finder is not a true bailee because he is not entrusted with the goods for a particular purpose. However, if he takes them into his possession he will be liable for loss or damage resulting from his negligence. (*Newman* v. *Bourne and Hollingsworth*, 1915.)[628]

A person cannot be made a bailee against his will. (*Neuwirth* v. *Over Darwen Industrial Co-operative Society*, 1894).[629] Where the receipt of the goods is involuntary it is unlikely that the recipient is under any higher duty than to refrain from intentional damage. However, he must not convert the goods, but although liability for conversion is usually strict, an involuntary recipient will only be liable if he acts intentionally or negligently. (*Elvin and Powell Ltd* v. *Plummer Roddis Ltd*, 1933.)[522]

The Unsolicited Goods and Services Acts, 1971 and 1975, are relevant in this connection. The Acts are designed to deal with selling techniques involving the sending of unsolicited goods, thus rendering the recipient an involuntary bailee. The Acts provide for fines to be made on persons making demands for payment for goods they know to be unsolicited. If the demand is accompanied by threats a higher scale of fines applies. Furthermore, unsolicited goods may be kept by the recipient without payment *after a period of thirty days* provided the recipient gives notice to the sender asking that they be collected, or *after six months* even if no notice has been given.

Obligations of the bailor

Where the bailment is gratuitous it has been said that the limit of the liability of the bailor is to communicate to the bailee defects in the article lent *of which he is aware*. However, the principle in *Donoghue* v. *Stevenson*, 1932,[399] may apply to gratuitous bailments so that the bailor would be liable if he had not taken reasonable care to ensure that the goods bailed were not dangerous, even though he had no actual knowledge of a defect in the chattels lent.

When the bailment is for reward there is an implied warranty on the part of the bailor that he has a title to the goods so that the bailee's possession will not be disturbed, and that the goods are fit and suitable for the bailee's purpose. This does not mean that the bailee is liable for all defects but only for those which skill and care can guard against. (*Hyman* v. *Nye*, 1881,[630] *Reed* v. *Dean*, 1949.)[631] However, the warranty as to fitness and suitability does not apply where the defect is apparent to the bailee and he does not rely on the skill or judgment of the bailor.

Obligations of the bailee

When Lord Holt, in *Coggs* v. *Bernard*, 1703,[116] established the liability of the bailee in negligence he laid down different duties of care for different kinds of bailments. Thus, in a bailment for the sole benefit of the bailee, such as a gratuitous loan, the bailee's duty of care was much higher than in a bailment for the benefit of both parties such as a hiring. However, in more recent times there has been disapproval of Lord Holt's different standards of care (*Houghland* v. *R. Low (Luxury Coaches) Ltd*, 1962),[632] and it is now the better view that the standard of care required of a bailee is to take reasonable care in all the circumstances of the case, which equates his duty with that owed by any person in the law relating to negligence, though the burden of disproving negligence is on the bailee. (*Global Dress Co.* v. *Boase & Co.*, 1966.)[633]

The *main* circumstances which the court is likely to consider when deciding the question of negligence in a bailee are—

(a) The type of bailment
Although some current legal opinion is against a legal distinction between bailment for reward and gratuitous bailment, reward or lack of reward will continue to be an *important circumstance* in the matter of the bailee's negligence. A gratuitous bailee must take the same care of the property bailed as a reasonable man would take of his own property. It is no defence for a bailee to show that he kept the goods with as much care as his own because the test of reasonableness is objective. (*Doorman* v. *Jenkins* 1834.)[634] In a bailment for reward the duty of care tends to be somewhat higher. (*Brabant* v. *King*, 1895.)[635]

(b) The expertise of the bailee
If the bailee's profession or situation implies a certain expertise he will be liable if he fails to show it. (*Wilson* v. *Brett*, 1843.)[636]

(c) The property bailed
If the goods bailed are, to the knowledge of the bailee fragile or valuable, a high standard of care will be expected. (*Saunders (Mayfair) Furs* v. *Davies*, 1965.)[637]

A bailee may be liable in negligence if he does not give notice to the bailor of a loss or try to recover lost or stolen property. (*Coldman* v. *Hill*, 1919.)[638]

A bailee is vicariously liable for the torts of his servants, but a servant who became a thief was not regarded as acting within the scope of his employment. (*Cheshire* v. *Bailey*, 1905.)[639] However, in *Morris* v. *C. W. Martin & Sons Ltd*, 1965,[427] it was held that a bailee for reward cannot necessarily escape liability for loss of goods stolen by his servant because theft is not necessarily beyond the scope of employment (see further p. 358).

A bailee may attempt to exclude his liability by an exemption clause in the contract of bailment. This matter must now be considered in the light of the rules of construction of contracts and the Unfair Contract Term Act, 1977 (pp. 258–60).

Delegation by bailee

Whether a bailee can delegate performance of the contract to another depends upon the nature of the bailment and the particular contract which may authorize delegation. Contracts involving the carriage, storage, repair or cleaning of goods often assume personal performance by the bailee. (*Davies* v. *Collins*, 1945;[640] *Edwards* v. *Newland*, 1950.)[641] Where there is a delegation, even though unknown to the bailor, the delegate is a bailee and owes a duty of care directly to the bailor. (*Learoyd Bros* v. *Pope*, 1966.)[642]

Estoppel and interpleader

A bailee is estopped at common law from denying the title of his bailor and if the bailor demands the return of the goods it is no defence for the bailee to plead that the bailor is not the owner. However, a bailee may defend an action for non-delivery of the goods—

(*a*) by showing that he has delivered them under an authorization by the bailor;

(*b*) by showing that he has not got the goods because he has been dispossessed by a person with a better title, as in a bailment of stolen goods which are reclaimed by the owner;

(c) if he still retains possession he may allege that a third party has a better title but he must defend the action on behalf of, and with the authority of, the true owner. (*Rogers, Sons & Co.* v. *Lambert & Co.*, 1891.)[643]

Where adverse claims are made against the bailee by the bailor and a third party, the bailee should take interpleader proceedings under the Rules of the Supreme Court. The effect of this will be to bring the bailor and the third party together in an action which will decide the validity of their claims. The bailee can then hand over the goods to whichever party has established his claims and will not risk liability for wrongful interference.

Lien

A bailee may, in certain circumstances, have a lien on the goods and the general nature of a lien is described on p. 461.

LAND LAW

Estates in land.

Since the Norman Conquest absolute ownership of land has been impossible. William the Conqueror considered himself owner of all land in England and parcelled it out to his barons who became his tenants. In return for this 'honour' the barons had to render to the Crown certain services, either of a military or other public nature, but an exception was made in the case of land held by the Church. The ecclesiastics were not able to provide military services, and special spiritual tenures were introduced.

In order to assist themselves in supplying the services required by the King, the barons began to subgrant part of the land, and a series of tenures sprang up, all persons holding as tenants of the Crown in the last analysis.

It is outside our scope to pursue the rise and fall of the system of tenures, but all land is now held on a single tenure called 'common socage', and all obligations to the Crown have disappeared, except for certain ceremonials preserved because of their antiquity. Even today, however, a person does not own land; he holds an estate in land. The *tenure* answers the question 'How is the land held?' The term *estate* answers the question 'For how long is the land held?'

The legislation of 1925

Before this legislation which is described below there were many different ways of holding land referred to as estates in land. The existence of so many estates in land made the transfer of land most complicated. There might be a large number of legal owners of the same piece of land, and before the land could be conveyed to a purchaser all the interests had to be got in. Other problems arose on intestacy, because the rules for intestate succession were not the same for realty and personalty. In 1925 a thorough reform of land law was undertaken and was eventually achieved by the following statutes: The Law of Property Act, 1925; The Settled Land Act, 1925; The Administration of Estates Act, 1925; The Land Charges Act, 1925; and the Land Registration Act, 1925.

Legal estates
The Law of Property Act, 1925, reduced the number of legal estates which can exist over land to two, and the number of legal interests or charges in or over land to five. All other estates, interests, and charges in or over land take effect as equitable interests, and can exist only behind a trust, the trustees having the legal fee simple estate.

The difference between a legal estate and a legal interest is that the owner of the legal estate is entitled to the enjoyment of the whole of the property, either in possession or receiving rents, whereas the owner of a legal interest has a limited right in or over the land of another.

The two legal estates possible today are—

(1) *A fee simple absolute in possession*; and
(2) *A term of years absolute.*

The word *fee* implies that the estate is an estate of inheritance, and the word *simple* shows that the fee is capable of descending to the general class of heirs, and is not restricted to heirs of a particular class. The word *absolute* distinguishes a fee simple which will continue for ever, from a fee which may be determinable. The fee simple must be *in possession*, although this does not imply only physical possession but also the right to receive rents and profits. Even if a landlord has granted a lease he may still have a fee simple in possession because he is entitled to the rent reserved by the lease.

The *term of years absolute* is what is normally understood by a lease. But a term of years includes a term for less than a year, or for a year or years and a fraction of a year, or even a tenancy from year to year. The essential characteristic is that a term of years has a minimum period of certain duration. It seems, therefore, that a lease for life is no longer a legal estate; nor is a tenancy at will or sufferance since there is no certainty as to the period of their continuance. A term of years may be absolute notwithstanding that it may be determined by notice, re-entry, or operation of law or other event.

Legal interests and charges
We have seen that there are, since 1926, only two possible legal estates: a fee simple absolute in possession and a term of years absolute, but the Law of Property Act, 1925, also lays down a number of legal interests in land. The most important are—

(i) An easement, right or privilege for an interest equivalent to either of the above estates. Thus an easement for life would not be a legal interest. (See further p. 440.)

(ii) A charge by way of legal mortgage.

EQUITABLE INTERESTS

All estates, interests or charges over land except those outlined above take effect as equitable interests only and must exist behind a trust. Life interests for example, are equitable.

The two major trust arrangements over land are called settled land and trusts for sale.

Settled land

Settlements created after 1925 other than by will require, under the Settled Land Act, 1925, two deeds to be executed—the vesting deed and the trust instrument. The vesting deed must contain a description of the settled land, a statement that the settled land is vested in the tenant for life upon the trusts for the time being affecting the settled land, the names of the trustees of the settlement, and a statement of any larger powers granted to the tenant for life in addition to his statutory powers.

The trust instrument must contain the appointment of the trustees, the names of the persons entitled to appoint new trustees, a statement of any additional powers conferred by the settlement in extension of the statutory powers, and the trusts of the settlement. Where a settlement is created by will, the will is regarded as the trust instrument, and the personal representatives must execute a vesting instrument, vesting the legal estate in the tenant for life. Thus a purchaser of settled land is only concerned with the vesting deed or assent, since it is from such documents that he derives his title. The trusts can remain secret since the trust instrument need not be produced on sale.

Under the settlement the person obtaining the benefit from the estate is usually an adult with a life interest and he is called the *tenant for life*. It is his function to manage the estate and he has power to sell or exchange the settled land or any part of it with an adjustment of any difference in value in the case of exchange. He may grant leases subject to certain restrictions, but in the absence of a contrary provision in the settlement, he has no power to mortgage or charge the legal estate for his own benefit, although he can mortgage or assign his own beneficial life interest.

He has other powers which he can only exercise with the consent of the settlement trustees or the court, e.g. the power to sell or otherwise dispose of the principal mansion house, the power to cut and sell timber, the power to compromise claims and sell settled chattels. He has the power to make improvements at his own expense, or the cost may be borne by the capital money if he complies with the provisions of the Act. He has also power to select investments for capital money.

The tenant for life is in a strong position, for he is subject to no control in the exercise of his powers except that he must give notice to the trustees of his intention to exercise the most important ones, he must obtain the consent of the trustees or leave of the court in certain cases, and he is in fact himself a trustee for the other beneficiaries. There may be joint tenants for life under a settlement and, where this is so, they must usually agree as to the exercise of their joint powers. The court will exercise a power, e.g. by ordering a sale of property, but only if the joint tenant who does not agree to sell is acting in bad faith. (*Barker* v. *Addiscott*, [1969] 3 All E.R. 685.)

It is clear that under a settlement a proper balance must be preserved between the tenant for life and the persons who will be entitled to the land or the proceeds of the land after his death. He is not allowed, therefore, to run down the estate during his lifetime in order to increase his own income, but is only allowed to take from the land the current income and must pass on the estate substantially unimpaired.

Trusts for sale

A trust for sale is an immediate binding trust for sale whether or not exercisable at the request or with the consent of any person, and with or without a power at discretion to postpone the sale. Such a trust for sale may be either express or by operation of law. Trusts for sale are governed by the Law of Property Act, 1925, and not by the Settled Land Act, 1925.

An express trust for sale is almost always created by two documents— a conveyance to trustees on trust for sale and a trust instrument. But even where a trust for sale is embodied in a single document, a purchaser of the legal estate is not concerned with the trusts affecting the rents and profits of the land until sale, or with the proceeds of the sale provided he obtains a receipt for the purchase money signed by at least two trustees or a trust corporation.

There are cases where a trust for sale is imposed by statute. These are—

(*a*) where a person dies intestate,

(*b*) where two or more persons are entitled to land as joint tenants or tenants in common,

(*c*) where trustees lend money on mortgage and the property becomes vested in them free from the right of redemption. (See further p. 451.)

CO-OWNERSHIP

Two persons may own land simultaneously. In such a case they are either joint tenants or tenants in common. Where they are joint tenants there

is no question of a share of the property—each is the owner of the whole..
Where there is a tenancy in common, each is regarded as owning an
individual share in the property, but that share has not positively been
marked out. Tenants in common hold property in undivided shares.

A joint tenancy arises where land is conveyed to two or more persons
and no words of severance are used. A tenancy in common arises when
there are words of severance. Thus a conveyance 'to A and B' would
create a joint tenancy, whilst a conveyance 'to A and B equally' would
create a tenancy in common. The right of survivorship or *jus accrescendi*
is a distinguishing feature of joint tenancies, and upon the death of one
joint tenant, his share in the property passes to the survivors until there
is only one person left and he becomes the sole owner of the property.
The *jus accrescendi* does not apply to tenancies in common and such a
tenant may dispose of his share by will. It will be appreciated also that
the conveyance (or a will) may actually state the type of co-ownership
e.g. 'to A and B as joint tenants'.

Both types of co-ownership have advantages and disadvantages. The
jus accrescendi as applied to joint tenancies prevents too many interests
being created in the land, because a joint tenant cannot leave any part
of the property by will and so the number of interests decreases. When
the land is sold the number of signatures on the conveyance will not be
excessive. On the other hand joint tenancies are unfair in that eventual
sole ownership depends merely on survival. Where there is a tenancy in
common, each tenant can leave his interest by will possibly by dividing
it between two or more persons, thus the number of interests increases
and on sale many interests must be got in.

The common law preferred the joint tenancy, but Equity preferred the
tenancy in common and would in certain circumstances treat persons as
tenants in common rather than joint tenants regardless of words of
severance. For instance where two persons lend money on mortgage,
Equity regards them as tenants in common of the interest in the land
subject to the mortgage; also where joint purchasers of land put up the
purchase money in unequal shares; and in the case of partnership land,
the partners are treated as tenants in common in Equity.

The Law of Property Act, 1925, has combined the best features of both
types of co-ownership by providing that where land is owned by two or
more persons they, or the first four of them if there are more than four,
should be treated as holding the legal estate as trustees and joint tenants,
for the benefit of themselves and other co-owners (if any) in Equity. Thus
a purchaser of the property is never required to get more than four
signatures on the conveyance, and the trusts attach to the purchase
money for the benefit of the co-owners. However, the Act does not state
what shares the co-owners are to have and this should be dealt with
specifically in the conveyance otherwise the court may have to decide in
a case of dispute. It does not follow from the provisions of the Act that
the co-owners share in equity equally. The statutory trusts on which the
property is held are: to sell the property with power to postpone the sale;

and to hold the proceeds of sale, and the rents and profits until sale, for those beneficially entitled under the trust.

It should be noted that although the provisions set out in the above paragraph deal with the problems which formerly arose in conveying land which was in joint ownership, it is still possible to create a joint tenancy in both the land and the proceeds of sale. Where such a joint tenancy exists the *jus accrescendi* will apply to the equitable interests of the joint tenants in the proceeds of sale, unless there has been a severance of the joint tenancy since the creation of the estate. Severence is possible under s. 36(2) of the Law of Property Act, 1925, which provides that—

> . . . where a legal estate (not being settled land) is vested in joint tenants beneficially, and any tenant desires to sever the joint tenancy in Equity, he shall give to the other joint tenants a notice in writing of such desire or do such other acts or things as would, in the case of personal estate, have been effective to sever the tenancy in Equity, and thereupon under the trust for sale affecting the land the net proceeds of sale, and the net rents and profits until sale, shall be held upon the trusts which would have been requisite for giving effect to the beneficial interest if there had been an actual severance.

A notice of severance may be regarded as properly served if sent by post even if it is not received by the addressee. (*Re 88 Berkeley Road, London N.W.9; Rickwood* v. *Turnsek*, [1971] 1 All E.R. 254.)

The better view is that severance of a joint tenancy may be effected unilaterally by one party other than by giving notice. (*Re Draper's Conveyance*, 1967.)[644] Before leaving this topic it should be noted that one tenant in common is not entitled to rent from another tenant in common, even though that other occupies the whole of the property. (*Jones (A.E.)* v. *Jones (F.W.)*, [1977] 2 All E.R. 231.)

A LEASEHOLD OR A TERM OF YEARS

The major characteristics of a term of years are that the lessee is given exclusive possession of the land and that the period for which the term is to endure is fixed and definite. It is open to the parties to decide whether their agreement shall be a lease or licence, though the words used by the parties are not conclusive. If there is no right to exclusive possession then there is a mere licence and not a lease. (*Shell-Mex* v. *Manchester Garages*, 1971.)[645] For example, a guest in a hotel does not normally have a lease, because the proprietor retains general control over the room.

The duration of leases

Leases may be for a fixed period of time, and in this case the commencement and termination of the lease must be ascertainable before the lease takes effect. Thus a lease 'for the life of X' would not come under this heading. A lease may be for an indefinite period in the sense that it is to end when the lessor or lessee gives notice. Even so such an arrangement would operate as a valid lease, since the duration of the term can be made certain by the parties giving notice.

In the absence of agreement, the period of a lease may be determined by reference to the payment of rent. Thus if a person takes possession of the premises with the owner's consent for an indefinite period, but the owner accepts rent paid say weekly, monthly, quarterly or annually, then the term may be based on that period, though from early times there has been a presumption that the payment and acceptance of rent shows an intention to create a yearly tenancy but not if the rent is received by mistake. (*Legal and General Assurance Society* v. *General Metal Agencies*, 1969.)[184] A yearly tenancy requires half a year's notice to terminate it if there has been no agreement on the matter. Other periodical tenancies, in the absence of agreement, are determined by notice for the full period. Even where there has been a definite term, a periodical tenancy can arise. Where X is granted a lease of twenty-one years and stays on after the expiration of that term with the owner's consent, then there is a new implied term based on the period of payment of rent.

However, where the tenant is permitted to stay in possession on the understanding that there are to be negotiations for a new lease there is a tenancy at will.

A *tenancy at will* may also arise *by agreement* where a person takes possession of property with the owner's consent, the arrangement being that the term can be brought to an end by either party giving notice. However, the court will look at the transaction in order to ascertain its true nature and will not be put off by ambiguous or wrong terminology. (*Binions* v. *Evans*, 1972.)[646] If there is no agreement as to rent, the tenancy can become a periodical tenancy if the tenant pays and the owner accepts rent paid at given periods of time. A tenancy at will may also arise *by implication* from the conduct of the parties. For example, a prospective purchaser of land who is allowed to take possession before completion occupies the property as a tenant at will until completion.

Where a tenant stays on after the expiration his term without the consent of the owner, there is a *tenancy by sufferance*. No rent is payable under such a tenancy, but the tenant must compensate the owner by a payment in respect of the use and occupation of the land. This compensation is referred to as *mesne profits*. Such a tenancy can be brought to an end at any time, thought it may become a periodical tenancy if the owner accepts a payment of rent at given intervals of time.

It should be noted that the law bases the duration of a periodic tenancy on the intervals of time at which the rent has been paid and accepted, on the ground that this is evidence of the parties' intention. If there is other evidence of intention, then the court will also take this into account, e.g. there may be a prior lease which negatives the intention to create the sort of periodic tenancy which the payment of rent suggests.

Creation of leases

Leases are normally created by a document under seal. However, where the lease is not to exceed three years, a written or oral lease will suffice, so long as the lease takes effect in possession at once at the best rent obtainable. Where a tenancy is in excess of three years then, if the agreement is not under seal, it will operate at common law as a yearly tenancy if the tenant enters into possession and pays rent on a yearly basis, i.e. by reference to a year, even if the rent is paid in quarterly instalments.

The position in Equity is rather different. In Equity, if a person has entered into an agreement for a lease but has no document under seal, then, if he has entered and paid rent or carried out repairs, i.e. if there is a sufficient act of part performance, Equity will insist that the owner of the property execute a formal lease under seal. The equitable maxim, 'Equity looks upon that as done which ought to be done,' applies. This principle is known as the Rule in *Walsh* v. *Lonsdale*, 1882.[647]

It may seem that this rule makes an agreement for a lease as effective as a lease under seal, and certainly, as between the parties to the agreement, absence of a seal is not vital.

However, the rights of the tenant under the rule are equitable and not legal rights, and the tenant can be turned out by a third party to whom the landlord sells the legal estate, if the third party purchases the property for value with or without notice of the existence of the lease.

Nevertheless, since the property legislation of 1925, the tenant can register the agreement as an Estate Contract, and, once the agreement is so registered, all subsequent purchasers of the legal estate are deemed to have notice of the lease and are bound to honour it. (See further p. 457.)

A lease which is to commence from the date of the lease is called a lease *in possession*. However, a *reversionary lease* may be created under which the term is to commence at some future date. A restriction is imposed by s. 149(3) of the Law of Property Act, 1925 which provides that the creation of a reversionary lease which is to take effect more than 21 years from the execution of the lease, e.g. a lease signed in 1984 for a term of ten years to run from 2020, is void. This does not effect the granting of a lease with an option to renew in the future.

Rights and liabilities of landlord and tenant

The rights and liabilities of the parties depend largely upon the lease though a landlord has a special right at common law to distrain for rent, i.e. to move in on the tenant's personal property and remove it for sale to satisfy the amount owing for rent. Where the lease is by deed, the deed will usually fix the rights and liabilities by express clauses which are called covenants. Certain covenants are also implied by law where there is no provision in the lease. The most usual express covenants are covenants to pay rent, covenants regarding repairs and renewals, and a covenant that the tenant will not assign or sub-let.

The main *implied* covenant is that the landlord will not disturb the tenant's quiet enjoyment of the property, or make the use or enjoyment of the land difficult or impossible, i.e. the landlord undertakes not to *derogate from the grant*. As regards furnished houses, the landlord covenants that the property is fit for human habitation. A covenant to keep in repair, whether implied by statute or express, does not impose any liability on a landlord to remedy a latent defect until he becomes aware of it. (*O'Brien* v. *Robinson*, 1973.)[648] The following tenant's covenants are implied by law: a covenant to pay rent, rates and certain taxes, and to repair. The tenant must in general keep the premises wind- and watertight, and must not commit waste, i.e. he must not to deliberate damage to the premises.

Breach of covenant by the tenant can result in forfeiture of the lease. A landlord's covenant to repair can be enforced by specific performance. (*Jeune* v. *Queen's Cross Properties Ltd*, [1973] 3 All E.R. 97.) However, since specific performance is a discretionary remedy it is advisable for tenants to rely on doing their own repairs and recouping from the rent for relatively trivial breaches rather than to approach the courts for specific performance.

The Leasehold Reform Act, 1967

This Act (as amended) enables tenants to buy the freehold of the property which they are leasing. In order to qualify the tenancy must have been granted for more than 21 years (*Roberts* v. *Church Commissioners for England*, 1971)[649] with a rateable value not exceeding £1500 in London and £750 elsewhere. The yearly ground rent must not amount to more than two-thirds of the annual rateable value of the property, i.e. £1000 in London and £500 elsewhere. It must be the tenancy of a house, not a flat, and the tenant must have occupied the house as his only, or main, residence during the past five years, or for periods amounting in total to five years within the past ten years.

A tenant pays the value of the property in the open market but on the assumption that it is subject to a 50-year lease.

Instead of buying the freehold, the tenant can ask for a new lease of 50 years to take effect after the existing lease expires.

SERVITUDES

Servitudes are rights over the property of another and may be either *easements* or *profits à prendre*.

Easements

An easement may be defined as a right to use or restrict the use of the land of another person in some way. There are various classes of easements and these include—

(a) rights of way,
(b) rights of light,
(c) righs to abstract water,
(d) rights to the support of buildings.

To be valid an easement must satisfy the following conditions—

There must be a dominant and servient tenement
The land in respect of which, and for the benefit of which, the easement exists is called the dominant tenement, and the land over which the right is exercised is called the servient tenement. A valid easement cannot exist 'in gross', i.e. without reference to the holding of land (*Hill* v. *Tupper*, 1863),[650] and the grant of a right of way over his land by a landowner to be exercised by the grantee personally, and without reference to any land capable of deriving benefit from the right of way, is merely a licence and not an easement.

The easement must accommodate the dominant tenement
The easement must confer some benefit on the land itself so as to make it a better and more convenient property; it is not enough that the owner obtains some personal advantage. A right of way over contiguous land generally benefits the dominant tenement, and an easement can exist even where two tenements do not actually adjoin, provided it is clear that the easement benefits the dominant tenement.

The dominant tenement and the servient tenement must not be both owned and occupied by the same person
Thus, if P owns both Blackacre and Whiteacre and habitually walks over Blackacre to reach Whiteacre, he is not exercising a right of way in respect of Blackacre, but merely walking from one part of his land to another. For this rule to apply, P must have simultaneously both ownership and possession of the two properties concerned. It is not enough the he owns the two if they are leased to different tenants, or that he is the tenant of both if they are owned by different owners.

The easement must be capable of forming the subject of a grant
This means that the right must be sufficiently definite. (*Bass* v. *Gregory*, 1890.)[651] There must be a capable grantor and a capable grantee, and the right must be within the general nature of the rights capable of existing as easements. An easement is a right to use or restrict the use of a neighbour's land which should not normally involve him in doing any work or

spending any money, though in *Crow* v. *Wood*, 1970,[652] the Court of Appeal recognized an easement of fencing.

The categories of easements are not closed and new rights have from time to time been recognized as easements (*Re Ellenborough Park*, 1956),[653] though in general the courts are still reluctant to extend the categories. (*Phipps* v. *Pears*, 1964.)[654] An easement of unlimited storage within a confined or defined space is probably not capable of existing as a matter of law. (*Grigsby* v. *Melville*, 1972.)[655]

Profits à prendre

A profit à prendre is the right to take something of legal value from the land of another, e.g. shooting, fishing, and grazing rights; the right to cut turf or take wood for fuel. The exception is a right to take water from a stream which is treated as an easement because running water cannot be privately owned and is not therefore a thing of legal value.

A profit necessarily involves a servient tenement but there may or may not be a dominant tenement, for a profit can exist *in gross*. A profit may be a several profit, where enjoyment is granted to an individual as is often the case with shooting and fishing rights; or a profit may be in common which may be enjoyed by more than one person, as is often the case with grazing rights and the right to take various materials for use as fuel.

Acquisition of servitudes

Servitudes may be acquired (*a*) by statute, (*b*) by express or implied grant, (*c*) by prescription, (*d*) by equitable estoppel. (See *Crabb* v. *Arun District Council*, 1975 at p. 593.)

Easements created by statute are usually in connection with local Acts of Parliament.

When land is sold, a servitude may be expressly reserved in favour of another tenement of the seller, or may be expressly granted in similar circumstances by deed; and under the Law of Property Act, 1925, s. 62 a conveyance, if there is no contrary express intention operates to convey servitudes appertaining to the land conveyed. (*Crow* v. *Wood*, 1970.)[652]

Where an owner of two plots conveys one of them, then certain easements are implied. These are *easements of necessity*, as where the piece of land would be completely surrounded and inaccessible without a right of way; *intended easements*, which would be necessary to carry out the common intentions of the parties; *ancillary easements*, which would be necessary in view of the right granted, as the grant of the use of water implies the right of way to reach the water. Where part of a tenement is granted, then the grantee acquires easements over the land which are continuous and apparent, are necessary to the reasonable enjoyment of the land granted, and have been and are used by the grantor for the benefit of the part granted. (*Ward* v. *Kirkland*, 1966.)[656] An example of this is a window enjoying light.

Prescription

Prescription may be based on a presumed grant or alternatively may be established by user as of right.

Prescription at common law depended on user since time immemorial, which at law means since 1189. Clearly in most cases it is out of the question to show continuous user for this period, and so the courts were prepared to accept twenty years' continuous user as raising the presumption of a grant. This presumption may be rebutted by showing that at some time since 1189 the right could not have existed, and it follows that an easement of light cannot be claimed by prescription at common law in a building erected since 1189. This serious difficulty was met in part by the presumption of a lost modern grant, and juries were told that if there had been user during living memory or even for twenty years, they might presume a lost grant or deed, and this ultimately become mandatory, even though neither judge nor jury had any belief that such instrument had ever existed. (*Tehidy Minerals* v. *Norman*, 1971.)[657]

The position is now clear under the Prescription Act, 1832, which was passed to deal with the difficulties arising under the common law. Under this Act, which supplements the common law, we must distinguish easements other than light from easements of light and easements from profits.

Easements other than light

Twenty years' uninterrupted user as of right will establish an easement. User as of right means *nec vi, nec clam, nec precario*, i.e. without force, stealth or permission. The law of prescription rests upon the acquiescence of the owner of the servient tenement. Thus he must have knowledge of the exercise of the right claimed. (*Diment* v. *N. H. Foot*, 1974.)[658] If the owner of the so-called servient tenement can prove that he has given verbal permission, i.e. that the easement is *precario*, then it cannot be claimed (and see *Goldsmith* v. *Burrow Construction Ltd*, 1987 at p. 850). Nevertheless forty years' similar user will establish the easement, and in this case, if the owner of the servient tenement wishes to prove that the right was exercised by permission, he must produce a written agreement to that effect. To establish a right of way by prescription, periods of user of an original and a substituted way may be added together. (*Davis* v. *Whitby*, 1974.)[659]

Easements of light

These can be established by twenty years' user, the defences being that the owner of the servient tenement gave permission and that there is a deed or written agreement to this effect, or that the owner of the servient tenement interrupted the enjoyment of the right for a continuous period of a year by erecting something which blocked the light. Under the Rights of Light Act, 1959 (as amended by the Local Land Charges Act, 1975), it is no longer necessary to erect something of this nature; the owner of the servient land may now register on the local land charges register a statutory notice indicating where he would have put up a screen, and this operates as if the access of light had been restricted for one year. User as of right is not necessary, and oral consent will not bar the claim even if the claimant has made regular money payments for the use of the right.

The right can only be claimed having regard to the type of room affected. A bedroom does not require the amount of light that other rooms do, and if the claimant has used the bedroom to repair watches for twenty years, he will still only be able to claim that amount of light appropriate to a bedroom. There is no right to receive unlimited light but in *Ough* v. *King*, [1967] 3 All E.R. 859, the Court of Appeal held that in determining whether there was an infringement of a right to light regard must be had to the nature of the locality and to the higher standard of lighting required in modern times.

However, in *Allen* v. *Greenwood*, [1979] 2 W.L.R. 187 the Court of Appeal held that the measure of light which can be acquired by prescription can, so far as a greenhouse used for its normal purposes is concerned, include the right to an extraordinary amount of light, and also to the benefits of that light, including the rays of the sun. Nevertheless, there is no claim to a view or a prospect which can be seen from a window.

Profits à prendre

The general period for prescription here is thirty years under the Act of 1832, though twenty years is enough if the court is presuming a lost modern grant. (*Tehidy Minerals* v. *Norman*, 1971.)[657]

If an easement is denied or threatened, it would be necessary to ask the court for an injunction to prevent the owner of the servient tenement from acting contrary to the easement, and its existence would have to be proved under one of the headings given above. The court may then—

(*a*) find the easement not proved; or

(*b*) grant an injunction to restrain the owner of the servient tenement from acting contrary to it; or

(*c*) if the infringement is not serious the court may award once for all damages, in which case the servient owner will have bought his right to act contrary to the easement.

Termination or extinguishment of servitudes

Servitudes may be extinguished by statute, or by express or implied release. At law a deed is necessary for express release, but in Equity an informal release will be effective if it would be inequitable for the dominant owner to claim that the right still exists.

If the dominant owner shows by his conduct an intention to release an easement, it will be extinguished. The demolition of a house to which an easement of light attaches may amount to an implied release, but not if it is intended to replace the house by another building. Mere non-user is not enough, although it may be some evidence of intention to abandon the right. (*Tehidy Minerals* v. *Norman*, 1971.)[657] There is no fixed time but twenty years' non-user usually constitutes abandonment.

We have already seen that an easement is extinguished when the dominant and servient tenements come into simultaneous ownership and possession of the same person, since a person cannot have an easement over his or her own land.

RESTRICTIVE COVENANTS

A restrictive covenant is essentially a contract between two owners of land whereby one agrees to restrict the use of his land for the benefit of the other. We are not concerned here with covenants in leases, which are governed by separate rules already outlined.

Such covenants were not adequately enforced by the common law because the doctrine of privity of contract applied, and as soon as one of the parties to the covenant transferred his land, the covenant was not enforceable by the transferee because he had not been a party to the original contract. However, the common law realized that this was rather too rigid and went so far as to allow a transferee to enforce the benefit of the covenant against the original party to it. Thus if A, the owner of Blackacre, agreed with B, the owner of Whiteacre, that he would not use Blackacre for the purposes of trade, then if B sold Whiteacre to C, C could enforce the covenant against A. However, if A sold Blackacre to D, C could not enforce the convenant against D, because the common law would not allow D to bear the burden of a covenant he did not make.

Equity takes a different view, and allows C to enforce the sort of covenant outlined above by injunction, if the following conditions are fulfilled—

(i) The covenant must be substantially negative
Much depends upon the words used in the covenant, and an undertaking which seems *prima facie* to be positive may imply a negative undertaking and this may then be enforced. (*Tulk* v. *Moxhay*, 1848.)[133] A covenant to use a house as a dwelling house implies that it will not be used for other purposes, and would be enforceable in the negative sense. If the covenant requires the covenantor to spend money, it is not a negative covenant.

(ii) The covenant must benefit the land
It is often said that the covenant must 'touch and concern' the land and must not be merely for the personal benefit of the claimant. Restrictive

covenants usually endeavour to keep up the residential character of the district and benefit the land by preserving value and amenities as a residential property.

(iii) The person claiming the benefit must retain land which can benefit from the covenant taken

If X owns a piece of land which he splits up into two plots, selling one plot to Y and taking a restrictive covenant in favour of the plot he has retained, then he can enforce the covenant so long as he retains the land to be benefited. If X now sells the plot he had retained, he will not be able to enforce the covenant for the future, although the purchaser from X will be able to do so. (*Kelly* v. *Barret*, 1924.)[660]

There is an exception to this rule in the case of *building schemes* involving an estate of houses. Here the covenants are taken by the owner of the land from each person purchasing a house, and although the owner does not retain any of the land, the covenants may be enforced by the purchasers as between themselves. However, a building scheme will not be implied simply because there is a common vendor and the existence of common covenants. It was at one time thought that there must be a defined area and evidence of laying out in lots (*Re Wembley Park Estate Co. Ltd's Transfer*, [1968] 1 All E.R. 457). However, in *Re Dolphin's Conveyance*, [1970] 2 All E.R. 664, Stamp, J., held that so long as the covenants held in the conveyances were, as a matter of construction, intended to give the purchasers of the parcels mutual rights, this was sufficient to make them enforceable and there was no need, in particular, to consider lotting.

Since restrictive covenants are in general enforceable only in Equity, the question of notice arises. In fact, restrictive covenants created after 1925 are void against a purchaser of the legal estate, even one who has notice of them, unless they are registered as land charges. (See further p. 457.) There is an exception as regards covenants between lessor and lessee. These cannot be registered and will be binding only if known to an assignee of the lease. In practice it is usual for an assignee to inspect the lease. As regards covenants created before 1 January, 1926, they bind all persons who acquire the land which is subject to them with the exception of a purchaser for value of the legal estate in the land without notice, actual or constructive, of the covenants.

Under s. 84 of the Law of Property Act, 1925 (as amended by s. 28(1) and Sch. 3 of the Law of Property Act, 1969), the Lands Tribunal has power, on the application of any person interested, to discharge or modify a restrictive covenant.

Whether a covenant runs with the land depends upon the words. In *Roake* v. *Chadha*, [1983] 3 All E.R. 503 the covenant between plots of land was that no more than one house should be built on each plot. The covenants were expressed to pass *only if specifically assigned*. A plot was sold to the defendant but the covenant was not assigned. He proposed to build more than one house on the plot and the plaintiff, who owned an adjacent plot, tried to enforce the 'one house' covenant. It was held that he could not do so because the covenant had not been specifically assigned as the agreement required.

THE TRANSFER OF LAND

It is usual, when a disposition of land is contemplated, to draw up a contract. For a contract of sale to be valid both parties must have contractual capacity, the contract must be legal, there must be clear agreement on all the essential terms, and acceptance of the offer must be unconditional. Where one accepts an offer to sell 'subject to contract', no contract is effected until a formal contract is approved.

Under s. 40 of the Law of Property Act, 1925, it is provided that no action may be brought upon any contract for the sale or other disposition of land, or any interest in land, unless the agreement upon which such action is brought, or some memorandum or note thereof, is in writing and signed by the party to be charged or some other person lawfully authorized. In the absence of a note or memorandum the contract is unenforceable, though the equitable doctrine of part performance may sometimes be invoked.

When a valid contract for sale exists, the purchaser acquires an equitable interest in the property and the vendor is in effect a qualified trustee for him. Thus if the property increases in value between contract and completion, the purchaser is entitled to the increase and similarly he must bear any loss. This is particularly important in cases where property is destroyed by fire between contract and completion, since the purchaser would still have to pay the purchase money, even though he only received a conveyance of the land with the useless buildings on it. It is now provided by s. 47 of the Law of Property Act, 1925, that in such a case the purchaser may become entitled to money payable on an insurance policy maintained by the vendor. However, it is prudent for the purchaser to take out his own insurance in case the vendor has none or his policy is defective.

The vendor has a lien on the property sold to the extent of the unpaid purchase money and may enforce this by an order for sale; this lien may be registered as a general equitable charge. The purchaser has a similar lien in respect of money paid under the contract prior to conveyance.

On a sale of land it is usual to use a standard form of contract prepared by The Law Society since this saves much trouble in drafting. In what is called an open contract for the sale of land the vendor must under s. 23 of the Law of Property Act, 1969, show a title for a least fifteen years, beginning with a good 'root of title', i.e. a document dealing with the whole legal and equitable interests in the land. It may be necessary to go back more than fifteen years in order to find such a document. The vendor prepares an abstract of title, listing all the relevant documents in connection with its establishment, and he must produce these documents in order to justify the abstract of title he has prepared. It should be noted that all the above matters are attended to by the parties' solicitors.

The Administration of Justice Act, 1985 has removed the monopoly on conveyancing which has been possessed by solicitors for many years. (See further p. 109.)

A contract for the sale of land will normally contain a completion date which is the time by which the transaction must be concluded. The transfer of land involves the following stages—

(a) The preparation of the contract.

(b) The exchange of contracts between the vendor's and purchaser's solicitors, when the purchaser pays a deposit, usually ten per cent of the purchase money. The purpose of this exchange is to provide each party with a written, signed agreement which will satisfy s. 40 of the Law of Property Act, 1925 and allow an action to be brought should one party fail to complete.

(c) The delivery by the vendor's solicitors of an abstract of title, or as is more usual today, copies of the documents, e.g. previous conveyances, upon which the vendor bases his title.

(d) The examination of this title by the purchaser's solicitors and the checking of the abstract against the actual deeds to see that it is correct.

(e) After all outstanding queries have been solved, a conveyance is prepared by the purchaser's solicitors which is sent to the vendor's sol-icitors for approval. The draft conveyance may be exchanged a number of times before agreement is reached. Where the land is registered, a simpler form of transfer deed is used.

(f) Just before completion the purchaser's solicitors will make the necessary searches in the Land Charges Register and in the Register maintained by the appropriate local authority to see what encumbrances are registered in respect of the property.

(g) An appointment is then arranged for completion and the purchaser hands over the money, the vendor handing over the conveyance, which he has signed, together with the title deeds. This brings the transaction to a conclusion. There need not be attendance at an office. Completion is very often carried out by post.

The above procedure refers to unregistered land where the need to examine title is to some extent cumbersome and expensive. The Land Registration Act, 1925, provides that the title to land can be examined by and registered with the state followed by the issue of a certificate guar-anteeing ownership. Where there is a sale of registered land the certifi-cate is handed over and the name of the new owner registered. A transfer, rather than a conveyance, is prepared. This is a more simple procedure than the one outlined above for unregistered land and the legal fees for the transaction are less.

PERSONAL PROPERTY

We have already mentioned that personal property is divided into two classes—*choses in action* and *choses in possession*, the latter being divided into *chattels real* (i.e. leaseholds) and *chattels personal*. We have already dealt with leaseholds, and the sale of chattels personal has been codified by the Sale of Goods Act, 1979, a study of which would not be appropriate to a book of this nature. The assignment of choses in action is considered on p. 464.

MORTGAGES OF LAND

Legal mortgage of freeholds

Under the 1925 legislation the mortgagor (the borrower) does not divest himself of his legal estate, but grants to the mortgagee (the lender) a demise for a term of years absolute. Thus, if X owns Blackacre and borrows money on mortgage from Y, he will grant Y a term of usually three thousand years in Blackacre, both agreeing that the term of years will end when the loan is repaid. X will also agree to pay interest on the loan at a stipulated rate.

Alternatively, under the provisions of s. 87 of the Law of Property Act, 1925, it is possible to create a legal mortgage of freeholds by means of a short deed stating that a charge on the land is created. Such a charge does not give a term of years, but the mortgagee has the same rights and powers as if he had received a term of years under a mortgage by demise.

Before 1926 mortgages were created by conveying the freehold to the mortgagee. Since 1925 an attempt to create a mortgage by this method operates as a grant of a mortgage lease of 3000 years, subject to cesser on redemption. (Section 85, Law of Property Act, 1925.)

Legal mortgage of leaseholds

If X, the owner of a ninety-nine years lease of Blackacre, borrows money on mortgage from Y, he may grant Y a sub-lease of (say) ninety-nine years less ten days, both agreeing that when the loan is repaid the term shall cease. X also agrees to pay interest. Such a term is known as a *mortgage by demise*.

Alternatively a legal mortgage of leaseholds may be created by a charge by way of legal mortgage under s. 87 of the Law of Property Act, 1925, if made by deed. No sub-lease is created but the remedies of the mortgagee are the same as if it had been.

When a person has borrowed money by mortgaging property, he may still be able to borrow further sums, if the amount of the charge is not equal to the full value of the property and there seems to be adequate security for further loans. The owner of freehold land may grant a term of three thousand years plus one day to another mortgagee, whilst the owner of a lease may grant a second sub-lease of (say) ninety-nine years less nine days. Alternatively, a second charge by way of legal mortgage may be created by a further deed.

The only limit to further borrowing on second and subsequent mortgages is that of finding a lender who is prepared to become a second, third, or fourth mortgagee.

Equitable mortgage

A mortgagee who receives a mere equitable interest in the land is said to have an equitable mortgage. Thus if the borrower's interest is equitable, e.g. a life interest, then any mortgage of it is necessarily equitable. Such an interest may be mortgaged by lease or charge, as in legal mortgages, or by a deposit of title deeds with the lender, usually accompanied by a memorandum explaining the transaction. Such mortgages must be in writing and signed by the borrower or his agent. (Section 53, Law of Property Act, 1925.)

An informal mortgage of a legal estate or interest creates an equitable mortgage, e.g. an attempt to create a legal mortgage otherwise than by deed.

Where there is a binding agreement to create a legal mortgage, but the formalities necessary to do so have not been carried out, Equity regards the agreement as an equitable mortgage. The agreement can be enforced by specific performance so that the mortgagee can obtain a legal mortgage from the borrower under the Rule in *Walsh* v. *Lonsdale*, 1882.[647] Before there is a binding agreement there must be either written evidence of the agreement, signed by the borrower or his agent, or a sufficient act of part performance by the lender.

Rights of the mortgagor or borrower

The main right of the mortgagor is the right to redeem (or recover) the land. Originally at common law the land became the property of the lender as soon as the date decided upon for repayment had passed, unless during that time the loan had been repaid. However, Equity regarded a mortgage as essentially a security, and gave the mortgagor the right to redeem the land at any time on payment of the principal sum, plus interest due to the date of payment. What is more important, this rule applied even though the common law date for repayment had passed. This right, which still exists, is called the *Equity of Redemption*, and there are two important rules connected with it—

(a) Once a mortgage always a mortgage
This means that Equity looks at the real purpose of the transaction and does not always have regard to its form. If Equity considers that the transaction is a mortgage, the rules appertaining to mortgages will apply,

particularly the right to redeem the property even though the contractual date for repayment has passed, or has not yet arrived. In the latter case, however, the mortgagor must generally give six months' notice of his intention to redeem, or pay six months' interest in lieu, so that the mortgagee may find another investment. However, if the parties contract at arm's length, and there is no evidence of oppression by the mortgagee, the court will endeavour to uphold the principle of sanctity of contract and will enforce any reasonable restriction on the right to redeem. (*Knightsbridge Estates Trust Ltd* v. *Byrne*, 1939.)[661]

(b) There must be no clog on the equity of redemption
This means—

(i) that the court will not allow postponement of the repayment period for an unreasonable time; and

(ii) the property mortgaged must, when the loan is repaid, be returned to the borrower in the same condition as when it was pledged. (*Noakes* v. *Rice*, 1902.)[662]

Nevertheless, particularly in modern times, so long as the parties are at arm's length when the loan is negotiated, Equity will allow a collateral transaction. (*Kreglinger* v. *New Patagonia Meat and Cold Storage Co.*, 1914,[663] and *Cityland and Property (Holdings) Ltd.* v. *Dabrah*, 1967.)[664]

It is worth noting that the mortgagor may, where he is in possession of the land, grant leases to third parties subject to any special agreement to the contrary.

(c) A term must not amount to an extortionate credit bargain
Sections 137 to 139 of the Consumer Credit Act, 1974 deal with extortionate credit bargains. The Court may re-open and revise the terms of such bargains to do justice to the borrower.

(d) A term must not be in restraint of trade
This has already been considered in Chapter 7 where the case of *Esso* v. *Harper's Garage*, 1967[311] was discussed.

Powers and remedies of the legal mortgagee

A legal mortgagee (the lender) has the following concurrent powers and remedies—

(a) To take possession
This right does not depend upon default by the mortgagor, but the mortgagee will normally only enter into possession of the property under the term of years granted to him, or under the charge by way of legal mortgage, when he is not being paid the sum due, and when he wishes to pay himself from the proceeds of the property. In addition, the court will grant a possession order where an insurance policy which is the security

has been allowed to lapse by the borrower. (*Western Bank* v. *Schindler*, [1976] 2 All E.R. 393.) This is not a desirable remedy, however, because when the mortgagee takes possession he is strictly accountable to the mortgagor, not only for what he has received but for what he might have received with the exercise of due diligence and proper management. (*White* v. *City of London Brewery Co.*, 1889.)[665] If the mortgagee is simply concerned to intercept rents, where the mortgaged property is let and the mortgagor is a landlord, he will do better to appoint a receiver under the Law of Property Act, 1925, s. 109. Most mortgagees who ask for a possession order do so in order to sell with vacant possession. The Administration of Justice Act, 1970, which is concerned, amongst other things, with mortgage possession actions, reinstates the old practice of the Chancery masters by allowing the court to make an order adjourning the proceedings, or suspending or postponing a possession order provided it appears that the mortgagor is likely to be able to pay within a reasonable time any sums due under the mortgage (s. 36). However, the court cannot suspend the execution of an order for possession indefinitely and must specify the period of suspension. (*Royal Trust Co. of Canada* v. *Markham*, [1975] 3 All E.R. 433.)

The Act applies wherever a mortgage includes a dwelling house even though part may be used for business purposes. Unfortunately, it was held in *Halifax Building Society* v. *Clark*, [1973] 2 All E.R. 33, that where, as is often the case, the mortgage provided that the whole sum should become payable on default by the mortgagor, the court's power to adjourn or stay execution under s. 36 could only be exercised if it appeared likely that the mortgagor could pay the *whole* sum within a reasonable period. This plainly defeated the intention of the 1970 Act in most cases as the period of the stay envisaged is short, and the likelihood of the mortgagor being able to repay the entire redemption figure, remote. Accordingly, s. 8 of the Administration of Justice Act, 1973, now provides that a court may treat as due under the mortgage only those instalments actually in arrear, but shall not exercise the power to postpone the order for possession unless the mortgagor will be able to catch up within a reasonable period. This means that not only must he be able to pay the instalments due month by month but also the arrears within a reasonable time.

It should be noted that where a house is owned by a husband and is mortgaged to secure the loan, the interest of the wife occupying the home overrides the lender's claim under the mortgage and the court may refuse a possession order. (*Williams & Glyn's Bank Ltd* v. *Boland*, 1980 (see further p. 853).)

(b) Foreclosure
The mortgagee may obtain a foreclosure order from the court if the mortgagor fails to pay for an unreasonable time. The first order is a *foreclosure order nisi* providing that the debt must be paid within a stated time. If it is not so paid, the order is made *absolute* and the property

becomes that of the mortgagee, the mortgagor's equity of redemption being barred, and the property vesting in the mortgagee, free from any right of redemption either in law or Equity. Such orders are seldom used, for it is still open to the court to re-open the foreclosure, i.e. to give the mortgagor a further opportunity to redeem. S. 36 of the Administration of Justice Act, 1970, excluded the power to postpone a foreclosure order because it was considered that the court's power to give the mortgagor time to redeem when granting the decree *nisi* was an adequate remedy. The Payne Committee recommended including actions for foreclosure, and they are now included by the Administration of Justice Act, 1973, s. 8(3). Thus the courts now have power to postpone an order for foreclosure.

(c) Right of sale
Normally this is the most valuable right of the mortgagee. Subject to certain conditions he can, on the default of the mortgagor, sell and convey to a purchaser the whole of the mortgaged property, and recoup himself out of the proceeds. Unless the mortgagee is a building society (Building Societies Act, 1986 Sch. 4), he is not a trustee of the power of sale for the benefit of the mortgagor. However, he must not fraudulently, wilfully or recklessly sacrifice the property of the mortgagor (*Kennedy* v. *De Trafford*, [1897] A.C. 180) and in addition owes a duty to the mortgagor to take reasonable care to obtain the best price that can be had in the circumstances. (*Cuckmere Brick Co. Ltd* v. *Mutual Finance*, [1971] 2 All E.R. 633.)

The general rule is that a mortgagee cannot sell to himself or to his nominee. Although a mortgagee is not a trustee of the power of sale and need not get the best possible price (though a building society must) the conflict of interest where he sells to himself is one which Equity generally forbids. However, it is thought that the mortgagee could purchase the property, subject to the mortgage, if he had leave from the court, which is the general rule for trustees who wish to buy the trust property, and provided the mortgagor did not object and possibly also if no other purchaser at an adequate price could be found. It is also probable that a mortgagee could buy the property at an auction since in that event the sale is not directly to himself but through an intermediary, i.e. the auctioneer, and given that there is no collusion between the mortgagee and the auctioneer there would seem to be no good reason why the mortgagee should not buy the property in.

In *Tsi Kwong Lam* v. *Wong Chit Sen*, [1983] 3 All E.R. 54, the Privy Council decided that a sale by a mortgagee exercising his power of sale to a company in which he had an interest would not necessarily be banned by the law provided the sale was made in good faith and that the mortgagee had taken reasonable precautions to obtain the best price reasonably obtainable at the time, namely by taking expert advice as to the methods of sale and the steps which ought reasonably to be taken to make the sale a success.

(d) To sue for the money owing

The mortgage is a pledge for the repayment of the money, but mortgagors almost invariably give a personal covenant to repay. This is of value should the property be destroyed or lose its value. When the date fixed for redemption is passed, the mortgage money is due and the mortgagee can sue for it. He will rarely do so, for in most cases the other remedies will be more satisfactory.

(e) The right to appoint a receiver

The Law of Property Act, 1925, s. 109, gives the mortgagee the right to appoint a receiver to receive the rents and profits on the mortgagee's behalf in order to pay the money due. The receiver is deemed to be the agent of the mortgagor, who is liable for his acts and defaults unless otherwise provided by the mortgage. The mortgagee thus avoids the disadvantage of strict accountability to which he would be subject if he entered himself.

Remedies of equitable mortgagees

Where the mortgage is equitable and is created by deed, then the mortgagee has virtually the same remedies as have been set out above. Otherwise, if the mortgage is by a mere deposit of title deeds, them the mortgagee must ask the court—

    (*a*) for an order to sell; or
    (*b*) for an order appointing a receiver.

Other rights of mortgagees

A mortgagee has other rights and he may, where the mortgage is created by deed, insure the mortgaged property against loss by fire up to two-thirds of its value, and charge the premiums on the property in the same way as the mortgage money.

A mortgagee has a right to the title deeds of the property, and if the mortgage is redeemed by the mortgagor, the mortgagee must return the deeds to him in the absence of notice of a second or subsequent mortgage, in which case the deeds should be handed to the next mortgagee.

There are two other important rights which a mortgagee may exercise in appropriate circumstances—the right to consolidate and the right to tack.

Consolidation

Where a person has two or more mortgages, he may refuse to allow one mortgage to be redeemed unless the other or others are also redeemed. This right is particularly valuable where property might fluctuate in value, and where a mortgagor might redeem one mortgage where the security was more than adequate, leaving the mortgagee with a debt on the other property not properly secured.

Consolidation is only possible if the right to consolidate was reserved in one of the mortgage deeds. The contractual date for redemption must have passed on all mortgages and they must have been created by the same mortgagor, though not necessarily in favour of the same mortgagee. Nevertheless in such cases, where it is proposed to consolidate two mortgages, both the mortgages must have been vested in one person at the same time as both the equities of redemption were vested in another.

Tacking

The right to tack may bring about a modification of the priority of mortgages. It is now confined to the tacking of further advances. Thus, where a man has lent money on a first mortgage and there are second and third mortgages, if the first mortgagee agrees to advance a further sum, he may tack this to his first mortgage and thus get priority over the second and third, which would normally rank before the tacked mortgage. This can now only be done if the intervening mortgagees agree, or if the further advance is made without notice of an intervening mortgage, or if the prior mortgage imposed an obligation to make further advances.

Attornment clause

Many mortgages contain an attornment clause by which the borrower attorns or acknowledges himself as a tenant at will, or from year to year, of the lender at a nominal rent such as a peppercorn. The advantage of such a clause was that it entitled the lender to evict the borrower for failure to pay the mortgage instalments and so obtain possession more speedily. However, changes in the rules of court from 1933–1937 made a speedy procedure available to mortgagees as such, and there is now no substantial advantage in an attornment clause.

Priority of mortgages

The Land Charges Act, 1925, introduced the principle of registering charges on land. The object of searching the Land Charges Register is to discover the rights, if any, of third parties which are enforceable against the land. It is a general principle that a purchaser or mortgagee of land is deemed to have actual notice of all third-party rights capable of registration and actually registered, whereas he acquires his interest in the land free from third-party rights capable of registration and not registered. There are five separate registers kept in the Land Charges Department of the Land Registry. Search is usually done by filling in an appropriate form and sending it to the Land Charges Superintendent. This results in an *official search certificate*.

Where there is a mortgage of a legal estate with deposit of title deeds, the mortgage ranks from the date of its creation and such a mortgage cannot be registered.

Where there is a mortgage of legal estate without deposit of title deeds, the mortgage ranks from its date of registration as a land charge.

Regarding mortgages of equitable interests, the question of priority is based on the rule in *Dearle* v. *Hall* (1828), 3 Russ. 1, and such mortgages rank from the date on which the mortgagee gave notice of his mortgage to the trustees of the equitable interest, though such notice will not postpone a previous mortgage of which the mortgagee giving notice was aware. Equitable mortgages of interests other than equitable interests rank in priority according to the date of creation. Thus, an equitable mortgage created in January, 1989, would take priority over one created in May, 1989, Legal mortgages take precedence over equitable mortgages, but an equitable mortgagee who obtains a legal interest does not thereby gain priority over an equitable interest of which he has constructive notice. Thus if A obtains an equitable interest in property, e.g. a contract to purchase land, in January, 1989, and fails to register it as an estate contract until May, 1989, and B in February, 1989, obtains an equitable mortgage over the land which is converted into a legal mortgage in April, 1989, at a time when B knows or ought to know that A has an interest, as where A is on the land and carrying out works, then B's mortgage, although legal will not rank over A's equitable interest. (*McCarthy and Stone* v. *Julian S. Hodge & Co.*, [1971] 2 All E.R. 973.)

The Leasehold Reform Act, 1967

Where, under the provisions of this Act, a leaseholder buys the freehold, the conveyance automatically discharges the premises from any mortgage even though the lender is not a party to the conveyance. (S. 12(1).) However, the leaseholder must apply the money which he is using to buy the freehold, in the first instance, in or towards the payment (or redemption) of the mortgage. (S. 12(2).) If the lender raises difficulties the tenant may, in order to protect his interest, pay the money into court. (S. 13.) The lender (or mortgagee) must accept not less than three months' notice to pay off the whole or part of the principal secured by the mortgage, together with interest to the date of payment regardless of any provisions to the contrary in the mortgage. (S. 12(4).)

The court is also given power, under s. 36, to alter the rights of the parties to a mortgage in order to mitigate any financial hardship which may arise as a result of the purchase of a freehold under the provisions of the Act.

If it is desired that a mortgage of the former leasehold interest should be extended to cover the freehold, this may be done by requesting the borrower to execute a deed of substituted security. If a tenant acquires an extended lease a lender is entitled to possession of the documents of title relating to the new lease (s. 14(6)) and should ask for them when the borrower obtains an extended lease. The borrower should also be required to execute a mortgage of the extended lease.

REGISTRATION OF LAND CHARGES

The Land Charges Act, 1925, and the Land Registration Act, 1925, introduced the principle of registering charges on land. The object of searching the Land Charges Register is to discover the rights, if any, of third parties which are enforceable against the land. It is a general principle that a purchaser or mortgagee of land is deemed to have actual notice of all third-party rights capable of registration and actually registered, whereas he acquires his interest in the land free third-party rights capable of registration and not registered.

The injustice to a purchaser of this rule lay in the fact that in practice there is no investigation of the title prior to the formation of the contract. In consequence, if a vendor did not actually disclose to a purchaser that there were charges over the land, then, if the charges were registered, the purchaser was unable to rescind the contract since he was deemed to know that they existed. However, under s. 24 of The Law of Property Act, 1969, the purchaser will be affected *as against his vendor* only by land charges of which he had *actual* knowledge at the time of entering into the contract. If he completes the contract the purchaser remains bound by registered land charges *as against the holder of the charge* whether or not he has actual knowledge of them.

The present system of registration of land charges at the Land Registry is governed by the Land Charges Act, 1972, in the case of unregistered land, and by the Land Registration Act, 1925, in the case of registered land. Prior registration of a land charge does not of itself confer priority; it merely gives notice to everyone dealing with the property so that they will take subject to the charge as purchasers with notice of it. Failure to register a land charge merely means that upon completion of a purchase the charge will be void against the purchaser. Right up to completion the person with the benefit of a land charge can preserve his rights by registering the charge.

The most important search is in the Registers of the Land Registry, though local land charges appear in registers kept by local authorities. A common example of a local land charge is road charges, i.e. charges against land which the local authority has in regard to the cost of making up a road which adjoins that land. Search may be in person at some Land Registry offices, of which there are 16 in England and Wales, or may be done by filling in the details on the appropriate form and sending it to the Land Registry in London. This results in an official search certificate.

It is now possible to ask for search by telephone or telex, the applicant receiving a printed result of the search by post. The Land Charges Act, 1972, introduced a number of changes designed to simplify the procedure. These include changes made necessary by computerization.

The registers are basically registers of names, not properties. Search is therefore under the name of the vendor. Thus a charge affecting

Whiteacre, a property situated in Birmingham and owned by John Jones, will be indexed under John Jones, provided he was owner of Whiteacre when the charge was created. Sometimes charges are registered in the name of the property but now that search is by computer this does not give rise to difficulties.

The Land Registration Act, 1988 allows members of the public to go to Land Registry offices in England and Wales and inspect the relevant registers to see who owns land.

The Matrimonial Homes Act, 1967 (see now Matrimonial Homes Act, 1983), created a new type of land charge. It was passed to restore the legal position to what it was before the decision of the House of Lords in *National Provincial Bank Ltd* v. *Ainsworth*, [1965] 2 All E.R. 472. In that case it was decided that a deserted wife had no special right or 'equity' to continue to occupy the matrimonial home though there had formerly been such a right. The effect of the decision in *Ainsworth's Case* was that a husband who was the owner of the matrimonial home could, having deserted his wife and children, sell or mortgage the house to a third party who would in most cases be able to get an order for possession in order to enforce his rights. In these circumstances the deserted wife and children would have to give up occupation of the matrimonial home and find other accommodation.

The 1983 Act provides that where one spouse owns or is the tenant of the matrimonial home, the other spouse has certain 'rights of occupation' (s. 1(1)) and cannot be evicted without an order of the court. Where a spouse is not in occupation of the matrimonial home he or she has a right, with the leave of the court, to enter and occupy the house. However, the court may order a spouse who is occupying the matrimonial home by reason of the Act to make periodical payments to the other spouse in respect of that occupation. It should be noted that the Act protects husbands as well as wives.

It should be noted that s. 1 of the Matrimonial Homes Act, 1983, provides that either of the spouses may apply to the court for an order prohibiting, suspending, or restricting the exercise by either spouse of the right to occupy the dwelling house or requiring either spouse to permit the exercise by the other of that right.

The Matrimonial Homes Act provides that the rights of occupation provided for in s. 1(1) are a charge on the estate or interest of the other spouse (s. 2(1)), registrable as a new type of land charge (Class F) under the Land Charges Act, 1972. Where the land is registered land a notice or caution must be registered under the Land Registration Act, 1925. A purchaser or mortgagee is deemed to have notice of rights of occupation which have been properly registered. Rights of occupation may be registered on marriage though in most cases registration will not take place unless and until the marriage breaks down.

Where a spouse registers rights of occupation, the house is unlikely subsequently to be an acceptable security for a loan because the rights of occupation represent a prior charge on the property which cannot be sold with vacant possession. However, a spouse who is entitled to rights of occupation may, under s. 6(3) of the Act, agree in writing that any other charge shall rank in priority to his or her charge.

However, even if the spouse's right of occupation is not registered it may still be recognized by the court. (*Williams & Glyn's Bank Ltd* v. *Boland*, 1980.)[666]

Searching applies to encumbrances over unregistered land, but in many parts of the country land registration is compulsory, e.g. in London, Middlesex and Surrey. The system of registration of title to land is similar to registration of title to shares. However, in place of the share register which a company keeps there is a register of land holdings which is maintained by the State and instead of a share certificate there is a land certificate. When the land is transferred the registered owner hands over the land certificate together with a deed of transfer signed by him to the purchaser who then registers these documents with the Registrar who amends the land register and the land certificate and returns the latter to the transferee.

In general terms the State guarantees the accuracy of the register and if there is an error the register will be rectified and an indemnity paid to anyone who suffers loss, e.g. a person does not, in fact, get a good title to the land. The only interests in respect of which title may be registered are legal estates in land, i.e. a fee simple absolute in possession or a term of years absolute. As regards other interests in the land, all registered land is deemed to be subject to overriding interests listed in s. 70 of the Land Registration Act, 1925, whether these are on the register or not. Some of the more important overriding interests are easements and profits which exist over the land, and the interest of a wife in occupying the matrimonial home. (See *Williams & Glyn's Bank Ltd* v. *Boland*, 1980.)[666] Other interests may be protected by requiring an entry of, e.g. a caution on the register. This entitles the person who asks for the caution to be notified by the Registrar of any proposed dealings with the land and to object within a specified period of time. Thus a purchaser under an estate contract could protect himself against further sales of the property in a situation where he had purchased it but had not yet received the land certificate from the registered proprietor.

It is expected that the compulsory registration system will, broadly speaking, be extended to all areas of the country within the next few years.

MORTGAGES OF PERSONAL CHATTELS

Just as land can be used as a means of securing debts, so also can personal chattels. There are two principal ways in which this can be done—

(a) By mortgage

In this case the borrower retains possession of his goods but transfers their ownership to the lender to secure the loan.

This raises a problem because, since the borrower retains the chattels, he also retains an appearance of wealth, and this may mislead others into giving him credit. Accordingly the Bills of Sale Acts, 1878–82, were passed, and under the statutory provisions, where chattels are retained by the mortgagor, a bill of sale must be made out. Where ownership of the chattel passes to the mortgagee conditionally upon its being re-conveyed to the mortgagor on repayment of the loan, the Bill of Sale is called a conditional bill. An absolute Bill of Sale in one which transfers completely the ownership in chattels by way of sale, gift or settlement.

All Bills of Sale must be attested and registered within seven days of execution. Registration is in the Central Office of the Supreme Court. Conditional Bills of Sale must be re-registered every five years if they are still operative.

A conditional Bill of Sale is totally void if it is not registered, whilst an unregistered absolute Bill of Sale is void against the trustee in bankruptcy and judgment creditors of the grantor so that the chattels represented by the Bill are available to pay the grantor's debts. However an absolute bill of sale will not be void for want of registration unless the chattels remain in the sole possession, or apparent possession, of the transferor (or grantor) of the bill. (*Koppel* v. *Koppel*, 1966.)[667]

(b) By pledge, or 'pawn'

In this case the lender obtains possession of the goods, the borrower retaining ownership. Thus there is no danger that the borrower will obtain credit on the strength of his possession of the chattels, and the law relating to pledges is mainly concerned to protect the interests of the borrower (or pledger) against dishonest pawnbrokers.

MORTGAGES OF CHOSES IN ACTION

It is possible to use a chose in action as security for a loan, and mortgagees frequently take life assurance policies as security, e.g. a bank in the case of an overdraft. However, shares in companies are perhaps the commonest chose in action to be used as security.

Shares may be made subject to a legal mortgage, but here the shares must actually be transferred to the mortgagee so that his name is in fact on the company's share register. An agreement is made out in which the mortgagee agrees to re-transfer the shares to the mortgagor when the loan is repaid.

It is also possible to have an equitable mortgage of company shares, and this is in fact the usual method adopted. The share certificate is deposited with the mortgagee, together with a blank transfer signed by the registered holder, the name of the transferee being left blank. The shares are not actually transferred, but the agreement accompanying the transaction allows the mortgagee to sell the shares by completing the form of transfer and registering himself as the legal owner if the mortgagor fails to repay the loan.

OTHER FORMS OF SECURITY

A security is some right or interest in property given to a creditor so that, if the debt is not paid, the creditor can obtain the amount of the debt by exercising certain remedies against the property, rather than by suing the debtor by means of a personal action on his promise to pay. Securities, therefore, create rights over the property of another and since we have already discussed mortgages of land, chattels and choses in action it remains only to consider the lien.

LIEN

A lien is a right over the property of another which arises by operation of law and independently of any agreement. It gives a creditor the right (*a*) to retain possession of the debtor's property until he has paid or settled the debt, or (*b*) to sell the property in satisfaction of the debt in those cases where the lien is not possessory. Where the parties agree that a lien shall be created, such agreement will effectively create one.

Possessory or common law lien

To exercise this type of lien the creditor must have actual possession of the debtor's property, in which case he can retain it until the debt is paid or settled. It should be noted that the creditor cannot ask for possession of the debtor's goods in order to exercise a lien.

A common law lien may be particular or general—

(a) Particular lien
This gives the possessor the right to retain goods until a debt arising in connection with those goods is paid.

(b) General lien
This gives the possessor the right to retain goods not only for debts specifically connected with them, but also for all debts due from the owner of the goods however arising.

The law favours particular rather than general liens.

If X sends a clock to R to be repaired at a cost of £5, R may retain the clock under a particular lien until the £5 is paid. If, however, X owed R £10 for the earlier repair of a watch, R cannot retain the clock to enforce the payment of £15 unless, as is unlikely, he can claim a general lien.

The following are cases of *particular lien*—

(i) A carrier can retain goods entrusted to him for carriage until his charges are paid.

(ii) An innkeeper has a lien over the property brought into the inn by a guest and also over property sent to him while there, even if it does not belong to him. (*Robins* v. *Gray* 1895.)[668] The lien does not extend to motor cars or other vehicles, or to horses or other animals.

(iii) A shipowner has a lien on the cargo for freight due.

(iv In a sale of goods, the unpaid seller has a lien on the goods, if still in his possession, to recover the price.

(v) Where a chattel is bailed in order that work may be done on it or labour and skill expanded in connection with it, it may be retained until the charge is paid. Such liens may arise, e.g. in favour of a car repairer over the car repaired; by an arbitrator on the award and by an architect over plans he has prepared.

A *general lien* may arise out of contract or custom, and the following classes of persons have a general lien over the property of their customers or clients—factors, bankers, solicitors, stockbrokers, and in some cases insurance brokers. (*Caldwell* v. *Sumpters*, 1971.)[669] In the course of their professional work accountants have at least a particular lien for unpaid fees over any books, files and papers delivered to them by clients and also over any other documents which come into their possession while acting for clients. (See *Woodworth* v. *Conroy*, [1976] 1 All E.R. 107.)

Although a common law lien normally gives no power of sale, there are some exceptional cases in which a right of sale is given by statute. Such a right is given to innkeepers (Innkeepers Act, 1878), unpaid sellers of goods (Sale of Goods Act, 1979), and bailees who accept goods for repair or other treatment for reward (Torts (Interference with Goods) Act, 1977). Briefly, the latter Act provides for the sale of goods accepted for repair or other treatment or for valuation or appraisal or for storage and warehousing provided the bailee gives notice to the bailor specifying the date on or after which he proposes to sell the goods. The period between the notice and the date specifying sale must be such as will afford the bailor a reasonable opportunity of taking delivery of the goods. However, if he does not do so the bailee may sell them but must account to the bailor for the balance of the proceeds of sale after deduction of charges and expenses.

It should also be noted that the High Court has a discretion to order the sale of goods if it is just to do so, e.g. where the goods are perishable. (And see *Larner* v. *Fawcett*, 1950.)[670]

A common law lien is discharged—

(a) by payment of the sum owing;
(b) by parting with the possession of the goods or other property upon

which the lien is being exercised (but see *Caldwell* v. *Sumpters*, 1971.)[669];

(*c*) By an agreement to give credit for the amount due;

(*d*) by accepting an alternative security for the debt owing.

Maritime lien

A maritime lien does not depend on possession. It is a right which attaches to a ship in connection with a maritime liability. It travels with the ship and may be enforced by the arrest and the sale of the ship through the medium of a court having Admiralty jurisdiction. Examples of such liens are—

(*a*) Liens of salvors.

(*b*) The lien of a master for his outgoings.

(*c*) Liens which arise from damage due to collision.

(*d*) Liens of bottomry bond holders. A bottomry bond is a form of security under which a ship and/or its cargo is pledged for the repayment of money borrowed for the purposes of a voyage.

The order of attachment is important and depends on circumstances.

Successive salvage liens attach in inverse order, later ones being preferred to earlier ones, since the earlier lien would be useless if the later salvage had not preserved the ship from loss. Claims for collision damage are treated as of equal rank. Liens for wages, in the absence of salvage liens, have priority over other liens; however, liens for wages earned before a salvage operation are postponed to the lien for salvage, since the value of such a lien has been preserved by the salvage operation.

If a ship which is subject to lien is sold, the purchaser takes it subject to the lien and is responsible for discharging it.

Equitable lien

An equitable lien is an equitable right, conferred by law, whereby one person acquires a charge on the property of another until certain claims have been met. It differs from a common law lien which is founded on possession and does not confer a power of sale. An equitable lien is independent of possession and may be enforced by a judicial sale.

An equitable lien may arise out of an express provision in a contract or from the relationship between parties. Thus a partner has an equitable lien upon the partnership assets for the purpose of ensuring that they are applied, on dissolution, to paying partnership debts. Furthermore, an *unpaid* vendor of land has an equitable lien on the property even after conveyance of ownership to the purchaser, or a third party who has taken it with notice of the lien, under which he may ask the court for an order to sell the property so that he may obtain the purchase money owing to him.

An equitable lien can, like all equitable rights, be extinguished by the owner selling the property to a *bona fide* purchaser for value who has no notice of the lien.

An equitable lien differs from a mortgage. A mortgage, as we have seen, is always created by the act of parties, and an equitable lien may arise by operation of law.

Banker's lien

At common law a banker has a general possessory lien on all securities, and e.g. bills of exchange, promissory notes and bonds, deposited with him by customers in the ordinary course of business unless there is an agreement, express or implied, to the contrary. The lien does not extend to property or securities deposited for safe custody. However, a customer may deposit a security as collateral for a loan, in which case the banker has rights over it, but the transaction is an equitable mortgage rather than a lien.

A banker's lien gives a right of sale, at least of negotiable securities subject to the lien, because s. 27 of the Bills of Exchange Act, 1882, provides that a person having a possessory lien over a bill is deemed a holder for value to the extent of the lien, and can, therefore, sell and transfer the bill.

ASSIGNMENTS OF CHOSES IN ACTION

The common law does not recognize assignments of choses in action, but Equity does and so does statute.

Assignment by act of parties

There are four possible categories—

(a) A legal assignment of a legal chose under s. 136 of the Law of Property Act, 1925

To be effective such an assignment, e.g. the goodwill of a business, must be absolute and not partial; must be in writing signed by the assignor; and must be notified in writing to the debtor, generally by the assignee. If the above requirements are complied with, the assignee can sue the debtor without making the assignor a party to the action. Failure to give notice to the debtor means that there is no legal assignment; the debtor can validly pay the assignor, and the assignee is liable to be postponed to a later assignee for value who notifies the debtor. However, it is not necessary for the date of the assignment to be given in the notice of assignment as long as the letter, or other form of written notice, states clearly that there has been an assignment and identifies the assignee.

(*Van Lynn Developments Ltd* v. *Pelias Construction Co. Ltd*, [1968] 3 All E.R. 824.)

(b) Equitable assignments of legal choses

(c) Equitable assignments of equitable choses

The difference between a legal and an equitable chose is historical in that an equitable chose is a right which, before 1875, could only be enforced in the Court of Chancery, e.g. the interest of a beneficiary under a trust fund.

In equitable assignments of legal choses the assignor must be made a party in any action against the debtor, but if the chose is equitable this is not necessary. No particular form is required; all that is necessary is evidence of intention to assign. Notice should be given to the debtor or the trustees, as the case may be, in order to preserve priority as outlined above.

Thus the transfer of a debt by word of mouth, although invalid under statute, may nevertheless be good and enforceable in Equity.

(d) Equitable assignments of mere expectancies

These are mere hopes of future entitlement, e.g. a legacy under the will of a living testator. The rules regarding such assignments are the same as those set out in (*b*) and (*c*) above, but no notice to the debtor can be given because there is none. Value is not needed for assignments within s. 136 of the Law of Property Act, 1925, or for equitable assignments of equitable choses in action. It is probably not needed for an equitable assignment of a legal chose, though the position is not clear. Value is needed for the assignment of mere expectancies; a document under seal is not enough. Value is also needed to support an agreement to assign an equitable chose, but if the assignee lawfully takes delivery of the property assigned, the assignor cannot recover it.

Assignments are said to be 'subject to equities'; the person to whom the right is assigned takes it subject to any right of set off which was available against the original assignor. So if X assigns to Z a debt of £10 due from Y, and X also owes Y £5, then in any action brought by Z for the money, Y can set off the debt of £5. But the assignee is not subject to purely personal claims which would have been available against the assignor, e.g. damages for fraud, though the remedy of rescission is available against the assignee where the assignor obtained the contract by fraud.

Assignments of certain choses in action are governed by special statutes so that the rules outlined above do not apply. In such cases the special statute must be complied with. Examples are—

(*a*) Bills of exchange, cheques and promissory notes—Bills of Exchange Act, 1882.

(*b*) Shares in companies registered under the Companies Act, 1985, and previous Acts—The Companies Act, 1985.

(*c*) Policies of Life Assurance—Policies of Assurance Act, 1867.

Rights of a personal nature under a contract cannot be assigned. If X contracts to write newspaper articles for a certain newspaper, it cannot assign its rights under the contract to another. The right to recover damages in litigation cannot be assigned, for reasons of public policy. Liabilities under a contract cannot be assigned; the party to benefit cannot be compelled by mere notice to accept the performance of another, though a liability can be transferred by a novation (a new contract), if the party to benefit agrees.

Assignment by operation of law

The involuntary assignment of rights and liabilities arises in the case of death and bankruptcy.

(i) Death

The personal representatives of the deceased acquire his rights and liabilities, the latter to the extent of the estate. Contracts of personal service are discharged.

(ii) Bankruptcy

The trustee in bankruptcy has vested in him all the rights of the bankrupt, except for actions of a purely personal nature which in no way affect the value of the estate, e.g. actions for defamation. The trustee is liable to the extent of the estate for the bankrupt's liabilities, though the trustee has a right to disclaim onerous or unprofitable contracts.

10 Negotiable instruments

The major characteristics of a negotiable instrument are as follows—

(*a*) The rights represented by the instrument are transferable merely by delivering it to another, though bills made payable to order require indorsement.

(*b*) Unlike the assignee of an ordinary contractual right, the transferee of a negotiable instrument does not, unless the instrument is issued 'not negotiable', take subject to equities, and he is not affected by defects in the title of his predecessor provided he is what is known as a *holder in due course*.

(*c*) The acceptor of a bill of exchange, or the banker in the case of a cheque, is under a duty to pay the *holder for the time being* of the instrument. So, upon transfer of the instrument, there is no need to notify the acceptor or the banker of a change of ownership, as there is on a legal assignment of other choses in action under the Law of Property Act, 1925.

(*d*) The holder of a bill of exchange can sue upon it in his own name. This can be done with a legal assignment, but not with an equitable one.

Types of instrument

The most important negotiable instruments are bills of exchange, promissory notes and cheques, and these three types are the subject-matter of the Bills of Exchange Act, 1882. Nevertheless, certain other instruments are negotiable namely—

(1) Treasury bills
That is, bills issued by the British Government.

(2) Share warrants
If they are to bearer but not otherwise.

(3) Dividend warrants.

(4) Bonds
Issued by English companies are negotiable if payable to *bearer*, and

bonds issued by a foreign government, or indeed by a foreign corporation, may be negotiable if they are negotiable in the country of issue and also negotiable by custom in England.

(5) Debentures
Payable to bearer.

Postal orders, Share Certificates and Share Transfers are not negotiable instruments, nor is a bill of lading.

THE BILLS OF EXCHANGE ACT, 1882

The law relating to bills of exchange has been codified in the Bills of Exchange Act, 1882, and *all section references on this subject are to this Act unless otherwise indicated*.

The nature of a bill of exchange

A bill of exchange is an unconditional order in writing, addressed by one person to another, signed by the person giving it, requiring the person to whom it is addressed to pay on demand, or at a fixed or determinable future time, a sum certain in money to, or to the order of, a specified person or to bearer. (Bills of Exchange Act, 1882, s. 3.)

The example on p. 469 is a bill of exchange which is addressed by Richard Brown to G. Green, and requires him to pay £400 to J. White, or his order, six months after the date of the bill which is 1 January, 1989. Richard Brown is called the *drawer*, G. Green is called the *drawee*, and J. White is called the *payee*.

The advantages of a bill of exchange

Although bills of exchange are used mainly in overseas and not in UK transactions it is worth examining why they are used at all.

(1) A bill of exchange provides a creditor with a better remedy
It is advisable to sue upon a bill of exchange (including a cheque) (1) because it makes the debt certain—it is a promise to pay a sum certain in money; (2) the bill provides good evidence of the promise to pay; and (3) the defendant to an action on a bill may not normally set up a counter-claim. He must pay the bill in full and bring a separate action if he has any complaint, e.g. about the quality of goods supplied in exchange for which he gave the bill. The only defence to an action on a bill is fraud, illegality, or total failure of consideration.

(2) Bills of exchange may be discounted
Thus anybody who holds the bill, and is entitled to claim the money on the due date, can discount the bill by taking it to a bank or discounting

house. The bank will, in many cases, be willing to take the bill off the holder's hands, pay the holder the present value of the bill and collect the money when due.

(3) A bill may be negotiated

Anyone who holds a bill of exchange can transfer it to a creditor in payment and White could, if he chose, use the bill in this manner to settle a debt with Gray.

THE PARTIES

The parties to the bill are Brown, the *drawer*; Green, the *drawee*; and White, the *payee*. If Green signs the bill he becomes the *acceptor*, and if White indorses the bill over to Gray, White becomes an *indorser* and Gray an *indorsee* and holder of the bill. Indorsement is effected by signing the bill on the back.

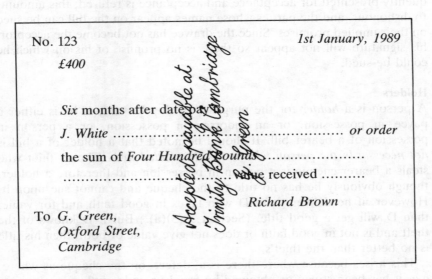

No. 123   *1st January, 1989*

£400

Six months after date pay to

J. White .... *or order*

the sum of *Four Hundred Pounds* ....

.... value received ....

                                        Richard Brown

To *G. Green,*
Oxford Street,
Cambridge

Accepted payable at Trinity Bank Cambridge
G. Green

Each of the parties to a bill makes certain promises which are implied by law. The drawer on signing the instrument promises that, if the bill is dishonoured, he will pay the amount thereof to the holder and that, if an indorser is called upon to pay the holder, he (the drawer) will indemnify that indorser.

The indorser on signing undertakes that, if the bill is dishonoured, he will pay the amount thereof to the holder and that, if a subsequent indorser is called upon to pay the holder, he (the prior indorser) will indemnify the subsequent indorser.

The acceptor on signing promises that he will pay the amount of the bill to the holder on maturity.

There are now three signatures on the specimen bill above: those of Brown as drawer, Green as acceptor, and White as indorser. The bill matures when six months have elapsed, i.e. on 1 July, 1989. On this date Gray, the holder, will present it to Green and demand payment. If Green pays, all parties are satisfied; but if Green dishonours the bill by non-payment, Gray has the following remedies—

(a) He can sue for the enforcement of Green's promise to pay when the bill matures;

(b) He can sue for the enforcement of Brown's promise to pay if the bill is dishonoured;

(c) He can sue for the enforcement of White's promise to pay if the bill is dishonoured.

Gray has thus three rights of action to obtain the money due to him. If he chooses to sue White, then White can recover from Brown on his promise to indemnify any indorser who has to pay the holder.

A bill may get into circulation without being accepted. If it is subsequently presented for acceptance and acceptance is refused, this amounts to dishonour, and the parties whose names appear on the bill can be sued on their implied promises. Since the drawee has not become the acceptor, his signature will not appear so there is no promise of his on which he could be sued.

Holders

A person is a *holder* for the purposes of the Act only if he is either a payee in possession, or an indorsee in possession, or a person in possession of a bearer bill. It should be noted that a holder of a bill is *not necessarily the person who is legally entitled to it*. Thus a thief who steals a bearer cheque is a person in possession and therefore a holder, though obviously he has no title to the cheque and cannot sue upon it. However, if he delivers it to D who takes in good faith and for value, then D will get a good title. (Section 38(3)(a).) But if D knows of the theft and is not in good faith or does not give value or both, then his title is no better than the thief's.

This arises because where there is a 'defect' on the cheque as where, e.g. it has been stolen or obtained by fraud or undue influence, then no one can sue upon it and obtain its face value unless he has taken it in good faith for value and without knowledge of previous defects. (*See* holder in due course, below.)

A *holder for value* is a person in possession as above of a bill for which at any time value has been given. He is a holder for value as regards all parties prior to himself.

A *holder in due course* is a holder (as defined above) who has taken the bill complete and regular on the face of it (*Arab Bank Ltd* v. *Ross*, 1952);[671] before it was overdue; for value and in good faith; without notice of any defect in the title of his transferor; and if it has been dishonoured, then without notice of dishonour. Every one of these requirements must be satisfied if a holder is to be a holder in due course.

A bill is deemed overdue in the following circumstances—

(*a*) If it has been drawn so that it is payable a fixed number of days, weeks or months after date, the bill is overdue when the relevant period has expired.

(*b*) If the bill is payable a fixed number of days, weeks or months after sight, the period is calculated from the date on which the bill is presented for acceptance. The bill is overdue when the relevant period has expired, and no days of grace are now to be added.

(*c*) If the bill is payable at sight, or on demand, it is overdue when it has been in circulation for an unreasonable length of time. What is unreasonable has never been legally defined, but with regard to cheques it has been suggested that they are stale, from the point of view of taking free from equities, after ten days. With regard to payment by a banker, a cheque is usually held stale after six months, though the drawer is still liable to the holder for the limitation period of six years if the holder sues upon the cheque.

Consideration

A bill must be supported by consideration, and under s. 27(1)(a) any consideration adequate to support an ordinary contract will support a bill. (*Pollway Ltd* v. *Abdullah*, 1974.)[672]

Under s. 27(1)(b) an antecedent debt or liability, i.e. a form of past consideration, is enough to support a bill of exchange or cheque. This is essential, particularly in the case of cheques, many of which are based on past consideration. Thus, if S sells goods to B a debt comes into being payable in legal tender when the contract is made so that when B decides to pay S by cheque, the cheque is based on a previous or antecedent debt or liability and is for past consideration. However, this concept would not have assisted Mrs McCardle in the case of *Re McCardle*, 1951[124] if she had been paid by cheque which was not met, because what she had done did not create an antecedent debt or liability.

Section 27(2) provides that consideration need not have moved from the holder of a bill or cheque so that the doctrine of privity of contract does not apply. Therefore, if P signs a cheque in favour of Q for the price of goods sold by Q to P and Q indorses the cheque to R as a gift, R may not sue Q on the cheque but he may sue P—R is a holder for value to that extent under s. 27(2). As between immediate parties absence of consideration prevents an action on the bill.

By reason of s. 27(2) it is not essential that consideration has passed from one party to a cheque to another party to the *same* cheque. (See *Diamond* v. *Graham*, 1968.)[673] But it must if the holder relies on a past consideration. (See *Oliver* v. *Davis and Another*, 1949.)[674]

ORDER IN WRITING

A bill of exchange is an unconditional order in writing addressed by one person to another. We will now consider these elements.

A bill of exchange is a written document and in this context writing includes print. (S. 2.) The person who originates it is called the *drawer*, and he must have capacity to incur liability and this is co-extensive with capacity to contract. (S. 22.)

The order must be unconditional

An instrument which orders any act to be done in addition to the payment of money is not a bill of exchange. (S. 3(2).) An order to pay out of a particular fund is not unconditional, e.g. out of the money due to me from P when received. An unqualified order to pay, coupled with an indication of a particular fund out of which the drawee is to reimburse himself, or a particular account to be debited with the amount, is regarded as unconditional, e.g. a cheque drawn on No. 2 A/c. (S. 3(3).) (And see *Bavins* v. *London and South Western Bank Ltd*, 1900[675] and *Nathan* v. *Ogdens Ltd*, 1905.)[676]

The bill of exchange must be signed

No person is liable as drawer, indorser, or acceptor of a bill, who has not signed it as such. The following cases should be noted—

(a) Where a person signs a bill in a trade or assumed name, he is liable on it as if he had signed in his own name.

(a) The signature of the name of a firm is equivalent to the signature by the person so signing of the names of all the persons liable as partners in that firm. (S. 23.) (*Ringham* V. *Hackett*, 1980.)[677]

(3) A signature by procuration (e.g. per pro B. Brown, J. Jones), operates as notice that the agent has a limited authority to sign, and the principal is only bound by such signature if the agent so signing was acting within the actual limits of his authority. (S. 25.)

Where a person signs a bill as a drawer, indorser, or acceptor, and adds words to his signature indicating that he signs for or on behalf of a principal or in a representative character, he is not personally liable thereon; but the mere addition to his signature of words describing him as an agent, or as filling a representative character, does not exempt him from personal liability. (*Childs* v. *Monins and Bowles*, 1821.)[678]

(4) Section 349 of the Companies Act, 1985, has effect upon representative signatures on behalf of companies. The relevant law is illustrated by *Durham Fancy Goods Ltd* v. *Michael Jackson (Fancy Goods) Ltd*, 1968[143] and *Hendon* v. *Adelman*, 1973.[679]

(5) A 'signature' is not defined in the Act but it would seem to permit a mechanically produced signature, and certainly a mark may be used if there is evidence that the person signing by mark habitually so signs. A bank will take an indemnity from a customer using cheques which bear a printed facsimile reproduction of an official signature.

Where a signature on a bill is forged or unauthorized

It is wholly inoperative and no rights can be acquired through or under that signature, unless the party against whom it is sought to retain or enforce payment of the bill is *precluded* from setting up the forgery or want of authority. A forgery will not pass a good title to the bill. A forged signature is in effect no signature at all and cannot pass any title. It is also worth noting that a forged signature can never be overcome. However, an unauthorized signature not amounting to a forgery may be ratified. (S. 24.) Thus, if a cheque is made payable to a company and a clerk in the company's employ without authority endorses the cheque on behalf of the company to a creditor of the company, and, where, say, the company disputes the debt or the debt is not yet due, then the creditor has no title to the cheque, but the company can ratify the unauthorized endorsement and the creditor (the endorsee) could then sue the company on the cheque. If the clerk had endorsed the cheque over to his private creditors to clear his own debts, the company would not normally wish to ratify his acts but could not do so in any case because the law does not allow ratification of a forgery or fraud.

Nevertheless, a person may be estopped from pleading forgery or an unauthorized signature if he has known of the forgery but has failed to notify, e.g. his bank, within a reasonable amount of time. (*Greenwood v. Martins Bank Ltd*, 1933.)[680]

ACCEPTANCE

When the drawee signs the bill he becomes the acceptor, and promises to pay the holder the amount of the bill on maturity provided the acceptance is unqualified. *A general acceptance* assents without qualification to the order of the drawer.

An acceptance must not express that the drawee will perform his promise by any other means than the payment of money, and the acceptance must be written on the bill and signed by the drawee. The drawee's signature without additional words is sufficient and he need not sign with his own hand; the signature may be written by some other person by or under his authority.

A bill may be accepted before it has been signed by the drawer or while otherwise incomplete. (S. 18(1).) Incompleteness does not invalidate a bill and a bill is not invalid by reason (*a*) that it is not dated; (*b*) that it does not specify the value given, or that any value has been given therefor; (*c*) that it does not specify the place where it is drawn or the place where it is payable. (S. 3(4).)

When a bill lacks a material particular, the person in possession of it has *prima facie* authority to fill up the omission in any way he thinks fit.

Qualified acceptance

The acceptor may qualify his acceptance. In the case of a bill for £1000 drawn six months after date, the acceptor may introduce a *qualification as to amount*: 'Accepted for five hundred pounds only.' The acceptor can then only be sued for £500. He may also sign thus: 'Accepted nine months after date.' The acceptor cannot then be sued until nine months have expired, and this is known as a *qualification as to time*. An acceptance 'Payable at my office and there only' would amount to a *qualification as to place*. Finally, an acceptance 'subject to security being provided' would be a *general conditional acceptance*.

Qualified acceptance amounts to dishonour and gives a right of action against the parties immediately, but the person presenting the bill may agree to the qualification. In this case, if he wishes to retain his rights against the drawer and prior indorsers, he must obtain their assent, except in the case of qualification as to amount when he need only serve notice on them.

Accommodation bills

Sometimes a bill is what is called an *accommodation bill*, and an accommodation party to such a bill is one who has signed it as drawer, acceptor, or indorser, without receiving value for it. His object is to lend his name and credit to some other person.

An accommodation party is liable on the bill to a holder for value; and it is immaterial whether, when such a holder took the bill, he knew the party to be an accommodation party or not. (S. 28.) Thus, if A is in business and requires capital to purchase a new van but will not be able to pay for it out of the profits of the business for three months he may ask B to accept a bill drawn by A on B for, say, £2000 and payable 'three months after date'. If B is willing he will accept the bill but receives no value for it. However, A can now discount the bill at his bank and if B is a prosperous person the bank will probably give a good price for it. Where a drawee accepts a bill for the accommodation of the drawer, it is understood that the drawer will make available funds to meet the bill on maturity, and, if he does not do so, and the acceptor has to pay the bill, the drawer must indemnify the acceptor. This is, however, of no concern to the banker, who can sue B on his acceptance even though he knew that B was an accommodation party. However, B is not liable to A because no consideration was given by A to B.

Presentment for acceptance

Where a bill expressly stipulates that it shall be presented for acceptance, or where a bill is drawn payable elsewhere than at the residence or place of business of the drawee, it must be presented for acceptance before it can be presented for payment. When a bill is payable after sight presentment is clearly necessary in order to fix the maturity of the instrument. The presentment must be made *by or on behalf of the holder to the drawee, or to some person authorized to accept or refuse acceptance on his behalf*, at a reasonable hour on a business day and before the bill is overdue.

When a bill is duly presented for acceptance and is not accepted within the customary time (usually twenty-four hours), the person presenting it must treat it as dishonoured by non-acceptance.)

In case of such dishonour, the holder has an immediate right of recourse against the drawer and indorsers, and no presentment for payment is necessary. He must, however, give them notice of dishonour without delay otherwise they are discharged not only from liability on the bill but also on the consideration given for it.

PAYMENT

Where a bill is not payable to bearer, *the payee* must be named or otherwise indicated therein with reasonable certainty. A bill may also be made payable to the holder of an office for the time being, e.g. the Treasurer of the Barchester Football Club. Instruments made out in a form 'pay wages' or 'pay cash' are not payable to a specified person and cannot be regarded as cheques. Such an instrument is not therefore negotiable but it is, under the Cheques Act, 1957 a mandate to the bank concerned to pay unless countermanded. Thus, unless the instrument is countermanded by the drawer the bank may properly pay out on it and debit the drawer's account. Where the payee is a fictitious or non-existent person, the bill may be treated as payable to bearer. (S. 7.) The payee is considered existing where the drawer knows of his existence and intends him to benefit. (*Vinden* v. *Hughes*, 1905.)[681] The payee is considered fictitious when his name is inserted by the drawer by way of a pretence and without any intention that the named payee should obtain payment. (*Bank of England* v. *Vagliano Bros*, 1891.)[682] The payee is considered non-existent where the drawer does not connect the payee's name with any person to whom he owes or might owe money, though there may very well be a person in existence with that name. (*Clutton* v. *Attenborough*, 1879.)[683] These concepts are somewhat artificial but are designed to ensure that those who carelessly allow employees or others to obtain by way of fraud signatures on cheques or bills, should not escape liability on the instruments.

The sum payable by a bill is a *sum certain* although it is required to be paid with interest, by stated instalments, or according to an indicated rate of exchange. (S. 9(1).)

Where the sum payable is expressed in words and also in figures, and there is a discrepancy between the two, the sum denoted by the words is the amount payable, though a bank will usually return such a cheque marked 'words and figures differ'. (S. 9(2).)

Presentment for payment

A bill must be duly presented for payment, otherwise the drawer and indorsers are discharged from liability.

(*a*) Where the bill is not payable on demand, presentment must be made on the day it falls due.

(*b*) Where the bill is payable on demand, presentment must be made within a reasonable time after its issue in order to render the drawer liable, and within a reasonable time after its indorsement to render the indorser liable.

The bill must be presented by the holder or by some person authorized to receive payment on his behalf, at a reasonable hour on a business day, at the proper place. Where it is authorized by agreement or usage, a presentment through the post office is sufficient. (S. 45.)

Presentment for payment is dispensed with—

(*a*) Where, after the exercise of reasonable diligence, it cannot be effected;

(*b*) Where the drawee is a fictitious person;

(*c*) Where the acceptor is an accommodation party;

(*d*) By waiver of presentment, express or implied.

Time of payment

A bill is payable on demand (*a*) which is expressed to be payable on demand, or at sight, or on presentation, or (*b*) in which no time for payment is expressed.

A bill is payable at a fixed or determinable future time when it is expressed to be payable (i) at a fixed period after date or sight; (ii) on or at a fixed period after the occurrence of a specified event which is certain to happen, though the time of happening may be uncertain. An instrument expressed to be payable on a contingency is not a bill, and the happening of the event does not cure the defect. (S. 11.) Suppose a bill runs 'Pay B. Brown or Order Five Hundred Pounds on the marriage of his daughter Jane to William Smith.' This would not be a valid bill, even though the wedding took place shortly afterwards. The words 'on or before' a given date import an element of contingency and an instrument ordering payment in this form is not a valid bill. (*Williamson* v. *Rider*, 1962.)[684]

A bill is not invalid by reason only of the fact that it is ante-dated, post-dated, or dated on a Sunday. (S. 13.)

Where a bill expressed to be payable at a fixed period after date is issued undated, or where the acceptance of a bill payable at a fixed period after sight is undated, any holder may insert therein the true date of issue or acceptance, and the bill will be payable accordingly.

Where the holder in good faith and by mistake inserts the wrong date, and in every case where a wrong date is inserted and the bill comes into the hands of a holder in due course, the bill is valid and the date so inserted is deemed to be the true one. (S. 12.)

In calculating the due date of a bill not payable on demand the period is determined by excluding the day from which time begins to run and including the day of payment. All bills whose payment falls due on non-business days, i.e. Saturdays, Sundays and Bank Holidays, are payable on the succeeding business day. (Banking and Financial Dealings Act, 1971.)

NEGOTIABILITY

When a bill contains words prohibiting transfer, or indicating an intention that it should not be transferable, it is valid as between the parties thereto, but is not negotiable. An example of this would be a bill made payable to *G. Green only*. Where a bill is negotiable, it may be payable either to order or to bearer, and a bill is payable to bearer which is expressed to be so payable, or on which the only or last indorsement is an indorsement in blank. Bills and cheques payable to fictitious and/or non-existing payees are also regarded as payable to bearer.

A bill is negotiated when it is transferred from one person to another in such a manner as to constitute the transferee the holder of the bill. A *bill payable to bearer is negotiated by delivery; a bill payable to order is negotiated by the indorsement of the holder completed by delivery*.

Where a bill is negotiable in its origin, it continues to be negotiable until it has been (*a*) restrictively indorsed; or (*b*) discharged by payment or otherwise. Where an *overdue bill* is negotiated, it can only be negotiated subject to any defects of title affecting it at maturity, and thenceforward no person who takes it can acquire or give a better title than that which the person from whom he took it had. *Future holders cannot be holders in due course.*

While it is true to say that the attribute of negotiability allows a person to obtain a good title to a negotiable instrument from a thief, the concept of negotiability after a theft is very restricted and applies in practice only to bearer bills. Before an instrument can be negotiated in such a way as to give the transferee a better title than the transferor it must be in a negotiable state. A bearer bill is in a negotiable state without endorsement. However, since most cheques are order cheques payable to (or to the order of) a particular person, they are not in a negotiable state unless they are endorsed. If, therefore, they are stolen, they can only be passed on without endorsement or by means of a forged endorsement and in both these instances the transferee will not get a good title even if he takes for value with no notice of defects in the title of the transferor.

For example, if T steals a bearer cheque from A and transfers it to B for value, B having no notice of the theft, then B's title will be good. If, however, the cheque was made payable to A, B's title will be incomplete because he will either take the cheque without an endorsement or as a result of T forging A's endorsement and in either event B's title will be affected adversely. A forged endorsement does not pass on the drawer's promise to pay 'to order' under s. 55 of the 1882 Act.

Valid indorsement

An indorsement, in order to operate as a negotiation, must comply with the following conditions, namely—

(1) *It must be written on the bill itself* and be signed by the indorser. The simple signature of the indorser on the bill, without additional words, is sufficient. An indorsement on a copy of the bill, in countries where copies are recognized, is valid.

(2) *It must be an indorsement of the entire bill.* A partial indorsement which purports to transfer to an indorsee a part only of the amount payable, or which purports to transfer the bill to two or more indorsees severally, does not operate as a negotiation of the bill.

(3) Where a bill is payable to the order of *two or more payees* or indorsees who are not partners, *all must indorse* unless the one indorsing has authority to indorse for the others.

(4) Where, in a bill payable to order, the *payee or indorsee is wrongly designated*, or his name is mis-spelt, he may indorse the bill as therein described adding, if he wishes, his proper signature.

(5) *Where there are two or more indorsements* on the bill, each indorsement is deemed to have been made in the order in which it appears on the bill until the contrary is proved.

(6) *An indorsement may be made in blank or special.* It may also contain terms making it restrictive. (S. 32.)

(a) Conditional indorsement

Where a bill purports to be indorsed conditionally, e.g. 'pay X when he delivers the bill of lading', the condition may be disregarded by the payer, and a payment made to the indorsee is valid whether the condition has been fulfilled or not. (S. 33.) Nevertheless the indorsee is bound by the condition and holds the money in trust for the indorser until the condition is fulfilled.

(b) Special indorsement

An indorsement in blank specifies no indorsee, and a bill so indorsed becomes payable to bearer. *A special indorsement* specifies the person to whom, or to whose order, the bill is to be payable. When a bill has been indorsed in blank, any holder may convert the blank indorsement into a special indorsement, by writing above the indorser's signature a direction to pay the bill to, or to the order of, himself or some other person. (S. 34.)

(c) Restrictive indorsement

An indorsement is restrictive which prohibits the further negotiation of the bill, or which expresses that it is a mere authority to deal with the bill as thereby directed and not a transfer of the ownership thereof, e.g. 'Pay D only.' or 'Pay D for the Account of Y.' or 'Pay D or order for collection.' A restrictive indorsement could be used where X, the payee of a cheque, owes a debt to an overseas supplier, P, and wishes to indorse the cheque over to P's agent A in England but wishes to make it clear that A is not the beneficial owner of the cheque; X can indorse 'Pay A for the account of P'. A can now obtain payment and must then account to P, though A cannot transfer the bill.

Delivery

Section 21(1) provides that every contract on a bill, whether it be a drawer's or an indorser's, is incomplete and revocable until delivery of the instrument. Thus, where an indorsement or other signature is required the mere fact that a signature is placed upon the instrument is not enough; there must also be delivery, which would not be the case where an order instrument was stolen after indorsement. The indorser must deliver it. However, there are certain presumptions of delivery as follows—

(*a*) under s. 21(2) valid delivery by all prior parties is *conclusively* presumed in favour of a holder in due course but not if the bill is inchoate (see below).

(*b*) under s. 21(3) valid delivery is presumed *until the contrary is proved* in the case of other holders.

Thus presumption of valid delivery of a complete bill cannot be disproved against a holder in due course but it may be as regards other holders.

Inchoate bills

These are bills lacking in some material particular(s) such as the names of the parties other than the drawer and the amount of the bill. Problems may arise, e.g. from completion of a cheque in excess of authority given by the drawer. Section 20 applies and requires 'delivery by the signer in order that it may be converted into a bill'. The law does not presume delivery under s. 21 because two elements are required—

(*a*) delivery, and

(*b*) the intention in the signer that the order be converted into a bill.

Thus, if A signs a cheque form and does not complete it and it is stolen from his desk and filled in, A is under no liability to anyone on his signature, not even to a holder in due course, because he did not deliver it *in order that it might be converted into a bill*.

However, if A signs a blank cheque and gives it to his gardener to buy a lawn mower and the gardener fills it in and pays a private debt, then A would be liable to a holder in due course because he did deliver it with the intention that it should be converted into a bill. The gardener's lack of authority is a 'defect' so far as a holder for value is concerned and A would not be liable to him. It should be noted, however, that a payee cannot be a holder in due course because the instrument is *issued* to him not *negotiated* to him. It is the first indorsee who takes it 'in due course'. (*Jones Ltd* v. *Waring & Gillow*, 1926).[685] Thus if the gardener made it payable to X to settle a private debt, X would not be able to sue A because as a payee he could not be a holder in due course and would take it subject to the defect, i.e. the gardener's lack of authority. Thus before anyone could sue A on the cheque there would have to be an indorsement by the first payee to an indorsee who might then be able to set up the fact that he was a holder in due course.

DISCHARGE

A bill of exchange is discharged in the following ways—

(*a*) *By payment in due course* by or on behalf of the acceptor.

(*b*) *By express waiver*, where the holder absolutely and unconditionally renounces his rights against the acceptor. The waiver must be in writing unless the bill is delivered up to the acceptor.

(*c*) *By material alteration* except as against a party who has himself made, authorized, or assented thereto, and against subsequent indorsers.

The following alterations are material, namely (i) any alteration of the date, the sum payable, the time of payment, the place of payment; and (ii) the addition of a place of payment without the acceptor's assent, where a bill has been accepted generally. (S. 64(2).) An alteration may be material even if the change is beneficial. (*Gardner* v. *Walsh*, 1855.)[686]

Examples of immaterial alterations are (i) changing a bill payable to *Jones or Bearer* into *Jones or Order*; (ii) striking out of the words *or Order*; (iii) the alteration of the drawee's name, when it is wrong, to agree with a name correctly signed by way of acceptance.

(*d*) *By intentional and apparent cancellation* by the holder or his agent.

(*e*) *By negotiation back to the acceptor*, sometimes called merger or discharge by circuity. Suppose A has accepted a bill for £1000 and has sold goods worth £1000 to H. If a subsequent indorser I negotiates the bill to H, and H negotiates it back to A in settlement, the bill is discharged.

(*f*) *By the bill becoming statute barred*. A bill of exchange is a simple contract and becomes statute barred six years from the cause of action, i.e. dishonour.

DISHONOUR

A bill may be dishonoured by non-acceptance or by non-payment, and the holder can sue prior parties on their implied promises. A bill is dishonoured by non-payment—

(a) When it is duly presented for payment and payment is refused or cannot be obtained; and

(b) When presentment is excused and the bill is overdue and unpaid. When a bill is dishonoured by non-payment, an immediate right of recourse against the drawer and indorsers accrues to the holder. (S. 47.)

Notice of dishonour

When a bill has been dishonoured by non-acceptance or by non-payment, notice of dishonour must be given to the drawer and each indorser, and any drawer or indorser to whom such notice is not given is discharged. Notice, in order to be valid and effectual, must be given in accordance with the rules laid down in the Bills of Exchange Act, 1882.

(a) Where the notice is given on behalf of the holder it operates for the benefit of subsequent holders, and all prior indorsers who have a right of recourse against the party to whom it is given.

If D is the drawer, P the payee, I_1, I_2, I_3, subsequent indorsers and H the holder, then if H gives notice to P, this would retain the liability of P, not only to H and subsequent holders, but also to I_1, I_2 and I_3, *although these latter three would not be liable to H.*

(b) Where notice is given by or on behalf of an indorser entitled to give notice, it operates for the benefit of the holder, and all indorsers subsequent to the party to whom notice is given.

If I_2 gives notice to P, then P is liable to I_1, I_2, I_3, H and subsequent holders.

(c) Actually if H gives notice to I_3, the chances are that I_3 will give notice to I_2, I_2 to I_1, I_1 to P, and P to D, since otherwise the person breaking the chain would lose his right of recourse though remaining liable himself. However, since one of these might fail to give notice and lose the right of recourse both for himself and for subsequent parties, the safest way is for H to notify all prior parties.

Notice must be given when the bill is dishonoured but not before. However, in *Eaglehill Ltd.* v. *J. Needham Builders Ltd*, 1972[687] it was held by the House of Lords that provided that the notice is received after dishonour it is valid regardless of when it was sent off.

Noting and protesting

It is convenient at this point to mention that, when a bill is dishonoured, it is sometimes obligatory and often desirable to *note* and *protest* the bill for non-acceptance or non-payment. Many solicitors carry out the office of *notary public*, and this office is universally recognized throughout the world.

In order to *note* the bill, the notary makes a formal demand upon the drawee for acceptance, or upon the acceptor for payment, as the case may be, and if the demand is refused, he writes a minute on the face of the bill consisting of the date, the noting charges, a reference to his register, and his initials. He also attaches to the bill a ticket giving the answer received to the request for acceptance or payment. To evidence these transactions the notary makes in his register a full copy of the bill, and a note of the answer, if any, received to his request.

The *protest* is against any loss sustained by the non-acceptance or non-payment of the bill, and is embodied in a solemn declaration made on behalf of the holder by a *notary public* who signs it. Where it is necessary to protest a bill and no notary is available, the function can be performed by a house-holder or substantial resident who gives a certificate of dishonour attested by two witnesses.

A protest must contain a copy of the instrument and must state the person who has requested the protest, the place and date of the protest, the reason for the protest, the demand made and the answer received, if any. Alternatively it may state that the drawee or acceptor cannot be found, if this is the case. The protest must be signed by the notary.

It is not necessary to note or protest inland bills, but there are certain advantages derived from noting a bill, and the costs of noting are recoverable as damages. The notary knows clearly what measures must be taken when a bill is dishonoured; he is the best witness at a trial that proper steps were taken; and his minute on the bill is the best record of dishonour for the purpose of notifying parties to the bill that they have acquired liability.

PROMISSORY NOTES

Definition

A promissory note is an unconditional promise in writing, made by one person to another, signed by the maker, engaging to pay, on demand or at a fixed or determinable future time, a sum certain in money to, or to the order of, a specified person or to bearer. (S. 83(1).)

A promissory note is inchoate and incomplete until delivery is made to the payee or to bearer.

Such an instrument has only two parties—the maker and the payee—and does not require acceptance. The relevant rules governing bills of exchange are applicable to promissory notes.

CHEQUES

A cheque is defined in s. 73 of the Bills of Exchange Act, 1882, as 'A bill of exchange drawn on a banker payable on demand'. The relevant provisions of the Act applicable to bills of exchange payable on demand apply also to cheques. However, the provisions regarding acceptance have no application to cheques and the rules relating to crossings on cheques do not apply to other bills. A crossing is an instruction to a banker on which the cheque is drawn. However, the words or crossing 'not negotiable' can be used on cheques and other bills because they are not addressed to a banker but mean that those who take the bill or cheque will do so subject to equities (or defects). Further, a delay in presenting a cheque for payment will not, in itself, discharge the drawer. (S. 74). If a banker pays a cheque bearing a forged or unauthorized indorsement he is nevertheless discharged, although in a similar case the acceptor of a bill would not be. There are also certain special obligations which arise in the case of cheques because of the contract between banker and customer.

The words 'on demand' are not usually printed on cheques but under the provisions of s. 10(1)(*b*) they are implied. A post-dated cheque, which is a cheque dated later than issue, is not, of course, payable on demand. A banker may pay a post-dated cheque in law but in practice if a post-dated cheque is presented for payment it will be returned 'post-dated'. A banker will not pay it or hold it until the due date, or hold funds for it, and he is under no duty to do so. The banker's risk if he pays before the due date is that he cannot debit the drawer's account until the date arrives and not then if the drawer has countermanded payment.

A cheque need not take any particular form unless there is a contrary agreement between banker and customer. Normally it is an implied term of the contract between banker and customer that the bank's cheque forms will be used.

Notice of dishonour of a cheque is not required to the drawer but notice to indorsers is required in order to make them liable. The reason that notice of dishonour need not be given to the drawer is that non-payment is usually because there are no funds in the account or that the drawer has countermanded the cheque and s. 50(2)(c) excuses notice in those cases.

RELATIONSHIP OF BANKER AND CUSTOMER

The relationship between a banker and a customer is that of *debtor and creditor* and is not fiduciary. Where a customer deposits money in a bank, this money is under the control of the banker and is not held by the banker in the form of a trust although he has obligations in connection with it. There are, however, some duties of a fiduciary type which arise in particular where a banker is taking a security. (See further p. 676.)

Banker's obligation to repay

The banker can invest the money and deal with it as he pleases, but he is answerable for the amount deposited by the customer, and is under an obligation to pay it on demand, or to pay it to third parties on the order of the customer. The banker is not an agent or a factor, he is a debtor who promises to repay the money or any part of it at the branch of the bank where the account is kept, during banking hours, against the written order of the customer presented at, or addressed to, the bank at that branch. The bank must honour a customer's cheques up to the amount of the customer's deposit or alternatively up to the amount of an agreed overdraft, but not without enquiry in unusual cases. (*Karak Rubber Co. Ltd* v. *Burden*, 1972.)[688]

The banker is under *no obligation to pay cheques in part*, and if a customer with a deposit or agreed overdraft of £400 draws against it a cheque for £500, the bank is not empowered to pay it as to £400, but should either pay it in full or refuse payment altogether.

Banker's obligation not to disclose

The bank has a further contractual obligation, by reason of an implied term, not to disclose information concerning the customer's affairs. (*Tournier* v. *National Provincial and Union Bank of England*, 1924.)[689] The obligation extends to all facts discovered by the banker while acting in that capacity and is not confined merely to the state of the account. Failure to comply with this obligation will render the banker liable to damages which will, however, be nominal unless actual loss can be proved.

The duty of non-disclosure is not absolute but qualified. On principle disclosure is excusable—

(*a*) *Under compulsion of law*, for example, under s. 7 of the Bankers' Books Evidence Act, 1879, the court may by order authorize a party to an action to inspect and copy entries in a banker's books, although the power is exercised with caution. (*Williams* v. *Summerfield*, 1972.)[690] Under s. 17 of the Taxes Management Act, 1970 a bank must report to the Revenue interest paid to a customer of £25 or more. In practice, only accounts showing £400 p.a. interest or more are sent automatically, though the Revenue may request a statement to be made in respect of interest in excess of £25 p.a. or more.

(*b*) *Where there is a duty to the public to disclose*, as where a customer is trading with the enemy in wartime. In addition, information may be given to the police. The police are asked to address a letter to the bank saying that information is necessary for due administration of justice and undertaking that the information will not be given in evidence unless the bank is ordered to give it by the court.

(*c*) *Where the interests of the bank require disclosure*, as where the bank is in the process of enforcing an overdraft, or a guarantee of an overdraft, where the amount of the overdraft will be stated on the face of the writ.

(*d*) *Where the disclosure is made with the express or implied consent*

of the customer. (Sunderland v. *Barclays Bank Ltd*, 1938.)[691]
(e) *Where enquiries are being made by sequestrators. (Eckman* v. *Midland Bank*, 1972.)[692]

There is a growing practice of making credit enquiries, and bankers' references are commonly given and asked for. If the customer gives the bank's name as a reference, the position is clear enough, but in the absence of the customer's express or implied consent the general practice may not be justifiable merely on the ground that it is an existing usage to supply such information to another bank. It should be noted that the Younger Committee on Privacy said that banks should tell their customers of a reference system in use and get a standing consent or ask for consent each time there was a disclosure. A misleading and negligent reference may render the banker liable in damages. (*Hedley Byrne & Co. Ltd* v. *Heller and Partners Ltd*, 1963.)[215]

Customer's obligation of care

The customer on his part undertakes to exercise reasonable care in drawing up his written orders so as not to mislead the bank or facilitate forgery. (*London Joint Stock Bank Ltd* v *Macmillan and Arthur*, 1918;[693] *C. H. Slingsby* v. *District Bank*, 1931.)[694] In addition he owes a duty to inform the bank of any forgery of his signature *of which he is aware*. He does not owe a duty to the bank in contract or in tort to take precautions to prevent forged or unauthorized cheques being presented to his bank for payment. (See *Tai Hing Cotton Mill Ltd* v. *Liu Chong Hing Bank Ltd*, 1985 at p. 860) where the Privy Council decided that the bank could not debit the account of a company with cheques on which the company's managing director's signature had been forged by a clerk.

Although a customer receives from time to time a bank statement he is not under a duty to check it and is not bound by any errors in it which he does not find. (*Tai Hing Cotton Mill Ltd* v. *Liu Chong Hing Bank Ltd*, 1985 at p. 860.) However, a bank may, by reason of estoppel, have to pay a cheque drawn by a customer who has relied upon an incorrect credit balance on his bank statement. (*United Overseas Bank* v. *Jiwani*, [1977] 1 All E.R. 733.)

Wrongful dishonour

A banker has a duty to honour a customer's cheques up to the amount of his credit balance or agreed overdraft. (But see *Karak Rubber Co. Ltd* v. *Burden*, 1972.)[688] This duty is owed to the customer only and not to any other party. If a banker wrongfully dishonours the cheque of a customer, and if the customer is a man of business, the harm to his credit might lead to the award of substantial sums in an action for damages. Where, however, the customer is not in business, he will only receive nominal damages unless he can prove special damage. (*Gibbons* v. *West-*

minster Bank Ltd, 1939.)[695] In certain cases there may indeed be a possible action for libel, as distinct from wrongful dishonour, against the bank. (*Davidson* v. *Barclays Bank Ltd*, 1940,[696] and *Jayson* v. *Midland Bank Ltd*, 1968.)[697]

Presentment of cheque for payment

Since a cheque is payable on demand against funds which are already provided, presentment for acceptance is quite unnecessary and would indeed have no significance. The cheque must, however, be presented for payment, and if not so presented within a reasonable time of its issue, and if the drawer or the person on whose account it is drawn had the right at the time of such presentment as between him and the banker to have the cheque paid, and suffers actual damage through the delay, he is discharged to the extent of such damage. In determining what is a reasonable time regard is had to the nature of the instrument, the usage of trade and of bankers, and the facts of the particular case.

The holder of such cheque as to which such drawer or person is discharged shall be a creditor, in lieu of such drawer or person, of such banker to the extent of such discharge, and is entitled to recover the amount from him. (S. 74.)

The effect of s. 74 is that the drawer of a cheque is liable on it for the usual limitation period of six years, but he will be discharged before then if the holder does not present it for payment within a reasonable time and the drawer suffers actual damage because of the delay.

For example, if D has £500 in his banking account and draws a cheque in favour of P for £300, and P is dilatory in presenting it so that before he does so D's bank goes into liquidation and is only able to pay fifty pence in the pound, D will be regarded as a creditor of the bank for £200 and P for £300. Thus D will receive £100 and P £150 in the liquidation. It is obviously, therefore, in the interest of payees to present cheques for payment without undue delay. Quite apart from the question of loss on liquidation (which is not really likely) a cheque may go *stale*. A cheque under banking practice is usually regarded as stale if it has not been presented for payment within six months of the date on which it was drawn. A bank might be reluctant to pay a stale cheque since such a payment would not be in the usual course of business and might well insist on it being re-drawn.

Revocation of banker's authority

The duty and authority of a banker to pay a cheque drawn on him by his customer are determined by—

(1) Countermand of payment;
(2) Notice of the customer's death. (S. 75.)

Countermand of payment must be brought to the notice of the banker in unambiguous terms if it is to be effective. (*Curtice* v. *London, City and Midland Bank Ltd*, 1908.)[698]

It should be noted that a countermand notice sent to one branch of a bank does not operate as notice to another branch. (*Burnett* v. *Westminster Bank*, 1965.)[699] A banker's authority to pay a cheque is determined by notice of the customer's death, and to this may be added notice of the customer's mental disorder, notice of an act of bankruptcy on which a bankruptcy petition could be presented against him, or that a receiving order has been made, or that he is an undischarged bankrupt, or on service of a garnishee order nisi.

A garnishee order issues only on a judgment debt. The order *nisi* is addressed to the customer against whom a judgment has been obtained asking if there is any good reason why the judgment debt has not been paid. A copy of this order is sent to the bank. An order *absolute* will be made if the customer cannot show good cause as to why he has not paid and then the bank will be ordered to pay the money out of the account to the plaintiff. Where the customer is a limited company, notice of a petition for compulsory winding up or a resolution for voluntary winding up will terminate the banker's duty to honour cheques. The banker need not, as we have seen, pay cheques where a customer has an insufficient balance to cover the cheque, or has not previously arranged an adequate overdraft, and the banker should not pay if he has notice of any defect in the title of the person presenting the cheque.

Payment without authority

A banker is liable for wrongfully dishonouring the cheques of his customers but may also be liable if he pays a cheque when he should not have done so. Thus, a banker will not be able to debit the customer's account if he pays a countermanded cheque, a cheque void for material alteration, or a cheque on which the drawer's signature is forged.

However, where the customer has been *negligent* in drawing up his cheque so as to mislead the bank or facilitate forgery, the bank may debit his account. (*London Joint Stock Bank* v. *Macmillan and Arthur*, 1918)[693] Further, if the drawer's signature has been forged and he gets to know of the forgery, he may, if he does not inform the bank promptly and the bank is put to loss, be *estopped* from asserting the forgery. (*Greenwood* v. *Martins Bank Ltd*, 1933.)[680]

Where the wrongful payment by the bank actually satisfies a debt due from a customer to his creditor, the customer would make a profit by reason of the restoration rule. For example, if the bank paid a countermanded cheque which A, a customer, had drawn in favour of B, to whom A owed money, the result of the restoration rule would be that A's debt to B would be satisfied and A's balance at the bank would have to be restored. To prevent this profit being made the bank, on restoring A's account, is *subrogated* to B's rights against A, and can recover from A by this means.

Limitation

The six-year limitation period applicable to simple contract debts does not run against the customer of a bank from the date of payment in, for there is no cause of action until the customer demands the money and the demand is not met. For example, if A deposited £100 with his bank in 1981 and did not draw cheques against the account until 1989, there would be no question of the bank pleading the Limitation Act as an excuse for not paying it. However, if a cheque was not paid by the bank time would then begin to run against A and he would have to sue the bank in respect of their failure to pay within six years.

Joint accounts

In *Brewer* v. *Westminster Bank*, [1952] 2 All E.R. 650, McNair, J., decided that in the case of a joint account, the bank's duties were owed to the account holders *jointly* and *not severally*. The result of this decision was that where one account-holder forged the other's signature on cheques drawn on the account and then added his own signature, the innocent account-holder had no action against the bank.

However, in *Jackson* v. *White and Midland Bank Ltd*, [1967] 2 Lloyd's Rep. 68, where one joint account-holder forged the signature of the other, Park, J., declined to follow *Brewer's* case, holding that where there was a joint account with say, A and B, the bank in effect agreed with A and B *jointly* that it would honour cheques signed by them both and with A *separately* that it would not honour cheques unless signed by him, and with B *separately* that it would not honour cheques unless signed by him. Thus, where the bank honours a cheque on which B has forged A's signature, A should be able to sue the bank because it is in breach of the separate agreement with him.

The reasoning in *Jackson's* case seems to be more satisfactory and makes better commercial sense. It was applied in *Catlin* v. *Cyprus Finance Corporation* (*London*) *Ltd*, [1983] 1 All E.R. 809. Mr and Mrs Catlin had a joint deposit account with the defendants. Withdrawals required the written instructions of them both. They separated in 1972. At that time there was £21,642 in the account. In 1975 the bank let Mr Catlin take various sums from the account on his signature alone. Mrs Catlin eventually discovered this. The account then stood at £897. Mrs Catlin claimed against the bank for the money withdrawn on the grounds that they had failed to observe the mandate. Mr Catlin was not joined in the action either as co-plaintiff or co-defendant. Could Mrs Catlin succeed on her own? Bingham, J. preferred the type of reasoning in *Jackson*. Therefore Mrs Catlin succeeded in her claim. The judge said, amongst other things: 'The duty could, in theory, have been owed jointly, but in my mind to make sense it has to be owed severally. The only possible purpose of requiring two signatures is to obviate the possibility of independent action by one account holder to the detriment of the other.

The duty on the bank which can only be performed jointly with Mr Catlin would be worthless to Mrs Catlin in practical terms and would deprive her of any remedy.' Thus joint account holders also have *several actions* against the bank.

Generally

Banks often accept valuable property for safe custody and are liable as ordinary bailees in this respect, i.e. they must take reasonable care for the safety of the property. Should the banker misdeliver the goods to the wrong person, then he is liable for wrongful interference even though there was no negligence on his part.

Bankers nowadays often give advice on investment to customers and potential customers and, if the giving of such advice forms part of the banker's business, he will be liable in damages if his advice is negligent. (*Woods* v. *Martins Bank*, 1958.)[700] If such advice is not part of the business of a particular banker, the person who gave the advice might be personally liable for negligence. (*Hedley Byrne & Co. Ltd* v. *Heller & Partners Ltd*, 1963.)[215]

In the absence of express instructions, it is not part of a banker's duty to consider a customer's tax liability when crediting an account with a dividend. (*Schioler* v. *Westminster Bank Ltd*, 1970.)[701]

Bankers have a fiduciary type of duty of disclosure, particularly when arranging a security for themselves in respect of a loan or overdraft facility. (*Lloyds Bank* v. *Bundy*, 1974.)[272]

CROSSED CHEQUES

Nature of crossing

The Act provides—

(1) Where a cheque bears across its face an addition of—

(*a*) The words 'and company' or any abbreviation thereof between two parallel transverse lines, either with or without the words 'not negotiable'; *or*

(*b*) Two parallel transverse lines simply, either with or without the words 'not negotiable', *that addition constitutes a crossing and the cheque* is *crossed generally*. (S. 76(1).)

Where there is a general crossing the banker must pay the cheque to another banker and must not cash the cheque across the counter. The expression 'and Co.' is a relic of earlier banking days and it is no longer necessary to add it to a crossing.

(2) Where a cheque bears across its face an addition of the name of a banker, either with or without the words 'not negotiable,' that addition

constitutes a crossing, and *the cheque is crossed specially and to that banker*. (S. 76(2).) Where there is a special crossing the cheque must be paid to the banker named in the crossing.

General and special crossings give additional protection to holders in the case of theft, for the thief may not have a bank account and, even if he has, the extra time involved in clearing the crossed cheque may enable the drawer or holder to stop payment.

In addition to the crossings specified in the Act, it is not uncommon for the drawer to add the words 'Account payee', and this is regarded as an instruction to the collecting banker to collect only for the account of that payee. The crossing 'Account payee' is not provided for in the 1882 or other Act. It is an instruction to the collecting banker, addressed to him by a person who has no contract with him, and it would be negligence in a banker if he collected the money for some other account, for a person with no title. The crossing has no effect on a paying banker since it merely states what is to happen to money after receipt. The crossing does not prevent the cheque from being transferred or indeed from being negotiable. (*National Bank* v. *Silke*, [1891] Q.B. 435. Obviously, no banker would normally collect the money for an endorsee but the drawer would remain liable on the instrument and would have to pay the amount of the cheque to an endorsee.

Bankers will sometimes collect a cheque crossed 'Account payee' for someone other than the payee, particularly if the cheque is for a small amount and the customer is one of long standing.

Crossing procedure

Section 77 of the Act lays down the following rules—

(1) A cheque may be crossed generally or specially by the drawer.

(2) Where a cheque is uncrossed, the holder may cross it generally or specially.

(3) Where a cheque is crossed generally, the holder may cross it specially.

(4) Where a cheque is crossed generally or specially, the holder may add the words 'not negotiable'.

(5) Where a cheque is crossed specially, the banker to whom it is crossed may again cross it specially to another banker for collection.

(6) Where an uncrossed cheque, or a cheque crossed generally, is sent to a banker for collection, he may cross it specially to himself. (S. 77.)

There is no reason why the payee cannot also add 'Account payee'.

A crossing authorized by the Act is a material part of the cheque and it is not lawful for any person to obliterate or, except as authorized by the Act, to add to or alter the crossing. (S. 78.) A crossed cheque cannot be converted into an uncrossed one except by the drawer.

Duties of banker as to crossed cheques

Section 79 provides that if a paying banker receives a cheque—

(i) crossed specially to more than one banker he must not pay it; however, if one of the bankers named is acting as an agent for collection for the other, the cheque may be paid to the agent bank; collection through an agent is rare today, but was more frequent when there were a number of small banks using a major London bank as agents for collection;

Examples of Crossings on Cheques

(ii) crossed specially to a named banker, he must pay only the named banker (or the named banker's agent for collection, if any);

(iii) crossed generally, it cannot be paid except through a banker, though payment through any banker will suffice.

If a banker fails to observe the above rules he is liable to the true owner for loss incurred because the cheque was not paid as directed by the crossing. There are two possible sets of circumstances to consider.

(*a*) *The banker may, in fact, have paid the true owner* in which case there can be no claim against him. However, Lord Cairns once said of such a cheque '. . . the drawers might refuse to be debited with it as having been paid contrary to their mandate.' (*Smith* v. *Union Bank of London*, (1875) 1 Q.B.D. 31 at p. 36.)

(*b*) *Payment may have been made to a person who is not the true owner*. In the case of an uncrossed cheque, the banker may be protected by s. 59 of the Act if the person he pays is the holder, and by s. 60 if the person to whom payment was made was in possession under a forged or unauthorized indorsement.

Thus, if a bearer cheque is stolen from its owner by T, and the drawee bank pays him, it has no liability to the true owner because T is the holder and s. 59 applies. Furthermore, if A draws a cheque on his bank payable to C and it is stolen by T who forges C's indorsement and negotiates it to E, who is paid by the bank in good faith and in the ordinary course of business, s. 60 will apply and the bank will not be liable to the true owner, C.

However, if, in the examples just given, the cheque had been crossed and the banker had not observed the instructions on the crossing, he would be liable to the true owner in each case and could not derive protection from ss. 59 and 60.

Protection against alterations and obliterations

Where a cheque is presented for payment which does not at the time of presentment *appear to be crossed*, or to have had a crossing which has been obliterated, or to have been added to or altered otherwise than as authorized by the Act, *the banker paying the cheque in good faith and without negligence shall not be responsible or incur any liability*. Nor shall the payment be questioned *even if the cheque had been crossed*, or if the crossing had been obliterated or been added to or altered otherwise than as authorized by the Act, or if payment had been made otherwise than to a banker or to the banker to whom the cheque was crossed, or to his agent for collection being a banker, as the case may be. (S. 79.)

Effect of crossing 'not negotiable'

Where a person takes a crossed cheque which bears on it the words 'not negotiable', he shall not have and shall not be capable of giving a better title to the cheque than that which the person from whom he took it had. (S. 81.)

While the words 'not negotiable' do not prevent the cheque from being transferred, they do have a serious effect on the title of subsequent holders. It was held in *Redmond* v. *Allied Irish Banks plc*, [1987] F.L.R. 307 that a bank is not under a duty to warn a customer of the danger of accepting a cheque crossed 'Not negotiable' *when he pays it in*. If he turns out to have no title and the bank is sued in conversion by the true owner or voluntarily reimburses him, the bank can obtain an indemnity from the customer. The bank would seem to be under a duty of care to a customer, however, who actually asked for advice about the nature of 'not negotiable' cheques.

The process of negotiation

(1) Order cheques
To negotiate an order cheque, an appropriate indorsement must be made. If such a cheque were lost or stolen, then any such indorsement would be forged and no subsequent holder could obtain a title, *even a holder in due course*. A forged or unauthorized indorsement is wholly

inoperative and anyone taking the bill after such an indorsement has no title to it, or right to sue on it, even though he may have no knowledge that the indorsement is forged or unauthorized. However, if the party against whom it is sought to retain or enforce the payment of the bill is precluded (i.e. estopped) from setting up the forgery or want of authority, he will be liable on the instrument (*Greenwood* v. *Martins Bank Ltd*, 1933.)[680] In addition, an unauthorized signature may be ratified unless it amounts to a forged signature. Thus, as we have seen, if a cheque is made payable to a company and a clerk in the company's employment without authority indorses the cheque on behalf of the company to creditors of the company, on the face of it the creditors have no title to the cheque, but the company could ratify the unauthorized indorsement if not put on for a fraudulent purpose, and the creditors could then sue on the cheques. In this context one must also consider s. 55(2) of the Act of 1882 which provides that the indorser of a bill by indorsing it—(*a*) engages that on due presentment it should be accepted and paid according to its tenor, and that if it be dishonoured he will compensate the holder or subsequent indorser who is compelled to pay it, provided that the requisite proceedings on dishonour be duly taken; (*b*) is precluded from denying to a holder in due course the genuineness and regularity in all respects of the drawer's signature on all previous indorsements; (*c*) is precluded from denying to his immediate or subsequent indorsee that the bill was at the time of his indorsement a valid and subsisting bill and that he had a good title thereto. Thus, suppose that a cheque is drawn in favour of C and indorsed by C to D. It is then stolen from D by a thief who forges D's indorsement and negotiates the cheque to E, who indorses it to F, who indorses it to G. G has no knowledge of the forgery and in all respects complies with the definition of a holder in due course, i.e. he would be a holder in due course but for the forgery. It is clear that G has no title to the bill because it rests on a forgery. However, he will have rights against E or F by virtue of s. 55. When E indorsed the cheque to F he impliedly guaranteed that it was a valid bill and that the signatures on it of the drawer and the previous indorsers were valid signatures. F gave an undertaking to the same effect when he indorsed the cheque to G. Therefore, because one of the earlier indorsements (D's) was forged, E is liable for the amount of the cheque to G or if G chooses to claim it from F, E is then liable to indemnify F. The addition of the words 'not negotiable' does not affect the position.

(2) Bearer cheques

A bearer cheque is negotiable by transfer without indorsement and a person taking such a cheque might have a title as a holder in due course even if a previous holder had none.

Since a bearer cheque can be transferred without indorsement, the person who transfers it does not give the 'guarantees' of an indorser under s. 55 (referred to above) in regard to the validity of the cheque. Instead s. 58 of the Act applies to the transferor of a bearer cheque who is called a transferor by delivery and under s. 58 warrants to his immediate transferee, being a holder for value, *and him alone*, that the cheque is valid; that he has the right to transfer it; that he is not aware at the time of transfer that it has become valueless, e.g. as where payment has been stopped. Thus if a bearer cheque apparently drawn by A is negotiated to B, who negotiates it to C, who negotiates it to D, then if A's signature is forged, D cannot sue A on it, nor can he sue B or C on the cheque. He can only sue C for breach of warranty.

The addition of the words 'not negotiable' to a bearer cheque protects the rights of the true holder against a subsequent holder, and if such a cheque were stolen and transferred to an innocent third party who obtained payment, the true owner could demand restitution within the limitation period of six years.

The words 'not negotiable' can be written on a crossed cheque when making the crossing or subsequently. A cheque crossed 'not negotiable' is still transferable subject to defects in title. A bill of exchange so crossed is not even transferable. This is because the meaning generally given to the word 'negotiable' is 'transferable free from equities' but in s. 8(1) the draughtsman has used it to mean 'transferable' and therefore a bill of exchange payable to 'G. Green only' or marked 'not negotiable' is not even transferable. Thus if A draws a bill on B payable 'to C only' or the bill is marked 'not negotiable' it is valid as between A, B and C but C cannot transfer it. (*Hibernian Bank* v. *Gysin & Hanson*, 1939.)[702] If the words 'not negotiable' appear on a cheque otherwise than as part of the crossing, the better view is that they are of no effect.

Account payee

We have seen that, although such a crossing is not authorized by the Act, it is not uncommon for the drawer of a cheque to include in the crossing the words 'A/c payee' or 'A/c payee only' (see p. 490).

Application of crossings rules

The crossings rules apply not only to cheques but also—

(i) to the instruments other than cheques specified in s. 4 of the Cheques Act, 1957 (see below, p. 496); and
(ii) to dividend warrants. (S. 95, Bills of Exchange Act, 1882).

BANKER'S PROTECTION

Paying bankers

If a banker pays one of his customer's cheques to the wrong person then he is liable to the true owner for wrongful interference by conversion for the face value of the cheque and he cannot debit the customer's account.

However, the following statutory provisions may provide the banker with a defence—

(a) Under s. 59
Payment by the banker to the holder at or after maturity in good faith and without notice of any defect in his title discharges the bill, frees the banker from all liability and enables him to debit the customer's account. However, the person paid *must be the holder*, and a person holding an order bill by means of a forged or unauthorized indorsement is not a holder. Therefore payment to him would not discharge the bill or free the banker from liability. The section would provide a defence where a banker paid the bearer of a bearer cheque.

(b) Under s. 60
If a banker on whom a cheque is drawn pays it, in good faith and in the ordinary course of business, he is deemed to have paid it in due course and is not prejudiced by the fact that the *indorsement* was forged or made without authority. The section applies only to indorsements on cheques and does not apply where the drawer's signature has been forged, nor where the cheque is void for material alteration.

(c) Where a cheque is crossed
Where the banker, on whom a crossed cheque is drawn, in good faith and without negligence pays it, if crossed generally, to a banker, and if crossed specially, to the banker to whom it is crossed (or his agent for collection being a banker), *the banker* paying the cheque, *and*, if the cheque has come into the hands of the payee, *the drawer shall* respectively be entitled to the same rights and *be placed in the same position as if payment of the cheque had been made to the true owner* thereof. (S. 80.)

For example, A draws a cheque on the B Bank payable to C. C, on receipt of the cheque, crosses it generally. The cheque is then stolen by T who opens an account at the Z Bank in the name of C. The Z Bank presents the cheque to the B bank which pays in good faith and without negligence. The B Bank is protected by s. 80 from liability to C, and C cannot sue A.

(d) Cheques Act, 1957, s. 1
Although cheques are bills of exchange, most of them have a very short life, being sent by the drawers to the payees who promptly pay them straight into their banking accounts. Prior to the Act, although there was no transfer by the payee to an indorsee, such cheques required indorsement, a laborious and rather useless process.

Section 1 of the Cheques Act, 1957, provides—

> Where a *paying banker* in good faith and in the ordinary course of business pays a cheque drawn on him which is not indorsed or is irreg-

ularly indorsed, he does not, in doing so, incur any liability by reason only of the absence of, or irregularity in, indorsement, and he is deemed to have paid it in due course.

The same protection is extended to him if he pays—

(i) A document issued by a customer of the bank which, though not a bill of exchange, is intended to enable a person to obtain from the bank the sum mentioned in the document; or

(ii) A draft payable on demand drawn by him on himself, whether payable at the head office or some other office of the bank.

The Committee of London Clearing Bankers announced, shortly after the Act was passed, that they would still require indorsement of cheques other than those paid into a banking account for the credit of the payee. Accordingly, if the payee pays a cheque into his own account there is no need for him to indorse it. However, if a payee or indorsee presents a cheque for payment over the counter (the cheque being uncrossed), the person receiving payment will have to indorse it. Where a crossed cheque is negotiated and paid into a bank by the last indorsee, the banker will require the indorsement of all indorsers but not that of the last indorsee who is paying in.

Whilst the decisions of the Committee of London Clearing Bankers are not law, it is thought than a banker who pays a cheque without obtaining an indorsement where the Committee says he should would not be acting in the ordinary course of business and would not, therefore, be protected by s. 1 of the Cheques Act, 1957, nor by s. 60 of the Bills of Exchange Act, 1882. He would probably also be negligent and be unable to claim the protection of s. 80.

Further, it is assumed that where the Committee requires an indorsement it must be a regular indorsement, and payment of a cheque with an irregular indorsement would be negligent and not in the ordinary course of business, so that there could be no statutory protection if there was a wrongful payment.

Bankers collecting cheques

The Cheques Act, 1957, s. 4, extends protection to *bankers who collect payment* on the following instruments—

(i) Cheques.

(ii) Any document issued by a customer of a banker which, though not a bill of exchange, is intended to enable a person to obtain payment from that banker of the sum mentioned in the document.

(iii) Any document issued by a public officer which is intended to enable a person to obtain payment from the Paymaster General or the Queen's and Lord Treasurer's Remembrancer of the sum mentioned in the document but which is not a bill of exchange.

(iv) Any draft payable on demand drawn by a banker upon himself, whether payable at the head office or some other office of the bank. (S. 4(2).)

Where a banker, *in good faith and without negligence—*

(*a*) receives payment for a customer of one of the above instruments; or

(*b*) having credited a customer's account with the amount of such an instrument receives payment thereof for himself; *and the customer has no title, or a defective title*, to the instrument, the banker does not incur any liability to the true owner of the instrument by reason only of having received payment thereof. (S. 4(1).)

A banker is not to be treated for the purposes of the section as having been negligent by reason only of his failure to concern himself with absence of, or irregularity in, indorsement of an instrument. (S. 4(3).)

This section repeals, replaces and extends s. 82 of the Bills of Exchange Act, 1882, and provides *protection for the collecting banker against an action for wrongful interference by conversion* if he collects for someone with no, or a defective title. (For wrongful interference generally see p. 383.)

Section 4 applies to all cheques, whether crossed or not, and also extends to a range of other instruments. However, an instrument on which the drawer's signature is forged is not a cheque nor is it an instrument which has become void for material alteration, and no protection is given in respect of the collection of such instruments.

The section applies only where the banker collects payment for a *customer* and acts without negligence, and in the matter of negligence the onus of proof is on him. Thus there must be an account, but it seems to be enough that the customer has opened it with the cheque which is in dispute.

The main areas of a collecting banker's negligence are as follows—

(1) Failure to obtain the name of the husband's employer when an account is opened for a married woman. (*Lloyds Bank Ltd* v. *E. B. Savory & Co.*, 1933.)[703]

(2) Failure to obtain references or follow them up on opening an account. (*Lumsden & Co.* v. *London Trustee Savings Bank*, 1971.)[704]

(3) Failure to obtain the name of the customer's employer. (*Lloyds Bank Ltd* v. *E. B. Savory & Co.*, 1933.)[703] It would appear, however, from the case of *Orbit Mining and Trading Co.* v. *Westminster Bank*, 1962[705] that the bank need not update this information.

(4) Collecting for the private account of a partner or a director cheques payable to the firm or to the company. (*Underwood* v. *Bank of Liverpool*, [1924] 1 K.B. 775.)

(5) Collecting for an employee cheques payable to his employer or drawn by his employer. (*Lloyds Bank Ltd* v. *E. B. Savory & Co.*, 1933.)[703]

(6) Collecting for the private account of an agent cheques which he

received only as an agent. (*Bute (Marquis)* v. *Barclays Bank Ltd*, [1954] 3 All E.R. 365.)

(7) Collecting cheques payable to a limited company for an account other than that of the company. (*London and Montrose Shipbuilding and Repairing Co. Ltd* v. *Barclays Bank Ltd*, (1926) 31 Com. Cas. 182.) However, the matter is not beyond doubt because in *Penmount Estates Ltd* v. *National Provincial Bank* (1945), 173 L.T. 344 a bank in a similar situation successfully defended itself in an action in conversion. However, it can be said that a bank would not collect a cheque payable to a limited company for an account other than that of the company without very strict inquiry. This makes it difficult for companies to negotiate cheques payable to them.

(8) Collecting 'Account Payee' cheques for someone other than the payee.

It should be noted, however, that the above decisions represent the high-water mark of judicial severity in the matter of bankers' negligence and in two recent cases, *Orbit Mining and Trading Co.* v. *Westminster Bank*, 1962,[705] and *Marfani & Co.* v. *Midland Bank*, 1967[706] the judiciary seems to have accepted that bank employees cannot be highly inquisitive if they are to deal promptly with the large number of cheques which are cleared every day, and the standard of care required has been lowered, possibly too far.

Collecting banker as holder in due course

Where a banker collects payment of a cheque for a person who is not the true owner, he may be liable for wrongful interference by conversion although, as we have seen, he may derive protection from s. 4 of the Cheques Act, 1957. However, he may also escape liability if he can prove that he has become a holder in due course of the cheque. Where this is so the banker will obtain a good title to the cheque even if the title of the transferee was non-existent or defective, and in spite of his own negligence, if any.

A banker, like any other person, must give *value* before he can become a holder in due course, and this may happen in *three* ways—

(i) where the customer pays in a cheque to reduce his overdraft, if the banker forgoes interest;

(ii) where there is an express or implied agreement between banker and customer under which the customer can and does draw against the cheque before it has been cleared: where there is no prior agreement it seems that the banker does not give value; and

(iii) where the banker cashes a cheque for a person who is not a customer and therefore *buys* it from that person rather than *collecting* it for him.

A banker cannot become a holder in due course if an *essential* indorsement is forged but he can, by virtue of s. 2 of the Cheques Act, 1957, become the holder in due course of an order cheque, even though it is not indorsed to him. The banker will, therefore, have the right to sue the drawer if the cheque is dishonoured.

The section provides that a *collecting banker* who gives value for, or has a lien on, a cheque payable to order which the holder delivers to him for collection without indorsing it, has such (if any) rights as he would have had if, upon delivery, the holder had indorsed in blank.

The section provides an exception to s. 31 of the Bills of Exchange Act, 1882, in that it allows an order cheque to be negotiated without indorsement. It should also be noted that the section applies only to cheques and not to analogous instruments, as do ss. 1 and 4, and that it does not deal with the case in which an indorsement exists and is irregular. Presumably, where this is so the cheque is not complete and regular on the face of it and the banker will not be a holder in due course. The cases of *Westminster Bank Ltd* v. *Zang*, 1965,[707] and *Barclays Bank Ltd* v. *Astley Industrial Trust Ltd*, 1970,[708] are illustrative of some of the problems arising out of the operation of s. 2.

Unindorsed cheques as evidence of payment

Section 3 of the Cheques Act provides that an unindorsed cheque which appears to have been paid by the banker on whom it is drawn is evidence of the receipt by the payee of the sum payable by the cheque. Prior to the Act such an indorsed cheque was *prima facie* but not conclusive evidence that the payee had received the sum payable; the Act merely confirms that in future an unindorsed cheque can fulfil the same function. Nevertheless, by drawing attention to this virtue of a cheque, it has led to a widespread practice among business men of dispensing with the issue of receipts where payment is by cheque, with a consequent saving in effort, time and money.

Banking Ombudsman

In January 1986 19 banks combined to set up and fund an Ombudsman. His role is to provide an independent body which will receive and resolve complaints by customers about the banking practices of the banks involved, which include all the big English and Scottish clearing banks.

The Ombudsman can make an award of up to £50,000 to customers who sustain a complaint. The award binds the bank provided the customer is willing to accept it in full and final settlement of the claim.

Complaints can be made about most aspects of personal banking: this includes the insurance and trustee services which the banks provide. However, complaints about refusal of an overdraft or loan would appear to be excluded by the scheme, as would complaints about charges. The first report of the Ombudsman indicates that cashcard machines are causing more complaints than any other banking service.

11 **The nature of crime**

CRIME AND CIVIL WRONGS DISTINGUISHED

The distinction does not lie in the *nature of the act* itself. For example, if a railway porter is offered a reward to carry A's case and runs off with it, then the porter has committed one crime, that of theft, and two civil wrongs, i.e. the tort of wrongful interference and a breach of his contract with A. Again, a signalman who carelessly fails to operate the signals so that a fatal accident occurs will have committed one crime, i.e. manslaughter, if persons are killed, and two civil wrongs, the tort of negligence in respect of those who died and those who are merely injured, and a breach of his contract of service with British Rail in which there is an implied term to take due care. It should also be noted that in this case the right of action in tort and the right of action in contract are vested in different persons.

The distinction does depend on the *legal consequences* which follow the act. If the wrongful act is capable of being followed by what are called criminal proceedings that means that it is regarded as a crime. If it is capable of being followed by civil proceedings that means that it is regarded as a civil wrong. If it is capable of being followed by both it is both a crime and a civil wrong. Criminal and civil proceedings are usually easily distinguishable, they are generally brought in different courts, the procedure is different, the outcome is different and the terminology is different. A major consequence of classifying proceedings as criminal is that the burden of proof is on the Crown. (*Woolmington* v. *DPP*, 1935.)[709]

TERMINOLOGY AND OUTCOME OF CRIMINAL AND CIVIL PROCEEDINGS

In criminal proceedings a prosecutor prosecutes a defendant. If the prosecution is successful it results in the conviction of the defendant. After the conviction the court may deal with the defendant by giving him a custodial sentence, e.g. prison or detention centre; or a non-custodial sentence, e.g. probation, or community service order. In rare cases the court may discharge the defendant without sentence.

As regards *civil proceedings*, a plaintiff *sues* (brings an action against) a defendant. If the plaintiff is successful this leads to the court entering judgment ordering, for example, that the defendant pay a debt owed to the plaintiff or damages. Alternatively, it may require the defendant to transfer property to the plaintiff or to do or not to do something (injunction) or to perform a contract (specific performance). Some of these remedies are legal, others equitable. The matter of remedies for breach of contract and for torts has already been dealt with in detail in the chapters on those topics.

NULLA POENA SINE LEGE

This important maxim leads to the proposition that a person should not be made to suffer criminal penalties except for a clear breach of *existing* criminal law, that law being precise and well defined.

The maxim thus prohibits—

(i) the introduction of new crimes which operate retrospectively under which a person might be found guilty of a crime for doing an act which was not criminal when he did it;

(ii) wide interpretation of precedents to include by analogy crimes which do not directly fall within it. Thus the extension of the criminal law in the way, for example, in which the civil law of negligence has been extended (see p. 393) is undesirable;

(iii) the formulation of criminal laws in wide and vague terms.

The last rule has in general terms been observed in England with perhaps the major exception of the law of conspiracy under which there has been a tendency to charge persons with criminal conspiracy rather than with specific criminal offences. Thus a conviction might be obtained for conspiracy to do an act even though there were doubts as to whether the act was or ought to be criminal. (See *Shaw* v. *DPP*, 1961.)[710]

Under ss. 1–5 of the Criminal Law Act, 1977, the offence of conspiracy at common law is abolished and the new statutory offence of conspiracy is restricted to agreements to commit criminal offences, though the common law offences of conspiracy to defraud and conspiracy to corrupt public morals are retained.

CRIMINAL ACTS

A criminal offence results from the action of a human being, or his failure to act, which is referred to as the *actus reus* of the crime. This act or omission must, at least at common law, be accompanied by an appropriate state of mind which is referred to as the *mens rea*.

Actus reus

The *actus reus* may consist of voluntary conduct or an omission and matters of causation arise.

Voluntary conduct

The defence of automatism may be raised as where, for example, the accused person pleads that he acted during a stroke or epileptic fit in order to show that there was no voluntary act. However, it must be said that in general terms the defence is difficult to establish. (*Hill* v. *Baxter*, 1958.)[711] This is particularly so where the state of automatism is induced by drink or drugs, though automatism induced in such a way may be a defence to a crime requiring a specific intent, such as murder, but not to manslaughter where a specific intent is not a requirement. (See *A-G* v. *Gallagher*, 1963[712] and *R.* v. *Lipman*, 1969.)[713] Automatism may be non-insane (*R.* v. *Charlson*, 1955)[714] or insane (*R.* v. *Kemp*, 1956).[46]

Omissions

Some modern statutes make failure to act criminal. For example, the Road Traffic Act, 1972, s. 25, imposes a duty to stop after an accident. The cases regarding liability for omissions *at common law* are concerned with manslaughter (see *R.* v. *Instan*, 1893)[715] and it does not seem likely that any significant developments outside the field of manslaughter are likely at common law. (But see *R.* v. *Miller*, 1983 at p. 878.)

Causation

The act of the accused must be *the cause* of the crime, though it is a general rule that the accused must take his victim as he finds him (see *R.* v. *Hayward*, 1908),[716] and that the accused must be regarded as having intended the natural consequences of his acts. However, this concept is rather different in modern law a comparison being provided by *R.* v. *Martin*, 1881[717] and *R.* v. *Moloney*, 1985 at p. 879. The matter of causation has given rise to difficulties some of which are illustrated by comparing *R.* v. *Jordan*, 1956[718] and *R.* v. *Smith*, 1959.[719] As regards causation, *R.* v. *Malcherek*, [1981] 2 All E.R. 422 is of interest. In that case two victims of assaults were placed on life support machines and in both cases doctors, having diagnosed brain death, discontinued treatment and disconnected the life support system. It was held by the Court of Appeal that there was no evidence in either case that the original injury was other than the continuing operating cause of death. The discontinuance of treatment did not break the chain of causation between initial injury and death.

It is not necessary for the Crown to establish which of the accused's actions caused the death. Thus in *Attorney-General's Reference* (No. 4 of 1980), [1981] 1 W.L.R. 705 the accused pushed his girlfriend downstairs and, believing her to be dead, dragged her upstairs by a rope around her neck, cut her throat, and dismembered and disposed of the body. He was charged with manslaughter and it was held by the Court of Appeal that he could be convicted, provided the jury was satisfied that one of the actions did cause the death, notwithstanding that it was impossible to say which of the culpable acts did so.

THE MENTAL ELEMENT—GENERAL PRINCIPLES

The *actus reus* must be accompanied by an appropriate state of mind which is referred to as *mens rea*. The *mens rea* and the *actus reus* must coincide in order to constitute a crime. (*Thabo Meli* v. *The Queen*, 1954.)[720]

Motive
As in torts the motive, i.e. the reason why the accused did the act, is irrelevant in regard to his guilt or innocence if his direct intention was to commit the offence. (*Chandler* v. *DPP*, 1962.)[721]

Intention, recklessness and negligence
The *mens rea* of a crime may be the existence in the mind of the accused of an *intention* to commit the act as where A shoots at B foreseeing and desiring or wishing that B will be killed, or as where A deliberately fails to feed an aged parent, B, in the hope and expectation of bringing about B's death. In this connection it should be noted that the House of Lords in *R.* v. *Cunningham*, [1981] 2 All E.R. 863 reaffirmed and approved its earlier decision in *Hyam* v. *DPP*, [1974] 2 All E.R. 41 that where a person unlawfully kills another intending only to cause him grievous bodily harm, he is none the less guilty of murder. These cases must now be read in the light of the decision of the House of Lords in *R.* v. *Moloney*, 1985. (See p. 879.)

It may in some cases be sufficient that the accused was *reckless*, as where when late for work A drives his car at an excessive speed through a crowded street where there is a chance that someone may be injured but not desiring or wishing injury to occur. Recklessness has always been regarded as a mental state adequate for crime, e.g. for manslaughter.

However, *negligence* is not a mental state and consists more in failure to foresee consequences which an ordinary person would be expected to foresee. Obviously, in negligence there is no wish or desire to injure.

Thus negligence is not generally regarded as *mens rea* at common law but if it is of a sufficiently high degree, as where lack of foresight reveals in a particular set of circumstances a very low standard of care so that it might be called *gross* negligence, then it may be enough to provide the necessary mental state for the crime of manslaughter.

In recent times there has been a development to the point where *inadvertent negligence* would seem sufficient as a mental state, at least for the crime of criminal damage. This has followed from the judgment of Lord Diplock in *R.* v. *Caldwell*, [1981] 1 All E.R. 961 at p. 967 (a case of criminal damage) where he said: 'A person . . . is 'reckless' . . . if (1) he does an act which in fact creates an obvious risk that property will be destroyed or damaged and (2) when he does the act he either has not given any thought to the possibility of there being any such risk or has recognized that there was some risk involved and has nonetheless gone on to do it.'

Although these words were spoken in regard to recklessness for the statutory offence of criminal damage, it seems from other parts of his judgment and what he said in *R.* v. *Lawrence*, [1981] 1 All E.R. 974 (a case of reckless driving) that they might apply to the construction of criminal statutes generally and to recklessness at common law, e.g. for manslaughter. The principles laid down as regards recklessness in *Caldwell* and *Lawrence* were applied in *Elliott* v. *C.*, 1983.[722]

Malice

This may also be a necessary mental state in certain crimes. It does not require any animosity towards the person or persons affected. (See *R.* v. *Martin*, 1881.)[717]

Mistake

The way in which a normal, sane and sober person sees the facts of a situation may be affected by mistake and may have an effect upon liability for crime. (*R.* v. *Levett*, 1638.)[723]

Mistake is not always relevant so that, for example, in sexual offences with young girls, the fact that the accused was mistaken as to the age of the girl, she being younger than he thought, may not as a matter of policy be a defence. As would be expected, mistake as to law is no defence. (*R.* v. *Bailey*, 1800.)[724]

Mens rea in statutory offences

The principles applied in regard to *mens rea* where the offence is set out in a statute are somewhat different from those applied in common law offences. The topic may be considered under the headings which follow.

Mens rea implied

As Lord Reid said in *Sweet* v. *Parsley*, 1969:[725] '. . . there has for centuries been a presumption that Parliament did not intend to make criminals of persons who were in no way blameworthy in what they did. This means that whenever a section of an Act is silent as to the requirement of *mens rea* there is a presumption that, in order to give effect to the will of Parliament, we must read in words appropriate to require *mens rea*.' (See also *R.* v. *Tolson*, 1889.)[726]

However, statutes which regulate public conduct and which cannot be enforced effectively if *mens rea* is required, e.g. pollution of the environment, are sometimes excepted from the rule that statutory crimes require *mens rea* by implication. (See *Alphacell* v. *Woodward*, 1972[727] and *Cundy* v. *Le Cocq*, 1884.)[728]

Particular words connoting *mens rea*

The use of words such as 'maliciously', 'knowingly', 'wilfully', 'permitting' and 'suffering' in a statute is usually an indication that *mens rea* is required to establish the offence. However, the absence of such words does not necessarily mean that no *mens rea* is required as we have seen from cases recently considered. The construction put upon these words in cases coming before the courts can be seen in *R.* v. *Cunningham*, 1957;[729] *Gaumont British Distributors Ltd* v. *Henry*, 1939;[730] *R.* v. *Lowe*, 1973[731] and *Somerset* v. *Wade*, 1894.[732]

Vicarious liability

If the offence is one which does not require *mens rea* so that it is an *absolute offence* an employer may be liable where an employee commits the offence in the course of his employment. It is no defence for the employer to say that he had no *mens rea* because none is required. (See *Griffiths* v. *Studebakers Ltd*, 1924.)[733]

However, if the offence requires *mens rea* as where, for example, it is one involving 'permitting', an employer will not be liable vicariously if it is the employee who does the permitting. (*James and Son Ltd* v. *Smee*, 1955.)[734]

If a person carries on a business which requires a licence which is issued subject to the observance of certain conditions, he cannot escape liability by delegating the duty of seeing that those conditions are observed to either an employee or a stranger. However, where the offence requires *knowledge* the holder of the licence will not be liable for the acts of his delegate unless the delegation is of the whole function of the licensee as where he leaves the premises to take a holiday so that the management of the business is in the hands of the delegate. (*Vane* v. *Yiannopoullos*, 1965.)[735]

An employer cannot, it would appear, be liable vicariously for *aiding and abetting* an offence unless he has knowledge of the offence. The knowledge of an employee in regard to such a charge is not imputed to the employer in order to make him liable. (*Ferguson* v. *Weaving*, 1951.)[736]

THE MENTAL ELEMENT—CORPORATIONS

In October 1987 an application was made for leave to apply for judicial review against the decision of the coroner for East Kent made on 18 and 19 September 1987 in the course of an inquest into the deaths of 188 people arising out of the capsize on 6 March 1987 of the *Herald of Free Enterprise*. (See *ex parte Spooner and Others; ex parte de Rohan and Another, The Times*, 10 October, 1987.)

As we have seen, application can be made to the Queen's Bench Divisional Court for judicial review to correct an alleged defect in a proceeding in a lower court, tribunal or public body. The coroner had decided as a matter of law that—

1. A corporate body could not be guilty of manslaughter.
2. Where the individual acts or omissions of individuals employed by a corporate body or engaged in its management were insufficient to render them guilty of manslaughter, those acts or omissions could not be aggregated in order to make the corporate body guilty.
3. The acts and omissions of the company, Townsend Car Ferries Ltd, were not the direct cause of the deaths.

The applicants, who were seeking to have the coroner's decisions reviewed, relied on three points made against the company in the Sheen Report published in July 1987 following an enquiry under Mr Justice Sheen. These were that—

(1) the company had failed to consider seriously a proposal to fit a warning light system on the ferry;
(2) five or six previous incidents of ferry doors being left open had not been properly reported and collated by the company; and
(3) it lacked any proper system to ensure that the highest standards of safety were observed.

In hearing the application for judicial review, Lord Justice Bingham said that he was prepared tentatively to accept that a corporate body was capable of being found guilty of manslaughter and Mr Justice Mann and Mr Justice Kennedy agreed.

However, the Court refused leave to apply for judicial review. No substantial case had been made against named directors of the company and in any case the Court was always reluctant to intervene in inquests.

So far the proceedings may seem to have been rather ordinary and straightforward but in fact the tentative acceptance of corporate liability for serious crime is far from innocuous. Up to now corporations have been convicted of crimes as follows—

(i) those for which no guilty mind (*mens rea*) or even recklessness as to consequences is necessary. Some Acts of Parliament which regulate public conduct cannot be enforced effectively if an intentional or reckless state of mind is required, either in an individual or a corporation, e.g. statutory crimes relating to the pollution of the environment are sometimes excepted from the rule that even statutory crimes require *mens rea*, either expressly or by implication even though no state of mind is mentioned in the statute.

Thus in *Alphacell Ltd* v. *Woodward*, 1972[727], A Ltd was the owner of papermaking mills. In the course of manufacture effluent passed into two tanks on the banks of a river. Pumps were used to remove the effluent from the tanks but it was inevitable that if the pumps failed the effluent would enter the river and pollute it. As a result of foliage blocking the pump inlet such an overflow occurred and A Ltd was charged with 'causing' polluting matter to enter the river under s. 2(1) of the Rivers

(Prevention of Pollution) Act, 1951. The House of Lords decided that A Ltd was guilty of that offence even though it had clearly not intended it or even been reckless as to whether it occurred or not. An intervening act of trespass or an Act of God would have been a defence but there was no such trespass or Act of God in this case.

(ii) Crimes which require a state of mind. Here, if the appropriate human decision-making organ within the company has the necessary state of mind the company may be found guilty. Examples are to be found in *Director of Public Prosecutions* v. *Kent & Sussex Contractors Ltd*, [1944] 1 All E.R. 119 where a company was convicted under statutory defence regulations for using a document with *intent* to deceive and for making a false statement, since those managing the company had the necessary state of mind.

Again, in *R.* v. *ICR Haulage Ltd*, [1944] KB 551 the company was successfully prosecuted for a *common law* conspiracy to defraud because of the state of mind of its managing director.

Finally, in *Moore* v. *Bresler Ltd*, [1944] 2 All E.R. 515 a company was successfully prosecuted for using a document with *intent* to defraud when the acts and state of mind were those of the company secretary and a branch manager, not those of the directors.

The requirements were clearly laid down by Lord Denning in *H.L. Bolton (Engineering) Ltd* v. *T.J. Graham & Sons Ltd*, [1956] 3 All E.R. 624 where he said: 'A company may in many ways be likened to a human body. It has a brain and nerve centre which controls what it does. It also has hands which hold the tools and act in accordance with directions from the centre. Some of the people in the company are mere servants and agents who are nothing more than hands to do the work and cannot be said to represent the mind or will. Others are directors and managers who represent the directing mind and will of the company and control what it does. The state of mind of these managers is the state of mind of the company and is treated by the law as such.'

Although it is not the intention here to consider whether the ferry company in the Zeebrugge case or its management, agents, and employees were guilty or innocent in the circumstances, or whether any of the allegations made are true or false, a prosecution for manslaughter against a company, if brought in such circumstances, would have to resolve a problem never before decided in the criminal courts of this country. That problem is whether there is a third category of corporate liability for crime where, although an appropriate state of mind is required, the individuals involved are not sufficiently guilty, as single units among many, to be convicted or to provide the necessary state of mind for corporate liability in class (ii), referred to above.

If there is to be a third category of corporate liability it would be based upon the fact that although no single individual is criminally culpable, he or she is nevertheless part of a complex and collective corporate mind which, when aggregated, gives the necessary culpability. These non-culpable people may be regarded by the courts in the future as part of a group lacking, say, a proper system of control and supervision to ensure observance of safety elements which, in a particular case, could lead to a conviction of the organization involved—the company—for a crime as serious as manslaughter where death of a person or persons has ensued. Since manslaughter is punishable by a fine, which is at the discretion of the court and has no limit, there would be no problem in punishing the corporation.

If such a prosecution were successful, it would bring *Salomon* v. *Salomon*, 1897[52] full circle. Since that case people have accepted gradually that it is *companies that do things*, such as make contracts and obtain licences and so on. The last frontier is the corporate doing of a crime where the necessary state of mind is not derived from any particular individual but from all those individuals involved in the failure of the system in general. The admission by the Court in *ex parte Spooner and Others* (above) that a corporate body is capable of being guilty of manslaughter suggests that if appropriate circumstances arise the law will take the final leap in the personification of corporate entities.

Cases and materials

THE DEVELOPMENT OF ENGLISH LAW

Where common law and equity are in conflict equity prevails

(1) *The Earl of Oxford's case* (1615), 1 Rep. Ch. 1

Merton College, Oxford, had been granted a lease of Covent Garden for 72 years at £9 a year, and some 50 years later sold the lease to the Earl for £15 a year. Later the college retook possession of part of it, on the ground that a statute of Elizabeth prevented the sale of ecclesiastical and college lands so that the conveyance to the Earl was void. The Earl brought an action to eject the college from the land, and the common law judges found in favour of the college, saying that they were bound by the statute. The Earl filed a Bill in Equity for relief, and Lord Ellesmere granted it, stating that the claim of the college was against all good conscience. This brought law and Equity into open conflict and resulted in the ruling of James I that, where common law and Equity are in conflict, Equity should prevail. This principle now appears in s. 49 of the Supreme Court Act, 1981.

The court must apply an Act of Parliament and cannot declare it illegal

(2) *Cheney* v. *Conn*, [1968] 1 All E.R. 779

Cheney objected to his tax assessments under the Finance Act, 1964, on the ground that the government was applying part of the tax collected to the making of nuclear weapons. Cheney alleged that this was contrary to the Geneva Conventions—which had been incorporated into the Geneva Conventions Act, 1957—and conflicted with international law. *Held*—that even if there was a conflict between the 1964 and 1957 Acts, the 1964 Act gave clear authority to collect the taxes in question and being later in time prevailed. 'It is not for the court to say that a parliamentary enactment, the highest law in this country, is illegal.' (*Per* Ungoed-Thomas, J.)

A statute remains law until repealed by Parliament

(3) *Prince of Hanover* v. *Attorney-General*, [1957] 1 All E.R. 49

A statute of Anne in 1705 provided for the naturalization of Princess Sophia, Electress of Hanover, and the issue of her body. The statute was repealed by the British Nationality Act, 1948, s. 34(3), but by s. 12 a person who was a British subject immediately before the commencement of the Act (1 January, 1949) became a citizen of the United Kingdom and Colonies. The plaintiff was born in 1914 in Hanover and was lineally descended from the Electress. He now claimed a declaration that he was a British subject immediately before the commencement of the British Nationality Act. It was necessary for him to establish this in order to make a claim on a fund, put up by the Polish Government, to compensate Britons who had lost property in Poland because of nationalization. Vaisey, J., held at first instance that the statute had not lost its force merely because of its age, but thought that, although the statute was unqualified and plain in its meaning, its words taken alone produced an absurd result, since, under the statute, the Kaiser would have been a British subject. Parliament must, therefore, have intended some limitation on the operation of the words used. By referring to the preamble it seemed possible to draw the conclusion that the purpose of the Act was to be effected in the lifetime of Anne, and that after that time its purpose was spent and the plaintiff was not entitled to his declaration. On reaching the Court of Appeal, *it was held* that the appellant was a British subject under the statute of Anne which had remained law until repealed by the 1948 Act, the statute being so clear in its meaning that it was unnecessary to apply rules of interpretation to it. Rules of interpretation were to be used only in case of ambiguity or doubts as to meaning. The decision of the Court of Appeal was affirmed by the House of Lords.

Parliament may specifically abolish or alter statute law by a later enactment. This will take place by implication if the later enactment is wholly inconsistent with the former

(4) *Vauxhall Estates Ltd* v. *Liverpool Corporation*, [1932] 1 K.B. 733

In 1928 the Minister of Health made a Street Improvement Scheme Order for a certain area of Liverpool. The Order required the compulsory purchase of property, and the question of compensation payable to owners arose. Under s. 2 of the Acquisition of Land (Assessment of Compensation) Act, 1919, the plaintiffs would receive £2370, but if s. 46 of the Housing Act, 1925, applied, the plaintiffs would receive £1133. A provision in the Act of 1919 stated that other statutes inconsistent with the 1919 Act were not to have effect. *Held*—The 1925 Act impliedly repealed the 1919 Act. It was inconsistent with it. Compensation was to be assessed under the latest enactment.

Comment. It was held by Farwell, J. in *Re Berrey*, [1936] 1 Ch. 274 at p. 279 that the court will not construe a later Act as repealing an earlier Act by implication unless it is *impossible* to make the two Acts, or certain sections of them, stand together, i.e. if a section of the later Act can only be given a sensible meaning, as in *Vauxhall*, if it is treated as impliedly repealing the relevant section of the earlier Act.

Legal texts may be a source of law

(5) *Boys* v. *Blenkinsop*, [1968] Crim. L.R. 513

Mrs Nellie Blenkinsop was charged at Lewes with having 'permitted' her son Donald to drive a car without third-party insurance contrary to s. 201 of the Road Traffic Act, 1960 (see now s. 143, Road Traffic Act, 1972). The registered owner of the car was the driver's father whose insurance policy did not cover driving by his son. However, it appeared that the son had asked his mother's permission to drive and she had given it and had said she was the owner when asked by a constable. The defence submitted that there was no case to answer because only the registered owner could permit use of the vehicle. The prosecution submitted that this was wrong because Mrs Blenkinsop might have been, if not joint owner, at any rate responsible for care, management or control of the car within *Lloyd* v. *Singleton*, [1953] 1 All E.R. 291. The prosecuting inspector had asked the justices to refer to *Wilkinson's Road Traffic Offences* (5th ed. 1965, p. 202) which in relation to that case stated 'A person may "permit" though he is not the owner.' Counsel for the defence objected that unless the justices were referred to the case itself they were not allowed to look at the textbook. The inspector did not have a report of the case with him. The justices dismissed the case and the prosecution appealed to the Divisional Court. The Court allowed the appeal and remitted the case to the justices to continue the hearing of it. Parker, L.C.J., said 'They are entitled to and should look at the textbook; and if they then feel in doubt they should, of their own motion, send for the authority, and if necessary, adjourn for it to be obtained.'

THE COURTS OF LAW

An arbitration reference in the county court may be rescinded where, e.g. the no costs rule could produce hardship for a party

(6) *Pepper* v. *Healey*, [1982] R.T.R. 411

Mrs Pepper, whose car was only insured for third party, was driving her car in Maghull, Merseyside. She was in collision with another car driven by Mrs Healey who had a comprehensive insurance cover. Mrs Pepper alleged that Mrs Healey was negligent. She issued a summons in the Liverpool County Court claiming £138 for repairs, and £5 for shock. Mrs Healey sent the summons to her insurers who took over the defence and instructed their solicitors. The claim, being for less than £500, was automatically referred to arbitration. It appeared that expert witnesses, along with other witnesses were to be called. This placed Mrs Pepper in a difficult position. In view of the complexity of the evidence which was to be introduced, she could not carry on without a solicitor. Furthermore the hearing would not be over quickly and so her solicitor's fee might well be more than she could afford. Yet even if she won she could not claim costs against Mrs Healey's insurance company because of the no-costs rule which applies in arbitration references.

The Registrar decided that the contest was unequal and rescinded the arbitration reference. There was an appeal by the insurers to the circuit judge. He upheld the Registrar. The insurers appealed to the Court of Appeal and they upheld the Registrar. The matter would have had to be tried in the county court where at least Mrs Pepper would have obtained costs if she had won. However, the insurers made a payment into court for the full amount of the claim, including Mrs Pepper's costs.

Arbitration in the county court—not unreasonable conduct to take advantage of the no-costs rule

(7) *Newland* v. *Boardwell and MacDonald* v. *Platt*, [1983] 3 All E.R. 179

Mrs Newland and Mr MacDonald in two separate actions involving identical questions, brought proceedings in the Liverpool County Court to recover damages which had resulted from car accidents. The defendants had passed the claims to their respective insurance companies who had taken over the defence. The claims were for damages not exceeding £500. Such claims are automatically referred to arbitration once a defence is filed. In these actions the insurance companies filed defences solely to cause the claim to be referred to arbitration and take advantage of the no-costs rule by avoiding the possibility of payment of extra costs by the insurance companies if they lost. The insurance companies admitted negligence but merely disputed the amount of damages in order to get a defence together. Under the county court rules where a case goes to arbitration, the only solicitors' costs allowed to a successful plaintiff are the costs on the summons, the costs of enforcing the award, and such costs as are certified by the arbitrator to have been incurred through the unreasonable conduct of the opposite party in relation to the proceedings. Was the conduct of the insurance companies unreasonable?

The County Court Registrar ruled that the defences were unreasonable and ordered the insurance companies to pay costs. The decision was upheld by the Circuit Judge on appeal to him. However, the Court of Appeal reversed the decision, ruling that Mrs Newland and Mr MacDonald were not entitled to any solicitors' costs not referred to in the summons, since the charges accruing after the filing of the defences had not been incurred through the unreasonable conduct of the defendant. Both plaintiffs had restricted their claims to the County Court Small Claims procedure, and they must be taken to have known that if a defence was filed, the case would automatically be referred for arbitration, and if they continued to use solicitors after the filing of the defence, they would not be able to recover their charges from the other party. Each plaintiff would therefore recover against the defendants only the solicitors' charges referred to in the summons.

CRIMINAL AND CIVIL PROCEDURE

Excessive reporting of criminal proceedings: no need to show prejudice to accused

(8) *The Eastbourne Herald Case, The Times*, 12 June, 1973

The *Eastbourne Herald* published an article upon the committal proceedings of a case in which a man was charged with unlawful sexual intercourse. The prosecution of the editor and proprietors which followed was based on the following matters which appeared in the articles—

(i) a headline reading 'New Year's Day Bridegroom Bailed';
(ii) a description of the offence charged as being 'serious';
(iii) a description of the alleged offender as 'bespectacled and dressed in a dark suit';
(iv) a note to the effect that he had been 'married at St. Michael's Church on New Year's Day';
(v) a reference to the way in which the prosecuting solicitor had handled the case.

The editor and proprietors were each found guilty by the Eastbourne Magistrates on the five counts relating to these different passages and were each fined a total of £2000 and ordered to pay £37.50 costs. This strange decision stems initially from the fact that liability may be incurred under what is now s. 8(4) of the Magistrates' Courts Act, 1980 where a report of committal proceedings contains any details other than those permitted by s. 8(4) and quite irrespective of whether or not the details are potentially prejudicial in nature. All that the prosecution is required to show is—

(i) that the defendant published a report of committal proceedings to which the restrictions apply, and
(ii) that the report contained matters for which no specific provision is made in s. 8(4).

Thus in this case it was an offence under the Act to describe unlawful sexual intercourse as a 'serious' offence for s. 8(4) permits of no such qualifying adjective. Equally, it was an offence to describe the defendant as 'bespectacled and dressed in a dark suit' for s. 8(4) only provides for reference to his name, address, and occupation. Furthermore, it is not necessary for the prosecution to show that the offending item purported to be an account of what transpired in court, provided only that it is contained within a report of committal proceedings. Thus, in this case the magistrates held that it was an offence under the Act to refer to the fact

English Law

that the defendant had been married at St Michael's Church on New Year's Day although this piece of background information does not appear to have been adduced as evidence in court.

OTHER COURTS AND TRIBUNALS AND THE LEGAL PROFESSION

The courts can control the defective jurisdiction of a tribunal or administrative authority by the doctrine of *ultra vires*

(9) *Attorney-General* v. *Fulham Corporation*, [1921] 1 Ch. 440

The local authority was authorized by the Baths and Wash-houses Acts, 1846–1878 to establish a wash-house where people could come and wash their own clothes. The Corporation decided to run a municipal laundry where people could bring their clothes to be washed by employees of the Corporation. *Held*—that the statutory powers did not cover running a laundry. The action of the authority was, therefore, *ultra vires* and an injunction was granted to prevent the Corporation from running the laundry.

Comment. (i) The *ultra vires* principle was used in *Bromley London Borough Council* v. *Greater London Council*, [1982] 1 All E.R. 129, where the House of Lords decided that the Labour-controlled GLC had no power under the Transport (London) Act, 1969 to pass resolutions to enforce a 25% cut in London's bus and tube fares. It was also decided that a public authority is under a *fiduciary duty* to hold the balance fairly between the various interests of those who are within its care, i.e. in this case between the ratepayers and the transport users. The effect of the resolutions was to pass on the cost of the reduction to ratepayers. The Labour Party's manifesto, which had advocated a reduction in fares, was no justification. It could not be assumed that all who voted Labour agreed with the whole of the manifesto. A manifesto is not a binding contract between a party and its supporters.

(ii) In *R.* v. *Lewisham B.C. ex p. Shell UK, The Independent*, 22 December, 1987, the Council passed a resolution to boycott all Shell products where suitable alternatives were available as part of the Council's anti-apartheid policy and on the basis of alleged activities by Shell in South Africa. The court granted Shell a declaration that the resolution was *ultra vires*. The Council had *no power* to put pressure on Shell in this way no matter how reasonable its desire to promote good race relations might be.

The supervisory jurisdiction of the High Court cannot normally be invoked if other and more appropriate procedures for appeal exist

(10) *R.* v. *Brighton Justices, ex parte Robinson*, [1973] 1 W.L.R. 69

The defendant was convicted and ordered to pay a fine in her absence for failing to give information about a driver's identity. She applied for *certiorari* on the grounds that she had not received the summons. *Held*—

by Queen's Bench Divisional Court—that the application would be granted but the court would not be minded to grant *certiorari* in such cases in the future since a statutory procedure existed under s. 24(3) of the Criminal Justice Act, 1967. (See now s. 14(1), Magistrates' Courts Act, 1980.)

Comment. (i) Section 14(1) provides that the defendant may make a statutory declaration that he did not know of any summons or proceedings until after the trial commenced. The statutory declaration must be served on the clerk to the justices within 14 days of the date when the defendant came to know of the proceedings whereupon the summons and subsequent proceedings are void.

(ii) Judicial review may be granted in exceptional cases. Thus in *R.* v. *Inspector of Taxes ex p. Kissane*, [1986] 2 All E.R. 37 taxpayers were granted leave to apply for judicial review against the decision of a tax inspector, even though they could have appealed to the Special Commissioners, because they could not recover costs on an appeal to the Commissioners.

An application for judicial review will not be granted unless the applicant has a sufficient interest in the matter to which the application relates

(11) *Inland Revenue Commissioners* v. *National Federation of Self-Employed and Small Businesses Ltd*, [1981] 2 All E.R. 93

The Federation asked for an order of *mandamus* on the Commissioners of Inland Revenue to assess and collect arrears of income tax said to be due from casual employees on national newspapers. The long-standing practice of Fleet Street employers had been to pay the casuals without deduction of tax and for the casuals to supply fake names and addresses when drawing their pay in order to avoid tax. Their true identities were known only to their union which operated a closed shop and controlled all casual employment on the newspapers. *Held*—by the House of Lords—that the Federation could not be granted the order of *mandamus*. The Federation had no *locus standi*. 'The total confidentiality of assessments and of negotiations between individuals and the Revenue is a vital element in the working of the system. As a matter of general principle I would hold that one taxpayer has no sufficient interest in asking the court to investigate the tax affairs of another taxpayer or to complain that the latter has been underassessed or overassessed; indeed there is a strong public interest that he should not. And this principle applies equally to groups of taxpayers: an aggregate of individuals each of whom has no interest cannot of itself have any interest.' (*Per* Lord Wilberforce.)

Certiorari **is available to control tribunals which have acted beyond their powers**

(12) *R.* v. *London County Council, ex parte Entertainments Protection Association Ltd*, [1931] 2 K.B. 215

The county council granted a new licence, under s. 2 of the Cinematograph Act, 1909, in respect of a cinema called the Streatham Astoria. One of the conditions contained in the Act was that the premises were not to be opened on Sundays, Christmas Day or Good Friday. Subsequent to the grant of the licence, a committee of the council considered an application that the Streatham Astoria be allowed to open on the above-mentioned days. The committee resolved that 'no action be taken for the present in the event of the premises being opened ... on Sundays, Christmas Day and Good Friday', subject to the applicants paying a sum of money to a selected charity. The Association challenged the ruling of the committee by *certiorari*. *Held*—The council was usurping its jurisdiction in breaking a condition of the licence, and that this was prohibited by the Act of 1909. *Certiorari* lay to quash the committee's ruling.

A court or other authority must not act if there is bias in the sense of any substantial pecuniary, personal or proprietory interest in the dispute before it. Natural justice also embraces the right to be heard

(13) *Dimes* v. *Grand Junction Canal* (1852), 3 H.L.C. 759

Dimes was the Lord of a manor through which the canal passed, and he had been concerned in a case with the proprietors of the canal in which he disputed their title to certain land. Dimes had obtained an order of ejectment, but the canal company approached the Lord Chancellor (Lord Cottenham) to prevent Dimes enforcing the order and to confirm the company's title. The Lord Chancellor granted the relief sought. Dimes now appealed to the House of Lords on the ground that the Lord Chancellor was a shareholder in the company and was therefore biased. *Held*—The Lord Chancellor's order granting the relief must be quashed because, although there was no evidence that his pecuniary interest had influenced him, yet it should not appear that any court had laboured under influences of this nature.

(14) *R.* v. *Bingham Justices, ex parte Jowitt, The Times*, 3 July, 1974

In announcing the conviction of the defendant for speeding the chairman of the justices said: 'Quite the most unpleasant cases that we have to decide are those where the evidence is a direct conflict between a police officer and a member of the public. My principle in such cases has always been to believe the evidence of the police officer, and therefore we find the case proved.' Mr Jowitt applied to the Divisional Court for *certiorari* and it was *held* that the attitute of the chairman clearly amounted to bias and the conviction was quashed.

Comment. (i) More recently, in *R.* v. *Liverpool City Justices, ex parte Topping*, [1983] 1 All E.R. 440, a conviction by magistrates was quashed by *certiorari* on the basis of bias where it was shown that they had gone on to try a case of criminal damage after becoming aware from court computer sheets of T's previous convictions.

(ii) As regards the right to be heard see *R. v. Wear Valley District Council ex p. Binks*, [1985] 2 All E.R. 699 where B operated a hot-food take-away caravan at a market under an informal arrangement with the council. She was given notice to quit without reasons or warning. Taylor, J. quashed the Council's decision on the grounds of denial of natural justice. B had a right to be heard and to prior notification and reasons.
(iii) Again in *R. v. Board of Governors of London Oratory School ex p. R., The Times*, 17 February, 1988 the rules of natural justice were applied to an expulsion of a child from school. The child must have an opportunity to state his case and know the nature of the accusations.

Although public tribunals will normally allow legal representation, in domestic tribunals the matter is basically within the discretion of the tribunal. However a rule forbidding legal representation in all circumstances is probably invalid

(15) *Enderby Town Football Club Ltd v. The Football Association Ltd*, [1971] 1 All E.R. 215

The football club, which had been censured by a local county football association for negligent administration, appealed to the F.A. and asked for representation. Two rules of the F.A. were brought into question. One was rule 38(*b*) which excluded legal representation and the other was rule 40(*b*) which said that legal proceedings should only be taken as a last resort and then only with the consent of the Council of the Association. The football club asked for an injunction restraining the hearing of the appeal unless the club was allowed legal representation. It was *held*—by the Court of Appeal—

(*a*) the points of law raised in the appeal were difficult and should be brought before the ordinary courts of law for a declaration of rights. These courts were the most appropriate place for such matters to be litigated. Rule 40(*b*) did not prevent this course of action since it was invalid in that it attempted to oust the jurisdiction of the courts, but;

(*b*) if the Club did not want to go to the ordinary courts but chose to raise the matter before the F.A., then it must abide by rule 38(*b*) and could not have legal representation.

'In many cases it may be a good thing for the proceedings of a domestic tribunal to be conducted informally without legal representation. Justice can often be done in them better by a good layman than by a bad lawyer. This is especially so in activities like football and other sports . . . But I would emphasize that the discretion must be properly exercised. The tribunal must not fetter its discretion by rigid bonds. A domestic tribunal is not at liberty to lay down an absolute rule: "We will *never* allow anyone to have a lawyer to appear for him". The tribunal must be ready, in a proper case, to allow it. That applies to anyone in authority who is entrusted with a discretion. He must not fetter his discretion by making an absolute rule from which he will never depart . . .' (*Per* Lord Denning, M.R.)

English Law

Rules of natural justice need not be applied where matters of national security are involved

(16) *R. v. Secretary of State for Home Department, ex parte Hosenball,* [1977] 3 All E.R. 452

Mr Hosenball was an American journalist working in London. He received a letter from the Home Department saying that the Home Secretary had decided to deport him in the interests of national security. The statement said that Mr Hosenball had tried to obtain and, indeed, had obtained, information harmful to the security of the United Kingdom and that that information had included information prejudicial to the safety of servants of the Crown. Mr Hosenball was given no further particulars and was told that he could not appeal but might make representations and appear before an independent advisory panel. Mr Hosenball did so but he did not see the panel's report, though the Home Secretary gave it his personal consideration. A deportation order was made under the Immigration Act, 1971, s. 5, and Mr Hosenball applied for an order of *certiorari* to quash the Home Secretary's decision. The Court of Appeal *held* unanimously that the application would be refused. Mr Hosenball had not been given enough information to enable him to meet the charge made against him. However, this was a case in which national security was involved and where the State was in danger even the rules of natural justice must take second place.

In addition, there was no infringement of Article 6 of the Convention for the Protection of Human Rights and Fundamental Freedoms. The European Commission of Human Rights in the case of Mr Philip Agee, whose deportation had been ordered by the Home Secretary at the same time as Mr Hosenball, had considered his application against the United Kingdom under the Convention as manifestly illfounded. The Commission considered that where the public authorities of a state decided to deport an alien on grounds of security that constituted an act of state falling within the public sphere and did not constitute a determination of his civil rights or obligations within the meaning of Article 6.

Comment. In *R. v. Secretary of State for the Foreign and Commonwealth Office, ex parte The Council of Civil Service Unions, The Times,* 23 November, 1984 (and [1984] 3 All E.R. 935) the House of Lords decided that the Government, in preventing its employees at Government Communication Headquarters (GCHQ) from joining trade unions, was acting in the interests of national security, and was entitled to act irregularly as regards procedure by not consulting its employees. Procedural propriety must give way to national security, when personal rights taken away by the action of the executive conflict with that security.

The decision of a tribunal acting in breach of the rules of natural justice (or *ultra vires*) is void

(17) *Ridge* v. *Baldwin*, [1963] 2 All E.R. 66

Mr Ridge, who was the Chief Constable of Brighton, had been acquitted on a charge of conspiring with other police officers to obstruct the course of justice, though the trial judge, Donovan, J., said that Mr Ridge had not given the necessary professional or moral leadership to the Brighton Police Force. The Brighton Watch Committee subsequently dismissed Mr Ridge from his post as Chief Constable under a power in the Municipal Corporations Act, 1882, giving them a right to dismiss 'any constable whom they think negligent in the discharge of his duty or otherwise unfit for the same'. Ridge was not given a chance to answer the charges or appear before the Watch Committee. *Held*—by the House of Lords—the dismissal was void; Mr Ridge should have been heard.

Mandamus lies to compel the exercise of a discretionary power but not in any particular way

(18) *R.* v. *Commissioner of Police of the Metropolis, ex parte Blackburn*, [1973] 1 All E.R. 324

Blackburn sought an order of *mandamus* requiring the Commissioner of Police to secure the enforcement of the law against pornography upon various publishers and booksellers, and to reverse his decision that no prosecution should be undertaken without the prior consent of the Director of Public Prosecutions. *Held*—by the Queen's Bench Divisional Court—that although the evidence showed that pornography was widely available, the Commissioner, because of an under-manned force, had to decide an order of priorities to deal with various offences. In these circumstances it was perfectly proper for the Commissioner to seek the Director's advice before embarking on a prosecution, so long as he did not consider himself bound to follow his advice, and, accordingly, the situation in London was not attributable to any breach of legal duty by the Commissioner and the court would not interfere with the legitimate exercise of his discretion in the matter of police powers.

Mandamus is not available against the Crown itself but it can issue against a minister

(19) *R.* v. *Secretary of State for Social Services, ex parte Grabaskey, The Times*, 15 December, 1972

A dentist treating a patient with a broken tooth, claimed payment not only for crowning the tooth but also for an amalgam filling. The latter claim was disallowed by the Dental Estimates Board and the Minister dismissed the appeal as unarguable under the proviso to reg. 18 of the National Health Service (Service Committees and Tribunals) Regulations, 1956. *Held*—by the Queen's Bench Divisional Court—that the dentist's case was reasonably arguable and accordingly the Minister had no jurisdiction to dismiss the appeal and *mandamus* would be granted requiring him to refer the matter to two dental referees.

Comment. In *Padfield* v. *Minister of Agriculture, Fisheries and Food*, [1968] 1 All E.R. 694 the House of Lords decided that an order of *mandamus* should issue to the Minister of Agriculture, requiring him to refer a complaint by milk producers against the working of a Milk Marketing Board Scheme to a committee of investigation in the exercise of a discretionary power conferred on him by s. 19 of the Agricultural Marketing Act, 1958.

A simple declaration of what the law on a particular matter is may sometimes be an appropriate remedy against an administrative authority

(20) *Laker Airways* v. *Department of Trade*, [1977] 2 All E.R. 182

The Civil Aviation Authority granted Laker Airways a licence for ten years from 1973 for a cheap passenger service between the UK and the USA called 'Skytrain'. Laker Airways was then designated as an airline under the Bermuda Agreement of 1946 made between the UK and the USA. Such designation was essential to get 'Skytrain' across the Atlantic. The Civil Aviation Act, 1971, gave the Secretary of State for Trade wide powers to revoke licences without reference to anyone and subject only to questions being asked in Parliament. However, these powers were restricted to time of war or great national emergency or where international relations might be affected. This part of the Act could not, therefore, have been applicable in regard to the revocation of the licence granted to Laker Airways. The Act also gave the Secretary of State power to give policy guidance in regard to civil aviation and it was under this power that the Secretary of State announced in 1976 by a White Paper that future policy would be to licence only one UK airline on any given long route. Paragraphs 7 and 8 of the White Paper contained an instruction to the Civil Aviation Authority to revoke the licence for 'Skytrain'. Laker Airways now claimed a declaratory judgment that paras 7 and 8 were *ultra vires* and that the Secretary of State was not entitled to withdraw their licence. Mocatta, J. granted the declaration sought, holding among other things that the power given to the Secretary of State to issue policy guidance did not extend to the revocation of licences in this way. On appeal to the Court of Appeal by the Department of Trade it was held, dismissing the appeal, the Laker Airways were entitled to the declaration sought. The Secretary of State could not lawfully use the procedure of 'guidance' for the revocation of licences.

(21) *Congreve* v. *Home Office*, [1976] 1 All E.R. 697

The plaintiff, on discovering that the price of the television licence was about to be increased, bought a new licence at the old rate before the expiry of his old licence, thus saving himself about £6. 25,000 other people did the same thing. The Home Secretary, in order to frustrate the scheme, threatened that unless the extra £6 was paid, the licences would be revoked under s. 1(4) of the Wireless Telegraphy Act, 1949. The plaintiff refused to pay the £6 and brought an action against the Home

Office claiming a declaratory judgment that revocation of the licences would be unlawful, invalid and of no effect. It was *held*—by the Court of Appeal—that although the Home Secretary had an undoubted discretion under s. 1(4) of the 1949 Act to revoke a TV licence, that discretion was fettered to the extent that the courts would intervene if it was exercised arbitrarily or improperly. The Minister's action was unfair, unjust, and unlawful. It was an improper exercise of the discretionary power as a means of levying money which the executive had no authority to demand and the court could, and should, intervene to declare the proposed revocation unlawful, invalid and of no effect.

Where discretionary powers are entrusted to the executive by statute, the courts may examine the exercise of those powers in order to ensure that they have not been exercised mistakenly or improperly

(22) *Secretary of State for Education and Science* v. *Tameside Metropolitan Borough Council*, [1976] 3 All E.R. 665

Tameside, a local education authority, submitted proposals for a comprehensive system of education to the Secretary of State in March, 1975. These proposals were approved and Tameside planned to implement them by September, 1976. In May, 1976, local elections were held and the membership of Tameside changed from a Labour to a Conservative authority. The Conservative council decided not to implement the scheme for comprehensive education fully and on 7 June, 1976, notified the Secretary of State of that intention. The Secretary of State was given a supervisory role by s. 68 of the Education Act, 1944. The section provides 'If the Secretary of State is satisfied, either on complaint by any person or otherwise, that any local education authority or the managers or the governors of any county or voluntary school have acted or are proposing to act unreasonably with respect to the exercise of any power conferred or the performance of any duty imposed by or under this Act, he may, notwithstanding any enactment rendering the exercise of the power or the performance of the duty contingent upon the opinion of the authority or of the managers or governors, give such directions as to the exercise of the power or the performance of the duty as appear to him to be expedient'. On 11 June the Secretary of State replied to Tameside saying that they had acted, or were proposing to act, unreasonably within s. 68 of the 1944 Act and accordingly directed Tameside to implement the 1975 scheme. Tameside refused, so the Secretary of State applied for *mandamus*. The Divisional Court of Queen's Bench granted the order but the Court of Appeal and the House of Lords reversed that decision. Before giving directions, under s. 68 the Secretary of State had to be satisfied that Tameside were acting unreasonably, i.e. that their conduct was such that no authority could reasonably engage in it. It had been alleged that there was insufficient time to carry out the necessary selection procedure for entry into grammar school. However, the House of Lords said that there were no grounds for concluding that the authority were acting unreasonably in taking the view that there was sufficient time available to carry out the necessary selection procedure. Although the Secretary of State might legitimately take the view that the authority's proposal to retain the grammar schools and to implement the selection procedure for the two schools where places were available was misguided or wrong, there were no grounds which could justify a conclusion that the proposal was such that no education authority, acting reasonably, would carry it out. It followed that the Secretary of State's direction was *ultra vires* and of no effect.

Barristers are not liable for negligence in connnection with litigation. This immunity is, however, extended only to the trial itself and to any pre-trial work which is intimately connected with a case in court

(23) *Saif Ali* v. *Sydney Mitchell & Co.*, [1978] 3 All E.R. 1033

The plaintiff, Mr Ali, sought damages for alleged professional negligence against Sydney Mitchell & Co., a firm of solicitors, and a barrister. His allegations against the barrister were that he had advised Mr Ali to bring an action against the husband of a woman driving the family car who, so Mr Ali said, had injured him by negligent driving. Subsequently it appeared that the wife was not driving as her husband's agent and so he was not the proper defendant. As a result Mr Ali's action had to be discontinued and before another action could be commenced the limitation period had expired and it was too late for Mr Ali to proceed against the wife. It was *held*—by the House of Lords—that although public policy required that a barrister should be immune from suit for negligence in respect of his acts or omissions in the conduct and management of litigation which caused damage to his client, such immunity was an exception to the principle that a professional person who held himself out as qualified to practise that profession was under a duty to use reasonable care and skill and was not to be given any wider application than was absolutely necessary in the interests of the administration of justice. A barrister's immunity from suit, therefore, extended only to those matters of pre-trial work which were so intimately connected with the conduct of the case in court that they could fairly be said to be preliminary decisions affecting the way that case was conducted when it came to a hearing. Inasmuch as the barrister's advice and settling of the pleadings in fact prevented the plaintiff's cause from coming to court in this case that advice could not be said to have been intimately connected with the conduct of the plaintiff's case in court, and was therefore not within the sphere of a barrister's immunity from suit for negligence. The appeal was allowed so that Mr Ali could proceed with his claim.

Comment. A solicitor acting as an advocate in court enjoys the same immunity as a barrister *per* Lord Wilberforce, Lord Diplock and Lord Salmon.

(24) *Rondel* v. *Worsley*, [1967] 3 All E.R. 993

The appellant was charged with causing grievous bodily harm and was tried and convicted. He was represented at the trial by the respondent barrister who had appeared on a 'dock brief'. The appellant later issued a writ and statement of claim against the respondent claiming damages for professional negligence in the respondent's presentation of the case and in his dealing with the evidence. The statement was ordered to be struck out by the Master as disclosing no cause of action and this order was upheld by Lawton, J., and the Court of Appeal. On further appeal to the House of Lords it was *held* that the appeal must be dismissed. A barrister's conduct and management of litigation either in court or at an earlier stage could not give rise to a claim for professional negligence. This ruling arose out of public policy in that—

(*a*) a barrister should be able to carry out *his duty to the court* independently and without fear;

(*b*) actions against barristers would amount in effect to a retrial of the case in which it was suggested negligence arose; this would prolong litigation contrary to the public interest; and

(*c*) barristers are obliged to accept any client if a proper fee is paid and cannot refuse clients on any other ground.

Lords Reid, Morris of Borth-y-Gest and Upjohn were of the opinion that public policy did not require the extension of this immunity to the non-litigious aspects of a barrister's work, and along with Lord Pearce thought that a solicitor should be given the same immunity in litigious work which could have been done by a barrister as the latter would have had if engaged.

Comment. In *Saif Ali* v. *Sydney Mitchell & Co.*, 1978[23] the majority in the House of Lords were of the opinion that *Rondel* v. *Worsley* was concerned only with matters taking place in court which resulted in an outcome unfavourable to the client. So far as the speeches in *Rondel* contained observations as to the extent of barristers' immunity for matters taking place outside court and in barristers' chambers, these, the House of Lords said, had only the status of *obiter dicta*.

Criminal conduct cannot be prevented by injunction unless the Attorney-General is prepared to take or agree to the taking, of civil proceedings

(25) *Gouriet* v. *Union of Post Office Workers*, [1977] 1 All E.R. 969

Under ss. 58 and 68 of the Post Office Act, 1953, it is an offence punishable by fine and imprisonment for persons employed by the Post Office wilfully to delay or omit to deliver packets and messages in the course of transmission and for any person to solicit or endeavour to procure another to commit such an offence. The Council of the Union of Post

Office Workers called on its members not to handle mail to South Africa for a week because they disapproved of South Africa's policies. The plaintiff, who was the Secretary of the National Association for Freedom, asked the Attorney-General for his consent to act as plaintiff in relator proceedings for an injunction to restrain the Union from soliciting or endeavouring to procure any person wilfully to detain or delay a postal packet in the course of transmission to South Africa. The Attorney-General refused. The plaintiff issued the writ of summons in his own name and applied to a judge in chambers for an injunction. The judge refused, saying he had no jurisdiction to grant relief where the Attorney-General had refused consent. The plaintiff appealed to the Court of Appeal who granted him an interim injunction against the Union. At a subsequent hearing the plaintiff amended his pleadings to claim permanent injunctions against the Union and a declaration that the Attorney-General, by refusing his consent, had acted improperly and wrongfully exercised his discretion. The Attorney-General stated that his discretion in relator proceedings was absolute and could not be reviewed by the courts. Furthermore, he did not have to give reasons and the courts could not enquire into them. He was answerable only to Parliament and he applied for the declaration claim to be struck out. It was *held*—by the Court of Appeal—that although the Attorney-General's refusal could not be reviewed or questioned, the Court was not without power to provide a remedy. It could grant a member of the public without any special interest in the matter a declaration and an interim injunction pending its final determination. The interim injunctions were in fact sufficient to stop the interference with mail to South Africa. Lord Denning, M.R., in a dissenting judgment, said that the Attorney-General had no prerogative, by which he alone could say whether or not the criminal law shall be enforced in the courts and if the court can grant a declaration, there is no reason why it should not be able to grant a permanent injunction.

Comment. The House of Lords decided [1977] 3 All E.R. 70 that proceedings to prevent the infringement of public rights can only be instituted by consent of the Attorney-General unless any individual has a special interest as where his private rights are threatened. Mr Gouriet had no such interest and was not entitled to the relief sought. Presumably, a company which dealt on a regular basis with South Africa by mail would have had the necessary *locus standi*.

LAW IN ACTION

The courts cannot disregard an Act of Parliament, whether public or private, nor can they examine the proceedings of Parliament to see whether an Act can be regarded as invalid on the grounds that it was obtained by some irregularity or fraud

(26) *British Railways Board* v. *Pickin*, [1974] 1 All E.R. 609

Section 259 of the Bristol and Exeter Railway Act, 1836, provides that if the railway, which it set up, should at any time be abandoned, the land acquired for the track should vest in the adjoining landowners; the same provision was contained in the Act setting up the Yatton to Clevedon line. The British Railways Board, in whom the railways had become vested, closed the line in the early 1960s and took up the tracks in 1969. A private Act of Parliament, the British Railways Act, was passed in 1968 cancelling the effect of s. 259 and vesting the track in the Board; the Act's preamble recited that plans and books of reference had been deposited with Somerset County Council. Pickin, who objected to the closing of the line, purchased a few feet of land adjoining the track in 1969 and sought a declaration that he owned the land as far as the middle of the track, the railway having been abandoned within s. 259. In reply to the Board's defence that the land was vested in them by virtue of s. 18 of the Act of 1968, Pickin pleaded that that Act had contained a false recital in that the requisite documents had not been deposited, that the Board had misled Parliament in obtaining the Act *ex parte* (in effect without hearing other views) and that it was ineffective to deprive him of his land. It was *held*—by the House of Lords—that the courts had no power to disregard an Act of Parliament, whether public or private, nor had they any power to examine proceedings in Parliament in order to determine whether the passing of an Act was obtained by means of any irregularity or fraud, so that Mr Pickin failed.

Comment. The decision of the House of Lords in *Anisminic Ltd* v. *Foreign Compensation Commission*, [1969] 1 All E.R. 208 shows that by interpretation the courts can in effect disregard the provisions of a statute. In that case A Ltd applied to the Commission for compensation for property sequestered by Egypt in 1956 at the time of the Suez crisis. The statute which set up the Commission, i.e. the Foreign Compensation Act, 1950, said that a decision of the Commission 'shall not be called into question in any court of law'. The Commission did not accept that A Ltd was entitled to any compensation but in arriving at that decision misinterpreted the statutory provisions. The House of Lords held that the decision was *ultra vires* and void and therefore not a decision as such. They could, therefore, call it into question, in spite of what the Act said, and declared the decision to be void.

The provisions of the Treaty of Rome are directly enforceable in the High Court under s. 2(4) of the European Communities Act, 1972 provided it is clear from the Treaty what the rights given are. A Directive normally requires UK legislation to implement it but may exceptionally be directly applicable, again, if clear. The provision in s. 2(4) of the 1972 Act directing the court to apply Community law has the effect of preventing the court from applying any earlier or later UK legislation which is inconsistent with Community law

(27) *Van Duyn* v. *The Home Office*, [1974] 3 All E.R. 178

Yvonne Van Duyn, a Dutch national, was a Scientologist who tried to enter the United Kingdom on 9 May, 1973. She was refused entry on the grounds that the Secretary of State considered it undesirable to give anyone leave to enter the United Kingdom on the business of, or in the employment of, the Church of Scientology because its activities were considered contrary to public policy. Miss Van Duyn did not appeal under the Immigration Act of 1971 but sought a declaration in the Chancery Division that she was entitled to enter the country. She claimed that Art. 48 of the Treaty which allowed nationals of member states to accept offers of employment and to remain in a member state for the purposes of employment applied in her case. She conceded that these rights were subject to 'limitation justified on grounds of public policy, public security or public health' (Art. 48(3)), but said that Art. 3 of Directive 64/221 of 25 February, 1964, provided that measures taken on grounds of public policy should be based exclusively on the personal conduct of the individual concerned and not merely on the basis of employment by a given organization. In the Chancery Division the Vice Chancellor (Sir John Pennycuick) made the first reference to the European Court (i.e. the Court of Justice of the European Communities) under the Rules of the Supreme Court Order 114. Among the matters referred was the question whether or not the directive of 1964 was 'directly applicable so as to confer on individuals rights enforceable by them in the courts of the United Kingdom'. The Court of Justice decided ([1975] 3 All E.R. 190)— (i) that obligations imposed on member states by Art. 48(1) and (2) of the Treaty to abolish discrimination based on nationality as regards employment were directly applicable so as to confer on individuals rights enforceable by them in the courts of member states, since those provisions imposed on member states precise obligations which did not require the adoption of any further measures by the Community or member states; (ii) although Art. 189 of the Treaty provided that regulations were to 'be directly applicable' in member states, it did not follow that directives could not be applicable also. In order to determine whether a directive was directly applicable it was necessary to examine whether the nature, general scheme and wording of the provision were capable of having a direct effect on the relations between member states and individuals. On that basis Art. 3(1) of Directive 64/221 was directly applicable since it laid down an obligation which was not subject to any exception or condition and which did not require any further act or measure for its implementation, and (iii) its function was to impose a limitation of the power of member states to implement a provision which was contrary to one of the fundamental principles of the Treaty in favour of individuals, i.e. the freedom of movement for workers.

However, the Court of Justice decided that the Home Secretary had power to do what he had done because the voluntary act of an individual in associating with a particular organization which involved participation in its activities and identification with its aims, could properly be regarded as a matter of 'personal conduct' within Art. 3(1) of directive 64/221. A member state was therefore permitted under Art. 48 of the Treaty and

Art. 3(1) of the Directive to prohibit, on the grounds of public policy, an individual from entering its territory where the individual was associated with an organization which the member state considered to be socially harmful and the individual was proposing to enter the territory of the member state in order to take up employment with that organization. It was immaterial that the organization was not subject to any restrictions under the law of the member state and that nationals of that state were permitted to take up employment with the organization.

(28) *Amies* v. *Inner London Education Authority*, [1977] 2 All E.R. 100

In October, 1975 Mrs Amies applied for a post as head of department of a school but her application was rejected and a man was appointed to the post. The Sex Discrimination Act, 1975, came into force on 29 December, 1975, as regards all acts of discrimination committed on or after that date. Mrs Amies brought a complaint before an industrial tribunal arguing, amongst other things, that although the appointment had taken place before the Act came into force, she was entitled to relief under Article 119 of the Treaty of Rome which had direct effect in the English courts. Article 119 concerned itself mainly with equal pay for equal work and there was no other article which dealt with discrimination based on sex other than that relating to pay. It was *held*—by the Employment Appeal Tribunal—that Mrs Amies had no claim because—(i) the act of which she complained was one which had occurred before the 1975 Act came into force and therefore an industrial tribunal had no jurisdiction to entertain her application. (ii) As regards the Treaty of Rome, a major consideration in determining whether one of its provisions was intended to create an 'enforceable Community right' for the purposes of s. 2(1) of the European Communities Act, 1972, was that a municipal court of a member state should need nothing more precise than the terms of the Treaty itself in order to determine whether the right it created had been infringed. Since Article 119 did not define the right which Mrs Amies alleged had been infringed, it could not be construed as conferring on her any enforceable right in respect of discrimination based on sex, other than in relation to equal pay. (iii) Even if Article 119 did confer an enforceable right on Mrs Amies, an industrial tribunal had no jurisdiction to give effect to that right since industrial tribunals were the creatures of statute and therefore their jurisdiction was limited to the jurisdiction conferred on them by statute. They had no statutory jurisdiction to give effect to rights directly conferred by the Treaty of Rome; such rights could only be enforced in the High Court.

(29) *Macarthys Ltd* v. *Smith*, [1981] 1 All E.R. 111

This case concerned a conflict between Art. 119 of the Treaty of Rome and the UK Equal Pay Act, 1970. An employee, Mrs Smith, was claiming that she had been discriminated against on the ground of sex because she was paid less per hour for the same work than her male predecessor.

The Equal Pay Act, 1970 is concerned with equality of contracts between men and women *in the same employment at the same time*. However, counsel for Mrs Smith submitted that Art. 119 of the Treaty of Rome said that *a woman might receive the same pay as a man whom she followed in a job*.

Counsel for her employer claimed that Art. 119 envisaged men and women working at the same time for the same employer, but the European Court, to which the case was referred, held that the provisions of Art. 119 had priority over anything in a UK statute which was inconsistent with it, and that that priority was given to it by reason of the European Communities Act, 1972. The European Court said that there was no need for contemporaneity: the Article was applicable when a woman was employed after a man had left, and that interpretation had priority. Mrs Smith was entitled to the same amount of pay as her predecessor.

Comment. (i) For more recent regulations on equal pay see p. 325.

(ii) In this case both UK law (Equal Pay Act, 1970) and EEC law (Treaty of Rome) provided for equal pay; they were merely inconsistent. Section 3 of the European Communities Act, 1972 says that EEC law overrules domestic law which is *inconsistent with it*. Some members of the judiciary have not been prepared to declare English law null and void under the 1972 Act provisions. Thus in *Farrall* v. *Secretary of State for Transport, The Times*, 16 October, 1982, Stephen Brown, J. refused to declare s. 85 of the Road Traffic Act, 1972 (requirement for driving test) null and void in favour of Mr F who had a Luxembourg licence which he wanted to exchange for a British one without a driving test. Art. 84 of the Treaty provides for free movement of workers within the Community and cases before the European Court have decided that internal rules on the issue of driving licences are against the principles of Art. 84. Here there was not mere inconsistency between the Treaty and the Road Traffic Act, 1972; there was a direct conflict. The Treaty said that people in Mr Farrall's position should be given a licence but the Road Traffic Act said not so without a test. '. . . when he seeks a declaration that s. 85 of the Road Traffic Act, 1972 should be regarded as null and void as against nationals of Member States of the Community who have successfully passed driving tests in a Member State other than the United Kingdom, I think he is seeking a declaration which it would be impossible to grant. It is a misunderstanding that any statute can be regarded as null and void because of the European Treaty. What is required is that the Member States shall introduce regulations or legislation which shall give effect to decisions which are binding because of the treaty.' (*Per* Stephen Brown, J.)

The matter is now dealt with by the Driving Licences (Community Driving Licence) Regulations 1982 (SI 1982/1555) which allows holders of driving licences here to apply for a Community driving licence. There are reciprocal arrangements in other parts of the Community.

Delegated legislation—judicial control: the application of the doctrine of
ultra vires

(30) *Hotel and Catering Industry Training Board* v. *Automobile Proprietary Ltd*, [1969] 2 All E.R. 582

This was a test case brought by the Board to decide whether the Industrial Training (Hotel and Catering Board) Order 1966 made by the Minister of Labour pursuant to powers conferred upon him by the Industrial Training Act, 1964, was *ultra vires* in so far as it purported to extend to any members' clubs. If the order was *ultra vires*, the R.A.C. club in Pall Mall was not liable to pay a levy to the Board by reason of its activities in providing midday and evening meals and board and lodging for reward. The relevant order was made under s. 1(1) of the Act of 1964, which provides that the Minister may 'for the purpose of making better provision for . . . training . . . for employment in any activities of industry or commerce' make an order specifying 'those activities', and establishing a board to exercise the functions of an industrial training board. The 1966 order specified 'the activities' as including the supply of main meals and lodging for reward by a members' club. *Held*—by the House of Lords—the general object of the Act of 1964 was to provide employers in industry and commerce with trained personnel and to finance the training by a levy on employers in the industry, and that it was not intended to allow a levy to be made on private institutions like members' clubs. Although such institutions might pursue activities not unlike those of an hotel keeper, they could not be regarded as within the phrase 'activities of industry or commerce'.

(31) *R.* v. *Immigration Appeal Tribunal, ex parte Joyles*, [1972] 3 All E.R. 213

In this case an applicant for *certiorari* alleged that certain regulations made under the Immigration Appeals Act, 1969 had not been properly laid before Parliament as required by s. 24(2) of the 1969 Act. A Divisional Court of the Queen's Bench relied on letters from the Clerks of the Journal to the Commons and Lords stating that the rules had been duly presented and laid. The Court was not prepared to go further and examine the internal proceedings of Parliament.

Comment. This ruling is similar to that in *British Railways Board* v. *Pickin*, 1974,[26] though Pickin's case applied to Acts of Parliament, whereas this one is concerned with delegated legislation.

Local authority by-laws can be challenged in the courts as being unreasonable

(32) *Denithorne* v. *Davies* [1967] 2 Lloyd's Rep. 489

Fishermen were charged with using edible crab as bait in their lobster pots contrary to a bye-law made by the Eastern Sea Fisheries Joint

Committee under the Sea Fisheries Regulation Acts, 1888 to 1894. The bye-law prohibited the use of any edible crab of whatever size for bait but under the general law only the taking of crabs under four-and-a-half inches in width is prohibited. However, the bye-law was made because the breaking of the crab's shell before using it for bait made it impossible to tell what size it had been before being used as bait. The accused contended that the bye-law was unreasonable and therefore unenforceable because only edible crab of less than four-and-a-half inches in width required protection. The justices accepted this contention. The prosecution appealed to the Divisional Court of Queen's Bench which allowed the appeal and directed the justices to convict. A court should only interfere with the bye-laws of a public body if they were patently oppressive. The magistrate's finding, that the difficulty in proving that edible crabs under four-and-a-half inches in width had been used as bait was an insufficient justification for the absolute prohibition, could not be supported in the light of *Kruse* v. *Johnson*, [1898] 2 Q.B. 91, because although drastic it was not unreasonable.

Comment. (i) In *Kruse* v. *Johnson*, Lord Russell of Killowen laid it down that a court will not treat the bye-laws of a public authority as unreasonable unless they are manifestly oppressive.

(ii) Suppose, for example, a local authority made a bye-law under an enabling Act of Parliament providing for payment of a fine of £100 in respect of cars left too long in a parking place. If they tried to recover such a fine in the courts they would presumably be unable to do so because such a bye-law would be unreasonable in terms of the fine imposed.

Since its declaration of 1966 the House of Lords is not bound by its own decisions: application of the declaration

(33) *Schorsch Meier Gmbh* v. *Hennin*, [1975] 1 All E.R. 152

The plaintiffs, who carried on business in West Germany, had sold goods to the defendants in England. They had not been paid in full for the goods and DM 3756 remained owing. At the date of the invoice the sterling equivalent of this sum was £452 but between the invoice date and the date of the County Court summons sterling had been devalued so that the value of £452 was only £266. Consequently, the plaintiffs asked for judgment in deutschmarks. The difficulty facing the plaintiffs was that the House of Lords had decided in *Re United Railways of Havana*, [1960] 2 All E.R. 332 that an English court could not give judgment for an amount in foreign currency. The plaintiffs challenged this on the grounds that the *Havana* case ran contrary to Article 106 of the EEC Treaty. The County Court judge held that he was bound by the *Havana* case and could only give judgment in sterling. On appeal, however, the Court of Appeal with Lord Denning, M.R., came to a different decision and found for the plaintiffs on two grounds—(i) as an English court had since *Beswick* v. *Beswick* 1967 (see p. 581) the power to order specific performance of a contract to make a money payment there was no longer a justification for the rule in *Havana* that judgment could only be given for a sum of money in sterling; (ii) secondly, that the effect of Article 106 of the EEC Treaty was to require the English courts to give judgment in favour of a creditor of a member state in the currency of that state.

(34) *Miliangos* v. *George Frank (Textiles) Ltd*, [1975] 3 All E.R. 801

This case was concerned with a contract for the sale of polyester yarn and in particular the money of payment and the money of account in the contract were in Swiss francs. The Swiss seller, who was unpaid, was allowed in view of the decision in *Schorsch Meier*[33] to claim payment in Swiss francs. Sterling had fallen in value against the Swiss franc and if the new rule in *Schorsch*[33] were to be applied the plaintiff stood to gain £60,000 as opposed to £42,000 under the *Havana* principle. At first instance Bristow, J., held that the decision in *Schorsch*[33] had been decided *per incuriam*, the Court of Appeal having been bound by the *Havana* case. Consequently, he felt able to give a judgment only in sterling. From his judgment an appeal was made to the Court of Appeal and his decision was reversed by a court presided over by Lord Denning, who had been in the majority in the Court of Appeal when *Schorsch* was decided. From the judgment of the Court of Appeal a further appeal was made to the House of Lords. Their Lordships quickly reached the conclusion that the *Havana* case had not been overruled, since the only means by which that could have been done was by the House of Lords itself under the declaration of 1966 and, accordingly, the Court of Appeal should have felt bound by the case. It was, however, now open for the House of Lords to re-examine its previous decision in *Havana*. The House of Lords concluded that as the situation regarding currency stability had substantially changed since 1961 when the *Havana* case was decided, there was justification for a departure from that decision under the 1966 declaration. Accordingly, the House refused to follow the *Havana* case and held that an English court may give judgment in a foreign currency. However, the majority of their Lordships were highly critical of the wide interpretation of Article 106 adopted by the Court of Appeal, Switzerland not being a member of the Common Market, and it remains to be seen when the matter comes before the courts again whether that Article is adequate to sustain the view taken in *Schorsch*.

Precedent: Court of Appeal Criminal Division: considerations applying on a criminal appeal

(35) *R.* v. *Gould*, [1968] 1 All E.R. 849

The appellant was convicted of bigamy although when he remarried he believed on reasonable grounds that a decree nisi of divorce in respect of his previous marriage had been made absolute which it had not, so that he was still married at the time of the second ceremony. The Court of Criminal Appeal in *R.* v. *Wheat and Stocks*, [1921] 2 K.B. 119, had decided on similar facts that a reasonable belief in the dissolution of a previous marriage was no defence. In this appeal to the Court of Appeal (Criminal Division) the court quashed the conviction *holding* that in spite of the decision in *R.* v. *Wheat and Stocks*, a defendant's honest belief on reasonable grounds that at the time of his second marriage his former marriage had been dissolved was a good defence to a charge of bigamy. Diplock, L.J., giving the judgment of the court, said that in its criminal jurisdiction the Court of Appeal does not apply the doctrine of *stare decisis* as rigidly as in its civil jurisdiction, and if it is of the opinion that the law has been misapplied or misunderstood it will depart from a previous decision.

Comment. In this case a three-judge court expressly overruled *Wheat and Stocks* which was itself a decision of a five-judge Court of Criminal Appeal.

Exceptions to the rule of binding precedent: where the previous decision is one of several conflicting decisions at the same level

(36) *Tiverton Estates Ltd* v. *Wearwell Ltd*, [1974] 1 All E.R. 209

Tiverton Estates Ltd was the registered proprietor of leasehold property. The company entered into an oral agreement on 4 July, 1973, to sell it to Wearwell Ltd. The same day Wearwell's solicitors wrote to Tiverton's solicitors saying 'We understand that you act for the vendor in respect of the proposed sale of (the property) to our clients . . . £190,000 subject to contract. We look forward to receiving the draft contract for approval.' On 9 July Tiverton's solicitors replied 'We refer to your letter dated July 4th upon which we have taken our client's instruction. We now send you a draft contract for approval . . . We await hearing from you.' Wearwell claimed that the oral contract was enforceable, sufficient note or memorandum for the purposes of s. 40(1) of the Law of Property Act, 1925, being the draft contract, read in conjunction with the letter from Wearwell's solicitors. *Held*—by the Court of Appeal—for the purposes of s. 40(1) the note or memorandum relied on must contain not only the terms of the contract but also express an implied recognition that a contract had in fact been entered into. Documents which are part of a correspondence expressed subject to contract could not, therefore, constitute a sufficient memorandum.

The earlier decision by the Court of Appeal in *Law* v. *Jones*, [1973] 2 All E.R. 437, to the effect that it was unnecessary for the memorandum to acknowledge the existence of the contract, was not binding on the Court because it was in conflict with earlier decisions of equal authority. Although in general the Court of Appeal was bound to follow its earlier decisions, it was not bound to do so where the decision was in conflict with another decision of the court.

Comment. The law relating to the s. 40 memorandum is explained on p. 215.

Interpretation Act, 1978: application to statutory interpretation

(37) *Hutton* v. *Esher Urban District Council*, [1973] 2 All E.R. 1123

The Council proposed to construct a sewer to drain surface water from houses and roads and also to take flood water from a river. The most economical line of the sewer would take it straight through the plaintiff's bungalow which would have to be demolished but might be rebuilt after the sewer had been constructed. The Public Health Act 1936 empowered the Council to construct a public sewer 'in, on, or over any land not forming part of a street'. The plaintiff argued that the expression 'land' did not include buildings and therefore the Council had no power to demolish his bungalow. However, s. 3 of the Interpretation Act of 1889 (see now s. 5 and Sch. 1 of the Interpretation Act, 1978) provided that unless a contrary intention appears the expression 'land' includes messuages, tenements and hereditaments, houses and buildings of any tenure. It was *held*—by the Court of Appeal—that the Interpretation Act was applicable and 'land' therefore included buildings. In consequence the Council had the power to demolish the plaintiff's bungalow.

Judicial interpretation of statutes: the Mischief Rule: a statute is to be construed so as to suppress the mischief in the common law and advance the remedy

(38) *Gardiner* v. *Sevenoaks R.D.C.* (1950), 66 T.L.R. 1091

The local authority served a notice under the Celluloid and Cinematograph Film Act, 1922, on the occupier of a cave where film was stored, requiring him to comply with certain safety regulations. Obviously, the common law had no such rules. The cave was described in the notice as 'premises'. Gardiner, who was the occupier, appealed against the notice on the ground that a cave could not be considered 'premises' for the purpose of the Act. *Held*—Whilst it was not possible to lay down that every cave would be 'premises' for all purposes, the Act was a safety Act and was designed to protect persons in the neighbourhood and those working in the place of storage. Therefore, under the 'Mischief Rule' this cave was 'premises' for the purposes of this Act.

Comment. The mischief rule is very close to the more recent recommendation of the Law Commission for a purposive interpretation of statutes. (See p. 147.)

The Golden Rule of interpretation: extends the Literal Rule where the application of that Rule leads to an absurd result: ejusdem generis rule

(39) *Keene* v. *Muncaster*, [1980] R.T.R. 377

Regulation 115 of the Motor Vehicles (Construction and Use) Regulations, 1973 provide that a motorist may only park a motor vehicle on the road during the hours of darkness with the nearside of the vehicle to the kerb. There is an exception to this if he has the permission of a police officer in uniform to do otherwise. The defendant, a police officer in uniform, parked his vehicle with the offside to the kerb during the hours of darkness. When he was charged with an offence under reg. 115, he claimed that he had given himself permission to park in that way. He was convicted by the magistrates and appealed to the Divisional Court of Queen's Bench. *Held*—dismissing the appeal—that under the Golden Rule of interpretation the word 'permission' meant permission had to be requested by one person from another. The permission could not be given by the person whose vehicle was parked with the offside to the kerb.

(40) *Lane* v. *London Electricity Board*, [1955] 1 All E.R. 324

The plaintiff was an electrician employed by the defendants to install additional lighting in one of their sub-stations. While inspecting the substation, he tripped on the edge of an open duct and fell, sustaining injuries. The plaintiff claimed that the defendants were in breach of their statutory duty under the Electricity (Factories Act) Special Regulations in that the part of the premises where the accident occurred was not adequately lighted to prevent 'danger'. *Held*—It appeared that the word 'danger' in the regulations meant 'danger from shock, burn or other injury'. Danger from tripping was not *ejusdem generis*, since the specific words related to forms of danger resulting from contact with electricity.

Comment. This summary is concerned only with the plaintiff's claim under the Regulations. The failure of this claim did not prevent a claim for damages for negligence at common law.

The *expressio unius est exclusio alterius* Rule of Statutory Interpretation: the expression of one thing implies the exclusion of another

(41) *R.* v. *Immigration Appeals Adjudicator, ex parte Crew, The Times*, 26 November, 1982

An Immigration Appeals Tribunal had in interpreting the Immigration Act, 1971 ruled that a woman who was born in Hong Kong of a Chinese mother and putative English father, was not entitled to a certificate of patriality. (A certificate allowing immigration). There was an appeal to the Court of Appeal where the sole question was whether the word 'parent' used in the 1971 Act included the father of an illegitimate child. The father in this case was unknown. It was held that since the definition section in the 1971 Act specifically mentioned the mother alone in the context of an illegitimate child, the Rule *expressio unius est exclusio alterius* served to exclude the father of an illegitimate child for these purposes as a 'parent'. The appeal was dismissed.

The *noscitur a sociis* Rule of Statutory Interpretation: the meaning of a word may be gathered from its context

(42) *Muir* v. *Keay* (1875), L.R. 10 Q.B. 594

Section 6 of the Refreshment Houses Act, 1860, stated that all houses, rooms, shops or buildings, kept open for public refreshment, resort and entertainment during certain hours of the night, must be licensed. The defendant had premises called 'The Cafe', and certain persons were found there during the night when the cafe was open. They were being supplied with cigars, coffee and ginger beer which they were seen to consume. The justices convicted the defendant because the premises were not licensed. He appealed to the divisional court by case stated, suggesting that a licence was required only if 'entertainment' in terms e.g. of music or dancing was going on. The divisional court, applying the *noscitur a sociis* rule, *held*—That 'entertainment', because of the context in which it appeared in the Act of 1860, meant matters of bodily comfort and not matters of mental enjoyment such as theatrical or musical performances with which the word 'entertainment' is so often associated in other contexts. The justices were therefore right to convict.

LAW OF PERSONS AND FUNDAMENTAL CONCEPTS

Domicil of origin and choice: effect on taxation

(43) *IRC* v. *Bullock*, [1976] 3 All E.R. 353

Mr Bullock was born in Nova Scotia in 1910 and had his domicil of origin there. In 1932 he came to England to join the RAF, intending to go back to Canada when his service was completed. In 1946 he married an Englishwoman and they went on a number of visits to Mr Bullock's father in Canada. In 1959 Mr Bullock retired from the RAF and took up civilian employment in England. In 1961 he was able to retire fully, having become entitled to·money from his father's estate on the latter's death. Mr Bullock had always tried to persuade his wife to live in Canada but she would not do so. Even so, Mr Bullock always hoped she would change her mind. In 1966 he made a will subject to Nova Scotia law under which he said that his domicil was Nova Scotia and that he intended to return and remain there if his wife died before him. The Crown claimed that he had acquired a domicil of choice in England and that all his income from Canada was chargeable to Income Tax. If Mr Bullock was not domiciled in England then tax would be chargeable only on that part of the income from his father's estate which was actually sent to him in England. This was less than all the income. It was *held*—by the Court of Appeal—that the fact that Mr Bullock had established a matrimonial home in England was evidence of his intention; but was not conclusive. On the evidence of his retention of Canadian citizenship and of the terms of a declaration as to domicil̇ in his will, it was impossible not to hold that Mr Bullock had always maintained a firm intention to return to Canada in the event of his surviving his wife, and there was a sufficiently substantial possibility of his surviving his wife to justify regarding the intention to return as a real determination to do so, in that event, rather than a vague hope or aspiration. Accordingly, Mr Bullock could not be said to have formed the intention to acquire an English domicil of choice. Thus he could be taxed only on that part of the Canadian estate which was remitted to England.

Domicil: a person who abandons a domicil of choice without acquiring another reverts to the domicil of origin

(44) *Tee* v. *Tee*, [1973] 3 All E.R. 1105

The parties were married in England in November, 1946 when the husband was a domiciled Englishman and the wife was an American citizen. In 1951 they went to the United States and in 1953 the husband became an American citizen and acquired a domicil of choice in that country. In 1960 the husband was posted to Germany by his employers, and in 1965 he left his wife and set up home with a German woman by whom he had two children. Some time during 1966/67 the husband decided to make his permanent home in England but it was not until November, 1972, that the husband with his mistress and children actually took up residence in the house he had bought in England in May, 1972. The husband had been granted a permit to work in England in 1969. In July, 1972, he presented a petition for divorce. The wife challenged the jurisdiction of the English Court to hear this petition and the question for the court was whether the husband was domiciled in England in July, 1972. *Held*—by the Court of Appeal—that the husband was domiciled in England. He had left the United States in 1960 and the intention not to return there was formed over the period 1966/67. In consequence the two elements necessary to establish the abandonment of a domicil of choice had been proved. When a domicil of choice was lost, the domicil of origin revives; the fact that the husband did not actually take up permanent residence in England until 1972 was immaterial since it is not necessary for the revival of a domicil of origin that residence should also be taken up in that country.

Domicil: evidence of change

(45) *Steiner* v. *Inland Revenue Commissioners*, [1973] STC 547

Steiner was born in the former Austro/Hungarian Empire. He lived in Berlin from 1906 but was driven out of Germany by the Nazis in 1939 and came to England. He acquired a flat in London in 1941 and by the end of 1948 had established a business in England and was naturalized in 1948. From 1948 to 1963 he spent six months of each year in Berlin where he had a property. He was assessed to Income Tax for the years 1960/61 to 1966/67 on rents on properties in West Berlin, the Special Commissioners holding that he had acquired an English domicil of choice. He appealed. *Held*—by the Court of Appeal—that the appeal would be dismissed; there were no grounds for holding the Special Commissioners' decision to be erroneous in law. The Court refused to grant leave to appeal to the House of Lords.

Comment. (i) If a person is domiciled and resident in England and Wales, tax is charged on the full amount of income arising within a given year wherever made or received. (Income and Corporation Taxes Act, 1988, s. 165(1).)

(ii) See also *IRC* v. *Bullock*, 1976[43] for other examples of evidence of change of domicil, e.g. by a will.

M'Naghten Rules: disease of the mind

(46) *R.* v. *Kemp*, [1956] 3 All E.R. 249

The accused struck his wife with a hammer without, so he said, being conscious of doing so and was charged with causing grievous bodily harm. He was an elderly man of good character who suffered from arteriosclerosis. Medical opinions differed as to the precise effects of this disease on his mind. It was *held* that, whichever medical opinion was accepted, arteriosclerosis was a disease capable of affecting the mind, and was thus a disease of the mind within the M'Naghten Rules, whether or not it was recognized medically as a mental disease.

Comment. In *R.* v. *Sullivan*, [1983] 2 All E.R. 673 the House of Lords held that the definition of insanity in *M'Naghten* could apply to a person suffering from epilepsy. Mr Sullivan admitted inflicting grievous bodily harm on a friend of his at a time when he was recovering from a minor epileptic seizure. His defence was automatism which could have resulted in an acquittal (see further p. 502) but the judge ruled that the defence amounted to one of insanity which would, if successful, have led to Mr Sullivan's immediate detention in a special institution. Mr Sullivan changed his plea to guilty of occasioning actual bodily harm and was convicted and sentenced to probation with medical supervision.

Previously it had been thought that for *M'Naghten* to apply the mind had to be working but not as it should. It seems from this decision that *M'Naghten* applies even if, as in this case, the mind is not working at all.

Racial discrimination: employment: s. 4, Race Relations Act, 1976

(47) *Johnson* v. *Timber Tailors (Midlands)*, [1978] I.R.L.R. 146

When the plaintiff, a black Jamaican, applied for a job with the defendants as a wood machinist the defendants' works manager told him that he would be contacted in a couple of days to let him know whether or not he had been successful. Mr Johnson was not contacted and after a number of unsuccessful attempts to get in touch with the works manager, was told that the vacancy had been filled. Another advertisement for wood machinists appeared in the paper on the same night as Mr Johnson was told that the vacancy had been filled. Nevertheless, Mr Johnson applied again for the job and was told that the vacancy was filled. About a week later he applied again and was told that the job had been filled although a further advertisement had appeared for the job on that day. It was *held* by an industrial tribunal that the evidence established that Mr Johnson had been discriminated against on the grounds of race.

Racial discrimination: inducement to discriminate on racial grounds

(48) *The Commission for Racial Equality* v. *Imperial Society of Teachers of Dancing*, [1983] I.C.R. 473

The Society wished to employ a filing clerk. A telephone call was made to a local girls' school to find a suitable applicant. During the course of the phone call it was made clear that a coloured girl would be out of place because there were no other coloured employees. It was held by the Employment Appeal Tribunal that the words 'to induce' in s. 31 of the Race Relations Act, 1976 meant to persuade or to prevail upon or to bring about, and the words used did constitute an attempt to induce the head of careers at the girls' school not to send a coloured girl. In consequence the Society had contravened s. 31.

Sex discrimination: indirect discrimination: requirements or conditions applied to all workers but the ability of some persons to comply because of sex considerably smaller

(49) *Price* v. *The Civil Service Commission* [1977] I.R.L.R. 291

The Civil Service required candidates for the position of executive officer to be between $17\frac{1}{2}$ and 28 years. Belinda Price complained that this age bar constituted indirect sex discrimination against women because women between those ages were more likely than men to be temporarily out of the labour market having children or caring for children at home. It was *held*—by the Employment Appeal Tribunal—that the age was indirect discrimination against women. The court held that the words 'can comply' must not be construed narrowly. It could be said that any female applicant could comply with the condition in the sense that she was not obliged to marry or to have children or to look after them—indeed she may find someone else to look after them or, as a last resort, put them into care. If the legislation was construed in that way it was no doubt right to say that any female applicant could comply with the condition. However, in the view of the court to construe the legislation in that way appeared to be wholly out of sympathy with the spirit and intention of the Act. A person should not be deemed to be able to do something merely because it was theoretically possible; it was necessary to decide whether it was possible for the person to do so in practice as distinct from theory.

Sex discrimination: facilities and services: refusal to serve drinks to women on the same terms as men: ss. 1(1)(a) and 29(1), Sex Discrimination Act, 1975

(50) *Gill* v. *El Vino Co Ltd*, [1983] 1 All E.R. 398

The plaintiffs, both women, entered a wine bar and stood at the bar and ordered wine. They were refused service under house rules but were told that if they would sit at a table their drinks would be brought to them. The plaintiffs brought an action alleging breach of the 1975 Act. It was *held*—by the Court of Appeal—that applying the simple words of the Act the defendants had failed to provide the plaintiffs with facilities afforded to men and by doing so they had treated women less favourably than men contrary to the 1975 Act.

Sex discrimination: credit: a requirement that a woman must have her husband's guarantee is unlawful

(51) *Quinn* v. *Williams Furniture Ltd*, [1981] I.C.R. 328

Mrs Quinn wanted to buy certain goods from a shop on hire-purchase terms. She was told by the shop assistant that if she took out a hire-purchase agreement her husband would have to give a guarantee for the credit allowed, but if he took out the agreement she would not be required to give a guarantee of his liability. She bought the goods and took out the agreement herself, her husband acting as guarantor. She then complained that the shop's refusal to give her credit facilities on the same basis as they would to a man in her position was a breach of the Sex Discrimination Act, 1975. The Court of Appeal held that it was. On the facts Mrs Quinn had not been allowed credit facilities in the same way as they would normally be offered to men. Even a suggestion or advice such as this to get her husband's guarantee was unlawful. There did not have to be an outright refusal of credit.

    Comment. The case shows that credit restrictions based on sex, at one time usual in business, may now infringe the 1975 Act.

The registered company has a separate legal entity

(52) *Salomon* v. *Salomon & Co.*, [1897] A.C. 22

Salomon carried on business as a leather merchant and boot manufacturer. In 1892 he formed a limited company to take over the business. The Memorandum of Association was signed by Salomon, his wife, daughter and four sons. Each subscribed for one share. The company paid £38,782 to Salomon for the business and the mode of payment was to give Salomon £10,000 in debentures, secured by a floating charge, 20,000 shares of £1 each and £8782 in cash. The company fell on hard times and a liquidator was appointed. The debts of the unsecured creditors amounted to nearly £8000, and the company's assets were approximately £6000. The unsecured creditors claimed all the remaining assets on the ground that the company was a mere alias or agent for Salomon. *Held*—The company was a separate and distinct person. The debentures were perfectly valid and therefore Salomon was entitled to the remaining assets in part payment of the secured debentures held by him.

A member may obtain an injunction to restrain a company from acting in a manner inconsistent with its constitution

(53) *Jenkin* v. *Pharmaceutical Society*, [1921] 1 Ch. 392

The defendant society was incorporated by Royal Charter in 1843 for the purpose of advancing chemistry and pharmacy and promoting a uniform system of education of those who should practise the same, and also for the protection of those who carried on the business of chemists or druggists. *Held*—The expenditure of the funds of the society in the formation of an industrial committee, to attempt to regulate hours of work and wages and conditions of work between masters and employee members of the society, was *ultra vires* the charter, because it was a trade union activity which was not contemplated by the Charter of 1843. Further, the expenditure of money on an insurance scheme for members was also not within the powers given in the charter, for it amounted to converting the defendant society into an insurance company. The plaintiff, a member of the society, was entitled to an injunction to restrain the society from implementing the above schemes.

Disclosure of documents: Crown or public interest privilege

(54) *Norwich Pharmacal Co.* v. *Commissioners of Customs and Excise*, [1973] 2 All E.R. 943

The plaintiffs held the patent of a chemical compound used in animal foods, which they discovered was being infringed by unknown importers. The Commissioners of Customs and Excise were allowing the importation and charging duty thereon, and consequently knew the identity of the importers concerned. The plaintiffs brought proceedings against the Commissioners for infringement of their patent, and for an order that they disclose the identity of the importers. The order was granted by the judge but reversed by the Court of Appeal. On appeal to the House of Lords by the plaintiffs it was *held*—allowing the appeal—that the interests of justice outweighed any public interest in the confidential nature of such information. The Commissioners were under a duty to assist a person wronged by disclosing the identity of the wrongdoer.

(55) *Alfred Crompton Amusement Machines* v. *Customs and Excise Commissioners (No. 2)*, [1973] 2 All E.R. 1169

The appellants had paid Purchase Tax on the wholesale value of amusement machines for some years on the basis of a formula negotiated with the Commissioners of Customs and Excise. The appellants claimed that the assessments were too high and thereupon the Commissioners investigated the appellants' books and obtained from customers and other sources information bearing on the ascertainment of the wholesale value of the machines. The appellants did not agree with the opinion of the Commissioners as to the way in which the Tax should be computed and in subsequent arbitration proceedings Crown privilege was claimed in respect of documents received by the Commissioners from third parties. It was *held*—by the House of Lords—that the considerations for and against disclosure were evenly balanced. In these circumstances it was held that the court ought to uphold the claim to privilege and trust the Executive to mitigate the ill-effects of non-disclosure.

Comment. It seems that where there is a doubt in regard to disclosure the benefit of the doubt is unfortunately to be allowed in favour of the Executive and against discovery. On considering the issue of Crown privilege their Lordships indicated by way of preface that the title is a misnomer; a more accurate term would be privilege on the ground of 'public interest'.

THE LAW OF CONTRACT

Deeds: the doctrine of estoppel by deed does not stand in the way of rectification of a deed in appropriate circumstances

(56) *Wilson* v. *Wilson*, [1969] 3 All E.R. 945

In 1961 the defendant wished to buy a freehold property in Battersea but his income was not sufficient to qualify him for a building society loan. Accordingly his brother, the plaintiff, joined him in the application to the building society but paid no part of the purchase price, nor any of the costs and expenses, or the mortgage repayments. The transfer of the property declared that the plaintiff and defendant were joint owners and the title was registered in their joint names as was the charge in favour of the building society.

In March, 1967, the plaintiff commenced an action claiming a half share in the property. The defendant alleged that it was never intended that he and his brother should be beneficial joint owners but that the property was held on trust by the defendant and his brother for the sole benefit of the defendant. The defendant asked, amongst other things, for rectification of the deed of transfer. *Held*—by Buckley, J.—that the court would order rectification of the deed by striking out that part of it which declared beneficial interests so as to show the true intention of the parties, i.e. that the beneficial ownership of the property was in the defendant alone. In the course of his judgment Buckley, J., said '. . . where a deed is rectifiable (that is to say, ought to be rectified), the doctrine of estoppel by deed will not bind the parties to it. . . .'

Offer and invitation to treat—generally

(57) *Carlill* v. *Carbolic Smoke Ball Co.*, [1893] 1 Q.B. 256

The defendants were proprietors of a medical preparation called 'The Carbolic Smoke Ball'. They inserted advertisements in various newspapers in which they offered to pay £100 to any person who contracted influenza after using the ball three times a day for two weeks. They added that they had deposited £1000 at the Alliance Bank, Regent Street, 'to show our sincerity in the matter'. The plaintiff, a lady, used the ball as advertised, and was attacked by influenza during the course of treatment, which in her case extended from 20 November, 1891 to 17 January, 1892. She now sued for £100 and the following matters arose out of the various defences raised by the company. (*a*) It was suggested that the offer was too vague since no time limit was stipulated in which the user was to contract influenza. The court said that it must surely have been the intention that the ball would protect its user during the period of its use, and since this covered the present case it was not necessary to go further. (*b*) The suggestion was made that the matter was an advertising 'puff' and that there was no intention to create legal relations. Here the court took the view that the deposit of £1000 at the bank was clear evidence of an intention to pay claims. (*c*) It was further suggested that this was an attempt to contract with the whole world and that this was impossible in English law. The court took the view that the advertisement was an offer to the whole world and that, by analogy with the reward cases, it was possible to make an offer of this kind. (*d*) The company also claimed that the plaintiff had not supplied any consideration, but the court took the view that using this inhalant three times a day for two weeks or more was sufficient consideration. It was not necessary to consider its adequacy. (*e*) Finally the defendants suggested that there had been no communication of acceptance but here the court, looking at the reward cases, stated that in contracts of this kind acceptance may be by conduct.

Comment. (i) An offer to the public at large can only be made where the contract which eventually comes into being is a unilateral one, i.e. where there is a promise on one side for an act on the other. An offer to the public at large would be made, for example, where there was an advertisement offering a reward for services to be rendered such as finding a lost dog. It is interesting to note that an invitation to treat may be put to the world at large but an offer cannot be unless designed to produce a unilateral contract.

(ii) Most business contracts are bilateral. They are made by an exchange of promises and not, as here, by the exchange of a promise for an act. Nevertheless, *Carlill's* case has occasionally provided a useful legal principle in the field of business law. (See, e.g. *The New Zealand Shipping Co. Ltd* v. *A.M. Satterthwaite & Co. Ltd*, [1974] 1 All E.R. 1015 at p. 664.)

As regards motive, presumably Mrs Carlill used the ball to prevent influenza and not to recover £100. However, she had seen the offer and her motive was immaterial.

(iii) A deposit of money from which to pay claims is not essential. In *Wood* v. *Lectrik Ltd, The Times*, 13 January, 1932 the defendants who were makers of an electric comb had advertised 'What is your trouble? Is it grey hair? In ten days not a grey hair left. £500 Guarantee.' Mr Wood used the comb as directed but his hair remained grey at the end of ten days of use. All the comb had done was to scratch his scalp. There was no bank deposit by the company but Rowlatt, J. held that there was a contract and awarded Mr Wood the £500.

(58) *Pharmaceutical Society of Great Britain* v. *Boots Cash Chemists (Southern) Ltd*, [1953] 1 Q.B. 401

The defendants' branch at Edgware was adapted to the 'self service' system. Customers selected their purchases from shelves on which the goods were displayed and put them into a wire basket supplied by the defendants. They then took them to the cash desk where they paid the price. One section of shelves was set out with drugs which were included in the Poisons List referred to in s. 17 of the Pharmacy and Poisons Act, 1933, though they were not dangerous drugs and did not require a doctor's prescription. S. 18 of the Act requires that the sale of such drugs shall take place in the presence of a qualified pharmacist. Every sale of the drugs on the Poisons List was supervised at the cash desk by a quali- fied pharmacist, who had authority to prevent customers from taking goods out of the shop if he thought fit. One of the duties of the Society was to enforce the provisions of the Act, and the action was brought because the plaintiffs claimed that the defendants were infringing s. 18. *Held*—The display of goods in this way did not constitute an offer. The contract of sale was not made when a customer selected goods from the shelves, but when the company's servant at the cash desk accepted the offer to buy what had been chosen. There was, therefore, supervision in the sense required by the Act at the appropriate moment of time.

Comment. (i) The fact that a price ticket is not regarded as an offer is somewhat archaic, being based, perhaps, on a traditional commercial view that a shop is a place for bargaining and not a place for compulsory sales. However, since there is no bargaining in the United Kingdom in modern times the rule could be a hardship to those purchasers who quite rightly think that the ticket represents the price and not merely an invi- tation to treat.

(ii) Although a trader can *refuse to sell* at his wrongly advertised price, if he actually sells to the customer at more than the wrongly advertised price he commits a criminal offence under s. 11 of the Trade Descriptions Act, 1968.

(iii) The relevant provisions of the 1933 Act are now in ss. 2 and 3 of the Poisons Act, 1972.

(iv) See also *Esso Petroleum Ltd* v. *Customs and Excise Commissioners*, [1976] 1 All E.R. 117 where the House of Lords decided that price indications at a petrol filling station were invitations to treat.

(59) *Spencer* v. *Harding* (1870), L.R. 5. C.P. 561

The defendants had sent out a circular in the following terms: 'We are instructed to offer to the wholesale trade for sale by tender the stock-in-trade of Messrs Gilbeck and Co., amounting as per stock-book to £2503 13s. 1d. and which will be sold at a discount in one lot. Payment to be made in cash. The stock may be viewed on the premises up to Thursday the 20th instant, on which day, at 12 o'clock noon precisely, the tenders will be received and opened at our offices.' The plaintiffs suggested that the circular was an offer to sell the stock to the person who made the highest bid for cash, and that they had sent the highest bid which the defendants had refused to accept. *Held*—The circular was an invitation to treat and not an offer, and the defendants need not accept a tender unless they wished to do so. Willes, J., said of the circular: 'It is a mere attempt to ascertain whether an offer can be obtained within such a margin as the sellers are willing to accept.'

Comment. If the tender is for an indefinite amount of goods the concept of the standing offer comes into play. (See *G.N. Railway* v. *Witham*, 1873 at p. 555.)

(60) *Partridge* v. *Crittenden*, [1968] 2 All E.R. 421

Mr Partridge inserted an advertisement in a publication called *Cage and Aviary Birds* containing the words 'Bramblefinch cocks, bramblefinch hens, 25s each'. The advertisement appeared under the general heading 'Classified Advertisements' and in no place was there any direct use of the words 'offer for sale'. A Mr Thompson answered the advertisement enclosing a cheque for 25s. and asking that a 'bramblefinch hen' be sent to him. Mr Partridge sent one in a box, the bird wearing a closed ring.

Mr Thompson opened the box in the presence of an RSPCA inspector, Mr Crittenden, and removed the ring without injury to the bird. Mr Crittenden brought a prosecution against Mr Partridge before the Chester magistrates alleging that Mr Partridge had offered for sale a brambling contrary to s. 6(1) of the Protection of Birds Act, 1954, the bird being other than a close-ringed specimen bred in captivity and being of a species which was resident in or visited the British Isles in a wild state.

The justices were satisfied that the bird had not been bred in captivity but had been caught and ringed. A close-ring meant a ring that was completely closed and incapable of being forced or broken except with the intention of damaging it; such a ring was forced over the claws of a bird when it was between three and ten days old, and at that time it was not possible to determine what the eventual girth of the leg would be so that the close-ring soon became difficult to remove. The ease with which the ring was removed in this case indicated that it had been put on at a much later stage and this, together with the fact that the bird had no perching sense, led the justices to convict Mr Partridge.

He appealed to the Divisional Court of the Queen's Bench Division where the conviction was quashed. The court accepted that the bird was a wild bird, but since Mr Partridge had been charged with 'offering for sale', the conviction could not stand. The advertisement constituted in law an invitation to treat, not an offer for sale, and the offence was not, therefore, established. There was of course a completed sale for which Mr Patridge could have been successfully prosecuted but the prosecution in this case had relied on the offence of 'offering for sale' and failed to establish such an offer.

Comment. The case shows how concepts of the civil law are sometimes at the root of criminal cases.

Offer an invitation to treat—alleged contracts for the sale of land

(61) *Harvey* v. *Facey*, [1893] A.C. 552

The plaintiffs sent the following telegram to the defendant: 'Will you sell us Bumper Hall Pen? Telegraph lowest cash price.' The defendant telegraphed in reply: 'Lowest price for Bumper Hall Pen £900.' The plaintiffs then telegraphed: 'We agree to buy Bumper Hall Pen for £900 asked by you. Please send us your title deeds in order that we may get early possession.' The defendant made no reply. The Supreme Court of Jamaica granted the plaintiffs a decree of specific performance of the contract. On appeal the Judicial Committee of the Privy Council *held* that there was no contract. The second telegram was not an offer, but was in the nature of an invitation to treat at a minimum price of £900. The third telegram could not therefore be an acceptance resulting in a contract.

(62) *Clifton* v. *Palumbo*, [1944] 2 All E.R. 497

The plaintiff who was the owner of a very large estate wrote to the defendant as follows: 'I am prepared to offer you or your nominee my Lytham estate for £600,000. I also agree that a reasonable and sufficient time shall be granted to you for the examination and consideration of all the data and details necessary for the preparation of the Schedule of Completion.' The defendant purported to accept this offer, but later the plaintiff thought the price too low and brought this action for a declaration that there was no binding contract between himself and the defendant. The defendant counterclaimed for specific performance. *Held*—The plaintiff's letter was an invitation to treat and not an offer, so that the defendant's purported acceptance did not give rise to a binding contract between the parties. Findlay, L.J. (following Lord Green, M.R.), said of the plaintiff's letter: 'It is quite possible for persons on a half sheet of notepaper, in the most informal and unorthodox language, to contract to sell the most extensive and most complicated estate that can be imagined. That is quite possible, but, having regard to the habits of the people in this country, it is very unlikely.'

Comment. The matter of invitation to treat and offer in the context of the alleged sale of land produced the most interesting case of *Gibson* v.

Manchester City Council, [1979] 1 All E.R. 972. The City Treasurer wrote to Mr Gibson saying that the Council 'may be prepared' to sell the freehold of his council house to him at £2,725 less 20%, i.e. £2,180. The letter said that Mr G should make a formal application, which he did. Following local government elections three months later the policy of selling council houses was reversed. The Council did not proceed with the sale to Mr Gibson. He claimed that a binding contract existed. The House of Lords said that it did not. The Treasurer's letter was only an invitation to treat. Mr G's application was the offer, but the Council had not accepted it. In the Court of Appeal Lord Denning said that there was an 'agreement in fact' which was enforceable. It was not always necessary, he said, to stick to the strict rules of offer and acceptance in order to produce a binding agreement. The House of Lords would not accept this and Lord Denning's view has not, as yet, found a place in the law.

Offer and invitation to treat—auction sales

(63) *Harris* v. *Nickerson* (1873), L.R. 8 Q.B. 286

The defendant, an auctioneer, advertised in London newspapers that a sale of office furniture would be held at Bury St Edmunds. A broker with a commission to buy furniture came from London to attend the sale. Several conditions were set out in the advertisement, one being: 'The highest bidder to be the buyer.' The lots described as office furniture were not put up for sale but were withdrawn, though the auction itself was held. The broker sued for loss of time in attending the sale. *Held*— He could not recover from the auctioneer. There was no offer since the lots were never put up for sale, and the advertisement was simply an invitation to treat.

Comment. A sensible decision, really. The statement 'I *intend* to auction some office furniture' is not the same as an offer for sale, and in any case there seems to be no way of accepting the 'offer' in advance of the event.

(64) *British Car Auctions* v. *Wright*, [1972] 3 All E.R. 462

The company carried on the business of auctioneers of second-hand motor vehicles and conducted the auction sale of an unroadworthy car which was driven away. The company was convicted on an information which charged that it did 'offer for sale' the car for delivery contrary to what is now s. 60 of the Road Traffic Act, 1972. There was an appeal by way of case stated to the Queen's Bench Divisional Court contending that in the auction situation there was no 'offer to sell'. *Held*—allowing the appeal—that although colloquially an auctioneer offered to sell the goods auctioned, strictly in the law of contract he invited those present to make offers to buy, the offer came from the bidder and acceptance was communicated by the fall of the hammer, so that it was technically incorrect to describe an auctioneer as offering goods for sale. In the face of *Partridge* v. *Crittenden*, 1968,[60] the court regretfully was required to apply the strict and not the colloquial meaning to 'offer to sell' in the relevant section of the Road Traffic Act. Accordingly, the conviction was quashed.

Acceptance of no effect until communicated to the offeror: agreement may be inferred from conduct

(65) *Brogden* v. *Metropolitan Railway* (1877), 2 App. Cas. 666

The plaintiff had been a supplier of coal to the Railway Company for a number of years, though there was no formal agreement between them. Eventually the plaintiff suggested that there ought to be one, and the agents of the parties met and a draft agreement was drawn up by the Railway Company's agent and sent to the plaintiff. The plaintiff inserted several new clauses into the draft, and in particular filled in the name of an arbitrator to settle the parties' differences under the agreement should any arise. He then wrote the word 'Approved' on the draft and returned it to the Railway Company's agent. There was no formal execution, the draft remaining in the agent's desk. However, coal was supplied according to the prices mentioned in the draft, though these were not the market prices, and prices were reviewed from time to time in accordance with the draft. The parties then had a disagreement and the plaintiff refused to supply coal to the Railway Company on the grounds that, since the Railway Company had not accepted the offer contained in the amended draft, there was no binding contract. *Held*—

(i) The draft was not a binding contract because the plaintiff had inserted new terms which the Railway Company had not accepted; but

(ii) the parties had indicated by their conduct that they had waived the execution of the formal document and agreed to act on the basis of the draft. There was, therefore, a binding contract arising out of conduct, and its terms were the terms of the draft.

Conditional assent: acceptance must be absolute and unconditional

(66) *Winn* v. *Bull* (1877), 7 Ch. D. 29

The defendant had entered into a written agreement with the plaintiff for the lease of a house, the term of the lease and the rent being agreed. However, the written agreement was expressly made 'subject to the preparation and approval of a formal contract'. It appeared that no other contract was made between the parties. The plaintiff now sued for specific performance of the agreement. *Held*—The written agreement provided a memorandum sufficient to satisfy s. 4 of the Statute of Frauds, 1677 (now s. 40 of the Law of Property Act, 1925), but there was no binding contract between the parties because, although certain covenants are normally implied into leases, it is also true that many and varied express covenants are often agreed between the parties. The words 'subject to contract' indicated that the parties were still in a state of negotiation, and until they entered into a formal contract there was no agreement which the court could enforce.

Comment. It should be noted that the court is not bound to accept that the words 'subject to contract' have resulted in a conditional acceptance and therefore no contract. Thus in *Alpenstow Ltd* v. *Regalian Properties plc*, [1985] 2 All E.R. 545, the parties had been in negotiations regarding the sale of property for some five months. The plaintiffs then sent a letter to the defendants containing quite detailed terms of the contract but said to be subject to contract. The arrangements set out in the letter were accepted by the defendants who then sought specific performance on the contract as a counter-claim in an action brought by the plaintiffs alleging that no contract existed. Nourse, J. refused to give the words 'subject to contract' their usual meaning and he held that a contract existed. His judgment indicates that the circumstances of the case are all-important and in particular that he would not have expected to find the words 'subject to contract' except in the primary stage of a negotiation, and not as in this case, some four to five months on. Nor would he have expected to find them, as he did here, in a detailed and conscientiously drawn document.

(67) *Filby* v. *Hounsell*, [1896] 2 Ch. 737

Property had been offered for sale by auction but had not been sold. An offer was then made to buy the property, stating that if the offer was accepted the purchaser would sign a contract 'on the auction particulars'. This offer was accepted 'subject to contract as agreed'. *Held*—The parties were bound by a contract drafted on the auction particulars, although they had not signed a formal contract.

(68) *Michael Richards Properties* v. *Corporation of Wardens of St Saviour's Parish, Southwark*, [1975] 3 All E.R. 416

In this case the words 'subject to contract' were included by the defendants by mistake on a document accepting a full and complete tender for the purchase of a piece of land which had been submitted by the plaintiffs. It was *held* that the agreement was binding and the phrase 'subject to contract' could be ignored as meaningless (*Nicolene Ltd* v. *Simmonds*, 1953 (see p. 552) applied). Mr Justice Goff said that he hoped that he was not sounding warning bells in solicitors' offices, and certainly the decision does not affect the general practice of heading standard correspondence before a draft contract is approved and exchanged with the words 'subject to contract'. The decision shows only that no protection can be achieved by using these words when a binding and evidenced agreement has been entered into. The case of a tender is a special one because the contract is normally constituted by the tender document itself, when fully completed, and the written acceptance.

Conditional assent: recovery of money paid under a 'subject to contract' arrangement

(69) *Chillingworth and another* v. *Esche*, [1923] All E.R. Rep. 97

By a document, dated 10 July, 1922, Chillingworth and Cummings agreed to purchase the defendant's nursery gardens at Cheshunt, Herts., for £4800 'subject to a proper contract to be prepared by the vendor's solicitors'. The plaintiffs paid a deposit of £240. After the solicitors on both sides had agreed on the terms of a contract the plaintiffs refused, without reason, to go on and claimed a declaration that the document of 20 July, 1922, was not binding and that the deposit must be repaid. *Held*—by the Court of Appeal—that the document was nothing more than a conditional offer and a conditional acceptance and would only ripen into a binding agreement when a formal document was signed. Further, on the construction of the documents and in the circumstances, the plaintiffs were entitled to the repayment of the deposit. The plaintiffs' solicitors were not agents of their clients, so as to bind them, when they agreed with the defendant's solicitors on the terms of the contract.

Conditional assent: effect of phrase 'without prejudice'

(70) *Tomlin* v. *Standard Telephones and Cables Ltd*, [1969] 3 All E.R. 201

The plaintiff was a fitter employed to help on board H.M. telecommunications ship *Alert*. In the course of his duties he strained his back and claimed against the defendants, his employers, for damages in respect of that accident. The plaintiff's solicitor and the employers' insurers negotiated an agreement that liability would be accepted on a 50 per cent basis. In this action the defendants alleged that they were not bound by the agreement entered into by their representatives the insurers, because it appeared that the letters constituting the agreement were headed 'Without Prejudice'. *Held*—by the Court of Appeal—that on a proper construction of the letters written by the defendants' representatives there was a definite and binding agreement to pay half the damages though the actual amount was left for further negotiation.

A point that arises is that all the letters written by the agent of the insurance company bore the words, 'Without Prejudice'. The point is taken that, by reason of those words, there could not be any binding agreement between the parties . . . *Walker* v. *Wilsher* (1889), 23 Q.B.D. 335. . . . Lindley, L.J., said at p. 337 'What is the meaning of the words "Without Prejudice"? I think they mean without prejudice to the position of the writer of the letter if the terms he proposes are not accepted. If the terms proposed in the letter are accepted a complete contract is established and the letter, although written without prejudice, operates to alter the old state of things and to establish a new one.' That statement of Lindley, L.J., is of great authority and seems to me to apply exactly to the present case if in fact there was a binding agreement, or an agreement intended to be binding, reached between the parties; and, accordingly, it seems to me that not only was the court entitled to look at the letters although they were nearly all described as 'Without Prejudice', but it is quite possible (and in fact the intention of the parties was) that there was a binding agreement contained in that correspondence. (*Per* Danckwerts, L.J.)

Vague or incomplete agreements: treatment by the courts

(71) *Hillas & Co. Ltd* v. *Arcos Ltd*, [1932] All E.R. Rep. 494

The plaintiffs had entered into a contract with the defendants under which the defendants were to supply the plaintiffs with '22,000 standards of soft wood (Russian) of fair specification over the season 1930'. The contract also contained an option allowing the plaintiffs to take up 100,000 standards as above during the season 1931. The parties managed to perform the contract throughout the 1930 season without any argument or serious difficulty in spite of the vague words used in connection with the specification of the wood. However, when the plaintiffs exercised their option for 100,000 standards during the season 1931, the defendants refused to supply the wood, saying that the specification was too vague to bind the parties, and the agreement was therefore inchoate as requiring a further agreement as to the precise specification. *Held*—by the House of Lords—that the option to supply 100,000 standards during the 1931 season was valid. There was a certain vagueness about the specification, but there was also a course of dealing between the parties which operated as a guide to the court regarding the difficulties which this vagueness might produce. Since the parties had not experienced serious difficulty in carrying out the 1930 agreement, there was no reason to suppose that the option could not have been carried out without difficulty had the defendants been prepared to go on with it. Judgment was given for the plaintiffs.

Comment. In these cases the defendant is trying to avoid damages for failing to perform the contract by saying 'I would like to perform the contract but I don't know what to do'. If there are, e.g. previous dealings, then he does know what to do and the defence fails.

(72) *Foley* v. *Classique Coaches Ltd*, [1934] 2 K.B. 1

F owned certain land, part of which he used for the business of supplying petrol. He also owned the adjoining land. The company wished to purchase the adjoining land for use as the headquarters of their charabanc business. F agreed to sell the land to the company on condition that the company would buy all their petrol from him. An agreement was made under which the company agreed to buy its petrol from F 'at a price to be agreed by the parties in writing and from time to time'. It was further agreed that any dispute arising under the agreement should be submitted 'to arbitration in the usual way'. The agreement was acted upon at an agreed price for three years. At this time the company felt it could get petrol at a better price, and the company's solicitor wrote to F repudiating the petrol contract. *Held*—although the parties had not agreed upon a price beyond three years, there was a contract to supply petrol at a reasonable price and of reasonable quality, and although the agreement did not stipulate the future price, but left this to the further agreement of the parties, a method was provided by which the price could be ascertained without such agreement, i.e. by arbitration.

Comment. The court awarded the plaintiff damages, a declaration that the agreement was binding, and an injunction restraining the company from buying petrol elsewhere, thus giving the company an enormous incentive to agree a price or go to arbitration as the contract provided. Generally speaking, of course, if the contract is silent as to price, the court is prepared to use s. 8(2) of the Sale of Goods Act, 1979 and imply and ascertain 'a reasonable price'. It would not have been appropriate in *Foley* to use this provision of sale of goods legislation (which in those days was in the 1893 Act) because the contract in *Foley* was not in fact silent as to price.

A similar problem arose in *F. & S. Sykes (Wessex)* v. *Fine-Fare*, [1967] 1 Lloyd's Rep. 53. In that case producers of broiler chickens agreed with certain retailers to supply between 30,000 and 80,000 chickens a week during the first year of the agreement and afterwards 'such other figures as might be agreed'. The agreement was to last for not less than five years, and it was agreed that any differences between the parties should be referred to arbitration. Eventually the retailers contended that the agreement was void for uncertainty. *Held*—by the Court of Appeal—it was not, because in default of the further agreement envisaged the number of chickens should be such reasonable number as might be decided by the arbitrator.

(73) *Brown* v. *Gould and Others*, [1971] 2 All E.R. 1505

A lease contained an option to renew 'at a rent to be fixed having regard to the market value of the premises at the time of exercising the option taking into account to the advantage of the tenant any increased value of such premises attributable to structural improvements made by the tenant'. The landlords maintained that the option was void for uncertainty. *Held*—by Megarry, J.—it was not. The parties had laid down a formula by which the rent might be ascertained. Although there was no machinery (e.g. arbitration) for resolving a dispute as to the application of the formula, the court could provide that machinery and determine the rent. The option was therefore valid and enforceable.

(74) *Scammell (G.) and Nephew Ltd* v. *Ouston*, [1941] A.C. 251

Ouston wished to acquire a new motor van for use in his furniture business. Discussions took place with the company's sales manager as a result of which the company sent a quotation for the supply of a suitable van. Eventually Ouston sent an official order making the following stipulation, 'This order is given on the understanding that the balance of the purchase price can be had on hire-purchase terms over a period of two years.' This was in accordance with the discussions between the sales manager and Ouston, which had taken place on the understanding that hire purchase would be available. The company seemed to be content with the arrangement and completed the van. Arrangements were made with a finance company to give hire-purchase facilities, but the actual terms were not agreed at that stage. The appellants also agreed to take Ouston's present van in part exchange, but later stated that they were not satisfied with its condition and asked him to sell it locally. He refused and after much correspondence he issued a writ against the appellants for damages for non-delivery of the van. The appellants' defence was that there was no contract until the hire-purchase terms had been ascertained. *Held*—The defence succeeded; it was not possible to construe a contract from the vague language used by the parties.

Comment. If there is evidence of a trade custom, business procedure or previous dealings between the parties, which assists the court in construing the vague parts of an agreement, then the agreement may be enforced. Here there was no such evidence.

(75) *Nicolene Ltd* v. *Simmonds*, [1953] 1 All E.R. 882

The plaintiffs alleged that there was a contract for the sale to them of 3000 tons of steel reinforcing bars and that the defendant seller had broken his contract. When the plaintiffs claimed damages the seller set up the defence that, owing to one of the sentences in the letters which constituted the contract, there was no contract at all. The material words were 'We are in agreement that the usual conditions of acceptance apply'. In fact there were no usual conditions of acceptance so that the words were meaningless but the seller nevertheless suggested that the contract was unenforceable since it was not complete. *Held*—by the Court of Appeal—that the contract was enforceable and that the meaningless clause could be ignored.

> In my opinion a distinction must be drawn between a clause which is meaningless and a clause which is yet to be agreed. A clause which is meaningless can often be ignored, whilst still leaving the contract good; whereas a clause which has yet to be agreed may mean that there is no contract at all, because the parties have not agreed on all the essential terms. . . . In the present case there was nothing yet to be agreed. There was nothing left to further negotiation. All that happened was that the parties agreed that 'the usual conditions of acceptance apply'. That clause was so vague and uncertain as to be incapable of any precise meaning. It is clearly severable from the rest of the contract. It can be rejected without impairing the sense or

reasonableness of the contract as a whole, and it should be so rejected. The contract should be held good and the clause ignored. The parties themselves treated the contract as subsisting. They regarded it as creating binding obligations between them; and it would be most unfortunate if the law should say otherwise. You would find defaulters all scanning their contracts to find some meaningless clause on which to ride free. (*Per* Denning, L.J.)

Comment. In this case there was no evidence of any usual conditions either in the trade or between the parties as a result of previous dealings. Therefore the expression 'the usual conditions of acceptance apply' had to be regarded as meaningless.

Counter-offer: if an offeree makes a counter-offer he cannot then effectively accept the original offer: the offeror can accept a counter-offer: what constitutes a counter-offer

(76) *Hyde* v. *Wrench* (1840), 3 Beav. 334

The defendant offered to sell his farm for £1000. The plaintiff's agent made an offer of £950 and the defendant asked for a few days for consideration, after which the defendant wrote saying he could not accept it, whereupon the plaintiff wrote purporting to accept the offer of £1000. The defendant did not consider himself bound, and the plaintiff sued for specific performance. *Held*—The plaintiff could not enforce this 'acceptance' because his counter-offer of £950 was an implied rejection of the original offer to sell at £1000.

(77) *Northland Airlines Ltd* v. *Dennis Ferranti Meters Ltd* (1970), 114 Sol. J. 845

Ferranti offered to sell Northland an aircraft by a telegram in the following terms—'Confirming sale to you—aircraft—£27,000 fob Winnipeg. Please remit £5000 for account of . . . (a bank account was named).'

Northland replied by telegram as follows—'This is to confirm your cable and my purchase—aircraft on terms set out in your cable. Price £27,000 delivered fob Winnipeg. £5000 forwarded your bank in trust for your account pending delivery. Balance payable on delivery. Please confirm delivery to be made 30 days within this date.' Ferranti did not regard this as an acceptance and disposed of the aircraft elsewhere. Northland sued for damages for breach of contract. *Held*—by the Court of Appeal—that the second telegram was not an acceptance because the deposit was not paid over outright as requested but left in trust pending delivery and Northland had inserted a delivery date whereas the offer did not mention one. These were new terms so that the second telegram was a counter-offer and not an acceptance.

(78) *Butler Machine Tool Co.* v. *Ex-cell-O Corp.* (*England*), [1979] 1 All E.R. 965

In this case a sellers' quotation for machinery included a price variation clause. The buyers' order was on their terms and conditions which included no variation clause. The sellers acknowledged the order on the buyers' form and supplied the machinery. It was *held*—by the Court of Appeal—that the buyers had made a counter-offer which had been accepted and the contract contained no variation clause. (*Hyde* v. *Wrench*, 1840[76] applied.)

Comment. The above principles of contract law are of increasing importance because of the modern commercial practice of making quotations and placing orders with conditions attached, so that the terms and conditions of the contract which may eventually be made may not be those which the original offeror put forward, since these may have been changed as a result of a 'battle of forms' between the parties.

(79) *Stevenson* v. *McLean* (1880), 5 Q.B.D. 346

On Saturday the defendant offered to sell to the plaintiffs a quantity of iron at 40s. nett cash per ton open till Monday (close of business). On Monday the plaintiffs telegraphed asking whether the defendant would accept 40s. for delivery over two months, or if not what was the longest limit the defendant would give. The plaintiffs did not necessarily want to take delivery of the goods at once and pay for them. They would have liked to have been able to ask for delivery and pay from time to time over two months as they themselves found buyers for quantities of the iron. The defendant received the telegram at 10.1 a.m. but did not reply, so the plaintiffs, by telegram sent at 1.34 p.m., accepted the defendant's original offer. The defendant had already sold the iron to a third party, and informed the plaintiffs of this by a telegram despatched at 1.25 p.m. arriving at 1.46 p.m. The plaintiffs had therefore accepted the offer before the defendant's revocation had been communicated to them. If, however, the plaintiffs' first telegram constituted a counter-offer, then it would amount to a rejection of the defendant's original offer. *Held*—The plaintiffs' first telegram was not a counter-offer, but a mere inquiry for different terms which did not amount to a rejection of the defendant's original offer, so that the offer was still open when the plaintiffs accepted it. The defendant's offer was not revoked merely by the sale of the iron to another person.

Comment. The case shows that a distinction must be drawn between a rejection by counter-offer and a request for information. A common example of this distinction occurs in business when an offer to sell at a stated price is not regarded as rejected, where, as here, the seller is asked whether he is prepared to give credit or even whether he is prepared to reduce the price.

Acceptance of an offer may operate retrospectively

(80) *Trollope & Colls Ltd* v. *Atomic Power Constructions Ltd*, [1962] 3 All E.R. 1035

The plaintiffs were sub-contractors for the civil engineering aspects of the building of a new power station. The defendants were the main contractors, the Central Electricity Board being the employing authority. The plaintiffs had submitted a tender in 1959 in which they had said that the price for their part of the work would be nine million pounds. Part A of this tender contained a price adjustment clause allowing the plaintiffs to adjust the price tendered according to variations, if any, in the cost of labour and materials during the course of completing the work. Numerous changes were made in this part of the tender and in the price adjustment clause by the Central Electricity Board, but at a meeting of the parties on 11 April, 1960, the tender as amended was agreed by the plaintiffs. The plaintiffs had by this time already done a considerable amount of work on the site.

Later the plaintiffs regretted the agreement of 11 April, 1960, and claimed that they were free to terminate operations at any time and asked for a *quantum meruit* for their services up to 11 April, 1960. The Board claimed that a binding contract existed between themselves and the plaintiffs on the terms of the agreement of 11 April, 1960, and that this agreement, when made, operated retrospectively to cover the work done by the plaintiffs up to 11 April and subsequently. The plaintiffs then alleged that the agreement of 11 April could only operate for the future, and that work done up to 11 April, 1960, should be assessed by the court on a *quantum meruit*, or alternatively be based on an implied contract on the terms of the tender of 1959 before amendments. *Held*—The agreement of 11 April, 1960, operated retrospectively so that the plaintiffs were entitled to payment for work done prior to 11 April only on the basis of the amended tender and were also bound to operate for the future on the same basis.

Comment. The action was one in which many parties were joined, and the Central Electricity Board was in fact one of the defendants.

Effect of accepting a tender for the supply of goods of an indefinite amount: the standing offer

(81) *Great Northern Railway* v. *Witham* (1873), L.R. 9 C.P. 16

The company advertised for tenders for the supply for one year of such stores as they might think fit to order. The defendant submitted a tender in these words: 'I undertake to supply the company for twelve months with such quantities of (certain specified goods) as the company may order from time to time.' The company accepted the tender, and gave orders under it which the defendant carried out. Eventually the defendant refused to carry out an order made by the company under the tender, and this action was brought. *Held*—The defendant was in breach of contract. A tender of this type was a standing offer which was converted into a series of contracts as the company made an order. The defendant might revoke his offer for the remainder of the period covered by the tender, but must supply the goods already ordered by the company.

Communication of acceptance: ineffective unless by a person authorized to make it

(82) *Powell* v. *Lee* (1908), 99 L.T. 284

The defendants were managers of a school and wished to appoint a head-master. Powell applied for the position and together with two other applicants was selected for the final choice of the managers. The managers passed a resolution appointing Powell but gave no instructions that this decision was to be communicated to him, although D (one of the managers) was instructed to inform one of the other candidates (Parker) that he had not been appointed. D, without authority, also informed Powell that he had been selected. The matter was then re-opened and Parker was properly appointed. Lee then informed the plaintiff that this appointment had been made. The plaintiff now sued the six managers for damages for breach of contract. *Held*—There was no contract because there was no authorized communication of the intention to contract by the managers.

If an offer states that acceptance may be by silence an offeree who does not respond to it will not normally be bound

(83) *Felthouse* v. *Bindley* (1862), 11 C.B. (N.S.) 869

The plaintiff had been engaged in negotiations with his nephew John regarding the purchase of John's horse, and there had been some mis-understanding as to the price. Eventually the plaintiff wrote to his nephew as follows: 'If I hear no more about him I consider the horse is mine at £30 15 s.' The nephew did not reply but, wishing to sell the horse to his uncle, he told the defendant, an auctioneer who was selling farm stock for him, not to sell the horse as it had already been sold. The auctioneer inadvertently put the horse up with the rest of the stock and sold it. The plaintiff now sued the auctioneer in conversion, the basis of the claim being that he had made a contract with his nephew and the property in the animal was vested in him (the uncle) at the time of the sale. *Held*—The plaintiff's action failed. Although the nephew intended to sell the horse to his uncle, he had not communicated that intention. There was, therefore, no contract between the parties, and the property in the horse was not vested in the plaintiff at the time of the auction sale.

Comment. The rule that silence cannot amount to acceptance does not necessarily mean that words of acceptance have to be spoken or written to the offeror. In a unilateral contract situation such as *Carlill's case*[57] an acceptance may be inferred from the way in which the offeree behaves and communication of acceptance may be dispensed with. However, in this case the contract was bilateral so that the conduct of John Felthouse in removing the horse from the sale was not relevant, as it might have been in a unilateral situation. In a bilateral situation the rule against acceptance by silence means only that the offeror is unable to impose on the offeree a stipulation that the offeree will be bound if he merely ignores the offer.

(84) *Fairline Shipping Corporation* v. *Adamson*, [1974] 2 All E.R. 967

Under an agreement made with Game and Meat Products Ltd, Fairline stored goods in a refrigerated store belonging to Mr Adamson, who was the managing director of Game and Meat. Game and Meat used the refrigerated store from time to time on an informal basis but never had a proper lease. Initially Fairline were doing business in regard to the storage of the goods with Game and Meat but prior to the arrival of the goods in the store Fairline received a letter and an invoice for the costs sent on behalf of Mr Adamson indicating that he regarded the storage as his own venture. As a result of Mr Adamson's negligence in that it was not discovered that there had been a breakdown in one of the fans distributing cold air into the store, Fairline's goods were damaged. Since Game and Meat was about to go into liquidation Fairline brought an action against Mr Adamson for breach of contract and negligence. As regards the claim for breach of contract, Kerr, J. decided that there was no contract between the plaintiffs and Mr Adamson. If the letter which he wrote could be regarded as an offer then there had been no acceptance of that offer by Fairline and the uncommunicated acceptance of an offer could not have the effect of binding the offeror. (*Felthouse* v. *Bindley*, 1862[83] applied.) As regards Mr Adamson's position as a bailee, one could be a bailee without the need for a contract. However, it was difficult to establish from the evidence whether at the time the goods were damaged Game and Meat were in exclusive possession or whether Mr Adamson was, and the judge was not persuaded by the proposition of counsel for Fairline that the case might be regarded as one of joint bailment of Game and Meat and Mr Adamson. In any case the judge was of the opinion that the refinements of the concepts of legal possession and bailment were unnecessary in order to determine liability in the tort of negligence. The real answer to the plaintiffs' case was a straightforward action in negligence. There was evidence to show that whatever the contractual position or the bailment position might be Mr Adamson had, by his letter, assumed a duty of care in respect of the goods and he was in breach of that duty so that the plaintiffs succeeded and damages were awarded against Mr Adamson.

Where the offeror prescribes the method of acceptance, the offeree must in general comply, but there are exceptions

(85) *Eliason* v. *Henshaw* (1819), 4 Wheat. 225 (Supreme Court USA)

Eliason & Co. sent an offer to purchase 300 barrels of flour at $9.50 a barrel in a letter sent by wagon to Henshaw. In the letter they asked for an answer by return of the wagon which was to Harpers Ferry. Instead, Henshaw sent his acceptance by post to Georgetown, where Eliason also had an office. As it happened the letter arrived later than a reply by the waggoner would have done but this was immaterial. The Supreme Court of the United States *held* that there was no contract since not only had the letter not been sent by the method required, it had not been sent to the place required.

Comment. English law has never gone as far as the Supreme Court in *Eliason's* case. In *Tinn* v. *Hoffman* (1873), 29 L.T. 271, it was held that an acceptance 'by return of post' did not mean exclusively by letter by return of post 'A telegram or verbal message or . . . any means not later than a letter written and sent by return of post' was sufficient.

(86) *Manchester Diocesan Council for Education* v. *Commercial and General Investments Ltd*, [1969] 3 All E.R. 1593

The plaintiffs, a corporate body, were the owners of a freehold property known as Hesketh Fletcher Senior Church of England School. The property was vested in the plaintiffs on a condition that it would be sold subject 'to the approval of the purchase price' by the Secretary of State for Education and Science. Late in 1963 the plaintiffs decided to sell the property by tender, the conditions requiring that tenders be sent to the plaintiffs' surveyor by 27 August, 1964. Clause 4 of the form of tender stated 'The person whose tender is accepted shall be the purchaser and shall be informed of the acceptance of his tender by letter sent to him by post addressed to the address given in the tender. . . .' The following events then occurred—

(i) On 25 August, 1964, the defendants completed the form of tender and stated that they agreed to its conditions.

(ii) On 26 August, 1964, the completed tender was sent to the plaintiffs' surveyor.

(iii) On 1 September, 1964, the plaintiffs' surveyor informed the defendants' surveyor that he would recommend acceptance of the defendants' offer and would write again as soon as he had formal instructions.

(iv) On 14 September, 1964, the defendants' surveyor replied saying that he looked forward to receiving formal acceptance and naming the solicitors who would act for the defendants.

(v) On 15 September, 1964, the plaintiffs' solicitors acknowledged this letter by correspondence with the defendants' surveyor which also stated that the 'sale has now been approved', and that instructions had been given to obtain the approval of the Secretary of State.

(vi) On 18 November, 1964, the approval of the Secretary of State was obtained.

(vii) On 23 December, 1964, the plaintiffs' solicitors wrote to the defendants' solicitors stating that the contract was now binding on both parties.

(viii) The defendants' solicitors replied to the effect that they did not agree that there was any binding contract.

(ix) On 7 January, 1965, the plaintiffs' solicitors wrote to the defendants at the address given in the tender giving formal notice of acceptance.

The question in issue in this case whether the offer contained in the tender lapsed before 7 January, 1965, by reason of lapse of time between 25 August, 1964, and 7 January, 1965. It was *held*—by Buckley, J.—

(i) That the letter of 15 September, 1964, looked at in the light of earlier correspondence, was communication to the defendants that their offer had been accepted. The failure to inform the defendants of the acceptance in the manner laid down in Clause 4 did not nullify acceptance of the offer since Clause 4 did not say that a letter addressed to the address given in the tender was the only mode of acceptance and acceptance by any other equally advantageous method was valid. (*Tinn* v. *Hoffman* (1873), 29 L.T. 271 applied.)

(ii) Alternatively, if the letter of 15 September, 1964, did not constitute an acceptance, the offer had not lapsed because the plaintiffs had not by any conduct refused the offer. In fact the letter of 15 September, 1964, showed a continuing intention to accept and there was no evidence of a change of mind before 7 January, 1965. Thus the offer was still open to be accepted on 7 January, 1965. (*Ramsgate Victoria Hotel Co.* v. *Montefiore*, 1866, (see p. 563) *distinguished*.)

(87) *Yates Building Co.* v. *R.J. Pulleyn & Sons* (*York*), (1975), 119 S.J. 370

An option to purchase a certain plot of land was expressed to be exercisable by notice in writing by or on behalf of the intending purchaser to the intending vendor 'such notice to be sent by registered or Recorded Delivery post'. It was *held*—by the Court of Appeal—that the form of posting prescribed was directory rather than mandatory, or alternatively permissive rather than obligatory, and the option was validly exercised by a letter from the purchaser's solicitors to the vendor's solicitors sent by ordinary post and received within the option period.

Use of post, telephone and telex as a means of communicating acceptance and also offer

(88) *Entores Ltd* v. *Miles Far Eastern Corporation*, [1955] 2 Q.B. 327

The plaintiffs, who conducted a business in London, made an offer to the defendants' agent in Amsterdam by means of a teleprinter service. The offer was accepted by a message received on the plaintiffs' teleprinter in London. Later the defendants were in breach of contract and the plaintiffs wished to sue them. The defendants had their place of business in New York and in order to commence an action the plaintiffs had to serve notice of writ on the defendants in New York. The Rules of Supreme

Court allow service out of the jurisdiction when the contract was made within the jurisdiction. On this point the defendants argued that the contract was made in Holland when it was typed into the teleprinter there, stressing the rule relating to posting. *Held*—Where communication is instantaneous, as where the parties are face to face or speaking on the telephone, acceptance must be received by the offeror. The same rule applied to communications of this kind. Therefore the contract was made in London where the acceptance was received.

Comment: (i) The suggestion was made that the doctrine of estoppel may operate in this sort of case so as to bind the offeror, e.g. suppose X telephones his acceptance to Y, and Y does not hear X's voice at the moment of acceptance, as where there is a break in the line or Y simply puts the phone down on his desk for a while without telling X, then Y may be estopped from denying that he heard X's acceptance and may be bound in contract. It is thought that the conversation prior to the acceptance which is not heard must suggest the possibility of an impending acceptance. It should be noted that this estoppel theory amounts to an exception to the rule that silence cannot amount to acceptance.

(ii) The House of Lords approved the *Entores* decision in *Brinkibon* v. *Stahag Stahl*, [1982] 1 All E.R. 293. The plaintiff wanted leave to serve a writ out of the jurisdiction, as in *Entores*. The message accepting an offer had been sent by telex from London to Vienna. The House of Lords held that the writ could not be served because the contract was made in Vienna and not London.

(89) *Household Fire Insurance Company* v. *Grant* (1879), 4 Ex.D. 216

The defendant handed a written application for shares in the company to the company's agent in Glamorgan. The application stated that the defendant had paid to the company's bankers the sum of £5, being a deposit of one shilling per share on an application for one hundred shares, and also agreed to pay nineteen shillings per share within twelve months of the allotment. The agent sent the application to the company in London. The company secretary made out a letter of allotment in favour of the defendant and posted it to him in Swansea. The letter never arrived. Nevertheless the company entered the defendant's name on the share register and credited him with dividends amounting to five shillings. The company then went into liquidation and the liquidator sued for £94 15 s., the balance due on the shares allotted. It was *held* by the Court of Appeal that the defendant was liable. Acceptance was complete when the letter of allotment was posted on the ground that, in this sort of case, the Post Office must be deemed the common agent of the parties, and that delivery to the agent constituted acceptance. Bramwell, L.J., in a dissenting judgment, regarded actual communication as essential. If the letter of acceptance does not arrive, an unknown liability is imposed on the offeror. If actual communication is required the *status quo* is preserved, i.e. the parties have not made a contract.

Comment. Not all lawyers would accept the point that the Post Office is the common agent of the parties. Those who do not accept this point would say that the Post Office cannot be an agent for communication since the Post Office and its servants do not know what is in the letter.

(90) *Re London and Northern Bank, ex parte Jones*, [1900] 1 Ch. 220

Dr Jones, who lived in Sheffield, applied for shares in the bank. He then sent a letter of revocation which was received by the bank at 8.30 a.m. on 27 October. The bank's letter of allotment was taken to the GPO at St Martins-le-Grand at 7 a.m. on 27 October, but was handed to a postman. Evidence showed that the letter did not go straight into the system. The allotment letter to Jones was delivered at 7.30 p.m. on 27 October, the postmark showing that it was posted at a branch office, not at the GPO. If the letter had been posted at 7.30 a.m., it would have gone to Sheffield on the 10 a.m. train. Evidence showed that it went by the 12 o'clock train. *Held*—The letter was not posted when it was handed to the postman. The evidence did not show with any clarity when the letter was posted, but, since the burden of proof was on the company, it was possible to say that they had not shown the letter of acceptance was posted before 8.30, or even before 9.30 a.m., when the bank's secretary opened the letter of revocation.

An additional point is that evidence given for the Post Office showed that, under the terms of the Post Office Guide, a town postman is not allowed to take letters in this way, and would be disciplined if he did. The position may be different in the country where the custom of taking letters in this way is perhaps better established.

(91) *Holwell Securities Ltd* v. *Hughes*, [1974] 1 All E.R. 161

By an agreement of 19 October, 1971 Dr Hughes, a medical practitioner of Wembley, had granted to the plaintiffs an option to purchase his premises in Wembley for £45,000. The agreement provided that the option should be exercisable 'by notice in writing' to Dr Hughes at any time within six months of the date of the agreement. On 14 April, 1972, the plaintiffs' solicitors sent to Dr Hughes by ordinary post a written notice exercising the option. That notice was never delivered to Dr Hughes nor left at his address. *Held*—by the Court of Appeal—on a construction of the agreement—that notice in writing had to be given to Dr Hughes in the sense that he had either to have actually received it or to be deemed to have received it under s. 196 of the Law of Property Act, 1925 which provides for service of notices by registered post, or within the Recorded Delivery Service Act, 1962, which applies a similar rule to Recorded Delivery. This was not a case, said Russell, L.J., where the basic principle of the need for communication to the offeror was displaced by the artificial concept of communication by the act of posting: the language of the agreement 'notice . . . to' was inconsistent with the theory that acceptance could be constituted by posting and s. 196 of the Law of Property Act, 1925 also impliedly excluded such a mode of acceptance.

Comment. The case illustrates that the rule of acceptance by post does not apply in all situations to which it might logically be applied. As the court said in this case the rule would not be applied where it led to 'manifest inconvenience and absurdity'. In each case, therefore, it is a matter of fact for the court to decide whether the rule should be applied, the test being whether it produces, on balance, a convenient and reasonable result.

(92) *Adams* v. *Lindsell* (1818), 1 B. & A. 681

The defendants were wool dealers in business at St Ives, Huntingdon. By letter dated 2 September they offered to sell wool to the plaintiffs who were wool manufacturers at Bromsgrove, Worcestershire. The defendants' letter asked for a reply 'in course of post' but was misdirected, being addressed to Bromsgrove, Leicestershire. The offer did not reach the plaintiffs until 7 p.m. on 5 September. The same evening the plaintiffs accepted the offer. This letter reached the defendants on 9 September. If the offer had not been misdirected, the defendants could have expected a reply on 7 September, and accordingly they sold the wool to a third party on 8 September. The plaintiffs now sued for breach of contract. *Held*—Where there is a misdirection of the offer, as in this case, the offer is made when it actually reaches the offeree, and not when it would have reached him in the ordinary course of post. The defendants' mistake must be taken against them and for the purposes of this contract the plaintiffs' letter was received 'in course of post'.

Comment. The position may be different if the fact of delay is obvious to the offeree so that he is put on notice that the offer has lapsed, e.g. A writes to B offering to sell him certain goods and saying that the offer is open until 30 June. If A misdirects the offer so that it does not reach B until 2 July, it is doubtful whether B could accept it.

Revocation of an offer must be communicated. It is not effective on posting

(93) *Byrne* v. *Van Tienhoven* (1880), 5 C.P.D. 344

On 1 October the defendants in Cardiff posted a letter to the plaintiffs in New York offering to sell them tin plate. On 8 October the defendants wrote revoking their offer. On 11 October the plaintiffs received the defendants' offer and immediately telegraphed their acceptance. On 15 October the plaintiffs confirmed their acceptance by letter. On 20 October the defendants' letter of revocation reached the plaintiffs who had by this time entered into a contract to resell the tin plate. *Held*— (*a*) that revocation of an offer is not effective until it is communicated to the offeree, (*b*) the mere posting of a letter of revocation is not communication to the person to whom it is sent. The rule is not, therefore, the same as that for acceptance of an offer. Thus the defendants were bound by a contract which came into being on 11 October.

(94) *Dunmore* (*Countess*) v. *Alexander* (1830), 9 Sh (Ct. of Sess.) 190

In this case a letter accepting an offer of employment was followed by a further letter withdrawing the acceptance. Both letters were received by the offeror by the same post. *Held*—The acceptance was validly cancelled.

Revocation of offer: the effect of an option

(95) *Routledge* v. *Grant* (1828), 4 Bing. 653

The defendant made an offer to take a lease of the plaintiff's premises: 'a definitive answer to be given within six weeks from 18 March, 1825'. On 9 April the defendant withdrew his offer and on 29 April the plaintiff purported to accept it. The Court of Common Pleas held that there was no contract. Best, C.J. *held* that the defendant could withdraw at any moment before acceptance, even though the time limit had expired. The plaintiff could only have held the defendant to his offer throughout the period, if he had bought the option, i.e. given consideration for it.

Revocation of offer: may be by a third party if a reasonable person would rely on that party's knowledge of the facts

(96) *Dickinson* v. *Dodds* (1876), 2 Ch.D. 463

The defendant offered to sell certain houses by letter stating, 'This offer to be left over until Friday, 9 a.m.' On Thursday afternoon the plaintiff was informed by a Mr Berry that the defendant had been negotiating a sale of the property with one Allan. On Thursday evening the plaintiff left a letter of acceptance at the house where the defendant was staying. This letter was never delivered to the defendant. On Friday morning at 7 a.m. Berry, acting as the plaintiff's agent, handed the defendant a duplicate letter of acceptance explaining it to him. However, on the Thursday the defendant had entered into a contract to sell the property to Allan. *Held*—Since there was no consideration for the promise to keep the offer open, the defendant was free to revoke his offer at any time. Further Berry's communication of the dealings with Allan indicated that Dodds was no longer minded to sell the property to the plaintiff and was in effect a communication of Dodds' revocation. There was therefore no binding contract between the parties.

Comment. The question of whether the person who communicates the revocation is a reliable source is a matter of fact for the court, but it could, e.g. be a mutual friend of the offeror and offeree or, as in this case, the offeror's agent.

Lapse of offer after a reasonable time

(97) *Ramsgate Victoria Hotel Co.* v. *Montefiore* (1866), L.R. 1 Exch. 109

The defendant offered by letter dated 8 June, 1864, to take shares in the company. No reply was made by the company, but on 23 November,

1864, they allotted shares to the defendant. The defendant refused to take up the shares. *Held*—His refusal was justified because his offer had lapsed by reason of the company's delay in notifying their acceptance.

Comment. The question of 'reasonable time' is a matter of fact to be decided by the court on the basis of the subject matter of the contract and the conditions of the market in which the offer is made. Offers to take shares in companies are normally accepted quickly because the price fluctuates in the market.

Conditional offer: termination on failure of condition

(98) *Financings Ltd* v. *Stimson*, [1962] 3 All E.R. 386

On 16 March, 1961, the defendant saw a motor car on the premises of a dealer and signed a hire-purchase form provided by the plaintiffs (a finance company), this form being supplied by the dealer. The form was to the effect that the agreement was to become binding only when the finance company signed the form. It also carried a statement to the effect that the hirer (the defendant) acknowledged that before he signed the agreement he had examined the goods and had satisfied himself that they were in good order and condition, and that the goods were at the risk of the hirer from the time of purchase by the owners. On 18 March the defendant paid the first instalment and took possession of the car. However, on 20 March, the defendant, being dissatisfied with the car, returned it to the dealer though the finance company were not informed of this. On the night of 24–25 March the car was stolen from the dealer's premises and was recovered badly damaged. On 25 March the finance company signed the agreement accepting the defendant's offer to hire the car. The defendant did not regard himself as bound and refused to pay the instalments. The finance company sold the car, and now sued for damages for the defendant's breach of the hire-purchase agreement. *Held*—The hire purchase agreement was not binding on the defendant because—

(i) he had revoked his offer by returning the car, and the dealer was the agent of the finance company to receive notice;

(ii) there was an *implied* condition in the offer that the goods were in substantially the same condition when the offer was accepted as when it was made.

Death of offeror before acceptance

(99) *Bradbury* v. *Morgan* (1862), 1 H. & C. 249

The defendants were the executors of J. M. Leigh who had entered into a guarantee of his brother's account with the plaintiffs for credit up to £100. The plaintiffs, not knowing of the death of J. M. Leigh, continued to supply goods on credit to the brother, H. J. Leigh. The defendants now refused to pay the plaintiffs in respect of such credit after the death of

J. M. Leigh. *Held*—The plaintiffs succeeded, the offer remaining open until the plaintiffs had *knowledge* of the death of J. M. Leigh.

Comment. This was a continuing guarantee which is in the nature of a standing offer accepted piecemeal whenever further goods are advanced on credit. Where the guarantee is not of this nature, it may be irrevocable. Thus, in *Lloyds* v. *Harper* (1880), 16 Ch.D. 290, the defendant, while living, guaranteed his son's dealings as a Lloyds underwriter in consideration of Lloyds admitting the son. It was *held* that, as Lloyds had admitted the son on the strength of the guarantee, the defendant's executors were still liable under it, because it was irrevocable and was not affected by the defendant's death. It continued to apply to defaults committed by the son after the father's death.

Death of offeree before acceptance

(100) *Re Cheshire Banking Co., Duff's Executors' Case* (1886), 32 Ch.D. 301

In 1882 the Cheshire and Staffordshire Union Banking Companies amalgamated, and Duff received a circular asking whether he would exchange his shares in the S Bank for shares in the C Bank which took the S Bank over. Duff held 100 £20 shares on which £5 had been paid, but he did not reply to the circular and died shortly afterwards. The option was exercised on behalf of his executors, Muttlebury, Bridges and Watts, and a certificate was made out in their names and an entry made in the register in which they were entered as shareholders, described as 'executors of William Duff, deceased'. The executors objected to having the share certificate in their names, so the directors of the Cheshire Banking Co. cancelled the certificate and issued a fresh one in the name of William Duff. On 23 October, 1884, the company went into liquidation. *Held*—The liquidator acted rightly when he restored the executors' names to the register. The executors wished to enter into a new contract which had not previously existed. They could not make a dead man liable and so could only make themselves personally liable. Their names were improperly removed and must be restored. Although they had a right of indemnity against the estate, they were personally liable for the full amount outstanding on the shares, regardless as to whether the estate was adequate to indemnify them.

Comment. This case probably has more to do with the liability of personal representatives in the law of succession than the law of contract. Personal representatives, like receivers, can be personally liable on contracts which they make, subject to a right of indemnity from the estate. The benefit of the contract is held on trust for the estate. This personal liability rule is essential in order to ensure that personal representatives cannot subject the estate to further debt without risk to themselves. There seems to be no direct contract law authority as to the effect of the death of the offeree. In *Reynolds* v. *Atherton*, (1922) 127 L.T. 189, Warrington, L.J. said: 'The offer having been made to a living person who ceases to be a living person before the offer is accepted, there is no longer an offer at all. The offer is not intended to be made to a dead person, nor to his executors, and the offer ceases to be an offer capable of acceptance.' There is, however, some Canadian authority. In *Re Irvine*, [1928] 3 D.L.R. 268 an offeree gave his son a letter of acceptance to post. The son did not post it until after the offeree's death. The Supreme Court of Ontario held that the acceptance was invalid.

Offer and acceptance not essential: the collateral contract

(101) *Clarke* v. *Dunraven*, [1897] A.C. 59

The owners of two yachts entered them for the Mudhook Yacht Club Regatta. The rules of the Club, which each owner undertook in a letter to the Club Secretary to obey, included an obligation to pay 'all damages' caused by fouling. While manoeuvring for the start the *Satanita* fouled the *Valkyrie* and sank her. The owner of the latter sued the owner of the former for damages. The defendant argued that his only liability was under the Merchant Shipping Act (Amendment) Act, 1862, s. 54(1) whereby his responsibility was limited to £8 per ton on the registered tonnage of his yacht. The plaintiff replied that the fact of entering the competition in accordance with the rules of the club created a contract between the respective competitors and that by these rules the defendant had bound himself 'to pay all damages'. The vital question therefore was whether any contract had been made between the two owners: their immediate relations were not with each other but with the Yacht Club. It was held both by the Court of Appeal and the House of Lords that a contract was created between them either when they entered their yachts for the race or at latest when they actually sailed. The competitors had accepted the rules as binding upon each other.

(102) *Rayfield* v. *Hands*, [1958] 2 All E.R. 194

The articles of a private company provided by Art. 11 that 'Every member who intends to transfer his shares shall inform the directors who will take the said shares . . . at a fair price'. The plaintiff held 725 full-paid shares of £1 each, and he asked the directors to buy them but they refused. *Held*—The directors were bound to take the shares. Having regard to what is now s. 14(1) of the Companies Act, 1985, Art. 11 constituted a binding contract between the directors, as members, and the plaintiff, as a member, in respect of his rights as a member. The word 'will' in the article did not import an option in the directors. Vaisey, J., did say that the conclusion he had reached in this case may not apply to all companies, but it did apply to a private company, because such a company was an intimate concern closely analogous with a partnership.

Comment. Although the articles placed the obligation to take shares of members on the directors, Vaisey, J., construed this as an obligation falling upon the directors in their capacity as members. Otherwise the contractual aspect of the provision in the articles would not have applied, since the articles are not a contract between the company and the directors.

Contractual intention: domestic agreements between husband and wife are in general terms unenforceable

(103) *Balfour* v. *Balfour*, [1919] 2 K.B. 571

The defendant was a civil servant stationed in Ceylon. In November, 1915, he came to England on leave with his wife, the plaintiff in the present action. In August, 1916, the defendant returned alone to Ceylon because his wife's doctor had advised her that her health would not stand up to a further period of service abroad. Later the husband wrote to his wife suggesting that they should remain apart, and in 1918 the plaintiff obtained a decree nisi. In this case the plaintiff alleged that before her husband sailed for Ceylon he had agreed, in consultation with her, that he would give her £30 per month as maintenance, and she now sued because of his failure to abide by the said agreement. The Court of Appeal *held* that there was no enforceable contract because in this sort of situation it must be assumed that the parties did not intend to create legal relations. The provision for a flat payment of £30 per month for an indefinite period with no attempt to take into account changes in the circumstances of the parties did not suggest a binding agreement. Duke, L.J., seems to have based his decision on the fact that the wife had not supplied any consideration.

Comment. Although this may seem unfair on the wife it should be remembered that if the husband was regarded as contracting to pay a housekeeping allowance, his wife could be sued for inadequate management of the household.

Contractual intention: agreements between husband and wife designed to regulate the terms of their separation are usually regarded as binding contracts

(104) *Merritt* v. *Merritt*, [1970] 2 All E.R. 760

After a husband had formed an attachment for another woman and had left his wife, a meeting was held between the parties on 25 May, 1966, in the husband's car. The husband agreed to pay the wife £40 per month maintenance and also wrote out and signed a document stating that in consideration of the wife paying all charges in connexion with the matrimonial home until the mortgage repayments had been completed, he would agree to transfer the property to her sole ownership. The wife took the document away with her and had herself paid off the mortgage. The husband did not subsequently transfer the property to his wife and she claimed a declaration that she was the sole beneficial owner and asked for an order that her husband should transfer the property to her forthwith. The husband's defence was that the agreement was a family arrangement not intended to create legal relations. *Held*—by the Court of Appeal—

(i) That the agreement, having been made when the parties were not living together in amity, was enforceable. (*Balfour* v. *Balfour*, 1919,[103] *distinguished.*)

(ii) The contention that there was no consideration to support the husband's promise could not be sustained. The payment of the balance of the mortgage was a detriment to the wife and the husband had received the benefit of being relieved of liability to the building society.

Accordingly the wife was entitled to the relief she claimed.

Contractual intention: family agreements other than those between husband and wife

(105) *Simpkins* v. *Pays*, [1955] 3 All E.R. 10

The defendant and the defendant's granddaughter made an agreement with the plaintiff, who was a paying boarder, that they should submit in the defendant's name a weekly coupon, containing a forecast by each of them, to a Sunday newspaper fashion competition. On one occasion a forecast by the granddaughter was correct and the defendant received a prize of £750. The plaintiff sued for her share of that sum. The defence was that there was no intention to create legal relations but that the transaction was a friendly arrangement binding in honour only. *Held*—There was an intention to create legal relations. Far from being a friendly domestic arrangement, the evidence showed that it was a joint enterprise and that the parties expected to share any prize that was won.

Comment. A family agreement which went the other way was *Julian* v. *Furby* (1982), 132 N.L.J. 64. J was an experienced plasterer who helped F, his son-in-law and his wife (J's favourite daughter) to buy, alter, and furnish a house for them. They later quarrelled and J sued for £4440. This included materials supplied and F was prepared to pay for these but not for J's labour which, it was understood, would be free. It was held by the Court of Appeal that there was never an intention to create a legal relationship between the parties in regard to the labour which J and F jointly provided in refurbishing the house.

(106) *Snelling* v. *John G. Snelling Ltd*, [1972] 1 All E.R. 79

The plaintiff and the second and third defendants were brothers and co-directors of John G. Snelling Ltd. Prior to 1967 the company had been financed by loans from each of them. In 1968 additional finance was required and a finance company agreed to provide it and the brothers agreed with the finance company not to reduce their loans to John G. Snelling Ltd until the loan from the finance company had been repaid. The brothers also made a separate agreement between themselves that if any of them voluntarily resigned before the loan from the finance company was repaid, the money due to him from John G. Snelling Ltd should be forfeited. The company John G. Snelling Ltd was not a party to this agreement. The plaintiff resigned voluntarily and sued the company for the return of his loan. His brothers were joined as co-defendants and counter-claimed for a declaration that the loans to the plaintiff had been forfeited. It was *held*—by Ormrod, J.—

(i) That the agreement between the brothers was intended to affect the legal rights of them all and was intended to create legal relations even though made by members of a family. This was not a 'family' situation like that in *Balfour* v. *Balfour*, 1919[103] because here the family relationship had already been destroyed by disagreements and nothing but the biological tie remained between them;

(ii) that the company could not rely directly on the agreement between the brothers since it was not a party to it;

(iii) that although the company could not rely on the agreement, the plaintiff brothers could enforce it being parties;

(iv) that their appropriate remedy was either to apply for an injunction before the plaintiff issued a writ (as had happened) or, after issue of the writ, to apply for a stay of proceedings under s. 41 of the Supreme Court of Judicature (Consolidation) Act, 1925 (see now s. 49(3) of the Supreme Court Act, 1981), which allows the court, if it thinks fit, to direct a stay of proceedings in any matter before it;

(v) that since all the parties were before the court and also that the reality of the matter was that the plaintiff's case failed, the proper order to make was one dismissing the plaintiff's claim and not one which merely stopped his action.

Comment. (i) In a way this case follows a standard exception to the doctrine of privity, i.e. a compromise between creditors which is what, in effect, the brothers were, under which any creditor who is a party to the compromise can obtain an order to stay the action of any other creditor provided he is a party to the compromise, against the debtor for the balance of the debt (see further p. 211).

(ii) This case does not affect the basic rule of privity but shows an additional method of avoiding the operation of the rule. It could, for example, have been used in cases such as *Adler* v. *Dickson*, [1955] 1 Q.B. 158 since if, as in that case, A makes a contract with B under which B excludes the liability of his servants, it may be possible to enforce that clause because B could apply to the court which could stay any action by A against B's servants and dismiss A's claim under s. 41 of the 1925 Act (see now s. 49(3) of the Supreme Court Act, 1981). The only qualification would seem to be that the promise not to sue should be clear and unambiguous (*Per* Ormrod, J.).

(107) *Parker* v. *Clark*, [1960] 1 All E.R. 93

The plaintiffs, Mr & Mrs Parker, were a middle-aged couple and lived in their own cottage in Sussex. The defendants, Mr & Mrs Clark, who were aged 77 and 78 respectively, lived in a large house in Torquay. Mrs Parker was the niece of Mrs Clark. In 1955 the plaintiffs visited the defendants and, as a result of certain conversations held at that time, Mrs Clark wrote to Mrs Parker suggesting that the plaintiffs should come to live in the defendants' house in Torquay, setting out detailed financial terms as to the sharing of expenses. Mrs Clark also suggested that the plaintiffs' cottage might be sold and the proceeds invested, and that the defendants would leave the house in Torquay, and its major contents, to Mrs Parker, her sister and her daughter. Mrs Parker wrote accepting this offer and the cottage was sold. After the mortgage was paid off, £2000 of the remaining money was lent to their daughter to enable her to buy a flat. The plaintiffs then moved into the defendants' house in Torquay. For a time all went well and Mr Clark executed a will leaving the property as agreed. In 1957 differences between the parties arose, and after much unpleasantness Mr Clark told the plaintiffs to go and they left in December, 1957. The plaintiffs claimed damages for breach of contract. *Held*—There was an intention to create legal relations arising from the circumstances. In view of the fact that the plaintiffs had sold their home and lent £2000 to their daughter, it was obvious that, having 'burned their boats', they must have relied on the agreement. The letter from Mrs Clark was an offer sufficiently precise and detailed; it was not merely a statement of terms for a future agreement. Further it was a sufficient memorandum to satisfy s. 40 of the Law of Property Act, 1925. Finally, the fact that Mr Clark had altered his will indicated that he regarded the agreement as binding.

The damages awarded were divided as follows

(i) Damages of £1200 plus costs, in favour of the parties jointly, based on the value per annum of living rent free in the house. (£300 multiplied by four because of the expectation of life of the defendants.)

(ii) Damages of £3400, in favour of Mrs Parker separately, in respect of the value to her of inheriting a share in the defendants' house on their death.

Comment. Although there was a family relationship in this case which would normally have gone to negative contractual intent, yet the court thought that the major importance of the steps taken by the Parkers gave rise to an inference of contractual intention which overrode the non-contractual inference arising from the family relationship.

Contractual intention: family agreements: effect of vagueness

(108) *Jones* v. *Padavatton*, [1969] 2 All E.R. 616

In 1962 the plaintiff, Mrs Jones, who lived in Trinidad, made an offer to the defendant Mrs Padavatton, her daughter, to provide maintenance for her at the rate of £42 a month if she would leave her job in Washington in the United States and go to England and read for the Bar. Mrs Padavatton was at that time divorced from her husband having the custody of the child of that marriage. The agreement was an informal one and there was uncertainty as to its exact terms. Nevertheless the daughter came to England in November 1962, bringing the child with her, and began to read for the Bar, her fees and maintenance being paid for by Mrs Jones. In 1964 it appeared that the daughter was experiencing some discomfort in England occupying one room in Acton for which she had to pay £6 17s. 6d. per week. At this stage Mrs Jones offered to buy a large house in London to be occupied partly by the daughter and partly by tenants, the income from rents to go to the daughter in lieu of maintenance. Again there was no written agreement but the house was purchased for £6000 and conveyed to Mrs Jones. The daughter moved into the house in January, 1965, and tenants arrived, it still being uncertain what precisely was to happen to the surplus rent income (if any) and what rooms the daughter was to occupy. No money from the rents was received by Mrs Jones and no accounts were submitted to her. In 1967 Mrs Jones claimed possession of the house from her daughter, who had by that time married again, and the daughter counter-claimed for £1655 18s. 9d. said to have been paid in connection with running the house. At the hearing the daughter still had one subject to pass in Part I of the Bar examinations and also the whole of Part II remained to be taken.

Held—by the Court of Appeal—

(i) That the arrangements were throughout family agreements depending upon the good faith of the parties in keeping the promises made and not intended to be rigid binding agreements. Furthermore, the arrangements were far too vague and uncertain to be enforceable as contracts. (*Per* Danckwerts and Fenton Atkinson, L.JJ.)

(ii) That although the agreement to maintain while reading for the Bar might have been regarded as creating a legal obligation in the mother to pay (the terms being sufficiently stated and duration for a reasonable time being implied), the daughter could not claim anything in respect of that agreement which must be regarded as having terminated in 1967, five years being a reasonable time in which to complete studies for the Bar. The arrangements in relation to the home were very vague and must be regarded as made without contractual intent. (*Per* Salmon, L.J.)

The mother was therefore entitled to possession of the house and had no liability under the maintenance agreement. The counter-claim by the daughter was left to be settled by the parties.

Comment. In this case there was an inference of contractual intent in the mother's promise because it caused Mrs Padavatton to leave one job to study for another, but the vagueness of the arrangement negatived that intent as in *Gould* v. *Gould*, [1969] 3 All E.R. 728 (see p. 202).

Contractual intent: assumed in business agreements unless excluded by the parties

(109) *Jones* v. *Vernon's Pools Ltd*, [1938] 2 All E.R. 626

The plaintiff said that he had sent to the defendants a football coupon on which the penny points pool was all correct. The defendants denied having received it and relied on a clause printed on every coupon. The said clause provided that the transaction should not 'give rise to any legal relationship . . . or be legally enforceable . . . but . . . binding in honour only'. The court *held* that this clause was a bar to any action in a court of law.

Comment. This case was followed by the Court of Appeal in *Appleson* v. *Littlewood Ltd*, [1939] 1 All E.R. 464, where the contract contained a similar clause.

(110) *Rose and Frank Co.* v. *Crompton (J.R.) & Brothers Ltd*, [1925] A.C. 445

In 1913 the plaintiffs, an American firm, entered into an agreement with the defendants, an English company, whereby the plaintiffs were appointed sole agents for the sale in the USA of paper tissues supplied by the defendants. The contract was for a period of three years with an option to extend that time. The agreement was extended to March, 1920, but in 1919 the defendants terminated it without notice. The defendants had received a number of orders for tissues before the termination of the contract, and they refused to execute them. The plaintiffs sued for breach of contract and for non-delivery of the goods actually ordered. The agreement of 1913 contained an 'Honourable Pledge Clause' drafted as follows: 'This arrangement is not entered into nor is this memorandum written as a formal or legal agreement and shall not be subject to legal jurisdiction in the courts of the United States of America or England. . . .' It was *held* by the House of Lords that the 1913 agreement was not binding on the parties, but that in so far as the agreement had been acted upon by the defendants' acceptance of orders, the said orders were binding contracts of sale. Nevertheless the agreement was not binding for the future.

Definition of consideration: consideration must move from the promisee: the doctrine of privity of contract.

(111) *Dunlop* v. *Selfridge*, [1915] A.C. 847

The appellants were motor tyre manufacturers and sold tyres to Messrs Dew & Co. who were motor accessory dealers. Under the terms of the contract Dew & Co. agreed not to sell the tyres below Dunlop's list price, and as Dunlop's agents, to obtain from other traders a similar undertaking. In return for this undertaking Dew & Co. were to receive special discounts, some of which they could, if they wished, pass on to retailers who bought tyres. Selfridge & Co. accepted two orders from customers for Dunlop covers at a lower price. They obtained the covers through Dew & Co. and signed an agreement not to sell or offer the tyres below list price. It was further agreed that £5 per tyre so sold should be paid to Dunlop by way of liquidated damages. Selfridges supplied one of the two tyres ordered below list price. They did not actually supply the other, but informed the customer that they could only supply it at list price. The appellants claimed an injunction and damages against the respondents for breach of the agreement made with Dew & Co., claiming that Dew & Co. were their agents in the matter. *Held*—There was no contract between the parties. Dunlop could not enforce the contract made between the respondents and Dew & Co. because they had not supplied consideration. Even if Dunlop were undisclosed principals, there was no consideration moving between them and the respondents. The discount received by Selfridge was part of that given by Dunlop to Dew & Co. Since Dew & Co. were not bound to give any part of their discount to retailers the discount received by Selfridge operated only as consideration between themselves and Dew & Co. and could not be claimed by Dunlop as consideration to support a promise not to sell below list price. (See now Resale Prices Act, 1976, s. 26.)

Comment. It was in this case that the House of Lords adopted the definition of consideration given by Sir Frederick Pollock, i.e. 'An act of forbearance of one party, *or the promise thereof* is the price for which *the promise* of the other is bought, and *the promise* thus given for value is enforceable.'

Consideration need not be adequate so long as it has some economic value.

(112) *Thomas* v. *Thomas* (1842), 2 Q.B. 851

The plaintiff's husband had expressed the wish that the plaintiff, if she survived him, should have use of his house. He left a will of which his brothers were executors. The will made no mention of the testator's wish that his wife should be given the house. The executors knew of the testator's wish and agreed to allow the widow to occupy the house on payment of £1 per year for so long as she remained unmarried. The plaintiff remained in possession of the house until the death of one of the executors, Samuel Thomas. The other executor then turned her out. She sued him for breach of contract. It was held that the plaintiff's promise to pay £1 per year was consideration and need not be adequate. The action for breach of contract succeeded.

Comment. The rule that consideration need not be adequate allows virtually gratuitous promises to be binding even though not under seal.

(113) *White* v. *Bluett* (1853), 23 L.J. Ex. 36

This action was brought by White who was the executor of Bluett's father's estate. The plaintiff, White, alleged that Bluett had not paid a promissory note given to his father during his lifetime. Bluett admitted that he had given the note to his father, but said that his father had released him from it in return for a promise not to keep on complaining about the fact that he had been disinherited. *Held*—The defence failed and the defendant was liable on the note. The promise not to complain was not sufficient consideration to support his release from the note.

Comment. This case illustrates the general point that on formation of contract consideration must be capable of expression in terms of value. On its facts, of course, the case is concerned with consideration on discharge of contract, i.e. the promissory note, where the rule is the same. In addition, the decision seems to be based upon the fact that the son had no right to complain of his disinheritance, so he was not giving up anything which he had a right to do. 'The son had no right to complain, for the father might make what distribution of his property he liked; and the son's abstaining from doing what he had no right to do can be no consideration'. (*Per* Pollock, C.B.)

(114) *Chappell & Co. Ltd* v. *Nestlé Co. Ltd*, [1959] 2 All E.R. 701

The plaintiffs owned the copyright in a dance tune called 'Rockin' Shoes', and the defendants were using records of this tune as part of an advertising scheme. A record company made the records for Nestlés who advertised them to the public for 1s. 6d. each but required in addition three wrappers from their 6d. bars of chocolate. When they received the wrappers they threw them away. The plaintiffs sued the defendants for infringement of copyright. It appeared that under the Copyright Act of 1956 a person recording musical works for *retail* sale need not get the permission of the holder of the copyright, but had merely to serve him with notice and pay 6¼ per cent of the retail selling price as royalty. The plaintiffs asserted that the defendants were not retailing the goods in the sense of the Act and must therefore get permission to use the musical work. The basis of the plaintiff's case was that retailing meant selling entirely for money, and that as the defendants were selling for money plus wrappers, they needed the plaintiff's consent. The defence was that the sale was for cash because the wrappers were not part of the consideration. The House of Lords by a majority gave judgment for the plaintiffs. The wrappers were part of the consideration since the offer was to supply a record in return, not simply for money, but for the wrappers as well. On the question of adequacy Lord Somervell said: 'It is said that, when received, the wrappers are of no value to the respondents, the Nestlé Co. Ltd. This I would have thought to be irrelevant. A contracting party can stipulate for what consideration he chooses. A peppercorn does not cease to be good consideration if it is established that the promisee does not like pepper and will throw away the corn.'

Comment. There seems to be no doubt that the wrappers could on their own have formed the consideration.

Adequacy of consideration: forbearance to sue can support a promise

(115) *Horton* v. *Horton*, [1961] 1 Q.B. 215

The parties were husband and wife. In March, 1954, by a separation agreement under seal the husband agreed to pay the wife £30 a month. On the true construction of the deed the husband should have deducted income tax before payment but for nine months he paid the money without deductions. In January, 1955, he signed a document, not under seal, agreeing that instead of 'the monthly sum of £30' he would pay such a monthly sum as 'after deduction of income tax should amount to the clear sum of £30'. For over three years he paid this clear sum but then stopped payment. To an action by his wife he pleaded that the later agreement was unsupported by consideration and that the wife could sue only on the earlier deed. The Court of Appeal held that there was consideration to support the later agreement. It was clear that the original deed did not implement the intention of the parties. The wife therefore might have sued to rectify the deed and the later agreement represented a compromise of this possible action. Whether such an action would have succeeded was irrelevant; it sufficed that it had some prospect of success and that the wife believed in it.

Adequacy of consideration: gratuitous promises are not enforceable unless under seal, but a gratuitous bailee of goods is liable in tort for intentional or negligent damage to them

(116) *Coggs* v. *Bernard* (1703), 2 Ld. Ray. 909

The defendant had agreed to take several hogsheads of brandy, belonging to the plaintiff, from the cellar of one inn to another. One of the casks was broken and the brandy lost and the plaintiff alleged that this was due to the defendant's carelessness. The defendant denied liability on the grounds that there was no consideration to support the agreement to move the casks. *Held*—the plaintiff's claim succeeded. The court made an attempt to find consideration by saying that when the plaintiff entrusted the goods to the defendant this was sufficient consideration to oblige him to be careful with them. However, it is hard to see how such a 'trusting' can amount to consideration for it was not a benefit to the defendant, nor was it a detriment to the plaintiff because he wished his goods to be carried. It does not appear to have been the price of any promise and the case seems to have been decided on the ground that once the relationship of bailor and bailee is established certain duties fall upon the bailee independently of any contract.

Comment. It should be borne in mind, of course, that if a person agrees to take charge of goods gratuitously he could not be sued if he fails to take them into his custody. The duty seen in this case arises only when the goods are in the custody of the gratuitous bailee.

(117) *Gilchrist Watt and Sanderson Pty* v. *York Products Pty*, [1970] 1 W.L.R. 1262

Two cases of German clocks were bought by the respondents and shipped to Sydney. The shipowners arranged for the appellant stevedores to unload the ship. The goods were put in the appellants' shed but when the respondents came to collect them one case of clocks was missing. It was admitted that this was due to the appellants' negligence. *Held*—by the Privy Council—that the appellants were liable. Although there was no contract between the parties an obligation to take due care of the goods was created by delivery and voluntary assumption of possession under the sub-bailment.

Sufficiency of consideration: promise to perform or performance of an existing public or contractual duty will not support a further promise: acts in excess of the duty may

(118) *Collins* v. *Godefroy* (1831), 1 B. & Ad. 950

The plaintiff was subpoenaed to give evidence for the defendant in an action to which the defendant was a party. The plaintiff now sued for the sum of six guineas which he said the defendant had promised him for his attendance. *Held*—The plaintiff's action failed because there was no consideration for the promise. Lord Tenterden said: 'if it be a duty imposed by law upon a party regularly subpoenaed to attend from time to time to give his evidence, then a promise to give him any remuneration for loss of time incurred in such attendance is a promise without consideration'.

(119) *Vanbergen* v. *St Edmunds Properties Ltd*, [1933] 2 K.B. 223

The plaintiff owed the defendants £208 and the defendants had issued a bankruptcy notice to be served on 7 July. On 6 July the plaintiff told the defendants' solicitors that he hoped to raise the money at Eastbourne, but that he could not do so until 8 July. The solicitors agreed to put off the service of the notice until noon on 8 July, in return for the plaintiff's promise to pay the money into an Eastbourne bank by that time. The plaintiff paid the money in as directed on 7 July, but his letter advising the solicitors went astray. They thereupon served the bankruptcy notice. The plaintiff now sued for damages for breach of contract. *Held*—The action could not be sustained because the plaintiff was already bound to pay the sum of £208 long before 8 July and was not supplying consideration by paying it into the bank on 7 July. The solicitors were in order in serving the notice.

(120) *Stilk* v. *Myrick* (1809), 2 Camp. 317

A sea-captain, being unable to find any substitutes for two sailors who had deserted, promised to divide the wages of the deserters among the rest of the crew if they would work the ship home shorthanded. *Held*—The promise was not enforceable because of absence of consideration. In sailing the ship home the crew had done no more than they were already bound to do. Their original contract obliged them to meet the normal emergencies of the voyage of which minor desertions were one. Compare *Hartley* v. *Ponsonby* (1857), 7 E. & B. 872, where a greater remuneration was promised to a seaman to work the ship home when the number of deserters was so great as to render the ship unseaworthy. *Held*—This was a binding promise because the sailor had gone beyond his duty in agreeing to sail an unseaworthy ship. In fact the number of desertions was so great as to discharge the remaining seamen from their original contract, leaving them free to enter into a new bargain.

(121) *Glasbrook Bros Ltd* v. *Glamorgan County Council*, [1925] A.C. 270

In 1921 the Glamorgan police were asked to provide 100 police officers to be billeted on the premises of Glasbrook's colliery near Swansea because it was feared that striking miners were going to prevent safety men going into the mine with the consequence that it would be flooded. The owners of the mine signed a document saying that they would not only pay for the services of the officers but also their travelling expenses. Glasbrook's also undertook to provide them with food and sleeping accommodation. Eventually a bill amounting to £2200 11s. 10d. was rendered to the police authority, by the Glamorgan County Council, for the above services. Glasbrook's refused to pay the bill, alleging that the police were doing no more than was their duty and therefore there was no consideration for Glasbrook's written promise to pay for the protection which they had had. *Held*—by the House of Lords—that Glasbrook's promise was binding on them on the ground that the number of constables provided was in excess of what the local police superintendent thought was necessary and therefore provided consideration over and above the obligation resting on the police to take all steps necessary for protecting property from criminal injury. In the course of his judgment Viscount Cave, L.C. said—

> 'No doubt there is an absolute unconditional obligation binding the police authorities to take all steps which appear to them to be necessary for keeping the peace, preventing crime, or for protecting property from criminal injury; and the public, who pay for this protection through the rates and taxes, cannot lawfully be called upon to make a further payment for that which is their right. . . . But it has always been recognized that, where individuals desire that services of a special kind which, though not within the obligations of a police authority, can most effectively be rendered by them, should be performed by members of the police force, the police authorities may . . . "lend" the services of constables for that purpose in consideration of payment. Instances are the lending of constables on the occasions of large gatherings in and outside private premises, as on the occasions of weddings, athletic or boxing contests or race meetings, and the provision of constables at large railway stations.'

Comment. This case was applied in *Harris* v. *Sheffield United Football Club, The Times*, 4 April, 1986 where Boreham, J. held that the provision of policemen at a football ground to keep law and order was the provision of special services by the police. The police authority is under a duty to protect persons and property against crime or threatened crime for which no payment is due. However, the police have no public duty to protect persons and property against the mere fear of possible future crime. The claim of the police authority for some £70,000 for police services provided at the defendants' football ground over 15 months was allowed.

(122) *Ward* v. *Byham*, [1956] 2 All E.R. 318

An unmarried mother sued to recover a maintenance allowance by the father of the child. The defence was that, under s. 42 of the National Assistance Act, 1948, the mother of an illegitimate child was bound to maintain it. However, it appeared that in return for the promise of an allowance the mother had promised—

(*a*) to look after the child well and ensure that it was happy; and
(*b*) to allow it to decide whether it should live with her or the father.

Held—There was sufficient consideration to support the promise of an allowance because the promises given in (*a*) and (*b*) above were in excess of the statutory duty, which was merely to care for the child.

Comment. 'Is a promise to make a child happy adequate consideration?' (Compare *White* v. *Bluett*, 1853.)[113] This point is not taken in the case and shows the considerable power which judges have to find or not to find contractual obligations.

Sufficiency of consideration: performance of a contractual duty owed by X to Y can support a promise made by Z to X

(123) *Shadwell* v. *Shadwell* (1860), 9 C.B. (N.S.) 159

The plaintiff was engaged to marry a girl named Ellen Nicholl. In 1838 he received a letter from his uncle, Charles Shadwell, in the following terms: 'I am glad to hear of your intended marriage with Ellen Nicholl and, as I promised to assist you at starting, I am happy to tell you that I will pay you one hundred and fifty pounds yearly during my life and until your income derived from your profession of Chancery barrister shall amount to six hundred guineas, of which your own admission will be the only evidence that I shall receive or require.' The plaintiff duly married Ellen Nicholl and his income never exceeded six hundred guineas during the eighteen years his uncle lived after the marriage. The uncle paid twelve annual sums and part of the thirteenth but no more. On his death the plaintiff sued his uncle's executors for the balance of the eighteen instalments to which he suggested he was entitled. *Held*—The plaintiff succeeded even though he was already engaged to Ellen Nicholl when the promise was made. His marriage was sufficient consideration to support his uncle's promise, for, by marrying, the plaintiff had incurred responsibilities and changed his position in life. Further the uncle probably derived some benefit in that his desire to see his nephew settled had been satisfied.

Comment. (i) In this case the consideration is a little dubious in that it is in part a sentimental benefit to the uncle. This type of consideration, e.g. the 'love and affection' variety, has often been regarded as ineffective to support a contract. Nevertheless, the principle of the case is a good one and makes more sense in a business context. (See *New Zealand Shipping Co. Ltd* v. *Satterthwaite*, 1974 at p. 664.)

(ii) An engagement to marry is no longer binding as a contract, see s. 1 Law Reform (Miscellaneous Provisions) Act, 1970.

Past consideration: where a particular activity is undertaken without any promise of payment a subsequent promise to pay is not actionable. If there is a request to carry out the act in a commercial situation where a promise to pay can be implied, the subsequent promise may be enforceable

(124) *Re McArdle*, [1951] Ch. 669

Certain children were entitled under their father's will to a house. However, their mother had a life interest in the property and during her lifetime one of the children and his wife came to live in the house with the mother. The wife carried out certain improvements to the property, and, after she had done so, the children signed a document addressed to her stating: 'In consideration of your carrying out certain alterations and improvements to the property . . . at present occupied by you, the beneficiaries under the Will of William Edward McArdle hereby agree that the executors, the National Provincial Bank Ltd, . . . shall repay to you from the said estate when so distributed the sum of £488 in settlement of the amount spent on such improvements. . . .' On the death of the testator's widow the children refused to authorize payment of the sum of £488, and this action was brought to decide the validity of the claim. *Held*—Since the improvements had been carried out before the document was executed, the consideration was past and the promise could not be enforced.

Comment. The rule applied also in *Roscorla* v. *Thomas* (1842), 3 Q.B. 234 where a horse was sold and the seller *after the sale* gave a warranty as to its quality, i.e. that it was not vicious whereas it was. There was no action on the warranty by the buyer.

(125) *Re Casey's Patents, Stewart* v. *Casey*, [1892] 1 Ch. 104

Patents were granted to Stewart and another in respect of an invention concerning appliances and vessels for transporting and storing inflammable liquids. Stewart entered into an arrangement with Casey whereby Casey was to introduce the patents. Casey spent two years 'pushing' the invention and then the joint owners of the patent rights wrote to him as follows: 'In consideration of your services as the practical manager in working both patents we hereby agree to give you one-third share of the patents.' Casey also received the letters patent. Some time later Stewart died and his executors claimed the recovery of the letters patent from Casey, suggesting that he had no interest in them because the consideration for the promise to give him a one-third share was past. *Held*—The previous request to render the services raised an implied promise to pay. The subsequent promise could be regarded as fixing the value of the services so that Casey was entitled to a one-third share of the patent rights.

Privity of contract: effect of doctrine: remedies (if any) available to a person not in privity

(126) *Jackson* v. *Horizon Holidays*, [1975] 3 All E.R. 92

Mr Jackson had booked a four-week holiday in an hotel in Ceylon for himself and his family, everything to be 'of the highest standard'. The brochure issued by the defendants described the hotel as enjoying many facilities including a mini golf course, a swimming pool, and beauty and hairdressing salons. None of these in fact materialized and the food was distasteful. It was *held* that Mr Jackson could sue on the contract not only for his own loss and disappointment but also for that of his family. The decision was not based on the fact that Mr Jackson was a trustee for the others but on the basis that he had entered into the contract partly for their benefit. On that basis an award of damages of £1100 was not excessive. In the course of his judgment Lord Denning, M.R. said: 'The case comes within the principle stated by Lush, L.J. in *Lloyd's* v. *Harper*, [1880] 16 Ch.D. 290 at p. 321: '. . . I consider it to be an established rule of law that where a contract is made with A for the benefit of B, A can sue on the contract for the benefit of B and recover all that B could have recovered if the contract had been made with B himself. ' Speaking of these words, Lord Denning said: 'I think they should be accepted as correct, at any rate so long as the law forbids the third persons themselves to sue for damages. It is the only way in which a just result can be achieved.'

Comment. This judgment of Lord Denning has been much criticized since it infringes a very old rule of English contract law which states that if A contracts with B in return for B's promise to do something for C, then if B repudiates the contract, C has no enforceable claim, and A is restricted to an action for nominal damages by reason of his having suffered no loss. The judgment in *Jackson* was criticized by the Lords in *Woodar* v. *Wimpey* [1980] 1 All E.R. 571 and they assumed that only nominal damages were available in *Beswick* (see below) so that it must be regarded with caution.

The House of Lords said that the *Jackson* case could be justified on the basis that Mr Jackson *actually saw* his family suffering discomfort and disappointment. Their Lordships would not, however, accept that there was a general rule in contract that A could recover damages from B in respect of loss suffered by C.

(127) *Beswick* v. *Beswick*, [1967] 2 All E.R. 1197

A coal merchant agreed to sell the business to his nephew in return for a weekly consultancy fee of £6 10s. payable during his lifetime, and after his death an annuity of £5 per week was to be payable to his widow for her lifetime. After the agreement was signed the nephew took over the business and paid his uncle the sum of £6 10s. as agreed. The uncle died on 3 November, 1963, and the nephew paid the widow one sum of £5 and then refused to pay her any more. On 30 June, 1964, the widow became the administratrix of her husband's estate, and on 15 July, 1964, she brought an action against the nephew for arrears of the weekly sums and for specific performance of the agreement for the future. She sued in her capacity as administratrix of the estate and also in her personal capacity. Her action failed at first instance and on appeal to the Court of Appeal, [1966] 3 All E.R. 1, it was decided amongst other things that—

(i) specific performance could in a proper case be ordered of a contract to pay money;

(ii) 'property' in s. 56(1) of the Law of Property Act, 1925, included a contractual claim not concerned with realty and that therefore a third party could sue on a contract to which he was a stranger. The widow's claim in her personal capacity was therefore good (*per* Denning, M.R., and Danckwerts, L.J.);

(iii) the widow's claim as administratrix was good because she was not suing in her personal capacity but on behalf of her deceased husband who had been a party to the agreement;

(iv) that no trust in her favour could be inferred.

There was a further appeal to the House of Lords, though not on the creation of a trust, and there it was *held* that the widow's claim as administratrix succeeded, and that specific performance of a contract to pay money could be granted in a proper case. However, having decided the appeal on these grounds their Lordships went on to say that the widow's personal claim would have failed because s. 56 of the Law of Property Act, 1925, was limited to cases involving realty. The 1925 Act was a consolidating not a codifying measure, so that if it contained words which were capable of more than one construction, effect should be given to the construction which did not alter the law. It was accepted that when the present provision was contained in the Real Property Act, 1845, it had applied only to realty. Although s. 205(1) of the 1925 Act appeared to have extended the provision to personal property, including things in action, it was expressly qualified by the words: 'unless the context otherwise requires', and it was felt that Parliament had not intended to sweep away the rule of privity by what was in effect a sidewind.

Comment. Here the problem of whether or not to award nominal damages to the plaintiff referred to in *Jackson's* case[126] was overcome because the court awarded specific performance. However, four Law Lords said that if damages had been awarded they would have been nominal only, though Lord Pearce would have awarded substantial damages. Furthermore, it is unlikely that s. 56 does have a very wide application. The subsection says that a person may take the benefit of an agreement although he is not 'named as a party'. The legislation does not say that he need not *be a party*. There are those who take the view, therefore, that s. 56(1) is designed to cover the situation where there is a covenant over land in favour of, say, 'the owner of Whiteacre', so that the owner of Whiteacre could benefit from the covenant, provided he could be ascertained, even though he was not named in the instrument creating the covenant. If this interpretation is correct then s. 56(1) of the 1925 Act has little effect on the law of contract generally.

(128) *Tweddle* v. *Atkinson* (1861), 1 B. & S. 393

William Tweddle the plaintiff was married to the daughter of William Guy. In order to provide for the couple, Guy promised the plaintiff's father to pay the plaintiff £200 if the plaintiff's father would pay the plaintiff £100. An agreement was accordingly drawn up containing the above-mentioned promise, and giving William Tweddle the right to sue either promisor for the sums promised. Guy did not make the promised payment during his lifetime and the plaintiff now sued Guy's executor. *Held*—The plaintiff's action failed because he had not given any consideration to Guy in return for the promise to pay £200. The provision in the agreement allowing William Tweddle to sue was of no effect without consideration.

(129) *Dunlop* v. *New Garage & Motor Co. Ltd*, [1915] A.C. 79

The facts of this case are somewhat similar to case 111 mentioned above except that here the wholesalers obtained an undertaking from the respondents by means of a written agreement in which the wholesalers were clearly described as the agents of Dunlop. There was therefore a direct contractual relationship between the parties, and the appellants could enforce the agreement not to sell below the list price. The case is also concerned with the distinction between liquidated damages and a penalty, because it was suggested that the sum of £5 per tyre was not recoverable because it was not a genuine pre-estimate of loss, but it was inserted to compel performance by the respondents. There is, of course, a presumption that where a single sum is payable on the occurrence of one or more or all of several events then the sum stipulated is a penalty because it is unlikely that all the events can attract the same loss. The contract in this case listed five events on the occurrence of which the sum of £5 was payable. Even so the House of Lords *held* that the presumption need not always apply, and that it did not apply in this case. Where precise estimation is difficult as it was here, then any contractual provision is likely to represent the parties' honest attempt to provide for breach, and the court will follow it.

Certain points of interest arise out of cases 111 and 129—

(i) In neither case did the court regard a re-sale price maintenance agreement as illegal because it was in restraint of trade. The decisions are therefore based on privity.

(ii) *Dunlop* v. *Selfridge*[111] illustrates that restrictive covenants do not run with chattels though they may with land. (Compare *Tulk* v. *Moxhay*, (1848), p. 584.)

Privity of contract: promises in the nature of a trust are enforceable: the rule of privity does not apply in general to trusts

(130) *Les Affréteurs Reunis Societe Anonyme* v. *Walford*, [1919] A.C. 801

The respondent Walford was a broker and he had negotiated a charter party between the owners of a ship the S.S. *Flore* and a fuel oil company. One of the clauses in the charter party stated that the owners of the ship promised the charterers that they would pay the broker (Walford) a certain commission on a figure estimated to be the gross amount of hire. In an action for the commission it was *held*—Although Walford was not a party to the contract, which was between the owners and the charterers, there was nevertheless a trust created in his favour and the commission was recoverable.

Comment. The case was, with the agreement of the appellants, dealt with as if the charterers were co-plaintiffs though they had not in fact been joined.

Privity of contract: acknowledgment or recognition of a third party's rights may produce a remedy in quasi-contract.

(131) *Shamia* v. *Joory*, [1958] 1 Q.B. 448

The defendant, an Iraqi merchant having a business in England, employed the plaintiff's brother as an agent in Baghdad. At the end of 1952 the defendant admitted that he owed his agent £1300, and was requested, and agreed, to pay £500 of this as a gift to the plaintiff, who was the agent's brother and a student in England. The agent informed his brother of the defendant's promise. The plaintiff then wrote to confirm this promise, and the defendant sent a cheque which was not paid because it was not properly drawn. The defendant asked for the return of the cheque to correct it, but shortly afterwards repudiated all liability to the plaintiff having, by this time, reason to doubt the account presented by the plaintiff's brother. The plaintiff now sued to recover the sum of £500 as money had and received to his use (an action in quasi-contract) and Barry. J., *held*—He must succeed.

Privity of contract: exceptions in the case of benefits and burdens attaching to land

(132) *Smith and Snipes Hall Farm Ltd* v. *River Douglas Catchment Board*, [1949] 2 K.B. 500

In 1938 the defendants entered into an agreement with eleven persons owning land adjoining a certain stream, that, on the landowners paying some part of the cost, the defendants would improve the banks of the stream and maintain the said banks for all time. In 1940 one landowner sold her land to Smith, and in 1944 Smith leased the land to Snipes Hall Farm Ltd. In 1946, because of the defendants' negligence, the banks burst and the adjoining land was flooded. *Held*—The plaintiffs could enforce the covenant given in the agreement of 1938 even though they were strangers to it. The covenants were for the benefit of the land and affected its use and value and could therefore be transferred with it.

(133) *Tulk* v. *Moxhay* (1848), 2 Ph. 774

The plaintiff was the owner of several plots of land in Leicester Square and in 1808 he sold one of them to a person called Elms. Elms agreed, for himself, his heirs and assigns, 'to keep the Square Garden open as a pleasure ground and uncovered with buildings'. After a number of conveyances, the land was sold to the defendant who claimed a right to build on it. The plaintiff sued for an injunction preventing the development of the land. The defendant, whilst admitting that he purchased the land with notice of the covenant, claimed that he was not bound by it because he had not himself entered into it. *Held*—An injunction to restrain building would be granted because there was a jurisdiction in Equity to prevent, by way of injunction, acts inconsistent with a restrictive covenant on land, so long as the land was acquired with notice of the covenant, and the plaintiff retains land which can benefit from the covenant.

Comment. (i) Such notice may now be constructive where the covenant is registered under land charges legislation.

(ii) It was held in *Roake* v. *Chadha*, [1983] 3 All E.R. 503 that whether a covenant runs with the land depends upon its wording. If the words used in it prevent the benefit of the covenant, in this case that the plot holder of land would not build more than one house on it, passing to a subsequent owner of the land unless specifically assigned to him by the present owner, then the covenant would not run with the land as such but would depend upon assignment.

Privity of contract and performance bonds

(134) *Edward Owen Engineering Ltd* v. *Barclays Bank International Ltd*, *The Times*, 1 July, 1977

In 1976 Edward Owen made a contract with the executive authority for Jabel El Akhaar to supply and erect glasshouses covering two hectares in Libya. The price of £502,030 was payable in Libyan dinars by instalments and payment of 20 per cent was guaranteed by the Umma Bank of Libya. The contract was governed by Libyan law and any disputes were to be brought before a Libyan court. The buyers agreed to open through the Umma Bank an irrevocable letter of credit in favour of Barclays International on behalf of Owens. Owens promised a performance guarantee and told their bankers, Barclays, to set it up to the value of £50,203. Barclays instructed Umma to issue a performance bond to the buyers for that sum, Barclays giving Umma a guarantee to pay it 'on demand' without proof or conditions. Owens gave Barclays a counterguarantee. Owens did not receive what they regarded as a suitable letter of credit from Umma on behalf of the buyers and, perhaps understandably, did not go on with the contract. However, the Libyan buyers demanded payment from Umma on the performance bond and Umma in turn made a demand for payment on Barclays. Owens obtained an interim injunction to stop Barclays honouring their obligation (which they wished in good faith to do) to Umma. When the matter came to trial Mr Justice Kerr discharged the injunction against Barclays which would have allowed them to pay Umma but Owens appealed. The Court of Appeal decided that Barclays were right in seeking to honour their obligation to Umma. A performance bond was like the more common letter of credit given on behalf of the buyer to the seller and it was decided in *Malas* v. *British Imex*, [1958] 1 All E.R. 262, that banks must honour letters of credit even where there is a dispute between buyer and seller as to the performance of the contract. If banks were prevented from honouring obligations of this kind confidence would be lost and international trade would suffer. As regards disputes between buyer and seller, these were not the concern of the bank but must be dealt with by the parties themselves (in this case presumably by Libyan law in a Libyan court, which is in fact almost impossible because of the problem of getting visas). However, a bank ought not to honour a letter of credit or performance bond where there is fraud of which the bank is aware, as where one of the parties has to the bank's knowledge deliberately misled the other as to the quality of the goods. There was, however, no fraud in this case, the issues being in the nature of contractual disputes between the parties. Mr Justice Kerr had been right in discharging the injunction and the appeal by Owens was dismissed leaving Barclays free to honour the obligation to Umma.

Comment. (i) Although banks always honour obligations of the kind described above, there are technical difficulties if they ever had to be sued because there is no contract between them and the seller (letter of credit) or the buyer (performance bond). The issue is unlikely to arise but it might if a bank went into liquidation when the liquidator might be obliged to raise technical difficulties of this kind. If he did the court would hold the bank bound to the seller or buyer as the case may be on the basis of commercial custom, giving rise to an exception to the concept of privity of contract.

(ii) In *Potton Homes* v. *Coleman Contractors*, (1984) 128 S.J. 282, the Court of Appeal emphasized the difference between performance bonds and letters of credit such as the one in issue in *Malas* v. *British Imex*, [1958] 1 All E.R. 262. In the former case the underlying contract was to be taken into consideration when establishing the seller's right to prevent a call on the bond. In the event of a lawful avoidance of the contract or a total failure of consideration by the buyer, the buyer would be restrained from exercising his rights under the bond. This statement by the Court of Appeal is interesting because it suggests that a performance bond is not as the *Edward Owen* case might suggest independent of the underlying contract. It appears that the bond need not be met if the buyer is in breach of his part of the contract. As we have seen in *Owen*, the seller did not perform because the buyer had not made proper arrangements to pay the seller, but nevertheless the buyer was entitled to collect on the bond. It would appear from *Potton Homes* that the Court might now have restrained the buyer from exercising his rights under the bond.

(iii) That fraud was also relevant to performance bonds was affirmed by the Court of Appeal in *United Trading Corporation* v. *Allied Arab Bank, The Times*, 23 July, 1984, though the Court said that the banker must pay on the bond unless there was clear evidence that the demand for payment was based upon a fraud and that the banker *knew* it was.

The common law doctrine of accord and satisfaction: agreed variations in contractual obligations are generally unenforceable without consideration

(135) *Foakes* v. *Beer* (1884), 9 App. Cas. 605

Mrs Beer had obtained a judgment against Dr Foakes for debt and costs. Dr Foakes agreed to settle the judgment debt by paying £500 down and £150 per half-year until the whole was paid, and Mrs Beer agreed not to take further action on the judgment. Dr Foakes duly paid the amount of the judgment plus costs. However, judgment debts carry interest by statute, and while Dr Foakes had been paying off the debt, interest amounting to £360 had been accruing on the diminishing balance. In this action Mrs Beer claimed the £360. *Held*—She could do so. Her promise not to take further action on the judgment was not supported by any consideration moving from Dr Foakes.

Comment. In view of the possible development of Equity envisaged by Lord Denning in the *D & C Builders* case,[136] it might be better to restrict the application of this case to situations where the promise has been extorted and not freely given. If this were so, *Foakes'* case would be reconcilable with any development of the equitable rule of promissory estoppel on the lines envisaged by Lord Denning in the *D & C Builders* case.

Accord and satisfaction: payment by cheque is not substituted performance: promissory estoppel may, in appropriate circumstances, extinguish as distinct from suspend contractual rights

(136) *D. & C. Builders Ltd* v. *Rees*, [1965] 3 All E.R. 837

D. & C. Builders, a small company, did work for Rees for which he owed £482 13s. 1d. There was at first no dispute as to the work done but Rees did not pay. In August and October, 1964, the plaintiffs wrote for the money and received no reply. On 13 November, 1964, the wife of Rees (who was then ill) telephoned the plaintiffs, complained about the work, and said, 'My husband will offer you £300 in settlement. That is all you will get. It is to be in satisfaction.' D. & C. Builders, being in desperate straits and faced with bankruptcy without the money, offered to take the £300 and allow a year to Rees to find the balance. Mrs Rees replied: 'No, we will never have enough money to pay the balance. £300 is better than nothing.' The plaintiffs then said: 'We have no choice but to accept.' Mrs Rees gave the plaintiffs a cheque and insisted on a receipt 'in completion of the account'. The plaintiffs, being worried about their financial position, brought an action for the balance. The defence was bad workmanship and also that there was a binding settlement. The question of settlement was tried as a preliminary issue and the judge, following *Goddard* v. *O'Brien*, [1880] 9 Q.B.D. 33, decided that a cheque for a smaller amount was a good discharge of the debt, this being the generally accepted view of the law since that date. On appeal it was *held* (*per* The Master of the Rolls, Lord Denning) that *Goddard* v. *O'Brien* was wrongly decided. A smaller sum in cash could be no settlement of a larger sum and 'no sensible distinction could be drawn between the payment of a lesser sum by cash and the payment of it by cheque'.

In the course of his judgment Lord Denning said of *High Trees*: 'It is worth noting that the principle may be applied, not only so as to suspend strict legal rights, but also so as to preclude the enforcement of them.

This principle has been applied to cases where a creditor agrees to accept a lesser sum in discharge of a greater. So much so that we can now say that, when a creditor and a debtor enter on a course of negotiation, which leads the debtor to suppose that, on payment of the lesser sum, the creditor will not enforce payment of the balance, and on the faith thereof the debtor pays the lesser sum and the creditor accepts it as satisfaction: then the creditor will not be allowed to enforce payment of the balance when it would be inequitable to do so. . . . But he is not bound unless there has been truly an accord between them.' In the present case there was no true accord. The debtor's wife had held the creditors to ransom, and there was no reason in law or Equity why the plaintiffs should not enforce the full amount of debt.

Comment. The case also illustrates the requirement of equality of bargaining power in the negotiation (or as here, the renegotiation) of a contract. (See also *Lloyds Bank* v. *Bundy*, 1974 at p. 676.)

Accord and satisfaction: compromises between creditors

(137) *Good* v. *Cheesman* (1831), 2 B. & Ad. 328

The defendant had accepted two bills of exchange of which the plaintiff was the drawer. After the bills became due and before this action was brought, the plaintiff suggested that the defendant meet his creditors with a view perhaps to an agreement. The meeting was duly held and the defendant entered into an agreement with his creditors whereby the defendant was to pay one-third of his income to a trustee to be named by the creditors, and that this was to be the method by which the defendant's debts were to be paid. It was not clear from the evidence whether the plaintiff attended the meeting, though he certainly did not sign the agreement. There was, however, evidence that the agreement had been in his possession for some time and it was duly stamped before the trial. No trustee was in fact appointed, though the defendant was willing to go on with the agreement. *Held*—The agreement bound the plaintiff and the action on the bills could not be sustained. The consideration, though not supplied to the plaintiff direct, existed in the forbearance of the other creditors. Each was bound in consequence of the agreement of the rest.

Comment. (i) The better view is that the basis of this decision is to be found not in the law of contract but in tort, in the sense that once an agreement of this kind has been made it would be a *fraud* on the other creditors for one of their number to sue the debtor separately.

(ii) These arrangements would more usually be made today under the Insolvency Act, 1986. Section 260 of that Act states that such an arrangement binds every creditor if it is approved by a meeting of creditors at which three-quarters in value vote in favour of the arrangement. Therefore, s. 260 really provides an exception to the rule of accord and satisfaction.

Accord and satisfaction: payments by third parties

(138) *Welby* v. *Drake* (1825), 1 C. & P. 557

The plaintiff sued the defendant for the sum of £9 on a debt which had originally been for £18. The defendant's father had paid the plaintiff £9 and the plaintiff had agreed to take that sum in full discharge of the debt. *Held*—The payment of £9 by the defendant's father operated to discharge the debt of £18.

Comment. Here again the basis of the decision is that it would be a fraud on the third party to sue the original debtor. 'If the father did pay the smaller sum in satisfaction of this debt, it is a bar to the plaintiff's now recovering against the son; because by suing the son, he commits a fraud on the father, whom he induced to advance his money on the faith of such advance being a discharge of his son from further liability.' (*Per* Lord Tenterden, C.J.)

Promissory estoppel: variation of contractual rights without consideration: the approach of equity

(139) *Central London Property Trust Ltd* v. *High Trees House Ltd*, [1947] K.B. 130

In 1937 the plaintiffs granted to the defendants a lease of ninety-nine years of a new block of flats at a rent of £2500 per annum. The lease was under seal. During the period of the war the flats were by no means fully let owing to the absence of people from the London area. The defendant company, which was a subsidiary of the plaintiff company, realized that it could not meet the rent out of the profits then being made on the flats, and in 1940 the parties entered into an agreement which reduced the rent to £1250 per annum, this agreement being put into writing but not sealed. The defendants continued to pay the reduced rent from 1941 to the beginning of 1945, by which time the flats were fully let, and they continued to pay the reduced rent thereafter. In September, 1945, the receiver of the plaintiff company investigated the matter and asked for arrears of £7916, suggesting that the liability created by the lease still existed, and that the agreement of 1940 was not supported by any consideration. The receiver then brought this friendly action to establish the legal position. He claimed £625, being the difference in rent for the two quarters ending 29 September and 25 December, 1945. *Held*—(i) A simple contract can in Equity vary a deed (i.e. the lease), though it had not done so here because the simple contract was not supported by consideration. (ii) As the agreement for the reduction of rent had been acted upon by the defendants, the plaintiffs were estopped in Equity from claiming the full rent from 1941 until early 1945 when the flats were fully let. After that time they were entitled to do so because the second agreement was only operative during the continuance of the conditions which gave rise to it. To this extent the limited claim of the receiver succeeded. If the receiver had sued for the balance of rent from 1941 he would have failed.

(140) *Tool Metal Manufacturing Co. Ltd* v. *Tungsten Electric Co. Ltd*, [1955] 2 All E.R. 657

The appellants were the registered proprietors of British letters patent. In April, 1938, they made a contract with the respondents whereby they gave the latter a licence to manufacture 'hard metal alloys' in accordance with the inventions which were the subject of patent. By the contract the respondents agreed to pay 'compensation' to the appellants if in any one month they sold more than a stated quantity of metal alloys.

Compensation was duly paid by the respondents until the outbreak of war in 1939 but thereafter none was paid. It was found as a fact that in 1942 the appellants agreed to suspend the enforcement of compensation payments pending the making of a new contract. In 1944 negotiations for such new contracts were begun but broke down. In 1945 the respondents sued the appellants for breach of contract and the appellants counter-claimed for payment of compensation as from 1 June, 1945. As regards the arguments on the counter-claim, it was eventually *held* by the Court of Appeal that the agreement of 1942 operated in equity to prevent the appellants demanding compensation until they had given reasonable notice to the respondents of their intention to resume their strict legal rights and that such notice had not been given.

In September, 1950, the appellants themselves issued a writ against the respondents claiming compensation as from 1 January, 1947. The respondents pleaded the equity raised by the agreement of 1942 and argued that reasonable notice of its termination had not been given. When this action reached the House of Lords it was *held*—affirming *Hughes* v. *Metropolitan Railway Co.* and the *High Trees Case*, that the agreement of 1942 operated in equity to suspend the appellants' legal rights to compensation until reasonable notice to resume them had been given. However, the counter-claim in the first action in 1945 amounted to such notice and since the appellants were not now claiming any compensation as due to them before 1 January, 1947, the appellants succeeded in this second action and were awarded £84,000 under the compensation clause.

Promissory estoppel: the meaning of reliance upon the promise

(141) *W.J. Alan & Co.* v. *El Nasr Export and Import Co.*, [1972] 2 All E.R. 127

A contract for the sale of coffee provided for the price expressed in Kenyan shillings to be paid by irrevocable letter of credit. The buyers procured a confirmed letter expressed in sterling and the sellers obtained part payment thereunder. While shipment was in progress sterling was devalued and the sellers claimed such additional sum as would bring the price up to the sterling equivalent of Kenyan shillings at the current rate. Orr, J. *held* that the buyers were liable to pay the additional sum as the currency of account was Kenyan shillings. On appeal by the buyers it was *held*—allowing the appeal—that the sellers by accepting payment in sterling had irrevocably waived their right to be paid in Kenyan currency or had accepted a variation of the sale contract, and that a party who has waived his rights cannot afterwards insist on them if the other party has acted on that belief differently from the way in which he would otherwise have acted; and the other party need not show that he has acted to his detriment. In the course of his judgment Lord Denning, M.R. said: '. . . if one party, by his conduct, leads another to believe that the strict rights arising under the contract will not be insisted on, intending that the other should act on that belief, and he does act on it, then the first party will not afterwards be allowed to insist on the strict legal rights when it would be inequitable for him to do so. . . . There may be no consideration moving from him who benefits by the waiver. There may be no detriment to him acting on it. There may be nothing in writing.

Nevertheless, the one who waives his strict rights cannot afterwards insist on them. His strict rights are at any rate suspended so long as the waiver lasts. He may on occasion be able to revert to his strict legal rights for the future by giving reasonable notice in that behalf, or otherwise making it plain by his conduct that he will thereafter insist on them. . . . I know that it has been suggested in some quarters that there must be a detriment. But I can find no support for it in the authorities cited by the judge. The nearest approach to it is the statement by Viscount Simonds in the *Tool Metal* case that the other must have been led "to alter his position" which was adopted by Lord Hodson in *Emmanuel Ayodeji Ajayi* v. *R. T. Briscoe (Nigeria) Ltd.'* [1964] 3 All E.R. 556. But that only means that he must have been led to act differently from what he otherwise would have done. And, if you study the cases in which the doctrine has been applied, you will see that all that is required is that one should have "*acted* on the belief induced by the other party". That is how Lord Cohen put it in the *Tool Metal* case and it is how I would put it myself.'

Comment. Since as in *High Trees* a tenant who only pays one-half of the rent cannot be said to be 'acting to his detriment' then 'detriment' cannot be a requirement of equitable estoppel. It is a requirement of estoppel at common law.

Promissory estoppel: does not operate to create new contractual rights but merely to suspend existing ones

(142) *Combe* v. *Combe*, [1951] 2 K.B. 215

The parties were married in 1915 and separated in 1939. In February, 1943, the wife obtained a decree *nisi* of divorce, and a few days later the husband entered into an agreement under which he was to pay his wife £100 per annum, free of income tax. The decree was made absolute in August, 1943. The husband did not make the agreed payments and the wife did not apply to the court for maintenance but chose to rely on the alleged contract. She brought this action for arrears under that contract. Evidence showed that her income was between £700 and £800 per annum and the defendant's was £650 per annum. Byrne, J., at first instance, held that, although the wife had not supplied consideration, the agreement was nevertheless enforceable, following the decision in the *High Trees*[139] case, as a promise made to be acted upon and in fact acted upon. *Held*— (i) That the *High Trees*[139] decision was not intended to create new actions where none existed before, and that it had not abolished the requirement of consideration in the formation of simple contracts. In such cases consideration was a cardinal necessity. (ii) In the words of Birkett, L.J., the doctrine was 'a shield not a sword', i.e. a defence to an action, not a cause of action. (iii) The doctrine applied to the modification of existing agreements by subsequent promises and had no relevance to the formation of a contract. (iv) It was not possible to find consideration in the fact that the wife forbore to claim maintenance from the court, since no such contractual undertaking by her could have been binding even if she had given it. Therefore this action by the wife must fail because the agreement was not supported by consideration.

Comment. Since the equitable doctrine is a 'shield not a sword' the sailors in *Stilk* v. *Myrick* (1809)[120], could presumably not have sued upon a promise to pay them extra wages even though they acted upon it.

Promissory estoppel: other applications

(143) *Durham Fancy Goods Ltd* v. *Michael Jackson (Fancy Goods) Ltd*, [1968] 2 All E.R. 987

On 18 September, 1967, the plaintiffs drew a bill of exchange on the first defendants in the following form, 'M. Jackson (Fancy Goods) Co.' The bill was signed by Mr Jackson who was the director and company secretary. The bill was dishonoured and the plaintiffs brought an action against Mr Jackson contending that by signing the form of acceptance he had committed a criminal offence under s. 108 of the Companies Act, 1948 and had made himself personally liable on the bill because he should either have returned the bill with a request that it be re-addressed to Michael Jackson (Fancy Goods) Ltd, or he should have accepted it 'M. Jackson (Fancy Goods) Ltd p.p. Michael Jackson (Fancy Goods) Ltd, Michael Jackson'. It was *held*—by Donaldson, J.—that the misdescription was in breach of s. 108 of the Companies Act, 1948, and that Mr Jackson was personally liable, under the section, to pay the bill. However, since the error was really that of the plaintiffs they were estopped from enforcing Mr Jackson's personal liability. The principle of equity upon which the promissory estoppel cases were based was applicable and barred the plaintiff's claim. That principle was formulated by Lord Cairns in *Hughes* v. *Metropolitan Railway Co.* (1877), 2 App. Cas. 439 at p. 448, and although in his enunciation Lord Cairns assumed a pre-existing contractual relationship between the parties, that was not essential provided that there was a pre-existing legal relationship which could in certain circumstances give rise to liabilities and penalties. Such a relationship was created by s. 108.

Comment. A holder other than the plaintiffs might have been able to bring an action against Mr Jackson under s. 108 since such a holder would not have been affected by the equity in that he would not have drawn the bill in an incorrect name. The provisions are now in s. 349, Companies Act, 1985.

(*Note:* s. 108 provided: '(1) every company . . . (c) shall have its name mentioned in legible characters . . . in all bills of exchange . . . purporting to be signed by or on behalf of the company . . . (4) If an officer of the company or any person on his behalf . . . (b) signs . . . on behalf of the company any bill of exchange . . . wherein its name is not mentioned in manner aforesaid . . . he shall be liable to a fine not exceeding £50, and shall further be personally liable to the holder of the bill of exchange . . . for the amount thereof unless it is duly paid by the company.')

Comment. A further application of the doctrine occurred in *Crabb* v. *Arun District Council*, [1975] 3 All E.R. 865 where Arun represented to Mr Crabb that he had a right of way across Arun's land which gave access to the public highway. It was held by the Court of Appeal that Arun could not go back on that promise after Mr Crabb had sold some of his land and had left himself without access to the public highway except by the right of way across Arun's land. He was granted an injunction to enforce the right. When promissory estoppel is used in this situation a plaintiff can raise it and indeed base his action upon it. Thus the expression of Birkett, L.J. in *Combe* v. *Combe*, 1951,[142] that the doctrine is 'a shield not a sword', is not always applicable where estoppel is used in situations other than the variation of contract rights.

Formalities: contracts which must be evidenced in writing: guarantee and indemnity: s. 4, Statute of Frauds, 1677

(144) *Mountstephen* v. *Lakeman* (1871), L.R. 7 Q.B. 196

The defendant was chairman of the Brixham Local Board of Health. The plaintiff, who was a builder and contractor, was employed in 1866 by the Board to construct certain main sewage works in the town. On 19 March, 1866, notice was given by the Board to owners of certain homes to connect their house drains with the main sewer within twenty-one days. Before the expiration of the twenty-one days Robert Adams, the surveyor of the Board, suggested to the plaintiff that he should make the connections. The plaintiff said he was willing to do the work if the Board would see him paid. On the 5 April, 1866, i.e. before the expiration of the twenty-one days, the plaintiff commenced work on the connections. However, before work commenced it appeared that the plaintiff had had an interview with the defendant at which the following conversation took place—

Defendant: 'What objection have you to making the connections?'
Plaintiff: 'I have none, if you or the Board will order the work or become responsible for the payment.'
Defendant: 'Go on Mountstephen and do the work and I will see you paid.'

The plaintiff completed the connections in April and May, 1866, and sent an account to the Board on 5 December, 1866. The Board disclaimed responsibility on the ground that they had never entered into any agreement with the plaintiff nor authorized any officer of the Board to agree with him for the performance of the work in question. It was *held*—that Lakeman had undertaken a personal liability to pay the plaintiff and had not given a guarantee of the liability of a third party, i.e. the board. In consequence Lakeman had given an indemnity which did not need to be in writing under s. 4 of the Statute of Frauds, 1677. The plaintiff was therefore entitled to enforce the oral undertaking given by the defendant.

Comment. Section 4 of the Statute of Frauds, 1677 provides that 'No action shall be brought . . . whereby to charge the defendant upon any special promise to answer for the debt default or miscarriage of another person . . . unless the agreement upon which such action shall be brought or some memorandum or note thereof shall be in writing and signed by the party to be charged therewith or some other person thereunto by him lawfully authorized'. It was held in *Birkmyr* v. *Darnell*, (1704) 1 Salk. 27 that the words 'debt default or miscarriage of *another person*' meant that the section applied only where there was some person other than the surety who was primarily liable.

Sale of Land: s. 40, Law of Property Act, 1925: memorandum in writing: description of parties

(145) *Carr* v. *Lynch*, [1900] 1 Ch. 613

The defendant was lessor of the Warden Arms, Kentish Town, which was leased to Charles Smith. In September, 1898, the premises were assigned to Arthur Jayne for the residue of the term. On the expiration of the lease Jayne applied to the defendant to grant him a further lease, and the defendant consented on condition that Jayne paid him £50. When Jayne paid the money he produced a memorandum which he had prepared and the defendant signed it. The memorandum read as follows: 'Dear Sir, In consideration of you having this day paid me the sum of £50, I hereby agree to grant you or your assigns a further lease of 24 years.' Before the new lease was to commence Jayne assigned the lease to the plaintiff, Arthur Carr, but the defendant refused to grant the new lease to Carr. This action was for specific performance of the agreement for a lease, and the defence was that the memorandum did not satisfy the Statute of Frauds because it did not sufficiently identify the parties. *Held*—The plaintiff succeeded. The memorandum was sufficient because the defendant had admitted that Jayne had paid him £50 on the day in question and the person who had paid was the person to get the lease according to the document. Therefore Jayne was adequately identified, and Carr, being Jayne's assignee, was entitled to a lease.

(146) *F. Goldsmith (Sicklesmere), Ltd* v. *Baxter*, [1969] 3 All E.R. 733

By an agreement dated 9 April, 1968, the defendant agreed to purchase a piece of land, cottage and buildings known as 'Shelley', Stanstead, Suffolk, from the plaintiff company. The memorandum of agreement was signed by a Mr Brewster, one of the company's directors, 'for and on behalf of Goldsmith Coaches (Sicklesmere) Limited'. Mr Brewster thought that this was the company's name and it did carry on business under that description. The property known as 'Shelley' was described in the particulars of sale and the memorandum of agreement stated that the vendor company, described as Goldsmith Coaches (Sicklesmere) Ltd, was the beneficial owner of it. The defendant's solicitors were subsequently unable to trace a company called Goldsmith Coaches (Sicklesmere) Ltd and the defendant refused to complete the purchase of property on the ground that since there was no vendor there was no contract. The company thereupon sued for specific performance. *Held*— by Stamp, J.—that specific performance would be granted. A contract was to be construed by reference to the surrounding circumstances or in the light of known facts. Accordingly it was clear that the name inserted in the memorandum of sale as being that of the vendor was merely an inaccurate description of the plaintiff company which was therefore a party to the contract and could easily be identified as such by reference to other characteristics.

'Looking at the memorandum alone, and without regard to the surrounding circumstances, I find that the person—the *persona ficta*— said to be the vendor has the following characteristics:

   (i) it is named Goldsmith Coaches (Sicklesmere), Ltd;
  (ii) its registered office is said to be at Sicklesmere;
 (iii) it has an agent called Brewster who claims to act for it;
 (iv) it is the beneficial owner of 'Shelley'.

Then, applying the rule that a contract is to be construed by reference to the surrounding circumstances, or in the light of the known facts, I find first, that there is no limited company which in law has the name Goldsmith Coaches (Sicklesmere), Ltd, but that the plaintiff company is often known as 'Goldsmith Coaches' and carries on business as a bus and coach contractor, and does so at Sicklesmere. Then I find, secondly, that the plaintiff company's registered office is at Sicklesmere, in the very place at which it carries on the bus and coach business. Thirdly, I find that the plantiff company has an agent called Brewster; and, fourthly, that it is the beneficial owner of 'Shelley'. I find in addition that there is no other company having those characteristics. Applying this process, if it be permissible, I conclude beyond peradventure that Goldsmith Coaches (Sicklesmere), Ltd, is no more, nor less than an inaccurate description of the plaintiff company, F. Goldsmith (Sicklesmere), Ltd. . . . In the absence of authority constraining me to do so—and none has been cited—I would find it impossible to hold that a company incorporated under the Companies Acts has no identity but by reference to its correct name, or that, unless an agent acts on its behalf by that name, or a name so nearly resembling it that it is obviously an error for that name, he acts for nobody. A limited company has in my judgment characteristics other than its name by reference to which it can be identified: for example, a particular business, and a particular place or places where it carries on business, particular shareholders, and particular directors.'

Sale of land: s. 40, Law of Property Act, 1925: the memorandum must contain all material terms: the concept of waiver

(147) *Tweddell* v. *Henderson*, [1975] 2 All E.R. 1096

Mr Henderson, a builder, agreed with Miss Tweddell, a potential purchaser, that she should buy a house when built on a plot of land at Tintagel for £8700. There was an oral agreement that Miss Tweddell should pay the purchase price in four instalments, the first when the footings of the house were built. Mr Henderson wrote to Miss Tweddell at a later stage saying that he had asked his solicitor to get a contract drawn up but this letter did not mention the system of payment. After a draft contract had been drawn up Mr Henderson said he could not go ahead with the sale unless Miss Tweddell could pay £9500 which she refused to do and Mr Henderson sold the house to somebody else. Miss Tweddell now claimed damages for breach of contract. It was *held*—by Plowman, V.C.—That the contract was not enforceable because there was not a sufficient memorandum in writing. In the course of his judgment Plowman, V.C. said: 'It seems to me that the provision that the purchase money was to be paid, not at the end of the day, when the bungalow had been completed and was ready for handing over, but by the four stages to which I have referred, is a material term in every relevant sense, and there is no reference to it anyway in the alleged memorandum.

'Accordingly, with some regret, because I think the plantiff has been hardly treated, I have come to the conclusion that the defence of s. 40 must succeed.'

(148) *Hawkins* v. *Price*, [1947] Ch. 645

On 31 January, 1946, the plaintiff and defendant entered into a bargain for the sale of a freehold bungalow and land. The plaintiff paid a deposit of £100, and the defendant signed a deposit receipt thus: 'Received of H.H. the sum of £100 being deposit on bungalow named "Oakdene", Station Road, Stoke Mandeville, Bucks, sold for £1000.' The plaintiff now sued for specific performance of the agreement, and it was discovered that there was a term that vacant possession be given by 31 March, 1946. This term was not mentioned in the deposit receipt. Nevertheless the plaintiff claimed that the said receipt was a sufficient memorandum to satisfy s. 40 of the Law of Property Act, 1925. *Held*—It was not, because—

(i) The deposit receipt did not contain reference to the fact that the sale was with vacant possession. Although it is not necessary that the memorandum should contain every term, it must at least contain all material terms. In the view of the court the question of vacant possession was material and not collateral.

(ii) The plaintiff suggested that since the term was solely for his benefit he could waive it. The court decided that the term was not solely for his benefit because, although it governed the date on which he could take possession, it also informed Mrs Price of how long she might remain in possession.

(iii) It was difficult for the plaintiff to waive the term because he was suing for specific performance with vacant possession.

Comment. It should be noted that in a subsequent case (*Farrell* v. *Green* (1974), 232 *Estates Gazette* 587 the court decided differently. The action was for specific performance of an oral contract for the sale of land supported by a memorandum in writing. Pennycuick, V.-C. decided that the memorandum need not contain terms which were implied by law; these were, he said, (1) completion within a reasonable time, and (2) vacant possession on completion. Although the memorandum was silent as to both, Pennycuick, V.-C. made an order for specific performance. This case suggests that although vacant possession is material, it will be implied, and that a written memorandum need not contain it.

(149) *Scott* v. *Bradley*, [1971] 1 All E.R. 538.

The plaintiff and defendant agreed that the defendant would sell her freehold property to the plaintiff for £5000. The plantiff agreed to pay half the defendant's legal costs but this was not recorded on the receipt. The plaintiff sought to enforce the contract and offered to pay half the defendant's legal costs of the sale. *Held*—by Plowman, J.—than on making this offer the plaintiff could enforce the contract.

Comment. This case illustrates that if the material term which is omitted is for the exclusive benefit of the defendant, then the court will allow the plaintiff to enforce the contract if he agrees to perform that omitted term.

Sale of land: s. 40, Law of Property Act, 1925: memorandum must be signed by the defendant

(150) *Caton* v. *Caton* (1867), L.R. 2 H.L. 127

A Mr Caton and a Mrs Henley proposed to marry, and decided to enter into a marriage settlement. A document was drafted as a basis for the marriage settlement and the names Caton and Henley appeared in it, but only for the purpose of showing what Mr Caton was to do and what Mrs Henley was to have under the agreement. The document was not signed by either of the parties. At the time when this action was brought a marriage settlement had to be evidenced in writing under the provisions of the Statute of Frauds, 1677, and this document was produced as a memorandum. *Held*—It was not a sufficient memorandum because, although the names of the parties appeared in the document, they did not appear as signatures intended to subscribe it.

Sale of land: s. 40, Law of Property Act, 1925: memorandum may be in a number of connected documents.

(151) *Pearce* v. *Gardner*, [1897] 1 Q.B. 688

The plaintiff brought this action to recover damages for breach of a contract by the defendant under the terms of which the defendant had agreed to sell the plaintiff certain gravel which was *in situ* on the land. At the trial the plaintiff put in evidence a letter signed by the defendant and commencing 'Dear Sir'. The letter did not contain the plaintiff's name. The plaintiff then put in evidence an envelope which had been used to post the letter, which showed the plaintiff's name and address. *Held*—The letter and the envelope together provided a memorandum sufficient to satisfy the Statute of Frauds.

Comment. Before documents can be connected so as to provide a memorandum, they must be *prima facie* connected as in the case of a letter and an envelope. (See also *Williams* v. *Lake* (1860), 2 E. & E. 349.) In this case the plaintiff put in evidence as a memorandum a letter similar to the one put forward in the above case. He was not able to produce an envelope, however, and the court *held* that the letter was not a memorandum sufficient to satisfy the Statute of Frauds.)

(152) *Timmins* v. *Moreland Street Property Ltd*, [1958] Ch. 110

The defendants agreed to buy certain property belonging to the plaintiff for £39,000 and gave him a cheque for £3900 as a deposit, the cheque being made payable to his solicitors. The plaintiff made out a signed deposit receipt which stated that the sum of £3900 was a deposit for the purchase of the property which was adequately described, and that the plaintiff agreed to sell for £39,000. Subsequently the defendants stopped the cheque and repudiated the contract. The plaintiff sued for breach of contract and the defendants pleaded absence of a memorandum under s. 40 of the Law of Property Act, 1925. The plaintiff claimed that a sufficient memorandum existed if the deposit receipt were read together with the cheque containing the defendants' signature. *Held*—The two documents could not be connected, because the cheque was made payable to the plaintiff's solicitors and there was no necessary connection between it and the deposit receipt.

Comment. (i) In addition the cheque contained no reference to the deposit receipt. It is unlikely that a cheque will ever refer to another document or transaction.

(ii) It is not necessary for one document to specifically refer to the other. Jenkins, L.J. said in *Timmins*: '. . . It is still indispensibly necessary, in order to justify the reading of documents together . . . that there should be a document signed by the party to be charged which, while not containing in itself all the necessary ingredients of the required memorandum, does contain some reference express or implied, to some other document or transaction.'

This passage was taken to be a correct statement of the modern law by the Privy Council in *Elias* v. *George Sahely & Co.*, [1982] 3 All E.R. 801. The case concerned the purchase of a property in Swan Street,

Bridgetown, Barbados. There was a letter containing all the material terms but this was not signed by the party to be charged,. i.e. the defendant. However, a deposit receipt was signed by his agent. If the letter and receipt could be connected there was an adequate memorandum. The Privy Council held that they could be connected. The deposit receipt did not refer specifically to the letter but it did refer to the transaction, being worded as follows: 'Received from Fauzi Elias the sum of $39,000 being deposit on property at Swan Street, B, town agreed to be sold by George Sahely & Co. B,dos Ltd to Fauzi Elias and/or his nominees.'

Sale of land: s. 40, Law of Property Act, 1925: effect at common law of absence of memorandum

(153) *Monnickendam* v. *Leanse* (1923), 39 T.L.R. 445

The plaintiff orally agreed to buy a house from the defendant and paid a deposit of £200. Later the plaintiff refused to go on with the contract and pleaded lack of memorandum in writing, though the defendant was always willing to complete. The plaintiff now sued to recover the deposit. *Held*—He could not recover the deposit.

Comment. The case illustrates that the difficulties arising out of the absence of a memorandum in writing are procedural rather than substantive. The contract, though unenforceable, is not wholly without effect, for in the above case the contract was raised as a defence to an action for the deposit. It is essential of course that the vendor be prepared to complete the bargain; he cannot deny the enforceability of the contract and yet claim its existence as a defence to the action for recovery of the deposit.

Sale of Land: s. 40(2), Law of Property Act, 1925: acts of part performance: nature of

(154) *Wakeham* v. *MacKenzie*, [1968] 2 All E.R. 783

Some two years after his wife's death a widower aged 72 orally agreed with the plaintiff, a widow of 67, that if she would move into his house and look after him for the rest of his life she should have the house (of which he was the owner) together with the contents on his death. It was also agreed that the plaintiff should pay her own board and buy her own coal.

The plaintiff gave up her council flat and moved into the widower's house and looked after him as agreed, paying for her board and coal. He died in February, 1966, but did not leave the house or contents to her. The executor of the widower's estate contended that if there was a contract no action could be brought upon it at common law because there was no memorandum in writing as required by s. 40 of the Law of Property Act, 1925, which was accepted. However in respect of the plaintiff's claim for the equitable remedy of specific performance the adequacy of her acts of part performance was in question. On this matter Stamp, J., *held*—

> I conclude from *Kingswood Estate Co. Ltd* v. *Anderson* [1962] 3 All E.R. 593 first that it is not the law that the acts of part performance relied on must be not only referable to a contract such as that alleged, but referable to no other title, the doctrine to that effect laid down by Warrington, L.J., in *Chaproniere* v. *Lambert* [1917] 2 Ch. 356 having been exploded; and secondly that the true rule is that the operation of acts of part performance requires only that the acts in question be such as must be referred to some contract and may be referred to the alleged one; that they prove the existence of some contract and one consistent with the contract alleged.

His Lordship accordingly made an order for specific performance of the oral agreement on which the plaintiff relied.

Comment. However, the agreement must not have been made 'subject to contract'. It was decided in *Cohen* v. *Nessdale Ltd*, [1981] 3 All E.R. 118 that a payment of ground rent by the purchaser under a contract to buy a lease was an act of part performance but the agreement could not be enforced by specific performance since it had been made 'subject to contract'.

(155) *Steadman* v. *Steadman*, [1973] 3 All E.R. 977

A husband and wife were married in 1962 and in 1963 bought a house which was conveyed into their joint names. Following proceedings in a magistrates' court in which the husband was ordered to pay maintenance, and a subsequent divorce, the wife applied under s. 17 of the Married Women's Property Act, 1882, for the house to be sold and that she should receive half the proceeds. Before the hearing, the parties made an oral agreement under which the wife would sell her interest in the house to the husband for £1500, that he would pay her £100 in respect of arrears of maintenance, the balance of the arrears being remitted and the maintenance order should be discharged except as to the payments in respect of the child. The magistrates varied the maintenance order and the husband paid the agreed £100 of the arrears. The Court of Appeal was asked to decide whether the husband could enforce the agreement for the transfer of the wife's interest in the house in consideration of his paying £1500. It was *held* that the husband's claim succeeded. (Edmund Davies, L.J. dissenting.) The agreement was one for the disposition of land within s. 40 of the Law of Property Act, 1925, but there had been sufficient acts of part performance by the husband in paying the agreed £100 of the maintenance arrears *together with announcing the agreement before magistrates*. That payment was unequivocally referable to some contract between the parties and evidence could be adduced to show what the contract was and that it included a term disposing of an interest in land. Dealing with the question of a payment of money as an act of part performance, Scarman, L.J. said—

> Accepting, as I believe we must, that the payment of purchase money is on the authorities not a sufficient part performance to let in oral evidence of a contract for the sale of land, I think this payment of £100 is to be distinguished from a payment of purchase money. Unlike purchase money it is not certain to be recovered if the contract fails to go forward; for it is paid on account of arrears of maintenance and would be greatly at risk if in the absence of an agreement the justices should be required to consider the husband's application for the remission of arrears. The husband by undertaking to pay this money on account of arrears altered his position significantly on the faith of the oral agreement.

Comment. This decision was affirmed in the House of Lords [1974] 2 All E.R. 977, their Lordships saying in particular that there was no general rule that the payment of a sum of money could never constitute part performance. There were, of course, other acts of part performance in *Steadman*, e.g. announcing the agreement to magistrates.

(156) *Re Gonin (deceased)*, [1977] 2 All E.R. 720

In this case a daughter tried to claim a contract under which she was to have her mother's house. There was no memorandum in writing and she pleaded acts of part performance. These were that she had left her lodgings in Stroud to come to live with her mother in her mother's home at Bromley and to look after her on the basis (she said) of a contract for the property. Her mother died intestate and did not leave her the property by will so that the daughter's only method of getting the property was to establish a contract. It was *held*—by Walton, J.—that her acts of part performance did not necessarily suggest the existence of a contract. In the course of his judgment he said: 'Anyway, I do not think that there can be any doubt whatsoever but that the learned judges' alternative ground in *Wakeham* v. *Mackenzie*, 1968[154], namely that the conduct of a stranger in giving up a council tenancy and moving into the house of somebody else pointed irresistibly to the fact that there was some contract in relation to the secured occupation of that house by the stranger so moving in, is undeniably correct.

'Applying the law as I see it, therefore, to the present case, are the acts done by Miss Gonin such as in themselves must be referable to some contract concerning The Gables? I regret that in my opinion they are not. Here, . . . Miss Gonin had no home of her own to give up, she was simply billetted out at Stroud, and she did not move into the house of strangers, she went back to the house which had, down to 1940, been and doubtlessly still was in her mind's eye, home, back to her parents, back to the same kind of position and standing which she had had before she had left home because of the call of the war. This does not seem to me to indicate the likelihood of any contract at all, let alone one concerning land.'

Minors: necessaries: the general test

(157) *Nash* v. *Inman*, [1908] 2 K.B. 1

The plaintiff was a Savile Row tailor and the defendant was an infant undergraduate at Trinity College, Cambridge. The plaintiff sent his agent to Cambridge because he had heard that the defendant was spending money freely, and might be the sort of person who would be interested in high-class clothing. As a result of the agent's visit, the plaintiff supplied the defendant with various articles of clothing to the value of £145 0s. 3d. during the period October, 1902 to June, 1903. The clothes included eleven fancy waistcoats. The plaintiff now sued the infant for the price of the clothes. Evidence showed that the defendant's father was in a good position, being an architect with a town and country house, and it could be said that the clothes supplied were suitable to the defendant's position in life. However, his father proved that the defendant was amply supplied with such clothes when the plaintiff delivered the clothing now in question. *Held*—The plaintiff's claim failed because he had not established that the goods supplied were necessaries.

(158) *Elkington* v. *Amery*, [1936] 2 All E.R. 86

The defendant was an infant and the son of a former cabinet minister. He purchased from the plaintiffs an engagement ring and an eternity ring, the court treating the latter as a wedding ring. He also purchased a lady's gold vanity bag. The Court of Appeal treated the two rings as being necessaries, but did not accept that the vanity bag was a necessary because there was no evidence to show that it was purchased in respect of the engagement.

Minors: beneficial contracts

(159) *Roberts* v. *Gray*, [1913] 1 K.B. 520

The defendant wished to become a professional billiards player and entered into an agreement with the plaintiff, a leading professional, to go on a joint tour. The plaintiff went to some trouble in order to organize the tour, but a dispute arose between the parties and the defendant refused to go. The plaintiff now sued for damages of £6000. *Held*—The contract was for the infant's benefit, being in effect for his instruction as a billiards player. Therefore the plaintiff could sustain an action for damages for breach of contract, and damages of £1500 were awarded.

(160) *Chaplin* v. *Leslie Frewin (Publishers)*, [1965] 3 All E.R. 764

The plaintiff, the infant son of a famous father, made a contract with the defendants under which they were to publish a book written for him, telling his life story and entitled 'I Couldn't Smoke the Grass on my Father's Lawn'. The plaintiff sought to avoid the contract on the ground that the book gave an inaccurate picture of his approach to life. *Held*— Amongst other things—that the contract was binding if it was for the infant's benefit. The time to determine that question was when the contract was made and at that time it was for the infant's benefit and could not be avoided.

Comment. (i) Although this was not a contract of service it could be regarded as analogous to one, and was for the plaintiff's benefit because although he had a ghost writer the publishing contract could have helped him to make a start as an author. So the court still felt it necessary to use the contract of service analogy and not merely say that the contract was beneficial because it made Mr Chaplin money.

(ii) In *Denmark Productions* v. *Boscobel Productions* (1967), 111 Sol. J. 715 Widgery, J., held that a contract by which a minor appoints managers and agents to look after his business affairs is, in modern conditions, necessary if he is to earn his living and rise to fame, and if it is for his benefit it will be upheld by analogy with a contract of service.

Minors: trading contracts are not binding on a minor unless exceptionally they are analogous to a contract of service

(161) *Mercantile Union Guarantee Corporation* v. *Ball*, [1937] 2 K.B. 498

The purchase on hire-purchase terms of a motor lorry by an infant carrying on business as a haulage contractor was *held* not to be a contract for necessaries, but a trading contract by which the infant could not be bound.

Comment. (i) It would be possible for the owner to recover the lorry without the assistance of s. 3 of the Minors' Contracts Act, 1987 because a hire-purchase contract is a contract of bailment not a sale. Thus, ownership does not pass when the goods are delivered.

(ii) It can be assumed from this case that the minor would not have been liable either for breach of a contract of carriage of goods in his lorry.

Beneficial contracts: the subject matter of the contract is not decisive

(162) *De Francesco* v. *Barnum* (1890), 45 Ch. D. 430

Two infants bound themselves in contract to the plaintiff for seven years to be taught stage dancing. The infants agreed that they would not accept any engagements without his consent. They later accepted an engagement with Barnum and the plaintiff sued Barnum for interfering with the contractual relationship between himself and the infants, and also to enforce the apprenticeship deed against the infants and to obtain damages for its breach. The contract was, of course, for the infants' benefit and was *prima facie* binding on them. However, when the court considered the deed in greater detail, it emerged that there were certain onerous terms in it. For example the infants bound themselves not to marry during the apprenticeship; the payment was hardly generous, the plaintiff agreeing to pay them 9d. per night and 6d. for matinee appearances for the first three years, and 1s. per night and 6d. for matinee performances during the remainder of the apprenticeship. The plaintiff did not undertake to maintain them whilst they were unemployed and did not undertake to find them engagements. The infants could also be engaged in performances abroad at a fee of 5s. per week. Further the plaintiff could terminate the contract if he felt that the infants were not suitable for the career of dancer. It appeared from the contract that the infants were at the absolute disposal of the plaintiff. *Held*—The deed was an unreasonable one and was therefore unenforceable against the infants. Barnum could not, therefore, be held liable, since the tort of interference with a contractual relationship presupposes the existence of an enforceable contract.

(163) *Clements* v. *L. & N.W. Railway*, [1894] 2 Q.B. 482

Clements, a minor, became a porter with the railway company and agreed to join the company's insurance scheme and to forego his rights under the Employers' Liability Act, 1880. He sustained an injury at work and claimed under the company's scheme. He now made a claim under the Act on the grounds that the contract was not for his benefit since it deprived him of an action under the Act. The company's scheme was on the whole a favourable one because it covered more injuries than the statute but the scale of compensation was lower. *Held*—The contract as a whole was for the infant's benefit and was binding on him. He had no claim under the Act.

Comment. (i) A minor cannot expect that every term in a contract will be beneficial. In this case the terms offered to the minor were the *usual terms* of employment offered to all porters with the company and they were not harsh and oppressive as they were, e.g. in *De Francesco* v. *Barnum*.[162]

(ii) Although a contract of service is binding on a minor as a beneficial contract, some employment protection benefits are not available to him, e.g. by reason of s. 81, Employment Protection (Consolidation) Act, 1978 a minor is not entitled to a redundancy payment. He can, however, make a claim for unfair dismissal.

Title to property: non-necessary goods

(164) *Stocks* v. *Wilson*, [1913] 2 K.B. 235

An infant obtained furniture from the plaintiff by falsely stating that he was of full age. *Held*—The property in the furniture passed to the infant, under the Infants Relief Act, 1874. Even if he sold the property the infant could not be sued in conversion. The infant had sold part of the furniture to a third party for £30, and Lush, J., *held* that the plaintiff could recover this sum from the infant by applying the equitable principle of restitution.

Comment. Pearce v. *Brain*,[168] supports *Stocks* v. *Wilson* because, if the property in the car had not passed to the infant, there would have been total failure of consideration, thus enabling him to recover his motorcycle. Although a contract for non-necessary goods is absolutely void, the property in the goods passes by delivery coupled with the seller's intention to pass the ownership to the minor. Where a contract is void, e.g. for mistake as to the identity of the other party, then ownership in the goods does not pass (see p. 229) because in that case the seller has no intention to pass the property to the person who receives it.

Minors: contracts binding unless repudiated

(165) *Steinberg* v. *Scala (Leeds) Ltd*, [1923] 2 Ch. 452

The plaintiff, Miss Steinberg, purchased shares in the defendant company and paid certain sums of money on application, on allotment and on one call. Being unable to meet future calls, she repudiated the contract whilst still an infant and claimed—

(*a*) rectification of the Register of Members to remove her name therefrom, thus relieving her from liability on future calls; and

(*b*) the recovery of the money already paid.

The company agreed to rectify the register and issue was joined on the claim to recover the money paid.

Held—The claim under (*b*) above failed because there had not been total failure of consideration. The shares had some value and gave some rights, even though the plaintiff had not received any dividends and the shares had always stood at a discount on the market.

(166) *Davies* v. *Beynon-Harris* (1931), 47 T.L.R. 424

An infant took a lease of a flat a fortnight before attaining his majority. Three years later he was sued for arrears of rent and claimed that he could avoid the contract. *Held*—He was liable to pay the rent because the lease was voidable not void, and was now binding on him because he had not repudiated it during minority or within a reasonable time thereafter.

Comment. An infant cannot take a legal estate in land (s. 1(6), Law of Property Act, 1925). This prevents him from taking a lease at law. However, he does obtain an equitable interest and must observe the covenants in the lease so long as he retains a beneficial interest in the property.

(167) *Goode* v. *Harrison* (1821), 5 B. & Ald. 147

A partner who was a minor, took no steps to avoid a partnership contract upon attaining his majority, and was held liable for the debts of the firm incurred after he came of age.

Minors: legal consequences of contracts

(168) *Pearce* v. *Brain*, [1929] 2 K.B. 310

Pearce, an infant, exchanged his motor-cycle for a motor-car belonging to Brain. The infant had little use out of the car, and had in fact driven it only 70 miles in all when it broke down because of serious defects in the back axle. Pearce now sued to recover his motor-cycle, claiming that the consideration had wholly failed. *Held*—(*a*) That a contract for the exchange of goods, whilst not a sale of goods, is a contract for the supply of goods, and that if the goods are not necessaries, the contract was void if with a minor. (Now voidable Type A). (*b*) The car was not a necessary good and therefore the contract was void. (*c*) Even so the infant could only recover the motor-cycle in the same circumstances as he could recover money paid under a void contract, i.e. if the consideration had wholly failed. The court considered that the infant had received a benefit under the contract, albeit small, and that he could not recover the motor-cycle.

(169) *Corpe* v. *Overton* (1833), 10 Bing. 252

An infant agreed to enter into a partnership and deposited £100 with the defendant as security for the due performance of the contract. The infant rescinded the contract before the partnership came into being. *Held*—He could recover the £100 because he had received no benefit, having never been a partner.

Comment. It should not be assumed that because the partnership begins and the minor then avoids it that he cannot recover any of his capital. The partnership suffers a technical dissolution and the rules of dissolution prevail. In *Lovell and Christmas* v. *Beauchamp*, [1894] A.C. 607, Lord Herschell, L.C. said that a minor partner was not personally liable for the debts of the firm because they would not be for necessaries. However, he might get some of his capital back. As Lord Herschell said: 'The adult partner is, however, entitled to insist that the partnership assets shall be applied in payment of the liabilities of the partnership and that until these are provided for no part of them shall be received by the infant partner. . . .'

(170) *Leslie (R) Ltd* v. *Sheill*, [1914] 3 K.B. 607

Sheill, an infant, borrowed £400 from R. Leslie, Ltd, moneylenders, by fraudulently representing that he was of full age. The contract was void under s. 1 of the Infants Relief Act, 1874 (now repealed) and the plaintiffs sued for the return of the money, either as damages for the tort of deceit, or as money had and received to the plaintiff's use, this latter being an action in quasi-contract. *Held*—Neither claim could succeed because they were attempts to circumvent the Act and the infant was entitled to retain the money advanced. With regard to the equitable doctrine of restitution, it was suggested that, since the money had been spent and could not be precisely traced, restitution was not possible; for to order restitution would mean that the infant would have to pay an equivalent sum out of his present or future resources, and this would be closer to enforcing a void contract than to granting equitable restitution. The court in this case suggested that 'Restitution ends where repayment begins', i.e. unless the actual property passing under the contract can be recovered, the remedy of restitution does not lie to recover money or property received in its stead.

Comment. (i) In this sort of case s. 3 of the Minors' Contracts Act, 1987 would allow restitution subject to the difficulty of tracing the money.

(ii) In *Burnard* v. *Haggis* (1863), 14 C.B.N.S. 45 Haggis was an undergraduate and hired the plaintiff's mare for riding. The plaintiff warned the defendant that the mare was not to be used for 'jumping or larking'. The defendant allowed a friend to ride the mare and the latter put the mare at a fence, in consequence of which the mare was impaled on a stake and died. The plaintiff sued the defendant in trespass. *Held*— The infant was liable, though the trespass actually happened because there had been a contract, yet the act of jumping the mare was just as distinct from the contract as if the defendant had run a knife into her and killed her. Therefore the defendant's infancy, which might have been a defence in contract, did not apply in this action for pure tort.

Burnard v. *Haggis* shows that a minor who hires a car and damages it by negligence in the course of a normal journey is liable for breach of contract and also in tort. If the contract of hiring is not regarded as a necessary contract the law will not allow an action for damages for breach of contract, nor will it allow the action in tort because that would circumvent the Minors' Contracts Act, 1987 if the contract has not been ratified after the age of majority has been reached. However, if as in this case, the minor does something which is wholly outside the acts which the contract envisages, as where, e.g. he hires a car and enters it for a racing event, such as a hill climb thus causing it damage, or if he sells it, then obviously an action in tort would be allowed.

(171) *Coutts & Co.* v. *Browne-Lecky*, [1947] K.B. 104

The first defendant, an infant, had been permitted to overdraw his account with the plaintiffs, who were bankers. The overdraft was guaranteed by the second and third defendants, who were adults. The overdraft was not repaid and the plaintiffs now sued the adult guarantors. *Held*—Since the loan to the infant was void under the Infants Relief Act, 1874 (now repealed) the infant could not be in default because he was not liable to repay the loan. Since the essence of a guarantee is that the guarantor is liable for the default or miscarriage of the principal debtor, it followed that the adult guarantors could not be liable. The action therefore failed.

Comment. (i) Had the contract been one of indemnity the adult defendants would have been liable, because, under a contract of indemnity, the person giving the indemnity is in effect the principal debtor and his liability does not depend on the default of any other person. (See *Yeoman Credit Ltd* v. *Latter*, [1961] 1 W.L.R. 828.)

(ii) In any case s. 2 of the Minors' Contracts Act, 1987 renders even a guarantee enforceable.

Registered companies: capacity to contract: *ultra vires* rule: application of s. 35 Companies Act, 1985

(172) *International Sales & Agencies* v. *Marcus*, [1982] 3 All E.R. 551

The second defendant in this case, Bentinck Securities Ltd which was owned by Mr Marcus, made a loan of £30,000 to a Mr Fancy. Mr Fancy was a major shareholder in International Sales & Agencies and also in the second plaintiff, Janthorpe Properties Ltd. He was the dominant director in both companies. Mr Munsey, who was also a shareholder and a director of ISA and Janthorpe, was a friend of Mr Marcus. Mr Fancy died insolvent. The loan of £30,000 was not repaid. However, Mr Fancy had told Mr Marcus prior to his death that Mr Munsey would see that the loan was repaid if anything happened to Mr Fancy. Shortly after Mr Fancy's death his widow and their son Ismat were made directors of ISA and Janthorpe but Mr Munsey assumed control of the companies and become the dominant director. He arranged for cheques to be drawn on ISA and Janthorpe to the value of £30,000 to repay Bentinck. Mrs Fancy and Ismat, together with other shareholders, on discovering what had been done brought the two companies into court to recover the money.

Mr Justice Lawson had no difficulty in deciding that the payments were *ultra vires*. The company had a standard form objects clause allowing it to draw cheques but the payment of money is not an independent transaction. It is always related to something else and here the payment was a mere handout. The company's money had not been used for its business but had been given away to a person who was in no way connected with it. This was *ultra vires*. The transactions were void and the money recoverable.

Furthermore, Mr Munsey was in breach of his fiduciary duty to the company as a director. He was, in effect, a constructive trustee of its funds and he broke that trust in making the payments. Mr Marcus was aware, and Bentinck was also aware through him, of this breach and therefore both Mr Marcus and Bentinck were also liable to replace the companies funds as constructive trustees having intermeddled with what was in effect trust property. In Mr Justice Lawson's view this decided the matter and allowed the company to recover its money. However, an amended defence had been entered on the basis that the defendants were protected by what is now s. 35, Companies Act, 1985. The judge held that the section did not apply to situations of constructive trust but since the section had been raised he made a number of observations on it as set out below.

(*a*) Since the defendants were not 'dealing' with ISA and Janthorpe, the section could not apply. They were dealing with Mr Munsey. The company's cheques were a mere vehicle of his personal generosity to Mr Marcus.

(*b*) The defendants were not acting in good faith. The burden of proof in this matter was upon the plaintiffs and not upon the defendants. However, a lack of good faith can be found, said the judge, in proof of a person's actual knowledge that the transaction is *ultra vires*, or where it can be shown that in all the circumstances the person concerned could not have been unaware that he was party to an *ultra vires* transaction. There was ample evidence in this case of a lack of good faith which, again, would prevent the section from applying.

(*c*) However, and most importantly, the judge did decide that in the circumstances of the case the transaction had been decided on by the directors within the meaning of what is now s. 35, although, of course, only one director had made the decision. Nevertheless, as the dominant director who was the sole effective director to whom all actual authority to act for the companies had been effectively delegated, the judge felt that this aspect of the section had been satisfied in terms of the cheques written by Mr Munsey. This is an important ruling and one which should help outsiders when dealing with a dominant director in a company's management.

Comment. The decision in *Rolled Steel*[178] would operate here to say that the 'power' to write cheques was in fact an object and that the cheques had not been written in an *ultra vires* way. However, they were for an improper purpose and not for the benefit of the company and since Mr Marcus and Bentinck knew this, the amount of the cheques could have been recovered by the company. If they had not known, *Rolled Steel*[178] would have prevented recovery of the money.

Registered companies capacity to contract: the *ultra vires* rule: the principles of the common law

(173) *Ashbury Railway Carriage & Iron Co.* v. *Riche* (1875), L.R. 7 H.L. 653

The company bought a concession for the construction of a railway system in Belgium, and entered into an agreement whereby Messrs Riche were to construct a railway line. Messrs Riche commenced the work, and the company paid over certain sums of money in connection with the contract. The company later ran into difficulties, and the shareholders wished the directors to take over the contract in a personal capacity, and indemnify the shareholders. The directors thereupon repudiated the contract on behalf of the company, and Messrs Riche sued for breach of contract. The case turned on whether the company was engaged in an *ultra vires* activity in building a complete railway system, because if so, the contract it had made with Messrs Riche would be *ultra vires* and void, and the claim against the company would fail. The objects clause of the company's memorandum stated that it was established—

'to make or sell or lend on hire railway carriages, wagons and all kinds of railway plant, fittings, machinery and rolling stock; to carry on the business of mechanical engineers and general contractors, to purchase and sell as merchants timber, coal, metal and other materials, and to buy and sell such materials on commission or as agents.'

The House of Lords *held* that the purchase of the concession to build a complete railway system from Antwerp to Tournai was *ultra vires* and void because it was not within the objects of the company. The words empowering the company to carry on the business of general contracting must be construed *ejusdem generis* with the preceding words, and must therefore be restricted to contracting in the field of plant, fittings and machinery only. The contract with Messrs Riche was therefore void, and the directors were entitled to repudiate it. It was also stated that even if all the shareholders had assented to the contract, it would still have been void because there can be no ratification of an *ultra vires* contract.

Comment. This strict interpretation of an objects clause contrasts sharply with the more modern approach seen in *Re New Finance and Mortgage Co. Ltd*, [1975] 1 All E.R. 684. In that case the memorandum of N Ltd stated its objects to be to carry on business as 'Financiers, capitalists, concessionaires, bankers, commercial agents, mortgage brokers, financial agents and advisers, exporters and importers of goods and merchandise of all kinds and merchants generally'. N Ltd carried on a petrol filling service station business which went into liquidation owing Total some £24,000 for petrol. The liquidator rejected T's proof as *ultra vires*. It was *held* that the words 'and merchants generally' were wide enough to cover the petrol filling service station business. T's claim was therefore good. It should also be noted that the decision in *Ashbury* would almost certainly go in favour of Riche now since the transaction was decided on by the directors and presumably s. 35 of the Companies Act, 1985 would apply.

(174) *Re Jon Beauforte*, [1953] Ch. 131

The company was authorized by its memorandum to carry on the business of costumiers, tailors, drapers, haberdashers, milliners and the like. It decided to manufacture veneered wall panels, and for this purpose had a factory erected, and ordered and was supplied with veneers. It was clear that the contracts for the erection of the factory and supply of veneers were *ultra vires* and void, but one of the questions before the court was whether the liquidator of the company had been correct in disallowing a claim made by a supplier of coke. The supplier argued that the coke might have been used in the good side of the business, and that he did not know that the coke was to be used for an *ultra vires* purpose. The court decided against him because the order for coke was given on headed paper describing the company as 'veneered panel manufacturers'. From this the coke supplier was deemed to know that the contract was *ultra vires*, because everyone is deemed to know the contents of the memorandum of association of a registered company, which is registered at the Companies' Registry, Cardiff, and can be inspected.

Comment. (i) This doctrine of constructive notice of a company's objects is now well established and yet it is based on the assumption that, because inspection is possible, it should always be made before contracts are entered into. However, business would grind to a halt if this sort of inquiry were made every time a contract was made; it does not accord, therefore, with normal business practice.

(ii) Where the transaction is decided on by the directors (as it was here) so that s. 35 of the Companies Act, 1985 can be applied, there is no constructive notice of the contents of the memorandum and articles. The coke supplier would now have succeeded.

(175) *Deuchar v. The Gas Light and Coke Co.*, [1925] A.C. 691

The plaintiff was a shareholder in the defendant company and was also the secretary of a company which supplied the defendants with caustic soda. The plaintiff sought a declaration from the court that the manufacture of caustic soda and chlorine by the defendants, and the erection of a factory for the purpose, was *ultra vires* the company. He also asked for an injunction to restrain the defendants from manufacturing caustic soda and chlorine. Astbury, J., at first instance, had found that the activities were fairly incidental to the powers given in the objects clause, and the Court of Appeal affirmed this decision. On appeal to the House of Lords it appeared that the defendants derived their powers from a special Act of Parliament, the Gas Light and Coke Companies Act, 1868, which gave them power to make and supply gas and deal with and sell by-products. The Act authorized the conversion of the by-products into a marketable state. One of the residuals of gas-making was naphthalene which could be converted into beta-naphthol and profitably sold, conversion being by the use of caustic soda. The company had formerly purchased this from the company of which the plaintiff was secretary, but later erected a factory on their land and began to make it themselves, though they only made what they required for their own use and did not make caustic soda for resale. Chlorine was a by-product of the manufacture of caustic soda, and the chlorine, it was admitted, was converted into bleaching powder and sold. The House of Lords *held* that the manufacture of caustic soda was fairly incidental to the company's powers, and although the sale of the bleaching powder was not incidental, the matter was trivial and on the basis of the maxim *de minimis non curat lex* (the law takes no account of trifling matters) the court would not interfere.

Registered companies: the *ultra vires* rule: evasion by means of concluding clauses in the memorandum of association

(176) *Cotman* v. *Brougham*, [1918] A.C. 514

The parties to this action were liquidators. Cotman was liquidator of the Essequibo Rubber Estates Ltd, and Brougham was liquidator of Anglo-Cuban Oil Co. It appeared that E underwrote the shares in A-C although the main clause of E's objects clause was to develop rubber estates abroad. However, a sub-clause allowed E to promote companies and deal in the shares of other companies and gave numerous other powers, though as it stood this would have given only a power to invest in companies concerned in the development of rubber production. However, the final clause of E's objects clause said in effect that each sub-clause should be considered as an independent main object. The E Company, not having paid for the shares which it had agreed to under-write, was put on the list of contributories of A-C, and E's liquidator asked that his company be removed from that list because the contract to underwrite was *ultra vires* and void. *Held*—by the House of Lords—that it was not, and that the E Company was liable to pay for the shares underwritten. The final clause of E's objects clause meant that each object could be pursued alone, because the Registrar had accepted the memorandum in this form and had registered the company. All the judges of the House of Lords deplored the idea of companies being registered with an objects clause in this wide form, and thought that the matter ought to have been raised by *mandamus* by the Registrar refusing to register the company. However, since the certificate of incorporation had been issued, it was conclusive; and matters concerning the company's registration could not be gone into.

(177) *Bell Houses Ltd* v. *City Wall Properties Ltd*, [1966] 2 All E.R. 674

The plaintiff company claimed £20,000 as commission under an alleged contract with the defendant company for the introduction of the latter to a financier who would lend the defendant company £1,000,000 for property development. As a preliminary issue the defendant company alleged that the contract was *ultra vires* and could not be enforced against them.

The principal business of the plaintiff company was the development of housing estates, and therefore the occasional raising of finance formed a necessary part of its activities. In consequence the company had obtained valuable knowledge of various sources of finance and because of this the company was able to arrange finance for the defendants. The defendants contended that the plaintiff company, in arranging finance for an outside organization, was, in effect, embarking on a new type of business, i.e. 'mortgage broking', and since this was not expressly included in the objects, nor reasonably incidental thereto, it was *ultra vires*. One of the sub-clauses in the objects clause of the plaintiff company was as follows: 'To carry on any other trade or business *whatsoever* which can *in the opinion of the board of directors* be *advantageously* carried on by (the company) in connection with, or as ancillary to, any of the above businesses or the general business of the (company).' *Held*—by the Court of Appeal—that the alleged contract was *intra vires* in particular because of the clause set out above. In the court's view the *bona fide* opinion of the board, in this case represented by the managing director who arranged the finance, that the contract could be advantageously carried on with the company's principal business, was enough no matter how unreasonable in the *objective* sense that opinion might seem to be.

Comment. The case illustrates that infringement of the *ultra vires* rule can be pleaded by both parties since the plaintiffs were claiming commission on a loan procured for the defendants under a contract and it was the defendants who pleaded (unsuccessfully) that the contract was *ultra vires*.

(178) *Rolled Steel Products (Holdings) Ltd* v. *British Steel Corporation*, [1985] 2 W.L.R. 908

In this case the Court of Appeal decided that a guarantee of a debt by Rolled Steel which another company, Scottish Sheet Steel, owed to the British Steel Corporation was *intra vires* because, although the guarantee was in no way for the purposes of Rolled Steel and not for its benefit, the clause in its objects clause allowing it to give guarantees had been converted into an object because of a *Cotman*-type clause which was also contained in the memorandum. However, since British Steel Corporation knew that the guarantee was not for the benefit of Rolled Steel but was only given to support a personal guarantee of the managing director of Scottish Sheet Steel of the debt of that company, it was not enforceable. The transaction was therefore *intra vires*, i.e. within the company's capacity, but invalid because made for an improper purpose known to British Steel Corporation. The transaction was not, therefore, *ultra vires* and void. If it had been then it would be unenforceable by anyone, whether they knew of the improper purpose or not.

This decision, then, makes the transaction good except for those who know of the improper purpose and it goes a long way to eliminate the *ultra vires* rule.

Comment. (i) Since modern companies have very long objects clauses and since this case decides that each clause is an object, companies will have *capacity* to do anything human beings can do. Even if the directors exercise the company's objects for improper purposes the transaction will still be good unless the other party *knows* of the improper purpose which often he will not.

(ii) In view of the decision in *Rolled Steel*, s. 35 would seem to be redundant in that it only operates when a transaction is *ultra vires*. As we have seen, the modern company with its long objects clause and a concluding *Cotman* or *Bell Houses* clause will, it seems, hardly ever do anything *ultra vires*.

However, s. 35 does have a place, as the case of *TCB* v. *Gray*, [1986]

1 All E.R. 587 shows. In that case a director delegated his power to issue a debenture giving a security to a lender over the company's property, to an agent. The articles of the company said that a debenture should be *signed by a director personally*. The loan was nevertheless good under what is now s. 35. The lender had no constructive notice of the articles, nor had he actual notice and acted in good faith. He could assume, therefore, that the security was valid. Section 35 is, therefore, still useful to overcome internal irregularities which have nothing to do with activities which are beyond the company's objects clause.

Contractual mistake: an operative mistake must be one of fact not law

(179) *Sharp Bros and Knight* v. *Chant*, [1917] 1 K.B. 771

Landlord and tenant agreed that the rent of a certain small house should be increased by the sum of 6d. per week. The tenant paid this increased rent for some time and it was then discovered that Rent Restriction legislation prevented the landlord from recovering any increase in rent he might make on certain properties of which the small house in question was one. *Held*—The tenant had paid the extra rent under a mistake of law, and could not sue for its return or deduct it from future payments of rent.

Comment. Here the court said that there was a mistake of law but see *Solle* below where the majority of the Court of Appeal held in somewhat similar circumstances that there was an actionable mistake of fact.

Common mistake: approach of equity to common mistake: rescission on terms

(180) *Solle* v. *Butcher*, [1949] 2 All E.R. 1107

Butcher had agreed to lease a flat in Beckenham to Solle at a yearly rental of £250, the lease to run for seven years. Both parties had acted on the assumption that the flat, which had been substantially reconstructed so as to be virtually a new flat, was no longer controlled by the Rent Restriction legislation then in force. If it were so controlled, the maximum rent payable would be £140 per annum. Nevertheless Butcher would have been entitled to increase that rent by charging 8 per cent of the cost of repairs and improvements which would bring the figure up to about £250 per annum, the rent actually charged, if he had served a statutory notice on Solle before the new lease was executed. No such notice was in fact served. Actually they both for a time mistakenly thought that the flat was decontrolled when this was not the case. Solle realized the mistake after some two years, and sought to recover the rent he had overpaid and to continue as tenant for the balance of the seven years as a statutory tenant at £140 per annum. Butcher counter-claimed for rescission of the lease in Equity. It was *held* by a majority of the Court of Appeal that the mistake was one of *fact* and not of law, i.e. the fact that the flat was still within the provisions of the Rent Acts, and this was a bilateral mistake as to quality which would not invalidate the contract at common law. However, on the counter-claim for rescission, it was *held* that the lease could be rescinded even though it had been executed. In order not to dispossess Solle, the court offered him the following alternatives—

(*a*) to surrender the lease entirely; or

(*b*) to remain in possession as a mere licensee until a new lease could be drawn up after Butcher had had time to serve the statutory notice which would allow him to add a sum for repairs to the £140 which would bring the lawful rent up to £250 per annum.

Comment: It is impossible to say at the present time what are the limits of this case. Equitable remedies are discretionary and it is not certain whether it applies to a contract for the sale of goods, nor whether it requires some form of sharp practice before it is implemented.

(181) *Cooper* v. *Phibbs* (1867), L.R. 2 H.L. 149

Cooper agreed to take a lease of a fishery from Phibbs, his uncle's daughter. Unknown to either party, because of a mix-up in family property, Cooper already had a life interest in the fishery and now brought this action to set aside the lease and for delivery up of the lease. *Held—* The agreement must be set aside on the grounds of common or identical bilateral mistake. However, since Equity has the power to give ancillary relief, Phibbs was given a lien on the fishery for the improvements she had made to it during the time she believed it to be hers. This lien could be discharged by Cooper paying Phibbs the value of the improvements.

Comment. This is an example of the grant of rescission on terms. Although in this case a person had bought his own property and could successfully ask for rescission, he was required to pay for the improvements. A further example of rescission on terms is seen in *Solle* v. *Butcher*[180] in view of the alternatives offered to Solle.

Mistake: documents mistakenly signed: relevance of signer's negligence

(182) *Saunders (Executrix of the Estate of Rose Maud Gallie)* v. *Anglia Building Society*, [1970] 3 All E.R. 961

Mrs Gallie, a widow aged 78 years, signed a document which a Mr Lee told her was a deed of gift of her house to her nephew, Walter Parkin. She did not read the document but believed what Lee had told her. In fact the document was an assignment by sale of her leasehold interest in the house to Lee who had arranged to get the money for Walter. Lee later mortgaged that interest to a building society but did not pay over the money to Mrs Gallie or Walter. In an action by Mrs Gallie against Lee and the building society it was *held*—(i) that the assignment was void and did not confer a title on Lee, (ii) although the plaintiff had been negligent she was not estopped from denying the validity of the deed against the building society for she owed it no duty. The Court of Appeal, in allowing an appeal by the building society, *held* that the plea of *non est factum* was not available to the plaintiff. The transaction intended and carried out was the same, i.e. an assignment.

Mrs Gallie died and an appeal to the House of Lords was brought by the executrix of her estate. The House of Lords affirmed the decision of the Court of Appeal but took the opportunity to restate the law relating to the avoidance of documents on the ground of mistake as follows—

(*a*) The plea of *non est factum* will rarely be available to a person of full capacity who signs a document apparently having legal effect without troubling to read it.

(*b*) A mistake as to the identity of the person in whose favour the document is executed will not normally support a plea of *non est factum* though it may do if the court regards the mistake as fundamental (Lord Reid and Lord Hodson). Neither judge felt that the personality error made by Mrs Gallie was sufficient to support the plea.

(*c*) The distinction taken in *Howatson* v. *Webb*, [1908] 1 Ch. 1 that the mistake must be as to the class or character of the document and not merely as to its contents was regarded as confusing and illogical. A better test would be whether the document which was in fact signed was 'fundamentally different', 'radically different' or 'totally different'. This test is vaguer but more flexible than the character/contents one and yet it still restricts the operation of the plea of *non est factum*. Under the character/contents rule a person who signed a guarantee for £2000 thinking that it was an insurance policy would escape all liability, though a person who signed a guarantee for £5000 believing it to be a guarantee for £500 would be fully liable for the larger sum. However, under the new test the court may regard the guarantee for the larger sum as being void on the basis that it is radically or essentially, or fundamentally, or substantially different.

(*d*) *Carlisle and Cumberland Banking Co.* v. *Bragg*, [1911] 1 K.B. 489, was overruled. Henceforth carelessness on the part of a person signing a document will prevent him from raising the plea. In addition the person claiming to have taken proper care bears the burden of proving that he did.

(183) *Foster* v. *Mackinnon* (1869), L.R. 4 C.P. 704

The plaintiff was a person entitled to receive payment on a bill of exchange for £3000; the defendant was an endorser of the bill and was *prima facie* liable on it. The evidence showed that the defendant was an old man of feeble sight, and that he had signed the bill under the mistaken impression that it was a guarantee. *Held*—The defendant was not in the circumstances negligent in signing the bill and his plea of mistake was successful so that he was not liable on it.

Unilateral mistake: ingredients: A is mistaken and B, the other party to the contract, knows he is

(184) *Legal and General Assurance Society* v. *General Metal Agencies*
(1969), 113 S.J. 876

Legal and General, who were the landlords of General Metal Agencies, served a statutory notice of termination of the tenancy. General Metal applied to the County Court for a new tenancy but Legal and General opposed the application on the grounds of persistent late payment of rent and it was dismissed. However, Legal and General subsequently sent by mistake a computerized demand for the next quarter's rent in advance over the signature of their general manager. General Metal sent a cheque for the rent and this was presented to the bank and paid. In this action Legal and General claimed possession of the premises and General Metal contended that Legal and General by demanding and accepting the next quarter's rent in advance had by implication created a new tenancy. It was *held*—by Fisher, J.—

(i) that Legal and General were entitled to show that the demand was sent and the rent received by mistake. There was no intention to create a new tenancy, the use of a computer making no difference to the established common law principle;

(ii) that, in consequence, Legal and General were entitled to possession of the premises.

(185) *Higgins (W.) Ltd* v. *Northampton Corporation*, [1927] 1 Ch. 128

The plaintiff entered into a contract with the corporation for the erection of dwelling houses. The plaintiff made an arithmetical error in arriving at his price, having deducted a certain rather small sum twice over. The corporation sealed the contract, assuming that the price arrived at by the plaintiff was correct. *Held*—The contract was binding on the parties. Rectification of such a contract was not possible because the power of the court to rectify agreements made under mistake is confined to common not unilateral mistake. Here, rectification would only have been granted if fraud, misrepresentation or unlawful concealment had been present.

Comment. (i) In this case the mistake did not produce a ridiculously small price for the erection of the dwelling houses. Higgins' mistake was therefore not known to the corporation, nor was it so obvious that it ought to have been known to them. This case should be compared with *Hartog* v. *Collin & Shields*, [1939] 3 All E.R. 566 where a seller of skins intended to offer them at a fixed price per piece and the buyer accepted the offer at a certain price per pound. There were three pieces to the pound and the value of the piece was therefore approximately one third of that of a pound. It was held that the buyer must, in view of market prices and conditions, have known that the seller could not have intended the quoted price to apply to pounds but only to pieces. In consequence the contract was void for unilateral mistake.

(ii) Reference should also be made to *Centrovincial Estates* v. *Merchant Investors Assurance*, 1983 at p. 197.

(iii) Since this case was decided the courts have moved away from the idea that rectification of a contract for unilateral mistake is permissible only if there is some form of sharp practice. (*See Thomas Bates & Sons Ltd* v. *Wyndham's (Lingerie) Ltd*, (1981) at page 234.) Even so, rectification would not have been granted in this case because Northampton Corporation were not aware of the plaintiff's error which is still a requirement for rectification.

Unilateral mistake: effect at common law: contract void: two entities rule: effect on third parties

(186) *Cundy* v. *Lindsay* (1878), 3 App. Cas. 459

The respondents were linen manufacturers with a business in Belfast. A fraudulent person named Blenkarn wrote to the respondents from 37 Wood Street, Cheapside, ordering a quantity of handkerchiefs but signed his letter in such a way that it appeared to come from Messrs Blenkiron, who were a well-known and solvent house doing business at 123 Wood Street. The respondents knew of the existence of Blenkiron but did not know the address. Accordingly the handkerchiefs were sent to 37 Wood Street. Blenkarn then sold them to the appellants, and was later convicted and sentenced for the fraud. The respondents sued the appellants in conversion claiming that the contract they had made with Blenkarn was void for mistake, and that the property had not passed to Blenkarn or to the appellants. *Held*—The respondents succeeded; there was an operative mistake as to the party with whom they were contracting.

Comment. As between the parties to the 'contract' (X and Y) the question whether the mistake has rendered the contract void is of little practical importance. Y's pretence will generally amount to fraud so that the contract (if any) between X and Y will be voidable because of that fraud. However, the question of mistake is of major importance where, as in this case, Y obtains the goods without paying for them and sells them on to Z who buys them in good faith. Where the contract between X and Y is void for mistake no title passes to Y who thus cannot give a title to Z. Therefore Z will have to give the goods up to X or be sued in conversion. However, if the contract between X and Y is merely voidable for fraud, Y will get a title to the goods which X will not be able to avoid once Z has acquired the goods *bona fide* and for value. A decision rendering the contract void for mistake is, therefore, greatly prejudicial to innocent third parties and that is why rules such as the two entities rule have been devised by the judiciary so that mistake is not too often found.

(187) *King's Norton Metal Co. Ltd* v. *Edridge, Merrett & Co. Ltd* (1897), 14 T.L.R. 98

The plaintiffs were metal manufacturers in Worcestershire, the defendants being metal manufacturers at Birmingham. In 1896 the plaintiffs received a letter from a firm called Hallam & Co., Soho Wire Works, Sheffield. The letter was written on headed paper, the heading depicting a large factory, and in one corner was a statement that the company had depots and agencies at Belfast, Lille and Ghent. The letter requested a quotation for the supply of brass rivet wire, and a quotation was sent and later an order was received and the goods dispatched. These goods were never paid for. It later emerged that a person named Wallis had set up in business as Hallam & Co. and had fraudulently obtained the goods by the above methods. Wallis sold the goods to the defendants who bought *bona fide* and for value. The plaintiffs had previously done business with Wallis's firm, Hallam & Co., and had been paid by cheque signed Hallam & Co. The plaintiffs sued the defendants in conversion, regarding this as a better action than the one for fraud against Wallis. In order to sustain the action in conversion, the plaintiffs had to establish that the contract with Hallam & Co. was void for mistake, and that because of this the defendants had no title to the wire. *Held*—The plaintiff's claim failed because the contract with Hallam & Co. was voidable for fraud but not void for mistake. The firm Hallam & Co. was a mere alias for Wallis, and since there was no other firm of Hallam & Co. with whom the plaintiffs had previously done business, they were really dealing with one person who from time to time used different names, i.e. Wallis or Hallam & Co. Although the contract was voidable for fraud, it had not been avoided when the goods were sold to the defendants; their title was good and they were not liable in conversion.

  Comment. (i) Since the plaintiffs sent goods on credit to a customer who was completely unknown to them in a credit sense without taking steps to find out whether the customer was creditworthy, the decision is obviously a very reasonable one.

  (ii) The Court of Appeal held, in effect, that the plaintiffs had intended to contract with the writer of the letter. They had no personal knowledge of any other Wallis or any other Hallam & Co.

(188) *Phillips* v. *Brooks Ltd*, [1919] 2 K.B. 243

A fraudulent person named North went into the plaintiff's jeweller's shop and selected goods to the value of £3000. He then asked whether he could take away one of the items (a ring) which he said he wanted for his wife's birthday. He said, no doubt to reassure the jeweller, that he was Sir George Bullough of St James's Square. The plaintiff had heard of the name and, on referring to a directory and finding the address was correct, he allowed North to take away the ring in return for a cheque. Then North, using the name Firth, pledged the ring with the defendants, who were pawnbrokers. They took the ring in good faith and advanced £350 upon it. North was subsequently convicted of obtaining the ring by false pretences, and this action was brought by the plaintiff who claimed that he was mistaken in his contract with North, and that since the contract was void the property had not passed. He, therefore, asked that the ring be returned to him or that he be paid £450, its value. *Held*—The contract between Phillips and North was not void for mistake and Brooks obtained a good title to the ring. The representation by North that he was Sir George Bullough only affected the taking away of the ring and the acceptance by Phillips of the cheque. By that time the sale had taken place and so far as the sale was concerned the identity of the purchaser was not important to Phillips.

(189) *Ingram and others* v. *Little*, [1961] 1 Q.B. 31

The plaintiffs, three ladies, were the joint owners of a car. They wished to sell the car and advertised it for sale. A fraudulent person, introducing himself as Hutchinson, offered to buy it. He was taken for a drive in it and during conversation said that his home was at Caterham. Later the rogue offered £700 for the car but this was refused, though a subsequent offer of £717 was one which the plaintiffs were prepared to accept. At this point the rogue produced a cheque book and one of the plaintiffs, who was conducting the negotiations, said that the deal was off and that they would not accept a cheque. The rogue then said that he was P.G.M. Hutchinson, that he had business interests in Guildford, and that he lived at Stanstead House, Stanstead Road, Caterham. One of the plaintiffs checked this information in a telephone directory and, on finding it to be accurate, allowed him to take the car in return for a cheque. The cheque was dishonoured, and in the meantime the rogue had sold the car to the defendants and had disappeared without trace. The plaintiffs sued for the return of the car, or for its value as damages in conversion, claiming that the contract between themselves and the rogue was void for mistake, and that the property had not passed. At the trial judgment was given for the plaintiffs, Slade, J., finding the contract void. His judgment was affirmed by the Court of Appeal, though Devlin, L.J., dissented, saying that the mistake made was as to the creditworthiness of the rogue, not as to his identity since he was before the plaintiffs when the contract was made. A mistake as to the substance of the rogue would be a mistake as to quality and would not avoid the contract. Devlin, L.J., also suggested that legislation should provide for an apportionment of the loss incurred by two innocent parties who suffer as a result of the fraud of a third.

(190) *Lewis* v. *Averay*, [1971] 3 All E.R. 907

Mr Lewis agreed to sell his car to a rogue who called on him after seeing an advertisement. Before the sale took place the rogue talked knowledgeably about the film world, giving the impression that he was the actor

Richard Green in the 'Robin Hood' serial. He signed a dud cheque for £450 in the name of 'R.A. Green' and was allowed to have the log-book and drive the car away late the same night when he produced a film studio pass in the name of 'Green'. It was *held*—by the Court of Appeal—that Mr Lewis had effectively contracted to sell the car to the rogue and could not recover it or damages from Mr Averay, a student, who had bought it from the rogue for £200. The contract between Mr Lewis and the rogue was voidable for fraud but not void for unilateral mistake.

Comment. (i) The distinctions drawn in some of these cases are fine ones. It is difficult to distinguish *Ingram*[189] from *Phillips*[188] and *Lewis*. The question for the court to answer in these cases is whether or not the offeror at the time of making the offer regarded the identity of the offeree as a matter of vital importance. The general rule seems to be that where the parties are face to face when the contract is made identity will not be vital and the contract voidable only. *Ingram* would appear to be the exceptional case.

(ii) It is thought the contract would be void for mistake in a case such as this if the dishonest person assumed a disguise so that he appeared physically to be the person he said he was.

Unilateral mistake: effect in equity: refusal of specific performance and rescission

(191) *Webster* v. *Cecil* (1861), 30 Beav. 62

The parties had been negotiating for the sale of certain property. Later Cecil offered by letter to sell the property for £1250. Webster was aware that this offer was probably a slip because he knew that Cecil had already refused an offer of £2000, and in fact Cecil wished to offer the property at £2250. Webster accepted the offer and sued for specific performance of the contract. The court refused to grant the decree.

Common mistake: mistake must exist when the contract is made: frustration: application to contracts for the sale of land

(192) *Amalgamated Investment & Property Co. Ltd* v. *John Walker & Sons Ltd*, [1976] 3 All E.R. 509

The defendants sold a warehouse to the plaintiffs for £1,710,000 which the plaintiffs wanted, as the defendants knew, for redevelopment. Both parties knew that planning permission would be required. On 25 September, 1973, the Department of the Environment wrote informing the defendants that the warehouse had been placed on a list of buildings regarded as being of special architectural or historic interest. Development was not therefore possible without a listed building consent which would be difficult to obtain. If it was not obtained the value of the property would be £200,000. The plaintiffs claimed rescission of the contract on the ground of common mistake or that the contract had been frustrated. The Court of Appeal had no doubt that common mistake did not upset the contract. On this Buckley, L.J. said: 'So the alleged common mistake was that the property was property suitable for and capable of being developed. . . . For the application of the doctrine of mutual mistake as a ground for setting aside the contract it is of course necessary to show that the mistake existed at the date of the contract. . . . But at the date when the contract was entered into I cannot see that there is any ground for saying that the parties were then subject to some mutual mistake of facts relating to the circumstances surrounding the contract. . . .'

On the question of frustration the court said that the obligation of the defendants was to sell the property at the contract price and to show a good title. The defendants had given no warranty that planning permission could be obtained. The subsequent listing of the property was not a frustrating event. It was a risk that the purchaser of property had to take and loss resulting from that risk would have to lie where it fell.

Comment. It is not certain whether the doctrine of frustration is capable of applying to contracts for the sale of land. (*Hillingdon Estate Co.* v. *Stonefield Estates Ltd*, [1952] 1 All E.R. 853.) The point was not argued in this case. Buckley, L.J. and Lawton, L.J. referred to it but did not pronounce upon it. However, they were prepared to assume for the sake of argument that such contracts were subject to the frustration principle.

Common mistake: *res extincta* contract void

(193) *Couturier* v. *Hastie* (1856), 5 H.L.C. 673

Messrs Hastie dispatched a cargo of corn from Salonica and sent the charterparty and bill of lading to their London agents so that the corn might be sold. The London agents employed Couturier to sell the corn and a person named Callander bought it. Unknown to the parties the cargo had become overheated, and had been landed at the nearest port and sold, so that when the contract was made the corn was not really in existence. Callander repudiated the contract and Couturier was sued because he was a *del credere* agent, i.e. an agent who, for an extra commission, undertakes to indemnify his principal against losses arising out of the repudiation of the contract by any third party introduced by him. *Held*—The claim against Couturier failed because the contract presupposed that the goods were in existence when they were sold to Callander.

Comment. The rule of law in this case is reinforced by s. 6 of the Sale of Goods Act, 1979, which provides that where there is a contract for the sale of specific goods and the goods without the knowledge of the seller have perished at the time when the contract is made, the contract is void.

Common mistake: *res extincta:* exceptionally the court may decide one party impliedly warrants the existence of the goods

(194) *McRae* v. *The Commonwealth Disposals Commission*, [1951] Argus
L.R. 771

The defendants had invited tenders for the purchase of a tanker, said to
be lying on the Jourmand Reef off Papua, together with the oil it was
said to contain. The plaintiff submitted a tender of £285 which the
defendants accepted. The plaintiff went to considerable trouble and
expense to modify a ship which he owned for salvage work, and also
bought equipment and engaged a crew. In fact there was no tanker
anywhere near the latitude and longitude given by the defendants, and
there was no such place as the Jourmand Reef. The plaintiff sued for
damages for breach of contract. The High Court of Australia *held* that
the plaintiff succeeded because the defendants had impliedly warranted
that the goods existed. The court distinguished *Couturier* v. *Hastie*
(1856)[193] on the ground that in that case the goods had existed but had
perished whereas in the present case the goods had never existed at all.

The implied term solution is not too sound because when the court
implies a term it generally does so on the ground that the parties would
have included it had they addressed themselves to the matter. It is by no
means certain in this case that the defendants would have agreed to such
a term. However, there would now be a possible solution in tort if the
plaintiff chose to sue in negligence because since the decision of the
House of Lords in *Hedley Byrne* v. *Heller and Partners* (1963) (see
p. 635), there is a liability for careless mis-statements resulting in
monetary loss if negligence can be proved.

Common mistake: *res sua:* contract void

(195) *Cochrane* v. *Willis* (1865), 1 Ch. App. 58

Cochrane was the trustee in bankruptcy of Joseph Willis who was the
tenant for life of certain estates in Lancaster. Joseph Willis had been
adjudicated bankrupt in Calcutta where he resided. The remainder of the
estate was to go to Daniel Willis, the brother of Joseph, on the latter's
death, with eventual remainder to Henry Willis, the son of Daniel.
Joseph Willis had the right to cut the timber on the estates during his life
interest, and the representative of Cochrane in England threatened to cut
and sell it for the benefit of Joseph's creditors. Daniel and Henry wished
to preserve the timber and so they agreed with Cochrane through his
representatives to pay the value of the timber to Cochrane if he would
refrain from cutting it. News then reached England that when the above
agreement was made Joseph was dead, and therefore the life interest had
vested in Daniel, i.e. was owned by him. In this action by the trustee to
enforce the agreement it was *held* that Daniel was making a contract to
preserve something which was already his and the court found, applying
the doctrine of *res sua*, that the agreement was void for an identical or
common mistake.

'It would be contrary to all the rules of Equity and common law to give effect to such an agreement.' *Per* Knight Bruce, L.J.

Common mistakes as to quality: no effect at common law

(196) *Bell* v. *Lever Bros Ltd*, [1932] A.C. 161

Lever Bros had a controlling interest in the Niger Company. Bell was the chairman, and a person called Snelling was the vice-chairman, of the Niger Company's Board. Both directors had service contracts which had some time to run. They became redundant as a result of amalgamations and Lever Bros contracted to pay Bell £30,000 and Snelling £20,000 as compensation. These sums were paid over and then it was discovered that Bell and Snelling had committed breaches of duty during their term of office by making small but secret profits on a cocoa pooling scheme. They could, therefore, have been dismissed without compensation. Lever Bros sought to set aside the payments on the ground of mistake. *Held*—The contract was not void because Lever Bros had got what they bargained for, i.e. the cancellation of two service contracts which, though they might have been terminated, were actually in existence when the cancellation agreement was made. The mistake was as to the quality of the two directors and such mistakes do not avoid contracts.

Comment. (i) The case is also authority for the proposition that the contract of service is not of utmost good faith. An employee is not bound to disclose his wrongdoing to his employer.

(ii) In order to regard the case as one of common mistake the court had to accept (which it did) that Bell and Snelling thought they were entitled to compensation in spite of the taking of secret profits. Evidence showed that they had forgotten their breaches of duty by insider dealing.

(iii) However, Bell and Snelling were director/employees and as directors had a duty of disclosure to their company. In *Horcal* v. *Gatland*, [1983] I.R.L.R. 459 it was held that a company could avoid an agreement to pay a director a golden handshake if at the time the agreement was reached the director had failed to disclose a breach of his duty to the company, which in *Horcal* was an alleged appropriation of the company's profits to his own use. In *Bell* v. *Lever Bros* the directors concerned had received golden handshakes from Lever, although they had made secret profits during their term of office against their company (Niger) which Lever had acquired. They kept the compensation and were not required to disclose their wrongdoing to Lever because they were not directors of Lever, but only of Niger. The *Horcal* case, however, confirms that a director of, say, company A, is under a duty to disclose his wrongdoing, if any, towards company A where he receives his compensation from company A itself.

(iv) It is worth mentioning that an employee is under a duty to disclose breaches of duty/conduct of subordinate employees, even though he is not under a duty to disclose to his employer his own misconduct or breaches of duty. This follows from the decision of the Court of Appeal in *Sybron Corporation* v. *Rochem Ltd*, [1983] 2 All E.R. 707.

(197) *Leaf* v. *International Galleries*, [1950] 2 K.B. 86

In 1944 the plaintiff bought from the defendants a picture of Salisbury Cathedral for £85. The defendants said that the picture was by Constable. Five years later the plaintiff tried to sell the picture and was told that this was not so. He now sued for rescission of the contract. The decision in the county court was that rescission could not be granted because the representation was innocent and the contract had been executed. The appeal to the Court of Appeal was concerned with the question of the right to rescind; no claim for damages was made. The following points of interest emerged: (i) it was possible to restore the *status quo* by the mere exchange of the picture and the purchase money so that rescission was not prevented by inability to restore the previous position. (ii) The mistake made by the parties in assuming the drawing to be a Constable was a mistake as to quality and did not avoid the contract. (iii) The statement that the picture was by Constable could have been treated as a warranty giving rise to a claim for damages, but it was not possible to award damages because the appeal was based on the plaintiff's right to rescind. (iv) The court, therefore, treated the statement as a representation and, finding it to be innocent, refused to rescind the contract because of the passage of time since the purchase.

Comment. (i) The plaintiff may now have had a successful action for damages for negligent misrepresentation under the Misrepresentation Act of 1967 provided the action is brought within the six-year limitaton period. (See further p. 237.)

(ii) Although this case was decided after *Solle* v. *Butcher*[180], there was presumably no need for the equitable relief of rescission in regard to the common mistake. After all, Leaf had paid only £85 for the drawing and the court may have regarded the contract as a speculation, each party taking a risk as to the authenticity of the drawing.

(iii) Mr Leaf might well have recovered damages even at the time if he had sued for these under what is now s. 13 of the Sale of Goods Act, 1979 (sale by description—goods described as by Constable) (*see further* page 249).

Common mistake: *res sua:* the approach of equity

(198) *Jones* v. *Clifford* (1876), 3 Ch.D. 779

Clifford agreed to buy from Jones some freehold and leasehold land, thinking that Jones was the owner. Before Clifford actually completed the contract, he entered into an agreement with a sub-purchaser for the sale of the property. The sub-purchaser discovered, whilst searching the title, that Clifford was in fact the true owner of the property, having derived his title from a conveyance to one of his ancestors in 1781. Clifford, on learning this, refused to complete, and Jones now sued for specific performance. *Held*—Specific performance would not be granted because the contract was affected by an identical bilateral or common mistake. The court also ordered an investigation into the title.

Common mistake: equity may treat the contract as voidable and grant rescission either with or without terms

(199) *Grist* v. *Bailey*, [1966] 2 All E.R. 875

In September, 1964, the defendant agreed to sell to the plaintiff a freehold dwelling house for £850 'subject to the existing tenancy'. Both parties believed at that time that the property was occupied by a tenant who was protected by the Rent Acts. In fact both the tenant and her husband had died before the contract was made and since the rent had always been paid to the vendor's agent he was not aware of the true position. The house was occupied by the son of the former tenant, but he was not protected by the Rent Acts and gave up possession. The plaintiff sought specific performance of the contract of sale and the defendant asked for rescission. *Held*—by Goff, J.—applying the dictum of Denning, L.J., in *Solle* v. *Butcher*, 1950,[180]—there was a jurisdiction in Equity to set aside an agreement for common mistake of a fundamental fact. Had the defendant known the true state of affairs she would not have agreed to sell at such a low price. However, being a case of equitable relief it could be granted unconditionally or on terms, and a term offered by the defendant was imposed, i.e. that, if required, she would enter into a fresh contract with the plaintiff at a proper price for vacant possession.

Comment. In *Magee* v. *Pennine Insurance Co. Ltd*, [1969] 2 All E.R. 891 an insurance company which agreed to settle a claim following a car accident under what was believed by the company and the driver to be a valid insurance policy, was held by the Court of Appeal to be voidable in equity. An incorrect statement in the proposal form that the driver had a licence when he did not rendered the policy invalid, though the driver did not know that this was the effect of the incorrect statement when the contract was made. The agreement by the insurance company to settle the claim would have been valid at common law because it was based on a common mistake as to the validity of the insurance policy. However, it could be rescinded in equity.

Rectification: equity can rectify mistakes made by the parties in recording their agreement provided the written contract does not express what the parties had previously agreed

(200) *Joscelyne* v. *Nissen*, [1970] 1 All E.R. 1213

The plaintiff, Mr Joscelyne, sought rectification of a written contract made on 18 June, 1964, under which he had made over his car-hire business to his daughter, Mrs Margaret Nissen. It had been well understood during negotiations that in return for the car-hire business Mrs Nissen would pay certain expenses including gas, electricity and coal bills but the agreement on these matters was not expressly incorporated into the written contract. The parties had also agreed that no concluded contract was to be regarded as made until the signing of a formal written document.

Mrs Nissen failed to pay the bills and the plaintiff brought an action in the Edmonton County Court claiming amongst other things a declaration that Mrs Nissen should pay the gas, electricity and coal bills and alternatively that the written agreement of 18 June, 1964, should be rectified to include a provision to that effect. The County Court judge allowed the claim for rectification and Mrs Nissen appealed to the Court of Appeal on the ground that the judge had misdirected himself, in ordering rectification, in view of his finding that there was no complete antecedent agreement in the sense of an oral contract between the parties on the issue of payment of the expenses. The Court of Appeal, after considering different expressions of judicial views upon what was required before a contractual instrument might be rectified by the court, *held* that the law did not require a binding antecedent contract provided there was some outward expression of agreement between the contracting parties, which there was in this case. Mrs Nissen's appeal was dismissed.

(201) *Frederick Rose (London) Ltd* v. *William Pim & Co. Ltd*, [1953] 2 Q.B. 450

The plaintiffs received an order from an Egyptian firm for feveroles (a type of horse bean). The plaintiffs did not know what was meant by feveroles and asked the defendants what they were and whether they could supply them. The defendants said that feveroles were horse beans and that they could supply them, so the plaintiffs entered into a written agreement to buy horse beans from the defendants which were then supplied to the Egyptian firm under the order. In fact there were three types of horse beans: feves, feveroles and fevettes, and the plaintiffs had been supplied with feves, which were less valuable than feveroles. The plaintiffs were sued by the Egyptian firm and now wished to recover the damages they had had to pay from the defendants. In order to do so they had to obtain rectification of the written contract with the defendants in which the goods were described as 'horsebeans'. The word 'horsebeans' had to be rectified to 'feveroles', otherwise the defendants were not in breach.

Held—

(i) Rectification was not possible because the contract expressed what the parties had agreed to, i.e. to buy and sell horsebeans. Thus the supply of any of the three varieties would have amounted to fulfilment of the contract.

(ii) The plaintiffs might have rescinded for misrepresentation but they could not restore the *status quo*, having sold the beans.

(iii) The plaintiffs might have recovered damages for breach of warranty, but the statement that 'feveroles are horsebeans and we can supply them' was oral, and warranties in a contract for the sale of goods of £10 and upwards had in 1953 to be evidenced in writing. (Sale of Goods Act, 1893, s. 4.) The plaintiff would now have a remedy because s. 4 was repealed by the Law Reform (Enforcement of Contracts) Act, 1954. (See p. 215.)

(iv) The defence of mistake was also raised, i.e. both buyer and seller thought that all horsebeans were feveroles. This was an identical bilateral or common mistake, but since it was not a case of *res extincta* or *res sua* it had no effect on the contract.

Comment. This case is quite complex on its facts but to put the rule in a simpler context, if A and B orally agreed on the sale of A's drawing of Salisbury Cathedral, thought to be by John Constable but not in fact by him, and then put that into a written contract for the sale of a drawing by John Constable, the contract could not be rectified simply because A and B thought that the drawing was by John Constable. The written contract and the oral one would be the same, as in the above case.

Mutual mistake: bilateral non-identical: effect at common law and in equity: court may enforce the contract if it can ascertain the sense of the promise: does the contract identify the agreement?

(202) *Henkel* v. *Pape* (1870), L.R. 6 Ex. 7

The parties to this action had been negotiating for the sale of certain rifles. No contract was made but later the purchaser ordered three rifles by telegram. Owing to the telegraph clerk's negligence the message was transmitted as 'the' rifles. From previous negotiations this was understood to mean fifty rifles and that number was dispatched. *Held*—there was no contract between the parties.

(203) *Wood* v. *Scarth* (1858), 1 F. & F. 293

The plaintiff was suing for damages for breach of contract alleging that the defendant had entered into an agreement to grant the plaintiff a lease of a public house, but had refused to convey the property. It was shown in evidence that the defendant intended to offer the lease at a rent, and also to include a premium on taking up the lease of £500. The defendant had told his agent to make this clear to the plaintiff, but the agent had not mentioned it. After discussions with the agent the plaintiff wrote to the defendant proposing to take the lease 'on the terms already agreed upon' to which the defendant replied accepting the proposal. There was a mutual or non-identical bilateral mistake. The defendant thought that he was agreeing to lease the premises for a rent plus a premium, and the plaintiff thought he was taking a lease for rental only because he did not know of the premium. The plaintiff had sued for specific performance in 1855, and the court in the exercise of its equitable jurisdiction had decided that specific performance could not be granted in view of the mistake, as to grant it would be unduly hard on the defendant. However, in this action the plaintiff sued at common law for damages, and damages were granted to him on the ground that in mutual or non-identical mistake the court may find the sense of the promise and regard a contract as having been made on these terms. Here it was quite reasonable for the plaintiff to suppose that there was no premium to be paid. Thus a contract came into being on the terms as understood by the plaintiff, and he was entitled to damages for breach of it. The contract identified the agreement.

Comment. This case shows that equitable remedies are discretionary and not available as of right. Also note the benefits of the Judicature Acts, 1873–1875. In this case which pre-dates those Acts the action for specific performance was brought in Chancery in 1855 and the action at common law for damages in 1858. Common law and equitable remedies could not be granted in one and the same action until the Judicature Acts were passed.

(204) *Raffles* v. *Wichelaus* (1864), 2 H. & C. 906

The defendants agreed to buy from the plaintiffs 125 bales of cotton to arrive '*ex Peerless* from Bombay'. There were two ships called *Peerless* sailing from Bombay, one in October and one in December. The defendants thought they were buying the cotton on the ship sailing in October, and the plaintiffs meant to sell the cotton on the ship sailing in December. In fact the plaintiffs had no cotton on the ship sailing in October. The defendants refused to take delivery of the cotton when the second ship arrived and were now sued for breach of contract. *Held—* Since there was a mistake as to the subject matter of the contract there was in effect no contract between the parties. There were no circumstances which would clearly indicate to a disinterested bystander that the contract made more sense if the cotton in the October ship was the subject matter than if the contract in the December ship was. Consequently it was impossible to determine the sense of the promise.

Comment. (i) The problem of categorizing this sort of case as mutual mistake, i.e. where both parties are mistaken but each has made a different mistake, is that the seller here was not mistaken at all since he always intended to sell cotton in the December ship. Mutual mistake would seem to be a category of unilateral mistake where the ordinary rules of unilateral mistake cannot be applied because although one party is mistaken (here the buyer) the other party (here the seller) does not know it. Nevertheless the contract must be regarded as void because there is obviously lack of consensus and the contract does not identify an agreement.

(ii) The principle of mutual mistake can also be applied where the mistake of a party is induced by the negligence of the other. Thus in *Scriven Bros & Co.* v. *Hindley & Co.*, [1913] 3 K.B. 564, Hindley's agent made a bid for bales of hemp. The bales contained tow, a cheaper product. The auction particulars were most unclear as to what was being put up and this induced the mistake. It was held that the contract was void.

(205) *Tamplin* v. *James* (1880), 15 Ch.D. 215

James purchased a public house following an auction sale, at which it was not sold. The property was adequately described in the particulars of sale and by reference to a plan. James thought he knew the property and did not bother to refer to the particulars. In fact a field which had been occupied by the publican, and which James thought to be included in the sale, was held under a separate lease and was not part of the lot offered. Tamplin sued for specific performance and James raised this mistake as a defence. *Held*—Specific performance would be granted. Although the parties were not at one on the question of the subject matter, James had by his conduct raised an implication that he was prepared to buy the property offered. The contract identified the agreement.

Comment. The £750 paid by James was presumably regarded as a fair price for the public house alone otherwise specific performance would not have been granted on the grounds of undue hardship to the defendant. (See *Wood* v. *Scarth*, 1858.)[203]

Misrepresentation: statements of intention, opinion, or belief as actionable statements of fact

(206) *Edgington* v. *Fitzmaurice* (1885), 29 Ch.D. 459

The plaintiff was induced to lend money to a company by representations made by its directors that the money would be used to improve the company's buildings and generally expand the business. In fact the directors intended to use the money to pay off the company's existing debts as the creditors were pressing hard for payment. When the plaintiff discovered that he had been misled, he sued the directors for damages for fraud. The defence was that the statement they had made was not a statement of a past or present fact but a mere statement of future intention which could not be the basis of an action for fraud. *Held*—The directors were liable in deceit. Bowen, L.J., said: 'There must be a mis-statement of an existing fact; but the state of a man's mind is as much a fact as the state of his digestion. It is true that it is very difficult to prove what the state of a man's mind at a particular time is, but if it can be ascertained, it is as much a fact as anything else. A misrepresentation as to the state of a man's mind is, therefore, a mis-statement of fact.'

(207) *Smith* v. *Land and House Property Corporation* (1884), 28 Ch. D. 7

The plaintiffs put up for sale on 4 August, 1882, the Marine Hotel, Walton-on-the-Naze, stating in the particulars that it was let to 'Mr Frederick Fleck (a most desirable tenant) at a rental of £400 for an unex-

pired term of $27\frac{1}{2}$ years'. The directors of the defendant company sent
the Secretary, Mr Lewin, to inspect the property and he reported that
Fleck was not doing much business and that the town seemed to be in
the last stages of decay. The directors, on receiving this report, directed
Mr Lewin to bid up to £5000, and in fact he bought the hotel for £4700.
Before completion Fleck became bankrupt and the defendant company
refused to complete the purchase, whereupon the plaintiffs sued for
specific performance. It was proved that on 1 May, 1882, the March
quarter's rent was wholly unpaid; that a distress was then threatened, i.e.
the landlord was threatening to remove property from the hotel to pay
the rent, and that Fleck paid £30 on 6 May, £40 on 13 June, and the
remaining £30 shortly before the sale. No part of the June quarter's rent
had been paid. The chairman of the defendant company said that the
hotel would not have been purchased but for the statement in the particulars that Fleck was a most desirable tenant. *Held*—Specific performance
would not be granted. The description of Fleck as a most desirable tenant
was not a mere expression of opinion, but contained an implied assertion
that the vendors knew of no facts leading to the conclusion that he was
not. The circumstances relating to the unpaid rent showed that Fleck was
not a desirable tenant and there was a misrepresentation. Bowen, L.J.,
said—

> It is material to observe that it is often fallaciously assumed that a
> statement of opinion cannot involve the statement of a fact. In a case
> where the facts are equally well known to both parties, what one of
> them says to the other is frequently nothing but an expression of
> opinion. The statement of such opinion is in a sense a statement of a
> fact about the condition of the man's own mind, but only of an irrel-
> evant fact, for it is of no consequence what the opinion is. But if the
> facts are not equally known to both sides, then a statement of opinion
> by the one who knows the facts best involves very often a statement
> of a material fact, for he impliedly states that he knows facts which
> justify his opinion.

Comment. What was being misrepresented here was a fact, namely the
state of the seller's belief in the statement. Sometimes, however, opinion
is not actionable in this way. For example in *Bissett* v. *Wilkinson*, [1927]
A.C. 177 a vendor of land stated that it could support 2000 sheep and
when sued by the purchaser because this was not the case, it was held
that the vendor was not liable because he had no personal knowledge of
the facts, the land having never been used to support sheep, and because
the buyer knew this the court assumed that the buyer must have understood that the seller could only be stating his belief or opinion.

Misrepresentation: the effect of a statement which is only partially true

(208) *Curtis* v. *Chemical Cleaning and Dyeing Co.*, [1951] 1 K.B. 805

The plaintiff took a wedding dress, trimmed with beads and sequins, to the defendant's shop for cleaning. She was asked to sign a receipt which contained the following clause: 'The company is not liable for damage howsoever arising.' The plaintiff asked what the effect of the document was, and the assistant told her that it exempted the company from liability in certain ways, and particularly that in her case she would have to take the risk of damage to beads and sequins. Thereupon the plaintiff signed the document without reading it. The dress was returned stained, and the plaintiff sued for damages. The company relied on the clause. *Held*—The company could not rely on the clause because the assistant had misrepresented the effect of the document so that the plaintiff was merely running the risk of damage to the beads and sequins.

Misrepresentation: effect of change of circumstances making a statement untrue

(209) *With* v. *O'Flanagan*, [1936] Ch. 575

The defendant was a medical practitioner who wished to sell his practice. The plaintiff was interested and in January, 1934, the defendant represented to the plaintiff that the income from the practice was £2000 a year. The contract was not signed until May, 1934, and in the meantime the defendant had been ill and the practice had been run by various other doctors as *locum tenentes*. In consequence the receipts fell to £5 per week, and no mention of this fact was made when the contract was entered into. The plaintiff now claimed rescission of the contract. *Held*— He could do so. The representation made in January was of a continuing nature and induced the contract made in May. The plaintiff had a right to be informed of a change in circumstances, and the defendant's silence amounted to a misrepresentation.

Comment. Presumably this case would not be followed where the original representation was so old that it was unreasonable for the party misled to rely on it.

Misrepresentation: constructive fraud: available in any situation where one party has taken unfair advantage of the other

(210) *Tate* v. *Williamson* (1866), 2 Ch. App. 55

An extravagant Oxford undergraduate who was being pressed for money by his creditors sought financial advice from Williamson who recommended the sale of the undergraduate's estate in Staffordshire. Williamson then offered to buy it himself for £7000 without disclosing the existence of minerals under the land which made the undergraduate's interest worth at least £14,000. The offer was accepted and a conveyance executed but some years later the sale was set aside by the court at the instance of the undergraduate's heir. Williamson had been guilty of constructive fraud in that he had exploited to his own advantage the confidence placed in him.

Misrepresentation: must induce the contract

(211) *Peek* v. *Gurney* (1873), L.R. 6 H.L. 377

Peek purchased shares in a company on the faith of statements appearing in a prospectus issued by the respondents who were directors of the company. Certain of the statements were false and Peek sued the directors. It appeared that Peek was not an original allottee, but had purchased the shares on the market, though he had relied on the prospectus. *Held*—Peek's action failed because the statements in the prospectus were only intended to mislead the original allottees. Once the statements had induced the public to be original subscribers, their force was spent.

Comment. (i) The above rule will not apply where the person making the representation intended that it should be passed on. In *Pilmore* v. *Hood* (1838), 5 Bing. N.C. 97 H wanted to sell a public house and told a potential purchaser, A, that the takings were £180 p.a. This was not true but in the event A was not able to buy the public house for financial reasons. However, with H's knowledge A persuaded P to buy it by repeating H's misrepresentation to him. It was held that H was liable in damages to P for fraudulent misrepresentation. This rule does not apply if, as in *Gross* v. *Lewis Hillman Ltd and Another*, [1969] 3 All E.R. 1476, A sells a property to B under a misrepresentation and B, having purchased the property, sells it on to C, repeating the same misrepresentation. In these circumstances C can only sue B for misrepresentation.

(ii) The decision has a somewhat unfortunate effect because at those times when public issues are over-subscribed it is most likely that persons who did not receive an allotment or an adequate allotment as subscribers will try to purchase further shares within a short time on the stock exchange. These people will clearly be relying on the prospectus, but in view of this decision would have no claim in respect of false statements in it.

(iii) A claim in tort for damages for negligent misstatement should be available under *Hedley Byrne*[215] in that those who publicly advertise a prospectus must surely in the modern context foresee that it will be relied upon by subscribers *and* by those who purchase from subscribers on the stock market for a reasonable time after the issue of the prospectus.

(iv) So far as the context of a public issue of shares goes, s. 150(1) of the Financial Services Act, 1986 provides that an action can be brought by '. . . any person who has acquired any of the securities in question and suffered loss in respect of any of them.' This would seem to include subsequent purchasers in the market but only within a reasonable time of the issue of the prospectus because eventually the true position will become public knowledge.

(212) *Redgrave* v. *Hurd* (1881), 20 Ch.D. 1

The plaintiff was a solicitor who wished to take a partner into the business. During negotiations between the plaintiff and Hurd the plaintiff stated that the income of the business was £300 a year. The papers which the plaintiff produced showed that the income was not quite £200 a year, and Hurd asked about the balance. Redgrave then produced further papers which he said showed how the balance was made up, but which only showed a very small amount of income making the total income up to about £200. Hurd did not examine these papers in any detail, but agreed to become a partner. Later Hurd discovered the true position and refused to complete the contract. The plaintiff sued for breach and Hurd raised the misrepresentation as a defence, and also counter-claimed for rescission of the contract. *Held*—Hurd had relied on Redgrave's statements regarding the income, and not his own skill and judgment, so the contract could be rescinded. It did not matter that Hurd had the means of discovering their untruth; he was entitled to rely on Redgrave's statement.

Comment. (i) A contrast is provided by *Attwood* v. *Small* (1838), 6 Cl. & Fin. 232 where A offered to sell a mine to S, making representations as to the earnings of the mine. S was willing to buy it provided A would allow S's agents to investigate the earning capacity of the mine. Experienced agents appointed by S inspected the mine and received all possible help from A. The agents made a report to the effect that A's representations as to earnings were true and S made the contract. The representations as to the earnings were not true but the House of Lords held that S could not rescind the contract. He had relied on his own investigations and not upon the representations of A.

(ii) There were no allegations of fraud in *Attwood*. Where a statement is fraudulent relief will not be denied merely because the plaintiff's attempt to discover the truth has failed. (See *S. Pearson & Son Ltd* v. *Dublin Corporation*, [1907] A.C. 351.) Otherwise skilful and well-planned deceptions would succeed.

(213) *Smith* v. *Chadwick* (1884), 9 App. Cas. 187

This action was brought by the plaintiff who was a steel manufacturer, against Messrs Chadwick, Adamson and Collier, who were accountants and promoters of a company called the Blochairn Iron Co. Ltd. The plaintiff claimed £5750 as damages sustained through taking shares in the company which were not worth the price he had paid for them because of certain misrepresentations in the prospectus issued by the defendants. The action was for fraud. Among the misrepresentations alleged by Smith was that the prospectus stated that a Mr J. J. Grieves, M.P., was a director of the company, whereas he had withdrawn his consent the day before the prospectus was issued. It was *held* that the statement regarding Mr Grieves was untrue but was not material to the plaintiff, because the evidence showed that he had never heard of Mr Grieves. His action for damages failed.

Misrepresentation: fraud: definition and burden of proof

(214) *Derry* v. *Peek* (1889), 14 App. Cas. 337

The Plymouth, Devonport and District Tramways Company had power under a special Act of Parliament to run trams by animal power, and with the consent of the Board of Trade by mechanical or steam power. Derry and the other appellants were directors of the company and issued a prospectus, inviting the public to apply for shares in it, stating they had power to run trams by steam power, and claiming that considerable economies would result. The directors had assumed that the permission of the Board of Trade would be granted as a matter of course, but in the event the Board of Trade refused permission except for certain parts of the tramway. As a result the company was wound up and the directors were sued for fraud. The court *decided* that the directors were not fraudulent but honestly believed the statement in the prospectus to be true.

Comment. (i) This case gave rise to the Directors' Liability Act, 1890, now s. 67 of the Companies Act, 1985, which makes directors liable to pay compensation for misrepresentation in a prospectus, subject to a number of defences. The latest provisions are in s. 150 Financial Services Act, 1986. (See p. 238.)

(ii) There was, of course, a certain amount of negligence in this case but carelessness is not fraud, though it may be actionable, either under the Misrepresentation Act or under the doctrine of *Hedley Byrne*.[215] However, no particular dishonesty is required for fraud. Thus if an agent sells his principal's goods to T knowingly and intentionally for a price less than that agreed between P and A, then T will not obtain a contract with P and can sue A for fraud and this even though A believed that P would accept the lower price and therefore that T would not be prejudiced. (*Polhill* v. *Walter* (1832). 3 B. & Ad. 114.)

(iii) It is difficult to prove fraud because the burden of proof is to the criminal standard, i.e. that the defendant was fraudulent beyond a reasonable doubt. The civil standard is on a balance of probabilities.

(iv) Fraud involves a degree of dishonesty not mere absence of reasonable grounds for believing the statement to be true as in negligent misrepresentation.

Misrepresentation: the contribution of the tort of negligence

(215) *Hedley Byrne & Co. Ltd.* v. *Heller & Partners Ltd*, [1963] 2 All E.R. 575

The appellants were advertising agents and the respondents were merchant bankers. The appellants had a client called Easipower Ltd who were customers of the respondents. The appellants had contracted to place orders for advertising Easipower's products on television and in newspapers, and since this involved giving Easipower credit, they asked the respondents, who were Easipower's bankers, for a reference as to the creditworthiness of Easipower. Heller's replied: 'without responsibility on the part of the bank or its officials' that Easipower was a 'respectably constituted company, considered good for its ordinary business engagements. Your figures are larger than we are accustomed to see'. In fact bankers normally use careful terms when giving these references, but Heller's language was so guarded that only a very suspicious person might have appreciated that he was being warned not to give credit to the extent of £100,000. In fact Heller's were trying to warn the plaintiffs off because Easipower had an overdraft with Heller's which Heller's knew they were about to call in and that Easipower might have difficulty in meeting the payment. One week after the reference was given Heller's began to press Easipower to reduce their overdraft. However, relying on this reply, the appellants placed orders for advertising time and space for Easipower Ltd, and the appellants assumed personal responsibility for payment to the television and newspaper companies concerned. Easipower Ltd went into liquidation, and the appellants lost over £17,000 on the advertising contracts. The appellants sued the respondents for the amount of the loss, alleging that the respondents had not informed themselves sufficiently about Easipower Ltd before writing the statement, and were therefore liable in negligence. *Held*—In the present case the respondents' disclaimer was adequate to exclude the assumption by them of the legal duty of care, but, in the absence of the disclaimer, the circumstances would have given rise to a duty of care in spite of the absence of a contract or fiduciary relationship. The dissenting judgment of Denning, L.J., in *Candler* v. *Crane, Christmas*, 1951 (see p. 813), was approved, and the majority judgment in that case was disapproved.

Comment. (i) The need for a special relationship cut down the number of claims for negligent mis-statements. The courts required that the person making the statement should *know* the person or persons who would rely on it, as Heller's knew Hedley Byrne would. However, in *JEB Fasteners* v. *Marks Bloom*, 1981 (see p. 815) it was decided that the test of knowledge should give way to a test of *foresight* and that in a contract to take over a company the purchasers could sue the accountants who had prepared, it was alleged negligently, the annual accounts of the company. These accounts were alleged to have influenced the purchasers and although the accountants did not know that they would be used by those considering a takeover, the court held that it was within their foresight. The accounts suggested that the company would require finance before its next annual accounts were completed and it was held to be within the accountants' foresight that the accounts might be used by a lender or an investor, or a purchaser of the company. This is a much wider test for duty of care in negligence than was contemplated in *Hedley Byrne* or *Esso Petroleum* v. *Mardon* (see p. 815) where the representee had to be *known* to the maker of the statement.

(ii) Disclaimers of the kind seen above must now satisfy the 'reasonableness' test of the Unfair Contract Terms Act, 1977. (See p. 260.) In this connection it was held in *Smith* v. *Eric S. Bush*, [1987] 3 All E.R. 179 to be unreasonable for a surveyor to rely on a general disclaimer of negligence where he had been asked by a building society to carry out a reasonably careful visual inspection of the property for valuation purposes (paid for by the would-be purchaser) when the valuer knew that the purchaser would be likely to rely on his report and not get another one. The house was purchased but, because of defects, turned out to be unfit for habitation. The surveyors when sued could not escape liability for damages on the basis of disclaimer.

The case suggests that insofar as such disclaimers are still used by professional persons they may not be effective, at least as regards ordinary consumers of professional services.

Misrepresentation: tort of deceit: measure of damages

(216) *Doyle* v. *Olby (Ironmongers) Ltd and Others*, [1969] 2 All E.R. 119

In 1963 the plaintiff wished to buy a business. He saw an advertisement in *Dalton's Weekly* and obtained particulars of an ironmonger's business in Epsom belonging to the first defendants. The price asked for the lease, the business and goodwill was £4500, the stock to be taken at valuation. In 1964 after negotiations with various members of the Olby family the plaintiff purchased the business paying £4500 covering goodwill and fixtures and fittings, and £5000 for the stock. He also needed a longer lease and so surrendered the existing lease taking on a longer one at an increased rent. The owner of the shop who benefited from this transaction was another member of the Olby family. In order to pay the money the plaintiff put up all the cash he had, i.e. £7000 and borrowed £3000 on mortgage. When he went into occupation he discovered that the defendants had made a number of false statements relating to the business. In particular the plaintiff discovered that half the trade was wholesale which could only be obtained by employing a traveller to go round to the customers. The plaintiff could not afford to employ a traveller and all the wholesale trade was lost. The second defendant had told the plaintiff in the course of negotiations that all the trade was over the counter.

The plaintiff was most dissatisfied and in May, 1964, he brought an action for damages for fraud and conspiracy against Olby (Ironmongers) Ltd and several members of the Olby family who had been involved in the sale of the Epsom business. At the trial the judge awarded damages on a contractual basis as if the statement 'the trade is all over the counter. There is no need to employ a traveller' had been a term of the contract. In consequence the judge accepted that the proper measure of foreseeable damage was, in accordance with *Hadley* v. *Baxendale* 1854 (see p. 724), the reduction in the value of goodwill due to the mis-statement. The goodwill was valued at £4000 and since 50 per cent of the turnover was wholesale goodwill would have been reduced by 35 to 40 per cent giving £1500 as a round figure for damages.

In the Court of Appeal Lord Denning, M.R., said on this point:

On principle the distinction seems to be this: in contract, the defendant has made a promise and broken it. The object of damages is to put the plaintiff in as good a position, as far as money can do it, as if the promise had been performed. In fraud, the defendant has been guilty of a deliberate wrong by inducing the plaintiff to act to his detriment. The object of damages is to compensate the plaintiff for all the loss he has suffered, so far, again, as money can do it. In contract, the damages are limited to what may reasonably be supposed to have been in the contemplation of the parties. In fraud, they are not so limited. The defendant is bound to make reparation for all the actual damage directly flowing from the fraudulent inducement. The person who has been defrauded is entitled to say: 'I would not have entered into this bargain at all but for your representation. Owing to your fraud, I have not only lost all the money I have paid you, but, what is more, I have been put to a large amount of extra expense as well and suffered this or that extra damages.' All such damages can be recovered: and it does not lie in the mouth of the fraudulent person to say that they could not reasonably have been foreseen. For instance, in this very case the plaintiff has not only lost the money which he paid for the business, which he would never have done if there had been no fraud; he put all that money in and lost it; but also he has been put to expense and loss in trying to run a business which has turned out to be a disaster for him. He is entitled to damages for all his loss, subject, of course, to giving credit for any benefit that he has received. There is nothing to be taken off in mitigation: for there is nothing more that he could have done to reduce his loss. He did all that he could reasonably be expected to do.

Accordingly damages were assessed by the Court of Appeal at £5500 being made up as follows—

	£	£	
Cost of acquiring business		4500	
Cost of acquiring stock		5000	
		9500	
Less: Cash received by Doyle when business sold in 1967	3500		
Cash received on sale of stock	800		
Value of living accommodation during the three years	2500	7000	(as a round figure)
		2500	
Loss			
Additional damages for strain and worry and interest on loans and bank overdraft		3000	
Damages awarded		**£5500**	

Misrepresentation: tort of deceit: exemplary (punitive) and aggravated damages

(217) *Mafo* v. *Adams*, [1969] 3 All E.R. 1404

In July, 1965, the plaintiff, a Nigerian, was granted a weekly tenancy in Richmond by the defendant, a West Indian. On 10 December, 1965, the defendant gave the plaintiff notice to quit though the plaintiff appeared to have been a good tenant. The plaintiff then claimed the benefit of the Rent Acts and refused to leave. On 15 February, 1966, the plaintiff was invited to see alternative accommodation at Norbury and saw a lady who posed as Mrs Williams. The plaintiff arranged to move into the accommodation at Norbury and paid Mrs Williams £6 10 s. representing two weeks' rent in advance, though the cheque was never cashed. The plaintiff and his pregnant wife then left the Richmond tenancy but were unable to obtain entry to the Norbury accommodation. It later emerged that Mrs Williams was in fact Adams' wife, from whom he was separated, and that he and she had combined in a piece of trickery to get the plaintiff out of the Richmond tenancy. The plaintiff was unable to resume possession of the Richmond accommodation and subsequently suffered physical inconvenience but no financial damage although it appeared that the accommodation he found was unlikely to be as securely protected by the Rent Acts as the Richmond flat had been. On appeal by the landlord from an award to the tenant of £100 for breach of covenant of quiet enjoyment and £100 exemplary damages for deceit it was *held*—by the Court of Appeal—

   (i) £100 was a proper figure for compensatory damages;

   (ii) that Lord Devlin's statements in *Rookes* v. *Barnard*, [1964] 1 All E.R. 367, at p. 411, that 'Exemplary damages can properly be awarded whenever it is necessary to teach a wrongdoer that tort does not pay' *might* well have extended the number of cases in which exemplary damages could potentially be awarded. However, assuming that exemplary damages could be awarded in an action for deceit, the plaintiff was not entitled to them because there was no finding that the landlord had acted in such a way as to bring himself within Lord Devlin's statement. Exemplary damages are in the main to be awarded in cases where the defendant realizes that he is breaking the law, and that damages may be awarded against him, but nevertheless makes what has been described as a cynical calculation of profit and loss and says that he will flout the powers of the court because on a purely cash basis he can show a profit. Where exemplary damages were claimed the court must be careful to see that the case for punishment was as well established as in other penal proceedings. The plaintiff was not therefore entitled to exemplary damages.

   Comment. In *Archer* v. *Brown*, *The Times*, 2 November, 1983, fraudulent misrepresentations were made to the plaintiff causing him to buy shares in a company and to conclude a service agreement. The shares were bought for a total of £30,000. It was held by the High Court that the plaintiff was entitled to the return of the £30,000 plus interest; £13,528 overdraft charges incurred as a result of the transactions; £2500 loss of earnings, and £1000 expenses. He was also entitled to aggravated damages in deceit for injury to feelings in the sum of £500.

A further point of interest which arises from the case is that the defendant had conceded the plaintiff's right to rescind but contended that the plaintiff could not, therefore, claim damages for deceit. The Court held that a right to rescind a contract does not rule out a claim for deceit. A plaintiff is not bound to rescind but can claim damages for fraud instead.

Misrepresentation: negligent misrepresentation: principal but not agent liable to a third party for the agent's negligent misrepresentation

(218) *Gosling* v. *Anderson, The Times*, 6 February, 1972

Miss Gosling, a retired schoolmistress, entered into negotiations for the purchase of one of three flats in a house at Minehead owned by Mrs Anderson. Mr Tidbury, who was Mrs Anderson's agent in the negotiations, represented to Miss Gosling by letter that planning permission for a garage to go with the flat had been given. Mrs Anderson knew that this was not so. The purchase of the flat went through on the basis of a contract and a conveyance showing a parking area but not referring to planning permission which was later refused. Miss Gosling now sought damages for misrepresentation under s. 2(1) of the Misrepresentation Act, 1967. *Held*—the facts revealed an innocent misrepresentation by Mr Tidbury made without reasonable grounds for believing it to be true (which could alternatively be called negligent misrepresentation). Mrs Anderson was liable for the acts of her agent and must pay damages under the Act of 1967. The court ordered an inquiry as to damages before the local county court judge.

Comment. (i) It was decided in *Resolute Maritime Inc* v. *Nippon Kaijji Kyokai*, [1983] 2 All E.R. 1 that in a situation such as *Gosling* the agent could not be sued by the third party since s. 2(1) of the 1967 Act requires that the action be brought against 'the other party to the contract', i.e. in this context the principal. The principal may sue the agent for loss caused, i.e. payment of the damages, by the agent's negligence.

(ii) As regards proving reasonable grounds, an expert will be expected to verify his statements in a professional way. However, those without relevant technical knowledge will often find that the court will accept a statement as made innocently if the maker of the statement had been induced to purchase the goods himself by the same statement.

Thus in *Humming Bird Motors* v. *Hobbs*, [1986] R.T.R. 276, H was a young man whom the judge found to be an amateur doing a bit of 'wheeling and dealing' in the motor trade. He bought a car from a dealer who told him that the mileage recorded, 34,900 miles, was correct. H sold the car on to the plaintiffs making the same statement, i.e. that the recorded mileage was, to the best of his knowledge and belief, correct. The plaintiffs discovered that the vehicle had done 80,000 miles and tried to claim damages for negligent misrepresentation. The Court of Appeal decided that H was not negligent; he was an amateur and merely repeating what he himself believed.

(iii) In order for a statement to be fraudulent an element of dishonesty is required. For example, if Mr Tidbury in the *Gosling* case had *known* that there was no planning permission for the garage but had nevertheless gone on to state that there was, then the element of dishonesty would have been present and he would have been guilty of fraud.

Misrepresentation: effecting rescission

(219) *Car & Universal Finance Co. Ltd* v. *Caldwell*, [1963] 2 All E.R. 547

On 12 January, 1960. Mr Caldwell sold a motor car to a firm called Dunn's Transport, receiving a cheque signed 'for and on behalf of Dunn's Transport, W. Foster, F. Norris'. Caldwell presented the cheque to the bank but it was dishonoured, and so he went to see the police and asked them to recover the car. He also saw officials of the Automobile Association and asked them to trace the car by their patrols. The car was found on 20 January, 1960, in the possession of a director of a firm of car dealers called Motobella & Co. Ltd. The company claimed to have bought it on 15 January from Norris and to have a good title. On 29 January, the defendant's solicitors demanded the car from Motobella and at the same time Norris was arrested and pleaded guilty to obtaining the car by false pretences. The defendant sued Motobella & Co. Ltd for the return of the car and obtained judgment, but when he tried to repossess the car, a finance house, Car & Universal Finance Co. Ltd, claimed that it belonged to them. It appeared that Motobella had transferred the ownership to a finance house called G. & C. Finance on 15 January, 1960, and they had transferred it to the plaintiffs on 3 August, 1960, the latter company taking the vehicle in good faith. In this action the plaintiffs claimed the car. It was *held* that Caldwell was entitled to it because, amongst other things, he had avoided the contract of sale to Norris when he asked the police to get the car back for him so that later sales of the car to Motobella and to G. & C. Finance did not pass the property.

Comment. (i) This case is of little practical importance because a buyer in possession of goods will give a good title to a third party under s. 9 of the Factors Act, 1889, and/or s. 25 of the Sale of Goods Act, 1979 because the fraudulent person is a buyer in possession who is allowed by both of the above-mentioned Acts of Parliament to give a good title to an innocent third party for value. Thus in *Newtons of Wembley Ltd* v. *Williams*, [1965] 1 Q.B. 560, where the facts were similar to *Caldwell*, the third party obtained a good title under what is now s. 25 of the Sale of Goods Act, 1979. *Caldwell* was distinguished because it appears that the first buyers from the fraudulent person (i.e. Motobella) were on notice of the fraud in the sale by Mr Caldwell to Dunn's Transport.

(ii) The distinction seems also to be between a *direct* and an *indirect* sale. In *Caldwell* the fraudsman did not sell direct to the purchaser. The first sale was to Motobella which had notice of the defect in title and so s. 25(1) did not apply, said the court, to give a good title to the finance house. In the *Newtons* case the sale was direct by the fraudsman to the innocent third party and the latter got a good title under s. 25(1). The distinction between a direct and an indirect sale is somewhat illogical and the Law Commission recommended in its 12th Report, Cmnd 2958 1966, that until the person deceived actually got in touch with the fraudsman all sales direct or indirect should give a good title to innocent purchasers.

Misrepresentation: loss of right to rescind: affirmation: inability to restore the parties to their original positions: accrual of third party rights

(220) *Long* v. *Lloyd*, [1958] 2 All E.R. 402

The plaintiff and the defendant were haulage contractors. The plaintiff was induced to buy the defendant's lorry by the defendant's misrepresentation as to condition and performance. The defendant advertised the lorry for sale at £850, the advertisement describing the vehicle as being in 'exceptional condition'. The plaintiff saw the lorry at the defendant's premises at Hampton Court on a Saturday. During a trial run on the following Monday the plaintiff found that the speedometer was not working, a spring was missing from the accelerator pedal, and it was difficult to engage top gear. The defendant said there was nothing wrong with the vehicle except what the plaintiff had found. He also said at this stage that the lorry would do 11 miles to the gallon.

The plaintiff purchased the lorry for £750, paying £375 down and agreeing to pay the balance at a later date. He then drove the lorry from Hampton Court to his place of business at Sevenoaks. On the following Wednesday, the plaintiff drove from Sevenoaks to Rochester to pick up a load, and during that journey the dynamo ceased to function, an oil seal was leaking badly, there was a crack in one of the road wheels, and he used 8 gallons of petrol on a journey of 40 miles. That evening the plaintiff told the defendant of the defects, and the defendant offered to pay half the cost of a reconstructed dynamo, but denied any knowledge of the other defects. The plaintiff accepted the offer and the dynamo was fitted straight away. On Thursday the lorry was driven by the plaintiff's brother to Middlesbrough, and it broke down on the Friday night. The plaintiff, on learning of this, asked the defendant for his money back, but the defendant would not give it to him. The lorry was subsequently examined and an expert said that it was not roadworthy. The plaintiff sued for rescission. *Held*—at first instance, by Glyn-Jones, J.—that the defendant's statements about the lorry were innocent and not fraudulent because the evidence showed that the lorry had been laid up for a month and it might therefore have deteriorated without the defendant's precise knowledge. The Court of Appeal affirmed this finding of fact and made the following additional points—

(1) The journey to Rochester was not affirmation because the plaintiff was merely testing the vehicle in a working capacity.

(2) However, the acceptance by the plaintiff of the defendant's offer to pay half the cost of the reconstructed dynamo, and the subsequent journey to Middlesbrough, did amount to affirmation, and rescission could not be granted to the plaintiff.

Comment. (i) Damages could now be obtained for negligent misrepresentation under the Misrepresentation Act, 1967, s. 2(1), for how could the seller say he had reasonable grounds for believing that the lorry was in exceptional condition or first class condition?

(ii) It seems remarkable that Glyn-Jones, J., did not find fraud. However, fraud must be proved according to the criminal standard, i.e. beyond a reasonable doubt and not according to the civil standard which is on balance of probabilities. Fraud is therefore difficult to prove and in this case there was presumably a reasonable doubt in the mind of the judge on the issue of fraud.

(iii) The Court of Appeal would not accept that the statement that the lorry was in first class condition was a term of the contract but decided that it was only a misrepresentation.

(221) *Clarke* v. *Dickson* (1858), E.B. & E. 148

In 1853 the plaintiff was induced by the misrepresentation of the three defendants, Dickson, Williams and Gibbs, to invest money in what was in effect a partnership to work lead mines in Wales. In 1857 the partnership was in financial difficulty and with the plaintiff's assent it was converted into a limited company and the partnership capital was converted into shares. Shortly afterwards the company commenced winding-up proceedings and the plaintiff, on discovery of the falsity of the representations, asked for rescission of the contract. *Held*—Rescission could not be granted because capital in a partnership is not the same as shares in a company. The firm was no longer in existence, having been replaced by the company, and it was not possible to restore the parties to their original positions.

Comment (i) It should be noted that in addition to the problem of restoration, third-party rights, i.e. creditors, had accrued on the winding up of the company and this is a further bar to rescission.

(ii) In this case the property had totally changed in nature but where the property has merely deteriorated the court may allow rescission with a cash adjustment. Thus in *Erlanger* v. *New Sombrero Phosphate Co.* (1878), 3 App. Cas. 1218 a person who had purchased a phosphate-bearing island had extracted some of the phosphate but not all of it. He asked for rescission on the basis of misrepresentation and the House of Lords held that he could rescind provided that he restored the island and accounted to the sellers for any profit that he had made in the operation of his phosphate mining activities.

Misrepresentation: negligent misrepresentation under s. 2(1), Misrepresentation Act, 1967: damages to be assessed on tort principles: Estoppel

(222) *Chesneau* v. *Interhome Ltd, The Times*, 9 June, 1983.

In this case the Court of Appeal decided that damages for misrepresentation under s. 2(1) of the Misrepresentation Act, 1967 were to be assessed on the same principles as damages in tort. The defendants had represented that a holiday villa for rental was in a quiet location when it was in fact part of a commercial complex. Lord Justice Eveleigh (sitting with Lord Justice O'Connor) said that he took the use of the word 'so' in 'that person shall be so liable notwithstanding that the misrepresentation was not made fraudulently' in s. 2(1) to mean liable as he would have been had the misrepresentation been made fraudulently.

Misrepresentation: a mis-statement may raise an estoppel

(223) *Henderson & Co.* v. *Williams*, [1895] 1 Q.B. 521

The plaintiffs were sugar merchants at Hull. The defendant was a warehouseman at Hull and Goole. On 3 June, 1894, a fraudulent person named Fletcher, posing as the agent of one Robinson, negotiated a purchase of sugar from Messrs Grey & Co., who were Liverpool merchants. The sugar was lying in the defendant's warehouse at Goole, and Messrs Grey & Co. sent a telegram and later a letter advising the defendant that the sugar was to be held to the order of Fletcher, and the defendant entered the order in his books. Robinson was a reputable dealer and a customer of Messrs Grey & Co., and of course Fletcher had no right to act on Robinson's behalf. Fletcher sold the goods to the plaintiffs who, before paying the price, got a statement from the defendant that the goods were held to the order of Fletcher. The defendant later discovered Fletcher's fraud and refused to release the sugar to the plaintiffs who now sued in conversion. *Held*—The defendant was estopped from denying Fletcher's title and was liable in damages based on the market price of the goods at the date of refusal to deliver. Further the true owners, Messrs Grey & Co., could not set up their title to the sugar against that of the plaintiffs, since they had allowed Fletcher to hold himself out as the true owner.

Comment. The plaintiff's action was not based on estoppel but upon the defendant's refusal to deliver. However, the estoppel operated to prevent the successful defence of the action on the grounds that the goods did not belong to Fletcher who had purported to sell them.

Misrepresentation: equity does not award damages but can order the payment of a monetary indemnity as part of the process of rescission

(224) *Whittington* v. *Seale-Hayne* (1900), 82 L.T. 49

The plaintiffs were breeders of prize poultry and they took a lease of the defendant's premises. The defendant innocently misrepresented that the premises were in a sanitary condition but in fact the water supply was poisoned, and this caused the illness of the plaintiff's manager. In addition, certain of their poultry died or became valueless for breeding purposes. The local authority required the plaintiffs to carry out certain work in order to render the premises sanitary, the plaintiffs having agreed in the lease to do such work if it became necessary. The plaintiffs now asked for rescission of the contract and for an indemnity against the following losses: Stock lost, £750; loss of profit on sales, £100; loss of breeding season, £500; removal of stores and rent, £75; medical expenses, £100. *Held*—The lease could be rescinded, but the plaintiffs' indemnity was restricted to the losses necessarily incurred by taking a lease of the premises, i.e. rent, rates and the cost of the repairs ordered by the local authority.

Comment. The reason for restricting the indemnity in this sort of case seems to be based on the fact that although Equity is prepared to rescind contracts for non-fraudulent misrepresentation, thus providing a remedy where the common law does not, Equity will not circumvent the law by making an indemnity (the object of which is to help restore the *status quo*) the equivalent of damages for fraud.

Contractual terms: admission of oral evidence where contract written: the oral evidence rule

(225) *Pym* v. *Campbell* (1856), 6 E. & G. 370

The defendants agreed in writing to buy from the plaintiff a share in an invention. There was an oral agreement that the contract should not operate unless and until a Mr Abernethie, an engineer, had inspected and approved the invention, which was a crushing machine. He inspected it and did not approve. The plaintiff now sued upon the written contract. It was held that oral evidence was admissible to show that the written contract had not come into operation, because the condition precedent, i.e. Mr Abernethie's approval, had not, in fact, taken place.

(226) *Quickmaid Rental Services Ltd* v. *Reece* (1970), *The Times*, 22 April, 1970

In 1967 a saleman named Burbridge persuaded Mr Reece to install on his service station premises in Ashton New Road, Manchester, a Quickmaid machine which supplied coffee, tea and other beverages to travellers by putting coins into a slot. Mr Reece was asked to sign two written agreements, one for the machine itself and the other for a canopy. It was to be for five years. Mr Reece paid £37 10s. deposit for the machine and was to pay monthly rentals thereafter. But before he agreed or signed anything Mr Burbridge made an important statement to him. He said that he would not install any other such machine on Ashton New Road. That stipulation induced Mr Reece to sign the documents. Mr Burbridge realized that any other machine would affect Mr Reece's business considerably. Later he made a memorandum saying he would not sell any more machines in that particular road.

However in May, 1968, Mr Reece discovered that in January the company, through another salesman, had installed another machine up the road. That was within two and a half months of the promise to him; and the second machine was in a more advantageous position for getting custom. On discovering that, Mr Reece, who had had trouble with his machine, stopped his banker's order for the rental. The company thereupon sued Mr Reece in the County Court for £73 15s., being the instalments from June to October, 1968. *Held*—by the Court of Appeal—that the company's claim failed. The proper way to approach the case was to regard it as a contract made partly in writing by the signed documents and partly by word of mouth, by what was said at the time. The stipulation about no other machine being in the road was most important; it was a term which amounted to a condition; and when it was broken it was broken in a manner which went to the root of the contract. It destroyed the profitable basis of the contract. Breach of that condition gave Mr Reece the right to say he would no longer go on; nor on the evidence did he affirm the contract after discovering the breach. The appeal should be dismissed. (*Per* Lord Denning, M.R.)

Contractual terms: representations and terms distinguished

(227) *Bannerman* v. *White* (1861), 10 C.B.(N.S.) 844

The defendant was intending to buy hops from the plaintiff and he asked the plaintiff whether sulphur had been used in the cultivation of the hops, adding that if it had he would not even bother to ask the price, by which he meant he would not make the contract. The plaintiff siad that no sulphur had been used, though in fact it had. It was *held* that the plaintiff's assurance that sulphur had not been used was a term of the contract and the defendant was justified in raising the matter as a defence to an action for the price.

(228) *D'Mello* v. *Loughborough College of Technology, The Times*, 17 June, 1970

In 1961 the college advertised a one-year postgraduate course in economics and administration in the oil industry. The plaintiff, who was then working for an oil company in India saw the advertisement and wrote asking for further details. The college sent him a prospectus containing a syllabus of the course and a college calendar for 1961/62 and 1962/63 together with an application form. In due course the college accepted him for the course and in September, 1963, he joined four other students who had already begun their studies. All the other students completed the course but D'Mello gave up early in 1964 because he said that the course was different from the one in the prospectus and in particular did not have sufficient relevance to the oil industry. He now claimed damages for breach of contract. *Held*—by O'Connor, J.—that the prospectus was part of the contract but the plaintiff failed in that he had not shown that the college was in breach of it. It was a matter for the college authorities to decide as a matter of skill and judgment how to conduct the course and there was no evidence to show that they were in breach of their duty to the plaintiff in this regard.

Comment. In *Routledge* v. *McKay*, [1954] 1 All E.R. 855 the plaintiff and defendant were discussing the possible purchase and sale of the defendant's motorcycle. Both parties were private persons. The defendant, taking the information from the registration book, said on October 23 that the cycle was a 1942 model. On October 30 a written contract of sale was made. The actual date of the cycle was later found to be 1930. It was held by the Court of Appeal that this was a mere innocent misrepresentation and rescission having been lost by affirmation, the buyer's claim for damages on the basis that it was a warranty, failed. This case illustrates that the issue of whether a statement is a misrepresentation or a term is really a matter of fact for the court to decide on the circumstances of the case.

(229) *Oscar Chess Ltd* v. *Williams*, [1957] 1 W.L.R. 370

In May, 1955, Williams bought a car from the plaintiffs on hire-purchase terms. The plaintiffs took Williams's Morris car in part exchange. Williams described the car as a 1948 model and produced the registration book, which showed that the car was first registered in April, 1948, and that there had been several owners since that time. Williams was allowed £290 on the Morris. Eight months later the plaintiffs discovered that the Morris car was a 1939 model, there being no change in appearance in the model between 1939 and 1948. The allowance for a 1939 model was £175 and the plaintiffs sued for £115 damages for breach of warranty that the car was a 1948 model. Evidence showed that some fraudulent person had altered the registration book but he could not be traced, and that Williams honestly believed that the car was a 1948 model. *Held*—The contract might have been set aside in Equity for misrepresentation but the delay of eight months defeated this remedy. This mistake was a mistake of quality which did not avoid the contract at common law and in order to obtain damages the plaintiffs must prove a breach of warranty. The court was unable to find that Williams was in a position to give such a warranty, and suggested that the plaintiffs should have taken the engine and chassis number and written to the manufacturers, so using their superior knowledge to protect themselves in the matter. The plaintiffs were not entitled to any redress. Morris, L.J., dissented, holding that the statement that the car was a 1948 model was a fundamental condition.

Comment. It is unlikely that Mr Williams would have been liable for negligent misrepresentation under the Misrepresentation Act, 1967, because he would presumably have had reasonable grounds to believe that his statement that the car was a 1948 model was true, since it had been sold to him on that basis. An interesting contrast to *Oscar Chess* is *Dick Bentley Productions Ltd* v. *Harold Smith (Motors) Ltd*, [1965] 2 All E. R. 65 where a dealer sold a Bentley to a customer, the vehicle's instruments showing that it had done only 30,000 miles since having a replacement engine fitted, whereas in fact it had covered 100,000 since that time. The seller, who was a dealer, was held liable for breach of what is now s. 13 of the Sale of Goods Act, 1979, whereas in *Oscar Chess*, where the seller was not a dealer, it was held that s. 13 did not apply.

Contractual terms: conditions and warranties distinguished

(230) *Poussard* v. *Spiers and Pond* (1876), 1 Q.B.D. 410

Madame Poussard had entered into an agreement to play a part in an opera, the first performance to take place on 28 November, 1874. On 23 November Madame Poussard was taken ill and was unable to appear until 4 December. The defendants had hired a substitute, and discovered that the only way in which they could secure a substitute to take Madame Poussard's place was to offer that person the complete engagement. This they had done, and they refused the services of Madame Poussard when she presented herself on 4 December. The plaintiff now sued for breach of contract. *Held*—The failure of Madame Poussard to perform the contract as from the first night was a breach of condition, and the defendants were within their rights in regarding the contract as discharged.

Comment. This case merely illustrates the availability of repudiation for serious breach of contract. Madame Poussard was not liable to pay damages because, unlike the defendants in *Gill and Duffus S.A.* (see p. 246), she could not help the breach, the contract being also frustrated. (*See p.* 300.)

(231) *Bettini* v. *Gye* (1876), 1 Q.B.D. 183

The plaintiff was an opera singer. The defendant was the director of the Royal Italian Opera in London. The plaintiff had agreed to sing in Great Britain in theatres, halls and drawing rooms for a period of time commencing on 30 March, 1875, and to be in London for rehearsals six days before the engagement began. The plaintiff was taken ill and arrived on 28 March, 1875, but the defendant would not accept the plaintiff's services, treating the contract as discharged. *Held*—The rehearsal clause was subsidiary to the main purposes of the contract, and its breach constituted a breach of warranty only. The defendant had no right to treat the contract as discharged and must compensate the plaintiff, but he had a counter-claim for any damage he had suffered by the plaintiffs' late arrival.

Comment. This case and *Poussard* are good examples of breaches of contract amounting, in *Poussard's* case, to a breach of condition excusing further performance by Spiers and Pond, and in *Bettini's* case, to a breach of warranty not excusing non-acceptance of further performance by Gye. Bettini was liable in damages; Madame Poussard was not. Presumably, therefore, unless the illness frustrates the contract, as it may if a condition is not complied with, then a party is liable for a breach he could not help but commit.

(232) *Harling* v. *Eddy*, [1951] 2 K.B. 739

The plaintiff purchased a heifer at an auction sale. The auction sale was subject to certain conditions which were printed in the catalogue issued to potential buyers. One of the conditions stated that no warranties were given regarding animals purchased unless such warranties appeared on the purchaser's account. When the heifer was brought into the ring, potential buyers showed little interest, and no bids were made until the auctioneer, with the authority of the owner, said: 'There is nothing wrong with her. I will guarantee her in every respect and I will take her back if she is not what I say she is.' The plaintiff thereupon purchased the animal, no warranties being given on the account. The heifer gave little milk and died of tuberculosis four months after purchase. The plaintiff sued for damages and the defence was the exemption clause in the auctioneer's catalogue. *Held*—The plaintiff succeeded. The following points arise out of the judgment in the Court of Appeal—

(*a*) A statement that an animal is sound in every respect would *prima facie* have been no more than a warranty, but the auctioneer's statement that he would take the animal back implied a right in the purchaser to reject the animal, thus making the statement a condition and not a warranty so that the exemption clause was not effective to exclude it. However, since the plaintiff had sued for breach of warranty, it was necessary also to treat the statement of the auctioneer as a warranty in which case it was possible to take the view that the statement was not incorporated into the original contract but was a collateral contract. This conclusion could be reached by bearing in mind the initial silence which greeted the entry of the animal into the ring; and the fact that the bidding only began when the statement had been made suggested that the defendants were not contracting on the auction particulars but on the auctioneer's statement. (*Per* Evershed, M.R.)

(*b*) Denning, L.J., proceeded on the assumption that the statement was a warranty and held that, even so, the exemption clause did not exclude it because 'the party who is liable in law cannot escape liability by simply putting up a printed notice or using a printed catalogue containing exempting conditions. He must go further and show affirmatively that it is a contractual document and accepted as such by the party affected'.

(233) *Behn* v. *Burness* (1863), 3 B. & S. 751

A ship, the *Martaban*, was chartered to carry coal from Newport to Hong Kong. The charterparty described the ship as 'now in the port of Amsterdam' whereas in fact the ship was at Niewdiep about 62 miles from Amsterdam. She was late in arriving at Newport and the charterers refused to load her. *Held*—The charterers were justified in repudiating the contract. In a charterparty the situation of the ship when the charter was made was a term of great commercial importance and must be treated as a condition.

(234) *Hong Kong Fir Shipping Co. Ltd* v. *Kawasaki Kishen Kaisha*, [1962] 1 All E.R. 474

Under a charterparty the owners chartered a ship to the defendants for 24 months from February 1957, the charterparty providing 'She being in every way fitted for ordinary cargo service.' The owners also agreed to 'maintain her in a thoroughly efficient state.' When the ship was delivered the engine room was undermanned for the age of the machinery and the staff were incompetent. On the first voyage it was found that the engines were in a bad state and when she arrived at her destination in May 1957 it was discovered that it would take 15 weeks to make the ship seaworthy. The charterers wrote to the owners in June 1957 repudiating the charter because of the breaches of contract by the owners which, as alleged, were failure to provide a seaworthy ship and negligently failing to maintain it in a proper state. The ship was likely to be, and indeed was, ready by September 1957. It was held by the Court of Appeal that the breaches did not entitle the charterers to repudiate the contract since neither the unseaworthiness, nor the delay, entitled them to do so. The unseaworthiness and failure to maintain were not breaches of conditions and had not in this case caused damage which went to the root of the contract. Furthermore, the delay had not frustrated the commercial purpose of the venture.

Comment. The court is always reluctant to allow a party to repudiate a contract as a means of getting rid of a bad bargain. It appears that the charterer in this case was motivated to repudiate the contract because freight rates had fallen since the charterparty was entered into and he could have chartered other ships more cheaply. However, the evidence did not show that he had suffered any loss because, while the ship was undergoing repairs, he did not under the terms of the contract have to pay the very high rate of agreed hire and could during that period have sent his goods at cheaper freight rates. The case is also a leading authority for the doctrine of the intermediate term, i.e. the term may be classified as a condition or warranty by looking at the nature and effect of its breach *after the event*.

(235) *L. Schuler A.G.* v. *Wickham Machine Tool Sales*, [1973] 2 All E.R. 39

Schuler, a German company, entered into a contract with Wickham, an English company, giving Wickham the sole rights to sell Schuler's panel presses in England. Clause 7(b) provided that 'it shall be a condition of this agreement' that Wickham's representatives should visit six named firms each week to solicit orders. Wickham's representatives failed on a few occasions to do so. Schuler claimed to be entitled to repudiate the agreement on the basis that a single failure was a breach of condition, giving them an absolute right to treat the contract as at an end. *Held*— by the House of Lords—that such a breach did not entitle Schuler to repudiate, since such a construction of the clause was so unreasonable that the parties could not have intended it. Furthermore, in construing a contract, whether to resolve an ambiguity or for any other purpose, a court is not entitled to take into account the conduct of the parties subsequent to the execution of the contract as throwing light on the meaning to be given to it.

Contractual terms: intermediate or innominate terms

(236) *Cehave NV* v. *Bremer Handelsgesellschaft, mbH—The Hansa Nord*, [1975] 3 All E.R. 739

The defendants sold citrus pulp pellets to the plaintiffs. A term of the contract was 'shipment to be made in good condition'. The goods were not delivered all at once but in consignments, and when a particular consignment arrived at Rotterdam the market price of the goods had fallen and it was found that 1260 tons of the goods out of a total consignment of 3293 tons were damaged. The plaintiffs rejected the whole cargo on the grounds that the shipment was not made in good condition. They then claimed the recovery of the price which amounted to £100,000. In the event, a middle man bought the goods at the price of £33,720 and resold them to the plaintiffs at the same price. The plaintiffs then used the pellets for making cattle food as was the original intention. The total result of the transaction, if it had been left that way, was that the plaintiffs had received goods which they had bought for £100,000 for the reduced price of £33,720. The Court of Appeal decided in favour of the sellers. The court *held* that the contractual term 'shipment to be made in good condition' was not a condition within the meaning of the Sale of Goods Act, but was an intermediate term. As Lord Denning, M.R. said: 'If a small portion of the whole cargo was not in good condition and arrived a little unsound, it should be met by a price allowance. The buyers should not have the right to reject the whole cargo unless it was serious or substantial.'

Comment. In *Bunge Corporation, New York* v. *Tradax Export SA Panama*, [1981] 2 All E.R. 540 the House of Lords recognized that intermediate clauses can exist but only as part of the principles of construction of a contract. There is no sense in law in which such a clause can exist; it is a matter for the judge in each case to look at the circumstances. In *Bunge* there was an instalment contract for the sale of goods under which the buyers had to give notice to the sellers of their readiness to load the goods on board ship. On one occasion the buyers failed to give notice of their readiness and the sellers repudiated the contract. The buyers argued that the clause was neither a condition, nor a warranty, but an intermediate clause. Whether or not the other party was entitled to repudiate depended entirely upon whether they had been deprived of the whole benefit of the contract. The House of Lords rejected that argument and construed the notice clause as a condition of the contract. Businessmen should know what their rights were at once and should not have to wait to see the results of a breach before knowing what their position was.

Contractual terms: waiver of express terms

(237) *Heron Garage Properties Ltd* v. *Moss*, [1974] 1 All E.R. 421

Moss contracted to sell part of his land to Heron Garage Properties. Heron wanted to develop the property, and the contract was therefore made conditional upon Heron obtaining detailed planning permission. The contract further stipulated that if permission was not forthcoming within a six-month period either Moss or Heron might serve notice determining the contract. Shortly before the sixth-month period expired Heron wrote to Moss purporting to waive the benefit of these terms of the contract. Shortly after the expiry of the six-month period (no planning permission having been received) Moss gave notice purporting to determine the contract according to its terms. Heron now sued for specific performance. *Held*—by Brightman, J.—that since the planning permission was expressed to be a condition fundamental to the enforceability of the agreement as a whole, it could not be waived by Heron unilaterally. Heron could not show that the stipulation was exclusively for their benefit and therefore had no right to waive it without the consent of Mr Moss. The obtaining of planning permission was not expressed as a condition which was precedent only to the liability of the plaintiffs as purchasers but was expressed to confer rights on both parties. The action was dismissed.

Contractual terms: terms implied by custom

(238) *Hutton* v. *Warren* (1836), 150 E.R. 517

The plaintiff was the tenant of a farm and the defendant the landlord under a written lease. At Michaelmas, 1833, the defendant gave the plaintiff notice to quit on the Lady Day following. The defendant insisted that the plaintiff should cultivate the land during the period of notice which he did. The plaintiff now asked for a fair allowance for seeds and labour of which he had no benefit having left the farm before harvest.

It was proved that by custom a tenant was bound to farm for the whole of his tenancy and on quitting was entitled to a fair allowance for seeds and labour. *Held*—the plaintiff succeeded.

We are of opinion that this custom was, by implication, imported into the lease. It has long been settled, that, in commercial transactions, extrinsic evidence of custom and usage is admissible to annex incidents to written contracts, in matters with respect to which they are silent. The same rule has also been applied to contracts in other transactions of life, in which known usages have been established and prevailed; and this has been done upon the principle of presumption that, in such transactions, the parties did not mean to express in writing the whole of the contract by which they intended to be bound, but to contract with reference to those known usages. (*Per* Parke, B.)

Comment. (i) Custom may, as in *Hutton*, add to a written contract a provision in respect of which it is silent. It may also, as in *Smith* v. *Wilson* (1832), B. & Ad. 728, contradict the normal meaning of words in the contract. In *Smith's* case a local custom was admitted to show that 1000 rabbits meant 1200 rabbits.

(ii) Michaelmas Day is 29 September and is a quarter day for payment of rent as well as a Christian feast. Lady Day is 25 March. It is also a quarter day for the payment of rent and is so called because it is a Christian feast.

Statutory implied terms: seller's right to sell

(239) *Rowland* v. *Divall*, [1923] 2 K.B. 500

In April, 1922, the defendant bought an 'Albert' motor car from a man who had stolen it from the true owner. One month later the plaintiff, a dealer, purchased the car from the defendant for £334, repainted it, and sold it for £400 to Colonel Railsdon. In September, 1922, the police seized the car from Colonel Railsdon and the plaintiff repaid him the £400. The plaintiff now sued the defendant for £334 on the grounds that there had been a total failure of consideration since the plaintiff had not obtained a title to the car. *Held*—The defendant was in breach of s. 12 of the Sale of Goods Act, which implied conditions and warranties into a sale of goods relating to the seller's right to sell, and there had been a total failure of consideration in spite of the fact that the car had been used by the plaintiff and his purchaser. The plaintiff contracted for the property in the car and not the mere right to possess it. Since he had not obtained the property, he was entitled to recover the sum of £334 and no deductions should be made for the period of user.

Comment. (i) Although the court purported to deal with this case as a breach of s. 12(1) of the Act, it would appear that in fact they operated on common law principles and gave complete restitution of the purchase price because of total failure of consideration arising out of the seller's lack of title. The condition under s. 12(1) had by reason of the plaintiff's use of the car and the passage of time become a warranty when the action was brought and if the court had been awarding damages for breach of warranty it would have had to reduce the sum of £334 by a sum representing the value to the plaintiff of the use of the vehicle which he had had.

(ii) The Law Reform Committee (1966 Cmnd 2958 para. 36) recommends that subject to further study of the law relating to restitution, an allowance in respect of use and enjoyment should be deducted from the purchase price and the balance returned to the plaintiff. The difficulty in this approach is that the seller gets an allowance in respect of use of a car which he, the seller, does not own.

(iii) It is also relevant to say that the court felt an allowance for use should not be made because the plaintiff had paid the price for the car to become its *owner*, and not merely to have *use* of it. So why should he be subject to an allowance for use when that is not what he wanted or bargained for? As Bankes, L.J. said: '. . . . he did not get what he paid for—namely a car to which he would have title.'

(240) *Microbeads A.C.* v. *Vinhurst Road Markings*, [1975] 1 All E.R. 529

In this case A sold road marking machines to B. After the sale C obtained a patent on the machine so that their continued use by B was in breach of that patent and C was bringing an action against B in respect of this. In a claim by A against B for the purchase price, B wished to include in their defence breach of s. 12(2) of the Sale of Goods Act, which deals with quiet possession. It was *held*—by the Court of Appeal— that s. 12(2) applied but there was no breach of s. 12(1) which deals with the right to sell. There had been no breach of s. 12(1) at the time of sale because A had the right to sell and had not infringed that subsection, but since B's quiet possession had been disturbed after sale A was in breach of s. 12(2). Therefore when the case came to trial it would be right for B to raise the breach as a defence in an action for the price of the goods.

Statutory implied terms: sale by description

(241) *Beale* v. *Taylor*, [1967] 1 W.L.R. 1193

The defendant advertised a car for sale as being a 1961 Triumph Herald 1200 and he believed this description to be correct. The plaintiff answered the advertisement and later visited the defendant to inspect the car. During his inspection he noticed, on the rear of the car, a metal disc with the figure 1200 on it. The plaintiff purchased the car, paying the agreed price. However, he later discovered that the car was made up of the rear of a 1961 Triumph Herald 1200 welded to the front of an earlier Triumph Herald 948. The welding was unsatisfactory and the car was unroadworthy. *Held*—by the Court of Appeal—that the plaintiff's claim for damages for breach of the condition implied in the contract by s. 13 of the Sale of Goods Act (i.e. sale by description) succeeded. The plaintiff had relied on the advertisement and on the metal disc on the rear and the sale was one by description even though the plaintiff had seen and inspected the vehicle.

Comment. (i) The seller in this case was also in breach of s. 14 of the Sale of Goods Act because the car, being unroadworthy, was neither fit for the purpose nor of merchantable quality. As an example of goods which infringe s. 13 alone, the case of *Dick Bentley Productions Ltd* v. *Harold Smith (Motors) Ltd*, [1965] 2 All E.R. 65 is instructive. In that case a dealer sold a car to a customer representing that it had done only 30,000 miles since a replacement engine was fitted when in fact it had covered 100,000 miles since that time. The seller was held to be in breach of s. 13. The engine state identified the vehicle.

(ii) It should be noted that the description must be an identifying description to come under s. 13. Statements regarding the state of a car's tyres, e.g. 'they were fitted 5,000 miles ago', are concerned more with quality and/or condition of the goods and s. 13 probably does not apply, the claim being for misrepresentation. If s. 13 did apply, then every trivial statement about the goods would be a breach of condition and the law relating to misrepresentation would have no place—a rather unlikely situation.

Statutory implied terms: fitness for purpose: merchantable quality: sales by sample

(242) *Godley* v. *Perry*, [1960] 1 All E.R. 36

The first defendant, Perry, was a newsagent who also sold toys and in particular displayed plastic toy catapults in his window. The plaintiff, who was a boy aged six, bought one for 6d. While using it to fire a stone, the catapult broke, and the plaintiff was struck in the eye, either by a piece of the catapult or the stone, and as a result he lost his left eye. The chemist's report given in evidence was that the catapults were made from cheap material unsuitable for the purpose and likely to fracture, and that the moulding of the plastic was poor, the catapults containing internal voids. Perry had purchased the catapults from a wholesaler with whom he had dealt for some time, and this sale was by sample, the defendant's wife examining the sample catapult by pulling the elastic. The wholesaler's supplier was another wholesaler who had imported the catapults from Hong Kong. This sale was also by sample and the sample catapult was again tested by pulling the elastic. In this action the plaintiff alleged that the first defendant was in breach of the conditions implied by s. 14(1) (now 14(3)) (i.e. fitness for purpose) and (2) (i.e. merchantable quality) of the Sale of Goods Act. The first defendant brought in his supplier as third party, alleging against him a breach of the conditions implied by s. 15(2)(c) (i.e. sale by sample), and the third party brought in his supplier as fourth party, alleging breach of s. 15(2)(c) against him. *Held—*

(i) The first defendant was in breach of s. 14(1) (now 14(3)) and (2) because—

(a) The catapult was not reasonably fit for the purpose for which it was required. The plaintiff relied on the seller's skill or judgment, this being readily inferred where the customer was of tender years. (S. 14(1) (now 14(3)).)

(b) The catapult, even though sold over the counter, was bought by description and was not merchantable. (S. 14(2).)

(ii) The third and fourth parties were both in breach of s. 15(2)(c) because the catapult had a defect which rendered it unmerchantable, and this defect was not apparent on reasonable examination of the sample. The test applied, i.e. the pulling of the elastic, was all that could be expected of a potential purchaser. The third and fourth parties had done business before, and the third party was entitled to regard without suspicion any sample shown to him and to rely on him and to rely on the fourth party's skill in selecting his goods.

Statutory implied terms: a retailer does not warrant the safety of goods when they are used by the purchaser after that purchaser knows of defects in them

(243) *Lambert* v. *Lewis*, [1981] 1 All E.R. 1185

Mr Lewis owned a Land Rover and a trailer. His employee, Mr Larkin, was driving it when the trailer broke away. It collided with a car coming from the opposite direction. Mr Lambert, who was driving that car, was killed and so was his son. His wife and daughter, who were also passengers, survived and then sued Mr Lewis for damages in negligence. He joined the retailer who sold him the towing hitch which had become detached from the trailer and was basically the cause of the collision. The retailer was sued under s. 14 (goods not fit for the purpose nor of merchantable quality). The Court found that the towing hitch was badly designed and a securing brass spindle and handle had come off it so that only dirt was keeping the towing pin in position. It had been like that for some months and Mr Lewis had coupled and uncoupled the trailer once or twice a week during that time and knew of the problem. The plaintiffs succeeded in their action against Mr Lewis. He failed in his claim against the retailer. The House of Lords decided that when a person first buys goods he can rely on s. 14. However, once he discovers that they are defective but continues to use them and so causes injury, he is personally liable for the loss caused. He cannot claim an indemnity under s. 14 from the retailer. The chain of causation is broken by the buyer's continued use of the goods while knowing that they are faulty and may cause injury.

Comment. The above summary does not concern itself with the possible liability of the manufacturers in terms of the design problem. However, a point of interest arises in connection with it. The issue of the manufacturer's liability was taken by an action in negligence. The court refused to construe a collateral contract between Mr Lewis and the manufacturer although he bought the hitch on the strength of the manufacturer's advertising. (Compare *Carlill*[57] where such a contract was rather exceptionally construed.)

Judicial implied terms

(244) *The Moorcock* (1889), 14 P.D. 64

The appellants in this case were in possession of a wharf and a jetty extending into the River Thames, and the respondent was the owner of the steamship *Moorcock*. In November, 1887, the appellants and the respondent agreed that the ship should be discharged and loaded at the wharf and for that purpose should be moored alongside the jetty. Both parties realized that when the tide was out the ship would rest on the river bed. In the event the *Moorcock* sustained damage when she ceased to be waterborne owing to the centre of the vessel settling on a ridge of hard ground beneath the mud. There was no evidence that the appellants had given any warranty that the place was safe for the ship to lie in, but it was *held*—by the Court of Appeal—that there was an implied warranty by the appellants to this effect, for breach of which they were liable in damages.

Now, an implied warranty, or, as it is called, a covenant in law, as distinguished from an express contract or express warranty, really is in all cases founded on the presumed intention of the parties, and upon reason. The implication which the law draws from what must obviously have been the intention of the parties, the law draws with the object of giving efficacy to the transaction and preventing such a failure of consideration as cannot have been within the contemplation of either side; and I believe if one were to take all the cases, and they are many, of implied warranties or covenants in law, it will be found that in all of them the law is raising an implication from the presumed intention of the parties with the object of giving to the transaction such efficacy as both parties must have intended that at all events it should have. In business transactions such as this, what the law desires to effect by the implication is to give such business efficacy to the transaction as must have been intended at all events by both parties who are business men; not to impose on one side all the perils of the transaction, or to emancipate one side from all the chances of failure, but to make each party promise in law as much, at all events, as it must have been in the contemplation of both parties that he should be responsible for in respect of those perils or chances. (*Per* Bowen, L.J.)

Comment. (i) In this sort of case the judge is implying a term *from the facts of the case* because it is reasonable to suppose that if the officious bystander had been asked whether the agreement was for a safe mooring, he would have said 'Oh, of course, it must be'. However, some terms which the judiciary imply are so complicated that the officious bystander would not normally consider them necessarily to be part of the contract. Thus in *Liverpool City Council* v. *Irwin*, [1977] A.C. 239, it was held that it was an implied term of a lease of a council maisonette in a block of such properties, that a landlord should take reasonable care to keep the 'common parts' of the block in a reasonable state of repair. This was obviously done because the court thought it was desirable to impose the obligation on the landlord. However, in that sort of case the court is implying a term *by law* and laying down that in *law* the parties should conduct themselves in a certain way. However, this tends often to improve the contract for one of the parties and it is regarded by some judges as an illegitimate extension of the jurisdiction to imply terms. It is said that the bystander test is the only legitimate one, i.e. that there is only a jurisdiction to apply terms *in fact*.

(ii) When *Irwin*'s case was in the Court of Appeal, Lord Denning, in deciding that there should be an implied term regarding maintenance, rejected the business efficacy test as the only test, saying that the court should imply a term whenever it was *just and reasonable* to do so, whether or not the term was strictly *necessary* to the performance of the contract. Although the House of Lords in *Irwin* implied a term relating to maintenance, they did not go along with the view of Lord Denning that the test should be reasonableness regardless of necessity. The Court of Appeal returned to the 'necessary' approach in *Mears* v. *Safecar Security*, [1982] 2 All E.R. 865 and refused to imply a term in a contract of service that payment should be made to an employee during sickness. Stephenson, L.J. was of opinion that the term could not be implied because although it might be *reasonable* to imply a term relating to sick pay, it was not *necessary* in a contract of employment. The term relating to maintenance in *Irwin* was in a sense not absolutely vital to performance of the contract in that the tenants could have walked up the stairs even in the dark to their flats if lift and light maintenance had not been carried out. However, it was much closer to being necessary to performance of the contract than was the sickpay term in *Mears*.

(iii) Although the court most often implies covenants or terms which are *positive*, i.e. the party concerned *has to do something, negative* covenants can be implied. Thus in *Fraser* v. *Thames Television Ltd*, [1983] 2 All E.R. 101 the members of a group called Rock Bottom brought an action alleging that Thames had broken an agreement with them about a TV series, an implied term of which was that Thames would not use the idea for the series, which was based on the history of the group and its subsequent struggles, unless the members of the group were employed as actresses in the series. Hirst, J. implied this negative term on the grounds that it was necessary to give business efficacy to the agreement between the parties.

(245) *Lister* v. *Romford Ice and Cold Storage Co. Ltd*, [1957] 1 All E.R. 125

The defendants' lorry driver negligently reversed the company's vehicle into another servant of the company (his father) who received damages from the company under the doctrine of vicarious liability. The defendants were insured against this liability and the insurance company paid the damages and, under the doctrine of subrogation, sued the lorry driver in the name of the company to recover what they had paid. It was unanimously *held* by the House of Lords that the lorry-driver, as a servant of the company, owed them a duty to perform his work with reasonable care and skill, and that a servant who involves his master in vicarious liability by reason of negligence is liable in damages to the master for breach of contract. This liability arises out of an implied term in the contract of service to indemnify the master for loss caused to him by the servant's negligence. The damages will in such a case amount to a complete indemnity in respect of the amount which the employer has been held vicariously liable to pay the injured plaintiff.

Comment. Although this case is an illustration of a judicial implied term, it should be noted that employers are not likely in ordinary circumstances to be required by their insurers to bring an action to enforce their right to an indemnity which was the position in *Lister's* case. A committee was set up to deal with the implications of the *Lister* case. As an outcome of its report all members of the British Insurance Association entered into an agreement to the effect that they would not enforce their rights of subrogation in an employer's liability policy, except where there was evidence of collusion or wilful misconduct on the part of the employee. A number of other insurance organizations have also entered into similar agreements. Under the Civil Liability (Contribution) Act, 1978, an employer who has paid damages as a result of a tort committed by his employee may be entitled to an indemnity or a contribution from the employee. Alternatively the employer may sue as in *Lister* for damages *at common law* for breach of an implied term.

(ii) The *Lister* implied term regarding competence was used successfully in *Janata Bank* v. *Ahmed*, [1981] I.C.R. 791. An assistant bank manager was alleged to have caused loss to the bank by allowing a customer for whom no enquiries were made as to credit-worthiness to overdraw some £5000 from his account shortly after the account was opened. The customer gave an hotel address and was not traced. The Court of Appeal decided that damages must be awarded against the assistant manager for breach of the implied term of competence.

(246) *Trollope & Colls Ltd* v. *North West Metropolitan Regional Hospital Board*, [1973] 2 All E.R. 260

The plaintiffs agreed to do some work for the defendants in three stages. The work on stage one was to be completed by April, 1969, subject to extensions caused by certain events. Work on stage three was to begin six months after stage one had been completed and was to be completed by April, 1972. There was the same provision for extending the completion date of stage three, but these events did not include any delay in the completion of stage one. Completion of stage one was delayed (mainly by events which under the terms of the contract, allowed for an extension of the completion date of stage one) and was not completed until June, 1970. Thus the plaintiffs were due to begin work on stage three in December. The House of Lords was asked by what date the plaintiffs were contractually bound to finish stage three. *Held*—that the plaintiffs were bound to complete by April, 1972. The contract expressly provided for what events would permit an extension to the completion date of stage three and these did not include any delay in the completion of stage one. A term could not be implied for allowing an extension of time in respect of such delays. 'The court will not . . . improve the contract which the parties have made, however desirable the improvement might be. . . . If the express terms are perfectly clear and free from ambiguity, there is no choice to be made between different possible meanings: the clear terms must be applied. . . .' (*Per* Lord Pearson at p. 267.)

Comment. This case shows what is perhaps a more legitimate approach to implying terms, i.e. that they can be implied only on the facts and not in law to improve the contract for one of the parties.

Exclusion clauses: the matter of communication

(247) *L'Estrange* v. *Graucob (F.)*, [1934] 2 K.B. 394

The defendant sold to the plaintiff, who owned a café in Llandudno, a slot machine for vending cigarettes inserting in the order form the following clause: 'Any express or implied condition, statement or warranty, statutory or otherwise, is hereby excluded.' The plaintiff signed the order form but did not read the relevant clause, and she now sued in respect of the unsatisfactory nature of the machine supplied. *Held*— The clause was binding on her, although the defendants made no attempt to read the document to her nor call her attention to the clause.

Comment. The ruling in this case would appear to apply even where the party signing cannot understand the document, as where the signer cannot read or does not understand the language in which the document is written. (*The Luna*, [1920] P. 22.) This would not, of course, apply if the person relying on the clause *knew* that the other party could not read. (*Geir* v. *Kujawa*, [1971] 1 Lloyd's Rep. 364.) It will of course, be realised that s. 6(3) of the Unfair Contract Terms Act, 1977 would now apply so that the clause could only be effective if reasonable.

(248) *Chapelton* v. *Barry Urban District Council*, [1940] 1 K.B. 532

The plaintiff Chapelton wished to hire deck chairs and went to a pile owned by the defendants, behind which was a notice stating: 'Hire of chairs 2d. per session of three hours.' The plaintiff took two chairs, paid for them, and received two tickets which he put into his pocket after merely glancing at them. Once of the chairs collapsed and he was injured. A notice on the back of the ticket provided that 'The council will not be liable for any accident or damage arising from hire of chairs.' The plaintiff sued for damages and the council sought to rely on the clause in the ticket. *Held*—The clause was not binding on Chapelton. The board by the chairs made no attempt to limit the liability, and it was unreasonable to communicate conditions by means of a mere receipt.

Comment. (i) The defendants would now have had to face an additional problem, i.e. was the clause reasonable?

(ii) This rule will not necessarily be applied if the term in the contract is particularly burdensome for the other party. In such a case the law may require that the burdensome clause is actually brought to the attention of the other party. This results from the decision of the Court of Appeal in *Interfoto Picture Library Ltd* v. *Stiletto Visual Programmes Ltd, The Times*, 14 November, 1987. In that case Interfoto sent some transparencies to Stiletto for them to make a selection. The delivery note which is a contractual document contained a clause that if the transparencies were not returned within 14 days Stiletto would pay £5 per day for each transparency retained after that. Stiletto delayed returning the transparencies for three weeks and ran up a bill of £3783. When Stiletto were sued for this sum the court said that it could not be recovered by Interfoto because the clause was not specifically drawn to the attention of Stiletto. The Court awarded damages of £3.50 per transparency per week but would not apply the clause.

(249) *Thompson* v. *L.M.S. Railway*, [1930] 1 K.B. 41

Thompson, who could not read, asked her niece to buy her an excursion ticket, on the front of which were printed the words, 'Excursion. For conditions see back.' On the back was a notice to the effect that the ticket was issued subject to the conditions in the company's timetables, which excluded liability for injury however caused. Thompson was injured and claimed damages. *Held*—Her action failed. She had constructive notice of the conditions which had, in the court's view, been properly communicated to the ordinary passenger. The railway ticket was a contractual document.

Comment. The Unfair Contract Terms Act, 1977 now outlaws exclusion clauses which exclude liability for death or personal injury. On its own facts, therefore, the above case is of historical interest only, though it is still relevant on the question of constructive notice. As we have seen, the position is different if the party relying on the clause knows that the other party cannot read it. Thus in *Geir* v. *Kujawa*, [1970] 1 Ll. Rep. 364 the driver of a car displayed a notice in English stating that passengers rode at their own risk but it was held that this did not bind the German passenger who, as the driver was aware, knew hardly any English. (See now Unfair Contract Terms Act, 1977.)

(250) *Richardson Steamship Company Ltd* v. *Rowntree*, [1894] A.C. 217

Rowntree booked a passage on the appellants' ship travelling from Philadelphia to Liverpool. The ticket was folded so that no writing was visible until it was opened. A clause printed on the ticket limited the appellants' liability for injury or damage to passengers or their luggage to $100. The clause was printed in rather small type and was rendered less obvious by a red ink stamp on the ticket. *Held*—Rowntree was not bound by the clause as she did not know of its existence, and there was no constructive notice because the shipowner had not given reasonable notice of the condition.

(251) *McCutcheon* v. *David MacBrayne*, [1964] 1 All E.R. 430

McCutcheon wished to have his motor car transported from Islay to the Scottish mainland, and McCutcheon's agent made a contract of carriage on behalf of McCutcheon with the respondent company. The ship sank owing to the respondents' negligent navigation and the appellant sued for damages. The respondents contended that they were not liable because of certain exemption clauses displayed on a notice in the booking office and also contained in a 'risk note' which was normally given to each customer, though one was not given to the appellant's agent in this case. However, on previous occasions when the parties had done business, 'risk notes' containing exemptions had sometimes been given either to the appellant or his agent. The appellant and his agent knew that some conditions were attached to the respondents' contract, but did not know specifically what they were. *Held*—by the House of Lords—allowing the appellant's appeal, that since this was an oral contract, the conditions relied on were not incorporated into it so as to exempt the respondents from liability in negligence. Lord Devlin was of opinion that previous dealings are relevant only if they prove actual and not constructive knowledge of the terms and also prove assent to them.

Comment. (i) There is in this case also the point that the previous dealings were not consistent in the sense that sometimes McCutcheon's agent had been asked to sign a written contract and sometimes MacBrayne's had been content with an oral one. It appears that if previous dealings are to pass through they must be consistent.

(ii) In *Hollier* v. *Rambler Motors Ltd*, [1972] 1 All E.R. 399 the plaintiff, who on five occasions during the previous five years had had his car repaired by the defendants, and had on some of those occasions signed a form which under the place for signature stated 'the company is not responsible for damage caused by fire to customers' cars' was not bound by the clause when on the sixth occasion he left his car for repair and was not asked to sign the form. The previous dealings did not bind him. Furthermore, the fire which damaged the plaintiff's car was caused by negligence and construing the clause under the *'contra proferentem'* rule, the Court said that it was only a warning that the garage would not be liable in the absence of negligence and did not cover the circumstances of this case. *Hollier* also illustrates that if previous dealings are to come through into a subsequent contract, the course of dealing must be regular. In this case the plaintiff had been to the garage just six times in the course of five years.

(252) *British Crane Hire Corporation* v. *Ipswich Plant Hire*, [1974] 1 All E.R. 1059

The plaintiff and defendant were both engaged in the business of hiring out earth moving equipment. The defendants were also involved in drainage work on marshy ground and urgently requiring a crane, agreed to hire such a crane from the plaintiffs, terms of payment being agreed but no mention being made of the plaintiffs' conditions of hire. The plaintiffs sent the defendants a copy of such conditions which provided, *inter alia*, that the hirer would be responsible for all expenses arising out of the crane's use. Before the defendant signed the form containing the conditions the crane sank into a marsh through no fault of the defendants and the plaintiffs claimed from the defendants the cost of recovering the crane. *Held*—by the Court of Appeal allowing the plaintiffs' claim—that the plaintiffs' conditions of hire applied since both parties were in the trade and of equal bargaining power and on the evidence the defendants and the plaintiffs both understood that the plaintiffs' conditions of hire would apply.

Comment. The terms which applied in this case were apparently drawn up by the trade association of those who were in the hiring business and should therefore have been known to all members of the trade association. In addition, it should be noted that this is not an exclusion clause but rather an indemnity clause, but the provisions regarding previous transactions apply equally to indemnity clauses.

(253) *Olley* v. *Marlborough Court Ltd*, [1949] 1 K.B. 532

Husband and wife arrived at an hotel as guests and paid for a room in advance. They went up to the room allotted to them; on one of the walls was the following notice: 'The proprietors will not hold themselves responsible for articles lost or stolen unless handed to the manageress for safe custody.' The wife closed the self-locking door of the bedroom and took the key downstairs to the reception desk. A third party took the key and stole certain of the wife's furs. In the ensuing action the defendants sought to rely on the notice as a term of contract. *Held*—The contract was completed at the reception desk and no subsequent notice could affect the plaintiff's rights.

Comment. It was said in *Spurling* v. *Bradshaw*, [1956] 1 W.L.R. 461, that if the husband and wife had seen the notice on a previous visit to the hotel it would have been binding on them, though this is by no means

English Law

certain in view of cases such as *Hollier* which suggest that in consumer transactions previous dealings are not incorporated unless they have been regular.

Exclusion clauses: the rule of privity of contract may be overcome: offer and acceptance not always identifiable

(254) *The New Zealand Shipping Co. Ltd* v. *A.M. Satterthwaite & Co. Ltd*, [1974] 1 All E.R. 1015

In this case the makers of an expensive drilling machine entered into a contract for the carriage of the machine by sea to New Zealand. The contract of carriage (the bill of lading) exempted the carriers from full liability for any loss or damage to the machine during carriage and also purported to exempt any servant or agent of the carrier, including independent contractors employed from time to time by the carrier. The machine was damaged by the defendants, who were stevedores, in the course of unloading, and the question to be decided was whether the defendant stevedores, who had been employed by the carrier to unload the machine, could take advantage of the exemption clause in the bill of lading since they were not parties to the contract. It was decided by the Privy Council that they could. The stevedores provided consideration and so became parties to the contract when they actually unloaded the machine. (*Carlill* v. *Carbolic Smoke Ball Co.*, 1893[57] applied.) The performance of services by the stevedores in discharging the cargo was sufficient consideration to constitute a contract, even though they were already under an obligation to the carrier to perform those services because the actual performance of an outstanding contractual obligation was sufficient to support the promise of an exemption from liability given by the makers of the drill, i.e. the shippers, who were, in effect, third parties to the contract between the carrier and the stevedores. (*Shadwell* v. *Shadwell*, 1860[123] applied.)

Exclusion clauses: contractual assent and *volenti non fit injuria*: the relationship

(255) *Burnett* v. *British Waterways Board*, [1973] 1 W.L.R. 700

Burnett was a lighterman working on his employer's barge. Due to the defendants' negligence a capstan rope parted while the barge was docking, injuring Burnett. At the dock office was a notice stating that persons availed themselves of the dock facilities at their own risk. Burnett had read the notice when he was a young apprentice. The defendants admitted negligence but claimed that Burnett had voluntarily undertaken the risk of injury. *Held*—by the Court of Appeal—that Burnett was an employee sent by his employer and it could not be said that he had freely and voluntarily incurred the risk of negligence on the part of the defendant. In the course of his judgment Lord Denning, M.R. said: 'If there was a contract with Mr Burnett, of course, the Board could rely upon it. But there was no contract with him. He was just one of the men working on the barges. The contract was with the barge owners. . . .'

Comment. If the defence of *volenti* succeeds then of course the plaintiff's claim fails.

Exclusion clauses: rules of construction: *contra proferentem* rule

(256) *Alexander* v. *Railway Executive*, [1951] 2 All E.R. 422.

Alexander was a magician who had been on a tour together with an assistant. He left three trunks at the parcels office at Launceston station, the trunks containing various properties which were used in an 'escape illusion'. The plaintiff paid 5d. for each trunk deposited and received a ticket for each one. He then left saying that he would send instructions for their dispatch. Some weeks after the deposit and before the plaintiff had sent instructions for the dispatch of the trunks, the plaintiff's assistant persuaded the clerk in the parcels office to give him access to the trunks, though he was not in possession of the ticket. The assistant took away several of the properties and was later convicted of larceny. The plaintiff sued the defendants for damages for breach of contract, and the defendants pleaded the following term which was contained in the ticket and which stated that the Railway Executive was 'not liable for loss misdelivery or damage to any articles where the value was in excess of £5 unless at the time of the deposit the true value and nature of the goods was declared by the depositor and an extra charge paid'. No such declaration or payment had been made. *Held*—The plaintiff succeeded because, although sufficient notice had been given constructively to the plaintiff, the term did not protect the defendants because they were guilty of a breach of a fundamental obligation in allowing the trunks to be opened and things to be removed from them by an unauthorized person.

Comment. (i) Devlin, J., said that a deliberate delivery to the wrong person did not fall within the meaning of 'misdelivery', and this may be regarded as the real reason for the decision, as it involves the application of the *contra proferentem* rule.

(ii) Note also that the receipt or ticket for the goods deposited was held to be a contractual document.

Exclusion clauses: rules of construction: repugnancy rule

(257) *Pollock & Co.* v. *Macrae*, [1922] S.C. (H.L.) 192

The defendants entered into a contract to build and supply marine engines. The contract carried an exemption clause which was designed to protect the defendant from liability for defective materials and workmanship. The engines supplied under the contract had a great many defects and could not be used. *Held*—by the House of Lords—that on a true construction of the contract the exemption clause did not apply because it was repugnant to the main purpose of the contract. Lord Dunedin said: 'Now, when there is such a congeries of defects as to destroy the workable character of the machine I think this amounts to a total breach of contract, and that each defect cannot be taken by itself separately so as to apply the provisions of the conditions of guarantee and make it impossible to claim damages.'

(258) *Karsales (Harrow) Ltd* v. *Wallis*, [1956] 2 All E.R. 866

The defendant inspected a Buick car which a Mr Stanton wished to sell him. The defendant found it to be in excellent condition and agreed to pay £600 for it, effecting the purchase through a finance company. The car was badly damaged before it was delivered to Wallis; the new tyres which were on the car when Wallis saw it had been replaced by old ones; the radio had been removed; the cylinder head was off; all the valves were burnt; and the engine had two broken pistons. Wallis would not agree to take delivery of the car but it was towed to his place of business and left there. The finance company originally involved assigned its rights under the agreement with Wallis to Karsales, and in this action Karsales were trying to recover the instalments due under the agreement. In so doing they relied on the following clause in the agreement assigned to them: 'No condition or warranty that this vehicle is roadworthy, or as to its age condition or fitness for any purpose, is given by the owner or implied therein.' The county court judge decided that the exemption clause was effective and ordered Wallis to pay. Wallis now appealed. The Court of Appeal held that Wallis was not liable because exemption clauses, no matter how widely expressed, only avail the party who includes them when he is carrying out his contract in its essential respects. Here there was a breach of a fundamental term amounting to non-performance. As Birkett, L.J., said: 'A car that will not go is not a car at all.'

Comment. (i) As the law has developed it would be better to consider this case as correct, but on the basis that the rules of construction were applied to the clause so that it did not apply, and that the rule of construction concerned was the repugnancy rule.

(ii) The contract was for a car in reasonable running order and what was delivered was a car that would not go. The clause purporting to excuse that sort of performance must be repugnant in a contract for a car in running order. It amounts, in effect, to saying 'we promise to sell you a car but all express promises are excluded'. If the exclusion clause was to be applied there is really nothing left of the contract. The whole transaction is excluded.

(iii) We should be careful about Birkett, L.J.'s statement. It really depends why the car will not go. This one was seriously defective but it might be reasonable to allow the contract to continue with the buyer suing merely for damages for breach if all that was preventing the car from going was, e.g. a flat battery.

(259) *Mendelssohn* v. *Normand Ltd*, [1969] 2 All E.R. 1215

The plaintiff left his car in the defendants' garage as he had done before. He was about to lock it as he had done on previous occasions when the attendant said that he could not do so. The plaintiff explained that there was a suitcase containing jewellery on the back seat and the attendant agreed to lock the car when he had moved it. He gave the plaintiff a ticket on the back of which was printed a statement that the proprietors would not 'accept responsibility for any loss sustained . . . no variation of these conditions will bind the (proprietors) unless made in writing signed by their duly authorized manager'. A conspicuous written notice at the reception desk exempted the defendants from loss or damage to the vehicle or its contents. When he returned the plaintiff found the car unlocked and the key in the ignition. It was later discovered that the suitcase had been stolen while the car was in the defendants' garage. In an action by the plaintiff for damages it was *held*—by the Court of Appeal—that

(*a*) The notice at the reception desk was of no effect. It was not seen by a driver until he came to collect his car. The plaintiff had seen it before but had not read it.

(*b*) The plaintiff must be taken to have agreed to the conditions on the ticket which were incorporated in the contract; but

(*c*) the defendants could not rely upon the ticket because—

(i) the attendant had ostensible authority to promise to lock the car and thus to see that the contents were safe. This promise was repugnant to and took priority over the printed condition; and

(ii) the defendants had through their employee agreed to keep the car locked and left it unlocked so performing the contract in an entirely different way from the manner agreed. The defendants were therefore liable.

(260) *J. Evans & Son (Portsmouth) Ltd* v. *Andrea Merzario Ltd*, [1976] 2 All E.R. 930

The plaintiffs imported machines from Italy. They had contracted with the defendants since about 1959 for the transport of these machines. Before the defendants went over to the use of containers the plaintiffs' machines had always been crated and carried under deck. When the defendants went over to containers they orally agreed with the plaintiffs that the plaintiffs' goods would still be carried under deck. However, on a particular occasion a machine being transported for the plaintiffs was carried in a container on deck. At the start of the voyage the ship met a swell which caused the container to fall off the deck and the machine was lost. The contract was expressed to be subject to the printed standard conditions of the forwarding trade which contained an exemption clause excusing the defendants from liability for loss or damage to the goods unless the damage occurred whilst the goods were in their actual custody and by reason of their wilful neglect or default, and even in those circumstances, the clause limited the defendants' liability for loss or damage to a fixed amount. The plaintiffs claimed damages against the defendants for loss of the machine alleging that the exemption clause did not apply. It was *held* by the Court of Appeal that it did not apply. The printed conditions were repugnant to the oral promise for, if they were applicable, they would render that promise illusory. Accordingly, the oral promise was to be treated as overriding the printed conditions and the plaintiffs' claim succeeded, the exemption clause being inapplicable.

Exclusion clauses: rules of construction: four corners rule

(261) *Thomas National Transport (Melbourne) Pty Ltd and Pay* v. *May and Baker (Australia) Pty Ltd*, [1966] 2 Ll. Rep. 347

The owners of certain packages made a contract with carriers under which the packages were to be carried from Melbourne to various places in Australia. The carriers employed a sub-contractor to collect the parcels and take them to the carriers' depot in Melbourne. When the sub-contractor arrived at the Melbourne depot it was locked and so he drove the lorry full of packages to his own house and left it in a garage there. This was in accordance with the carriers' instructions to their sub-contractors in the event of late arrival at the depot. There was a fire at nearby premises which spread to the sub-contractor's premises and some of the packages were destroyed. The owners sued the carriers who pleaded an exemption clause in the contract of carriage. *Held*—by the High Court of Australia—that the plaintiffs succeeded. There had been a fundamental breach of contract. The intention of the parties was that the goods would be taken to the carriers' depot and not to the sub-contractor's house, in which case the carriers could not rely on the clause.

Comment. (i) The decision, which was partly based on fundamental breach of contract, is perhaps better founded on the four corners rule, i.e. the exclusion clause is available only so long as the contract is being performed in accordance with its terms.

(ii) The alleged negligence of the carriers consisted in their instruction to sub-contractors to take the goods home.

Fundamental breach: does not prevent reliance on an exclusion clause in a non-consumer situation

(262) *Photo Production Ltd* v. *Securicor Transport Ltd*, [1980] 1 All E.R. 556

The defendants had agreed to provide security services to the plaintiffs' factory where there was a considerable amount of inflammable material since they were manufacturers of greetings cards. There were to be four visits every night of the week. On the night in question the defendants' employee, a man of 23 who was highly spoken of, entered the factory with keys provided and for no reason that could be shown dropped a lighted match on to a cardboard box. This may have been a prank or a form of idleness; the trial judge was unable to say. To the employee's surprise the fire spread quickly and it was soon clear that it was out of his control. He made frantic efforts to put it out in the course of which he lost his spectacles and his false teeth and suffered considerable burns. He dialled 999, having no intention of doing any harm, although the harm actually done was estimated at £600,000.

When sued, Securicor pleaded the exemption clause set out below

'Under no circumstances shall the company (Securicor) be responsible for any injurious act or default by any employee of the company unless such act or default could have been seen and avoided by the exercise of due diligence on the part of the company as his employer'.

The Court of Appeal found that the clause did not apply on the basis of the doctrine of fundamental breach and on the principles of construction of contracts. That decision was reversed by the House of Lords who said that the clause did apply so that Securicor was not liable for the damage. The following points should be noted—

(a) the House of Lords seemed to feel that if both parties are business organizations they should be left free to decide what their liability should be without interference from the court. A business liability is, or should be, covered by insurance and if the contract uses words appropriate to exclude breaches of fundamental terms, i.e. conditions, the clause should be allowed to apply. It should therefore be noted that those in business must read the small print most carefully.

(b) The House of Lords decided that even clauses excluding breaches of fundamental terms could be regarded as reasonable for the purposes of the Unfair Contract Terms Act, 1977, though the Act was not in force when the facts of the case occurred. Their Lordships commented that it was significant that Parliament had refrained in the 1977 Act from legislating over the whole field of contract by preventing exclusion clauses entirely. Exclusion clauses were not defeated by some rule of law; the matter was left to a judicial construction of particular contracts in the circumstances of each case within the general framework of reasonableness.

(c) The decision would appear to be set in the context of business liability and would not rule out the use of the 'reasonable' test by the courts to prevent exemption clauses applying to fundamental breach in consumer transactions.

Comment. (i) In *Harbutt's Plasticine Ltd* v. *Wayne Tank and Pump Co. Ltd*, [1970] 1 All E.R. 225, Lord Denning accepted that the principle which said that no exclusion clause could excuse fundamental breach was not a rule of law when the injured party carried on with (or affirmed) the contract. Where this was so the rules of construction must be used and the exclusion clause might have to be applied. However, if the injured party elected to repudiate the contract for fundamental breach and, as it were, pushed the contract away, the exclusion clause went with it, according to Lord Denning, and could never apply to prevent the injured party from suing for the breach. The same, Lord Denning said, was true where the consequences were so disastrous (as they were in *Photo Production*) that one could assume that the injured party had elected to repudiate. The *Photo Production* case overrules *Harbutt*, as does s. 9(1) of the Unfair Contract Terms Act, 1977. This provides that if a clause, as a matter of construction, is found to cover the breach and if it satisfies the reasonable test, it can apply and be relied on by the party in breach, even though the contract had been terminated by express election or assumed election following the disastrous results of the breach.

(ii) The House of Lords also allowed a *Securicor* exemption clause to apply in circumstances of fundamental breach in *Ailsa Craig Fishing Co. Ltd* v. *Malvern Fishing Co. Ltd.*, [1983] 1 All E.R. 101. In that case the appellant's ship sank while berthed in Aberdeen harbour. It fouled the vessel next to it which was owned by Malvern. The appellant sued Malvern. Securicor were the second defendants. Securicor had a contract with the appellant to protect the ship. The accident happened as a result of a rising tide. At the time the Securicor patrolman had left his post to become involved in New Year celebrations. Although there were arguments by counsel to the contrary, the House of Lords held that the exclusion clause covered the circumstances of the case provided the words were given their natural and plain meaning. It therefore applied to limit the liability of Securicor and the appellants failed to recover all their loss.

Exclusion clauses: Unfair Contract Terms Act, 1977: exclusion of statutory implied terms: reasonableness

(263) *Mitchell (George) (Chesterhall) Ltd* v. *Finney Lock Seeds Ltd*, [1983] 1 All E.R. 108

This case is a landmark. It was the last case heard by Lord Denning in the Court of Appeal. In it he gave a review of the development of the law relating to exclusion clauses in his usual clear and concise way. The report is well worth reading in full. Only a summary of the main points can be given here.

George Mitchell ordered 30 pounds of cabbage seed and Finney supplied it. The seed was defective. The cabbages had no heart; their leaves turned in. The seed cost £192 but Mitchell's loss was some £61,000, i.e. a year's production from the 63 acres planted. Mitchell carried no insurance. When sued Finney defended the claim on the basis of an exclusion clause limiting their liability to the cost of the seed or its replacement. In the High Court Parker, J. found for Mitchell. Finney appealed to the Court of Appeal. The major steps in Lord Denning's judgment appear below.

(1) *The issue of communication—was the clause part of the contract?* Lord Denning said that it was. The conditions were usual in the trade.

They were in the back of Finney's catalogue. They were on the back of the invoice. 'The inference from the course of dealing would be that the farmers had accepted the conditions as printed, even though they had never read them and did not realise that they contained a limitation on liability. . . .'

(2) *The wording of the clause*. The relevant part of the clause read as follows: 'In the event of any seeds or plants sold or agreed to be sold by us not complying with the express terms of the contract of sale or with any representation made by us or by any duly authorised agent or representative on our behalf prior to, at the time of, or in any such contract, or any seeds or plants proving defective in varietal purity we will, at our option, replace the defective seeds or plants, free of charge to the buyer or will refund all payments made to us by the buyer in respect of the defective seeds or plants and this shall be the limit of our obligation. We hereby exclude all liability for any loss or damage arising from the use of any seeds or plants supplied by us and for any consequential loss or damage arising out of such use or any failure in the performance of or any defect in any seeds or plants supplied by us or for any other loss or damage whatsoever save, for, at our option, liability for any such replacement or refund as aforesaid.'

Lord Denning said that the words of the clause did effectively limit Finney's liability. Since the Securicor cases (see *Photo Production* and *Ailsa Craig*, above) words were to be given their natural meaning and not strained. A judge must not proceed in a hostile way towards the working of an exclusion clause as was, for example, the case with the word 'misdelivery' in *Alexander* v. *Railway Executive*, 1951.[256]

(3) *The test of reasonableness*. Lord Denning then turned to the new test of reasonableness which could be used to strike down an exclusion clause even though it had been communicated and in spite of the fact that its wording was appropriate to cover the circumstances. On this he said: 'What is the result of all this? To my mind it heralds a revolution in our approach to exemption clauses; not only where they exclude liability altogether and also where they limit liability; not only in the specific categories in the Unfair Contract Terms Act, 1977, but in other contracts too. . . . We should do away with the multitude of cases on exemption clauses. We should no longer have to go through all kinds of gymnastic contortions to get round them. We should no longer have to harass our students with the study of them. We should set about meeting a new challenge. It is presented by the test of reasonableness.'

(4) *Was the particular clause fair and reasonable*? On this Lord Denning said: 'Our present case is very much on the borderline. There is this to be said in favour of the seed merchants. . . . The price of this cabbage seed was small: £192. The damages claimed are high: £61,000. But there is this to be said on the other side. The clause was not negotiated between persons of equal bargaining power. It was inserted by the seed merchants in their invoices without any negotiation with the farmers. To this I would add that the seed merchants rarely, if ever, invoked the

clause. . . . Next, I would point out that the buyers had no opportunity at all of knowing or discovering that the seed was not cabbage seed, whereas the sellers could and should have known that it was the wrong seed altogether. The buyers were not covered by insurance against the risk. Nor could they insure. But as to the seed merchants the judge said (Lord Denning here refers to Parker, J. at first instance): "I am entirely satisfied that it is possible for seedsmen to insure against this risk. . . ." To that I would add this further point. Such a mistake as this could not have happened without serious negligence on the part of the seed merchants themselves or their Dutch suppliers. So serious that it would not be fair to enable them to escape responsibility for it. In all the circumstances I am of the opinion that it would not be fair or reasonable to allow the seed merchants to rely on the clause to limit their liability.'

Oliver and Kerr, L.JJ. also dismissed the appeal.

The suppliers asked for leave to appeal to the House of Lords but the Court of Appeal refused. However, the House of Lords granted leave and affirmed the decision of the Court of Appeal. (See [1983] 2 All E.R. 737.)

Comment. This is in effect an application of s. 6(3) of the Unfair Contract Terms Act, 1977. It was actually brought under the Sale of Goods Act, 1979 which contained transitional provisions and s. 55(3) of the 1979 Act plus para. II of Sch. I applied to this contract. For contracts made after 31 January, 1978, s. 6(3) of the Unfair Contract Terms Act would apply.

Exclusion clauses: misrepresentation: s. 8, Unfair Contract Terms Act, 1977: reasonableness

(264) *Walker* v. *Boyle*, [1982] 1 All E.R. 634

The vendor of a house was asked in a pre-contract enquiry whether the boundaries of the land were the subject of any dispute. The vendor asked her husband to deal with the enquiry. He said that there were no disputes. There were, in fact, disputes, but the husband did not regard them as valid because he believed that he was in the right and his view could not be contradicted. His answers were nevertheless wrong and misleading. Contracts were later exchanged. These contracts were on the National Conditions of Sale (19th Edition) produced under the aegis of the Law Society. Condition 17(1) excluded liability for misleading replies to preliminary enquiries. The purchaser later heard of the boundary disputes and claimed in the High Court for rescission of the contract and the return of his deposit. Dillon, J. held that Condition 17(1) did not satisfy the requirements of reasonableness as set out in s. 3 of the Misrepresentation Act, 1967 (as substituted by s. 8(1) of the Unfair Contract Terms Act, 1977). The plaintiff therefore succeeded.

Comment. (i) The National Conditions of Sale have been revised and as regards misrepresentation, the contract now only attempts a total exclusion of the purchaser's remedies if the misrepresentation is not material or substantial in terms of its effect and is not made recklessly or fraudulently.

(ii) The provisions relating to inducement liability were also applied in *South Western General Property Co. Ltd* v. *Marton* [1983] 2 T.L.R. 14; the court held that conditions of sale in an auction catalogue which tried to exclude liability for any representations made, if these were incorrect, were not fair and reasonable. The defendant had relied upon a false statement that some building would be allowed on land which he bought at an auction, even though the facts were that the local authority would be most unlikely to allow any building on the land. The clauses excluding liability for misrepresentation did not apply and the contract could be rescinded.

Contracts of utmost good faith: insurance: effect of basis clauses

(265) *Dawsons Ltd* v. *Bonnin*, [1922] 2 A.C. 413

Dawsons Ltd insured their motor lorry against loss by fire with Bonnin and others, and signed a proposal form which contained the following as Condition 4: 'Material misstatement or concealment of any circumstance by the insured material to assessing the premium herein, or in connection with any claim, shall render the policy void.' The policy also contained a clause saying that the 'proposal shall be the basis of the contract and shall be held as incorporated therein'. Actually the proposal form was filled up by an insurance agent, and although he stated the proposer's address correctly as 46 Cadogan Street, Glasgow, he also stated that the vehicle would usually be garaged there, although there was no garage accommodation in the Cadogan Street address and the lorry was garaged elsewhere. Dawsons' secretary, who signed the proposal, overlooked this slip made by the agent. The lorry was destroyed by fire and Dawsons claimed under the policy. *Held*—on appeal, by the House of Lords—The statement was not material within the meaning of Condition 4. However, the basis clause was an independent provision, and since the statement, though not material, was untrue, the policy was void. Viscount Cave said: 'The meaning and effect of the basis clause, taken by itself, is that any untrue statement in the proposal, or any breach of its promissory clauses, shall avoid the policy, and if that be the contract of the parties, the question of materiality has not to be considered.'

Comment. (i) The Unfair Contract Terms Act of 1977 does not apply to contracts of insurance and so basis clauses cannot be struck down on that ground. However, the Director of Fair Trading has agreed codes of practice with insurance companies under which basis clauses are not to be used unreasonably, at least in consumer transactions.

(ii) However, even if we get rid of the basis clause problem, the rule of disclosure of material matters by the person seeking insurance remains a difficulty. It is based upon s. 18(2) of the Marine Insurance Act, 1906. This should not have been used as a basis for *all* insurances. Those seeking marine insurance are well aware of the risks they seek to insure.

Those seeking, e.g. domestic fire insurance are not. The Law Commission Report entitled *Non-Disclosure and Breach of Warranty* places a heavy onus on insurance companies to phrase their questions so as to elicit the kind and amount of information they want and not to leave it, as at present, to the person seeking insurance to make uninformed guesses as to what might be material to the insurers. The common law has already taken steps in this direction in *Hair* v. *Prudential Assurance*, (1983) 133 N.L.J 282, the court deciding in that case that if a person seeking insurance answered honestly all the questions put to him by the proposal for insurance he should not be required to disclose any other matters. The questions should reveal all material issues.

Contracts of utmost good faith: duty of disclosure in family relationships

(266) *Gordon* v. *Gordon* (1819), 3 Swan. 400

Two brothers made an agreement for division of the family estates. The elder supposed he was born before the marriage of his parents and was therefore illegitimate. The younger knew that their parents had been married before the birth of the elder brother and the elder brother was therefore legitimate and his father's heir. He did not communicate this information to his elder brother; 19 years afterwards the elder brother discovered that he was legitimate and the agreement was set aside at his suit. He would have had so case if at the time of the agreement both brothers had been in honest error as to the date of their parents' marriage.

Comment. If a family relationship has been, or is about to be terminated, as where husband and wife are separated or about to separate, the duty of disclosure does not apply. Thus in *Wales* v. *Wadham*, [1977] 1 All E.R. 125, a husband, after he had left his wife, offered her financial provision after she had told him that she would not re-marry. She accepted her husband's offer, having decided to re-marry, and it was held that the wife was not bound to disclose her change of mind.

Duress: effect upon gifts and contracts

(267) *Welch* v. *Cheesman* (1974), 229 Estates Gazette 99

Mrs Welch lived with Cheesman for many years in a house which she owned. Cheesman was a man given to violence and after threats from him Mrs Welch transferred her house to him for £300. Cheesman then died and his widow claimed the house which was worth about £3000. Mrs Welch sought to set aside the transfer on the grounds of duress and her claim succeeded.

(268) *Cumming* v. *Ince* (1847), 11 Q.B. 112

An old lady was induced to settle property on one of her relatives by the threat of unlawful confinement in a private mental home. *Held*—The settlement could be set aside on the ground of duress, i.e. the threat of false imprisonment.

Undue influence: effect upon gifts and contracts

(269) *Allcard* v. *Skinner* (1887), 36 Ch.D. 145

In 1868 the plaintiff joined a Protestant institution called the sisterhood of St Mary at the Cross, promising to devote her property to the service of the poor. The defendant Miss Skinner was the Lady Superior of the Sisterhood. In 1871 the plaintiff ceased to be a novice and became a sister in the order, taking her vows of poverty, chastity and obedience. By this time she had left her home and was residing with the sisterhood. The plaintiff remained a sister until 1879 and, in compliance with the vow of poverty, she had by then given property to the value of about £7000 to the defendant. The plaintiff left the order in 1879 and became a Roman Catholic. Of the property she had transferred, £1671 remained in 1885 and the plaintiff sought to recover this sum, claiming that it had been transferred in circumstances of undue influence. *Held*—The gifts had been made under pressure of an unusually persuasive nature, particularly since the plaintiff was prevented from seeking outside advice under a rule of the sisterhood which said, 'Let no sister seek the advice of any extern without the superior's leave.' However, the plaintiff's claim was barred by her delay because, although the influence was removed in 1879, she did not bring her action until 1885.

(270) *Lancashire Loans Ltd* v. *Black*, [1934] 1 K.B. 380

A daughter married at eighteen and went to live with her husband. Her mother was an extravagant woman and was in debt to a firm of money-lenders. When the daughter became of age, her mother persuaded her to raise £2000 on property in which the daughter had an interest, and this was used to pay off the mother's debts. Twelve months later mother and daughter signed a joint and several promissory note of £775 at eighty-five per cent interest in favour of the moneylenders, and the daughter created a further charge on her property in order that the mother might borrow more money. The daughter did not understand the nature of the trans-action, and the only advice she received was from a solicitor acting for the mother and the moneylenders. The moneylenders brought this action against the mother and daughter on the note. *Held*—The daughter's defence that she was under the undue influence of her mother succeeded, in spite of the fact that she was of full age and married with her own home.

(271) *Williams* v. *Bailey* (1866), L.R. 1 H.L. 200

A father agreed to make a mortgage of property to a bank in consider-ation of the return by the bank of certain promissory notes forged by his son. The banker concerned had suggested in conversation with the father that the son would be prosecuted if some agreement were not reached. The promise to make the mortgage was held invalid because of undue influence which, though not presumed in this case, had been proved.

Comment. The application of the presumption in a relationship which was not one of the established ones is also illustrated by *Goldsworthy* v. *Brickell*, [1987] 2 W.L.R. 133 where a contract to grant a tenancy of a farm advantageous to the defendant in that, e.g. it did not allow the landlord, G, to make any rent increases, was set aside. The defendant, B, who had become the tenant, was a neighbour of G's. G was 85 and had come to rely implicitly on the advice of B. Undue influence was presumed although neighbours are not within the established categories where undue influence is generally presumed.

Unconscionable bargains: protection against improper pressure and inequality of bargaining power

(272) *Lloyds Bank* v. *Bundy*, [1974] 3 All E.R. 757

The defendant and his son's company both banked with the plaintiffs, the defendant having been a customer for many years. The company's affairs deteriorated over a period of years and at the son's suggestion the bank's assistant manager visited the defendant and said that the bank could not continue to support an overdraft to the company unless the defendant entered into a guarantee of the account. The defendant received no independent advice, nor did the bank's assistant manager suggest that he should do so. The defendant charged his house as security for the over-draft and shortly afterwards the company went into receivership. The bank obtained possession of the house from the defendant in the county court where the assistant branch manager in evidence said that he thought that the defendant had relied upon him implicitly to advise him about the charge. The defendant appealed to the Court of Appeal in an attempt to set aside the guarantee and the security and it was *held*—allowing the defendant's appeal—that in the particular circumstances a special relationship existed between the defendant and the bank's assistant manager, as agent for the bank, and the bank was in breach of its duty of fiduciary care in procuring the charge which would be set aside for undue influence. The defendant, without any benefit to himself, had signed away his sole remaining asset without taking independent advice.

Comment. (i) While the majority of the Court of Appeal (Cairns, L.J. and Sir Eric Sachs) were content to decide the appeal on the conventional ground that a fiduciary relationship existed between the bank and its customer, which is to suggest that a new fiduciary relationship has come into being, Lord Denning took the opportunity to break new ground by deciding that in addition to avoiding the contract on the grounds of a fiduciary relationship Mr Bundy could also have done so on the basis of 'inequality of bargaining power'. Although inequality of bargaining power obviously includes undue influence, Lord Denning made it clear that the principle does not depend on the will of one party being dominated or overcome by the other. This is clear from that part of the judgment where he says: 'One who is in extreme need may knowingly consent to a most improvident bargain, solely to relieve the straits in which he finds himself.' This approach is, of course, at variance with the traditional view of undue influence which was that it was based on dominance resulting in an inferior party being unable to exercise independent judgment.

(ii) A further example of unequal bargaining power is to be found in *Cresswell* v. *Potter*, [1978] 1 W.L.R. 255 where an agreement by a wife in the course of divorce proceedings to transfer her share of the matrimonial home to her husband for an inadequate sum without independent advice was set aside by the Court.

(iii) Again, in *National Westminster Bank plc* v. *Morgan*, [1983] 3 All E.R. 85 the Court of Appeal set aside a charge over a wife's share in the matrimonial home after she executed it without legal advice in order to secure a loan from the bank to clear a building society mortgage, and after the bank manager had assured her that the charge would not be used to secure her husband's business advances whereas it did in fact extend to such advances. However, the bank had no intention of using the charge other than to secure the advance to clear the building society mortgage; nor did it.

The above decision which moved in the direction of saying that banks would have to ensure that all their customers had independent legal advice before taking out a bank mortgage was reversed by the House of Lords in *National Westminster Bank plc* v. *Morgan*, [1985] 1 All E.R. 821. Undue influence, the House of Lords said, was the use by one person of a power over another person to take a certain course of action generally to his or her disadvantage. A bank manager need not advise independent legal advice in a situation such as this. The manager in this case had stuck to explaining the legal effect of the charge which, though erroneous as to the terms of the charge, correctly represented his intention and that of the bank. The security represented no disadvantage to Mrs Morgan. It was exactly what she wanted to clear the building society loan on her home. The House of Lords also rejected the view that the court would grant relief where there was merely an inequality of bargaining power. Their Lordships rejected that view which was expressed by Lord Denning in *Bundy*. The courts will not, said the House of Lords, protect persons against what they regard as mistakes merely because of inequality of bargaining power. This is a much harder line.

(iv) In *Bundy*, therefore, the Court of Appeal held that the bank in not advising the person giving the security to get independent advice exercised undue influence and for this reason set the security aside. In *Morgan* the House of Lords held that no presumption of undue influence existed. In *Cornish* v. *Midland Bank*, [1985] 3 All E.R. 513 the Court of Appeal decided that the proper way to deal with these cases was not through undue influence but by using the law of negligence, though only where the bank had given wrong advice.

In *Cornish* the plaintiff had signed a second mortgage on a farmhouse jointly owned with her husband in order to secure £2,000 which her husband had borrowed from the bank. She did so because the bank clerk involved said that the mortgage was like a building society mortgage. It was not because unlike a building society mortgage it covered all future borrowing by the husband. The bank later tried to enforce the security. Eventually the Court of Appeal held that the bank was liable in negligence for the wrong advice of its clerk who made a negligent misstatement causing damage, i.e. that £2,000 was the borrowing limit when it was not. The mortgage was not set aside for undue influence so that the bank was entitled to the proceeds of the sale of the farmhouse but had to pay the plaintiff £11,231 damages plus interest for negligence. Thus, although it would be good practice for a bank to advise independent advice, it is not necessary for it to do so. The security will be good and there is no presumption of undue influence. However, if an employee of the bank *actually* gives negligent advice or fails to explain the consequences of the charge and/or fails to advise the taking of independent advice (See *Midland Bank plc* v. *Perry, The Times*, 28 May, 1987.) the bank will be able to enforce the security but will be liable in damages under the ruling in *Hedley Byrne* v. *Heller & Partners*, (1963) (See p. 635.)

Public policy: application of law to foreign contracts

(273) *Kaufman* v. *Gerson*, [1904] 1 K.B. 591

The defendant's husband had misappropriated money entrusted to him by the plaintiff, his employer. The defendant made a contract in writing with the plaintiff under which she agreed to make good the loss, the plaintiff agreeing not to prosecute. The events took place in France and the agreement was governed by French law, which did not regard the element of coercion in the case as a vitiating element. Nevertheless, the action being brought on the contract in an English court, it was dismissed because it was contrary to public policy for an English court to enforce a contract obtained in this way.

Comment. The court would, therefore, have set the contract aside if that had been the issue on the grounds of undue influence. It should be noted that the contract is not in fact affected by duress because the threats involved in duress must be unlawful, and if the threatened act is lawful it cannot be regarded as duress, though in the case of threats of criminal proceedings, the contract can be set aside on the ground of undue influence.

Public policy: judiciary: illegal contracts

(274) *Dann* v. *Curzon* (1911), 104 L.T. 66

An agreement was made for advertising a play by means of collusive criminal proceedings brought as a result of a pre-arranged disturbance at the theatre. The plaintiffs, who agreed to create the disturbance and did in fact do so, sued for the remuneration due to them under the agreement. *Held*—The action failed because it was an agreement to commit a criminal offence and was therefore against public policy.

(275) *Pearce* v. *Brooks* (1866), L.R. I. Exch. 213

The plaintiffs hired a carriage to the defendant for a period of twelve months during which time the defendant was to pay the purchase price by instalments. The defendant was a prostitute and the carriage, which was of attractive design, was intended to assist her in obtaining clients. One of the plaintiffs knew that the defendant was a prostitute but he said that he did not know that she intended to use the carriage for purposes of prostitution. The evidence showed to the contrary. The jury found that the plaintiffs knew the purpose for which the carriage was to be used and thereupon the court held that the plaintiffs' claim for the sum due under the contract failed for illegality.

Comment: The contract would, of course, have been valid if the plaintiffs had not *known* of the intended use of the carriage.

(276) *Regazzoni* v. *K.C. Sethia Ltd*, [1958] A.C. 301

The defendants agreed to sell and deliver jute bags to the plaintiff, both parties knowing and intending that the goods would be shipped from India to Genoa so that the plaintiff might then send them to South Africa. Both parties knew that the law of India prohibited the direct or indirect export of goods from India to South Africa, this law being directed at the policy of apartheid adopted by South Africa. The defendants did not deliver the jute bags as agreed and the plaintiff brought this action in an English court, the contract being governed by English law. *Held*—Although the contract was not illegal in English law, it could not be enforced because it had as its object the violation of the law of a foreign and friendly country in which part of the contract was to be carried out.

Comment. In an earlier case, *Foster* v. *Driscoll*, [1929] 1 K.B. 470, decided on this ground, the court held that a contract to smuggle whisky to the USA during the period of prohibition was illegal and void.

(277) *John* v. *Mendoza*, [1939] 1 K.B. 141

The defendant owed the plaintiff some £852. The defendant was made bankrupt and the plaintiff was intending to prove for his debt in the bankruptcy. The defendant asked him not to do so, but to say that the £852 was a gift whereupon the defendant would pay the plaintiff in full regardless of the sum received by other creditors. In view of the defendant's promise the plaintiff withdrew his proof, but in the event all the other creditors were paid in full and the bankruptcy was annulled. The plaintiff now sued for the debt. *Held*—There was no claim, for the plaintiff abandoned all right to recover on failure to prove in the bankruptcy, and the defendant's promise to pay in full was unenforceable, being an agreement designed to defeat the bankruptcy laws.

(278) *Parkinson* v. *The College of Ambulance Ltd and Harrison*, [1925] 2 K.B. 1

The first defendants were a charitable institution and the second defendant was the secretary, who fraudulently represented to the plaintiff, Colonel Parkinson, that the charity was in a position to obtain some honour (probably a knighthood) for him if he would make a suitable donation to the funds of the charity. The plaintiff paid over the sum of £3000 and said he would pay more if the honour was granted. No honour of any kind was received by the plaintiff and he brought this action to recover the money he had donated to the College. *Held*—The agreement was contrary to public policy and illegal. No relief could be granted to the plaintiff.

(279) *Napier* v. *National Business Agency Ltd*, [1951] 2 All E.R. 264

The defendants engaged the plaintiff to act as their secretary and accountant at a salary of £13 per week plus £6 per week for expenses. Both parties were aware that the plaintiff's expenses could never amount to £6 a week and in fact they never exceeded £1 per week. Income Tax was deducted on £13 per week, and £6 per week was paid without deduction of tax as reimbursement of expenses. The plaintiff, having been summarily dismissed, claimed payment of £13 as wages in lieu of notice. *Held*—The agreement was contrary to public policy and illegal. The plaintiff's action failed.

Comment. In an earlier case on this point (*Alexander* v. *Rayson*, [1936] 1 K.B. 169), Mrs Rayson took a lease of a service flat. The rent was £1200 per annum and she signed two forms: under one she agreed to pay £450 for the lease, under the other £750 for services provided by the plaintiff landlord. His purpose in splitting the transaction was to defraud the rating authorities who assessed the flat for rates on the basis of a rent of £450 p.a. which was all the plaintiff disclosed. This was unknown to the defendant. It was held that the contract was illegal. Mrs Rayson could not be sued for the rent. The service contract was also void.

Illegal contracts: consequences: is performance necessarily unlawful or not? The *in pari delicto* rule: the matter of repentance

(280) *Bowmakers Ltd* v. *Barnet Instruments Ltd*, [1944] 2 All E.R. 579

Bowmakers bought machine tools from a person named Smith. This contract was illegal because it contravened an Order made by the Minister of Supply under the Defence Regulations, Smith having no licence to sell machine tools. Bowmakers hired the machine tools to Barnet Instruments under hire-purchase agreements which were also illegal because Bowmakers did not have a licence to sell machine tools. Barnet Instruments failed to keep up the instalments, sold some of the machine tools and refused to give up the others. Bowmakers sued, not on the illegal hire-purchase contracts, but in conversion, and judgment was given for Bowmakers. The Court of Appeal declared the contracts illegal but, since Bowmakers were not suing under the contracts but as owners, their action succeeded. The wrongful sales by Barnet Instruments terminated the hire-purchase contracts.

Comment. Although the contract between Smith and Bowmakers was illegal ownership passed to Bowmakers by reason of delivery. When goods are delivered the person receiving them has some evidence of title by reason of possession and need not necessarily plead a contract. Where, in an illegal situation, the goods have not been delivered there may be difficulty in establishing ownership without relying on the illegal contract Nevertheless, ownership was established without delivery in *Belvoir Finance Co. Ltd* v. *Stapleton*, [1970] 3 W.L.R. 530. In this case A (a dealer) sold certain cars to B (a finance company) which let them on hire purchase to C (a car-hire firm). C did not pay the minimum deposit required by regulation to B; thus the hire-purchase contract was illegal. Later, C's manager, S, sold the cars to innocent purchasers. C did not pay the hire-purchase instalments and B sued S in conversion, the company C having gone into liquidation. It was *held* by the Court of Appeal that B succeeded. They were the owners of the cars and S had converted their property. The decision is of interest since B (the finance company) had never taken delivery of the cars; they were sent direct from A to C as is usual in these transactions. Nevertheless B was accepted as owner although the only means of proving ownership open to B seems to have been the illegal hire purchase contract with C. This was the only document which showed how B came to acquire ownership of the cars. On the assumption that this case means what it says, then the rule that there can be no enforcement of illegal contracts loses much of its practical value since the major remedy of claiming the goods back appears to be available equally against a hirer in default, whether the contract is legal or illegal.

(281) *Edler* v. *Auerbach*, [1950] 1 K.B. 359

The defendant leased premises to the plaintiff for use as offices. The lease was contrary to the provisions of the Defence Regulations of 1939, since the premises had previously been used as residential accommodation and should have been let as such. The local authority discovered the illegal use and would not allow it to continue. The plaintiff now sued for rescission of the lease together with rent paid under it. The defendant counter-claimed for rent due and for damage done to the premises, including the removal of a bath. *Held*—The landlord could not enforce the illegal lease but was entitled to damages for the plaintiff's failure to replace the bath.

(282) *Hughes* v. *Liverpool Victoria Legal Friendly Society*, [1916] 2 K.B. 482

John Henry Thomas, a grocer, had originally taken out five policies on customers who owed him money. It was agreed that Thomas had an insurable interest in the customers because they were his debtors. Thomas let the policies drop and an agent of the defendant company persuaded a Mrs Hughes to take them up, assuring her that she had an insurable interest which she had not. She now brought this action to recover the premiums paid. *Held*—The contract was illegal but the plaintiff could recover the premiums. She had been induced to take up the policies by the fraud of the defendants' agent.

Comment. In an earlier case on this point (*Atkinson* v. *Denby* (1862), 7 H. & N. 934), the plaintiff was insolvent and wished to compromise with his creditors by paying 25 p in the £1. One creditor would not agree unless the plaintiff paid him £50. This sum was paid and was later recovered by the plaintiff who had been forced to defraud his creditors. The money was then available for distribution to creditors generally.

(283) *Bigos* v. *Bousted*, [1951] 1 All E.R. 92

The defendant was anxious to send his wife and daughter abroad for the sake of the daughter's health, but restrictions on currency were in force so that a long stay abroad was impossible. In August, 1947, the defendant, in contravention of the Exchange Control Act, 1947, made an agreement under which the plaintiff was to supply £150 of Italian money to be made available at Rapallo, the defendant undertaking to repay the plaintiff with English money in England. As security, the defendant deposited with the plaintiff a share certificate for 140 shares in a company. The wife and daughter went to Italy but were not supplied with currency, and had to return sooner than they would have done. The defendant, thereupon, asked for the return of his share certificate but the plaintiff refused to give it up. This action was brought by the plaintiff to recover the sum of £150 which she insisted she had lent to the defendant. He denied the loan, and counter-claimed for the return of his certificate. In the course of the action the plaintiff abandoned her claim, but the defendant proceeded with his counter-claim saying that, although the contract was illegal, it was still executory so that he might repent and ask the court's assistance. *Held*—The court would not assist him because the fact that the contract had not been carried out was due to frustration by the plaintiff and not the repentance of the defendant. In fact his repentance was really want of power to sin.

(284) *Taylor* v. *Bowers* (1876), 1 Q.B.D. 291

The plaintiff was under pressure from his creditors and in order to place some of his property out of their reach he assigned certain machinery to a person named Adcock. The plaintiff then called a meeting of his creditors and tried to get them to settle for less than the amount of their debts, representing his assets as not including the machinery. The creditors would not and did not agree to a settlement. The plaintiff now sued to recover his machinery from the defendants who had obtained it from Adcock. *Held*—The plaintiff succeeded because the illegal fraud on the creditors had not been carried out.

(285) *Kearley* v. *Thomson* (1890), 24 Q.B.D. 742

The plaintiff had a friend who was bankrupt and wished to obtain his discharge. The defendant was likely to oppose the discharge and accordingly the plaintiff paid the defendant £40 in return for which the defendant promised to stay away from the public examination and not to oppose the discharge. The defendant did stay away from the public examination but before an application for discharge had been made the plaintiff brought his action claiming the £40. *Held*—The claim failed because the illegal scheme had been partially effected.

Illegal contracts: consequences: effect on collateral transactions

(286) *Fisher* v. *Bridges* (1854), 188 E.R. 713

The plaintiff agreed to sell the defendant certain land which the defendant intended to use as a prize in a lottery. The use of land for lotteries was forbidden by statute but the land was conveyed and the purchase price all but £630 was paid. Later the defendant entered into a deed with the plaintiff under the terms of which he agreed to pay the £630 and the plaintiff now sued upon that deed. *Held*—No action lay on the deed. Jervis, C.J., said: 'It is clear that the covenant was given for the payment of the purchase money. As it springs from, and is the creature of the illegal agreement, and as the law would not enforce the original illegal contract, so neither will it allow the parties to enforce a security for the purchase money which, by the original bargain, was tainted with illegality.'

(287) *Southern Industrial Trust* v. *Brooke House Motors* (1968), 112 Sol. J. 798

A customer wished to buy a car from the defendants who were dealers. The dealers and the customer inserted incorrect figures relating to price and deposit in the hire-purchase agreement so that it became illegal under statutory provisions then applying to such agreements. The car was then sold to the plaintiff finance company which was unaware of the true position. The finance company hired it out to the customer under the falsified hire-purchase agreement. The dealers had represented both to the customer and the finance company that the car was a 1962 model whereas in fact it was registered in 1958. When the customer discovered this he refused to pay any further instalments to the finance company and the company sued the dealers for breach of a warranty in the contract of sale to them, i.e. that the car was a 1962 model. It was *held*—by the Court of Appeal—that damages were recoverable notwithstanding the illegality of the hire-purchase agreement between the plaintiffs and the customer. The sale by the dealers to the finance company was collateral to that and was not tainted by the illegality in the other agreement.

Comment. It was held in a later case on this point (*Spector* v. *Ageda* (1971), 115 S.J. 426) that a loan of money was illegal and could not be recovered because the lender knew that it was going to be used to pay another illegal loan to a money-lender.

Illegal contracts: consequences: contract lawful on the face of it

(288) *Fielding and Platt Ltd* v. *Najjar*, [1969] 2 All E.R. 150

The plaintiffs entered into an agreement with a Lebanese company to make and deliver an aluminium press. Payment was to be made by six promissory notes given at stated intervals by the defendant personally. The defendant, who was the managing director of the Lebanese company, told the plaintiffs that they ought to invoice the goods as part of a rolling mill, his intention being to deceive the Lebanese import authorities into believing that the import of the press was authorized whereas in fact it was not. The first promissory note was dishonoured and the plaintiffs stopped work on the press and cabled a message to the Lebanese company to that effect. The second promissory note was then dishonoured and the plaintiffs sued upon the notes. The case eventually reached the Court of Appeal where it was *held*, that—

(i) since the first note covered work in progress there was no defence based on failure of consideration;

(ii) any illegality in connection with the importing of the press was not part of the contract or agreed to by the plaintiffs;

(iii) the plaintiffs' claim was not, therefore, affected by illegality;

(iv) since the plaintiffs had repudiated the contract before the second note was dishonoured they had no claim for the amount of the note as such but could only sue for damages—the defendant was not liable on the second note.

Comment. In an earlier case on this point (*Clay* v. *Yates* (1856), 1 H. & B. 73) it was held that a printer who had, without knowledge, printed a book containing libels could recover his charges.

(289) *Cowan* v. *Milbourn* (1867), L.R. 2 Ex. 230

A person hired a hall to deliver blasphemous lectures and then was refused possession of it. His action claiming possession was refused on the grounds that no relief could be granted by the court where the purpose of the contract was illegal.

(290) *Ashmore, Benson, Pease & Co. Ltd* v. *A. V. Dawson Ltd*, [1973] 2 All E.R. 856

The defendant haulage company agreed to carry some equipment for the plaintiff company. As the plaintiff's transport manager and his assistant watched but did not assist, the defendant company loaded their vehicles to a laden weight of 35 tons without objection being made. The maximum permitted laden weight was 30 tons under the Motor Vehicles (Construction and Use) Regulations, 1966. One of the vehicles toppled over, and the vehicle and its load were damaged. The plaintiff company claimed damages for negligent driving and negligence in placing the load on an unsuitable lorry. *Held*—that the contract, though lawful in its inception, was illegal in its carrying out to the knowledge and with the concurrence of the plaintiff company's servants. Thus damages were not recoverable, *Dictum* of Atkin, L.J., in *Anderson Ltd* v. *Daniel*, 1924 (see p. 282) applied.

(291) *Berg* v. *Sadler and Moore*, [1937] 1 All E.R. 637

The plaintiff was a hairdresser and sold tobacco and cigarettes. He was a member of the Tobacco Trade Association, the Association having as its object the prevention of price cutting. Manufacturers would supply tobacco to traders who agreed not to sell at less than the fixed retail price. The plaintiff sold tobacco at cut prices and was put on the manufacturers' stop list which meant that he could not obtain supplies. The plaintiff made contact with a person named Reece who was a member of the Association and Reece agreed to obtain goods from manufacturers and hand them over to the plaintiff, in return for which Reece was to receive a commission from the plaintiff. One such transaction was carried out. On a later occasion the plaintiff's assistant and a representative of Reece went to the defendant's premises to obtain a supply of cigarettes. The plaintiff's assistant handed over some £72 to Moore, who had some doubt about the matter and said he would send the goods direct to Reece's shop. Thereupon the plaintiff's assistant demanded the return of the money, Moore refused to give it back, and this action was brought to recover it. *Held*—This was an attempt by the plaintiff to obtain goods by false pretences and, since no action arises out of a base cause, the plaintiff's action failed.

Public policy: contracts to oust the jurisdiction of the courts: severance

(292) *Goodinson* v. *Goodinson*, [1954] 2 All E.R. 255

A contract made between husband and wife, who had already separated, provided that the husband would pay his wife a weekly sum by way of maintenance in consideration that she would indemnify him against all debts incurred by her, would not pledge his credit, and would not take matrimonial proceedings against him in respect of maintenance. The wife now sued for arrears of maintenance under this agreement. The last promise was admittedly void since its object was to oust the jurisdiction of the courts, but it was *held* that this did not vitiate the rest of the contract; it was not the sole or even the main consideration, and the wife's action for arrears succeeded, this promise being severable.

Comment. In a later case on this point (*Re Davstone Estates Ltd*, [1969] 2 All E.R. 849) it was decided that a clause in a lease providing that, as regards certain payments to be made by tenants for services to common parts, e.g. staircases, in a block of flats, the certificate of the landlord's surveyor was to be final and conclusive, could be regarded as void.

Public policy: restraint on employees against mere competition

(293) *Morris & Co.* v. *Saxelby*, [1916] 1 A.C. 688

On leaving school Saxelby entered the drawing office of a company engaged in the manufacture of lifting machinery, pulley blocks and travelling cranes. The company had its head office and works in Loughborough and branch offices in eight large cities. Eventually Saxelby became head of one of the company's departments at a salary of £3 17s. 6d. a week. He had entered into a covenant not to engage in a similar business in the United Kingdom for a period of seven years from the date of leaving the company's service. In this action the company sought to enforce that covenant and it was *held* by the House of Lords that it was unreasonably wide, having regard to Saxelby's interests because it would 'deprive him for a lengthened period of employing, in any part of the United Kingdom, that mechanical and technical skill and knowledge which, as I have said, his own industry, observation, and intelligence have enabled him to acquire in the very specialized business of the appellants, thus forcing him to begin life afresh, as it were, and depriving him of the means of supporting himself and his family': *Per* Lord Atkinson.

Furthermore, their Lordships were unanimously of the opinion that the covenant was wider than was necessary to protect those interests which the company was entitled to protect, being aimed at securing the appellants against all competition from Saxelby.

Comment. In a later case (*Wyatt* v. *Kreglinger and Fernau*, [1933] 1 K.B. 793) an employee was promised a pension on his retirement and agreed that it would not be paid if he competed against his employers who were in the wool trade. The pension was held void by the Court of Appeal. Two judges said that it was contrary to the public interest to deprive the community of services from which it might derive advantage.

Public policy: restraints on employees: trade secrets

(294) *Forster & Sons Ltd* v. *Suggett* (1918), 35 T.L.R. 87

The works manager of the plaintiffs who were mainly engaged in making glass and glass bottles was instructed in certain confidential methods concerning, amongst other things, the correct mixture of gas and air in the furnaces. He agreed that during the five years following the termination of his employment he would not carry on in the United Kingdom, or be interested in, glass bottle manufacture or any other business connected with glass making as conducted by the plaintiffs. It was *held* that the plaintiffs were entitled to protection in this respect and that the restraint was reasonable.

(295) *Commercial Plastics* v. *Vincent*, [1964] 3 All E.R. 546

The plaintiffs employed Vincent, a plastics technologist, to co-ordinate research and development in the production of their PVC (Poly-vinyl-chloride) calendered sheeting, which was made up into adhesive tape. Vincent's contract forbade him to seek employment with any of the plaintiffs' competitors in the PVC calendering field for one year after leaving their employment. Vincent had access to secret material, including certain mixing specifications recorded in code and, although he could not remember these, he could probably remember, in relation to any matter concerning adhesive tape, what was the problem and what was the solution, what experiments were made and whether the results were positive or negative. Vincent left his employment with the plaintiffs and proposed to take up employment with a competitor. The plaintiffs asked for an injunction to restrain Vincent from breaking the restraining term in his contract with them. *Held*—by the Court of Appeal—An injunction could not be granted. Although what Vincent could remember was sufficiently definite to be capable of protection by an appropriate condition or covenant, the term in the agreement was excessive. It was world-wide in scope, although the plaintiffs did not, on the facts of the case, require protection outside the United Kingdom. Furthermore, the term extended to the plaintiffs' competitors in the whole field of PVC whereas they required protection, so far as Vincent was concerned, only in relation to calendered sheeting for adhesive tape.

Public policy: restraints on employees: solicitation of customers and clients

(296) *Home Counties Dairies* v. *Skilton*, [1970] 1 All E.R. 1227

Skilton, a milk roundsman employed by the plaintiffs, agreed, amongst other things, not 'to serve or sell milk or dairy produce' to persons who within six months before leaving his employment were customers of his employers. Skilton left his employment with the plaintiffs in order to work as a roundsman for Westcott Dairies. He then took the same milk round as he had worked when he was with the plaintiffs. *Held*—by the Court of Appeal—This was a flagrant breach of agreement. The words 'dairy produce' were not too wide. On a proper construction they must be restricted to things normally dealt in by a milkman on his round. 'A further point was taken that the customer restriction would apply to anyone who had been a customer within the last six months of the employment and had during that period ceased so to be, and it was said that the employer could have no legitimate interest in such persons. I think this point is met in the judgment in *G. W. Plowman & Sons Ltd* v. *Ash*, 1964, where it was said that a customer might have left temporarily and that his return was not beyond hope and was therefore a matter of legitimate interest to the employer.' (*Per* Harman, L.J.)

Comment. (i) *Skilton* is a *solicitation* covenant (i.e. one preventing solicitation of customers) not an *area* covenant (i.e. one preventing an employee from working in a particular area in which customers are, or might be). The courts have tended to prefer solicitation covenants. Thus in *Financial Collection Agencies (U.K.)* v. *Batey* (1973), 117 S.J. 416, the Court of Appeal decided that covenants restraining debt collectors working in Birmingham for a period of six months after leaving employment from soliciting business for clients in Birmingham, Glasgow, Leeds, Liverpool, London, and Manchester were too wide and unenforceable because on the evidence the collectors had no contact with clients outside Birmingham.

However, much depends on the influence over customers and clients which an employee may have acquired and in *S.W. Strange* v. *Mann*, [1965] 1 All E.R. 1096, Stamp, J., drew a distinction between a credit business and a cash business. In a cash business the names of the customers are known only to the employees and are not recorded in the books of the firm. For this reason the employees in a cash business are more likely to have influence over the customers of the firm and the court may be more sympathetic towards a wider area restraint in respect of them, provided it does not exceed the area of the employer's trade.

Nevertheless, area covenants cannot be ruled out entirely and may still be upheld if the area is not too wide. Thus in *Fitch* v. *Dewes*, [1921] A.C. 158, the House of Lords decided that a restraint upon a solicitor's managing clerk prohibiting him from practising within seven miles of his employer's main office in Tamworth was valid, though this is thought to be an exceptional case perhaps not surviving the solicitation approach.

(ii) It was held by the Court of Appeal in *John Michael Design* v. *Cooke*, [1987] 2 All E.R. 332, after referring to *Plowman* v. *Ash* that a restraint in a contract of employment preventing an employee (A) from competing with his former employer (B) could be enforced by an injunction even to prevent the former employee from doing business with a customer (C) of his former employer who had make it clear that he would not do business with B again. There was always the possibility that C would change his mind.

(297) *Scorer* v. *Seymour Jones*, [1966] 3 All E.R. 347

Under a contract dated 2 June, 1964, between an estate agent and one of his unqualified employees who was the estate agent's clerk and negotiator, the employee agreed that he would not, for three years after leaving his employment, carry on or be employed or interested in the business of an auctioneer, surveyor or estate agent within five miles of the employer's premises at Kingsbridge and Dartmouth. The employee was the manager of the branch office at Kingsbridge and there were recurring customers at this branch. The employee was unsatisfactory and was dismissed in November, 1964; thereafter he practised on his own account as an estate agent in Salcombe within five miles of Kingsbridge, but outside a five-mile radius of Dartmouth. The employer Scorer asked for an injunction restraining his former employee Seymour Jones from practising within five miles of the Kingsbridge office. The injunction was granted at Kingsbridge County Court, and on appeal by the employee against the granting of an injunction it was *held* by the Court of Appeal that the injunction was rightly granted because the employer had many recurring clients and the restraint on practising within five miles of the Kingsbridge office was reasonable. Further, the restriction on practising within five miles of the Dartmouth office was not a reasonable restraint but was severable. *Per* Sellers, L.J., in considering whether the restriction was contrary to the public interest, it was proper to take into account the fact that the employee was unqualified and not controlled by professional rules.

(298) *White (Marion) Ltd* v. *Francis*, [1972] 3 All E.R. 857

In this case the Court of Appeal declared valid a covenant which restrained the defendant from being in any capacity whatsoever engaged, concerned or interested in ladies' hairdressing within one half-mile of the plaintiff's premises during the continuance of her employment or within 12 months of her employment ceasing.

(299) *T. Lucas & Co. Ltd* v. *Mitchell*, [1972] 3 All E.R. 689

In 1968 Mitchell entered into a service agreement as a sales representative with the plaintiffs, a subsidiary of Spillers Ltd. The plaintiffs' principal business was the manufacture and sale of articles, products and commodities used in the meat processing industry. Mitchell was allocated the Manchester district as his sales area and it was divided into six 'journeys' each of which normally took a week. In the course of each journey he visited all the plaintiff company's customers on the route so that each customer was normally visited once every six weeks. In clause 16 of the agreement the defendant undertook 'not for a period of one year after the determination of his employment either by effluxion of time or otherwise howsoever either directly or indirectly whether as principal, partner, agent, servant or assistant within the allocated districts as existing at the termination of his employment to deal in any goods similar to or capable of being used in place of any of the allocated articles or solicit orders for or supply any such goods to any person firm or company carrying on business within the allocated districts as existing at the termination of his employment hereunder to whom the (plaintiff) company has supplied any of the allocated articles during the twelve months preceding such a determination'. In February, 1972, the plaintiff company's head office became aware that the defendant, who had terminated his employment in December of the previous year had been active in canvassing a considerable number of their customers in the Manchester area on behalf of his new employers, a rival firm in the same business as the plaintiffs. A writ was issued claiming damages and an injunction restraining further breaches of clause 16 of the contract of service. At first instance Pennycuick, V.-C., following *Attwood* v. *Lamont*, 1920 (see p. 701), held that the clause in effect prohibited two things—(*a*) dealing in allocated articles in the Greater Manchester area; and (*b*) soliciting the company's customers in the area. It followed that as stipulation (*a*) was plainly wider than was necessary to protect the company's trade connection in that it prevented the defendant from visiting persons with whom he could have had no possible previous connection, the whole restraint was unreasonable and void, it being impossible to sever the two restraints. On the issue of severance Pennycuick, V.-C., took the view that the type of goods covered in part (*b*) of the restraint, i.e. goods similar to or capable of being used in place of any of the allocated articles, could only be ascertained by reference to part (*a*) of the restraint. In these circumstances it was not possible to treat the restrictions as entirely separate. The Court of Appeal, however, took a different view of the question of severance. In a judgment of the court read by Russell, L.J., it was found that the restraint was not a single restraint against dealng, soliciting or supplying, but in essence two separate obligations, one against dealing and the other against soliciting and supplying. This being so, the Court of Appeal, finding its own decision in *Scorer* v. *Seymour Jones*, 1966[297] to be inconsistent with *Attwood* v. *Lamont*, 1920 (see p. 701) preferred to follow the former case and allowed severance granting an injunction in respect of breaches of the clause restraining soliciting and supplying. It is perhaps unfortunate that *Scorer* was followed because in that case the restraint was clearly an attempt to protect the employers' several businesses and not his business as a whole, and as such, was more readily severable. In addition, the employee in *Scorer's* case had prior to dismissal, apparently been guilty of a particularly culpable breach of fidelity in the course of his employment.

Public policy: restraints on employees: effect of employer's breach of contract

(300) *General Billposting Co. Ltd* v. *Atkinson*, [1909] A.C. 118

Atkinson was manager to a Newcastle billposting company for a number of years upon terms that he should hold office subject to termination at twelve months' notice by either party, and with a restriction on his right to trade after termination of his employment. The restriction on trade was that he should not, whilst in the employment of the company or within two years afterwards, carry on a similar business within a certain radius of Newcastle without the company's permission. In 1906 Atkinson was dismissed without notice and he successfully sued the company for wrongful dismissal. Having recovered damages he began to trade as a billposter on his own account within the prohibited area. The General Billposting Co. Ltd, having taken over the company with which Atkinson was employed, brought an action for an injunction and for damages for breach of contract. *Held*—by the House of Lords—Atkinson was entitled to treat the dismissal as a repudiation of the contract and to sue for damages for breach of contract, and was no longer bound by the restriction on trade.

Public policy: restraints on employees: in regard to future activities of the employer

(301) *Bromley* v. *Smith*, [1909] 2 K.B. 235

The plaintiff was a baker at Clacton and it was his practice to send carts containing bread on various rounds to visit boarding houses and shops. In 1895 the plaintiff required an assistant to undertake what was known as the town round and by means of an advertisement he came into communication with the defendant, a young man of eighteen years, who lived some miles away at a place called Great Baddow. The defendant had since the age of twelve been engaged in the bakery trade. On 18 November, 1895, the plaintiff and defendant entered into an agreement under which the defendant agreed that he would not at any time within the space of three years after the date of leaving the plaintiff's service engage or be engaged in the business of miller, baker, hay, straw or corn dealer, or restaurant keeper, or in the manufacture of flour meal. Eventually the defendant terminated his employment by giving notice to the plaintiff and then in partnership with a man named Green he took over premises in Clacton, three miles from the plaintiff's premises, and commenced business as a baker and confectioner. Both before and after he left the plaintiff's employment the defendant, on his own admission, canvassed the plaintiff's customers and some of these customers gave their custom to the defendant. At the time of the agreement the plaintiff did not carry on any business other than that of a baker and confectioner but he was contemplating an extension of his business and was considering opening a restaurant. *Held*—by Channell, J.—The restraint must coincide with what is necessary for the protection of the existing business of the employer and the restriction relating to the business of restaurant keeper went further than was necessary. However, the restraint was severable because each of the prohibited trades was stated separately and those relating to the business of baker or confectioner were enforceable. Furthermore, the contract as severed was enforceable, even though the defendant was a minor when he made it. It was a contract for his benefit even though it contained restraints. 'A contract which contains only terms on which an infant can reasonably expect employment must, I think, be for his benefit.'

Public policy: non-contractual restraints on employees: the duty of fidelity

(302) *Printers and Finishers* v. *Holloway (No. 2)*, [1964] 3 All E.R. 731

The plaintiffs brought an action against Holloway, their former works manager, and others, including Vita-Tex Ltd, into whose employment Holloway had subsequently entered, claiming injunctions against Holloway and other defendants based, as regards Holloway, on an alleged breach of an implied term in his contract of service with the plaintiffs that he should not disclose or make improper use of confidential information relating to the plaintiffs' trade secrets. Holloway's contract did not contain an express covenant relating to non-disclosure of trade secrets. The plaintiffs were flock-printers and had built up their own fund of 'know-how' in this field. The action against Vita-Tex arose because Holloway had, on one occasion, taken a Mr James, who was an employee of Vita-Tex Ltd, round the plaintiff's factory. Mr James's visit took place in the evening and followed a chance meeting between himself and Holloway. However, the plant was working and James did see a number of processes. It also appeared that Holloway had, during his employment made copies of certain of the plaintiff's documentary material and had taken these copies away with him when he left their employ. The plaintiffs sought an injunction to prevent the use or disclosure of the material contained in the copies of documents made by Holloway.

Held—by Cross, J.—

(*a*) The plaintiffs were entitled to an injunction against Holloway so far as the documentary material was concerned, although there was no express term in his contract regarding non-disclosure of trade secrets.

(*b*) No injunction would be granted restraining Holloway from putting at the disposal of Vita-Tex Ltd his memory of particular features of the plaintiffs' plant and processes. He was under no express contract not to do so and the court would not extend its equitable jurisdiction to restrain breach of confidence in this instance. Holloway's knowledge of the plaintiffs' trade secrets was not readily separable from his general knowledge of flock printing.

(*c*) An injunction would be granted restraining Vita-Tex Ltd from making use of the information acquired by James on his visit.

Comment. (i) In *Faccenda Chicken Ltd* v. *Fowler*, [1986] 1 All E.R. 617 Mr Fowler was sales manager for Faccenda Chicken Ltd for seven years and set up a van sales operation whereby refrigerated vans travelled around certain districts offering fresh chicken to retailers and caterers. He left the company and set up his own business selling chickens from refrigerated vans in the same area. Eight of the company's employees went to work for him.

Each of the salesmen in the company knew the names and addresses of the customers, the route and timing of deliveries, and the different prices quoted to different customers.

The company unsuccessfully brought an action for damages in the High Court, and the Court of Appeal alleging wrongful use of confidential sales information and were also unsuccessful in a counter-claim for damages for breach of contract by abuse of confidential information in Mr Fowler's action against them for outstanding commission.

(ii) It is generally the case that rather more protection in terms of preventing an employee from approaching customers can be obtained by an express term which is reasonable in terms of its duration. In the absence of an express term, it is clear from this decision of the Court of Appeal that confidential information of an employer's business obtained by an employee in the course of his service may be used by that employee when he leaves the job unless, as the Court of Appeal decided, it can be classed as a trade secret or is of such a confidential nature that it merits the same protection as a trade secret. For example, there would have been no need for a term in the contract of service in *Forster*.[294] The Court could have prevented use of the secret process for a period without this. It should however, be noted that in *Faccenda* the Court of Appeal did say that if the employees had written down lists of customers, routes, etc, as distinct from having the necessary information in their memories, and presumably being unable to erase it, short of amnesia, they might have been restrained for a period from using the lists. This follows the case of *Robb* v. *Green*, (1895)[303] where the manager of a firm dealing in live game and eggs copied down the names of customers before leaving and then solicited these for the purposes of his own business after leaving the employment of the firm.

(303) *Robb* v. *Green*, [1895] 2 Q.B. 315

The plaintiff was a dealer in live game and eggs. The major part of his business consisted of procuring the eggs, and the hatching, rearing and sale of game birds. For the purpose of carrying on this business, the plaintiff occupied game farms at Liphook in Hampshire, and at Elstead near Godalming. His customers were numerous and for the most part were country gentlemen and their gamekeepers. The plaintiff kept a list of these customers in his order book. The defendant, who was for three years the plaintiff's manager, copied these names and addresses, and after leaving the plaintiff's employ set up in a similar business on his own and sent circulars both to the plaintiff's customers and their gamekeepers inviting them to do business with him. The plaintiff sought damages and an injunction. *Held*—by the Court of Appeal (affirming the judgment of Hawkins, J.)—Although there was no express term in the defendant's contract to restrain him from such activities, it was an implied term of the contract of service that the defendant would observe good faith towards his master during the existence of the confidential relationship between them. The defendant's conduct was a breach of that contract in respect of which the plaintiff was entitled to damages of £150 and an injunction.

(304) *Sanders* v. *Parry*, [1967] 2 All E.R. 803

In January, 1964, the defendant was engaged by the plaintiff solicitor as assistant solicitor. The defendant had been told by the plaintiff that he was to undertake the legal work of an important client, Mr Tully. The defendant took up his employment on 16 March, 1964. During August or September, 1964, the defendant and Tully agreed that the defendant would set up in practice on his account whereupon Tully would transfer all his legal business from the plaintiff to the defendant and this was done. In an action for damages for breach of an implied term of the contract that the defendant would serve the plaintiff faithfully, the defendant admitted the term but said that he was not in breach of it because the agreement between him and Tully had been initiated by Tully and he had merely accepted an offer which Tully had made. *Held*—That even if the agreement had not been initiated by the defendant, he had, in accepting the offer during the substance of his agreement with the plaintiff, acted contrary to the interests of the plaintiff and was in breach of the implied term of fidelity.

(305) *Hivac Ltd* v. *Park Royal Scientific Instruments Ltd*, [1946] 1 All E.R. 350

The plaintiffs were manufacturers of midget valves used in deaf aids, the work requiring a high degree of skill. The defendants were newcomers to the trade and concerned themselves mainly with the assembly of hearing aids. The plaintiffs' employees worked a five and a half day week, having Sunday free. Five such employees worked on Sundays for the defendants, assisting in the assembly of midget valves. The plaintiffs asked for an injunction to restrain their employees from carrying out such work. *Held*—In the special circumstances of the case an injunction would be granted, not because of any specific contractual restraint but because the conduct of the particular employees constituted a breach of the duty of fidelity which every servant owes to his master.

(306) *Initial Services* v. *Putterill*, [1967] 3 All E.R. 145

The first defendant was employed by the plaintiff launderers as their sales manager but he resigned and took a number of the plaintiffs' documents which he handed to reporters of the *Daily Mail*, who were the second defendants. He also gave the reporters of the same newspaper information about the company's affairs. The newspapers published articles alleging a liaison system between launderers to keep up their prices, and that the plaintiffs had increased their prices after the imposition of the Selective Employment Tax ostensibly to offset that tax, when in fact they were getting substantial extra profit. On the plaintiffs' action for breach of an implied term of the defendant's contract of service that he would not disclose to strangers confidential information obtained by him in the course of his employment, the defendant pleaded that the plaintiffs had agreements which ought to have been registered under the Restrictive Trade Practices Act, 1956 (see now Restrictive Trade Practices Act, 1976), that they ought to have been referred to the Monopolies Commission, and that they had issued misleading circulars about their reasons for raising their prices. *Held*—in interlocutory proceedings to strike out the defence—

(i) The servant was under no obligation not to disclose information which ought, in the public interest, to be disclosed to a person having a proper interest to receive it;

(ii) it was at least arguable that the information supplied by the defendant was in the above category;

(iii) the allegations in the defence could not be said to be so invalid that they ought to be struck out.

There was argument on the question as to whether the press was the proper authority for the receipt of confidential information but this doubt was not enough to invalidate the defence at this stage.

Public policy: restraints during employment: exclusive service contracts

(307) *A. Schroeder Music Publishing Co. Ltd* v. *Macauley*, [1974] 3 All E.R. 616

The plaintiff was a young songwriter who had made an exclusive service contract with some music publishers for five years and assigned to them the full copyright in all his songs both existing and those which he might compose in the five-year period. The publishers could at any time terminate the contract by one month's notice, they could assign the benefit of the contract and were under no obligation to exploit any of the compositions during the five years. The plaintiff asked for a declaration that the agreement was not binding on him. It was *held*—by the House of Lords—that this particular restraint was contrary to the public interest. Two matters appear to have influenced the decision of the court; the first was that the contract appeared to be almost totally one-sided: the second was that the particular contract did not appear to be in accordance with standard trade practice.

Comment. In the case of *Davis* v. *W.E.A. Records*, [1975] 1 All E.R. 237 the Court of Appeal followed the above case making the additional point that it was a restraint contrary to the public interest, as well as an example of inequality of bargaining power verging upon undue influence.

Public policy: restraint of trade: partnership restraints

(308) *Lyne-Pirkis* v. *Jones*, [1969] 3 All E.R. 738

The plaintiff and the defendant were medical practitioners in practice at Godalming. A clause in the partnership deed stated that if any partner retired he should not 'for a period of five years immediately following such retirement . . . engage in practice as a medical practitioner whether alone or jointly with any other person within a radius of ten miles of the Market House in Godalming'. The defendant terminated the partnership and the plaintiff asked for an injunction to prevent him from practising within the stated area. The patients of the partnership all lived within a radius of five miles. *Held*—by the Court of Appeal—that the covenant was not enforceable. It was wider than was reasonably necessary to restrict competition because it used the phrase 'medical practitioner' which could include medical consultant and was not limited to general practice. In these circumstances there was no need for the court to decide whether a radius of ten miles was too wide though Russell, L.J., thought it was.

Comment. In *Trego* v. *Hunt*, [1896] A.C. 7 the House of Lords decided that even though partners have sold a business and have been paid for goodwill, they cannot be prevented from carrying on a business competing with the purchaser. They can be prevented by injunction from actually soliciting old customers and from representing to the world that they are carrying on the actual business sold. However, the fact that they can compete does affect the value of the firm's goodwill. In consequence the law allows express agreements not to compete in this field but, as this case shows, care is needed in drafting such covenants because they must still not be wider than is reasonably necessary, so that in this case it was not necessary in order to protect the partnership that the restraint should preclude practice as a consultant.

Public policy: restraints on vendors of businesses

(309) *British Concrete Co.* v. *Schelff*, [1921] 2 Ch. 563

The plaintiffs carried on a large business for the manufacture and sale of 'B.R.C.' Road Reinforcements. The defendant carried on a small business for the sale of 'Loop Road Reinforcements'. The defendant sold his business to the plaintiffs and agreed not to compete with them in the manufacture or sale of road reinforcements. It was held that the covenant was void. All that the defendant transferred was the business of selling the reinforcements called 'Loop'. It was therefore only with regard to that particular variety that it was justifiable to curb his future activities.

Comment. A very wide restraint may be reasonable in some cases. In *Nordenfelt* v. *Maxim Nordenfelt Guns and Ammunition Co.*, [1894] A.C. 535 a world-wide restraint was upheld by the House of Lords on the seller of an ammunition business because the customers of the business were governments all over the world.

Public policy: restrictive trade practices: restraints on employees taken in a contract between their employers

(310) *Kores Manufacturing Co. Ltd* v. *Kolok Manufacturing Co. Ltd*, [1959] Ch. 108

The two companies occupied adjoining premises in Tottenham and both manufactured carbon papers, typewriter ribbons and the like. They made an agreement in which each company agreed that it would not, without the written consent of the other, 'at any time employ any person who during the past five years shall have been a servant of yours'. The plaintiffs' chief chemist sought employment with the defendants, and the plaintiffs were not prepared to consent to this and asked for an injunction to enforce the agreement. *Held*—by the Court of Appeal—

(*a*) A contract in restraint of trade cannot be enforced unless—
  (i) it is reasonable as between the parties, and
  (ii) it is consistent with the interests of the public.
(*b*) The mere fact that the parties are dealing on equal terms does not prevent the court from holding that the restraint is unreasonable in the interests of those parties.
(*c*) The restraint in this case was grossly in excess of what was required to protect the parties and accordingly was unreasonable in the interests of the parties.
(*d*) The agreement therefore failed to satisfy the first of the two conditions set out in (*a*) above and was void and unenforceable.

Public policy: restraints on distributors of merchandise

(311) *Esso Petroleum Co. Ltd* v. *Harper's Garage (Stourport) Ltd*, [1967] 1 All E.R. 699

The defendant company owned two garages with attached filling stations, the Mustow Green Garage, Mustow Green, near Kidderminster, and the Corner Garage at Stourport-on-Severn. Each garage was tied to the plaintiff oil company, the one at Mustow Green by a solus supply agreement only with a tie clause binding the dealer to take the products of the plaintiff company at its scheduled prices from time to time. There was also a price-maintenance clause which was no longer enforceable and a 'continuity clause' under which the defendants, if they sold the garage, had to persuade the buyer to enter into another solus agreement with Esso. The defendants also agreed to keep the garage open at all reasonable hours and to give preference to the plaintiff company's oils. The agreement was to remain in force for four years and five months from 1 July, 1963, being the unexpired residue of the ten-year tie of a previous owner. At the Corner Garage there was a similar solus agreement for twenty-one years and a mortgage under which the plaintiffs lent Harpers £7000 to assist them in buying the garage and improving it. The mortgage contained a tie covenant and forbade redemption for twenty-one years. In August 1964, Harpers offered to pay off the loan but Esso refused to accept it. Harpers then turned over all four pumps at the Corner Garage to V.I.P. and later sold V.I.P. at Mustow Green. The plaintiff company now asked for an injunction to restrain the defendants from buying or selling fuels other than Esso at the two garages during the subsistence of the agreements. *Held*—by the House of Lords—that the rule of public policy against unreasonable restraints of trade applied to the solus agreements and the mortgage. The shorter period of four years and five months was reasonable so that the tie was valid but the other tie for twenty-one years in the solus agreement and the mortgage was invalid, so that the injunction asked for by the plaintiffs could not be granted.

Comment. It appears from this case that the doctrine of restraint of trade applies to solus agreements where the petrol company lends money on mortgage to the garage proprietor, but does not apply to restrictions where property is sold or leased. In *Harper* Lord Reid said that 'A person buying or leasing land had no previous right to be there at all, let alone to trade there, and when he takes possession of that land subject to a negative restrictive covenant he gives up no right or freedom which he previously had.'

(312) *Cleveland Petroleum Co. Ltd* v. *Dartstone Ltd*, [1969] 1 All E.R. 201

The owner of a garage and filling station at Crawley in Sussex leased the property to Cleveland and they in turn granted an underlease to the County Oak Service Station Ltd. The underlease contained a covenant under which all motor fuels sold were to be those of Cleveland. There was power to assign in the underlease and a number of assignments took place so that eventually Dartstone Ltd became the lessees, having agreed to observe the covenants in the underlease. They then challenged the covenant regarding motor fuels and Cleveland asked for an injunction to enforce it. The injunction was granted. Dealing in the Court of Appeal with *Harper's Case*[311] Lord Denning, M.R., said—

'. . . it seems plain to me that in three at least of the speeches of their Lordships a distinction is taken between a man who is already in possession of the land before he ties himself to an oil company and a man who is out of possession and is let into it by an oil company. If an owner in possession ties himself for more than five years to take all his supplies from one company, that is an unreasonable restraint of trade and is invalid. But if a man, who is out of possession, is let into possession by the oil company on the terms that he is to tie himself to that company, such a tie is good.'

Comment. (i) The period of five years is based upon figures given for such ties in the Monopolies Commission Report on the Supply of Petrol (1965). The present practice as regards petrol stations is governed by undertakings which the oil companies gave after the Monopolies Commission Report. However, the decisions in *Esso* v. *Harper* and *Cleveland* are still of importance since they provide guidance as to the common law view in regard to the validity of exclusive dealing agreements in goods other than petrol and oil.

(ii) In *Alec Lobb (Garages) Ltd* v. *Total Oil G.B. Ltd*, [1985] 1 All E.R. 303 the plaintiff company borrowed from the defendant to develop a site. As part of the loan arrangements, the plaintiff agreed to buy the defendant's petrol for 21 years. Since the company was already in occupation of the garage and filling station when the agreement was made, it was subject to the doctrine of restraint of trade being a *contract* of loan and not a *sale or lease*. The High Court said that 21 years was too long and that the restraint was unenforceable. The Court of Appeal rejected that view and with it the opinion of the Monopolies Commission that it was not in the public interest that a petrol company should tie a petrol filling station for more than five years in the circumstances of this case.

The House of Lords in *Esso* v. *Harper's Garage* (see above) agreed with the Commission, but said that it would allow a restriction for more than five years if the petrol company could prove economic necessity. In the *Alec Lobb* case, Total did not try to prove economic necessity.

Therefore, the case seems to show that the courts may not be prepared to help the so-called weaker party, i.e. the garage owner, as they were in the past, particularly in Lord Denning's time. In *Alec Lobb*, the Court of Appeal said that each case must depend on its own facts.

In that case the loan by Total was a rescue operation greatly benefiting Lobb and enabling it to continue in business. There were also break clauses in the arrangement at the end of seven and 14 years if Lobb wished to use them. In view of the ample consideration offered by Total, the restraint of 21 years was not, according to the Court of Appeal, unreasonable and was therefore valid and enforceable.

Public policy: involuntary restraints on members of trade associations and professions

(313) *Pharmaceutical Society of Great Britain* v. *Dickson*, [1968] 2 All E.R. 686

The Society passed a resolution to the effect that the opening of new pharmacies should be restricted and be limited to certain specified services, and that the range of services in existing pharmacies should not be extended except as approved by the Society's council. The purpose of the resolution was clearly to stop the development of new fields of trading in conjunction with pharmacy. Mr Dickson, who was a member of the Society and retail director of Boots Pure Drug Company Ltd, brought this action on the grounds that the proposed new rule was *ultra vires* as an unreasonable restraint of trade. A declaration that the resolution was *ultra vires* was made and the Society appealed to the House of Lords where the appeal was dismissed, the following points emerging from the judgment.

(i) Where a professional association passes a resolution regulating the conduct of its members the validity of the resolution is a matter for the courts even if binding in honour only, since failure to observe it is likely to be construed as misconduct and thus become a ground for disciplinary action.

(ii) A resolution by a professional association regulating the conduct of its members is *ultra vires* if not sufficiently related to the main objects of the association. The objects of the Society in this case did not cover the resolution, being 'to maintain the honour and safeguard and promote the interests of the members in the exercise of the profession of pharmacy'.

(iii) A resolution by a professional association regulating the conduct of its members will be void if it is an unreasonable restraint of trade.

Public policy: restraints upon personal liberty

(314) *Horwood* v. *Millar's Timber Co.*, [1917] 1 K.B. 305

The plaintiff was a moneylender and he had lent money to a person named Bunyon who was employed as a clerk by the defendants. Bunyon owed £42 together with a sum of £31 as interest. Bunyon assigned to the plaintiff a policy of assurance on his life worth £100, and all the salary or wages due or to become due to him with the defendants or any other employer. The plaintiff attached certain conditions to the agreement and under these Bunyon agreed not to leave his job without the plaintiff's permission; to do nothing to get himself dismissed; not to borrow; not to sell, pledge or otherwise dispose of his property, and not to obtain credit. If Bunyon was in breach of any of the conditions the whole sum was immediately payable. The plaintiff now sued Bunyon's employers in respect of the salary assigned. *Held*—The contract was illegal, being against public policy, and it was therefore unenforceable. That part of the contract which dealt with the assignment of salary was not severable from the rest and so the action failed.

Comment. In an earlier case (*Neville* v. *Dominion of Canada News Co. Ltd*, [1915] 3 K.B. 556) a contract under which the owner of a trade journal agreed with the plaintiff for forgiveness of part of a debt not to comment on the dealings of the plaintiff's company was held void. It was an undue restriction on personal liberty, or a restraint of trade contrary to public policy since it could prevent the journal from revealing even fraudulent dealings.

(315) *Denny's Trustee* v. *Denny*, [1919] 1 K.B. 583

A young man with dissolute habits had fallen into the hands of money-lenders. A deed was entered into under the terms of which the son transferred all his property to the father, who agreed to pay all his debts and to make him a reasonable allowance. The deed provided that the son should not go within eighty miles of Piccadilly Circus without his father's consent, otherwise the annuity would be forfeited. The son became bankrupt and his trustee, wishing to set aside the deed and claim the property for the benefit of creditors. suggested that the deed constituted an illegal restraint. *Held*—The deed was good and could not be set aside; its purpose was to reform the son.

Public policy: contracts declared void by the judiciary: consequences: recovery of property and severance

(316) *Hermann* v. *Charlesworth*, [1905] 2 K.B. 123

C agreed that he would introduce gentlemen to Miss Hermann with a view to marriage. She agreed to make an immediate payment of £52 and a payment of £250 on the day of marriage. He introduced her to several gentlemen and corresponded with others on her behalf but no marriage took place. Miss Hermann now sued for the return of the £52 and succeeded.

(317) *Wallis* v. *Day* (1837), 2 M. & W. 273

The plaintiff was in business as a carrier and he sold that business to the defendant. The plaintiff agreed in return for a weekly salary of £2.19 to serve the defendant as assistant for life and further agreed that except as assistant he would not for the rest of his life exercise the trade of carrier. This action was brought by the plaintiff to recover eighteen weeks' arrears of salary. The defence was that the contract was void as being an unlawful restraint of trade and that no part of it was enforceable. It was unnecessary to decide this point because the court held, perhaps surprisingly in modern terms, that the restraint was reasonable but Lord Abinger, dealing with the defence, said: 'The defendants demurred on the ground that the covenant being in restraint of trade was illegal and therefore the whole contract was void. I cannot however accede to that conclusion. If a party enters into several covenants one of which cannot be enforced against him he is not therefore released from performing the others, and in the present case the defendants might have maintained an action against the plaintiff for not rendering them the services he covenanted to perform, there being nothing illegal in that part of the contract.'

(318) *Attwood* v. *Lamont*, [1920] 3 K.B. 571

Attwood carried on business as a draper, tailor and general outfitter in a shop at Kidderminster. The business was organized into different departments, each with a manager. Lamont was appointed as head cutter and manager of the tailoring department, and in his contract of service he agreed that he would not at any time, whether on his own account or on behalf of anybody else, carry on the trades of tailor, dressmaker, general draper, milliner, hatter, haberdasher, gentlemen's, ladies', or children's outfitter at any place within ten miles of Kidderminster. Some time later Lamont asked Attwood to release him from the covenant or to make him a partner, but Attwood refused to do this. Lamont left his employment and set up in business at Worcester, which was outside the ten-mile limit. However, he did do business with Attwood's customers and took orders in Kidderminster. Attwood now asked for an injunction to restrain Lamont in respect of his tailoring activities, claiming that that part of the covenant was severable, though admitting the covenant as a whole was too wide. *Held*—The part of the agreement concerning tailoring was not severable; and even if severable was invalid because it was a covenant against competition. Lamont was a rival largely because of his skill and not because of trade connection.

'The doctrine of severance has not, I think, gone further than to make it permissible in a case where the covenant is not really a single covenant but is in effect a combination of several distinct covenants. In that case and where the severance can be carried out without the addition or alteration of a word, it is permissible. But in that case only. Now here, I think, there is in truth but one covenant for the protection of the respondent's entire business, and not several covenants for the protection of his several businesses. The respondent is, on the evidence, not carrying on several businesses but one business, and in my opinion this covenant must stand or fall in its unaltered form.' (*Per* Younger, L.J.)

Comment. (i) Younger, L.J., in his second sentence, is referring to what is sometimes called the 'blue pencil' test; which states that it must be possible to sever the illegal part of a restraint by merely deleting words in the contract. The court will not either add words or substitute other words or rearrange words for this would be redrafting the contract. Thus a contract not to compete within 15 miles of, say Barchester Town Hall, cannot be severed by deleting 15 and substituting 3, even though a three-mile restraint would, in the court's view, have been perfectly reasonable. Furthermore, even where the 'blue pencil' test is satisfied, as it was in this case, the court will still not sever the promises if to do so would change the nature of the contract. In this case the Court of Appeal was of the opinion that the contract was for the protection of the respondent's entire business and was never intended to be seen as several covenants for the protection of his several businesses. The Court would not delete the invalid part of the restraint because it was the major part of the restraints imposed.

(ii) A contrast is provided by *Goldsoll* v. *Goldman*, [1915] 1 Ch. 292. In that case the defendant sold imitation jewellery and when he sold his business he agreed 'not for two years to deal in real or imitation jewellery in any part of the United Kingdom'. The Court was prepared to sever the words 'real or' in order to make the restraint valid and restrict the defendant from competing in imitation jewellery. Only two words needed to be deleted and this was a very small part of the restraint as a whole.

(319) *Kenyon* v. *Darwin Cotton Manufacturing Co.*, [1936] 2 K.B. 193

The plaintiff was employed by the defendants and joined a scheme under which the employees were to finance the company by taking up shares in it. Payment for the shares was to be made by deductions from wages and the employees signed documents agreeing to take the shares and authorizing a sum of money to be deducted from their wages. This second document was illegal under the Truck Act, 1831 (now repealed.) The plaintiff now sued to recover that part of her wages which had been applied in paying for shares, and the defendants counter-claimed for the amount due on the shares. The plaintiff succeeded because her action was a statutory one under the Truck Act of 1831. The defendants claimed that the agreement to take the shares was legal and should be severed from the part of the agreement dealing with the method of payment. *Held—* There could be no severance because that would leave a contract in which the employees agreed to pay for the shares not out of their wages but out of their assets generally, and this was an agreement which they did not intend to make.

Public policy: contracts impliedly illegal by statute

(320) *Shaw* v. *Groom*, [1970] 1 All E.R. 702

Mrs Groom was the tenant of a room in North London and Mrs Shaw was her landlord. The tenancy was a controlled one and Mrs Groom had occupied the room for some twenty years at a rent of 39p per week plus 12½p for electricity. Mrs Groom fell into arrears with her rent and Mrs Shaw brought this action to recover the money owing to her. Unfortunately Mrs Shaw had failed, during the tenancy, to comply with s. 4 of the Landlord and Tenant Act, 1962, which required that the tenant be provided with a rent book. Mrs Groom now alleged that Mrs Shaw could not recover the arrears of rent because her failure to provide a rent book was illegal performance of the contract. *Held*—by the Court of Appeal— that Mrs Shaw succeeded. The intention of the legislature was not to preclude the landlord from recovering rent due or to impose on him any forfeiture beyond the fines stipulated in the Act of 1962. It was accepted that the requirement of a rent book was to protect a class of persons of whom Mrs Groom was one. This did not, however, automatically prevent Mrs Shaw's claim. The rule that an illegal contract cannot be enforced by the guilty party must be sensibly restricted in its operation.

(321) *Kiriri Cotton Co.* v. *Dawani*, [1960] A.C. 192

A tenant paid a premium to his landlord in order to get possession of a flat. The acceptance of the premium was an offence under s. 3(2) of the Uganda Rent Restriction Ordinance, and the Ordinance did not provide for recovery of the premium. Both parties were ignorant of the Ordinance. In this action to recover the premium the Judicial Committee of the Privy Council *held* that the premium paid by the tenant must be recoverable because the object of the statute was to protect tenants.

Restrictive trade practices: power to investigate services

(322) *Ravenseft Properties Ltd* v. *Director-General of Fair Trading*, [1977] 1 All E.R. 47

In this case the High Court considered for the first time the application of restrictive trade legislation to services. In the case Ravenseft Properties Ltd were the leasehold owners of a shopping centre in Salford and sub-let the centre in units for use as business premises. The sub-leases also provided that Ravenseft should provide services for their tenants including maintenance, cleaning and porterage, and the tenants agreed to this and the payment of a service charge. Ravenseft were, in effect, asking the court to declare that the agreements regarding services in the under-leases did not constitute agreements to which restrictive practices legislation applied. The case was obviously important to property companies because there could be thousands of leases with service provisions which might have to be registered or become void and un-enforceable by property companies as landlords. It was *held*—by Mocatta, J.—that while all leases cannot be regarded as beyond the scope of restrictive practices legislation, these particular leases were because Ravenseft was not in *business* to supply services. Furthermore (following *Cleveland Petroleum Co. Ltd* v. *Dartstone Ltd*, 1969[312]) where, as in this case, a person takes possession of premises under a lease, not having been in possession before, and enters into a restrictive covenant tying him to take supplies or services from the lessor, the tie is normally valid and not a restriction for the purposes of restrictive practices legislation, though restrictions in the case of a sale and lease-back might be.

Comment. An example is also provided by *Agreement between the Members of the Association of British Travel Agents*, [1983] Com. L.R. 50. In that case it appeared that under the ABTA agreement no tour operator could sell foreign package tours through a non-ABTA agent. The Director General of Fair Trading thought that that was contrary to the public interest under the Restrictive Trade Practices Act of 1976 and took the agreement to the Restrictive Practices Court. However, the Court decided that the agreement was valid because (a) the accounting discipline imposed by ABTA in terms of financial statements and returns from their agents and operators was valuable in terms of the public interest, and (b) there were ABTA arrangements under which members of the Association would cope with those who had booked holidays with an operator or agent who had collapsed because of insolvency. This again was very much in the public interest.

Restrictive trade practices: resale prices: the public interest issue

(323) *Re Chocolate and Sugar Confectionery Reference*, [1967] 3 All E.R. 261

The Restrictive Practices Court was asked to make an order exempting chocolate, sugar confectionery, and related types of goods from the general ban on resale price maintenance. The case for the suppliers, i.e. virtually all of the major manufacturers, was that without resale price maintenance there would be a major shift in trade from confectionery shops to supermarkets as a result of price cutting. This would lead to a loss of sales since chocolate and similar goods were often bought on impulse from small outlets. This would lead to loss of variety and higher prices in the longer term.

That price cutting by supermarkets would take place was accepted by the court but the consequences were not regarded as inevitably those put forward by the suppliers. A normal shopper would not, for example, travel more than a short distance to buy a bar of chocolate for say, one new penny less than the recommended price. Some shops would go out of business, probably to the extent of 10 per cent of outlets, but in the view of the court this reduction would not cause the public significant inconvenience. Accordingly the court ruled that the suppliers had not established their case and that resale price maintenance for chocolates and sweets was unlawful.

A significant feature of the case was the acceptance by the court of evidence of economic principles and statistics. It marks the first real sign of co-operation between lawyers and economists; the arguments were economic and statistical rather than legal.

Treaty of Rome: application of competition laws: Arts. 85 and 86

(324) *Re German Ceramic Tiles Discount Agreement*, [1971] C.M.L.R.D. 6

Interessengemeinschaft was a company constituted under German law having as its members twelve German concerns producing ceramic tiles. The membership represented nearly all German producers of ceramic tiles, though two were not involved. Interessengemeinschaft gave a discount to buyers based on their purchases in the preceding year of tiles from any of the 12 member companies. They would not include for discount purposes purchases from the two non-member organizations except at the request of the purchaser who did not receive a full discount even then. *Held*—by the Commissioners of the European Community—that

(i) the agreement limited the freedom of economic action of producers and so restricted competition within the Community under Art. 85(1);

(ii) it tended towards a concentration of orders upon the producers of one country and restricted competition within the Common Market under Art. 85(1);

(iii) the agreement violated Art. 85(1) and, since exemption under Art. 85(1) could not be granted, must be terminated without delay.

Treaty of Rome: application of Art. 86 in the House of Lords

(325) *Garden Cottage Foods Ltd* v. *Milk Marketing Board*, [1983] 2 All E.R. 770

Garden Cottage (the company) was a middle man transferring butter from the Board to traders in the bulk market in Europe and the UK, taking a cut of the price. In March 1982 following some packaging problems which the company appeared to have overcome, the Board refused to supply direct. It said that supplies must be obtained from one of four independent distributors nominated by the Board.

These distributors were the company's competitors. The company would have to pay more to them for its supplies than if it bought direct from the Board. Therefore it could not compete on price and would be forced out of business.

The company alleged that the Board was in breach of Art. 86 of the Treaty of Rome. This provides: 'Any abuse by one or more undertakings of a dominant position within the Common Market or in a substantial part of it, shall be prohibited as incompatible with the Common Market insofar as it may affect trade between Member States. . . .'

The Court of Appeal granted an interlocutory injunction, i.e. an injunction until the trial, restraining the Board from refusing to maintain normal business relations contrary to Art. 86.

The Board appealed to the House of Lords against the injunction. Interlocutory injunctions were considered by the House of Lords in *American Cyanamid Co.* v. *Ethicon Ltd*, [1975] A.C. 396 (see further p. 316). It was decided in that case that if when the trial came on damages were likely to be regarded as an adequate remedy and the defendant could clearly pay any damages which might be awarded, then no interlocutory injunction would be granted.

That was the position here, said the majority of their Lordships. If the Board refused to supply the company direct and this meant the suspension of its butter business, the loss would be monetary, i.e. its cut of the price as middleman. There could hardly be a clearer case of damages being an adequate remedy and no insuperable difficulty of estimation had so far appeared. The injunction was therefore withdrawn. The House of Lords therefore thought that the eventual action would be for damages. However, it is in fact uncertain whether an infringement of Art. 86 gives rise in English law to an action for damages in this way. Their Lordships thought it did, but the case shows that there are still problems in terms of defining English law remedies for breach of EEC law.

Discharge of contract: by agreement: contracts requiring written evidence on formation: formalities on discharge

(326) *Moore* v. *Marrable* (1866), 1 Ch. App. 217

Under an original written agreement of 12 August, 1856, a house was let by A to B for 21 years. There were covenants by B to keep the premises in repair, to repaint the outside every three years and redecorate the inside every seven years according to a specification. On 12 October, 1859 an oral agreement was made under which C replaced B as tenant on the same terms, though B undertook to guarantee payment of the rent. It was *held* that the effect of this oral agreement was to relieve B of his liability under the original lease.

(327) *Goss* v. *Nugent* (1833), 5 B. and Ad. 58

The plaintiff, who was a vendor, brought this action to recover the purchase money due under a written contract for the sale of land. The defendant, who was the purchaser, pleaded that the title to part of the land was defective. This plea, which was true, would normally have been enough to defeat the action. It was replied, however, that by a later parol contract the purchaser had waived the defect and agreed to accept the actual title. *Held*—that the vendor could not rely on this parol variation and that his action must fail since he was unable to deliver the title that he had agreed to deliver by the original contract. The contract was no longer the original contract but the original contract as varied and there was no written evidence of the true agreement as it was ultimately made. The whole, not a mere part of the agreement must be evidenced by writing.

Discharge of contract: by performance: entire contracts

(328) *Moore & Co.* v. *Landauer & Co.*, [1921] 2 K.B. 519

The plaintiffs entered into a contract to sell the defendants a certain quantity of Australian canned fruit, the goods to be packed in cases containing 30 tins each. The goods were to be shipped 'per S.S. *Toromeo*'. The ship was delayed by strikes at Melbourne and in South Africa, and was very late in arriving at London. When the goods were discharged about one half of the consignment was packed in cases containing 24 tins only, instead of 30, and the buyers refused to accept them. *Held*—Although the method of packing made no difference to the market value of the goods, the sale was by description under s. 13 of the Sale of Goods Act, 1893, and the description had not been complied with. Consequently the buyers were entitled to reject the whole consignment by virtue of the provisions of s. 30(3) of the Sale of Goods Act, 1893 (see now s. 30(4) of the Sale of Goods Act, 1979).

Comment. The obligation in s. 30(4) of the Sale of Goods Act is entire since it provides 'Where the seller delivers to the buyer the goods he contracted to sell mixed with goods of a different description not included in the contract, the buyer may accept the goods which are in accordance with the contract and reject the rest, *or he may reject the whole*'.

(329) *Sumpter* v. *Hedges*, [1898] 1 Q.B. 673

The plaintiff entered into a contract with the defendant under the terms of which the plaintiff was to erect some buildings for the defendant on the defendant's land for a price of £565. The plaintiff did partially erect the buildings up to the value of £333, and the defendant paid him a part of that figure. The plaintiff then told the defendant that he could not finish the job because he had run out of funds. The defendant then completed the work by using material belonging to the plaintiff which had been left on the site. The plaintiff now sued for work done and materials supplied, and the court gave him judgment for materials supplied, but would not grant him a sum of money by way of *quantum meruit* for the value of the work done prior to his abandonment of the job. The reason was given that, before the plaintiff could sue successfully on a *quantum meruit*, he would have to show that the defendant had voluntarily accepted the work done, and this implied that the defendant must be in a position to refuse the benefit of the work as where a buyer of goods refuses to take delivery. This was not the case here; and the defendant had no option but to accept the work done, so his acceptance could not be presumed from conduct. There being no other evidence of the defendant's acceptance of the work, the plaintiff's claim for the work done failed.

Comment. (i) Obviously, the rule protects the aggrieved party against having to pay for a performance which is different from that envisaged by the contract. However, it can lead to injustice because, as in this case, a person can obtain a nearly completed building for nothing. The Law Commission in Working Paper 65, Part II, recommended that the party in breach should be able to recover the value to the other party of the performance actually rendered with an allowance for any loss suffered by the aggrieved party because of the failure to complete performance.

(ii) In a later case (*Heywood* v. *Wellers*, [1976] 1 All E.R. 300) the rule of entire contracts was applied where solicitors were not able to recover their costs when they failed to take the necessary steps to enforce a non-molestation injunction which they had obtained against a man who had molested the plaintiff so that her molestation continued. Lord Denning said that the law as to entire contracts was put vividly by Jessel, M.R., in *Re Hall and Barker* (1878), 9 Ch.D. 538 at p. 545 when he said: 'If a man engages to carry a box of cigars from London to Birmingham, it is an entire contract, and he cannot throw the cigars out of the carriage half-way there and ask for half the money; or if a shoemaker agrees to make a pair of shoes, he cannot offer you one shoe and ask you to pay half the price.' Applying those words to this case, Lord Denning said that if litigation is not carried through to the end the proceedings were as useless to the client as a single shoe.

(iii) In practice this form of injustice to the builder is avoided because a building contract normally provides for progress payments, thus making it a divisible agreement.

Discharge of contract: by performance: entire contracts: performance prevented

(330) *De Barnardy* v. *Harding* (1853), 8 Exch. 822

The plaintiff agreed to act as the defendant's agent for the purpose of preparing and issuing certain advertisements and notices designed to encourage the sale of tickets to see the funeral procession of the Duke of Wellington. The plaintiff was to be paid a commission of 10 per cent upon the proceeds of the tickets actually sold. The plaintiff duly issued the advertisements and notices, but before he began to sell the tickets, the defendant withdrew the plaintiff's authority to sell them and in consequence the plaintiff did not sell any tickets and was prevented from earning his commission. The plaintiff now sued upon a *quantum meruit* and his action succeeded.

Discharge of contract: by performance: effect of substantial performance

(331) *Hoenig* v. *Isaacs*, [1952] 2 All E.R. 176

The defendant employed the plaintiff who was an interior decorator and furniture designer to decorate a one-room flat owned by the defendant. The plaintiff was also to provide furniture, including a fitted bookcase, a wardrobe and a bedstead, for the total sum of £750. The terms of the contract regarding payment were as follows—'Net cash as the work proceeds and the balance on completion.' The defendant made two payments to the plaintiff of £150 each, one payment on the 12 April and the other on the 19 April. The plaintiff claimed that he had completed the work on 28 August, and asked for the balance, i.e. £450. The defendant asserted that the work done was bad and faulty, but sent the plaintiff a sum of £100 and moved into the flat and used the furniture. The plaintiff now sued for the balance of £350, the defence being that the plaintiff had not performed his contract, or in the alternative that he had done so negligently, unskilfully and in an unworkmanlike manner.

The Official Referee assessed the work that had been done, and found that generally it was properly done except that the wardrobe door required replacing and that a bookshelf was too short and this meant that the bookcase would have to be remade. The defendant claimed that the contract was entire and that it must be completely performed before the plaintiff could recover. The Official Referee was of the opinion that there had been substantial performance, and that the defendant was liable for £750 less the cost of putting right the above-mentioned defects, the cost of this being assessed at £55 18s. 2d. The court accordingly gave the plaintiff judgment for the sum of £694 1s. 10d.

(332) *Bolton* v. *Mahadeva*, [1972] 2 All E.R. 1322

The plaintiff, a plumbing and heating contractor, agreed to install a combined heating and domestic hot water system in the defendant's house for £560. There was a defect in the finished work which caused the system not to heat adequately and to give off fumes, and which would cost £174 to repair. The defendant refused to pay and the plaintiff sued him. The County Court judge held that there had been substantial performance of the contract and gave judgment for the plaintiff, subject to an appropriate set-off in favour of the defendant. On appeal by the defendant it was *held*—by the Court of Appeal—allowing the appeal—that having regard to the nature of the defects and the cost of remedying them, the plaintiff could not be said substantially to have performed the contract and he was not entitled to recover anything. (*Hoenig* v. *Isaacs*, 1952[331] distinguished.)

Discharge of contract: by performance: optional methods of performance

(333) *Narbeth* v. *James:* *(The Lady Tahilla)*, [1967] 1 Ll. Rep. 591

The plaintiff sold his motor-yacht to the defendant in April, 1960, for a price of £8000. The defendant paid £5000 and it was agreed that the balance be met at the defendant's option in one of three ways—(i) by allowing the plaintiff free use of the yacht for one month during each of the years 1962, 1963 and 1964, subject to the plaintiff giving the defendant three months' notice of the month in which he required the yacht; (ii) by paying the plaintiff £1000 for any year in which the yacht was not available for use under method (i); (iii) by payment in cash if the vessel was disposed of by the defendant. In April, 1960, the defendant secured the balance due from him by executing a mortgage in favour of the plaintiff. In 1966 the plaintiff sued the defendant for the whole balance with interest under the mortgage. The defendant denied liability and contended that the yacht was made available for the plaintiff in 1962, 1963 and 1964, but the plaintiff had not given notice of the month he required her. *Held*—by Brandon, J.—that the plaintiff was entitled to the £3000 plus interest. As a general proposition where A had an option to perform a contract in more than on way and the obligations of B depended on which way A chose and could only be effectively performed by B if he had notice beforehand, then A would be under an implied obligation to give B proper notice. Thus in the present case in order to give business efficacy to the contract it was necessary to imply a term that the defendant would give the plaintiff reasonable prior notice whether or not he was choosing method (i) in respect of any of the three relevant years. No notice had been given, therefore the mortgage remained undischarged and the plaintiff was entitled to the judgment.

Discharge of contract: by performance: time of performance

(334) *Bowes* v. *Shand* (1877), 2 App. Cas. 455

The action was brought for damages for non-acceptance of 600 tons (or 8200 bags) of Madras rice. The sold note stated that the rice was to be shipped during 'the months of March and/or April, 1874'. 8150 bags were put on board ship on or before 28 February, 1874, and the remaining 50 bags on 2 March, 1874. The defendants refused to take delivery because the rice was not shipped in accordance with the terms of the contract. *Held*—The bulk of the cargo was shipped in February and therefore the rice did not answer the description in the contract and the defendants were not bound to accept it.

Comment. The date of shipment is in fact regarded as part of the description of the goods so that the buyer may reject the goods for breach of condition as to description, whether or not he is prejudiced, because liability for breach of description is strict.

(335) *Chas. Rickards Ltd* v. *Oppenhaim*, [1950] 1 K.B. 616

The defendant ordered a Rolls-Royce chassis from the plaintiffs, the chassis being delivered in July, 1947. The plaintiffs found a coachbuilder prepared to make a body within six or at the most seven months. The specification for the body was agreed in August, 1947, so that the work should have been completed in March, 1948. The work was not completed by then but the defendant still pressed for delivery. On 29 June, 1948, the defendant wrote to the coachbuilders saying that he would not accept delivery after 25 July, 1948. The body was not ready by then and the defendant bought another car. The body was completed in October, 1948, but the defendant refused to accept delivery and counter-claimed for the value of the chassis which he had purchased. *Held*—Time was of the essence of the original contract, but the defendant had waived the question of time by continuing to press for delivery after the due date. However, by this letter of 29 June he had again made time of the essence, and had given reasonable notice in the matter. Judgment was given for the defendant on the claim and counter-claim.

Comment. There is no consideration for the promise of a buyer to accept a late delivery where, as here, the promise is made purely for the benefit of the seller because he cannot deliver on time. The waiver is therefore valid in law only by reason of the *High Trees* case[139] and s. 11 of the Sale of Goods Act, 1979.

(336) *Elmdore Ltd* v. *Keech* (1969), 113 Sol. J. 871

The plaintiffs agreed to print an advertisement in their plastic telephone directory cover which they said would be distributed within 120 days. The covers were distributed eleven days late. It was *held*—by the Court of Appeal—that since this was a mercantile contract the general rule that time was of the essence applied unless the circumstances showed otherwise. There were no special circumstances on the facts of the case and the plaintiffs' action for the price must be dismissed.

Discharge of contract: by performance: appropriation of payments:
Clayton's **case**

(337) *Deeley* v. *Lloyds Bank Ltd*, [1912] A.C. 756

A customer of the bank had mortgaged his property to the bank to secure an overdraft limited to £2500. He then mortgaged the same property to the appellant for £3500, subject to the bank's mortgage. It is the normal practice of bankers, on receiving notice of a second mortgage, to rule off the customer's account, and not to allow any further withdrawals, since these will rank after the second mortgage. In this case the bank did not open a new account but continued the old current account. The customer thereafter paid in moneys which at a particular date, if they had been appropriated in accordance with the rule in *Clayton's* case, would have extinguished the bank's mortgage. Even so the customer still owed the bank money, and they sold the property for a price which was enough to satisfy the bank's debt but not that of the appellant. *Held*—The evidence did not exclude the rule in *Clayton's* case, which applied, so that the bank's mortgage had been paid off and the appellant, as second mortgagee, was entitled to the proceeds of the sale.

Discharge of contract: by breach: express and implied repudiation: effect of anticipatory breach

(338) *Hochster* v. *De La Tour* (1853), 2 E. & B. 678

The defendant agreed in April, 1852, to engage the plaintiff as a courier for European travel, his duties to commence on 1 June, 1852. On 11 May, 1852, the defendant wrote to the plaintiff saying that he no longer required his services. The plaintiff commenced an action for breach of contract on 22 May, 1852, and the defence was that there was no cause of action until the date due for performance, i.e. 1 June, 1852. *Held*—The defendant's express repudiation constituted an actionable breach of contract.

(339) *Gorse* v. *Durham County Council*, [1971] 1 W.L.R. 775

The plaintiffs were school teachers employed by the defendants. Their contracts allowed suspension for misconduct without loss of salary if there was reinstatement. On the instruction of their union the plaintiffs refused to serve school meals whereupon the education office excluded them from the school and withheld their salaries. They were later reinstated and sued for the salary withheld. Cusack, J., *held*—that supervising meals was a normal part of a teacher's duties and refusal was an express repudiation of the contract. However, since the defendants had not accepted the repudiation but had reinstated the plaintiffs they must be regarded as having been suspended and were entitled under the terms of their contracts to the salary withheld.

(340) *Omnium D'Entreprises and Others* v. *Sutherland*, [1919] 1 K.B. 618

The defendant was the owner of a steamship and agreed to let her to the plaintiff for a period of time and to pay the second plaintiffs a commission on the hire payable under the agreement. The defendant later sold the ship to a purchaser, free of all liability under his agreement with the plaintiffs. *Held*—The sale by the defendant was a repudiation of the agreement and the plaintiffs were entitled to damages for breach of the contract.

Comment. The charterer would have no claim against the purchaser of the vessel because restrictive covenants do not pass with chattels (which a ship is) but only with land. Compare *Dunlop* v. *Selfridge*, (1915) (*see* page 572), and *Tulk* v. *Moxhay*, (1848) (*see* page 584).

(341) *Maredelanto Compania Naviera S.A.* v. *Bergbau-Handel GmbH, the Mihalis Angelos*, [1970] 3 All E.R. 125

The vessel *Mihalis Angelos*, which was owned by Maredelanto, was chartered by Bergbau-Handel under a charterparty dated 25 May, 1965. The charterparty provided—

(a) that the vessel should be ready to load about 1 July, 1965; and
(b) that if it was not ready to load on or before 20 July, 1965, the charterers should have the option of cancelling the contract.

The purpose of the charterparty was for the charterers to load mineral ore (apatite) in Haiphong in North Vietnam and transport it to Hamburg or another port in Europe. Sometime before 12 July, 1965, the railway which was to bring the ore to Haiphong was allegedly destroyed by American bombing. However, the *Mihalis Angelos* was in Hong Kong on 23 July and could not have reached Haiphong before 27 July. Instead of waiting until 20 July when they could have cancelled the contract legitimately, the charterers decided to repudiate it on 17 July on the grounds of *force majeure* because they thought the railway had been destroyed so that the apatite ore could not be transported to Haiphong, thus rendering the charterparty useless to them. The shipowners did not accept that *force majeure* applied and they sued for £4000 being damages for loss of the charter. At first instance Mocatta, J., held that the charterers were not entitled to repudiate on 17 July. The situation was not necessarily one of *force majeure* at that time. They were therefore in breach on 17 July and the owners were entitled to sue at that time. In addition they were entitled to damages of £4000 and it did not matter that they would have been unable to perform the contract at the due date, i.e. 20 July. In the Court of Appeal, however, it was decided that the owners were only entitled to nominal damages. The fact that the owners could not have performed the contract on 20 July was a contingency which had to be taken into account.

(342) *Avery* v. *Bowden* (1855), 5 E. & B. 714

The defendant chartered the plaintiff's ship and agreed to load her with a cargo at Odessa within forty-five days. The ship went to Odessa and remained there for most of the forty-five day period. The defendant told the captain of the ship that he did not propose to load a cargo and that he would do well to leave, but the captain stayed on at Odessa, hoping that the defendant would change his mind. Before the end of the forty-five-day period the Crimean War broke out so that performance of the contract would have been illegal. *Held*—The plaintiff might have treated the defendant's refusal to load a cargo as an anticipatory breach of contract but his agent, the captain, had waived that right by staying on at Odessa, and now the contract had been discharged by something which was beyond the control of either party.

Comment. A more modern application of the above rule can be seen in *Fercometal Sarl* v. *Mediterranean Shipping Co. Ltd, The Times*, 1 June, 1987. The plaintiffs chartered a ship to the defendants. The charter-party (i.e. the contract) provided that if the ship was not ready to load during the period 3–9 July the defendants could cancel the contract. On 2 July the defendants said they were not going on with the contract anyway but the plaintiffs did not accept that breach and provided the ship which was not ready to load until 12 July. The defendants said again that they would not go on with the contract. The plaintiffs sued for damages and failed. They could have based an action on the first breach but had not done so. Their action on the second 'breach' failed because the ship was not ready to load.

(343) *White and Carter (Councils) Ltd* v. *McGregor*, [1961] 2 W.L.R. 17

The respondent was a garage proprietor on Clydebank and on 26 June, 1957, his sales manager, without specific authority, entered into a contract with the appellants whereby the appellants agreed to advertise the respondent's business on litter bins which they supplied to local authorities. The contract was to last for three years from the date of the first advertisement display. Payment was to be by instalments annually in advance, the first instalment being due seven days after the first display. The contract contained a clause that, on failure to pay an instalment or other breach of contract, the whole sum of £196 4s. became due. The respondent was quick to repudiate the contract for on 26 June, 1957, he wrote to the appellants asking them to cancel the agreement, and at this stage the appellants had not taken any steps towards carrying it out. The appellants refused to cancel the agreement and prepared the advertisement plates which they exhibited on litter bins in November, 1957, and continued to display them during the following three years. Eventually the appellants demanded payment, the respondent refused to pay, and the appellants brought an action against him for the sum due under the contract. *Held*—The appellants were entitled to recover the contract price since, although the respondent had repudiated the contract, the appellants were not obliged to accept the repudiation. The contract survived and the appellants had now completed it.

Comment. (i) Although the respondent's agent had no actual authority, he had made a similar contract with the appellants in 1954, and it was not disputed that he had apparent authority to bind his principal.

(ii) The ruling of the House of Lords appears to conflict with the principle of mitigation of loss (see p. 309). In fact it does not, at least in law, because it has been laid down in a number of cases, e.g. *Shindler* v. *Northern Raincoat Co. Ltd*, [1960] 2 All E.R. 239, that there is no duty on a plaintiff to mitigate his damages before there has been any breach which he has accepted as a breach. In this case the plaintiffs did not accept the first breach but preferred to wait until he date of performance. During that time they were, according to the law, not obliged to mitigate loss.

(iii) The decision may result from the fact that Mr McGregor did not produce any evidence that the appellants could have mitigated their loss, in the sense of doing the advertising for someone else. He may therefore have had a 'legitimate interest' in going on with the contract. (*See* below.)

(iv) The line taken in *White & Carter* has been departed from in more recent times. Thus, in *Attica Sea Carriers Corporation* v. *Ferrostaal Poseidon Bulk Reederei GmbH*, [1976] 1 Ll. Rep. 250 the charterer of a ship agreed to execute certain repairs before he redelivered it to the owner and to pay the agreed hire until that time. He did not carry out the repairs but the owner would not take redelivery of the ship until they had been done and later sued for the agreed hire. It was held that the owner was not entitled to refuse to accept redelivery and to sue for the agreed hire. The cost of the repairs far exceeded the value which the ship would have had if they had been done and the owner had therefore no legal interest in insisting on their execution and the payment of the hire. The court held that he should have mitigated his loss by accepting re-delivery of the unrepaired ship so that his only remedy was damages and not for the agreed hire.

This line was followed also in the case of *Clea Shipping Corporation* v. *Bulk Oil International—The Alaskan Trader*, [1983] 1 Ll. Rep. 315. A vessel had been chartered by the plaintiff owners to the defendants, the hire charge having been paid in advance. However, the ship broke down and required extensive repairs. The charterers thereupon gave notice that they intended to end the contract. However, the plaintiffs decided to keep the agreement open and undertook the repairs and then informed the defendant that the vessel was at their disposal. The plaintiffs said they were exercising their right of election conferred upon the in-nocent party in such circumstances to keep the contract open, thus en-titling them to keep the hire money instead of suing for damages. Lloyd, J., denied the existence of an unfettered right of election for an innocent party to keep a contract running in such circumstances. He found that, in the absence of a 'legitimate interest' in the contract's perpetuation by the party faced with the repudiation, the party concerned could, though innocent, be forced to accept damages in lieu of sums falling due under the contract subsequent to the actual event. This restraint is founded on general equitable principles, to be based on what is reasonable on the facts of each case.

(344) *Allen* v. *Robles (Compagnie Parisienne de Garantie, Third Party)*, [1969] 3 All E.R. 154

The defendant, Mr Robles, drove his car in a negligent fashion and ran into the plaintiff's house. In an action at Nottingham Assizes the judge awarded the plaintiff damages against Mr Robles and the question arose as to whether Mr Robles could claim on his insurance policy with the French insurance company which was joined as third party in this action. Mr Robles was in breach of his contract of insurance because that contract provided that he must notify the insurance company of any claim made against him within five days of the claim. This he had not done. In fact he failed to inform the insurance company of the claim by the plaintiff until two months after he knew it had been made. On the other hand the insurance company did not repudiate their liability until some four months after Mr Robles informed them of the claim. It was *held*— by the Court of Appeal—that the insurance company had not lost its right to repudiate the contract. The delay was not so long as to indicate that they had accepted liability and it had in no way changed the circumstances of the case. It had not, for example, increased Mr Allen's loss or altered Mr Robles liability. There was thus no prejudice to those concerned.

(345) *Total Oil Great Britain Ltd* v. *Thompson Garages (Biggin Hill) Ltd*, [1971] 3 All E.R. 1226

The plaintiffs leased a garage to the defendants for 14 years on terms that the defendants would purchase all their fuel supplies from the plaintiffs and that payment was on delivery. Later the plaintiffs changed the method of payment to a banker's draft sent to the plaintiff's depot *before* delivery. This was a repudiation of the contract by the plaintiffs which was accepted by the defendants who went elsewhere for their fuel. The plaintiffs claimed, amongst other things, an injunction restraining the defendants from selling fuels other than those obtained from the plaintiffs. The plaintiffs also agreed to revert to the 'cash on delivery' system of payment. *Held*—by the Court of Appeal—that an injunction would be granted. A lease which conveys an interest in land does not come to an end like an ordinary contract by repudiation and acceptance of repudiation, and so was still in existence in the present case. The plaintiffs could insist upon the enforcement of the tie since they were now prepared to adhere to the terms of supply and payment.

Discharge of contract: by frustration: illustrations of the doctrine

(346) *Davis Contractors Ltd* v. *Fareham UDC*, [1956] A.C. 696

In July, 1946, the plaintiffs contracted with the defendants to build seventy-eight houses for £92,425 within a period of eight months. Owing to lack of adequate supplies of labour and building materials, it took the plaintiffs twenty-two months to complete the work. There was no provision in the contract regarding such eventualities. The extra expense incurred by the plaintiffs was £17,651, and they claimed that the original contract with the council was frustrated and that they were entitled to recover the total cost on a *quantum meruit*. *Held*—Events had made the contract more onerous to the plaintiffs but had not frustrated the contract. The eventuality should have been provided for. The only claim the plaintiffs had was for the sum agreed in the contract; *quantum meruit* was not available in the absence of frustration. 'It by no means follows that disappointed expectations lead to frustrated contracts.' *Per* Viscount Simmonds, L.C.

Comment. This case was followed in *Amalgamated Investment and Property Co. Ltd* v. *Walker*, 1975.[192] The case illustrates that the doctrine of frustration will not allow a party to escape from a contract because it has in the event become a bad bargain.

(347) *Re Shipton, Anderson & Co. and Harrison Bros. Arbitration*, [1915] 3 K.B. 676

A contract was made for the sale of wheat lying in a warehouse in Liverpool. Before the seller could deliver the wheat, and before the property in it had passed to the buyer, the Government requisitioned the wheat under certain emergency powers available in time of war. *Held*— Delivery being impossible by reason of lawful requisition by the Government, the seller was excused from performance of the contract.

(348) *Storey* v. *Fulham Steel Works* (1907), 24 T.L.R. 89

The plaintiff was employed by the defendants as manager for a period of five years. After he had been working for two years he became ill, and had to have special treatment and a period of convalescence. Six months later he was recovered, but in the meantime the defendant had terminated his employment. The plaintiff now sued for breach of contract, and the defendants pleaded that the plaintiff's period of ill-health operated to discharge the contract. *Held*—The plaintiff's illness and absence from duty did not go to the root of the contract, and was not so serious as to allow the termination of the agreement.

(349) *Mount* v. *Oldham Corporation*, [1973] 1 All E.R. 26

The plaintiff owned and was the headmaster of a school for maladjusted children. In July, 1970, he was arrested on a charge of indecency. He was released on bail but only on condition that he did not reside at the school and had no contact with the children. The rest of the staff attempted to carry on the school in the plaintiff's absence but nevertheless the defendants, who had sent four boys to the school, removed them. In December the plaintiff was acquitted and his character vindicated. As a result the defendants sent the boys back to school and the plaintiff now claimed the school fees for the period from July to December. *Held*—by the Court of Appeal—that the plaintiff was entitled to the fees. It was a trade usage that a parent could not withdraw his child from school but if he did so he had to give a term's notice or pay a term's fees in lieu. Although the defendants had acted reasonably in the circumstances, they had still committed a breach of contract by removing the four boys from the school without giving sufficient notice. The defendants would have been justified if the plaintiff committed a breach which went to the root of the contract but the plaintiff had not committed any breach of contract at all. Neither was the contract frustrated. The position of the headmaster in this school was not so personal and important that the school could not continue in his absence.

Comment. Lord Denning did say in the course of his judgment that if Mr Mount had been found guilty of the charges he would, of course, have been guilty of a breach going to the root of the contract and he could not have recovered any fees. That would have been the way of solving the problem if he had been found guilty because even if he had been found guilty his sentence would have been short and would not have frustrated the contract.

(350) *Hare* v. *Murphy Brothers*, [1975] 3 All E.R. 940

Hare, a foreman, after 25 years' service in Murphy's employment was sentenced to 12 months' imprisonment for unlawful wounding during an incident wholly unconnected with his work. Evidence was given at his trial that if Hare was not sent to prison he would get his job back; otherwise the question would have to be considered on his release. On his release he was told that his post had been filled and the company had no other vacancy for him. They did, however, make him an *ex gratia* payment of £150. Hare claimed redundancy payment. It was *held*—by the Court of Appeal dismissing the application—that the sentence was of such length and Hare's position of such importance that the sentence rendered it impossible for Hare to perform his part of the contract of employment and the contract was accordingly terminated as from the date of the sentence.

Comment. More recently, in *Norris* v. *Southampton City Council*, [1982] I.R.C.R. 141 the Employment Appeal Tribunal has taken the view that where an employee by his own fault makes the performance of the contract of employment impossible, the contract is not frustrated. The employee is in breach of contract and the employer may repudiate the contract and dismiss him. The facts of the case were that Mr Norris was employed as a cleaner by the defendant council. He was convicted of assault and reckless driving and was sentenced to a term of imprisonment. His employers wrote dismissing him and Mr Norris complained to an industrial tribunal that his dismissal was unfair. The tribunal held that the contract of employment was frustrated and that the employee was not dismissed and therefore not entitled to compensation. The employment appeal tribunal, to which Mr Norris appealed, laid down that frustration can only arise where there was no fault by either party. This had been the line taken by Lord Denning in a minority view in *Hare*. Where there was fault, such as deliberate conduct leading to an inability to perform the contract, there was no frustration but a repudiatory breach of contract. The employer had the option of whether or not to treat the contract as repudiated and if he chose to dismiss the employee he could do so, regarding the breach as repudiatory. The question then to be decided was whether the dismissal was fair. The case was remitted to the Industrial Tribunal for further consideration of whether there was unfair dismissal on the facts of the case.

(351) *Taylor* v. *Caldwell* (1863), 3 B. & S. 826

The defendant agreed to let the plaintiff have the use of the Surrey Gardens and Music Hall for the purpose of holding four concerts on four named days in June, July and August, 1861. Before the first concert was due to be held the music hall was destroyed by fire, and the plaintiff now sued for damages because of the defendant's breach of contract in not having the premises ready for him. *Held*—The contract was impossible of performance and the defendant was not liable.

Comment. The case illustrates that destruction of the subject matter need not be total. The Surrey Gardens seemed to have survived without damage. Thus destruction in the frustration context does not mean complete physical destruction but destruction in terms of the commercial viability of the subject matter.

(352) *Krell* v. *Henry*, [1903] 2 K.B. 740

The plaintiff owned a room overlooking the proposed route of the Coronation procession of Edward VII, and had let it to the defendant for the purpose of viewing the procession. The procession did not take place because of the King's illness and the plaintiff now sued for the agreed fee. *Held*—The fact that the procession had been cancelled discharged the parties from their obligations, since it was no longer possible to achieve the real purpose of the agreement.

(353) *Herne Bay Steamboat Co.* v. *Hutton*, [1903] 2 K.B. 683

The plaintiffs agreed to hire a steamboat to the defendant for two days, in order that the defendant might take paying passengers to see the naval review at Spithead on the occasion of Edward VII's Coronation. An official announcement was made cancelling the review, but the fleet was assembled and the boat might have been used for the intended cruise. The defendant did not use the boat, and the plaintiffs employed her on ordinary business. This action was brought to recover the fee of £200 which the defendant had promised to pay for the hire of the boat. *Held*— The contract was not discharged, as the review of the fleet by the Sovereign was not the foundation of the contract. The plaintiffs were awarded the difference between £200 and the profits derived from the use of the ship for ordinary business on the two days in question.

Comment. It may be thought that it is difficult to reconcile this case with *Krell*. (See above). However, whatever the legal niceties may or may not be, there is clearly a difference in fact. To cruise round the fleet assembled at Spithead, even though the figure of the Sovereign (miniscule to the viewer, anyway) would not be present, is clearly more satisfying as the subject-matter of a contract than looking through the window at ordinary London traffic.

(354) *Joseph Constantine Steamship Line Ltd* v. *Imperial Smelting Corporation Ltd*, [1942] A.C. 154

The respondents chartered a steamship to proceed to Port Pirie, Australia, to load a cargo. On the day before the ship was due to load her cargo, and while she was lying in the roads off Port Pirie, there was an explosion in one of her boilers. She was therefore unable to perform the charter as agreed, although she could have done so after rather extensive repairs. The respondents claimed damages for breach of contract. *Held*—The explosion frustrated the contract and the appellants were not liable. The cause of the explosion was unknown, and negligence could not be proved against the appellants; otherwise they would have been liable on the ground that the frustrating event would have been self-induced.

(355) *Jackson* v. *Union Marine Insurance Co.* (1874), L.R. 10 C.P. 125

The plaintiff was the owner of a ship which had been chartered to go with all possible dispatch from Liverpool to Newport, and there load a cargo of iron rails for San Francisco. The plaintiff had entered into a contract of insurance with the defendants, in order that he might protect himself against the failure of the ship to carry out the charter. The vessel was stranded in Caernarvon Bay whilst on its way to Newport. It was not re-floated for over a month, and could not be fully repaired for some time. The charterers hired another ship and the plaintiff now claimed on the policy of insurance. The insurance company suggested that since the plaintiff might claim against the charterer for breach of contract there was no loss, and the court had to decide if such a claim was possible. *Held*— The delay consequent upon the stranding of the vessel put an end, in the commercial sense, to the venture, so that the charterer was released from his obligations and was free to hire another ship. Therefore, the plaintiff had no claim against the charterer and could claim the loss of the charter from the defendants.

Discharge of contract: by frustration: where frustration is self-induced

(356) *Maritime National Fish Ltd* v. *Ocean Trawlers Ltd*, [1935] A.C. 524

The respondents were the owners and the appellants the charterers of a steam trawler, the *St Cuthbert*. The *St Cuthbert* was fitted with, and could only operate with, an otter trawl. When the charterparty was renewed on 25 October, 1932, both parties knew that it was illegal to operate with an otter trawl without a licence from the Minister. The appellants operated five trawlers and applied for five licences. The

Minister granted only three and said that the appellants could choose the names of three trawlers for the licences. The appellants chose three but deliberately excluded the *St Cuthbert* though they could have included it. They were now sued by the owners for the charter fee, and their defence was that the charterparty was frustrated because it would have been illegal to fish with the *St Cuthbert*. It was *held* that the contract was not frustrated, in the sense that the frustrating event was self-induced by the appellants and that therefore they were liable for the hire.

Comment. An otter trawl is a type of net which can, because of its narrow mesh, pick up small immature fish. Its use is restricted for environmental reasons.

Discharge of contract: by frustration: position prior to 1943

(357) *Chandler* v. *Webster*, [1904] 1 K.B. 493

The defendant agreed to let the plaintiff have a room for the purpose of viewing the Coronation procession on 26 June, 1902, for £141 15s. The contract provided that the money be payable immediately. The procession did not take place because of the illness of the King and the plaintiff, who had paid £100 on account, left the balance unpaid. The plaintiff sued to recover the £100 and the defendant counter-claimed for £41 15s. It was *held* by the Court of Appeal that the plaintiff's action failed and the defendant's counter-claim succeeded because the obligation to pay the rent had fallen due before the frustrating event.

Comment. (i) In a later decision, the *Fibrosa Case*, [1942] 2 All E.R. 122, the House of Lords overruled *Chandler* and decided that if, as in that case, there had been total failure of consideration, money paid could be recovered in quasi-contract. If money had been paid in advance to secure performance, said the House of Lords, it was right that it should be recoverable if there was no performance. However, the Law Reform (Frustrated Contracts) Act, 1943 was necessary to deal with the problems of frustration where the contract had been partly performed so that there was no total failure of consideration.

(ii) This case is included mainly to show how important the Law Reform (Frustrated Contracts) Act, 1943 really is.

Limitation of actions: effect of fraud, concealment, and mistake

(358) *Lynn* v. *Bamber*, [1930] 2 K.B. 72

In 1921 the plaintiff purchased some plum trees from the defendant, and was given a warranty that the trees were 'Purple Pershores'. In 1928 the plaintiff discovered that the trees were not 'Purple Pershores' and sued for damages. The defendant pleaded that the claim was barred by the Statutes of Limitation. *Held*—The defendant's fraudulent misrepresentation and fraudulent concealment of the breach of warranty provided a good answer to this plea, so that the plaintiff could recover.

Comment. (i) Examples of concealment are to be found in *Applegate*

v. *Moss* (1970), 114 Sol. J. 971. The plaintiff bought houses from the defendant estate developer in 1951. In 1965 it became obvious by the state of the houses that the foundations were inadequate. In this action it was held that the plaintiff's claim was not statute-barred. Time did not start to run until 1965. In a case on similar facts, *King* v. *Victor Parsons & Co.*, [1973] 1 All E.R. 206, Lord Denning, M.R., speaking of the nature of fraud and concealment for the purposes of what is now s. 32 of the Limitation Act, 1980, said 'It may be that he has no dishonest motive; but that does not matter. He has kept the plaintiff out of the knowledge of his right of action; and that is enough.'

(ii) In *Peco Arts Inc* v. *Hazlitt Gallery Ltd.* [1983] 3 All E.R. 193, the plaintiffs bought from the defendants in November 1970 what purported to be an original drawing in black chalk on paper 'Etude Pour Le Bain Turc' by J.A.D. Ingres for a price of $18,000. In 1976 it was revalued by an expert for insurance purposes. No doubts were cast upon its authenticity. However, on a valuation in 1981 it was discovered that the drawing was a reproduction. The plaintiff claimed rescission and recovery of the purchase price plus interest on the grounds of mutual, common, or unilateral mistake of fact. The trial was adjourned on the first day because the parties wished to simplify the issues. After this the only defence was the Limitation Act, 1980, i.e. that the plaintiff's claim was statute-barred. It was held that it was not and judgment was given for the plaintiff. Webster, J., decided that a prudent buyer in the position of the plaintiff would not normally have obtained an independent authentification but would have relied on the defendants' reputation, as the plaintiff had done. Further, the plaintiff was entitled to conclude that the drawing was an original as the valuers who had examined it in 1976 had not questioned its authenticity. There was no lack of diligence on the part of the plaintiff. Accordingly, the action was not time-barred and there would be judgment for the plaintiff.

The case does not decide what the effect of the mistake was, and to that extent does not go contrary to *Leaf*[197] and *Bell*.[196] These matters were not contested by the defendants. In *Leaf*[197] the Court was deciding how soon an action must be brought for rescission for *innocent misrepresentation*. The issue here was how soon must an action be brought where the plaintiff claims relief for the consequences of a mistake.

Discharge of contract: by operation of law: effect of bankruptcy on claims vested in the debtor

(359) *Wilson* v. *United Counties Bank*, [1920] A.C. 102

A business man left his business affairs in the hands of the bank whilst he went to serve in the war of 1914–18. The bank mismanaged his affairs, and he was eventually adjudicated bankrupt. The trader and his trustee brought this action against the bank for breach of their contractual duty.

Damages of £45,000 were awarded for loss of estate, and of £7500 for the injury caused to the trader's credit and business reputation. With regard to the damages the court *held* that the £45,000 belonged to the trustee for the benefit of creditors, and the £7500 went to the trader personally.

Damages: object of: to place the plaintiff in the same position financially as if the contract had been properly performed.

(360) *Sunley & Co. Ltd* v. *Cunard White Star Ltd*, [1940] 1 K.B. 740

The defendants agreed to carry a machine, belonging to the plaintiffs, to Guernsey, but because of delays for which the defendants were responsible, the machine was delivered a week late. The plaintiffs were not able to show that they had an immediate use for the machine, and could not prove loss of profit. However, it was *held* that, to compensate the plaintiffs for the defendant's breach of contract, they should recover £20 as one week's depreciation of the machine, and the sum of £10 as interest on the capital cost.

Comment. (i) This principle of compensation was applied in *Thake* v. *Maurice*, [1984] 2 All E.R. 513, where Peter Paine, J., decided that the parents of a healthy child were entitled to damages against a surgeon who contracted to sterilize Mr Thake. The operation was performed without negligence but fertility returned because of the particular way in which scar tissue developed. However, the Court said, perhaps exceptionally, that there was an implied term in the contract guaranteeing the success of the operation. If the operation had been successful the Thakes would not have had the expense of another child (their seventh). This was redressable in damages.

(ii) Again, in *C. & P. Haulage* v. *Middleton*, [1983] 3 All E.R. 94, M, an engineer, was ejected from his rented business premises before his contractual licence had expired. He then worked from home, rent free. The Court of Appeal would not give him damages for eviction. If they did he would have been better off.

(iii) An interesting point on assessment arises from *Paula Lee Ltd* v. *Robert Zehill & Co. Ltd*, [1983] 2 All E.R. 390. The plaintiffs made dresses and the defendants distributed them in the Middle East. The defendants agreed to take at least 16,000 dresses a season as required by the market. The defendants terminated the agreement when it had two seasons to run, and argued that the measure of damages they should pay was the plaintiffs' loss of profit on 32,000 of their cheapest dresses. Mustill, J., would not accept this. He decided that there was an implied term in the agreement that 32,000 garments would be selected in a reasonable manner from the various price ranges so as to yield the lowest price, and not the highest price that the defendants would have paid over a normal trading selection. The parties were asked by the judge to compromise their differences on this basis.

(361) *Beach* v. *Reed Corrugated Cases Ltd*, [1956] 2 All E.R. 652

This was an action brought by the plaintiff for wrongful dismissal by the defendants. The plaintiff was the managing director of the company and he had a fifteen-year contract from 21 December, 1950, at a salary of £5000 per annum. His contract was terminated in August, 1954, when he was fifty-four years old and the sum of money that he might have earned would have been £55,000, but the general damages awarded to him were £18,000 after the court had taken into account income tax, including tax on his private investments.

Comment. (i) The same principle has been applied to damages recoverable in tort for loss of earnings (*B.T.C.* v. *Gourley*, [1956] A.C. 185). (ii) The tax deducted does not go to the Revenue but merely reduces the defendant's liability. The same is true where the action is in tort.

Damages: object of: speculative damages may in principle be awarded but not invariably

(362) *Chaplin* v. *Hicks*, [1911] 2 K.B. 786

The defendant organized a beauty contest inviting the readers of certain newspapers to select fifty girls from whom the defendant would select twelve. The twelve successful entrants were to be offered theatrical engagements. The plaintiff was one of the fifty girls selected by the newspaper readers, but the defendant did not invite her to the final selection. She now claimed damages for breach of contract, and the defendant pleaded that, even if he had invited her to the final selection, it was by no means certain that she would have been one of the successful twelve, and therefore, the damages should be nominal. *Held*—Although it was difficult to assess damages, yet the plaintiff was entitled to an assessment, whereupon the jury awarded her £100.

Comment. In *Entertainments Ltd* v. *Great Yarmouth Borough Council* (1983), 134 N.L.J. 311, Cantley, J., awarded only nominal damages to the plaintiffs whose contract to put on summer shows at Great Yarmouth had been repudiated by the Council. The judge said that it had not been established as probable that the shows would have made a profit and after considering *Chaplin* v. *Hicks* (above), said that it was in these circumstances too speculative to put a value on the loss of a chance.

Damages: remoteness: damages will be awarded for loss which is proximate and not too remote

(363) *Hadley* v. *Baxendale* (1854), 9 Exch. 341

The plaintiff was a miller at Gloucester. The driving shaft of the mill being broken, the plaintiff engaged the defendant, a carrier, to take it to the makers at Greenwich so that they might use it in making a new one. The defendant delayed delivery of the shaft beyond a reasonable time, so that the mill was idle for much longer than should have been necessary. The plaintiff now sued in respect of loss of profits during the period of additional delay. The court decided that there were only two possible grounds on which the plaintiff could succeed—(i) That in the usual course of things the work of the mill would cease altogether for want of the shaft. This the court rejected because, to take only one reasonable possibility, the plaintiff might have had a spare or have been able to get one. (ii) That the special circumstances were fully explained, so that the defendant was made aware of the possible loss. The evidence showed that there had been no such explanation. In fact the only information given to the defendant was that the article to be carried was the broken shaft of a mill, and that the plaintiff was the miller of that mill. *Held*—That the plaintiff's claim failed, the damage being too remote.

However, loss of profits for non-delivery or delayed delivery are recoverable if foreseeable as a consequence of the breach. Thus in *Victoria Laundry Ltd* v. *Newman Industries Ltd*, [1949] 1 All E.R. 997, the defendants agreed to deliver a new boiler to the plaintiffs by a certain date but failed to do so with the result that the plaintiffs lost (*a*) normal business profits during the period of delay, and (*b*) profits from dyeing contracts which were offered to them during the period. It was *held* that (*a*) but not (*b*) were recoverable as damages. The general loss of profit in this case arose naturally from the breach and no further 'contemplation' or 'notice' test need be applied.

Comment. The defendant is not liable under the rule in this case unless he knows of the special circumstances, but it is not the case that he is liable merely because he does know of them. One must go further and say that there is not only knowledge but some form of *acceptance* of the liability (see *Weld-Blundell* v. *Stephens*, [1920] A.C. 956).

(364) *The Heron II (Czarnikow Ltd* v. *Koufos)*, [1967] 3 All E.R. 686

Shipowners carrying sugar from Constanza to Basrah delayed delivery at Basrah for nine days during which time the market in sugar there fell and the charterers lost more than £4000. It was held that they could recover that sum from the shipowners because the very existence of a 'market' for goods implied that the purchasers would re-sell the sugar and not use it in trade and that prices might fluctuate and a fall in sugar prices was reasonably foreseeable by the shipowners. In this case the House of Lords *held* that the correct criterion of liability is not whether the loss is reasonably foreseeable by the parties but whether it should have been within their reasonable contemplation at the time of the contract, having regard to their knowledge at that time. The difference between the two is probably slight, but in the view of the House of Lords 'foreseeability' and 'contemplation' are different concepts and the former is wider than the latter and should be restricted to cases of tort. When references are made to 'foresight' in contract it must appear, as the House of Lords said, that the loss which has resulted from the breach of contract was 'a serious possibility', or 'a real danger'.

Comment. (i) It would seem from this case that the House of Lords were of the opinion that the shipowners not only knew what the charterers' purpose was i.e. to sell the sugar but also accepted liability for the loss of the particular market because of undue delay.

(ii) The matter of narrowing the scope of damages in contract was considered by *H. Parsons (Livestock) Ltd* v. *Uttley Ingham & Co. Ltd*, [1978] 1 All E.R. 525. In that case Uttley supplied a pigfood hopper to the plaintiffs and having erected it left the ventilator in the closed position which was a breach of contract. The pigfood stored in the hopper became mouldy and the pigs which ate it died from a rare infection. The Court of Appeal held that the defendants were liable for the loss of the pigs. The decision follows *Heron II* because the Court was satisfied that there was 'a serious possibility' that this would happen. The illness and death of the pigs was not too remote so that even by applying the *Heron II* test a wide range of damage, e.g. for the rare disease in the pigs may be recoverable.

(365) *Horne* v. *Midland Railway Co.* (1873), L.R. 8 C.P. 131

The plaintiff had entered into a contract to sell 4595 pairs of boots to the French Army at a price above the market price. The defendants were responsible for a delay in the delivery of the boots, and the purchasers refused to accept delivery, regarding time as the essence of the contract. The plaintiff's claim for damages was based on the contract price, namely 4s. per pair, but it was *held* that he could only recover the market price of 2s. 9d. per pair unless he could show that the defendants were aware of the exceptional profit involved, and that they had undertaken to be liable for its loss.

Comment. In *Simpson* v. *London & North Western Rail Co.* (1876), 1 Q.B.D. 274 the plaintiff entrusted samples of his products to the defendants so that they could deliver them to Newcastle for an agricultural exhibition. The goods were marked 'Must be at Newcastle on Monday certain'. The defendants did not get them to Newcastle on time and were held liable for the plaintiff's prospective loss of profit arising because he could not exhibit at Newcastle. They had agreed to carry the goods knowing of the special instructions of the customer.

(366) *Pinnock Brothers* v. *Lewis and Peat Ltd*, [1923] 1 K.B. 690

The plaintiffs bought from the defendants some East African Copra Cake which, to the defendants' knowledge, was to be used for feeding cattle. The cake was adulterated with castor oil and was poisonous. The plaintiffs resold the cake to other dealers, who in turn sold it to farmers, who used it for feeding cattle. Cattle fed on the cake died, and claims were made by the various buyers against their sellers, the whole liability resting eventually on the plaintiffs. In this action the plaintiffs sued for the damages and costs which they had been required to pay. Two major defences were raised, the first being an exemption clause saying that the goods were not warranted free from defects, and the other that the damage was too remote. The court dismissed the exemption clause and *held* that, when a substance is quite different from that contracted for, it cannot merely be defective. Further the damage was not too remote, since it was in the implied contemplation of the defendants that the cake would at some time be fed to cattle.

Damages: the injured party must mitigate his loss

(367) *Brace* v. *Calder*, [1895] 2 Q.B. 253

The defendants, a partnership consisting of four members, agreed to employ the plaintiff as manager of a branch of the business for two years. Five months later the partnership was dissolved by the retirement of two of the members and the business was transferred to the other two who offered to employ the plaintiff on the same terms as before but he refused the offer. The dissolution of the partnership constituted a wrongful dismissal of the plaintiff and he brought an action for breach of contract seeking to recover the salary that he would have received had he served the whole period of two years. It was *held* that he was entitled only to nominal damages since it was unreasonable to have rejected the offer of continued employment.

(368) *Moore* v. *D.E.R. Ltd*, [1971] 3 All E.R. 517

In this case a dentist who ordered a new Rover 2000 to replace one which became a total loss in an accident instead of buying a second-hand car was *held* by the Court of Appeal to have acted reasonably. He had a busy practice and needed to be certain that his car was reliable. He was also entitled to the cost of hiring alternative transport for the time it took to obtain the new car even though he could have acquired a second-hand car much sooner.

(369) *Charter* v. *Sullivan*, [1957] 2 Q.B. 117

The plaintiffs, who were motor dealers, agreed to sell a Hillman Minx car to the defendant for £773 17s., which was the retail price fixed by the manufacturers. The defendant refused to complete the purchase and the plaintiffs resold the car a few days later to another purchaser at the same price. The plaintiffs sued for breach of contract and the measure of damages claimed was £97 15s., the profit the plaintiffs would have made on the sale if it had gone through. Evidence showed that the plaintiffs could have sold to a second purchaser another Hillman Minx which could have been ordered from the manufacturers' stock had the defendant taken the first Hillman Minx as agreed. The plaintiff's sales manager said in his evidence 'we can sell all the Hillman Minx cars we can get'. This evidence was accepted by the trial judge. The plaintiffs were really suggesting that but for the defendant's refusal to complete they would have sold two cars and not one, and in so doing would have made double the profit. *Held*—An award of nominal damages (i.e. forty shillings) would be made. The plaintiff's sales manager said the plaintiffs could always find a purchaser for every Hillman Minx car they could get from the manufacturers, and so the plaintiffs must have sold the same number of cars and made the same number of fixed profits as they would have made if the defendant had duly carried out his promise.

(370) *Lazenby Garages* v. *Wright*, [1976] 2 All E.R. 770

Lazenby's were dealers in new and second-hand cars. They bought a secondhand BMW for £1325. Wright agreed in writing to buy it for £1670 but before taking delivery changed his mind and refused to purchase the car. Six weeks later Lazenby's sold the same car for £1770 to someone else but still claimed damages from Wright in the sum of £345, being the loss of profit on the sale to him. It was *held*—by the Court of Appeal—that as Lazenby's had sold the car at a higher price they had suffered no loss on the transaction. The argument that Lazenby's might have sold a different car to the other purchaser was rejected.

(371) *Thompson (W.L.) Ltd* v. *Robinson (Gunmakers) Ltd*, [1955] Ch. 177

On 4 March, 1954, the defendants agreed in writing with the plaintiffs, who were motor car dealers, to purchase from them a Standard Vanguard car. On 5 March, 1954, the defendants said that they were not prepared to take delivery. The plaintiffs returned the car to their suppliers who did not ask for any compensation. The plaintiffs now sued for damages for breach of contract. The selling price of a Standard Vanguard was fixed by the manufacturers and the plaintiff's profit would have been £61 1s. 9d. When the agreement was made there was not sufficient demand for Vanguards in the locality as would absorb all such cars available for sale in the area, but evidence did not show that there was no available market in the widest sense, i.e. in the sense of the country as a whole. It was *held* that the plaintiffs were entitled to compensation for the loss of their bargain. i.e. the profit they would have made (being £61 1s. 9d.) because they had sold one car less than they would have done.—The decision depends to a large extent on the fact that in Yorkshire, at the time the contract was made, the supply of Standard Vanguards did exceed the demand. In fact, the car concerned was returned unsold by the retailers to the manufacturers. This distinguishes the case quite clearly from *Charter* v. *Sullivan* (p. 727).

(372) *Hoffberger* v. *Ascot International Bloodstock Bureau*, *The Times*, 30 January, 1976

After the defendants had broken their contract to buy a horse the plaintiff, who was the vendor, incurred considerable expense in keeping the animal in the hope of selling advantageously. Eventually the horse was sold for a much reduced figure. It was *held*—by the Court of Appeal—that the plaintiff had acted reasonably and was entitled as part of damages to the expenses of attempting to mitigate his loss, notwithstanding that his final claim exceeded the original sale price.

(373) *Luker* v. *Chapman* (1970), 114 Sol. J. 788

The plaintiff lost his right leg below the knee as a result of a traffic accident in which his motor cycle was in collision with the defendant's sports car. The accident was partly caused by the defendant's negligence. After the accident the plaintiff was unable to continue with his employment as a telephone engineer and refused a clerical job, taking up teacher training instead. *Held*—by Browne, J.—that the plaintiff was required to mitigate damages and should have accepted the clerical job. The defendant was not liable for the loss of income involved in the period of teacher training.

Damages: an award of aggravated damages is compensatory, not exemplary (or punitive)

(374) *Ansell* v. *Thomas, The Times*, 23 May, 1973

The plaintiff, the managing director of a company, was in dispute with his co-directors who alleged that he had resigned. When the plaintiff refused to leave the company's premises, the police were called and threatened to use force if the plaintiff did not leave. On the plaintiff's action against his co-directors for assault and conspiracy, the County Court judge awarded him £750 including aggravated damages. *Held*—by the Court of Appeal—that the plaintiff was, on the judge's findings of fact, entitled to aggravated damages to compensate for indignity, mental suffering, disgrace and humiliation. In addition, the defendants were liable for the conduct of the constables who were acting on their behalf.

Damages: must be a genuine pre-estimate of loss, not a penalty

(375) *Ford Motor Co. (England) Ltd* v. *Armstrong* (1915), 31 T.L.R. 267

The defendant was a retailer who received supplies from the plaintiffs. As part of his agreement with the plaintiffs the defendant had undertaken—

    (i) not to sell any of the plaintiffs' cars or spares below list price;
    (ii) not to sell Ford cars to other dealers in the motor trade;
    (iii) not to exhibit any car supplied by the company without their permission.

The defendant also agreed to pay £250 for every breach of the agreement as being the agreed damage which the manufacturer will 'sustain'. The defendant was in breach of the agreement and the plaintiffs sued. It was *held* by the Court of Appeal that the sum of £250 was in the nature of a penalty and not liquidated damages. The same sum was payable for different kinds of breach which were not likely to produce the same loss. Furthermore its size suggested that it was not a genuine pre-estimate of loss.

(376) *Cellulose Acetate Silk Co. Ltd* v. *Widnes Foundry Ltd*, [1933] A.C. 20

The Widnes Foundry entered into a contract to erect a plant for the Silk Co. by a certain date. It was also agreed that the Widnes Foundry would pay the Silk Co. £20 per week for every week they took in erecting the plant beyond the agreed date. In the event the erection was completed thirty weeks late, and the Silk Co. claimed for their actual loss which was £5850. *Held*—The Widnes Foundry were only liable to pay £20 per week as agreed. It was a genuine pre-estimate of loss.

Quantum meruit: **as a quasi-contractual remedy**

(377) *Craven-Ellis* v. *Canons Ltd*, [1936] 2 K.B. 403

The plaintiff was employed as managing director by the company under a deed which provided for remuneration. The Articles provided that directors must have qualification shares, and must obtain these within two months of appointment. The plaintiff and other directors never obtained the required number of shares so that the deed was invalid. However, the plaintiff had rendered services, and he now sued on a *quantum meruit* for a reasonable sum by way of remuneration. *Held*—He succeeded on a *quantum meruit*, there being no valid contract.

(378) *Gilbert and Partners* v. *Knight*, [1968] 2 All E.R. 248

The respondent Knight, agreed, in August, 1965, to pay Gilbert, who was a member of the appellant firm of surveyors, a fee of £30 to supervise specified building work estimated to cost £600. In May, 1966, when the builder started work, the respondent ordered some additional work which brought the cost to £2238. Gilbert supervised this additional work but made no request for an additional payment until the work was completed. He then rendered an account for £135 being the agreed £30 plus a scale fee of 100 guineas for supervising the additional work. The respondent paid only the agreed £30 and would not pay more. Gilbert and Partners' action against Knight was dismissed and they appealed. It was *held* by the Court of Appeal, dismissing the appeal, that the firm was entitled to £30 only. No *quantum meruit* claim lay for supervising the additional work unless a new contract to pay for that work had been made because the parties never discharged the original contract for one lump-sum fee of £30.

Specific performance and injunction generally: remedies granted where damages are not an adequate or a just remedy.

(379) *Sky Petroleum Ltd* v. *VIP Petroleum Ltd*, [1974] 1 All E.R. 954

Under a contract made in March, 1970, the plaintiff company agreed with the defendant that, for a minimum period of 10 years, it would buy all the petrol and diesel fuel it needed for its filling stations from the defendant. In November, 1973, the defendant purported to terminate the contract for an alleged breach of its terms by the plaintiff company. The plaintiff company brought an action against the defendant and sought an interlocutory injunction to restrain the defendant from withholding supplies of petrol and diesel from the plaintiff company. There was evidence that in November, 1973, the petroleum market was in an unusual state and that the plaintiff company would have little prospect of finding an alternative source of supply. Goulding, J., held that an interlocutory injunction would be granted and in the course of his judgment said: 'Now I come to the most serious hurdle in the way of the plaintiff company which is the well-known doctrine that the Court refuses specific performance of a contract to sell and purchase chattels not specific or ascertained. . . . I am entirely unconvinced by counsel for the plaintiff company when he tells me that an injunction in the form sought by him would not be specific enforcement at all. . . . It is, in my judgment, quite plain that I am for the time being specifically enforcing the contract if I grant an injunction. However, the ratio behind the rule is, as I believe, that under the ordinary contract for the sale of non-specific goods, damages are a sufficient remedy. . . . Here, the defendant company appears for practical purposes to be the plaintiff company's sole means of keeping its business going, and I am prepared so far to depart from the general rule as to try to preserve the position under the contract until a later date. I therefore propose to grant an injunction.'

Injunction: of a negative stipulation: generally and in contracts of service

(380) *Metropolitan Electric Supply Co.* v. *Ginder*, [1901] 2 Ch. 799

The defendant entered into a contract with the plaintiffs in which he agreed to take all the electricity he required from them. The plaintiffs sued for an injunction to prevent the defendant from obtaining energy elsewhere. *Held*—The plaintiffs succeeded since the agreement was in essence an undertaking not to take supplies of electricity from elsewhere, and could be enforced by injunction.

(381) *Whitwood Chemical Co.* v. *Hardman*, [1891] 2 Ch. 416

The defendant entered into a contract of service with the plaintiffs and agreed to give the whole of his time to them. In fact he occasionally worked for others, and the plaintiffs tried to enforce the undertaking in the service contract by injunction. *Held*—An injunction could not be granted because there was no express negative stipulation. The defendant had merely stated what he would do, and not what he would not do, and to read into the undertaking an agreement not to work for anyone else required the court to imply a negative stipulation from a positive one. No such implication could be made.

Comment. It is because of the fact that the granting of an injunction of a negative stipulation is so close to specific performance that it is restricted to cases where the negative stipulation is express.

(382) *Warner Brothers Pictures Incorporated* v. *Nelson*, [1937] 1 K.B. 209

The defendant, the film actress Bette Davis, had entered into a contract in which she agreed to act exclusively for the plaintiffs for twelve months. She was anxious to obtain more money and so she left America, and entered into a contract with a person in England. The plaintiffs now asked for an injunction restraining the defendant from carrying out the English contract. *Held*—An injunction would be granted. The contract contained a negative stipulation not to work for anyone else, and this could be enforced. However, since the contract was an American one, the court limited the operation of the injunction to the area of the court's jurisdiction, and although the contract stipulated that the defendant would not work in any other occupation, the injunction was confined to work on stage or screen.

Comment. Even where, as here, there is a negative stipulation, the court will not grant an injunction if the pressure to work for the plaintiffs is so severe as to be for all practical purposes irresistible. In this case it was said that Bette Davis could still earn her living by doing other work.

Injunction: used only to redress a continuing wrong

(383) *Desk Advertising Co. Ltd* v. *Société Civile De Participations Du Group S.T. Dupont and Others*, 1973, *The Times*, June 15.

Since 1953 the plaintiffs had acted as the exclusive distributors in Great Britain of cigarette lighters made by Dupont. The sole shareholder in Dupont had been SCP. In January, 1970, after negotiations for the purchase by Gillette of a substantial shareholding in Dupont, SCP agreed to procure the execution by Dupont before the shareholding control passed from SCP of a contract appointing the plaintiffs exclusive distributing agents in Great Britain on the existing terms for a term certain to December, 1976. Gillette acquired a substantial shareholding and SCP did not procure the promised contract for the plaintiffs, thus breaking their 1970 agreement. The plaintiffs sought injunctions to restrain the marketing of the lighters otherwise than through the plaintiffs' exclusive agency. It was *held*—by the Court of Appeal—that SCP's breach of contract was complete when control of Dupont passed from it; it was not, therefore, a continuing breach. Specific performance was based upon continuing contractual obligation. A mandatory injunction was based on a continuing wrong. The court was unaware of a remedy which in general terms required wrongdoers (other than by damages) to take steps to right a past wrong, and accordingly an injunction could not be granted.

Injunction: the obligation to be enforced must be certain

(384) *Bower* v. *Bantam Investments Ltd*, [1972] 3 All E.R. 349

The plaintiff, who wanted some land that he owned developed as a marina, sold the land to Bantam Investments Ltd. They formed a company to carry out the development and the land was bought by his company. The contract for sale to the defendants was conditional upon planning permission which would enable the marina 'to proceed as envisaged'. The marina was not built and the plaintiff, fearing that the land would be sold, brought an action for an injunction to prevent a further sale and so by implication require the marina to be built. It was *held* by Goff, J., that an injunction would not be granted. There was no express obligation in the contract to develop the land so the plaintiff could only rely on an implied term to this effect. An injunction would be given to restrain breach of an implied negative undertaking but it was necessary to indicate some specific thing which the defendant had impliedly agreed not to do and conduct inconsistent with contractual obligation does not suffice. The defendant's obligations were, at the most, to use their best endeavours to develop the site as a marina if this was practical, so that an injunction could not be granted.

Injunction: *quia timet*: to prevent a threatened injury

(385) *Hooper* v. *Rogers*, [1974] 3 All E.R. 417

Mr Hooper and Mr Rogers were tenants in common near Bude in Cornwall of steeply sloping land. At the top of the steep slope was Mr Hooper's farmhouse. In December, 1971, Mr Rogers, without warning and in a most high-handed manner, levelled and deepened a track which was owned and occupied by the two tenants and which cut across the slope, its nearest point being 80 feet from Mr Hooper's farmhouse. A surveyor, Mr Borton, inspected the site on behalf of Mr Hooper in January, 1972, and observed that there was erosion from the west of the track. He considered that there was a long-term danger to Mr Hooper's farmhouse by erosion aided by the prevailing westerly gales and rain. The result of the erosion and the fact that the natural repose of the hillside had been disturbed was likely to be that trees between the track and the farmhouse would lose their roothold and would no longer bind the soil together, the process ending with the footings of the farmhouse being deprived of earth support and the building being damaged and collapsing. Judge Chope at first instance awarded judgment for £750 based on the cost of reinstating the track to its former condition and consolidating it. Mr Rogers appealed on the ground that no damages based on the threat to the support of the farmhouse could be awarded. It was *held*—by the

Court of Appeal—that a mandatory injunction or damages in lieu could be ordered where there was a real probability that in time the action of deepening the track would result in actual damage to the house unless prevented by filling in and consolidation. Russell, L.J., said. 'The evidence of Mr Borton, which I accept, is that there is a real probability, not just a possibility, a real probability of prejudice to the plaintiff's house if nothing is done . . . and I find that there is a real risk.'

Comment. Although damages were awarded the Court of Appeal said that in the circumstances an injunction could have been awarded although no damage had actually occurred.

Specific performance: contract must be supported by consideration: adequacy

(386) *Mountford* v. *Scott*, [1974] 1 All E.R. 248

The defendant, an illiterate West Indian who had lived in England for 20 years, signed an agreement in consideration of £1 giving the plaintiff an option to purchase his house for £10,000 within six months. He sought to resile after some weeks because the value of the house had gone up but his solicitors wrote telling him that he could not do so and three months later the plaintiffs purported to exercise their option. They then issued a writ claiming specific performance. Brightman, J., *held* that an order for specific performance must be made and in the course of his judgment said: 'As the plaintiffs had made no more than a token payment for the defendant's promise, are the plaintiffs, so far as the equitable remedy of specific performance is concerned, in the position of volunteers who ought to be left to their remedy in damages? . . . An option to purchase land creates an equitable interest in the land. . . . Such equitable interest is an inevitable consequence of the existence of the option. It would seem immaterial to this concept that the option happened to be gratuitous. It is only necessary, as I see it, that the option should have been validly created. It is not the function of equity to protect only those equitable interests which have been created for valuable consideration. . . . In the result, therefore, I am of the opinion that the plaintiffs acquired an equitable interest in the defendant's land at the moment when the option agreement came to be signed and that such interest will be enforced subject only to the exercise of the option, as has been done in this case, and the payment of the purchase money due for the land. I therefore conclude that the plaintiffs are entitled to a decree for specific performance.'

Comment. This decision was affirmed by the Court of Appeal [1975] 1 All E.R. 198.

Specific performance and injunction: court must be able to supervise performance.

(387) *Ryan* v. *Mutual Tontine Westminster Chambers Association*, [1893] 1 Ch. 116

The defendants leased a residential flat to the plaintiff and also agreed to employ a porter who would be resident on the premises. The porter was to clean the flats and deliver parcels, take in articles for safe custody, and take charge of keys. The defendants appointed a porter but the man concerned was also a chef at a club in Westminster and was absent from the flats each day from 11 a.m. to 3 p.m., carrying out his duties as a chef. While he was away his duties were carried out in a most indifferent fashion by a number of boys and a charlady. These persons were not resident. The plaintiff now sued for breach of contract and asked for specific performance of the promise to appoint a full time porter. *Held*— Specific performance could not be granted because the court could not supervise the day-to-day performance of such an obligation. The plaintiff's remedy was an action for damages.

Comment. In *Posner* v. *Scott-Lewis*, [1986] 3 W.L.R. 531 Mervyn-Davies, J., decided that the tenants of a block of flats could enforce by specific performance an undertaking in their leases that the defendant landlords would employ a resident porter to keep the communal areas clear. The court had only to ensure that the appointment was made. The plaintiffs were not asking the court to supervise the porter's day-to-day work.

(388) *Hill* v. *C. A. Parsons & Co. Ltd*, [1971] 3 All E.R. 1318

The defendants capitulated to demands from a trade union (DATA) that certain of their employees should be required to join that union. The plaintiff, a chartered engineer aged 63 with 35 years' service, was accordingly told to join and when he refused was given one month's notice. He then started proceedings for, *inter alia*, an injunction to prevent the company from terminating his employment. The Court of Appeal (Stamp, L.J., dissenting) felt that six months would have been a proper period of notice and granted an injunction which in effect resulted in specific performance of the contract of service for that period of time.

Comment. The court was obviously influenced by the fact that by the time six months had elapsed the Industrial Relations Act, 1971 (now repealed), would be in force and give greater rights of compensation to the plaintiff. Nevertheless, Lord Denning, M.R., treated the decision as based on the principle *ubi jus ibi remedium* (where there is a right there is a remedy) and regarded Mr Hill's right to damages as inadequate, thus allowing the court to grant an injunction.

Injunction: of a negative stipulation: not granted to compel performance

(389) *Page One Records Ltd* v *Britton*, [1967] 3 All E.R. 822

By a written contract made in 1966 the defendants, a group of four musicians ('The Troggs'), appointed the plaintiffs to manage their professional careers for five years, they being persons of no business experience who were unlikely to survive as a 'pop' group without the services of a manager. The contract was world-wide. The plaintiffs agreed to use all their resources of knowledge and experience to advance the defendants' careers, and the contract further provided that the defendants would not engage any other person to act as manager or agent for them, and that they would not act themselves in such capacity. The plaintiffs were to receive twenty per cent of all moneys earned by the defendants during the period of the contract. The Troggs became an established group, earning as much as £400 per night. In 1967 the defendants signified their intention to repudiate the management contract, but the court held that there had been no breaches of duty by the plaintiffs to justify the repudiation. In fact the plaintiffs had supported the group in the fullest measure and were to a large extent responsible for the success of the group. The plaintiffs sued for damages for breach of contract and applied also for an interlocutory injunction restraining the defendants until trial from engaging any person, firm or corporation, other than the plaintiffs, as their manager. *Held*—by Stamp, J.—that the injunction must be refused because—

(i) The defendants had no business experience and had to have a manager. If an injunction was granted it would *compel* not merely *encourage* the defendants to carry out their contract with the plaintiffs. *Warner Bros* v. *Nelson*, 1937,[382] was distinguishable because Bette Davis was a person of intelligence, capacity and means and if she had chosen not to act at all rather than for Warner Bros, she would have been able to employ herself both usefully and remuneratively in other spheres of activity. Other similarly remunerative employment was not available to the 'Troggs'.

(ii) The injunction, if granted, would also have the effect of enforcing a contract for personal services of a fiduciary nature, because the plaintiffs were managers and it would be necessary for them to see, and be friendly with, the defendants for a further four years. In *Warner Bros* v. *Nelson*, 1937, the obligation of the plaintiffs was largely to pay money to Miss Davis; they were not involved in the much more intimate relationship of managing her career.

Specific performance and injunction: not granted if leading to further litigation or breach of another obligation

(390) *Wroth* v. *Tyler*, [1973] 1 All E.R. 897

A vendor entered into a contract for the sale of his house with vacant possession. After the contract and unknown to the vendor the vendor's wife registered notice of statutory right of occupation under s. 1 of the Matrimonial Homes Act, 1967. This meant that the vendor was unable to complete and the purchaser brought an action for specific performance. The wife refused to remove the notice from the register. It was *held* by Megarry, J., that specific performance must be refused. It was unreasonable to decree specific performance if it would result in litigation between the spouses. In these circumstances the plaintiffs were awarded damages of £5,500 representing the difference between the original sale price and the value of the property at the date of hearing.

(391) *Warmington* v. *Miller*, [1973] 2 All E.R. 372

The defendant held a lease of premises, the lease containing an absolute prohibition against assignment, underletting or parting with possession. The defendant orally agreed with the plaintiff to grant him an under-lease of part of the premises. He did not do so and the plaintiff brought an action for specific performance. *Held*—by the Court of Appeal—the action for specific performance must be dismissed. Specific performance of the contract to grant an under-lease would not be ordered since it would result in a breach of covenant by the defendant.

Quasi-contract: generally

(392) *Greenwood* v. *Bennett*, [1972] 3 All E.R. 586

In this case a thief stole a car from a company and sold it to the appellant who, in good faith and without notice of the defect in title, carried out extensive repairs. The repairs cost him £226. He sold the car to a finance company who let it out on hire purchase for £450. The police traced the car to the hirer and took possession of it. The Chief Constable then took out an interpleader summons to determine to whom he should return it. The County Court judge held that the company was entitled to possession of the car and that they did not have to reimburse the appellant with the money he had expended on repairs. The appellant appealed contending that he should be paid £226 by the company. *Held*—by the Court of Appeal—the appeal would be allowed. The appellant was entitled to be paid £226 by the company in respect of the improvements he had made to the car. If the police had not taken possession of it and the company had brought an action for conversion or detinue or for specific delivery of the car, the court would have ordered that an allowance should be made for the cost of the repairs. (See *Munro* v. *Wilmot*, [1948] 1 K.B. 295). In interpleader proceedings a similar course must be adopted in favour of an innocent claimant for otherwise the true owner would be unjustly enriched at his expense. It should be noted that the decision in this case applies only where the person who does the work honestly believes himself to be the owner of the property. Where the person who does the work knows or ought to know that the property does not belong to him then he will not normally be paid for his work on it.

Quasi-contract: actions for money paid

(393) *Brook's Wharf and Bull Wharf Ltd* v. *Goodman Bros*, [1936] 3 All
      E.R. 696

The plaintiff company had agreed to store in its warehouse goods
imported by the defendants. The defendants were liable by Act of
Parliament to pay customs duties but the Act also allowed the authorities
to recover these duties from the warehouseman. The goods were stolen
before the defendants had paid the customs duties and they refused to
do so. The authorities claimed the duties from the plaintiffs who paid
them. *Held*—by the Court of Appeal—that the plaintiffs could recover
the sums paid by way of duty from the defendants in quasi-contract.

(394) *Metropolitan Police District Receiver* v. *Croydon Corporation*,
      [1957] 1 All E.R. 78

A policeman had recovered damages for an accident resulting from the
defendants' negligence. The injuries were received while the policeman
was on duty and his wages were paid while he was unfit by the Police
Receiver who was required by Act of Parliament to make these
payments. In this action the Receiver was seeking to recover the amount
paid in wages on the ground that the defendants would have had to pay
more in damages to the policeman if he had not received his pay. *Held*—
by the Court of Appeal—that the action failed. The defendants were not
under a common and legal obligation to pay the policeman's wages so
that quasi-contract did not apply.

Quasi-contract: actions for money had and received: mistake of fact

(395) *Cox* v. *Prentice* (1815), 3 M. & S. 344

The defendant wished to sell a bar of silver to Cox but before the sale
the bar was weighed by an assay master. Cox paid £88 for the bar on the
basis of the weight ascribed to it by the assay master. It was later discovered that the weight was less than certified by the assay master who
had made a mistake in the weighing. *Held*—Cox could recover the excess
from Prentice since the money had been paid under a mistake of fact.

   Comment. Sometimes the rule of evidence called estoppel may override
and prevent an action for money paid under mistake of fact. Thus in
Avon County Council v. *Howlett*, [1983] 1 All E.R. 1073, H, a teacher,
was regularly overpaid whilst off sick. When the mistake was discovered
the Council sued to recover the extra payment of £1007 as money paid
under a mistake of fact. It was held by the Court of Appeal that although
this was so they were estopped from denying that H was entitled to the
money. H had relied on the Council's representation that he was entitled
to the money and had in fact spent nearly half of it. The Council could
not recover any of the overpayments.

LAW OF TORTS

Nature of tort: not all harm is actionable

(396) *Perera* v. *Vandiyar*, [1953] 1 All E.R. 1109

The plaintiff was the tenant of a flat in Tooting, and the defendant was the landlord. On 8 October, 1952, the landlord cut off the supply of gas and electricity to the flat in order to induce the plaintiff to leave. As a result, the plaintiff was forced to move out of the flat and lived elsewhere until the services were restored on 15 October, 1952. The plaintiff claimed damages for breach of implied covenant for quiet enjoyment, and also for eviction. *Held*—The plaintiff was entitled to damages for breach of the implied covenant, but punitive damages on the purported tort of eviction were not recoverable because the defendant had not committed a tort. It had not been necessary for the defendant to trespass on any part of the demised premises in order to cut off the services, and mere intention to evict was not a tort.

Comment. This kind of conduct by a landlord is now a criminal offence under s. 1, Protection from Eviction Act, 1977. However, there is no civil action for breach of the statutory duty. (*McCall* v. *Abelesz*, [1976] 1 All E.R. 727.)

(397) *Hargreaves* v. *Bretherton*, [1958] 3 W.L.R. 463

The plaintiff pleaded that the defendant had falsely and maliciously and without just cause or excuse committed perjury as a witness at the plaintiff's trial for certain criminal offences, and that as a result the plaintiff had been convicted and sentenced to eight years' preventive detention. A point of law arose because the plaintiff's action was in effect based on the purported tort of perjury. *Held*—No action lay on this cause, since there was no tort of perjury, and therefore the plaintiff's claim must be struck out.

(398) *Roy* v. *Prior*, [1969] 3 All E.R. 1153

The plaintiff, a doctor, sued the defendant, a solicitor, for damages alleging, amongst other things, that the defendant had caused his arrest and forcible attendance at court to give evidence in a criminal case by saying falsely in court that the plaintiff was evading a witness summons. The action failed. Lord Denning, M.R., saying in the course of his judgment—

It is settled law that, if a witness knowingly and maliciously tells untruths in the witness box, and as a result an innocent person is imprisoned, nevertheless no action lies against that witness. . . . The reason lies in public policy. Witnesses must be able to give their evidence without fear of the consequences. They might be deterred from doing so if they were at risk of being sued for what they said. So the law gives a witness the cloak of absolute immunity from suit. This applies not only to statements made by a witness in the box, but also to statements made whilst he is giving his proof to his solicitor beforehand. The reason is because the protection given to the witness in the box would be useless to him if it could be got round by an action against him in respect of his proof. . . .

Comment. The Criminal Justice Act 1988 gives prisoners whose convictions are quashed or pardoned a *right* to monetary compensation from the Government. The matter of compensation was formerly a matter for the discretion of the Home Secretary.

Nature of tort: expanding role of negligence from the Atkinian neighbour test

(399) *Donoghue (or M'Alister) v. Stevenson*, [1932] A.C. 562

The appellant's friend purchased a bottle of ginger beer from a retailer in Paisley and gave it to her. The respondents were the manufacturers of the ginger beer. The appellant consumed some of the ginger beer and her friend was replenishing the glass, when, according to the appellant, the decomposed remains of a snail came out of the bottle. The bottle was made of dark glass so that the snail could not be seen until most of the contents had been consumed. The appellant became ill and served a writ on the manufacturers claiming damages. The question before the House of Lords was whether the facts outlined above constituted a cause of action in negligence. The House of Lords *held* by a majority of three to two that they did. It was stated that a manufacturer of products, which are sold in such a form that they are likely to reach the ultimate consumer in the form in which they left the manufacturer with no possibility of intermediate examination, owes a duty to the consumer to take reasonable care to prevent injury. This rule has been broadened in subsequent cases so that the manufacturer is liable more often where defective chattels cause injury. The following important points also arise out of the case.

(i) It was in this case that the House of Lords formulated the test that the duty of care in negligence is based on the foresight of the reasonable man.

As Lord Atkin said: 'The liability for negligence, whether you style it such or treat it as in other systems as a species of 'culpa' is no doubt based upon a general public sentiment of moral wrongdoing for which the offender must pay. But acts or omissions which any moral code would censure cannot in a practical world be treated so as to give a right to every person injured by them to demand relief. In this way rules of law arise which limit the range of complainants and the extent of their remedy. The rule that you are to love your neighbour becomes in law, you must not injure your neighbour; and the lawyer's question, Who is my neighbour? receives a restricted reply. You must take reasonable care to avoid acts or omissions which you can reasonably foresee would be likely to injure your neighbour. Who, then, in law is my neighbour? The answer seems to be—persons who are so closely and directly affected by my act that I ought reasonably to have them in contemplation as being so affected when I am directing my mind to the acts or omissions which are called in question.'

(ii) Lord Macmillan's remark in his judgment that the categories of negligence are never closed suggests that the tort of negligence is capable of further expansion. That this has been so is revealed by the discussion of later cases at p. 813.

(iii) The duty of care with regard to chattels as laid down in the case relates to chattels not dangerous in themselves. The duty of care in respect of chattels dangerous in themselves, e.g. explosives, is much higher.

(iv) The appellant had no cause of action against the retailer in contract because her friend bought the bottle, so that there was no privity of contract between the retailer and the appellant. Therefore terms relating to fitness for purpose and merchantable quality, now implied into such contracts by the Sale of Goods Act, 1979, did not apply here.

Comment. A remedy under the Sale of Goods Act could have been given to the appellant if the reasoning of Tucker, J., in *Lockett* v. *A & M Charles Ltd*, [1938] 4 All E.R. 170 had been applied in *Donoghue*. In *Lockett* husband and wife went into an hotel for lunch. The wife ordered whitebait which was not fit for human consumption. She only ate a small amount of the whitebait and was then taken ill. In the subsequent action against the hotel, Tucker, J., held that although the husband ordered the meal there was an assumption in these cases that each party would be, if necessary, personally liable for what he or she consumed. There was therefore a contract between the hotel and the wife into which Sale of Goods Act terms could be implied and she was awarded damages because the whitebait was not fit for the purpose or of merchantable quality. This approach is surprisingly modern in spite of the fact that the case was decided in 1938.

Damage and liability: *damnum sine injuria*: **effect of malice and motive.**

(400) *Best* v. *Samuel Fox & Co. Ltd*, [1952] 2 All E.R. 394

Best was a workman at the defendants' factory and because of an accident caused by the defendants' negligence he was emasculated and thus rendered incapable of sexual intercourse. Best's claim for damages was successful but his wife also claimed damages for loss of her husband's *consortium* through the defendants' negligence. The House of Lords *held* that her claim failed because the *damnum* was not of a kind recognized by law. 'It is true that a husband is entitled to recover damages for loss of *consortium* against a person who negligently injures his wife, but this exceptional right is an anomaly at the present day. A wife . . . was never regarded as having any proprietary right in her husband. . . .' *per* Lord Morton of Henryton.

Comment. Some American jurisdictions allow such a claim. The *Best* case is in no sense antifemale. The House of Lords simply took the view that the right of *consortium* in both parties was an anachronism and took the opportunity to deny the right of *consortium* in the wife. The Law Commissioners recommended giving equal rights to husband and wife by abolishing the husband's right to compensation for loss of his wife's *consortium*. (See Report No. 56 on Personal Injury Litigation—Assessment of Damages (1973).) This has been achieved by s. 2(a), Administration of Justice Act, 1982.

(401) *Electrochrome Ltd* v. *Welsh Plastics Ltd*, [1968] 2 All E.R. 205

A lorry driver employed by the defendants drove the defendants' vehicle into a fire hydrant near to the plaintiff's factory. Water escaped from the damaged hydrant and the supply had to be cut off while repairs were carried out. The plaintiffs lost a day's work at their factory and sued for this loss. However, since they were not the owners of the hydrant it was *held* that no action lay. They had suffered loss but there had been no infringement of their legal rights.

Comment. (i) The case is a good example of the reluctance of a court to allow the law of tort to be used to compensate for economic loss, i.e. the mere loss of an opportunity to make a profit, perhaps on the grounds that the law of contract is more concerned with the loss of expectations. Furthermore, the decision in this case can be reached by way of *damnum sine injuria* or by saying that there was no duty of care or, if there was, that the damage was too remote.

(ii) In *Junior Books Ltd* v. *Veitchi Co. Ltd*, 1982 (see p. 804), the House of Lords decided that if a plaintiff was in sufficiently close proximity to the defendant he could recover foreseeable economic loss even though there was no physical damage either to a person or to property. It would, however, be unwise to assume that *Junior Books* covers all cases of economic loss, particularly where, as in the Electrochome case, proximity of the plaintiff and defendant does not exist in the *Junior Books* way.

(402) *Bradford Corporation* v. *Pickles*, [1895] A.C. 587

The corporation had statutory power to take water from certain springs. Water reached the springs by percolating (but not in a defined channel) through neighbouring land belonging to Pickles. In order to induce the corporation to buy his land at a high price, Pickles sank a shaft on it, with the result that the water reaching the corporation's reservoir was discoloured and its flow diminished. The corporation asked for an injunction to restrain Pickles from collecting the subterranean water. *Held*—An injunction could not be granted. Pickles had a right to drain from his land subterranean water not running in a defined channel. (This right of a landowner was established by the House of Lords in *Chasemore* v. *Richards* (1859), 7 H.L. Cas. 349). Any malice which he might have had in doing it did not affect that right, since English law knows no doctrine of abuse of rights. No use of property which would be legal if due to a proper motive can become illegal because it is prompted by an improper or malicious motive.

(403) *Langbrook Properties* v. *Surrey County Council*, [1969] 3 All E.R. 1424

The plaintiffs claimed that buildings on their land had suffered from subsidence caused by the defendants' conduct in pumping out excavations for the construction of a motorway near Sunbury-on-Thames. They claimed damages for nuisance and negligence. *Held*—by Plowman, J.—the claim disclosed no cause of action, a landowner being entitled to abstract underground percolating water as much as he wished regardless of resulting damage to his neighbour. (*Bradford Corporation* v. *Pickles*, 1895, *applied*.)

Comment. The *Bradford* and *Langbrook* cases were followed in *Stephens* v. *Anglian Water Authority, The Times*, 24 August, 1987. The water authority abstracted subterranean water flowing in undefined channels beneath its land and caused part of the plaintiff's property to collapse. Nevertheless her claim in negligence failed as would any other claim.

(404) *Wilkinson* v. *Downton*, [1897] 2 Q.B. 57

The defendant, 'as a practical joke', called on Mrs Wilkinson and told her that her husband had been seriously injured in an accident and had had both his legs broken. Mrs Wilkinson travelled to see her husband at Leytonstone, and believing the message to be true, sustained nervous shock and in consequence was seriously ill. This action was brought for damages for false and malicious representation. Damages were awarded. The court *held* that intentional physical harm is a tort even though it does not consist of a trespass to the person. Further, whether the act is malicious or by way of a joke is irrelevant.

Comment. Although it is often stated that trespass lies only for direct damage, trespass is felt to be the basis of this action and it clearly suggests that the tort of trespass is available for indirect physical damage caused wilfully.

Minors: liability as defendant

(405) *Williams* v. *Humphrey, The Times*, 20 February, 1975

The defendant, a youth of nearly 16, accompanied his friend and the friend's parents to a swimming pool. As part of the general fun the defendant pushed the friend's father, the plaintiff, a middle-aged man, into the shallow end of the pool, merely intending to cause a big splash.

The plaintiff's left foot struck the edge of the pool and he sustained severe injuries to his foot and ankle. He underwent five operations and ended up crippled. It was *held*—by Talbot, J.—that the plaintiff had not taken such part in the pool activities that he could be said to have willingly accepted the risk of personal injury and the defendant was guilty of both negligence and trespass to the person. The plaintiff succeeded.

Comment. It may be puzzling to the reader why this action was worthwhile in terms of the fact that the defendant would not have had a lot of money in his personal capacity. However, there was a household insurance policy available. Most modern household insurance policies have a public liability clause which provides cover, sometimes up to £250,000, for accidents caused by the householder or his family.

(406) *Ballett* v. *Mingay*, [1943] K.B. 281

The appellant was an infant and he borrowed from the respondent an amplifier and a microphone. When the respondent demanded the return of the articles, the appellant failed to do so having lent them to another. The infant was sued in detinue (now wrongful interference by conversion). It was suggested that in this action the respondent was seeking to make the appellant liable in tort for an act which was really a breach of contract and for which, as an infant, he could not be liable. *Held*—The infant was properly sued in tort because his action in parting with possession of the articles was not allowed by the contract of bailment and was therefore outside the terms of the contract.

Minors: liability of parents and others in charge of minors: negligent control

(407) *Donaldson* v. *McNiven*, [1952] 1 All E.R. 1213

The defendant lived in a densely populated area of Liverpool and allowed his thirteen-year-old son to have an air rifle on condition that he did not use it outside the house. The defendant's house had a large cellar and the boy was told to use the rifle there. Without the defendant's knowledge the boy fired the air rifle at some children playing near to the house, injuring the plaintiff, a child of five. *Held*—In the circumstances the precautions taken by the defendant were reasonable and would have been adequate but for the son's disobedience, which could not have been foreseen because the boy was usually obedient. The defendant was not guilty of negligence.

(408) *Bebee* v. *Sales* (1916), 32 T.L.R. 413

A father allowed his fifteen-year-old son to retain a shot gun with which he knew he had already caused damage. The father was *held* liable for an injury to another boy's eye.

Comment. Cases 407 and 408 were decided on the ordinary principles of negligence at common law. However, since the Air Guns and Shot

Guns Act, 1962 (see now Firearms Act, 1968), an action may lie against the parent for breach of statutory duty. The Act makes it a criminal offence to give an air weapon to a person under fourteen years, and restricts the use or possession of air weapons by young persons in public places except under supervision. In any case breaches of these statutory duties could be relied upon as evidence of negligence. Furthermore a person injured might now claim compensation from the Criminal Injuries Compensation Board. The age of the child causing the injury is not a bar to a claim against the Board because payments will be made even though the child inflicting the injury is below the age of criminal responsibility. In *Gorely* v. *Codd*, [1966] 3 All E.R. 891, the plaintiff was injured by a pellet from Codd's air rifle when they were larking about in a field in open country. Codd was sixteen-and-a-half years of age and when the plaintiff sued Codd's father the court found that he had given proper instruction to his son and was not liable at common law. Since the shooting did not occur in a public place there was no breach of the Air Guns and Shot Guns Act, 1962 (see now Firearms Act, 1968).

(409) *Carmarthenshire County Council* v. *Lewis*, [1955] 1 All E.R. 565

A boy aged four years was a pupil at a nursery school run by the appellants who were the local education authority. The boy and another were made ready to go out for a walk with the mistress in charge who left them for a moment in order to get ready herself. She did not return for ten minutes, having treated another child who had cut himself. During her absence the boy got out of the classroom and made his way through an unlocked gate, down a lane, and into a busy highway. He caused the driver of a lorry to swerve into a telegraph pole, as a result of which the driver was killed. His widow brought an action for damages for negligence. *Held*—In the circumstances of the case the mistress was not negligent so the liability of the local authority was not vicarious. However, they were negligent themselves because they had not taken reasonable precautions to keep the young children who used the premises from getting out into the highway.

(410) *Butt* v. *Cambridgeshire and Isle of Ely County Council* (1969), 119 N.L.J. 118.

The plaintiff was a pupil in a class of 37 girls of nine and ten years of age. She lost an eye when another girl in her class waved pointed scissors which the children were using to cut out illustrations. The teacher was giving individual attention to another child. *Held*—by the Court of Appeal—that her claim for damages failed. The teacher was not under a duty to require all work to stop while she was giving individual attention to members of the class. She was not negligent so that there was no vicarious liability in the local authority. The local authority was not liable for its own negligence in that evidence of experienced teachers showed that there was no fault in the system of using pointed scissors.

Mental patients: liability in tort

(411) *Morriss* v. *Marsden*, [1952] 1 All E.R. 925

The defendant took a room at an hotel in Brighton, and whilst there he violently attacked the plaintiff who was the manager of the hotel. Evidence showed that at the time of the attack the defendant was suffering from a disease of the mind. He knew the nature and quality of his act, but did not know that what he was doing was wrong. The plaintiff sued for damages for assault and battery. *Held*—Since the defendant knew the nature and quality of his tortious act, it did not matter that he did not know that what he was doing was wrong, and he was liable in tort.

Judicial immunity in tort

(412) *Law* v. *Llewellyn*, [1906] 1 K.B. 487

Law appeared at Bridgend magistrates' court to prosecute two persons for obtaining money by false pretences. He was advised by counsel that, in the absence of certain witnesses, it would not be possible to secure a conviction. Law agreed to withdraw the charges and, after he had done so, Llewellyn, who was a presiding magistrate, said words which meant that the plaintiff was a blackmailer and had brought unfounded criminal charges. He also added that a term of imprisonment would do the plaintiff good. Law brought this action against Llewellyn for defamation, and it was *held* that judicial immunity extended to Llewellyn and therefore Law's claim showed no reasonable cause of action.

Diplomatic immunity in tort: nature of

(413) *Dickinson* v. *Del Solar*, [1930] 1 K.B. 376

The plaintiff had been knocked down by a car driven by the defendant's servant. The defendant was the First Secretary of the Peruvian Legation in London. The Head of the Legation directed the defendent not to plead diplomatic privilege, and the defendant entered an appearance in the action. The plaintiff succeeded and the defendant's insurance company refused to indemnify their client, saying, in effect, that his diplomatic immunity was immunity from liability. *Held*—The insurers were liable to indemnify the defendant. Diplomatic agents are not immune from liability for wrongful acts, but are merely immune from suit. This immunity can be waived with the sanction of the sovereign of the state in question, or an offical superior of the person concerned. The defendant's act in entering an appearance operated as a waiver of diplomatic privilege, and judgment was properly entered against him.

Corporations: as plaintiffs in tort

(414) *D. & L. Caterers Ltd and Jackson* v. *D'Anjou*, [1945] 1 All E.R. 563

The plaintiffs owned a West-End restaurant called the 'Bagatelle'. The defendant made certain statements alleging that the restaurant was operated illegally and obtained its supplies on the Black Market. *Held—* The statements were defamatory and a limited liability company could sue for slander without proof of special damage. Where the slander related to its trade or business, the law implied the existence of damage to found the action.

Corporations: as defendants in tort

(415) *Poulton* v. *London and South Western Railway Co.* (1867), L.R. 2 Q.B. 534

The plaintiff was arrested by a station-master for non-payment of carriage in respect of his horse. The defendants, who were the employers of the station-master, had power to detain passengers for non-payment of their own fare, but for no other reason. *Held—*Since there was no express authorization of the arrest by the defendants, the station-master was acting outside the scope of his employment and the defendants were not liable.

(416) *Campbell* v. *Paddington Borough Council*, [1911] 1 K.B. 869

The defendants, in accordance with a resolution duly passed, erected a stand in Burwood Place in order that members of the council might view the funeral procession of King Edward the Seventh passing along the Edgware Road. The plaintiff, who occupied certain premises in Burwood Place, often let the premises for the purpose of viewing public processions passing along the Edgware Road. The stand obstructed the view of the funeral procession from the plaintiff's house and she was unable to let the premises for that purpose. *Held—*As the stand constituted a public nuisance, the plaintiff could maintain an action for the special damage which she had sustained through the loss of view. The corporation was properly sued, and the fact that the erection of the stand was probably *ultra vires* did not matter.

Comment. The damages in this case must be regarded as parasitical because the law does not recognize a right to a view or prospect and it must be accepted therefore that a plaintiff may recover as part of his damages for injury to a recognized interest a financial loss related to another interest which would not in itself be protected by law. (And see also *Spartan Steel and Alloys Ltd* v. *Martin & Co Ltd*, 1972; see p. 804.)

Vicarious liability: who is a servant? Control and other tests: transfer of employees

(417) *Garrard* v. *Southey (A.E.) and Co. and Standard Telephones and Cables Ltd*, [1952] 2 Q.B. 174

Two persons employed by electrical contractors were sent to work in a factory on electrical installations. The electrical contractors continued to employ the men, paying their wages, stamping their insurance cards, and retaining the sole right to dismiss them. The electricians worked exclusively at the factory and used the factory canteen. The occupiers of the factory supplied them with all materials, tools and plant, except for certain special tools belonging to the electricians themselves. They were supervised by a foreman employed by the occupiers and they followed the system laid down in the factory. One of the electricians was injured when he fell from a defective trestle owned by some building contractors who were also working in the factory. *Held*—The occupiers of the factory, and not the electrical contractors, owed the injured electrician the common law duty of a master to his servant (to provide proper plant and equipment) and they were liable to him for breach of that duty.

(418) *Mersey Docks and Harbour Board* v. *Coggins and Griffiths (Liverpool) Ltd and McFarlane*, [1947] A.C. 1.

A firm of stevedores had hired from the Harbour Board the use of a crane together with its driver, Mr Newall, to assist in loading a ship lying in the Liverpool docks. The contract of hire was subject to the Board's regulations, one of which contained the clause: 'The driver provided shall be the servant of the applicants.' The driver of the crane was a skilled man appointed and paid by the Board, and the Board alone had power to dismiss him. The stevedores told the driver what they wanted the crane to lift but had no authority to tell him how to work the crane. McFarlane, who was a checker employed by the forwarding agents, was noting the number and marks on a case which the crane had picked up when he was trapped because of the negligence of the crane driver in failing to keep the crane still.

The question to be determined was whether in applying the doctrine of vicarious liability the general employers of the crane driver or the hirers were liable for his negligence. The Board contended that, under the terms of the contract between the Board and the stevedores, the stevedores were liable. *Held*—by the House of Lords—

(i) The question of liability was not to be determined by any agreement between the general employers and the hirers, but depended on the circumstances of the case. The test to apply was that of control.

(ii) The Board, as the general employers of the crane driver, had not established that the hirers had such control of the crane driver at the time of the accident as to become liable as employers for his negligence. Although the hirers could tell the crane driver where to go and what to carry, they had no authority to tell him how to operate the crane. The Board were, therefore, liable for his negligence.

Comment. The answers given by Mr Newall to counsel's questions in this case were highly important. At one point he said: 'I take no orders from anybody.' Commenting on this, Lord Simonds said that it was '. . . a sturdy answer which meant that he was a skilled man and knew his job and would carry it out in his own way. Yet ultimately he would decline to carry it out in the appellants' way at his peril, for in their hands lay the only sanction the power of dismissal.'

(419) *Wright* v. *Tyne Improvement Commissioners (Osbeck & Co. Ltd, Third Party)*, [1968] 1 All E.R. 807

Tyne Improvement Commissioners hired a crane to Osbeck & Co. Ltd, under a written contract whereby the hirers agreed 'to bear the risk of and be responsible for all damage, injury or loss whatsoever, howsoever and whensoever caused arising directly or indirectly out of or in connection with the hiring or use of the said crane'. The plaintiff, who was a docker employed by Osbeck & Co., was injured when a wagon, in which he was standing to receive timber, was negligently moved forward by the capstan driver causing the plaintiff to collide with timber being lowered into the wagon by the crane. The plaintiff and the crane driver did all they could to avoid the accident but failed to do so and it was accepted that the capstan driver, who was employed by the Commissioners, was wholly to blame. Under the doctrine of vicarious liability the Commissioners were also to blame. When the action was tried at Newcastle upon Tyne Assizes, Waller, J., awarded the plaintiff damages of some £2985 against the Commissioners but dismissed a claim by the Commissioners against Osbeck & Co., as hirers of the crane, for an indemnity against the plaintiff's claim by virtue of the clause quoted above. The Commissioners now appealed against the dismissal of the claim for indemnity. *Held*—by the Court of Appeal—that as the accident arose directly or at least indirectly, out of or in connection with the use of the crane, the indemnity clause entitled the Commissioners to an indemnity against Osbeck & Co. even though the use to which the crane was being put was not a blameworthy cause of the accident.

(420) *Cassidy* v. *Ministry of Health*, [1951] 2 K.B. 343

The plaintiff's left hand was operated on at the defendant's hospital by a whole-time assistant medical officer of the hospital. After the operation the plaintiff's hand and forearm were put in a splint for fourteen days. During this time the plaintiff complained of pain but was merely given sedatives by the doctors who attended him. When the splint was removed, it was found that all four fingers of the plaintiff's hand were stiff, and that his hand was virtually useless. Someone, either the doctor, surgeon, or a nurse, had been negligent, but the plaintiff could not in fact point to which of these it was. The plaintiff sued the defendants for negligence. *Held*—The defendants were liable in spite of their absence of real control over the type of work done by the doctors employed by them. Denning, L.J., stated that only where the patient himself selects and employs the doctor will the hospital authorities escape liability for that doctor's negligence. If the person causing the harm is part of the organization, the employer is liable.

Comment. In this case Lord Denning used the doctrine of *res ipsa loquitur* (see p. 397) in order to help the plaintiff to establish his case. In other words, he presumed negligence, thus relieving the plaintiff of the burden of actually having to point to a particular employee of the Ministry who was negligent.

(421) *Ferguson* v. *John Dawson & Partners (Contractors)*, [1976] 3 All E.R. 817

The plaintiff, who was working 'on the lump' was injured whilst working for the defendants who were contractors. No deductions were made by the defendants for income tax or National Insurance contributions and the plaintiff had been told that he was working 'purely as a lump labour force'. The defendants' site agent was responsible for hiring and dismissing the workmen, including the plaintiff; he told them what to do and moved them from site to site. If tools were required for the work, the defendants provided them. The plaintiff was injured when he fell off a roof which had no guard rail and he brought this action against the defendants on the basis that they were liable as his employers for failing to provide a guard rail on the flat roof which was required by construction regulations. It was *held*—by the Court of Appeal—that whatever label was put on the parties' relationship, other factors should be considered, such as the fact that the defendants could dismiss the workmen, including the plaintiff, and tell them what to do and where to do it. Accordingly, the plaintiff was the employee of the defendants who were therefore liable under the construction regulations and must pay the plaintiff damages for breach of that statutory duty.

(422) *Lee (Catherine)* v. *Lee's Air Farming Ltd*, [1960] 3 All E.R. 420

In 1954 the appellant's husband formed the respondent company which carried on the business of crop spraying from the air. In March, 1956, Mr Lee was killed while piloting an aircraft during the course of top soil dressing, and Mrs Lee claimed compensation from the company, as the employer of her husband, under the New Zealand Workers' Compensation Act, 1922. Since Mr Lee owned 2,999 of the company's 3000 £1 shares and since he was its governing director, the question arose as to whether the relationship of master and servant could exist between the company and him. He was employed as the company's chief pilot under a provision in the articles at a salary to be arranged by himself. *Held*— Mrs Lee was entitled to compensation because her husband was employed by the company in the sense required by the Act of 1922, and the decision in *Salomon* v. *Salomon & Co.*[52] was applied.

Vicarious liability: improper performance of acts within scope of employment

(423) *Century Insurance Co. Ltd* v. *Northern Ireland Road Transport Board*, [1942] A.C. 509

A tanker belonging to the respondents, and driven by one of their employees, was delivering petrol to a garage in Belfast. While the tanker was discharging petrol at the garage, the driver lit a cigarette and threw away the lighted match. The resulting explosion caused considerable damage. The contract under which the petrol was being delivered said that the respondents' employees were to take their orders from a petrol company to which the tankers were hired, a firm named Holmes, Mullin and Dunn, though they were not by virtue of this to be deemed the hirers' employees. The appellants had insured the defendants against liability to third parties, and pleaded that no claim could be made on them because, although the driver was admittedly negligent, he was at the time the servant of the hirers. *Held*—The appellants must pay the third party claim because the terms of the contract as a whole did not involve a transfer of the employees to Holmes, Mullin and Dunn; therefore, the respondents were liable for the negligence of the driver and were entitled to claim under their insurance.

Comment. (i) It would seem that however improper the manner in which an employee is doing his work, whether negligently or fraudulently, or contrary to express orders, his employer is liable.

(ii) This case was followed in *Harrison* v. *Michelin Tyre Company*, [1985] 1 All E.R. 918 where the plaintiff, a tool grinder employed by the defendants, was injured at work when standing on a duckboard of his machine talking to a fellow-employee. Another employee was pushing a truck along a passage in front of the plaintiff and decided as a joke to suddenly turn it two inches outside the chalk lines of the passageway and push the edge under the plaintiff's duckboard. The duckboard tipped. The plaintiff fell off and suffered injury. In an action against the defendants he claimed that the employee had acted in the course of his employment and that they were vicariously liable. The defendants denied liability saying that the employee had embarked on a frolic of his own. It was held by Comyn, J., that the employers were liable. The test for determining vicarious liability was whether a reasonable man would say either that the employee's act was part and parcel of his employment, even though unauthorized or prohibited, or that it was so divergent as to be plainly alien to it. In this case the employee's act was part and parcel of the employment.

(424) *Limpus* v. *London General Omnibus Co.* (1862), 1 H. & C. 526

The plaintiff's omnibus was overturned when the driver of the defendants' omnibus drove across it so as to be first at a bus stop to take all the passengers who were waiting. The defendants' driver admitted that the act was intentional, and arose out of bad feeling between the two drivers. The defendants had issued strict instructions to their drivers that they were not to obstruct other omnibuses. *Held*—The defendants were liable. Their driver was acting within the scope of his employment at the time of the collision, and it did not matter that the defendants had expressly forbidden him to act as he did.

Comment. As we have seen, the matter to be decided in these cases is whether the employee was doing what he was employed to do. If he is not, then the employer is not liable. Thus in *Beard* v. *London General Omnibus Co.*, [1900] 2 Q.B. 530 a bus conductor who turned the bus round when the driver was absent and injured the plaintiff whilst he was doing this was held by the Court of Appeal to have been acting outside the course of his employment so that his employers were not liable.

(425) *Rose* v. *Plenty*, [1976] 1 All E.R. 97

Leslie Rose, aged 13, was given to helping Mr Plenty, a milkman, to deliver milk. Co-operative Retail Services Ltd, who employed Mr Plenty, expressly forbade their milkmen to take boys on their floats or to get boys to help them deliver the milk. On one occasion, while helping Mr Plenty, Leslie was sitting in the front of the float when his leg caught under the wheel. The accident was caused partly by Mr Plenty's negligence. It was *held*—by the Court of Appeal (Lord Denning, M.R. and Scarman, L.J.)—that Mr Plenty had been acting in the course of his employment so that his employers were liable to compensate Leslie Rose for his injuries. Lawton, L.J. (dissenting) said that the case of *Twine* v. *Bean's Express*, (1946) and similar cases were indistinguishable and that in giving Leslie a lift Mr Plenty had acted outside the *scope* of his employment.

Comment. There is really very little difference in the facts of *Rose* v. *Plenty* and *Twine* other than the fact that Leslie Rose was more than a mere hitch-hiker. His presence on the milk float was connected with the delivery of the milk which was a reason connected with the *scope* of employment and this is why Lord Denning and Scarman, L.J., felt able to distinguish *Twine* and other similar cases.

Vicarious liability: employee mixing employer's business with his own

(426) *Britt* v. *Galmoye and Nevill* (1928), 44 T.L.R. 294

The first defendant, who had the second defendant in his employment as a van-driver, lent him his private motor car, after the day's work was finished, to take a friend to a theatre. The second defendant by his negligence injured the plaintiff. *Held*—that as the journey was not on the master's business and the master was not in control, he was not liable for his servant's act.

Vicarious liability at civil law: for criminal conduct of employee

(427) *Morris* v. *C. W. Martin & Sons Ltd*, [1965] 2 All E.R. 725

The plaintiff sent a mink stole to a furrier for the purpose of cleaning. The furrier later told the plaintiff by telephone that he did not clean furs himself but intended to send the stole to the defendants, one of the biggest cleaners of fur in the country. The plaintiff knew of Martin & Sons and agreed that the stole be sent to them. Martin & Sons did work only for the fur trade and had issued to the furrier printed conditions which provided that goods belonging to customers were at customer's risk when on the premises of Martin & Sons, and that they should not be responsible for loss or damage however caused, though they would compensate for loss or damage to the goods during the cleaning process by reason of their negligence, but not by reason of any other cause. The furrier knew of these conditions when he handed the stole to the defendants and the defendants knew that it belonged to a customer of the furrier but they did not know that it was Morris. While in the possession of Martin & Sons the fur was stolen by a youth named Morrisey who had been employed by them for a few weeks only, though they had no grounds to suspect that he was dishonest. The plaintiff sued the defendants for conversion or negligence but the County Court Judge felt bound by *Cheshire* v. *Bailey*, 1905 (See p. 841) and held that the act of Morrisey, who had removed the stole by wrapping it round his body, was beyond the scope of his employment. In the Court of Appeal it was *held* that *Cheshire* v. *Bailey*, 1905 (see p. 841) had been impliedly overruled by *Lloyd* v. *Grace, Smith & Co.*, [1921] A.C. 716 (where it was held that a solicitor was liable for the criminal frauds of his managing clerk so long as the clerk was acting in the apparent scope of his authority). The defendants, as sub-bailees, were liable to the plaintiff, and on the matter of the exemption clause the Court of Appeal said that the terms of such a clause must be strictly construed, and since they referred only to goods 'belonging to customers' this could be taken to mean goods belonging to the furrier and not to the furrier's customer, and because of this ambiguity the clause was inapplicable.

Comment. (i) The above decision applies only to bailees for reward and only in circumstances where the servant is entrusted with, or put in charge of, the bailor's goods by his master. The mere fact that the servant's employment gave him the opportunity to steal the bailor's goods is not enough. Thus in *Leesh River Tea Co.* v. *British India Steam Navigation Co.*, [1966] 3 All E.R. 593 a stevedore stole a brass cover plate from the hold of a ship when he was unloading tea and the Court of Appeal held that he was not acting in the course of his employment on the grounds that his job had nothing to do with the cover plate. Perhaps if the plate had been stolen by someone who was sent to clean it, then that person would have been acting within the course of his employment.

(ii) The tortious or criminal act must be committed as part of the employment; i.e., as an act within the scope of the employment. In

Heasmans v. *Clarity Cleaning*, [1987] I.R.L.R 286 the Court of Appeal decided that the defendants were not liable when their employee, who was sent to the plaintiffs' premises to clean 'phones, made unauthorized calls on them to the value of £1,400. He was employed to *clean* 'phones, not to *use* them.

Vicarious liability: casual delegation to 'agents': liability of 'principal'

(428) *Ormrod* v. *Crossville Motor Services Ltd*, [1953] 2 All E.R. 753

By an arrangement between the owner of a motor car and his friend, the friend was to drive the car from Birkenhead to Monte Carlo in order that the owner, the friend and the friend's wife, might use the car during their holiday in Monte Carlo. The owner of the car was travelling to Monte Carlo in another car as a competitor in the Monte Carlo Rally. Owing to the friend's negligent driving, the car was involved in a collision in which a motor bus was damaged. The question of the liability of the owner of the car for the damage arose. *Held*—The friend was acting as the owner's agent in the matter. The owner had an interest in the arrival of the car at Monte Carlo, and the driving was done for his benefit. Accordingly the owner was vicariously liable for his friend's negligence.

(429) *Vandyke* v. *Fender*, [1970] 2 All E.R. 335

Mr Vandyke and Mr Fender were employed by the same firm and lived thirty miles from the business premises. The employer agreed to supply a car to Mr Fender and to pay him 50p a day for petrol for the journey. The journey could have been made by train but was more convenient by car. Two other employees who lived in the same area were also carried. On one occasion the car loaned to Mr Fender was not available and he was allowed to use a car belonging to the company secretary. While driving this car an accident occurred resulting in an injury to Mr Vandyke who claimed damages from the company. It was *held* that the company was liable because Mr Fender, though not a paid driver, *was driving the car as the company's agent* and they were liable for his negligence. The question then arose as to which of the insurance companies involved should indemnify the company. If the risk was to be borne by the employers' liability insurance it was necessary to show that the accident occurred during and in the course of Mr Vandyke's employment, otherwise the risk would be borne by a road traffic insurance policy of Mr Fender's which covered him while driving someone else's car. It was *held*—by the Court of Appeal—that a man going to or from work as a passenger in a vehicle provided by his employers for that purpose is not in the course of employment unless he is obliged by the terms of his employment to travel in that vehicle. If not then, as here, the liability must be borne by the road traffic insurers and not by the employers' liability insurers.

(430) *Nottingham* v. *Aldridge; Prudential Assurance Co.*, [1971], 2 All
E.R. 751.

In this case a Post Office trainee was returning to his normal work in his
father's van after spending the week-end at his home having attended a
training course the previous week. He was carrying another trainee,
Nottingham, as a passenger and was entitled to a mileage allowance from
the Post Office for himself and his passenger. Nottingham was injured
as a result of an accident caused by the defendant's negligent driving.
Held—by Eveleigh, J.—that the Post Office was not liable because the
two trainees were not in the course of employment while travelling to
work; *nor was Aldridge the agent of the Post Office for the purposes of
the journey.* The vehicle did not belong to the Post Office nor was it
provided by them. They had not prescribed the method of travel; admittedly a mileage allowance was payable but travelling expenses of any
other kind would have been paid, e.g. bus or train fare. The question of
agency was one of fact and on the facts of this case Aldridge was not an
agent. The company which had insured the van was therefore liable to
indemnify Aldridge in respect of his own liability to Nottingham.

(431) *Morgans* v. *Launchbury*, [1972] 2 All E.R. 606

In this case the family car was registered in the name of the wife though
it was used mainly by the husband who worked seven miles from home.
The wife had asked her husband not to drive the car home himself if he
had been drinking. On one occasion the husband had been drinking
heavily and asked a friend, C, to drive him home together with three
other passengers. There was an accident caused by the negligent driving
of C and the husband and he were killed. The three passengers were
injured and sued the wife claiming that she was liable vicariously for the
negligence of C, who had been appointed to drive on her behalf by her
husband. If the wife was held liable then her insurance company would
be liable to the plaintiffs. The House of Lords held that she was not
liable. The concept of agency required more than mere permission to use.
Use must be at the owner's request or on his instructions.

Comment. Before 1971 it was not compulsory for road traffic insurance
to cover passengers. In fact Mrs Launchbury had an insurance policy
which covered passengers but only in respect of accidents which occurred
while she or her agent was driving. The plaintiffs would have preferred
to get their money from the insurance company than to sue the estate
of C.

(432) *Rambarran* v. *Gurrucharran*, [1970] 1 All E.R. 749

In this case Rambarran, a chicken farmer in Guyana, owned a car which
was used by several of his sons, Rambarran himself being unable to drive.
One of his sons, Leslie, damaged Gurrucharran's car by negligently
driving the family car. The Privy Council found that Rambarran was not

liable for Leslie's negligence because he did not know that Leslie had taken the car since he was away from home at his chicken farm at the time in question. Furthermore, there was no evidence to show what the purpose of Leslie's journey was, but it was clearly not for any business or family purpose. Ownership of the vehicle was not enough in itself to establish liability.

(433) *Klein* v. *Calnori*, [1971] 2 All E.R. 701

The defendant, Calnori, was the manager of a public house at Sunbury-on-Thames. While he was busy at the bar a Mr Freshwater, who knew Calnori, took his car and drove it away without his permission. Later Freshwater telephoned Calnori and told him he had taken his car. Calnori told him to bring it back. On the way back to Sunbury Freshwater collided with Klein's stationary car severely damaging it. Klein alleged that Calnori was liable for this damage because Freshwater was his agent. By asking Freshwater to bring the car back Freshwater was driving it partly for Calnori's purposes. *Held*—by Lyell, J.—Calnori was not liable. If Freshwater had borrowed the car with Calnori's consent then the loan to Freshwater, for his own purposes, would have involved returning it. In these circumstances Calnori would not have been liable for an accident on the return journey. Therefore Calnori's liability could not be greater in circumstances in which the car had been taken without his consent and had been used solely for the taker's purpose.

Liability for the torts of independent contractors

(434) *Bower* v. *Peate* (1876), 1 Q.B.D. 321

The plaintiff and defendant were respective owners of two adjoining houses, the plaintiff being entitled to the support for his house of the defendant's land. The defendant employed a contractor to pull down his house and to rebuild it after excavating the foundations. The contractor undertook the risk of supporting the plaintiff's house during the work and to make good any damage caused. The plaintiff's house was damaged in the progress of the work because the contractor did not take appropriate steps to support it. *Held*—that the defendant was liable. The fact that the injury would have been prevented if the contractor had provided proper support did not take away the defendant's liability. A person employing a contractor to perform a duty cast upon himself, in this case a duty of support, is responsible for the contractor's negligence in performing it.

(435) *Salsbury* v. *Woodland*, [1969] 3 All E.R. 863

The defendant employed, as an independent contractor, an experienced tree-feller to fell a large tree in his front garden. The contractor was negligent and the tree fell towards the highway bringing down telephone wires on to the highway. A car came along too fast, and the plaintiff, who was a bystander watching the whole operation, was injured when he dived out of the way of the inevitable collision between the car and the wire. *Held*—by the Court of Appeal—the defendant was not liable though the contractor was. There was no special liability in the defendant merely because the contractor was employed to work near, as distinct from on, the highway.

Comment. In *Tarry* v. *Ashton* (1876), 1 Q.B.D. 314 the defendant employed an independent contractor to carry out repairs to a lamp which, though attached to his house overhung the highway. The contractor failed to secure the lamp properly and it fell, injuring the plaintiff. It was held that the defendant was liable because it was his duty to make the lamp safe and he was in breach of that duty because the contractor had not secured the lamp properly.

(436) *Padbury* v. *Holliday and Greenwood Ltd and Another* (1912), 28 T.L.R. 494

The defendants were employed to erect certain premises in Fenchurch Street, and the contract involved the employment by the defendants of sub-contractors to carry out the special work of putting metallic casements into the windows. While this work was being carried out an iron tool was placed by a servant of the sub-contractors on the window sill. The casement was blown by the wind and the tool fell and struck the plaintiff who was walking in the street below. The placing of the tool on the window sill was not the normal practice adopted in the work involved. *Held*—that the injuries were caused to the plaintiff by an act of collateral negligence on the part of a workman who was a servant of the sub-contractors and not of the defendants and that the latter were not, therefore, liable for the consequences of that negligence.

General defences: *volenti non fit injuria*

(437) *Simms* v. *Leigh Rugby Football Club*, [1969] 2 All E.R. 923

The plaintiff was a member of a visting team playing rugby football on the defendant club's ground when his leg was broken as he was tackled and thrown towards a concrete wall which ran at a distance of 7 ft 3 in from the touch line. The League's by-laws prescribed that the distance had to be at least 7 ft. *Held*—by Wrangham, J.—that the plaintiff must be taken willingly to have accepted the risks involved in playing on that field. The ground complied with the by-laws of the Rugby Football League and the defendants were not, therefore, liable under the Occupiers' Liability Act, 1957, or in general negligence by reason of the plaintiff's consent.

Comment. In this connection the decision of the Court of Appeal in *Condon* v. *Basi*, [1985] 2 All E.R. 453 is of interest. In that case the defendant made a late and reckless slide tackle upon the plaintiff resulting in the plaintiff sustaining a broken right leg and the defendant being sent from the field of play. The County Court judge awarded the plaintiff £4900 for damages for the injuries sustained and the Court of Appeal dismissed an appeal against that decision. It was decided by the Court of Appeal that participants in competitive sport owe a duty of care to each other to take all reasonable care having regard to the particular circumstances in which the participants are placed. If one participant injures another he will be liable in negligence for damages at the suit of the injured participant if it is shown that he failed to exercise the degree of care appropriate in all the circumstances or that he acted in a manner to which the injured participant could not have been expected to consent. The law is clearly having to respond to the increasing amount of unnecessary violence in certain sports.

(438) *Murray* v. *Harringay Arena Ltd*, [1951] 2 K.B. 529

David Charles Murray, aged six, was taken by his parents to the defendants' ice rink to watch a hockey match. They occupied front seats at the rink, and during the game the boy was hit in the eye by the puck. This action was brought against the defendants for negligence. *Held*—The risk was voluntarily undertaken by the plaintiffs. The defendants had provided protection by means of netting and a wooden barrier which, in the circumstances, was adequate, since further protection would have seriously interfered with the view of the spectators.

(439) *Hall* v. *Brooklands Auto-Racing Club*, [1933] 1 K.B. 205

The plaintiff paid for admission to the defendants' premises to watch motor car races. During one of the races a car left the track, as a result of a collision with another car, and crashed through the railings injuring the plaintiff. It was the first time that a car had gone through the railings, and in view of that the precautions taken by the defendants were adequate. In this action by the plaintiff for personal injuries, it was *held* that the danger was not one which the defendants ought to have anticipated, and that the plaintiff must be taken to have agreed to assume the risk of such an accident.

General defences: *volenti*: the plaintiff must know of the risk, though knowledge is not necessarily assent

(440) *White* v. *Blackmore*, [1972] 3 All E.R. 158

The husband of the plaintiff widow was a member of a 'jalopy' racing club. He went to a meeting organized by the defendants as a competitor but stood outside the spectators' ropes close to a stake. The wheel of a car caught on one of the ropes some distance away so that the stake was pulled up sharply and the husband was killed when he was catapulted some 20 feet. The defendants displayed notices warning the public of the danger and stating as a condition of admission that they were absolved from all liabilities for accidents howsoever caused. The widow claimed damages for breach of s. 2 of the Occupiers' Liability Act, 1957 and/or

general negligence. *Held*—by the Court of Appeal—(i) that even though
the deceased had been negligent in standing where he did, the defence
of *volenti* would not succeed as the deceased did not know of the risk that
had caused his death; (ii) however, the claim would fail as the defendants
were entitled to exclude their liability and this they had done by warning
notices.

Comment. It is true that the defendants could effectively exclude their
liability under the Occupiers' Liability Act, 1957, by warning notices and
without a contract. Section 2(1) of the Act of 1957 provides that an
occupier owes 'a common duty of care' to all his visitors but that this can
be restricted or excluded 'by agreement or otherwise'. However, as
regards the claim in general negligence, it ought not to be possible to
exclude liability for negligence unless the plaintiff assents in a contract.
But see now Unfair Contract Terms Act, 1977.

(441) *Baker* v. *James Bros* [1921] 2 K.B. 674

The defendants were wholesale grocers and they employed the plaintiff
as a traveller. He was supplied by the defendants with a motor car, the
starting gear of which was defective. The plaintiff repeatedly complained
about this to the defendants, but nothing was done to remedy the defect.
While the plaintiff was on his rounds, the car stopped, and he was injured
whilst trying to re-start. *Held*—Notwithstanding the plaintiff's knowledge
of the defect, he had never consented to take upon himself the risk of
injury from the continued use of the car. He was not guilty of any
contributory negligence and was entitled to recover damages.

(442) *Dann* v. *Hamilton*, [1939] 1 K.B. 509

The plaintiff had been with a party to see the coronation decorations in
London. They made the journey in the defendant's car. During the day
and evening the defendant had consumed a quantity of intoxicating
liquor, but he drove the party back to Staines where they all got out. The
plaintiff was at this point a 2d. bus ride from her home but she accepted
the defendant's invitation to take her there. During this part of the
journey there was an accident caused by the defendant's negligence, and
the plaintiff was injured. She now sued in respect of these injuries and
the defendant pleaded *volenti non fit injuria*. *Held*—That the defence did
not apply and the plaintiff succeeded. She had knowledge of a potential
danger, but that did not mean that she assented to it.

Comment. (i) The court left open the question where the driver was
'dead drunk' or 'very drunk'. In such a case the maxim might have
applied.

(ii) It should be noted that the defence of contributory negligence was
not pleaded in *Dann* although Asquith, J., encouraged counsel for the
defence to raise it but he would not be drawn. However, it is now
accepted that although *volenti* may not apply in a situation such as *Dann*
a plaintiff may be guilty of contributory negligence if he travels as a

passenger when he knows the driver has consumed enough alcohol to impair his ability to drive safely, or if he goes drinking with the driver knowing he will be a passenger later when the drink deprives him of his own capacity to appreciate the danger. (So decided in *Owens* v. *Brimmell*, [1976] 3 All E.R. 765.)

(443) *Smith* v. *Baker and Sons*, [1891] A.C. 325

Smith was employed by Baker and Sons to drill holes in some rock in a railway cutting. A crane, operated by fellow employees, often swung heavy stones over Smith's head while he was working on the rock face. Both Smith and his employers realized that there was a risk the stones might fall, but the crane was nevertheless operated without any warning being given at the moment of jibbing or swinging. Smith was injured by a stone which fell from the crane because of negligent strapping of the load. The House of Lords *held* that Smith had not voluntarily undertaken the risk of his employers' negligence, and that his knowledge of the danger did not prevent his recovering damages.

General defences: *volenti*: actions against employers based on breach of statutory duty

(444) *Imperial Chemical Industries Ltd* v. *Shatwell*, [1964] 2 All E.R. 999

George and James Shatwell were certificated and experienced shotfirers employed by ICI. Statutory rules imposed an obligation on them personally (not on their employers) to ensure that certain operations connected with shotfiring should not be done unless all persons in the vicinity had taken cover. They knew of the risks of premature explosion which had been explained to them; they knew of the prohibition; but on one occasion because a cable they had was too short to reach the shelter, they decided to test without taking cover rather than wait ten minutes for their companion Beswick who had gone to fetch a longer cable. James gave George two wires, and George applied them to the galvanometer terminals. An explosion occurred and both men were injured. At the trial it was found that James was guilty of negligence and breach of statutory duty for which the employers were held vicariously liable, damages being assessed at £1500 on a basis of 50 per cent contributory negligence. The Court of Appeal affirmed, but the House of Lords *reversed*, the decision and *held* that, although James's acts were a contributory cause of the accident to George, the employers were not liable.

(*a*) They were not themselves in breach of a statutory duty.

(*b*) They could plead *volenti non fit injuria* to a claim of vicarious liability.

(*c*) They had shown no negligence. They had instilled the need for caution, made proper provision, and even arranged a scale of remuneration in a way which removed a temptation to take short cuts.

(*d*) The Shatwell brothers were trained men well aware of the risk involved so the principle of *volenti non fit injuria* applied. Lord Pearce said: 'The defence (of *volenti non fit injuria*) should be available where the employer was not in himself in breach of a statutory duty and was not vicariously in breach of a statutory duty through the neglect of some person of superior rank to the plaintiff and whose commands the plaintiff was bound to obey or who has some special and different duty of care.'

Comment. If the employers had been compelled to rely on the defence of contributory negligence, they might have escaped liability if only one man were involved and treated as solely responsible, but where two men were involved, as here, they would have been vicariously liable for James's contribution to George's injury and for George's contribution to James's injury so they would have been compelled partially to compensate each man.

General defences: *volenti*: the rescue cases: generally

(445) *Haynes* v. *Harwood and Son*, [1935] 1 K.B. 146

The defendants' servant left his van unattended in a street. A boy threw a stone at the horses and they bolted with the van. The plaintiff was a police constable on duty in a police station and seeing the horses bolting into a crowded street, and realizing that, unless the horses were stopped, people in the street, including many children, would be likely to be injured, he darted out of the police station and, at great risk to himself, seized one of the horses and managed to bring them to a standstill. He was injured in doing so. It was *held* by the Court of Appeal that the defendants had been negligent in leaving the van unattended, that the plaintiff was not guilty of contributory negligence, and that the damage was not too remote. The defendants also alleged assumption of risk by the plaintiff, but the court decided that the plaintiff's knowledge of the risk was not a bar to his claim.

(446) *Baker* v. *T. E. Hopkins and Son Ltd*, [1959] 3 All E.R. 966

The defendants were building contractors and were engaged to clean out a well. Various methods had been used in order to pump out the water, including hand-operated pumps, but eventually a petrol-driven pump was employed. The exhaust from the engine on the pump resulted in a lethal concentration of carbon monoxide forming inside the well. Two of the defendants' employees went down the well to carry on the work of cleaning it and were overcome by the fumes. Baker was a local doctor and, on being told what had happened, he went along to give what assistance he could. He was lowered down the well on a rope, and on reaching the two men, he realized that they were beyond help. He then gave a pre-arranged signal to those at the top of the well and started his journey to the surface. Unfortunately the rope became caught on a projection and Dr Baker was himself overcome by fumes and died. His executors claimed damages in respect of Dr Baker's death. *Held*—The defendants were negligent towards their employees in using the petrol-driven pump and the maxim *volenti non fit injuria* did not bar the claim of Dr Baker's executors. Although Dr Baker may have had knowledge of the risk he was running, he did not freely and voluntarily undertake it, but acted under the compulsion of his instincts as a brave man and a doctor.

(447) *Cutler* v. *United Dairies (London) Ltd*, [1933] 2 K.B. 297

The defendants' carman left the defendants' horse and van, two wheels being properly chained, while he delivered milk. The horse, being startled by the noise coming from a river steamer, bolted down the road and into a meadow. It stopped in the meadow and was followed there by the carman who, being in an excited state, began to shout for help. The plaintiff, a spectator, went to the carman's assistance and tried to hold the horse's head. The horse lunged and the plaintiff was injured. In this action by the plaintiff against the defendants for negligence it was *held* that in the circumstances the plaintiff voluntarily and freely assumed the risk. This was not an attempt to stop a runaway horse so that there was no sense of urgency to impel the plaintiff. He therefore knew of the risk and had had time to consider it, and by implication must have agreed to incur it.

Comment. Evidence showed that the horse had bolted before and should not have been used on the milk round at all.

(448) *Hyett* v. *Great Western Railway Co.*, [1948] 1 K.B. 345

The plaintiff was employed by a firm of wagon repairers and he was on the defendants' premises with their authority to carry out his duties. While repairing a wagon he saw smoke rising from one of the defendants' wagons in the same siding and went to investigate. The floor of the wagon, which contained paraffin oil, was in flames. The plaintiff was trying to get the drums of paraffin oil out, when one of them exploded and injured him. Evidence showed that the defendants knew that there was a paraffin leakage in the wagon, but had nevertheless allowed it to remain in the siding. *Held*—The plaintiff was entitled to recover damages from the defendants, and the maxim *volenti non fit injuria* did not apply. A man may take reasonable risks in trying to preserve property put in danger by another's negligence.

General defences: *volenti*: duty to a rescuer

(449) *Videan* v. *British Transport Commission*, [1963] 2 All E.R. 860

A child managed to get on to a railway line and was injured by a trolley. The Court of Appeal *held* that the child's presence was not in the circumstances foreseeable and the defendants did not owe him a duty of care. However, a duty was owed to his father who was injured trying to rescue him.

Comment. It is difficult to follow the reasoning by which the Court of Appeal held that the defendants ought to have foreseen that a station-master would try to rescue a minor on the line (the minor being the son of the stationmaster) yet need not have foreseen the presence of that minor himself.

General defences: *volenti*: defence irrelevant unless the defendant has committed a tort

(450) *Wooldridge* v. *Sumner*, [1962] 2 All E.R. 978

A competitor of great skill and experience was riding a horse at a horse show when it ran wide at a corner and injured a cameraman who was unfamiliar with horses and who had ignored a steward's request to move outside the competition area. The rider was thrown, but later rode the horse again and it was adjudged supreme champion of its class. The cameraman brought an action for damages, and at the trial was awarded damages on the ground of negligence. *Held*—on appeal, that no negligence had been established because (i) any excessive speed at the corner was not the cause of the accident, and was not negligence but merely an error of judgment; and (ii) the judge's finding that the horse would have gone on to a cinder track without harm to the plaintiff if the rider had allowed it to, was an inference from primary facts and unjustified, and in any event an attempt to control the horse did not amount to negligence.

Per Diplock, L.J., 'If, in the course of a game or competition, at a moment when he has not time to think, a participant by mistake takes a wrong measure, he is not to be held guilty of any negligence. . . . A person attending a game or competition takes the risk of any damage caused to him by any act of a participant done in the course of and for the purposes of the game or competition, notwithstanding that such act may involve an error of judgment or a lapse of skill, unless the participant's conduct is such as to evince a reckless disregard of the spectator's safety. The spectator takes the risk because such an act involves *no breach of the duty of care* owed by the participant to him. He does not take the risk by virtue of the doctrine expressed or obscured by the maxim *volenti non fit injuria*. . . . The maxim in English law *presupposes a tortious act* by the defendant. The consent that is relevant is not consent to the risk of injury but consent to the lack of reasonable care than may produce that risk.'

(451) *Wilks* v. *Cheltenham Home Guard Motor Cycle and Light Car Club, The Times*, 25 March, 1971

The plaintiffs were father and daughter and they sued in negligence for injuries received as spectators at a motor cycle scramble at Withybridge on 21 September, 1966. They were in an enclosure fenced off with stakes and ropes designed to keep spectators in. Some ten feet away from this fence was another rope designed to keep any motor cycle from intruding into the enclosure. A competitor, Mr Ward, left the course, crashed through the safety rope and struck the plaintiffs. It was *held*—by the Court of Appeal—that Mr Ward was not negligent. He was going at about ten miles per hour when he left the track and although he lost control this could be expected in a scramble of this kind. A competitor in a race must use reasonable care. But that meant reasonable care having regard to the fact that he was a competitor in a race in which he was expected to go 'all out' to win. A batsman was expected to hit a six if he could, even if it landed among the spectators. So in a race a competitor was expected to go as fast as he could, as long as he was not foolhardy. In a race a reasonable man should do all that he could do to win, but he should not be foolhardy.

General defences: *volenti*: public policy: duty of care

(452) *Nettleship* v. *Weston*, [1971] 3 All E.R. 581

The plaintiff, a non-professional driving instructor, gave the defendant driving lessons after having first satisfied himself that the car was insured to cover injury to passengers. The defendant was a careful driver but on the third lesson she failed to straighten out after turning left and struck a lamp standard breaking the plaintiff's kneecap. The defendant was convicted of driving without due care and attention. *Held*—by the Court of Appeal—that since the plaintiff had checked on the insurance position he had expressly not consented to run the risk and there was no question of *volenti*. Furthermore, the duty of care owed by a learner-driver was the same as that owed by every driver and the defendant was liable for the damages. A learner-driver owes a duty to his instructor to drive with proper skill and care, the test being the objective one of the careful driver and it is no defence that he was doing his best.

Comment. (i) Nobody would suggest that a learner-driver can do any more than his best. However, the mere fact of learning to drive a motor car is dangerous, at least in its initial stages, and the risk of injury has to be upon the driver. This facilitates an insurance claim by the injured party. In addition, the application of an objective standard of care facilitates a speedier and cheaper settlement of the many road accident cases.

(ii) A passenger who knows that a driver is under the influence of drink or drugs may, if he is injured, be barred from recovering damages on the grounds of *public policy* since he is aiding and abetting a criminal offence. As Megaw, L.J., said in this case: 'There may in such cases sometimes be an element of aiding and abetting a criminal offence; or, if the facts fall short of aiding and abetting, the passenger's mere assent to benefit from the commission of a criminal offence may involve questions of *turpis causa*.' The phrase '*turpis causa*' denotes something dishonourable or immoral.

General defences: inevitable accident

(453) *Stanley* v. *Powell*, [1891] 1 Q.B. 86

The defendant was a member of a shooting party, and the plaintiff was employed to carry cartridges and also any game which was shot. The defendant fired at a pheasant, but a shot glanced off an oak tree and injured the plaintiff. *Held*—The plaintiff's claim failed. The defendant's action was neither intentional nor was it negligent.

(454) *National Coal Board* v. *Evans (J. E.) & Co. (Cardiff) Ltd and Another*, [1951] 2 K.B. 861

Evans & Co. were employed by Glamorgan County Council to carry out certain work on land belonging to the council. It was necessary to excavate a trench across the land, and Evans & Co. sub-contracted with the second defendants to do this work. An electric cable passed under the land, but the council, Evans & Co., and the sub-contractors had no knowledge of this and it was not marked on any available map. During the course of the excavation a mechanical digger damaged the cable so that water seeped into it causing an explosion. The electricity supply to the plaintiff's colliery was cut off, and they sued the defendants in trespass and negligence. Donovan, J., at first instance, found that the defendants were not negligent, but were liable in trespass. The Court of Appeal *held* the defendants were entirely free from fault and there was no trespass by them.

General defences: Act of God

(455) *Nichols* v. *Marsland* (1876), 2 Ex.D. 1

For many years there had existed certain artificial ornamental lakes on the defendant's land, formed by damming up of a natural stream the source of which was at a point higher up. An extraordinary rainfall 'greater and more violent than any within the memory of witnesses' caused the stream and the lakes to swell to such an extent that the artificial banks burst, and the escaping water carried away four bridges belonging to the county council. Nichols, the county surveyor, sued under the rule in *Rylands* v. *Fletcher*. *Held*—The defendant was not liable for this extraordinary act of nature which she could not reasonably have anticipated. The escape of water was owing to the Act of God, and while one is bound to provide against the ordinary operations of nature, one is not bound to provide against miracles.

   Comment. Although *Rylands* v. *Fletcher* liability is strict. Act of God is a defence. (See p. 421.)

General defences: necessity

(456) *Cresswell* v. *Sirl*, [1948] 1 K.B. 241

The defendant, a farmer's son, was awakened during the night by dogs barking, and on going out found certain ewe sheep in lamb, penned up by the dogs in a corner of a field. The dogs seemed about to attack the sheep and had been chasing them for an hour. A light was turned on the dogs, who then left the sheep and started for the defendant. When they were about 40 yards away, the defendant fired and killed one of the dogs. The owner of the dog sued the defendant for damages. In the county court, judgment was given for the owner of the dog on the ground that such a killing could be justified only if it took place while the dog was actually attacking the sheep. In the view of the Court of Appeal, however, the defendant could justify his act by showing that it was necessary to avert immediate danger to property. It was not necessary that the dog should actually be attacking the sheep. This decision is affirmed by s. 9 of the Animals Act, 1971, which now covers the situation.

(457) *Cope* v. *Sharpe (No. 2)*, [1912] 1 K.B. 486

The plaintiff was a landowner and he let the shooting rights over part of his land to a tenant. A heath fire broke out on part of the plaintiff's land and the defendant, who was the head gamekeeper of the tenant, set fire to patches of heather between the main fire and a covert in which his master's pheasants were sitting. His object was to prevent the fire spreading. In fact the fire was extinguished independently of what the defendant had done, and the plaintiff now sued the defendant for damages for trespass. *Held*—The defendant was not liable because when he carried out the act it seemed reasonably necessary, and it did not matter that in the event it turned out to be unnecessary.

Comment. In *Rigby* v. *Chief Constable of Northampton*, [1985] 2 All E.R. 985, R's shop was burnt out when the police fired a canister of C.S. gas into the building to force out a dangerous psychopath. R's claim in trespass failed on the grounds of the defence of necessity. His claim in negligence succeeded because there was, to the knowledge of the police, no fire-fighting equipment available.

General defences: mistake

(458) *Beckwith* v. *Philby* (1827), 6 B. & C. 635

In this case it was *held* that the mistaken arrest of an innocent man on suspicion of felony by an ordinary citizen is not actionable as false imprisonment, if the felony has been committed, and if there are reasonable grounds for believing that the person arrested is guilty of it.

General defences: act of state

(459) *Buron* v. *Denman* (1848), 2 Exch. 167

The captain of a British warship was *held* not liable for trespass when he set fire to the barracoon of a Spaniard slave trader on the West Coast of Africa and released the slaves. The captain had general instructions to suppress the slave trade, and in any case his conduct in this matter was afterwards approved by the Admiralty and the Foreign and Colonial Secretaries. It seems, therefore, that neither the official responsible nor the Crown can be sued for injuries inflicted upon others outside the territorial jurisdiction of the Crown, if these are authorized or subsequently ratified by the Crown.

(460) *Nissan* v. *Attorney-General*, [1967] 2 All E.R. 1238

The plaintiff, a British subject, was the tenant of an hotel in Cyprus. In December, 1963, the Government of Cyprus accepted an offer that British Forces stationed in Cyprus should give assistance in restoring peace to the island. The British troops occupied the plaintiff's hotel for some months and the plaintiff now sued the Crown for compensation. It was *held—inter alia* that the Crown was obliged to pay compensation and that a plea by the Crown of 'Act of State' was no defence as against a British subject.

(461) *Johnstone* v. *Pedlar*, [1921] 2 A.C. 262

Johnstone was the Chief Commissioner of the Dublin Metropolitan Police. He was the defendant in an action in which Pedlar sued for the detention of £124 in cash and a cheque for £4 15s. 6d. Pedlar was convicted of being engaged in the illegal drilling of troops in Ireland, and the above property was found on him at the time of his arrest. Pedlar, who was a naturalized citizen of the United States of America, sued for the return of his property, and the defence was 'Act of State'. A certificate given by the Chief Secretary for Ireland was put in at the trial, certifying that the detention of the property was formally ratified as an Act of State. *Held*—Pedlar was entitled to claim his property, because the defence of 'Act of State' cannot be raised against an alien who is a subject of a friendly nation.

General defences: statutory authority

(462) *Vaughan* v. *Taff Vale Railway* (1860), 5 H. & N. 679

The defendants were *held* not liable for fires caused by sparks from engines which they were bound by statute to run and constructed with proper care.

Comment. (i) By s. 1 of the Railway Fires Acts, 1905 as amended by s. 38 of the Transport Act, 1981, British Rail is under a liability of up to £3000 for damage to crops caused by fire by engines run under statutory authority, though the advent of diesel and electric trains makes the statute somewhat out of date.

(ii) Even if the authority to act is absolute, the damage will not be excused unless it is necessarily incidental. Thus it is not necessary to the processing of sewage that rivers be polluted. (*Pride of Derby and Derbyshire Angling Association* v. *British Celanese Ltd*, [1952] 1 All E.R. 1326.)

(463) *Penny* v. *Wimbledon Urban District Council*, [1899] 2 Q.B. 72

The defendants, acting under conditional powers conferred upon them by s. 150 of the Public Health Act, 1875, employed a contractor to make up a road in their district. The contractor removed the surface soil and placed it in heaps on the road. The plaintiff, while passing along the road in the dark, fell over one of the heaps, which had been left unlighted and unguarded, and was injured. She now sued for damages. *Held*—She succeeded. Although the council were operating under statutory powers they must, if they do acts likely to cause danger to the public, see that the work is properly carried out, and take reasonable measures to guard against danger. The council did not discharge this duty by delegating it to a contractor, and the local authority were liable for negligence.

(464) *Marriage* v. *East Norfolk Rivers Catchment Board*, [1950] 1 K.B. 284

In pursuance of their powers under s. 34 of the Land Drainage Act, 1930, the Catchment Board deposited dredgings taken from the river on the south bank of that river, so raising its height by one to two feet. When the river next flooded, the flood waters instead of escaping over the south bank, as they had always done, ran over the north bank and swept away a bridge leading to a mill owned by the plaintiff. Section 34(3) of the Land Drainage Act, 1930, provided that, in the event of injury to any person by reason of the exercise by a drainage board of any of its powers, the board concerned should make full compensation, disputes being settled by a system of arbitration. The plaintiff had issued a writ for nuisance against the board. *Held*—No action in nuisance lay; the plaintiff's only remedy was to claim compensation under s. 34(3).

Remoteness of damage: development of the foresight test

(465) *Re Polemis and Furness Withy and Co.*, [1921] 3 K.B. 560

Stevedores were unloading the hold of a vessel which contained drums of petrol. There was some leakage from certain of the drums and the hold was filled with highly inflammable vapour. Through the negligence of a stevedore a plank was knocked into the hold, where, in its fall, it struck a spark, setting the vapour alight. The ensuing fire destroyed the ship. It was *held*—that the employers of the stevedores were liable for the total loss, even though the negligent stevedore could not have reasonably foreseen that his act would destroy the ship, though he might have foreseen some damage. The destruction of the ship was a direct consequence of the negligent act, and damages were recoverable.

(466) *Liesbosch, Dredger* v. *S.S. Edison*, [1933] A.C. 449

The dredger *Liesbosch* was lost after being dragged into open sea from her mooring in Patras harbour. This was the result of the negligence of the navigator of the S.S. *Edison*. The *Liesbosch* was engaged in dredging Patras harbour, and the contract provided for heavy penalties for delay. The dredger could have been replaced by the purchase of a new one, but the owners of the *Liesbosch* were poorly placed financially and could not afford to do so immediately. They had, therefore, to hire a dredger (the *Adria*) in the meantime at great expense. The plaintiffs included this additional hiring in their claim for damages for the loss of the *Liesbosch*. *Held*—Damages in respect of the hiring were not recoverable under the rule in *Re Polemis*. This damage was not caused by the defendants' negligence but by the plaintiffs' poverty. However, the plaintiffs were entitled to the value of the *Liesbosch* as a going concern, not simply her value as a rather old dredger, on the basis that you take your victim as you find him.

(467) *Overseas Tankship (UK) Ltd* v. *Morts Dock and Engineering Co. Ltd (The Wagon Mound)*, [1961] A.C. 388

The appellants were the charterers of a ship called the *Wagon Mound*. While the ship was taking on furnace oil in Sydney harbour, the appellants' servants negligently allowed oil to spill into the water. The action of the wind and tide carried this oil some 200 yards and over to the respondents' wharf where the business of shipbuilding and repairing was carried on. The servants of the respondents were at this time engaged in repairing a vessel, the *Corrimal*, which was moored alongside the wharf, and for this purpose they were using welding equipment. The manager of the respondents, seeing the oil on the water, suspended welding operations and consulted the wharf manager who told him it was safe to continue work—a decision which was justified, because previous knowledge showed that sparks were not likely to set fire to oil floating on water. Work, therefore, proceeded with safety precautions being taken. However, a piece of molten metal fell from the wharf and set on fire a piece of cotton waste which was floating on the oil. This set the oil alight and the respondents' wharf was badly damaged. The Supreme Court of New South Wales held the appellants liable for the extensive damage by fire, and in doing so followed *Re Polemis*.[465] The case then came before the Judicial Committee of the Privy Council on appeal. *Held*—the appellants were successful in their appeal, the Judicial Committee holding that *Re Polemis*[465] should no longer be considered good law, and that foreseeability of the actual harm resulting was the proper test. On this principle, they held that the damage caused by the fire was too remote, though they would have awarded damages for the fouling of the respondents' slipways by oil, if such a claim had been made, since this was foreseeable.

Comment. In *Overseas Tankship (UK) Ltd* v. *Miller Steamship Property Ltd (The Wagon Mound (No. 2))*, [1966] 2 All E.R. 709, the same blaze had caused damage to the respondents' ship (they were the owners of the *Corrimal*). However, the Privy Council had by this time the decision of the House of Lords in *Hughes* v. *Lord Advocate*, 1963[468] before them. It said that the *precise* nature of the injury suffered need not be foreseeable so long as it was one of a kind that was foreseeable. Therefore the respondents recovered damages in negligence and also nuisance. The Privy Council *held* that in the case of nuisance, as of negligence, it is not enough that the damage was a direct result of the nuisance if the injury was not foreseeable.

(468) *Hughes* v. *Lord Advocate*, [1963] 1 All E.R. 705

Workmen opened a manhole in the street and later left it unattended having placed a tent above it and warning paraffin lamps around it. The plaintiff and another boy, who were aged 8 and 10 respectively, took one of the lamps and went down the manhole. As they came out the lamp was knocked into the hold and an explosion took place injuring the plaintiff. The explosion was caused in a unique fashion because the paraffin had vapourized (which was unusual) and been ignited by the naked flame of the wick. The defendants argued that although some injury by burning was foreseeable, burning by explosion was not. *Held*—by the House of Lords—that the defendants were liable. 'The cause of this accident was a known source of danger, the lamp, but it behaved in an unpredictable way. . . . This accident was caused by a known source of danger but caused in a way which could not have been foreseen and in my judgment that affords no defence.' (*Per* Lord Reid.) 'The accident was but a variant of the foreseeable. It was, to quote the words of Denning, L.J., in *Roe* v. *Minister of Health* (see p. 810) 'within the risk created by the negligence'. . . . The children's entry into the tent with the ladder, the descent into the hole, the mishandling of the lamp, were all foreseeable. The greater part of the path to injury had thus been trodden, and the mishandled lamp was quite likely at that state to spill and cause a conflagration. Instead, by some curious chance of combustion, it exploded and no conflagration occurred, it would seem, until after the explosion. There was thus an unexpected manifestation of the apprehended physical dangers. But it would be, I think, too narrow a view to hold that those who created the risk of fire are excused from the liability for the damage by fire because it came by way of explosive combustion. The resulting damage, though severe, was not greater than or different in kind from that which might have been produced had the lamp spilled and caused a more normal conflagration in the hole.' (*Per* Lord Pearce.)

Comment. (i) A good illustration of the rule in *Hughes* that the *precise* mechanics of the way in which harm occurs need not be foreseen if it is within the risk caused by the negligence is *Draper* v. *Hodder*, [1972] 2 All E.R. 210. The defendant owned 30 Jack Russell terriers which he kept on his ungated premises. The dogs could run into a nearby house which was owned by the plaintiff's parents. That house was also ungated. On one occasion the dogs ran into the yard of the nearby house and one or more of them attacked the plaintiff, a three-year-old boy and bit him. His action for damages succeeded. It was foreseeable immediately that the dogs would bowl over and scratch the child. Nevertheless, the fact that one or more of them bit him was within the risk created by the negligence.

(ii) In spite of the more liberal attitude taken to foresight in *Hughes*, some things are still too remote as consequences. For example in *Meah* v. *McCreamer* (No. 2), [1986] 1 All E.R. 943 the plaintiff had been injured in a car accident by reason of the defendant's negligence. The plaintiff alleged that he had suffered a personality change leading to him attacking women. He raped one and indecently assaulted another. The women recovered damages against him and he tried to recover them from the defendant. It was held that the alleged damage was too remote.

(469) *Bradford* v. *Robinson Rentals*, [1967] 1 All E.R. 267

In January, 1963, the plaintiff, a television engineer aged 57, was told by his employer to drive an old van from Exeter to Bedford, exchange it there for a new one and drive back to Exeter, a round journey of some 500 miles involving about 20 hours' driving.

The plaintiff protested because the weather was severe but he undertook the journey. The radiator of the old van had to be refilled frequently and neither of the vans had a heater so that the windscreen had to be kept open to prevent the formation of ice. The plaintiff took all reasonable precautions to protect himself from the cold but even so he sustained permanent injury to his hands and feet from frostbite. *Held*—that the defendant had been negligent and judgment was given for the plaintiff. Liability in negligence does not depend upon the precise nature of the injury being foreseeable. It is enough if the injury was of a kind that was foreseeable even though the form that it took was unusual. *Some* injury from cold was foreseeable.

(470) *Weiland* v. *Cyril Lord Carpets*, [1969] 3 All E.R. 1006

The plaintiff was injured when the bus on which she was travelling had to brake suddenly as a result of the negligent driving of the defendant's vehicle by one of their employees. As part of her treatment she had to have a collar fitted to her neck and in consequence was unable to use her bi-focal spectacles with her usual skill. At a later stage this caused her to fall down some stairs sustaining further injuries. *Held*—by Eveleigh, J.—that the second injury was attributable to the original negligence of the defendants and they were liable in damages. If an injury affects a person's ability to cope with the vicissitudes of life and thereby is the cause of another injury, the latter injury is a foreseeable consequence of the former within the terms of *the Wagon Mound*, 1961,[467] and *Hughes* v. *Lord Advocate*, 1963.[468]

(471) *Doughty* v. *Turner Manufacturing Co.*, [1964] 1 All E.R. 98

Doughty, a workman, was injured in a factory where he worked. A workman accidentally knocked an asbestos cement cover into a cauldron of sodium cyanide which was rendered molten by being raised to 800°C., eight times the heat of boiling water. The cover fell some four to six inches, and one or two minutes afterwards the heat caused a chemical change in the asbestos cement whereby it released water, which turned into steam and caused an explosion of the hot liquid which injured Doughty. Such an eruption was not expected, and indeed its cause was only discovered by subsequent experiments carried out by Imperial Chemical Industries Ltd, which revealed that the immersion of such a cover, or indeed any other object containing actual moisture, and its subjection to a temperature of 500°C., would cause such an eruption. Such a phenomenon could not have been known to the defendants beforehand. The Court of Appeal allowed an appeal by the Turner Manufacturing Co. against an award by the lower court of £150 damages to Doughty. It was *held* that a splash, such as was caused by the falling cover, would be a foreseeable danger and should be guarded against, but this was not the cause of the accident, and in any case the lid fell only a few inches and the heavy liquid would not travel far. Although the eruption had the same effect as a splash, it was quite unrealistic to regard it as a variant of the perils of splashing. The cause was quite different, it would be wrong to make such an inroad into the doctrine of foreseeability.

Comment. It might be thought that the plaintiff should have recovered damages in this case on the principles laid down in *Hughes* v. *Lord Advocate*, 1963.[468] It was a negligent act to fail to take reasonable care to prevent the cover from being knocked into the liquid. This being so it should not have mattered whether the cover caused a splash or an eruption. Injury caused by either event should have resulted in an award of damages.

(472) *Tremain* v. *Pike*, [1969] 3 All E.R. 1303

The plaintiff, who was a herdsman, contracted Weil's disease through handling hay and washing his hands in a water trough both of which were contaminated by the urine of rats with which the farm was badly infested. Weil's disease is rarely contracted by human beings, but when it is, it results from the skin coming into contact with the urine of rats. *Held—* by Payne, J.—that the plaintiff's employer was not liable. Although the defendant was negligent in that a prudent farmer would have called in a rodent officer to deal with the infestation, the resulting injury to the plaintiff was not foreseeable, though an injury arising from a rat-bite or food poisoning by consumption of food or drink contaminated by rats might have been. ('Weil's disease) . . . was entirely different in kind from the effect of a rat-bite, or food poisoning by the consumption of food or drink contaminated by rats. I do not accept that all illness or infection arising from an infestation of rats should be regarded as of the same kind.'

Comment. This decision seems to be out of line with *Hughes* v. *Lord Advocate*, 1963,[468] and *Bradford* v. *Robinson Rentals*, 1967.[469] An infestation of rats is a known source of danger to man. The fact that they attacked in an unusual and upredictable way should not have affected the right of the plaintiff to damages.

Remoteness of damage: the unusual plaintiff rule.

(473) *Smith* v. *Leech Braine & Co. Ltd*, [1962] 2 W.L.R. 148

The plaintiff was the widow of a person employed by the defendants. Mr Smith's work consisted of lowering articles into a galvanizing tank containing molten zinc. On one occasion he was struck on the lip by a piece of molten metal which caused a burn. This resulted in a cancer from which he died three years later. Mr Smith's work had given him a predisposition to cancer and the question arose whether, since the *Wagon Mound*, the so-called 'thin skull rule' had disappeared, so that the plaintiff had to show that the cancer was foreseeable. The Lord Chief Justice, Lord Parker, finding for the plaintiff, said in the course of his judgment: 'I am satisfied that the Judicial Committee of the Privy Council did not have what are called "thin skull" cases in mind. It has always been the common law that a tortfeasor must take his victim as he finds him.'

(474) *Martindale* v. *Duncan*, [1973] 1 W.L.R. 674

The plaintiff's car was damaged in a collision with the defendant's car because of the negligence of the defendant. The plaintiff delayed repairs to his car pending the approval of the defendant's insurers and also of his own. The defendant's insurers wished to seek the advice of independent engineers and did so. About nine weeks after the accident, the defendant's insurers approved the estimate. A few days later the plaintiff's insurers did so and the repairs were started one week afterwards. The District Registrar awarded the plaintiff damages including £220 for loss of use of his vehicle for ten weeks at the rate of £22 per week for hire of a substitute vehicle to cover the period during which he had delayed repairs pending approval of the estimate by the insurers. The defendant had argued that the repairs were not commenced as early as they could have been since the plaintiff was not himself able to pay for the repairs but had to wait to see what the position was as regards payment from an insurance company. On appeal by the defendant it was *held*—by the Court of Appeal—dismissing the appeal—that the plaintiff was not in breach of his duty to mitigate his loss and had acted reasonably in the circumstances. (*Liesbosch* v. *Edison*, 1933[466] distinguished.)

(475) *Morgan* v. *T. Wallis*, [1974] 1 Ll. Rep. 165

Mr Morgan, a lighterman on the River Thames, sustained back injuries in trying to avoid a wire rope thrown by a stevedore onto a barge where Mr Morgan was working. Liability for his injuries was admitted by the defendants, his employers, because they should have had a better system of working, but the amount of damages was disputed because Mr Morgan unreasonably refused to undergo tests and an operation because he genuinely feared both of these things. The highest estimate by a surgeon of the chances of success of such an operation was 90%. It was *held*—by Browne, J.—that the defendants had proved that Mr Morgan's refusal was unreasonable as to the investigations and that the operation would have been successful on a balance of probabilities. Where there was no prior disability, physical, mental or psychological, a defendant did not have to take a plaintiff as he found him.

Remoteness of damage: intended damage never too remote: *novus actus interveniens*: act of third party expected

(476) *Scott* v. *Shepherd* (1773), 2 Wm. Bl. 892

On the evening of a fair-day at Milborne Port, Shepherd threw a lighted squib on to the market stall of one Yates who sold gingerbread. Then one Willis, in order to protect the wares of Yates, threw it away and it landed on the stall of one Ryal. He threw it to another part of the market house where it struck the plaintiff in the face, exploded and put out his eye. *Held*—Shepherd was liable for the injuries to Scott because he intended the initial act and there was no break in the chain of causation. Shepherd should have anticipated that Willis and Ryal would act as they did.

Comment. The decision in this case is initially difficult to understand because Shepherd did not injure the plaintiff. It would seem that since battery is also a crime the maxim of the criminal law that a person intends the natural consequences of his acts was applied to produce the 'transferred intent' of the type seen in criminal cases.

Remoteness of damage: *novus actus* not materially causing or contributing to injury

(477) *Barnett* v. *Chelsea and Kensington Hospital Management Committee*, [1968] 1 All E.R. 1068

Mr Barnett drank tea which had, unknown to him, been contaminated with arsenic. He attended at the casualty department of a hospital saying that he had been vomiting for some three hours after drinking the tea. The casualty doctor failed to examine him but sent a message that he should report to his own doctor. Some five hours later Mr Barnett died and on his widow's action for damages, it was *held* that the hospital authority owed a duty of care and that the doctor was negligent in failing to examine and admit Mr Barnett and accordingly there had been a breach of that duty. However, on the facts the deceased's condition was such that he must have died despite any medical attention which the hospital could have given so that causation was not established and the widow's claim failed.

(478) *Robinson* v. *The Post Office, The Times*, 26 October, 1973

The plaintiff suffered a minor injury for which the defendants, his employers, admitted liability. As a result the plaintiff received an anti-tetanus injection which produced the rare complication of encephalitis, with grave consequences. Ashworth, J., held that the doctor had acted negligently in administering the injection in that he had failed to administer a test dose. However, it appeared that even if such a test had been made the plaintiff would have shown no reaction to it. Thus the doctor's negligence had had no causative effect, since even with proper precautions the encephalitis would not have been prevented. The defendants appealed and it was *held*—by the Court of Appeal—that the judge's conclusions on the question of the medical negligence were correct and that accordingly the defendant could not rely on that negligence as a *novus actus interveniens*. They were therefore liable for all the plaintiff's disabilities and the contention that these were too remote was to be rejected.

Remoteness of damage: duty to guard against *novus actus*

(479) *Davies* v. *Liverpool Corporation*, [1949] 2 All E.R. 175

The plaintiff was trying to board a tramcar belonging to the defendants at a request stopping place. An unauthorized person (a passenger) rang the bell, whereupon the car started, throwing the plaintiff off the platform and causing her injury. The conductor was on the upper deck collecting fares. Evidence showed that the car had been standing at the request stop for an appreciable time, and that the conductor had been upstairs for the whole of that time, though it was not a particularly busy period. In this action for negligence brought by the plaintiff, it was *held* that the defendants were liable for the negligent act of the conductor. He should have foreseen that if he was absent from the plaform of the car for an appreciable time, some passenger might ring the bell. The act of the passenger did not, therefore, break the chain of causation because it was just that sort of act which the conductor was employed to prevent.

Remoteness of damage: *novus actus* not anticipated by defendant

(480) *Cobb* v. *Great Western Railway*, [1894] A.C. 419

The railway company allowed a railway carriage to become overcrowded, and because of this the plaintiff was hustled and robbed of £89. He now sued the company in respect of his loss. *Held*—This was too remote a consequence of the defendants' negligence. The robbery was a *novus actus interveniens* breaking the chain of causation.

Comment. In *Stansbie* v. *Troman*, [1948] 2 K.B. 48 the owner of a house was obliged to leave a painter working alone on the premises. The owner told the painter to shut the front door when he left the house but in fact the painter left the house empty for about two hours in order to obtain some wallpaper and left the door unlocked. It was held that the painter was liable for the loss of jewelry stolen by a third party who entered the house in his absence because this was foreseeable as being just the kind of thing which might happen in the situation. It is difficult to reconcile *Stansbie* with *Cobb* and leads to the suggestion that *Cobb* may no longer be good law, though it has never been overruled.

Remoteness of damage: *novus actus* may be that of the plaintiff

(481) *Sayers* v. *Harlow U.D.C.*, [1958] 2 All E.R. 342

The defendants owned and operated a public lavatory. The plaintiff having paid for admission entered a cubicle. Finding that there was no handle on the inside of the door, and no means of opening the cubicle, the plaintiff had tried for some ten to fifteen minutes to attract attention. Having failed to do so, and wishing to catch a bus to London in the next few minutes, she tried to see if there was a way of climbing out. She placed one foot on the seat of the lavatory and rested her other foot on the toilet roll and fixture, holding the pipe from the cistern with one hand and resting the other hand on the top of the door. She then realized it would be impossible to climb out, and she proceeded to come down, but, as she was doing so, the toilet roll rotated owing to her weight on it and she slipped and injured herself. She sued the defendants for negligence. In the County Court the defendants were found negligent, but, as the plaintiff was in no danger on that account, and as she chose to embark on a dangerous act, she must bear the consequences. It was *held*—by the Court of Appeal—that her act was not a *novus actus interveniens*, and the damage was not too remote a consequence of the defendants' negligence. She was thirty-six years of age, and in her predicament her act was not unreasonable, though if she had been an old lady it might have been. However, the damages recoverable by the plaintiff would be reduced by one quarter in respect of her share of the responsibility for the damage.

(482) *McKew* v. *Holland and Hannen and Cubitts (Scotland) Ltd*, [1969] 2 All E.R. 1621

McKew sustained an injury during the course of his employment for which his employers were liable. The injury caused him occasionally and unexpectedly to lose the use of his left leg. On one occasion he left a flat and started to descend some stairs which had no handrail. His leg gave way and he sustained further injury. *Held*—by the House of Lords—that his conduct in trying to descend the stairs was unreasonable and thus broke the chain of causation. The subsequent injury was therefore too remote and the employers were not liable.

Remoteness of damage: *novus actus*: the intervener must intend the act

(483) *Philco Radio Corporation* v. *Spurling*, [1949] 2 All E.R. 882

Certain packing cases containing inflammable film scrap were delivered in error by the defendants to the plaintiff's premises. No warning as to their contents was given on the cases. The cases were opened by the plaintiffs' servants, and a foreman recognized the contents as inflammable, and gave instructions that the scrap was to be replaced, and that there was to be no smoking in the vicinity. He telephoned the defendants and arranged to have the cases delivered to their proper destination, 150 yards away. Before the cases had been moved, a typist employed by the plaintiffs negligently set light to the scrap with a cigarette, and it exploded causing damage. The defendants pleaded that the proximate cause of the damage was the typist's act and that the chain of causation was broken. *Held*—The defendants were negligent in not ensuring that such dangerous material was properly delivered. The act of the typist did not break the chain of causation; she did not intend to injure her employer, and when she approached the scrap with a cigarette she did so as a joke. Her act was not such a conscious act of violation as to relieve the defendants from liability, and in any case the act formed part of the very risk that was envisaged.

Remoteness of damage: nervous shock.

(484) *Dulieu* v. *White*, [1901] 2 K.B. 669

The defendant, who was driving a van negligently, ran into a public house. The plaintiff, who was pregnant, was in the public house and because of the shock became ill and gave birth to a premature and mentally deficient child. It was *held* that she could recover damages.

(485) *Hambrook* v. *Stokes*, [1925] 1 K.B. 141

The defendant left his lorry unattended on a sloping street and because of his negligence in failing to brake the vehicle properly, it began to run away. The plaintiff's wife had just left her children further down the street though they were in fact round a bend and not within her view. However, she saw the lorry moving and suffered shock, which resulted in her death, because she feared for the safety of her children. Her husband brought this action for loss of her services and was *held* entitled to recover damages provided that the shock was brought about by his wife's own experience and not by the accounts of bystanders.

(486) *Hinz* v. *Berry*, [1970] 1 All E.R. 1074

Mrs Hinz witnessed a car accident in which her husband was killed and her children injured. The accident was caused by the negligent driving of the defendant. As a result of seeing the accident Mrs Hinz, who had been a vigorous and lively woman, became morbid and depressed for years afterwards. *Held*—by the Court of Appeal—she was entitled to damages of £4000 for nervous shock. She was a woman of robust character who would probably have stood up to the strain if she had not *seen* the accident.

Somehow or other the court has to draw a line between sorrow and grief for which damages are not recoverable; and nervous shock and psychiatric illness for which damages are recoverable. The way to do this is to estimate how much the plaintiff would have suffered if, for instance, her husband had been killed in an accident when she was fifty miles away; and compare it with what she is now, having suffered all the shock due to being present at the accident. The evidence shows that she suffered much more by being present. (*Per* Lord Denning, M.R.)

Comment. (i) In *McLoughlin* v. *O'Brian*, [1981] 1 All E.R. 809 the plaintiff's husband and three children were involved in a road accident caused by the negligence of the defendant. One child was killed and the husband and the other two children were badly injured. At the time of the accident the plaintiff was at home two miles away and was told of the accident by a neighbour and taken to hospital where she saw the injured members of her family and the extent of their injuries and shock, and heard that her daughter had been killed. As a result of hearing and seeing the results of the accident the plaintiff suffered severe and persisting nervous shock and brought this action against the defendant for negligence. It was held by the Court of Appeal that the claim failed. Even though the plaintiff's nervous shock was a reasonable foreseeable consequence of the defendant's negligence, in accordance with precedent and social policy the duty of care owed by a driver of a motor vehicle was limited to persons and owners of property on the road or near it who might be directly affected by the driver's negligent driving and accordingly the defendant did not owe a duty of care to the plaintiff because she had not been in the physical proximity of the accident when it occurred.

(ii) The House of Lords, [1982] 2 All E.R. 278, reversed the Court of Appeal and upheld the plaintiff's claim, even though she was two miles from the accident. The argument that this would open the floodgates to many claims by people who had not actually seen the accident, which was a former restriction on claims of this sort, did not deter their Lordships. They all agreed that the plaintiff's nervous shock was a foreseeable event producing an identifiable mental illness. However, that part of the decision in *Hinz* v. *Berry* (above) which says that nervous shock does not cover sorrow or grief was upheld.

(iii) Following the decision in *McLoughlin* it would seem that damages for nervous shock are recoverable by those who see the accident (even perhaps on TV) and those who do not see the accident but see the state of the victims shortly afterwards. Whether it would be enough merely to read an account in a newspaper or hear it on radio is doubtful.

(iv) It was held in *Attia* v. *British Gas plc*, [1987] 3 All E.R. 456 that damages for nervous shock could be recovered where they were caused by damage to property. It need not result from the death or injury of a person. The plaintiff's shock in this case arose when, on returning home, she saw the whole of her house on fire as a result of the defendant's negligence.

(487) *Chadwick* v. *British Railways Board*, [1967] 1 W.L.R. 912

A serious railway accident was caused by negligence for which the Board was liable. A volunteer rescue worker suffered nervous shock and became psychoneurotic as a result. The plaintiff, as administratrix of his estate, claimed damages for nervous shock. It was *held* that—

(i) damages were recoverable for nervous shock even though the shock was not caused by fear for one's own safety or that of one's children;

(ii) in the circumstances injury by shock was foreseeable;

(iii) the defendants ought to have foreseen that volunteers might attempt rescue and accordingly owed a duty of care to those who did.

Comment.·If the plaintiff had merely read of this accident to strangers in his newspaper there would have been no claim for nervous shock if this had resulted. However, if the newspaper had reported some gruesome accident to, e.g. a relative, a claim would seem possible since *McLoughlin* v. *O'Brian*, 1982 (p. 778).

(488) *Owens* v. *Liverpool Corporation*, [1939] 2 K.B. 394

A funeral procession was making its way to the cemetery when a negligently driven tram owned by the defendants collided with the hearse and overturned the coffin. Several mourners who were following in a carriage suffered shock and it was *held* by the Court of Appeal that they were entitled to damages.

Remoteness of damage: nervous shock: there must be a duty of care

(489) *Hay (or Bourhill)* v. *Young*, [1943] A.C. 92

The plaintiff, a pregnant Edinburgh fishwife, alighted from a tramcar. While she was removing her fish-basket from the tram, Young, a motor cyclist, driving carelessly but unseen by her, passed the tram and collided with a motor car some fifteen yards away. Young was killed. The plaintiff heard the collision, and after Young's body had been removed, she approached the scene of the accident and saw a pool of blood on the road. She suffered a nervous shock and later gave birth to a stillborn child. The House of Lords *held* that her action against Young's personal representative failed, because Young owed no duty of care to persons whom he could not reasonably anticipate would suffer injuries as a result of his conduct on the highway.

Remoteness of damage: successive accidents and supervening events

(490) *Jobling* v. *Associated Dairies*, [1980] 3 All E.R. 769

The plaintiff, an employee in a butcher's shop, suffered a partially disabling accident at work in 1973. In 1976 before the trial in regard to that accident came on, the plaintiff was found to be suffering from a totally disabling but unconnected condition. At the trial in 1979 the judge took no account of the supervening disability. On appeal on amount of damages it was *held*—allowing the appeal—that where a plaintiff was subsequently injured by a non-tortious act the tortfeasor's damages were to be reduced by the extent of the plaintiff's further injuries and consequent loss. *Baker* v. *Willoughby* 1969[491] should not be extended further.

(491) *Baker* v. *Willoughby*, [1969] 3 All E.R. 1528

In September, 1964, the plaintiff was involved in an accident on the highway caused by the negligent driving of the defendant, but attributable as to one quarter to the plaintiff's contributory negligence. The plaintiff received serious injuries to his left leg, but after long hospital treatment he took up employment with a scrap metal merchant. On 29 November, 1967, while in the course of his employment, the plaintiff was the innocent victim of an armed robbery receiving gunshot wounds necessitating the immediate amputation of his left leg which was already defective because of the previous accident. The question of the amount of damages for the plaintiff's injuries in the road accident of September, 1964, came before the Court for assessment in February, 1968. *Held*—by the Court of Appeal—that no consequence of the accident of September, 1964 survived the amputation of the plaintiff's left leg and the defendant was liable only for loss suffered by the plaintiff up to 29 November, 1967. Damages are compensation for loss arising from a tortious act and cease when by reason of recovery, supervening disease, or further injury there is no continuing loss attributable to that act.

The House of Lords, [1969] 3 All E.R. 1529, reversed the Court of Appeal decision holding that damages are not merely compensation for physical injury but for the loss which the injured person suffers. This loss was not diminished by the supervening event and the second injury was irrelevant. '. . . The supervening event has not made the appellant less lame nor less disabled nor less deprived of amenities. It has not shortened the period over which he will be suffering. It has made him more lame, more disabled, more deprived of amenities. He should not have less damages through being worse off then he might have expected . . .' (*Per* Lord Pearson, L.J.)

(492) *Performance Cars Ltd* v. *Abraham*, [1961] 3 All E.R. 413

The plaintiffs owned a motor car which was damaged in a collision with a car driven by the defendant. The damage to the plaintiff's car was such that it would necessitate respraying the whole of the lower body. Two weeks before the accident the plaintiffs' car had been involved in another collision which had also made respraying of the lower body of the car necessary. The plaintiffs obtained judgment against the driver responsible for the first collision but that judgment was not satisfied and the car had not been resprayed at the time when the second collision took place. The court was asked to decide whether the plaintiffs were entitled to recover as damages from the defendant the cost of respraying the lower body of their car. *Held*—by the Court of Appeal—that the plaintiffs were not entitled to recover the cost of respraying from the defendant because that damage was not the result of his wrongful act.

(493) *Cutler* v. *Vauxhall Motors Ltd*, [1970] 2 All E.R. 56

In 1965 the plaintiff grazed his right ankle as a result of an accident at work for which the defendants were responsible. In 1966 the plaintiff had an operation for varicose veins in both legs. He would have had to have the operation a few years later had the grazing not occurred. The trial judge awarded £10 for the graze and nothing for the operation. *Held*— by the Court of Appeal—the sum awarded was adequate. The defendant's liability for the operation had not been established.

Cessation of liability: waiver

(494) *United Australia Ltd* v. *Barclays Bank Ltd*, [1941] A.C.1.

In November, 1934, certain debtors of United Australia sent to them a crossed cheque for £1900 payable to their order. On 12 November that cheque, purporting to have been indorsed in the name of United Australia by one A. H. Emons, their Secretary, in favour of MFG Trust, was presented at a branch of the respondent bank for payment into the account of MFG at that branch, and the amount was shortly collected, received and paid by the bank. On 13 May, 1935, the appellants, who alleged that Emons had no authority to indorse the cheque, issued a writ against MFG claiming £1900 a loan to MFG or as money had and received to the appellant's use (i.e. an action in quasi-contract.) This action never came to final trial and MFG afterwards went into liquidation. On 8 November, 1937, the appellants brought this action against the respondents for conversion of the cheque. *Held*—by the House of Lords—that the appellants by merely initiating proceedings against MFG in quasi-contract had not thereby elected to waive the tort of conversion by the bank and were not precluded from bringing the present action. It is judgment and satisfaction in the first action which constitutes a bar to a second action.

(495) *Verschures Creameries Ltd* v. *Hull and Netherlands Steamship Co. Ltd*, [1921] 2 K.B. 608

Certain boxes of margarine were delivered by the plaintiffs to the defendants, who were carriers and forwarding agents, to be carried by sea to Hull and thence forwarded to two customers in Liverpool and Manchester, S. Beilin and R. Beilin respectively. When the goods arrived at Hull the plaintiffs instructed the defendants not to deliver to the Beilins but to deliver to a Mr Schneiderman of Manchester, but in the event the goods were delivered to R. Beilin. The plaintiffs, having heard of the misdelivery, nevertheless invoiced the goods to R. Beilin and sued him and recovered judgment for the price of goods sold and delivered. Failing to get satisfaction from Beilin, the plaintiffs took proceedings in bankruptcy against him. *Held*—they could not afterwards sue the forwarding agents for negligence and breach of duty.

Limitation of actions in tort

(496) *Letang* v. *Cooper*, [1964] 2 All E.R. 929

In July, 1957, the plaintiff was run over by a motor car negligently driven by the defendant. She issued a writ on 2 February, 1961 (that is after the three years' period of limitation then provided by s. 2(1) of the Law Reform (Limitation of Actions, etc.) Act, 1954, had expired), claiming damages for personal injuries in negligence and in the alternative trespass to the person. Since the claim in negligence was statute-barred, she hoped to succeed in trespass to the person, believing the six-year limitation period to apply in this case. The action failed. It was *held*—by the Court of Appeal—that where the injury was not intentional, the only action is negligence not trespass. In the course of his judgment Lord Denning, M.R., said: 'The truth is that *the distinction between trespass and case is obsolete*. We have a different subdivision altogether. Instead of dividing actions for personal injuries into *trespass* (direct damage) or *case* (consequential damage), we divide the causes of action according as the defendant did the injury intentionally or unintentionally. . . . If intentional, it is the tort of assault and battery (or trespass to the person). If negligent and causing damage, it is the tort of negligence.'

Elsewhere Lord Denning made a point of interpretation: 'It is legitimate to look at a report of such a committee (in this case the Tucker Committee on the Limitation of Actions), so as to see what was the mischief at which the Act was directed. You can get the facts and surrounding circumstances from the report, so as to see the background against which the legislation was enacted. This is always a great help in interpreting it. But you cannot look at what the committee recommended, or at least, if you do look at it, you should not be unduly influenced by it. It does not help much, for the simple reason that Parliament may, and often does, decide to do something different to cure the mischief.'

Limitation of actions: fraudulent or negligent concealment of claim

(497) *Beaman* v. *A.R.T.S.*, [1949] 1 All E.R. 465

In November, 1935, Mrs Beaman, before leaving for Istanbul, deposited with the defendants several packages to be sent to her as soon as she gave notice requesting it. In May, 1936, the defendants at her request dispatched one of the packages but afterwards regulations made by the Turkish authorities prevented the dispatching of the other packages and Mrs Beaman asked the defendants to keep them in store pending further instructions. Three years later the defendants, who had not received instructions, wrote and asked the plaintiff to insure the contents of the packages. She did not do so but replied saying that she was hoping to return to England. However, the outbreak of war while she was still in Turkey prevented this.

On the entry of Italy into the war in 1940 the defendants, being a company controlled by Italian nationals, had their business taken over by the Custodian of Enemy Property. Wishing to wind up the business as soon as possible, the manager of ARTS Ltd examined the packages, reported that they were of no value and gave them to the Salvation Army. No steps were taken to obtain the plaintiff's consent. The plaintiff returned to England in 1946 and commenced proceedings more than six years after the packages were disposed of, claiming damages for conversion. The defendants set up the defence that the action was barred by the Limitation Act. The plaintiff relied on what is now s. 32 of the Limitation Act, 1980 which provides that where '(a) the action is based on fraud of the defendant . . . or (b) the right of action is concealed by the fraud of any such person . . . the period of limitation shall not begin to run until the plaintiff has discovered the fraud. . . .'
Held—

(i) That the action for conversion was not 'based on fraud' so that what is now s. 32(1)(a) had no application.

(ii) The conduct of the defendants constituted a reckless 'concealment by fraud' of the right of action within what is now s. 32(1)(b). Therefore the plaintiff's action was not barred.

Comment. It appears that it is not necessary to prove a degree of moral turpitude to establish fraud for the purposes of s. 32. Thus in *Kitchen* v. *Royal Air Force Association*, [1958] 1 W.L.R. 563, solicitors negligently concealed a payment of money on behalf of the plaintiff and this conduct was held to amount to 'fraud' for the purposes of what is now s. 32 even though the court accepted that the solicitors were not dishonest.

Trespass to the person: words may prevent an assault

(498) *Turbervell* v. *Savage* (1669), 2 Keb. 545

In this old case a man laid his hand menacingly on his sword, but at the same time said, 'If it were not assize time I would not take such language from you.' *Held*—This was not an assault because it was assize time, and there was no reason to fear violence.

Trespass to the person: battery may arise from a failure to act

(499) *Fagan* v. *Metropolitan Police Commissioner*, [1968] 3 All E.R. 442

Fagan was driving his car when he was told by a constable to draw into the kerb. He stopped his car with one wheel on the constable's foot and was slow in restarting the engine and moving the vehicle off. He was convicted of assault on the constable and Quarter Sessions dismissed his appeal. He then appealed to the Queen's Bench Divisional Court where it was *held*—dismissing his appeal—that whether or not the mounting of the wheel on the constable's foot had been intentional the defendant had deliberately allowed it to remain there when asked to move it and that constituted an assault. The decision seems to extend the law because there was no act but merely an omission. Furthermore, there was no intentional application of force but only a failure to withdraw it. A more appropriate charge might have been false imprisonment because the constable could not presumably have moved while the wheel remained on his foot.

Comment. This was a criminal prosecution for assault, an expression which is commonly used to mean battery also. In strict civil law terms the trespass to the policeman was a battery.

Trespass to the person: is not actionable in itself: the plaintiff must prove intention or negligence

(500) *Fowler* v. *Lanning*, [1959] 1 All E.R. 290

By a writ the plaintiff claimed damages for trespass to the person. In his statement of claim he alleged that on 19 November, 1957, at Vineyard Farm, Corfe Castle, in the County of Dorset, the defendant shot the plaintiff. By reason of the premises, the plaintiff sustained personal injuries and suffered loss and damage; particulars of the plaintiff's injuries were then set out. The defendant denied the allegations of fact and objected that the statement of claim disclosed no cause of action, because the plaintiff had not alleged that the shooting was either intentional or negligent. *Held*—In an action for trespass to the person, onus of proof of the defendant's intention or negligence lay on the plaintiff and the plaintiff must allege that the shooting was intentional or that the defendant was negligent, stating the facts alleged to constitute the negligence. The plaintiff's statement of claim, therefore, disclosed no cause of action.

Trespass to the person: false imprisonment

(501) *Bird* v. *Jones* (1845), 7 Q.B. 742

A bridge company enclosed part of the public footway on Hammersmith Bridge, put seats on it for the use of spectators at a regatta on the river, and charged admission. The plaintiff insisted on passing along this part of the footpath, and climbed over the fence without paying the charge. The defendant, who was the clerk of the Bridge Company, stationed two policemen to prevent, and they did prevent, the plaintiff from proceeding forwards along the footway in the direction he wished to go. The plaintiff was at the same time told that he might go back into the carriage way and proceed to the other side of the bridge if he wished. He declined to do so and remained in the enclosure for about half an hour. *Held*—There was no false imprisonment, for the plaintiff was free to go off another way.

(502) *Herd* v. *Weardale Steel, Coal and Coke Co. Ltd*, [1915] A.C. 67

The plaintiff was an employee of the defendant company and at 9.30 a.m. on 30 May, 1911, he descended the defendants' mine. In the ordinary way he would have been entitled to be raised at the end of his shift at 4 p.m. The plaintiff and two other men were given certain work to do which they believed to be unsafe, and they refused to do it. At about 11 a.m. they, and twenty-nine men acting in sympathy with them, asked the foreman to allow them to ascend the shaft. The foreman, acting on instructions from the management, refused this request. At about 1 p.m. the cage came down carrying men, and emptied at the bottom of the shaft. The twenty-nine men were refused permission to enter, but some got in and refused to leave the cage, which was left stationary for some twenty minutes. At 1.30 p.m. permission was given for the men to leave and the plaintiff was brought to the top. He now sued for false imprisonment. *Held*—There was no false imprisonment. There was a collective agreement regarding the use of the cage, and the plaintiff's right to be taken to the surface did not arise under the agreement until 4 p.m. The defendants were perfectly willing to let the plaintiff ascend, but were not required in the absence of any emergency to provide him with the means of doing so except in accordance with the agreement.

(503) *Meering* v. *Grahame White Aviation Co. Ltd* (1919), 122 L.T. 44

The plaintiff, being suspected of stealing a keg of varnish from the defendants, his employers, was asked by two works policemen to accompany them to the Works Office to answer questions. The plaintiff, not realizing that he was suspected, assented to the suggestion and even suggested a short cut. He remained in the office for some time during which the works policemen stayed outside the room without his knowledge. The plaintiff later sued for false imprisonment and the question arose as to whether the plaintiff must know that the defendant is restraining his freedom. *Held*—The plaintiff was imprisoned and his knowledge was irrelevant, though knowledge of imprisonment might increase the damages.

Trespass to the person: unlawful arrest

(504) *Christie* v. *Leachinsky*, [1947] A.C. 573

The appellants, without the necessary warrant, arrested the respondent for unlawful possession of a number of bales of cloth. They had reasonable grounds for thinking that the bales were stolen but did not disclose this until later. *Held*—by the House of Lords—that the arrest was unlawful.

(505) *R.* v. *Kulynycz*, [1970] 3 W.L.R. 1029

The defendant was convicted of possessing drugs contrary to the Drugs (Prevention of Misuse) Act, 1964. He resided in Cambridge and was suspected of supplying drugs to persons who 'pushed' them in King's Lynn. He was arrested in Cambridge by a police officer who told him that a warrant for his arrest had been issued at King's Lynn on suspicion of offences committed there. The offences were not specified and in fact no warrant had been issued. At the police station in Cambridge the full nature of the charge was made clear to the defendant. He was committed for trial to Norfolk Quarter Sessions on an indictment charging possession of drugs in Cambridge. Under s. 11(1) of the Criminal Justice Act, 1925, Norfolk Quarter Sessions had jurisdiction to try the case only if the defendant was 'in custody on a charge for the offence' in Norfolk. On that basis the question for decision was whether the defendant was in lawful custody when he appeared before Norfolk Quarter Sessions. It was *held* by the Court of Appeal (Criminal Division) that he was because although the original arrest was unlawful in that there was no specification of the offences (*Christie* v. *Leachinsky*, 1947),[504] the defendant was informed of these in sufficient detail at Cambridge police station. It was not necessary that he should be released and re-arrested. It did not matter that the police officer was wrong in saying that a warrant had been issued. An arrested person is not bound to know whether he is arrested on warrant or on reasonable suspicion.

(506) *Wheatley* v. *Lodge*, [1971] 1 All E.R. 173

The defendant's car collided with a parked vehicle. A constable saw him about an hour later and smelling alcohol on his breath, cautioned him and said that he was arrested for driving under the influence of drink contrary to what is now the Road Traffic Act, 1972. The defendant was deaf and could not lip read though the constable did not know this. Nevertheless the defendant got into a police car which the constable pointed to and was taken to the police station where he indicated his deafness. From then on the charge and all relevant matters were made clear to him by written and printed matter. On the question of the lawfulness of his arrest it was *held* by the Queen's Bench Divisional Court that the original arrest was valid. A police officer arresting a deaf person had to do what a reasonable person would do in the circumstances and the magistrates were clearly of the opinion that the constable had done so.

Comment. (i) Presumably on the basis of this decision if a person is arresting someone who cannot speak English he is not obliged to find an interpreter.

(ii) The Police and Criminal Evidence Act, 1984 confirms the common law rule that where an arrest is made by seizure of a person, words indicating that the person is under arrest should accompany the seizure. (S. 28(1).) However, the common law rule is modified by requiring that where an arrest is made by a policeman that the person arrested must be informed that he is under arrest even though that fact is obvious. The common law also requires that the person arrested be told the reason(s) for the arrest, and s. 23(3) confirms this rule but modifies it where there is an arrest by a constable, requiring that in such a case information regarding the ground for the arrest be furnished, regardless of whether it is obvious. (S. 28(4).) The section confirms the common law rule that there is no requirement to tell a person that he is under arrest or of the ground for his arrest if it is not reasonably practicable to do so, as where he has escaped from arrest before the information can be given. (S. 28(5).)

Trespass to land

(507) *Southport Corporation* v. *Esso Petroleum Co.*, [1954] 2 Q.B. 182

The Esso company's tanker became stranded in the estuary of the River Ribble. The master of the tanker discharged oil in order to re-float the ship. The action of the wind and tide took the oil on to the Corporation's foreshore and caused damage. The Corporation sued in trespass and negligence. Devlin, J., at first instance, thought that trespass would lie, but on appeal to the Court of Appeal, Denning, L.J., contended that there could be no trespass because the injury was not direct, but was caused by the tides and prevailing winds; in trespass the injury must be direct and not consequential. In the House of Lords, [1956] A.C. 218, Lord Tucker agreed with Denning, L.J., though in the House of Lords trespass was not pursued. The appeal was based on negligence and the defendants were *held* not liable.

Comment. This case illustrates the difficulties of trying to recover for oil pollution damage in negligence or trespass. The action for nuisance has similar difficulties. *Rylands* v. *Fletcher* does not apply because, among other things, the oil does not escape from the land but from the sea and the sea is the equivalent of a public highway. Oil pollution is now dealt with by the Merchant Shipping (Oil Pollution) Act, 1971, which provides a more straightforward method of making claims.

(508) *Kelson* v. *Imperial Tobacco Co.*, [1957] 2 All E.R. 343

The plaintiff was the lessee of a one-storey tobacconist's shop and brought this action against the defendants, seeking an injunction requiring them to remove from the wall above the shop a large advertising sign for cigarettes showing the words 'Players Please'. The sign projected into the air space above the plaintiff's shop by a distance of some eight inches. The plaintiff claimed that the defendants, by fixing the sign in that position, had trespassed on his air space. *Held*—The invasion of an air space by a sign of this nature constituted a trespass and, although the plaintiff's injury was small, it was an appropriate case in which to grant an injunction for the removal of the sign.

Comment. The plaintiff seemed prepared for the sign to remain until he became involved in a dispute with the defendants regarding the quota of cigarettes supplied to him. It was after the dispute that he brought this action, but the court found that the plaintiff's claim was not affected by his acts.

(509) *Woollerton and Wilson* v. *Richard Costain (Midlands) Ltd* (1969), .119 N.L.J. 1093

In this case the court granted to the owners of a factory and warehouse in Leicester an injunction restraining the defendants from trespassing on and invading air space over their premises by means of a swinging crane. The injunction was suspended for twelve months to enable the defendants to finish their work, the defendants having offered to pay for the right to continue to trespass and to provide insurance cover for neighbouring properties. It was also *held* that it was no answer to a claim for an injunction for trespass that the trespass did no harm to the plaintiff.

Comment. There has not been full support from the judiciary on the issue of postponing the injunction. In *John Trenbart Ltd* v. *National Westminster Bank Ltd* (1979), 123 S.J. 38 Walton, J., would not postpone the operation of an injunction in similar circumstances and refused to follow *Wollerton* saying it was wrongly decided.

(510) *Bernstein* v. *Skyviews & General*, [1977] 2 All E.R. 902

The plaintiff claimed damages for trespass against a firm which had taken an aerial photograph of his home from about 630 feet, crossing his land in order to do so. It was *held*—by Griffiths, J.—that an owner of land at common law had rights above his land to such height as was necessary for the ordinary use and enjoyment of the land and the structures upon it. The plane was therefore too high to be trespassing. In any case s. 40(1) of the Civil Aviation Act, 1949 (see now Civil Aviation Act, 1982, s. 76) provided a defence to such a claim where the height was reasonable. However, the judge did say that constant surveillance from the air with photographing might well be actionable nuisance.

Trespass to land: effect of revocation of licences

(511) *Wood* v. *Leadbitter* (1845), 13 M. & W. 838

Wood purchased a ticket for one guinea which entitled him to come into the stand, and the enclosure surrounding it, at Doncaster race course. The ticket was valid for the period of the race meeting. Lord Eglington was the steward of the Doncaster races and, while the races were going on, the defendant, who was Lord Eglington's servant, asked the plaintiff to leave. Wood refused to go and the defendant ejected him using no more than reasonable force. *Held*—It was lawful for Lord Eglington, without returning the guinea or giving any reason for his action, to order any holder of a ticket to leave the stand and enclosure, even though such holder had not misconducted himself. The plaintiff's licence to remain could, therefore, be revoked, so making him a trespasser. From then on he could be removed by the use of reasonable force.

(512) *Hurst* v. *Picture Theatres Ltd*, [1915] 1 K.B. 1

Hurst paid sixpence for an unreserved seat at the defendants' theatre. He was given a metal check, which he gave up at the door, and was then shown to a seat. Some time later he was asked if he had paid for admission and replied that he had. He was then asked to go and see the manager, but he refused to do so. Eventually the manager sent the door-keeper to eject the plaintiff, the police having refused to do so. The door-keeper lifted the plaintiff out of his seat, whereupon the plaintiff walked out quietly. He now sued for damages for assault and false imprisonment. The defendants contended that they were entitled, without giving reasons, to ask the plaintiff to leave, and if he did not do so, to remove him, using no more than reasonable force. *Held*—The plaintiff's claim succeeded. The defendants could not revoke the plaintiff's right in that way so as to make him a trespasser.

(513) *Winter Garden Theatre (London) Ltd* v. *Millenium Productions Ltd*, [1948] A.C. 173

The respondents were permitted by a contractual licence to use the Winter Garden Theatre, Drury Lane, which belonged to the appellants, for the purpose of producing plays, concerts or ballets in return for a weekly payment of £300. There was no express term in the licence providing that the appellants could revoke it. However, the appellants did revoke it, giving the respondents one month in which to quit the premises, but stating that they were prepared to give fresh notice for a later date if the respondents required further time in which to make other arrangements. The respondents contended that the licence could not be revoked so long as the weekly payments were continued. The appellants claimed that it was recovable on giving reasonable notice. *Held*—On a proper construction of the contract the licence was not intended to be perpetual, but nevertheless could only be determined by reasonable notice. What was reasonable notice depended on the commitments of the licensees and the circumstances of the parties. In this case the notice given by the appellants was reasonable and valid to determine the licence.

(514) *Hounslow London Borough Council* v. *Twickenham Garden Developments*, [1970] 3 W.L.R. 538

A building owner granted a licence under a building contract to a builder to enter on his land and do work there. The procedure for terminating the building contract involved an architect giving notice that the work was not being carried out properly. Such a notice was given but the building contractor refused to leave the land and carried on his work. The owner claimed an injunction and damages for trespass. *Held*—by Megarry, J.— in view of the fact that it was not certain whether the architect's notice had been given as a result of following proper procedures the contract had not necessarily been terminated and the builder was not, unless and until that was done, a trespasser. The owner's action failed.

Trespass to land: self-help

(515) *Hemmings* v. *Stoke Poges Golf Club*, [1920] 1 K.B. 720

The plaintiff was employed by the defendants and occupied a cottage belonging to them. Later he left the defendants' service and was called upon to given up possession. On refusal, he and his property were ejected with no more force than was necessary. *Held*—The defendants were not liable for assault or trespass.

Comment. Since this case concerns the eviction of an employee/occupier, it would seem to be overruled on its facts by s. 8(2) of the Protection From Eviction Act, 1977. Hemmings could now claim damages for breach of that Act. However, the principle behind the decision on the *Hemmings* facts is still revelant in that the occupier of property could eject a person not covered by the 1977 Act, e.g. a squatter, from his property by the use of reasonable force.

(516) *The Tubantia*, [1924] P. 78

The plaintiff, who was a marine salvor, was trying to salvage the cargo of the S.S. *Tubantia* which had been sunk in the North Sea. He had discovered the wreck and marked it with a marker buoy, and his divers were already working in the hold, when the defendant, a rival salvor, appeared on the scene and started to send divers down to salvage cargo from the wreck. *Held*—Whoever was the owner of the property salvaged, the plaintiff was sufficiently in possession of the wreck to found an action in trespass.

Conversion: may be based on a possessory title: finders of property

(517) *Parker* v. *British Airways Board*, [1982] 1 All E.R. 834

The plaintiff was in BA's first class lounge at Heathrow waiting for a flight. He found a gold bracelet on the floor and gave it to an employee of BA together with his name and address asking that it be returned to him if not claimed. It was not claimed but BA sold it. The plaintiff sued in conversion and the Court of Appeal held that the plaintiff was entitled to the proceeds of sale.

Comment. This principle was applied in two earlier cases, i.e. *Bridges* v. *Hawkesworth* (1851), 21 L.J. Q.B. 75 where the finder of some bank notes which were lying on the floor in the public part of a shop was held entitled to them as against the shopkeeper: and *Hannah* v. *Peel*, [1945] K.B. 509, where a soldier billeted in a house found a brooch lying loose in an upstairs room, and he was held entitled to it as against the free-holder of the property who had no knowledge of the brooch until the plaintiff found it.

Conversion: possessory title: goods on or attached to land or buildings

(518) *South Staffordshire Water Co.* v. *Sharman*, [1896] 2 Q.B. 44

The plaintiffs sued the defendant in detinue, claiming possession of two gold rings found by the defendant in the Minster Pool at Lichfield. The plaintiffs were owners of the pool and the defendant was a labourer employed by them to clean it. It was in the course of cleaning the pool that the defendant came across the rings. He refused to hand them to his employers, but gave them to the police for enquiries to be made to find the true owners. No owner was found and the police returned the rings to the defendant who retained them. *Held*—The rings must be given over to the plaintiffs. The plaintiffs were freeholders of the pool, and had the right to forbid anyone coming on the land; they had a right to clean the pool out in any way they chose. They possessed and exercised a practical control over the pool and they had a right to its contents.

Comment. It is also worth noting *Elwes* v. *Brigg Gas Co.* (1886), 33 Ch.D. 562 where it was held that a prehistoric boat found some six feet below the surface of the land belonged to the landowner and not to the finders. Similarly, in *Corporation of London* v. *Appleyard*, [1963] 2 All E.R. 834, owners of a building site were held entitled against workers of a demolition contractor to bank notes found in a wall safe in an old cellar.

Conversion: the relationship between the plaintiff and the goods

(519) *Jarvis* v. *Williams*, [1955] 1 All E.R. 108

Jarvis agreed to sell some bathroom fittings to Peterson and at Peterson's request delivered them to Williams. Peterson refused to pay the price and Jarvis agreed to take them back if Peterson would pay for collection. Peterson accepted this offer and Jarvis sent his lorryman, with a letter of authority, to collect the fittings but he was told that he could not take them, so he returned empty-handed. Jarvis claimed against Williams in conversion for the return of the goods. *Held*—On the delivery to Williams the property in the goods passed to Peterson, and the arrange-ment for re-collection did not re-vest the property in Jarvis. It follows that at the time of collection, Jarvis had no right of property in the goods to sustain an action in conversion.

Conversion: the defendant's conduct

(520) *Fouldes* v. *Willoughby* (1841), 8 M. & W. 540

The plaintiff had put his horses on the defendant's ferry boat and, a dispute having arisen, the defendant asked the plaintiff to take them off.

The plaintiff refused so the defendant did so, and since the plaintiff refused to leave the boat, the defendant ferried him across the river. The plaintiff sued in conversion. Maule. J., directed the jury that the putting of the horses ashore was a conversion, but on appeal, the Court of Exchequer *reversed* the decision and found there was no conversion. Lord Abinger, C.B., said: 'In order to constitute a conversion it is necessary either that the party taking the goods should intend some use to be made of them by himself or by those for whom he acts, or that owing to his act, the goods are destroyed or consumed to the prejudice of the lawful owner. The removal of the horses involved not the least denial of the right of the plaintiff to enjoyment or possession of them and was thus no conversion.'

(521) *Oakley* v. *Lyster*, [1931] 1 K.B. 148

Oakley, a demolition contractor, agreed to pull down an aerodrome on Salisbury Plain and reinstate the land, a process which involved disposing of 8000 tons of hard core and tar macadam. He thereupon rented three and a half acres of a farm on the opposite side of the road on which to dump it. He sold 4000 tons, but in January, 1929, there was still 4000 tons undisposed of when Lyster bought the freehold of the farm. Shortly afterwards Oakley found that some of the hardcore was being removed on Lyster's instructions, and Oakley saw him and was told that Lyster had bought the land and all that was on it, and on 9 July, 1929, his solicitors wrote to Oakley to this effect and forbade Oakley to remove the hard core otherwise he would become a trespasser on Lyster's land. Correspondence followed but at the trial it was admitted that Oakley was a lawful tenant and owner of the hard core. While the correspondence was continuing, Oakley agreed to sell that 4000 tons to Mr Edney, but in view of Lyster's claim, Edney withdrew and the stuff was undisposed of. The conversion alleged was the removal by Lyster of some of the hard core and the denial of title in the correspondence. *Held*—The defendant was liable in damages for conversion. In the correspondence Lyster was asserting and exercising dominion over the goods inconsistent with the rights of the true owner, Oakley. Nor was it sufficient to allow Oakley to resume dominion over the hardcore and remove it. He was entitled to damages of £300 for the loss of the sale to Edney.

Conversion: principle of liability: where the defendant has acted honestly

(522) *Elvin and Powell Ltd* v. *Plummer Roddis Ltd* (1933), 50 T.L.R. 158

A fraudulent person ordered a consignment of goods from the plaintiffs in the name of the defendants. He then telephoned the defendants in the plaintiff's name, saying that the goods had been dispatched to them in error and that they would be collected. The fraudulent person then himself collected the goods from the defendants and absconded with them. The plaintiffs now sued the defendants for conversion. *Held*—As involuntary bailees of goods, the defendants had acted reasonably in returning them, as they believed, to the plaintiffs, by a trustworthy messenger. They had not committed conversion.

Public nuisance: obstruction of the highway: dangerous activities near the highway

(523) *Attorney-General* v. *Gastonia Coaches, The Times*, 12 November, 1976

G, who were coach operators, owned 22 coaches of which 16 were parked in residential roads adjoining the Gastonia offices. No matter how carefully these coaches were parked they inevitably interfered with the free passage of other traffic. It was *held*—on a public relator action by the Attorney-General—that Gastonia were guilty of a public nuisance and would be restrained from parking the vehicles on the highway. Damages would also be awarded to private litigants who had suffered from the emission of exhaust gases, excessive noise and obstruction of drives.

(524) *Castle* v. *St Augustine's Links Ltd and Another* (1922), 38 T.L.R. 615

On 18 August, 1919, the plaintiff was driving a taxicab from Deal to Ramsgate when a ball played by the second defendant, a Mr Chapman, from the thirteenth tee on the golf course, which was parallel with the Sandwich Road, struck the windscreen of the taxicab. In consequence a piece of glass from the screen injured the plaintiff's eye and a few days later he had to have it removed. He then brought this action. *Held*—the plaintiff succeeded. Judgment for £450 damages was given by Sankey, J. The proximity of the hole to the road constituted a public nuisance. Compare *Bolton* v. *Stone*, [1951] A.C. 650, where cricket balls had been hit out of the ground and into the highway six to ten times in thirty-five years but had injured nobody. *Held*—no nuisance. See also *Miller* v. *Jackson*, [1977] 3 W.L.R. 20, where the Court of Appeal held that the public interest, which requires young people to have the benefit of outdoor games, may be held to outweigh the private interest of neighbouring householders who are the victims of sixes landing in their gardens so that it would be impossible to use the garden when cricket was being played. Thus no injunction was granted even though the sportsmen were held to be guilty of both nuisance and negligence.

Comment. In *Kennaway* v. *Thompson*, 1980 (see p. 800) the Court of Appeal refused to follow this approach on the matter of an injunction and said in effect that a court ought not to refuse an injunction if the tort is established merely because there is benefit to a section of the public.

(525) *Tarry* v. *Ashton* (1876), 1 Q.B.D. 314

A lamp projected from the defendant's premises over the highway. It fell and injured the plaintiff who then sued the defendant in respect of his injuries.

The defendant had previously employed an independent contractor, who was not alleged to be incompetent, to repair the lamp and it was because of the negligence of that contractor that the lamp fell. Even so the defendant was *held* liable and the decision suggests that there is strict liability in respect of injuries caused by artificial projections over the highway.

(526) *Dymond* v. *Pearce*, [1972] 1 All E.R. 1142

A lorry was left parked on a road subject to a 30 m.p.h. speed limit with its lights on beneath a street lamp. The plaintiff collided with the vehicle and suffered injury. He sued the defendants alleging negligence and nuisance. It was *held*—by the Court of Appeal—that the claim in negligence failed as there was no evidence to show that the driver had not acted reasonably in the circumstances. The claim in nuisance also failed, for although a nuisance had been created, the injury suffered resulted solely from the negligence of the motorcyclist himself. Of more importance than the actual decision are the comments made in the Court of Appeal regarding the relationship between negligence and nuisance in terms of fault. See in particular Edmund Davies, L.J., who said: 'But if an obstruction be created, here to, in my judgment, fault is essential to liability in the sense that it must appear that a reasonable man would be bound to realize the likelihood of risk to highway users resulting from the presence of the obstructing vehicle on the road.'

Nuisance: utility or benefit of activity no defence: nor is coming to the nuisance

(527) *Bliss* v. *Hall* (1838), L.J. C.P. 122

The defendant carried on the trade of a candle-maker in certain premises near to the dwelling house of the plaintiff and his family. Certain 'noxious and foul smells' issued from the defendant's premises and the plaintiff sued him for nuisance. The defence was that, for three years before the plaintiff occupied the dwelling house in question, the defendant had exercised the trade complained of in this present establishment. *Held*— This was no answer to the complaint and judgment was given for the plaintiff.

Comment. In *Miller* v. *Jackson*, [1977] 3 W.L.R. 20 the Court of Appeal decided that it was no defence to the claim in nuisance that the cricket ground only became a nuisance when the plaintiff built a house close by it.

(528) *Adams* v. *Ursell*, [1913] 1 Ch. 269

The plaintiff was a veterinary surgeon and he purchased a house in 1907 for £2370. In November, 1912, the defendant opened a fried fish shop at premises adjoining the plaintiff's house. Very soon after the commencement of the business, the plaintiff's house was permeated with the odour of fried fish, and the vapour from the stoves filled the rooms 'like fog or steam'. The plaintiff sued the defendant for nuisance, seeking an injunction. *Held*—An injunction would be granted because the defendant's activities materially interfered with the ordinary comfort of the plaintiff and his family; and it did not matter that the shop was in a large working-class district and therefore supplied a public need.

(529) *Dunton* v. *Dover District Council, The Times*, 31 March, 1977

The Council provided a play area for children of a housing estate on grazing land at the rear of the plaintiff's hotel. The playground was not fenced and there was no restriction on the age of the children using it. The plaintiff suffered noise and inconvenience and was awarded £200 damages and a continued injunction against the Council that the playground should only be open between 10 a.m. and 6.30 p.m. to children under 12.

Nuisance: modes of annoyance

(530) *Christie* v. *Davey*, [1893] 1 Ch. 316

The plaintiff was the occupier of a semi-detached house, and she and her daughter gave pianoforte, violin and singing lessons in the house, four days a week for seventeen hours in all. There was also practice of music and singing at other times, and occasional musical evenings. The defendant, a woodcarver and a versatile amateur musician, occupied the adjoining portion of the house, and he found the activities of the plaintiff and her family annoying. In addition to writing abusive letters, he retaliated by playing concertinas, horns, flutes, pianos and other musical instruments, blowing whistles, knocking on trays or boards, hammering, shrieking or shouting, so as to annoy the plaintiffs and injure their activities. *Held*—What the plaintiff and her family were doing was not an unreasonable use of the house, and could not be restrained by the adjoining tenant. However, the adjoining tenant was himself restrained from making noises to annoy the plaintiff, the court being satisfied that such noises had been made wilfully for the purpose of annoyance.

(531) *Hubbard* v. *Pitt*, [1975] 3 All E.R. 1

The defendants picketed in the road outside the offices of the plaintiff estate agents to protest against a particular property development. An interlocutory injunction was granted to restrain them from doing so. The Court of Appeal *held*—dismissing their appeal—(i) that the original ground for granting the injunction, namely, that street picketing other than in furtherance of a trade dispute was unlawful, was correct; (ii) that the balance of convenience required an injunction to be issued there being a serious issue to be tried. (*American Cyanamid Co.* case applied.)

Comment. As regards what is lawful picketing in a trade dispute, s. 15(1) of the Trade Union and Labour Relations Act, 1974, as amended by s. 16 of the Employment Act, 1980, provides: 'It shall be lawful for a person in contemplation or furtherance of a trade dispute to attend— (a) at or near his own place of work, or (b) if he is an official of a trade union, at or near the place of work of a member of that union whom he is accompanying and whom he represents, for the purpose only of peace-fully obtaining or communicating information, or peacefully persuading any person to work or abstain from working.' This provision would not appear to provide a defence if pickets approached and stopped vehicles.

Nuisance: duration of offending acts

(532) *British Celanese Ltd* v. *A.H. Hunt (Capacitors) Ltd*, [1969] 2 All E.R. 1252

The defendants allowed metal foil to escape from their land and foul the bus bars of overhead electric cables. The plaintiffs lost power and their machines were clogged up and time and material wasted. *Held*—by Lawton, J., that—

(*a*) the defendants were not liable under *Rylands* v. *Fletcher*, because there was no non-natural use of land;

(*b*) the defendants owed a duty of care to the plaintiffs and could be liable in negligence, the plaintiffs had a proprietory interest in the machines which were damaged and could recover loss flowing from that, pure economic loss was not involved;

(*c*) the defendants were liable in nuisance, an isolated happening such as this could create an actionable nuisance and the plaintiffs were directly and foreseeably affected.

Nuisance: effect of malice or evil motive

(533) *Hollywood Silver Fox Farm Ltd* v. *Emmett*, [1936] 2 K.B. 468

The plaintiffs were breeders of silver foxes and erected a notice board on their land inscribed: 'Hollywood Silver Fox Farm'. The defendant owned a neighbouring field, which he was about to develop as a building estate, and he regarded the notice board as detrimental to such devel-opment. He asked the plaintiffs to remove it, and when this request was refused, he sent his son to discharge a 12-bore gun close to the plaintiff's land, with the object of frightening the vixens during breeding. The result of this activity was that certain of the vixens did not mate at all, and others, having whelped, devoured their young. The plaintiff brought this action alleging nuisance, and the defence was that Emmett had a right to shoot as he pleased on his own land. *Held*—An injunction would be granted to restrain Emmett. His evil motive made an otherwise innocent use of land a nuisance.

Comment. (i) It seems at first sight difficult to reconcile the above case with *Bradford Corporation* v. *Pickles* (1895).[402] The difference probably is in the fact that *Hollywood Silver Fox Farm* v. *Emmett* was an action for nuisance by noise, so that the defendant's motive was relevant in establishing the tort. In *Bradford Corporation* v. *Pickles*, the action was really one for interference with a servitude or right over land, and motive was not relevant in establishing the rights of the parties.

(ii) In *Christie* v. *Davey*, 1893[530] also North, J., took into account the malice of the defendant by saying that the noise was 'made deliberately and maliciously for the purpose of annoying the plaintiff'.

Nuisance: act need not cause ill-health or diminish the value of property

(534) *Bone* v. *Seale*, [1975] 1 All E.R. 787

Over a period of 12½ years smells coming from a neighbouring pig farm owned by the defendant had caused a nuisance to properties owned by the plaintiff who claimed an injunction restraining the nuisance and damages. The judge found that no diminution in the value of the properties had resulted but granted an injunction and awarded over £6000 damages. The defendants appealed, saying, amongst other things, that the award was too high. It was *held*—by the Court of Appeal allowing the appeal against the award—that by drawing a parallel with loss of sense of smell as a result of personal injury the award was erroneous and £1000 for the plaintiff would be substituted.

Nuisance: who can sue? Who can be sued?

(535) *Malone* v. *Laskey*, [1907] 2 K.B. 141

The defendants owned a house which they leased to a firm named Witherby & Co., who sub-let it to the Script Shorthand Company. The plaintiff's husband was employed by the latter company, and was allowed to occupy the house as an emolument of his employment. A flush cistern in the lavatory of the house was unsafe, the wall brackets having been loosened by the vibration of the defendants' electric generator next door. The plaintiff told Witherby & Co. of the situation, and they communicated with the defendants who sent two of their plumbers to repair the cistern gratuitously. The work was carried out in an improper and negligent manner, and four months later the plaintiff was injured when the cistern came loose. The plaintiff sued the defendants (i) in nuisance, and (ii) in negligence. *Held*—There was no claim in nuisance against the defendants. The plaintiff was not their tenant, and in nuisance the tenant is the person to sue, not other persons present on the premises, though such persons may have a claim where the nuisance is a public nuisance. Further, there was no claim in negligence, because the defendants owed no duty of care: firstly, because there was no contractual relationship; secondly, because the defendants did not undertake any duty towards the plaintiff. They were under no obligation to carry out repairs but sent their plumbers merely as a matter of grace. This was a voluntary act and was not in any sense the discharge of a duty. The defendants were not in occupation of the premises and had not invited the plaintiff to occupy them.

Comment. The case still represents the law regarding nuisance. Regarding the claim for negligence it was overruled in *Billings* v. *Riden*, [1958] A.C. 240, where it was held that there may be liability in negligence, where premises are left in a dangerous condition by workmen so that injury results, even though the injured person is not the occupier but is a visitor to the premises.

(536) *Wilchick* v. *Marks and Silverstone*, [1934] 2 K.B. 56

Landlords who had let premises with a defective shutter, and had expressly reserved the right to enter the premises to do repairs, were *held* liable along with their tenant, to a passer-by injured by the shutter.

(537) *Mint* v. *Good*, [1951] 1 K.B. 517

Landlords were *held liable* to the infant plaintiff, who was injured when a wall on the premises, which they had let, collapsed on to the highway. They had not reserved the right to enter to do repairs, but the Court of Appeal stated that such a right must be implied, because the premises were let on weekly tenancies and it was usual to imply a right to enter to do repairs in such tenancies.

(538) *Harris* v. *James* (1876), 45 L.J.Q.B. 545

A landlord was *held* liable for the nuisance created by his tenant's blasting operations at a quarry because he had let the property for that purpose. The tenant, therefore, inevitably created a nuisance.

Comment: In *Tetley* v. *Chitty*, [1986] 1 All E.R. 663, a local authority granted a seven year lease to a go-kart club. T and others who were ratepayers living near the track obtained an injunction against the council to prevent the continuance of the nuisance by noise. Damages were an inadequate remedy.

(539) *Smith* v. *Scott*, [1972] 3 All E.R. 645

The local authority had placed in an adjoining house to the plaintiff's a family which it knew was likely to cause a nuisance but on conditions of tenancy which expressly prohibited the commission of such. These tenants had a large and unruly family and their conduct was in the words of Pennycuick, V.-C. 'Altogether intolerable both in respect of physical damage and noise.' The plaintiff and his wife, an elderly couple, found it impossible to live next door and moved away. Notwithstanding protests on the part of the plaintiff, the local authority took no effective steps to control the unruly family or to evict them. It was *held* by Pennycuick, V.-C., that, whatever the precise tests might be, it was impossible to apply the exception rendering a landlord liable for his tenants' acts in the present case. The exception was not based on cause and probable result apart from express or implied authority. The property had been let on conditions of tenancy which expressly forbade the commission of a nuisance and it would not be legitimate to say that the local authority had authorized the nuisance.

It should also be noted that the court held that the rule in *Rylands* v. *Fletcher* could not be applied and that the rights and liabilities of landowners had already been determined by the law and it was not open to the court to reshape those rights and liabilities by reference to the concept of duty of care. Thus the defendants were not liable in negligence. On the matter of *Rylands* v. *Fletcher* liability Pennycuick, V.-C., said: 'The rule in *Rylands* v. *Fletcher* was applied in *Attorney-General* v. *Corke* (see p. 833) against a defendant who brought caravan dwellers on to his land as licencees but so far as counsel has been able to ascertain the rule has never been sought to be applied against a landlord who lets his property to undesirable tenants and I do not think it can be properly applied in such a case. The person liable under the rule in *Rylands* v. *Fletcher* is the owner or controller of the dangerous "thing", and this is normally the occupier and not the owner of the land. . . . A landlord parts with possession of the demised property in favour of his tenant and could not in any sense known to the law be regarded as controlling the tenant on property still occupied by himself. I should respectfully have thought that *Attorney-General* v. *Corke* (see p. 833) could equally well have been decided on the basis that the landowner there was in possession of the property and was himself liable in nuisance for the acts of his licencees.'

Comment. It should be noted that in *O'Leary* v. *Islington London Borough Council, The Times*, 5 May, 1983 it was decided by the Court of Appeal that there was no implied term in a tenancy agreement obliging landlords to enforce a tenant's agreement not to cause nuisance to neighbours who were also their tenants, and the appropriate remedy for aggrieved tenants was to bring an action in tort against the tenant causing the nuisance.

(540) *Brew Brothers* v. *Snax (Ross)*, [1969] 3 W.L.R. 657

In June, 1965, the freehold owners of premises leased them for a term of 14 years. The lease contained covenants by the tenants regarding repairs, payment of maintenance expenses and viewing by the landlords. In November, 1966, one of the walls of the premises tilted towards the neighbouring premises which belonged to the plaintiff. It was shored up but caused an obstruction for 18 months. It appeared that the reason why the wall had tilted was the seeping of water from certain drains and the removal of a tree by the tenants. The plaintiffs sued the landlords and the tenants, and the landlords contended that the responsibility fell entirely on the tenants under the lease. *Held*—by the Court of Appeal—

(*a*) the tenants were responsible for repairing defects pointed out by the landlords but that the work required on the wall was not within the terms of the lease;

(*b*) the landlords must be presumed to know the state of the premises and were liable for nuisance in that they allowed the state of affairs to continue;

(*c*) the tenants were jointly liable in nuisance in that they failed to put the matter right, this liability was quite independent of their duties under the lease.

Nuisance: abatement

(541) *Sedleigh-Denfield* v. *O'Callagan and Others*, [1940] A.C. 880

One of the respondents (a college for training foreign missioners) was the owner of property adjoining the appellant's premises in Mill Hill. On the boundary of the property owned by the college there was a ditch and it was admitted that the ditch also belonged to the college. About 1934, when a block of flats was erected on the western side of the appellant's premises, the county council had laid a pipe and grating in the ditch but no permission was obtained and no steps were taken to inform the college authorities of the laying of the pipe. However, the presence of the pipe became known to a member of the college who was responsible for cleaning out the ditch twice a year. The council had not put a guard at the entrance to the pipe to prevent its being blocked by debris. The pipe became blocked and the appellant's garden was flooded. He claimed damages from the college on the ground that the pipe was a nuisance. *Held*—by the House of Lords—the college was liable because it appeared that they should have known about the pipe and realized the risk. Furthermore they had adopted the nuisance by using the pipe to drain their land.

Comment. This case was applied in *Page Motors* v. *Epsom and Ewell Borough Council*, (1981), 80 L.G.R. 337 where a site on an industrial estate was leased to a firm for the sale and repair of motor vehicles but was occupied by gypsies who caused a nuisance. The firm claimed damages against the council for the nuisance in the years 1973 until 1978 by which time the unauthorized gypsy caravans had all left the site. It was held by the Court of Appeal that the council was liable because they had adopted the nuisance by failing to take steps to move the gypsies on. Furthermore, the plaintiffs could recover damages for loss of business. This was a foreseeable result of having a gypsy site nearby.

Nuisance: the remedy of injunction

(542) *Kennaway* v. *Thompson*, [1980] 3 All E.R. 329

The defendants represented a club at which motorboat racing and water-skiing were carried on. In 1972 the plaintiff moved into a house which she had had built near to the lake on which the above activities were carried out, as they had been since the early 1960s. After the plaintiff moved in the nature of the club's activities increased in frequency and noise because large power boats took part in international meetings which were preceded by periods of noisy practice. The plaintiff sought damages for nuisance and an injunction but Mais, J., awarded her damages only— £1000 for the past nuisance and £15,000 in respect of future nuisance, since he regarded it as oppressive to issue an injunction to prevent the club from continuing its activities on the grounds that this was contrary to the public interest. The Court of Appeal allowed the plaintiff's appeal and awarded an injunction stating that the public interest should not prevail over the private interest of a person affected by a continuing nuisance, and accordingly the plaintiff was entitled to an injunction under which the club was ordered to curtail its activities, restricting noisy meetings to a limited number of occasions.

Nuisance: defences: prescription

(543) *Sturges* v. *Bridgman* (1879), 11 Ch. D. 852

For more than twenty years the defendant, a confectioner, had used large pestles and mortars in his premises in Wigmore Street. Then the plaintiff, a physician in Wimpole Street, built a consulting room in his garden abutting on the confectioner's premises. The noise and vibration made by the confectioner's activities interfered materially with the plaintiff's practice. He sued for an injunction to prevent the offensive activities and the defence was that the defendant had acquired a prescriptive right to commit the nuisance. *Held*—Though it was possible to acquire a right, the defendant had not done so, because the nuisance only arose when the consulting room was built.

Negligence: duty of care: the old 'two liabilities' rule

(544) *Earl* v. *Lubbock*, [1905] 1 K.B. 253

The plaintiff was employed by a firm of mineral water manufacturers, and the defendant, a wheelwright, had agreed with the plaintiff's employers that he would keep a certain number of their delivery vans in repair. The defendant failed to keep a certain van in repair, the result being that a wheel came off while the plaintiff was driving, and he suffered injuries. The plaintiff sued the defendant for negligence. *Held*—The plaintiff could not maintain an action against the defendant, since any duty the defendant had to repair the van properly was owed to the plaintiff's employer, with whom he had a contract, and not to the plaintiff.

Negligence: liability for omissions

(545) *Argy Trading Development Co. Ltd* v. *Lapid Developments Ltd*, [1977] 1 W.L.R. 444

In an under-lease for six years from 19 October, 1971 the tenant agreed to insure against fire for the full value of the premises, including two years' rent, and in the event of loss or damage by fire to reinstate the premises. In fact the landlords insured the premises under a block policy covering other property as well and the tenant paid the landlords the appropriate proportion of the premium. In 1973 there was a change in the control of the landlords and the landlords did not renew the block policy but failed to notify the tenant of its cancellation. In 1973, some months after the policy had lapsed, the premises were gutted by fire. Neither party wanted the premises, which were scheduled for redevelopment, to be reinstated. The landlords undertook not to enforce the covenant to reinstate but the tenant wished to recover damages from the landlords on the ground that it had been deprived of the insurance moneys, which it would otherwise have received, by the landlords failure to continue the insurance or to notify the tenant of its cancellation so that it had no opportunity to take out the policy. It was *held*—by Croom-Johnson, J.—that there was no implied term that the landlords would maintain their block policy or not cancel it without notifying the tenant. Nor was there any equitable estoppel such as was applied in the *High Trees* case[139] since there was no representation by the landlords intended to affect the legal relations of the parties. There was a special relationship between the parties which might have created a duty of care under the principle of *Hedley Byrne*[215] but that duty was not to *give* negligent information. The *failure* to give information which amounted to an omission was not within the principle of *Hedley Byrne*.[215]

Negligence: economic loss recoverable by way of parasitical damages

(546) *Weller & Co.* v. *Foot and Mouth Disease Research Institute*, [1965] 3 All E,R. 560

The defendants carried out experiments on their land concerning foot and mouth disease. They imported an African virus which escaped and infected cattle in the vicinity. As a consequence two cattle markets in the area had to be closed and the plaintiffs, who were auctioneers, sued for damages for loss of business. *Held*—by Widgery, J.—that so far as negligence was concerned the defendants owed no duty of care to the plaintiffs who were not cattle owners, and had no proprietary interest in anything which could be damaged by the virus. Furthermore, the defendants owed no absolute duty to the plaintiffs under *Rylands* v. *Fletcher*, 1868, because the plaintiffs had no interest in any land to which the virus could have escaped.

Comment. Had a duty of care been found, the liability in this case would have been endless. The closing of the market no doubt affected also the takings of cafes, car parks, shops, and public houses, amongst others. In spite of the decision of the House of Lords in *Junior Books*[549] it would not seem likely that the courts are yet ready to extend liability in this way.

(547) *SCM (United Kingdom) Ltd* v. *W.J. Whittall & Son Ltd*, [1970] 3
All E.R. 245

A workman employed by the defendants who were carrying out construction work near the plaintiffs' factory, cut into an underground electric cable so that the power to the plaintiffs' factory failed. The plaintiffs made typewriters and the lack of power caused molten materials to solidify in their machines which were *physically* damaged. The machines had to be stripped down and reassembled and production was brought to a halt for seven and a half hours. In the Court of Appeal the plaintiffs limited their claim to damages in respect of the physical damage to the machines and the financial loss *directly* resulting from that damage. This enabled the court to decide that the plaintiffs' property had foreseeably been damaged by the defendants' act so that the plaintiffs could recover for damage to the machines and the consequential financial loss flowing from it. Nevertheless the court went on to consider economic loss in the context of negligence and dealt in effect with the position as it might have been if the power cut had stopped production without damaging the machines. The following aspects of the judgments are important: *Per* Lord Denning, M.R.—

In actions of negligence, when the plaintiff has suffered no damage to his person or property, but has only sustained economic loss, the law does not usually permit him to recover that loss. Although the defendants owed the plaintiffs a duty of care, that did not mean that additional economic loss which was not consequent on the material damage suffered by the plaintiffs would also be recoverable; in cases such as *Weller & Co.* v. *Foot and Mouth Disease Research Institute*, 1965,[546] and *Electrochrome Ltd.* v. *Welsh Plastics Ltd*, 1968,[401] the plaintiffs did not recover for economic loss because it was too remote to be a head of damage, not because there was no duty owed to the plaintiffs or because the loss suffered in each case was not caused by the negligence of the defendants.

(*Per* Winn, L.J.)

Apart from the special case of imposition of liability for negligently uttered false statements, there is no liability for unintentional negligent infliction of any form of economic loss which is not itself consequential on foreseeable physical injury or damage to property.

Comment. The power shut-off lasted for some time and during that time the plaintiffs would normally have processed four more 'melts'; because they had been unable to do so they had lost the profits they would have made on them. However, this was regarded as economic loss not consequent upon the physical damage and therefore what was recoverable was only the loss of profit on the melt which was actually interrupted by the failure of electrical supplies.

(548) *Spartan Steel and Alloys Ltd* v. *Martin & Co. Ltd*, [1972] 3 All
E.R. 557

While digging up a road the defendants' employees damaged a cable
which the defendants knew supplied the plaintiffs' factory. The cable
belonged to the local electricity board and the resulting electrical power
failure meant that the plaintiffs' factory was deprived of electricity. The
temperature of their furnace dropped and so metal that was in melt had
to be poured away. Furthermore, while the cable was being repaired the
factory received no electricity so it was unable to function for some 14
hours. The Court of Appeal, however, allowed only the plaintiffs'
damages for the spoilt metal and the loss of profit on one 'melt'. They
refused to allow the plaintiffs to recover their loss of profit which resulted
from the factory being unable to function during the period when there
was no electricity. Lord Denning, M.R., chose to base his decision on
remoteness of damage rather than the absence of any duty of care to
avoid causing economic loss. However, he did make it clear that public
policy was involved. In the course of his judgment he said: 'At bottom
I think the question of recovering economic loss is one of policy. whenever the courts draw a line to mark out the bounds of duty, they do so
as a matter of policy so as to limit the responsibility of the defendant.
Whenever the courts set bounds to the damages recoverable—saying that
they are, or are not, too remote—they do it as a matter of policy so as
to limit the liability of the defendant.'

Negligence: economic loss: injury to person or property not always essential

(549) *Junior Books Ltd* v. *Veitchi Co. Ltd*, [1982] 3 All E.R. 201

Junior Books (J) owned a building. Veitchi (V) were flooring contractors
working under a contract for the main contractor who was doing work
on the building. There was no privity of contract between J and V. It was
alleged by J that faulty work by V left J with an unserviceable building
and high maintenance costs so that J's business became unprofitable. The
House of Lords decided in favour of J on the basis that there was a duty
of care. V were in breach of a duty owed to J to take reasonable care
to avoid acts or omissions, including laying an allegedly defective floor,
which they ought to have known would be likely to cause the owners
economic loss including loss of profits caused by the high cost of main-
taining the allegedly defective floor and, so far as J were required to
mitigate the loss by replacing the floor itself, the cost of replacement was
the appropriate measure of liability so far as this loss was concerned. The
standard of care required is apparently the contractual duty, and so long
as the work is up to contract standard, then the defendant in a case such
as this cannot be in breach of his duty. Lord Fraser of Tullybelton said:
'Where a building is erected under a contract with a purchaser, then
provided the building, or part of it, is not dangerous to persons or to

other property and subject to the law against misrepresentation, I can see no reason why the builder should not be free to make with the purchaser whatever contractual arrangements about the quality of the product the purchaser wishes. However jerry-built the product, the purchaser would not be entitled to damages from the builder if it came up to the contractual standards.'

Comment. (i) This case concerned damage to real property by alleged defective workmanship. Whether the same principle would apply to defective chattels which are unsatisfactory in their use is not absolutely certain. There would seem to be no insuperable difficulty in extending this case to chattels, but it may be some time before all the implications are known.

(ii) It should not be assumed from this case that all economic loss is recoverable. There are two main areas where economic loss is not recoverable. They are—

(*a*) where A, the owner of a ship, gives use of it to B under a contract, such as a time charter, and then the ship is damaged as a result of, say, a collision caused by the negligence of X. A can sue X because there is physical damage to A's property, the ship. B cannot recover his economic loss of profit caused by the non-availability of the ship for his cargo. (See the decision of the Privy Council in *Candlewood Navigation Corporation Ltd* v. *Mistui OSK Lines Ltd, The Times*, 9 July, 1985.)

(*b*) Where S sells good to B under an export contract and the ownership (or property) has not passed because B has not paid S, then if in transit the goods are lost or damaged by, say, the carrier's negligence, B can claim on his insurance policy but cannot sue the carrier for any economic loss which may have arisen because the goods were not available to him. This was decided by the House of Lords in *Leigh & Sillivan Ltd* v. *Aliakmon Shipping Co.*, [1986] 2 W.L.R. 902 where Lord Brandon said: '. . . there is a long line of authority for a principle of law that, in order to enable a person to claim in negligence for loss caused to him by reason of loss of or damage to property, he must have had either the legal ownership of or a possessory title to the property concerned at the time when the loss or damage occurred and it is not enough for him to have only contractual rights in relation to such property which have been adversely affected by the loss of or damage to it.'

It appears that in (*a*) and (*b*) above the risk is too wide and that at present public policy will not allow the remedy of negligence to be extended to cover it.

(iii) The effect of the decision in *Junior Books* was further whittled away in *Simaan General Contracting Co.* v. *Pilkington Glass Ltd, The Times*, 18 February, 1988. The plaintiffs (S Ltd) were the main contractors to construct a building in Abu Dhabi for a sheikh. The erection of glass walling together with supplying the glass was subcontracted to an Italian company (Feal). Feal bought the glass from the defendants

(P Ltd). The glass units should have been a uniform shade of green but some were various shades of green and some were red. The sheikh did not pay S Ltd. They chose to sue P Ltd in tort rather than Feal in contract for their loss i.e. the money the sheikh was withholding. *Held*—by the Court of Appeal—since there was no physical damage this was purely a claim for economic loss and P Ltd had no duty of care. S Ltd's claim failed. Feal would have been liable under the Supply of Goods and Services Act, 1982 (see p. 251) but for some reason were not sued. Economic loss can be recovered in contract.

Dillon L.J. said of *Junior Books* that it had 'been the subject of so much analysis and discussion that it cannot now be regarded as a useful pointer to any development of the law. It is difficult to see that future citation from *Junior Books* can ever serve any useful purpose.'

Negligence: negligent exercise of or failure to exercise a statutory power

(550) *Home Office* v. *Dorset Yacht Co. Ltd*, [1970] 2 All E.R. 294

The respondents' yacht was damaged by a number of Borstal boys who had escaped at night from an island when they were left uncontrolled by their guards. The respondents sued the Home Office for the amount of damage. *Held*—by the House of Lords—

(i) The officers guarding the boys owed a duty of care to the respondents. The fact that the boys might take nearby yachts was foreseeable. The Home Office was therefore liable vicariously for the negligence of the officers.

(ii) The fact that the Borstal was conducted under statutory authority did not warrant unreasonable acts or justify negligent conduct.

(iii) There was no ground in public policy for granting *complete* immunity from liability in negligence to the Home Office or its officers in respect of the acts of prisoners or other detainees.

(551) *Anns and Others* v. *Merton London Borough Council*, [1977] 2 All E.R. 492

Flats occupied by the plaintiffs had been built on inadequate foundations. This led to walls cracking and other damage. The plaintiffs sued the local authority alleging negligence and failing to carry out a statutory power of inspection and approval of the foundations. The local authority said that they were not under a duty to inspect and could not, therefore, be held liable. The House of Lords decided that the local authority's failure to address itself to a proper exercise of its public health functions and powers was *ultra vires* and that if, as alleged, in this case, that failure was negligent, there could be liability.

Negligence: breach of duty: behaviour as a reasonable man

(552) *Daniels* v. *R. White and Sons Ltd*, [1938] 4 All E.R. 258

The plaintiffs, who were husband and wife, sued the first defendants, who were manufacturers of mineral waters, in negligence. The plaintiffs had been injured because a bottle of the first defendants' lemonade, which they had purchased from a public house in Battersea, contained carbolic acid, presumably from the bottle-washing plant. Evidence showed that the manufacturer took all possible care to see that no injurious matter got into the lemonade. It was *held* that the manufacturers were not liable in negligence because the duty was not one to ensure that the goods were in perfect condition but only to take reasonable care to see that no injury was caused to the eventual consumer. This duty had been fulfilled.

(553) *Hill* v. *J. Crowe (Cases), The Times*, 19 May, 1977

The plaintiff was injured when he stood on a packing case whose boards collapsed causing him to fall. It was *held*—by MacKenna, J.—that the case had been badly made and the manufacturers owed a duty of care to the plaintiff. They could not escape liability by showing that they had a good system of work and proper supervision. *Daniels* v. *White and Sons*, (1938)[552] was not followed.

(554) *Greaves & Co. (Contractors)* v. *Baynham Meikle & Partners*, [1974] 3 All E.R. 666

The plaintiff, a builder, was instructed to build a warehouse and sub-contracted its structural design to the defendants who were a firm of consultant structural engineers. B knew, or by reason of the relevant British Standard Code of Practice, ought to have known, that as the warehouse was to carry loaded trucks there was a danger of vibration. The design was competent but inadequate for the purpose of carrying the trucks and it was *held*—by Kilner Brown, J., allowing the plaintiff's claim for breach of duty of care and breach of an implied term of the contract—that the duty of the defendants was not simply to exercise the care and skill of a competent engineer which they had done, but to design a building fit for its purpose in the light of the knowledge which they had as to its proposed use.

(555) *Paris* v. *Stepney Borough Council*, [1951] A.C. 367

The plaintiff was employed by the defendants on vehicle maintenance. He had the use of only one eye and the defendants were aware of this. The plaintiff was endeavouring to remove a bolt from the chassis of a vehicle, and was using a hammer for the purpose, when a chip of metal flew into his good eye so that he became totally blind. The plaintiff claimed damages from his employers for negligence in that he had not been supplied with goggles. The defendants showed in evidence that it was not the usual practice in trades of this nature to supply goggles, at least where the employees were men with two good eyes. The trial judge found for the plaintiff, but the Court of Appeal reversed the decision on the grounds that the plaintiff's disability could be relevant only if it increased the risk, i.e. if a one-eyed man was more likely to get a splinter in his eye than a two-eyed man. Having found that the risk was not increased they allowed the appeal. The House of Lords reversed the judgment of the Court of Appeal, holding that the gravity of the harm likely to be caused would influence a reasonable employer, so that the duty of care to a one-eyed employee required the supply of goggles, and Paris therefore succeeded.

(556) *Haley* v. *London Electricity Board*, [1964] 3 All E.R. 185

The appellant, Haley, a blind man who was on his way to his work as a telephonist, tripped over an obstacle placed by servants of the London Electricity Board near the end of a trench excavated in the pavement of a street in Woolwich. He fell and suffered an injury which rendered him deaf, and brought about his premature retirement from his employment. The guard was sufficient warning for sighted people but was by its nature inadequate to protect or warn the blind. It consisted of a hammer hooked in the railings and resting on the pavement at an angle of thirty degrees, and Haley's white stick, which he was properly using as a guide, did not encounter the obstacle with the result that instead of warning him he fell over it. Evidence was given that about one in five hundred people were blind and there were 258 registered blind people in Woolwich, many of whom were capable of walking in the streets alone, taking the normal precautions such blind persons were accustomed to take. The House of Lords *held*, reversing the decision of the Court of Appeal, that the London Electricity Board were liable in negligence. Those engaged in operations on the pavement of a highway must act reasonably to prevent danger to passers-by including blind people who must, however, also take reasonable care of themselves. The Board had not fulfilled this duty and were liable in damages for negligence which were assessed at £3000 general damages, and £2250 special damages, Haley's retirement being accelerated by four years.

(557) *Watt* v. *Hertfordshire County Council*, [1954] 2 All E.R. 368

A fireman was injured by a heavy jack which slipped while being carried in a lorry which was going to the scene of an accident. The lorry was not equipped to carry such a heavy jack but it was required to free a woman who had been trapped in the wreckage. No proper vehicle was available and it was *held* that the fire authority was not liable.

(558) *Latimer* v. *AEC Ltd*, [1953] 2 All E.R. 449

A heavy rainstorm flooded a factory and made the floor slippery. The occupiers of the factory did all they could to get rid of the water and make the factory safe, but the plaintiff fell and was injured. He alleged

negligence in that the occupiers did not close down the factory. *Held*—
the occupiers of the factory were not liable. The risk of injury did not
justify the closing down of the factory.

Negligence: *res ipsa loquitur*

(559) *Easson* v. *L.N.E. Railway Co.*, [1944] 1 All E.R. 246

The plaintiff, a boy aged four years, fell through the open door of a
corridor train seven miles from its last stopping place. It was *held* that
the defendants did not have sufficient control over the doors for *res ipsa
loquitur* to apply. In the course of his judgment Goddard, L.J., said: 'It
is impossible to say that the doors of an express corridor train travelling
from Edinburgh to London are continuously under the sole control of the
railway company . . . passengers are walking up and down the corridors
during the journey and get in and out at stopping places. The fact that
the door came open could as well have been due to interference by a
passenger as to the negligence of the defendants' servants.'

(560) *Byrne* v. *Boadle* (1863), 2 H. & C. 722

The plaintiff brought an action in negligence alleging that, as he was
walking past the defendant's shop, a barrel of flour fell from a window
above the shop and injured him. The defendant was a dealer in flour, but
there was no evidence that the defendant or any of his servants were
engaged in lowering the barrel of flour at the time. The defendant
submitted that there was no evidence of negligence to go to the jury, but
it was *held* that the occurrence was of itself evidence of negligence
sufficient to entitle the jury to find for the plaintiff, even in the absence
of an explanation by the defendant.

(561) *Scott* v. *London and St Katherine Docks Co.* (1865), 3 H. & C. 596

The plaintiff, a Customs officer, proved that when he was passing in front
of the defendant's warehouse six bags of sugar fell upon him. It was *held*
that the maxim *res ipsa loquitur* applied. In the course of his judgment
Erle, C.J., said: '. . . where the thing is shown to be under the management of the defendant, or his servants, and the accident is such as, in the
ordinary course of things, does not happen if those who have the
management use proper care, it affords reasonable evidence, in the
absence of explanation by the defendant, that the accident arose from
want of care.'

Comment. This case was followed in *Ward* v. *Tesco Stores*, [1976] All
E.R. 219, where the Court of Appeal held that an accident which had
occurred due to a spillage of yoghourt on a shop floor put an evidential
burden upon the defendant shopowners to show that the accident did not
occur through any want of care on their part. They were not able to
satisfy that burden and the plaintiff succeeded.

(562) *Roe* v. *Minister of Health*, [1954] 2 Q.B. 66

Two patients in a hospital had operations on the same day. Both operations were of a minor character and in each case nupercaine, a spinal anaesthetic, was injected by means of a lumbar puncture. The injections were given by a specialist anaesthetist, assisted by the theatre staff of the hospital. The nupercaine had been contained in sealed glass ampoules, stored in a solution of phenol. After the operations both patients developed symptoms of spastic paraplegia caused by the phenol, which had contaminated the nupercaine by penetrating almost invisible cracks in the ampoules. In the event, both patients became permanently paralysed from the waist down, and they now sued the defendants for negligence. *Held*—The defendants were vicariously liable for the negligence (if any) of those concerned with the operations, but on the standard of medical knowledge in 1947, when the operations took place, those concerned were not negligent. The cracks in the ampoules were not visible on ordinary examination, and could not be reproduced even by deliberate experiment. It was true that in 1954, when the case was brought, phenol used for disinfectant purposes was tinted so that it might be seen on examination, but the case must be decided on medical knowledge at the time when the operations were carried out. It was also suggested that once the accident has been explained, there is no question of *res ipsa loquitur* applying. Nor does the maxim apply when many persons might have been negligent. Denning, L.J., suggested that every surgical operation is attended by risk, and one cannot take the benefits of surgery without accepting the risks. Doctors, like the rest of us, have to learn by experience. Further, one must not condemn as negligence that which is only misadventure.

(563) *Pearson* v. *North-Western Gas Board*, [1968] 2 All E.R. 669

The plaintiff's husband was killed by an explosion of gas which also destroyed her house. It appeared from the evidence that a gas main had fractured due to a movement of earth caused by a severe frost. When the weather was very cold the defendants had men standing by ready to deal with reports of gas leaks, but unless they received reports there was no way of predicting or preventing a leak which might lead to an explosion. *Held*—by Rees, J.—that assuming the principle of *res ipsa loquitur* applied, the defendants had rebutted the presumption of negligence and the plaintiff's case failed.

Contributory negligence: some decisions on particular facts

(564) *O'Connell* v. *Jackson*, [1971] 3 All E.R. 129

The defendant, who was driving a car, came out of a minor road on to a major road and collided with the plaintiff who was riding a moped. The plaintiff was thrown on to the road and suffered severe head injuries.

Medical evidence showed that if the plaintiff had been wearing a crash helmet his injuries would have been much reduced. *Held*—the plaintiff's damages would be reduced by 15 per cent. Although it was accepted and admitted that the defendant was solely responsible for the accident, one must always take into account the possibility of others being careless, and by not wearing a crash helmet the plaintiff had contributed to the harm suffered.

(565) *Jones* v. *Lawrence*, [1969] 3 All E.R. 267

A boy aged seven years and three months ran out from behind a parked van across a road apparently without looking in order to get to a fun fair. He was knocked down by Lawrence who was travelling on his motorcycle at fifty miles per hour in a built-up area. The boy's injuries adversely affected his school work and he subsequently failed his eleven-plus examination. In action on his behalf for damages it was *held* by Cumming-Bruce, J.—that

(*a*) his conduct was only that to be expected of a seven-year-old child and could not amount to contributory negligence;

(*b*) the failure to obtain a grammar-school place and the permanent impairment of his powers of concentration affected his job attainment potential and were factors to be taken into account in assessing damages.

(566) *Oliver* v. *Birmingham Bus Co.*, [1932] 1 K.B. 35

A grandfather was walking with his grandchild aged four, when a bus approached quickly and without warning. The grandfather, being startled, let go the child's hand and the bus struck the child. It was *held* that the damages awarded to the child should not be reduced to take account of the grandfather's negligence.

Negligence: actions based on breach of statutory duty

(567) *Atkinson* v. *Newcastle and Gateshead Waterworks Co.* (1877), L.R. 2 Ex. D. 441

The plaintiff's timber yard caught fire and was destroyed, there being insufficient water in the mains to put it out. The defendants were required by the Waterworks Clauses Act, 1874, to maintain a certain pressure of water in their water pipes, and the Act provided a penalty of £10 for failure to keep the required pressure and 40s, for each day during which the neglect continued, the sums being payable to aggrieved ratepayers. The plaintiff sued the defendants for loss caused by the fire on the ground that they were in breach of a statutory duty regarding the pressure in the pipes. *Held*—The defendants were not liable. The statute did not disclose a cause of action by individuals for damage of this kind. It was most improbable that the legislature intended the company to be gratuitous insurers against fire of all the buildings in Newcastle.

(568) *Gorris* v. *Scott* (1874), L.R. 9 Exch. 125

A statutory order placed a duty on the defendant to supply pens of a specified size in those parts of a ship's deck occupied by animals. The defendant did not supply the pens, and sheep belonging to the plaintiff were swept overboard. The plaintiff claimed damages from the defendant for breach of statutory duty. *Held*—The plaintiff could not recover for his loss under breach of statutory duty, because the object of the statutory order was to prevent the spread of disease, not to prevent animals from being drowned.

Mis-statements: fraudulent mis-statements as to credit: Lord Tenterden's Act, 1828

(569) *Anderson (W.B.) and Sons* v. *Rhodes (Liverpool)*, [1967] 2 All E.R. 850

The plaintiff and the first defendant were wholesalers in the Liverpool fruit and vegetable market. In April, 1965, the manager of a newly formed company bought some potatoes for cash from Rhodes & Co. and later purchased potatoes from them on credit. The manager of Rhodes & Co. made no credit inquiries about the new company. The market rule was that payment should be made within seven days of invoice but at all material times substantial amounts were overdue as between Rhodes & Co. and the new company, but the salesman and buyer of Rhodes & Co. were not informed of this fact. Rhodes & Co. also acted from time to time as commission agents and their buyer, a man called Reid, later arranged sales on a commission basis between the new company and the plaintiffs. Reid represented orally to the plaintiffs that the new company was creditworthy and he acted throughout in good faith. The plaintiffs supplied goods on credit to the new company which then became insolvent and could not pay its debts. The plaintiffs sued Rhodes & Co. for negligence in representing that the new company was creditworthy. *Held*—by Cairns, J.—that the plaintiffs were entitled to recover damages against Rhodes & Co. because—

(i) Rhodes & Co. owed a duty of care to the plaintiffs in respect of Reid's representations acting as their servant or agent (*Hedley Byrne*[215] applied);

(ii) Rhodes & Co. were vicariously liable for the negligence of their manager who knew that the new company was not creditworthy even though Reid and not the manager made the representation;

(iii) Section 6 of the Statute of Frauds Amendment Act (Lord Tenterden's Act), was not a defence to a claim based on negligence as distinct from fraud.

Negligent statements: from knowledge to foresight

(570) *Candler* v. *Crane, Christmas & Co.*, [1951] 2 K.B. 164

The defendants, a firm of accountants and auditors, prepared the accounts and balance sheet of a limited company at the request of its managing director, knowing that they were required to induce the plaintiff to invest money in the company. The plaintiff, relying on the accounts, invested £2000 in the company. It was alleged that the accounts were negligently prepared and failed to give an accurate picture of the company's financial state in that certain leases shown as assets of the company either did not belong to it, but to its managing director, or had been forfeited for non-payment of rent. It was alleged that the auditors did not seek evidence as to the ownership of these leases. The company was wound up within a year and the plaintiff lost his money. He now sued the accountants in negligence. The Court of Appeal *held* that, in the absence of a contractual or fiduciary relationship between the parties, the defendants owed no duty of care to the plaintiff in preparing the accounts. Denning, L.J., thought that the defendants might be held liable because they knew that the accounts were to be shown to the plaintiff, though he would not have found them liable to complete strangers.

In his judgment, Denning, L.J., said: 'I think the law would fail to serve the best interests of the community if it should hold that accountants and auditors owe a duty to no-one but their client. There is a great difference between the lawyer and the accountant. The lawyer is never called on to express his personal belief in the truth of his client's case, whereas the accountant, who certifies the accounts of his client, is always called on to express his personal opinion whether the accounts exhibit a true and correct view of his client's affairs, and he is required to do this not so much for the satisfaction of his own client, but more for the guidance of shareholders, investors, revenue authorities and others who may have to rely on the accounts in serious matters of business. In my opinion, accountants owe a duty of care not only to their own clients, but also to all those whom they know will rely on their accounts in the transactions for which those accounts are prepared.'

(571) *Clayton* v. *Woodman & Son (Builders) Ltd and Others*, [1961] 3 All E.R. 249

The plaintiff was a bricklayer employed by the first defendants, Woodman & Son, a firm of builders. The builders had entered into a contract with the second defendants, a regional hospital board, to install a lift at a hospital. The work was carried out in accordance with the instructions given by a firm of architects who were made third defendants. An architect employed by the third defendants allowed the plaintiff to cut a chase or wide groove in an unsupported gable. This had the effect of weakening the gable and the architect should have known that it would fall if not supported. The plaintiff cut the chase, and the gable collapsed and injured him. The question of the liability of each of the defendants arose. At first instance Salmon, J., *held*—(*a*) The first defendants (the builders) were liable for negligence at common law because they had failed to provide a safe system of work. They were also liable for breach of their statutory duty under the Building (Safety, Health and Welfare) Regulations, 1948. (*b*) The second defendants (the hospital authorities) were not liable. They were not in breach of their duty under the Occupiers' Liability Act, 1957. Further, they were not vicariously liable for the negligence of the architect since he was an independent contractor. (*c*) The architects were liable. The decision in *Candler* v. *Crane, Christmas & Co.* (1951)[570] did not apply, because the architect was not making careless mis-statements, but was giving careless orders or instructions, and in any case the injury here was physical not financial.

Comment. In *Clayton* v. *Woodman & Sons (Builders) Ltd and Others*, [1962] 2 All E.R. 33, the Court of Appeal reversed the part of the above decision which found the architect liable, saying that the question of his liability did not arise for decision because: (*a*) The architect had not given orders to the bricklayer. All he had done was to refuse to allow the gable to be demolished, and he was bound to do this because he had instructions to preserve certain features of the building of which the gable was one. The cutting of the chase followed from that refusal. (*b*) From then on it was the duty of the plaintiff's employers to provide a safe system of doing the job, and they were solely responsible.

(572) *Mutual Life Assurance* v. *Evatt*, [1971] 1 All E.R. 152

Evatt had made certain investments in P. Ltd and wished to know whether he should retain these investments or expand them. P. Ltd and the assurance company were both subsidiaries of the same holding company, the only relationship between Evatt and the assurance company being that Evatt was one of their policy holders. On the basis of that and the assurance company's personal knowledge of P. Ltd's affairs Evatt sought the assurance company's advice as to P. Ltd's financial prospects. The advice was given, without any disclaimer, and Evatt invested accordingly. Soon afterwards the investments fell in value and Evatt claimed that the advice was given negligently. It was *held*—by the Judicial Committee of the Privy Council (Lords Reid and Morris dissenting) that there was no cause of action. The liability in the *Hedley Byrne* case was limited to persons who held themselves out as being skilled in the subject matter of the inquiry and, since it was no part of the business of an insurance company to give advice on the financial position of other companies the appeal was allowed.

It would not in their Lordships' view be consonant with the principles hereto accepted in the common law that the duty to comply with that objective standard should be extended to an advisor who, at the time when his advice is sought, has not let it be known to the advisee that he claims to possess the standard of skill and competence and is prepared to exercise diligence which is generally shown by persons who carry on the business of giving advice of the kind sought. He has given the advisee no reason to suppose that he is acquainted with the standard or capable of complying with it, or that he has such appreciation of the nature and magnitude of the loss which the advisee may sustain by reason of any failure by that advisor to attain that standard as a reasonable man would require before assuming a liability to answer for the loss. (*Per* Lord Diplock.)

Comment. It is interesting to note that even Lords Reid and Morris accepted that there should be no liability for advice, even if given by a person in business to advise, where the advice was given casually or socially.

(573) *Esso Petroleum* v. *Mardon*, [1976] 2 All E.R. 5

In this case it was held that the principle in *Hedley Byrne*[215] could apply even where the parties concerned were in a pre-contractual relationship, and, in addition, that the person who made the statement need not necessarily be in business to give advice. Mr Mardon was awarded damages for a negligent mis-statement by a senior sales representative of Esso in regard to the amount of petrol he could expect to sell per year from a petrol station which he was leasing from Esso. The facts of *Mardon* pre-dated the Misrepresentation Act, 1967 and the judge could not use it. The decision is obviously important, but where the facts have occurred since 1967, the Misrepresentation Act is likely to prove more popular to plaintiffs since they can ask the representor to show that he is not negligent. In *Hedley Byrne* claims the burden of proof is on the plaintiff to prove negligence. However, the fact that *Hedley Byrne* can be used in a pre-contractual relationship is of some importance because where there is a breach of contract, time, under the Limitation Act, runs from the breach, but in tort from the cause of action. Thus, for example, an accountant could be liable under *Mardon* even in retirement for accounts which were prepared in his first year of practice if the cause of action arose in tort from a person who relied upon them.

Comment. The senior sales representative was not a person who was in business to advise and yet he was held liable for a negligent statement and rendered his employer, Esso, vicariously liable. The advice was, of course, given in the way of business and was in no sense casual or social.

(574) *JEB Fasteners Ltd* v. *Marks Bloom & Co.*, [1981] 3 All E.R. 289

The plaintiff bought the entire share capital of a company called B G Fasteners in June 1975. He claimed to have relied on the audited accounts of the company for the year ended 31 October, 1974 prepared by the defendants who were the company's auditors and a firm of chartered accountants. The plaintiff alleged that the accounts did not give a true and fair view of the state of the company although they were given an unqualified audit certificate and that in consequence the plaintiff suffered loss because he had purchased a company which was not worth what it appeared from the accounts to be worth. Mr Justice Woolf (and later the Court of Appeal [1983] 1 All E.R. 583) held that the auditors owed a duty of care to the plaintiff but judgment was given for the defendants because the judge took the view that on the evidence the plaintiff would still have bought the company, even if the true position of the accounts had been known since the real object was to acquire the services of two directors in B G Fasteners. Thus the defendants' alleged negligence was not in fact the cause of the plaintiff's loss. The most significant part of the case, because it represents a broadening of the 'special relationship' concept set out in the *Hedley Byrne*[215] case, is that the judge found that a legal duty of care existed and was owed by the auditors to a person who was a complete stranger to them at the time of the audit and whom they did not know was intending to rely on the accounts which they produced.

However, the accountants must be regarded as foreseeing that B G Fasteners would require funds before the next accounts were prepared. It was therefore foreseeable that persons such as lenders of money, investors in the company's share capital, or those contemplating a take-over bid, might rely on the accounts.

Comment. An auditor owes no duty of care to a take-over bidder unless he already owns shares in the victim company. If he does not, there is no duty or liability for loss in the auditor of the victim company. (*Caparo Industries plc* v. *Dickman, The Times* 5 August 1988). This is a further retreat from *Anns*.[551]

Negligent statements: immunity: valuer or arbitrator

(575) *Sutcliffe* v. *Thackrah*, [1974] 1 All E.R. 859

The plaintiff had acquired a site and wished to have a house built on it. The defendants, a firm of architects, were employed to prepare designs. There was no formal contract but the defendants knew that builders would be employed under the RIBA form of contract and that they would be the architects supervising construction. The plaintiff entered into a contract with builders for the construction of the house. Under a clause in that contract the parties agreed, amongst other things, that at intervals which were specified the architects should issue interim certificates stating how much was due to the builders in respect of work properly executed and that the plaintiff would within 14 days pay the amounts so stated. There were delays in completion of the house. A number of interim certificates were issued to the builders by the defendants and the plaintiff paid the sums certified. Later the plaintiff terminated the builders' contract for reasons which it was accepted were sufficient. The builders later became insolvent. The plaintiff brought an action against the defendants claiming damages for negligence and breach of duty in the following respects—

(i) in the course of supervising the building, and

(ii) in certifying, in two of the interim certificates, for work not done or improperly done by the builders.

The Court of Appeal held that in issuing interim certificates, the defendants were acting in an arbitral capacity and provided they acted honestly were not therefore under any duty to the plaintiff to exercise care or professional skill. The plaintiff appealed to the House of Lords where it was *held*—

(i) that although every case depended on its own facts and on the particular provisions of the relevant contract, in general any architect or valuer would be liable to the person who employed him if he caused loss by reason of his negligence, but as an exception to that rule, immunity would be accorded to the architect or valuer if he could show that, by agreement, he had been appointed to act as an arbitrator or quasi-arbitrator, i.e. that he had been appointed to determine a specific dispute submitted to him, or define differences that might arise in the future, and there was agreement that his decision would be binding. Where, however a professional man was employed to make a valuation and, to his knowledge, that valuation was to be binding on his principal and another party under an agreement between them, it did not follow that, because he was under a duty to act fairly in making his valuation, he was acting in a judicial capacity and was therefore immune from liability to his principal for loss caused to him by a negligent valuation;

(ii) that the defendants were not immune from liability to the plaintiff for their negligent over-certification because (*a*) the giving of an interim certificate was not the decision of a dispute between the plaintiff and the builders, (*b*) there was no agreement to abide by the decision of the defendants as to the value of the work done, and (*c*) the defendants owed a duty to the plaintiff to exercise care and skill in the giving of certificates. The fact that the plaintiff became obliged to pay the amount certified by the defendants did not place them in the position of arbitrators; nor did the fact that the defendants could only properly perform their duties if they acted fairly as between the plaintiff and the builders.

Accordingly, the plaintiff's appeal would be allowed.

Negligent statements: to be actionable the statement must be in the nature of advice

(576) *McInerny* v. *Lloyds Bank*, [1973] 2 Ll. Rep. 389

P wished to sell his business to M. Payment was to be made over a period of time by P drawing bills of exchange on M. M asked Lloyds Bank to guarantee payment of the bills but they wrote to him saying that English banking regulations precluded guarantees by the bank of the payment of trade debts. They went on to say that they would establish irrevocable credit by an alternative method and stating that 'I think . . . P ought to be satisfied with this' and that the bank had 'agreed in principle to the amended terms of credit which we will not finally establish, under the advice to P from Barclays Bank until we receive your confirmation of the exact amount due on 3 March, 1968'. M asked the bank to send a copy of this letter to P and on the basis of it P signed the contract with M relying, so he said, on the fact that the bank was in some way to back the bills drawn on M. Later M failed to honour some of the bills of exchange. *Held*—by Kerr, J., that—

(i) it was impossible to infer any contract between the bank and P from the circumstances or their conduct and in any event no consideration in respect of such a contract had moved from P;

(ii) since it was unlikely that P would consider the sentence indicating that he should be satisfied as advice to him and since the whole contents of the letter were merely to inform P of the action the bank were prepared to take, there was no misrepresentation for the purposes of the rule in *Hedley Byrne* v. *Heller & Partners*, 1963.[215] The court should give great weight to the fact that the contents of the statement were primarily prepared for the purposes of and addressed to someone else; and

(iii) accordingly P's claim against the bank failed in contract and tort.

Occupiers' liability: two or more occupiers

(577) *Wheat* v. *E. Lacon & Co. Ltd*, [1966] 1 All E.R. 582

The manager of a public house was permitted by the owners, Lacon & Co., to take paying visitors who were accommodated in a part of the premises labelled 'Private'. The plaintiff's husband, while a paying visitor, was killed by a fall from a staircase in the private part of the premises. Lacon & Co. denied liability on the ground that they were not occupiers of the private part of the premises. *Held*—by the House of Lords—

(i) that the defendants retained occupation and control together with the manager;

(ii) the deceased was a visitor to whom the defendants owed a common duty of care;

(iii) on the facts the staircase, though not lit, was not dangerous if used with proper case.

Wheat's claim therefore failed because there was no breach of the duty of care.

Occupiers' liability: defective work of an independent contractor

(578) *Cook* v. *Broderip*, (1968), 112 S.J. 193

The owner of a flat employed an apparently competent contractor to put in a new socket. Mrs Cook, who was a cleaner, received an electric shock caused because the socket was faulty. It appeared that the contractor had negligently failed to test the socket for reversed polarity. *Held*—by O'Connor, J.—that Major Broderip, the owner of the flat, was not vicariously liable for the contractor's negligence and was not in breach of duty under the Occupiers' Liability Act, 1957. Damages of £3081 were awarded against the contractor who was the second defendant.

Comment. On the issue of inspection of the work done, the House of Lords stated in *Ferguson* v. *Welsh, The Times,* 30 October, 1987 that it would not ordinarily be reasonable to expect an occupier, having engaged a contractor, whom he believed on reasonable grounds to be competent, to supervise the contractor's activities. If he knew, however, that an unsafe system was being used it might be reasonable for the occupier to take steps to see that things were made safe. If not, he might be liable.

Occupiers' liability: effect of plaintiff's knowledge of danger

(579) *Bunker* v. *Charles Brand & Son,* [1969] 2 All E.R. 59

The plaintiff's employers were engaged as sub-contractors by the defendants who were the main contractors for tunnelling in connection with the Victoria Line. The plaintiff was required to carry out modifications to a digging machine. He had seen the machine *in situ* and was taken to have appreciated the danger in crossing its rollers when in operation. He was injured while attempting to cross the rollers in the course of his work and sued for damages. *Held*—by O'Connor, J.—that the defendants having retained control of the tunnel and the machine were the occupiers. They were not absolved from liability under the Act of 1957 merely because of the plaintiff's knowledge of the danger. Knowledge was not assent. However, the plaintiff's damages were reduced by 50 per cent on the ground of his contributory negligence.

Comment. It was held in *Salmon* v. *Seafarer Restaurants Ltd,* [1983] 3 All E.R. 729 that an occupier owes a duty to firemen attending his premises to put out a fire. A fire occurred in the defendants' fish and chip shop because of the negligence of an employee. The employee failed to turn off a gas heater prior to closing the shop. The plaintiff fireman was injured when attending the fire. The Court said that the defendants were vicariously liable. It was foreseeable that a fireman might be injured following the employee's negligence.

Occupier's liability and negligence liability: the special case of children

(580) *Yachuk* v. *Oliver Blais & Co. Ltd,* [1949] A.C. 386

In this appeal from the Supreme Court of Canada to the Judicial Committee of the Privy Council the facts were as follows: a servant of Oliver Blais & Co. Ltd had supplied five cents' worth of gasoline in an open lard pail to certain boys, aged nine and seven, who told him that they needed it for their mother's car, which had run out of petrol down the road. In fact they wanted it for a game of Red Indians. The boys dipped a bullrush into the pail and lit it. This set fire to the petrol in the pail and the boy Yachuk was seriously injured. The Judicial Committee *held* that the company was liable for the negligence of its servant in allowing the boys to take away the gasoline. The question of contributory negligence did not arise, because there was no evidence that the infants appreciated the dangerous quality of gasoline. The company was fully responsible even though the boys had resorted to deceit to overcome the supplier's scruples.

(581) *Gough* v. *National Coal Board*, [1954] 1 Q.B. 191

The defendants were owners of a colliery which included a small railway which was constantly in use. The railway lines were not fenced or guarded, although there were houses on both sides. The public had for a long time been permitted to cross the lines, and children often played on the wagons, although the defendants' servants had been told to keep children off. The plaintiff, a boy aged six and a half, was seriously injured when he jumped off a wagon on which he had been riding. At the trial the boy admitted that he knew he was not supposed to ride on the wagons, and that his father had threatened to punish him if he did. Nevertheless it was *held* that the defendants were liable. The fact that children had for many years played near the railway made them licensees, and although the boy was strictly speaking a trespasser as regards the wagon, he was allured by the slow-moving wagons which the defendants knew were an attraction to children.

(582) *Mourton* v. *Poulter*, [1930] 2 K.B. 183

The owner of certain land wished to carry out building operations on it, but before he could so do, it was necessary to fell a large elm tree. The land was unfenced, and children of the locality were in the habit of using it as a playground. During the process of felling, a large number of children gathered near the tree, and Poulter, who had been employed to fell the tree, warned the children of the danger likely to arise when the tree came down. He failed to repeat the warning when the tree was about to fall, and the plaintiff, a boy of ten, was crushed by the falling tree. *Held*—The defendant was liable. Even though the children were trespassers, he owed them a duty to give adequate warning.

(583) *Pannett* v. *McGuinness & Co.*, [1972] 3 All E.R. 137

The defendants were demolishing a warehouse in a heavily populated area near a park where children played. Three workmen were specially appointed to make a bonfire of rubbish and to keep a lookout for children and to see that they came to no harm. The plaintiff, a boy of five, got in while the three men were away and was severely burned. The men had frequently chased children away in the past and in particular the plaintiff on a number of occasions. The contractors contended that the plaintiff was a trespasser, that he had been warned off and that they were under no duty. *Held*—the contractors were in breach of the duty of care owed to the child, their workmen had failed to keep a proper look out.

Comment. Penny v. *Northampton Borough Council*, (1974), 72 L.G.R. 733, provides a contrast. In that case a child trespasser was not successful in recovering damages following injury from an aerosol can which exploded when it was thrown into a fire by another child. The accident took place in a discarded rubbish tip some 50 acres in area which resembled a rough field. The children had often been warned off the land by the council's workmen. The court considered the authority had behaved with commonsense and humanity and could not have known of the danger on the land so that it had discharged its duty of care. However, in *Harris* v. *Birkenhead Corporation*, [1975] 1 All E.R. 1001, a local authority was not successful in showing that it had discharged its duty of care to a child trespasser who had entered a derelict house which the Corporation had purchased under a compulsory purchase order. The child fell from an upstairs window and the authority was held to be the occupier since the previous owner had got out of the premises in view of the order. The authority was fixed with knowledge of the relevant facts and Kilner Brown, J., found for the plaintiff.

Highways Act, 1980: no defence unless authority has done what was reasonably required

(584) *Griffiths* v. *Liverpool Corporation*, [1966] 2 All E.R. 1015

The plaintiff tripped and fell on a flagstone which rocked on its centre. In this action against the highway authority for breach of s. 1(1) of the Highways (Miscellaneous Provisions) Act, 1961 (see now Highways Act, 1980), it appeared that a regular system of inspection was desirable but was not carried out because the authority could not get tradesmen to put right faults discovered. The present fault could, however, have been put right by a labourer and no shortage of labourers was alleged. *Held*—by the Court of Appeal—the authority had not brought itself within the statutory defence in s. 1(2) and damages should be awarded.

Comment. In *Pridham* v. *Hemel Hempstead Corporation* (1970), 69 L.G.R. 525 the authority proved that it had inspected the footpath of a minor residential road every three months and had kept a complaints book. The Court of Appeal held that this excluded the authority from liability for injury caused by a defect in the footpath.

Employer's negligence: effect of statutory duties of care

(585) *Millard* v. *Serck Tubes Ltd*, [1969] 1 All E.R. 598

The plaintiff operated a power drill during the course of his employment. The drill was fenced, but the guard was not complete in that there was a gap in it through which the operator's hand could be drawn. While the plaintiff's hand was resting on the guard a piece of swarf thrown out from the drill wound itself around the plaintiff's hand and drew it into the drill causing injury to the plaintiff. The defendant employers conceded that the drill had not been properly fenced but contended that they were not liable because the accident itself was unforeseeable. This defence was rejected by the Court of Appeal and the plaintiff succeeded in his claim for damages. Where a defendant has failed to fence dangerous machinery, as here, in breach of s. 14 of the Factories Act, 1961, he cannot escape liability for injury on the grounds that such injury occurred in a way that was not reasonably foreseeable. Thus a plaintiff might succeed when suing on a statutory duty and fail if suing on a common law one.

Torts against business interests: inducing a breach of contract

(586) *Lumley* v. *Gye* (1853), 2 E. & Bl. 216

The plaintiff, who was the manager of an opera house, made a contract with a *prima donna* Johanna Wagner for her exclusive services for a period of time. Gye induced Johanna Wagner to break her operatic engagement with the plaintiff and sing for him. It was *held* that whatever might have been the origin of the right to sue in such cases as this, it was not now confined to actions by masters for the enticement of their servants but extended to wrongful interference with any contract of personal service.

(587) *Daily Mirror Newspapers* v. *Gardner*, [1968] 2 All E.R. 163

The executive committee of the retailers' federation recommended their members to boycott the *Daily Mirror* for one week after that newspaper had announced that the retailers' discount rate was to be reduced when the price of the newspaper was increased. The newspaper asked for interlocutory injunctions requiring the committee to communicate with their members and withdraw the recommendation on the grounds—

(i) that it was an unlawful interference with the newspaper's contracts with the wholesalers because the wholesalers would not want to take copies of the *Daily Mirror* if the retailers would not take it; and
(ii) that it was equivalent to an agreement contrary to the public interest within s. 21(1) of the Restrictive Trades Practices Act, 1956 (see now the Restrictive Trades Practices Act, 1976).

Held—by the Court of Appeal—that a sufficient *prima facie* case had been made out on both grounds and the injunctions would be granted.

Civil conspiracy: the principles illustrated

(588) *Crofter Hand Woven Harris Tweed Co. Ltd* v. *Veitch*, [1942] A.C. 435

Veitch and the other defendants were officials of the Transport and General Workers Union. The dockers at Stornaway on the island of Lewis were all members of the union and so were most of the employees in the spinning mills on the island. The yarn when spun in the mills was woven into tweed cloth by crofters working at home, the woven cloth being finished in the mills. The tweed thus produced was sold by the owners of the mill as Harris Tweed. The Crofter Company also produced tweed cloth but their yarn was not spun on the island but was obtained more cheaply on the mainland. This cloth was sold as Harris Tweed but did not bear the trade mark in the form of a special stamp. The mill owners making the genuine Harris Tweed were being pressed by the union to increase wages but they said that they could not accede to union requests because of the damaging competition of the Crofter Company. Consequently Veitch and others acting in combination placed an embargo on the Crofter Company's imported yarn and exported tweed by instructing dockers at Stornaway to refuse to handle these goods. The dockers obeyed these instructions but were not on strike or in breach of contract. The Crofter Company sought an interdict (or injunction) against the embargo. The House of Lords *held* that the union officials were not liable in conspiracy because their purpose was to benefit the members of the union and the means employed were not unlawful.

Defamation: what is?

(589) *Byrne* v. *Deane*, [1937] 1 K.B. 818

The plaintiff was a member of a golf club in which there had been some gaming machines. The defendants, Mr and Mrs Deane, were proprietors of the club. As a result of a complaint being made to the police the machines were removed. Shortly afterwards, the following typewritten lampoon was placed on the wall of the clubhouse near to the place where the machines had stood—

> For many years upon this spot
> You heard the sound of the merry bell
> Those who were rash and those who were not,
> Lost and made a spot of cash
> But he who gave the game away,
> May he Byrne in hell and rue the day.   Diddleramus.

The plaintiff brought this action for libel alleging that the defendants were responsible for exhibiting the lampoon, and that the lampoon was defamatory in that it suggested that he was disloyal to his fellow club members. *Held*—The words were not defamatory because the standard was the view which would be taken by right-thinking members of society, and, in the view of the court, right-thinking persons would not think less of a person who put the law into motion against wrongdoers.

Defamation: libel or slander: form of publication

(590) *Youssoupoff* v. *Metro-Goldwyn-Mayer Pictures Ltd* (1934), 50 T.L.R. 571

The plaintiff was a member of the Russian Royal House. The defendants produced in England a film dealing with the life of Rasputin who had been the adviser of the Tsarina of Russia. The film also dealt with the murder of Rasputin. In the course of the film, a lady (Princess Natasha), who was affectionate towards the murderer of Rasputin, was also represented as having been raped by Rasputin, a man of the worst possible character. The plaintiff was married to a man who was undoubtedly one of the persons concerned in the killing of Rasputin. The plaintiff alleged that because of her marriage reasonable people would think that she was the person who was so raped. The action was for libel. *Held*— The action was properly framed in libel and the plaintiff succeeded.

Comment. This case is generally accepted as authority for the view that a defamatory talking film is always libel. However the rape of Princess Natasha was in the pictorial part of the film and not on the sound track. It is also uncertain whether a plaintiff can sue for a slanderous imputation of rape without proving special damage. The Slander of Women Act, 1891, provides that the 'words spoken and published . . . which impute unchastity or adultery to any woman or girl shall not require special damage to render them actionable'. However lack of consent, which is essential in rape, may mean that there is no imputation of unchastity.

Defamation: innuendo: illustrations from case law

(591) *Cassidy* v. *Daily Mirror Newspapers Ltd*, [1929] 2 K.B. 331

A man named Cassidy or Corrigan who was well known for his indiscriminate relations with women, allowed a racing photographer to take a photograph of himself and a lady, and said that she was his fiancée and that the photographer might announce his engagement. The photograph was published in the *Daily Mirror* with the following caption: 'Mr M. Corrigan, the race-horse owner, and Miss X whose engagement has been announced.' The plaintiff, Cassidy's lawful wife, who was also known as Mrs Corrigan, sued the newspaper for libel alleging as an innuendo that, if Mr Corrigan was unmarried and able to become engaged, she must have been co-habiting with him in circumstances of immorality. *Held*— Since there was evidence that certain of her friends thought this to be so, she was entitled to damages.

Comment. The case is authority for the view that a person may be liable for a statement which he does not actually know to be defamatory. It does not decide, nor does any other relevant case, that a person who has taken all possible steps to ensure the accuracy of his statement and could not, by reasonable enquiries have discovered that his statement was defamatory is or is not liable in defamation.

(592) *Morgan* v. *Odhams Press*, [1971] 2 All E.R. 1156

In 1965 *The Sun* reported that a kennel girl had been kidnapped by a dog-doping gang. In or about the relevant period various witnesses had seen her in the company of Mr Morgan whose friend she was. The newspaper article made no mention of Mr Morgan's name. Nevertheless he began an action against the newspaper pleading that he had been libelled by innuendo in that persons would think he was involved either in the kidnapping or the dog-doping, or both. *Held*—by the House of Lords—that—

(*a*) the newspaper article was not, by itself, capable of being so understood;

(*b*) an article to be defamatory of a person need not contain a 'key or pointer' showing it refers to him. Evidence is admissible to import a defamatory meaning to otherwise innocent words.

(593) *Tolley* v. *J.S. Fry & Sons Ltd*, [1931] A.C. 333

The plaintiff was a well-known amateur golfer. The defendants published an advertisement without the plaintiff's consent containing his picture and underneath the following words—

The caddy to Tolley said, 'Oh Sir,
Good shot, Sir! That ball, see it go, Sir.
My word, how it flies,
Like a cartet of Fry's,
They're handy, they're good, and priced low, Sir.'

The plaintiff brought an action for libel, alleging an innuendo. It was said that a person reading the advertisement would assume that the plaintiff had been paid for allowing the use of his name in it, and that in consequence he had prostituted his amateur status as a golfer. *Held*—The evidence showed that the advertisement was capable of this construction and the plaintiff was awarded damages.

(594) *Sim* v. *Stretch* (1936), 52 T.L.R. 669

The defendant had encouraged the plaintiff's housemaid to leave the plaintiff's employ and re-enter the defendant's. The defendant later sent the following telegram to the plaintiff: 'Edith has resumed her services with us to-day. Please send her possessions and the money you borrowed, also her wages.' The telegram was said to impute that the plaintiff was in financial difficulties and had in consequence borrowed from his housemaid, and that he had been unable to pay her wages, and was a person of no credit. The plaintiff succeeded at first instance and in the Court of Appeal, but the House of Lords reversed the judgment, *holding* that the telegram was incapable of bearing a defamatory meaning. In the words of Lord Atkin: 'It seems to me unreasonable that, when there are a number of good interpretations, the only bad one should be seized upon to give a defamatory sense to the statement.' It was also in this case that Lord Atkin suggested the following test of a 'defamatory' statement: 'Would the words tend to lower the plaintiff in the estimation of right-thinking members of society generally?'

(595) *Fulham* v. *Newcastle Chronicle and Journal*, [1977] 1 W.L.R. 651

In 1962 the plaintiff left the Catholic priesthood. He married in 1964, a child being born 14 months later. In 1973 he was appointed as deputy headmaster of a school in Teesside having previously lived in South Yorkshire. A Newcastle newspaper published by the defendants commented upon his appointment stating that he 'went off very suddenly' from Salford where he had been a priest 'about seven years ago' and had subsequently married. The plaintiff claimed that such statements contained a libellous imputation that he had married while still a priest and had fathered an illegitimate child. The particulars supplied by the plaintiff simply stated his date of marriage and the date of birth of his eldest child. The defendants sought to strike out his claim. It was *held*— by the Court of Appeal—that only those knowing of the dates of the plaintiff's marriage and/or the birth of his child could draw the imputation alleged and that since the defendants' newspaper did not circulate in the area where the plaintiff had been a priest or subsequently lived it was necessary for him to plead particulars of persons receiving the publication having the requisite knowledge and that unless he was able to do so his allegation of innuendo would be struck out.

(596) *Grappelli* v. *Derek Block (Holdings) Ltd*, [1981] 2 All E.R. 272

The plaintiffs, Mr Grappelli and Mr Disley, were jazz musicians with an international reputation. The defendants were their managers and agents. The defendants had, so the plaintiffs alleged, purported to book contracts for them without authority. Then it was said that one of these concerts had been cancelled because Mr Grappelli was seriously ill which was an entirely untrue story. It was said that that was defamatory, not as it stood, but because of an innuendo that people finding out that the plaintiffs were appearing at other concerts on the same dates as those cancelled would think that the plaintiffs had given a false story. It was held by the Court of Appeal that where a plaintiff relies on an innuendo he must prove that the words were published to a specific person who knew *at the time* of the publication of specific facts enabling him to understand the words in the innuendo meaning. Facts which came into existence afterwards did not make the statement defamatory. As Lord Denning said, the statement was not defamatory as it stood, since it is not defamatory of a person to say that he is seriously ill. At the time the statement was made those becoming aware of it would not have access to facts to suggest that it was wrong. Obviously, later on, when concerts were advertised in the *Sunday Times* on the same dates as those which had been cancelled it might have been possible to construe that Mr Grappelli and Mr Disley were not really ill and that the whole story was a put-up job. However, this information had to be available at the time of publication of the defamatory words since, according to Lord Denning, the cause of action arises in defamation when the words are published and they must be seen to be defamatory then, and not later.

Defamation: the words must refer to the plaintiff

(597) *E. Hulton & Co.* v. *Jones*, [1910] A.C. 20

A newspaper published an article descriptive of life in Dieppe in which one Artemus Jones, described as a churchwarden at Peckham, was accused of living with a mistress in France. All persons concerned contended that they were ignorant of the existence of any person of that name, and the writer of the article said that he had invented it. Unfortunately the name so chosen was that of an English barrister and journalist, and the evidence showed that those who knew him thought that the article referred to him. *Held*—The newspaper was responsible for the libel and the plaintiff was awarded damages.

Comment. (i) In cases of this kind the defence of offer of amends may be available under s. 4 of the Defamation Act, 1952. However, it is by no means certain that it would have been available on the actual facts of this case, because s. 4 applies only where the defendant can show that he and his servants or agents have taken all reasonable care with regard to the publication. On the facts of *Hulton* v. *Jones* it seems that the publication was attended by some carelessness.

(ii) In *Hayward* v. *Thompson*, [1981] 3 All E.R. 450 the defendants were the editor, a journalist on, and the proprietors and publishers of, a Sunday paper. In one article it was alleged that a wealthy benefactor of the Liberal Party was connected with an alleged murder plot but no name was given. In a later article the paper named the plaintiff reporting that the police wished to interview him in connection with the alleged murder plot which was not, of course, a defamatory allegation that he was involved in it as the first article had been. It was *held*—by the Court of Appeal—that the two articles could be connected. Thus the libel in the first article was of the plaintiff by reason of connection with the second one.

(598) *Knupffer* v. *London Express Newspaper Ltd*, [1944] A.C. 116

The plaintiff was head in the United Kingdom of a Russian Refugee organization, active in France and the United States of America, but having only twenty-four members in England. An article in the newspaper ascribed Fascism to this 'minute body established in France and the United States of America', but without mentioning the English branch. *Held*—The article was not defamatory of the plaintiff since he was not marked out by it, even assuming that it was defamatory to call someone a Fascist.

(599) *Schloimovitz* v. *Clarendon Press, The Times*, 6 July, 1973

The plaintiff by statement of claim alleged that the definitions of the word 'Jew' contained in three dictionaries published by the defendants were derogatory, defamatory and deplorable and sought an injunction restraining the defendants from publishing such definitions, at least without qualification, in any future editions of such dictionaries. *Held*— by Goff, J., that what was before the court was not whether the definitions were right or wrong or whether they were justly applied to any Jews, but whether in law the plaintiff had a cause of action to restrain the conduct of the defendant. No individual could maintain an action in respect of defamatory matter published about a body of persons unless in its terms, or by reason of the circumstances, it should and must be construed as a reference to him as an individual. There were two questions: (i) were the words defamatory? (ii) did they in fact apply to the plaintiff or were they capable in law of being so regarded? The plaintiff failed to satisfy the latter test and accordingly the defendants were entitled to have the writ and statement of claim struck out. (*Knupffer*[598] applied.)

Comment. It was decided in *Farringdon* v. *Leigh*, *The Times*, 10 December, 1987, that it was at least arguable that where defamatory words in a publication referred to an unidentified member or members of a group of persons, each of those persons had a cause of action in libel. In these circumstances an action by members of a team of seven police officers was allowed to proceed to trial where they alleged that certain articles in *The Observer* were defamatory of them in alleging that at least two of them, who were unnamed, had passed confidential information to journalists.

Defamation: defences: justification

(600) *Alexander* v. *The North Eastern Railway Co.* (1865), 6 B. & S. 340

The defendants published the following notice—

> North Eastern Railway. Caution. J. Alexander, manufacturer and general merchant, Trafalgar Street, Leeds, was charged before the magistrates of Darlington on 28th September, for riding on a train from Leeds, for which his ticket was not available, and refusing to pay the proper fare. He was convicted in the penalty of £9 1s., including costs, or three weeks' imprisonment.

In this action for libel, the plaintiff contended that the defence of justification could not lie because, although he had been convicted as stated, the alternative prison sentence was fourteen days not three weeks. *Held*—The substitution of three weeks for a fortnight did not make the statement libellous. It could be justified, since the rest of it was true.

Defamation: defences: fair comment

(601) *London Artists* v. *Littler*, [1969] 2 All E.R. 193

In 1965 four of the principal actors and actresses in a play called *The Right Honourable Gentleman* simultaneously wrote to the defendant, who was the producer of the play, terminating their engagement by four weeks' formal notice. This was, of course, highly unusual and the defendant wrote to the actors and actresses concerned wrongly accusing the plaintiffs, who were their agents, of conspiracy to close down the play. The defendant also communicated the letter to the press. The defendant was now sued for libel. It was *held*—by the Court of Appeal—that he had libelled the plaintiffs because although the subject matter of the allegations was of public interest, i.e. the fate of the play, the defence of fair comment did not apply to the allegation of a plot which was an allegation of fact. The allegation of a plot was defamatory and had not been justified. In fact it seemed that all the actors and actresses involved had their own good and different reasons for leaving the play. There was no evidence of combination.

Defamation: defences: qualified privilege

(602) *London Association for the Protection of Trade* v. *Greenlands*, [1916] 2 A.C. 15

The respondents were a limited company carrying on business as drapers and general furnishers at Hereford. The appellants were an unincorporated association consisting of about 6300 traders and had, as one of their objects, the making of private inquiries as to the means, respectability and trustworthiness of individuals and firms. A member of the association was about to sell goods to the respondents and he asked the association to report on them, and particularly to say whether the respondents were a good risk for credit of between £20 and £30. In the report submitted, the association declared that the respondents were a fair trade risk for the sum mentioned, but said that they had heavy mortgages charged on their assets, and that the assets barely covered the loans. In fact the mortgages were secured by a charge upon the real and leasehold property only, and all other assets were entirely free from any mortgage whatever, and constituted a large and valuable fund. The respondents were originally the plaintiffs in an action for libel contained in the statement about the mortgages, and the statement that they were only good for credit of between £20 and £30. *Held*—The occasion was privileged and thus the respondents had no claim in the absence of malice which they had not proved. Judgment was therefore given for the appellants.

(603) *Osborn* v. *Thomas Boulter & Son*, [1930] 2 K.B. 226

The plaintiff, a publican, wrote a letter to the defendants, his brewers, complaining of the quality of the beer. The defendants sent one of their employees to investigate and report. After receiving the report, Mr Boulter dictated a letter to his typist in which he suggested that the plaintiff had been adding water to the beer, and pointing out the penalties attaching to this if the plaintiff was caught. The plaintiff sued, alleging publication to the typist and certain clerks. *Held*—The occasion was privileged, and since the plaintiff could not prove malice in the defendants, his action failed.

(604) *Beach* v. *Freeson*, [1971] 2 W.L.R. 805

A member of Parliament wrote to the Law Society complaining of the conduct of a firm of solicitors reported to him by his constituents. He also sent a copy of the letter to the Lord Chancellor. *Held*—by Geoffrey Lane, J.—that both publications were protected by qualified privilege. The privilege arose out of a Member of Parliament's duty to his constituents and the responsibilities of the Law Society and the Lord Chancellor.

(605) *Cook* v. *Alexander*, [1973] 3 W.L.R. 617

The plaintiff sued the defendant for libel in respect of an account of a House of Lords debate which he had written for the *Daily Telegraph*. The debate had been about an approved school where the plaintiff had been a teacher and which had been closed partly because of the plaintiff's revelations as to the system of punishment there. The newspaper had published a précis of each speech on one of the inside pages, but the plaintiff objected to a report written by the defendant which appeared on the back page. In this report, known as 'Parliamentary Sketch', the writer gave his impression of the debate and emphasized the salient aspects of it, but there was a reference to the more detailed account on another page. The plaintiff alleged that the sketch was defamatory of him because it gave great prominence to a speech that was very critical of him and his conduct, while it dismissed in uncomplimentary terms a speech which defended his action. It was *held*—by the Court of Appeal—that such a Parliamentary sketch was protected by qualified privilege. A reporter was entitled to select from a debate those parts which seemed to him to be of public interest and provided that the account as a whole was fair and honest, such a Parliamentary sketch was protected by qualified privilege.

(606) *Horrocks* v. *Low*, [1972] 1 W.L.R. 1625

At a local authority council meeting Low made a speech defamatory of Horrocks who in answer to Low's defence of justification, fair comment and qualified privilege, alleged that Low had been actuated by express malice. *Held*—by the Court of Appeal—that malice could not be inferred. Low held an honest and positive belief in the truth of his statement and had not abused the privileged occasion. '(The defendant) is not to be held malicious merely because he was angry or prejudiced even unreasonably prejudiced, against the plaintiff, so long as he honestly believed what he said to be true. Such is the law as I have always understood it to be.' (*Per* Lord Denning, M.R.)

'What has to be proved is that the defendant was activated by malice in the popular meaning of the word: that is to say, in speaking as he did, he must have been actuated by spite or ill-will against the person defamed or by some indirect or improper motive.' (*Per* Edmund Davis, L.J.)

'When there is . . . (gross and unreasoning) prejudice there will often, perhaps usually, be reckless indifference whether what is said is true or false. But if there is honest belief that it is true, there cannot in any judgment be recklessness whether it be true or false.' (*Per* Stephenson, L.J.)

(607) *Egger* v. *Viscount Chelmsford*, [1964] 3 All E.R. 406

Mrs Egger, a judge of Alsatian dogs, was on the list of judges of the Kennel Club, and Miss Ross, the secretary of a dog club in Northern Ireland, wrote to the Kennel Club asking them to approve of Mrs Egger as a judge of Alsatians at a show. The assistant secretary of the Kennel Club, C. A. Burney, wrote to Miss Ross to say that the committee could not approve the appointment. Mrs Egger brought an action for libel against the ten members of the committee and the assistant secretary on the grounds that the letter reflected on her competence and integrity. There were two long trials at both of which the judge ruled that the occasion was privileged. The jury disagreed the first time, but at the second trial the jury found that the letter was defamatory and that five members of the committee were actuated by malice but three were not. The other two had meanwhile died. The judge gave judgment against all the defendants including the assistant secretary. *Held*—on appeal—The defence of qualified privilege is a defence for the individual who is sued, and not a defence for the publication. It is quite erroneous to say that it is attached to the publication. The three committee members innocent of malice were entitled to protection and were not liable. The assistant secretary also had an independent and individual privilege, and was not responsible or liable for the tort of those members of the committee who had acted with malice. Even in a joint tort, the tort is the separate act of each individual; each is severally answerable for it; and each is severally entitled to his own defence.

Defamation: consent of the plaintiff to publication

(608) *Chapman* v. *Lord Ellesmere and Others*, [1932] 2 K.B..431

The plaintiff was a trainer and one of his horses, after winning a race, was found to be doped. An inquiry was held by the Stewards of the Jockey Club, as a result of which they decided to disqualify the horse for future racing, and to warn the plaintiff off Newmarket Heath. The decision was published in the *Racing Calendar*. The plaintiff contended that the words were defamatory because they implied that he had doped the horse. The defendants, who were the proprietors of the *Racing Calender*, contended that the words were not defamatory, and meant simply that the plaintiff had been warned off for not protecting the horse against doping. Evidence showed that it was a condition of a trainer's licence that the withdrawal of that licence should appear in the *Racing Calendar*, which was also to be the recognized vehicle of communication for all matters concerning infringement of rules. *Held*—The plaintiff being bound by the terms of his licence, the doctrine of *volenti non fit injuria* applied as regards publication in the *Racing Calendar*, so that the plaintiff had no cause of action.

Defamation: damages: compensatory not punitive

(609) *Davis* v. *Rubin*, [1967] 112 Sol. J. 51

The plaintiffs were chartered accountants of good reputation and they wished to buy the lease of business premises. The defendants, who were the landlords, wrote to the holder of the lease saying that they would not accept the plaintiffs if the lease was assigned and referred in a defamatory fashion to the plaintiffs' business and references. The plaintiffs claimed damages in respect of the libel published in the letter, and were awarded £4000 each. The Court of Appeal, allowing the defendants' appeal, said that the damages were 'excessive, extravagant and exorbitant'. There had been publication to one person only and there was no evidence that the plaintiffs' reputation had been diminished in the minds of other persons. A reasonable sum would not have exceeded £1000 each and a new trial was ordered.

Rylands v. *Fletcher*: strict liability: escape of fire

(610) *Emanuel* v. *Greater London Council* (1970), 114 Sol. J. 653

A contractor employed by the Ministry of Public Building and Works removed prefabricated bungalows from the Council's land. The contractor lit a fire and negligently allowed sparks to spread to the plaintiff's land where buildings and goods were damaged. The plaintiff claimed against the G.L.C. and it was *held*—by James, J.—that—

(*a*) on the facts the Council remained in occupation of the site;

(*b*) the contractor was not a 'stranger' to the Council since they retained a power of control over his activities; and

(*c*) although the Council had not been negligent and were not vicariously liable for the contractors' negligence since they did not employ him, they were strictly liable under *Rylands* v. *Fletcher* for the escape of fire.

Rylands v. *Fletcher*: there must be an escape: whether the rule applies to personal injuries

(611) *Read* v. *J. Lyons & Co. Ltd*, [1947] A.C. 156

The appellant was employed by the Ministry of Supply as an Inspector of Munitions in the respondents' munitions factory. In the course of her employment there she was injured by the explosion of a shell which was in course of manufacture. She did not allege negligence on the part of the defendants, but based her claim on *Rylands* v. *Fletcher*. The trial judge found that there was liability under the rule, but the Court of Appeal and the House of Lords reversed this decision, *holding* that the rule did not apply since there had been no escape of the thing that inflicted the injury. In the words of Viscount Simon, L.C., 'Escape for the purpose of applying the proposition in *Rylands* v. *Fletcher* means escape from a place which the defendant has occupation of, or control over, to a place which is outside his occupation or control.' It was also suggested *obiter* in this case that the rule in *Rylands* v. *Fletcher* does not extend to personal injuries, but only to injury to property.

Comment. The *ratio* of the Court of Appeal in *Hale* v. *Jennings Bros*, [1938] 1 All E.R. 579 suggests that there may be liability for personal injuries. In that case a stallholder at a fair suffered personal injuries because of the escape of the defendants' chair-o-plane. It was held that she had a good claim under *Rylands* v. *Fletcher*.

Rylands v. *Fletcher:* does not depend on ownership of land: covers escapes of a variety of offensive and dangerous substances.

(612) *Charing Cross Electricity Supply Co.* v. *Hydraulic Power Co.*, [1914] 3 K.B. 772

The defendants' water mains under a public street burst and damaged the plaintiffs' cables which were also laid under the street. *Held*—The defendants were liable under the rule in *Rylands* v. *Fletcher*, because the rule was not confined to wrongs between owners of adjacent land and does not depend on ownership of land. Here it could be applied to owners of adjacent chattels.

(613) *Attorney-General* v. *Corke*, [1933] Ch. 89

The defendant was the owner of disused brickfields, and he permitted a number of gypsies to occupy them and live in caravans and tents. The gypsies threw slop water about in the neighbourhood of the fields and accumulated all sorts of filth thereabouts. The court *held* that *Rylands* v. *Fletcher* applied, and an injunction was granted against the defendant. While it was not unlawful to license caravan dwellers, it was abnormal use of land, since such persons often have habits of life which are offensive to those persons with fixed homes.

Rylands v. *Fletcher:* escape caused by act of stranger

(614) *Perry* v. *Kendricks Transport*, [1956] 1 W.L.R. 85

The defendants had placed on their parking ground a disused coach, having drained off the petrol and screwed a cap over the entrance pipe. The plaintiff, a boy of ten, was injured as he approached the parking ground by an explosion of petrol fumes from the coach. The trial judge found that the cap had been removed by some unknown person, and that a lighted match had been thrown in the tank, probably by one of two boys who hurried away as the plaintiff approached. The Court of Appeal *held* that the facts were within the rule in *Rylands* v. *Fletcher*, but the defendants were not liable because the escape was caused by the act of a stranger.

Rylands v. Fletcher: not applicable to escape of things naturally on land: other claims

(615) *Giles* v. *Walker* (1890), 24 Q.B.D. 656

The defendant wished to redeem certain forest land and ploughed it up. Thistles grew up on the land and thistle-seed was blown in large quantities by the wind from the defendant's land to that of the plaintiff. *Held*—There was no duty as between adjoining occupiers to cut things such as thistles which are the natural growth of the soil; therefore the defendant was not liable. Presumably if a person deliberately set thistles on his land he would be liable under the rule in *Rylands* v. *Fletcher*, for it is not usual to cultivate weeds on one's land.

   Comment. An action for nuisance would probably have succeeded here, because a person is liable for a nuisance on his land (even if he has not caused it) if he lets it continue (but note Weeds Act, 1959, p. 392).

(616) *Davey* v. *Harrow Corporation*, [1957] 2 All E.R. 305

The roots of the defendants' elm trees spread to the plaintiff's land and caused damage to the plaintiff's property. *Held*—The defendants were liable in nuisance, whether the trees were self-sown or not. It was no defence to an action for nuisance that the thing causing the nuisance was naturally on the defendants' land, though it might be a defence to liability under the rule in *Rylands* v. *Fletcher*.

Rylands v. Fletcher: defence of Act of God

(617) *Greenock Corporation* v. *Caledonian Railway Co.*, [1917] A.C. 556

The Corporation, in laying out a park, constructed a concrete paddling pool for children in the bed of a stream, thereby altering its course and natural flow. Owing to rainfall of extraordinary violence, the stream overflowed and poured down the street, flooding the railway company's premises. The House of Lords *held* that this was not an Act of God and the Corporation was liable. The House of Lords indicated the restricted range of the defence of Act of God and of the decision in *Nichols* v. *Marsland* (1876),[455] distinguishing that case on the grounds that whereas in *Nichols* v. *Marsland* the point at issue was the liability for storing water in artificial lakes, the point here was interference with the natural course of a stream, and anyone so interfering must provide even against exceptional rainfall.

Rylands v. Fletcher: defence: wrongful act of stranger.

(618) *Rickards* v. *Lothian*, [1913] A.C. 263

The defendant was the occupier of business premises and leased part of the second floor to the plaintiff. On the fourth floor was a men's cloak-room with a wash basin. The cloakroom was provided for the use of tenants and persons in their employ. The plaintiff's stock in trade was found one morning seriously damaged by water which had seeped through the ceiling from the wash basin on the fourth floor. Examination showed that the waste pipe had been plugged with various articles such as nails, penholders, string and soap, and the water tap had been turned full on. The defendant's caretaker found the cloakroom in proper order at 10.20 p.m. the previous evening. *Held*—The defendant was not liable under the rule in *Rylands* v. *Fletcher* because the damage had been caused by the act of a stranger.

Rylands v. *Fletcher*: defence: common benefit

(619) *Peters* v. *Prince of Wales Theatre (Birmingham) Ltd*, [1943] K.B. 73

The defendants leased to the plaintiff a shop in a building which contained a theatre. In the latter there was, to the plaintiff's knowledge, a sprinkler system installed as a precaution against fire and the system extended to the plaintiff's shop. In a thaw, following a severe frost, water poured from the sprinklers in the defendants' rehearsal room into the plaintiff's shop and damaged his stock. The plaintiff claimed damages for negligence, and under *Rylands* v. *Fletcher*. *Held*—There was no negligence on the part of the defendants and there was no liability under *Rylands* v. *Fletcher*, because the sprinkler had been installed for the common benefit of the plaintiff and defendants.

THE LAW OF PROPERTY

Ownership and possession: rights of owner paramount

(620) *Moffat* v. *Kazana*, [1968] 3 All E.R. 271

The plaintiff hid banknotes in a biscuit tin in the roof of his house. He sold the house to the defendant, one of whose workmen discovered the money. In this action by the plaintiff to recover the money it was *held*—by Wrangham, J.—that the plaintiff succeeded. He had never evinced any intention to pass the title in the money to anyone. Therefore his title was good, not only against the finder, but also against the new owner of the house.

Adverse possession or squatters' rights

(621) *Hayward* v. *Challoner*, [1967] 3 All E.R. 122

The predecessors in title of the plaintiff landowner let land to the rector of a parish at a rent of 10s. a year. The rent was not collected after 1942 and the plaintiff now sued for possession. *Held*—by the Court of

Appeal—that a right of action in respect of rent or possession must be held to have accrued when the rent due was first unpaid, and therefore was barred by what is now the Limitation Act, 1980. The rector as a corporation sole had acquired a good squatter's title.

(622) *Littledale* v. *Liverpool College*, [1900] 1 Ch. 19

The plaintiffs had a right of way for agricultural purposes over a strip of grass land belonging to the defendants. The plaintiffs put up gates which they kept locked at each end of the strip, and used the grass for grazing, keeping the hedges of the strip clipped. They now claimed ownership of the land by virtue of adverse possession. *Held*—The plaintiffs' acts could be construed as protecting the right of way, rather than excluding the owner, and were insufficient to establish the plaintiffs' title to the land.

(623) *Smirk* v. *Lyndale Developments Ltd*, [1974] 2 All E.R. 8

The plaintiff had a service tenancy of a house owned by the British Railways Board. In 1960 he took effective possession of an adjacent plot of land owned by the Board, though the Board was unaware of his action. The plaintiff did not communicate to the Board at any time that he disclaimed the Board's title. The Board sold the house and the plot to the defendants who granted a new tenancy of the house to Smirk on different terms not including the adjacent plot. The plaintiff claimed a possessory title to that plot. It was *held*—by Pennycuick, V.C.—that the plaintiff did not have a good possessory title to the plot.

Bailment: damage to goods: action by bailee

(624) *The Winkfield*, [1902] P. 42

This was an Admiralty action arising because a ship called the *Mexican* was negligently struck and sunk by a ship called the *Winkfield* The *Mexican* was carrying mail from South Africa to England during the Boer War. The Postmaster General made, among other things, a claim for damages in respect of the estimated value of parcels and letters for which no claim had been made or instructions received from the senders. The Postmaster General undertook to distribute the amount recovered when the senders were found. An objection was made that the Postmaster General represented the Crown and was not liable to the senders (see now Crown Proceedings Act, 1947). *Held*—As a bailee in possession the Postmaster General could recover damages for the loss of the goods irrespective of whether or not he was liable to the bailors.

Bailment and licence distinguished

(625) *Ashby* v. *Tolhurst*, [1937] 2 All E.R. 837

The plaintiff drove his car on to a piece of land at Southend owned by the defendants. He paid 1s. to an attendant who was the defendants'

servant and was given a ticket. He left the car with the doors locked. When he returned his car had gone, the attendant having allowed a thief, who said he was a friend of the plaintiff, to drive it away. The ticket was called a 'car-park ticket' and contained the words 'The proprietors do not take any responsibility for the safe custody of any cars or articles therein, nor for any damage to the cars or articles however caused nor for any injuries to any persons, all cars being left in all respects entirely at their owner's risk. Owners are requested to show a ticket when required.'
Held—

(i) The relationship between the parties was that of licensor and licensee, not that of bailor and bailee because there was in no sense a transfer of possession. There was, therefore, no obligation upon the defendants towards the plaintiff in respect of the car.

(ii) If there was a contract of bailment, the servant delivered possession of the car quite honestly under a mistake and the conditions on the tickets were wide enough to protect the defendants.

(iii) There could not be implied into the contract a term that the car should not be handed over without production of the ticket.

Comment. (i) Where the plaintiff hands over the key, the court may find a transfer of possession and a bailment, but the delivery of the key is not conclusive.

(ii) It was held in *Chappell (Fred)* v. *National Car Parks, The Times*, 22 May 1987, that where a vehicle was parked on NCP land for a fee but there was no barrier, the land was open and no keys to the vehicle were handed over, as the owner locked the vehicle and retained the keys, no bailment of the vehicle took place and NCP were not liable for its theft.

(626) *Ultzen* v. *Nicols*, [1894] 1 Q.B. 92

A waiter took a customer's overcoat, without being asked to do so, and hung it on a peg behind the customer. The coat was stolen and it was *held* that the restaurant keeper was a bailee of the coat and that there was negligence in supervision on the part of the bailee.

Comment. In this case the servant seems to have been regarded as taking possession, but it is unlikely that a bailment will arise if a customer merely hangs his coat on a stand or other device provided by the establishment.

(627) *Deyong* v. *Shenburn*, [1946] 1 All E.R. 226

An allegation that an actor who left his clothes in a dressing room had constituted the theatre owners bailees of the clothes was not sustained.

Bailment: finders and involuntary recipients

(628) *Newman* v. *Bourne & Hollingsworth* (1915), 31 T.L.R. 209

The plaintiff went into the defendant's shop on a Saturday in order to buy a coat. While trying on coats she took off a diamond brooch and put it on a show case. She left the shop having forgotten the brooch; an assistant found it and handed it to the shopwalker who put it in his desk. By the firm's rules the brooch ought to have been taken to their lost property office. The brooch could not be found on the following Monday. *Held*—There was evidence to support the trial judge's finding that the firm had become bailees and had not exercised proper care.

(629) *Neuwirth* v. *Over Darwen Industrial Co-operative Society* (1894), 70 T.L.R. 374

A concert hall was hired for an evening performance. No mention was made of rehearsal but the orchestra rehearsed in the hall during the afternoon without opposition from the proprietors or the keeper of the hall. After the rehearsel Neuwirth left his double-bass fiddle in an ante-room in such a position that when the hall keeper came to turn on the gas in the ante-room he could not do so without first moving the instrument. The fiddle fell and was badly damaged. *Held*—There was no contract of bailment between the parties. The care of musical instruments was outside the scope of the hall keeper's authority and there was no evidence that he had been guilty of negligence in the course of his employment.

Bailment: obligations of bailor

(630) *Hyman* v. *Nye* (1881), 6 Q.B.D. 685

The plaintiff hired a landau with a pair of horses and a driver for a drive from Brighton to Shoreham and back. The plaintiff was involved in an accident owing to a broken bolt which caused the carriage to upset so that the plaintiff was thrown out of it. *Held*—The trial judge's direction to the jury that the plaintiff must prove negligence was wrong. There was an implied warranty that the carriage was as fit for the purpose for which it was hired as skill and care could make it.

(631) *Read* v. *Dean*, [1949] 1 K.B. 188

The plaintiffs hired a motor launch called the *Golden Age* from the defendant for a family holiday on the Thames. The plaintiffs set sail at about 7 p.m. on 22 June, 1946, and at about 9 p.m., when they were near Sonning, they discovered that a liquid in the bilge by the engine was on fire. They attempted to extinguish the fire but were unable to do so, the fire-fighting equipment with which the launch was supplied being out of order. The plaintiffs had to abandon the launch and suffered personal injuries and loss of belongings. The plaintiffs admitted to a fireman after the accident that they might have spilt some petrol when the tank was refilled. *Held*—The plaintiffs succeeded because there was an implied undertaking by the defendant that the launch was as fit for the purpose for which it was hired as reasonable care and skill could make it. Further, as the launch had caught fire due to an unexplained cause, there was a presumption that it was not fit for this purpose. The defendant's failure to provide proper fire-fighting equipment was a breach of the implied warranty of fitness.

Bailment: obligations of bailee

(632) *Houghland* v. *R. Low (Luxury Coaches) Ltd*, [1962] 2 All E.R. 159

The defendants supplied a coach for the purposes of an old people's outing to Southampton. On returning the passengers put their luggage into the boot of the coach. During a stop for tea the coach was found to be defective and another one was sent for and the luggage was transferred from the first coach to the relief coach. The removal of the luggage from the first coach was not supervised, but the restacking of the luggage into the new coach was supervised by one of the defendants' employees. When the passengers arrived home a suitcase belonging to the plaintiff was missing and he brought an action against the defendants for its loss. It was *held*, by the Court of Appeal, that whether the action was for negligence or in detinue, the defendants were liable unless they could show that they had not been negligent. On the facts they had failed to prove this and were therefore liable. It was in this case that Ormerod, L.J., made some observations on bailments in general. The County Court Judge had found that the bailment was gratuitous and that the defendants were liable only for gross negligence. Dealing with this question, Ormerod, L.J., said 'For my part I have always found some difficulty in understanding just what was gross negligence, because it appears to me that the standard of care required in a case of bailment or any other type of case is the standard demanded by the circumstances of the particular case. It seems to me to try and put bailment, for instance, into a watertight compartment, such as gratuitous bailment on the one hand and bailment for reward on the other, is to overlook the fact that there might well be an infinite variety of cases which might come into one or other category.'

(633) *Global Dress Co.* v. *W. H. Boase & Co.*, [1966] 2 Ll. Rep. 72

B & Co. were master porters and had custody of thirty cases of goods belonging to G & Co. at a Liverpool dock shed. One case was stolen and G & Co. brought an action for damages against B & Co. B & Co. offered evidence of their system of safeguarding the goods and the County Court Judge at first instance found the system to be as good as any other in the Liverpool Docks, but notwithstanding this he found B & Co. liable. On appeal to the Court of Appeal it was *held* that if B & Co. could not affirmatively prove that their watchman was not negligent it was of no avail to show that they had an impeccable system, and the appeal should be dismissed. Thus the onus of proving that their servant was not negligent lay upon B & Co.

(634) *Doorman* v. *Jenkins* (1843), 2 Ad. & El. 256

The plaintiff left the sum of £32 10s. with the defendant, who was a coffee-house keeper, for safe custody and without any reward. The defendant put the money in with his own in a cash box which he kept in the taproom. The taproom was open to the public on a Sunday but the rest of the house was not and the cash was, in fact, stolen on a Sunday. Lord Denman *held* that the loss of the defendant's own money was not enough to prove reasonable care and the court found for the plaintiff.

(635) *Brabant* v. *King*, [1895] A.C. 632

This action was brought against the government of Queensland for damage to certain explosives belonging to the plaintiff which the government as bailees for reward had stored in sheds situated near the water's edge on Brisbane River. The water rose to an exceptional height and the store was flooded. The question of inevitable accident was raised and also the degree of negligence required. The Privy Council *held* that because of the nature of the site the bailees were required to place the goods at such a level as would in all probability ensure their absolute immunity from flood water, and the defendants were held liable. The Privy Council went on to say that in a case of a deposit for reward the bailees were 'under a legal obligation to exercise the same degree of care, towards the preservation of the goods entrusted to them from injury, which might reasonably be expected from a skilled storekeeper, acquainted with the risks to be apprehended from the character either of the storehouse or of its locality; and the obligations included, not only the duty of taking all reasonable precautions to obviate these risks but the duty of taking all proper measures for the protection of the goods when such risks were imminent or had actually occurred'. Counsel for the government suggested that a bailee was not liable for damage caused by the defects in his warehouse where these defects were known to the bailor, in this case the proximity of the warehouse to the Brisbane River. The Privy Council dismissed this argument on the grounds that it was a dangerous one, not supported by any authority. They said that the bailor could rely on the skill of the bailee in this matter. It will be seen from this decision that a bailee for reward is liable even in the case of uncommon or unexpected danger, unless he uses efforts which are in proportion to the emergency to ward off that danger.

(636) *Wilson* v. *Brett* (1843), 11 M. & W. 113

Wilson was in process of selling his horse and Brett volunteered to ride the horse in order to show it off to a likely purchaser. Brett rode the horse on to wet and slippery turf and the horse fell and was injured. Brett pleaded that he was not negligent but the court *held* that he had not used the skill he professed to possess when he volunteered to ride the horse and that he was liable.

(637) *Saunders (Mayfair) Furs* v. *Davies* (1965), 109, S.J. 922

The plaintiffs delivered a valuable fur coat to a shop belonging to the defendants, on sale-or-return terms. The defendants displayed it in their shop window and at 2.30 a.m. one morning the coat was stolen in a smash-and-grab raid. *Held*—That in all the circumstances and because of the valuable nature of the property, the defendants had taken an unreasonable risk and were negligent in leaving the coat on display in the window all night.

(638) *Coldman* v. *Hill*, [1919] 1 K.B. 443

The defendant was a bailee of cows belonging to the plaintiff. Two of these cows were stolen through no fault of the defendant, though he failed to notify the plaintiff and did not inform the police or take any steps to find the cows. The plaintiff now sued him for negligence and it was *held*—by the Court of Appeal—that it was up to the defendant to prove that, even if notice had been given, the cows would not have been recovered. In the circumstances of this case that burden had not been discharged and the defendant was liable.

(639) *Cheshire* v. *Bailey*, [1905] 1 K.B. 237

In this case jewellery had been deposited in a carriage by the hirer and was stolen by thieves. It transpired that the coachman, who was the servant of the person who let out the carriage, was in league with the thieves, but it was *held* that the owner of the carriage was not liable for the loss because the dishonesty of his servant was beyond the scope of employment.

Bailment: delegation by bailee

(640) *Davies* v. *Collins*, [1945] 1 All E.R. 247

An American Army officer sent his uniform to the defendants to be cleaned. It was accepted on the following conditions—'Whilst every care is exercised in cleaning and dyeing garments, all orders are accepted at owner's risk entirely and we are unable to hold ourselves responsible for damage.' The defendants did not clean the uniform but sub-contracted the work to another firm of cleaners. In the event the uniform was lost and the defendants were *held* liable in damages. The Court of Appeal took the view that the limitation clause operated to exclude the right to sub-contract because it used the words 'every care is exercised', which postulated personal service.

(641) *Edwards* v. *Newland*, [1950] 2 All E.R. 1072

The defendant agreed to store the plaintiff's furniture for reward. Later, without the plaintiff's knowledge, the defendant made arrangements with another company to store the plaintiff's furniture. The third party's ware-

house was damaged by a bomb and they asked the defendant to remove
the furniture but this was not done immediately because there was a
dispute about charges. Eventually the plaintiff removed his furniture but
some pieces were missing. *Held*—The plaintiff could recover from the
defendant because he had departed from the terms of the contract of
bailment by sub-contracting. However, the defendant was not entitled to
damages against the third party because the latter, though a bailee, had
not, in the circumstances, been negligent.

(642) *Learoyd Bros & Co.* v. *Pope & Sons*, [1966] 2 Ll. Rep. 142

The plaintiffs entered into an agreement with a carrier for the transport
of their goods. The carrier sub-contracted the work to the defendants,
who were also a firm of carriers, though the plaintiffs had no notice of
this arrangement. The lorry was stolen while the defendants' driver was
in the wharf office upon arrival at London Docks, and the carrier with
whom the plaintiffs had contracted paid some of the plaintiffs' loss and
the plaintiffs now sued the defendants for the balance. *Held*—That the
defendants were bailees to the plaintiffs, notwithstanding the absence of
any contract between them, and that the defendants' driver was negligent
in leaving the lorry unattended and therefore the defendants were liable
for the plaintiffs' loss.

**Bailment: actions against bailees for non-delivery: defence of superior
titles**

(643) *Rogers, Sons & Co.* v. *Lambert & Co.*, [1891] 1 Q.B. 318

The plaintiffs had purchased copper from the defendants but did not take
delivery of it and left it with the defendants as warehousemen. The plaintiffs then resold the copper to a third person. Some time later the plaintiffs asked for delivery of the copper from the defendants but the
defendants refused to deliver on the grounds that the plaintiffs no longer
had a title to it. *Held*—This was no defence to an action of detinue. The
defendants must show that they were defending the action on behalf, and
with the authority, of the true owner.

Co-ownership: severance of joint tenancy

(644) *Re Draper's Conveyance*, [1967] 3 All E.R. 853

In 1951 a house was conveyed to a husband and wife in fee simple as joint
tenants at law *and* of the proceeds of the trust for sale. In November,
1965, the wife was granted a decree *nisi* of divorce and this was made
absolute in March, 1966. In February, 1966, she applied by summons
under s. 17 of the Married Women's Property Act, 1882, for an order
that the house be sold and in her affidavit asked that the proceeds of sale
be distributed equally between her husband and herself. The court made
such an order in May, 1966, and in August, 1966, a further order was

made under the Act of 1882 that the former husband give up possession of the house. In spite of the order the former husband remained in possession until January, 1967, when a writ of possession was executed. Four days later he died without having made a will. The former wife now applied to the court to determine whether she held the proceeds of any sale absolutely (which would have been the case if she and her former husband had been joint tenants at his death) or for herself and the deceased's estate as tenants in common in equal shares (which would have been the case if there had been severance.) *Held*—Severance of a joint tenancy in a matrimonial home may be effected by the wife's issue of a summons under s. 17 of the Married Women's Property Act, 1882, and her affidavit in support. The affidavit had stated the former wife's wish for severance and had operated accordingly. Therefore she held any proceeds of sale as trustee for herself and the estate of her former husband as tenants in common in equal shares.

Leasehold: leases and licences distinguished

(645) *Shell-Mex and B.P. Ltd* v. *Manchester Garages Ltd*, [1971] 1 All E.R. 841

The plaintiffs by an agreement contained in a document called a licence, let the defendants into occupation of a petrol filling station for one year. The parties had some disagreements during this time and at the end of the year the plaintiffs asked the defendants to leave. The defendants refused claiming that the agreement gave them a business tenancy protected by the Landlord and Tenant Act, 1954, Part II, which deals with the method of terminating business tenancies. This method had not been followed by the plaintiffs. *Held*—by the Court of Appeal—it was open to parties to an agreement to decide whether that agreement should constitute a lease or a licence but the fact that it was called a licence was not conclusive. However, in this case it was a licence because the plaintiffs retained, under the agreement, the right to visit the premises whenever they liked and to exercise general control over the layout, decoration and equipment of the filling station. These rights were inconsistent with the grant of a tenancy.

Leasehold: exclusive possession of land not necessarily a tenancy in spite of agreement

(646) *Binions* v. *Evans*, [1972] 2 All E.R. 70

Mr Evans was employed as a chauffeur by the Tredegar Estate which owned a number of houses. His father and grandfather had also worked for the estate. Mr Evans died in 1965 and the trustees of the estate allowed Mrs Evans to continue to reside in a cottage which belonged to the estate, free of rent and rates. In 1968 the trustees made a formal agreement with Mrs Evans, the defendant in this case, who was then aged 76. The agreement purported to create a tenancy at will in order to provide her with a temporary home for the rest of her life free of rent without any right to assign, sub-let or part with possession. Two years later the trustees sold the cottage and other properties to Mr and Mrs Binions, the plaintiffs, expressly subject to the tenancy of Mrs Evans and because of that tenancy the trustees accepted a lower price. A copy of the trustees' agreement with Mrs Evans was given to the purchasers. Shortly afterwards the purchasers tried to evict Mrs Evans on the ground that her tenancy, being at will, was liable to determination at any time. She refused to vacate and the court was asked to decide whether her occupation was in the nature of a tenancy at will or a mere licence. *Held*—by the Court of Appeal—that the interest of the defendant was not a tenancy at will although it had been so described in the agreement. When the trustees created a right in her favour to live in the cottage for the rest of her life it could not be a tenancy at will liable to be terminated at any time. It was therefore a mere licence though Equity would not permit the plaintiffs to revoke it as long as the defendant was not in breach of the licence. The plaintiffs held on a constructive trust to give effect to the agreement with Mrs Evans.

Leaseholds: effect in equity of unsealed agreement for a lease: part performance: liability of landlord for latent defects

(647) *Walsh* v. *Lonsdale* (1882), 21 Ch.D. 9

The defendant agreed in writing to grant a seven years' lease of a mill to the plaintiff at a rent payable one year in advance. The plaintiff entered into possession without any formal lease having been granted, and he paid his rent quarterly and not in advance. Subsequently the defendant demanded a year's rent in advance, and as the plaintiff refused to pay, the defendant distrained on his property. At common law the plaintiff was a tenant from year to year because no formal lease had been granted, and as such his rent was not payable in advance. The plaintiff argued that the legal remedy of distress was not available to the defendant. *Held*—As the agreement was one of which the court could grant specific performance, and as Equity regarded as done that which ought to be done, the plaintiff held on the same terms as if a lease had been granted. Therefore the distress was valid.

Leaseholds: implied covenants: inapplicable to latent defects

(648) *O'Brien* v. *Robinson*, [1973] 1 All E.R. 583

The plaintiff was the tenant of a flat to which s. 32 of the Housing Act, 1961 (giving an implied covenant to repair) applied. In 1965 the plaintiff had complained about stamping on the ceiling above, but it was found that the landlord was not given notice that the ceiling was defective. In 1968 the ceiling fell and the plaintiff was injured. *Held*—by the House of Lords—that the defendant landlord was not liable for breach of covenant.

Comment. In *Sheldon* v. *West Bromwich Corporation*, (1973) 25 P. & C.R. 360, the Court of Appeal held the defendant landlords liable where a water tank in a council house had remained discoloured for some considerable time to the knowledge of the Council. The tank burst and the Council were in breach of their implied covenant under s. 32 of the Housing Act, 1961, to keep the installation for the supply of water in repair. The discolouration of the tank, which the Council knew about, meant that this was not a latent defect.

Leasehold Reform Act: tenancy must be for more than 21 years

(649) *Roberts* v. *Church Commissioners for England*, [1971] 3 All E.R. 703

In May, 1950, landlords granted a lease from 25 March, 1950, for 10¾ years to the tenant's predecessor at a ground rent of £10 per annum. Subsequently, by a lease dated 29 October, 1952, the landlords granted a lease for 21 years from 25 March, 1950, at a yearly rent of £29, the first instalment being deemed to have become due on 24 June, 1950. On the tenant's application for a declaration that she was entitled to acquire the freehold under the Leasehold Reform Act, 1967, it was *held*—by the Court of Appeal—that the Act could not be construed as extending to a relationship which ultimately produced a continuous relationship of landlord and tenant for over 21 years, nor a case where the parties to a short tenancy subsequently agreed to enlarge it retrospectively. To fulfil the definition of a long tenancy within s. 3(1) of the Leasehold Reform Act, 1967, a tenant must at some point of time be, or have been, in a position to say that he is or was entitled to remain tenant for the next 21 years, whether at law or in Equity.

Easements: cannot exist 'in gross' but only with reference to the holding of land

(650) *Hill* v. *Tupper* (1863), 2 H. & C. 121

Hill was the lessee of land on the bank of a canal. The land and the canal were owned by the lessor, and Hill was granted the sole and exclusive right of putting pleasure boats on the canal. Later Tupper, without authority, put rival pleasure boats on the canal. Hill now sued Tupper for the breach of a so-called easement granted by the owner of the canal. *Held*— The right to put pleasure boats on the canal was not an interest in property which the law could recognize as attaching to land. It was in the nature of a contractual licence which could not be enforced against the whole world. Tupper could have been sued by the owner of the canal, or by Hill, as lessee, if he had also been granted a lease of the canal.

Easements: right must be definite enough to form subject of grant

(651) *Bass* v. *Gregory* (1890), 25 Q.B.D. 481

The plaintiffs were the owners of a public house in Nottingham, and the defendant was the owner of some cottages and a yard adjoining the plaintiffs' premises. The plaintiffs claimed to be entitled, by user as of right, to have the cellar of their public house ventilated by means of a hole or shaft cut from the cellar to an old well situated in the yard occupied by the defendant. The plaintiffs claimed an injunction to prevent the defendant from continuing to block the passage of air from the well. *Held*—The right having been established, an injunction would be granted because the access of air to the premises came through a strictly defined channel, and it was possible to establish it as an easement.

Comment. In *Bryant* v. *Lefever* (1879), 4 C.P.D. 172, the plaintiff and defendant occupied adjoining premises, and the plaintiff's complaint was that the defendant, in rebuilding his house, carried up the building beyond its former height and so checked the access of the draught of air to the plaintiff's chimneys. The Court of Appeal held that the right claimed could not exist at law, because it was an attempt to claim special rights over the general current of air which is common to all mankind.

Easements: not necessarily negative

(652) *Crow* v. *Wood*, [1970] 3 All E.R. 425

This case arose out of damage done on a farm in Yorkshire by sheep which strayed on to it from an adjoining moor. The owner of the sheep, who was the owner of another farm adjoining the moor, raised, as a defence against an action for trespass, an obligation on the plaintiff to fence her own property to keep the sheep out. It was *held*—by the Court of Appeal—that a duty to fence existed as an easement and that it had passed under s. 62 of the Law of Property Act, 1925, when the defendant purchased his farm, even though his conveyance and previous ones had made no reference to the obligation of other farmers to keep up their fences. However, the right was appurtenant to the land sold and therefore became an easement in favour of the defendant and his successors in title.

Easements: categories capable of limited expansion

(653) *Re Ellenborough Park*, [1956] Ch. 131

Ellenborough Park was a piece of open land near the seafront at Weston-super-Mare. The park and the surrounding land was jointly owned by two persons. The surrounding land was sold for building purposes, and the conveyances granted an easement over the park in favour of the owners of the houses. The owners of the houses undertook to be responsible for some of the maintenance, and the owners of the park agreed not to erect dwelling houses or buildings, other than ornamental buildings, on the park. The park was later sold, and the question of the rights of the owners or occupiers of the houses fronting on to the park to enforce their rights over the park arose. It was contended that the rights created by the conveyances were not enforceable, because they did not conform to the essential qualities of an easement, and that they gave a right of perambulation which was not a right legally capable of creation. *Held*— The rights granted to the owners of the houses were enforceable as a legal easement.

(654) *Phipps* v. *Pears*, [1964] 2 All E.R. 35

A Mr Field owned two houses, Nos 14 and 16 Market Street, Warwick, and in 1930 he demolished No. 16 and built a new house with a wall adjacent to the existing wall of No. 14. In 1962, No. 14 was demolished under an order of Warwick Corporation, leaving exposed the wall of No. 16. This wall had never been pointed; indeed it could not have been because it was built hard up against the wall of No. 14. It was not, therefore, weatherproof, the rain got in and froze during the winter causing cracks in the wall. The plaintiff claimed for damage done, claiming an *easement of protection*. It was *held* by the Court of Appeal that there is no such easement. There is a right of support in appropriate cases, No. 16 did not depend on No. 14 for support; the walls, though adjoining, were independent. Lord Denning, M.R., said in the course of his judgment: 'A right to protection from the weather (if it exists) is entirely negative. It is a right to stop your neighbour pulling down his house. Seeing that it is a negative easement, it must be looked at with caution because the law has been very chary of creating any new negative easements. . . . If we were to stop a man pulling down his house, we would put a brake on desirable improvement. If it exposes your house to the weather, that is your misfortune. It is not wrong on his part. . . . The only way for an owner to protect himself is by getting a covenant from his neighbour that he will not pull down his house. . . . Such a covenant would be binding in contract; and it would be enforceable on any successor who took with notice of it, but it would not be binding on one who took without notice.'

(655) *Grigsby* v. *Melville*, [1962] 1 W.L.R. 1355

A Mr Holroyd owned two adjoining properties, consisting of a cottage and a shop which had recently been occupied in single occupation by a butcher. Beneath the drawing room of the cottage there was a cellar, the only practical means of access to which was by way of steps from the shop and which the butcher had used for storing brine in connection with the business of the shop. In 1962, Holroyd conveyed the cottage to Natinvil Builders Ltd, the predecessor in title of the plaintiff in this case. The conveyance accepted 'such rights and easements or quasi-rights and quasi-easements as may be enjoyed in connection with the . . . adjoining property'. A month later Holroyd conveyed the shop to a Mrs Melville. Mrs

Melville, who was a veterinary surgeon, began to use the cellar for storage. The plaintiff acquired the cottage in 1969 but did not realize the situation until 1971 when she heard hammering beneath her drawing room floor. She sought an injunction to prevent Mrs Melville from trespassing there. The defendants claimed that the cellar was excluded from the property conveyed, or alternatively that they enjoyed an easement of storage there equivalent to an estate in fee simple. *Held*—by Brightman, J.—(i) that the cellar, though not the steps leading to it, formed part of the property conveyed to Natinvil Builders Ltd; (ii) that the exclusive right of user claimed was so extensive as probably to be incapable of constituting an easement at law; (iii) that in any event on the facts use of the cellar for the purposes of the shop had ceased when the properties were divided, it had never been contemplated that such would be the case in the future and the defendants' claim to an easement failed. This decision was confirmed by the Court of Appeal [1973] 3 All E.R. 455.

Easements: acquisition: effect of s. 62, Law of Property Act, 1925

(656) *Ward* v. *Kirkland*, [1966] 1 All E.R. 609

The wall of a cottage could be repaired only from the yard of the adjoining farm. Before 1928 both properties belonged to a rector and the tenant of the cottage repaired the wall without seeking the permission of the tenant of the farm. In that year the cottage was conveyed to a predecessor in the title of Ward and in 1942 Mrs Kirkland became the tenant of the farm. From 1942 to 1954 work to the wall was done with her permission as tenant and in 1958 she bought the farm. In October, 1958, Ward did not make entry on to the farmyard to maintain the wall because Mrs Kirkland would not let him enter as of right. In this action, which was brought to determine, amongst other things, whether Ward was entitled to enter the farmyard to maintain the wall and for an injunction to prevent interference with drains running from the cottage through the farmyard, it was *held*—by Ungoed Thomas, J.—

(i) assuming such a right could exist as an easement it would not be defeated on the ground that it would amount to possession or joint possession of the defendant's property;

(ii) that although such a right was not created by implication because it was not 'continuous and apparent' yet the advantage having in fact been enjoyed it was transformed into an easement by s. 62 of the Law of Property Act, 1925;

(iii) no easement had arisen by prescription because permission had been given between 1942 and 1958;

(iv) permission having been granted by the rector to Ward to lay drains from the cottage through the farmyard and Ward having incurred expense in so doing it was assumed that the permission was of indefinite duration and an injunction would be granted to prevent interference with the drains by Mrs Kirkland.

Easements: acquisition: by prescription

(657) *Tehidy Minerals* v. *Norman*, [1971] 2 W.L.R. 711

The owners of a number of farms adjoining a down claimed to be entitled to grazing rights over it. The facts of the case were as follows—

(*a*) the farms and the down had been owned by one person until 19 January, 1920;

(*b*) the down had been requisitioned by the Government on 6 October, 1941;

(*c*) during the period of requisition the owners of surrounding farms had grazed cattle on the down by arrangement with the Ministry concerned;

(*d*) on 31 December, 1960, the down was derequisitioned and the association of farms which had made the arrangements with the Ministry entered into a further arrangement with the owner of the down for the maintenance of certain fences erected by the Ministry and grazing continued but under the control of the association of farmers.

On appeal from a decision of the County Court judge that the farmers were entitled to grazing rights over the down it was *held* by the Court of Appeal—that

(*a*) as there had been no enjoyment of the grazing rights between 6 October, 1941, and 31 December, 1960, except by permission of the Ministry, the farmers could not claim thirty years prescription which the Act of 1832 required for a profit to be established by user as of right;

(*b*) despite the extreme unreality of such a presumption it must be presumed that a modern grant, since lost, had been made of grazing rights at some time between 19 January, 1920, and 6 October, 1921, i.e. twenty years before the requisition; this presumption could not be rebutted by evidence that no such grant had been made but only by evidence—of which there was none—that it could not have been made;

(*c*) the period of twenty years applied to profits as well as to easements for the purposes of the law of lost modern grant although the Act of 1832 provided for different periods in the two cases;

(*d*) only the demonstration of a fixed intention never at any time to assert the right or to attempt to transmit it to anyone else could amount to an abandonment of an easement or profit, thus the acquiescence by the farmers in the arrangement under which the association controlled the grazing for a period of time did not amount to abandonment.

(658) *Diment* v. *N. H. Foot*, [1974] 2 All E.R. 785

A vehicular way across the plaintiff's field was claimed and had been used by the defendant from time to time without dispute between 1936 and

1967. The plaintiff, although the registered owner of the field throughout that period, had never farmed the land herself but had had tenants and during much of the time had lived far away or abroad. Until 1967 the plaintiff knew nothing of the way claimed. *Held*—by Pennycuick, V.-C.—(i) the law of prescription rested upon acquiescence for which knowledge was essential; (ii) the plaintiff had no actual knowledge and knowledge was not to be imputed to her either (*a*) because there was a gateway from the field to a parcel of the defendant's land to which there was no vehicular access; there were a number of possible explanations for it; or (*b*) because the plaintiff had not shown that her agents did not have knowledge of the use of the way or the means of knowledge. The presumption that long user was known to the owner was rebuttable and in the present case had been rebutted. It did not extend to the knowledge of agents. The burden of proving such knowledge or means of knowledge lay on the defendant and there was no evidence of either in the present case.

Comment. Even if the owner of the servient tenement (A) *knows* of the user the right will not arise if A *permits* the use. Thus in *Goldsmith v. Burrow Contruction Co. Ltd, The Times*, 31 July, 1987, the plaintiffs had used a path over the defendants' land for over 20 years. However, the defendants had a gate across the path and locked it from time to time. The Court of Appeal held that no easement had come into being. The plaintiffs' user depended on the permission of the defendants. They had shown this by locking the gate from time to time.

(659) *Davis* v. *Whitby*, [1974] 1 All E.R. 806

The plaintiff and his predecessors in title had enjoyed a right of way over the defendant's land by a certain route for 15 years and then by another route, substituted by agreement, for a further 18 years. On appeal by the defendant to the Court of Appeal against the decision that a right of way over the substituted route had been established by prescription, it was *held*—by the Court of Appeal—that the appeal should be dismissed. '. . . When you have a way used for some time and then afterwards a substituted way is used for the same purpose, both users being as of right, with the apparent consent or acquiescence of those concerned, then the original way and the substituted way should be considered as one.' *Per* Lord Denning, M.R.

Restrictive covenants: There must be land which can benefit

(660) *Kelly* v. *Barrett*, [1924] 2 Ch. 379

The owner of an estate in Hampstead developed it for building purposes. He made a new road through it, and sold plots of land along the road to a building firm who erected dwelling houses on the land. the purchasers undertook that the houses built should be used as private dwelling houses only. The owner of the estate did not retain any land except the road, which was afterwards taken over and vested in the local authority. A subsequent purchaser of two adjoining houses carried on a nursing and maternity home in them. The tenant for life under the former estate owner's will and one of the original purchasers claimed an injunction to restrain the defendant's activities. *Held*—No injunction could be granted because the agreement was not a valid building scheme, and the vendor's successor did not retain any interest capable of being affected by the restrictions.

Mortgages: equity of redemption: restraint on redemption enforced if parties at arm's length: collective transactions

(661) *Knightsbridge Estates Trust Ltd.* v. *Byrne*, [1939] Ch. 441

The plaintiffs were the owners of a large freehold estate close to Knightsbridge. This estate was mortgaged to a friendly society for a sum of money, which, together with interest, was to be repaid over a period of forty years in eighty half-yearly instalments. The company wished to redeem the mortgage before the expiration of the term, because it was possible for them to borrow elsewhere at a lower rate of interest. *Held*— The company was not entitled to redeem the mortgage before the end of the forty years because, in the circumstances, the postponement of the right was not unreasonable, since the parties were men of business and equal in bargaining power. A postponement of the right of redemption is not by itself a clog on the equity of redemption; much depends upon the circumstances. Further, the postponement did not offend the rule against perpetuities, which did not apply to mortgages.

(662) *Noakes* v. *Rice*, [1902] A.C. 24

The appellants were a brewery company and the respondent wished to become the purchaser of a public house owned by the company. The respondent borrowed money from the company in order to effect the purchase, and agreed that the company should have the exclusive right to supply the premises with malt liquors during the period of the mortgage and afterwards, whether any money was or was not owed. The respondent subsequently gave notice to the company that he was prepared to pay off the money secured by the mortgage, if the company would release him from the above-mentioned contract. This was refused and the respondent asked the court for relief. *Held*—The covenant was invalid as a clog on the equity of redemption in so far as it purported to tie the public house after payment of the principal money and interest due on the security.

(663) *Kreglinger* v. *New Patagonia Meat and Cold Storage Co.*, [1914] A.C. 25

The appellants were a firm of merchants and wool brokers. The respondents carried on the business of preserving and canning meat, and of boiling down carcasses of sheep and other animals. The appellants advanced money to the respondents, the loan being secured by a charge over all the respondents' property. The appellants agreed not to demand repayment for five years, but the respondents could repay the debt at an earlier period on giving notice. The agreement also contained a provision that the respondents should not sell sheepskins to anyone but the appellants for five years from the date of the agreement, so long as the appellants were willing to purchase the same at an agreed price. The loan was paid off before the expiration of the five years. *Held*—The option of purchasing the sheepskins was not terminated on repayment, but continued for the period of five years. The option was a collateral contract which was not a mortgage and in no way affected the right to redeem the property.

(664) *Cityland and Property (Holdings) Ltd* v. *Dabrah*, [1967] 2 All E.R. 639

A first mortgage of £2900 was granted by the seller of property to a purchaser and was expressed to be repayable in the sum of £4553 for which the property was charged. The £4553 was to be repaid over six years by equal monthly instalments and there was no mention in the mortgage of any interest. The whole of the balance of the £4553 became payable if the borrower defaulted and for this reason Goff, J., *held* that the premium amounting to £1653 was an unreasonable collateral advantage and therefore void under the principle in *Kreglinger's Case*, 1914.[663] The Judge having disallowed the premium was prepared to allow interest at seven per cent on a day-to-day basis which he thought to be somewhat more than market rates, but in fact it was far below market rates. The premium was an interest computation of nine-and-a-half per cent, non-reducing over six years and if it had been expressed as such in the mortgage it would appear that the court could not have set it aside since the court can only set aside unreasonable collateral advantages. However, in regard to interest rates, it appears that 'equity does not reform mortgage transactions because they are unreasonable', Greene, M.R., in *Knightsbridge Estates Trust Ltd* v. *Byrne*, 1939.[661] But this case was not cited to Goff, J. It would seem that for the future interest in mortgages should be expressed as such and not disguised as premium.

Remedies of legal mortgagee: taking possession: duty of mortgagee

(665) *White* v. *City of London Brewery Co.* (1889), 42 Ch.D. 237

The plaintiff had a lease of a public house in Canning Town, and he mortgaged it to the defendants to secure a loan of £900 with interest. One year later, no interest having been paid since the date of the mortgage, the defendants entered into possession of the public house. They later let the premises on a tenancy determinable at three months' notice under which the tenant was to take all his beer from the defendants. Eventually the lease was sold by the defendants, and the plaintiff asked the defendants to account and pay him what should be found due. *Held*—The defendants must account to the plaintiff for the increased rent they might have received if they had let the public-house without the restrictive condition regarding the sale of the defendants' beer, since a 'free house' would produce more rent than a 'tied house'.

Charges and encumbrances over land: spouses right of occupation

(666) *Williams & Glyn's Bank Ltd* v. *Boland*, [1980] 3 W.L.R. 138

A husband and wife lived together in the matrimonial home which was owned by the husband and subject to a mortgage with the bank. The husband was registered as the owner for the purposes of the Land Registration Act, 1925. It appeared that his wife had made a substantial contribution of money towards buying the house and that she had, accordingly, equitable rights in it. The husband failed to keep up the mortgage repayments and the bank asked the court for a possession order over the house with a view to selling it. The wife raised objection to the possession order, claiming that her rights and occupation gave her an 'overriding interest' in the home which overrode the bank's claim to possession under s. 70(1) of the Land Registration Act, 1925. Section 70 includes as an overriding interest 'The rights of every person in actual occupation . . .' The bank argued that the wife was not in actual occupation and also relied on s. 3 of the 1925 Act which provides that equitable rights such as the wife had, were not an overriding interest but a 'minor interest' and it was admitted that these would not have defeated the bank's claim. However, the House of Lords held that the wife's objection must be sustained and refused the bank an order for possession. The wife was in actual possession just as much as her husband and the fact that he was in occupation did not prejudice her right to be regarded as in occupation also. If she had not been in occupation apparently her equitable rights would have been a minor interest, but since she was also in occupation this fact converted them into an overriding interest.

Comment. (i) This decision has caused considerable concern to banks and building societies since the occupation of most houses is shared either with a wife or a mistress or relatives who have made some financial contribution towards the purchase.

(ii) The response of lending institutions has been to ask a spouse (or other relatives who may have rights of occupation) to sign a Deed of Postponement as s. 6(3) of the Matrimonial Homes Act, 1983 allows. This postpones the interest of an occupier to that of the lender.

Mortgages of chattels: bills of sale

(667) *Koppel* v. *Koppel*, [1966] 2 All E.R. 187

Mr Koppel, who was estranged from his wife, invited a Mrs Wide to come to his house and look after his children on a permanent basis. Mrs

Wide agreed to do so provided that Mr Koppel transferred the contents of his house to her to compensate for giving up her own home and disposing of her furniture. The transfer was recorded in writing. Later Mrs Koppel sought to levy execution on the contents of the house for her unpaid maintenance which amounted to £114. In proceedings resulting from Mrs Wide's claim to the property, the Registrar of the County Court held that the written transfer of the property to Mrs Wide was void as an unregistered bill of sale. *Held*—by the Court of Appeal—that the contents of the house were not in Mr Koppel's 'possession or apparent possession' within s. 8 of the Bills of Sale Act, 1878, because—

(i) Mr Koppel had transferred possession to Mrs Wide under the document which was an absolute bill of sale;

(ii) the grantor of the bill, Mr Koppel, had therefore neither possession nor apparent possession. He did not have apparent possession because Mrs Wide was living in the house with him and both had apparent possession of the property, not merely Mr Koppel;

(iii) Mrs Wide was therefore entitled to the property.

Lien: innkeepers

(668) *Robins & Co.* v. *Gray*, [1895] 2 Q.B. 501

The plaintiffs dealt in sewing machines and employed a traveller to sell the machines on commission. The plaintiffs' traveller put up at the defendant's inn in April, 1894, and stayed there until the end of July, 1894. During this time the plaintiffs sent the traveller machines to sell in the neighbourhood. At the end of July, the traveller owed the defendant £4 for board and lodging, and he failed to pay. The defendant detained certain of the goods sent by the plaintiffs to their traveller, claiming he had a lien on them for the amount of the debt due to him although the defendant knew that the goods were the property of the plaintiffs. *Held*— The defendant was entitled to a lien on the plaintiff's property for the traveller's debt.

Lien: insurance brokers

(669) *Caldwell* v. *Sumpters*, [1971] 3 All E.R. 892

The defendants, who were a firm of solicitors, were holding the title deeds to property recently sold by a former client, Mrs Caldwell, who had not paid their charges. They voluntarily released the deeds to another firm which had been instructed to take their place to complete the sale, stating that they did so on the understanding that the deeds would be held to their order until Mrs Caldwell had paid. The second firm of solicitors kept the deeds and refused to accept that understanding. *Held*—by Megarry, J.—Sumpters' lien was lost when they voluntarily parted with possession of the deeds and could not be retained by a one-sided reservation of the kind made. If the agreement of the second firm of solicitors had been obtained the lien would have been preserved as it would also if Sumpters had lost possession by trickery or other wrongdoing. The second firm was under no obligation to accept the reservation or to return the deeds.

Comment. The decision of Megarry, J., was reversed by the Court of Appeal (*Caldwell* v. *Sumpters*, [1972] 1 All E.R. 567), the court holding that Sumpters' lien was not lost when they parted with the deeds since—

(*a*) possession was given up on the clear and express understanding that the deeds were to be held to Sumpters' order; and

(*b*) solicitors as officers of the court could not be allowed to take advantage of this sort of situation even out of regard for any duty owed to a client.

Lien: power of court to order sale

(670) *Larner* v. *Fawcett*, [1950] 2 All E.R. 727

The defendant owned a racehorse and made an agreement with a Mr Davis under which it was agreed that Davis would train and race the filly and receive half of any prize money she might win. Davis, unknown to the defendant, agreed to let Larner have the animal to train. Larner did so, and when his charges had reached £125, he discovered that Fawcett was the true owner. Larner, being unable to recover the cost of training and feeding the filly from Davis, who had no funds, now applied to the court for an order for sale. Fawcett was brought in as defendant. *Held*, by the Court of Appeal, that Larner had a common law lien for his charges, and although such a lien does not carry with it a power of sale, the power given in the Rules of the Supreme Court to make an order for sale was appropriate here, particualrly since the filly was eating a great quantity of food. Fawcett had not made any attempt to get his property back but had clothed Davis with all the indicia of ownership. An order for sale would therefore be made unless Fawcett paid into court the amount of Larner's charges by a given date.

NEGOTIABLE INSTRUMENTS

Negotiable instruments: holder in due course: complete and regular bill

(671) *Arab Bank Ltd* v. *Ross*, [1952] 2 Q.B. 216

The plaintiffs claimed to be holders in due course of two promissory notes made by Ross and payable to 'Fathi and Faysal Nabulsy Company', a firm of which the two men named were the only partners. Ross alleged that he had been induced to make the notes by the fraud of the payees, and attempted unsuccessfully to show that the plaintiffs had knowledge of this fraud and had not taken the notes in good faith. The plaintiffs claimed to be holders in due course, but the point was taken that the indorsement on the notes was simply 'Fathi and Faysal Nabulsy' with the omission of the word 'Company' *Held*—by the Court of Appeal, that an indorsement could be valid to pass the property without being regular on the face of it. Regularity is different from validity. The Arab Bank were not holders in due course, because the indorsement was not regular, but were holders for value. Although the indorsers were in fact the only two partners, the word Company did not imply this, and therefore the indorsement was not manifestly regular by reference only to the instrument. The circumstances under which an indorsement gives rise to doubt is a practical matter and is best answered by the practice of bankers. This practice insists that the indorsement shall correspond exactly with the payee as named.

Negotiable instruments: consideration to support a bill; privity of contract does not apply

(672) *Pollway Ltd* v. *Abdullah*, [1974] 2 All E.R. 381

D contracted at an auction to purchase land from V.P, the auctioneer acting for V in the sale, signed the memorandum of the contract and, as agent for V, accepted D's cheque in payment of the ten per cent deposit. The payee named in the cheque was P.D wrongfully stopped the cheque and refused to pay the deposit, whereupon V exercised his right to treat the contract as repudiated. Was P a holder for value and thus able to enforce the cheque against D?

Yes, said the Court of Appeal (Megaw, Buckley and Roskill, L.JJ.). P was the holder of the cheque within the Bills of Exchange Act, 1882, s. 2. The consideration for the cheque was sufficient to support a simple contract, viz. either (*a*) P's warranty of his authority to sign the memorandum on V's behalf and to receive the cheque or (*b*) P's acceptance of a cheque in place of legal tender. Valuable consideration within the Bills of Exchange Act, 1882, s. 27(1) having been given, P could enforce payment against D.

Comment. In this case the vendors had not supplied consideration to the defendant because they had not gone on with the sale. The defendant had forfeited his deposit and the plaintiffs were the only ones who might have been in a position to claim consideration sufficient to enforce the cheque, which, in the event, the court held they had done. The cheque was, of course, also in the plaintiffs' name but if they had endorsed it over to the vendors this would not have enabled the vendors to sue because, as we have seen, they had not supplied consideration to the defendant.

(673) *Diamond* v. *Graham*, [1968] 2 All E.R. 909

A Mr Herman was anxious to borrow the sum of £1650 for immediate commitments and he asked a Mr Diamond whether he would lend him that sum. Mr Diamond agreed provided Mr Herman could repay by the

following Monday the sum of £1665. Mr Herman said that he would have
a cheque from a Mr Graham by that time which he would ask to be made
payable to Mr Diamond. Mr Diamond then drew a cheque for £1650 in
favour of Mr Herman. Mr Herman could not get a cheque from Mr
Graham on the following Monday because he was not available on that
day. However, Mr Herman presented the cheque for payment but Mr
Diamond countermanded payment and told the bank manager not to pay
it until authorized by Mr Diamond. Some days later Mr Herman obtained
a cheque from Mr Graham in favour of Mr Diamond. Mr Graham asked
who was providing Mr Herman with temporary relief and was told it was
the plaintiff. Mr Herman gave the cheque to Mr Diamond who paid it
into his bank and authorized payment of his cheque to Mr Herman.
However, the cheque drawn by Mr Graham was dishonoured. Mr
Herman had also drawn a cheque in favour of Mr Graham and this was
also dishonoured, Mr Diamond's cheque being the only one paid. Mr
Diamond now sued Mr Graham on his unpaid cheque. The defendant
argued that the plaintiff was not a holder for value within s. 27(2) of the
Bills of Exchange Act, 1882, because no value had passed between him
and Mr Graham. It was held by Danckwerts, L.J., that there was nothing
in s. 27(2) which required value to be given by the holder of a cheque
so long as value had been given by someone. Here value had been given
as follows—

(i) by Mr Herman who gave his own cheque to Mr Graham in return
for Mr Graham drawing a cheque in favour of Mr Diamond; and
(ii) by Mr Diamond when he released his cheque to Mr Herman.

Thus, Mr Diamond was a holder for value of the cheque and was
entitled to judgment and the appeal must be dismissed. Diplock and
Sachs, L.JJ., also dismissed the appeal.

Comment. The plaintiff in this case gave consideration after the
defendant's cheque was issued, i.e. he released his cheque to Mr
Herman.

(674) *Oliver v. Davis and Another*, [1949] 2 K.B. 727

On 18 July, 1947, the plaintiff lent £350 to William Davis and received
from him a cheque for £400, post-dated to 8 August, 1947. This was
presented on 19 August, 1947, and Davis was not able to meet it. Davis
persuaded a Miss Marjorie Woodcock (he was 'engaged' to her sister
although he was married) to draw a cheque of £400 in favour of the
plaintiff, and an envelope containing this cheque, but without any
covering letter, was left at the plaintiff's house.

The plaintiff was away at the time and returned on 22 August when
he received Miss Woodcock's cheque but did not know who had sent it.
Miss Woodcock, however, had discovered that Davis was a rogue and she
informed the plaintiff within an hour or two of his receiving the cheque
why she had sent it and also that she had stopped payment of it. On 23

August, the plaintiff presented Davis's cheque which was dishonoured and later presented Miss Woodcock's cheque which was returned marked, 'Stopped by order of the drawer'. In an action by the plaintiff against Miss Woodcock, suing her on the cheque, the plaintiff relied, *inter alia*, on s. 27(1)(b) of the Bills of Exchange Act, 1882. Miss Woodcock contended that there was no consideration for the cheque. *Held*— An antecedent debt or liability within the meaning of s. 27(1)(b) was a debt or liability due from the maker or negotiator of the instrument and not from a third party. The plaintiff, therefore, could not rely on s. 27(1)(b) but must show consideration sufficient to satisfy a simple contract under s. 27(1)(a). This he could not do because he had not given her any promise, express or implied, to forbear in respect of any remedy he might have against Davis, nor had he changed his position for the worse in regard to his claim on Davis's cheque. There was no evidence of any consideration and the plaintiff's action failed.

Comment. In this case the plaintiff did nothing after Miss Woodcock's cheque was issued which could be regarded as amounting to consideration to Davis or Miss Woodcock. If, for example, he had said after receiving Miss Woodcock's cheque that he would not sue Davis, he might have provided consideration sufficient to enable him to enforce Miss Woodcock's cheque since forbearance to sue can amount to consideration.

Negotiable instruments: unconditional order

(675) *Bavins* v. *London and South Western Bank Ltd*, [1900] 1 Q.B. 270

In the course of this action, the Court of Appeal had to deal with an instrument, in the form of a cheque, given to the plaintiffs by the Great Northern Railway Co. for work done. The instrument read as follows: 'The Great Northern Railway Company No.1 Accountants drawing account London, 7 July 1898. The Union Bank of London Limited. . . . Pay to J. Bavins, Jnr. and Sims the sum of Sixty-nine Pounds Seven Shillings. Provided the receipt form at the foot hereof is duly signed, stamped, and dated. £69.7s.' *Held*—That the instrument was not a cheque within the definition given by the Bills of Exchange Act, 1882, because it was not an unconditional order. The bank was not to pay the instrument unless the receipt was signed.

Comment. The bank lost its protection because the instrument was not a cheque and had been collected by the bank for a person who had stolen it. The bank was liable to the true owner, Bavins.

(676) *Nathan* v. *Ogdens Ltd* (1905), 94 L.T. 126

In the course of this action the Court of Appeal was dealing with an instrument on the face of which were printed the words 'The receipt at the back hereof must be signed, which signature will be taken as an indorsement of the cheque,' *Held*—The order to pay was unconditional and therefore the cheque was valid. The words could be taken as addressed to the payee and not to the bank.

Comment. It may now be settled that it is not a condition that a banker must obtain the payee's signature, on a receipt form, on a cheque before paying out. If the condition is regarded as addressed to the payee, the instrument is unconditional. However, bankers usually obtain an indemnity from customers having receipt forms on their cheques. This indemnity protects the bank if it incorrectly treats an instrument requiring a receipt as a cheque.

Negotiable instruments: signature by partner

(677) *Ringham* v. *Hackett* (1980), 124 S.J. 201

Mr Hackett and Mr Walsmley were partners and opened a bank account with Lloyds Bank. The cheque books were issued with 'Hackett/Walmsley Promotions' printed on each cheque and it was agreed with the bank that they would meet any cheque signed by one partner. Mr Hackett wrote and signed a crossed partnership cheque for £500 in favour of Paul Ringham in payment for two stage appearances. Mr Hackett then disappeared and Mr Walmsley, who had not agreed that the payment be made to Mr Ringham, instructed the bank not to honour any cheques drawn by his partner. Mr Ringham presented the cheque but did not obtain payment from the bank and sued the firm of Hackett/Walmsley. The Court of Appeal held that the firm was liable under s. 23. It was a necessary inference that a partner who signed his name under the printed name of the firm was making a cheque on the firm and/or its partners.

Negotiable instruments: procuration signatures

(678) *Childs* v. *Monins and Bowles* (1821), 2 Brod. and B. 460

The defendants were the executors of Thomas Taylor, and as such executors made a promissory note as follows: 'Ringwould, 28 December, 1816, as executors to the late Thomas Taylor, of Ringwould, we severally and jointly promise to pay to Mr Nathaniel Childs the sum of £200 on demand, together with lawful interest for the same. J. Monins, Phineas Bowles, executors.' *Held*—The executors were personally liable. The words 'on demand' implied that the executors had assets to satisfy the note. If they had meant to limit their liability, they should have added the words 'out of the estate of Thomas Taylor'. Burrough, J., said, 'The insertion of the words "as executors" cannot alter the case if, on the whole instrument, the parties appear liable.'

Negotiable instruments: representative signatures on behalf of companies

(679) *Hendon* v. *Adelman, The Times*, 16 June, 1973

A cheque signed on behalf of L. & R. Agencies omitted the ampersand in the company's name. *Held* by MacKenna, J., that the directors who had signed the cheque had not complied with what is now s. 349 of the Companies Act, 1985, and, accordingly, were personally liable.

Negotiable instruments: forged signatures: the doctrine of estoppel.

(680) *Greenwood* v. *Martins Bank Ltd*, [1933] A.C. 51

The appellant, who was a dairy man in Blackpool, opened with the respondents a joint account in the name of himself and his wife. Cheques drawn on this account were to bear the signature of them both. Later on the appellant opened a further account with the respondents in his own name, though the wife kept the pass books and cheque books in respect of both accounts. In October, 1929, Greenwood asked his wife to give him a cheque, saying he wanted to draw £20 from his own account. His wife then told him that there was no money in the bank, and that she had used it to help her sister who was involved in legal proceedings over property. He asked her who had forged his signature but she would not say. However, she did ask him not to inform the respondents of the forgeries until her sister's case was over. Greenwood complied with this request until 5 June, 1930, when he discovered that there were no legal proceedings instituted by his wife's sister and that his wife had been deceiving him. He told his wife that he intended to go the bank and reveal her forgeries, but before he actually made the visit she shot herself. Greenwood now claimed £410 6s. 0d. from the bank on the grounds that this sum had been paid out of his own account and the joint account by means of forged cheques. The bank pleaded ratification, adoption or estoppel. *Held*—There could be no ratification or adoption in this sort of case, but the essential elements of estoppel were present. The appellant's failure to inform the bank was a representation that the cheques were good. The bank had suffered a detriment because, if Greenwood had told the bank when his wife first confessed to forgery, they might have brought an action against her. Under the law *existing at that time* they could not bring such an action after her death. The bank had, therefore, a legal right to debit Greenwood's account with the amount of the forged cheques.

Comment. (i) Generally, knowledge by the customer of the forgery is required if an estoppel is to be successfully raised by the bank. In the USA an estoppel can be raised where the customer failed to examine and draw inferences from his bank statements on which the forged cheques are recorded. However, McNeil, J., refused to bring UK law into line on this in *Wealden Woodlands (Kent) Ltd* v. *National Westminster Bank Ltd* (1983), 133 N.L.J. 719. In that case cheques drawn on the plaintiffs' account required the signatures of two directors. One director got money from the company's account by forging the signature of another director. The Court held that the plaintiffs were not estopped from making a claim against the bank even though they might have discovered the fraud by diligent examination of the company's bank statement. They had not discovered the fraud in this way and the Court held that they could not be regarded as negligent because they had not done so.

(ii) The case of *Tai Hing Cotton Mill Ltd* v. *Liu Chong Hing Bank Ltd*, [1985] 2 All E.R. 947 is also of interest. In that case an accounts clerk employed by a company which was a customer of three banks forged the signature of the company's managing director on some 300 cheques to the value of 5.5 m Hong Kong dollars. He presented the cheques as appropriate to the three banks and they debited the company's current account with the amounts. The clerk's fraudulent activities lasted five years and were only discovered when a newly-appointed accountant began reconciling bank statements with the company's books.

The company sued the banks, claiming that the money was wrongly debited to the company's current account. The case eventually came to the Privy Council which decided that the company succeeded; the bank had no right to debit the cheques.

(iii) It should also be noted that if a bank pays a cheque on which the signature of its customer as drawer has been forged, the bank can sue the person to whom payment was made for restitution of the amount paid out, because the money with which payment was made was the property of the bank. A paying bank, merely by paying a cheque on which its customer's signature has been forged, does not thereby represent that the signature is genuine so as to estop itself from recovering the money paid to the recipient in quasi-contract. (*National Westminster Bank Ltd* v. *Barclays Bank International Ltd*, [1974] 3 All E.R. 834.)

Negotiable instruments: existing, fictitious, and non-existing payees

(681) *Vinden* v. *Hughes*, [1905] 1 K.B. 795

A clerk persuaded the plaintiff, his employer, to draw cheques in favour of his actual customers by saying the employer owed money to them which he did not. The clerk then forged the customers' indorsements and kept the proceeds. *Held*—These were existing payees and therefore order cheques and the defendants had no title.

Comment. This case was followed in *North & South Wales Bank* v. *Macbeth*, [1908] A.C. 137. It may be that the principle in *Vagliano's* Case[682] can never apply to a cheque, since the drawer of a cheque usually intends the payee to receive payment. However, the payee may be non-existent in which case the cheque is considered to be a bearer instrument. (See *Clutton* v. *Attenborough*, 1879.)[683]

(682) *Bank of England* v. *Vagliano Bros*, [1891] A.C. 107

Glyka, a clerk of Vagliano Bros, forged the signatures of Vucina and Petriai and Co. as drawer and payees of bills drawn on Vagliano Bros. The bills were accepted by Vagliano, since he knew the parties concerned and had done business with them. Glyka got possession of the bills and then forged indorsements in favour of fictitious persons whereby he was able to cash them with the Bank of England. Glyka was arrested and acknowledged the forgeries but the Bank had debited Vagliano Bros account with the sums paid out. Vagliano now sued the Bank for repayment. *Held*—by the House of Lords on appeal—Fictitious does not mean 'imaginary' but 'feigned' or 'counterfeit'. The bills were fictitious from beginning to end and all the persons were feigned or counterfeit persons put forward as real persons, and were not less fictitious because real persons did correspond to the names used. Since bills drawn payable to a fictitious payee can be treated as payable to bearer, the Bank of England was in order in paying them and Vagliano Bros failed in their action.

(683) *Clutton* v. *Attenborough & Son* [1879], A.C. 90

A clerk persuaded his employer to draw cheques in favour of one Brett by telling the employer that Brett had done work for the firm. The employer had never heard of Brett. The clerk then forged the indorsements. *Held*—Brett was a non-existing payee. Therefore the cheques were bearer cheques and the indorsee received a good title to them.

Negotiable instruments: bill payable upon a contingency

(684) *Williamson* v. *Rider*, [1962] 2 All E.R. 268

R signed a document in these terms 'In consideration of the loan of £100 from W., I, R, agree to repay W the sum of £100 on, or before, 31 December, 1956.' *Held*—This was not a promissory note because the option to pay at an earlier date created an uncertainty or contingency in the time of payment.

Negotiable instruments: the payee cannot be a holder in due course

(685) *Jones (R.E.) Ltd* v. *Waring and Gillow*, [1926] A.C. 670

A fraudulent person named Bodenham was indebted to Waring and Gillow in the sum of £5000 which he could not pay. He went to the plaintiffs and said that he was an agent for International Motors' new car the Roma, but they would have to take 500 cars and pay a deposit of £5000. The plaintiffs were interested in the deal but did not wish to pay Bodenham or International Motors because they did not know these parties. Bodenham then said that Waring and Gillow were the real backers and asked the plaintiffs to make out a cheque for £5000 to them, which the plaintiffs did. Waring and Gillow received payment of the cheque and when the fraud was discovered the plaintiffs sought to recover their money from Waring and Gillow. The House of Lords held that the plaintiffs succeeded because the money was paid under a mistake of fact and that the original payee of a bill of exchange is not a holder in due course.

Comment. However, an original payee may rely on the doctrine of estoppel. Thus in *Lloyds Bank* v. *Cooke*, [1907] 1 K.B. 794 Cooke signed his name on a blank promissory note and gave it to another person with authority to complete it for £250 payable to the plaintiffs as security for an advance made by them. The other person completed it for £1,000 and took the balance for himself. It was held that although the bank were payees and not holders in due course, Cooke was liable to them by estoppel. He had held out the other party as having authority.

Negotiable instruments: discharge: material alteration

(686) *Gardner* v. *Walsh* (1855), 5 E. & B. 83

This was an action against the defendant and Elizabeth Burton and Alice Clarke on a promissory note now overdue. The defendant agreed to be jointly and severally liable to pay to the plaintiff or his order the sum of £500. Evidence showed that Elizabeth Burton was indebted to the plaintiff and she agreed to get two sureties, the defendant and Alice Clarke, to join her in a joint and several promissory note to the plaintiff. Burton and Walsh signed the note together and gave it to the plaintiff. The plaintiff got Alice Clarke to sign it although the defendant did not know there was to be another party. In this action on the note Walsh alleged that the note was avoided by virtue of a material alteration after issue, namely the addition of another party without Walsh's knowledge. *Held*—The addition of Clarke's name was a material alteration and if made after the note was issued would avoid it.

Negotiable instruments: notice of dishonour: requirements

(687) *Eaglehill Ltd* v. *J. Needham Builders Ltd*, [1972] 3 All E.R. 895

The plaintiffs were holders for value of a bill of exchange for £7660 drawn by the defendants and accepted by Fir View Furniture Co. payable at a certain bank. The bill became due and payable on 31 December, 1970, but prior to that date Fir View Furniture Co. went into liquidation. By mistake, the plaintiffs posted their notice of dishonour dated 1 January, 1971, on 30 December, 1970, and it arrived at Fir View Furniture Co's office on 31 December. The Court of Appeal held that the notice was not subsequent to the dishonour within the Bills of Exchange Act, 1882, and was therefore invalid. On appeal by the plaintiffs it was *held*—by the House of Lords allowing the appeal—that a notice of dishonour was given when it was received, i.e when it was opened in the ordinary course of business or would have been if the ordinary course of business were followed. Provided that notice is received after dishonour it is valid regardless of when it is sent off. The notice was valid and the plaintiffs' action succeeded.

Banking: banker should not pay in unusual circumstances

(688) *Karak Rubber Co. Ltd.* v. *Burden (No. 2)*, [1972] 1 All E.R. 1210

A take-over transaction involved the purchase by a director of the company's issued share capital. The director used the company's assets to finance the purchase of the shares by borrowing money from a third party to buy them and repaying the third party by a cheque for £99,504 drawn on the company's account at Barclays Bank. The cheque was paid by the bank which was held liable to repay Karak for breach of their contractual duty because—

(*a*) although a bank was obliged to pay on demand a cheque which was in proper form and backed by adequate funds, it did not follow that a paying bank was under an absolute unqualified duty to pay without enquiry; it was, on the contrary, under a contractual duty to exercise such care and skill as would be exercised by a reasonable banker and that care and skill included, in appropriate circumstances, a duty to enquire before paying;

(*b*) in exercising its duty of care the paying bank was bound to make such enquiries as might, in given circumstances, be appropriate and practical, where it had, or a reasonable banker would have, grounds for believing that the authorized signatories were misusing their authority for the purpose of defrauding their principal or otherwise defeating his true intentions;

(*c*) the circumstances in which the Karak cheque came to be tendered to Barclays were so unusual and out of the ordinary course of banking business, the sum involved was so large, and the ground so solid for suspecting that someone was using Karak money to finance the takeover transaction, that a reasonable banker, in the interests of his customers, would have made further enquiries before inviting or allowing the customer's signatories to pay over £99,504 of the customer's money.

The bank was also liable as a constructive trustee. Although, in order to establish liability as a constructive trustee on the part of a third party who has assisted a trustee as his agent in a breach of trust, it was necessary to show that the third party had assisted with knowledge of a dishonest and fraudulent design on the part of the trustee, it was not necessary to show that the third party had actual knowledge; it was sufficient to show constructive knowledge, i.e. that the third party had knowledge of circumstances which would have indicated to an honest, reasonable man that such a design was being committed or would have put him on enquiry whether it was being committed.

Comment. This liability as a constructive trustee makes life difficult for bankers, particularly where the money of companies is misapplied in breach of trust by the directors, the relevant cheque(s) having been drawn within the mandate on which the account is operated. Consideration has already been given to the rule of *ultra vires* in *International Sales and Agencies* v. *Marcus*, 1982.[172] An additional point in that case was that the payment of the cheques of the companies by the director, Mr Munsey, was a breach of trust. The debt was not an obligation of the company and in an action brought on behalf of the company it succeeded in recovering the money paid by the bank from the bank.

Banking: banker's duty not to disclose customers' affairs

(689) *Tournier* v. *National Provincial and Union Bank of England*, [1924] 1 K.B. 461

Tournier banked with the defendants and, being overdrawn by £9 6s. 8d., signed an agreement to pay this off at the rate of £1 a week, disclosing the name and address of his employers, Kenyon & Co., with whom he had a three months' contract as a traveller. The agreement to repay was not observed and the bank also discovered, through another banker, that Tournier had indorsed a cheque for £45 over to a bookmaker. The manager of the bank thereupon telephoned Kenyon & Co. to find out Tournier's private address and told them that Tournier was betting heavily. Kenyon & Co., as a result of this conversation, refused to renew Tournier's contract of employment. Tournier sued the bank for slander and for breach of an implied contract not to disclose the state of his account or his transactions. Judgment was entered for the defendants but the Court of Appeal allowed Tournier's appeal and ordered a new trial. Bankes, L.J., laid down four qualifications to the duty of non-disclosure: (*a*) where the disclosure is under compulsion of law; (*b*) where there is a duty to the public to disclose; (*c*) where the interests of the bank require disclosure; (*d*) where the disclosure is made by the express or implied consent of the customer. Atkin, L.J., said: 'I do not desire to express a final opinion on the practice of bankers to give one another information as to the affairs of their respective customers, except to say it appears to me that if it is justified it must be upon the basis of an implied consent of the customer.'

(690) *Williams* v. *Summerfield*, [1972] 3 W.L.R. 131

Police issued summonses against employees alleging theft of sums of money from their employer. The defendants handed back £19,000. The justices granted an application by police to inspect the defendants' accounts, there being a large sum outstanding which the police could not specify without sight of them. On appeal by the defendants to the Divisional Court it was held that the appeal must be dismissed. Police investigating charges of theft may be granted permission to inspect defendants' bank accounts when otherwise unable to specify the sum stolen. However, an application for an order under s. 7 of the 1879 Act should be rejected if legal proceedings were started with the sole object of investigating a suspect bank account. It would be proper for justices faced with a difficult case to decline to make such an order on the ground that they feel that the concurrent jurisdiction of a High Court judge may be invoked instead.

(691) *Sunderland* v. *Barclays Bank Ltd* (1938), *The Times*, 25 November

Mrs Sunderland had drawn a cheque in favour of her dressmaker on an account containing insufficient funds. The cheque was returned because the bank knew she indulged in gambling and thought it unwise to grant her an overdraft. Mrs Sunderland complained to her husband and the manager of the bank informed him, over the 'phone, of the wife's transactions with bookmakers. Mrs Sunderland regarded this as a breach of the bank's duty of secrecy, but in fact the husband's telephone conversation was a continuation of one of her own in which she requested the bank to give an explanation to the husband concerning the return of the cheque. The bank pleaded implied authority to disclose. du Parcq, L.J., gave judgment for the defendants and affirmed the criteria relating to disclosure laid down in *Tournier* v. *National Provincial and Union Bank of England*, 1924.[689] However, each case must depend on its own facts. The relationship of husband and wife was a special one. The demand by Dr Sunderland for an explanation required an account of why the bank had done what it had done. It might be said that the disclosure was with the implied consent of the customer and the interests of the bank required disclosure. Since the husband had taken over conduct of the matter, the manager was justified in thinking that the wife did not object to the offer of an explanation. If judgment had been for the plaintiff, the damages were assessed at forty shillings—nominal damages.

(692) *Eckman* v. *Midland Bank, The Times*, 9 December, 1972

A union was fined £5000 for contempt of court and writs of sequestration were issued. The union's bankers refused to disclose assets and make payment unless a court order was made on the basis that until then they were not compelled to do so. *Held*—by the National Industrial Relations Court—that the bankers were not affected until they knew of the issue of the writ of sequestration but that thereafter their duty and their only duty was to refuse to take any action they knew to have as its object the frustration of the writ. A demand by sequestrators for disclosure of property must be complied with. However, since the bankers had not acted unreasonably in coming to court to clarify the position, no order would be made as to costs.

Banking: customer's duty of care: drawing cheques

(693) *London Joint Stock Bank Ltd.* v. *Macmillan and Arthur*, [1918] A.C. 777

Macmillan and Arthur were customers of the bank and entrusted their clerk with the duty of filling in cheques for signature. The clerk presented a cheque to a partner for signature, drawn in favour of the firm or bearer, and made out for £2 0s. 0d. in figures but with no sum in words. The clerk then easily altered the figures to £120 0s. 0d. and wrote 'one hundred and twenty pounds' in words, presenting the cheque to the bank and obtaining £120 in cash. The firm contended that the bank could only debit them with £2; the bank alleged negligence on the part of the firm. *Held*—by the House of Lords—that the relationship of banker and customer imposes a special duty of care on the customer in drawing cheques. A cheque is a mandate to the banker to pay according to the tenor. The customer must exercise reasonable care to prevent the banker being misled. If he draws a cheque in a manner which facilitates fraud, he is guilty of a breach of duty as between himself and the banker, and he will be responsible to the banker for any loss sustained by the banker as a natural and direct consequence of this breach of duty. If the cheque is drawn in such a way as to facilitate or almost to invite an increase in the amount by forgery if the cheque should get into the hands of a dishonest person, forgery is not a remote but a very natural consequence of such negligence. The bank could, therefore, debit Macmillan and Arthur with the full £120 0s. 0d.

Compare *Scholfield* v. *Earl of Londesborough*, [1896] A.C. 514, where it was held that the drawer of a bill of exchange owed no such duty to other parties.

(694) *Slingsby* v. *District Bank*, [1931] All E.R. Rep. 147

The executors of an estate drew a cheque payable to John Prust & Co. but left a space between the payee's name and the printed words 'or order'. A fraudulent solicitor named Cumberbirch wrote 'per Cumberbirch and Pott's' after the payee's name. He then indorsed the cheque and received payment. *Held*—There was no negligence on the part of the executors; it was not a usual precaution to draw lines before or after the name of the payee and the executors were entitled to recover the amount of the cheque from the bank.

Comment. If the precaution of filling in the gap after the payees' name is more usual now than in 1931, then a present-day court may not follow *Slingsby* because the question of what is usual is purely one of evidence. It should also be noted that this was an alteration other than to amount and because alterations other than to amount are less usual, the drawer may not be required to protect himself against them.

Banking: wrongful dishonour of cheques and defamation

(695) *Gibbons* v. *Westminster Bank Ltd*, [1939] 2 K.B. 882

The plaintiff drew a cheque for rent which she gave to her landlords and which was dishonoured in error. The bank had credited to another account funds paid in by the plaintiff sufficient to meet the cheque. The bank offered her £1 1s. 0d. in full satisfaction of her complaint, but the jury found that she did not accept this. As a result of the bank's action the plaintiff's landlords insisted thereafter that she pay her rent in cash. However, she did not claim special damage and was not allowed to amend her statement of claim during the trial. *Held*—The plaintiff was entitled to nominal damages of forty shillings. A trader is entitled to recover substantial damages for wrongful dishonour without pleading or proving actual damage, but a person who is not a trader is not entitled to recover substantial damages for the wrongful dishonour of a cheque, unless the damage he has suffered is alleged and proved as special damage.

Comment. Again, in *Rae* v. *Yorkshire Bank plc, The Times*, 12 October, 1987 where a bank, in breach of a contract to extend the overdraft facility of a customer who was not in trade, dishonoured his cheques, a customer was only entitled, said the Court of Appeal, to nominal damages unless he could prove special damage arising from the breach, which he could not. He was not entitled on an action for breach of such a contract to recover general damages for any mental or physical distress caused by having the cheques dishonoured. Parker, L.J., thought that the figure of damages awarded in the court below, i.e. £20, was too high a figure for nominal damages for the three breaches that had in fact occurred, but since it had not been challenged by the bank, he allowed it.

(696) *Davidson* v. *Barclays Bank Ltd*, [1940] 1 All E.R. 316

Davidson was both a cash and credit bookmaker who drew a cheque for £2 15s. 8d. on his account. The bank had previously paid a cheque for £7 15s. 9d. which Davidson had stopped by letter, and this wrongful payment made it appear that Davidson had no funds to meet the cheque for £2 15s. 8d. which was therefore returned marked 'Not sufficient' across its face. The plaintiff alleged libel in that the bank held him out to be a person who had drawn a cheque on an account without sufficient funds to meet it, and gave the impression that the plaintiff and his firm were unsafe to do business with or to deal with on credit. The bank pleaded that the words were published only to the payee to whom they owed an explanation as to why the cheque had not been met: that the words were published in the honest though mistaken belief that they were true; and that the occasion was privileged. *Held*—The bank had no duty to publish. There was no common interest requiring such a communication. The bank made a mistake in returning the cheque and this was the reason for the need for explanation. It was self-created. The case is essentially different from one where the bank might make an error in replying to a specific request for a reference, since then the occasion of privilege is already constituted. Judgment was given for the plaintiff for £250.

(697) *Jayson* v. *Midland Bank Ltd*, [1968] 1 L1. Rep. 409

The plaintiff claimed damages for breach of contract and libel against the bank who had returned two cheques drawn by her marked 'refer to drawer'. She alleged that the bank had agreed to pay the cheques if she paid £100 into her account the following week (which she in fact did). The bank's contention was that they had agreed to pay the cheques only if the plaintiff's overdraft limit of £500 were not exceeded (which it would have been if the cheques concerned had been paid). The action was tried before Blain, J., and a jury and the jury *found* as follows—

(i) the bank's contention was proved;

(ii) the effect of the words 'refer to drawer' was to lower the plaintiff's reputation in the eyes of right-thinking people and was defamatory—however, this did not avail the plaintiff because the bank was quite justified in its action; and

(iii) the plaintiff would have exceeded the overdraft if the cheques had been met.

An appeal to the Court of Appeal against judgment for the bank was dismissed.

Comment. This case goes some way towards removing the doubts which had previously existed regarding the defamatory nature of the words 'refer to drawer.' This decision supports the view that they are defamatory and unless the bank can plead justification, it would seem to be liable.

Banking: no constructive countermand: communication of countermand to branch on which the cheque is drawn

(698) *Curtice* v. *London, City & Midland Bank Ltd*, [1908] 1 K.B. 293

The plaintiff drew a cheque for £63 in favour of a Mr Jones to pay for some horses. When the horses were not delivered he stopped the cheque by a telegram to the bank which was delivered into the bank's letter box at 6.15 pm. The telegram was not noticed on the next day and the bank paid the cheque, only to find on the following day both the telegram which had been overlooked and a written confirmation of countermand which had been posted. The plaintiff was notified that the countermand was received too late to be effective, and he retorted by drawing a cheque on the bank for the whole of his funds, including the £63, which the bank naturally enough dishonoured. The plaintiff brought an action for money had and received. The county court gave judgment for the plaintiff; the Divisional Court dismissed the bank's appeal; but it was *held* by the Court of Appeal that there had been no effective countermand of payment and the bank were not liable for money had and received. They might have been held liable in negligence, but the damages would not then have been the same. Cozens-Hardy, M.R., said: 'There is no such thing as a constructive countermand in a commercial transaction of this kind.'

Comment. (i) Although damages would have been available in negligence, they would have been based upon the loss which the bank's negligence had caused and this would not necessarily have amounted to the full sum in the plaintiff's account. The court would have had to investigate what the real value of the horses was set against the amount which Mr Curtice was eventually made to pay for them by reason of the bank's negligence.

(ii) In practice a bank will normally act upon a customer's instructions in order to countermand an instrument, but require written confirmation immediately. There can be no stopping of a cheque issued under a cheque guarantee card. Where a customer has lost his cheque book and tells the bank they will put a stop on the remaining cheques. If a bank pays a stopped cheque it is liable to the customer and cannot recover from the payee, but it seems that where the cheque has been used to pay for goods the bank can claim the goods.

(699) *Burnett* v. *Westminster Bank*, [1965] 3 All E.R. 81

P had for a number of years had accounts at the X branch and the Y branch of the defendant bank. The bank then began to issue him with cheque books with a notice on the cover to this effect 'the cheques in this book will be applied to the account for which they have been prepared'. In the course of a transaction P used an X branch cheque but altered it as payable at Y branch and later stopped payment by giving notice to Y branch. The cheque was electronically sorted by a computer which was not equipped to read the alteration and the cheque went to X branch, which paid it. P sued the bank for the amount of the cheque. *Held*—The bank should not have debited P's account with the cheque and he succeeded.

Comment. P seems to have succeeded largely because he was an *existing* customer and the notice was on the cover. The court did say that if such a cheque book was in fact issued to a customer on opening an account, he might be bound by it, and any customer would have been bound by a notice printed on each cheque.

Banking: liability of banker for negligent financial advice: no duty to take into account the customer's tax liability in carrying out normal duties

(700) *Woods* v. *Martins Bank Ltd*, [1958] 3 All E.R. 166

The plaintiff claimed, amongst other things, damages against the defendant bank and Mr Joseph Johnson, the manager of the defendants' Quayside branch at Newcastle upon Tyne, and the case is reported only on the liability of the bank. The bank had advertised investment advice, saying 'the very best advice is available through our managers', and as a result of a request for financial advice by the plaintiff, who was a customer, the manager arranged for the plaintiff to invest £14,800 in a private company called Brocks Refrigeration, although, to the manager's knowledge, the company had a considerable overdraft and was in need of funds. The whole of this sum was eventually lost. The bank's defence was that the giving of financial advice was not part of a banker's business, relying on earlier decisions that had suggested this, and that they were not therefore vicariously liable for the negligence of their manager, since he was not acting within the scope of his employment. *Held*—By Salmon, J., (i) The limits of a banker's business could not be laid down as a matter of law. In this case the advertisement showed that the giving of financial advice was part of the business and therefore the bank was vicariously liable for the act of its servant, the manager. (ii) The duty to give proper and not negligent advice extended to potential customers as well as existing customers.

(701) *Schioler* v. *Westminster Bank Ltd*, [1970] 3 All E.R. 177

Mrs Schioler was Danish, residing in England but domiciled in Denmark. She opened an account in 1962 with a bank in Guernsey. Dividends were forwarded in sterling to the Guernsey branch by a Malaysian company and Mrs Schioler's account was credited without deduction of UK income tax to which she was not liable unless the dividends were sent to a branch in the United Kingdom. In 1969 the Malaysian company converted its shares from sterling units into Malaysian dollars. They also sent the 1967 dividend voucher and warrant to the Guernsey branch expressed in Malaysian dollars. The Guernsey branch lacked the facilities to realize the warrant so it was sent to the bank's stock officer in England for realization. The dividends thus became liable to UK income tax. In this action by the plaintiff for breach of contractual duty by the bank it was *held*—by Mocatta, J.—that in the absence of special arrangements bankers could not in discharge of their contractual duties in crediting an account with a dividend be obliged to consider the tax implications to the customer or consult him before acting in accordance with their ordinary practice.

Banking: cheques crossed 'not negotiable' are transferable: not so bills of exchange proper

(702) *Hibernian Bank* v. *Gysin and Hanson*, [1939] 1 All E.R. 166

A bill of exchange was drawn by the Irish Casing Co. on the defendants in the terms 'Payable to the order of the Irish Casing Co. only—not negotiable'. The defendants accepted the bill and the Casing Co. indorsed it to the plaintiffs who presented it for payment and it was dishonoured because the defendants were owed a greater sum of money by the Casing Co. and wished to set off. *Held*—The bill was not a negotiable instrument and the defendants were not liable to anyone but the Casing Co. The words 'to order' did not negative the crossing 'not negotiable' and the latter covered the whole legal position of the bill.

Banking: collecting banker's negligence

(703) *Lloyds Bank Ltd* v. *E. B. Savory & Co.*, [1933] A.C. 201

Two clerks, Perkins and Smith, stole bearer cheques from Savory & Co., their employers, who were stockbrokers, and paid them into branches of Lloyds Bank—Perkins into an account at Wallington, and Smith into his wife's account at Redhill and subsequently at Weybridge. The clerks paid in the cheques at other branches, using the 'branch credit' system, with the result that branches in which the accounts were kept did not receive particulars of the cheques. Neither bank made inquiries concerning the employers of Smith and Perkins. The frauds were discovered and Savory & Co. brought an action against the bank for conversion. The bank pleaded s. 82 of the Bills of Exchange Act, and denied negligence, since the 'branch credit' system was in common use by bankers. At first instance judgment was given for the bank, but this was reversed on appeal and the bank then appealed to the House of Lords. *Held*—The appeal should be dismissed as the bank had not been able to rebut the charge of negligence. With regard to the defence under s. 82, the court held that, although the branch credit system had been in use for forty years, it had 'an inherent and obvious defect which no reasonable banker could fail to observe'. Lord Wright said: 'Where a new customer is employed in some position which involves his handling, and having the opportunity of stealing, his employer's cheques, the bankers fail in taking adequate precautions if they do not ask the name of his employers. . . . Otherwise they cannot guard against the danger known to them of his paying in cheques stolen from his employers.' This is not the ordinary practice of bankers but that does not acquit them of negligence. Such inquiries should be made on the opening of an account even though they could turn out to be useless if the customer changed his employment immediately afterwards.

(704) *Lumsden & Co.* v. *London Trustee Savings Bank*, [1971] 1 Ll. Rep. 114

Stockbrokers employed a temporary accountant called Mr Blake. Blake opened an account with the bank in the fictitious name of 'Brown' and managed to divert to that account a sum of £5541 paid out by his employer ostensibly to other stockbrokers. When opening the account he gave the bank the name and address of a spurious referee and subsequently made up and submitted his own reference. The bank made no check on 'Brown's' business address nor did they obtain independent confirmation of his identity. The bank manager did ask for the address of the spurious referee's own bankers but drew no adverse conclusions when this information was not given to him. The stockbrokers claimed the value of the cheques from the bank. *Held*—by Donaldson, J.—that the bank was guilty of negligence and was not protected by s. 4(1) of the Cheques Act, 1957. However, the stockbrokers could only recover 90 per cent of the damages which would otherwise have been awarded because they had drawn their cheques in a negligent fashion, often omitting the initials of the payee; this had facilitated Blake's fraud.

Comment. This was the first reported case in which damages for conversion were reduced by apportionment under the Law Reform (Contributory Negligence) Act, 1945. Now a banker is specifically permitted by s. 47 of the Banking Act, 1979 to plead the contributory negligence of the customer. The doubts raised by some judicial decisions as to whether this was possible are now resolved in favour of the banker.

(705) *Orbit Mining and Trading Co. Ltd* v. *Westminster Bank*, [1962] 3 All E.R. 565

The plaintiff company had an account with the Midland Bank, and cheques drawn on this account had to be signed by two directors. One of these directors, A, was often abroad and had been in the habit of signing cheque forms in blank before going abroad, assuming that the other director authorized to sign, B, would use the cheques only for trading purposes.

B added his signature to three cheque forms and inserted the word 'cash' between the printed words 'Pay' and 'or order' and passed the cheques for collection to the Westminster Bank Ltd, where he had a private account. The Westminster Bank collected the sums due on the cheques and B used the money for his private purposes. The Westminster Bank did not know that B was connected with the plaintiff company since it had no up-to-date information as to his place of employment, and his signature on the cheques was, in any case, illegible. Each cheque form was crossed generally and was stamped 'for and on behalf of' the company under which appeared the signatures of A and B. *Held*—The three instruments in this case were not cheques, but were documents issued by a customer of a banker intended to enable a person to obtain payment from the banker within s. 4(2) of the Cheques Act, 1957, and since the bank had acted without negligence it was entitled to the protection of the Act in respect of the collection of an instrument to which the customer had no title.

(706) *Marfani & Co.* v. *Midland Bank*, [1967] 3 All E.R. 967

The managing director of the plaintiff company signed a cheque for £3000 drawn by the office manager Kureshy payable to Eliaszade and gave it to Kureshy for despatch. However, Kureshy opened an account with the cheque at the Midland Bank by falsely representing that he was Eliaszade and that he was about to set up a restaurant business. The bank asked for references and Kureshy gave the names of two satisfactory customers of the bank, and one of these references indicated, while on a visit to the bank, that Kureshy, whom he knew as Eliaszade, would be a satisfactory customer. The second referee did not reply to the bank's inquiry. Kureshy then drew a cheque for £2950 on the account and absconded. It appeared that the bank did not ask to see Kureshy's passport and his spelling of Eliaszade was inconsistent with the spelling on the cheque. Further the bank officials did not notice the similarity in handwriting between the cheque and the indorsement. The plaintiff company sued the bank for conversion and it was held that the bank had not fallen short of the standard ordinary practice of careful bankers and was protected by s. 4 of the Cheques Act, 1957.

Banking: collecting banker as holder in due course

(707) *Westminster Bank Ltd* v. *Zang*, [1965] 1 All E.R. 1023

Mr Zang, having lost heavily at seven-card rummy, drew a cheque for £1000 payable to 'J. Tilley or order', receiving from Mr Tilley £1000 in cash to pay part of his gambling debts. The £1000 cash belonged to Tilley's Autos Ltd, a company of which Mr Tilley was managing director. Tilley took Zang's cheque to his bank, asking them to credit the account of the company, which was overdrawn. Tilley did not indorse the cheque before paying it in. The cheque was dishonoured and the bank returned it to Tilley so that he could sue Zang. The action was commenced but discontinued and the cheque was returned to the bank who sued Zang as holder in due course or holder for value of the cheque. The bank failed in its claim. The reasons given in the Court of Appeal were—

(i) as the payee (Tilley) had asked the bank to credit the cheque to the account of a third party (Tilley's Autos), the cheque had not been received for collection within the meaning of the Cheques Act, 1957, s. 2, and as the cheque was not indorsed the bank were not 'holders' (*per* Denning, M.R.);
(ii) the cheque had been received for collection but the bank had not given value, so that s. 2 did not apply (*per* Salmon, L.J.);
(iii) the cheque had been received for collection but the bank in returning the cheque to Tilley lost their lien and consequently the protection of s. 2 (*per* Danckwerts, L.J.).

In the House of Lords their Lordships unanimously held that the cheque had been received for collection, but the bank had not given value.

The company's account was overdrawn, but it was hard to see how, by crediting the cheque to the account and reducing the overdraft, the bank gave value for it, because in fact interest had been charged on the original amount of the overdraft unreduced by the cheque. There was no agreement express or implied to honour the cheques of Tilley's Autos before they had been cleared, and consideration could not, therefore, be established in this way.

(708) *Barclays Bank Ltd* v. *Astley Industrial Trust, Ltd*, [1970] 1 All E.R. 719

Mabons Garage Ltd were motor dealers who banked with the plaintiffs and arranged hire-purchase transactions with the defendants. In November, 1964, the plaintiffs gave Mabons a temporary overdraft up to £2000 and on 18 November, when the account was £1910 overdrawn, cheques for £2673 drawn by Mabons were presented for payment. The bank manager agreed to pay them only after receiving an assurance from the directors of Mabons that cheques for £2850 in favour of Mabons and drawn by the defendants would be paid into the account the next day.

On 19 November, when Mabons overdraft stood at £4673, two further cheques for £345 drawn by Mabons were presented for payment and the bank manager refused to pay these until he had received the defendants' cheques for £2850. On 20 November the defendants stopped their cheques which it appeared they had been induced to draw by the fraud of Mabons' directors. In an action by the bank claiming to be holders in due course of the cheques, the defendants alleged that the bank had not taken them for value. *Held*—by Milmo, J.—that the bank was holder in due course since—

(*a*) a banker who takes a cheque as agent for collection can also be a holder in due course under s. 2 of the Cheques Act, 1957;

(*b*) the bank was a holder in due course. They were holders because they had a lien on the cheques and were entitled to hold them pending payment of the overdraft. The value was the overdraft of £4673. An antecedent debt would support a bill of exchange.

The bank was entitled to recover the amount of the cheques from the defendants.

THE NATURE OF CRIME

Crime and civil wrongs distinguished: the burden of proof in crime

(709) *Woolmington* v. *Director of Public Prosecutions*, [1935] A.C. 462

W had been charged with the murder of his wife. He had, on his own admission, shot her but said in his defence that the gun had gone off accidentally. The judge told the jury that so long as the prosecution had shown that the accused had caused the death malice was presumed and that the accused must prove that the killing was an accident. The jury convicted W who appealed to what was then the Court of Criminal Appeal where his conviction was upheld. However, on appeal to the House of Lords his conviction was quashed. 'Throughout the web of English Criminal Law one golden thread is always to be seen, that it is the duty of the prosecution to prove the prisoner's guilt subject to what I have already said as to the defence of insanity and subject also to any statutory exceptions. If, at the end of and on the whole of the case, there is a reasonable doubt created by the evidence given by either the prosecution or the prisoner, as to whether the prisoner killed the deceased with a malicious intention, the prosecution has not made out the case and the prisoner is entitled to an acquittal.' (*per* Viscount Sankey, L.C.)

Nulla poena sine lege: the common law offence of conspiracy

(710) *Shaw* v. *Director of Public Prosecutions*, [1961] 2 All E.R. 446

S published a booklet called '*The Ladies' Directory*' which contained the names and addresses of prostitutes. The entries gave telephone numbers and indicated that they were offering their services for sexual intercourse and some of them for the practice of sexual perversions. S was convicted of conspiracy to corrupt public morals and his appeal eventually reached the House of Lords. His appeal was dismissed and his conviction affirmed. However, Lord Reid, in a strong dissenting judgment, said that in his view there was no such general offence known to the law as conspiracy to corrupt public morals and the court in convicting S of it was creating a new crime on the basis of public mischief which is the criminal law equivalent of public policy. He thought that if the courts had stopped creating new heads of public policy in, for example, the civil law of contract, then they certainly should refrain from doing so in criminal law.

Actus reus: **is voluntary conduct required?**

(711) *Hill* v. *Baxter*, [1958] 1 All E.R. 42

The defendant had been charged with dangerous driving and failing to conform with a traffic sign under ss. 11 and 49(b) of the Road Traffic Act, 1930, respectively. He said in his defence that he had been unconscious at the time because a sudden illness had overtaken him. The magistrates accepted his defence and dismissed the charges and the prosecutor appealed. The appeal was allowed and the defendant therefore convicted. 'I agree that there may be cases where the circumstances are such that the accused could not really be said to be driving at all. Suppose he had a stroke or an epileptic fit, both instances of what may properly be called acts of God; he might well be in the driver's seat even with his hands on the wheel, but in such a state of unconsciousness that he could not be said to be driving. A blow from a stone or an attack by a swarm of bees I think introduces some conception akin to *novus actus interveniens*. In this case, however, I am content to say that the evidence falls far short of what would justify a court holding that this man was in some automatous state'. (*Per* Lord Goddard, C.J.)

   Comment. In *Moses* v. *Winder*, [1980] Crim. L.R. 232 the defendant had been a diabetic for 20 years. He felt a diabetic attack developing and took a dose of sugar which usually postponed the attacks for about an hour. However, whilst driving home he drove his car on the wrong side of the road, colliding with an oncoming car. He stopped a few minutes later in a daze, examined his car and then drove a further half mile. It was held by a Divisional Court that the defendant was nevertheless guilty of driving without due care and attention. His defence of automatism did not succeed and would rarely succeed without medical evidence. The defendant had not taken sufficient precautions to deal with the threat of a diabetic coma.

(712) *Attorney-General for Northern Ireland* v. *Gallagher*, [1963] A.C. 349

G was convicted of murdering his wife. In his defence he pleaded insanity under the M'Naghten Rules or, as an alternative, that he was too drunk at the time to form the necessary intent for murder so that he was only guilty of manslaughter. G had shown intention to kill his wife before taking the drink. The case eventually reached the House of Lords where Lord Denning gave a useful summary of the effect of drunkenness when he said: '1. If a man is charged with an offence in which a specific intention is essential (as in murder, though not in manslaughter), then evidence of drunkenness, which renders him incapable of forming that intention is an answer . . . 2. If a man by drinking brings on a distinct disease of the mind such as *delirium tremens*, so that he is temporarily insane within the M'Naghten Rules, that is to say, he does not at the time know what he is doing or that it is wrong, then he has a defence on the ground of insanity. . . .' However, G's original conviction for murder was upheld because he did not fit the above categories. As Lord Denning said: 'My Lords, I think the law on this point should take a clear stand. If a man, whilst sane and sober, forms an intention to kill and makes preparation for it, knowing it is a wrong thing to do, and then gets himself drunk so as to give himself Dutch courage to do the killing, and whilst drunk carries out his intention, he cannot rely on this self-induced drunkenness as a defence to a charge of murder, nor even as reducing it to manslaughter.'

Comment. In *R* v. *Tandy, The Times*, 23 December, 1987, an alcoholic mother who drank nine-tenths of a bottle of vodka before strangling her 11 year old daughter was convicted of murder. The defence of diminished responsibility (see p. 158) was not available if based on drunkenness.

(713) *R.* v. *Lipman*, [1969] 3 All E.R. 410

L was charged with murder of a girl but convicted of manslaughter. Both he and the girl had taken LSD together in her room and L said that while under the influence of the drug he had an illusion of being attacked by snakes and that he must have killed the girl during this time. The girl had received two severe blows on the head but the immediate cause of her death was asphyxia as a result of having part of a sheet pushed down her mouth. The Court of Appeal affirmed the conviction, saying that when the killing results from the unlawful act of the accused, no specific intent was to be proved to convict of manslaughter and mental states which are self-induced by drink or drugs are no defence to a charge of manslaughter.

(714) *R.* v. *Charlson*, [1955] 1 All E.R. 859

C had been charged with unlawfully and maliciously causing grievous bodily harm. He hit his small son with a mallet and then threw him out of a window. He could have been suffering from a cerebral tumour at the time and certainly there was no obvious motive or rage which would have caused him to do as he did. He said in defence that he was unconscious at the time. He was acquitted by the jury both on the charge mentioned above and on the more serious charges of causing grievous bodily harm with intent to do so and with intent to murder.

Actus reus: liability for failing to act

(715) *R.* v. *Instan*, [1893] 1 Q.B. 450

Instan lived with her 73-year-old aunt. The aunt seemed to be in reasonable health until shortly before her death. During the 12 days prior to her death she had gangrene in her leg and could not look after herself or summon help. That she was in this condition was a matter known only to Instan. It appeared that she had not given her aunt any food nor had she tried to obtain medical or nursing aid. Following the death of her aunt she was accused of manslaughter and convicted. The Court for Crown Cases Reserved (as it then was) affirmed the conviction. 'The prisoner was under a moral obligation to the deceased from which arose a legal duty towards her; that legal duty the prisoner has wilfully and deliberately left unperformed, with the consequence that there has been an acceleration of the death of the deceased owing to the non-performance of that legal duty. It is unnecessary to say more than that upon the evidence this conviction was most properly arrived at'. (*Per* Lord Coleridge, C.J.)

Comment. That liability for omissions is not restricted to cases of manslaughter is illustrated by *R.* v. *Miller*, [1983] 1 All E.R. 978. The defendant, who was a vagrant squatter, fell asleep after lighting a cigarette. He woke to find that his mattress was smouldering. He left it and went to sleep in another room. There was a fire and the defendant was charged with arson. He was found guilty and his appeal was dismissed by the House of Lords. His conviction was justified either on the basis that there was a continuous act or on the basis that the defendant owed a responsibility to try and undo the harm he had unwittingly done. The House of Lords felt that this latter basis, which is really an omission, would be easier to explain to juries.

Causation: illustrations from case law

(716) *R.* v. *Hayward*, (1908) 21 Cox 692

H came home one night in a violent state of excitement. He had said previously that he was going to 'give his wife something' when she returned home. When she arrived there were sounds of quarrelling and soon afterwards the wife ran out of the house followed by H. The wife fell onto the road and H kicked her on her left arm. She died and the medical examination showed that the kick was not the cause of her death. She was in good health apart from thymus gland trouble, on which the medical evidence was that a person with such a condition might die from the combined effects of fright, strong emotion and physical exertion. H was charged with manslaughter at Maidstone Assizes and found guilty. Ridley, J., said that the abnormal state of the deceased's health did not affect the question whether the prisoner knew or did not know of it, if it were proved to the satisfaction of the jury that the death was accelerated by the prisoner's illegal act.

(717) *R.* v. *Martin*, (1881) 8 Q.B.D. 54

Just before a theatrical performance came to an end M, intending to terrify people leaving the theatre, put out lights on the staircase which he knew a large number of people would use when leaving the theatre. He then placed an iron bar across an exit door. As a result of his actions several people were hurt as they tried to leave the theatre. M was convicted on a charge of unlawfully and maliciously inflicting grievous bodily harm. 'The prisoner must be taken to have intended the natural consequences of that which he did. He acted "unlawfully and maliciously", not that he had any personal malice against the particular individuals injured, but in the sense of doing an unlawful act calculated to injure, and by which others were in fact injured. Just as in the case of a man who unlawfully fires a gun among a crowd, it is murder if one of the crowd is thereby killed. The prisoner was most properly convicted'. (*Per* Lord Coleridge, C.J.)

Comment. The view taken by the House of Lords in *R.* v. *Moloney*, [1985] 2 W.L.R. 648 was that a person did not intend an act unless (in effect) he wanted it to exist or occur, is aware that it exists, or is almost certain that it exists or will exist or occur. Thus in murder cases intent is not now established by a kind of objective foresight of consequences. Moloney's conviction for murder of his father when larking about with guns, when both father and son were drunk, was reduced to manslaughter.

(718) *R.* v. *Jordan*, (1956) 40 Cr. App. R. 152

J stabbed his victim in the stomach; the victim was rushed to hospital where the wound was stitched, but he died a few days later. J was convicted of murder at Leeds Assizes. On his appeal he brought forward additional medical evidence which revealed that the stab wound had penetrated the intestine in two places but that these wounds were in the main healed at the time of death. A hospital doctor had administered terramycin to prevent infection but the victim was intolerant to it and its use was stopped. Two new witnesses said also that abnormal quantities of liquid had been given intravenously so that the victim's lungs became waterlogged and pulmonary oedema resulted. The Court of Criminal Appeal quashed J's conviction. 'It is sufficient to point out here that this was not normal treatment. Not only one feature, but two separate and independent features, of treatment were, in the opinion of the doctors, palpably wrong and these produced the symptoms discovered at the postmortem examination which were the direct and immediate cause of death, namely, the pneumonia resulting from the condition of oedema which was found.' (*Per* Hallett, J.)

(719) *R.* v. *Smith*, [1959] 2 All E.R. 193

The facts were that the victim of a barrack room brawl who was stabbed twice with a bayonet was dropped twice by those trying to get him to hospital and given artificial respiration when he got there although he was wounded in the lungs so that this was not advisable. Nevertheless these events were held not to break the chain of causation. However, it must be said that the events in this case, including the death of Private Creed who was the victim, all occurred within a period of some two hours. '. . . a man is stabbed in the back, his lung is pierced and haemorrhage results; two hours later he dies of haemorrhage from that wound; in the interval there is no time for a careful examination, and the treatment given turns in the light of subsequent knowledge to have been inappropriate and, indeed, harmful. In those circumstances no reasonable jury or court could, properly directed, in our view possibly come to any other conclusion than that the death resulted from the original wound. Accordingly the court dismisses this appeal.' (*Per* Lord Parker, C.J.)

Mens rea: **must coincide with** *actus reus*

(720) *Thabo Meli* v. *The Queen*, [1954] 1 All E.R. 373

In this case the accused persons planned to kill the victim in a hut and thereafter to roll his body over a cliff so that it would appear that he had died an accidental death. The victim was made unconscious in the hut by the attack and thinking him to be dead, the accused persons rolled him over a cliff. There was evidence that the victim was not in fact killed in the hut but that he died on account of exposure at the bottom of the cliff. 'The point of law which was raised in this case can be simply stated. It is said that two acts were necessary and were separable; first, the attack in the hut; and, secondly, the placing of the body outside afterwards. It is said that, while the first act was accompanied by *mens rea*, it was not the cause of death; but that the second act, while it was the cause of death, was not accompanied by *mens rea*; and on that ground it is said that the accused are not guilty of any crime, except perhaps culpable homicide.

'It appears to their Lordships impossible to divide up what was really one transaction in this way. There is no doubt that the accused set out to do all these acts in order to achieve their plan and as part of their plan; and it is much too refined a ground of judgment to say that, because they were under a misapprehension at one stage and thought that their guilty purpose had been achieved before in fact it was achieved, therefore they are to escape the penalties of the law. . . .' (*Per* Lord Reid.)

The appeal of the accused persons was therefore dismissed.

Mens rea: **motive: irrelevant to guilt or innocence**

(721) *Chandler* v. *Director of Public Prosecutions*, [1962] 3 All E.R. 142

In this case the accused impeded the operation of an airfield at

Wethersfield. Their object was to demonstrate against nuclear armament. 'In the result, I am of opinion that if a person's direct purpose in approaching or entering is to cause obstruction or interference, and such obstruction or interference is found to be a prejudice to the defence dispositions of the State, an offence is thereby committed, and his indirect purposes or his motives in bringing about the obstruction or interference do not alter the nature or content of his offence. . . . Is a man guilty of an offence, it was asked, if he rushes onto an airfield intending to stop an airplane taking off because he knows that a time-bomb has been concealed on board? I should say that he is not, for the reason that his direct purpose is not to bring about an obstruction but to prevent a disaster, the obstruction that he causes being merely a means of securing that end.' (*Per* Lord Radcliffe.)

Mens rea: inadvertent negligence as a criminal mental state

(722) *Elliott* v. *C*, [1983] 2 All E.R. 1005

C was a 14-year-old schoolgirl who was charged with criminal damage under s. 1(1) of the Criminal Damage Act, 1971, (destroying or damaging property without danger to life.) She spent one entire night awake and wandering around. She had entered a toolshed and there poured white spirit onto a carpet and set light to it, destroying the shed. The magistrates found that she did not appreciate just how inflammable the spirit was, and having regard to her extreme state of tiredness, that she did not in fact give any real thought to the risk of fire. In consequence the magistrates acquitted her. It was held by a Divisional Court of Queen's Bench, allowing the prosecutor's appeal, that the correct test was whether a reasonably prudent man would realize the dangers of fire in the circumstances, even though the particular accused might not appreciate them. In other words, it would appear that the test at criminal law has become an objective test of negligence to some extent in line with the civil standard, at least where criminal damage is concerned.

Comment. The civil standard approach was followed in *R.* v. *Sangha, The Times*, 2 February, 1988 where the Court of Appeal said that the test was '. . . would an ordinary prudent bystander have perceived an obvious risk that property of value and life would be endangered'. Sangha was convicted of *arson* under s. 1(2) of the Criminal Damage Act, 1971 because life was endangered.

Mens rea: effect of mistake of fact and law

(723) *R.* v. *Levett*, (1638) 79 E.R. 1064

L and his wife were in bed and asleep at night when their servant, having procured without their knowledge the services of a Frances Freeman to help her about the house, let Frances out at about midnight. She thought she heard thieves at the door offering to break in and in fear she ran to Mr and Mrs Levett and told them that she thought thieves were breaking down the door. On receiving this information Mr Levett arose and fetched a drawn rapier. At the same time the servant hid Frances Freeman in the buttery in case Mr Levett found her. Mrs Levett caught a glimpse of Frances Freeman in the buttery and turned to her husband in great fear and said: 'Here they be that would undo us'. Hearing this Mr Levett, not knowing that Frances was in the buttery, rushed in with a drawn rapier. It was dark and he thrust his rapier ahead giving Frances a mortal wound in the left breast from which she instantly died. It was resolved by the court that it was not manslaughter for what Mr Levett did he did ignorantly without intention of hurt to Frances.

(724) *R.* v. *Bailey*, (1800) 168 E.R. 651

Bailey, who was the captain of a ship, fired at another ship on the high seas without any justification and wounded one of the sailors on that other ship. He was charged under an Act of Parliament which made such a shooting on the high seas triable and punishable in this country. The following extract from the judgment of the court is relevant: 'It was then insisted that the prisoner could not be found guilty of the offence with which he was charged, because the Act of 39 Geo. 3, c. 37 upon which . . . the prisoner was indicted at this Admiralty Sessions, . . . only received the Royal Assent on 10 May, 1799, and the fact charged in the indictment happened on 27 June in the same year when the prisoner could not know that any such Act existed (his ship the *Langley* being at the time upon the coast of Africa). Lord Eldon told the jury that he was of opinion that he was, in strict law, guilty within the statutes . . . though if the facts laid were proved, though he could not then know that the Act of 39 Geo. 3, c. 37 had passed, and that ignorance of that fact, could in no other wise affect the case, than that it might be the means of recommending him to a merciful consideration elsewhere should he be found guilty. . . .'

Comment. At the next Admiralty Sessions the prisoner was pardoned.

Mens rea: **statutory offences**

(725) *Sweet* v. *Parsley*, [1969] 1 All E.R. 347

The magistrates had convicted Sweet of being concerned in the management of premises which were used for the purpose of smoking cannabis or cannabis resin, contrary to s. 5(b) of the Dangerous Drugs Act, 1965. The evidence showed that she had no knowledge whatever that the house was being used for the purpose of smoking cannabis or cannabis resin. She visited the premises only occasionally to collect letters and rent and though sometimes she stayed overnight, generally she did not. Section 5 of the 1965 Act provides 'if a person (*a*) being the occupier of any premises, permits those premises to be used for the purpose of smoking cannabis or cannabis resin or of dealing in cannabis or cannabis resin (whether by sale or otherwise); or (*b*) is concerned in the management of any premises used for any such purposes aforesaid; he shall be guilty of an offence under the Act'. The House of Lords, after holding that in spite of the wording of the Act *mens rea* must be implied, found that there was no *mens rea* in the accused in this case and that therefore her appeal should be allowed and her conviction quashed.

(726) *R.* v. *Tolson*, (1889) 23 Q.B.D. 168

Martha Ann Tolson, who married in September, 1880, was deserted by her husband in December, 1881. She made enquiries and learned from his elder brother that he had been lost at sea in a ship bound for America which sank with all hands. Believing herself to be a widow, she went quite openly through a ceremony of marriage on 10 January, 1887, with Y who was fully aware of the circumstances. It was held that she could not be convicted of bigamy under s. 57 of the Offences Against the Person Act, 1861, even though the opening part of that section says: 'Whosoever, being married, shall marry any other person during the life of the former husband or wife . . . shall be guilty of a felony. . . .' She had no *mens rea*. The object of Parliament was not to treat the marriage of widows as an act to be if possible prevented as presumably immoral. Mrs Tolson's conduct was not immoral but perfectly natural and legitimate. A statute may relate to such subject matter and may be so framed as to make an act criminal whether there has been any intention to break the law or not. In other cases a more reasonable construction requires the implication into the statute that a guilty mind is required.

(727) *Alphacell* v. *Woodward*, [1972] 2 All E.R. 475

A Ltd was the owner of paper-making mills. In the course of manufacture effluent passed into two tanks on the banks of a river. Pumps were used to remove the effluent from the tanks but it was inevitable that if the pumps failed the effluent would enter the river and pollute it. As a result of foliage blocking the pump inlets such an overflow occurred and A Ltd was charged with 'causing' polluting matter to enter the river under s. 2(1) of the Rivers (Prevention of Pollution) Act, 1951. It was *held*— by the House of Lords—that they were guilty of that offence even though they had not been negligent. The intervening act of a trespass or act of God would have been a defence but there was no such trespass or act of God in this case.

(728) *Cundy* v. *Le Cocq*, (1884) 13 Q.B.D. 207

C, who was a licensed victualler, sold liquor to a person who was drunk though C did not know this. He was, however, convicted of unlawfully selling liquor to a drunken person contrary to s. 13 of the Licensing Act, 1872, which provided that: 'If any licensed person . . . sells any intoxicating liquor to a drunken person he shall be liable to a penalty. . . .' It was *held*—by Stephen, J.—that knowledge of the condition of the person to whom the liquor was sold was not necessary to constitute the offence. 'Against this view we have had quoted the maxim that in every criminal offence there must be a guilty mind; but I do not think that maxim has so wide an application as it is sometimes considered to have. In old time, and as applicable to the common law or to earlier statutes, the maxim may have been of general application; but a difference has arisen owing to the greater precision of modern statutes. It is impossible now, . . . to apply the maxim generally to all statutes, and the substance of all the reported cases is that it is necessary to look at the object of each Act that is under consideration to see whether and how far knowledge is of the essence of the offence created. Here, as I have already pointed out, the object of this part of the Act is to prevent the sale of intoxicating liquor to drunken persons, and it is perfectly natural to carry that out by throwing on the publican the responsibility of determining whether the person supplied comes within that category. I think, therefore, the conviction was right and must be affirmed.'

(729) *R.* v. *Cunningham*, [1957] 2 All E.R. 412

C was convicted of unlawfully and maliciously causing to be taken by Sarah Wade a certain noxious thing, namely, coal gas, so as to endanger her life contrary to s. 23 of the Offences Against the Person Act, 1861. C had gone into an empty house and torn away the gas meter in the cellar in order to take the money it contained with the intention of stealing that money. However coal gas poured out of the pipe he had fractured and percolated into the house next door where it almost asphyxiated the occupant, Sarah Wade. C appealed and his appeal was allowed. '. . . we think it is incorrect to say that the word "malicious" in a statutory offence merely means wicked. We think the judge was, in effect, telling the jury that if they were satisfied that the appellant acted wickedly—and he had clearly acted wickedly in stealing the gas meter and its contents—they ought to find that he had acted maliciously in causing the gas to be taken by Mrs Wade so as thereby to endanger her life.

'In our view it should have been left to the jury to decide whether, even if the appellant did not intend to injure Mrs Wade, he foresaw that the removal of the gas meter might cause injury to someone but nevertheless removed it. We are unable to say that a reasonable jury, properly directed as to the meaning of the word "maliciously" in the context of s. 23, would without doubt have convicted.

'In these circumstances this court has no alternative but to allow the appeal and quash the conviction' (*Per* Byrne, J.).

(730) *Gaumont British Distributors Ltd* v. *Henry*, [1939] 2 K.B. 717

Gaumont British were charged under s. 1(a) of the Dramatic and Musical Performers' Protection Act, 1925, with knowingly making a record of a musical work without the written consent of the performers. No consent had actually been given but GB said, and it was accepted, that they had never thought about the question of consent. Nevertheless GB was convicted and appealed. The appeal was allowed. 'I desire to add emphatically that no colour can be obtained from this case, or from the argument, or from any opinion which is present to my mind, that the wholesome and fundamental principle *ignorantia juris neminem excusat* is in any degree to be modified or departed from. . . . I should be very sorry, directly or indirectly, even to appear to add any colour to the suggestion, if it were made—as I do not think it is—that in circumstances of this kind ignorance of the law might excuse. The way in which the topic of the appellants' knowledge came in was solely with reference to the words 'knowingly makes any record without the consent in writing of the performers', and the contention was a contention of fact. According to a true view of the evidence of fact in this case it was incorrect to say that the appellants did knowingly without the consent in writing of the performers that which was done'. (*Per* Lord Hewart, C.J.)

(731) *R.* v. *Lowe*, [1973] 1 All E.R. 805

Lowe was charged under s. 1 of the Children and Young Persons Act of 1933 as being a person who had the charge of a child and wilfully neglected it in a manner likely to cause it unnecessary suffering or injury to health. L's case was that the child's critical condition arose after he had told the woman he was living with, who was the child's mother, to take the child to a doctor and that she later falsely told him that she had done so. He was convicted and appealed. 'It did not matter what he ought to have realized as the possible consequences of his failure to call a doctor; the sole question was whether his failure to do so was deliberate and thereby occasioned the results referred to in s. 1(1) of the Act of 1933. We are quite satisfied that the conviction on count 2 was justified both on the law and the facts . . .' (*Per* Phillimore, L.J.)

(732) *Somerset* v. *Wade*, [1894] 1 Q.B. 574

Wade was charged with permitting drunkenness under s. 13 of the Licensing Act, 1872, which provides that if any licensed person permits drunkenness, or any violence, quarrelsome or riotous conduct to take place on his premises or sells any intoxicating liquor to any drunken person, he commits an offence. A drunken woman was actually found on Wade's premises but it was accepted that Wade did not know that she was drunk. The charge having been dismissed the prosecutor appealed. The appeal of the prosecutor failed and Wade was not convicted. '. . . but the word "suffers" is not distinguishable from "permits", which is the word used in s. 13, the section now before us. In a case where the defendant does not know that the person who was on his premises was in fact drunk, he cannot be said to permit drunkenness. In the present case the justices have found that the respondent did not know that the woman was drunk and there was evidence to support that finding.' (*Per* Mathew, J.)

Comment. In this case Mathew, J., was prepared to say that the word 'suffers' was the same as 'permits', i.e. a word requiring *mens rea* in the accused.

Vicarious liability in crime

(733) *Griffiths* v. *Studebakers Ltd*, [1924] 1 K.B. 102

Studebakers were holders of a limited trade licence and were charged with having used on a public road a motor car carrying more than two persons in addition to the driver, which was an offence under the Road Vehicles (Trade Licences) Regulations, 1922. At the time of the alleged offence the car was being driven by a servant of the respondents. He was in the course of his employment because he was giving a trial run to prospective purchasers of the car but by carrying more than two passengers he was infringing the express orders of his employers. The employers were convicted and appealed to the Divisional Court. 'It would be fantastic to suppose that a manufacturer, whether a limited company, a firm, or an individual, would, even if he could, always show cars to prospective purchasers himself; and it would defeat the scheme of this legislation if it were open to an employer, whether a company, or a firm, or an individual, to say that although the car was being used under the limited licence in contravention of the conditions upon which it was granted: "My hand was not the hand that drove the car." On these facts there ought to have been a conviction of the respondents and also the driver as aider and abettor.' (*Per* Lord Hewart, C.J.) Thus the conviction of Studebakers was affirmed by the Divisional Court.

(734) *James and Son Ltd* v. *Smee*, [1955] 1 Q.B. 78

Under the Motor Vehicles (Construction and Use) Regulations in force at the time the alleged offence occurred the braking system of a vehicle or trailer used on the road had to be in efficient working order and further anyone who used or caused or permitted to be used on the road a motor vehicle or trailer where the braking system was not in efficient working order was liable to a fine. James and Son Ltd sent out in the charge of their employee a lorry and trailer the braking system of which was in efficient working order. However, during the course of his rounds the employee had to disconnect the braking system of the trailer and forgot to connect it up again. James and Son were convicted of 'permitting to be used' the trailer in contravention of the regulations then in force. However, their appeal was allowed by the Divisional Court. 'In other words, it is said that in committing the offence of the user in contravention of the regulations he at the same time made his master guilty of the offence of permitting such user. In our opinion this contention is highly artificial and divorced from reality. We prefer to view that before the company can be held guilty of permitting a user in contravention of the regulations it must be proved that some person for whose criminal acts the company is responsible permitted as opposed to committed the offence. There was no such evidence in the present case.' (*Per* Parker, J.)

(735) *Vane* v. *Yiannopoullos*, [1965] A.C. 486

Section 22(1) of the Licensing Act, 1961, which was relevant in this case provided 'If—(*a*) the holder of a Justices' on-licence knowingly sells or supplies intoxicating liquor to persons to whom he is not permitted by the conditions of the licence to sell or supply it . . . he shall be guilty of an offence.' Y was the licensee of a restaurant and had been granted a justices on-licence subject to a condition that intoxicating liquor was to be sold only to those who ordered meals. He employed a waitress and he instructed her to serve drinks only to customers who ordered meals but on one occasion whilst Y was in another part of the restaurant the waitress did serve drinks to two youths who had not in fact ordered a meal. Y did not know of that sale. He was charged with knowingly selling intoxicating liquor on the premises to persons to whom he was not permitted to sell contrary to s. 22(1)(a) of the Act. The magistrates dismissed the information and the prosecutor appealed eventually to the House of Lords. The appeal of the prosecutor was dismissed and there was therefore no conviction of Y. 'So far, however, as the present case is concerned, I feel no doubt that the decision of the Divisional Court was right. There was clearly no "knowledge" in the strict sense proved against the licensee: I agree also with the Lord Chief Justice that there was no sufficient evidence of such "delegation" on his part of his powers, duties and responsibilities to render him liable on that ground. I would therefore without hesitation dismiss the appeal.' (*Per* Lord Evershed.)

(736) *Ferguson* v. *Weaving*, [1951] 1 All E.R. 412

Section 4 of the Licensing Act, 1921, which was relevant in this case, made it an offence for any person, except during permitted hours, to consume intoxicating liquor on any licensed premises. In a large public house of which W was the manager customers were found consuming liquor outside permitted hours and were convicted of an offence under the section. The evidence did not show that W knew that the liquor was being consumed. It had in fact been supplied to customers by waiters employed by her who had neglected to collect the glasses in time. A charge against W of aiding and abetting the customers' offence was dismissed and the prosecutor appealed. The appeal was dismissed. 'There can be no doubt that this court has more than once laid it down in clear terms that before a person can be convicted of aiding and abetting the commission of an offence he must at least know the essential matters which constitute the offence. . . .' (*Per* Lord Goddard, C.J.)

General index